CHRONOLOGY OF
20TH-CENTURY
EASTERN
EUROPEAN
HISTORY

CHRONOLOGY OF
20TH-CENTURY
EASTERN
EUROPEAN
HISTORY

Gregory C. Ference

Editor

Foreword by

Drs. Charles and Barbara Jelavich

 *Gale Research Inc.*

DETROIT • WASHINGTON, D.C. • LONDON

Gale Research Inc. Staff

Allison McNeill-Gudenau, Carol DeKane Nagel, *Developmental Editors*
Kelle Sisung, Peg Bessette, *Contributing Editors*
Lawrence W. Baker, *Senior Developmental Editor*

Mary Beth Trimper, *Production Director*
Evi Seoud, *Assistant Production Manager*
Shanna P. Heilveil, *Production Assistant*

Cynthia Baldwin, *Art Director*
Barbara J. Yarrow, *Graphic Services Supervisor*
Mary Krzewinski, *Cover and Page Designer*
Willie Mathis, *Camera Operator*

Benita L. Spight, *Data Entry Services Manager*
Gwendolyn S. Tucker, *Data Entry Supervisor*
LySandra Davis, *Data Entry Associate*
Margaret Chamberlain, *Picture Permissions Supervisor*
Susan Brohman, *Permissions Assistant*

Cover photos courtesy of German Information Center; U.S.S.R. State Archival Fund

∞™ This book is printed on acid-free paper that meets the minimum requirements of American National Standard for Information Sciences—Permanence Paper for Printed Library Materials, ANSI Z39.48-1984.

ISBN 0-8103-8879-0
Library of Congress Catalog Card Number 94-77453

Printed in the United States of America by Gale Research Inc.
Published simultaneously in the United Kingdom
by Gale Research International Limited
(An affiliated company of Gale Research Inc.)

10 9 8 7 6 5 4 3 2 1

The trademark **ITP** is used under license.

Contents

Highlights

The *Chronology of 20th-Century Eastern European History* is a reference source designed for users seeking information on important people, places, and events in the history of Eastern Europe from 1900 through the end of 1993. This work features separate chronological histories of:

- Albania
- Bulgaria
- Hungary
- Poland
- Romania

as well as the former nations of

- Czechoslovakia
- East Germany
- Soviet Union
- Yugoslavia

The *Chronology of 20th-Century Eastern European History* provides an abundance of information, and its orderly format makes it easy to use. Special features include:

- Overview of each country's history up to 1900 at the beginning of each chapter
- Timeline of major events in Eastern Europe and across the globe
- Over 70 brief biographical sketches of significant Eastern European figures
- Annotated bibliography
- Glossary
- Keyword index listing important names, places, and events
- Over 100 photos and maps

Foreword

Given the role that Eastern Europe has played in the twentieth century, one cannot minimize its importance not only for European history but for the world. Both World Wars had their immediate origins there—the first, in 1914, involved Serbia, Sarajevo, and the Yugoslav movement; and the second, in 1938–1939, Munich, Czechoslovakia, and Poland. Furthermore, Eastern Europe which, at best, had been of secondary concern to the United States before 1939, became a focus of American foreign policy as Washington, together with its Western Allies, sought to contain the Soviet Union and limit its domination of the region. Most recently the world has witnessed the collapse of the Communist system and the violent breakup of Yugoslavia and the partition of Czechoslovakia. Today the nations of Eastern Europe are struggling to establish democratic governments after four decades of Communist rule. At present, the United States and other governments are giving their support to the democratic revival of these nations.

For Americans in general, however, Eastern Europe commanded little interest before 1945. The wave of immigrants coming to the U.S. from that region between 1890 and 1914 tended to alienate Americans, especially when they heard the multiplicity of languages spoken by people with different manners, customs, and dress who also added to the religious diversity of the nation by practicing Orthodoxy, Judaism, Islam, and Catholicism, among others. In fact, before the Second World War there were at most only about a half dozen professors in all the American universities whose primary research interests were the lands of Eastern Europe. Today the number is several thousand and East European subjects are taught in hundreds of American educational institutions. Now, for example, Polish, Czech, and Serbo-Croatian are taught on a regular basis in about a dozen universities, and other languages—Hungarian, Slovak, Romanian, Bulgarian— are offered sporadically at other institutions.

The history of Eastern Europe is rich, complicated, and detailed. Although the years of Communist domination—1945 to 1990—are perhaps the period best known to Americans generally, they were in fact an aberration in the historical development of the area. The multitude of political, economic, social, religious, and cultural problems that plague the region today in many cases antedate the contemporary era. Ironically, however, it is the concept of modern nationalism that led to the desire to create independent states. Today, this desire adds to the complexities of those areas where ethnic boundaries cannot be clearly delineated and where national antagonisms are often as old as the nations themselves.

Extensive research and thousands of books and articles have been published in the last four decades on Eastern Europe. And while some books contain brief historical chronologies for individual countries or for limited periods of history, we still do not have in English a readily available chronology that covers the major events of the twentieth century for all Eastern European countries. Hence the present undertaking, a general reference work covering all the nations of Eastern Europe in what promises to be a useful tool for teaching and research. The work is further enhanced by the inclusion of a comprehensive timeline, an annotated bibliography, as well as biographical sketches of some of the more prominent individuals in each nation. Although this publication is primarily aimed at the student and general public, it will also be a welcomed reference work for scholars who need rapid access to dates, events, and personalities.

Barbara and Charles Jelavich
Professors Emeriti
Indiana University

vii

Introduction

The *Chronology of 20th-Century Eastern European History* is the product of a group of nationwide scholars who specialize in the study of the region. This ready-reference source is intended to provide the reader with a concise look at the major political, economic, and cultural events that have shaped the history of Eastern Europe from the turn of the century to the end of 1993. In doing so, this volume is meant to provide researchers, students, and general readers with an easy-to use compendium of information regarding a largely neglected area of the globe.

Prior to 1989, Eastern Europe was viewed by many as a mere appendage of the Soviet Union, under whose domination most of the countries fell in 1945. As a result, unfortunately, the uniqueness of the area was ignored. In fact, the peoples and countries of the area have had an independent existence from their neighbor to the east both prior to World War II and again since 1989. With the fall of communism and the rise of democracy in the countries of East Central and Southeastern Europe, the West began to notice the distinctiveness of these nations. Since 1989, moreover, events in this part of the world have been highlighted almost daily in the news. For example, as recently as five years ago, relatively few people had ever heard of Bosnia or even knew where it was. Today, such is not the case.

Historical Coverage of Nine Countries

The nine chapters in *Chronology of 20th-Century Eastern European History* focus on the nations of Albania, Bulgaria, Hungary, Poland, and Romania, as well as the former countries of Czechoslovakia, East Germany, and Yugoslavia. Due to its immense influence in the region, especially from 1945 to 1989, a chapter on the former Soviet Union is also included. Each chapter begins with a brief overview of the history of the country and peoples prior to the twentieth century. This is followed by an annual chronological format of significant developments that is further broken down into a day-by-day format for the most important events of each country (*e.g.,* the 1968 "Prague Spring" in Czechoslovakia and the 1956 Hungarian Revolution). The chronologies for Albania, Bulgaria, Hungary, and Romania start around 1900 since all were independent/semi-independent prior to World War I. As the creation of Czechoslovakia, Poland, and Yugoslavia resulted directly from the First World War, and East Germany was the direct product of the Second World War, these chronologies begin with these wars. The chapter on the Soviet Union starts with the Revolutions of 1917, two of the most dramatic and influential episodes in the history of this century because of their role in sparking the Communist regime in Eastern Europe.

Special Features Enhance Volume

This reference volume features a foreword by Drs. Barbara and Charles Jelavich, two of the best, and most well-known scholars on Eastern European history. A comprehensive timeline provides readers with a quick overview of each country's main events in relation to one another and the world. In addition, over 70 brief biographies profile some of the important personalities in the development of their respective countries. An annotated bibliography for each country guides the reader to more specific sources covering the individual countries and the important events discussed therein. Sprinkled throughout the text are over 100 photos and maps that help bring the material to life. The maps, especially, illustrate more vividly the frequent and sometimes drastic geographical changes that have swept this region throughout the century. Included are present-day maps of Albania, Bulgaria, Hungary, Poland, and Romania. The former countries of Czechoslovakia, East Germany, and Yugoslavia each have maps depicting their former configurations, as well as current maps depicting the Czech Republic and Slovakia, united Germany, and the nations of Bosnia and Herzegovina, Croatia, Macedonia, Montenegro, and Slovenia. A current map is also provided detailing the 12 former Soviet republics. Land comparison maps of each country in relation to the United States, excluding the Soviet Union, are provided giving readers an overall perspective of each country.

Acknowledgments

For their interest and support of this project I would like to thank the Drs. Jelavich. Thanks are also extended to the contributors to this project for their hard work, and also to my editors at Gale Research, Allison McNeill and Carol Nagel.

Suggestions Are Welcome

The editor and publisher of the *Chronology of 20th-Century Eastern European History* appreciate suggestions for correction of factual materials and additions or changes that will make future editions of this book more accurate and useful. Please send comments to:

Editor
Chronology of 20th-Century Eastern European History
Gale Research Inc.
835 Penobscot Bldg.
Detroit, MI 48226
Phone: (313)961-2242
FAX: (313)961-6741
Toll-free: 1-800-347-GALE

Gregory C. Ference
June 1994

Contributors

Albania	Dr. Alexandros K. Kyrou *Indiana University—Purdue University at Fort Wayne*	Hungary	Dr. Melissa K. Bokovoy *University of New Mexico*
Bulgaria	Dr. Gregory C. Ference *Salisbury State University*	Poland	Dr. Peter Wozniak *Auburn University at Montgomery*
	Dr. Alexandros K. Kyrou *Indiana University—Purdue University at Fort Wayne*	Romania	Dr. Mari A. Firkatian-Wozniak *American University in Bulgaria*
Czechoslovakia	Dr. Gregory C. Ference *Salisbury State University*	Soviet Union	Bradley L. Schaffner *University of Kansas*
East Germany	Dr. Melvin T. Steely *West Georgia College*	Yugoslavia	Dr. Nicholas J. Miller *Boise State University*

Credits

Photographs appearing in *Chronology of 20th-Century Eastern European History* were received from the following sources:

L'Illustration/Sygma: **p. 17**; Sovfoto: **p. 32**; Keystone/Sygma: **p. 38**; ATA/Eastfoto: **p. 51**; Aldo Pavan/Gamma: **pp. 52, 53**; © 1940/Gamma: **p. 56**; Nikos Economopoulos/ Magnum Photos: **pp 57, 58, 99**; © 1993 Mark Simon/ Black Star: **p. 59**; UPI/Bettmann: **pp 72, 146, 204, 238, 241, 274**; Zentralfoto/Eastfoto: **p. 82**; Christian Vioujard/Gamma: **p. 86**; Alain-Buu/Gamma: **p. 95**; © Patrick Forestier/Sygma: **p. 96**; © 1991 Paul Miller/Black Star: **p. 100**; courtesy of Library of Congress: **pp. 107, 282, 353, 362**; The Granger Collection, New York: **pp. 115, 220, 312**; Photoworld/FPG International: **p. 117**; Eupra-Bildarchiv: **p. 137**; © Josef Kondolka/Magnum Photos, Inc.: **p. 138**; Camera Press London: **p. 139**; Archive Photos/LDE: **pp. 141, 242, 246**; Reuters/Bettmann Newsphotos: **pp. 154, 207, 208, 390, 423**; AP/Wide World Photos: **pp. 156, 174, 189, 244, 245, 250, 251, 278, 288,** **293, 294, 378, 380, 409**; Walter Sanders, *Life Magazine* © Time Warner: **p. 171**; German Information Center: **pp. 188, 201, 205**; © Erich Lessing/Magnum Photos: **p. 243**; Dever from Black Star: **p. 271**; © Raymond Depardon/ Magnum Photos: **p. 273**; Chris Niedenthal/ Black Star © 1981: **p. 291**; Chris Niedenthal/Black Star © 1982: **p. 292**; Robert Capa/Magnum: **p. 295**; Ria-Novosti/Sovfoto: **p. 317**; Rompres/Eastfoto: **pp. 322, 329, 336**; MTI/Eastfoto: **p. 332**; P. Vauthey-Sygma: **p. 333**; Gilles Saussier/Gamma: **p. 334**; Tass from Sovfoto: **p. 342**; Archive Photos/Archive France: **p. 365**; Vlstimir Shone/Gamma Liaison: **p. 371**; © V. Ivleva/Magnum Photos: **p. 373**; © Henry Gris 1993/ FPG International: **p. 381**; Archive Photos: **pp. 408, 415**; Reuters/Bettmann: **p. 422**; © Tom Stoddart/KATZ/ SABA: **p. 431**; © Jon Jones/Sygma: **p. 434**; Nigel Chandler/Sygma: **p. 435**.

Maps appearing in *Chronology of 20th-Century Eastern European History* were received from the U.S. Central Intelligence Agency.

Timeline

1901–09 Theodore Roosevelt serves as U.S. president.

1903 Russia's Social Democratic party splits into two wings—the moderate Mensheviks and the revolutionary Bolsheviks.

1904–05 The Russo-Japanese War.

1905–06 Demonstrations in St. Petersburg, Russia, are crushed by police; known as "Bloody Sunday," the incident touches off the Russian Revolutions.

1908 Francis Joseph I of Austria annexes two Turkish provinces, Bosnia and Herzegovina.

July 24. The rebel group, The Young Turks, forcibly establish a constitutional regime, proclaiming liberty and equality for all nationalities within the Ottoman Empire.

1909–13 William Howard Taft serves as U.S. president.

1912 *October 8.* The First Balkan War begins.

November. Albania declares independence; Turkish rule ends.

1913 *May 7.* A peace conference in St. Petersburg, Russia, marks the end of the First Balkan War.

June 29. The Second Balkan War begins.

1913–21 Woodrow Wilson serves as U.S. president.

1903
Russia's Social Democratic party splits into two wings—the moderate Mensheviks and the revolutionary Bolsheviks.

1908
Francis Joseph I of Austria annexes two Turkish provinces, Bosnia and Herzegovina.

1912
Albania declares independence; Turkish rule ends.

1900   **1904**   **1908**   **1912**

1914

June 28. Archduke Franz Ferdinand, the heir apparent of Austria-Hungary, and his wife are assassinated in Sarajevo. As a result, Austria-Hungary declares war on Serbia. Soon all the major European powers become entangled in what develops as the First World War.

October 10. King Carol, ruler of Romania since 1866, dies; Ferdinand succeeds his uncle Carol as king of Romania.

December 7. The Serbian government issues its Nis Declaration, in which it announces its war aim—unification of all of the South Slavs in one state.

1914–18   World War I

1917

February and October. Russian Revolutions take place.

March. Tsar Nicholas II of Russia abdicates.

April 6. The United States enters World War I.

December 6. The Truce of Focsani is signed ceasing hostilities between the Central Powers and Romania.

1917–22   Russian Revolution and Civil War.

1918

Germany's Wilhelm II abdicates; German Republic proclaimed; Polish Republic proclaimed; Hungary proclaimed an independent republic.

January 7. Vladimir Lenin assumes leadership of the Russian government.

January 8. U.S. president Woodrow Wilson gives his famous Fourteen Points speech outlining American war aims.

March 3. The peace treaty of Brest-Litovsk is signed between Russia and the Central Powers.

May 7. Romania signs the Treaty of Bucharest with the Central Powers.

October 3. King Ferdinand of Bulgaria abdicates leaving his son, Boris III, to succeed him.

October 28. The Czechoslovak republic is proclaimed.

October 29. Croatia declared an independent state.

November 11. World War I ends; Emperor Charles of the Habsburg monarchy steps down from control of the government of Austria-Hungary.

December 3. The National Council passes the act of unification of December 1 officially creating Yugoslavia.

1919

Admiral Miklos Horthy becomes regent of Hungary and rules until 1944.

March 2–7. To facilitate the international spread of Communism, Russian Bolsheviks establish the Communist International (Comintern).

September 10. Yugoslavia signs the Treaty of St. Germain, the peace treaty with Austria after World War I. As a result, Yu-

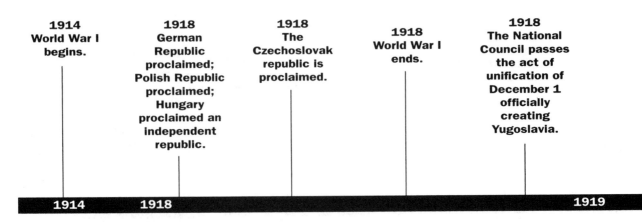

1914
World War I
begins.

1918
German
Republic
proclaimed;
Polish Republic
proclaimed;
Hungary
proclaimed an
independent
republic.

1918
The
Czechoslovak
republic is
proclaimed.

1918
World War I
ends.

1918
The National
Council passes
the act of
unification of
December 1
officially
creating
Yugoslavia.

1914   1918   1919

goslavia officially receives Bosnia-Herzegovina, Slovenia, and Dalmatia.

1919–20 Paris Peace Conference; Treaty of Versailles signed; Adolf Hitler joins German Workers' Party, which becomes the National Socialist (Nazi) Party; Russo-Polish War.

1920 *January 10.* The League of Nations is founded.

April–October. The Polish-Soviet war.

June 4. In the Trianon Palace at Versailles, the Allies and Hungary sign the Trianon Peace Treaty.

August 14. Czechoslovakia and Yugoslavia form a mutual defensive alliance against Hungary by pledging to uphold the Treaty of Trianon marking the beginnings of the Little Entente.

September 14. Romania joins the League of Nations.

1921 *June 7.* The Romanian-Yugoslav alliance is signed, officially forming the Little Entente between Romania, Yugoslavia, and Czechoslovakia.

June 29. Communists attempt to assassinate Serbian Crown Prince Aleksandar.

August 16. Serbia's King Petar Karađorđević dies.

November 6. Prince Aleksandar Karađorđević is crowned king of the Kingdom of Serbs, Croats, and Slovenes.

1921–23. Warren G. Harding serves as U.S. president.

1922 *April 3.* Joseph Stalin becomes general secretary of the Soviet Russian Communist party.

October 15. King Ferdinand and Queen Marie are crowned as the rulers of greater Romania.

December 30. The Bolshevik government establishes the Union of Soviet Socialist Republics through the federation of the republics of Russia, Ukraine, Belorussia, Transcaucasia, Khorezm, Bokhara, and the Far Eastern Republic.

1923–29 Calvin Coolidge serves as U.S. president.

1924 Albanian Republic founded.

January 21. Soviet leader Vladimir Lenin dies.

1925 Hitler organizes Nazi Party; SS formed.

April. Cathedral of Sofia in Bulgaria is bombed.

1926 *December 10.* Serbian and Yugoslav statesman Nicola Pasić dies. His death begins a period of unstable political maneuvering ultimately leading to the dictatorship of King Aleksandar in 1929.

1927 *June 24.* The fascist, terrorist organization known as the Iron Guard is formed in Romania.

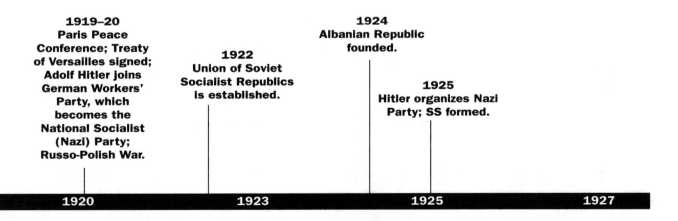

1919–20
Paris Peace Conference; Treaty of Versailles signed; Adolf Hitler joins German Workers' Party, which becomes the National Socialist (Nazi) Party; Russo-Polish War.

1922
Union of Soviet Socialist Republics is established.

1924
Albanian Republic founded.

1925
Hitler organizes Nazi Party; SS formed.

| 1920 | 1923 | 1925 | 1927 |

1928   Stalin becomes leader of the Soviet Communist Party; Albania proclaimed kingdom; Zog I elected king.

1929   *January 6.* Serbia's King Aleksandar proclaims a royal dictatorship and suspends the constitution, dissolves parliament, and abolishes all religious or ethnically-based parties.

October 3. The Kingdom of Yugoslavia is proclaimed by King Aleksandar.

1929–33   Herbert Hoover serves as U.S. president.

1930s   Europe is hit hard by the Great Depression.

1933   Adolph Hitler becomes Chancellor of Germany.

1933–45   Rise of the Third Reich; Nazis take control; all opposition parties banned; civil rights suspended; operation of concentration camps begins for political opponents, Jews, and others, known as the Holocaust.

Franklin D. Roosevelt serves as U.S. president.

1934   *February 8.* The Balkan Pact is concluded between Romania, Yugoslavia, Greece, and Turkey.

October 9. Serbia's King Aleksandar and the French foreign minister are assassinated in Marseilles.

1936–38   Stalin carries out widespread purges within the Soviet Communist Party.

1937   *May 21.* A Soviet plane lands at the North Pole to establish a weather station. The next day, the USSR claims the North Pole as its permanent possession.

1937–40   British prime minister, Neville Chamberlain, attempts policy of appeasement toward Nazi Germany.

1938   *August 23.* The Little Entente dissolves.

September 29. The Munich Conference takes place between Chamberlain, Hitler, Premier Edouard Daladier of France, and Benito Mussolini, the dictator of Italy.

October 1–10. German troops occupy the Sudetenland.

October. Kristallnact; "the night of broken glass."

1939   *March 15.* Hitler nullifies Munich Pact by invading Czechoslovakia.

April. Italian invasion and occupation of Albania; Hitler's armies prepare for "Case White," the invasion of Poland.

August 23. The Nazi-Soviet Nonagression Pact—also known as the Molotov-Ribbentrop Pact, is signed.

August 26. Croatia becomes its own province within Yugoslavia.

September 1. World War II begins with the Nazi invasion of Poland.

1928
Stalin becomes leader of the Soviet Communist Party.

1933
Adolph Hitler becomes Chancellor of Germany.

1933–45
Rise of the Third Reich and the Holocaust.

1939
The Nazi-Soviet Nonagression Pact—also known as the Molotov-Ribbentrop Pact, is signed.

1939
World War II begins with the Nazi invasion of Poland.

| 1928 | 1933 | 1939 |

December 14. The Soviet Union is expelled from the League of Nations.

1939–45 World War II

Late 1940s Soviets engineer Communist takeovers in most East European countries.

1940 Concentration camps, including Auschwitz, are established around Poland; thousands of Jews are confined to the Warsaw ghetto.

July 10. Romania withdraws from the League of Nations.

October 19–23. Josip Broz's (Tito) position as head of the Communist Party of Yugoslavia is secured.

1941 *March 1.* The Tripartite Pact is signed in Vienna.

March 25. Yugoslavia joins the Tripartite Pact.

April 10. The Independent State of Croatia is proclaimed.

April 14–16. King Petar II and the royal Yugoslav government go into exile in Athens.

May 6. Joseph Stalin assumes the post of Soviet Union premier or chairman of the Council of People's Commissars.

June 22. "Operation Barbarossa:" Germany invades the Soviet Union. Italy also declares war on Soviet Union.

December 7. Great Britain and U.S. declare war on Japan.

1941–45 Ante Pavelić's regime institutes a policy of elimination of the Serbian Orthodox minority of Croatia through expulsion, conversion to Roman Catholicism, and extermination. Gypsies, Jews, and Croatian opponents of the regime are also exterminated.

1943 Wladyslaw Gomulka becomes the leader of the Polish Communist Party.

April–May. The Warsaw Ghetto Uprising.

November 28. The Teheran Conference convenes U.S. president Franklin Delano Roosevelt, British prime minister Winston Churchill, and Soviet dictator Joseph Stalin.

1944 *June 6.* United States, Canadian, and British forces invade the beaches at Normandy, signalling the Allied invasion of western Europe; known as D-Day.

July 23. Death camps are first discovered by Allied forces.

August–October. The Warsaw Uprising.

October. Enver Hoxha, commander in chief of the Albania National Liberation Army and acknowledged ACP leader, is named premier.

October 9. Winston Churchill meets with Soviet leader Joseph Stalin in Moscow where the two divide up the Balkans.

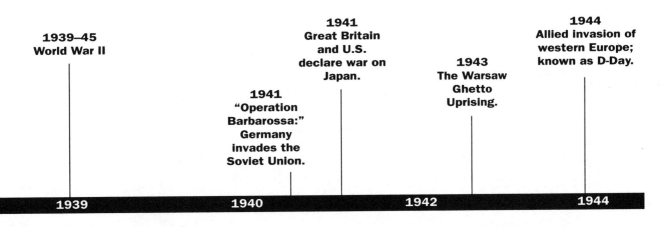

1939–45
World War II

1941
Great Britain and U.S. declare war on Japan.

1941
"Operation Barbarossa:" Germany invades the Soviet Union.

1943
The Warsaw Ghetto Uprising.

1944
Allied invasion of western Europe; known as D-Day.

1939   **1940**   **1942**   **1944**

1944–45 Soviet troops trounce Germans in Poland, Hungary, and most of Czechoslovakia and occupy all three countries.

1945 The Soviet Union invades Bulgaria.

January 17. Soviet forces liberate Warsaw.

February 4–11. The Yalta Conference takes place between Winston Churchill, Franklin Roosevelt, and Joseph Stalin in the Crimea.

March 7. Tito becomes prime minister of Yugoslavia.

April 11. The Yugoslav government signs a 20-year treaty of friendship and mutual aid with the Soviet Union.

April 13. Soviet forces capture Vienna.

May 7. Germany surrenders to the Americans at Reims.

May 8. The German army unconditionally surrenders to the Allies, officially ending the European theater of the Second World War; known as VE Day.

July 17. Harry S Truman, Winston Churchill and Clement Attlee meet with Stalin at the Potsdam Conference to discuss the specifics of the occupation and the future of Germany.

August 6. First atomic bomb dropped on Hiroshima, Japan.

August 8. The Soviet Union declares war on Japan.

August 9. Second atomic bomb dropped on Nagasaki, Japan.

September 2. Japan surrenders; known as VJ Day.

November 29. The Federal People's Republic of Yugoslavia is proclaimed by the Constituent Assembly. The Karađorđević dynasty is banished and the monarchy is abolished.

1945–53 Harry S Truman serves as U.S. president.

1946 *March 5.* Winston Churchill delivers his "Iron Curtain" speech in Fulton, Missouri.

July 9. The Yugoslav-Albanian Treaty of Friendship, Cooperation, and Mutual Assistance is concluded in Tirana.

1946–47 Soviet Union's control of Eastern Europe leads to increasing East-West tensions and beginning of Cold War.

1947 Meeting of Big Four (U.S., USSR, Great Britain, and France) on divided Germany's economic future; People's Republic of Romania proclaimed.

February 10. The signing of peace treaties in Paris formally terminates the state of war between the Allies and Italy, Finland, Romania, Bulgaria, and Hungary.

March 12. Truman unveils the Truman Doctrine which supports the rights of nations to formulate their own destinies.

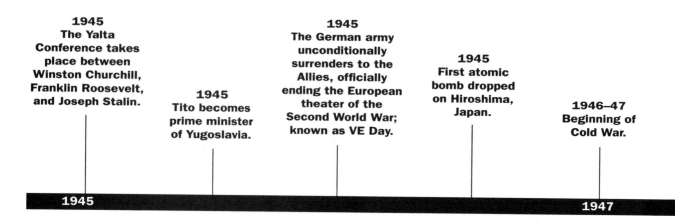

1945
The Yalta Conference takes place between Winston Churchill, Franklin Roosevelt, and Joseph Stalin.

1945
Tito becomes prime minister of Yugoslavia.

1945
The German army unconditionally surrenders to the Allies, officially ending the European theater of the Second World War; known as VE Day.

1945
First atomic bomb dropped on Hiroshima, Japan.

1946–47
Beginning of Cold War.

1945 **1947**

October 5. The Communist Information Bureau (Cominform) is established.

1948   *February 25.* Communists legally take control of the Czechoslovak government in what is referred to as the "February Coup."

June 28. Yugoslavia is expelled from the Soviet Bloc, marking the complete break between Stalin and Tito.

October 10. The Soviets test launch the first long-range guided missile.

1948–49   The Soviet and East German blockade of West Berlin requires Western airlift efforts. The Blockade is lifted after 328 days in May, 1949.

1948–52   Defection of Yugoslavia from the Soviet bloc provokes extensive purges in Eastern Europe's Communist Parties.

1949   Federal Republic of Germany (West Germany) created from U.S., British, and French occupation zones; Konrad Adenauer elected its first chancellor.

January 25. The Council for Mutual Economic Aid (CMEA or Comecon) is established.

April 4. The North Atlantic Treaty is signed in Washington D.C., establishing a defensive alliance, NATO, aimed at the Soviet bloc.

September 25. The Soviet news agency TASS reports the testing of the first Soviet atomic bomb.

October. Yugoslavia is elected to a seat on the United Nations Security Council.

July 13. The Vatican excommunicates all members and sympathizers of the Communist party from the Roman Catholic Church.

1949–71   Walter Ulbricht is made leader of the German Democratic Republic (East Germany).

1950–52   Soviet pacts declaring friendship and economic collaboration are signed with Communist China.

1950–53   Korean War

1953   *January 13.* Tito is made the president of the Republic of Yugoslavia, a position abolished upon his death in 1980.

March 5. Joseph Stalin dies.

April 3. Carol II, former king of Romania, dies in exile in Portugal.

August 12. The Soviet Union test explodes a hydrogen bomb.

September 13. Nikita S. Khrushchev becomes the first secretary of the Communist party.

1953–61   Dwight D. Eisenhower serves as U.S. president.

1954   *June 30.* The Soviets announce the operation of the first atomic electric power plant in the USSR.

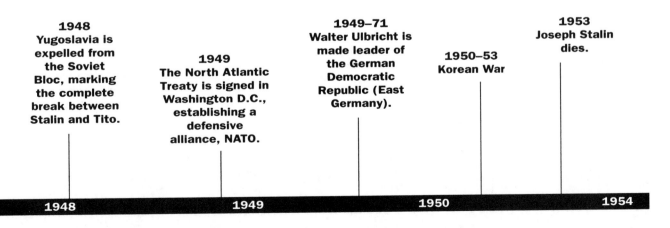

1948
Yugoslavia is expelled from the Soviet Bloc, marking the complete break between Stalin and Tito.

1949
The North Atlantic Treaty is signed in Washington D.C., establishing a defensive alliance, NATO.

1949–71
Walter Ulbricht is made leader of the German Democratic Republic (East Germany).

1950–53
Korean War

1953
Joseph Stalin dies.

1948   1949   1950   1954

1955

May 9. West Germany is formally admitted into NATO.

May 14. The Warsaw Pact Treaty is signed by the USSR, Albania, Bulgaria, Czechoslovakia, Hungary, Poland and Romania.

May 15. The Austrian State Treaty is signed and the Soviets withdraw their troops soon after.

December 15. Albania is admitted as a member of the United Nations.

1956

Mid–February. Khrushchev formally initiates the policy of de-Stalinization in his speech to the Twentieth Congress of the Communist Party of the Soviet Union.

April 17. The Cominform is dissolved.

October 19. The Soviet government and Japan sign a joint declaration ending the state of war between the two nations and establishing diplomatic ties.

October–November. Hungarian Revolution explodes in the streets of Budapest. Uprising is soon crushed by a massive deployment of Soviet troops; Janos Kádár appointed head of new, Soviet-backed government to replace regime of Imre Nagy.

1957

European Economic Community established.

August 26. The Soviet government announces that it has successfully tested an intercontinental multi-stage ballistic missile.

October 4. The Soviet Union launches the first successful space satellite, *Sputnik.*

1958

October 23. The Nobel Prize for Literature is awarded to Soviet writer Boris Pasternak for his novel *Doctor Zhivago,* which will not be published in the Soviet Union until the end of the 1980s.

1959

May 11. The conference of foreign ministers (U.S., France, Great Britain, and USSR) opens in Geneva to discuss the German question.

July 24. The "Kitchen Debate" takes place between Khrushchev and American vice-president Richard Nixon at a U.S. exhibition in Moscow.

1960

May 1. Soviet forces shoot down a U.S. U-2 spy plane and capture its pilot, Francis Gary Powers.

1961

April 12. Soviet cosmonaut, Yuri Gagarin, becomes the first person successfully to orbit the earth.

April 30. The Soviet Union awards the 1960 Lenin Peace Prize to Cuban Prime Minister Fidel Castro.

August 13. The Berlin wall is erected.

November 1. Ivo Andrić, a Bosnian Serb writer, receives the Nobel Prize for Literature.

December 3. The Soviet Union breaks diplomatic relations with Albania, with-

---

1955
The Warsaw Pact Treaty is signed by the USSR, Albania, Bulgaria, Czechoslovakia, Hungary, Poland and Romania.

1956
Hungarian Revolution explodes in the streets of Budapest.

1957
The Soviet Union launches the first successful space satellite, *Sputnik.*

1961
The Berlin wall is erected.

1955   **1957**   **1959**   **1961**

drawing all Soviet personnel from the country—an act without precedent in the history of the Communist camp.

1961–63 John F. Kennedy serves as U.S. president.

1962–63 The Cuban Missile Crisis.

1962–73 The Vietnam War.

1963 The USSR signs the Nuclear Test-Ban Treaty with Great Britain.

June 16. Soviet cosmonaut Valentina Tereshkova becomes the first woman to travel in outer space.

June 20. The United States and Soviet Union agree to establish a "hot line," a direct phone line between the White House and the Kremlin. It is installed on August 31.

June 27. American president John F. Kennedy delivers his "Ich bin ein Berliner" speech at Berlin's Tegel Airport.

November 22. John F. Kennedy is assassinated in Dallas, Texas.

1963–69 Lyndon B. Johnson serves as U.S. president.

1964 *June 12.* Khrushchev and East German president Walter Ulbricht sign a 20-year treaty of friendship that asserts the legal existence of the Communist party in East Germany.

October 14–15. Khrushchev is forced to resign as premier of the Soviet government and as first secretary of the Communist party. Leonid I. Brezhnev is appointed first secretary and Aleksei Kosygin, premier.

1965 *March 19.* Nicolae Ceausescu becomes Romania's first secretary of the Workers' party.

October 15. Soviet author Mikhail Sholokov is awarded the Nobel Prize for Literature.

1966 *February 3.* The Soviet spacecraft *Luna 9,* launched on January 13, completes the first successful "soft" landing without damage on the moon and begins transmitting signals to earth.

1967 *October 30.* The Soviet Union accomplishes the first unmanned docking of two satellites in space.

1968 Alexander Dubček introduces liberal reforms in Czechoslovakia known as Prague Spring.

March 23. Warsaw Pact leaders warn the Czechoslovak leaders, Alexander Dubček, Jozef Lenárt, and others, not to let their liberalizing program get out of hand.

July 1. Sixty-two nations, including the Soviet Union, sign the nuclear nonproliferation treaty.

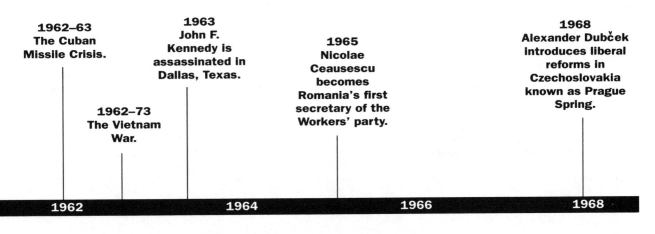

July 15. Pan American World Airways and Aeroflot, the Soviet national airlines, open the first direct flights between the United States and the Soviet Union.

August 20–21. Warsaw Pact invasion of Czechoslovakia.

September 13. Albania formally withdraws from the Warsaw Pact.

September 26. Pravda reports on the ideological doctrine used to justify the invasion of Czechoslovakia. This doctrine subsequently comes to be known as the "Brezhnev Doctrine."

1969 Willy Brandt becomes chancellor of West Germany.

January 16. As a protest against the Soviet military occupation of Czechoslovakia and the abandonment of the reforms, philosophy student Jan Palach sets himself on fire in Wenceslas Square in Prague, and dies three days later.

March 2. Soviet and Chinese forces battle over Damanskii (Chenpao) Island, disputed territory in the Ussuri river. During 1969 there will be over four hundred skirmishes along the Sino-Soviet border resulting in no change of territory.

November. In Helsinki, the U.S. and USSR begin the first round of Strategic Arms Limitations Talks (SALT).

November 24. Soviet president Nikolai Podgorny and American president Richard Nixon sign the nuclear nonproliferation treaty.

1969–74 Richard M. Nixon serves as U.S. president.

1970 *January 15–17.* The "Croatian Spring," as it will come to be known, is a movement motivated by a desire of Croatians to see Croatia autonomous.

June 19. The Soviet spacecraft *Soyuz 9* returns to earth after a record-setting flight of seventeen days.

October 8. Soviet novelist Alexandr I. Solzhenitsyn wins the Nobel Prize for Literature.

October 29. American and Soviet officials sign the first cooperative space effort agreement.

December. Lenin Shipyard massacre in Gdańsk, Poland.

1971 *June 30. Soyuz 11* cosmonauts are found dead in their reentry capsule after completing a new space endurance record.

September 11. Former Soviet leader Nikita S. Khrushchev dies in Moscow.

November 14. Romania becomes a member of GATT (General Agreement on Trade and Tariffs).

1972 *May 22–30.* President Nixon arrives in Moscow for the first official visit of a U.S. president to the Soviet Union. Brezhnev and Nixon sign the first Strategic Arms Limitations Treaty (SALT I).

June 3. The Soviet Union, the United States, France, and Great Britain sign the

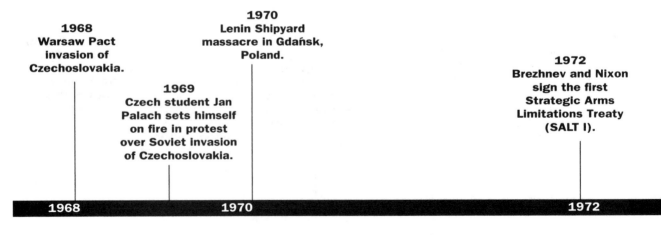

1968
Warsaw Pact invasion of Czechoslovakia.

1970
Lenin Shipyard massacre in Gdańsk, Poland.

1969
Czech student Jan Palach sets himself on fire in protest over Soviet invasion of Czechoslovakia.

1972
Brezhnev and Nixon sign the first Strategic Arms Limitations Treaty (SALT I).

1968   **1970**   **1972**

"final protocol" of the Quadripartite Agreement on Berlin.

1973   *April 19.* The Soviets launch the *Intercosmos-Copernicus 500,* a joint endeavor of Czechoslovakia, Poland, and the USSR, that will measure the sun's radiation and the earth's ionosphere.

May 10. The West German parliament (Bundestag) ratifies the treaty that will establish formal relations between East and West Germany.

1974   *March 28.* The Grand National Assembly elects Nicolae Ceausescu president of the Socialist Republic of Romania.

1974–77   Gerald R. Ford serves as U.S. president.

1975   *July 17–19.* The Soviets and Americans conduct joint space maneuvers. An *Apollo* and *Soyuz* spacecraft link together on July 17.

July 30–August 1. The Final Act of the Conference on Security and Cooperation in Europe, known as the Helsinki Accords, is signed by 35 nations.

October 9. Andrei Sakharov wins the Nobel Peace Prize for his work in fighting for civil liberties and human rights. He becomes the first Soviet citizen to win the prize.

1976   *July 1.* The prime minister of India, Indira Gandhi, arrives in East Berlin on the first official visit to East Germany by the leader of a noncommunist government.

1977   Charter 77 manifesto in Czechoslovakia criticizes government for violating 1975 Helsinki Accords guarranteeing human rights.

March 4. An earthquake strikes Romania destroying large sections of Bucharest.

1977   *June 16.* Brezhnev becomes the first Soviet leader to hold both the post of party general secretary and president at the same time.

1977–81   James Carter serves as U.S. president.

1978   Polish Cardinal Wojtyla is elected pope and takes the name John Paul II.

June 16–18. Brezhnev and Jimmy Carter hold a summit meeting in Vienna. On June 18, they formally sign the SALT II treaty, but it still needs to be ratified by the U.S. Senate.

1979   *December 27.* The Soviet Union invades Afghanistan. Afghan president Hafizullah Amin is ousted and murdered in a Soviet-backed coup.

1980   Lech Walesa begins organizing the Polish independent trade union that will come to be known as Solidarity (Solidarnos).

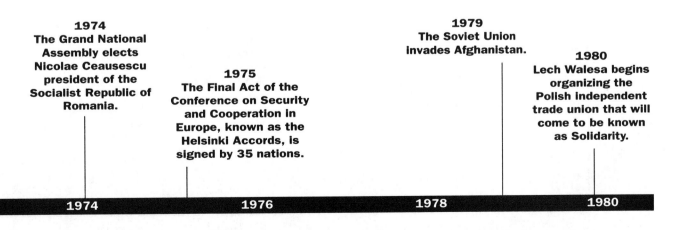

1974
The Grand National Assembly elects Nicolae Ceausescu president of the Socialist Republic of Romania.

1975
The Final Act of the Conference on Security and Cooperation in Europe, known as the Helsinki Accords, is signed by 35 nations.

1979
The Soviet Union invades Afghanistan.

1980
Lech Walesa begins organizing the Polish independent trade union that will come to be known as Solidarity.

1974   **1976**   **1978**   **1980**

January. As a result of the Soviet invasion of Afghanistan, further consideration of SALT II by the Senate is halted; Carter also restricts grain sales to the Soviet Union.

May 4. Yugoslav president Josip Tito dies.

July 19. The XXII Summer Olympic Games open in Moscow. Many nations, including the United States and West Germany, boycott the Games in protest of the 1979 Soviet invasion of Afghanistan.

1981   *April 24.* President Reagan lifts the U.S. embargo on the sale of grain to the Soviet Union.

December. Martial law is declared in Poland. It is suspended one year later.

December 29. Reagan imposes sanctions against the USSR for the imposition of martial law in Poland.

1981–89   Ronald Reagan serves as U.S. president.

1982   Poland bans Solidarity.

November 10. Leonid Brezhnev dies.

1984   *February.* The 1984 Winter Olympics are held in Sarajevo. Forty-nine countries participate in the first Games to be held in Eastern Europe.

July 28. The XXIII Summer Olympic Games open in Los Angeles, California.

The Soviet Union, East Germany, and Bulgaria refuse to participate because of "inadequate security." In actuality their refusal stems from the U.S. boycott of the 1980 Games in Moscow.

August 18. Friendship '84, the Soviet Union's sport festival for nations who pulled out of the Summer Olympics, begins in Moscow.

1985   *February.* Mikhail Gorbachev announces that the Soviet Union must follow a policy of glasnost (openness).

March 11. Gorbachev is declared general secretary of the Communist party.

April. Albanian leader Enver Hoxha dies at the age of 76. Ramiz Alia is named party first secretary.

April 26. Representatives of Bulgaria, Czechoslovakia, Hungary, Poland, Romania, and the Soviet Union sign a 20-year extension of their Warsaw Pact treaty.

November 19–21. Mikhail Gorbachev and Ronald Reagan meet in Geneva, Switzerland for the first summit between American and Soviet leaders since 1979.

1986   *April–May.* An accident at the Chernobyl nuclear power plant in the Ukraine kills twenty people. Thousands more will subsequently die as a result of the radiation leak. Radiation is detected worldwide.

June 20. A report by the human rights organization Helsinki Watch accuses Bul-

1980
The XXII Summer Olympic Games open in Moscow.

1981
Martial law is declared in Poland.

1985
Mikhail Gorbachev is declared general secretary of the Communist party.

1986
Accident at the Chernobyl nuclear power plant in the Ukraine.

| 1980 | 1982 | 1984 | 1986 |

garia of killing up to 1,500 Bulgarian Turks since 1984 in its attempt to Slavicize and Christianize them.

1987   *September 7–12.* Erich Honecker visits West Germany and is greeted by Helmut Kohl thereby becoming the first East German leader to visit West Germany.

December 8. Gorbachev and Reagan sign the INF (Intermediate Nuclear Forces) treaty abolishing intermediate-range nuclear missiles.

1988   Gorbachev becomes president of Soviet Union.

May 15. Soviet troops begin to leave Afghanistan.

August 17. The U.S. and USSR conduct a joint nuclear test in Nevada.

December 7. An earthquake destroys several cities in Armenia SSR.

1989   *April 25.* The USSR begins its military reduction in Eastern Europe by removing 31 heavy tanks from Hungary.

May 2. Hungary is the first country to dismantle the barbed wire fence ("iron curtain") along its border with Austria.

May 15–18. Gorbachev becomes the first Soviet leader to visit China since 1959.

June. Pro-democracy demonstrators occupy Tiananmen Square in Peking, China; the occupation lasts seven weeks un-

til the government imposes martial law; it is believed that thousands die.

June 8. Due to the oppression of the Bulgarian Turks, Turkey opens its border allowing over 300,000 refugees to stream in until late August when the border is again closed.

August 23. Two million people form a human chain across Estonia, Latvia, and Lithuania to commemorate the 50th anniversary of the Soviet occupation of the countries.

August 24. Tadeusz Mazowiecki forms Poland's first non-Communist government in more than 40 years.

September. Hundreds of East Germans flee over the Hungarian border into Austria, signifying that Hungary is no longer a member of the Soviet bloc.

October 26. Gorbachev abandons the "Brezhnev Doctrine" and states that the Soviet Union has no moral or political right to interfere with the events taking place in Eastern Europe.

November–December. The Velvet Revolution in Czechoslovakia.

November 9. The Berlin Wall, a symbol of the Cold War and Communist repression, is taken down, resulting in free travel between East and West Germany.

November 10. In Bulgaria, Todor Zhivkov, who has controlled the country since 1954, resigns as president of the

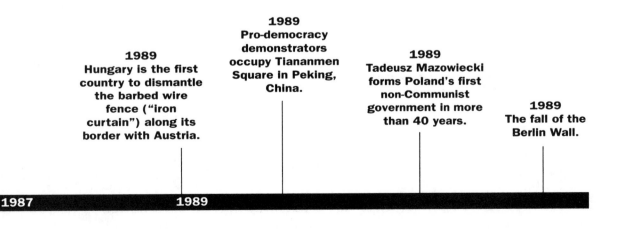

country and general secretary of the Communist party.

December 4. Five members of the Warsaw Pact jointly condemn the 1968 invasion of Czechoslovakia.

December 20. The Lithuanian Communist party declares itself independent of the Communist party of the Soviet Union.

December 22. The famous Brandenburg Gate, the symbol of Germany, reopens.

December 25. Romanian leader Nicolae Ceausescu and his wife Elena are found guilty of genocide against the Romanian people and sentenced to death; they are shot immediately. The proceedings are videotaped and broadcast worldwide.

1989–93 George Bush serves as U.S. president.

1990 *January–December.* Stalinism comes to an end in Albania as the Alia regime attempts to quell growing unrest through concessions.

May 9. The Estonian Soviet Socialist Republic changes its name to the Republic of Estonia and reinstates its prewar constitution.

May 29. Boris Yeltsin becomes president of the Russian Soviet Federated Socialist Republic.

July 5–6. During a meeting in London, the leaders of NATO declare that the Cold War is over.

October 3. Germany is officially reunited.

December. Lech Walesa becomes president of Poland.

1991 *January–April.* The Persian Gulf War.

March 16. The Serbian region of Croatia declares independence from Croatia; the region is now called the Serbian Autonomous Region of Krajina.

June. Croatia and Slovenia declare independence from Yugoslavia; the USSR and Czechoslovakia sign an agreement formally ending the twenty-three-year Soviet occupation of the country.

June 28. Comecon, the economic equivalent of the Warsaw Pact founded in 1949, officially ends.

July 1. The Warsaw Pact is formally dissolved.

July 30–31. Gorbachev and Bush meet in Moscow to sign the Strategic Arms Reduction Treaty (START).

August 19. The Soviet Vice-President Gennadi I. Yanayev and seven other members of a State Committee for the State of Emergency in the USSR take over the government in an attempted coup. A state of emergency is declared.

August 20. Estonia proclaims its independence from the Soviet Union.

August 21. The August 19 Soviet coup collapses.

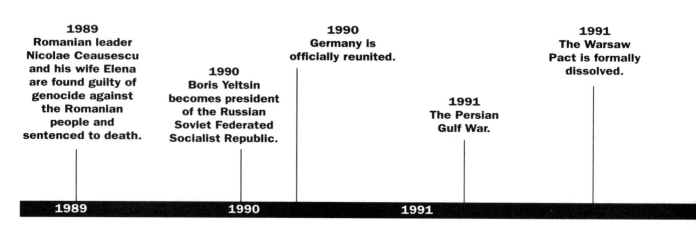

1989
Romanian leader
Nicolae Ceausescu
and his wife Elena
are found guilty of
genocide against
the Romanian
people and
sentenced to death.

1990
Boris Yeltsin
becomes president
of the Russian
Soviet Federated
Socialist Republic.

1990
Germany is
officially reunited.

1991
The Persian
Gulf War.

1991
The Warsaw
Pact is formally
dissolved.

1989   1990   1991

August 24. Ukraine declares independence from the Soviet Union.

August 25. Belorussia declares independence from the Soviet Union.

August 27. Moldavia declares independence from the Soviet Union. Georgia, Armenia, and the Central Asian republics soon follow.

September 25. The United Nations Security Council places an embargo on arms shipments to all parts of the former Yugoslavia.

December 8. Yeltsin and the leaders of eleven of the former Soviet republics sign an agreement creating the Commonwealth of Independent states to replace the Union of Soviet Socialist Republics. Georgia, Estonia, Latvia, and Lithuania do not join.

December 21. Serbian leaders in Bosnia and Herzegovina declare their intention to form a Yugoslav republic of the Serbian areas of Bosnia and Herzegovina.

December 25. Gorbachev resigns as president of the USSR and the Soviet Union formally ceases to exist.

1992

January 9. The self-proclaimed Serbian Assembly of the Autonomous Region of Bosanska Krajina declares its independence from Bosnia and Herzegovina.

February 1. Meeting at Camp David, George Bush and Boris Yeltsin declare a formal end to the Cold War.

March. McDonald's opens its first restaurant in Prague, Czechoslovakia.

April. Serbia and Montenegro proclaim a new Federal Republic of Yugoslavia and claim the new state is the legitimate successor to the old Yugoslavia.

May 14. The first accusations of massacres between Serbs and Muslims surface in former Yugoslavia.

October 28. The last Soviet combat troops stationed in Poland leave.

1993

Warring factions in Bosnia sign a Christmas cease-fire that is to last until January 15, 1994. Nonetheless, the fighting continues.

January 1. Czechoslovakia ceases to exist and splits into two independent parts: the Czech Republic and Slovakia.

January 9. Bosnia and Herzegovina's Deputy Prime Minister Hakija Turajlić is murdered by Serb gunmen.

February 11. Warren Christopher, the U.S. secretary of state, announces the United States' six-point support plan for Bosnia and Herzegovina.

April 8. Macedonia becomes the 181st member of the United Nations and is called the Former Yugoslav Republic of Macedonia.

June 22. The European Community formally invites the Czech Republic, Slovakia, Bulgaria, Hungary, Poland, and Romania to apply for membership.

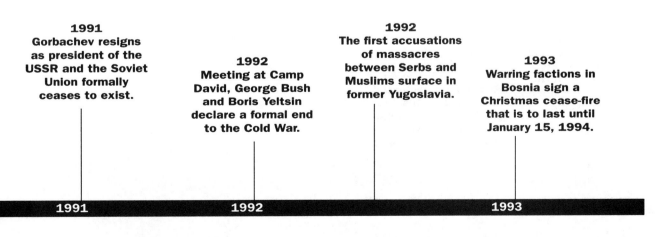

1991
Gorbachev resigns as president of the USSR and the Soviet Union formally ceases to exist.

1992
Meeting at Camp David, George Bush and Boris Yeltsin declare a formal end to the Cold War.

1992
The first accusations of massacres between Serbs and Muslims surface in former Yugoslavia.

1993
Warring factions in Bosnia sign a Christmas cease-fire that is to last until January 15, 1994.

1991   1992   1993

September 2. The United States and Russia agree to develop an international space station.

October 5. Yeltsin begins to rule Russia by presidential decree. The Russian White House is sealed off and a state of emergency is declared.

November 17. The Yugoslav war crimes tribunal meets for the first time at the Hague.

1993– William Clinton serves as U.S. president.

1993
Czechoslovakia ceases to exist and splits into two independent parts: the Czech Republic and Slovakia.

1993
Yeltsin begins to rule Russia by presidential decree. The Russian White House is sealed off and a state of emergency is declared.

1993

Chapter One

ALBANIA

The Albanians call themselves Shqiptarë (Sons of the Eagle) and their country Shqipëria (Land of the Eagle), but the term Albanian derives from Albanoi, the Greek name for these people. The name Albanoi first appeared in the second century A.D. referring only to one tribe of people north of Tirana, but by the eleventh century the Byzantine Greeks called all Albanians Albanoi. The Indo-European ancestors of the Albanians, the ancient Illyrians, entered the Balkan peninsula probably before the arrival of the Greeks in the second millennium B.C. The Illyrian tribes settled in most of the northwestern Balkans and united into a kingdom in the third century B.C. with its center at Shkodër (Scutari).

In 167 B.C. the Illyrian kingdom was conquered by Rome. For many centuries the Illyrians were a major source of military manpower and leadership for the Roman Empire. In the early Byzantine period the Slavs, then a new force, pressured the Illyrians. Crossing the Danube River in the late sixth century, Slavic tribes for the next five centuries pushed the Illyrians progressively south, until their lands were reduced to the area roughly constituting modern Albania. The Byzantines crushed the Slavs in the early eleventh century and reasserted their control over Albania. Nevertheless, from the late eleventh century to the fourteenth century Albania was a battleground between the Angevins, Bulgars, Byzantines, Greek Byzantine successor states, Normans, Serbs, and Venetians, who each successively invaded and dominated the region. With the collapse of Stephen Dusan's Serbian Empire in the mid-fourteenth century, this chaotic period of foreign rule ended, and Albania passed to the control of native lords.

Before the independent feudal lords were able to form a cohesive Albanian state the country was invaded again, this time by the Ottoman Turks in 1385. In 1444 local lords formed the Albanian league. The lords elected to unite their forces under a single leader, George Kastrioti, the celebrated Skënderbeg (Common Alexander, after Alexander the Great). Skënderbeg successfully expelled the Turks from Albania in a series of brilliant campaigns from 1444 to his death in 1468. Resistance continued, but gradually the Turks extended their rule over all of Albania. A mass exodus followed the Ottoman victories in the late fifteenth and early sixteenth centuries. Refugees established large settlements in southern Italy and Sicily, where modern Albanian nationalism emerged four centuries later.

Ottoman Turkish rule contributed to the religious and social differences among the Albanians. Whereas Albanians before the Turkish conquest were Greek Orthodox in the center and south and Roman Catholic in the north of the country, the majority gradually converted to Islam. Some forced conversions took place in the seventeenth century, but most Albanians embraced Islam voluntarily to gain advantages from the Ottoman Empire's religion-based system of administration and taxation, which favored Muslims.

The Albanians were, and are, divided between two subgroups, the Ghegs in the north and the Tosks in the south, with the Shkumbi River separating them. The two groups speak dialects that differ considerably, and under Turkish rule the Ghegs and Tosks experienced dissimilar patterns of government and social development. In northern Albania, the converted Muslim tribal chiefs were accepted as de facto rulers of their country in exchange for

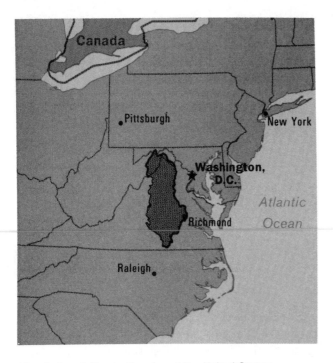

Albania in relation to the size of the United States.

military service. The Ghegs in the north, therefore, enjoyed considerable freedom in the management of their own affairs due to their great geographic isolation, whereas the Tosks in the south were not afforded the same level of self-government. Southern Albania was dominated by large landowners, rather than by autonomous tribal chiefs. Whereas the Ghegs provided military contingents to the Turks in time of war, the Tosks were increasingly prominent in the Ottomans' administrative and diplomatic services.

Despite some challenges to the authority of the sultan in the beginning of the nineteenth century, the Albanians remained the Ottomans' loyalist Balkan subjects. The Albanians' position in the Ottoman Empire did not change until the late nineteenth century. Beginning in the 1860s, intellectuals in the Albanian communities in Italy stimulated national consciousness and pride through patriotic literature. Albanian leaders in the homeland, influenced by the nationalist awakening in Italy, were shocked by the March 1878 Treaty of San Stefano, concluding the Russo-Turkish War of 1877–78, which awarded considerable Albanian territory to Bulgaria. On June 10, 1878, Albanian leaders met in the city of Prizren in Kosovo and organized the Albanian League for the Defense of the Rights of the Albanian Nation, commonly known as the League of Prizren. The league sought two objectives: to resist any foreign attempt to annex Albanian

land, and to obtain an autonomous status for Albania within the Ottoman Empire. Meanwhile, to keep a large Bulgarian state from being realized, the Western Great Powers intervened to reverse San Stefano.

In a subsequent international conference and treaty—the Berlin Congress and the Treaty of Berlin of July 1878—the Great Powers assigned much less territory to Bulgaria than proposed at San Stefano. Regardless, the League of Prizren complained that the new frontiers drawn by the Treaty of Berlin assigned Albanian territory to Montenegro. The Great Powers dismissed the league's protests, and in response the Albanians successfully took up arms against Montenegrin forces. With the sanction of the Great Powers, the Turks dispatched an army to subdue the Albanians and in November 1880 delivered the disputed territory to the Montenegrins. While fighting the Montenegrins in the north, the league opposed Greek expansionism in the south. The Greek representatives at the Congress of Berlin demanded Epirus and Thessaly from the Ottoman Empire, and the league organized a considerable force in Epirus to stop any potential Greek advance. In 1881 the Greeks acquired most of Thessaly but only a small portion of southern Epirus.

While the new frontiers were being drawn, the league turned to its second objective, autonomy for Albania. The Albanian leaders demanded that all predominantly Albanian lands be united into one autonomous region within the Ottoman Empire. The Turks opposed the proposal, and the league responded by resisting Ottoman authority. The Turks, in turn, sent an army into Albania and imposed rule by force. Although the Turks suppressed the league in 1881, its program continued to influence Albanian nationalist thought and revolutionary activity during the remainder of the nineteenth century and beyond. Until 1892 Albanian nationalists in exile in Bulgaria, Egypt, and Romania organized committees promoting the cause of Albanian autonomy.

Meanwhile in 1879 the Society for the Printing of Albanian Writings (the Society of Istanbul) was founded in Constantinople. The Society won permission from the Ottoman authorities to publish a monthly periodical in Albanian, *Drita* (Light), later titled *Dituria* (Knowledge), which first appeared in August 1884. The society's work was officially linguistic and cultural, but its true mission was to instill nationalist political sentiment in the struggle for autonomy. In the following year the Ottoman government permitted the first entirely Albanian-language school in Korcë (Korytsa), opened by the Istanbul Society. Between 1895 and 1897 the Albanian National Society was

founded in the Italo–Albanian colonies and established branches in every Albanian community in southern Italy and Sicily. The society began publication of *La Nazione Albanese,* its official organ, in which Italo-Albanian and homeland Albanian writers collaborated.

1900

The Italian government establishes a chair of Albanian language and literature at the Instituto Orientale in Naples.

1902

The Ottoman government takes increasingly extreme measures to suppress the growing autonomy movement. The Turks close the Albanian School of Korcë, arrest a number of teachers, and ban all Albanian books and correspondence in the Albanian language.

1905

November Responding to Ottoman oppression, a secret revolutionary organization, the Committee for the Freedom of Albania, is founded by a group of young nationalists in Bitola (Monastir). Under the leadership of the teacher Bajo Topulli, the committee establishes clandestine cells in a number of Albanian towns. Closely connected to the Albanian nationalist societies abroad, the committee favors complete independence.

1906

January Topulli organizes the first armed bands of the Committee for the Freedom of Albania in the mountains in the district of Korcë.

March 1906–July 1908 Armed bands of the Committee for the Freedom of Albania expand throughout southern Albania. They conduct increasingly aggressive raids on Ottoman police and army detachments and also attack rival Greek bands and the Greek minority, especially in the districts of Gjirokastër (Argyrokastron) and Korcë.

1908

March Platon, the Russian archbishop of New York, establishes the Albanian Orthodox Church of America.

The Albanian church is organized as a missionary church under the jurisdiction of the Russian Orthodox church. With the appointment of Fan Stylian Noli as its bishop, the Albanian Orthodox Church of America is elevated to an independent diocese in 1919.

July Inspired by reformist intellectuals and resentful of the increasingly inefficient and corrupt imperial administration, elements of the Ottoman army revolt against the government. The Young Turks, as the rebels are called, force the sultan to accept a liberal constitution on July 24, establishing a constitutional regime and proclaiming liberty and equality for all nationalities within the Ottoman Empire.

July 1908–April 1909 Liberalization under the Young Turks unleashes nationalism in Albania and leads to an outburst of educational activities. Approximately 60 schools are established, and a National Board of Education is created at a congress held at Elbasan in August. At the same time, four Albanian-language printing presses and 17 newspapers begin publication. In November a congress of representatives from all parts of Albania and the Albanian communities abroad convenes at Bitola to decide on a common alphabet. Instead of the Arabic script or Greek, used by most Muslim and Orthodox Albanians, respectively, the congress unanimously adopts the Latin alphabet, thus promoting Albanian unity.

1909

April 1909–February 1910 The Young Turks, alarmed by the magnitude of the Albanian national awakening, are committed to a centralization of the Ottoman Empire and are opposed to further fragmentation along national lines. Reacting to a failed counterrevolution against them, the Young Turks vigorously enforce their policy of centralization founded on the Turkification of all groups within the Ottoman Empire. The Young Turks now require Turkish to be the language of instruction in all Albanian schools and in all schools in the Ottoman Empire. They also impose compulsory military service and regular taxation upon all Albanians.

1910

March Discontent with the Young Turks leads to clashes between Albanians and Turkish forces in Priština. Armed bands attack the Turks in the district of Peje (Peć), and the entire Kosovo area revolts. The rebellion spreads to the Shkodër region.

April–June Turkish reinforcements arrive in Kosovo and crush the revolt.

July The Albanian revolt against the Young Turks collapses when Turkish forces converge on the rebel bands in the Shkodër region, causing 12,000 refugees to flee into neighboring Montenegro. Martial law is imposed on all the Albanian lands. For the first time, international sympathy develops for the plight of the Albanians, in particular the refugees living in miserable conditions in Montenegro.

July 1910–February 1911 In order to suppress the rising movement for autonomy fearing a fragmentation of the empire along ethnic lines, the Turks treat the Albanian lands as conquered territory. Nationalist associations, private schools, and Albanian newspapers are suspended. Hundreds of Albanian activists are arrested, and the Turkish army conducts a policy of terror and intimidation throughout the countryside. Meanwhile, the Young Turk government in Constantinople launches an international public relations campaign to convey the impression abroad that the Albanian people do not really want autonomy.

1911

March The Catholic highlanders of northern Albania revolt, and they are joined by refugee bands in Montenegro crossing the border back into Albania. The rebellion is in large part instigated and supported by King Nicholas of Montenegro, who hopes to gain territory in northern Albania.

April–May Turkish forces advance against the rebels, destroy a number of armed bands, but fail to end the revolt. The fighting continues and draws the concern of the Great Powers as well as European public sympathy for Albania.

June Fearing the Albanian revolt may lead to a disruption of the status quo, the Great Powers—Austria-Hungary and Russia in particular—pressure the Turkish government to stop the uprising by peaceful means. The Young Turks, accordingly, offer substantial concessions to the northern Albanians: an amnesty for all insurgents, the opening of Albanian schools, and a limit on military service.

June 23 Northern Albanian leaders respond to the Turks' proposal with a memorandum demanding autonomy for all the Albanian lands as a condition to end the revolt.

July 21 An armed gathering of southern Albanian bands is held outside Gjirokastër, where they demand that all concessions granted by the Turks to the northern Albanians be extended to include southern Albania.

August The Turkish government and the rebels reach a settlement ending the revolt. The Albanians do not win autonomy; however, the Turks agree to extend their original proposal of concessions to all Albanians.

September–October Italy rapidly defeats the Ottoman Empire in a war for the conquest of Tripoli. In order to avoid disturbances in Albania while engaged in war with Italy, the Turkish government abides by most of the terms of the August settlement. However, the Turks do not fulfill the key promise of a general amnesty and many Albanians remain in prison.

November A new political party, Liberty and Entente, is founded to challenge the Young Turks' control of the government. The opposition party advocates a policy of decentralization of the administration and recognition of constitutional rights to the national provinces of the empire. The 26 Albanian deputies in the Turkish parliament establish close relations with the opposition party, and they interpret its agenda to favor Albanian autonomy.

December Led by Ismail Kemal of Vlorë (Valona), a prominent Ottoman official since 1860 and a liberal Albanian nationalist, the Albanian deputies spark a series of heated arguments in the Turkish parliament, where they demand that the government acknowledge nationality rights and grant administrative autonomy to Albania. The much more numerous Turkish deputies denounce the Albanian members of parliament and refuse to consider their demands for autonomy. On Kemal's initiative a meeting of prominent Albanian political leaders, including the popular nationalist deputy from Kosovo, Hasan Prishtina, is held in Constantinople. The leaders, known simply as the Central Committee, decide to organize a general insurrection in Albania for the coming spring.

1912

February–March While the Young Turks plan to solidify their control of the government, Albanian political leaders prepare for a general uprising. Kemal travels throughout Europe procuring funds and weapons from governments sympathetic to the Albanian movement and from Albanian communities abroad. Prishtina returns to Kosovo to ready his allies for the revolt. In addition to Kosovo, by March the Central Committee has coordinated bands to prepare for action in Berat, Durrës (Durazzo), Krujë (Croia), Tirana, and Vlorë.

April After the Young Turks win 215 of the 222 seats in the Ottoman parliament through fraud and intimidation, the Albanian Central Committee meets in Constantinople at the end of April and resolves to begin the revolution. In the meantime, various Albanian immigrant associations in the United States combine in Boston, Massachusetts, to form the Pan-Albanian Federation, Vatra (The Hearth), which publishes literature and sponsors activities designed to promote Albanian identity and national interests.

May Clashes between Albanian insurgents and Turkish forces break out in Kosovo.

June The uprising spreads throughout Kosovo and extends quickly over most of the Albanian lands. Albanian soldiers and officers begin to desert from the Ottoman army and many join the rebels.

Mid-July The 50,000-strong rebel army is in control of most of Albania, although many Albanian leaders are divided on their ultimate objectives.

July 30 The rebel Albanian Central Committee presents its demands to the Turkish government, including union of the vilayets (provinces) of Bitola, Kosovo, Ioannina (Yannina), and Shkodër into a single autonomous Albanian state within the Ottoman Empire; Albanian soldiers to serve only in Albania during peacetime; Albanian to be the language of administration and education in Albania; local revenues to be expended locally; and certain politicians in Constantinople to be impeached for their past oppression of the Albanians. In addition, the committee demands that the Ottoman parliament be dissolved within 48 hours.

August 5 The Turkish government dissolves parliament, but the Albanian rebels make it clear to the government that their insurrection will continue until all their demands are met.

August 12 The city of Skopje (Üsküb) falls to the rebel forces, and the Albanian leaders threaten to continue their advance on to Thessaloniki (Salonika).

August 18 Under rebel pressure, the Turkish government unofficially informs the Albanian Central Committee that it accepts their demands, with two exceptions, namely the impeachment of Ottoman officials and the demand for regional military service.

September 4 The Turkish government officially accepts the Albanian conditions, with the two exceptions of August 18. The Turkish government, in order to demonstrate its intention to carry out the terms it has agreed upon, begins to fill administrative posts in the four vilayets with Albanian leaders. Although the Albanians insist on accept-

ance of all terms, the concessions in general are accepted by the insurgents as satisfactory.

October Before the Albanian leaders and the Turkish government can resolve their remaining differences, war erupts in the Balkans. The Balkan nations are emboldened by Turkey's weakness in its war with Italy in 1911. Consequently, Bulgaria, Greece, Montenegro, and Serbia conclude a series of alliances in the spring of 1912. In spite of the opposition of the Great Powers, the Balkan allies declare war on the Ottoman Empire in order to divide between them the territories still held by the Turks in southeastern Europe. According to the plans of the Balkan allies, after the expulsion of Turkey from Europe, the Albanian territories will be parceled out among Greece, Montenegro, and Serbia.

November The rapid succession of allied victories abruptly ends Turkish rule in the Balkans. The Albanians are thus compelled to give up their autonomy policy and to strike out for full independence in order to safeguard their own national security.

November 26–27 While the Greek, Montenegrin, and Serbian armies advance into Albanian territory, a national congress of 83 Christian and Muslim delegates from all parts of the country hastily assembles in Vlorë.

November 28 The national congress of Vlorë proclaims the independence of Albania and hoists the flag of Skënderbeg (the common Alexander, George Kastrioti). It elects a cabinet of seven Christian and Muslim ministers, with Ismail Kemal as president of the Albanian provisional government. A few hours after the proclamation of independence, Kemal sends a telegram to Constantinople and the Great Powers announcing the political independence of Albania. At the same time, Kemal informs the Great Powers that Albania is neutral in the present conflict and that he requests their protection against foreign invasion. Kemal makes this appeal to the Great Powers because it is increasingly evident that the Balkan allies intend to partition Albania.

Late November–early December The Great Powers are divided on the issue of Albanian independence. Austria-Hungary and Italy favor an independent Albania as a barrier to Serbian expansion towards the Adriatic Sea. On the other hand, France and Russia oppose Albanian aspirations, because they prefer a strong Serbia as a counterbalance against Austro-Hungarian and Italian influence in the Balkans. Only Germany and Great Britain remain nonpartisan. In the meantime, the Balkan allies of Serbia, Montenegro, Greece, and Bulgaria continue their offensives. The Serbs overrun Kosovo and push on towards the

Adriatic. Serbian forces unite with the Montenegrin army in northern Albania, and they jointly occupy Durrës and lay siege to Shkodër. Greek troops besiege Ioannina and advance northwards towards Gjirokastër and Sarandë (Santi Quaranta). Fighting breaks out between the Albanian and Greek communities in the area of Himarë (Chimara). At that point, and with the total defeat of Turkey by December 3, the Great Powers decide to hold a conference in London for the consideration of the Albanian problem and the other questions arising from the war.

December 17 The Great Powers open the Conference of Ambassadors in London, which is concerned with four principal matters: drawing Albania's boundaries; deciding its status as a state; determining its form of government; and choosing its ruler. The conference continues until August 1913.

December 20 The Conference of Ambassadors announces that they agree to the principle of Albanian autonomy in which the Albanians will run their own local affairs, to be guaranteed and controlled by the six Great Powers, under the sovereignty of the Ottoman sultan. At this time, despite the fact that Albania has already declared its independence, the conference recognizes it as an autonomous state under the authority of the sultan and the Ottoman government and not as an independent state with complete control of all its affairs.

1913

January From the first sessions at the Conference of Ambassadors the frontier issue is particularly complex. The Albanian leaders seek a large Albania, a goal that Austria-Hungary and Italy favor. The Russians, in contrast, support Montenegrin and Serbian claims to lands that are predominantly Albanian; the Serbs are committed to maintaining the outlet to the Adriatic Sea that they hold, and the Montenegrins want to incorporate Shkodër. For its part, the Greek government seeks to annex most of southern Albania, a region the Greeks call Northern Epirus. The Greeks are supported by Russia and France and opposed by Austria-Hungary and Italy.

February 3 Following a month-long deadlock, peace negotiations between Turkey and the Balkan allies fall apart. Fighting resumes on all fronts, and Albanian territory is further threatened. The Greeks renew their attacks on besieged Ioannina and continue to advance in Epirus. The Montenegrins and Serbs launch operations in northern Albania. The scattered and besieged Turkish units are reinforced by Albanian forces.

March 6 Despite Albanian support, the Turkish garrison in Ioannina surrenders the city to the Greek army.

March 15–21 Greek forces occupy the towns of Gjirokastër and Tepelenë. The capture of Gjirokastër completes the occupation of the territories they seek for a western frontier with Albania.

March 22 After delicate negotiations, the Conference of Ambassadors announces its decision to give Shkodër and the surrounding region to an autonomous Albania. Most of northern Albania is occupied by Montenegrin and Serbian forces; therefore, in exchange for Shkodër, the Great Powers award Kosovo and Debar (Dibër) to Serbia, and Peć and border areas around Lake Shkodër to Montenegro. In short, in order to remove the Serbs from the Adriatic, the Great Powers give to Serbia other areas that are overwhelmingly Albanian. As a result, more than one-third of the Albanian population (740,000 out of a total of approximately 2.1 million) is excluded from the autonomous Albania and placed under the control of Serbia and Montenegro.

March–April Despite the decision of the Great Powers to award Shkodër to Albania, Montenegro intensifies its effort to capture the city.

April 22 Ending seven months of siege, Esad Pasha Toptani, the Shkodër defense garrison commander, surrenders the city to the Montenegrins in exchange for the support of Montenegro in his effort to form a new government for Albania to replace the one headed by Ismail Kemal. Toptani's ultimate goal is to become king of Albania.

Late April–early May Under the pretext that he is fulfilling the Ottoman sultan's right of sovereignty over Albania, still recognized as valid by the Great Powers, Toptani seeks to achieve his goals. He withdraws from Shkodër the forces under his command, one Albanian and one Turkish division, and takes them to Durrës and Tirana in central Albania, which are under Serbian occupation. Here Toptani establishes a separate administration without regard to the Albanian provisional government in Vlorë.

May 4 After Austria-Hungary threatens military action against Montenegro for its occupation of Shkodër, King Nicholas agrees to place the disputed city in the hands of the Great Powers (*see* April 22).

May 14 Montenegrin forces withdraw from Shkodër. Instead of being placed under Albanian authority, troops of the Great Powers establish international control over the city.

Mid–late May Fearing that Toptani's rival administration will try to overthrow the government in Vlorë under the guise of Ottoman sovereignty, Kemal urges the Conference of Ambassadors to recognize the full independence of Albania. Kemal reasons that if the Great Powers recognize Albanian independence and officially end Ottoman sovereignty over the country, Toptani will not be able to claim that his actions represent the interests of the sultan. Moreover, Toptani's divisions, which are still part of the Ottoman army, will have to leave Albania or be disbanded, thus rendering him powerless to challenge the authority of the Vlorë government.

May 30 After exerting pressure on the Turks and the Balkan allies alike, the Great Powers compel them to sign the Treaty of London. Included in the treaty are clauses relating to the Albanian problem. According to the treaty, the boundaries of Albania and all other questions concerning Albania are left to the decisions of the Great Powers. With the signing of the Treaty of London, Britain's foreign minister announces to the conference that there remain two questions relating to Albania to be settled: the organization of a government for Albania and the drawing of a frontier between Greece and Albania; borders with Montenegro and Serbia had already been decided on March 22.

July 29 The Conference of Ambassadors approves the organization and status of the Albanian state. Albania is recognized as an independent state under the guarantee of the Great Powers. At the head of the state there will be a sovereign prince, to be elected by the Great Powers. The control by the Great Powers will last 10 years and will be exerted by an International Control Commission, consisting of one representative of each of the six Great Powers and one Albanian, which oversees the civil and financial administration of the country. The Great Powers likewise decide that domestic security and order will be maintained by a gendarmerie, or police, headed by Swedish and later Dutch officers. Although the July 29 decision by the Great Powers recognizes the independence of a state that has nominally existed since November 28, 1912, the influence of the Great Powers through the International Control Commission places great limitations on Albania's actual independence.

August–September Despite recognition by the Great Powers, Albania remains in a state of great anarchy. The authority of Kemal's government in Vlorë extends only to the district of Berat. Its authority in central Albania is blocked by Toptani's army and rival administration. Furthermore, Toptani has the support of a considerable number of Muslim large landowners who are anxious to see the reestablishment of Ottoman rule in the country. To that end they organize a movement in favor of a Muslim prince

under the suzerainty, or overlordship, of the sultan. Besides Kemal's government in Vlorë and Toptani's government in Durrës, there are several areas in Albania controlled by different authorities: Shkodër continues to be administered by the Great Powers; the Catholic Albanian Malissori clans along the Montenegrin frontier control their lands independently; the Muslim mountaineer tribesmen in the north do not accept the authority of any Albanian government; the Serbs continue to occupy much of central and northern Albania, from which they are only very slowly withdrawing; and the Greeks control the districts of Gjirokastër and Korcë.

August 11 After much discussion, the Conference of Ambassadors settles Albania's southern boundary. The district of Korcë will go to Albania, and the remaining disputes concerning territory between Himarë to the north and the Kalamas River to the south will be decided by a commission. This commission will be empowered to draw the frontier between Albania and Greece after it investigates the ethnological and geographical features of the disputed area. The commission will begin its work on September 1, 1913, and conclude it on November 30, 1913.

September 26 In the Albanian territories still occupied by Serbian troops, a number of tribes revolt against Serbian oppression.

Late September–early October The revolt spreads rapidly into territories assigned to Serbia by the Great Powers. The Albanian insurgents overwhelm the Serbian defenses and capture Debar; Albanian rebels also advance on Djakovica (Gjakove) and Prizren in Kosovo.

Early–mid October Alarmed by the expanding revolt against their occupation in Kosovo, the Serbs launch a massive counteroffensive. After crushing the insurgents, the Serbs invade Albania and again advance towards the Adriatic. Their intent is to destroy Kemal's government in Vlorë and set up Toptani, the Serb's proxy, as the ruler of Albania. Accordingly, as soon as the Serbian army enters Albania, Toptani prepares to overthrow the Vlorë government. He announces that he recognizes the suzerainty of the sultan, and he sends a memorandum to the Great Powers calling for the removal of the Kemal government. He also calls directly for the breakup of the Vlorë government and the formation of a new national government based at Durrës.

October 12 Kemal rejects Toptani's demands, and in response Toptani establishes a national government of his own in Durrës, which he calls the Senate of Central Albania.

Mid-October   The Austro-Hungarian government repeatedly warns Serbia to recall its troops from Albania, but the Serbs refuse to comply.

October 18   The Austro-Hungarian foreign minister dispatches an ultimatum to Serbia demanding complete evacuation of Albania within eight days. He threatens to take military action against Serbia if his demand is not met. The Serbs reluctantly withdraw and inform the Austrians two days later that their evacuation from Albania is complete.

Mid–late October   After the formation of his government in Durrës, consisting of a senate of representatives from Durrës, Krujë, Shijak, and Tirana, Toptani establishes his authority firmly between the Mat and the Shkumbi Rivers. In these circumstances the International Control Commission recognizes both governments—Kemal's government in Vlorë and Toptani's government in central Albania—as equals.

October 1913–January 1914   The Bekir Grebeneja Affair takes place. The anarchy in Albania encourages the Turkish government in October to send Major Bekir Grebeneja there. His mission is to spread the idea of recognizing a Muslim prince, Izzet Pasha, the Turkish minister of war, who is of Albanian origin. The Turks' objective is to restore Turkish suzerainty over Albania and to use the country as a future military base for operations against Greece and Serbia. In early November Grebeneja contacts Easd Pasha Toptani, who initially agrees to support him but changes his position and expels him from Durrës in the middle of December. Undaunted, Grebeneja proceeds to Vlorë and meets with Ismail Kemal. Kemal agrees to support the Turkish designs against Greece and Serbia, in exchange for the Turks' promise of Greek and Serbian territory. In addition, Kemal accepts the plan to make Izzet Pasha prince of Albania. Kemal's secret negotiations and agreement with Grebeneja become known to the International Control Commission, which denounces the entire affair as destabilizing and illegal. Grebeneja is arrested by the commission in Vlorë on January 8, 1914, and sentenced to death before a court martial conducted by Dutch officers (his sentence is later changed to life imprisonment). After the arrest of Grebeneja, the International Control Commission resolves that measures should be taken to unite Albania under one government.

December 17   Meeting in Italy, the International Control Commission decides the boundary between Albania and Greece in the Protocol of Florence. The two focal points in the territorial dispute, the districts of Gjirokastër and Korcë, go to Albania. The southern frontier with Greece is far more equitable than Albania's northern and eastern frontiers with Montenegro and Serbia. Although an Albanian minority is left under Greek rule, predominantly in the Tsamouria (Camëri) region, a numerically comparable, albeit proportionally more considerable, Greek minority is left in southern Albania. Despite the fact that none of the concerned parties—Albania, Greece, Montenegro, and Serbia—are satisfied with the outcome, the borders established by the Great Powers in 1913 are to remain essentially unchanged.

1914

January 11   In view of the division of the country between two governments and taking into account his declining credibility with the Great Powers following the Grebeneja Affair, Kemal declares that he is prepared to resign on one condition: that the International Control Commission assumes control of the whole of Albania.

January 22   Kemal resigns as president of the provisional Albanian government of Vlorë and leaves for Western Europe. Before departing Vlorë, he hands over his powers to the International Control Commission, which now controls most of Albania.

February 12   Under increasing pressure from the International Control Commission, Toptani resigns and hands over his government in Durrës to the commission, thereby nominally uniting Albania with the exception of the southern districts under Greek occupation.

February 13   The Great Powers agree on a schedule for the withdrawal of the Greek army from southern Albania, beginning on March 1 from the district of Korcë, and to end on March 31 with the departure of Greek troops from the Delvinë (Delvino) area. The Greek government reluctantly agrees to the plan. At the same time, the Panepirotic Assembly, a body representing Greeks in Northern Epirus (which the Albanians consider southern Albania), meets in Gjirokastër, where it announces that, short of incorporation with Greece, it demands either local autonomy or an international occupation of Great Power forces for the districts of Gjirokastër and Korcë.

February 28   George Zographos, a former foreign minister of Greece, proclaims at Gjirokastër the establishment of the Autonomous Republic of Northern Epirus, with Zographos as president. He notifies the International Control Commission that his government has been established, because the Great Powers have not provided the Greeks in southern Albania any guarantees for the protection of life, property, religious freedom, and ethnic existence. Zographos warns that his government will resist any attempt by the

Albanian gendarmerie to enter the autonomous republic's territory, which already include the towns of Delvinë, Gjirokastër, Himarë, Sarandë, and Përmet (Permeti).

March 7 Prince William of Wied lands at Durrës, united Albania's capital, where he is enthusiastically welcomed as the successor to Skënderbeg, the medieval Albanian leader. In accord with their July 29, 1913, decision to appoint a sovereign prince over Albania, William is the Conference of Ambassadors' choice for the position. A 35-year-old German army officer, William is the nephew of Queen Elizabeth of Romania. Immediately after arriving in Durrës, Prince William orders the Dutch commander of the Albanian gendarmerie to negotiate with the autonomous government in Gjirokastër.

March 10 Representatives of Prince William's government and the autonomous government meet on Corfu. William's government proposes limited local administration for Northern Epirus under a Christian governor and religious and educational freedoms. The Greek government, learning about the proposal, urges the autonomists to accept the offer, but Zographos rejects the proposal.

Mid-March–April Once the Corfu negotiations break off and the Greek army evacuates southern Albania, fighting erupts between the autonomist forces and the Albanians. In late March a revolt takes place in Korcë. After five days of street fighting the Albanian gendarmerie crush the autonomist rebellion and restore order. Meanwhile, autonomist forces take Ereskë (Ereska) and advance towards Korcë.

April The International Control Commission, to which one more Albanian member has been added, completes the draft of a state constitution. Albania is to be a sovereign principality whose neutrality will be guaranteed by the Great Powers. A national assembly will be composed of three representatives from each of the country's seven administrative divisions, to be elected by direct suffrage, and 10 delegates will be appointed by the prince with all delegates serving four-year terms. In addition, certain notables, the heads of the Catholic, Muslim, and Orthodox faiths, and the commissioner for the prospective national bank are to be members by virtue of their prominent positions. The prince has the power to appoint the cabinet, or his council of ministers, which will be directly responsible to him.

May 5 Unable to defeat the autonomist forces, the Albanian government decides to negotiate, with the International Control Commission acting as intermediary. The autonomist government immediately accepts the mediation of the commission and suspends hostilities.

May 9–17 The International Control Commission and Zographos conduct negotiations on Corfu, resulting in an agreement known as the Protocol of Corfu. By its terms Northern Epirus is granted complete autonomy under the nominal hegemony (influence over the state) of Prince William. The Albanian government maintains the right to appoint and dismiss governors and high officials, but virtually all other positions and decisions are left to self-administration in the autonomous districts of Gjirokastër and Korcë. The agreement also provides for a local gendarmerie, religious and educational freedom, and the recognition of Greek as an official language. Moreover, the Great Powers are to guarantee the execution and maintenance of the agreement.

Mid–late May Prince William is confronted by a rival to the throne, Esad Pasha Toptani. After arriving in Durrës in March, William has attempted to pacify Toptani by giving him the key cabinet posts of minister of the interior and minister of defense. However, instead of appeasing him, these positions give him a better opportunity to intrigue and foster dissension throughout the country. With Italian support, Toptani secretly distributes arms to his followers in central Albania and incites the people against William. The peasantry is alienated by William's support of the large landowners, and the Muslim religious leaders fear that the new regime will discriminate against the country's Muslim majority. Inspired by economic and social motives, a revolt against William erupts in central Albania. The insurgents take Tirana, and on May 18 their forces appear outside Durrës. William has Toptani arrested as a traitor on May 19, but Rome intervenes on Toptani's behalf, and William allows him to leave for Italy.

June Although Toptani is banished, the insurrection spreads still further. While Durrës is besieged, the rebels extend their authority over most of central Albania. A new rival administration is established by an assembly of insurgents in Shijak.

June 23 The Albanian government agrees to the Protocol of Corfu, and the International Control Commission notifies the autonomists that Prince William and his government unconditionally accept the agreement. The Great Powers approve the protocol on July 1.

July 26 After much discussion at a meeting in Delvinë, the autonomist assembly approves the Protocol of Corfu, but before the agreement can be applied and before Prince William's government can effectively exercise its authority, the First World War breaks out, and Albania once again falls into a state of anarchy.

August The outbreak of the First World War in early August adds to the country's growing chaos. The authority of William's government is confined only to Durrës and Vlorë, while the insurgents' assaults against the government in Durrës gain momentum.

September 1 Vlorë falls to the insurgents.

September 3 Deprived of all support from the Great Powers, including his former patron, Austria-Hungary, William leaves Albania on the advice of the International Control Commission. Thus after six months, Prince William's regime comes to an end, and although he does not formally abdicate, William never returns to Albania.

September 5 The rebel forces enter Durrës.

Mid–Late September With the departure of William and the collapse of the central government, Albania disintegrates into divisions corresponding to its geographic configuration, each under a separate administration: Shkodër and its environs under a local committee; Durrës and central Albania under the insurgent government hostile to the regime of former Prince William; Vlorë and its hinterland under the International Control Commission, with insurgent forces in occupation; southern Albania under the Greek autonomist forces; and the remote mountain areas of northern Albania under local chieftains.

October Hoping to take advantage of the unstable conditions in Albania, Toptani emerges from exile and raises an armed force in Debar, with Italian and Serbian support.

October 2 Toptani's forces enter Durrës unopposed.

October 5 Toptani takes the title of president and commander in chief of the Albanian republic. His control over central Albania, however, declines under increasing local resistance, as the leaders of the opposition join together in a loose alliance that becomes known as the Union of Krujë. The union insurgents advocate reunification with the Ottoman Empire or the establishment of an Ottoman principality in Albania. They also receive the support of many tribal chieftains who are threatened by Toptani's goal of a centralized government.

October 31 Italy occupies the strategic island of Sazan (Saseno) in the Gulf of Vlorë, under the pretext that such an occupation will protect Albania's neutrality in the war. The Greek government determines this act to be the first step in the Italian conquest of Albania, and accordingly the Greeks dispatch Greek forces to protect the autonomist government in southern Albania (Northern Epirus), occupying Gjirokastër and Sarandë.

December Toptani's influence is confined to Durrës. Outside the city a military stalemate exists between his forces and the insurgents.

December 16 Using the excuse of anarchy in Albania and of an appeal from the Toptani government in Durrës for the maintenance of order, Italian forces occupy Vlorë. The Italian government declares the occupation to be only temporary, and states that it has no intention of expanding its occupation any further in Albania.

1915

January The leaders of the Union of Krujë dispatch a communication to the Great Powers, which is repeated in February and March in which they announce their neutrality in the world war and emphasize that their objective is merely anti-Toptani. Xaxhi Kamil, a pro-Ottoman chieftain from the Sharri district of Tirana, is elected by the insurgents as their commander in chief. Led by Kamil, the insurgents attack the large landowners presumed to support Toptani and confiscate their estates. In addition, they resume their assaults against Toptani's forces still besieged in Durrës.

January–April Italy, still neutral, enters into secret negotiations with both warring camps in Europe—the Central Powers (Austria-Hungary, Germany, and Turkey) and the Entente Powers, or Allies (Great Britain, Belgium, France, Japan, Montenegro, Russia, and Serbia). Italy decides to enter the war on the side of the Allies, which it considers has more chance of victory, and which has given Rome assurances for more territorial gains than those promised by the Central Powers. Italy's negotiations and decision to enter the war on the Allied side have immense consequences for the future of Albania.

April 26 The Italian government signs the secret Treaty of London (not to be confused with the May 30, 1913 Treaty of London) by which Italy joins the Allies. In addition to promises of Austro-Hungarian territories, Britain, France, and Russia give Italy considerable concessions in Albania, including the right to annex Vlorë and its hinterland together with the island of Sazan. The treaty further stipulates that part of Shëngjin is to be annexed by Montenegro, while Britain, France, and Russia have the right to grant the northern and southern regions of Albania to Serbia and Greece respectively. According to the treaty, what is to remain of Albania is essentially central Albania. In addition this truncated state, with its capital in Durrës, is to be autonomous and neutral, and its foreign affairs will be conducted by Italy. With the Treaty of London, the Great

Powers scrap their July 29, 1913, commitment to guarantee the independence of Albania.

May   Although the Treaty of London is officially kept secret even after Italy enters the war on May 23, Serbia learns of its contents. Dissatisfied that the treaty does not grant them as much influence in Albania as Italy has, the Serbs prepare to invade Albania. The Serbian military is also motivated to secure its rear from Albanian insurgents led by the Union of Krujë. The Serbs suspect the insurgents of allying with Austria-Hungary, which has been at war with Serbia since July 1914.

June 2   The Serbian army invades Albania and routs Kamil's forces at Kukës.

Early–mid June   Encountering little organized resistance, Serbian forces rapidly overrun northern and central Albania. However, in the face of pressure from the Allies, who do not want the Serbs to interfere with Italian designs on Albania, the Serbs halt their advance before entering Durrës. In the meantime, the Serbian army and Toptani's forces, relieved by the Serbs from their besiegement in Durrës, destroy the Union of Krujë insurgency. Kamil is arrested by Esad Pasha Toptani and hanged.

Mid–late June   Montenegro, with the aim of annexing Shkodër, invades Albania and captures the city (*see* May 14, 1913).

July   Serbia withdraws its army from Albania as the position of its puppet, Toptani, stabilizes.

July–August   Toptani retaliates against the former insurgents with a campaign of terror aimed at much of the peasantry.

1916

January   With Serbia being overrun by the Central Powers, the Serbian army retreats through the mountains of northern Albania. The remnants of the Serbian army reach the Adriatic and are evacuated in Allied ships to Corfu. The Allies also evacuate Toptani and his government to Corfu. Following the retreating Serbs, Austro-Hungarian forces advance into Albania from the north, and by the end of January they occupy northern and central Albania.

January 11   Deputies from Northern Epirus are seated in the Greek parliament in an attempt at claiming international recognition for the union of that area with Greece.

February   The Greek government proceeds to substitute civil officers for the military authorities of occupation in southern Albania (Northern Epirus).

March   King Constantine of Greece signs a royal decree uniting Northern Epirus with Greece, which the Allies do not accept.

August   Toptani, his government, and his one battalion of infantry arrive in Thessaloniki. The French commander of the Allied forces on the Salonika Front officially recognizes Toptani as the president of the Albanian republic. Representatives of the Allied governments in Thessaloniki, however, treat Toptani with suspicion (*see* January).

September–November   Italian forces spread out from Vlorë over most of southern Albania, while French forces from Thessaloniki occupy the Korcë district. The Italians treat their occupation zone as a colony by taking complete control of its financial administration, criminal jurisdiction, and trade and customs.

Early December   The French military authorities in Korcë hand over the administration of the city to the Greek government. The Albanian majority in the Korcë district protest, viewing it as French support for Greek annexation of the area. Albanian bands launch attacks against Greek communities in the area and against each other. The nationalist leader of the Orthodox Albanians in Korcë, Themistokli Germenji, convinces the French that they can enjoy order in the region only if Greek administration is removed and Albanian independence is promoted.

December 10   Responding to local opposition to Greek administration, the French military authorities agree to Albanian demands and sign the Protocol of December 10, 1916, in Korcë. According to the protocol, government authority in the "Autonomous District of Korcë," both legislative and executive, is vested in a commission of 14 members, of whom half are Orthodox Christians and half Muslims. Albania is declared the official language; a gendarmerie and militia are established, which, in case of military necessity, will be placed under French command; Greek schools are replaced by Albanian schools. The administration of the Autonomous District of Korcë is placed under the protection of the French military authorities. Geremnji emerges as the leader of the Autonomous District of Korcë, or "Republic of Korcë," as the Albanians prefer to call it. The concession of Albanian autonomy is significant, because it obliges France to reject the claims of the Greeks on Korcë. In addition, local autonomy under the French gives the Albanians of Korcë an opportunity to learn self-government by experience.

1917

January The establishment of the Autonomous District of Korcë is a stimulus for Albanian nationalists under foreign occupation in other parts of the country to fight for similar autonomy. Under the pressure of these demands, the Austro-Hungarian occupation authorities make concessions in administration to the Albanians and promise to acknowledge Albania's autonomy and territorial integrity as soon as the war is ended.

June In order to check growing pressure against them, Italian military authorities make concessions in administration to the Albanians in their area of occupation. Like the Austro-Hungarians, the Italians promise to acknowledge Albanian autonomy and territorial integrity once the war ends. Meanwhile, as an inducement to the Greeks to enter the war on the Allied side, the French military authorities begin to violate the Protocol of December 10, 1916. After a six-month existence, the Autonomous District of Korcë is eliminated. French authorities arrest Germenji and transport him to Thessaloniki to await trial before a French military tribunal. Greece will enter the war on the side of the Allies on July 2.

November 9 Germenji is executed in Thessaloniki after being found guilty of espionage by a French military tribunal, on the basis of false evidence.

1918

February 16 The Protocol of December 10, 1916, is annulled by the French commander of the Allied forces on the Salonika Front, and the entire district of Korcë comes under the direct administration of the French military.

September The two-year-long military stalemate in Albania is broken when the combined Allied forces in Thessaloniki launch a massive offensive against Bulgarian and German forces in occupied Serbia. Simultaneously, the Allied armies in southern Albania attack the Austro-Hungarian forces to the north. The Italian forces advance from Vlorë and break through the Austro-Hungarian lines, after fierce fighting in and around Fier. The French army marches out from Korcë and encounters strong resistance from the Austro-Hungarian forces before defeating them near Pogradec.

September 29 Bulgaria surrenders to the Allies forces, with the Austro-Hungarians to evacuate Albania through early November.

November 5 The Austro-Hungarians complete their evacuation of Albania, and combined Allied forces enter Shkodër.

November 11 With the armistice ending the First World War, the victorious Allies possess Albania. The French hold Korcë, the Greeks control the rest of Northern Epirus, the Serbs are deployed on the left bank of the Drin River, and the Italians occupy all the other territories. The Allies agree to continue this occupation arrangement until the future peace conference settles Albania's fate. The First World War leaves behind enormous human loss and material destruction in Albania; nearly 70,000 persons were killed or died of starvation during the fighting, occupation, and anarchy, and the economy—which was poor and acutely underdeveloped before the conflict—is now completely ravaged.

December The conclusion of the First World War, instead of marking the end of conflict in Albania, sees the beginning of a new period of troubles. The Bolsheviks, or Communists, who seized power in Russia in November 1917, publicize the content of the secret treaties concluded between the Allies during the war, including the April 26, 1915, Treaty of London. Albanian leaders, still counting on the 1912 guarantee of the Great Powers to protect Albanian independence, learn for the first time that the Allies have agreed to partition the country.

December 28 Albanian leaders convene in Durrës to discuss measures to safeguard their national interests. Forty-eight delegates from all parts of Albania attend the Congress of Durrës. The Italian occupation authorities grant permission to call the Congress of Durrës on the condition that it not appoint a national government but only a national council. Nevertheless, once in session the congress elects a national government with Turhan Pasha, the former prime minister of Prince William's regime, as its president. Further, the congress appoints a delegation to defend Albania's interests at the peace conference in Paris. Although discontented with the congress, the Italian occupation authorities do not interfere with Turhan Pasha's government in order to avoid causing a rebellion.

1919

January 18 At the Paris Peace Conference, Albania's neighbors present their territorial claims: Greece demands Northern Epirus (the districts of Gjirokastër and Korcë); Italy demands the district of Vlorë together with the island of Sazan, and it insists that the rest of Albania become an

Italian protectorate; Montenegro claims Shkodër; and Serbia claims the northern districts of Albania.

Late January–May The Albanian government delegation at the peace conference, led by Turhan Pasha, is joined by delegates from Albanian communities in Bulgaria, Egypt, Romania, Turkey, and the United States. The Allies, however, do not allow Albania to be represented. Austria-Hungary, Albania's principal defender in the prewar years, no longer exists, and Italy insists that it has the right to represent Albania at the peace conference. In spite of its position, the Albanian delegation remains at the conference, where it hopes to restore Albania's frontiers drawn by the Conference of Ambassadors in 1913 and to secure recognition of Albanian independence.

June Frustrated by his delegation's inability to be heard and under mounting pressure from the Italians, Turhan Pasha changes policy. In order to avoid partition he proposes an Italian mandate over all of Albania, on the condition that the country's 1913 boundaries be maintained. Turhan Pasha is denounced by his government, and under a storm of protest he resigns from the presidency and is replaced by Bp. Juigj Bumci as head of the conference delegation.

July 20 Greece and Italy sign the secret Venizelos-Tittoni agreement, by which Italy agrees to support Greek claims in Northern Epirus and oppose Turkey, while Greece agrees to support Italian claims for the remainder of Albania. Britain and France are willing to accept this arrangement in order to facilitate territorial settlements elsewhere.

August–December Albania's position at the conference steadily declines. It is generally treated as a trading chip in complicated negotiations over other more significant territorial issues.

1920

January 14 Great Britain, France, and Italy agree that Rome, and not Yugoslavia, should have all of Istria and Fiume (former territory of Austria-Hungary) in the north Adriatic, and that Yugoslavia (Serbia's successor state) in return should receive northern Albania. Further, they agree that the rest of the country should be partitioned as stated in the Venizelos-Tittoni agreement.

January 28 Turhan Pasha's willingness to place Albania under an Italian protectorate does harm to the credibility of the Congress of Durrës by causing Albanian leaders to lose faith in it and to organize a national government to liberate the country. Fifty delegates convene a national congress at Lushnjë, where the government of Durrës attempts to disperse the national congress but, without any support, it fails and dissolves a few days later.

January 31 After four days of deliberations, the national congress ends and proclaims its resolutions, including the dismissal of the Durrës government and the appointment of a new national government under the moderate Suleyman Bey Delvina as prime minister. The congress approves provisional laws, the Lushnjë Statutes, in force until general elections take place and a legislative constituent assembly can meet. In accordance with the Lushnjë Statutes, the congress elects a supreme council, composed of four members, to direct state affairs. The congress also informs the Allies that the Albanians are determined to fight all foreign powers in order to defend their country's independence and territorial integrity. Further, by sanctioning the Lushnjë Statutes, the national congress rejects the 1913 Conference of Ambassadors, which places Albania under the control of the Great Powers. The national congress, by opposing the partition plans of the Allies and by deposing the Durrës government, decides that the Albanian people should exercise self-determination.

February 11 The supreme council establishes its offices in Tirana, in the center of the country, and the town of 12,000 is chosen as the capital of Albania. From Tirana the supreme council demands that all foreign armies withdraw from Albania or face conflict.

Italy abandons its occupation of most of Albania but concentrates its forces in the Vlorë area.

March 6 Albania is saved from seemingly inevitable partition by the intervention of the American president Woodrow Wilson. Wilson opposes giving Albanian lands to Yugoslavia as compensation for Adriatic territories that Yugoslavia would relinquish to Italy (*see* January 14). Wilson's position ends British, French, Greek, and Italian plans for the partition of Albania. No other agreement is concluded for a partition of Albania, and the country maintains its territorial integrity by default.

March 27 Thirty-seven elected deputies meet in Tirana as a National Legislative Assembly, or national council, establishing Albania's first genuine parliament. Two immediate problems confront Prime Minister Delvina and the national council: the liberation of the district of Vlorë, and the defeat of an Italian-sponsored rebellion on behalf of Esad Pasha Toptani. Delvina's government decides to organize an uprising against the Italians and plans military operations against the Toptani forces.

May 20 The Delvina government's secret rebel organization in Vlorë, the Committee of National Defense, issues orders to its members to prepare for an armed uprising against the Italian occupation.

June 3 The Committee of National Defense sends an ultimatum with a 24-hour limit to the Italian commander to withdraw his troops from Vlorë.

June 5–11 With no Italian response to the Albanian ultimatum, the Committee of National Defense launches its uprising throughout the Vlorë district. Armed bands quickly overrun the smaller Italian garrisons in the countryside and liberate most of the district. The Italian forces withdraw to the fortified defenses outside Vlorë, and the Albanians besiege the city. In the meantime, Delvina's forces crush Toptani's rebel movement.

June 13 Toptani is assassinated in Paris by a revolutionary nationalist student, Avni Rustem.

July 20 After repeated counterattacks, the Italian forces fail to lift the siege of Vlorë.

August 2 Unable to secure a military victory in Vlorë, the Italian government signs the Preliminary Protocol of Tirana in which it agrees to withdraw its troops from Albania within one month, with the exception of the island of Sazan; to renounce all its claims to annex Vlorë; and to respect the independence and territorial integrity of Albania.

September 2 The last Italian troops leave Albania.

September 3 Albanian forces enter Vlorë and unite it with independent Albania.

November 14 The Delvina government, believing that its mandate has come to an end, resigns. Although Delvina's government has secured a number of considerable achievements, Albania faces grave economic, political, and social problems. The country is acutely underdeveloped: there is virtually no transportation infrastructure; industry is limited to handicrafts; mineral resources lay unexploited; agricultural methods are inefficient; and living standards are abysmal. Illiteracy is the norm, and there is no standard educational system to replace the ones formerly dominated by Greeks, Italians, and other foreigners. Tribal chieftains maintain their local power in defiance of the central government. Land reform is blocked by Muslim large landowners, which adds to the considerable friction between Christians and Muslims, particularly in southern Albania. The economic and social divisions in Albania are also reflected in the country's emerging political parties. One is the Progressive party led by Shefqet Bey Vërlaci of central Albania, the country's largest landowner. The Progressives are opposed to land reform and wish to preserve as much as possible of the old economic and social order of the Ottoman period. The other party, the Popular (or Reform) party, is led by Orthodox bishop Fan Stylian Noli, the leader of the Albanian-American community and their elected representative in the National Legislative Assembly in Tirana. Noli is a democratic idealist committed to economic and social reform. Another leader of the Popularists is Ahmed Bey Zogolli, the chief of the Muslim Mati clan in northern Albania. Apart from establishing a heroic reputation as a nationalist fighter and clever politician during the First World War, Zogolli is a senior officer in Albania's small army. He is as much a patriot as Noli, but, unlike Noli, Zogolli is interested primarily in power for himself.

November 19 A new cabinet is formed under the presidency of Ilias Vrioni, the son of a great landowner; Vrioni was a delegate to the National Congress of Lushnjë (*see* January 31).

December 5 The Vrioni government publishes the law on elections, drafted in such a way as to benefit large landowner candidates.

December 5, 1920–April 5, 1921 The election campaign for a new parliament takes place and the chief differences between the Progressive party and the Popular party crystallize.

December 17 Albania becomes a full member of the League of Nations.

1921

June–August A rebellion breaks out against the expanding authority of the central government. Gjon Marka Gjoni, the leader of the Mirdite tribe dominating the area between the Drin and Mat Rivers, proclaims the establishment of the Republic of Mirdita, which receives financial and military aid from Yugoslavia.

September The Vrioni government puts down but does not entirely destroy the Mirdite rebellion.

October Yugoslav troops violate Albania's frontiers in a series of border raids and occupy territory in the Puka region.

October 11 The Popular party, together with a number of Progressive party members, forces the Vrioni cabinet out of power.

October 16 A new cabinet is formed under the leadership of Pandeli Evangjeli.

November 9 The Conference of Ambassadors in Paris reconfirms Albania's southern frontier set in 1913, forcing Greece to withdraw its army from southern Albania. In the north, however, the Conference of Ambassadors makes changes in the boundaries to the disadvantage of Albania. Certain small border areas, in particular the district of Gora, are ceded to Yugoslavia.

November 20   The Evangjeli cabinet signs the order to begin military operations against Yugoslav bands in Albanian territory. In addition, the government assigns Colonel Zogolli to destroy the Mirdite rebellion. Zogolli, who has started to call himself Zogu (Zog), uses his command position to strengthen his personal power.

December 6   Alarmed by the growing power of Zog and his influence over Evangjeli, the supreme council dismisses Evangjeli's cabinet and approves the formation of an anti-Zogist government, with Qazim Koculi as prime minister.

December 7   Confronted by strong opposition from pro-Zogist ministers, the Koculi government resigns and is replaced by a new anti-Zogist cabinet, led by Hasan Prishtina.

December 10   With Zog threatening the government with civil war, the Prishtina cabinet resigns.

December 14   Zog enters Tirana at the head of his troops, proclaims martial law, and forces the supreme council, his chief opponents, to resign.

December 24   A new supreme council is elected under Zog's guidance. It is dominated by Zog's cronies, and he assumes the post of minister of the interior.

1922

January–February   As minister of the interior Zog takes a series of measures in order to strengthen his power. On the pretext of establishing order, he begins to disarm the population, while directing his real efforts against those hostile to him.

March   Bp. Fan Noli resigns from his post as foreign minister in protest against Zog's trend towards dictatorship. Noli leads the democratic wing of the Popular party in a parliamentary fight against the Zogist clique.´

Provoked largely by Zog's attempt to disarm them, a number of highlander tribes in the north revolt.

March 22   Part of the rebel forces enter Tirana; however, the movement is ill-organized and quickly fails. During the crisis, the British minister to Albania negotiates on his behalf with the rebels. Meanwhile, Zog is the only member of the government to remain in the capital during the crisis, and his reputation is greatly enhanced by his repeated demonstrations of courage.

April–June   Government retaliation against opponents follows the uprising by purging the army and the bureaucracy of anti-Zogist elements and imprisoning hundreds. Zog also suspends parliament until September.

September   Parliament reconvenes. However, despite Zog's police measures, opposition to him grows within the parliament.

November   Besides dissent within parliament, opposition to Zog is organized by Avni Rustem, the charismatic assassin of Esad Pasha Toptani. Rustem forms a liberal opposition movement, the Union of Young Albanians (*see* June 13, 1920).

December 2   Despite mounting opposition, Zog becomes premier. In his speech to parliament he declares his intention to establish a civilized Western state based on democratic principles. However, Zog already exercises dictatorial power, and his personal associations seem to favor the privileged large landowners. Zog's opponents put little faith in his pledges.

December 24   Zog forms a new cabinet, with himself holding the position of interior minister.

Late December   Noli and other democratic reformers leave the Popular party and organize an opposition bloc in parliament. It draws strong support from the Orthodox population in the south, which is increasingly disillusioned with the government's economic and tax policies.

1923

January–July   Noli's opposition bloc expands, but Zog maintains majority support in the parliament.

August–September   The conflict between Zog and the opposition takes shape around the government's parliamentary election bill. The pro-Zogist bloc supports the bill, which provides indirect two-phase elections, while the opposition denounces the bill in debates and demands modifications so that voting should be direct and in one phase.

September 28   After prolonged debate, the pro-Zogist majority in the parliament passes the government's indirect election bill without any amendments.

October–December   The electoral campaign is marred by violence and police intimidation, as Zog's government takes measures to deter any support for the opposition.

December 27   The parliamentary elections are completed. In spite of voting fraud, Zog fails to win a majority. Of the 95 seats in parliament, Zog's faction secures only

King Zog I and his military staff.

40; the opposition led by Noli wins 35; the remaining 20 seats go to independent candidates.

1924

February 2   The new parliament opens amidst growing political tension. In violation of the constitution, Zog fails to resign as prime minister and is denounced by the opposition, which demands his resignation and a new government.

February 24   Zog escapes an assassination attempt by a member of the Union of Young Albanians while walking up the steps of the parliament building.

February 25   After 14 months in office, Zog resigns as prime minister (*see* February 2).

March 3   After heated debate in the parliament, a new government is formed led by Prime Minister Shefqet Vërlaci, Zog's fiancée's father. In order to appease the opposition, Zog does not place himself in the cabinet but continues to control the government from behind the scenes.

April 22 Avni Rustem, the leader of the Union of Young Albanians and a member of Noli's parliamentary opposition, dies after being shot by attackers in Tirana on April 20. There is no question that Zog is behind the murder, given Rustem's implication in the assassination attempt on Zog in February. Rustem's assassination arouses a wave of anger throughout Albania (*see* November 1922).

May 1 The body of Rustem is buried in Vlorë amid mass public mourning. After the funeral, 43 opposition delegates send an ultimatum from Vlorë to the cabinet in Tirana, demanding that Rustem's murderers, including Zog, be punished. The government does not reply.

May 2–24 The opposition boycotts the parliament, leaving it without a quorum, and issues a proclamation stating that Zog still dominates the government and demanding that he leave Albania. The highland tribes of the north and other disaffected groups throw their support to the opposition movement.

May 25 An armed uprising against the government begins in the Kukës district and quickly spreads.

May 31 The army garrisons in Përmet and Shkodër join the insurgents.

June 2 Most of northern and southern Albania falls into the hands of the rebels.

June 9 The insurgents, along with 7,000 Albanian army troops, close in on Tirana. Zog calls on the citizens of the capital to come to his support, but they do not.

June 10 Zog flees to Yugoslavia, and the insurgents enter Tirana.

June 16 Bp. Fan Noli becomes prime minister and forms a liberal government.

June 19 Prime Minister Noli announces a 19-point reform program, including eradication of the feudal land-tenure system; definite establishment of democracy; emancipation of the peasantry; judicial reform; tax reform; simplification of the state bureaucracy; and reorganization of education.

Late June–early December Noli's cabinet ministers, although united with him against Zog, are divided over the reform program. Noli's government flounders as his plans are stifled by his own allies. In the meantime, Zog, in exile in Belgrade, secures the support of the Yugoslav government, which assumes that he can be manipulated to serve its future interests in Albania.

December 13–17 With considerable assistance from mercenaries and the Yugoslav army, Zog's forces invade Albania.

December 24 Zog enters Tirana. Noli, part of his cabinet, and approximately 500 supporters flee from Vlorë to Italy.

1925

January–June Zog conducts punitive operations against the supporters of the former democratic government: martial law is imposed, hundreds are imprisoned, court martials issue scores of death sentences, political organizations and clubs are banned, and police censorship is placed on the press. Zog's agents track down and assassinate prominent democratic opponents outside Albania.

January 6 A new cabinet is formed under Zog. He also assumes the positions of commander in chief of the armed forces and minister of the interior.

January 21 Zog calls the remnants of the parliament elected at the end of 1923 to meet in Tirana. This assembly proclaims the establishment of the Albanian republic.

January 31 The weak assembly officially proclaims Zog as the president of the Albanian republic for a term of seven years.

March 2 A new constitution is approved, giving the president extensive powers: he directs state policy, nominates and dismisses ministers, has the right to veto all legislative bills, has the sole right to propose laws concerning budgetary increases and transfers, and has complete control over appointments and dismissals in the military and over all senior civil employees.

March 15 Looking for economic support to develop Albania, Zog concludes an agreement with Rome. This agreement begins the first stage of Italian penetration in Albania by providing that Italian interests will have the exclusive right to issue currency and negotiate government and municipal loans on behalf of Albania. In addition, Italian companies gain the right to research and exploit natural resources within specified areas of the country.

September 2 The National Bank of Albania is constituted in Rome.

October The Italian-directed National Bank of Albania organizes the Company for Economic Development of Albania (SVEA) to grant loans to the Albanian government for a program of public works.

November 1925–November 1926 Italian capital begins to flow into Albania through the National Bank of Albania and SVEA. Albania profits economically from these arrangements with Italy. For the first time the country has a national currency, and the interest burden on loans is insignificant. Italian economic aid to Albania, however, is politically inspired. Rome's loans are to be used as a means to eventually gain control of the country.

1926

November 20 An insurrection against Zog erupts in the northern district of Dukagjini, which is quickly suppressed.

November 27 Alarmed by the Dukagjini rebellion, Zog signs the Italo-Albanian Pact of Friendship and Security, or the Tirana Pact, with fascist leader Benito Mussolini. According to the pact, Italy undertakes to protect the political, juridical, and territorial status quo in Albania.

December 1926–November 1927 In Belgrade the Tirana Pact is interpreted as an anti-Yugoslav alliance. Yugoslavia consequently adopts a strong anti-Albanian policy, and relations between the two countries deteriorate. Meanwhile, Italian commercial concerns deepen their penetration of the Albanian economy.

1927

November 22 Zog responds to Yugoslavia's anti-Albanian policy by signing the Second Pact of Tirana with Mussolini, which is a 20-year defensive military alliance. With the signing of the pact, Albania becomes Italy's stepping stone for the penetration of the Balkans. Italy gains increasing control over Albania's armed forces: Italian arms are introduced; an Italian military mission reorganizes the Albanian army; Albanian officers go to Italy for advanced training; and Italian fascist instructors train Albanian youth in paramilitary drills. Moreover, the port of Durrës is enlarged and modernized to make it suitable for large-scale landings and supply operations.

December 1927–May 1928 Italian support enables Zog to consolidate his power. At the same time that Zog restructures Albania's army, he inaugurates a program of administrative and social reform. The most outward vestiges of the old Ottoman Turkish state system are replaced by a newer, more Western, model. The common practices of the vendetta and the carrying of arms are outlawed. National education and public works projects make progress.

1928

June Zog summons the parliament and forces it to pass a bill providing for its dissolution. In addition, the bill calls for the election of a special assembly to revise the constitution. These and subsequent parliamentary actions during the summer are orchestrated by Zog to create a monarchy for himself.

July–mid-August During the electoral campaign for the special assembly, Zog prompts demonstrations to propose that the future assembly offer him the crown.

August 17 The elections for the special assembly take place. Given police interference, the disorganization of the opposition, and the elimination of the opposition leadership through exile or assassination, Zog's victory is absolute.

September 1 The new assembly unanimously proclaims Albania a democratic, parliamentary, and hereditary kingdom, with Zog becoming "Zog I, King of the Albanians." The period of monarchy is characterized by a combination of despotism and Western reforms. Zog continues practices inherited from the Ottoman Turks, such as direct interference in the courts and nepotism. Elections are reduced to automatic ratifications of Zog's own personally chosen candidates. Nevertheless, some substantial reforms are enacted: a penal code based on the Italian model, a civil code patterned after the Napoleonic Code, and a commercial code modeled on French and Italian examples are adopted, in 1928, 1929, and 1932 respectively. This period also sees the introduction of modern facilities and some Western technology, although generally limited to Tirana and a few other cities. At the same time, the central government consolidates control over local administration through the ministry of the interior. Albania is divided into 10 administrative units or prefectures (provinces): Berat, Debar, Durrës, Elbasan, Gjirokastër, Korcë, Kukës, Shkodër, Tirana, and Vlorë. Every level of local administration is directly responsible to both its immediate administrative superior and the minister of the interior.

September 5 Koco Kota—a former minister in the pro-Zogist Vrioni government, a commander in Zog's December 1924 invasion force, and a prominent official during Zog's presidency—becomes prime minister.

December 1 A monarchical constitution is adopted. The king is given extraordinary state power, and all legislative power is exercised jointly by the king and a parliament of 56 members. The king has the authority to appoint and dismiss ministers, command the armed forces, declare war, veto legislation, and suspend legal procedures for political crimes. He has the right to direct policy and conclude agreements with other countries, informing parliament so far as state interests permit. The constitution, in short, establishes a royal dictatorship in Albania.

1930

May 3 Zog decrees the enactment of the Agrarian Reform Law approved by the parliament on April 17, which is officially intended to redistribute land from the large landowners to the peasantry. The law provides for the expropriation, with compensation, of one third of all land held in excess of 100 acres. The land acquired by the state is to be resold on favorable terms to the peasants. However, the agrarian reform is applied only on a limited area. Altogether merely 11,600 acres of the 130,000 acres that belong to the state and 8,500 acres of the 255,000 acres that belong to the large landowners are redistributed. Moreover, full implementation of the agrarian law is postponed from year to year until it is ignored entirely. As a result, the large landowners maintain their dominant economic status and continue supporting Zog, whereas the peasants, 40 percent of whom are landless, become increasingly dissatisfied.

1931

February 20 An assassination attempt is made on Zog's life in Vienna. The two assassins are both Albanian émigrés, former officers in the Albanian gendarmerie, and members of the Bashkimi Kombëtar (National Union), a nationalist émigré opposition movement with close ties to the Yugoslav government. It is discovered during the subsequent trial of the assassins in the Austrian courts that Bashkimi Kombëtar forces were positioned on the border waiting to invade Albania once Zog was killed.

1932

June–August Due to the assassination attempt made on him in the previous year, Zog is convinced that an insurrection is being planned by revolutionary groups in Albania, although no proof exists. Consequently, a group of Vlorë intellectuals is arrested for sedition. The intellectuals are part of a nationalist organization that is not even directly opposed to Zog. Nevertheless, Zog insures that the court passes severe verdicts on all 49 defendants as an example to deter any potential internal opposition.

September–October Zog takes measures to appease widespread discontent with his policy towards Italy.

Albanian nationalists resent Italy's increasing involvement in the country. Moreover, Zog realizes that the Italians plan to extend their sovereignty to Albania through economic manipulation. Thus, Zog rejects a proposal for a customs union with Italy. In order to stress his determination against further concessions to Italy, Zog makes preparations to nationalize education and close the Italian schools opened by Rome in Albania.

1933

April 1933–December 1934 Zog implements the nationalization of education, targeting mainly Italian schools, but all private and foreign schools are affected. New legislation makes it a criminal offense for parents to send their children to foreign schools in or outside Albania. The four Italian technical schools are taken over by Albanian staffs, as are the few other foreign facilities in the country. The 17 Roman Catholic schools in the north are closed. The scores of Greek schools in the south are also closed, and many teachers and Greek minority leaders are arrested after complaining to the League of Nations.

April 1 Mussolini responds to Zog's new policy of independence from Rome by suspending all financial assistance to Albania. Rome begins the withdrawal of all Italian civil and military personnel, and all shipments of arms and equipment to the Albanian army stop. The Italians plan to force Albania to concede by placing it under economic duress. Since Zog's presidency in the 1920s, the Albanian government has grown increasingly dependent on economic support from Rome. The suspension of Italian loans and investments creates an extremely difficult situation for the government. The state treasury is depleted, so that civil servants can not be paid for several months. The National Bank of Albania, in the hands of Italian managers, reduces the money supply, which stifles economic activity. As a result, unemployment increases dramatically, the prices of agricultural products collapse, and the peasantry is financially ruined.

1934

June 23 Mussolini increases the pressure on Albania with a demonstration of Italian military power. Six Italian cruisers and 13 destroyers approach the port of Durrës without any previous notice, and without asking for permission they drop anchor in the port. The Albanians prepare for war.

June 30 The Italian fleet withdraws from Durrës. During the squadron's week-long stay, however, the Italian foreign ministry proposes the resumption of normal relations. Zog does not agree immediately, but his determination to maintain his independent policy begins to weaken.

August Zog enters into negotiations with Mussolini's government with the aim of restoring normal relations. The Italians demand a virtual protectorate over Albania in exchange for badly needed economic help, whereas the Albanians want to preserve their independence and make as few concessions as possible in exchange for aid.

September 1934–March 1936 Negotiations between Rome and Tirana progress, as the Italians modify some of their demands limiting Albanian independence. A rapprochement becomes certain as the Albanian economy continues its decline.

1935

August 14–15 Due to growing discontent and economic hardship of the peasantry, an anti-Zogist insurrection takes place in Fier. After seizing Fier, the insurgents advance towards Lushnjë but are dispersed by government forces. The revolt is small and poorly led but is sufficient enough to cause Zog to overreact. A reign of terror follows in the area of Fier, where over 500 show trials are staged in order to intimidate any potential opposition.

October 21 Realizing that his overreaction to the Fier insurrection provoked more opposition than it suppressed, Zog makes a major concession. He appoints as prime minister Mehdi Bey Frashëri, an accomplished historian and jurist who for years has been Albania's representative to the League of Nations. Because Frashëri is known to advocate Western democratic liberalism, his appointment is generally seen as a shift in Zog's domestic policy towards the moderate political center. This view is reinforced when Frashëri forms a new cabinet composed of youthful, dedicated reformers.

October 26 Frashëri's cabinet presents its reform program, which pledges to improve and consolidate the administration and develop art and education. Nepotism and corruption are to be rooted out and the independence of the courts protected. What governmental resources are available are to be used to develop the road system and improve agriculture. In addition, the liberal government guarantees the freedom of speech and of the press, excluding criticisms of the king and foreign policy. As a result, the Frashëri government gains a good deal of popular support.

1936

February–March Taking advantage of the apparent liberalization policy of the Frashëri government, workers in Korcë demand permission to form labor unions. Labor strikes take place principally for better working conditions and against unemployment. The government crushes the strikers with the violent intervention of the gendarmerie. For the first time Communists are involved in organizing workers, but there is as yet no Communist party, but rather small uncoordinated groups in Korcë and Tirana.

March A comprehensive agreement between Albania and Italy is announced. In exchange for considerable economic aid, the Albanians agree to grant Italy a series of showy, insignificant concessions. In reality, however, Italian financial support is accompanied by Italian control. In the following years Italian influence in the army and the national economy steadily increases (*see* September 1934–March 1936).

November 7 King Zog dismisses the liberal Frashëri cabinet. From the start Frashëri's reform program threatened conservative interests and quickly made many enemies in and out of parliament. With little cooperation from both the parliament and the bureaucracy, Frashëri's program floundered and his leadership became increasingly ineffectual. Zog, therefore, returns to his old methods.

November 9 The new cabinet, headed by Zog's lackey, Koco Kota, takes office. The Kota government signals the end of Zog's brief period of concession to liberal reform and the return to royal dictatorship. Emphasizing the return to his former policies, Zog allows the Italians to expand their influence in Albania.

1937

May 15–17 The former minister of the interior in Frashëri's government, Efthem Toto, leads a rebellion in the Delvinë area. Toto's force is repulsed as it advances towards Vlorë, Toto is killed, and the insurrection is quickly suppressed. Zog concludes the need for further stability, for which he turns to Italy.

1938

April 27 Zog marries the Hungarian countess Geraldine Apponyi, during which Italian foreign minister and son-in-law of Mussolini, Count Galeazzo Ciano, acts as best man. Zog's betrothal to Shefqet Bey Vërlaci's daughter ended long ago, because marriage to a commoner is considered unsuitable for a king.

May   On his return to Italy, Ciano proposes the annexation of Albania to Mussolini. Ciano regards annexation to be the logical outcome of Italy's methodical decade-long penetration of Albania. Moreover, both are encouraged by the fact that there appears to be little support for the royal dictatorship.

1939

January 18–23   Ciano meets with Yugoslavia's foreign minister in Belgrade, where he obtains assurances that the Yugoslav government will not oppose Italian annexation of Albania. With this guarantee, Mussolini's government decides to prepare for the military conquest of Albania.

March 25   The Italian government sends to Zog's regime the draft of an agreement for an Italian protectorate over Albania in which Albanian independence would end, and in essence make Albania an Italian province.

March 27   Rome dispatches an ultimatum demanding an answer to the terms of March 25 before April 7. It is made clear to Zog that, if he refuses, Italian forces will invade Albania.

March 28   In an attempt to delay, Zog informs Ciano that he supports the Italian demands but his cabinet refuses to agree.

March 31   Ciano concludes that Zog does not intend to sign the agreement for a protectorate.

April 2   Zog presents Ciano with a revised plan incorporating some but not all of the points of the Italian ultimatum. Zog refuses to accept those demands that compromise Albania's independence and integrity. The Italian government ignores Zog's proposal and responds only with the granting of a delay of 12 hours for the expiration of its ultimatum. Mussolini decides to proceed with the invasion if Zog does not cave in.

April 3–6   Although Zog's government denies that a crisis exists between it and Rome, rumors abound that invasion is imminent. Public demonstrations break out throughout Albania, demanding that the government inform the nation of the crisis and that action be taken to defend the country from Italian attack.

April 5   Crown Prince Leka is born in Tirana to King Zog and Queen Geraldine. Zog appeals to the Western democracies for support against Italy, but to no avail.

April 6   A special cabinet and parliamentary meeting votes to reject the Italian demands and to resist the Italian invasion.

April 7   At 5:30 A.M., 40,000 troops, 400 aircraft, and dozens of warships attack Durrës, Sarandë, Shëngjin, and Vlorë. The Italians encounter strong resistance in Durrës but occupy the town by the early afternoon. Fighting is sporadic and insignificant elsewhere. Queen Geraldine and Crown Prince Leka flee Tirana for Greece. Close to noon, Zog makes a final effort to come to a negotiated settlement with the Italians, but the talks prove unsuccessful. Zog abandons the idea of continuing resistance and decides to follow his family into exile. Zog does not abdicate, but his monarchy, established on September 1, 1928, ends abruptly.

April 8   Italian forces enter Tirana. Organized Albanian resistance collapses. Zog joins his wife and son in Greece.

April 9   Gjirokastër and Shkodër are occupied by Italian forces.

April 10   All of Albania is under Italian occupation.

April 12   Ciano arrives in Tirana and convenes the Albanian parliament. The parliament obediently votes to abolish the 1928 constitution and proclaims the union of Albania with Italy by offering the crown to the Italian monarch, Victor Emmanuel III. The new king is represented by a viceroy, or royal lieutenant, Francesco Jacomoni, the former Italian minister to Albania. A puppet government is formed under the presidency of Shefqet Bey Vërlaci.

April 20   President Vërlaci signs a series of political and economic conventions with the Italian government, according to which Albania constitutes with Italy one single land under a customs union, linked currencies, and co-equal citizenship.

April 21   The Albanian Fascist party is established under political opportunist Tefik Mborja, who becomes minister of fascism in the puppet government. The Albanian population, however, responds with indifference to the new ministry's efforts to promote fascism.

May 2   The Albanian royal family, accompanied by some 80 followers, leaves Greece by special train for Turkey.

June 3   The Italian government issues a new de facto constitution for Albania designed to institutionalize Italian domination. Albania no longer has a parliament, and King Victor Emmanuel III is entrusted with executive, legislative, and judicial authority. The Albanian armed forces and the diplomatic corps are incorporated into those of Italy.

1940

October 28   Italy's main objectives in occupying Albania are to secure control over the strategic Strait of Otranto, commanding the entry to the Adriatic, and to establish a bridgehead in the Balkans for an invasion of Greece. A hastily organized but large Italian army attacks Greece from bases in southern Albania. As a pretext for its aggression, and in order to enlist the support of Albanian nationalists, the Italian government claims to be taking action against Greece on behalf of Albanian irredenta in Tsamouria. Albania is automatically at war with Greece.

October 28–November 14   Suffering heavy losses, the Italian invasion force makes only marginal gains in its offensive across the Greek frontier. Two battalions of Albanian recruits sent to the front refuse to fight. They are withdrawn and confined to the Shijak concentration camp in central Albania. Although some Albanians fight alongside the Italians, many desert and join the Greeks.

November 14–December 28   The Greek army launches a counteroffensive, defeating the Italians and pushing them back across the frontier. Greek forces penetrate deep into the territory of Albania, capturing Korcë on November 22 and Gjirokastër in the beginning of December. By the end of their counteroffensive, the Greeks hold the southern fourth of Albania.

December 28, 1940–April 6, 1941   The Greek forces in southern Albania are initially welcomed as liberators, but the establishment of Greek administration in the occupied regions causes disillusionment among the Albanians. In the meantime, Mussolini masses twenty-five divisions in Albania and launches an enormous offensive in March in order to break the center of the Greek front in the area of Tepelenë, but it fails.

1941

April 6   German führer (leader) Adolf Hitler is forced to rescue Mussolini from military disaster in the Balkans. The German army attacks Greece and Yugoslavia from positions in Bulgaria and Hungary.

April 21   The Greek army capitulates to the Germans, as it withdraws from southern Albania.

Late April   With the approval of Germany, Italy incorporates into Albania the province of Kosovo as well as other districts of southwestern Yugoslavia, and the area of Tsamouria in Greek Epirus. Fascist propaganda heralds the claim that Albania has secured its ethnic frontiers, thanks to German and Italian intervention. With the annexations, the territory and population of Albania almost doubles. Given that the annexed region of Kosovo is more productive, Albania's chronic deficit in agricultural production is solved at once. The Italians and Vërlaci's puppet government exploit these facts in their propaganda campaigns in order to persuade Albanian public opinion that the existence of a greater Albania depends on the victory of the Axis powers, and that with the victory of the Western powers, whose allies are Greece and Yugoslavia, the very survival of Albania would be put in question. The propaganda campaign is also promoted by anti-Zogist personalities who have returned from exile, in particular Mustafa Merlika Kruja, a nationalist and longtime, well-known opponent of the large landowners. Despite the efforts of the Italian and puppet propagandists, Albanian public opinion is not won over to the Axis cause. As testament to this fact, nationalist Vasil Laci makes an attempt on the life of King Victor Emmanuel during the monarch's visit in Tirana.

November 8   The Albanian Communist party (ACP) is formed in Tirana. Before 1941 communism is an insignificant factor in Albanian politics. At the time of the Italian invasion there were fewer than 200 Communists in Albania, and the movement is handicapped by very serious problems: it lacks leadership and discipline; it has no popular support; it is organized on a purely local basis; and despite its small size, the Albanian Communist movement is split into contending factions of Marxist-Leninists, nationalist Communists, and Trotskyists. The Axis invasion of the Soviet Union in summer 1941 provides the necessary impetus to form a unified party. The task of organizing an Albanian Communist party is assigned to two emissaries of Yugoslav Partisan leader Josip Broz Tito—Dusan Mugosa and Miladin Popovic, members of the regional committee of the Yugoslav Communist party for Kosovo. Mugosa and Popovic meet with representatives of the various Albanian groups clandestinely in Tirana, where they unite to form the Albanian Communist party. The delegates elect an 11-member Central Committee and choose Enver Hoxha, a 33-year-old former school teacher from Gjirokastër, as provisional secretary. The majority of the ACP leadership and the bulk of the 130 original party members are young intellectuals and students of middle-class origins. From its inception the ACP is dependent on the Yugoslav Communist party. In fact, it begins its history as essentially a branch of the older and much larger organization. Further, Tito's emissaries remain in Albania throughout the war, and they are the real leaders of the ACP, with Mugosa as the military organizer and Popovic as the political organizer of the Communist movement in Albania.

October 28 A nationalist demonstration against Italian occupation takes place in Tirana in front of Verlaci's office.

December Given the failure of Italian propaganda to win the support of the Albanian public, and the emergence of resistance against Italian occupation, Rome shifts policy. Following directives from Rome for the inclusion in the Tirana government of new and more representative officials, a cabinet is formed under Kruja. In addition, Rome makes some concessions toward Albanian autonomy.

can and champions the objective of an ethnic Albania. Its armed bands welcome all Albanians except Communists.

December 10 Albanians are encouraged when U.S. secretary of state Cordell Hull announces that the American government acknowledges the independence of Albania and leaves it up to the Albanian people to decide their form of government at the end of the war.

December 17 The British announce that they support the American position on postwar Albania and that the question of Albania's postwar boundaries will be discussed at the peace conference after the war. The Soviet government gives similar assurances the next day.

1942

January–September Despite Rome's concessions, resistance to Italian occupation increases. Encouraged by the example of Greece and Yugoslavia, guerrilla bands begin armed resistance in the mountains.

September 16 The Pezë Conference convenes. In order to promote their image and stimulate support, the Communists resort to a popular front strategy aimed at appealing to Albanian nationalism. They organize the conference to which a diverse number of groups are invited. The ACP plans to present the conference as a union of nationalists and Communists and so gain legitimacy and control of the entire resistance movement. However, the few nationalists at the conference see through the popular front ploy and do not sign the resolution that proclaims the formation of the National Liberation Front. Nevertheless, the Communists claim that the union between them and the nationalists is complete and that they will fight the occupation forces together. As a tactical maneuver the Communists include Abaz Kupi, the pro-Zogist chieftain of Krujë, in the National Liberation Council, which is to direct the resistance activities of the National Liberation Front and its military, the Albanian National Liberation Army. As the only organized political party in the National Liberation Front, the Communists are able to dominate the organization by placing their members in key leadership positions. Behind the facade of the National Liberation Front, the ACP prepares for revolution under the guise of patriotic resistance.

November The Balli Kombëtar (National Front) emerges under the leadership of Midhat Frashëri. Frashëri, a democratic nationalist and writer, formed a secret resistance movement centered at Tirana during the first days of the Italian occupation that becomes national in scope by the autumn of 1942. The Balli Kombëtar is essentially republi-

1943

January–July Armed bands of the Balli Kombëtar and the National Liberation Front wage war both on the Italians and with each other. The Balli Kombëtar forces are larger, but the National Liberation Front is more effective in fighting the occupiers and publicizing its successes. The Balli Kombëtar is hampered by its decision to reduce its military operations against the Italians during the early summer in order to lessen the loss of civilian life and to conserve its forces as a counterbalance to the Communists. However, this policy weakens the Balli Kombëtar's popular support and upsets the British military advisers present in Albania since May seeking to expand the Albanian resistance.

January 10 Dissatisfied with their inability to pacify the growing resistance movements, the Italians force Kruja and his cabinet to resign.

February 22 The Italians install a new cabinet led by Maliq Bushati, a former parliamentary deputy and an opponent of King Zog.

March 17–22 Regional delegates of the National Liberation Front assemble at a conference in the village of Labinot near Elbasan, where the Albanian Communist party (ACP) makes the decision to intensify military operations against the Italians. More importantly, the ACP resolves that efforts should be made to incorporate all other resistance organizations into the National Liberation Front. However, if it proves impossible to unite the Balli Kombëtar with the National Liberation Front and thus subordinate it to the ACP, the goal will be to brand the nationalist resistance as traitorous and destroy it through military action. This policy decision is of course kept secret. The official announcements emphasize patriotic clichés and make appeals to national unity in the common struggle against Axis occupation.

July 10 The General Council of the National Liberation Front establishes a supreme command for its armed forces. A general staff for the National Liberation Army is formed under guerrilla leader Spiro Moissiu, acting as military commander, and Enver Hoxha as political commissar. The approximately 11,000-man-strong army is organized into 30 regional partisan battalions.

August 1–3 With the urging of British military advisers, representatives of the Balli Kombëtar and the National Liberation Front meet at Mukaj, near Tirana, in an effort to establish a united resistance. The chief obstacle to an agreement is the question of Kosovo; the Balli Kombëtar refuses to consider cooperation unless the National Liberation Front joins in the demand that Kosovo not be returned to Yugoslavia but be retained by Albania after the war. Ultimately the emissaries of the National Liberation Front accept these terms and agree to form a joint Committee of National Salvation to direct united resistance against the Italians. However, ACP leader Hoxha and the National Liberation Council refuse to ratify the agreement. They reject the plan, because it seriously diminishes the prospect for an armed takeover following the liberation of Albania by creating a new resistance organization, in which power would be shared equally by both the Balli Kombëtar and the National Liberation Front. Moreover, the ACP's Yugoslav superiors, Mugosa and Popovic, veto the agreement.

September 4 Regional delegates of the National Liberation Front meet again in Labinot where, realizing that efforts to unite the Balli Kombëtar with the National Liberation Front have failed, they decide to destroy the Balli Kombëtar.

September 8 Italian capitulation to the Allies marks the end of that country's rule in Albania, forcing the Germans to take over the occupation of Albania and rush in troops. Nonetheless, the National Liberation Front manages to disarm two Italian divisions and obtains large quantities of supplies. The Germans cannot spare a large occupation force, so they control the cities and main transportation routes, leaving the rest of the country to the resistance.

September 11 The German occupation authorities in Tirana announce their support for Albanian independence, neutrality, and territorial integrity, with the intention of pacifying resistance and helping in the building of an anti-Communist nationalist coalition.

October Strengthened by captured Italian arms, the National Liberation Front launches a full-scale attack against the Balli Kombëtar.

October 18 A German-sponsored nationalist parliament convenes in Tirana.

October 20 The collaborationist parliament establishes a four-member Council of Regents. As with the parliament, the Council of Regents represents a nationalist anti-Communist coalition. Its members are Anton Arapi, a Catholic priest; Fuad Dibra, a member of the Balli Kombëtar; Lef Nosi, an independent nationalist; and Mehdi Frashëri, the former prime minister of Zog held in Italian confinement during Rome's occupation of Albania and now returned to the country by the Germans.

November Communist hostilities against the Balli Kombëtar leads to the defection of Abaz Kupi from the National Liberation Front. Kupi and his forces form the Legality Organization, which favors the restoration of King Zog.

December The Germans take advantage of the Albanian civil war by launching an offensive against the National Liberation Front. The guerrillas, however, evade the Germans and increase their numbers as a result of German terrorism against the rural population.

1944

January–April Despite heavy losses inflicted by the Germans, the National Liberation Front resumes attacks against both the occupation forces and rival resistance organizations. The British military mission makes repeated efforts to arrange a truce among the contending resistance factions but is unsuccessful. Meanwhile, the ACP's aggressive pursuit of the war against the Germans and its successful propaganda campaign against the resistance organizations causes popular support to shift to the National Liberation Front, particularly in central and southern Albania.

May 24–28 Nearly 200 delegates of the National Liberation Front meet in Përmet for the Antifascist National Liberation Congress. King Zog is formally deposed and forbidden to return to Albania. The congress creates the 78-member Antifascist Council of National Liberation and declares that this body is the representative of the Albanian people. The council elects an 11-member cabinet, the Antifascist National Liberation Committee, headed by Enver Hoxha, who is appointed commander in chief of the National Liberation Army.

Late May–late August The Germans, along with the forces of the Balli Kombëtar and Abaz Kupi's Legality Organization, launch a major offensive against the now 35,000-man-strong National Liberation Front. The National Liberation Army suffers heavy casualties, but its numbers swell with thousands of new volunteers. Conversely, the Balli Kombëtar and the Legality Organization are seriously weakened during the course of the campaign.

September The advance of the Soviet Red Army into the Balkans forces the Germans to prepare to evacuate Albania, while the National Liberation Army launches a counteroffensive. As German withdrawal becomes imminent, the Balli Kombëtar and the Legality Organization are further reduced in strength by mounting desertions.

Late September–October The Albanian minority in Tsamouria flees Greek Epirus into southern Albania, fearing retribution from the Greeks for having actively collaborated with the Axis occupation forces in Greece. They withdraw into Albania alongside the retreating Germans.

September 12 Berat is liberated by the National Liberation Army.

September 18 Gjirokastër is liberated.

October 16 Vlorë is liberated.

October 20–23 The National Liberation Front convenes the second meeting of the Antifascist Council of National Liberation in Berat. On October 22 the Communists transform the Anti-Fascist National Liberation Committee into a de facto government, the Provisional Democratic Government of Albania. Hoxha, commander in chief of the National Liberation Army and acknowledged ACP leader, is named premier. On October 23, the Congress of Berat, as the meeting becomes known, issues a Declaration of the Rights of the Albanian People, pledges to hold free elections for a constituent assembly, and expresses its intention to maintain close ties with the Allies—Great Britain, the Soviet Union, and the United States.

October 24 Korcë is liberated.

October 29 The National Liberation Army launches an attack on Tirana, liberating it on November 17 after intense fighting.

November 28 The Provisional Democratic Government enters Tirana and installs itself in the capital as the government of Albania, with Hoxha as premier.

November 29 With the German evacuation of Albania complete, the National Liberation Army enters Shkodër; Albania is now under the control of the Communist government in Tirana.

December The Hoxha regime faces many serious problems: (1) the economy and infrastructure are in a shambles; (2) there is considerable opposition to the new regime in northern Albania, especially among the Catholic and pro-Zogist population; (3) the Yugoslavs continue their domination of the ACP and encourage the activities of a particularly subservient faction, which Belgrade hopes will replace Hoxha with its openly pro-Yugoslav deputy, Koci Xoxe. Belgrade, furthermore, reincorporates Kosovo into Yugoslavia and suppresses Albanian irredentism there. Meanwhile, Athens, which refuses to recognize Albania as an Allied state and maintains that a state of war exists between the two countries because of the October 1940 invasion, renews its claims to Northern Epirus.

1945

January 4 The Albanian government requests recognition on the part of Great Britain, the Soviet Union, and the United States.

January 27 A special tribunal opens in Tirana with the alleged objective of trying ''war criminals'' and ''people's enemies.'' Similar tribunals are created throughout the country. Their real purpose is to eliminate political opponents of the regime. The trials last for more than a year and lead to hundreds of death sentences and thousands of imprisonments.

March 22 An enormous tax is imposed on businessmen for alleged war profiteering. The taxes are so high that they are unable to pay them. As a result, their property is confiscated and the merchants are imprisoned or sent to labor camps; the new regime succeeds in liquidating the merchant class.

April 29 Yugoslavia recognizes the Albanian government.

May 8 An informal U.S. mission to Albania enters Tirana to survey conditions.

July 14 The government forms consumer goods cooperatives, followed by similar organizations for service tradespeople.

August 2 Transportation is nationalized, and the nationalization of all industry begins.

August 5 The Hoxha regime changes the name of the National Liberation Front to the Democratic Front in a ploy intended to win Western recognition.

August 29 The Agrarian Reform Law goes into effect, with the official objective of the redistribution of the large landowner estates to the peasantry. In reality the law is the first step in a long-term program aimed at the collectivization of agriculture.

November 10   The Soviet Union establishes diplomatic relations with Albania. The British and American governments express their readiness to recognize the Tirana regime on the condition that free elections take place for the Constituent Assembly.

December 2   Elections for the Constituent Assembly take place. In order to create the impression of free elections, the government provides for the casting of opposition ballots. However, since no organized opposition exists because of state terror, the Democratic Front wins 93 percent of the votes, according to official returns.

1946

January 11   The newly elected Constituent Assembly formally abolishes the monarchy and proclaims Albania a people's republic.

March 14   A constitution, patterned on the Yugoslav one, which legitimizes the ACP's control of the country, is ratified by the Constituent Assembly.

April   With the Communists in firm control, the government adopts new measures: all building enterprises, agricultural machinery, mines, and remaining private industries are nationalized; merchants are forced to surrender their merchandise to the state; state and cooperative enterprises replace private retailers; medical facilities are nationalized; and the sale of agricultural property is prohibited. The leading force behind these policies is Hoxha, who serves simultaneously as secretary general of the ACP, president of the Democratic Front, prime minister, foreign minister, defense minister, and commander in chief of the armed forces.

April 17   Hoxha threatens drastic measures against persons opposing the government's policies. Mass arrests take place within the army, the Democratic Front, the bureaucracy, and the ACP.

July 9   The Yugoslav-Albanian Treaty of Friendship, Cooperation, and Mutual Assistance is concluded in Tirana, which envisions the merger of Albanian and Yugoslav economic interests.

July 29   The U.S. Senate passes the Pepper Resolution, which places the Senate on record as favoring the award of Northern Epirus to Greece. This presents the ACP with a tool on which to build up anti-Western sentiment. Although the U.S. government secures the withdrawal of the Northern Epirus question from the agenda of the Paris Peace Conference, the ACP continues and intensifies its anti-American propaganda.

August 29   The United Nations rejects Albania's application for membership due to outstanding unresolved differences between Albania and the United States causing Washington to veto the application.

August 30   The Ministry of the Interior is given the right to regulate the movement of all citizens and foreigners, enforced through its secret police apparatus, the Sigurimi (State Security Police).

October 22   Two British destroyers are damaged and suffer heavy casualties from mines placed in the Corfu Channel near the Albanian coast. London breaks off relations with Tirana when it concludes that the mines were placed in the path of the British vessels with the knowledge of the Albanian government.

November 6   Confronted with the growing hostility of the Albanian regime and its refusal to recognize prewar treaties between it and Tirana, the United States recalls its diplomatic mission, breaking relations.

November 27   The Albanian and Yugoslav governments sign the Treaty on the Coordination of Economic Plans, the Customs Union, and Equalization of Currencies. This treaty details the plan for economic integration established with the July 9, 1946, Treaty of Friendship, Cooperation, and Mutual Assistance. The new treaty provides for an agency to coordinate the economic plans of Belgrade and Tirana, for the standardization of the Albanian and Yugoslav monetary systems, and for the creation of a common price system and customs union. In essence, the two economies are to be merged. The Albanians hope that this association will enable them to become economically independent, while Yugoslavian head of state Josip Tito hopes to strengthen his grip on Albania by making it dependent upon Yugoslavia. Tito, in effect, plans to ultimately incorporate Albania into Yugoslavia as a federal republic. Given their conflicting interests with regard to the treaty, misunderstandings and tensions arise between the two countries.

1947

January–May   Relations between Albania and Yugoslavia become increasingly strained. The Yugoslavs refuse to discuss Albanian proposals for developmental aid until Tirana agrees to the formation of a joint commission to coordinate the economic plans of the two nations, as stipulated by the July 1946 treaty. Premier Hoxha, however, rejects the Yugoslav demand. He and other members of the Albanian Communist party (ACP) become suspicious of Belgrade when the Yugoslav government proposes that the two states sign a secret pact, which would protect Yugoslav interests in Albania in the event of a change in regime in Tirana. Hoxha is convinced that Tito is more interested in incorporating Albania into Yugoslavia than in strengthening the Communist regime in Tirana.

February 10 The treaties formally ending the war between Italy and the Allies are signed at the Paris Peace Conference, requiring Italy to pay $5 million and to surrender the island of Sazan to Albania.

March 25 The United Nations Security Council condemns Albania for collusion in the damaging of two British destroyers on October 22, 1946.

May 20 Acting through their chief supporter, Interior Minister Koci Xoxe, the Yugoslavs launch an attack against those elements in the ACP considered hostile to their interests. Nine members of the Constituent Assembly, known for their opposition to the Yugoslavs, are arrested, tried, and convicted of plotting against the state. Xoxe's actions are designed to intimidate Hoxha and others in the ACP who have displayed a reluctance to accept the Yugoslav plan for Albania.

May 27 The Commission of Investigation of the United Nations Security Council concludes that Albania is participating in efforts to overthrow the Greek government by supporting Communist guerrillas in Greece. Albania, in fact, is serving as the main base of operations and refuge for the Greek Communists.

June–August Hoxha turns to the Soviet Union for assistance to lessen the dependency of his government on Yugoslavia and to serve as a counterbalance to Belgrade's increasing influence in Albania. The Soviet Union grants some credits to Albania and takes diplomatic actions to warn Tito that the final decision concerning the future of Albania will be made in Moscow, not Belgrade.

November Fearing that their position in Albania is seriously threatened, the Yugoslavs dispatch a strong letter to the Central Committee of the ACP, singling out opponents of Belgrade for criticism and demanding Albanian conformity with Yugoslavia.

November 17 The Albanian government announces the completion of the private agricultural property reform and the initiation of agricultural collectivization (*see* August 29, 1945).

December In order to refute Tito's contention that Yugoslavia holds a privileged position in Albania, Hoxha travels to Sofia, Bulgaria, where he concludes a Treaty of Friendship, Cooperation, and Mutual Assistance. Xoxe attempts to disrupt the effort but is not successful.

1948

February 26–March 8 The Eighth Plenum of the Central Committee of the ACP takes place, marking the high tide of Yugoslav influence in Albania. The decisions of the Eighth Plenum represent a victory for Xoxe and the pro-Yugoslav wing of the ACP by expelling a number of anti-Yugoslav members from the party. Hoxha survives the purge and is able to retain his position as secretary general of the ACP only by changing his views and expressing support for Xoxe's policies. Before ending, the Plenum approves Xoxe's proposals to merge the Albanian and Yugoslav economies and armed forces.

April Xoxe, now confident that he has beaten Hoxha, calls a meeting of the Politburo. He proposes that Albania petition Yugoslavia for admission as a federal republic, but the majority in the Politburo rejects the plan. In response, Xoxe launches a propaganda and terror campaign through the Ministry of the Interior and the secret police.

May–June Xoxe's terror campaign comes too late, and Yugoslav influence and prestige in Albania declines as Tito's ambitions in the Balkans draw Stalin's condemnation. Hoxha takes advantage of the worsening Soviet-Yugoslav dispute to reassert his power by challenging Xoxe. Hoxha now openly criticizes the Yugoslavs and their supporters in the ACP.

June 28 Yugoslavia is expelled from the Soviet Bloc, marking the complete break between Stalin and Tito. Hoxha uses the split to shake Albania from Tito's grasp.

July 1 Albania becomes the first of the Eastern European Communist states to condemn Yugoslavia. The ACP breaks off economic relations with Yugoslavia and expels Yugoslav experts sent to Albania under the economic integration treaties of 1946, while the Albanian press launches a propaganda offensive against Tito.

September Moscow concludes an economic agreement with Tirana to compensate for the loss of Yugoslav aid. Confident of Soviet support, Hoxha attacks the pro-Yugoslav elements in the ACP at a meeting of the Central Committee, which also changes the name of the ACP to the Albanian Party of Labor (APL).

October 3 Xoxe is removed as minister of the interior and transferred to the Ministry of Industry.

October 31 Xoxe and his followers are stripped of their government posts.

November 8–22 The First Congress of the APL meets in Tirana attended by 862 delegates representing over 45,000 party members. Enver Hoxha is renamed secretary general, and a new Central Committee composed of 21 Hoxha supporters is chosen. The Central Committee unleashes a purge of Xoxe and his followers and expels them from the party.

1949

February 8 Albania becomes a member of the Council of Mutual Economic Assistance (COMECON, or CMEA). As a result, the other East Bloc states are required to aid the Soviet Union in the development of the Albanian economy, as Soviet and East Bloc technical advisers are dispatched to Albania to fill the gaps created by the expulsion of Yugoslav specialists.

May 11–June 8 Koci Xoxe is arrested, and his trial takes place in secret. He is found guilty of "Titoist" and "Trotskyite" activities and is sentenced to death, which is carried out on June 11.

August 26 The National Committee for a Free Albania is formed in Paris and is led by the democratic nationalist and leader of the Balli Kombëtar, Midhat Frashëri. The National Committee is composed of émigrés opposed to the Communist regime and enjoys the support of Britain and the United States.

August 28 The head of the Albanian Orthodox church, Abp. Kristofer Kisi, is removed from his post by the government and later imprisoned.

September 21 The United Nations Special Committee on the Balkans advises the General Assembly to declare the Albanian government primarily responsible for the threat to peace in the Balkans, based on Albania's aggressive role in the Greek civil war (*see* May 27, 1947).

November 12 Yugoslavia repudiates the Friendship, Cooperation, and Mutual Aid Treaty with Albania, the only pact with Yugoslavia not denounced by Tirana after the Stalin-Tito break (*see* June 28, 1948).

November 26 The government enacts a law imposing greater restrictions on religious communities and obliging them to profess loyalty to the People's Republic.

1950

January 1950–December 1952 The Soviet government constructs a major naval complex in the Vlorë-Sazan area, with a Soviet fleet of 12 submarines and several auxiliary surface vessels stationed here.

April Hoxha convenes a conference of the APL to expel his remaining opponents. After the conclusion of the conference, a series of trials of Titoists are staged throughout the nation.

June 1950–September 1951 The purge of Titoists enters a new phase, when all members of the APL are required to submit their credentials for reevaluation. Approximately 4,000 individuals are expelled from the party.

July 4 A new constitution, amended along the lines of that of the Soviet Union, is approved by the Constituent, now People's, Assembly.

1951

February A new wave of party purges is unleashed after the Soviet legation in Tirana is bombed.

August 3 The government forces the Roman Catholic church in Albania to sever all connections with the Vatican.

1952

March 31–April 7 The Second Congress of the APL meets in Tirana. Hoxha is reelected secretary general, and the APL condemns Titoism, reaffirms its support for the program of rapid industrialization, and calls for a drive to popularize the collectivization of agriculture.

September 1 A new penal code embodying the basic principles of Soviet justice goes into effect. It grants considerable latitude to state prosecutors in their persecution of political opponents and suspects. It imposes the death penalty on anybody twelve years old or older for conspiracy against the state, damaging state property, and economic sabotage. Furthermore, all those who criticize the Albanian government or the Soviet Union are to be jailed.

1953

March 5 Hoxha is informed of the death of Stalin. Hoxha, who has enthusiastically embraced Stalinism, agrees to implement the concept of collective leadership, as has taken place in the Soviet Union, by gradually relinquishing all his official government positions through July 1954.

July 11 While meeting in Athens, the foreign ministers of the Balkan Pact (Greece, Turkey, and Yugoslavia) make the declaration ''that the independence of Albania would constitute an important element for the peace and stability of the Balkans.''

August 2 Since the Athens declaration recognizes the independence of Albania but not its territorial integrity, it draws the condemnation of the Albanian government. In a speech before the People's Assembly, Hoxha denounces the Balkan Pact as an instrument of aggression and attacks the declaration as a program for dismembering Albania and subjugating it to Greece and Yugoslavia.

August 4 Albania and the Soviet Union raise their respective legations to the status of embassies.

August 27 In a letter to the National Committee for a Free Albania, U.S. secretary of state John Foster Dulles expresses official American friendship for the Albanian people, sympathy with them in their plight, and support for the establishment of a free and representative government.

December 22 Under pressure from Moscow—which, since Stalin's death, is pursuing better relations with Tito—Albania resumes diplomatic relations with Yugoslavia.

1954

July 20 Hoxha officially completes the transition to collective leadership by resigning as prime minister (*see* March 5, 1953). He is succeeded by the Moscow-trained general, Mehmet Shehu, who quickly becomes a member of Hoxha's inner circle. Although Hoxha now holds no government office, he still exercises control over the state by retaining his positions as head of the APL and the Democratic Front. In that capacity the former title of secretary general of the APL is replaced by first secretary of the Central Committee of the APL.

October While outwardly demonstrating support for Stalin's successor, Nikita Khrushchev, the Albanian leadership is privately concerned with the Soviet Union's reduction in aid and by the thawing of relations between Moscow and Belgrade. Taking advantage of Khrushchev's relaxed grip on the satellite states, Hoxha and Shehu seek new sources of aid to compensate for Soviet and East Bloc cutbacks in economic support. Accordingly, Tirana and Beijing sign a series of agreements providing for cultural, scientific, and technical cooperation. The October Beijing-

Tirana agreements mark the first step in the formation of the Albanian-Chinese alliance.

December Beijing presents Tirana with a gift of approximately $2.5 million worth of various commodities. This gift is to be followed by Chinese loans totaling $12.5 million for the next five years, 1955–60.

1955

March 4 The U.S. government offers a donation of $850,000 worth of food to ease shortages in Albania, which Tirana rejects three days later because of its anti-American stance.

May 14 Albania becomes a charter member of the Warsaw Treaty Organization (Warsaw Pact), a military alliance with Bulgaria, Czechoslovakia, Hungary, Poland, Romania, and the Soviet Union.

June 24 Fearing that a Soviet-Yugoslav rapprochement may result in their removal from power, Hoxha and Shehu attack their principal opponents within the government, relieving them of their posts for ''inefficiency.'' However, in his denunciation of them, Hoxha does not brand them as Titoists, in deference to Moscow's new policy towards Yugoslavia.

July 1955–May 1956 Forced to conform to Khrushchev's new line, Hoxha and Shehu reluctantly improve relations with Yugoslavia. In addition, the government initiates a modest domestic liberalization program: some economic reforms are launched; the power of the secret police is reduced; freer discussion within the Albanian Party of Labor (APL) is encouraged; and the role of the APL is minimized in certain areas of public life.

July 3 In a message to Athens, through the secretary of the United Nations, Tirana expresses the desire to establish normal diplomatic relations.

August 3 Athens expresses willingness to end the official state of war between the countries and to establish normal diplomatic relations subject to certain conditions: a settlement of territorial issues, an end of Albanian aid to Greek Communist agents, and a return to Greece of the Greek hostages taken into Albania by the Communists during the Greek civil war. Tirana rejects these demands, and relations are not established.

December 15 Albania is admitted as a member of the United Nations; the United States abstains from voting.

1956

Mid–February Khrushchev formally initiates the policy of de-Stalinization. In his speech to the Twentieth Congress of the Communist Party of the Soviet Union (CPSU), Khrushchev denounces his predecessor and calls for reform within the party. Emboldened by these pronouncements, the small and hitherto silent anti-Hoxha faction of the APL criticizes party policies.

March With the active support of Belgrade and the tacit approval of Moscow, the anti-Hoxha faction of the APL begins a movement to seize the party.

April The anti-Hoxha faction makes its bid for power at the Tirana city party conference. A large and vocal group of delegates denounces the government's leadership practices and economic and diplomatic policies. In addition, they call for the rehabilitation of Xoxe and other victims of the Titoist purges. The APL dissidents try to obtain backing for a program of de-Stalinization, but Hoxha is able to assert his authority and suppresses the opposition.

May 25–June 3 The Third Congress of the APL meets in Tirana. In his speech to the congress, Hoxha reaffirms his support for Khrushchev's policies. Nevertheless, the congress witnesses Hoxha's first public defiance of Moscow when he refuses to rehabilitate victims of the Titoist purges. Moreover, the congress elects a Central Committee composed largely of Stalinists who are completely loyal to the reelected First Secretary Hoxha. The weakness of the anti-Stalinist faction in the APL insures that the Albanian government will soon end its reluctantly initiated de-Stalinization program. The Third APL Congress thus marks the point at which Hoxha fully consolidates his hold on the party.

November 8 In an article published in the official newspaper of the Soviet Communist party, *Pravda* (Truth), to commemorate the fifteenth anniversary of the founding of the Albanian Communist party, Hoxha denounces Titoism as the cause of the recent anti-regime disturbances in Poland and the revolution in Hungary. Privately, Hoxha fears that the experiences of Poland and Hungary confirm that any substantial deviation from the Stalinist model will eventually lead to rebellion, and that in the case of Albania such a development would provide the Soviets and Yugoslavs with an excuse to intervene and impose a regime in Tirana more to their liking. This fear, shared by the Albanian leadership in general, fuels the deterioration of Albanian-Soviet relations over the next five years.

November 11 In a speech at Pula, Yugoslavian leader Tito attacks Hoxha and attributes the Hungarian revolution and the disturbances in Poland to Stalinism.

December 29 Hoxha receives support from Beijing in his escalating war of words with Tito. The Chinese publish a lengthy text appealing to Communist unity while denouncing Titoism as a threat to Bloc solidarity and reaffirming the achievements of Stalinism.

1957

February 13 In a fiery speech before the Central Committee of the APL, Hoxha attacks Tito and the anti-Stalinists in the Soviet Union and the Eastern Bloc.

April Hoxha and Prime Minister Shehu are summoned to Moscow by Khrushchev. Realizing that they have no choice but to give in to Soviet demands, the Albanian leaders renew their pledge of loyalty to Moscow. The Albanians are rewarded for their cooperation with material concessions: the Soviets cancel the $105 million due them from outstanding credits and agree to furnish Tirana with approximately $7.75 million worth of food during 1958.

May A Soviet delegation arrives in Tirana to advise the Albanian government in the preparation of its Fifteen-Year Prospective Plan (1961–75) for economic development.

August Through Soviet coordination, Tirana signs trade agreements with Budapest and Prague that provide for industrial equipment and manufactured goods to Albania in exchange for agricultural and mineral products.

October Economic conditions in Albania improve to the point where the government is able, for the first time since World War II, to abolish food rationing, reduce food prices, and raise most wages.

November The Albanian economy is further strengthened with a new long-term credit of $40 million from Moscow.

1958

May Tirana renews its attack on Tito as a revisionist shortly after the Yugoslavs adopt a new reform program.

June Hoxha attempts to create an anti-Tito coalition within the East Bloc by strengthening Albania's ties with

The Albanian government delegation in Moscow, dedicated to the friendship between the Soviet Union and the People's Republic of Albania.

the two most outspoken opponents of Yugoslav revisionism in Eastern Europe—Bulgaria and Czechoslovakia. Second only to the Albanians in hostility toward the Yugoslavs in the Communist world are the Chinese, whose position on this question strengthens their bonds with Albania.

August Tension between Albania and Yugoslavia reaches new heights when Tirana brands Tito a fascist who has sold out to American imperialism and accuses Tito's regime of practicing genocide against the Albanian population of Kosovo.

December Hoxha is frustrated by Khrushchev's foreign and economic policies. Specifically, Hoxha is concerned both by Khrushchev's unwillingness to denounce and make a final break with Tito and by his long-term economic plans for Albania stressing agriculture, which undermine Tirana's program of rapid industrialization.

1959

March The Yugoslavs withdraw their minister in Tirana.

May 25–June 4 Alarmed by the ongoing controversy between Belgrade and Tirana, and by the expanding ties between Beijing and Tirana, Khrushchev visits Albania. In order to gain Albanian cooperation, Khrushchev promises new economic concessions to Tirana. In turn Hoxha assures Khrushchev that Albania will seek better relations with Yugoslavia.

August Despite his pledge to Khrushchev of friendlier relations with Yugoslavia, Hoxha resumes open attacks against Belgrade.

December As the rift between Moscow and Tirana grows, the foundations for a Beijing-Tirana axis are laid. The Albanian and Chinese governments find themselves increasingly in agreement in opposition to the Soviet Union on the issues of de-Stalinization, global strategy, and Yugoslav revisionism. Nevertheless, First Secretary Hoxha and Prime Minister Shehu continue to officially support Khrushchev's policy by paying lip service to Moscow, because Albania still depends on the Soviet Union for economic support. Moreover, Hoxha and Shehu are reluctant to jeopardize their own positions by precipitating a break with Moscow.

1960

June 5–9 The General Council of the World Federation of Trade Unions meets in Beijing. The conference marks the first international confrontation where Albanian support for Beijing in the Chinese-Soviet dispute publicly emerges. By attempting to form an opposition group at the conference, the Chinese challenge Soviet organizational supremacy in international Communism. The Albanian delegation joins with the Chinese in their opposition to the Soviet Union. Nevertheless, it is doubtful that Hoxha, before the meeting, wanted to take sides totally with Beijing against Moscow. But given Beijing's public pronouncements and open challenge to Moscow, Hoxha has no choice but to side with China.

Mid-June Khrushchev reacts to the Albanian gestures of defiance by attempting to force Hoxha to capitulate to Moscow. Khrushchev undertakes an intimidating diplomatic maneuver by meeting with Greek liberal politicians to discuss the possibility of obtaining at least cultural autonomy for the Greek population in southern Albania. Hoxha views this move as an implicit threat to partition Albania, and it causes an increase in Albanian hostility towards the USSR.

June 20–25 At the Third Congress of the Romanian Communist party in Bucharest, Khrushchev attempts to secure condemnation of China. Khrushchev's speech at the congress makes clear his opposition to China's foreign policy direction and interpretations of Marxism-Leninism. All of the East European delegations at the congress support the Soviets and denounce the leader of China, Mao Zedong, except the Albanians. While the leader of Tirana's delegation, Hysni Kapo, does not take a clear-cut stand on the Chinese-Soviet dispute, it is obvious that Albania's loyalty lies with China. At this point Khrushchev decides that, since the Albanian leadership will not voluntarily retreat from its anti-Soviet stand, it will have to be overthrown.

July–August Moscow launches a campaign to topple the Hoxha regime and replace it with a pro-Soviet one. Khrushchev begins by cutting Soviet aid and wheat shipments promised to the Albanians, in the midst of a severe drought. The Soviet embassy in Tirana openly encourages the pro-Soviet faction in the Albanian Party of Labor (APL) to work against the pro-Chinese orientation of the Albanian leadership. Meanwhile, the Soviets are secretly involved in the preparation of a coup and armed uprising by disillusioned elements within Albania. Despite the intense pressures against them, Hoxha and Shehu survive. China dispatches wheat shipments to Albania, thus saving the country from famine and making it possible for Tirana to continue defying Moscow. In addition, the insurrection and coup plots are uncovered by the Sigurimi, and the conspirators are arrested. Hoxha is able to withstand the serious challenge because of his tight control over the party machinery, which in turn is able to maintain its firm grip on the police and armed forces, the mainstays of the Hoxha regime.

August 13 Realizing that his campaign to overthrow Hoxha has failed, Khrushchev shifts his tactics. The Central Committee of the Soviet Communist party sends a message to its Albanian counterpart, calling for bilateral talks and reconciliation. Two weeks later Tirana rejects the proposal.

Early September The Albanian delegation to the Congress of the North Vietnamese Communist party in Hanoi comes out strongly in favor of Beijing in the worsening Chinese-Soviet dispute.

Late September Khrushchev openly snubs Shehu, while demonstrating friendship for Tito at the opening sessions of the United Nations General Assembly. The Albanians respond by opposing the Soviet-backed Bulgarian proposal for total disarmament in the Balkans.

November 10 The International Conference of the world's 81 Communist parties convenes in Moscow with the Albanian delegation being led by Hoxha and Shehu.

November 12 Khrushchev meets with the Albanian delegation but neither side demonstrates a willingness to compromise, and the meeting ends without result.

November 16 Hoxha delivers a speech against Khrushchev to the Moscow conference. He repeats the Chinese position on the major ideological, organizational, and political issues that divide Beijing and Moscow. Addressing the crisis in Albanian-Soviet relations, Hoxha accuses Moscow of numerous offenses: failing to consult Tirana concerning policy towards Yugoslavia; encouraging Greek irredentism in southern Albania; fomenting revolt in the APL and Albanian armed forces; attempting to disrupt Albanian–Chinese relations; applying economic extortion against Albania; and threatening to expel Albania from the Warsaw Pact. Hoxha's speech ends all remaining chances of a reconciliation between Moscow and Tirana.

November 25 Fearful of their own boldness in attacking the Soviets, Hoxha and Shehu leave Moscow a week before the end of the conference.

December 20 After two months of haggling, negotiations concerning economic issues break down between Moscow and Tirana.

1961

January–October Albanian-Soviet relations continue to deteriorate. The period is marked by escalating insults and exchanges of condemnations. The Soviets halt work on the Tirana Palace of Culture, withdraw their specialists, and praise Tito repeatedly in public. The Albanians, meanwhile, publicly honor Stalin, subject Soviet personnel to severe security checks and harassment, and routinely denounce Tito. As the tension continues, Beijing increases its support of Albania.

January 7 Beijing dispatches an economic mission to Tirana.

February 2 Beijing and Tirana conclude an agreement whereby China pledges $123 million in aid and credits for the years 1961–65, which represents approximately 90 percent of the amount promised by the Soviet Bloc for the same period. The terms of accord are not disclosed until April 1961.

February 13–20 At the Fourth Congress of the APL in Tirana, Hoxha and Shehu challenge the primacy of Moscow in the Communist movement. Most of the foreign delegations are stunned by Hoxha and Shehu's pronouncements, and the European delegations condemn the APL when the Greek delegate to the congress is refused permission to address that body. The congress not only intensifies the Moscow-Tirana split but alienates the APL from Europe's other Communist parties.

April 9 After suffering from ill health for more than a decade, the exiled King Zog dies outside Paris.

April 15 Leka, son of the late King Zog, ascends to the nonexistent Albanian throne in ceremonies held in a Paris hotel.

April 25 One day after the terms of the February 2 Albanian-Chinese economic accords are made public, Moscow officially notifies Tirana that all Soviet economic aid programs in Albania have ended.

Late May The Soviets begin to dismantle their naval complex at Vlorë, and Albanian forces attempt to prevent the withdrawal of the 12 Soviet submarines based there. After bitter negotiations, the Soviets are permitted to evacuate their positions, but only after agreeing to leave behind four submarines and considerable military equipment. In retaliation the Soviets seize several Albanian surface vessels undergoing repairs at the Black Sea port of Sevastopol.

October 17 In his opening address to the Twenty-second Congress of the Soviet Communist party, Soviet leader Khrushchev scolds the Albanian leadership, and he urges the Albanian Party of labor (APL) to renounce its position and return to Soviet conformity.

October 20 The APL Central Committee reacts to Khrushchev's speech by issuing a statement condemning Khrushchev as a Judas and an anti-Marxist in the service of imperialists and Yugoslav revisionists.

October 27 The Soviet anti-Albanian campaign reaches its climax. Khrushchev delivers his concluding speech to the Soviet congress, where he again denounces the APL and calls upon the Albanian people to overthrow First Secretary Hoxha and Prime Minister Shehu.

November 7 In a sharp rebuke to Khrushchev, Hoxha lists the ideological differences and political issues that have driven Albania and the Soviet Union apart. Hoxha insists that Moscow's de-Stalinization policy and its friendship with Tito are aiding the opponents of Communism and threatening the unity of the socialist camp. Hoxha holds Khrushchev personally responsible for the crisis in Albanian-Soviet relations and the problems in Communist solidarity.

November 8 The Central Committee of the Chinese Communist Party issues a statement declaring that the Albanian leadership is ideologically correct and asserts that Albanian-Chinese unity ''can be shaken by no force on earth.''

November 11 The Central Committee of the APL sends a note to its Soviet counterpart urging it to repudiate the alleged anti-Marxist actions of Khrushchev and his clique.

December 3 The Soviet Union breaks diplomatic relations with Albania, withdrawing all Soviet personnel from the country—an act without precedent in the history of the Communist camp.

1962

January 10 In an attempt to offset its increasing isolation from the East Bloc, Tirana expresses a desire to improve diplomatic and trade relations with capitalist countries. There is no response from the West; the only Western nations maintaining relations with Albania are Austria, France, and Italy.

January 14 In a declaration, the Soviets insist that Albania's leadership has become an enemy of the Communist movement and can no longer be considered a member of the socialist world. The Soviets blame Albania's departure on narrow nationalist and egoistic interests fostered by Hoxha and Shehu.

January 30–February 1 Albania is excluded from a Prague meeting of the Warsaw Pact's defense ministers; Tirana reacts with angry protest.

February 22 Moscow dispatches a note to Beijing calling on the Chinese to stop their criticisms of the Soviet Union and to withdraw their support from Albania.

April 7 Beijing agrees to curb its anti-Soviet pronouncements but makes it clear that it will not abandon the Albanians. Instead the Chinese urge the Soviets to take the initiative in normalizing relations with Albania.

May 31 Moscow rejects Beijing's conditions regarding Albania by stressing that there can be no reconciliation with Tirana until the Albanians change their position.

July 16 After a three-month suspension of polemics against Moscow, Tirana resumes its attacks on Khrushchev. Hoxha and Shehu end the Chinese-inspired lull once the Soviets openly court Yugoslavia's friendship and exclude Albania from the June East Bloc economic summit meeting.

November–December Albania's anti-Soviet stand isolates it completely from the Communist world, save China. Tirana attacks Moscow for bowing before American pressure during the October Cuban missile crisis. The Albanians allege that Khrushchev's response proves that the Soviet leadership has betrayed the world Communist movement and is conspiring with the imperialists to destroy it. Consequently, the Albanian leadership and its policies are condemned almost universally by the Communist nations, with the exception of China—rendering the country a virtual outcast.

1963

January 1963–December 1970 Albania is reduced to a secondary role in the Chinese-Soviet dispute. Moscow makes a deliberate effort to downgrade the importance of Albania in its controversy with Beijing. The

Soviets intentionally ignore Tirana, communicating almost exclusively with the Chinese on matters involving Albania. Hoxha resents the Soviet attempt to portray Albania as a mere dependent of China.

The Chinese continue to fill most of the void created by the cessation of Soviet and East European aid. In particular, Tirana depends on China for wheat, due to its increasingly serious grain shortages. Chinese advisers and specialists insist that agricultural development is paramount, and self-sufficiency in wheat is made the country's prime goal. In the industrial sector, priority goes to the export of oil and mining resources and to the development of metallurgical plants and power stations. By 1967 the collectivization of agriculture is completed, and the size of private plots is reduced to approximately one-half acre in an effort to eliminate all vestiges of capitalism in farming. By 1970 drainage programs double the prewar figure of land area available for agriculture. Nevertheless, given the shortcomings of the collectivized system, Albanian agriculture consistently realizes only about half of its centrally planned goals. By comparison, industrial output during the same period progresses well at an annual growth rate of 10 percent. With Chinese financial and technical assistance, Albania successfully extends its hydroelectric network, constructs oil refineries, builds ore-processing plants, develops its chemical and machine tool industries, and expands its consumer-goods, textile, and food-processing industries. All the same, Tirana remains dependent on Chinese aid to sustain its economic programs.

December 31, 1963–January 9, 1964 A high-ranking Chinese delegation led by Prime Minister Zhou Enlai tours Albania, visiting every major city and virtually every significant industrial facility in the country. On January 8, at a mass rally in Tirana, Zhou praises the Albanian government and people for their successful struggle against American imperialism and Yugoslav revisionism. He congratulates the leadership of the APL for preserving the independence of Albania and for remaining true to the principles of Marxism-Leninism.

1964

February 24 Authorities seize the Soviet embassy in Tirana, causing Albanian-Soviet hostility to reach a new peak. Although the embassy buildings were built at Soviet expense on land donated by Albania, Tirana claims it has seized them because Moscow refuses to pay for their cost.

April 3 The Central Committee of the Soviet Communist party publishes a report recommending an international Communist conference to resolve the problems plaguing the socialist world. The report infuriates the Albanian leadership by dismissing them as mere tools of the Chinese.

May 17 Tirana responds to the Soviet report calling for an international Communist conference by blaming Khrushchev for starting the Chinese-Soviet dispute. The Albanians reject the Soviet assertion that they are tools of the Chinese by setting forth the conditions under which they would be willing to participate in a conference of world Communist parties, including that Yugoslavia be excluded from such a conference and that Khrushchev and his allies in Eastern Europe publicly admit the errors they have committed in their relations with Albania. These terms are unacceptable to Moscow.

October 14 Soviet leader Khrushchev falls from power. Tirana hails this development as a great victory for the forces of Marxism-Leninism and a heavy blow to revisionists and American imperialism.

Early November Tirana outlines its conditions to the new Soviet leadership for an Albanian-Soviet reconciliation. Albanian first secretary Hoxha and prime minister Shehu demand that Moscow rehabilitate Stalin, repudiate revisionism, restore Marxist-Leninist norms in the Soviet Union, and overthrow Yugoslavian leader Tito.

November 28 The Albanians conclude that there is no possibility of reaching an agreement with Moscow, since the new Soviet leaders have no intention of giving serious consideration to the Albanian conditions for reconciliation. Hoxha responds by renewing the Albanian anti-Soviet propaganda campaign with a violent personal attack against Khrushchev's successor, Leonid Brezhnev.

1965

January 15 Tirana rejects a Soviet offer to participate in an upcoming meeting of Warsaw Pact partners. The Albanians urge the member states to condemn Soviet actions against Albania and insist that Moscow compensate Tirana for the economic and military aid they have lost due to the Albanian-Soviet break. The other Warsaw Pact countries do not respond.

March 13 Fan Stylian Noli—the bishop of the Albanian Orthodox Church in America, former liberal Albanian premier, and rival of Zog—dies in Fort Lauderdale, Florida.

April 26–June 8 A 15-man Albanian delegation visits China and obtains a credit agreement estimated to amount to $214 million.

May 24 The official newspaper of the Albanian Party of Labor (APL), *Zëri i Popullit* (The Voice of the People), accuses the Soviet Union of stealing eight Albanian submarines from Albania, referring to the submarines removed by the Soviets from the Vlorë-Sazan base in late May 1961.

1966

February 1966–December 1969 Albania's "Ideological and Cultural Revolution" takes place in response to growing popular dissatisfaction and major domestic problems. By the end of 1965 the APL leadership is more concerned about the emergence of revisionist tendencies within Albania than abroad. Hoxha is convinced that Albania is threatened internally in several areas: there is a serious breakdown in party discipline as local APL elites use their positions for personal advantage; a new humanist wave of literary activity breaks away from the standards of socialist writing; and state planning failures contribute to growing hardship for most of the population. Consequently, feeling that the leadership's power is being undermined, Hoxha launches an Ideological and Cultural Revolution to prevent the emergence of revisionism and the restoration of capitalism, eliminate potential alternative power centers that threaten APL control over society, and forestall the emergence of a new elite class by reducing the bureaucracy.

No sector of Albanian society is left untouched. A purge of the bureaucracy replaces a large number of executive administrators and some 15,000 functionaries. The salaries of party and state officials are lowered to reduce the disparities between different kinds of work. Numerous party officials and intellectuals are sent to work in the countryside. The military is especially hard hit by the Cultural Revolution; all military ranks are abolished, party committees are established in army units, and political commissars are introduced into the military. The military's role in the state is decreased, and ideology and economics are given priority over military professionalism. The aim of the military reforms is to strengthen the APL's role in the armed forces, and as a result the position of the Ministry of Defense is seriously undermined. Other ministries are eliminated altogether, reducing the total from 19 to 13 by 1969. In 1966, for instance, the Ministry of Justice is done away with on the grounds that the establishment of socialist legality in Albania is complete.

In the social sphere, the APL begins a campaign to emancipate women by eliminating socially conservative attitudes, viewed by the APL as an obstacle to the construction of a socialist society, and promoting a greater female presence in the labor force. The Cultural Revolution also abolishes religion by banning religious worship. Other noteworthy results of the Cultural Revolution include the strengthening of the ideological component of instruction at all levels of the educational system and a reduction in the size of collective farmers' private plots to one-quarter of an acre.

When China phases out its Great Proletarian Cultural Revolution in 1969, Hoxha follows suit. Although it is widely believed that Albania's Cultural Revolution is inspired by Mao's Cultural Revolution, there are significant differences between the two movements. In contrast to China, the Albanian Cultural Revolution does not result in a weakening of the party and its mass organizations, considerable violence, economic disruption, or increased diplomatic isolation. Distinct from its Chinese counterpart, the Albanian Cultural Revolution is not a power struggle within the party, but represents a unified effort by the APL leadership to reaffirm its authority over the local party organizations, rally the people behind the regime, and reestablish the party's control over all aspects of Albanian society.

April 28–May 12 A delegation headed by Prime Minister Shehu pays a visit to China. The Albanian delegation is accorded a spectacular reception and a private audience with Mao, reflecting the importance that China attaches to its only European ally. At the conclusion of the visit, a joint statement reaffirms the close alliance between Beijing and Tirana and is highly critical of the Soviet Union, the United States, and Yugoslavia. The document portrays Albania and China as the defenders of Marxist-Leninist purity and the leaders of the struggle against imperialism and revisionism.

June Zhou Enlai, the Chinese premier, makes another visit to Albania, which reinforces Albanian-Chinese for-

eign policy. The United States is regarded as their primary capitalist adversary, bent on dominating the world and committed to destroying the Albanian and Chinese regimes, while the Soviet Union is believed to have entered into an alliance with the United States to contain and isolate China. As a result the Soviet Union and the United States represent equally dangerous enemies. Accordingly, Albania and China commit themselves to a two-front struggle against revisionism and imperialism.

November 1–8 The Fifth Congress of the APL meets in Tirana where First Secretary Hoxha reaffirms the Albanian-Chinese alliance and calls on all the Marxist-Leninist parties to join Beijing and Tirana in forming a united front to combat the forces of revisionism in the Communist camp. Hoxha also devotes a substantial portion of his address to praise the objectives of the Cultural Revolutions in Albania and China. The congress concludes by reelecting Hoxha party first secretary and enthusiastically endorsing his policies.

1967

July 25 The Bulgarian ambassador is expelled from Tirana for ''slanders'' against Albania. Romania thus remains the only East European country maintaining ambassadorial-level relations with Albania.

September Tirana announces that all of the country's 2,169 churches, monasteries, and mosques are closed, and that as a result Albania has become ''the first atheist State in the world.'' Hoxha remarks that ''the faith of an Albanian is Albanianism.'' The antireligious drive is accompanied by the murder or imprisonment of many mullahs and priests. In this, as well as in other mass campaigns that take place during the Cultural Revolution, young people play a very prominent part, imitating in a number of ways the activities and behavior of the Red Guards in China. However, whereas the Chinese Red Guards are more or less self-appointed agents of revolution, the young people in Albania act under strict party control. This wave of religious oppression results in very little open resistance in Albania.

October On the occasion of the eighteenth anniversary of the establishment of the People's Republic of China, Albanian's prime minister Shehu tours China. At the

President of Albania Enver Hoxha arm in arm with Zhou Enlai in July, 1966.

conclusion of his visit, a joint communique is issued in which Shehu characterizes China's leader, Mao, as a "great Marxist-Leninist" and "a worthy successor and heir" to Marx, Engels, Lenin, and Stalin.

1968

August 22 An official statement from Tirana condemns the Soviet-led invasion of Czechoslovakia by troops of five Warsaw Pact members as a fascist attack. The Albanian government claims that the pact has lost is original defensive character and has become an instrument of aggression against the socialist countries. However, as both the Czechoslovak and Soviet leaders are considered by the Albanians to be revisionists, they are criticized with equal fury, the one for committing an act of aggression against an ally, the other for failing to resist the invasion.

September 13 Tirana announces that it has formally withdrawn from the Warsaw Pact. The Albanian leadership is alarmed by the Soviet invasion of Czechoslovakia and concerned that the Soviets might use the Warsaw Pact Treaty to justify intervention in Albania. Hoxha argues that Albania has nothing to lose by leaving an alliance from which it had de facto been expelled in 1961. Hoxha insists that the invasion of Czechoslovakia necessitates significant changes in foreign policy. Long at odds with other European nations and dependent on a distant ally, Albania now finds itself vulnerable to Soviet military pressure. Hoxha thus moves Albania towards a new regional foreign policy. Yugoslavia is transformed from an Albanian enemy into a potential ally against Soviet aggression, and better relations are pursued with Greece. Despite ideological and political differences with Belgrade, Hoxha now sees Albania and Yugoslavia engaged in a common struggle against Moscow. He views Yugoslavia as a barrier against Soviet aggression and is confident the Yugoslavs would resist a Soviet attack. As a result, Tirana softens its anti-Yugoslav propaganda. Although Tirana does not enter into direct negotiations with Belgrade to form a military alliance, Albania recognizes that its fate is closely related to that of Yugoslavia.

Late September–early October   A military delegation visits Beijing and is received by Mao. Beijing provides Albania a new $200 million interest-free loan, but in discussions concerning military aid, the Chinese inform the Albanians that no matter how much Chinese military assistance it might receive, Albania is in no position to defend itself alone against Soviet aggression. Therefore, the Chinese suggest that the only way for Albania to cope with the possibility of a Soviet attack is join a military alliance with Yugoslavia.

Late November   In order to demonstrate Beijing's commitment to Tirana, a Chinese military delegation pays a weeklong visit to Albania, but the Chinese admit that they cannot guarantee Albania's security against Soviet aggression.

Late November–December   Tirana's new policy of security with Yugoslavia produces a cautious and mild Albanian reaction to nationalist disturbances in Kosovo. Fearing that the destabilization of Yugoslavia will give the Soviets a pretext to intervene in the Balkans, Tirana shows little interest in the Albanian demonstrations in Kosovo. Although Hoxha's regime has long portrayed itself as the advocate and protector of ethnic Albanian rights, Tirana does not endorse the protesters' demands that the province of Kosovo be granted the status of a republic within the Yugoslav federation.

1969

April 11   While noting the profound ideological differences between Tirana and Belgrade, an editorial in the Albanian Party of Labor (APL) newspaper, *Zëri i Popullit,* pledges solidarity with Yugoslavia and Romania against Soviet aggression.

September 4   *Zëri i Popullit* reaffirms Tirana's solidarity with Belgrade and Bucharest, while expressing an unusually friendly attitude towards Yugoslavia.

1970

January   Fearing Soviet aggression, Hoxha seeks a reconciliation with Greece. The Greek government facilitates the Athens-Tirana rapprochement by implicitly renouncing territorial claims against southern Albania. After 30 years Albania and Greece resume trade relations. At the same time, the APL leadership decides to expand diplomatic and commercial ties with selected West European and Third World nations.

April   Albania establishes diplomatic relations with Denmark.

May 30   Addressing a rally in Bajram Curri, Hoxha calls for better relations with Yugoslavia. Although he notes the irreconcilable ideological conflict with Belgrade, Hoxha places strong emphasis on the Albanian and Yugoslav peoples' common security interests.

June   China and Yugoslavia normalize relations, followed by Chinese declarations of support for Yugoslavia's independence and sovereignty. The Albanians are apprehensive about the Chinese-Yugoslav rapprochement, but Hoxha, citing the common Soviet threat, indicates Tirana is interested in improving relations with Belgrade despite ideological differences.

June 2   A four-man Albanian trade mission concludes a two-week visit to Athens that results in joint commercial orders.

July   Albania establishes diplomatic relations with Switzerland.

July 29   Indicating improved relations between Albania and Yugoslavia, a delegation headed by the deputy rector of the State University of Tirana is warmly received in Priština, capital of the province of Kosovo, where discussions about academic cooperation and faculty exchanges with Priština University take place.

August 7   Yugoslavian leader Tito responds to Hoxha's May 30 speech while speaking in Montenegro by recalling the success of wartime cooperation between the Albanian and Yugoslav partisans. He insists that renewed cooperation between Belgrade and Tirana can be successful in preserving the independence of both countries.

September In order to defuse border tensions, Beijing agrees to open talks with Moscow indicating to Tirana that China's national interests will supersede its ideological concerns in foreign policy. For his part, Hoxha rejects Soviet proposals for normalization of relations and indicates that Albania will not compromise with Soviet revisionists. Beijing's moves with Moscow creates uncertainty in Albanian-Chinese relations, and Albania fears a Chinese-Soviet reconciliation. In this regard, Beijing's failure to consult with Tirana in advance about Chinese-Soviet negotiations arouses mistrust in Albania.

October 16 Despite Tirana's misgivings about Beijing's new foreign policy, it continues to be dependent on Chinese economic and technical aid. In new loan and trade agreements signed in Beijing, Albania receives a long-term interest-free loan estimated at $400 million, the amount needed to implement Tirana's 1971–75 economic plan.

November Albania establishes diplomatic relations with Belgium and the Netherlands.

November 5 Tirana announces the completion of its program of electrification of all rural areas in the country.

November 7 Albania and Greece open direct telegraphic links for the first time since 1940.

1971

February 5 Albanian and Yugoslavia announce their intention to raise their diplomatic representation to the ambassadorial level.

May 6 Although Albania and Greece are technically still in a state of war because of their failure to sign a peace treaty after the Second World War, they agree to resume diplomatic relations on the ambassadorial level.

July In order to cope with the Soviet threat, Beijing advocates the normalization of American-Chinese relations. Accordingly, the U.S. president, Richard M. Nixon, is invited to visit China. In its rapprochement with Washington, Beijing acts without consulting or informing Albania in advance. While sharing Beijing's concern about

the Soviet threat, Albania insists that there are no changes in the threat posed by the United States to justify a change in policy. The Chinese take advantage of Mao's theory of differentiating among adversaries and cooperating with enemies of secondary importance (now the United States) against the principal enemy (the Soviet Union), but the Albanians still view the two superpowers as equally dangerous. Albanian first secretary Hoxha refuses to endorse the American-Chinese rapprochement and expresses concern about the preservation of Marxist-Leninist purity.

August In a letter to the Chinese party Central Committee, the Albanians express their opposition to the American-Chinese rapprochement by stating that China is embarking upon a revisionist path and is abandoning "the genuine socialist countries, the Marxist-Leninist movement, the revolution and the national-liberation struggle of the peoples."

September 29 In a speech Hoxha implicitly denounces China for deviating from the Marxist-Leninist approach in international affairs.

October The United Nations General Assembly adopts an Albanian resolution assigning China's seat in the world organization to Beijing in place of Taiwan. Beijing now begins to play a more active role in international affairs, and Tirana finds itself competing with other countries for Beijing's economic, military, and political support.

November 1–7 The Sixth Congress of the Albanian Party of Labor (APL) meets in Tirana. The Chinese express their dissatisfaction with Albania's defiance of their new foreign policy by refusing to send a delegation. In his opening address, Hoxha bitterly denounces American imperialism and Soviet revisionism, insisting that both are equally dangerous. In addition, he publicly rejects, for the first time, Chinese suggestions for the establishment of an Albanian-Romanian-Yugoslav alliance. Hoxha also resumes ideological attacks against Belgrade. While defying China on several major foreign policy issues, Hoxha is careful not to provoke a break with Beijing. Because Chinese aid is indispensable to the Albanian economy, Hoxha continues to emphasize the importance of its alliance with Beijing.

November 13 To facilitate the restoration of full diplomatic relations, Athens renounces its intention to annex Northern Epirus by announcing that "the Greek side wishes to restore confidence and cooperation with Tirana especially because Greece harbors no territorial designs on Albania." Three days later full diplomatic relations are restored between Athens and Tirana.

1972

January 1972–July 1978 Albania's refusal to accept China's new foreign policy of closer ties to the United States causes Beijing to reduce economic and military aid to Albania. The Albanians respond by trying to reduce dependence on the Chinese by diversifying trade, diplomatic, and cultural relations, especially with Western Europe. Tirana expands its foreign relations and establishes ties with most West European and many Third World countries. However, except for trade relations and cultural exchanges, primarily with Greece, Turkey, and the Albanian-populated areas of Yugoslavia, the level of contact remains low. There is no change in relations with Eastern Europe; Tirana repeatedly rejects Soviet and East Bloc offers to normalize relations. By the mid-1970s, Tirana succeeds in decreasing its dependence on Beijing by diversifying its trade and diplomatic relations to the extent that transactions with Beijing are no longer of vital importance.

October 30 A trade pact with Greece calls for exchanges worth $8 million annually.

1973

March 1973–November 1976 Widespread purges take place within the APL as Hoxha eliminates officials who represent threats to his policies. Hoxha believes that the gradual opening towards neighboring states and selected West European nations is destabilizing the country. Hoxha is distressed by the growing calls for liberalization that seem to be stimulated by increased foreign contact; there are demands for a relaxation of party controls, greater reforms, and an acceleration of the diversification of external relations. Moreover, Hoxha feels threatened by the increasingly open challenge to his policies by Albania's cultural, economic, and military elites.

Hoxha's purges first target the cultural elite and youth leadership. Hoxha is alarmed by reports of poor discipline by students and young workers, and by the growing challenge to socialist standards by artists and writers. There are major leadership changes in the country's artistic, literary, and youth organizations. Hoxha then turns his attention to the military. This next phase of the purge takes on a new urgency after Hoxha suffers a heart attack in October 1973. During the early 1970s tension developed between the APL leadership and the military over the army's desire to decrease party influence in the armed forces and over

defense strategy. Hoxha fears the emergence of a professional army dominated by a career officer class with only loose ties to the APL. As such, Hoxha believes the military could become strong enough to overthrow the regime. Consequently, in July 1974 he purges the defense minister, and within six months the senior leadership of the military is eliminated. Third on Hoxha's purge list are his Politburo colleagues and ministers who manage the economy. Hoxha has serious differences with the Ministry of Trade, which advocates reducing Albania's dependence on China by expanding trade and accepting loans from Western Europe. Instead, Hoxha emphasizes national self-reliance and beginning in 1975 rejects increasing trade with the West. Hoxha ends demands for reforms by purging Albania's economic and managerial elite, which also provides Hoxha with convenient scapegoats for Albania's failure to realize its 1971–75 development plan.

Hoxha's mid-1970s purges are accompanied by the dismissals of numerous party and state bureaucrats and their replacement with individuals who hold politically conformist views rather than professional qualifications. Although the new party and state appointees are unquestionably loyal to Hoxha, they lack the experience and ability to effectively perform their duties, and, furthermore, they do not enjoy the respect and confidence of the masses.

November Archbishop Damnian, head of the Albanian Orthodox church, dies in prison, where he has been held since 1967.

1975

April During a visit to Kosovo, Yugoslavian leader Tito states that the establishment of friendly relations between Yugoslavia and Albania is hampered by Tirana's persistent attacks on Yugoslav domestic policies.

September 9 A decree, adopted by the People's Assembly, orders ''all Albanian citizens [chiefly Greeks] who have inappropriate names in view of the political, ideological and moral standards to change their names,'' which is directed against the rapidly growing Greek minority in the South.

November 17 The People's Assembly unanimously approves a 51-member commission to draft a new constitution, with Hoxha as chair. The Politburo states that a new constitution is needed to replace the 1946 one, due to the profound social, economic, and political changes Albania has undergone during socialist rule.

1976

January 26 Albania declines to attend the first conference on Balkan cooperation since the Second World War, stating that it prefers to develop relations on a bilateral, rather than regional, basis.

September Mao Zedong's death causes a good deal of uncertainty and anxiety in Tirana about the future of its alliance with Beijing. In its message of condolence to China, the APL leadership expresses the hope that Mao's support of the Beijing-Tirana alliance will continue to be a source of inspiration in the post-Mao era.

October The first supply of Albanian steel is produced at the Elbasan metallurgical plant, marking a major industrial achievement.

November 1–7 The Seventh Congress of the APL meets in Tirana, where First Secretary Hoxha stresses Albanian self-reliance, indicating a move away from ideological and material dependence on China. While expressing gratitude to Beijing for its support, Hoxha does not endorse the new Chinese government since its purge of the Maoists in the Chinese Communist party, the faction Hoxha most identifies with. Moreover, without directly mentioning China, Hoxha denounces its foreign policy reorientation. Hoxha speaks publicly for the first time about the purges begun in 1973. He states that a number of high party officials were dismissed because of their involvement in economic, ideological, and industrial sabotage as well as other antistate activities. This public announcement marks the end of the purges.

December In an effort to discourage any further opposition to his policies, Hoxha promulgates a new constitution. The document changes the official name of the country from the People's Republic of Albania to the People's Socialist Republic of Albania. The constitution abolishes private property except for personal residences and articles for private use; the government is prohibited from granting concessions to foreign companies or states and forbidden to seek and obtain foreign loans and credits; the regime's 1967 decision to abolish religion is reaffirmed; Marxism-Leninism is proclaimed as the nation's official ideology; the one-party system is sanctioned; and, in contrast to other socialist countries, the first secretary is designated as the commander in chief of the armed forces, thus showing the party's determination to hold the military under its direct control.

Albanian citizens are officially guaranteed certain civil rights, including freedom of speech, press, organization, association, assembly, and public demonstration. In reality, Albanians enjoy only very limited liberties, because the constitution stresses that citizen rights cannot be exercised if they are in opposition to the state order. Furthermore, the penal code contains enough provisions to provide a legal basis for suppressing and punishing any dissident opinion.

December 8 Beijing protests Hoxha's criticism of Chinese foreign policy and warns Tirana that continued political defiance will harm Albanian-Chinese friendship.

1977

May A Chinese parliamentary delegation visits Romania and Yugoslavia but not Albania, arousing grave suspicions in Albania.

June Tirana loses hope that the radicals can reassert their authority in Beijing and return China to its former policies, when it is reported that the rehabilitation of moderate Chinese leader Deng Xiaoping—denounced publicly by the Albanians as a revisionist—is imminent. Moreover, Beijing announces that Tito has been invited to visit—a personal insult to Hoxha, who has not been invited to visit China in more than 20 years.

July 7 A turning-point for Albanian-Chinese relations comes with the publication of an editorial in the Albanian Party of Labor's (APL) official newspaper, *Zeri i Popullit,* titled "The Theory and Practice of Revolution." The 8,500-word editorial, probably written by Hoxha, contains a sharp rebuttal of the theory of the Three Worlds, expressed by Mao, and the driving force behind China's foreign policy reorientation. The theory envisages the world divided into three broad groupings: first, the two super powers, the Soviet Union and the United States; second, the industrialized states of Western Europe, Canada, and Japan; and, third, the developing nations of Africa, Asia, Europe, and Latin America. This analysis maintains that Communist regimes and parties should foster ties between the Second and Third Worlds in order to thwart the imperialist ambitions of the two super powers and in order to promote revolutionary change. The *Zeri i Popullit* editorial objects to this theory, stating that it creates dangerous illusions: that the nations of the Second and Third World really share common interests; that the United States is less aggressive than the Soviet Union; and that the nonaligned countries are genuinely independent. Furthermore, the editorial characterizes the theory as a flagrant departure from Marxism-Leninism. According to the Albanian view, the theory preaches social peace and collaboration with the bourgeoisie and is intended to curb revolution and defend capitalism. These ideological arguments indicate that Tirana refuses to follow China's example of opening to the United States or of establishing closer ties with Yugoslavia. According to Tirana, such policies can only hurt Marxism-Leninism and threaten the stability of the Hoxha regime. The Albanian embassy in Beijing takes the highly provocative step of delivering copies of the editorial to other embassies and to foreign correspondents, and the article consequently receives worldwide publicity.

September 2   In a move intended to embarrass the Chinese, Tirana reprints and distributes an article entitled "Khrushchev Kneels Before Tito," written by Hoxha and first published in 1963, with the purpose of demonstrating that by receiving Tito on a visit, the Chinese leaders are pursuing Khrushchev's policy and thus acting as revisionists.

November 17–18   The Third Plenum of the APL Central Committee decides to inform party members of the disagreements with China and prepare the country for a break by launching a propaganda barrage against China.

November 29   In a bitter attack on China, Albanian prime minister Shehu uses strong, unprecedented language to denounce Beijing's foreign policy direction.

1978

March 28–30   The Greek commerce minister visits Tirana, where he concludes an expanded Albanian-Greek trade agreement. An agreement is also signed, establishing a new air route from Athens to Tirana; the weekly flight between the two capitals makes Greece the only Western nation with a direct air route to Albania. In another unusual step on the part of the Albanian authorities, the Greek official is permitted to visit several Greek communities in southern Albania.

April–May   Tirana's propaganda campaign against Beijing intensifies, as the Albanian Foreign Ministry complains that Chinese experts were deliberately harming Albania's economy.

June 24   An editorial in *Zëri i Popullit* expresses Albanian support for Vietnam in its conflict with Cambodia. This is a serious affront to Beijing, which is supporting Cambodia against Vietnam, Beijing's rival in Indochina.

July 7   Exactly one year after the publication of the *Zëri i Popullit* editorial denouncing Beijing's foreign policy, the Chinese government informs Tirana that it is ending all economic and military assistance and recalling all 513 Chinese technicians and specialists. The Chinese charge

that the Albanian leadership has maligned Beijing's economic and military aid, thus ending the Albanian-Chinese alliance that since 1954 has supplied Albania with some 6,000 technicians and aid amounting to $5 billion dollars.

July 29   In a 56-page letter to the Chinese Communist party, Tirana denounces the end of aid as proof of Beijing's reactionary and revisionist path. The APL accuses the Chinese of megalomania and betrayal of communism. Although the Albanians downplay the role of China's assistance in their country's economic development, they allege that China is seeking to damage the Albanian economy and defense capacity by suspending aid. Finally, Tirana accuses the Chinese leadership of interfering in the internal affairs of Albania, thereby sabotaging the cause of revolution and socialism.

The disintegration of the alliance, however, does not result in a break of diplomatic relations between Beijing and Tirana. Albanian first secretary Hoxha makes it clear that the dispute with China will not lead to Albania's alliance with another bloc. Hoxha now insists that Albania is the only real socialist state in the world.

September 1978–December 1985   With the loss of Chinese aid, Albania is without an economic patron for the first time in the postwar period. Since Tirana is barred by the 1976 constitution from seeking loans or credits from capitalist countries, and since Hoxha is unwilling to turn to the Soviet Union and the East Bloc for support, the Albanians attempt to sustain their economic development programs through self-reliance. As a result, Albania becomes more dependent than ever on international trade. Emphasis is placed on finding means of exploiting national resources, with Tirana relying heavily on its ability to increase its exports of surplus electric power and minerals. New trade agreements are concluded with several countries, and special efforts are made to expand economic and technical cooperation with Yugoslavia, which quickly becomes Albania's principal trading partner. All these efforts, however, cannot sustain the 10 percent average annual growth rate in industry that had been achieved between 1961 and 1975. With the withdrawal of Chinese aid, the annual growth rate in industry falls by more than half. As industrial growth slows, it becomes increasingly plagued with problems related to complexity, poor planning, and declining efficiency. In short, the Albanian strategy of self-reliance does not solve the serious economic problems created by the withdrawal of Chinese aid.

December   Tirana announces that it intends to expand trade with France, Greece, Italy, Yugoslavia, and the smaller countries of Western Europe.

1979

January 27 Hoxha publishes the first of three books to be released in 1979 (*Imperialism and Revolution, Reflections on China,* and *With Stalin*) in which he expresses his political ideas vis-à-vis China. His main argument is that only his regime, of all the Communist ones, has remained faithful to the principles of the Marxist-Leninist doctrine. Hoxha also delivers his sharpest attack on China since the start of his quarrel with Beijing, charging that Mao was not a true Marxist-Leninist and that he had run China as if it were his personal fief.

February A Montenegrin delegation visits Albania to discuss cooperation in transport, telecommunications, the regulation of the water resources of Lake Shkodër and the Bojanë River, and the export of Albanian electric power to Yugoslavia.

April 15 A major earthquake hits northern Albania and Montenegro. On the Albanian side, 35 people are killed, approximately 400 are injured, 17,000 homes and buildings are destroyed, and over 100,000 people are left homeless. Unlike Yugoslavia, which receives considerable international relief, Albania—maintaining its isolationist stance in international affairs—makes no appeal for outside help.

September With the death of Hysni Kapo, one of Hoxha's most trusted associates, Hoxha, who is in declining health, becomes increasingly preoccupied with the task of choosing his successor.

October The Albanian and Yugoslav ministers of foreign trade meet in Tirana and agree to build a railway line in 1983 between the Albanian town of Shkodër and the Yugoslav town of Titograd. This would be the first railway between the two countries and would create a link for Albania with the European railway system via Yugoslavia.

1981

Early April Violent unrest follows several weeks of demonstrations by Albanians in Kosovo. The protesters, centered in Priština, demand the upgrading of Kosovo's status from an autonomous province within Serbia to a full republic within the Yugoslav federation. The Yugoslav authorities respond with armed force, martial law, and mass arrests and imprisonments. Belgrade blames Tirana for the disturbances and rejects what the Albanian-majority Kosovars claim are the real causes of the unrest: national oppression, discrimination and the subordination of Albanians, and the province's depressed economic conditions.

April 8 An article in *Zëri i Popullit,* the official newspaper of the Albanian Party of Labor (APL), states that it was not Albania that had caused the rioting in Kosovo but the wretched economic and political conditions of the Albanian population in the province. The article criticizes the use of force against the demonstrators, and, in addition, claims that while Albania has never interfered in Yugoslavia's internal affairs, it cannot refrain from protesting when the legitimate rights of Albanians living in that country are being violated.

May 24 Two bombs explode at the Yugoslav embassy in Tirana; the Albanian government denies any involvement in the incident.

November 1–8 The Eighth Congress of the APL meets in Tirana, where the issue of Kosovo is taken up by Hoxha during his address to the congress. Hoxha denies that Albania is making any territorial claims on Kosovo, where approximately 80 percent of the population is Albanian. Hoxha supports the demonstrators' demands that Kosovo should become a separate republic within Yugoslavia, and he dismisses the pronouncements of Yugoslav officials who fear that such a move would be the first step toward dismembering the multinational state.

December 4 Belgrade dispatches a note to Tirana protesting interference in Yugoslavia's internal affairs by the APL congress, which Albania rejects.

December 17 Hoxha bitterly denounces his longtime friend and ally, Prime Minister Shehu, at a meeting of the Politburo, reflecting Hoxha's decision to chose senior party official Ramiz Alia over Shehu as his successor. Hoxha concludes that Shehu, who has health problems of his own, is not the logical person to succeed him. Aside from the issues of his age and health, Shehu is disliked and feared by many party members. Moreover, because of sharp differences with him over priorities in domestic economic development and foreign trade relations, Hoxha lacks confidence in Shehu's ability to oversee the administration of the bureaucracy and the nation's increasingly problem-plagued agricultural and industrial sectors. Initially, Hoxha attempts to lure Shehu into a privileged retirement. However, after failing to convince Shehu to step aside voluntarily in favor of Alia, Hoxha forcibly dislodges him.

December 18 An official government statement announces that Shehu has committed suicide "in a moment of nervous crisis." It remains uncertain as to whether Shehu committed suicide or was executed by Hoxha's direction.

Late December 1981–November 1982 Following Shehu's death, Hoxha initiates a purge of the late prime minister's allies. Hoxha moves swiftly and successfully to neutralize any potential opposition from within the military and security forces that had traditionally supported Shehu. The regime also unleashes a propaganda campaign designed to defame Shehu, his family, and his associates. The attacks against Shehu and his supporters climax with Hoxha's stunning declaration in November that Shehu, one of his closest collaborators for more than three decades, had all along been a foreign spy working simultaneously for the American, British, Soviet, and Yugoslav intelligence services. Although Hoxha maintains that he has proof to support the allegations against Shehu, no such evidence is produced. Going further, Hoxha claims that Shehu had received instructions from Belgrade to kill him and other Albanian leaders, and when confronted with the evidence of his treason, Shehu committed suicide.

1982

January 14 Longtime Politburo member and first deputy prime minister under Shehu, Adil Carcani, is named prime minister.

September 25 A group of heavily armed exiles land on the Adriatic coast of Albania but are destroyed by security forces. The claimant to the Albanian throne, Leka, while not directly involved, admits to his acquaintance with the rebel's leader, Xhevdet Mustafa. The Albanian authorities assume that the invaders are part of the National Liberation Army, an émigré monarchist force.

November 10 During a speech in Tirana, First Secretary Hoxha protests the repression of Albanians in Kosovo and Yugoslav Macedonia. He characterizes Belgrade's policy as genocide, and he rejects Belgrade's allegations that the Albanian regime is encouraging rebellion among the inhabitants of Kosovo. Hoxha concludes his attack by accusing the Yugoslav government of being responsible for the abortive incursion on the Albanian coast in September.

November 14 According to the state news agency, all 1,627,968 eligible Albanians vote in the elections for a new People's Assembly. Consistent with the pattern established by previous official national outcomes under the Hoxha regime, only one Albanian reportedly votes against the Democratic Front and eight ballots are declared invalid, while 1,627,959 votes are cast for the single-slate Democratic Front candidates.

November 22 Following the general elections, the People's Assembly meets, and Ramiz Alia—a member of the Politburo, the party secretariat, and Hoxha's hand-picked successor—is elected chairman of the People's Assembly. Alia's new position makes him the nominal head of state, and, keeping with Hoxha's plans for a smooth transition of power, it provides him with broader domestic and international exposure. Adil Carcani, who has acted as prime minister since January, is formally confirmed.

November 23 Carcani announces the formation of a new government in which 10 cabinet ministers are dismissed including the minister of defense, the brother-in-law and close ally of Shehu. These changes are designed to further rid the government of the late Shehu's allies and to promote loyal, younger officials of the APL.

1983

January 1983–April 1985 As Hoxha's health continues to decline, he increasingly limits his own political activity and goes into semiretirement. Alia, in turn, gradually assumes more of the day-to-day administration of the nation's affairs. Although personally chosen by Hoxha to be his successor, Alia lacks Hoxha's charisma and wields considerably less power, but Alia begins to play a preeminent role in the governing of Albania, which enables him to build his authority.

June Alia announces that Albania has embarked upon a more pragmatic foreign policy. He indicates that Albania will shift away from interaction with Yugoslavia and towards greater relations with Greece, Italy, and Turkey. Tirana takes gradual steps to emerge from its self-imposed isolation and limit the adverse consequences of the deterioration of relations with Belgrade.

October Albania signs an agreement with Italy to establish a regular maritime line linking the ports of Durrës and Trieste. Frustrated by the Yugoslavs' failure to complete construction of their section of the Shkodër-Titograd railway, Tirana considers rerouting its entire trade with Western Europe through Italy. Concurrently, following a discreet visit to Albania by a Chinese trade delegation, Beijing and Tirana reestablish commercial ties. The Albanians agree to resume the sale of chromium to China in exchange for badly needed spare parts for Chinese-supplied machinery and military equipment.

October 16 Enver Hoxha's 75th birthday is celebrated throughout Albania amidst an official campaign of public adulation.

December The Durrës-Trieste maritime line begins operating. The line is to be used mainly for the transportation of trucks and postal freight and is intended to provide Albanian exports with an access to the markets of Western Europe.

1984

November In a major policy address, Alia reaffirms Albania's interest in expanding relations with other countries, especially those of Western Europe.

December Albania and Greece sign a long-term economic accord as well as agreements on a host of other interests: cultural exchanges; postal services; road transportation; scientific and technological cooperation; and telecommunications. The Albanians also agree to establish a Department of Greek Studies at the Tirana Pedagogical Institute.

1985

January 12 Albania and Greece reopen the Kakavija (Kakavia) Pass on the main road linking the two countries, closed since 1940 when Italy used it to invade Greece.

February–July The government publicly expresses concerns over the increasing alienation, low morale, and restlessness of the country's youth. Officials insist that Albania's young people are being adversely influenced by foreign television broadcasts, commercial advertising, and personal contacts with tourists from abroad. The regime is also clearly troubled by a religious revival among the country's youth.

April 11 Enver Hoxha dies at the age of 76 from complications resulting from diabetes. The public mourns this loss.

April 13 Ramiz Alia is named party first secretary.

April 15 During Hoxha's funeral in Tirana, Alia pledges that he will uphold the policies of his predecessor. Following the policy of isolationism in international affairs, no foreign delegations are permitted to attend the funeral, and a Soviet message of condolence is rejected.

June–July Owing to the growing severity of economic problems, meat and other foodstuffs and consumer goods are rationed throughout the country. Hoxha's policy of isolation, designed in part to protect Albania from political, social, and cultural "contamination," is now working against the country's vital interests. Despite their reluctance, sheer economic necessity forces Hoxha's successors to expand foreign trade. Hence, Tirana publishes posthu-

mously a book by Hoxha, the main thesis of which supports Alia's view that opening up to the outside world is acceptable if it is consistent with the country's national interests. However, international trade relations and economic development are still hampered by the regime's constitutionally bound inability to accept credits and loans from foreign states and companies.

August Displaying a degree of openness in the sphere of cultural policy, Alia calls for a new standard of toleration of literature during a meeting with artists and writers in Korcë. Although he does not relax censorship, his comments spark a lively debate and a plea for freedom of expression.

In a speech, Alia denounces the Yugoslavs and accuses them of following a racist policy of oppression against the Albanian Kosovars.

Albania and Great Britain hold secret talks in an attempt to settle their 40-year-old diplomatic rift. London claims over $1 million in compensation for two destroyers mined off the Albanian coast, with the loss of more than 40 British lives on October 22, 1946. Tirana refuses to pay until Britain returns Albanian gold looted by the Germans during the Second World War, which is held jointly by Britain, France, and the United States and valued at over $60 million. The discussions reach a deadlock and break off.

September Prime Minister Carcani welcomes to Tirana the French deputy foreign minister who is accompanied by a large group of Western executives interested in trade with Albania. After a number of discussions, the Albanians and French agree to establish a joint commission to study ways of expanding trade.

1986

March Alia appoints Enver Hoxha's widow, Nexhmije Hoxha, to the chair of the General Council of the Democratic Front. The appointment is intended as a kind of outward reassurance that her late husband's policies will continue. Yet at the same time, her position is one of high visibility but little power and is also intended to keep her from a senior party or state post.

June East Germany's minister of foreign trade, accompanied by a trade delegation, visits Albania in the first official visit by a representative of an East Bloc country since the Albanian-Soviet break in 1961.

July 23 The Albanian government announces that the nation has failed to meet the goals set in the last five-year economic development plan: production targets for copper, chromium, gas, and oil have not been reached, and serious failures in grain production and dairy farming are noted. These problems are attributed to poor management and organization, declining worker discipline and efficiency, and distribution difficulties caused by an inadequate transportation system.

August 6 After a delay of three years, the Shkodër-Titograd railway is opened. Despite this accomplishment, there is no real improvement in the general relations between Albania and Yugoslavia, which remain icy since the Kosovo riots of 1981 and their aftermath.

October Albania and Spain establish diplomatic relations.

November 3–8 The Ninth Congress of the Albanian Party of Labor (APL) meets in Tirana. Although Alia announces that there will be no departure from Hoxha's policies regarding the party and its leading role in society, he clearly indicates that Albania will soften its isolationism. With the intensification of the ethnic conflict in Kosovo, Belgrade has resorted to economic, political, and military pressures on Tirana, which it considers directly responsible for the escalation of problems. Hence, a major objective of Alia's foreign policy is the prevention of the establishment of an anti-Albanian-Balkan coalition directed by Belgrade. Therefore, Alia emphasizes the stabilization and strengthening of relations with other countries, particularly Greece and Bulgaria, as a counterbalance to Yugoslavia.

Most of the Congress energies, however, are spent on addressing Albania's economic problems. Ambitious production targets in agriculture and industry are announced for the next five-year development plan (1986–90), and great stress is placed on the urgent need to modernize Albanian technology. However, Alia ignores two key obstacles: constitutional bans on foreign loans and credits continue to restrict the country's technology imports, and the shortage of qualified Albanian experts to fully utilize new technology.

November 29 The official newspaper of the Soviet Communist party urges Tirana to normalize relations, which the Albanian leadership ignores.

1987

April In a speech at the Third Central Committee Plenum, Alia expresses concerns about the increasing disparity between production and the population's material needs and purchasing power. Alia recognizes the importance of private plots in helping to alleviate the country's acute food

shortages. Alia ends the consolidation of the collective ownership system, and he stops the transformation of agriculture cooperatives into state farms. However, he stops short of sanctioning the expansion of private plots and permitting small-scale private enterprise. Instead, Alia encourages granting greater economic autonomy to agricultural brigades—cooperative groupings of agricultural collectives. More than 80 percent of the cultivated area is in the hands of collective farms, 18 percent in the hands of state farms, and less than 2 percent is in private plots. Although measures are promised to improve the situation, Alia concludes his speech on a pessimistic note by stating that Albania will continue to face serious food shortages because of its high birthrate and the gradual reduction of arable land owing to the rapid expansion of urban and industrial areas.

July Alia announces that the production of chromium, Albania's main hard-currency export, is thousands of tons below planned quotas and that there are serious failures in the country's oil industry. These disclosures are accompanied by official statements and newspaper articles with suggestions about introducing wage incentives and bringing about a limited degree of decentralization in order to stimulate production.

Although the government's proposals represent a bold departure from Hoxha's rigid economic principles, they are more an attempt at tinkering with the country's economic problems than a signal that the leadership is determined to face realities. This fact is shown in the regime's propaganda campaign against the reformist policies of Mikhail Gorbachev in the Soviet Union which labels him a revisionist, capitalist, and counterrevolutionary.

August The Greek government ends the state of war with Albania in existence since 1940. In announcing the lifting of the technical state of war, Athens emphasizes its expectation that the decision will contribute to an improvement of the position of the Greek minority in Albania, which Tirana numbers approximately 60,000, while Athens claims the number to be 400,000.

October Following negotiations lasting several years, Albania and West Germany establish diplomatic relations. For years Tirana has demanded reparations for destruction in Albania during the German occupation in the Second World War. Albania's decision to drop these claims paves the way for the normalization of relations, with which Tirana hopes that Bonn will make much-needed advanced technology available to Albania.

October 26 Tirana denounces Belgrade's October 25 dispatch of federal paramilitary police units to Kosovo, saying that it will worsen the already strained relations between Belgrade and Tirana.

November   Accompanied by West German economic and industrial experts, the Bavarian prime minister visits Albania and signs an agreement in Tirana, whereby the Albanian government is granted a gift of DM 6 million (marks) to purchase any West German goods it chooses, except weapons and police vehicles. The aid is granted as a gift in order to bypass the Albanian constitutional ban on foreign credits and loans.

The Greek foreign minister visits Tirana and signs a series of agreements, including a five-year agreement on economic, industrial, and scientific cooperation. The Albanian and Greek governments also sign an agreement on expanding cultural exchanges, a four-year agreement for cooperation in the health sector, and a protocol on banking cooperation.

1988

February 23–26   After some initial reluctance, Albania takes part in a conference of the Balkan foreign ministers meeting in Belgrade, which represents Albania's departure from Hoxha's strict opposition to multilateral relations in foreign affairs.

March   The authorities report that widespread corruption and crime are responsible for the many shortcomings of Albanian society. The problem of crime is officially labeled an alien symptom and is attributed to foreign influences.

March 5   For the first time since 1954 the anniversary of Stalin's death is not commemorated in Tirana, indicating a relaxation of Stalinist ideals in Albania.

April   Albania and Canada establish diplomatic relations.

April 17   Albania and Greece sign an agreement to encourage local trade across their 154-mile border, and the two countries also sign an accord on the establishment of a ferry line between Corfu and Sarandë.

June   Albania and West Germany sign an agreement on economic, industrial, and technical cooperation.

July   The Politburo meets to discuss Albania's worsening agricultural crisis. Although Alia concedes that the centralized economic management system has led to an absence of initiative and is unsuited to tackle the country's agricultural problems, he gives no indication what measures the government intends to take to improve efficiency and productivity.

September   Albania and West Germany sign an agreement on the exchange of scholars, scientists, and specialists, as well as cooperation in art, literature, radio, and television.

October   First Secretary Alia takes steps to cope with the state's increasing problems stemming from bribery, influence peddling, and favoritism by hoping to ensure good administration. All managers or officials in charge of local housing, labor, and residence permit bureaus who have served more than five years in the same position are replaced. Alia also indicates that officials occupying such positions will be replaced every five years.

1989

January   Tirana hosts the meeting of Balkan deputy foreign ministers.

March   The West German government grants Albania a gift of DM 20 million to invest in the oil, iron, and steel industries, and in livestock breeding.

March 3   Tirana dismisses Yugoslav allegations that it is planning a revolt in Kosovo. It denounces Belgrade's recent arrests of scores of Albanian political and business leaders in Kosovo. Tirana accuses Belgrade of planning to hand over Kosovo to Serbia.

March 15–16   Albania participates in a conference of the economic ministers of the Balkan states meeting in Ankara, where it is agreed to implement a dozen proposals aimed at easing regional trade barriers and promoting economic contacts.

March 23–29   After Kosovo's legislature votes to give Serbia direct control of the province, Albanians riot throughout Kosovo. The Yugoslav government attributes the wave of violence to pro-Tirana separatists.

September   In a speech to the Albanian Party of Labor (APL) Central Committee meeting in Tirana, Alia denounces the political changes taking place in the East Bloc. He revives the late First Secretary Hoxha's doctrine that Albania is in a permanent state of political, ideological, and military encirclement, designed to intimidate those who may be enticed by the freedom movements that are bringing down the Communist regimes in the rest of Eastern Europe. The Soviet leader Mikhail Gorbachev's reforms are attacked, and he is accused of undermining the very foundations of the Communist system. It is stressed that the APL will never compromise its monopoly of power nor will it ever tolerate pluralism. The party is urged to meet all dangers to its position by appropriate political indoctrination and propaganda.

October Young workers and students in the predominantly Greek-inhabited region of Sarandë stage protests against the regime's policies of labor incentives, which amount to higher production quotas for less pay. Scores of people are arrested and—adding to Albania's horrendous record of human rights—four Greeks are publicly tortured and killed by authorities, following their attempt to escape across the border to Greece.

November 17 With the approach of the 45th anniversary of Albania's liberation from Nazi occupation, a November 20 amnesty is declared for certain prisoners, including a number of political detainees, some imprisoned for attempting to flee the country and others convicted on charges of agitation and propaganda against the state.

Late December Encouraged by the events in Eastern Europe that caused the fall of communism, the pretender to the throne, Leka, from exile in South Africa, urges the Albanians to revolt and emulate the people of Romania in ousting the country's Communist leadership. Leka's pleas are met with no response in Albania.

December 28 The Yugoslav official news agency reports that an antigovernment demonstration has been crushed by Albanian security forces in Shkodër and that many people have been arrested and sent to labor camps. Albanian officials deny the reports and there is no independent confirmation of the incident.

1990

January–December Stalinism comes to an end in Albania as the Alia regime attempts to quell growing unrest through concessions, with each concession serving merely to encourage further demands for liberalization. Initially the contest is between reformist and hard-line Stalinist factions within the APL, but following major public upheavals in July it is also openly a struggle against the party.

January 11–14 The unrest that broke out in Shkodër in December 1989 continues, as 7,000 demonstrators are reported to take part in further protests. Yugoslav sources allege that numerous arrests are made and that public hangings take place. The Albanian government places Shkodër off limits to foreign visitors and tightens border security with Greece and Yugoslavia (*see* December 28, 1989).

January 22–23 The APL Central Committee holds a Plenary Session in Tirana. In a departure from the party's

policies, which emphasize rigid Marxist-Leninist orthodoxy, the Central Committee endorses a program for limited economic and political reforms. While continuing to deny the reports of unrest, First Secretary Alia announces that the reform package is aimed at stabilizing the country. However, Alia stresses that the APL will not give up its political monopoly nor will the government embrace the democratization that is sweeping the rest of Eastern Europe. He characterizes these changes as a tragedy brought on by ruling cliques that have fallen prey to revisionism. The Alia reform program includes: decentralization within the party, with local organizations gaining more decision making powers; multicandidate elections, although the leading role of the APL is to be upheld—no more than two candidates can seek each post, and only party-approved candidates can run; decentralization of the management of state enterprises; the introduction of wage and price incentives into the economy to promote production; allowing agricultural cooperatives to market products free of fixed prices; and the right to appeal court verdicts and state decrees.

April Further displays of public discontent take place, with protestors being critical of the antireformist elements within the APL, particularly Nexhmije Hoxha, the wife of the late First Secretary Enver Hoxha. Industrial unrest appears with a strike by 2,000 textile workers at a factory in Berat.

April 17 Alia announces that, due to recent international developments, Albania will seek the reestablishment of diplomatic relations with the Soviet Union and the United States.

May 2 Unsanctioned pro-democracy protests in support of Alia's liberal reforms take place in Durrës, Elbasan, Korcë, and Vlorë. The targets of the mainly young protestors include the Sigurimi, local Communist officials, and Nexhmije Hoxha, who is widely believed to be the de facto head of the APL's hard-line antireform faction.

May 8 The People's Assembly approves extensive reforms of the judicial system shortly before a visit to Tirana by the United Nations secretary general. The Ministry of Justice is reestablished, and the number of offenses punishable by execution is reduced from 34 to 11, with antistate agitation and propaganda ceasing to be such a crime. Although Albania is to remain an atheist state, "religious propaganda" will henceforth be tolerated. Furthermore, Albanians are to be granted the right to obtain passports to travel abroad, while the penalty for attempting to flee the country is reduced. The assembly also approves measures ending the constitutional ban on foreign credits and loans.

These concessions mark the victory of the reformists over the Stalinists within the APL, but by no means put an end to the country's upheavals.

June 6 After some preliminary statements in May, Tirana formally announces that it will sign the Helsinki Final Act and that it will join the 35-nation Conference on Security and Cooperation in Europe.

June 28–July 8 A series of pro-democracy, antigovernment demonstrations in Tirana on June 28–29, July 2–3, and July 6 turn into clashes with the security forces. When riot police fire on the crowds and violently disperse them, a number of Albanians flee to the West German embassy in search of asylum. Within days, more than 3,000 Albanian citizens follow, while others seek refuge in the embassies of Czechoslovakia, France, Greece, Hungary, Italy, Poland, and Turkey, the total exceeding 5,000. The Albanian government denounces the refugees and initially blocks off the embassies, refusing to allow shipments of food to be delivered into the compounds. Nevertheless, on July 8 the authorities grant permission for the refugees to leave the country. A multinational relief operation, coordinated by the United Nations, facilitates the evacuation of the Albanians, most of whom travel to Italy and West Germany.

July 7–9 The Alia regime dismisses hard-liners from the Politburo and replaces them with reformists in an attempt to defuse the growing unrest.

July 30 Albania and the USSR restore diplomatic relations after 29 years as a result of a thawing in both countries' foreign relations policies.

July 31 The Presidium of the People's Assembly ends the ban on foreign investment and joint enterprises and grants Albanians a limited right to conduct public demonstrations.

October 24–25 The foreign ministers of the six Balkan nations hold a summit meeting in Tirana, where the Greek foreign minister calls for the participating nations to respect religious, political, and economic freedoms, which is taken to be directed at Albania's dreadful human rights record.

October 25 Albania's most prominent author and deputy chairman of the Democratic Front, Ismail Kadare, defects during a visit to France. He declares there is no prospect of legal opposition in Albania and that the government is not serious with its reforms.

September 28 Alia addresses the United Nations General Assembly in New York, where he states that Albania welcomes closer relations with its European neigh-

bors, but he warns against foreign interference in his country's domestic affairs. It is also disclosed that Albania and the United States have been quietly conducting talks since April on a possible restoration of diplomatic relations.

November 8 Against mounting pressure for the pace of reform to be accelerated, Alia urges in a speech to the Central Committee that the leading role of the Albanian Party of Labor (APL) be redefined and proposes a multiparty system.

November 13 The People's Assembly confirms the new electoral law endorsed by Alia, which allows secret ballots and independent candidates for the legislature. It also requires at least two candidates for every post.

A special commission is established for the purposes of studying possible changes in the constitution.

Early December Alia's November concessions are not sufficient to pacify the mounting unrest. In large demonstrations in cities, students and workers demand that more than one political party be allowed to participate in the national elections scheduled for February 10, 1991.

December 11 Alia removes five hard-liners from the Politburo, and he agrees to permit the establishment of independent political parties and their participation in the forthcoming elections.

December 12 The Democratic Party of Albania (DPA), under the leadership of an academic, Gramoz Pashko, is formed in Tirana. Alia makes a nationally televised appeal for calm, but to no avail. Following three days of clashes between students and riot police at Enver Hoxha University (the name formally given to the State University of Tirana after the first secretary's death in 1985), riots erupt outside the capital, beginning in Krujë.

December 13–14 Anti-Communist riots erupt in Durrës, Elbasan, and Shkodër. In Shkodër protesters attack government and party buildings and destroy a statue of Enver Hoxha, while in Elbasan crowds stone the police and make bonfires from copies of Hoxha's memoirs. The government dispatches thousands of riot police and army troops, including armored units, into the troubled areas where mass arrests follow.

December 19 The government officially recognizes the Democratic Party of Albania.

December 20 Nexhmije Hoxha, the de facto leader of the hard-line faction of the APL, resigns from her post as head of the Democratic Front.

December 21 Underscoring the end of Stalinism, the Albanian government orders the removal of all statues and symbols of the former Soviet leader in the country.

Toppling of the Enver Hoxha monument in Tirana.

December 25 In Shkodër, Albania's leading Catholic activist, Fr. Simon Jubani, who has been recently released from 25 years' imprisonment, conducts the first public celebration of mass since 1967.

December 30 Tirana announces that Albania's approximately 1,000 Jews will be allowed to emigrate.

December 30–31 At least 3,000 Albanians, mostly Greeks, cross the Greek border seeking political asylum. Faced with the refugee influx, the Greek government appeals to the Greeks to stay in Albania and wait for "the inevitable" democratization there.

1991

January 7 Albanian border guards fire on several hundred Albanians attempting to cross into Yugoslavia near Shkodër.

January 13–14 Tirana allows the Greek prime minister to tour several Greek villages in southern Albania. Following discussions on the refugee issue, the Greek and Albanian prime ministers jointly announce that citizens of either country may freely cross their borders. The number of Albanian refugees, mostly Greeks, in Greece is estimated at 11,000. Despite the continuing exodus, the Albanians reject a Greek request to institute measures to benefit its Greeks in order to induce them to stay in Albania. Athens fears that Tirana is making an effort to expel the Greek population from southern Albania, since border guards in the north of the country have been stopping attempts by Albanians to flee across the frontier, whereas border guards in the south have apparently been ordered since December 1990 to ignore such movements. Furthermore, the Catholic and Muslim communities have been granted the right to public worship, but the Alia regime continues its harassment of the Orthodox in the south, as well as its repression of the Greek language.

January 16 Greeks in Albania form a political party, Omonoia (Concord), or Democratic Union of the Greek Minority.

First Secretary Alia bends to an opposition demand to postpone the national elections, originally scheduled for February 10, until March 31, with runoffs on April 7 and 14.

Tirana crowd during the announcement of the Democratic Party recognition.

January 18 The restoration of Muslim worship is symbolized by the reopening of the great Etem Bey mosque in central Tirana.

February 6 Pro-democracy unrest in the Albanian capital begins anew with rallies and a mass student strike at the Enver Hoxha University in Tirana. Protest leaders demand liberal economic and political reforms, the resignation of major government officials, and the removal of Hoxha's name from the university.

February 18 With most of Enver Hoxha University's 10,000 students boycotting classes, an estimated 700 students and faculty begin a hunger strike to push their pro-democracy demands.

February 20 More than 5,000 students and workers stage a demonstration in Tirana in support of the university hunger strikers. The protest also marks the start of a general strike by thousands of workers in the capital, called by the pro-democracy movement. Hundreds of protesters topple a giant statue of Hoxha in Tirana's central Skënderbeg Square before being suppressed by police backed with armed tanks. Conceding to one of the demonstrators' demands, the government announces that Hoxha's name

will be removed from the university. In order to further pacify the protesters, Alia sacks Prime Minister Carcani, replacing him with reformist economist Fatos Nano.

February 21 Demonstrators storm a bookstore in Tirana devoted to the writings of Hoxha and burn hundreds of volumes in the street. In a related incident, security forces fire warning shots to disperse a crowd of protesters marching on an exclusive district of Tirana that houses the Albanian Party of Labor (APL) elite.

February 22–24 Violence and the death toll in the capital escalate as the state security forces are reinforced with army units.

March 4–7 About 24,000 Albanians seek political asylum in Italy. The refugees commandeer scores of fishing trawlers and freighters at the ports of Durrës, Shëngjin, and Vlorë and force the crews to sail to Italy. The Italian government is slow to help the refugees, many of whom are starving or ill, and threaten to have all the refugees rounded up and sent back to Albania.

In an attempt to curb further unrest, on March 7 the Albanian government places Durrës' port facilities under

Dismantling of the Stalin statue, Tirana.

military control and bans mass gatherings in Tirana, Durrës, Shëngjin, and Vlorë.

March 10–11 Goaded by international criticism, the Italian government takes measures to help the Albanian refugees quarantined in its southeastern ports. Meeting in Tirana, Italian deputy premier offers Albania $9 million in economic aid in return for Alia's pledge to halt the flow of refugees. Meanwhile, Albanian refugees continue to stream into Greece at a rate of more than 100 a day.

March 15 Albania and the United States reestablish diplomatic relations after a 45-year break.

March 17–18, 30 Fulfilling a preelection pledge, the Albanian government frees 433 political prisoners, but the opposition maintains that others remain in custody.

March 31 Albania's first postwar multiparty national elections take place. Approximately 95 percent of the country's roughly 1.9 million eligible voters go to the polls. About 250 foreign observers monitor the voting, but their presence is limited mainly to urban areas. Communist terror and intimidation characterize the electoral process in the countryside.

April 2 The first-round election results are reported, with the Communists retaining power as the Albanian Party of Labor (APL) captures 66 percent of the popular vote and 162 seats in the 250-member People's Assembly. Even though Alia and other prominent Communists are personally defeated in their Tirana constituencies, they do not resign their government offices. Widespread protests ensue, and in Shkodër, where the local APL headquarters is set ablaze, four people are killed, including the city's Democratic Party of Albania (DPA) leader, and at least 30 are wounded when security forces open fire on demonstrators.

April 14 Runoff elections for a total of 19 races are completed. According to final election results, the Albanian Party of Labor (APL) wins 169 of the 250 seats in the People's Assembly, the DPA gets 75 seats, the Omonoia wins 5 seats, and 1 seat goes to a Communist front organization, the Veterans Committee.

April 15 The opening session of the new People's Assembly is boycotted by the DPA members, pending the establishment of an inquiry into the April 2 Shkodër killings.

April 17 Following the formation of a parliamentary commission to investigate the April 2 Shkodër killings, the DPA ends its boycott of the assembly.

April 29 Under an interim constitution adopted by the legislature, the country is renamed the Republic of Albania.

April 30 Alia is confirmed as president of the Republic of Albania. The opposition, holding only one-third of the 250 seats in the assembly, does not put forth a candidate and abstains from presidential voting.

May 4 Alia renounces his APL posts, including first secretary, keeping with a new constitutional provision that bars the national president from holding a position in any political party.

May 9 Prime Minister Nano unveils a new 25-member cabinet composed entirely of members of the APL.

May 13 Tirana drops its long-standing demand that London return gold looted from Albania by the Germans during the Second World War as a precondition for the restoration of relations (*see* August 1985).

May 15 The newly established Union of Independent Trade Unions of Albania (UITUA) initiates a crippling nationwide strike, with half of the country's 700,000 workers leaving their jobs. The strikers demand a 50 percent wage increase, better conditions for working women, arrests in connection with the violent suppression of anti-Communist protests in Shkodër in April, and the resignation of the government.

May 22 As a result of the strike, President Alia agrees to appoint a caretaker government, headed by Ylli Bufi, when the government finally resigns. Bufi's nomination is approved by the DPA, and according to an agreement reached by both factions, Bufi is to select a 24-member cabinet drawn in equal parts from the Albanian Party of Labor (APL) and the opposition.

May 29 Tens of thousands of protesters attend a demonstration in Tirana in support of the UITUA strikers.

June 4 Beset by UITUA's crippling strike, Prime Minister Nano's Communist government resigns. Nano announces that a nonpartisan interim ''government of national salvation'' will be appointed, which will prepare the country for new elections in mid-1992. The DPA opposition agrees to support the interim government.

June 10–12 The Tenth Congress of the APL meets in Tirana, where the party, displaying deep divisions, takes some steps toward reform. In an attempt to show a new orientation, the party's 1,400 delegates expel 9 former members of the Politburo from the APL, and the APL changes its name to the Albanian Socialist party (ASP), with former Prime Minister Fatos Nano as its leader.

June 12 The People's Assembly confirms the Bufi cabinet, known as the ''government of national salvation.'' Prime Minister Bufi promises rapid privatization of land, economic liberalization, and the depoliticization of state institutions, the police, and education. Adhering to the May 22 accord, 12 of the new coalition government's 24 ministers come from the opposition, including members of the DPA, the Albanian Republic party (ARP), the Social Democrat party (SDP), and the Agrarian party (AP). Keeping also with the May 22 agreement, all members of the cabinet withdraw from their party affiliations.

June 13   The Italian foreign minister visits Tirana and pledges $50 million in emergency economic aid for Albania.

June 19   Albania is admitted as a member nation in the Conference on Security and Cooperation in Europe.

June 22   U.S. secretary of state James A. Baker III visits Albania. A crowd estimated at 200,000 to 300,000 people enthusiastically responds to his address in Skënderbeg Square. Later Baker meets with Alia and Bufi, and pledges $6 million in American emergency aid to Albania. Baker also confers with Albanian opposition leaders.

July 23   Responding to an Albanian plea to the international community to help ease the country's mounting shortages of food, the European Community announces a plan to send 50,000 tons of grain to Albania.

August 8   An estimated 18,000 Albanian refugees flee to Italy, causing Albania to place all its ports under military rule. Italy declares a state of emergency on its southeastern coastline. The Albanian freighter *Vlorë,* overcrowded with about 10,000 refugees, forces its way into the Italian port of Bari despite an attempt by Italian naval vessels to block the harbor.

August 9–12   The Italian government quickly repatriates 12,000 of the new Albanian refugees. In Bari, where more than 2,000 Albanians refuse to leave Italy, clashes erupt between Italian riot police and refugees. Many of the Albanians have been placed in a soccer stadium under police guard, and hundreds of others are confined to a wharf area with no sanitation facilities or shelter. All refugees are given a bare minimum of food and water.

August 12   Italy begins a $70 million emergency airlift of food to Albania.

August 17–18   After breaking their resistance, Italy forcibly repatriates the last of an estimated 18,000 Albanian refugees who had arrived on August 8.

August 19   Albania and Israel establish diplomatic relations; Albania appeals to Israel for agricultural, financial, and medical aid.

Late August   The government begins measuring out land in preparation for its return to those dispossessed under collectivization. Nonetheless, the economy has come to a standstill, as agricultural and industrial output decline

by roughly half the preceding year's figures. Demonstrations are renewed.

September 7   Albania and the Vatican establish diplomatic relations.

Mid-September   Tens of thousands of protesters gather in central Tirana, demanding the arrest of former APL leaders, full freedom of the media, and the abolition of the secret police.

October   Opposition to the government increases due to a serious decline in food supplies, which in turn leads to increasing anarchy in the countryside. By month's end, parts of the northeast of the country are beyond state control. Demonstrators at a rally in Fier demand the resignation of President Alia.

November   The Democratic Party of Albania (DPA) threatens to withdraw from the coalition government unless various demands, including the holding of new elections by February 1992, are satisfied.

November 29   In a concession to the DPA, the cabinet agrees to hold general elections within three months, several months earlier than originally planned.

December 4   The Bufi coalition government collapses when the DPA announces that it will withdraw its seven ministers from the cabinet. The fall of the cabinet comes as dwindling food and fuel supplies are causing nationwide unrest. DPA chairman Sali Berisha, announcing his party's withdrawal from the government, accuses cabinet members from the Albanian Socialist party (ASP; formerly APL) of blocking needed economic and political reforms.

December 6   In an attempt to keep the DPA in the cabinet, the government arrests several former hard-line Communists, including Nexhmije Hoxha, the widow of the late First Secretary Hoxha.

December 7   Defections from his cabinet, together with more opposition demonstrations in Tirana, persuade Prime Minister Bufi to resign. Responding to reports of food riots in towns in northern Albania, President Alia authorizes the army to use force against looters, while police take control of bread distribution throughout the country.

December 9–11   Thousands of demonstrators gather in Tirana to protest continued Communist influence in the government. They call for Alia's resignation and blame Communist administrators and bureaucrats for ongoing shortages of food and fuel.

December 10   President Alia names Vilson Ahmeti, a nonpartisan intellectual, to replace Ylli Bufi. Alia announces that the new government will work to ensure

Riots in Tirana illustrating civil unrest.

adequate food supplies and political stability until the next elections.

At least 35 people are killed in Fushe-Arrez, north of Tirana, when a mob that is raiding a food warehouse accidentally sets fire to the building.

December 23   To prevent an expected flood of Albanian refugees into Greece, Athens reinforces its northwest border with more troops and steps up massive food shipments to southern Albania. Athens has allowed 40,000 Albanians to enter Greece legally in 1991, but thousands of other refugees have slipped across the border.

1992

January   Widespread food riots continue as public order breaks down.

Thousands of Albanian refugees pour across the border into Greece.

Early February   The People's Assembly approves a new electoral law in which the legislature is to consist of 100 members to be elected by majority vote from single-member constituencies, while 40 deputies are to be elected according to a system of proportional representation. The law also bans political parties representing ethnic minorities. These provisions are directed against the large Greek population in the south and are intended to prevent the Omonoia from taking part in the March elections. Once the assembly codifies political repression against the country's Greek minority, Albanian nationalists attack and ransack Omonoia headquarters in Tirana and local offices in southern Albania. These actions provoke widespread protest from the Greek minority and, in an act of opposition, prompt the withdrawal of the Albanian National Unity party (the former Democratic Front) from the election campaign.

February 28   The government closes the port of Durrës and orders all ships out of the harbor to prevent a recurrence of the 1991 exodus to Italy.

March 22   The Democratic Party of Albania (DPA) routes the former Communists in the country's first-round elections. The DPA captures about 62 percent of the vote, compared with 25 percent for the ASP; the remaining 13 percent of the vote is divided among nine other political parties.

Kavakia on the Greek Albanian border in 1991. Albanians try to pass into Greece with false visas and passports, or with no papers at all, and are stopped by Greek army border control units.

March 24 Sali Berisha, leader of the DPA, addresses 50,000 jubilant supporters in Tirana's Skënderbeg Square. He announces: ''We are saying farewell to Communism once and for all. It will never return.''

March 29 With the completion of the second and final round of the general elections, the DPA wins 92 of the People's Assembly's 140 seats, while the ASP receives 38 seats, the SDP 7 seats, the Union for Human Rights 2 seats, and the ARP 1 seat.

April The escalating conflict in the former Yugoslavia further strains Tirana's already tense relations with Belgrade. In protest against the repression of the Albanian population in Kosovo, Tirana withdraws its ambassador from Belgrade.

The United States pledges $35 million in aid to Albania.

April 3 Following the defeat of the ASP, Ramiz Alia resigns as president.

April 4 The People's Assembly elects Sali Berisha president by a vote of 96 to 35. Berisha, a 47-year-old cardiologist, becomes Albania's first non-Marxist leader since the Second World War. Berisha nominates Alexan-

der Meksi, a 53-year-old engineer, to replace Prime Minister Ahmeti.

Mid-April Prime Minister Meksi's cabinet, consisting of 15 members of the DPA, one each from the ARP and the SDP, and two independents, is formally sworn in.

April 17 President Berisha meets with Ibrahim Rugova, the leader of the Albanian Kosovars, in Tirana, where he endorses Rugova's efforts for Kosovo's independence from Yugoslavia.

April 20 The Meksi government introduces an economic reform package that entails privatization of land and industrial enterprises, banking restructuring, and the reduction of price controls.

May Berisha addresses the Council of Europe's Parliamentary Assembly in Strasbourg and meets with a number of economic and finance ministers in Brussels. Albania and the European Community sign a 10-year agreement on trade and cooperation.

June Greece pledges $70 million in aid to Albania for agricultural development. The United States pledges $60

On March 24, 1992, Sali Berisha is cheered on by crowds in front of the Democratic Party headquarters upon winning the elections.

million in aid to Albania, in addition to the aid package promised in April.

Albania, together with 10 other countries, signs a Black Sea economic cooperation pact, which envisages the creation of a Black Sea economic zone that will complement the European Community.

July Although the anarchy of the preceding months subsides, major strikes continue. The government declares many of them illegal and insists that they are being fomented by former Communists.

July 10 Albanian court officials announce that high-ranking former Communists will be tried for abuse of public funds, including Nexhmije Hoxha and former Prime Minister Adil Carcani.

July 16 An amendment to the law on political organizations outlaws Stalinist and ''Enverist'' (referring to Enver Hoxha) political parties. The last head of the now defunct APL, Hysni Milloshi, is arrested in Tirana and charged with illegally carrying a gun.

August 2 Albania's first local postwar elections, with their first round held on July 26, are completed. The DPA

secures most votes, but wins only a narrow plurality of 43 percent to the ASP's 41 percent. Although the DPA controls most urban areas, including Tirana, the ASP makes a strong showing in the countryside as well as in the north. In the south the Human Rights Union receives overwhelming support from the Greek minority. The decline of the DPA reflects disillusion with the performance of the Berisha administration. Furthermore, Berisha's party is hurt by an internal power struggle at the top, leading to the expulsion from the DPA of one of the organization's founders, Gramoz Pashko.

A Greek national, Anastasios Yanoulatos, becomes the head of the Albanian Orthodox church in a ceremony in Tirana. Regardless of the lack of qualified Albanian Orthodox clerics after 25 years of repression, Archbishop Anastasios' inauguration draws protests from some Albanians who believe the post should have gone to an Albanian.

September 15 Ramiz Alia is placed under house arrest in Tirana on charges of corruption.

September 28 The finance ministers of the European Community announce a grant of $95 million to Albania.

Women from the Northern Albanian village of Bicaj mourning a woman's son—killed crossing the Kosoua border.

October Strikes break out at the Bulqize chromium mines and the oil-processing plant at Ballsh.

November Although most land is redistributed five months earlier, in June, and is under de facto private ownership, legislation for the official decollectivization of agricultural land is introduced in the People's Assembly.

Athens grants $24 million in credits to Albania.

November 8 Tension develops between Tirana and Skopje, following unrest in the former Yugoslav republic of Macedonia. Three ethnic Albanians are killed, 30 people are injured, and more than 100 are arrested by police during rioting in Skopje. Approximately 25 percent to 30 percent of the republic's population of 2.1 million are ethnic Albanians, the overwhelming majority of whom demand political and cultural autonomy from Skopje; Tirana supports these demands.

December 3 Albania establishes diplomatic relations with Saudi Arabia and is granted membership in the Organization of the Islamic Conference.

December 16 Albania applies for membership in the North Atlantic Treaty Organization (NATO) during a visit by President Berisha to Brussels. Albania wants NATO

membership as a security hedge against a possible spread of the Yugoslav civil war to Kosovo.

December 28 Tirana expresses satisfaction with Washington's warning to Belgrade not to attack Kosovo.

1993

January 27 Nexhmije Hoxha is sentenced in Tirana to nine years in prison for having misappropriated funds worth $55,000 between 1985 and 1991.

April 25 Pope John Paul II visits Albania, where about 10 percent of the population of 3.2 million is Catholic. The pontiff is accompanied by Mother Teresa, the Albanian 1979 Nobel Peace laureate. In his addresses in Shkodër and Tirana, Pope John Paul II pays tribute to Albanians who had suffered religious and political persecution during the country's Communist era. He also cautions his audiences against violent solidarity with the Albanians in neighboring Kosovo and assails nationalism.

May 17 Albania's appeal court increases the jail term for Nexhmije Hoxha to 11 years, after finding her guilty on further charges of misappropriating state funds.

May 26   President Berisha urges NATO and the United States to send troops to Kosovo to prevent Serbia from engaging in the "ethnic cleansing"—forced removal or extermination of the non-Serbian population—of the province, which is approximately 90 percent Albanian.

June 25   The Albanian government expels a senior Orthodox cleric, Archimandrite Chrysostomos Maidonis, charging him with fomenting separatist nationalist feeling among the Greeks in southern Albania. In further action against Orthodox clerics, the Albanian government prohibits three recently appointed Greek auxiliary bishops to Archbishop Anastassios from entering the country. These moves prompt the Greek authorities to begin deporting the more than 200,000 illegal Albanian immigrants in Greece, which is a very serious measure, because the refugees' earnings remitted from Greece have become the mainstay of the Albanian economy during the last two years.

July 14   After weeks of worsening tension between Athens and Tirana, Greek Prime Minister Constantine Mitsotakis establishes terms for improving relations. Mitsotakis sets out six conditions: the return of Archimandrite Chrysostomos to his parish in Gjirokastër, the restoration of all Orthodox Church property forcibly seized during Communist rule, and free practice of Orthodox Christianity and liturgical use of the Greek language when so desired; permission for public and private minority schools, with access to Greek language instruction; unhindered operation of Greek community, cultural, and political organizations; an end to harassment and arbitrary dismissals of ethnic Greeks employed in Albania's public services, and the assurance of equal opportunity in the state administration; permission for Greek families expelled during the Communist era to return to Albania and claim their property; and the institution of programs to discourage prejudice towards Greek and other minorities. Mitsotakis states that Greece will continue to expel illegal immigrants, but is ready to sign an agreement for Albanians to come to Greece legally as seasonal workers. Mitsotakis reminds Tirana that Greece had been the first country to provide aid to Albania after the fall of communism and that Greece had been the only country willing to receive tens of thousands of Albanian refugees during the mass exodus of 1991–92.

July 17   Tirana rejects all conditions set by the Greek government.

August   Albanian security forces launch a wave of attacks on ethnic Greeks who have gathered to discuss their minority rights in connection with a visit to Albania by the Conference on Security and Cooperation in Europe High Commissioner for National Minorities. Tension escalates between Athens and Tirana as the Greek government enters a formal protest with the Albanian government against its use of violence against ethnic Greeks.

September   A delegation of Albanian parliamentary deputies visits Athens. Much to the embarrassment of the Berisha government, members of the delegation express publicly the view that the constitutional provisions defending minority rights in Albania are not being put into practice. Moreover, the deputies claim that the Berisha government is engaging in the systematic intimidation and harassment of the Greek population in Albania.

October 14   Albanian Defense Minister Safet Zhulali signs an agreement, initialled six days earlier by United States Defense Secretary Les Aspin, providing for military cooperation between their two countries. Although the Tirana-Washington agreement is not an official treaty but a memorandum of understanding that is not binding on either side, its provisions foresee expanded contacts between both nations. The agreement also calls for exchanges of officers and for the United States to offer training programs for Albanian military personnel. Underscoring the new orientation of the Albanian military toward the United States, Zhulali has already ordered all active-duty personnel in the armed forces to learn English over the next year.

October 26   After the beating to death of an elderly Greek woman and reports of other violent attacks on ethnic Greeks in southern Albania, the Greek government submits a formal protest to the Albanian ambassador in Athens. The Greek government expresses concern about the mounting wave of hate crimes and governmental abuse on ethnic Greeks, asserting that the actions are part of a design to put pressure on Athens to legalize the status of the illegal Albanian migrants that infiltrate Greece's borders hourly, and to destroy the morale of the Greek minority in Albania.

November 19   The would-be king of Albania, Leka I, returns to the country he left as an infant (*see* April 7, 1939), to commemorate the 50th anniversary of the founding of a monarchist movement during World War II. After Albanian authorities ask him to leave, he complies early the next day.

Chapter Two

BULGARIA

The modern Bulgarians are principally descendants of Slavic tribes that entered the Balkans in the late sixth and early seventh centuries and occupied the lands peopled by the ancient Thracians. These Slavs were conquered during the second half of the seventh and eighth centuries by a Turkic people known as the Bulgars, or proto-Bulgars, from Central Asia. The Bulgars were fewer in number than the Slavs, and in a relatively short time the Bulgar minority became culturally and linguistically assimilated. By the tenth century the early Slavs and the Bulgars had consolidated into a unified Slavic people who maintained the name Bulgarians.

The Bulgars/Bulgarians organized two powerful states in the central Balkans during the medieval period. During the First Bulgarian Empire (681–1018) the leader, Khan Boris I Michael (852–889), personally accepted Orthodox Christianity, made it the official religion of Bulgaria in 865, and promoted its transmission through the work of missionaries. The First Bulgarian Empire reached its zenith during the reign of Boris' son, Symeon (893–927). Bulgarian architecture, literature, and the arts flourished in imitation of Byzantine models. This period also marked the height of Bulgaria's territorial expansion as its frontiers included what is now Bulgaria, Serbia, Albania, northern Macedonia, and portions of Romania. Despite the growing cultural affinity between Bulgaria and the Byzantine Empire, constant political rivalry between the two empires led to a series of bitter wars; by the end of the tenth century the Bulgarians were in retreat and by 1018 the Byzantine Empire's victory was complete. However, by the late twelfth century the Bulgarians were able to profit from the decline of Byzantine power by organizing a successful revolt that freed them from Byzantine domination in 1185. The Second Bulgarian Empire lasted from 1186 to 1393. During the reign of Ivan Assen II (1218–1241), Bulgaria was the leading power in southeastern Europe. Ivan's weak and ineffectual successors, however, were unable to maintain this position. In 1330 the declining and fragmented empire was defeated by the Serbs, and Bulgaria was reduced to a vassal state, politically subservient to Serbia.

Serbian domination over Bulgaria was eclipsed by the rising power of the Ottoman Turks who destroyed the final remnants of Bulgarian political independence in 1393 when the capital of Turnovo fell to the Ottomans. In 1767 the Ottomans abolished the national Bulgarian Orthodox Church founded by Boris I and placed it under the control of the Patriarchate of Constantinople. Thus, along with ecclesiastical administration, education in Bulgaria passed to the control of the Greeks. As a result, early Bulgarian nationalists regarded Greek dominance of higher culture as great a threat to their aspirations as Ottoman political control. Consequently, the first step towards national liberation was the revival of Bulgarian education in the early nineteenth century. In 1835 the first Bulgarian-language schools were established. The second step towards liberation was the freeing of the Bulgarian Church from Greek influence which was accomplished in 1870 when the Ottomans agreed to establish the Bulgarian Exarchate Church.

The final step towards Bulgarian national liberation was political independence from the Ottoman Empire. The opportunity for revolt came in 1875 when an uprising against Ottoman rule broke out among the Slavs in the

Bulgaria in relation to the size of the United States.

provinces of Bosnia and Hercegovina. The rebellion spread quickly and drew the Balkan principalities of Montenegro and Serbia into war with the Ottomans. The Bulgarians joined the revolt in the spring of 1876 but were brutally crushed by the Ottoman forces. Stirred in part by public opinion against the Turkish atrocities in Bulgaria, Russia intervened in the Balkans in April 1877. After a difficult military campaign Russia forced the Ottoman Empire to sign the Treaty of San Stefano on March 3, 1878. Among other things, the treaty called for the creation of a large Bulgarian state which was to include not merely the lands where the national revolt had taken place, but most of Macedonia as well. However, the Western Great Powers of Austria-Hungary, France, Germany, and Great Britain feared that a large Bulgaria would be little more than a Russian puppet. After a period of international tension Russia agreed to submit to a revision of the treaty. Accordingly, the Treaty of Berlin, signed on July 13, 1878, replaced the Treaty of San Stefano. By its provisions the size of Bulgaria was reduced to one-third that of San Stefano; Bulgaria proper (Sofia and the lands north of the Balkan Mountains) was made an autonomous principality; Eastern Rumelia (the land between the Balkan Mountains and Thrace) was to be administered by a Christian governor under Ottoman authority; and Macedonia was to remain under direct Ottoman administration. The Bulgarians

were bitterly disappointed with the Treaty of Berlin that greatly reduced the size of their state, and in subsequent years the restoration of the boundaries established by the Treaty of San Stefano became the chief foreign policy goal of all Bulgarian nationalists.

Despite their territorial frustration, the Bulgarians did at least obtain a state of their own. On April 29, 1879, the new nation's political leaders adopted a liberal constitution which guaranteed civil liberties and provided for a parliament elected by almost universal manhood suffrage. Alexander of Battenberg (1857–1893), related by marriage to both the English royal family and the Russian tsar, was elected Prince of Bulgaria the day after the constitution was accepted. In September 1885 nationalists in Eastern Rumelia revolted and declared their union with Bulgaria. Against the express wishes of Tsar Alexander III, Prince Alexander endorsed the union and accepted the leadership of the nationalist movement in the province. Meanwhile, concerned that a greater Bulgaria would upset the balance of power in the region, Serbia declared war on Bulgaria on November 13, 1885. However, the rapid victory of the Bulgarian army ensured that the union of Eastern Rumelia with Bulgaria would not be undone. In January 1886 the Ottoman government accepted Alexander as governor of Eastern Rumelia, thereby making possible a personal union of the province with Bulgaria. A final agreement was signed on April 5, 1886, and the merger of the principality and Eastern Rumelia was thus formally recognized by the Great Powers as the foundation of a single unified Bulgarian state.

1886

August Prince Alexander is abducted by Russian conspirators and forced to abdicate. Several days later, the President of the *Subranie* (parliament) puts down the coup, takes control of the government, and urge Alexander to return to Bulgaria. Eventually, due to unrelenting Russian pressure, Alexander formally abdicates and leaves Bulgaria.

1887

July Ferdinand of Saxe-Coburg-Gotha (1861–1948), an officer in the Habsburg army, is crowned Prince of Bulgaria. The *Subranie* unanimously elects him to the throne without the sanction of Russia and the Great Powers, who withhold their official recognition. Until mid-1894 repeated Russian attempts to unseat Ferdinand and to set up a Russophile regime in Bulgaria fail.

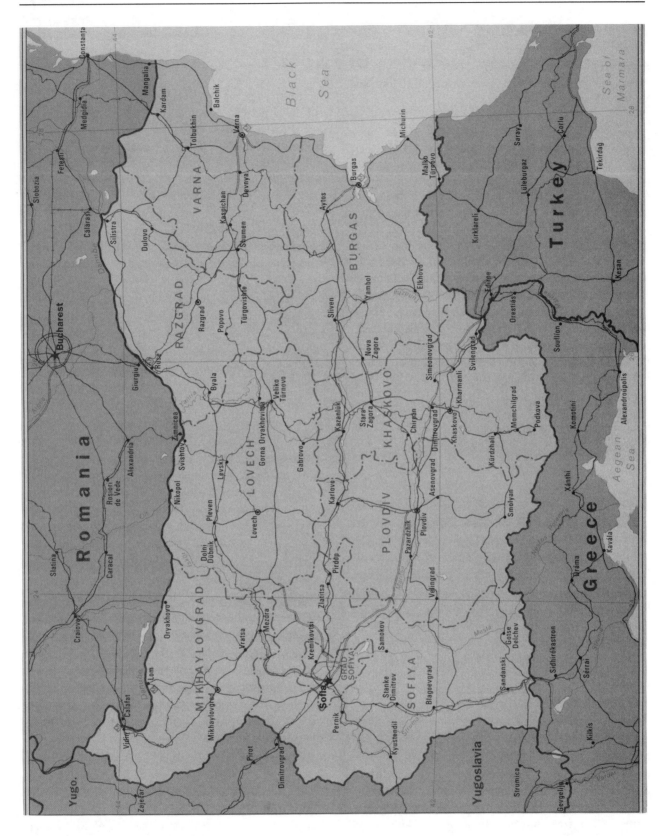

1896

February Relations are restored between Bulgaria and Russia, and the other Great Powers recognize Ferdinand shortly thereafter.

1894

August The Internal Macedonian Revolutionary Organization (IMRO) is organized in the western Macedonian town of Resen (Resna). Led by ethnic Bulgarians, IMRO opposes any partitioning of Macedonia along ethnological lines. Instead the organization's different factions seek either autonomy for the entire region within the Ottoman Empire; autonomy within an independent South Slav federation consisting of Bulgaria, Macedonia, and Serbia; or some kind of union with Bulgaria. Although the Bulgarian government is generally sympathetic to the activities of IMRO, Ferdinand prefers that the revolutionary movement in Macedonia be solely committed to the goal of union with Bulgaria. Toward this end, as a rival to IMRO, the Macedonian External Organization, also known as the Supreme Committee, or the Supremists, is organized in Sofia where it advocates the annexation of Macedonia by Bulgaria.

1895

June 1895–August 1903 The fate of Macedonia leads to bitter and escalating armed rivalries within the region. Despite Supremist terrorist attacks in Ottoman-held Macedonia, Bulgarian aspirations in the region do not remain uncontested. The growing Bulgarian guerilla movements in Macedonia are forced to compete with Greek and, to a lesser extent, Serbian bands. The wave of inter-community violence in the region is compounded by Macedonia's complex ethnological composition: the majority of the population in northern Macedonia (north of the line Bitola [Monastir]-Kavadarci-Sandanski) consists of ethnic Bulgarians; Greeks are a majority in southern Macedonia (south of the line Kastoria-Édhessa-Serres); and Muslims, mainly Turks, constitute a plurality in the intensely mixed area of central Macedonia. In addition, Albanians are settled in large numbers in the Northwest, Serbs in the area immediately north of Skopje, and Armenians, Gypsies, Jews, Vlachs, and other groups are scattered throughout the region.

1900

July 22 Stefan Mihaileanu, the prominent Vlach professor and opponent of IMRO, is murdered in Bucharest by Supremist assassins. The Mihaileanu affair brings Romania and Bulgaria to the brink of war. The situation is quelled only after the Russians pressure the Bulgarian government to arrest Boris Sarafov, the leader of the Supremists.

1901

August Sarafov is tried in Sofia, acquitted, and released.

September–March 1902 An IMRO band abducts Ellen Stone, an American missionary posted to Bulgaria, as she and a Bulgarian Protestant companion travel in the company of others in eastern Macedonia. The United States government refuses to negotiate with the captors who demand a ransom in exchange for Stone's release. She is finally freed only after IMRO receives $66,000 from the American Missionary Board. Most of the money extorted by IMRO is used to purchase arms.

1902

October–November Supremist forces invade eastern Macedonia from positions in Bulgaria. The attack ends in failure and the Supremists retreat back across the border. Despite Ferdinand's efforts to control the Supremists through loyal officers, the organization causes the Bulgarian government significant embarrassment.

1903

May A new government comes to power under the leadership of General Racho Petrov, an associate of the Agrarian party. Upon taking office the predominantly Agrarian cabinet makes it apparent that Macedonia, and not any domestic issue, is its major concern. Accordingly, the Petrov government is committed to improving relations with the Ottoman Empire while simultaneously strengthening the Bulgarian army.

July–December The escalating wave of terrorism and violence in Macedonia culminates in the IMRO Ilinden (St. Elijah's Day) Uprising. The rebels seize most of the province of Bitola, where they organize a revolutionary council and attempt to liberate the rest of Macedonia. Armed bands enter Macedonia from Bulgaria and join the insurgents as tension escalates between Constantinople and Sofia. Despite a number of border clashes with Ottoman forces and popular demands for Bulgarian intervention, Sofia is unprepared for war and fears defeat in the event of unilateral action against the Turks. Meanwhile, the Ottoman forces are reinforced and gain the initiative against the IMRO forces by the end of August. The revolt is suppressed with great loss of life and property. The Bulgarian cause in Macedonia is seriously weakened by the unsuccessful uprising, a situation Greek and Serbian bands quickly take advantage of.

1904

March A Turco-Bulgarian treaty is signed in which Bulgaria promises to prevent armed bands from crossing into Ottoman territory, to control anti-Turkish agitation in Bulgaria, and to punish those guilty of such actions. For their part, the Turks promise to implement a Great Powers' reform plan for Macedonia, to end trade restrictions on Bulgarian goods, to grant amnesty to some 4,000 political prisoners, and to extend other concessions to the Christians within the empire. The treaty reduces tensions between Bulgaria and Turkey and in effect ends the danger of a war.

April 12 Bulgaria and Serbia conclude a secret military alliance providing for mutual aid in case of attack from any nation.

1905

May–October Frustrated by Greek advances in Macedonia, Bulgarian nationalists stage anti-Greek demonstrations throughout the principality and the Bulgarian government imposes certain restrictions on its Greek communities.

June 22 Bulgaria and Serbia conclude an economic treaty establishing virtually free trade between the two countries and foreseeing the creation of a customs union in 1917.

July The Radical Democratic party is founded whose aims are to limit the authority of Ferdinand.

1906

May–September The anti-Greek movement in the principality assumes the form of a pogrom—or organized persecution and murder—as Bulgarian extremists destroy Greek communities and property. Despite a massive wave

of emigration following the violent attacks, considerable numbers of Greeks remain in the Plovdiv area and they continue to dominate the Burgas coastline.

December 1906–March 1907 The Bulgarian government is confronted by urban unrest. Goaded by deplorable working and living conditions, as well as a socialist intelligentsia, railwaymen launch a crippling strike. Tensions between the strikers and the government escalate as students join the railwaymen and use the opportunity to denounce Prince Ferdinand. The government responds by closing the University of Sofia, sacking its faculty, and imposing austere political restrictions on all teachers. Despite intense criticism of its policies in the press and *Subranie,* the Agrarian government remains in power and ends the strike in March 1907 by agreeing to increase wages.

1907

February 11 Nikola Petkov, the leader of the Agrarian government since 1906, is assassinated in Sofia.

December Factional conflicts escalate among the Bulgarian Macedonian nationalist movements. IMRO, increasingly disunited since the Ilinden failure, is divided into two wings: one Rightist which favors cooperation with the Supremists and integration of Macedonia into Bulgaria; and one Leftist which opposes the Supremists and is committed to Macedonian autonomy. Supremists also suffer fragmentation as armed rivalry develops between the supporters of the former Supremist leader, Boris Sarafov, and the official Supremist organization in Sofia. To add to the organization's problems, the Bulgarian government, having lost control of the Supremists, launches a campaign of suppression. Sarafov and Ivan Garvanov, a prominent figure in IMRO's right-wing, are assassinated in Sofia.

1908

January 21 Stigmatized by widespread corruption the Agrarian cabinet is replaced by the Democratic party.

Late January–March 1911 The Bulgarian government is led by the Democratic party under Alexander Malinov. Once in office, Malinov's longtime struggle against Ferdinand's personal regime comes to an end. In fact, Malinov's government presides over developments that considerably strengthen Ferdinand's power and prestige, but on the other hand is able to concurrently enact a broad spectrum of reforms. Malinov realizes many of the promises he makes to the electorate to reverse the reactionary policies of the Stambulovists: increase democracy by instituting proportional representation in local elections; guarantee the constitutional freedoms of speech, assembly and association; reform the bureaucracy and the educational system; make taxation more equitable; and pursue more responsible budgetary practices. Opposition to the Democratic party in the Subranie is disunited and insignificant, save the 24-member bloc of Agrarians under the leadership of the charismatic Alexander Stamboliiski.

October 5 Taking advantage of the confusion in the Ottoman Empire caused by the Young Turk Revolt, the Malinov government and Ferdinand proclaim the full independence of Bulgaria in Turnovo's Church of the Forty Martyrs. Ferdinand assumes the title King of the Bulgarians.

1910

March An incident involving Christian-Muslim tension in the northern town of Ruse sets off a series of intercommunal disturbances throughout Bulgaria.

1911

March Continued and increasing unrest in European Turkey points to the apparently inevitable collapse of Ottoman rule. Malinov's policy of good relations with the Ottoman Empire coupled with the fact that his policies seem to jeopardize Bulgaria's claims on Macedonia lead to the fall of the Democratic party government. Malinov, therefore, is dropped and his government is replaced by a coalition cabinet composed of members of the Nationalist party and Progressive Liberal party. They, unlike Malinov are prepared to form regional alliances with Bulgaria's chief competitors in Macedonia in order to eliminate Ottoman rule in the Balkans. The Nationalist party leader Ivan Evstratiev Geshov becomes head of the government and Minister of Foreign Affairs and Stoyan Danev, leader of the Progressive Liberal party, becomes president of the *Subranie.*

1912

March 13 Bulgaria and Serbia take the first step toward the formation of an anti-Ottoman Balkan League. A secret treaty is signed between the two countries. Belgrade and Sofia agree to aid each other in the event that either is attacked, and to take joint action against any Great Power which might attempt to occupy any Ottoman territory in the Balkans. The treaty also outlines the prospective division of Ottoman territory between Bulgaria and Serbia agreed to earlier by both: Bulgaria is to annex that part of Macedonia south and east of a line running from Ohrid to Veles to Kriva Palanka. The fate of the remainder of northern Macedonia to the Shar Mountains—the Macedonian contested zone—is to be determined by future negotiations.

May 29 The Balkan League is expanded as Bulgaria and Greece conclude an alliance. However, conflicting aspirations in Macedonia, particularly over the city of Thessaloníki, preclude any territorial agreements.

October 6 Montenegro becomes the last nation to join the Balkan League as it concludes an alliance with Serbia, mirroring a pact signed with Bulgaria in late September. Underlying the actual intent behind the recent flurry of diplomatic activity among the Balkan states, Montenegro's secret pacts with Bulgaria and Serbia are avowedly offensive in character—they require the signatories to begin hostilities against the Ottoman Empire.

October 8 The First Balkan War begins. Disregarding Austrian and Russian threats that the Great Powers will not recognize any changes in the territorial integrity of the Ottoman Empire, Montenegro declares war on Turkey.

October 18 Bulgaria, Greece, and Serbia join Montenegro in the war against the Turks.

October 22 The Bulgarian army, which because of geography is forced to assume the brunt of the fighting against the Ottoman forces, wins a decisive battle at Kirk-Kilissa, forcing the Turks to withdraw deep into Eastern Thrace.

October 23–29 The Bulgarians begin their siege of Edirne (Adrianople) and continue their advance through Eastern Thrace to the defense lines outside Constantinople. Concurrently, Bulgarian forces overrun most of Western Thrace and penetrate eastern Macedonia.

October 30–November 8 As the Bulgarians intensify their siege of Edirne, the Greek and Serbian armies make rapid advances in the west. Serbian troops march beyond their assigned sphere of influence and occupy considerable territory in Macedonia south of the Ohrid-Veles-Kriva Palanka line.

November 8 Greek units liberate the city of Thessaloníki, beating the Bulgarians to the city by one day.

December 3 The Turks conclude an armistice with Bulgaria and Serbia while the Greeks continue their operations.

December 16–January 22, 1913 Peace negotiations in London conclude with the Turks agreeing to relinquish all European territory except Constantinople and most of Eastern Thrace.

1913

January 30 The extreme nationalist Young Turks refuse to accept the loss of most of European Turkey and renew hostilities after removing the Turkish premier in a coup.

January 30–March 26 The Turkish counteroffensive ends in disaster with the Ottoman forces being routed and virtually all their remaining positions overrun. Edirne falls to the Bulgarians on March 26. At this point the Great Powers intervene to halt the hostilities.

April 16 An armistice is concluded between the Ottoman Empire and the Balkan allies.

May 7 A great power conference in St. Petersburg, Russia, awards Romania Silistra and a small piece of southern Dobrudja—a region on the Black Sea south of the Danube River—which Romania demanded for its neutrality in the First Balkan War. Romania occupies the territory the same day.

May 20 The Turks sign the Treaty of London thus ending the First Balkan War. The Ottoman Empire relinquishes all territory west of Constantinople and its surrounding area. The status of Macedonia, the remainder of Thrace, and Albania remains undetermined, presumably to be decided by the Great Powers.

May 20–June 29 Dissension develops among the Balkan allies over the division of the former Ottoman territories. Because considerable territory, which in the original Bulgarian-Serbian pact had been assigned to Serbia, is now reserved by the Great Powers for Albania, Belgrade demands that its share of Macedonia be extended beyond the Ohrid-Veles-Kriva Palanka line. Accordingly, the Serbian government refuses to withdraw its forces from the lands in Macedonia it has occupied beyond the original demarcation (*see* March 13; October 30–November 8, 1912). In addition, although the prewar treaty between Bulgaria and Greece said nothing of Macedonia, Sofia is laying claim to Greek-held Thessaloníki (*see* May 29, 1912).

June 1 Apprehensive of Sofia's new predominant position in the region, and under pressure from repeated sorties by Bulgarian forces in Macedonia, Greece and Serbia sign a secret treaty of alliance. They agree to seek a common frontier in Macedonia west of the Vardar River, to ask for the mediation of the Great Powers if there should be disagreement with Sofia over the delimitation of frontiers, and to aid each other in the event of war. Soon thereafter, both powers gain the support of Montenegro and Romania.

June 28 With the knowledge and approval of Danev and Geshov, King Ferdinand orders the Bulgarian army to attack the Greek and Serbian lines in Macedonia. As a result of diplomatic bungling Bulgaria is left without any regional allies or supporters among the Great Powers. Public opinion in Bulgaria is emphatically in favor of war; the Bulgarian Macedonian groups even threaten Danev and Ferdinand with assassination if they seek a peaceful resolution. The army general staff and the government are convinced of Bulgaria's military superiority. Finally, Sofia aspires to annex all of Macedonia.

June 29–30 The Bulgarian army mounts a surprise attack on Greece and Serbia, thereby starting the Second Balkan War. Montenegro immediately joins Serbia against Bulgaria.

July 10 As the Greek and Serbian armies halt the Bulgarian advances and launch successful counteroffensives, Romania enters the conflict by declaring war on Bulgaria. Units of the Romanian army move into the poorly defended southern Dobrudja.

July 13–15 Taking advantage of Bulgaria's weak position, Turkey enters the war and its forces attack westward into Thrace. Meanwhile the Greek army advances north through the Struma valley, and the Serbs continue their push east. Simultaneously, large numbers of Romanian forces cross the Danube and march south towards Vratsa. The Bulgarian army collapses on all fronts.

July 17 Overwhelmed by its military catastrophe, the Danev-Geshov government falls. It is replaced by a coalition of various liberal factions headed by Vasil Radoslavov.

July 31 An armistice is concluded between Bulgaria and its enemies.

August 10 The Treaty of Bucharest is signed, ending hostilities between Bulgaria on the one hand and Greece, Montenegro, Romania, and Serbia on the other. Greece acquires all of southern Macedonia; Romania gains a larger section of southern Dobrudja; Serbia is granted northern and central Macedonia; and Bulgaria retains only a small portion of eastern Macedonia. The disaster of the summer of 1913 leaves Bulgaria embittered toward, and alienated from, its former allies. Whereas Bulgaria refuses to accept the peace terms as final, Greece, Romania, and Serbia are equally determined to maintain them.

September 29   Bulgaria and the Ottoman Empire sign the Treaty of Constantinople by which Turkey regains Eastern Thrace and Bulgaria acquires Western Thrace.

November   Radoslavov's coalition government fails to win a majority in the *Subranie* following Bulgaria's first postwar general election. Radoslavov's coalition receives 97 parliamentary seats to the combined opposition's 109. The opposition delegates are divided among nine parties, the most influential being the Agrarians with 47 seats. The voting clearly reflects widespread disillusion with the parties responsible for the nation's recent military humiliations. Despite the election results, Radoslavov continues to lead the government with the confidence of Ferdinand.

1914

January   Radoslavov's attempts to gain the parliamentary support of Alexander Stamboliiski's Agrarian party ends in failure and the *Subranie* is therefore dissolved.

March   New national elections are held for seats in the *Subranie*. Amidst enormous government tampering Radoslavov's coalition secures a majority in the *Subranie*, with 132 seats to the opposition's 107.

July 28   Austria-Hungary declares war on Serbia. By August 6 the Central Powers of Austria-Hungary and Germany are fighting the Triple Entente (Great Britain, France, and Russia) and its allies (Belgium, Serbia, and Montenegro) in the First World War.

1915

June   After being courted for almost a year by the Triple Entente and the Central Powers, Ferdinand and Radoslavov decide to bring Bulgaria into the First World War on the side of the Central Powers of Germany, Austria-Hungary, and the Ottoman Empire.

July 22   Austro-Hungarians and Germans persuade the Turks to immediately hand over to Bulgaria a small portion of Thrace as a preliminary reward to Sofia for joining its side.

September 3   The Entente Powers make a frantic last-minute attempt to win Bulgaria's support by offering it Eastern Thrace and Serbian Macedonia, the latter being territory of an Entente ally.

September 6   Bulgaria signs a series of agreements with Austria-Hungary and Germany. Bulgaria is to join in an Austro-Hungarian and German attack on Serbia for which it will receive all of Serbian Macedonia and part of Serbia proper. Bulgaria is also promised Greek and Romanian territories in the event that either intervenes in the war on the side of the Entente.

September 17   In an audience with King Ferdinand the leaders of the opposition party express their disapproval of Bulgaria's alliance with the Central Powers. Stamboliiski warns Ferdinand that if he persists in his plans to break Bulgaria's neutrality he risks losing his life as well as his throne.

Late September–October   The Bulgarian government imprisons Stamboliiski, closes opposition newspapers, postpones the meeting of the *Subranie,* and institutes a general policy of repression to stifle all dissent.

October 11   Bulgaria enters the First World War. The Bulgarian army attacks Serbia from the east as Austro-Hungarian and German forces overrun the country from the north and west. Sofia officially declares war on Serbia three days later.

November–December   As the remnants of the Serbian army retreat toward Albania and the Adriatic Sea, the Bulgarian forces advance rapidly in eastern Serbia and Serbian Macedonia, stopping their march at the Greek border. The advancing forces are greeted as liberators in Serbian Macedonia where the Slavic population is overwhelmingly Bulgarian.

December 28   Emboldened by the recent victory over Serbia, and confident of public support, Ferdinand and Crown Prince Boris open the *Subranie*. Both the king and the crown prince are given an enthusiastic reception from all the delegates but the Agrarians and Socialists.

1916

August–September   Romania enters the war on the side of the Entente on August 18 but is quickly overrun by the armies of the Central Powers. As Austro-Hungarian and German forces invade Romania from the west, Bulgarian units, with Turkish support, recapture southern Dobrudja and cross the Danube.

September 1   Bulgaria and Ottoman Turkey declare war on Romania.

Late September   The Bulgarians suffer their first serious setback of the war as Entente forces operating from bases in northern Greece launch successful attacks across the border into Bulgarian-occupied Serbian Macedonia.

November The Serbian army, reorganized and reequipped in Greece, wins an important victory against the Bulgarians by retaking Bitola.

December–June 1918 As the tide of the fighting shifts against Sofia, the Bulgarian government is subjected to increasing criticism. Because of declines in production and systematic expropriations by Germany, shortages of food and other necessities intensify. The acute lack of supplies dampens the morale of the army and produces war-weariness among the civilian population. Nevertheless, Radoslavov continues in power because of two factors: first, the opposition to his government is split and incapable of forming a united movement; second, Radoslavov is able to appeal to nationalist sentiments by arguing that his regime has in effect realized the borders of the Treaty of San Stefano from 1878 (*see* Bulgaria introduction).

1918

June 20 Overwhelmed by swelling popular discontent and insurmountable domestic problems, Radoslavov resigns his premiership under Ferdinand's urging. The task of forming a new government is given to Alexander Malinov, who attempts to form a broad coalition. Malinov declares his rule will have two objectives: prosecution of the war to final victory and honest and legal administration.

July–August Despite Malinov's pledge to organize efficient and honest government, his regime's control over the nation and its institutions begins to dissolve under the pressure of a famine caused by the war.

September 15 Bulgaria's final collapse is precipitated by the launching of a massive Entente offensive in Macedonia.

September 17 The Bulgarian front in Macedonia collapses. Bulgarian forces retreat in disorder, suffering heavy casualties. The Bulgarian High Command reports that the army is disintegrating and discipline has evaporated.

September 24 Enraged troops attack the Bulgarian General Headquarters at Kiustendil.

September 25 British, French, and Greek forces enter Bulgaria proper. In the meantime, Malinov releases Stamboliiski from prison in the hope that he will participate in a broad coalition to calm the nation and begin peace talks.

September 28 Raiko Daskalov, one of Stamboliiski's Agrarian party lieutenants, declares a republic under Stamboliiski's presidency. From his position in the town of Radomir, Daskalov issues an ultimatum to the government in Sofia. He threatens to march on the capital with rebel army units the following day if power is not handed to him.

September 29 Bulgaria signs an armistice with the Entente command in Thessaloníki.

September 30 Daskolov's attack on Sofia is repulsed by loyal Bulgarian troops, IMRO bands, and some German units while Stamboliiski publicly denies any association with the Radomir republic. Nonetheless, the government issues an order for the arrest of Stamboliiski, who follows Daskalov into hiding.

October 3 Ferdinand abdicates leaving his son, Boris III, to succeed him. His life at risk, and guarded by German troops, Ferdinand leaves for Germany by train.

October 18 Malinov forms a new coalition government including members of the Agrarian, Broad Socialist, and Nationalist parties, as well as the existing coalition partners, the Democrats and Republicans.

November Malinov's government collapses. Todor Todorov, the deputy leader of the Nationalist party, forms a new government with support from the Agrarians, Broad Socialists, Democrats, and Nationalists. A cabinet post is reserved for Stamboliiski who is granted a pardon.

1919

August The electorate's anger against the traditional political parties, which are generally held responsible for Bulgaria's wartime deprivations and humiliating defeat, are reflected in the country's first postwar national election. The vote is overwhelmingly in favor of the radical parties, which poll approximately 60 per cent of the total ballots and secure 72 percent of the seats in the *Subranie*. The Agrarians win 85 parliamentary seats, the Narrow Socialists (renamed Communists in March 1919) 47 seats, and the Broad Socialists 36. The strongest of the traditional parties, the Democrats, gain only 28 seats. With the Agrarians holding a plurality of the parliamentary seats, Stamboliiski emerges as the new premier.

October 6 King Boris calls on Stamboliiski to form a government. However, commanding only 85 seats out of 223 in the *Subranie*, Stamboliiski needs a coalition to govern. After failing to organize a government with the other radical parties, which seek excessive concessions, the new premier forms a coalition with two of the traditional parties.

November 27 Stamboliiski signs the Neuilly Treaty, ending hostilities with the Entente powers. Southern Dobrudja is restored to Romania thereby recognizing the old border established after the Second Balkan War in 1913. In the west Bulgaria loses four small but strategically valuable pieces of territory to the Kingdom of the Serbs, Croats, and Slovenes (Yugoslavia). The treaty also requires Bulgaria to cede Western Thrace to Greece. In addition to these territorial losses, Bulgaria is forced to limit its army to 33,000 men and to pay reparations totalling $450,000,000 over a period of 38 years. Although the Neuilly Treaty seems finally to be the destruction of a greater Bulgaria as envisioned by the 1878 San Stefano Treaty (*see* December–June 1918), the nationalist dream of a large Bulgarian state remains strong. Bulgarians generally, and IMRO emphatically, continue to regard a San Stefano Bulgaria as the country's chief foreign policy goal. Fixated overwhelmingly on Yugoslav Macedonia—the region outside Bulgaria where the ethnic Bulgarian population constitutes a majority—nationalists remain committed to the unification of this region with the mother country.

December The Bulgarian Communist party clashes with the Stamboliiski government. The Communists, who are very active in labor agitation, launch a series of anti-government strikes that culminate in a massive one-week walkout of transport and communications workers. Stamboliiski responds by militarizing the facilities and bringing out the Agrarian Orange Guard, peasant units armed with clubs, which are used to break up Communist-led strikes and demonstrations. The strike is defeated, but the Communists remain locked in a political war with the Agrarians. The Communists' younger leaders, Georgi Dimitrov (a printer who rose in the labor movement in Sofia), Vasil Kalarov (a lawyer educated in Switzerland), and others viciously condemn Stamboliiski in the press and the *Subranie*.

1920

March To put through his reform program Stamboliiski holds a general election. The Agrarians win 110 seats out of the total of 229, and the Communists come in second with 51 seats. Since he is short of a majority, Stamboliiski invalidates 13 seats on the basis of a strict interpretation of

the election laws. He is thus able to form an entirely Agrarian government in May that rests on a small majority in the *Subranie*. With this support, Stamboliiski proceeds to implement his political program. The dozens of reforms that Stamboliiski proposes are intended to modernize the countryside and make Bulgaria a model agricultural state in a projected twenty years of Agrarian rule. He wants to marginalize the importance of the cities and his plan cuts the bureaucracy to a minimum. He ultimately hopes to create a strong peasant-based republic. Moreover, in the political system Stamboliiski plans, Boris will be unable to build the sort of personal regime that his father Ferdinand had.

1923

March Stamboliiski signs the Treaty of Nish. Stamboliiski's foreign policy is founded on the principle of peaceful coexistence with Bulgaria's neighbors. The linchpin of this policy is *rapprochement,* or the establishment of friendly relations, with Yugoslavia. IMRO, acting without deference to government authorities in Bulgarian Macedonia, continues the practice of organizing raids from Bulgaria into Yugoslav Macedonia. Obviously, Stamboliiski understands that he has to restrict IMRO incursions into Yugoslavia before better relations can be established between Belgrade and Sofia. Hence, in the Treaty of Nish Bulgaria and Yugoslavia agree that both sides of their common frontier will be cleared of brush to a depth of approximately 100 yards and that other major efforts will be taken to prevent the crossing of armed bands. For the signing of this pact Stamboliiski receives a death sentence from IMRO, which has already assassinated Stamboliiski's interior and police minister as well as other officials.

April The Stamboliiski government employs repressive methods to help secure a significant majority in a new general election. The Agrarians win 212 parliamentary seats, the Communists 16, and a Rightist bloc 14. With such an enormous majority Stamboliiski lays out plans to change the constitution, end the party system, and, as rumor has it, abolish the monarchy.

May–June A diverse assortment of Rightist forces emerge, united to overthrow Stamboliiski. Led by IMRO and the Military League composed of active and inactive officers of the old political order, the anti-Agrarian coalition plans a coup.

June 9 The coup proceeds according to plan. Army units, IMRO bands, and armed civilians seize Sofia without resistance. Stamboliiski, in his home village near Pazardzhik, tries to organize a local force.

June 14 After being captured by an IMRO band, Stamboliiski is tortured, mutilated (his right hand is hacked off in revenge for signing the Nish agreement), and finally decapitated by his Bulgarian Macedonian tormentors.

Mid–Late June The chief coup plotters organize a new right-wing government with the academic, Alexander Tsankov, as premier. A coalition of parties calling itself the Democratic Alliance provides Tsankov the support necessary in the *Subranie* to govern.

Late June–December A wave of terror follows the Rightist coup as Tsankov's government eliminates Stamboliiki's chief supporters.

September Acting under Soviet instructions, the Bulgarian Communist party attempts to exploit the popular resentment against the Rightist wave of terror. Ill-prepared, the Communist uprising is quickly suppressed, leaving 5,000 casualties.

November Tsankov's coalition of parties wins a majority in a new general election.

1924

January The government outlaws the Communist party. Nevertheless, it continues to function underground. Following banning of the party, Communists launch a campaign of assassinations and other terrorist attacks against political opponents.

1925

April The more than year-long Communist wave of violence climaxes with the bombing of the Cathedral of Sofia. The explosion misses King Boris, its primary target, but kills some 150 persons and wounds 500. Tsankov and his cabinet members escape with minor injuries. The attack is followed by police reprisals which further escalate the violence throughout Bulgaria.

October Following a series of IMRO raids into Greece and other border disturbances, units of the Greek army invade and occupy portions of southern Bulgaria. The League of Nations intervenes and compels the Greeks to withdraw and to pay an indemnity to Bulgaria.

1926

January 4 Unable to achieve domestic peace, Tsankov resigns. The new Cabinet is led by another leader of the coalition, the Bulgarian Macedonian, Andrei Liapchev.

January–June 1931 Premier Liapchev's five years in power are spent trying to realize his objective of internal peace. Toward this goal, Liapchev relaxes repressive measures, enacts a series of amnesties, and allows the Communists to reenter political life under the guise of the Bulgarian Workers' party, which is formed in February 1927. Despite the Communists earlier wave of violence, IMRO remains the greatest source of instability and terrorism in Bulgaria. Moreover, IMRO in effect functions as a state within a state and its oppressive control over Bulgarian Macedonia supersedes the authority of the government. Liapchev is unable to deal with IMRO, and the uncontrolled activities of the organization further isolate Bulgaria in the international community and engender hostility among Bulgaria's Balkan neighbors. In addition to these political problems, Liapchev's government is faced with serious economic challenges as the effects of the Great Depression begin to reach Bulgaria.

1930

May 14 Bulgaria and Czechoslovakia sign a treaty of friendship and nonaggression.

1931

June 21 Growing discontent with the Liapchev government culminates in an election victory for the opposition parties. The winner is the so-called Peoples, or Popular Bloc, composed of the Democratic party, the Centrist Agrarians, the Liberals, and the Radicals.

June 29 A new government is formed by the Democratic leader, Alexander Malinov.

June 29–May 19 1934 The Democratic-led coalition governments do not bring about significant changes. The parties and leadership within the coalition are preoccupied with fighting over political spoils. Meanwhile IMRO still rules unchallenged in Bulgarian Macedonia and engages in murders and terrorist attacks with impunity.

Bombing of the Cathedral of Sofia, April 1925.

October 12 Another Democratic premier, Nikola Mushanov, succeeds Malinov.

1934

February 4 Sofia is further isolated diplomatically. To protect themselves against Bulgarian revisionism, Greece, Romania, Turkey, and Yugoslavia form the Balkan Entente, a mutual defense bloc. Bulgaria's weak diplomatic position convinces many that a radical change in foreign

policy is necessary. But this remains out of the question so long as IMRO is allowed to act freely. The pact is formally signed four days later.

May 19 The combination of diplomatic, economic, and political problems that beset the nation lead to another coup. The two chief architects of the coup are Colonel Kimon Georgiev and Colonel Damian Velchev. Velchev, one of the organizers of the 1923 coup which overthrew Stamboliiski, leads the Military League, which includes a large proportion of the army officers. Velchev is also connected with Zveno (Link), a small political circle of reformers whose leader, Georgiev, was Velcev's co-conspirator in the 1923 coup. Velchev and Georgiev are alienated by the terrorism, inefficiency, and instability that marks Bulgarian political life. They are convinced that the existing political parties are corrupt and incapable of effective governing and that the army's high command is unwilling to halt the activities of IMRO terrorists. Both the Military League and Zveno wish to abolish political parties and establish a government capable of suppressing IMRO and coping with the country's economic and moral crises. Taking advantage of a cabinet emergency, the Military League carries out a bloodless coup and installs a government under Georgiev; Velchev does not take an official post.

May–January 1935   Once in power the coup leaders implement the Zveno program. The new leaders attempt to make radical changes in the political institutions that they believe to be the cause of the nation's chief problems. The "Nineteenth of May Government," as it is officially called, proclaims a program of social renewal to be achieved by authoritarian rule. The constitution is abolished, the *Subranie* is dissolved, censorship is imposed on the press, and all political parties and activities are banned. Georgiev and Velchev do not attempt to create a government party or an official coalition, instead the regime governs by decree. The government reduces peasant debts, reorganizes the credit system, and establishes a new state bank. It also attempts to reorganize education and improve rural conditions. The new regime reveals that previous governments, despite their routine protestations, had lacked the will rather than the means to cope with IMRO. In fact, the new government destroys the entire IMRO apparatus in Bulgaria within a few days. With IMRO out of the way, Sofia is finally free to pursue an independent foreign policy. Accordingly, Bulgaria moves diplomatically closer to the Western democracies, opens relations with the Soviet Union, and seeks reconciliation with Yugoslavia and the other countries of the Balkans.

1935

January   Frustrated by his inability to exert any influence over the "Nineteenth of May Government," and fearing that Velchev and Georgiev are planning to abolish the monarchy, King Boris takes steps to undermine the new regime. Boris wins the support of royalist officers in the Military League on the issue of the alleged republican plot. Under pressure from royalist officers Velchev withdraws from politics and Georgiev resigns the premiership. Boris

chooses Minister of War General Pencho Zlatev as the new premier. Zlatev declares in his policy statement that he is an enemy of republicanism, that the monarchy is the only form of government suited to the Bulgarian people, and that the Bulgarian monarchy is a state above classes and parties. Zlatev, in effect, obediently helps Boris establish a royal dictatorship. From this point until his death in August 1943, Boris presides over a personal government administered through receptive officers and civilian nonentities without a political base of their own.

April   To avoid the appearance of a military regime, Boris replaces Zlatev with a civilian, Andrei Toshev.

April 21   Boris issues a manifesto announcing the reestablishment of his authority. He declares that political parties will remain prohibited, but there will be some form of representative government in the future. In short, Boris makes it understood that he will allow the people a certain degree of participation in government but with no actual authority.

November 23   Boris' closest friend, career diplomat Georgi Kioseivanov, replaces Toshev as premier.

1937

March   To avoid the appearance of personal rule, Boris allows a general election to take place. The elections, however, are held entirely on Boris' terms: no one identified with the banned political parties is allowed to run; the candidates, screened by the courts and under tight censorship, run solely as individuals without ideological affiliation; and the 274 seats of the Subranie are reduced to the more manageable size of 160. The election results are in keeping with Boris' expectations—Kioseivanov continues in office with a majority of approximately 100 seats, made up of nationalists and admirers of fascist Italy and Nazi Germany.

June 16   Crown Prince Symeon is born.

October 21   Boris issues an electoral law that forbids candidates to run as members of political parties.

1938

July 31   An agreement is concluded in Thessaloníki between Bulgaria and the Balkan Entente recognizing the right of Bulgaria to rearm. Furthermore, the states agree to abstain from the use of force against one another. By this accord, Greece, Romania, Turkey, and Yugoslavia hope to draw Bulgaria closer to the Balkan Entente and promote peace and stability in the region. However, the Thessaloníki Agreement has the opposite effect. By erasing the disarmament clauses of the Neuilly Treaty (*see* November 27, 1919), the Thessaloníki Treaty of Friendship and Nonaggression with Bulgaria stimulates a new outburst of revisionist sentiment in Sofia. This growing revisionism provides the Nazi Germans with their most effective enticement for eventually winning over the Bulgarian regime to Axis policy.

1939

July   With the Second World War approaching, Kioseivanov visits Berlin. Despite the absence of any formal commitments, Kioseivanov assures Hitler that Bulgaria is Germany's natural ally.

September 16   Fifteen days after the outbreak of the Second World War Boris announces Bulgaria's official neutrality in the conflict.

October 23   Boris directs Kioseivanov to reorganize the cabinet, dissolve the *Subranie,* and call a new election for the end of the year. Boris's objective is to rid himself of undesirable personalities in the *Subranie* and strengthen the compliant majority.

1940

February 15   Having lost confidence in Kioseivanov, Boris replaces him with a new premier—the president of the Bulgarian Academy of Sciences, and ardent Germanophile, Bogdan Filov.

February 24   Despite the increased pro-German orientation of the cabinet under Filov, Boris states in his speech at the opening of the new, and even more submissive, *Subranie* that there will be no change in Bulgaria's policy of neutrality. Unofficially, however, there is little sympathy for the Allies but great admiration for Germany.

June 15   Filov officially reaffirms Bulgaria's official policy of neutrality. Nevertheless, Bulgaria continues to strengthen its ties with Germany. Economically, Bulgaria has become a German satellite. Cultural ties are vastly expanded by German-sponsored academic exchange programs. The Gestapo, the German secret police, is allowed to operate freely in Bulgaria. Private contact with Western diplomatic missions is discouraged, and anti-Semitic activities increase.

September 7   Romania, under German and Soviet pressure since mid-August, cedes southern Dobrudja to Bulgaria (*see* November 27, 1919).

September 20   Boris publicly thanks Hitler and Mussolini for their support of Bulgarian claims in the Dobrudja. Streets are renamed in Bulgaria in honor of the Axis leaders.

November 17   Hitler invites Boris to join his alliance system with Italy and Japan, the Tripartite Pact. Boris, however, is reluctant to commit Bulgaria openly to the Axis because of Greece's recent successes against the Italian army in Albania.

November 18   Boris declines to commit Bulgarian troops to an invasion of Greece, but consents to Hitler's request to use Bulgaria as a base against Greece in the event of an invasion.

1941

January   The *Subranie* passes and Boris promulgates the Law on the Protection of the Nation that establishes repressive state measures against Bulgaria's Jews.

January 12   Prime Minister Bogdan Filov states Bulgaria will remain neutral in the European war and remain friendly towards both Nazi Germany and the Soviet Union.

February 12   German troops in civilian clothes begin entering Bulgaria.

February 17   Bulgaria and Turkey sign a treaty of friendship and nonaggression.

February 22   Student demonstrations against the presence of German troops in Bulgaria take place.

February 24   Bulgaria orders the start of national blackouts against possible air attacks.

March 1   Filov signs the Tripartite Pact in Vienna thus officially bringing Bulgaria into the Axis camp. As a reward Bulgaria is to receive territory in Greek Macedonia and Thrace. German forces, clothed as civilians, begin crossing the Danube to take up positions in southern Bulgaria.

March 2   German radio announces that German troops have entered Bulgaria to prevent the war in the Balkans from spreading from Greece.

The Bulgarian ambassador in London resigns in protest over his country signing the Tripartite Pact.

March 3   Citing German forces in the country, Turkey revokes its friendship and nonaggression treaty with Bulgaria from February 17.

The Soviet government denounces the presence of German troops in Bulgaria.

The American government freezes $100,000 in Bulgarian assets in the United States to prevent possible takeover by the Germans.

March 5   Great Britain severs relations with Bulgaria after a series of blatant Bulgarian provocations against British diplomatic personnel and property in Sofia.

April 6   The German army attacks Greece and Yugoslavia. Although Bulgaria declines to participate directly in the invasion, its role as a German staging area makes it a target for British air attacks.

April 18   As the German army advances through Greece and Yugoslavia, Boris meets with Hitler in Vienna to determine the boundaries of the Bulgarian occupation zones in both countries. The Bulgarians are given eastern Greek Macedonia, all but the most eastern prefecture of Greek Thrace, most of Yugoslav Macedonia, and a portion of eastern Serbia. The attainment of a greater Bulgaria produces universal euphoria in the country.

May 14   Bulgaria formally annexes the occupied portions of Greece and Yugoslavia. Germany does not raise any objections but does not recognize the annexations.

June 24   Two days after the German invasion of the Soviet Union the underground Bulgarian Communist party forms a Central Military Commission and calls for an armed struggle against the Germans and Boris's regime. However, the Communist leadership is decimated by police arrests and there is considerable popular support for Boris's nationalist triumphs. Consequently the growth of an effective partisan movement is hampered.

September   The Bulgarian occupation authorities in Greek Macedonia and Thrace proceed to implement a policy of terror against the local population. Whereas the Bulgarian policy in Yugoslav Macedonia is to win the loyalty of the predominantly ethnic Bulgarian population, the policy in Greek Macedonia and Thrace is to forcibly Bulgarize, and expel or exterminate the overwhelmingly Greek population. Eventually approximately 50,000 Greeks are killed and 250,000 are deported. Bulgarian colonists are encouraged to settle on land expropriated from Greeks, in the hope that a Bulgarian majority can be created in the region to insure permanent Bulgarian control.

September 20   The government proclaims martial law throughout the country thereby giving military authorities control over civilians.

October 14   Eleven alleged Communists are condemned to death for sabotage plots, and they are executed several days later.

November 25   Bulgaria signs the Anti-Comintern Pact aimed at international communism. This agreement was formulated in the mid-1930s among Germany, Japan, and Italy and was meant to strengthen their alliance. Later, states in the Nazi camp, such as Bulgaria, adhered to it.

December 13   Satisfying its obligations under the Tripartite Pact, Bulgaria declares war on the United States and Great Britain. The two countries reciprocate on June 5, 1942, and December 13, 1941, respectively.

December 25   Eleven are sentenced to death (six in absentia including Georgi Dimitrov, leader of the Comintern—the international Communist movement controlled by the Soviets) with 22 others given long prison sentences after having been convicted of plotting to overthrow the government.

1942

January   The Germans urge Bulgaria to join the war against the Soviet Union. Realizing this would be an unpopular move, Boris refuses to commit the Bulgarian army to the Eastern Front. He insists that the Bulgarian armed forces are not yet prepared for such a mission and that they are already serving a useful purpose as both an occupation force and a strategic reserve force in the Balkans.

March 26   Delegates in the *Subranie* cause a commotion after it is announced that King Boris orders its suspension starting on March 28 until late October.

April 11   Premier Filov reshuffles his government placing more pro-Germans in office.

June   The underground political opposition is formed into a coalition called the Fatherland Front. The idea of such a coalition is urged by the exiled Georgi Dimitrov in the Soviet press and radio, and becomes the program of a Soviet secret radio station broadcasting in Bulgarian. The Fatherland Front is led by the Communists, but, in order to appear as a democratic movement, it also includes some republicans and Leftist Agrarians. The Fatherland Front fails to win any popular following.

June 1   General Vladimir Zaimov, a former minister of the interior, is executed on charges of spying for the USSR.

August 13   An armed clash takes place between Bulgarian troops on one hand and Italian and Albanian forces on the other over contested occupation positions in western Yugoslav Macedonia.

September 14 Allied bombers based in Egypt carry out a mission over Sofia.

September 15 The Soviet ambassador protests a police raid on the Soviet consulate in Varna.

October A series of armed clashes erupt between Bulgarian and Italian occupation forces in Yugoslav Macedonia.

1943

February 13 The former minister of war and *Subranie* member General Hristo Lukov, an extreme Germanophile and an advocate of Bulgarian participation in the war against the Soviet Union, is killed in Sofia by unknown assassins. This is the latest in the growing waves of opposition to the war which, over the past several months, have included riots. Unrest continues to increase over the next months.

March The Bulgarian occupation authorities in Greece and Yugoslavia implement the Nazi's plan for a final solution of the "Jewish question." The approximately 11,400 Greek and Yugoslav Jews under Bulgarian occupation are deported for extermination. After some hesitation, Boris sanctions an alternative policy for Jews in Bulgaria proper. Following the state confiscation of their properties, Bulgaria's approximately 48,000 Jews are expelled to the countryside in heavy labor teams and makeshift camps.

March 24 The Greek Office of Information in Washington, D.C. accuses the Bulgarian occupation authorities of having killed approximately 20,000 Greeks.

April 9 King Boris takes personal command over foreign affairs.

April 15 The pro-German editor of the newspaper *Slovo* (The Word) and the chairman of the Foreign Affairs Committee of the *Subranie,* Sotir Yanev, are killed by unknown assailants.

May 1 Massive anti-German demonstrations take place in Sofia where it is reported that the authorities arrest approximately 700.

May 3 Terrorists strike again in the capital, this time killing Colonel Pantev, the former director of the state police and chairman of the Sofia Military Tribunal. The government proclaims martial law when rioting takes place after his funeral two days later.

May 5 Suspecting that the sudden rash of attacks on prominent state officials is the work of Communists, the government blockades the entire city of Sofia and a house-to-house search is conducted. Fifty known Communists are discovered in hiding.

June–August Encouraged by the Soviet victory at Stalingrad in January 1943, the demoralized Bulgarian Communists are revived and lead renewed partisan activities. The most successful partisan band operates in the Sredna Mountains east of Sofia and north of the Maritsa Valley. Other bands emerge in the Balkan Mountain range and in the southwestern mountains. Although the partisans, all under command of the Communist-led Fatherland Front, increase they never expand to more than 10,000 and they are an almost insignificant force throughout the war.

August 14–15 Boris, who has met with Hitler more times than any other European leader, confers for the last time with the German dictator at his headquarters in East Prussia. They meet amid rumors that the Allies are preparing to invade the Balkans and that, with Italy about to surrender, Germany's satellites are secretly negotiating their way out of the war. Although no record is kept, some accounts suggest the meeting is stormy because Hitler suspects Boris of collaboration with the Allies.

August 28 King Boris III dies in Sofia. The death certificate cites natural causes from complications of a heart attack, but immediately conspiracy theories abound that he is the victim of foul play, having been poisoned by the Germans or others. Boris is succeeded by his six-year-old son who becomes King Symeon II. Due to the new ruler's age, a government committee governs in his name until a regency council is appointed.

August 29 Mourning demonstrations in Sofia turn anti-war and anti-German.

September 14 The Council of Regents is appointed consisting of Boris's brother, Prince Kiril, Premier Filov, and Minister of War General Nikola Mikhov. A new cabinet under Minister of Finance Dobri Bozhilov consists of conservative loyalists who harbor no thoughts of ending Bulgaria's alliance with Germany.

November 14–March 30, 1944 In order to convince the Bulgarians that the war is real and not merely symbolic, the Allies conduct a bombing campaign against Sofia. The city suffers heavy losses of life and enormous physical damage, while the government and communications are repeatedly paralyzed. As a result of the Allied air raids, the Bulgarian people lose nearly all their faith in German power, and the Bulgarian leaders are discredited for having entered into the alliance with the Axis.

December–February 1944 Despite contacts and peace feelers between United States agents in Istanbul and Bulgaria's ambassador to Turkey, the Bulgarian government refuses to sanction discussions with the Allies. The government is unwilling to change its policy because it still clings to the hope of retaining the occupied Greek and Yugoslav territories and is fearful of German reprisals.

1944

January 23 A Soviet-controlled All-Slavic Committee in Moscow, consisting of Soviet Slavs and pro-Soviet Poles and Czechoslovaks, warns the Bulgars that the war is coming closer to Bulgaria and urges them to leave the Axis alliance and oust the German forces from the country.

March 29 *Izvestia,* the newspaper of the Soviet government, warns Bulgaria to break its ties to Nazi Germany or share Germany's fate.

May 12 A joint Allied communiqué urges Bulgaria and other German allies to leave the war as Germany's partners, stop aiding the Nazis, and contribute to the Allied cause.

May 21 Frustrated by the government's inability to cope with the major problems facing the country—Allied bombing raids, inflation, popular disaffection, political disunity, the threat of invasion—the Council of Regents dismisses the Bozhilov cabinet.

June 1 The Council of Regents appoints Ivan Bagrianov, a Rightist Agrarian and a longtime friend of the late King Boris, to the premiership. Bagrianov hopes to remain on good terms with the Germans while working behind the scenes for a favorable armistice with the Allies. He plans to arrange the armistice with the Allies but to refrain from implementing it until the Germans withdraw from the Balkans. Bulgaria, according to Bagrianov's plans, will then change sides in the war and mobilize along its frontiers to discourage either a German or Soviet invasion.

June 20 The Bulgarian consul in Istanbul is authorized to begin armistice discussions with Americans in Turkey.

Late June–Mid-August After lengthy secret deliberations the Allies and the Bulgarians fail to reach an armistice agreement. The main difficulty remains the territorial question: the Bulgarians insist they be allowed to continue their occupation of Greek lands; the Allies demand that the pre-war Greek borders be restored.

August 17 Bagrianov officially denounces the policies of his predecessors in a speech before the *Subranie*. He announces that henceforth Bulgaria will follow a policy of strict neutrality. Bagrianov thus attempts to take Bulgaria out of the war not by surrendering and withdrawing from its occupied territories, but by simply declaring the country

neutral and continuing its occupation of Greek and Yugoslav lands. The *Subranie* greets the new policy with the same enthusiasm it had given the former pro-Axis policy.

August 23–August 30 Bagrianov's government conducts another round of fruitless negotiations with the Allies in Ankara, Turkey and Cairo, Egypt.

August 25 Great Britain announces that Bulgaria will surrender unconditionally pending the outcome of negotiations.

August 26 The Soviets report that Bulgaria will disarm German forces on its territory, while Bulgarian radio states that the Bulgarian government has requested Allied peace terms which are sent two days later.

August 30 The Soviet Union announces that it refuses to accept Bulgaria's declaration of neutrality. The advancing Soviet forces now in Romania stream south from Bucharest towards the Danube, the Bulgarian frontier.

September 1 As Bulgaria's situation continues to deteriorate Bagrianov and his government resign.

Peace negotiations in Cairo between Bulgaria and the Allies break off.

September 2 The Council of Regents appoints Konstantin Muraviev, the late Stamboliiski's nephew and former Agrarian government official, to the post of premier.

September 3 After failing to form a broad representative government that would include, among others, members of the Fatherland Front, Muraviev establishes a more narrowly based cabinet consisting of only a few political parties. The new government issues an executive order halting the execution of political prisoners.

September 4 Muraviev announces a 12-point political reform program that includes the following provisions: a constitutional administration is promised; all fascist institutions are to be abolished; a complete amnesty is offered to those who had opposed the royal dictatorship; the *Subranie* will be dissolved; and negotiations for an armistice with the Allies will be given priority. Muraviev reaffirms Bagrianov's strategy by insisting on a policy of neutrality toward all belligerents.

September 4–7 A series of violent Communist strikes and demonstrations erupt in Sofia, Pernik, Pleven, Plovdiv, Silistra, and Varna. The demonstrators denounce Muraviev as a Nazi agent. Adding to the heightened political tension, a number of military uprisings are reported among the occupation troops in Greece.

September 5 The Soviet Union declares war on Bulgaria. The Soviets announce that they are taking this action because of Sofia's failure to declare war on Germany. The Soviets are also motivated by the desire to enable the Red

Army to enter Bulgaria and assist in the creation of a Communist regime.

Premier Muraviev asks the Soviets for a truce and breaks diplomatic relations with Nazi Germany.

September 6   Soviet radio urges the Bulgarian population to overthrow the government.

September 7   The Bulgarian government claims that German forces in the country have been disarmed.

September 8   Soviet forces cross the border into Bulgaria. The Bulgarian forces do not offer any resistance to the Red Army. The military garrison at Burgas rebels against the Bulgarian government and arrests its own officers. The authority of the Muraviev government collapses. Bulgaria declares war on Nazi Germany, while the pro-German regent and former prime minister Bogdan Filov is forced to resign from the Regency Council.

September 9   At two o'clock in the morning, a force of rebellious soldiers, cadets from the Sofia Military Academy, and partisan detachments occupy strategic positions in the capital before the Red Army reaches Sofia. The coup is led by the Communist party organization in Sofia and the 1934 coup organizers Kimon Georgiev and Damian Velchev. At six o'clock in the morning, Georgiev announces on the radio that the Muraviev government has been overthrown and that he is now the prime minister of a new government formed by the Fatherland Front. Georgiev immediately dismisses regents Prince Kiril and General Mihov and replaces them with Todor Pavlov, the leader of the Communist party, and the pro-Soviet Professor Venelin Ganev. The real power of the new government, however, is in the hands of the Communists.

As Soviet troops continue to occupy sections of Bulgaria, the USSR and Bulgaria announce an armistice.

September 11   Bulgaria begins releasing all Allied prisoners of war.

Mid-September–November 1945   The Communists increase their grip on the state. With their control of the strategic ministries of the interior and justice in the Georgiev government, the Communists launch a wave of terror to destroy their opponents. For more than a year mass arrests and executions take place. These arrests and executions reflect the Communist strategy to attain complete political domination over the country.

September 21   The Bulgarian Communist authorities arrest Prince Kiril and former prime ministers Bogdan Filov and Dobri Bozhilov.

The Georgiev government proclaims women's equality, religious freedom and tolerance, civil marriage, and the separation of church and state.

October 3   The government establishes "people's courts" for the trying of war criminals. If convicted, punishment would result in the death sentence or heavy penalties without any form of appeal. These courts, established three days later, are in place by the end of the year and are meant to purge all classes of enemies of the Fatherland Front.

October 14   Bulgarian troops help liberate the Yugoslav city of Nish from the Germans.

October 28   As the Bulgarian army continues fighting alongside the Soviet army in Yugoslavia and Hungary against Sofia's former ally, Nazi Germany, Bulgaria signs an armistice with the Allies. The armistice includes the following terms: to surrender all occupied regions of Greece and Yugoslavia taken in 1941; to supply relief aid to the two above former occupied areas; to supply the Allies with war materiel; and to restore or pay for confiscated property of Allied nationals. An Allied Control Commission consisting of Americans, Soviets, and British will oversee the terms.

December 24   Trials begin in Sofia against *Subranie* deputies, government ministers, military officers, and royal advisers.

1945

January 15   The government and Stefan, the Bulgarian Orthodox metropolitan (archbishop) of Sofia, end the schism with the parent church and the patriarch of Constantinople (Istanbul). This schism, in effect since 1870 when the Bulgarians declared their church independent of Constantinople, is healed with the help of the Russian patriarch. Stefan is then elected exarch, or head, of the Bulgarian Orthodox Church.

January 20   The government establishes forced labor camps to be filled with those sentenced by the people's courts.

February 1   Prince Kiril, former regent General Mihov, former premiers Filov, Bozhilov, and Bagrianov, 22 former cabinet ministers, and 11 royal advisers are sentenced to death on charges of treason and war crimes. Furthermore, each receives a heavy fine and has his property confiscated. The executions are carried out on January 21. Former prime minister Muraviev receives life imprisonment. During the next several months a number of others are also convicted of war crimes and treason across Bulgaria. According to official statistics, when the trials end in March, approximately 11,000 persons are found guilty— more than 2,100 are executed with others receiving prison sentences ranging from one year to life.

March 15 Georgi Dimitrov returns to Bulgaria from the USSR where he has been in exile since the mid-1930s, and becomes a member of the Fatherland Front.

April 15 The government enacts a law providing for the collectivization of agriculture, where individual peasant farms are forcibly consolidated into large, state owned and controlled enterprises.

April 19 A government decree grants the police greater powers.

May The Communists score a major victory by splintering their primary opposition, the Agrarian party, into two factions.

July After splitting the Social Democrats (the other chief opposition party) in the spring, the Communist-led faction takes over the party organization.

July 31 Nikola Petkov—deputy premier, leader of the Agrarian party, and son of Premier Nikola Petkov who was assassinated on February 11, 1907—and several other non-Communist members of the government resign in protest over Communist policies, and join the opposition.

August 18 The United States charges that the Georgiev government does not represent the majority of the Bulgarian people nor is it taking measures to ensure fair and free elections. The British support the American charges.

August 25 As a result of American and British protests, general elections scheduled for August 28 are postponed until November 18.

September 8 Under American and British pressure, the government legalizes four opposition parties and takes some superficial steps to give the appearance of free elections scheduled for November 18.

October 11 The opposition announces it will boycott the elections.

October 26 Members of the Fatherland Front and opposition groups battle each other in Sofia.

November 7 Georgi Dimitrov takes command of the Communist election campaign.

November 9 Martial law officially ends, and the government begins demobilization of its military forces.

November 18 With the opposition abstaining from the general election in protest, the Communists win a major electoral victory for seats in the *Subranie* which had been

dissolved in 1944. The results produce an 86 percent majority for the government. The second-ranking Bulgarian Communist, Vasil Kalorov, becomes president of the *Subranie*. Dimitrov, although he now dominates the political life of Bulgaria, does not assume the premiership for another year.

December 27 The foreign ministers of Great Britain, the United States, and the USSR meet in Moscow and request that two opposition representatives be included in the Bulgarian government after which the United States and Great Britain agree to extend diplomatic recognition. Bulgaria accepts the proposition the next day.

1946

January 9 Opposition leaders Nikola Petkov and Kosta Lulchev refuse to join the government as stipulated in the December 27, 1945 plan. They demand more posts in the government and new elections to parliament.

February 22 The United States demands that the Bulgarian government include two representatives from the opposition. The British back the U.S. in early March.

March 21 The Georgiev government resigns, but Georgiev remains to form another government that he states will not include any members from the opposition.

March 28 The Soviets tell the Bulgarian government that Petkov's and Lulchev's demands from January 9 go against the December 27, 1945 Moscow plan, therefore the opposition can be ignored.

March 31 A new government consisting of only Fatherland Front ministers takes office under the leadership of Georgiev.

April 2 Great Britain and the United States announce they will not recognize the Bulgarian government.

April 22 Greece asks the Allies for over 4,000 square miles of the Rhodope Mountains in southern Bulgaria, claiming strategic reasons. The request will be rejected.

June 7 Hristiu Pastukhov, the leader of the Socialist party, is tried on false charges and sentenced to five years in prison where he dies in 1950. Through 1946 the government will try members of the opposition and distrusted military officers and government officials on trumped-up charges.

June 9 The law for agrarian reform passes which limits the amount of land that can be owned by farmers, increases the number of farm cooperatives, establishes a State Land Fund out of public and expropriated lands, and provides for the resettlement of people onto redistributed land from the State Land Fund.

July 2 To weaken the independence of the army and to bring it under Communist dominance, the government passes a law that gives it full control over the army thereby lessening the power of the minister of war and the officer corps.

July 12 Georgi M. Dimitrov, former leader of the Agrarian party and no relation to the Communist Georgi Dimitrov, receives a life sentence in absentia.

August 5 Colonel A. Krustev, leader of the military opposition group "Tsar Krum," is convicted of treason and executed. The military is purged of untrustworthy elements during the rest of 1946 and 1947 after which the military becomes sovietized.

August 17 In another purge trial, 25 members of the oppositional Internal Macedonian Revolutionary Organization are convicted of treason and executed.

August 24 The Compulsory Labor Service decree goes into effect. This law states that all young people of draft age who do not go into the military will serve three years in construction, production, and other activities without pay. In reality it is a means to get free labor and to deal with unloyal elements in society.

September 8 In a referendum that allows no expressive opinion, over 92 percent vote to abolish the monarchy and establish a republic. Nine-year-old King Symeon II and his family leave for exile in Egypt the next day.

September 15 Bulgaria officially becomes a people's republic.

October 25 Communist leader Georgi Dimitrov renounces his Soviet citizenship so he can serve officially in the government after the elections.

October 27 *Subranie* elections result in a victory for the Fatherland Front which takes 366 seats out of 465 despite the fact that the opposition received approximately 30 percent of the vote. Great Britain and the United States later charge election intimidation and fraud.

November 21 Georgi Dimitrov forces the Georgiev government to resign.

November 22 Communist leader Georgi Dimitrov becomes premier and forms a new government controlled by the Communists and their allies.

November 28 Bulgaria denies Greek allegations that it is aiding Communist guerrillas in Greece.

December In a move against foreign ministry elements loyal to the old regime, the government orders all Bulgarian diplomats to return home by March 15, 1947, or they will lose their citizenship.

1947

February 10 Bulgaria signs a peace treaty with the Allied powers that ends Bulgaria's involvement in World War II. Under its provisions Bulgaria agrees to limit its army to 55,000 soldiers, navy to 3,500 sailors and just over 72,000 tons for ships, and air force to 5,200 men; pay reparations at $50 million to Greece and $25 million to Yugoslavia; partial to full demilitarization along the Greek frontier. Bulgaria loses no territory and keeps Southern Dobrudja.

February 12 Great Britain extends recognition to the Bulgarian government.

Twenty-three high ranking military officers receive sentences of up to 15 years in prison for allegedly plotting to overthrow the government. More military officers are arrested throughout the year. Most plead guilty.

April 1 The government enacts a Two-Year Plan in an attempt to fix the war damage, restoring industry to its prewar level so further industrialization is possible in the future.

April 19 In order to lower prices on goods, the government orders an across-the-board price cut of 10 to 30 percent.

June 5 The authorities arrest the leader of the opposition, Nikola D. Petkov, on charges of plotting a coup. Both the United States and Great Britain protest this action by the Bulgarian government. He is indicted on the charges in July.

June 10 Prime Minister Dimitrov accuses foreign powers of aiding Petkov in his plot, and declares that Bulgaria will never become a base for attack on the USSR.

June 12 The *Subranie* expels 23 members from the Agrarian party claiming they are Petkov's stooges.

June 14 United States president Harry S Truman signs the ratification of the Bulgarian peace treaty, but characterizes the Bulgarian government as undemocratic and tyrannical. He signs the actual treaty in September.

August 2 Bulgaria and Yugoslavia conclude an agreement which calls for a customs union of the two countries and common policy in foreign affairs.

August 16 Nikola D. Petkov is sentenced to death after a brief trial during which he denies his guilt and insists that he was framed. Both the United States and Great Britain condemn the conviction.

August 25 The parliament unanimously approves the June 14 peace treaty although speakers condemn it as unfairly harsh.

The government announces that the Agrarian party will be dissolved and its representatives in the national legislature dismissed since the party has become a "hotbed" of fascism.

September 23 The government executes Petkov by hanging.

September 30 The United States grants Bulgaria full diplomatic recognition with a warning about its past actions.

October 5 Bulgaria becomes a founding member of the Communist Information Bureau (Cominform), a Soviet-dominated organization that coordinates the international Communist movement and is a successor to the Comintern.

October 25 The Fatherland Front announces that it will reorganize as one party.

December 4 With the adoption of an almost exact model of the 1936 Soviet constitution, sometimes called the "Dimitrov constitution," Bulgaria officially becomes the People's Republic of Bulgaria.

December 11 As a result of the new constitution, Prime Minister Dimitrov forms a new government dominated by Communists.

December 15 The USSR announces the withdrawal of its occupation forces from Bulgaria.

December 24 The government nationalizes (takes ownership) of mines and industry. Two days later it nationalizes banking.

Late December The Fatherland Front forms a committee to aid the Communist guerrillas fighting in the Greek Civil War.

1948

January 12 Dimitrov reminds several *Subranie* deputies, including the leader of the opposition Socialists, Kosta Lulchev, about the fate of Petkov after they refuse to support his budget (*see* September 23, 1947). In November nine opposition deputies receive prison terms of 10–15 years on charges of aiding the West.

January 16 In light of the Greek Civil War, Dimitrov characterizes Greece as a threat to peace and stability in the Balkans after signing a treaty of friendship with Romania.

January 17 Dimitrov predicts a federation of the USSR and its East European allies. The idea is quickly denied by the Soviets, who have no plans to incorporate any more territory into the USSR and fear that the West might overreact to Dimitrov's idea.

February 4 At the second congress of the Fatherland Front, it becomes a uniform political organization that guarantees control by the Communists.

February 9 Bulgaria claims to have shot down two Turkish air force planes over its territory.

February 18 The parliament passes legislation for the nationalization of all land, houses, apartments, and buildings not belonging to workers, as well as extensive inventory owned by uncollectivized farmers.

March 5 The ambassador to Belgium quits after he denounces the Bulgarian Communist regime. The ambassador to Great Britain follows suit two days later. On March 8, the Bulgarian government deprives both of their citizenship.

March 18 Bulgaria and the USSR sign a 20-year friendship and mutual aid treaty. Similar pacts with Poland and Czechoslovakia are signed in the coming months.

March 25 The Act on the People's Militia goes into effect that divides the police into three groups under the control of the Ministry of the Interior, militarizes it, gives it control of all prisons, and allows it to establish forced labor camps.

April 16 After a trial of several weeks, peasant leader Dimiter Gichev receives a sentence of life in prison after being convicted on charges of terrorism and sabotage.

May 8 The Bulgarian Church Diocese of the Americas and Australia announces it will not accept the decision of the mother church in Sofia to dismiss its leader, Bishop Andrey, who is unwilling to follow orders from the Communist-dominated church in Bulgaria.

May 21 Bulgaria protests in the United Nations against what it claims are unceasing border incidents by Greeks.

June 30 Anti-Communist hijackers kill a member of the crew and force a plane with 20 aboard to Istanbul, Turkey where they seek asylum.

August 11 The Socialists in the Fatherland Front merge with the Communists thereby ending any political independence the group enjoyed prior to the time.

September 5 The Bulgarian government announces that, in July, it had demanded the recall of an American diplomat for spying.

Prime Minister Georgi Dimitrov addresses a crowd of millions in Sofia on the occasion of the signing of a 20-year friendship and mutual aid treaty between Bulgaria and the USSR.

September 6 Feeling that Stefan I is becoming too independent, the government forces the Exarchate of the Bulgarian Orthodox Church and Bishop of Sofia to resign. He is banished to a monastery.

September 10 Ferdinand, the former king of Bulgaria, dies in German exile at the age of 87.

November In a further move against private ownership of farmland, the amount of land in private plots on collective farms is reduced to between two and five decares (1 decare equals ten acres) and the amount of livestock is limited to one cow, two pigs, two goats, and five sheep. There are no limitations on poultry, rabbits, or beehives. By the end of 1948, however, the amount of land in the collective farms is only a little over 6 percent.

November 15 Kosta Lulchev, the leader of the opposition Socialists, receives a life prison sentence after being arrested in July.

November 26 Bulgaria recognizes the independent state of Israel. Since 1947 the government has "encouraged" Jews to leave Bulgaria for Israel in an attempt to limit ethnic diversity. By 1954 almost 40,000—or about 90

percent—of Bulgarian Jews have left the country. Other nationalities "encouraged" to leave are the Gypsies, Armenians, and Turks.

November 27 In a 47 to 6 vote, the United Nations General Assembly charges Bulgaria, Albania, and Yugoslavia with aiding Greek revolutionaries, and demands that they stop.

December 19–26 The 5th Congress of the Bulgarian Communist party takes place where Dimitrov asserts that the "dictatorship of the proletariat" has been established in the country.

December 29 The first Five-Year Plan (1949–53) calls for increases and development in industrial production by over 100 percent and agriculture output by 57 percent.

1949

January 25 Bulgaria becomes a founding member of the Council for Mutual Economic Assistance (CMEA, COMECON). This Soviet-dominated organization of Eastern Bloc nations coordinates their economic cooperation with the USSR, and is in response to the U.S.-sponsored Marshall Plan in Western Europe that aims to rebuild the war-torn countries with American aid.

February 10   The government arrests 15 Bulgarian Protestant ministers on spying and other charges. The 15 Baptist, Congregationalist, Methodist, and Pentecostal ministers are all leaders in a state-run association. As a result, two days later the government announces that it is planning a new, ''trustworthy'' blanket organization for the country's 8,000 Protestants.

February 17   The *Subranie* passes a law to close foreign religious missions and congregations and transfer their assets to the state.

February 19   The People's Union Zveno, a political party in the opposition, dissolves and its members join the Fatherland Front.

March 1   A law goes into effect putting organized religion under control of the state.

March 6   The opposition Radical party dissolves and its members join the Fatherland Front. As a result only the Agrarian party, controlled by Communists, remains as an opposition group.

March 8   After a trial starting on February 25, the 15 Protestant churchmen are found guilty of spying for the United States and Great Britain and receive sentences from one year to life; four get life, the rest 15 years or less.

April 4   The government announces that Traicho Kostov, vice premier and head of economic affairs, lost his government positions and was arrested on charges of nationalistic ''deviation'' after a Central Committee meeting in March. This marks the beginning round in the Bulgarian purge trials. He is expelled from the Communist party in June.

April 14   To dispel rumors that Premier Dimitrov has been ousted, the government announces that the 66-year-old leader has been in Moscow for medical treatment since January.

May 15   In local elections the Fatherland Front claims 92 percent of the vote.

June 25   A United Nations Special Commission on the Balkans levels charges against Bulgaria and Albania for giving large amounts of aid to the Greek rebels.

July 2   Georgi Dimitrov, Communist leader of Bulgaria since 1946, dies near Moscow from diabetes.

July 13   Vasil Kolarov, the foreign minister and acting premier since April 14, succeeds the late Dimitrov as premier.

Parliament expels Traicho Kostov from his seat.

October 1   Copying the USSR, Bulgaria revokes its friendship and mutual aid treaty with Yugoslavia since Yugoslavia refuses to follow the USSR completely in all matters.

December 8   Kostov and 10 other former high ranking Communist officials are tried on charges of treason and espionage for Yugoslavia and the West. Out of the 11 defendants, Kostov denies he is guilty.

Bulgaria leaves the World Health Organization claiming it is a front organization for anti-Communist activities of the West.

December 11   The embalmed body of Georgi Dimitrov is placed on view in a white stone mausoleum in Sofia.

December 14   The government hands down convictions in its case against 11 leading former Communists. Five receive life sentences, five get 8 to 15 years, and Kostov alone is sentenced to hang. The purge trials continue until the early 1950s.

December 16   Traicho Kostov is executed.

December 18   In nationwide *Subranie* elections that feature a single slate of candidates, the Fatherland Front claims over 97 percent of the vote.

December 21   Bulgaria renames the Black Sea port of Varna, as well as a mountain, school, and hydroelectric dam in honor of Soviet dictator Joseph Stalin's 70th birthday.

1950

January 19   Bulgaria demands that the United States remove its ambassador who had been implicated in spying during recent purge trials. The next day America denies the allegations and responds that relations might be broken off if the demand is not rescinded.

January 20   Seven more leading Communists are purged.

January 23   Premier Kolarov dies.

February 1   Vulko Chervenkov, the brother-in-law of Georgi Dimitrov and former vice premier and secretary of the Communist party, becomes prime minister. Chervenkov continues the purge of the party and government by placing Communists loyal to the USSR in power.

February 20   The United States breaks relations with Bulgaria after members of the American embassy staff are systematically harassed and terrorized, and Bulgaria refuses to drop espionage allegations against the American ambassador, Donald R. Heath. The United States announces that its quarrel is with the Bulgarian government not the people.

Bulgaria announces the indictments of five on charges of espionage for the United States including two former Bulgarian employees of the American embassy, Mihail Shipkov and Kivka Rindova.

February 24 Claiming that Bulgaria has not paid American citizens for nationalizing their property in Bulgaria, the United States freezes Bulgarian assets in America.

February 27 The United States forbids its citizens from visiting Bulgaria.

March 8 After a two-day trial, eight Bulgarians accused of spying for the United States are found guilty and sentenced from 4 1/2 to 15 years in prison. Mihail Shipkov, a translator at the American embassy, receives 15 years, while Kivka Rindova, a phone operator at the American embassy, gets 12 years.

August 16 In a diplomatic note, Bulgaria announces that it will allow 250,000 Bulgarian Turkish Moslems to emigrate to Turkey over the next three months.

August 27 The United Nations Special Commission on the Balkans states that Bulgaria remains a threat to Greek independence and that none of the over 28,000 children taken by guerrillas to Bulgaria during the Greek Civil War from 1946–49 have been returned.

September 10 Citing humanitarian and economic reasons, Turkey closes its border with Bulgaria to prevent a flood of ethnic Turks leaving Bulgaria for political reasons.

November 7 A decree allows Soviet citizens to hold positions in the Bulgarian government.

November 11 Chervenkov is elected leader of the Bulgarian Communist party.

December 2 Turkey reopens its border with Bulgaria, and by early May 1951 approximately 110,000 Turkish refugees arrive from Bulgaria.

1951

January 1 The government passes a law that raises the Bulgarian Orthodox Church from exarchate to patriarchate status thereby gaining complete recognition as an independent church.

February 13 A new criminal code based upon the Soviet model becomes effective.

March 21 The government announces an end to rationing that began during World War II and reduces prices on manufactured goods, while at the same time increasing wages and pensions.

August 1 President Truman curbs American trade with Bulgaria and other Communist countries.

September 17 The United States prohibits trade concessions with Bulgaria to become effective one month later.

November 8 Turkey closes the border with Bulgaria after several people try to enter with forged passports.

November 13 Parliament passes a new labor law based on the Soviet model.

December 9 All laws passed before the Communists took power are repealed.

1952

January 1 Collectivization of agriculture reaches 47.5 percent of all farmland by the end of 1951 (*see* September 10, 1948).

March 23 A Bulgarian Red Cross medical brigade, consisting of 15 people, arrives in Communist North Korea to help in the Korean War. They will return in April 1953.

May 10 Bulgaria devalues its currency, the lev, to bring it into line with the Soviet ruble. Between one-half to four new levs are equal to 100 old levs depending on how much money a person has; people who have large amounts of money will receive the lesser amount while those with very little savings will be able to exchange at the higher rate.

May 30 Premier Chervenkov becomes the president of the Fatherland Front at its third congress meeting since May 28.

June 16 A witness to the United Nations Special Commission on Forced Labor reports that Bulgaria has 30 labor camps with about 100,000 inmates.

August 5 In the Cominform magazine, Todor Zhivkov, secretary of the Communist party, admits that there has been widespread resistance to collectivization by the peasantry.

July 27–August 7 After the Marica (Evros) River changes its course on the ten-mile section that forms the Bulgarian-Greek border in the east, Bulgarian forces occupy the eight-acre Gamma Island that they claim now belongs to them. Greece issues an ultimatum to evacuate the island and attacks on August 7; the Bulgarians leave without returning fire. Clashes will continue over the next year.

September 22   In a move to undermine the Roman Catholic Church in Bulgaria, 40 Bulgarian Roman Catholics, including 28 priests, are placed on trial for treason. Early in October, a bishop and three priests receive the death penalty, while the others receive prison sentences.

1953

February 21   After 14 months Turkey reopens its border with Bulgaria when Bulgaria agrees to take back 132 gypsies who crossed the border illegally back in November 1951.

March 6   The death of Soviet leader Joseph Stalin is marked by five minutes of silence followed by blaring sirens and cannonades.

May 10   Kiril, the metropolitan of Plovdiv, is elected the first patriarch of the Bulgarian Orthodox Church.

May 19   The United States government reports that 60 American citizens are held by Bulgaria. These people had all emigrated to the United States, received American citizenship, and eventually returned to their native Bulgaria where the Communist regime views them as traitors.

July 1   A law proscribes imprisonment or fines for workers or apprentices who leave their positions without permission. It is canceled in November.

July 10   Bulgaria and Greece settle their dispute over Gamma Island by granting it to Greece (*see* July 27–August 7, 1952).

September 9   On the ninth anniversary of the Communist takeover of Bulgaria, the government announces an amnesty for political prisoners.

December 9   The government reduces the penalty for fleeing the country from death to 10 to 15 years in prison.

December 18   Prime Minister Chervenkov states he wishes to restore diplomatic relations with the United States broken since February 20, 1950.

December 20   One slate elections are held for the 249 seats of the *Subranie*. In this style of election the voters have no choice for candidates but instead are presented a ballot with just one name for every position.

1954

February 25–March 3   At the 6th Congress of the Bulgarian Communist party, Todor Zhivkov becomes party secretary replacing Chervenkov.

May 24   Bulgaria and Greece resume diplomatic relations broken since 1941.

1955

March 1   Bulgaria officially ends its state of war with Germany.

May 14   The Warsaw Pact, a treaty of friendship, cooperation, and mutual assistance, is signed in Warsaw, Poland by Bulgaria, Albania, Czechoslovakia, Hungary, Poland, Romania, East Germany, and the Soviet Union. This Soviet-controlled defensive alliance is meant to counter the Western alliance of NATO.

June 19   In a show of relaxation in tensions between the two countries, the United States approves a deal to sell 500 Chevrolet automobiles to Bulgaria for over $1 million. Citing a company rule against sales to Communist countries, General Motors will cancel the deal in August.

July   Hoping to improve relations with the United States, the government releases all those convicted in the Shipkov case (*see* March 8, 1950).

July 27   Bulgarian fighters shoot down an Israeli airliner killing all 58 persons aboard. The London-Tel Aviv flight had strayed over Bulgarian territory near the Greek-Yugoslav-Bulgarian border.

July 29   Bulgaria expresses regret over shooting down the Israeli airliner. Four days later it states those responsible for the shooting will be punished, promises to prevent similar occurrences in the future, and offers to pay damages to the families of the victims.

August 12   Showing a warming in relations, in a diplomatic note to the United States Bulgaria apologizes for the death of 12 Americans in the Israeli airline incident.

September 20   The government announces that it will cut its military by 18,000 men before the end of the year.

December 14   When the criteria for membership changes and the United States no longer vetoes its request for admission, Bulgaria is finally admitted to the United Nations after trying for seven years.

1956

January 1   As of the end of 1955 collectivization of agriculture now stands at 62.5 percent of all farmland (*see* January 1, 1952).

February 14   Israel asks for over $2.5 million from Bulgaria in the July 29, 1955 airline shooting.

April 11   Traicho Kostov, executed in the 1949 purges, is posthumously rehabilitated (*see* December 14, 1949).

April 17   In a move against Communist, and following the lead of Soviet leader Nikita Khrushchev who attacked Stalin and his excesses at the twentieth Soviet party congress in February, Chervenkov is demoted to deputy prime minister from prime minister on charges of promoting a cult of personality. Anton Yugov replaces him.

The Central Committee of the Communist party posthumously exonerates Traicho Kostov of all charges.

May 26   Despite a relaxation in tensions between the two countries, the United States reports that it spurned attempts by Bulgarian diplomats at the United Nations to wholly restore diplomatic relations.

September 7   The Central Committee restores party membership to the late Kostov and most of the others convicted in the late 1940s purge trials.

September 22–October 7   Todor Zhivkov makes an official visit to Yugoslavia where on the last day of his visit the two countries re-establish diplomatic relations broken since 1948.

1958

February 5   The authorities move thousands of "hooligans" and unemployed youths from urban areas to the countryside for farm work.

March 15   The Bulgarian Orthodox Church issues a directive ordering its clergy to completely support the policies of the Zhivkov regime especially in its move to completely collectivize agriculture at an estimated 87 percent.

May 27   In a communiqué following a meeting of the Warsaw Pact in Moscow, Bulgaria announces it will reduce its military by 23,000 men.

September 4   Former King Symeon II enrolls at the Valley Forge Military Academy outside Philadelphia, Pennsylvania.

December 20   The government orders all government employees to annually "volunteer" 30 days farming in industry.

1957

January 1   As of the end of 1956 collectivization of agriculture amounts to over 77 percent of land suitable for farming (*see* January 1, 1956).

February   Reports note that 1,500 students at the University of Sofia have been expelled and 200 university and high school students have been sent to labor camps for sympathizing with the Hungarian revolution in October 1956 which aimed to take Hungary out of the Eastern Bloc.

July 11–12   Following a series of purges on all levels of the party throughout the country to strengthen Zhivkov's control, senior hard-line party officials Yonko Panov, Dobri Terpeshev, and Georgi Chankov are removed from the Central Committee.

August 5   Bulgaria offers $1,000 in damages for each victim of the July 27, 1955 Israeli airliner shooting. Israel rejects the offer.

September 5   The United States allows limited travel to Bulgaria.

October 17   Israel sues Bulgaria at the International Court at The Hague for full compensation from the 1955 airliner incident. The United States files a similar claim against Bulgaria on October 29.

Todor Zhivkov (c. 1958)—Tenure as leader of the Bulgarian Communist party spanned from 1954 through the 1980s.

1959

January 20 In a speech to parliament, Todor Zhivkov announces a major reorganization of the government which will abolish numerous ministries thereby releasing approximately 140,000 people to work in industry and agriculture.

March 16 Bulgaria announces it is not subject to the findings of the World Court in the 1955 Israeli airliner incident. The World Court rules ten days later that it has no jurisdiction in the case (*see* October 17, 1957).

March 27 After Bulgaria agrees to withdraw espionage charges against former U.S. ambassador Donald R. Heath and to not harass embassy personnel, the United States and Bulgaria agree to restore diplomatic ties broken since February 21, 1950.

May 12 The United States ends its travel ban on Bulgaria.

May 15 Greece presents Bulgaria with a $18 million bill for damages from World War II.

July 22 To deflect attention from Greece's request for monetary compensation in May, Bulgaria offers Greece a 20-year nonaggression pact which the Greeks reject.

December 22 Parliament is told that only one-third of the expected agriculture output for 1959 has been achieved.

December 25 In an address to the national legislature, Zhivkov suggests that both Greece and Bulgaria reduce their military to a level of border guards; Greece ignores the proposal.

1960

March 19 The government reports that collectivization of agriculture is 95 percent complete (*see* January 1, 1957).

1961

April 18–19 Government-sponsored demonstrators attack the American embassy in Sofia protesting the April 17 unsuccessful Bay of Pigs invasion by American-backed rebels who attempt to overthrow the Communist regime in Cuba.

August 16 Bulgaria completes building the Rastan Dam on the Ortones River in western Syria showing the importance of friendship between Bulgaria (and other Communist states) and the Arab world.

November 29 Deputy Premier Vulko Chervenkov is expelled from the Politburo, the principal policy-making and executive committee of the Communist party, after Todor Zhivkov accuses him of wrongdoing during his term as premier from 1950 to 1956.

December 18 Vulko Chervenkov loses his deputy premiership.

1962

January 20 A Bulgarian air force MIG fighter jet crash-lands near Bari, in southeastern Italy, on what is believed to be a spy mission on a NATO base. The Bulgarian government denies the charge and demands both the plane and the pilot back the next day.

February 1 Italy files espionage charges against the pilot of the MIG jet that crashed on January 20.

July 29 In an attempt to stop food hoarding and shortages, the government raises the price of basic food products an average of 32 percent for dairy items, 24 percent for meat, 27 percent for poultry, and 11 percent for eggs. The government also lowers the salaries of top paid employees and increases the wages of poorly paid agricultural workers in an attempt to boost morale and thereby increase agricultural output.

September 27 The government announces that during reshuffling deputy premier Todor Zhivkov has taken on the additional position of head of the state planning commission.

November 5–14 The 8th Congress of the Bulgarian Communist party takes place. In his opening speech, First Secretary Todor Zhivkov announces that Chervenkov, Premier Anton Yugov, and six others were expelled from the Central Committee, ending a power struggle between Zhivkov who favors Soviet Premier Khrushchev's policy of de-Stalinization and the Stalinists Yugov and Chervenkov. There now remain no major rivals of Zhivkov in the top levels of government and the party.

November 14 At the end of the congress Zhivkov is reelected as leader. In a move to consolidate his position in the party, the congress also approves the purging of numerous members from party leadership.

November 19 Todor Zhivkov becomes premier.

November 27 Zhivkov increases his control of the government by revising the cabinet and reorganizing ministries.

1963

January 3 Italy drops espionage charges against a Bulgarian MIG pilot who crash-landed in Italy the year before (*see* February 1, 1962).

February 12 Police attack a demonstration of African students who are protesting the arrest of their student leaders, racial prejudice, Communist propaganda, and the Bulgarian government's decision to ban their just established All-African Student Union. Two days later African students begin leaving the country.

May 17 The government announces that it centralized several governmental agencies to make them more efficient. In order to carry out this program of centralization, more bureaus are created on May 24.

June 2 After seven years Bulgaria pays Israel $195,000 in damages resulting from the death of 22 Israeli passengers in the airline incident from 1955 (*see* March 16, 1959).

September Ivan-Assen Khristov Georgiev, a former Bulgarian diplomat to the United Nations from 1956–1961, is arrested on charges of espionage for the United States.

November 5 The Kremikovtski Metallurgical Combine is dedicated. This combine, close to Sofia, becomes the showpiece of industrialization for the Bulgarian Communist party. The party has been pushing to change the economy from an agricultural based one to an industrialized society where it feels the strength of socialism lies.

December 26 Georgiev goes on trial and pleads guilty to spying for the United States.

December 27 A government-orchestrated demonstration, in conjunction with the Georgiev trial, takes place outside the American embassy in Sofia leading to minor attacks on the building and the destruction of several embassy automobiles.

December 31 Georgiev is found guilt of espionage and sentenced to death.

1964

January 5 Georgiev is executed by firing squad.

February 17–19 During an official visit to Moscow, Zhivkov signs an agreement in which the USSR grants Bulgaria $333 million in economic credits over the next five years in return for Bulgaria agreeing to join a joint Soviet-Bulgarian economic, technical, and scientific cooperation commission.

March 14 Traicho Kostov and three other Communist leaders executed during the purge trials in the 1950s are proclaimed heroes of Bulgaria (*see* September 7, 1956).

May 3 Clashes occur between Easter worshipers and police after the authorities attempt to prevent Christians from celebrating midnight mass at Sofia's main cathedral.

June 28 Bulgaria and Greece work out an agreement to settle reparations from World War II. Bulgaria refused to pay the $50 million in damages awarded to Greece in 1946. Under the new agreement, Bulgaria will send Greece $7 million in goods, do approximately $15 million in flood control work on the Arda River, and improve all relations with Greece.

October 18 Bulgaria becomes the first Communist country to officially approve of the coup against Soviet leader Nikita Khrushchev during October 14–15.

1965

February 15 Several hundred Bulgarian and foreign students pelt the American embassy in Sofia in protest over American involvement in Vietnam.

March 6 Anti-American demonstrations take place in Sofia against United States policy in Vietnam.

April 7 Three prominent party members and officials are arrested for conspiracy to overthrow Zhivkov at an upcoming April 14 meeting of the Central Committee. At least seven other alleged conspirators are arrested or commit suicide during the month.

June 19 The government announces that nine "pro-Chinese" Bulgarians, five military officers, and four civilians, have been sentenced from three to 15 years in prison for their roles in the abortive coup attempt.

September 22–23 Yugoslav leader Josip Broz Tito visits Bulgaria for the first time since 1947 marking a warming in relations.

1966

February 27 Reportedly over 99 percent of the electorate cast their ballots in elections for 416 seats in the *Subranie*. The single slate of Fatherland Front candidates receives 99.85 percent of the vote.

May 1 A dam bursts at Vratsa killing a reported 50 people.

November 24 A Bulgarian airliner, flying from Prague to Sofia, crashes in the Carpathian Mountains killing all 82 people aboard.

November 28 The United States raises its diplomatic relations with Bulgaria from ministerial to ambassador rank thereby establishing full relations.

1967

May 10–16 After talks between Zhivkov and Soviet leader Leonid Brezhnev in Sofia, the 1948 20-year Treaty of Friendship and Mutual Aid and Cooperation is renewed.

June 10 Bulgaria breaks diplomatic relations with Israel due to the Six Day (Arab-Israeli) War in which the Israelis defeat the Arabs and seize large amounts of territory. For a number of years the Communist bloc has had close, friendly relations with the Arab world and has viewed Israel as a tool of the West.

October 10 Bulgaria joins 84 other nations in banning nuclear weapons from outer space.

1968

March 23 In Dresden, East Germany, leaders of Bulgaria, East Germany, Hungary, Poland, and the Soviet Union warn Czechoslovak leaders not to let their liberalizing program get out of hand. The program aims to lessen Communist control in the country.

May 8 Bulgarian, East German, Hungarian, and Polish Communist party leaders confer in Moscow about the liberalizing events in Czechoslovakia, which they fear might spread to their own countries.

July 1 Bulgaria joins 62 other nations in signing the nuclear non-proliferation treaty.

July 14–16 The Communist leaders of Bulgaria, East Germany, Hungary, Poland, and the USSR, fearful of the repercussions in their own countries from the Czechoslovak liberalizing movement, meet in Warsaw and send a virtual ultimatum to the Czechoslovak Communist party demanding an end to the reforms. The five countries back up their resolution with troop movements near the Czechoslovak borders.

July 25 Zhivkov calls for greater economic ties to the USSR and closer economic cooperation with the West.

July 28–August 6 The 9th World Youth Festival takes place in Sofia. Although carefully planned by the Bulgarian government, it quickly turns into a melee between non-Communist, Western Communist, progressive Communist, Soviet-back Communist, and Maoist Communist youths. The authorities handle any opposition brutally causing the conference to fall apart.

August 3 The leaders of Bulgaria, East Germany, Hungary, Poland, and the Soviet Union meet in Bratislava, Czechoslovakia to ratify the Čierna plan, a compromise worked out between Czechoslovakia and the USSR between July 29 and August 1, in which Czechoslovakia agrees to limit its reforms in relation to the media. Despite the compromise, the various Communist leaders feel that the Czechoslovak reforms have gone too far.

August 20–21 Bulgarian troops take part, along with forces from Poland, Hungary, and East Germany, in the Soviet-led invasion of Czechoslovakia, crushing the liberal program of the Prague Spring, as the Czechoslovak reform movement is called.

August 30 Due to Bulgaria's participation in the invasion of Czechoslovakia, the United States cancels the American exhibit at a September trade fair in Bulgaria. A complete cultural exchange ban takes place in September, but is removed on December 20.

September 3 A Bulgarian airliner en route from Dresden, East Germany to Burgas, Bulgaria crashes near Burgas leaving 50 out of 89 passengers dead.

October 29 Bulgarian forces depart from Czechoslovakia.

December 27 Parliament approves a plan by Zhivkov to reorganize several governmental agencies.

1969

January 31 A campaign begins against Western influences and "revisionism" in Bulgarian culture.

April 1 A banking reorganization plan goes into effect with the creation of two new institutions, the Bulgarian Industrial Bank and the Bulgarian Agricultural and Trade bank, to encourage profits in the economy. It is hoped that by lending money to modernize industry and agriculture, Bulgarian goods will be able to compete in the world market.

August 19 In an attempt to reduce its ethnic Turkish population, Bulgaria and Turkey exchange ratified agreements. The agreements permit approximately 30,000 ethnic Turks in Bulgaria with close relatives in Turkey, who left Bulgaria in 1949–1951, to leave between April 1 and November 30 each year at the rate of 300 per week (*see* November 26, 1948).

September 9 Nationwide celebrations mark the 25th anniversary of the Communist takeover. In conjunction with the anniversary, the government pardons or partially pardons over 12,000 prisoners.

November 25 Citing corruption, the government abolishes the Commercial Maritime Agency, an industrial enterprise engaged in shipbuilding, food processing, and other endeavors, and transfers its duties to other bureaus.

December 8–12 During an official visit to Yugoslavia, the Bulgarian foreign minister keeps relations between the two countries very cool by stating that his country has no territorial designs on Yugoslavia, but that the Macedonians are descended from Bulgarians and thus part of Bulgaria.

1970

April 1 In an attempt to end discrepancies in wages, the basic minimum wage of 60 levs takes effect.

Late spring Bulgaria, only somewhat affected by flood waters of the Danube and its tributaries due to an exceptionally wet spring, sends approximately $800,000 in aid to flood-ravaged Romania.

August 22 Due to a cholera outbreak in the region, border officials announce that all visitors from Turkey will not be able to come into the country unless they can prove at least five days have passed since their second immunization shot against the disease.

1971

January 18 A Bulgarian airliner crashes in heavy fog near the airport at Zurich, Switzerland, killing all but two of the 35 passengers.

March 7 Kiril, the first patriarch of the Bulgarian Orthodox Church elected on May 10, 1953, dies in Sofia.

March 30 The government publishes the draft of a new constitution that would provide for a State Council to replace the Presidium of Subranie. The State Council would represent the country in international relations and would be headed by the new office of president. Authorities state that a new constitution is needed due to the great socialist strides made in the country.

April 20–25 During the 10th Congress of the Bulgarian Communist party Todor Zhivkov is reelected as first secretary, and delegates approve the draft of the new constitution.

May 16 A national referendum approves the new constitution.

July 7 Todor Zhivkov resigns as prime minister, and is elected president of the country; he remains first secretary of the Communist party. Stanko Todorov succeeds Zhivkov as premier.

July 19 Bulgaria denies that its embassy played an important role in an attempted leftist coup in Sudan.

September 26 Brezhnev presents Todor Zhivkov with the Order of Lenin (one of the highest awards granted by the USSR) during a brief visit to Sofia.

1972

March 12 Italy expels two Bulgarian diplomats, a Czechoslovak diplomat, and a Polish diplomat on charges of spying.

May 3 Bulgaria grants political asylum to four Turkish skyjackers who forced a Turkish airliner to land in Sofia, after their demands are not met by the Turkish government. The Bulgarian government will later reverse its decision and sentence the four to three years in prison on charges of hijacking.

October 23 Another four Turkish skyjackers are granted political asylum in Sofia after the Turkish government refuses to meet their demands.

1973

March 1 The government decrees that on June 1 the minimum wage for all categories of work will increase 23.2 percent. Furthermore, it orders that wages be increased approximately 16 percent for physicians, school teachers, miners, and artists.

May 4 Due to the declining birth rate of the ethnic Bulgarian population, abortions are restricted to married women with two or more children and to unmarried women over 18 years old if the pregnancy is life-threatening to the mother.

May 20 The government announces that it will reduce the work week to five days and from 46 to 42.5 hours starting in 1975.

December 14 Due to the world-wide energy crisis, Bulgaria imposes gasoline rationing which restricts drivers to 10 gallons a month at 85 cents per gallon with additional gallons costing double.

December 21 After negotiations in Bonn on July 31 and August 1, West Germany and Bulgaria establish diplomatic relations.

1974

January 26 The United States Coast Guard seizes a Bulgarian fishing trawler for fishing within American territorial waters. The captain is fined $20,000 on February 2.

February 5 The Sofia newspaper *Uchitelski Delo* reports that an ethnic Turk is sentenced to 20 months in prison for advocating Turkish nationalism and libeling Bulgaria.

March Eighteen ethnic Turkish Bulgarians ask for asylum while visiting Istanbul, Turkey.

June 1 Bulgarian economist Henrich N. Schpeter, who worked at the United Nations from 1966 to 1972, receives the death penalty after being found guilty of spying.

June 3 The government reports shortages in consumer goods and basic food items during the first six months of 1974.

August 22 After an international outcry from numerous United Nations agencies and other international organizations over the Schpeter death sentence, Bulgarian authorities release him, and Schpeter flies to Israel.

September 2 A gas pipeline between Bulgaria and the USSR opens.

September 9 Bulgaria agrees to stop jamming Voice of America broadcasts.

October 31 In an attempt to lure foreign investors, parliament passes a law that permits foreign companies a share in Bulgarian management and profits for joint business ventures.

November 15 The government decrees that all tourists from non-socialist lands must exchange at least $10 daily while in Bulgaria.

1975

June 27 Todor Zhivkov meets with Pope Paul VI in the Vatican indicating a thaw between the Vatican and the officially atheistic Bulgarian regime.

June 28 A Bulgarian airliner on a domestic flight is skyjacked to Salonika, Greece, where the hijacker is granted asylum.

August 5 Due to Zhivkov's meeting with the pope on June 27, Bulgaria permits the appointment of two bishops for Bulgaria's approximately 70,000 Roman Catholics.

Early December A census reports that the population has grown by 6 percent in ten years to 8.73 million people with 58 percent in urban areas.

1976

March 29–April 2 The 11th Congress of the Bulgarian Communist party reelects Zhivkov as party first secretary

September 8 It is reported that Bedford Trucks, a British subsidiary of General Motors, signed a deal to provide Bulgaria with trucks in exchange for forklifts.

1977

February 23 A Bulgarian exile group based in Vienna urges the Communist parties of France, Italy, and Spain to support dissidents in Bulgaria.

March 4 An earthquake measuring 7.5 on the Richter scale centered north of Bucharest, Romania, kills 50 in Bulgaria.

October 1 Argentine naval vessels fire on and seize two Bulgarian fishing vessels and arrest their crews for fishing within its territorial waters.

1978

April 29 Due to agricultural declines of 6 percent from 1976 to 1977, the government dismisses the minister of agriculture, two deputy premiers connected with agriculture, and several other officials.

August 26 Bulgarian dissident Vladimir Kostov becomes ill after being stabbed in the back by an unknown assailant in Paris. A microscopic metal pellet is removed from his back.

September 11 Georgi Markov, an exiled Bulgarian writer who works for the Bulgarian section of the BBC and Radio Free Europe, dies four days after being stabbed by a man with an umbrella. An autopsy on September 12 rules the death suspicious after poison is found in his blood. On September 29, British authorities rule it a murder when a microscopic metal ball is found embedded in Markov's skin. Markov had recently been describing corruption within the Bulgarian government and Communist party;

the Bulgarian government denies any involvement with the death.

1979

March 19 Citing health risks, the government forbids physicians and nurses from bringing cigarettes to work in hospital.

April 10–12 Major Georgi Ivanov becomes the first Bulgarian cosmonaut during a Soviet mission in space.

May 21 Due to the continued energy crisis, Bulgaria raises the price of gasoline to $4.25 per gallon (official exchange rate) and introduces a plan barring cars with odd numbered license plates from the road on certain days and even numbers on others.

July 16 Due to failures in agriculture, a government report recommends decentralizing the system and allowing market forces a greater role in agriculture. Suggestions include agricultural worker wages to be tied to productivity, production quotas eliminated, collective farms will become more autonomous in making contracts, and surpluses to be sold abroad.

1980

January 23 Bulgaria issues its annual economic report for the previous year. However, key figures for a number of areas are left out indicating poor performance.

March 25 To aid the ailing economy, the government enacts a law which permits foreign business to establish joint companies in Bulgaria. Foreign ownership is expected to be between 40 and 60 percent of a company and the foreign firms are permitted to take part in management, as well as take their profits out of Bulgaria.

October 21 After a long illness Vulko Chervenkov, called the "Little Stalin" and prime minister from 1950 to 1956, dies at the age of 80 in Sofia.

December 31 It is estimated that by the end of 1980 Bulgaria's total accumulated debt to the West stands at $3.8 billion.

1981

April 4 The 12th Congress of the Bulgarian Communist party reelects Zhivkov as party leader.

May 23–June 3 Bulgaria celebrates the 1,300th anniversary of its founding with commemorations throughout the year. An international conference of scholars is held in Sofia covering Bulgarian history and culture to celebrate the event.

June 16 Stanko Todorov, premier since July 1971, is replaced by Grisha Filipov. Filipov will soon be replaced by Georgi Stanchev.

1982

January–February A number of economic reforms are enacted in an attempt to improve production, including wages linked to output and monies given to companies only after their products are sold.

August 17 Western new sources release reports that link the Bulgarian secret service to the unsuccessful assassination attempt on Pope John Paul II on May 13, 1981, by the Turk Mehmet Ali Agca. Bulgaria denies the allegations.

November 25 Serge Ivanov Antonov, the manager for the Bulgarian airlines in Rome, is arrested by Italian police as an accomplice in the May 1981 shooting of Pope John Paul II. Two employees of the Bulgarian embassy in Rome are also implicated, but have returned to their country. Bulgaria protests his arrest and the accusations against the other two.

December 9 Due to the cooling of relations over the alleged assassination attempt on the pope, Bulgaria recalls its ambassador from Italy. Italy recalls its ambassadors two days later.

December 22 In an apparent link to the icy relations between Bulgaria and Italy, two Italians go on trial in Sofia on charges of spying; they were arrested in August.

1983

February 28 Bulgaria calls Italian investigations into four Bulgarians' involvement in a 1981 plot to kill Polish Solidarity leader Lech Wałęsa in Rome "absurd." The investigation is dropped by Italian officials in October 1984.

July 8 Mehmet Ali Agca, convicted of trying to kill the pope, tells reporters in Rome that terrorist experts trained him in Bulgaria and that the Bulgarian secret service and Sergei Ivanov Antonov were both part of the plot.

December 21 For health reasons, Sergei Ivanov Antonov is released from prison and put under house arrest in the Bulgarian embassy.

1984

March 16 After three months under house arrest Antonov goes back to an Italian jail. In June, Antonov is again placed under house arrest due to poor health.

April 6 and 9 Bulgaria and Italy exchange new ambassadors after 16 months.

May 9 Following the Soviet lead, Bulgaria announces that it will not attend the Summer Olympics in Los Angeles for "security reasons." In actuality, this action is in response to the United States' boycott of the 1980 Summer Games in Moscow due to the Soviet invasion of Afghanistan in late 1979. Instead, in August, Bulgaria attends a rival competition—the Friendship Games—in Moscow.

August A bombing campaign begins when 14 people die as a result of an explosion in the Plovdiv railroad station. Bombings take place in Varna, Targoviste, Ruse, and elsewhere until March 1985. The authorities suspect the Turkish minority although it cannot find any evidence.

October 26 Italian officials charge three Bulgarians, including Sergei Ivanov Antonov, and four Turks in the plot to assassinate the pope in May 1981. Bulgaria denounces the indictments. The trial opens in May 1985.

1985

February 15 Turkey recalls its ambassador over Bulgaria's drive to Slavicize its Turkish population since 1983. Fearing that the larger Turkish birthrate will eventually destabilize the country, the government forces ethnic Turks to Bulgarize their names in an attempt to assimilate them.

March 16 A Bulgarian airliner taking off from Sofia for Warsaw crashes killing all 73 people aboard.

March 21 Nearly 40,000 people demonstrate in Istanbul concerning Bulgaria's abuse of its ethnic Turks.

March 26 Bulgaria rejects Turkey's request for talks regarding a possible mass emigration of ethnic Turks from Bulgaria.

April 3 Western news sources report that nameless Bulgarian dissidents issued a statement called Declaration 78 in which they demand freedom of the press, religion, and travel; independent trade unions; higher living standards; and the abolition of special privileges for high officials.

April 26 The members of the Warsaw Pact, including Bulgaria, sign a 20-year extension of this military alliance (*see* May 14, 1955).

May 19 Due to a wave of bombings since August 1984, the *Subranie* enacts a law to increase penalties for terrorism with prison sentences up to 20 years for conspiracy and possession of illegal arms, death penalty for setting off explosions, and grants increased powers to the police and border authorities to search suspected terrorists.

June 15 In a speech in Blagoevgrad, Zhivkov states that Bulgaria has no designs on Yugoslav territory, but makes no mention of Macedonians thereby inferring that Macedonians in Yugoslavia are still considered to be Bulgarians. His statement keeps Yugoslav-Bulgarian relations icy.

1986

February 11 The official Bulgarian news service, BTA, denies Turkish charges that Bulgaria is oppressing its ethnic Turkish minority.

March 21 Georgi Atanasov replaces Georgi Stanchev as prime minister.

March 29 An Italian court acquits three Bulgarians indicted for helping in the 1981 assassination attempt on Pope John Paul II thereby leaving the Bulgarian connection in the case uncertain. The official Bulgarian news agency lauds the verdict as proof that Bulgaria had no role in the attempt on the pope's life (*see* October 26, 1984).

April 2–5 At the 13th Congress of the Bulgarian Communist Party, Zhivkov states that the country must undergo economic changes. This is seen as a move by Bulgaria to follow Soviet leader Mikhail Gorbachev's policies of perestroika, which is an attempt to transform and restructure the lagging economy of the USSR. Zhivkov remains unhappy about events in the Soviet Union and Bulgarian-Soviet relations continue to be cool.

May 7 Due to the accident at the Soviet Chernobyl nuclear power plant in late April, the European Community bans agricultural imports from Bulgaria and other East European countries until May 31.

June 20 A report by the human rights organization Helsinki Watch accuses Bulgaria of killing up to 1,500 Bulgarian Turks since 1984 in its attempt to Slavicize and Christianize them.

September 11 Bulgaria signs a nonaggression pact with Greece. The agreement states that the two countries will consult on matters of mutual security and will not allow their countries to be used as a base of aggressive operations against the other.

October 17 The International Olympic Committee chooses Albertville, France, for the 1992 winter games over Sofia, Bulgaria.

November 1 Due to lax safety standards an explosion at a chemical plant near the city of Varna kills 17 and injures 19.

1987

March 21 Bulgaria grants the British fast food chain Wimpy International the right to open 20 restaurants.

July 28 In a speech to a plenum (general assembly of all members) of the Central Committee, Zhivkov calls for political and economic reforms which include less party interference in the government and the economy, and a restructuring of the government.

November 7 Zhivkov attends ceremonies in Moscow marking the 70th anniversary of the Bolshevik or Communist revolution in Russia.

1988

January 28–29 A national Communist party meeting, postponed from December 1987, decides to move slowly on economic reforms outlined on July 28, 1987.

February 23–26 The foreign ministers of Bulgaria, Albania, Romania, Greece, Turkey, and Yugoslavia meet in Belgrade for talks. Bulgarian Foreign Minister Petur Mladenov demands that the Balkans become a nuclear and chemical weapons free zone. Furthermore, Mladenov meets with his Turkish counterpart and the two agree to try to improve relations cooled over Bulgaria's treatment of its ethnic Turkish minority.

February 29 Reportedly over 98 percent of the population votes in elections where more than one candidate can run for an office. However, all candidates have to receive approval from the Communist party before they can run.

June 7–17 Alexander Alexandrov, a Bulgarian cosmonaut, takes part in a research mission in the Soviet space station Mir. He is Bulgaria's second cosmonaut.

July 19–20 Four top officials of the party are removed from the Central Committee. This purge at a Central Committee meeting is viewed as Zhivkov's attempt to control reformist elements in the party.

September 15 Sofia again loses a bid to hold the Winter Olympics, this time in 1994 (*see* October 17, 1986).

1989

January 11 The authorities arrest a number of human rights activists.

January 27 The government announces it will cut its military budget by 15 percent during 1990–91, while reducing the budget for 1989 by 12 percent. In addition, the number of military personnel is to drop by 10,000 and military hardware reduced by the end of 1990.

February–March Due to continued government attempts to Slavicize the over 1 million Turks in Bulgaria, over 200,000 of them flee to Turkey for refuge. Reportedly Bulgarian officials are seizing their valuables and harassing them at the border. Another 100,000 to 150,000 leave from late May through mid-August when the Turkish government closes the border.

February 11 The independent trade union *Podkrepa* (Support) applies to the government for official status. Thousands join thereafter.

February 21 At a meeting of the Politburo, Zhivkov asserts that any attempts to change socialism in the country will never be permitted.

March 15–16 The economic ministers of Bulgaria, Albania, Greece, Romania, Turkey, and Yugoslavia meet in Ankara, Turkey and agree to ease trade barriers.

May 4 During a plenum of the Central Committee, Todor Zhivkov announces plans for land reform in which large collective farms are dissolved and individual farmers can lease the land. Furthermore, Zhivkov states that no great steps have been taken for the economic reforms announced in 1987 (*see* January 28–29, 1988).

May 5 The authorities arrest several dissidents, including the philosopher Zheliu Zhelev, for distributing a document demanding democratic changes in Bulgaria.

May 19–27 After some Turks began a hunger strike on May 6 in Razgrad to protest against the government's attempt to Slavicize or assimilate them, the movement spreads to south and northeast Bulgaria. The authorities brutally put down the demonstrations and report that six are killed. Unofficial Western sources put the death toll at much higher.

After years of repression at the hands of the Bulgarians, thousands of ethnic Turks attempt to flee the country for asylum in Turkey. Pictured are refugee camps along the Turkish border.

June 8 Due to the oppression of the Bulgarian Turks, Turkey opens its border allowing over 300,000 refugees to stream in until late August when the border is again closed.

June 22 Due to labor shortages caused by the emigration of Bulgarian Turks, the government increases working hours, urges retired persons to return to work, and forces students into agrarian jobs.

June 24 Rallies in Turkey call for an invasion of Bulgaria due to its treatment of its Turkish population.

August 29 The United States recalls its ambassador from Sofia in protest over Bulgaria's treatment of its Turks.

September 29 United State Secretary of State James A. Baker III meets secretly in the United Nations with Foreign Minister Mladenov where he tells the Bulgarian leader that relations between the two countries depends on Bulgaria improving its human rights record.

October 26 Police beat and detain members of the dissident, environmental group Eco-Glasnost as they try to collect signatures on a petition in Sofia. This is just one of a number of demonstrations in Sofia that have publicly taken place in the capital since October 16 when a European conference on environmental issues opened; the demonstrations will continue after the end of the meeting on November 1.

October 29   In a statement to the Communist party newspaper *Rabotnichesko Delo* (Worker's Accomplishment), Zhivkov admits that his attempt at reforming the economy of the country have failed.

October 30   Talks between Bulgaria and Turkey begin over the issue of Bulgaria's treatment of and the mass emigration to Turkey by its ethnic Turkish population.

November 3   Nearly 10,000 people take part in anti-government demonstrations led by Eco-Glasnost in Sofia demanding free elections and democracy.

November 10   After massive protests and under pressure from reformists in the Communist party who are attempting to prevent a collapse of communism in Bulgaria, Zhivkov, who has controlled the country since 1954, resigns as president of the country and general secretary of the party. A compromise candidate, Foreign Minister Petur T. Mladenov replaces him as general secretary of the party.

November 13   The government recognizes opposition parties and groups.

November 16   In a move to calm the demonstrations, the Communist party announces it will begin to purge itself of Zhivkov supporters.

November 17   Mladenov is elected president of Bulgaria.

Throughout December   The government ends it discrimination toward and drops its attempt to Slavicize its Turkish population. It also asks those who fled in the last year to return; an estimated 200,000 Bulgarian Turks will come back in the following months.

December 4   The leaders of the Warsaw Pact, including Bulgaria, jointly denounce their countries' invasion of Czechoslovakia in August 1968.

December 7   Nine political groups and others form the Union of Democratic Forces (UDF), an opposition coalition political party that includes Eco-Glasnost. Zheliu Zhelev serves as the UDF's chairperson.

December 8   A number of Zhivkov's supporters are purged from the Central Committee and the Politburo. Other purges began shortly after Zhivkov was forced from office on November 10.

December 10   Approximately 50,000 pro-democracy demonstrators rally in freezing temperatures in Sofia.

December 11–12   During a plenum of the Central Committee, Mladenov states that he supports an end to the Communist party's dominant role in society and free nationwide elections. He notes furthermore, that the country is in deep economic trouble with an over $10 billion foreign debt and the possibility of runaway inflation in the future.

December 13   The Bulgarian Communist party expels Zhivkov and votes to end its monopoly on power.

December 14   Twenty thousand students and others demonstrate in Sofia near the parliament building demanding an end to Communist rule. The crowd shouts down President Mladenov when he attempts to address it.

December 15   Over 15,000 pro-democracy demonstrators protest at the state-run television building in Sofia.

The *Subranie* repeals laws that provide penalties for anti-Communist activities and grants an amnesty for those convicted of such crimes.

A young Bulgarian is just one of thousands of demonstrators who converge throughout 1989 to spur the collapse of communism and to denounce longtime Communist head, Todor Zhivkov.

The parliament votes to set up a special committee to investigate the corruption of former leader Zhivkov and his government.

December 16   Nearly 6,000 Bulgarian Turks rally in favor of religious freedom in the southwest Bulgarian city of Goce Delchev.

December 27   The Communist party and the Union of Democratic Forces agree to begin talks in January on sharing power.

1990

January 1–8   Bulgarian nationalists hold nationwide anti-Turkish rallies after the government ends its assimilation policies toward the Bulgarian Turks (*see* throughout December 1989).

January 8–12   Nationalist demonstrations against the Turks end as peace talks begin. The end result is the 11-point plan that includes the freedom of religion, the right to choose one's own name, and Bulgarian as the official language of the country. The *Subranie* passes the plan on January 15.

January 10   After flying to Sofia and meeting with officials, the widow of Georgi Markov states that the government has agreed to investigate her husband's murder (*see* September 11, 1978).

January 14   More than 50,000 pro-democracy demonstrators brave sub-freezing temperatures in Sofia's central square.

January 15   Parliament abolishes the special status of the Communist party in Bulgarian society as stated in the constitution. It also rehabilitates members of the opposition killed, imprisoned, or exiled in the 1940s, 1950s, and 1960s.

January 16   The Communist party begins power-sharing talks with the Union of Democratic Forces (UDF) (*see* December 7, 1989).

January 26   The government announces that the Communist party is no longer in control of the military and police.

January 29   The government announces that former leader Todor Zhivkov has been placed under formal arrest, after earlier being under house arrest, and sent to a prison in Sofia. The government also indicts Zhivkov's son-in-law, Ivan Slavkov, and an aide, Milko Balev, on charges of misuse of power.

January 30–February 2   An emergency meeting of the Communist party is held during which Mladenov unsuccessfully attempts to get the opposition to join the government. The party votes to change its ideology on February 1, and on February 2, Aleksandur Lilov replaces Mladenov as secretary general. The party also votes to restructure itself.

February 1   Discredited by its association with Zhivkov in the past, the government of Premier Georgi Atanasov resigns.

February 2   Former leader Zhivkov is hospitalized for an unknown aliment. He is later released on house arrest.

February 3   Andrey Lukanov, a reformist Communist, becomes premier and forms a government made up of all Communists.

February 7   The Interior Ministry announces the abolition of the secret police.

February 10   United States Secretary of State James A. Baker III visits Sofia where he hold talks with Bulgarian leaders and receives a warm welcome.

February 11   Disgruntled reformist members of the Communist party leave and form their own political organization, the Alternative Socialist Alliance.

February 19–20   The government passes laws allowing farmers the right to grow and export what they want, and establishing a bank to provide loans to create small farms and food processing businesses.

February 25   In a move organized by the UDF, over 80,000 pro-democracy protestors demonstrate in Sofia.

March 2   Another pro-democracy demonstration takes place in Sofia, consisting of about 20,000 people.

March 29   The authorities arrest a former deputy interior minister for allegedly running concentration camps for political opponents in the 1950s where hundreds reportedly died.

Due to a lack of money and a declining economy Bulgaria suspends its repayment of its $10 billion Western debt.

March 30   Talks between the Communist party, the UDF, and other opposition groups lead to an agreement on political reform for the country.

April 3   The Bulgarian Communist party changes its name to the Bulgarian Socialist party.

The *Subranie* sets June 10 and June 17 as the dates for free parliamentary elections, and passes a constitutional amendment to create a presidency to which Mladenov is elected. Mladenov then resigns as secretary general of the Socialist (Communist) party. The new presidency is more powerful than the before more honorary position. Another constitutional amendment removes the terms "communist" and "socialist" from the constitution.

May 3   Bulgaria restores diplomatic ties to Israel after 23 years.

May 21   Thirty-five political groups, including the UDF, refuse to sign an agreement to hold fair political campaigns for the June elections claiming that the accord is a propaganda tool for the Socialists; 45 other organizations, including the Socialists, sign.

June 10   Over 80 percent of the people vote in free elections to decide 400 seats in parliament; the Socialists (Communists) win over 47 percent of the vote (172 seats); and the UDF wins over 36 percent (107 seats)

June 11   Thousands of people demonstrate in Sofia claiming that the Socialists used deceit and scare tactics in the election. Protests continue on June 13.

June 17   The Socialist (Communist) party wins a total of 211 out of 400 parliamentary seats in the second round and runoff election, making it the majority party; the UDF takes 144. The next day, Premier Lukanov calls for a coalition government which is rejected by the UDF.

July 4   The Group of 24—the foreign ministers of the 24 most advanced industrialized countries—meet in Brussels, Belgium, and agree to provide economic aid for Bulgaria, Czechoslovakia, Yugoslavia, and East Germany whose faltering economies are seen as destabilizing.

July 6   Due to anti-government protests against the Socialist (Communist) regime, Mladenov resigns as president.

July 17–21   Nationalists strike near the southern city of Kardzhali over what they claim is the growing power of Bulgarian Turks in the largely Turkish region.

July 18   Zhivkov agrees to appear before the *Subranie* to address questions regarding his years in power. On July 30 he reverses his decision.

Authorities remove and cremate the embalmed body of Communist leader Georgi Dimitrov from Sofia mausoleum where it had been on display since 1949. A memorial procession for Dimitrov draws about 150,000 people five days later.

July 19   The USSR reports it has sharply reduced its oil and gas shipments to Eastern Europe. As a result, Bulgaria begins oil and electricity rationing in the coming weeks.

July 23   The government orders an end to all anti-government protests which have taken place for months; the decree does little to stop the demonstrations.

August 1   Despite a Socialist majority in parliament, Zheliu Zhelev, the leader of the UDF opposition, is elected president.

August 8   The *Subranie* votes to reduce mandatory military service from two years to 18 months.

August 13   Parliament subpoenas Zhivkov to testify about his years in control of Bulgaria.

August 26   A protest against the red star on top of the Socialist (Communist) headquarters in Sofia turns into a violent anti-government riot which sets fire to and destroys the building. In September 20 people are charged with arson.

August 27   In a radio address President Zhelev condemns the August 26th riot.

September   Due to the faltering economy that has disrupted distribution services, sugar and cheese join a long list of other food items that are rationed. In mid-month the government bans the export of all foods.

September 17   The UDF hold an anti-government rally in which over 30,000 people take part.

September 22   Hard line Socialists who wish to see a return to the "old days" replace many reformers at a Socialist (Communist) party congress. Nonetheless, the delegates reelect Lilov as party chairperson.

October 25   Iraq releases 700 Bulgarian advisers and technicians who have been prevented from leaving the country due to international pressure on Iraq after its invasion of Kuwait. Due to the international embargo placed on Iraq energy shortages become commonplace in Bulgaria.

November 9   Seventeen Socialist deputies form their own political organization, but the Socialist still retain a majority in the *Subranie*.

November 29   After a general strike and several weeks of anti-government protests the Lukanov Socialist government falls. Spontaneous celebrations greet the news.

December 6   Bulgaria and the Vatican reestablish diplomatic relations.

December 7   Dimitur Popov, a lawyer without political party affiliation, becomes prime minister of a coalition government that takes control on December 20.

1991

January 21   Police overpower a Soviet airline hijacker after the plane makes an emergency landing in Burgas, Bulgaria.

The effects of a nation poised on the brink of democracy; people stand in line waiting to buy bread.

February 1 In a move aimed at turning Bulgaria into a free market economy, government price controls and subsidies on energy and public transportation end causing prices to increase by as much as 12 percent.

February 6 The Bulgarian National Bank announces that it will raise interest rates from 15 to 45 percent in an attempt to curb the almost 50 percent inflation rate in 1990.

February 25 The corruption trial of former leader Todor Zhivkov begins in Sofia. Zhivkov pleads not guilty to charges of misappropriating government funds to his family and friends in the way of cash and material items such as automobiles and housing (*see* August 13, 1990).

The Bulgarian foreign and defense ministers, along with their counterparts from Czechoslovakia, Hungary, Poland, Romania, and the Soviet Union, sign an agreement in Budapest to dissolve the Warsaw Pact by March 31, 1991. It will not take place, however, until July.

February 28 The Socialist (Communist) party agrees to turn over nearly $52 million in property and other possessions to the government. In mid-December the

government orders the confiscation of all property owned by the party since 1944 when it came to power.

June 28 Comecon, the economic equivalent of the Warsaw Pact founded in 1949, officially ends (*see* January 25, 1949).

July 1 The Warsaw Pact is formally dissolved.

July 14 A new constitution takes effect which guarantees human rights and private property. The document is signed by 307 of the 400 parliamentary deputies. Several opposition deputies, who claim that the new constitution will allow the Socialists to consolidate their control, go on a nine-day hunger strike in protest. Pro- and anti-constitution demonstrations involving some violence take place over the next several days.

August 5 The World Bank announces it will loan $250 million to Bulgaria to be used for importing essential items.

August 23 A nine-day-old coal, lead, and zinc miner strike involving over 27,000 workers ends after the government signs an accord with the miners' union to hold negotiations on wages and better working conditions.

September 3 Authorities close down two nuclear reactors at the Kozlodui power plant after the International Atomic Energy Commission states they were unsafe in June and several problems were discovered in July. The reactors are of the same design as the one involved in the 1986 USSR Chernobyl accident.

October 13 Approximately 85 percent of eligible voters cast their ballots in the second free national elections giving the opposition party UDF a victory for the new 240-seat *Subranie*. The UDF wins over 34 percent of the vote thereby receiving 110 seats in parliament; the Socialists earn 106 seats with just over 33 percent of the vote. The remaining seats go the Movement for Rights and Freedom, a Turkish party, that takes 7.5 percent of the vote.

October 23 The trial of former leader Todor Zhivkov continues after a five-month recess due to his health.

November 5 Filip Dimitrov, the leader of the UDF, forms a new government that contains no Socialists.

December 6 A Bulgarian investigator on the Markov case claims that former leader Zhivkov was involved in the

A Bulgarian casts his ballot in the country's second national free election.

plot to kill the Bulgarian author in 1978. Zhivkov denies he had any role in the murder (*see* January 10, 1990).

1992

January 6 General Stoyan Savov, a former deputy interior minister and a chief suspect in the Georgi Markov murder investigation, dies of an apparent self-inflicted gunshot wound two days before he was scheduled to go on trial for removing files on the Markov case.

January 8 Former interior minister General Vladimir Todorov goes on trial for removing government files concerning the Georgi Markov murder case.

January 12 An estimated 70 percent of the electorate cast ballots in the direct presidential elections. Since none of the 21 candidates receives a majority, the top two candidates face a runoff election.

January 15 Bulgaria grants diplomatic recognition to the former Yugoslav republics of Bosnia and Hercegovina, Croatia, Macedonia, and Slovenia.

January 19 President Zhelev is reelected as president in a runoff election with approximately 53 percent of the vote, defeating the candidate of the Socialist party, Velko Valkanov.

January 20 Indicating a cooling in relations, Bulgaria and Greece begin informal talks after the January 15 move by Bulgaria to recognize Macedonia. Greece wants to isolate Macedonia diplomatically until it changes its name claiming that the name Macedonia infers territorial designs on Greece.

February 1 Bulgaria exchanges ambassadors with the Union of South Africa.

March 25 Bulgaria is one of 25 countries in Europe, North America, and the former USSR that signs an ''Open Skies'' agreement that allows a limited number of surveillance flights annually over its territory.

April 3 Bulgaria joins 26 other countries in signing an agreement to better oversee the transfer of nuclear technology so that it cannot be used for military purposes.

April 24 Authorities arrest Georgi Atanasov, premier from 1986 to 1990, and a former minister of the economy for diverting public funds from an orphan's organization. He receives a ten-year prison sentence after being convicted in November.

May 20 Dimitrov replaces several members of his government.

June 25 Leaders from 11 countries of the Balkan Peninsula (Turkey, Greece, Romania, Bulgaria, and Albania) and the former Soviet Union (Russia, Ukraine, Georgia, Moldova, Azerbaijan, and Armenia) sign the Declaration of Black Sea Economic Cooperation in Istanbul, Turkey, where the participants agree to increase economic contacts.

July 9 Andrei Lukanov, premier briefly in 1990, is arrested on charges of misusing government monies.

July 14 The authorities arrest Georgi Stanchev, premier from 1981 to 1986, on charges of embezzlement and government corruption.

August 3 The government announces that, due to the poor economy, an estimated 140,000 ethnic Turks have left the country since the fall of communism.

August 23 Due to rebel attacks on the city Bulgaria closes its embassy in Kabul, Afghanistan.

September 4 Still claiming innocence, former leader Todor Zhivkov receives a seven-year prison sentence—with time served deducted—after being convicted of embezzlement and misuse of state funds. He is allowed to remain under house arrest at the estate built for his daughter, Ludmila, outside of Sofia (*see* February 25, 1991).

October 6 For the first time since 1990, the government announces that it made a $10 million interest payment on its foreign debt of approximately $12 billion.

October 28 The government of Prime Minister Dimitrov falls.

December 17 The government announces that it plans to sell a maximum of 49 percent of the national airline, Balkan Air, to foreigners.

December 30 Lyuben Berov, an economic adviser to President Zhelev, forms a new government.

1993

February 12 Bulgaria and Greece agree to try to keep the violence in former Yugoslavia from spreading into Macedonia.

February 14 Bulgaria and Albania sign a friendship agreement.

April Four Bulgarian soldiers, part of the UN peacekeeping force in Cambodia, are killed by the Communist Khmer Rouge guerrillas.

June 21–22 The European Community leaders, meeting in Copenhagen, invite Bulgaria to apply for EC membership. Nevertheless, it is considered unlikely that Bulgaria will be able to fulfill the economic and political

conditions required for full EC membership before the year 2000.

June 30 The Bulgarian government announces that it will stop interest payments on its debts to foreign commercial banks. Bulgaria owes over nine billion dollars to more than 300 foreign banks, and approximately four billion dollars to foreign governments. Sofia states that it will again begin paying debt interest only if its creditors acknowledge the losses that Bulgaria has incurred by officially observing international economic sanctions against Yugoslavia. The Bulgarians claim that these losses amount to almost two billion dollars since the sanctions went into effect in May 1992.

Bulgaria, Russia, Ukraine, Georgia, Romania, and Turkey meet in Varna, Bulgaria, and draw up a three-year plan to deal with pollution in the Black Sea.

August 6 Bulgaria's last Communist premier, Andrei Lukanov, is charged with diverting state funds totalling $60 million to leftist governments and foreign Communist parties in the late 1980s (*see* July 9, 1992)

August 23 Bulgarian monarchists bury a heart presumed to be that of King Boris III in the Rila Monastery. The heart, discovered in 1991 in a glass jar located in the garden of a former royal palace, is thought to have been separated from the body when the secret police destroyed Boris' grave in 1954.

September 3 Former Communist Premier Georgi Atanasov begins serving a ten-year prison sentence for embezzlement of state funds (*see* April 24, 1992).

September 10 In an effort to protect its fragile domestic economy from imported goods, the Bulgarian government erects new barriers to foreign trade. The government sets minimum prices on foreign products and announces that import licenses are subject to amendment or cancellation.

October 4 The Bulgarian parliament passes legislation to introduce an 18 percent value-added tax (VAT) beginning April 1, 1994. The tax, which exempts some basic goods for three years, is approved to raise state revenues. Furthermore, the International Monetary Fund has made the tax a condition both on the new loan and of further credits. Bulgaria however, has yet to fulfill other conditions for the loan, such as an acceleration of the pace of privatization (or the selling of state-owned businesses and companies to private individuals).

November 11 Kraft Jacobs Suchard, a division of the Philip Morris Company, agrees to purchase 80 percent of Republika Confectionary, the state-owned candy maker, with the remaining 20 percent being bought by Republika employees.

November 25 The Bulgarian government reaches a tentative debt reduction agreement with its more than 300 commercial bank creditors. The deal, negotiated through the London Club of Commercial Banks, provides for a down payment of not more than $865 million and annual payments averaging less than $300 million in the first seven years of the payment. Although it is not yet approved by the Bulgarian parliament, the accord, if accepted, will reduce Bulgaria's over $9 billion foreign debt by as much as half.

December 9 Parliament votes to declassify secret police files.

December 11 After an 11-day strike involving over 20,000 ore miners, the Confederation of Independent Trade Unions, the country's largest union, reaches an agreement with the government on paying overdue wages and the reorganization of the mining industry.

December 13 Podkrepa, the second largest trade union, launches a strike of coal miners and medical workers. The union demands foreign investment and higher pensions for the miners and increased government funds for medical services.

December 28 The government orders Vladimir Zhirinovskii, the Russian ultra-nationalist, to leave the country within 24 hours after he publicly states in Sofia on December 26 that President Zhelev should resign in favor of Svetoslav Stoilov, Zhirinovskii's Bulgarian-born advisor on European economic affairs.

December 29 In a press conference, President Zhelev labels Zhirinovskii a fascist, but expresses Bulgaria's continued support for the democratic process in Russia.

Chapter Three

CZECHOSLOVAKIA

A Czechoslovak state never existed prior to its creation out of the ruins of the Austro-Hungarian Empire on October 28, 1918. However, precedents for its establishment reach back as far as the ninth century. The ancestors of the Czechs and Slovaks united in the Great Moravian Empire around A.D. 830 until its destruction by invading Magyars, or Hungarians, in 906.

With the fall of Great Moravia, the Kingdom of Hungary incorporated Slovakia, where the Slovaks remained as peasants. The Czech Lands of Bohemia, Moravia, and Silesia eventually formed a separate kingdom under a Czech Přemyslide dynasty that became part of the Holy Roman Empire. As a result, the Slovak and Czech peoples developed under different social, political, and economic systems for the next one thousand years.

During brief periods in the thirteenth and fifteenth centuries, the Luxembourg and Habsburg dynasties united the kingdoms of Hungary and Bohemia. In 1526 the Bohemian and Hungarian kingdoms once again came under the control of the Habsburg family, where they remained until 1918. Yet, the two kingdoms retained most of their traditional rights and privileges, and they continued to develop along their separate paths ruled by Czech and Hungarian nobilities; they were united only under the Habsburg monarch.

The Habsburgs destroyed the native Czech nobility after the mobility attempted to depose the Habsburgs in 1618 at the beginning of the Thirty Years War. The Czech lands became integral parts of the Habsburg possessions, the nobility was replaced with non-Czechs sympathetic to the Habsburgs, and the Czech language and culture was reduced to that of the peasantry. The Hungarians continued to retain their special privileges and protected their separate existence under the Habsburg ruler. Habsburg Emperor Joseph II attempted to make his empire stronger by consolidating the various kingdoms and provinces which, although unsuccessful, stimulated nationalism among the various peoples of the empire including the Czechs and Slovaks.

During the revolutions of 1848, the idea of a "Czechoslovakia" again arose. Several times various Czech leaders suggested a reorganization of the empire based along ethnic lines, including a Czechoslovak entity consisting of the Czech-speaking regions of Bohemia, Moravia, and Silesia, and the Slovak-speaking areas of Hungary. The authorities rejected the plans as too radical, while the Slovaks, distrustful of potential Czech domination under such plans, wanted to work for equal rights within the framework of the Hungarian state.

1914

June 28 Archduke Franz Ferdinand, the heir apparent of Austria-Hungary, and his wife are assassinated in Sarajevo, the capital of the Austro-Hungarian province of Bosnia.

July 28 As a result of the assassination of the archduke and, suspecting that Serbia had a part in it, Austria-Hungary declares war on Serbia. Soon all the major European powers become entangled in what develops into the First World War.

October 2 The French government grants "trustworthy" Czechs and Slovaks in France the same rights as those

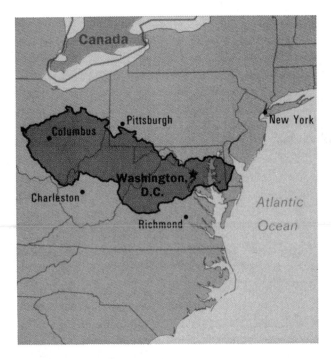

The former Czechoslovakia in relation to the size of the United States.

enjoyed by citizens from Allied nations living in France, thereby no longer considering them enemy aliens.

December 17 Tomáš G. Masaryk, a professor of philosophy at Charles University in Prague and a deputy in the Austrian parliament, leaves Austria-Hungary to work in Allied countries for the independence of the Czechs and Slovaks. He keeps in touch with the people and events back in the empire through an underground organization called the Maffia.

1915

July 6 In a speech marking the four hundredth anniversary of the burning at the stake of the Czech religious reformer and martyr Jan Hus by Roman Catholic authorities, Masaryk calls for the downfall of the Habsburg Monarchy and the creation of Czechoslovakia.

July 27 The Czech Action Committee Abroad is founded in Paris by Masaryk, Milan Rastislav Štefánik, Edvard Beneš, and Josef Dürich. The purpose of this ill-defined association is to disseminate propaganda among the Allies concerning the liberation movement. Štefánik and Beneš remain in Paris to handle the committee's affairs, while Masaryk goes to London and Dürich heads for Russia as

the organization's spokesmen. Beneš, a Czech, was a lecturer and writer on sociology and economics at Charles University in Prague before leaving Austria-Hungary. Dürich, another Czech, was also a writer and a politician, who represented the Old Czech and Agrarian parties in the Austrian parliament before going into exile. Štefánik, a Slovak, had left Hungary in his teens and earned a reputation as an explorer and astronomer while in the French service.

October 19 Great Britain no longer considers Czechs and Slovaks on its soil as enemy aliens.

October 22 Representatives of the Bohemian National Alliance and the Slovak League, claiming to speak on behalf of the Czech and Slovak communities in the United States, meet in Ohio and sign the Cleveland Agreement. This document becomes the first formal accord calling for the union of the Czechs and Slovaks in an independent federative state.

November 14 Representatives of Czech and Slovak organizations in the Allied countries of Great Britain, France, and Russia, as well as the United States, issue the Manifesto of the Czech Action Committee Abroad. This document highlights the reasons behind the drive for independence and the dismemberment of Austria-Hungary claiming that the Habsburgs had become dictators and have neglected the interests of the empire's people.

1916

January 13 The Družina, a military unit of Czechs and Slovaks in Russia, becomes a regiment. This unit of immigrants, led by Russian officers, was formed in September 1914 and was attached to the Russian army.

February 3 French Premier Astride Briand receives Tomáš G. Masaryk, leader of the Czech Action Committee Abroad. Briand, the first Allied leader to meet with Masaryk, listens to and sympathizes with Masaryk's plan for independence.

February 6 The loosely defined Czech Action Committee Abroad transforms itself into a more formal organization called the Czechoslovak National Council to facilitate its work for independence. The Council is a quasi government-in-exile, with Masaryk as president, Edvard Beneš as the general secretary, Josef Dürich as the vice president, and Milan Rastislav Štefánik as the representative for Slovakia.

April 17, 1916–January 4, 1917 The Russian government agrees to the formation of a Czechoslovak

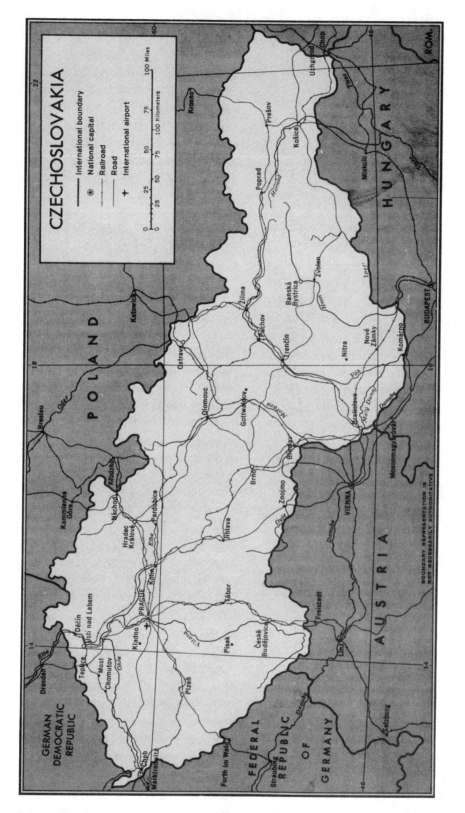

The former Czechoslovakia.

brigade in the Russian army consisting of former prisoners of war. Russian czar Nicholas II withdraws his approval but later agrees to the proposal.

1917

January 10 In their response to U.S. president Woodrow Wilson's December 16, 1916 note asking for a definition of war aims, the Allies demand as one of their conditions that the Czechs and Slovaks be set free from foreign domination.

March 12 The Russian legislature, the Duma, declares a provisional government. Three days later the czar abdicates.

March 23 During a press conference, Paul Miliukov, the Russian foreign minister of the provisional government, becomes the first Allied official to openly support an independent Czechoslovak state.

March 24 Miliukov confirms the regulations for the formation of a Czechoslovak brigade in Russia made up of former Czech and Slovak prisoners of war. However, the opposition of other provisional Russian governmental officials keeps the brigade from fully materializing.

April 6 The United States enters World War I.

May Masaryk travels to Russia and successfully negotiates with the provisional government for the organization of Czech and Slovak prisoners of war into an independent army known as the Czecho-Slovak Legion to fight the Central Powers of Germany, Austria-Hungary, Turkey and Bulgaria.

May 30 On the opening day of the Austrian parliament, the Czech representatives demand the union of the Czechs and Slovaks in a reorganized, federated Habsburg Empire of equal nationalities.

June 13 Due to the unstable conditions in Russia, Masaryk concludes an agreement with the French government for the transfer, via Vladivostok, of 30 thousand Czech and Slovak prisoners of war to France, where they can fight alongside the Allies.

Early July During the Brusilov Offensive near the small town of Zborov (Zborow), the Czecho-Slovak Legion performs bravely against the Austro-Hungarian army and is commended for its actions.

July 13 As a result of the Czecho-Slovak Legion's successes, the provisional Russian government allows the formation of an independent army made up of former Czech and Slovak prisoners of war.

August 18 The Russian branch of the Czechoslovak National Council issues a loan of 20 million French francs to support its army in Russia.

October 4 The Italian government allows the formation of a labor unit consisting of former Czech and Slovak prisoners of war.

November 6 The Bolsheviks, or Communists, seize power in Russia.

December 16 The French government permits the formation of a Czecho-Slovak Legion, an autonomous army unit in France under the authority of the French High Command but ''politically'' under the control of the Czechoslovak National Council. The unit is composed of Czechs and Slovaks already serving in the French army or volunteers from other countries.

1918

January 6 The Czech representatives in the Austrian parliament, the Czech members of the provincial diets, or legislatures, and leading Czech intellectuals and businessmen issue the Epiphany Declaration, demanding independence for the Czech Lands and Slovakia.

January 8 President Woodrow Wilson lists his Fourteen Points, a peace program calling for an end to World War I, to a joint session of the U.S. Congress. Article X states that the nationalities of Austria-Hungary should be free to develop autonomously in that country.

March 3 Communist Russia leaves the First World War by signing the Treaty of Brest-Litovsk with the Central Powers. With Russia out of the war, Masaryk holds successful talks with the Bolsheviks concerning the transfer of the Czecho-Slovak Legion to the western front via Siberia.

March 22 Fearing a potential threat to their position in Russia, the Soviets plan to stop and disarm the Czecho-Slovak Legion. The Legion is traveling eastward along the Trans-Siberian Railway to Vladivostok, where it will board ships to reenter the war on the Western Front.

May 1 In Liptovský Svätý Mikuláš the Slovak Social Democratic party issues a resolution that includes the right of self-determination for the Slovaks in Hungary.

May 24 Since it is still too dangerous to publicly demand the destruction of Hungary, a secret gathering of representatives of all Slovak political parties, except the socialists, meet in Turčiansky Svätý Martin and adopt the idea of an independent Czechoslovakia.

May 26 Fighting erupts between the Czecho-Slovak Legion and the Soviets after they attempt to disarm the Legion as it moves out.

May 30 Masaryk meets in Pittsburgh Pennsylvania, with representatives of the Bohemian National Alliance and the Slovak League, who want him to sign the Cleveland Agreement from October 1915. He deems it out of date and draws up another document, the Pittsburgh Pact, which assures autonomy for Slovakia in a Czechoslovakia.

June The ease with which the Czecho-Slovak Legion seizes the Trans-Siberian Railway convinces many that the Bolshevik government is weak, and helps cause the Russian Civil War and Allied intervention in Russia.

June 22 President Wilson alters Article X of the Fourteen Points, which now calls for the liberation of all Slavs from under Austro-Hungarian domination.

Summer The Allied powers recognize the Czechoslovak National Council as the future government of a Czechoslovakia. A Czechoslovak National Committee is formed in Prague, and shortly thereafter Slovak leaders establish a Slovak National Committee in Budapest.

October 18 In Washington D.C. Masaryk issues the Czechoslovak Declaration of Independence in an attempt to ward off efforts by the Habsburg ruler to keep his empire intact.

October 21 The Sudeten German regions of Bohemia, Moravia, and Silesia vote to join German Austria. Czechoslovak forces will occupy these areas almost without incident in late November.

October 28 Representatives of the Prague National Committee peacefully take control of Bohemia and Moravia, establish a provisional government, and proclaim the Czechoslovak republic.

October 30 Unaware of events in Prague, Slovak leaders meet in Turčiansky Svätý Martin and agree to join in a common state with the Czechs.

November 5 Under orders from the National Committee in Prague to establish a Czechoslovak presence in Slovakia, the Slovak Vavro Šrobár sets up a government in Skalica, in western Slovakia, where it controls a small amount of territory.

The Czechs and Poles in Těšín (Teschen, Cieszyn) divide this region of Silesia along ethnic lines, awaiting the final result of the impending peace conference that will assign boundaries. As a result Czechoslovakia loses many coal reserves and one of two railway lines that link Slovakia with the Czech Lands.

November 11 World War I ends.

November 13 A provisional constitution is adopted providing for the creation of a unicameral national legislature, the National Assembly. Other provisions include that the prime minister and other governmental leaders are to be elected by the National Assembly, and that the president, as head of state, has limited powers.

November 13–15 Hungarian troops reoccupy most of Slovakia, disband the organization formed by Slovak leaders in Turčiansky Svätý Martin, and force the Skalica government to flee to Moravia.

November 14 The National Assembly holds its first session and elects Tomáš G. Masaryk, who is still in the United States, as the first president of the Czechoslovak republic.

December 19 Father Andrej Hlinka establishes the Slovak People's, or L'udák, party to work for Slovak autonomy within Czechoslovakia as outlined in the Pittsburgh Pact from May 30, 1918. The party will be renamed in 1925 as the Hlinka Slovak People's party (HSL'S) to honor its founder.

The first president of Czechoslovakia, Tomáš Masaryk.

Under Allied pressure Hungary agrees to evacuate Slovakia, and by January 20, 1920, Czechoslovak forces take control of all of Slovakia.

December 20 President Masaryk returns to Prague from exile.

1919

January 18 The Paris Peace Conference, meeting to decide the peace settlement for World War I, admits Czechoslovak representatives as a victorious Allied state, represented by Karel Kramář and Edvard Beneš.

January 23 Czechoslovak troops occupy the Polish-held regions of Těšín with the intent of showing the Paris Peace Conference that this region is Czech before the meeting can decide on its fate. The Poles, fighting territorial disputes in the east and west, do little.

January 29 The Council of Ten—the main deliberating body of the Paris Peace Conference consisting of the presidents/prime ministers and foreign ministers of the five chief powers, the United States, Great Britain, France, Italy, and Japan—demands an explanation of the Těšín crisis from the Czech and Polish delegates.

January 31 The Supreme Allied Council—consisting of the leaders and representatives of the United States, France, Great Britain, and Italy at the Paris Peace Conference—appoints a commission to investigate the Těšín crisis.

February 1 The Council of Ten forces the Czech and Polish delegates to sign an agreement that ends the Těšín crisis by redividing the region along the lines drawn in 1918. This agreement will hold until the matter can be resolved by the conference.

The Slovak government formally takes office in Bratislava after Czechoslovak troops liberate the city at the end of January.

February 5 The Těšín crisis is temporarily resolved with Czechoslovak and Polish regions being defined.

February 25 Czechoslovakia enacts a currency reform that distinguishes Czechoslovak money from that of other successor states to the Habsburg Empire, stabilizing its finances and keeping the country from undergoing further inflation.

March 21 The Danube River is internationalized for commerce.

April 4 Great Britain, France, the United States, and Italy agree at the Paris Peace Conference to incorporate German areas in the Sudetenland along the borders of Bohemia and Moravia in Czechoslovakia, thereby putting a sizeable minority of Germans, numbering about three million, in the new state.

April 16 The government enacts the Land Expropriation Act, which introduces land reform by dividing up the great estates over 150 hectares (370 acres).

May 1–June 23 The Hungarian Red Army, under the Communist Béla Kun, invades Czechoslovakia, taking all of eastern and large sections of central Slovakia.

May 4 General Milan Rastislav Štefánik, the Slovak leader in the independence movement abroad, dies as a result of an airplane accident near Bratislava as he was returning from his wartime efforts to take up his position as minister of defense in the Czechoslovak government.

May 8 The leaders of Ruthenia agree to join Czechoslovakia as its eastern province.

May 25 With support from the Communist Hungarian regime, a Slovak Soviet Republic is established in Prešov. It quickly falls apart when the Hungarian Red Army leaves in mid-June.

June 6 The National Assembly, the parliament of Czechoslovakia, establishes the first Slovak institution of higher learning at Bratislava, Comenius University.

June 28 The Treaty of Versailles between the Allies and Germany recognizes the independence of Czechoslovakia.

July 8 The first Czechoslovak government, in office since October 1918 and led by the old politician Karel Kramář, resigns, and a new government headed by Vlastimil Tusar, the Social Democrat leader, takes control.

July 17 The government enacts a child labor law to protect children from being exploited by businesses.

August 27 Andrej Hlinka and several other Slovaks leave for the Paris Peace Conference where they will unsuccessfully submit a memorandum requesting Slovak autonomy, guaranteed by the Allies, in Czechoslovakia. Hlinka will be arrested for his actions in October, but released in the spring of 1920 without going to trial.

September 10 The Treaty of St. Germain between the Allies and Austria recognizes Czechoslovakia as an independent state. The treaty also grants landlocked Czechoslovakia duty-free commercial zones in the ports of Hamburg and Stettin for 99 years. Czechoslovakia also signs two other treaties with the Allies: the first providing for equal rights and protection for ethnic minorities in Czechoslovakia under the protection of the League of Nations, and the second calling for Czechoslovakia to pay a portion of the former Austro-Hungarian debt as a successor state.

December 12   The government passes a law requiring all foreign owned companies in Czechoslovakia to establish headquarters in the country with the purpose of keeping the nation from foreign economic domination.

1920

January 10   Czechoslovakia becomes a founding member of the League of Nations, an international organization created to preserve peace in the world and to settle disputes through negotiations rather than war.

February 19   Poland and Czechoslovakia sign an armistice concerning Těšín.

February 29   The National Assembly adopts a six-part, democratic constitution based on the American and French models, with a president as the chief of state of the republic. Provisions of the constitution provide for a bicameral legislature, the National Assembly, which includes a Chamber of Deputies, or lower house, numbering 300 persons elected to six-year terms, and the Senate, or upper house, consisting of 150 people chosen for eight years. Both houses are elected by direct, secret ballot by universal suffrage (voting rights), and the president of the country is elected every seven years by a joint session of the National Assembly. The government is responsible for its actions to the Chamber of Deputies. The president, with the consent of the National Assembly, may declare war, and he appoints all higher officials. The constitution guarantees freedom of the press and speech, with the right to vote for all citizens over 21 years of age, with anyone over the age of 30 eligible to run for elected office. Furthermore, it allows for an independent judiciary and for the protection of ethnic and religious minorities. With its adoption, the provisional National Assembly will dissolve on April 15, to allow for elections to a new National Assembly as outlined in the new constitution.

March 7–11   Conflict erupts again with the Poles over Těšín.

April 14   The government passes a law authorizing a national bank.

April 18   First elections for the lower house of the National Assembly are held, with approximately eight million out of 14 million people voting for 23 political parties. The elections for the Senate will be held seven days later.

May 18   A riot breaks out in the town of Těšín.

May 21   Polish miners in the Karvin district of Těšín strike.

May 25   Prime Minister Tusar forms a new government based upon the results from the April elections.

May 27   In its opening session, the new National Assembly reelects Masaryk as president of the republic.

June 4   The Treaty of Trianon between the Allies and Hungary recognizes Czechoslovakia and its incorporation of the former Hungarian areas of Slovakia and Ruthenia.

June 28   Czechoslovakia and Poland sign another armistice in Paris regarding the disputed region of Těšín.

July 28   The Conference of Ambassadors, which succeeds the Council of Ten—consisting of a French delegate and the ambassadors to France from the United States, Great Britain, Italy, and Japan—at the Paris Peace Conference announces its findings and establishes the border between Poland and Czechoslovakia in the disputed regions of Těšín, Orava, and Spiš.

August 10   The New States Treaty of the Allies recognizes the independence and the borders of Czechoslovakia, Poland, and Romania.

August 14   Czechoslovakia and Yugoslavia form a mutual defensive alliance against Hungary by pledging to uphold the Treaty of Trianon. This marks the beginnings of the Little Entente (*see* April 23 and June 7, 1921).

August 17   Romania unofficially joins the Czechoslovak-Yugoslav alliance.

September 14   The Tusar government falls, and on the following day Jan Černý, the provincial leader of Moravia, forms a new non-party cabinet.

October 28–November 16   Troops are called in to quiet Czech-German violence in Prague and several other areas of Bohemia.

December   Workers strike and riot as a result of problems and the subsequent split between the left and right wings of the Social Democratic party. The government intervenes forcefully, ending the strikes by December 15; however, their actions result in the deaths of over 11 people and the arrest of over three thousand others.

1921

February 15   The first official census of Czechoslovakia lists a total population of 13,613,172 persons, including 6,670,582 in Bohemia, 2,622,884 in Moravia, 672,268 in Silesia, 3,000,870 in Slovakia, and 606,568 in Ruthenia. The census divides the population ethnically into 8,760,937

Czechoslovaks, 3,123,568 Germans, 745,431 Magyars or Hungarians, 461,879 Ruthenians or Rusyns, 180,855 Jews, and 75,853 Poles.

March 10   Austria and Czechoslovakia sign an agreement establishing a definitive common boundary.

April 23   In response to ex-Emperor Charles's attempt to return to the Hungarian throne, Czechoslovakia and Romania form an alliance to uphold the Treaty of Trianon and to render mutual military aid in case of unprovoked attack by a third country, meaning Hungary.

May 14–16   The Communist Party of Czechoslovakia (KSČ) is formed.

June 7   With the signing of a Romanian-Yugoslav alliance, the Little Entente is officially formed (*see* August 14, 17, 1920).

July 1   Rationing and price controls established by Austria-Hungary during the First World War are lifted.

August 12   The government enacts a law providing for unemployment compensation benefits, which will not become effective until 1925 after funds are built up to support the program.

September 26   The Černý government falls, and Edvard Beneš, the foreign minister, is appointed by Masaryk as the new prime minister; Beneš then forms a new government.

October 27   Czechoslovakia and Yugoslavia begin mobilization over the second return and attempted restoration of the last Habsburg Emperor Karl (Charles) to the throne of Hungary. His earlier try failed in April 1921.

November 6   Czechoslovakia and Poland sign an agreement ending their bitter relations over the Těšín issue.

1922

January   The Chamber of Deputies, the lower house of the National Assembly, passes a law forbidding the sale of alcoholic beverages to anyone under age 16, with spirits being reserved for those older than 18.

Monsignor Andrej Hlinka, leader of the Slovak People's party, unsuccessfully introduces a bill into the National Assembly that would allow for Slovak autonomy based upon the Pittsburgh Pact from May 30, 1918.

February   President Masaryk issues a general amnesty that sets free the people arrested in connection with the December 1920 strikes and riots.

Airline passenger service is established between Prague, Vienna, and Bratislava.

February 2–10   Coal miners strike over a proposed 25 percent wage cut. The strike is settled by a compromise over the wage issue.

February 4   Poland and Czechoslovakia sign an agreement settling their border disputes as delineated in July 1920.

August 31   Czechoslovakia and Yugoslavia sign a 5-year alliance at Mariánské Lázně (Marienbad), allowing the two countries to work jointly in foreign affairs on matters concerning their common interests, thereby strengthening the Little Entente.

October 7   Edvard Beneš resigns as prime minister and retakes his former position as foreign minister in the government of his successor Antonín Švehla, leader of the Agrarian party.

October 20   Czechoslovakia and Poland sign a commercial agreement to ease the flow of goods between their countries.

October 28   Czechoslovakia and Hungary agree on a common boundary.

1923

January 5   Alois Rašín, the minister of finance and the author of many of Czechoslovakia's successful economic reforms, is shot and dies in February from his wounds.

May   A commercial airline company begins regular flights, carrying passengers, mail, and cargo between Prague, Warsaw, Paris, and Istanbul.

May 5   A Czechoslovak commission leaves for the United States to work out arrangements for the repayment of approximately $106 million owed to the United States for aid granted during the First World War.

May 7   Czechoslovakia and Romania sign a three-year defensive military treaty.

June 7   An alleged Hungarian spy ring is discovered in Bratislava and reportedly two hundred people are arrested.

Late June   The Slovak People's party demands that the country be renamed Czecho-Slovakia. The government refuses and keeps the unhyphenated name of Czechoslovakia.

Late August   The Austro-Czechoslovak Boundary Commission finishes its work by placing some five thousand border-stone markers between the two countries.

October 28   In conjunction with the fifth anniversary of the founding of the republic, President Masaryk makes official visits to Paris, Brussels, and London.

1924

January 25 France and Czechoslovakia sign an alliance and friendship treaty that provides no definite military commitments, but it does allow for common action for the maintenance of Austrian independence and against any attempted Habsburg restorations. The treaty also calls for mutual consultations on issues that threaten the postwar peace settlements and for safeguarding common interests in case they are threatened.

March 16 First-time elections for eight deputies to the National Assembly are held in Ruthenia.

April 8 The newly elected deputies from Ruthenia take their oaths of office in a variety of languages: three in Ukrainian or Rusyn, two in Magyar, and one each respectively in Czech, Slovak, and Russian, emphasizing the fact that Czechoslovakia is indeed a multiethnic state.

May 19 During a state visit to Italy, President Masaryk signs a treaty of friendship and alliance, which allows for much the same terms as the Franco-Czechoslovak accord of January 25, 1924.

July 5 Italy and Czechoslovakia sign a treaty of friendship.

October 30 The National Assembly passes old age and further workmen's compensation insurance laws, which will become effective in 1926 after funds build up to support the programs (*see* July 1, 1926).

1925

April 23 Czechoslovakia and Poland sign a treaty calling for the peaceful resolution of all mutual disputes except those involving territory.

July 5 President Masaryk and most of the government leaders officially attend a rally commemorating the burning of Jan Hus, an early Czech religious reformer, at the stake in 1415. In the next few days, as a result of this celebration, the Vatican recalls its representative from Prague, and Czechoslovakia breaks off relations with the Holy See.

August 12 The government nationalizes the spa at Mariánské Lázně (Marienbad) hitherto owned by the Roman Catholic church.

October 5–16 The Locarno Conference results in an agreement that includes an arbitration treaty between Czechoslovakia and Germany in which the two countries agree to settle differences peacefully, and a mutual guarantee between Czechoslovakia, France, and Poland, in case of aggression by Germany.

October 9 Czechoslovakia and the United States agree on a plan to repay the Czechoslovak debt to the United States. The estimated $185 million debt, including interest, is to be repaid in 62 years. However, Czechoslovakia will only pay about $20,000 of the entire loan.

November 15 and 22 General elections for the National Assembly are held.

December 9 As a result of the November general elections, Antonín Švehla, the Agrarian leader, forms his second government based upon a coalition of political parties.

1926

February 8 The Czechoslovak government officially recognizes the Soviet Union.

March 5 Edvard Beneš, the foreign minister, signs a 10-year arbitration agreement in Vienna with Austria, which calls for mandatory arbitration on every difference between the two countries, with the right of appeal to the World Court in The Hague.

March 17 The Švehla government resigns due to problems among the various members of the coalition.

March 18 Jan Černý again accepts the position of prime minister and once again forms a non-party government.

March 30–31 The Austrian chancellor, Dr. Rudolf Ramek, officially visits Prague, returning the earlier March visit of Edvard Beneš to Vienna, marking the rapprochement of the two countries.

April 1 The Czechoslovak National Bank opens.

May 28 Nine thousand Slovak Ľudáks, or members of the Slovak People's party, attend a meeting in Hronský Svätý Beňadik where they pledge their lives to work for their the preservation of Slovak autonomy and the Roman Catholic faith.

June 13 Czechoslovakia, Romania, and Yugoslavia renew the Little Entente treaties.

July 1 The social security program goes into effect providing for old age pensions and workmen's compensation (*see* October 30, 1924).

July 2 After months of rumors of an attempted coup d'etat by fascists led by the chief of staff of the Czechoslovakian army, General Rudolf Gajda, he is relieved of his command and retires from the military for a career in politics as the leader of the National Fascist Community, a Czech political party.

October 12   The Černý government resigns; Antonín Švehla forms his third government, with the first-time support of the Sudeten Germans and representatives of the Slovak People's party, who join the cabinet.

1927

May 27   A joint session of the National Assembly reelects Tomáš G. Masaryk as president for a second term of seven years. His only opposition comes from a Communist candidate who receives very few votes.

July 1   The government passes an administrative reform bill that legally divides the country into four provinces: Bohemia, Moravia, Slovakia, and Ruthenia or Carpatho-Russia.

1928

January 20   Czechoslovakia and the Vatican end their feud from July 1925, after the Vatican agrees to change the Catholic church administrative boundaries to correspond with those of Czechoslovakia, thereby removing sections of the country that had been under the jurisdiction of foreign bishops.

July 4   A statue of Woodrow Wilson is unveiled in Prague with the American ambassador in attendance.

July 16   Czechoslovakia and the United States sign a naturalization agreement that recognizes the new citizenship of their former nationals and releases them from their former allegiances and duties.

August 27   Czechoslovakia signs the Paris Anti-War Pact, or Kellogg-Briand Pact, which renounces war as an instrument of national policy.

October 28   The 10th anniversary of the founding of the republic is greeted with much fanfare and celebration throughout the country.

December 2   General elections signal a victory for Prime Minister Švehla and his Agrarian party.

December 20   The Slovak parliamentary deputy, a member of the Slovak People's party and an advocate of Hungarian revisionist propaganda, Professor Vojtech Tuka, loses his parliamentary immunity. He is arrested in early January 1929 on charges of treason and Hungarian irredentist agitation. His arrest causes ill feelings in Slovakia.

1929

February 1   Švehla resigns because of ill health, and his minister of war, František Udržal, succeeds him without changing the cabinet.

February 20   Foreign Minister Edvard Beneš declares that the country will not pay the amount awarded to the Habsburg Archduke Frederick by the Arbitral Tribunal at The Hague in compensation for lands confiscated by the Czechoslovak government. Beneš furthermore states that Czechoslovakia would no longer permit any non-Czechoslovak court to decide similar cases.

February 26   The Czechoslovak government refuses the exiled Russian Bolshevik leader Leon Trotsky's request to settle in the country.

May 21   Czechoslovakia, Romania, and Yugoslavia renew the treaties of the Little Entente, adding a further agreement to settle peacefully all disputes between the three countries.

Early July   Relations between Czechoslovakia and Hungary become strained after the Hungarian authorities arrest a Czechoslovak railway worker on charges of espionage. In reprisal the Czechoslovaks close the Budapest-Košice railway, which reopens on July 24 even though the Hungarians continue to detain the worker.

September 25   Premier Udržal dissolves the National Assembly due to problems between the Czech parties in his cabinet and threats of the Slovak People's party to withdraw from his coalition if Tuka is found guilty (*see* December 20, 1928). Udržal calls for general elections on October 27.

October 5   After several months the trial of Professor Vojtech Tuka ends with his conviction for spying and treason and for aiding and abetting Hungarian irredentists who want to seize Slovakia. He receives a 15-year prison sentence, and the Slovak People's party members of the Udržal government resign.

October 27   Approximately 90 percent of the eligible population votes in the third general elections, which result in no one majority party. Attempts are made to form a government through early December.

November 7   Czechoslovakia joins the gold standard by backing its currency, the koruna (Kčs), or crown, with gold.

December 7   Udržal, remaining as prime minister, forms a new government consisting of 12 Czechs, two Slovaks, and two Germans.

1930

March 7 On the occasion of President Masaryk's 80th birthday, the National Assembly grants him a special 20 million crown (Kčs) fund to aid philanthropic causes.

March 9 A letter from President Masaryk to Father Andrej Hlinka, leader of the Slovak People's party, is made public, in which Masaryk scolds Hlinka for intransigence in the government.

April The court of appeals confirms the prison sentence of Professor Tuka (*see* October 5, 1929).

May 8 The Slovak People's party deputies in the National Assembly unsuccessfully attempt to reintroduce legislation granting autonomy to Slovakia.

May 14 Bulgaria and Czechoslovakia sign a treaty of friendship and nonaggression.

August 18 Some 150,000 acres of land pass from the Prince of Liechtenstein, who is also the largest landowner in Czechoslovakia, to the government for redistribution.

Late September President Masaryk states in an interview that he is not opposed to border revisions, which members of the government quickly renounce.

October 2 The National Assembly officially repudiates any ideas regarding Masaryk's earlier statement on border revisions.

December 2 The government takes a new census. The population of Czechoslovakia consists of 14,726,158 persons divided in the following categories: 7,345,137 Czechoslovaks, 3,088,530 Germans, 119,469 Magyars, 458,094 Rusyns, 120,277 Jews, and 80,182 Poles; with 238,808 resident aliens. The Germans and Magyars (the dominant people of Hungary) charge enumeration fraud, claiming they are being undercounted.

1931

March 21 Czechoslovakia, France, and Italy protest the announced Austro-German customs union. The World Court rejects the union after the question of the customs union is referred to it later in May.

May 3–5 The Little Entente holds a conference in Bucharest at which the major topic revolves around the proposed Austro-German customs union announced in March.

1932

February 11 A new banking bill is passed placing greater safeguards on deposits by requiring a bank director to make good any losses of deposits caused by any fault on his part, and also to guarantee the deposits to the extent of one-fourth of 1 percent of the bank's total capital or 50,000 Kčs, whichever is higher.

March The government dissolves the Sudeten German fascist organization Volksport on the charge it has become a paramilitary group and a threat to the safety of the republic.

May 9 The Little Entente treaties are renewed.

June 25–26 Slovak political leaders and intellectuals gather at Trenčianske Teplice to discuss Slovakia's precarious social and economic conditions made even worse by the worldwide depression.

July 12 Tomáš Baťa, a Czech shoe manufacturer and the leading Czechoslovak industrialist, dies in an airplane accident.

August The government tries seven German youths in Brno on charges of conspiracy against the republic.

October 16 The Slovak members of the Czechoslovak National Democrat party break off to form their own party, which agrees to work with the Slovak People's party for autonomy for Slovakia.

October 24 The Udržal government resigns due to the illness of the prime minister. Jan Malypetr, speaker of the lower house of the National Assembly, forms a new government with only three changes in governmental ministers.

1933

January 21–22 In an unsuccessful coup d'état, a small group of Czech fascists attack an army base in Brno.

February 16 The Little Entente of Czechoslovakia, Romania, and Yugoslavia meet in Geneva and reorganize the alliance with a permanent council to harmonize economic relations and to devise a unified foreign policy in the wake of Nazi successes in Germany.

April 19 Citing the rise of Nazism, the government prohibits the publication of Nazi speeches broadcast from Germany to all except the owners of radio sets who can receive the speeches directly over the air.

May 8 The government bans 334 newspapers for spreading Nazi propaganda.

June 6 In response to the worldwide depression, the National Assembly grants the government wider powers to regulate the stalled economy.

June 20 In London the members of the Little Entente discuss plans for a Danubian customs union.

July 4 The members of the Little Entente sign a nonaggression pact with the Soviet Union.

July 10 The National Assembly passes a law calling for the suspension or suppression of the newspapers that advocated subversive measures against the republic; it is aimed primarily at the Sudeten Germans.

September 25 With the Czechoslovak Foreign Minister Edvard Beneš in attendance, a diplomatic meeting of the Little Entente is held in Sinaia, Romania, where relations with Poland, a proposed Danubian customs union, and general solidarity are discussed.

October 2 Konrad Henlein, a gymnastic instructor and the leader of the Nazi Sudetenland Germans, calls for a single German political party in Czechoslovakia under his leadership.

October 4 The government abolishes the German National Socialist and German Nationalist parties by decree because of Nazi tendencies.

October 25 The National Assembly enacts a law aimed at the Sudeten Germans allowing for the suspension of subversive political parties.

1934

January 9 With Beneš as chair, the economic council of the Little Entente adopts resolutions intending to keep 50 percent of their 1934 foreign trade among themselves.

February 10 In an attempt to stimulate exports, the government suggests the devaluation of the currency, the koruna (Kčs), by 16.66 percent. The National Democrats oppose the move and leave the Malypetr government, causing its collapse.

February 14 Prime Minister Malypetr forms his second cabinet.

February 17 In response to the worldwide depression, Czechoslovakia devalues its currency, the koruna, by one-sixth in order to compete in the world market with nations off the gold standard.

March 16–17 Austria, Italy, and Hungary sign the Rome Protocols in which the three countries agree to cooperate in foreign affairs. The agreements are aimed

against the Little Entente of Czechoslovakia, Romania, and Yugoslavia.

May 24 Despite poor health, the 84-year-old Tomáš G. Masaryk is reelected president for a third time by a joint session of the National Assembly. The Czech Communist Klement Gottwald, Masaryk's only opponent, receives a small number of votes.

June 9 Czechoslovakia opens diplomatic relations with the Soviet Union.

November 24–26 Serious clashes occur between Czech and German students at the University of Prague, a dual Czech and German institution, after the government orders the German university to hand over its insignia to the Czech university.

1935

May 16 Czechoslovakia and the Soviet Union sign a mutual assistance pact, which provides aid in case of unprovoked attack provided France honors its obligation to its mutual assistance treaties with the Soviet Union from May 2 and with Czechoslovakia from 1925.

May 19 The Sudeten German party, a Nazi front organization led by Konrad Henlein, becomes the strongest German party in the fourth national elections by winning 66 percent of the German vote. As a result, it places 44 deputies and 23 senators in the National Assembly.

June 6 As a result of the national general elections, Prime Minister Malypetr forms his third government.

November 5 Milan Hodža, the Slovak leader of the Agrarian party, becomes the first Slovak prime minister of the country and forms a new government when Malypetr takes the position of the Speaker of the Chamber of Deputies of the National Assembly.

December 14 After announcing his decision in November, Masaryk resigns as president due to age and poor health. He supports his protege, Foreign Minister Edvard Beneš, as his successor.

December 18 Beneš is overwhelmingly elected over another candidate by the National Assembly as Czechoslovakia's second president.

1936

March 10 An Austro-Czechoslovak trade agreement is signed.

Czechoslovak statesman Edvard Beneš.

September 10 Germany accuses Czechoslovakia of harboring Soviet aircraft.

1937

September 14 Tomáš G. Masaryk, the "liberator-president" of Czechoslovakia, dies at the age of 87.

September 21 At the state funeral for Masaryk, President Beneš delivers the eulogy reconfirming Masaryk's ideals of democracy.

October 17 Riots break out in the Sudetenland between Czechs and Germans.

November 29 Sudeten German deputies walk out of the parliament following a governmental ban on political meetings in the Sudetenland.

1938

March 12 The Anschluss, or Germany's incorporation of Austria, takes place almost engulfing Czechoslovakia

on three sides. After this event, fearing the growing power of Nazi Germany, several independent Sudeten German political parties merge with the Nazi Sudeten German party.

March 28 Konrad Henlein, leader of the Nazi Sudeten German party, meets with Adolf Hitler, the chancellor of Germany, and the two agree on the destruction of Czechoslovakia with the Sudeten Germans acting as obstructionists in talks with the Czechoslovak government.

April 23–24 Henlein demands full autonomy for the Germans in the Sudetenland and proposes that Czechoslovakia become a confederation of nationalities.

May 19–20 Rumors spread that German troops are going to occupy the Sudetenland. Czechoslovakia responds by ordering partial mobilization of its military; France and Great Britain support Czechoslovakia in its action, but they realize that such moves could lead to war with Germany, which neither wants to fight. As a result, Britain and France urge the Czechoslovak government to be more conciliatory in negotiations with the Sudeten Germans.

May 30 Hitler signs a secret order calling for war against Czechoslovakia by October 1.

Late May–early June The Slovak People's party commemorates the twentieth anniversary of the signing of the Pittsburgh Pact on May 30, 1918, which called for autonomy for Slovakia, with rallies and by displaying the original document brought to Slovakia by American-Slovaks.

July 25 The British government's fact-finding mission on the Sudeten problem, led by Lord Walter Runciman, goes to Prague where it reports in early August in favor of Sudeten Germans' and Germany's demands for autonomy in the Sudetenland.

August 16 Monsignor Andrej Hlinka, leader of the Slovak People's party, dies at the age of seventy-four. Monsignor Jozef Tiso, leader of the moderate L'udáks, succeeds Hlinka to become party chairman on August 31.

August 19 The Slovak People's party unsuccessfully attempts for the third time to introduce legislation for Slovak autonomy in the National Assembly.

August 23 Signaling the end of the alliance between Czechoslovakia, Romania, and Yugoslavia, the Little Entente recognizes Hungary's right to rearm realizing they are powerless to stop Hungary, which now has close ties to Nazi Germany.

September 7 Czechs and Sudeten Germans clash in Moravská Ostrava, allowing the Sudeten German negotiators to use this event as an excuse to break off talks with the government. Sporadic violence and fighting erupts in the Sudetenland over the next few days.

September 15   As a result of the fighting between Czechs and Germans, British Prime Minister Neville Chamberlain meets with Adolf Hitler at Berchtesgaden to discuss the Sudeten problem. Hitler states he is determined to annex the Sudetenland on the principle of self-determination.

September 19   The British and French propose solutions to the Sudeten problem by urging the Czechoslovaks to hand over those areas of the Sudetenland with a majority of Germans to Germany; Czechoslovakia rejects this plan on the following day.

September 21   The British and French demand that Czechoslovakia unconditionally accept their suggestions from September 19. The Czechoslovak government debates the issue and decides that if it were to resist it would mean an invasion and the end of Czechoslovakia. It agrees to the British and French terms on the condition that the two countries guarantee the integrity of a rump Czechoslovakia (the area remaining after the Sudetenland is turned over to Germany). Spontaneous demonstrations against the decision take place throughout the country.

Taking advantage of Czechoslovakia's isolation during the Sudetenland crisis, Poland demands that the Czechs cede the Těšín region to the Poles.

September 22   The government of Prime Minister Hodža resigns over the unpopular decision to capitulate in the Sudetenland crisis. A nonparty government is formed by General Jan Syrový, the inspector general of the army, who orders general military mobilization on September 23.

September 22–23   British Prime Minister Chamberlain again meets with Hitler regarding the crisis in Czechoslovakia, but the two disagree on what steps to follow.

September 26   In a fiery speech Hitler demands that the Sudetenland be given to Germany immediately or war will result on October 1.

September 29   In order to end the possibility of war breaking out on October 1, the Munich Conference takes place between Chamberlain, Hitler, Premier Edouard Daladier of France, and Benito Mussolini, the dictator of Italy. They grant Germany the Sudetenland and other border regions of Bohemia and Moravia with a majority of Germans. Furthermore, the four leaders agree to guarantee the remaining territory, or the rump state of Czechoslovakia; no representatives from Czechoslovakia are invited to the meeting.

September 30   The four-power Munich Agreement is presented to the Czechoslovak government. Not wishing to

fight alone against the Germans if it rejects the document, the government accepts it.

October   The radical members of the L'udák, or Slovak People's party (HSL'S), establish the Hlinka Guards, a paramilitary group based on Italian fascist and Nazi models. The Guard is anti-Czech, anti-Semitic, and pro-German.

October 1   Czechoslovakia accepts the Polish ultimatum to cede Těšín and begins its evacuation the next day.

October 1–10   German troops occupy the Sudetenland, which contains Czechoslovakia's most modern defenses. As a result, Bohemia and Moravia lose about 38 percent of their territory and 34 percent of their total population.

October 5   Edvard Beneš resigns as president of the republic and goes into exile in Great Britain.

October 6   Due to the weakness of the central government after the Munich Agreement, the leaders of the People's party and several other Slovak political parties meet in Žilina, demand autonomy, and present their program to the Syrový government, which agrees to it on the same day. Slovakia receives autonomy, which becomes official on November 23 when the national legislature approves it, thereby making Czechoslovakia a federal republic. Czechoslovakia officially becomes Czecho-Slovakia. Monsignor Jozef Tiso, the chairman of the L'udák party (HSL'S), becomes prime minister of Slovakia. Tiso, a moderate L'udák, wants gradual independence from the Czech Lands.

October 11   Prague grants autonomy to Ruthenia, which takes the name of Carpathian Ukraine.

October 21   Under pressure from Germany, Czechoslovakia terminates its pact with the Soviet Union from May 1935. Despite the Munich Agreement, Hitler secretly tells his military to be ready at any time for the destruction of the remainder of Czechoslovakia.

November 2   The Vienna Award grants lands of Czechoslovakia with majorities of Hungarians to Hungary; Slovakia and Ruthenia lose approximately 5,000 square miles and a population of 1,040,000; including 592,000 Magyars, 290,000 Slovaks, 37,000 Ruthenes, and 14,000 Germans. In another agreement, Poland receives two small border regions of northern Slovakia. The two countries occupy these regions over the next few days.

November 8   The L'udák party becomes the only legal political party in Slovakia; all others are suppressed.

November 30   Dr. Emil Hácha, a respected judge, is elected president of the rump Czechoslovak state, and the Syrový government resigns.

Nazi troops parade through the occupied Sudetenland.

December 1 Rudolf Beran, leader of the Agrarian party, forms a new government.

December 25 Czechoslovakia's greatest writer, Karel Čapek, the author of *R.U.R* and *War with the Newts,* dies at the age of 48.

December 27 After the government bans its activities in October, the Communist Party of Czechoslovakia dissolves. A month earlier, the chairman, Klement Gottwald, and other leaders of the party began to leave for exile in the Soviet Union.

1939

January Wanting to destroy the remainder of Czechoslovakia, Hitler orders German intelligence to urge Slovak extremists to declare the independence of Slovakia in mid-March.

January 18 The Slovak parliament opens.

February 12 Hitler receives Professor Vojtech Tuka, the leader of the radical wing of the L'udák party that demands immediate Slovak independence. In their conversations, Hitler hints at the imminent destruction of Czechoslovakia.

March 7 The Nazi governor of Austria, Artur Seyss-Inquart, arrives in Bratislava to discuss with Tiso and other Slovak leaders the need for proclaiming independence for Slovakia.

March 10 Due to German intrigues, leaders in Prague dismiss the government of Monsignor Jozef Tiso in Slovakia, reinforces the police in Bratislava, and occupies all public buildings in Slovakia with troops. Professor Tuka and other radical members of the L'udák party are arrested, while Radio Vienna calls for a Slovak uprising.

March 11 Karol Sidor, a moderate L'udák and member of the central government in Prague, replaces Monsignor Tiso as prime minister of Slovakia.

March 12 Special envoys sent by Hitler arrive in Bratislava. They urge Sidor to proclaim independence, which he refuses. They meet next with Monsignor Tiso and invite him to speak with Hitler in Berlin. Hitler gives the final orders for the invasion of Bohemia and Moravia on March 15.

March 13 Hitler tells Monsignor Tiso that the time for independence has arrived, and if the Slovaks want it, they must act immediately. If they do so, Hitler will guarantee Slovak independence; if not, he will let events take their course, meaning a partition between Hungary, Germany, and Poland. Monsignor Tiso calls for a special meeting of the Slovak parliament on the following day to deal with the matter.

March 14 Slovakia proclaims its independence. Sidor resigns and Tiso becomes the prime minister. Eventually 27 countries, including France, Great Britain, and the USSR, will recognize independent Slovakia.

Hungary occupies Ruthenia with German approval. The Ruthenian government unsuccessfully attempts to halt the occupation by proclaiming independence and placing the province under German protection.

With the eastern provinces no longer in existence, President Hácha leaves Prague for a meeting with Hitler to discuss the situation.

March 15 In a three-hour early morning confrontation, Hitler tells Hácha that he ordered German troops to occupy the Czech Lands of Bohemia and Moravia. Threatened with the air destruction of Prague if the Czechoslovak army puts up a struggle, Hácha orders his army not to resist. German troops march into Bohemia and Moravia, and Hitler arrives triumphantly in Prague. German troops occupy the western portion of the Slovak republic.

March 16 Hitler declares Bohemia and Moravia as protectorates and integral parts of the German Reich, with Dr. Emil Hácha remaining as president of the protectorates.

While in Chicago, Edvard Beneš denounces the destruction of Czechoslovakia and sends notes of protest to the governments of Great Britain, France, the Soviet Union, and the United States.

March 17–18 Great Britain, France, the Soviet Union, and the United States send official notes to the German government announcing that they refuse to accept the destruction of Czechoslovakia.

March 18 Hitler appoints Baron Konstantin von Neurath, a moderate former German foreign minister, as Reich protector of Bohemia and Moravia, the chief political position of the protectorates, who will take control of the government on April 16. Until then Bohemia and Moravia are ruled by martial law. To financially exploit the protectorates, the government establishes an exchange rate of one reichsmark to ten Czechoslovak korunas (Kčs), which is half the going exchange rate prior to March 15, 1939.

March 19 The German army, showing its strength, holds a parade in St. Wenceslas Square in Prague.

March 20 The United States recalls its ambassador from Germany to protest the destruction of Czechoslovakia.

March 21 The official languages of Bohemia and Moravia become German and Czech. President Hácha dissolves the parliament of former Czechoslovakia and in its place sets up a national council. Hácha also forbids the activity of all hitherto legal political parties, replacing them with a front organization called the National Assemblage. Both the National Council and the National Assemblage serve under the "good will" of the protectorate government.

March 23 The Slovak Republic signs a protection treaty and an economic agreement with Germany, making Slovakia a puppet state of the Third Reich.

May The Soviets instruct the Slovak Communists to form the Slovak Communist party (KSS).

June 21 A decree forbids the Jews of Bohemia and Moravia to dispose of or to purchase land.

August 21 On the 508th anniversary of the defeat at Domažlice of German crusaders by the Hussites, early Czech religious reformers, the citizens of Prague express their nationalism by boycotting the streetcars.

September 1 World War II begins with the German invasion of Poland. Units of the Slovak Republic also take part despite widespread opposition, and for their action, Slovakia receives land it lost to Poland in July 1920 and November 1938.

September 5 The Slovak government requires all male Slovaks between the ages of six and 60 to join either the Hlinka Youth or some organization of the Hlinka Guard.

September 15 Showing their displeasure for Slovakia's part in the invasion of Poland, about 3,500 Slovak soldiers refuse to follow orders to take part in the German attack on Poland.

September 30 On the first anniversary of the Munich Agreement, the people of Prague again boycott streetcars as an expression of nationalism.

October 2 France allows the formation of a Czechoslovak army on its territory.

October 26 Monsignor Jozef Tiso is elected the president of Slovakia.

October 28 On the 21st anniversary of the independence of Czechoslovakia, the Czechs in Prague tear down street signs written in Czech and German, heckle German officials, and demonstrate. The police open fire on the crowds, killing one student and wounding another who dies on November 12.

November 2 The pro-Nazi Professor Vojtech Tuka becomes the prime minister of Slovakia.

November 14 France recognizes the Czechoslovak National Committee, an exile organization in London headed by Beneš, as the official voice for Czechoslovakia.

November 16–17 As the result of some minor nationalistic manifestations by students after the funeral of the student seriously wounded in the October 28 demonstrations, the Nazi authorities occupy four student dormitories and arrest approximately 1,800 Czech students and teachers; nine student leaders are immediately shot.

November 17 Using the charge of subversion, Hitler orders the closing of all Czech universities and colleges for three years. They will not reopen until after the end of the German occupation in 1945.

December 20 Great Britain, following France's lead from November 14, also recognizes the Czechoslovak National Committee as the spokesman for Czechoslovak affairs.

1940

January 30 Slovakia signs a treaty that allows the Germans to control its entire weapons industry.

February 24 Prime Minister Neville Chamberlain states that both Polish and Czechoslovak independence will be restored after the war.

July 21 Great Britain recognizes the Czechoslovak National Committee in London as the provisional government, or government-in-exile, of Czechoslovakia, thereby upgrading its status diplomatically and politically to other countries, with Edvard Beneš as president and Jan Masaryk, son of Tomáš G. Masaryk, as foreign minister.

July 28 In a meeting with Slovak leaders in Salzburg, Hitler reorganizes the Slovak government. The moderate Monsignor Tiso remains as president, but the pro-German faction receives many important positions.

July 30 Professor Tuka, the pro-German Slovak prime minister and after July 28 also the Slovak foreign minister, declares the beginning of Slovak National Socialism in an attempt to turn Slovakia into a copy of Nazi Germany.

August Slovakia agrees to the German demand that it "resettle" its Jewish population in Nazi-occupied Poland.

Fall The German authorities dissolve the Czechoslovak Boy Scouts.

October 1 All customs barriers between Germany and Bohemia and Moravia are removed.

November 24 Slovakia joins the Axis powers, headed by Germany, Italy, and Japan, by signing the Tripartite Pact.

November 25 Slovakia signs the Anti-Comintern Pact aimed at the USSR.

December 3 The Polish government-in-exile agrees with Beneš's plan for the establishment of a Polish-Czechoslovak confederation after the war, which would act as a bulwark against Germany.

1941

Summer Several strikes in Prague and other industrial cities take place as a means of slowing down the German war effort.

June 22 Nazi Germany invades the USSR. Several Slovak units, eventually consisting of about fifty thousand men, will take part on the Eastern Front fighting the Soviets.

Mass arrests of Czech Communists begin. They counter with acts of sabotage and resistance against the Germans.

July 18 Great Britain grants full recognition to the Czechoslovak government-in-exile in London. The Soviet Union also extends recognition.

July 31 The United States officially recognizes the Czechoslovak government-in-exile.

September 10 The pro-German Slovak leaders, led by Professor Tuka, railroad through parliament a Jewish code based upon the Nazi model. These laws allow for the property confiscation, internment, and deportation of Slovak Jews.

September 27 Hitler appoints Reinhard Heydrich, head of the German Reich Security Office, as the deputy Reich protector of Bohemia and Moravia. In actuality he replaces the moderate Baron Konstantin von Neurath, who, due to "ill health," receives a leave of absence. Heydrich declares martial law in large sections of Bohemia and Moravia, and he embarks upon a policy of oppressing all forms of Czech nationalism.

October 1 Numerous restrictions are placed upon the Jewish population in Bohemia and Moravia, and deportation begins to concentration camps.

November Terezín (Theresienstadt), a fortress town near Litoměřice, becomes a ghetto for Jewish families from Bohemia and Moravia and for German Jews who receive "preferential" treatment for their past national service.

December 1 Heydrich ends martial law after a number of show trials and executions of Czech intellectuals and leaders.

December 12 Slovakia declares war on the United States and Great Britain.

1942

January 19 The Polish government-in-exile and the Czechoslovak government-in-exile sign an agreement formalizing the postwar union of both states, which also holds out the possibility of including other countries (*see* December 3, 1940).

May 27 Czechoslovak paratroopers from Great Britain ambush Reinhard Heydrich near Prague wounding him. The paratroopers escape, and on June 4 Heydrich dies from wounds received in the raid. As a result, the Germans proclaim martial law and pursue heavy-handed tactics in which over one thousand people will be executed.

June 9–10 In retaliation for the assassination of Heydrich, the Germans destroy the Czech village of Lidice near Kladno. The Germans accuse the village of sheltering the paratroopers and shoot all its 199 men, send all its women to concentration camps, and those children with Aryan, or German, characteristics are sent to be raised by German families, while the others arrive at concentration camps. The village is then razed. The Germans officially announce this deed in Prague.

June 9 The USSR states that it recognizes Czechoslovakia as including its pre-Munich Agreement borders.

June 18 Seven Czechoslovak paratroopers, including those involved in the Heydrich assassination, are killed after a battle in an Orthodox church in Prague. As a result the Nazis dissolve the Orthodox church in Bohemia and Moravia and execute its leaders.

June 24 The Nazis destroy the village of Ležáky near Prague and shoot its 33 inhabitants, claiming that the Czechoslovak paratroopers responsible for the death of Heydrich found aid there.

July After first sending mixed signals on the proposed Polish-Czechoslovak confederation (*see* January 19, 1942), the USSR opposes the move, which in effect kills the plan.

July 3 The Nazis remove martial law in Bohemia and Moravia imposed after the assassination of Heydrich. The Czechs then pursue a policy of passive resistance.

August President Tiso stops the deportation of Slovak Jews after the Vatican protests and points out that the Jews are being exterminated rather than being resettled.

August 5 Great Britain repudiates the Munich Agreement, which it signed in September 1938, and agrees to Beneš's plan for the removal of Germans from Czechoslovakia after the war.

September 29 The Free French government in Great Britain also revokes the Munich Agreement, which France signed along with Great Britain.

October 23 In an attempt to break down the strength of the pro-German faction of the Slovak People's party led by Prime Minister Tuka, President Tiso has the Slovak parliament proclaim him leader, or fuhrer, of the country and political party along the German model.

December 25 In his Christmas radio address, Beneš urges the Slovaks to greater resistance against the Tiso regime.

1943

January 12 Tuka resigns as the vice-president of the Slovak People's party, marking a success for the moderates led by President Jozef Tiso.

May–June While visiting the United States, Beneš receives President Franklin Delano Roosevelt's approval for the transfer of Czechoslovakia's German population to Germany after the war.

June 5 The Soviet government also agrees that Czechoslovakia can remove its German population after the war.

August 20 Baron Konstantin von Neurath is officially replaced as Reich protector of Bohemia and Moravia by Wilhelm Frick.

Fall The German government forces approximately thirty thousand Czech laborers to Germany to work in its defense industries.

October 30 Approximately 2,200 Slovak troops defect from the Axis side to the Soviets on the Eastern Front. The majority of them will later join the Czechoslovak army in the USSR.

November 20 After several months of negotiations, the leaders of the outlawed Slovak political parties, including the Communists, agree to establish a clandestine Slovak National Council to destroy the Slovak puppet state and restore a democratic Czechoslovakia. Several high-ranking Slovak military officers involved with the secret operation plan a mutiny of the Slovak military to join the Allies.

While on a state visit to Moscow, Beneš unsuccessfully offers two cabinet positions to the Czechoslovak Communists in exile in the USSR in an attempt to placate them.

December 12 Beneš signs a treaty of friendship and alliance with the USSR in Moscow.

December 17 Under pressure from the Nazis, President Emil Hácha of the Protectorate of Bohemia and Moravia issues a protest against the Soviet-Czechoslovak alliance of December 12.

1944

April 8 The Red Army reaches the Czechoslovak border, but advances no further for several months.

May 15 The Slovak parliament passes a law forbidding the deportation of Slovak Jews for ''resettlement'' and confines them to Slovak camps.

August 12 As a result of growing partisan activity in the mountainous areas of central and northern Slovakia, the government proclaims martial law.

August 25 The government-in-exile appoints a delegation, which heads to Moscow to organize the administration of liberated territory.

August 27–28 Slovak partisans capture and execute a German military mission, led by General Paul von Otto, returning from Romania.

August 29 The German army is ordered to occupy Slovakia as a result of the execution of General Otto.

August 29–October 27 Fearing German occupation in the wake of greater partisan activity on Slovak territory, the Slovak National Council proclaims the Slovak National Uprising in Banská Bystrica against the Nazis and the Slovak fascist regime. The National Council furthermore announces the restoration of the Czechoslovak sovereignty in Slovakia. Joining the uprising are Czechs, Yugoslavs, Hungarians, Poles, Soviets, French, and Americans, among others. The Slovak army forms the basis of the uprising and is recognized by the Czechoslovak government-in-exile as the First Czechoslovak Army; the majority of the Slovak air force, however, defects to the Soviets. Without expected Soviet aid, the uprising fails after German troops quickly enter Slovakia after October 16. After the failure of the uprising, the Germans carry out harsh retributions against the insurgents and civilians alike. However, guerrilla bands continue operating in the mountains until the arrival of the Red Army.

September 5 As a result of the Slovak National Uprising, the Germans force the reorganization of the Slovak government, which now completely follows orders from Germany.

October 4 The Allies bomb Prague for the first time.

October 18 Soviet troops enter Ruthenia and Slovakia through the passes in the Carpathian Mountains.

October 27 The Red Army takes Užhorod, the capital of Ruthenia.

October 28 The delegation sent by the Czechoslovak government-in-exile to administer liberated territories sets up headquarters in Chust, Ruthenia.

November 11 The Ruthenian People's Committee, a front organization established by the Soviets, sends a telegram to the Czechoslovak government-in-exile in London demanding that Ruthenia be incorporated into the USSR as part of the Ukraine.

November 23 The Czechoslovak government-in-exile submits a plan to the Allies for the removal of the German population after the war.

November 29 The Soviet Union approves the government-in-exile's plan for the transfer of the German population from Czechoslovakia to Germany after the war.

1945

January Joseph Stalin, the Soviet leader, advises Klement Gottwald and other leaders of the Czechoslovak Communist party (KSČ) to cooperate with the Beneš government.

January 23 Joseph Stalin sends Beneš a letter in which he suggests that the fate of Ruthenia with its large Ukrainian population should be negotiated.

February 4–11 The Yalta Conference takes place between Winston Churchill, Franklin Roosevelt, and Joseph Stalin in the Crimea, where the three agree on the post-war settlement. The settlement stipulates, among other things, that the East European governments will be freely elected but pro-Soviet, meaning that they will come under Soviet influence.

March 17 Beneš arrives in Moscow from London to await a return to a liberated Czechoslovakia.

March 22–30 A meeting of several Czech and Slovak political parties takes place in Moscow to work out the future government and fate of Czechoslovakia. Beneš feels the need to reassure the Soviet Union about the orientation of postwar Czechoslovakia by placing Communists in several key positions of the postwar government, including the ministries of the interior, information, education, agriculture, and social welfare.

April Guerrilla warfare by partisan bands in Bohemia and Moravia becomes more widespread as the war nears its end.

April 1 Edvard Beneš appoints a National Front government, a collective government dominated by three socialist parties (Communist, National Socialist, and Social Democrat), with the Social Democrat Zdeněk Fierlinger as premier. Fierlinger, the Czechoslovak ambassador in Moscow, is pro-Soviet and anti-West. As the Soviet military occupies more Czechoslovak territory, the role of the Czechoslovak Communist party (KSČ) becomes more important in the government.

April 3 Beneš and the Czechoslovak government arrive in the eastern Slovak city of Košice from the Soviet Union.

April 4 The Red Army takes Bratislava.

April 5 The Czechoslovak government adopts the Košice Program, which accepts the Slovaks as a distinct people and allows for Slovak autonomy in a reconstituted Czechoslovakia. It establishes a National Front government of all ''acceptable'' political parties, including Communists, and orders a planned economy as well as the nationalization of large and key industries and businesses. It promises to hold elections as soon as possible, to outlaw the Agrarian party and the Slovak People's party, to punish those Czechs and Slovaks who collaborated with the Nazis, and to expel the German and Hungarian minorities. Furthermore, the program reorganizes the military along Soviet models and bases foreign policy on cooperation with the USSR.

Late April–early May The American army, under General George S. Patton, takes western Bohemia. He stops at a pre-agreed line, running from Karlovy Vary to Česke Budějovice, to await Soviet forces.

May 1 Spontaneous uprisings against the Germans, followed by harsh German reprisals, take place throughout Bohemia and Moravia as Soviet and American forces come closer.

May 5–8 After scattered fighting with German forces, an uprising takes place in Prague without any Allied help, even though the American army is about 50 miles away. Approximately two thousand citizens of the city lose their lives.

May 8 The German army in Prague surrenders.

President Tiso and the Slovak government surrender to the Allies in Austria.

May 9 The Red Army takes Prague; the city welcomes it.

May 10 The Czechoslovak government-in-exile returns to Prague, and the purge of Nazi collaborators begins in the city.

May 16 President Beneš returns to Prague.

May 19 The government decrees the seizure of German property in Czechoslovakia. Further laws on June 21 and October 25 clarify the issue.

June 19 Polish troops seize Těšín, and the Soviet Union invites the Czechoslovaks and Poles to Moscow to discuss this and other matters affecting their mutual relations. Poland eventually returns the region that had been seized by the Germans when they invaded Poland on September 1, 1939.

June 21 A government order allows for the seizure of the property of German, Hungarian, Czech, and Slovak collaborators. The Communist-controlled Ministry of Agriculture will redistribute the land.

June 29 Czechoslovakia cedes Ruthenia, its eastern heavily Ukrainian- populated province, to the Soviet Union, creating a common Soviet-Czechoslovak border.

July 17–18 The Central Committees of the Czechoslovak Communist party (KSČ) and the Slovak Communist party (KSS) meet together in Prague. The two decide on the continued existence of the Slovak Communist party, which in actuality will have little independence from the Czechoslovak Communist party.

July 23 Beneš issues a decree abolishing all German and Hungarian laws for the territory of Czechoslovakia imposed from 1938 to 1945.

August 3 The Czechoslovak government revokes the citizenship of Germans and Hungarians in the country.

October 24 A presidential decree nationalizes heavy industry, firms dealing with natural resources, banks, insurance companies, and large food and drink companies, totaling approximately 61 percent of the work force.

October 28 The provisional National Assembly, or national parliament, meets for the first time and affirms Beneš as president.

December 1 American and Soviet occupation forces complete their withdrawal from Czechoslovakia.

1946

January 25 The removal of the German population of Czechoslovakia begins and will continue into November, involving approximately 1,500,000 persons.

February 27 Despite earlier Slovak attempts to remove all Hungarians from Slovakia after the war, negotiations between Czechoslovakia and Hungary agree to a mutual exchange of populations, which affects only about 68 thousand out of a total Hungarian population of approximately five hundred thousand in Czechoslovakia.

May 22 Several days before the first free elections since the end of World War II, the Soviet Union announces that it will move troops from Hungary and Austria through Czechoslovakia to the Soviet-occupied zone of Germany. After the Czechoslovaks disapprove of this plan as an attempt to influence voters, the Soviets postpone the order, but the event shows that the Red Army will always be very close to the country.

May 26 Free general elections are held without incident. The Communist party wins a plurality with 38 percent of the total vote. In the Czechs Lands, the Communist party wins approximately 40 percent of the vote, and its allies, the National Socialist and Social Democrat parties, earn about 39 percent. In Slovakia the Democratic party earns about 60 percent of the vote, while the Communist party earns only 30 percent.

June The United States grants Czechoslovakia a $50 million credit to buy surplus American war equipment in Europe. It is suspended in September due to a growing anti-American press and greater Czechoslovak friendship with the USSR.

June 27 Despite the Košice Program (*see* April 5, 1945), Slovakia is again placed under the central government control of Prague.

July 2 The government is changed to allow for the results of the May 26 election. The Communist leader Klement Gottwald becomes prime minister, and of 25 cabinet posts, the Communists receive eight.

July 26 Prime Minister Gottwald and other Czechoslovak leaders return from Moscow and announce that the Soviet Union has agreed to support Czechoslovak claims at the upcoming Paris Peace Conference; has relinquished any attempts to take German assets from Czechoslovakia; and will provide economic aid.

November Josef Beran is appointed archbishop of Prague and primate of the country.

December 3 The treason trial of Monsignor Jozef Tiso, the former president of the Slovak Republic from 1939–1945, begins in Bratislava.

1947

January 1 A planned economy begins with the implementation of the Two-Year Economic Act for 1947–1948. It includes provisions for a 10 percent increase in the 1937 level of industrialization and for a lessening of the difference between industrialized regions, such as Bohemia, and less developed areas, such as Slovakia.

March Tiso is convicted of treason and sentenced to death.

April 18 Tiso is hanged after appeals for commuting his sentence to life imprisonment fail.

July 4–7 The Czechoslovak government unanimously agrees to send representatives to Paris for the opening meeting of the Marshall Plan, a coordinated effort by the United States and many nations of Europe for the rebuilding of Europe.

July 9 In response to Czechoslovakia's favorable reaction to the Marshall Plan, Soviet leader Joseph Stalin tells Prime Minister Gottwald and other government leaders, who are visiting Moscow, that they must choose either an Eastern or Western orientation, but not both. The next day, the Czechoslovak government reverses its decision to attend the Marshall Plan meeting. Czechoslovakia thereby further enters the Soviet bloc, although it still has a democratic government.

Fall A drought results in about half of the expected harvest, causing the Communist party, as the leading party in the government, to lose public support.

September 10 Unsuccessful assassination attempts on the lives of Jan Masaryk, the foreign minister, and two other non-Communist government members are announced. The three had received packages containing bombs, but the Communist interior minister and Communist-dominated police do little to investigate the plots.

September 14 The Communist-dominated police announce the discovery of an alleged plot to assassinate President Beneš in Slovakia led by former members of the outlawed L'udák party. More than five hundred people will be arrested in this move by the Communists to weaken the Democratic party in Slovakia.

October 15 Czechoslovakia receives a small amount of territory, or a bridgehead, at the expense of Hungary. The territory, across the Danube River from Bratislava, is acquired as a result of the Hungarian peace treaty signed in February.

November 18 After several weeks of negotiations, and with the help of police intimidation, the Communists successfully reconstitute the Slovak regional government more in their favor by removing the Democratic party majority.

Late November Communist party membership reaches an all time high of 1,250,000 people.

1948

February 12 After weeks of slowly increasing their control of Czechoslovakia, the Communists appear ready to grab control of the government. The Communist-dominated Revolutionary Trade Union Movement (ROH) asks workers' councils to assemble in Prague on February 22, which many see as the beginnings of a coup.

February 13 The majority non-Communist government ministers demand that the Communist minister of the interior reinstate eight high-ranking non-Communist police officers and prevent him from making any further changes in the police.

February 20 A minority of the non-Communist government ministers resign from the government after the Communist minister of the interior refuses to carry out their demands from February 13. They expect President Beneš will not accept their resignations, but that he will call for early, new general elections instead. General elections are scheduled for May, in which the Communists are expected to do poorly.

February 21 The Communist prime minister, Klement Gottwald, addresses a mass rally in Prague where he accuses the resigned ministers of obstructionism in the government and insists that they be replaced by others who are willing to cooperate, meaning Communists or their allies.

The Communist-dominated police take over the radio stations, post offices, telegraph offices, and railroad stations in Prague.

The Communist chair of the Slovak regional government, Gustáv Husák, removes the remaining members of the Democratic party from the government and fills it with Communists and collaborators, assuring Communist control of Slovakia.

February 24 Communist armed workers from the Workers' Militia patrol the streets of Prague to guard against counter-revolutionaries.

February 25 Under Communist threats of bloodshed if he does not comply, the ill President Beneš agrees to accept the resignations of the non-Communist ministers from February 20 and to appoint a new government chosen by Prime Minister Gottwald. Thus, the Communists legally take control of the government in what is referred to as the ''February Coup.''

The police disperse a student protest march against the new government.

February 26 A joint American-British-French communique condemns the actions of the Communist party in Czechoslovakia.

February 27 President Beneš swears in the new Communist-dominated government. Although still president, Beneš retires from active politics to his country home.

March 10 Jan Masaryk, the non-Communist foreign minister and son of the first president, Tomáš G. Masaryk, is found dead beneath the window of his residence. The Communist authorities rule it a suicide, although many suspect that the Communists murdered him.

The Czechoslovak representative to the United Nations requests an investigation into the Communist coup; his request is refused.

April 16 The National Assembly passes a new electoral law in which the voters will be presented in the upcoming May elections with either a single slate of candidates or a blank piece of paper if they disapprove of the single slate, thereby negating their votes.

Local governments receive the authority to disqualify those people from voting who have engaged in ''anti-democratic'' and ''anti-government'' actions, meaning those people who do not support the Communists or their allies.

April 26 The National Assembly enacts a law nationalizing all businesses with over 49 employees. Two days later another law is passed nationalizing the construction industry, apartment buildings, and radio stations.

May 5 The National Assembly rearranges the number of seats allocated to the political parties to allow the Communist party an overwhelming majority.

May 9 The National Assembly approves a new constitution, based on the Soviet model that proclaims Czechoslovakia as a People's Democratic Republic, thereby legalizing Czechoslovakia as a communist state.

May 30 The government reports in the general elections that 89 percent of the people voted for the single slate of candidates dominated by the Communist party.

June 7   The ailing Edvard Beneš resigns as president of the republic rather than sign the new constitution into law. Klement Gottwald, the Communist prime minister, becomes temporary president, and he will sign the constitution into law two days later.

June 14   The National Assembly unanimously elects Klement Gottwald to succeed Beneš as president. Antonín Zápotocký, the Communist leader and chair of the unified trade union, becomes the new prime minister.

To mark his inauguration as president, Gottwald attends a *Te Deum* in St. Vitus Cathedral in Prague presided over by Cardinal Beran.

June 27   The Social Democratic party, which had cooperated with the Communists since the 1946 elections, merges into the Communist party.

July 15   Being in control of the country and not needing large numbers, the Communist party begins a selected recruitment of members, no longer granting membership to anyone who wants to join.

August 5   The government announces that approximately 93 percent of all industry has been nationalized, with a little less than half occurring since June.

September 3   Former president Edvard Beneš dies and is given a state funeral.

October 25   The National Assembly enacts a law establishing forced labor camps for people who refuse to work with the new Communist system.

October 27   The government announces Czechoslovakia's first Five-Year Plan for a planned economy.

November   The Communist-dominated Youth League begins a purge of university students by checking into their family and political backgrounds.

December 3   The provinces of Bohemia, Moravia, and Slovakia are abolished as relics of a bourgeois past, being replaced with 19 districts instead.

December 22   The National Assembly strips the judiciary of its independence.

1949

January 25   The Council for Mutual Economic Aid (CMEA or Comecon), a Communist bloc trading organization, is established in Moscow, consisting of Czechoslovakia, Bulgaria, Hungary, Poland, Romania, and the USSR.

January 28   General Heliodor Píka, the former assistant chief of staff of the Czechoslovak army and former

commander of the Czechoslovak-Moscow military mission, is sentenced to death on charges of spying for Great Britain. He is executed on June 21.

March   The authorities arrest the British military permit officer for the western zones of occupied Germany on charges of espionage.

The government passes the Publishing Act, which gives full control over the book publishing and market trade to the Ministry of Information and Public Culture.

April 16   Czechoslovakia and Hungary sign a treaty of friendship and mutual assistance.

May 9   The U.S. Department of State releases documents indicating that the halting of American forces at Plzeň in 1945 was a military consideration that had no political significance in light of the subsequent Communist takeover.

May 16   General Karel Kutlvašr, leader of the May 1945 anti-Nazi uprising in Prague, receives a life sentence for spying for the West.

May 25–29   The Communist party holds its ninth congress in Prague.

June 9   The government establishes the Roman Catholic Committee, a Communist-controlled organization, in an attempt to convince Roman Catholics that the government is respecting and safeguarding Catholicism in the country, while the Pope and bishops, as tools of the West, are trying to prevent an agreement between church and state. Three days later Archbishop Beran proclaims that the Roman Catholic Committee—a government-sponsored organization to control the Roman Catholic Church—is dividing the church in Czechoslovakia between those loyal to the committee and those loyal to the Vatican, and orders all Roman Catholic clergy to avoid it.

June 11   Czechoslovakia breaks off economic relations with Yugoslavia, which left the Soviet bloc in 1948.

June 19   A group of Communist hecklers from the Workers' Militia keep Abp. Josef Beran from delivering his sermon in St. Vitus Cathedral in Prague. From this day on, Beran is placed under house arrest in his official residence in Prague.

June 26   In a pastoral letter, the Czechoslovak Roman Catholic hierarchy accuses the government of persecuting the church.

June 27   Due to the June 26 Roman Catholic pastoral letter, the government bans such letters and the assembly of Roman Catholic clergy without government approval.

July 3 The government announces that Slovak peasants are forcibly opposing steps taken to control the Roman Catholic church.

July 4 Czechoslovakia signs a one-year cooperative agreement with Finland, Poland, and the Soviet Union for the exchange of goods.

July 7 The government announces a law for all religious denominations in the country, putting all religious organizations under government control.

July 13 The Vatican excommunicates all members and sympathizers of the Communist party.

August 17 Archbishop Josef Beran accuses the government of interfering in the internal affairs of the Roman Catholic church, of depriving him of his civil liberties, and preventing him from performing his ecclesiastic duties.

August 28 The government accuses Archbishop Beran and other Roman Catholic bishops of aiding subversive elements in Czechoslovakia.

August 30 The government announces that it discovered and thwarted a coup attempt by an unnamed Western power. Subsequently, 10 people receive sentences of life imprisonment and six are executed.

Late September–mid-October Approximately 10 thousand non-Communist professionals, businessmen, small shopkeepers, priests, military officers, and government officials are arrested on charges of Titoism (the political, economic, and social policies associated with Yugoslav leader Josip Broz Tito), or deviating from the Soviet model of communism.

October The authorities arrest the American embassy member Samuel Meryar on charges of spying.

October 14 Two laws are enacted to place further controls on religion by requiring all religious organizations to become financially and administratively dependent on the state, while the government takes control of all parochial schools to spread Marxist-Leninist ideology among the students.

December 4 Roman Catholic bishops inform the government that they will not follow any laws that attempt to control church affairs by destroying religious freedom.

1950

January 10 All books published before May 5, 1948 in Czechoslovakia are banned.

Late February The government announces that due to the opposition of wealthy peasants, agricultural collectivization—where all land, equipment, and animals are owned by the state—is proceeding more slowly than anticipated.

March 15 The government relieves the Slovak Vladimír Clementis of his post of foreign minister, which he held since June 1948. The Slovak Viliam Široký replaces him.

April 18 Claiming a housing shortage, the government confiscates all monasteries and convents, concentrating all the monks and nuns in a few buildings throughout the country. It furthermore restricts the number of people who can join these orders.

April 19 The Czechoslovak government charges the U.S. Information Service libraries in Prague and Bratislava with being centers of propaganda and spying and orders them closed. It also demands that the American press attache leave the country. This sets off a diplomatic war between the two countries.

April 21 In retaliation for the closing of the U.S. Information Service libraries in Prague and Bratislava, the American government orders Czechoslovakia to close its Chicago consulate, but recalls its press attache from Prague.

May 5 Gustáv Husák, chair of the Slovak Board of Commissioners, the local government of Slovakia, is relieved of his post.

May 12 Claiming that British Broadcasting Corporation (BBC) broadcasts are prejudiced against Czechoslovakia, the government orders the British Information Office and British Council offices closed.

May 13 As the diplomatic war escalates, the American government orders Czechoslovakia to close its consulates in Cleveland and Pittsburgh and to reduce its diplomatic staff in the United States by two-thirds.

May 16 The Czechoslovak delegate at the United Nations resigns and requests asylum in the United States.

May 23 The government splits the Ministry of the Interior and establishes a new Ministry of National Security.

May 24–27 At the ninth congress of the Slovak Communist party in Bratislava, four leading members, including Gustáv Husák and the former foreign minister Vladimír Clementis, are charged with being bourgeois nationalists. Husák and the other three admit their guilt and lose their positions in the Central Committee, although they still keep their party memberships.

May 27 The American government orders Czechoslovakia to close its consulate in New York City.

May 30 The government charges 13 Czechoslovaks with spying for the West. Named in the indictment are 21

Western diplomats and correspondents, including the former American ambassador, Laurence Steinhardt.

May 31 The government hangs former parliamentary deputy and Czech socialist leader, Milada Horaková, after she is found guilty of espionage for the West.

June In an attempt to "Sovietize" the military, the Ministry of Defense grants greater authority to military commissars and recommends stronger political action in the military by the Communist party and youth organizations.

June 21 The Communist East German leader, Walter Ulbricht, visits Prague and signs a treaty stating that the current borders between the two countries are permanent.

July The Czechoslovak government accuses the United States of attempting to destroy its agriculture by dropping beetles from aircraft.

August The authorities take control of the training of all religious personnel by closing all seminaries and theological schools.

September 4 At a miners' union meeting in Ostrava, Premier Antonín Zápotocký urges greater coal production, since the output of coal in 1950 was less than before World War II.

October 4 A coal mine explosion kills 36 miners near Ostrava.

November 3 Czechoslovakia and the USSR sign a five-year trade agreement that will further integrate Czechoslovakia's economy into that of the Soviet Union.

1951

Late January Several former leaders of the Communist party, including the Slovak Vladimír Clementis, are arrested without being charged with any crimes (*see* March 15; May 24–27, 1950).

February 21–24 At the meeting of the Czechoslovak Communist Party Central Committee, three former leaders, including Vladimír Clementis, are accused of treason by being involved in an alleged plot to remove President Gottwald and the secretary general of the Communist party, Rudolf Slánský, and replace them with a pro-Western group.

March 2 The purge of about six hundred thousand Czechoslovak and Slovak Communist party members begins. The purge helps keep the growing Communist party membership in control, thus keeping better control of the country.

March 10 The government exiles Archbishop Beran from Prague and fines him for not cooperating with the Roman Catholic Committee, the government office in charge of the church. He has been under house arrest since June 19, 1949.

July 4 The American Associated Press correspondent William N. Oatis receives a 10-year prison sentence for espionage after being arrested in April. The United States protests the conviction and imposes economic sanctions.

September 6 The Communist party is reorganized by abolishing the post of secretary general and transferring its duties to a party chair, while membership in the Central Committee is reshuffled.

September 7 A major reorganization of the government causes numerous changes in the cabinet. Rudolf Slánský, the secretary general of the Czechoslovak Communist party, loses his post and becomes deputy prime minister of the country.

November 23 The government arrests Rudolf Slánský on charges of treason.

December 6 As a result of Slánský's arrest, membership in the Central Committee is reorganized.

1952

February 27 In a speech to scientific workers, the minister of information attacks Jan Masaryk, the late foreign minister and son of the first president, and Edvard Beneš, the late president, as enemies of the USSR.

March 21 The government announces an austerity program so that more money can be channeled into national defense, with a 44 percent increase in its budget. The money will be raised by reducing wages and increasing productivity, thus leading to a further decline in the standard of living of the Czechoslovak people, which has steadily declined since the 1948 Communist takeover.

March 24 The budget for 1952 is released, and for the first time it follows the Soviet example by covering the entire economy in a planned manner.

May 17 Leading Boy Scout officials receive heavy sentences for "attempting" to overthrow the government. Trials of other Scout leaders will follow. The organization is denounced as a bourgeois tool of the West and will eventually be banned.

June 7 Prime Minister Zápotocký admits in a radio address that the country is suffering economic hard times due to coal shortages, failures in agricultural collectivization, and lack of skilled labor since industrial production increased too rapidly. In an attempt to end the labor problems, the government begins removing politically "untrustworthy" Czechoslovaks from urban areas to work in industrial and mining complexes. This mass relocation of workers intensifies through 1953.

July 1   The government announces that the judiciary will be reorganized along the Soviet model, which will subordinate the courts to the state prosecutors.

November 20–27   The treason trials of Rudolf Slánský, former secretary general of the Communist party and deputy prime minister; Vladimír Clementis, former foreign minister; and 12 other leading Communists begin. The government charges them with spying for the West, plotting to overthrow the government, Titoism (advocating a Yugoslav style of communism), Trotskyism (a radical form of mainstream communism championing immediate worldwide revolution), and Zionism (supporting an international Jewish movement). Slánský, Clementis, and nine others are sentenced to death, while the others receive life sentences. All but Clementis are of Jewish descent.

December 3   The execution of the 11 defendants sentenced to death in the "Slánský Trial" takes place. Purge trials will continue throughout the 1950s.

1953

January 31   The government reorganizes itself along the Soviet model, placing power in a presidium, or a collective leadership, consisting of the prime minister and nine deputy prime ministers.

March 10   Two Czechoslovak air force fighters shoot down an American air force jet over the U.S.-occupied zone of Germany. The United States protests this action, which the Czechoslovak government rejects.

March 14   Nine days after the death of Soviet leader Joseph Stalin, President Klement Gottwald dies in Prague at age 56 from pneumonia that he caught while attending Stalin's funeral in Moscow.

March 15   Drawing deliberate attention to its communist regime, the Czechoslovak government announces the death of President Gottwald through diplomatic channels by using the Russian language instead of the traditional French in its communiqués to foreign embassies in Prague and foreign governments.

March 21   The National Assembly unanimously elects Antonín Zápotocký, the prime minister, as president. President Zápotocký appoints Viliam Široký, a Slovak, as prime minister.

March 24   Six Czechoslovaks hijack a Czechoslovak airliner with 23 other people aboard and force it to fly to the U.S.-occupied zone of Germany, where they seek asylum.

May   The government reduces or cancels the pensions of large sections of the middle class, particularly those formerly involved in business, claiming that they are remnants of capitalism.

May 2   Czechoslovak police begin wearing uniforms modeled on those worn by Soviet policemen or militiamen.

May 15   After an exchange of notes between President Eisenhower of the United States and President Zápotocký with the promise of lifting the economic sanctions if the American correspondent William N. Oatis is released, Zápotocký pardons Oatis. The United States responds by lifting its embargo against Czechoslovakia (*see* July 4, 1951).

May 30   The government enacts drastic currency and wage devaluations whereby one new koruna is exchanged for five old. The purpose of the reform is to deprive wealthier peasants, better paid workers, and the middle class of their savings. Furthermore, the Czechoslovak koruna becomes tied to the Soviet ruble.

The currency reform sparks widespread demonstrations and riots throughout the country, with the heaviest scuffles taking place in Plzeň where pictures of Stalin and Gottwald are destroyed. The government responds by removing a statue of President Masaryk in Plzeň and arresting numerous people. Ten will be tried in the fall on charges of sedition by acting on behalf of the United States, receiving prison terms from six years to life.

June   The government classifies foreign trade data, agricultural output, and the national budget as state secrets.

June 10   In a surprising move, President Zápotocký admits during a speech that there has been widespread unrest due to the May 30 currency reform.

June 18   The Slovak Academy of Sciences is established.

July 1   The government enacts a law that provides heavy penalties for absenteeism in the workplace. Due to heavy negative public opinion, and still recovering from the fallout over the May 30 currency reform, the government cancels the law on July 6.

July 25   Eight Czechoslovaks flee to West Germany in a homemade armored car, which the border guards mistake for a Czechoslovak military vehicle. The eight are granted asylum in West Germany.

September 11 The Communist party is reorganized with Antonín Novotný becoming the first secretary.

October 1 In an attempt to quiet the population, the government reduces food prices up to 20 percent and on some items of clothing by 40 percent.

December The government bars the bishop of Brno from carrying out his church functions because he refuses to follow the orders of the government-controlled Roman Catholic Committee.

1954

February 6 The government announces that President Zápotocký has returned to his official duties after a "serious illness." Rumors abound that he was recovering from an assassination attempt in late 1953.

April 20–24 The trial of the former chair of the Slovak government, Gustáv Husák, and four other leading Slovak Communists on charges of Slovak nationalism and Zionism results in their convictions. Husák is sentenced to life in prison and the others receive long prison terms.

May 16 In local and municipal elections, the single slate of Communist candidates receives less than 96 percent of the vote and, in some areas, as low as 86 percent. Prior to the election, newspapers claim that anyone who does not vote for the candidates are enemies of the people. Yet, over a million voters do not place their ballots in the boxes in protest against the Communist regime.

June 12–13 The Soviet leader, Nikita S. Khrushchev, attends the 10th Czechoslovak Communist Party Congress, where he hears First Secretary Novotný state that the Czechoslovak economy will become more in line with that of the Soviet Union. Furthermore, the 22-member presidium of the party is replaced by a nine-member politburo, or executive committee.

July 16 Czechoslovakia and Austria sign a treaty allowing their ships to freely traverse each other's territory on the Danube River.

July 23 The bishop of Litoměřice and three other Roman Catholic priests receive long prison sentences for spying for the Vatican.

August 21 In a speech, President Zápotocký admits that the purges of "bourgeois" personnel in the economic sector have gone too far, causing numerous breakdowns and delays.

November 28 In nationwide elections the Communists claim a 99 percent favorable vote for its single list of candidates to the National Assembly.

December 12 In a token move due to the general elections in November, Prime Minister Široký "reorganizes" the government, trying to make it look democratic by reflecting the results of the elections.

1955

February 3 The government announces that its state of war with Germany has ceased and that peaceful relations can resume.

May 1 The largest statue in the world of Joseph Stalin is unveiled in Prague as part of the official May Day celebrations.

May 9 To commemorate the 10th anniversary of the liberation of the country by the Red Army, the government grants a general amnesty to any person who has fled the country provided they return within six months.

May 14 Czechoslovakia joins the Warsaw Pact, a mutual defense alliance aimed at the West, by signing the East European Defense Treaty in Warsaw with Albania, Bulgaria, East Germany, Hungary, Romania, and the USSR.

June 19 The Garden of Peace and Friendship opens containing thousands of rose bushes donated by 32 countries to commemorate the Nazi destruction of the village of Lidice in 1942 (*see* May 27, 1942).

October 28 In order to avoid celebrating Czechoslovak independence day, the government proclaims "Nationalization Day," to celebrate the 10th anniversary of nationalizing large sections of the economy after World War II.

1956

January 1 In his New Years address, President Zápotocký states that Czechoslovakia had gone too far in its attacks on Yugoslavia after it split from the Soviet bloc in 1948, thereby seeking to renew friendship with that country. In addition, he recognizes the West German state and says he wants normalized, friendly relations with it.

The second Five-Year Plan calls for a 50 percent increase in heavy industrial output and a 31 percent increase in agricultural production, with the percentages at 61 and 40 respectively for Slovakia.

February 2 The government releases one of the three defendants of the "Slánský Trial" sentenced to life imprisonment. The two remaining defendants are released later in 1956 and in 1960 (*see* November 20, 1952).

April Several speakers at the Second Congress of Czechoslovak Writers, an organization controlled by the government, openly criticize the Communist regime.

May 15 University students in Prague and Bratislava demonstrate against the government's administrative and educational policies. Their demands include greater academic freedom, the end of censorship, and less official admiration for the USSR. As a result, the government permits Western publications to be sold in international hotels, to which very few Czechoslovaks have access, and orders that the Soviet flag no longer fly beside the Czechoslovak flag on public buildings except during official celebrations.

August 1 The National Assembly grants greater powers to the Slovak regional government.

Mid-August One hundred sixty thousand citizens of German descent receive the right to immigrate to West Germany.

October 1 The work week is reduced to 46 hours from 49 hours.

November 3 As a result of the Hungarian Revolution, which is attempting to remove Hungary from under Soviet dominance and socialism, President Zápotocký warns that his regime will not tolerate any threats to the socialist system in Czechoslovakia.

December 25 The state radio ends the use of the Soviet national anthem as its sign-off each midnight, which had been played along with the Czechoslovak anthem since mid-1948.

1957

January 1 In response to the October Hungarian Revolution, a new law goes into effect strengthening the penal code to allow for enhanced socialist legality and presence in Czechoslovakia. This move allows the government greater ability to arrest people for any alleged anti-socialist activity.

January 29 Czechoslovakia and the USSR agree to integrate production in selected key industries such as nuclear power and to cooperate fully in economic planning.

March 2 Seven Czechoslovaks receive prison sentences of up to seven years on the alleged charges that they planned demonstrations against the Soviet invasion of Hungary in October 1956.

July 9–16 After Khrushchev defeats his rivals for control of the Soviet government, he visits Czechoslovakia for a week, where the leadership stresses its undivided support for him and the Soviet Union.

October 2 The Rapacki Plan, a resolution supported by Czechoslovakia, East Germany, and Poland, calling for a nuclear-free zone in Central Europe, is proposed to the United Nations. The West rejects the resolution in April 1958 since it would hamper its ability to defend West Germany in case of a conventional war.

October 13 Youths stage an anti-government demonstration in Prague. Unlike its actions following the May 15, 1956 demonstrations, the government retaliates in the following weeks by arresting and sentencing many to prison.

November 13 President Antonín Zápotocký dies at the age of 72.

November 19 The National Assembly unanimously elects Antonín Novotný as president, allowing him to retain his post as first secretary of the Czechoslovak Communist party. To mark his election, Novotný grants a general amnesty for minor criminal offenses.

December 31 Following a brief thaw in the tight control over the press and literature after Khrushchev's speech in 1956—which attacked the excesses of the Stalin era—the government appoints a committee, led by a hard-line Stalinist, to further censor publications.

1958

January 1 In his New Year's address, President Novotný urges his people to work harder, sacrifice, and eliminate waste in the workplace in an attempt to stimulate the economy.

February 23 The government marks the 10th anniversary of taking power with huge celebrations throughout the country.

May 17 The government calls for an increased effort to destroy the influence of religion in society and to spread atheism.

July 15 President Novotný states that he would like to establish diplomatic relations with West Germany.

September 27 On the 20th anniversary of the signing of the Munich Agreement, Czechoslovakia and East Germany issue a joint declaration denouncing it as a shameful plot against the USSR.

October 23 A law is passed forcing Gypsies and other people who travel from place to place peddling their wares and services—an estimated 50,000 people—to settle down and become "productive" citizens or face stiff penalties.

1959

January 1 The government announces the complete socialization of medicine by noting that the private practice of medicine has been officially eliminated. Citizens must now visit public clinics.

March 8 The government orders price reductions on basic food items and some consumer goods in an attempt to raise the standard of living.

July The government furthers its hard-line stance against literature by ordering all publishers to follow the party line and to allow no political or ideological ambiguities. Earlier in the year the government banned Josef Škvorecký's book, *The Cowards,* claiming it was politically unsound and tainted with petty bourgeoisism (*see* December 31, 1957).

December 28 The government announces that 95 percent of the national productivity output comes from publicly owned enterprises and that 84 percent of agriculture has been collectivized.

1960

March 7 The United States releases two postage stamps honoring the first president of Czechoslovakia, Tomáš G. Masaryk, in the "Champion of Liberty" series. Czechoslovakia either returns the letters and packages bearing such stamps or removes them in violation of international mail agreements.

June 12 General and local elections take place with a single slate of candidates presented, and with the number of seats in the National Assembly being reduced from 368 to 300. As a result of these general elections, a new government is formed, which remains virtually the same as before.

Mid-June For economic reasons the government reorganizes the country administratively from 19 regions into 10 and from 270 districts to 108. It hopes to make each of the divisions integral economic units so that industry and agriculture can balance each other in the new units and be decentralized nationally to stimulate production.

July 6–7 A Communist Party Congress unanimously approves a new constitution and the third Five-Year Plan (1961–65). The Plan envisions higher wages, a 40-hour, five-day work week, more schools and apartments, and a 56 percent increase in industrial production. The new constitution changes the name of the country from the Czechoslovak Republic to the Czechoslovak Socialist Republic, which becomes a centralized state ruled from Prague. The document proclaims the fraternal coexistence of the Czechs and Slovaks as the basis of the state, but Slovak provincial ministries are transferred to Prague, the Slovak board of commissioners (the government of Slovakia) is dissolved, and ethnic minorities (Hungarians, Poles, and Ukrainians, but not Germans) are granted the right to use their own languages in public life. Furthermore, it spells out the roles of the president, National Assembly, and government; describes the Communist party as the guiding force in society; and guarantees personal property, freedom of assembly, religion, and speech, and the inviolability of the home and the mails; these guarantees are ignored.

1961

April 27–28 During a visit to Czechoslovakia, Major Yuri A. Gagarin, the Soviet cosmonaut and the first man to orbit the earth, receives the "Hero of Labor" medal from the government.

July A mine disaster at Dolná Súča claims the lives of 108 miners. The government admits later that the drive to increase coal production led to a lapse in mine safety.

September 2 Due to the crisis over Berlin in which the Western powers reject Soviet attempts to make Berlin a free city, the military is placed on alert and partially mobilized.

Mid-September Czechoslovak troops mass on the border where East and West Germany meet. Twenty thousand reservists are activated, and the government recalls retirees and women to fill their jobs during the crisis so that the economy will not lag any further.

October 23 The government extends the military service of certain personnel expected to be released in 1961.

November 16–18 In a token attempt at de-Stalinization that is following the Soviet lead, the Central Committee of the Communist party orders all streets and enterprises named after the late Joseph Stalin to be renamed, the destruction of the world's largest statue of Stalin in Prague, and the removal from its mausoleum and burial of the embalmed body of the first Communist president, Klement Gottwald.

1962

February 8   Deputy prime minister Rudolf Baŕak loses his position and is expelled from the Communist party on charges of embezzlement, for which he receives a prison sentence of 15 years. In actuality, he urged complete de-Stalinization in the country and challenged Novotný for control of the party.

April 29   The government reverses its mid-June 1960 decision and decides to recentralize the economic structure of the country after the economy continues to slump. The Five-Year Plan is abandoned since collectivized agriculture has difficulty feeding the population, causing shortages in meat and other food products, and the overextended and overcommitted heavy industry lags way behind in the official estimates.

May 1   Protests against meat shortages by approximately 300 students quickly turn anti-government. The police restore order by arresting 18 people who later receive prison sentences ranging from seven months to three years.

October 12   The world's largest statue of Joseph Stalin is blown up in Prague.

1963

April   The government retracts the sentences against the 14 defendants in the "Slánský Trial," despite the fact that 11 were executed in 1952 (*see* November 20–27, 1952; February 2, 1956).

May 1   Due to the poor economy, youths again take part in anti-government demonstrations in Prague; over 20 students are arrested.

May 9–11   Youths attack African students studying in Czechoslovakia in protest against foreign aid while the country suffers economic woes. Czechoslovakia grants the second largest amount of foreign aid in the Communist bloc, after the USSR, to Third World nations.

September 21   In the wake of continued economic problems, Prime Minister Široký is dismissed along with several other government ministers. He is replaced by the Slovak Communist, Jozef Lenárt.

September 25   In his address to the National Assembly, Prime Minister Lenárt urges harder work to combat the weak economy.

October 4   The authorities release from house arrest the prelate of Czechoslovakia, Archbishop Beran, after 12 years of imprisonment (*see* March 10, 1951).

December 10   Czechoslovakia and the USSR renew their 1943 friendship treaty by extending it another 20 years.

1964

February 29   The Communist party rehabilitates and readmits to membership Vladimír Clementis, Gustáv Husák, and two others. Clementis was executed in 1952, while Husák and the two others received long prison sentences and were released in the late 1950s and in 1960. On June 27, the Slovak Communist party will follow suit for Clementis, Husák, and one other former member (*see* November 20–27, 1952; April 20–24, 1954).

March   The Czechoslovak military stops wearing its Soviet-style uniforms and goes back to the uniforms and insignia from the pre-Communist days.

Mid-April   Due to the continued poor showing of the economy, the government considers alternative styles of economic management and planning to that of the Stalinist, totally centralized model.

May 1   For the third straight year, anti-government protests in Prague are broken up by riot police; 31 demonstrators are arrested. In June 12 receive sentences of three to 14 months in prison.

May 8   A leading member of the Communist party criticizes the mass media and writers for advocating greater freedom and for the removal of Stalinism. He also warns that stern measures will be taken against those who do not follow the party line. Despite the tough talk, the relaxation of controls continues due to the economic slump.

May 28   President Novotný states in a speech that during the next two years the government will move to turn around the economy by changing wage and price policies, reallocating investment monies, and strengthening the authority of enterprise directors and managers. He also stresses a slow process to shift away from reliance on heavy industry to the chemical industry and foreign trade with the West, better quality control, and small private businesses. Many of his announced reforms are adopted in late October.

June 14   In parliamentary, local, and municipal elections, the single slate of Communist candidates receives 99.4 percent of the vote. However, many staunch Stalinists are replaced by younger, more reform-minded Communists on the candidates' list.

August 27–September 4 Soviet leader Nikita S. Khrushchev attends celebrations marking the 20th anniversary of the Slovak National Uprising against the Nazis. In an August 29 ceremony in Banská Bystrica, Khrushchev presents medals to 50 former Slovak partisans, including Gustáv Husák, the former chair of the Slovak Board of Commissioners, who was purged and jailed as a nationalist during the Stalin era.

October 11 Approximately 1,000 people take part in an anti-government demonstration in Wenceslas Square in Prague.

October 19 The Communist Party of Czechoslovakia expresses shock at the removal of Soviet leader Khrushchev on October 16. It stresses continued support of him, and states that his removal should be only due to poor health and age. Despite the fall of Khrushchev, the Czechoslovak government asserts that it will continue with its economic reforms and will not revert to the ways of the Stalinist era.

November 12 President Novotný is reelected as president for a second term of five years.

1965

January 29 The Communist party passes a resolution aimed at revitalizing the economy by allowing the mobility of workers, technological advances, profit incentives, and the interplay of prices, credit, and interest. It stresses that the consumer is the first priority, but that the economic changes will not weaken socialism.

June The government grants permits to open small businesses for such occupations as tailors, hair dressers, shoe repair, auto mechanics, carpenters, and interior decorators.

November 11 The government is reorganized by placing some economic reformers in some high governmental positions in a move to support the economic reforms.

December 18 The government publicizes the budget for 1966 that counts on the country's economic reforms working. In it the government will grant greater production control and market decisions to enterprise managers and reduce its support to heavy industry by 10 percent.

December 22 In an attempt to win public approval for its economic reforms, the Communist party issues a document in which it criticizes itself for making poor economic decisions in the past that have cost the country heavily.

1966

January 1 In his New Year's address, President Novotný promises a better economy, but he stresses it will not mean a return to the capitalism that existed in Czechoslovakia prior to the Communist takeover in 1948.

April 18 The Czechoslovak film *The Shop on Main Street* wins the Academy Award for best foreign picture for 1965.

May 30–June 4 At the Thirteenth Congress of the Communist party, the Central Committee is expanded from 95 to 109 members, with some hard-line Stalinists being dropped; President Novotný is reelected as first secretary of the party.

October 31 Vladimír Kazan-Komárek, a Czech-born, naturalized American citizen, is arrested while aboard a Soviet airliner that makes an unscheduled stop in Prague. He is charged with treason, murder, and working with counterrevolutionary groups before leaving his native country in 1948. His arrest leads to very strained Czechoslovak-U.S. diplomatic relations.

1967

January The U.S. government stops issuing visas to Czechoslovaks in retaliation for the arrest of Kazan-Komárek in late October.

February 1 Vladimír Kazan-Komárek receives an eight-year prison sentence after his trial in late January on charges of subversion. After much American pressure, he is expelled from the country the same day.

March 1 Czechoslovakia and Poland renew their friendship and mutual assistance pact from 1947 for another 20 years. The treaty, aimed at West Germany, furthermore declares the borders of both countries as inviolable and the Munich Agreement from 1938 as null and void.

June 5–11 The Slovak author, Ladislav Mňačko, is expelled from the Communist party for publicly condemning Czechoslovak support for the Arabs in the Six Day War (or the Arab-Israeli conflict).

June 27–29 Several Communist writers denounce the domestic and foreign policies of the Novotný government during the Fourth Congress of the Czechoslovak Writers' Union in Prague. The concluding address by Jan Procházka states that struggle for freedom of expression will continue.

Mid-August Ladislav Mňačko visits Israel to show his support in the wake of the Six Day War. As a result, the Czechoslovak government strips him of his citizenship.

Mid-September The government curtails the economic reforms after wholesale prices shoot up about 30 percent. It orders excess profits to be returned to the state and begins greater crackdowns in the areas of religion, art, and literature.

September 27 The government moves against Jan Procházka by dismissing him from the Central Committee of the Communist party. Other writers who voiced their opinions during the June writers' congress are expelled from the party. In an attempt to quash the writers' movement, the newspaper *Literární Noviny* (Literary News) is censored by the Ministry of Education and Culture.

October 30 Students openly demonstrate against poor housing conditions in student hostels.

December 8 The Soviet leader Leonid I. Brezhnev flies to Prague to intervene personally on behalf of President Novotný, who is under threat of removal by the Czechoslovak Communist Party Central Committee. Novotný has been under attack for the last two months from the Slovak members of the presidium, including Prime Minister Lenárt and the first secretary of the Slovak Communist party, Alexander Dubček, who claim the president blocked economic reform, took excessive repressive measures in cultural areas, and discriminated against Slovakia. Brezhnev gets the committee to agree to keep Novotný for the time being.

December 22 In a bid to remain as president and first secretary, Novotný calls for a meeting of the Central Committee in January.

1968

January 3–5 The Czechoslovak Communist party meets and separates the position of first secretary from the president of the republic. The party then elects a compromise candidate, Alexander Dubček, the moderate leader of the Slovak Communist party, as its first secretary, removing the Stalinist Antonín Novotný, who remains president of the republic.

February 25 Major General Jan Šejna, a Warsaw Pact commander, defects to the United States.

February 28 The supreme commander of the Warsaw Pact, Soviet Marshal Ivan Yakubovsky, flies to Prague to ascertain if General Šejna took any secrets with him.

The National Assembly makes Bratislava the capital of Slovakia.

March 5 The government relaxes censorship and begins to work on changing the laws overseeing strict control of publications.

March 14 The Slovak National Council, the government for Slovakia, calls for a decentralized Czechoslovakia along federal lines.

March 19 The Czechoslovak Communist party daily newspaper, *Rudé Právo,* calls for the resignation of Antonín Novotný as president of the country.

March 22 Under great pressure from the reformers and humiliated by and blamed for the Šejna defection, Antonín Novotný resigns as president and goes into retirement.

March 23 In Dresden, East Germany, the Czechoslovak leaders, Alexander Dubček, Jozef Lenárt, and others are warned by the leaders of Bulgaria, East Germany, Hungary, Poland, and the Soviet Union not to let their liberalizing program get out of hand.

March 30 The moderate General Ludvík Svoboda is overwhelmingly elected president by the National Assembly.

April 3 The government announces it will investigate the mysterious circumstances surrounding the death of former Foreign Minister Jan Masaryk, son of the first president Tomáš G. Masaryk, shortly after the Communist takeover in March 1948.

April 4 The Communist party elects a new presidium consisting mainly of reformers.

April 5 A plenary session of the Central Committee of the Communist party adopts the idea for a Czech-Slovak federative state and a 24,000-word Action Program, which outlines reforms for "a new road to socialism," guaranteeing political plurality, freedom of the press, speech, assembly, organization, religion, and employment, the right to personal property and a fair trial, and small scale private businesses. As a result, the Czechoslovak Stalinists begin to lose power. This liberalizing program becomes known as the Prague Spring.

April 6 The hard-line Communist Jozef Lenárt is ousted as premier and his government falls; Oldřich Černík succeeds him.

April 9 Černík forms a reformist government, forcing the Stalinists out of power.

April 10 The Slovak Communist party demands a federative Czechoslovakia.

April 24 Černík presents his reformist program to the National Assembly which approves the reformist Action Program and plans for a federative state on May 3.

Soviet Marshal Ivan Yakubovsky again visits Prague; this time to discuss preparations for the June Warsaw Pact maneuvers in Czechoslovakia.

April 26 Ladislav Mňačko, the Slovak writer, gets his Czechoslovak citizenship back (*see* Mid-August 1967).

April 29 Czech and Slovak economists meet in Bratislava to discuss the effects that federalization might have on the country. A commission to work out the economic arrangements for a federative Czechoslovakia will be appointed on June 1.

May 1 The government orders the full rehabilitation and exoneration, as well as the restoration of Communist party membership to, the 14 defendants of the "Slánský Trial" (*see* November 20–27, 1952). Other Communists and non-Communists purged after the Communist takeover in 1948 will also be rehabilitated in the coming months.

May 4 Alexander Dubček and other leaders hold talks with their Soviet counterparts in Moscow where sharp disagreements surface over the Czechoslovak reforms are reported.

May 7 The Soviets protest after an article appears in *Rudé Právo,* the newspaper of the Czechoslovak Communist party, that implicates Soviet agents in the death of Foreign Minister Jan Masaryk in 1948.

May 8 Bulgarian, East German, Hungarian, and Polish Communist party leaders confer in Moscow about the liberalizing events in Czechoslovakia.

May 9 President Svoboda grants amnesty to mainly political prisoners on the anniversary of the liberation of Prague from the Nazis in 1945.

May 10 Joint Soviet-Polish military maneuvers take place in Poland near the Czechoslovak frontier, while Soviet troop movements take place near the Czechoslovak border in the east.

May 17–25 Soviet Premier Aleksei Kosygin visits Prague for discussions concerning the reform movement, but he ends his mission early and returns to Moscow after he is unable to slow the pace of reforms. However, Czechoslovakia agrees to allow Warsaw Pact military exercises on its territory in June.

May 19 The Soviet Communist party newspaper, *Pravda,* criticizes developments in Czechoslovakia.

May 30 Antonín Novotný and other hard-line Communists are ousted from the Czechoslovak Communist party.

June 5 Railway workers strike in Žilina to force management changes.

June 14 Showing some understanding for the Czechoslovak reform program, Hungary renews its friendship treaty with Czechoslovakia.

June 20–July 2 Joint Soviet-Polish-Hungarian-East German military maneuvers take place and move into Czechoslovakia. Soviet forces, however, remain until August 3, one month later than scheduled.

June 24–27 The National Assembly passes many liberal reforms including the abolition of press censorship, the federalization of the country into two states, and the rehabilitation of people unjustly persecuted, arrested, and sentenced for political reasons since 1948.

July 4 The Warsaw Pact nations, minus Romania, call for joint talks with Czechoslovakia over the issue of the reforms. On July 8 Dubček rejects this proposal unless the discussions are bilateral with each of the countries.

July 9 The National Assembly passes legislation permitting all Czechoslovaks the right to own a passport, thereby allowing them unlimited travel abroad.

July 14–16 The Communist leaders of Bulgaria, East Germany, Hungary, Poland, and the USSR, fearful of the repercussions in their own countries from the Czechoslovak liberalizing movement, meet in Warsaw and send a virtual ultimatum to the Czechoslovak Communist party demanding an end to the reforms, including the banning of all non-Communist political organizations, controls on the media, and a strengthened military. The five countries back up their resolution with troop movements near the Czechoslovak borders.

July 15 General Václav Prchlík, head of the Communist Party Central Committee military section, criticizes the continued presence of Soviet troops in Czechoslovakia. In an attempt to placate the Soviet Union, Prchlík is removed from his position on July 25.

President Nicolae Ceaușescu of Romania gives his public support for the events in Czechoslovakia.

July 18 The Communist Party of Yugoslavia declares its support for the reformist program in Czechoslovakia. Four days earlier, President Tito of Yugoslavia expressed his support for the Czechoslovak reforms.

July 19 The Central Committee of the Communist party gives its unanimous support to its leaders to resist pressure from the Soviets and the four other Warsaw Pact countries. Dubček announces that he remains committed to the Action Program from April.

July 21 At a rally President Svoboda states that Czechoslovakia remains committed to the Warsaw Pact.

July 23 In an attempt to intimidate Czechoslovakia, the Soviets undertake military exercises near the frontier of Slovakia and the Soviet Union.

July 27 In response to the July 16 note from the five Warsaw Pact countries, Alexander Dubček pledges in a radio and television address that the country will carry out its reforms to the end and will not back down the slightest bit.

July 27–August 6 Czechoslovak delegates to the Ninth World Youth Festival held in Sofia, Bulgaria, are given a very cold reception, which warms up after the Čierna Accord is ratified on August 3.

July 29–August 1 Czechoslovak leaders meet with Soviet leaders in the Slovak town of Čierna and Tisou to discuss the current situation in Czechoslovakia. At the end of the meeting, both parties declare that a compromise has been reached. This compromise states that both sides will refrain from mutual criticism if Czechoslovakia limits its reforms, especially with regard to the media.

August 3 The leaders of Bulgaria, East Germany, Hungary, Poland, and the Soviet Union meet in Bratislava to ratify the Čierna Plan.

August 4 In a televised speech, Alexander Dubček declares that no secret deals were made at Čierna and Bratislava with the other Warsaw Pact countries and that Czechoslovakia's independence is secure.

August 9–11 As a gesture of support for the Czechoslovak reforms, President Tito of Yugoslavia visits Czechoslovakia and receives a warm welcome.

August 10 The Soviets announce new Warsaw Pact maneuvers along the Czechoslovak frontier beginning the next day.

August 12–13 Fearful of Czechoslovakia's liberalizing program spilling over into his country, East German hard-line Communist leader Walter Ulbricht meets with Alexander Dubček in Karlovy Vary and demands that the reforms cease and the old hard-line ways be restored. Dubček refuses.

August 15–16 To give moral support to Czechoslovakia, President Nicolae Ceauşescu of Romania visits Prague and renews a 20-year treaty of friendship.

August 20–21 Without warning the Warsaw Pact countries, minus Romania, invade Czechoslovakia at 11:00 P.M. with combined forces totaling around 200,000 men. The government orders the people and army not to resist. The population remains calm, although there is passive resistance and sporadic civilian resistance throughout the country that results in loss of life. Dubček, Černík, Josef Smrkovský, and some other leaders of the government are arrested and taken to Moscow. This marks the beginning of the end of the Prague Spring reform movement.

August 21 The Communist party holds a secret congress where it reelects Dubček as first secretary.

The National Assembly meets, condemns the invasion, and vows not to adjourn until foreign troops leave the country.

The Soviet Union justifies the invasion by stating that unnamed Czechoslovak governmental and Communist party leaders asked for assistance.

August 21–24 Some members of the United Nations Security Council attempt to persuade the general secretary to send a special envoy to Prague to seek the release and guarantee the safety of the detained Czechoslovak leaders. The Czechoslovak delegate asks on August 27 that the council remove the item from the agenda after the Czechoslovak leadership returns from Moscow on the same day.

August 23 An hour-long general strike is held throughout the country to protest the invasion.

A United Nations Security Council resolution condemning the invasion of Czechoslovakia and demanding the withdrawal of all foreign troops from the country is vetoed by the USSR.

August 23–26 President Ludvík Svoboda flies to Moscow for discussions with the Soviets regarding matters caused by the invasion. He refuses to begin the talks until Dubček and the others are released and restored to leadership.

The Soviets allow the Czechoslovak regime to remain in power, but they force it to sign an agreement that halts the reforms and establishes tighter controls over many spheres of society. Furthermore, Soviet troops will remain temporarily until the situation has normalized, with the Soviet government deciding when this normalization has occurred.

August 25 Representatives of the other Warsaw Pact nations that invaded Czechoslovakia take part in the Moscow discussions between Czechoslovakia and the Soviet Union.

A small number of Soviet intellectuals wave pro-Czechoslovak banners in Red Square and are immediately arrested. They receive stiff sentences in November.

August 27 The Czechoslovak leaders return from Moscow and Dubček urges his country to remain calm and to support the Moscow agreement.

East German leader Walter Ulbricht (l.) meets with Alexander Dubček in an attempt to quell the reforms sweeping Czechoslovakia.

Soviet troops begin leaving the center of Prague.

August 28 The National Assembly declares the Soviet-led invasion illegal and demands a specific date for the withdrawal of all foreign troops.

August 31 The Communist party elects a new presidium that includes only two, out of 18, members against reforms.

September 2 The government bans three anti-communist journals due to Soviet complaints that the journals were critical of Soviet actions.

September 3 Under pressure from the Soviet Union, deputy premier Ota Šik, the architect of many of the economic reforms, resigns.

September 8 A 59-year-old Polish bookkeeper, Ryszard Siwiec, sets himself on fire at a fall festival in a major stadium in Warsaw to protest the invasion of Czechoslovakia. He dies four days later. This event goes unnoticed until 1991, after the fall of communism in Eastern Europe, when a film about the incident, *Cry for Freedom*, is released.

September 10 A government proclamation assures the population of continued reforms and the security of its personal freedom.

While visiting Moscow to sign economic agreements, Premier Černík tries to reassure his country of continued civil liberties and free access with the West.

September 11 Soviet tanks begin to withdraw from Prague.

September 13 Although it had not participated actively in several years, Albania formally leaves the Warsaw Pact citing Soviet aggression in Czechoslovakia as its reason.

The government reinstitutes direct press censorship, but Premier Černík asserts that there will still be room for criticism.

September 14 Alexander Dubček goes on television to urge his people not to provoke the occupation troops.

September 19 Under pressure from the Soviets, the foreign minister is removed.

Smoke and flames fill the streets of Prague during the August 1968 Warsaw Pact invasion. Soviet tanks and soldiers soon become a common, though unwelcome, sight to the citizens of Czechoslovakia.

October 2   During a speech at the opening of the United Nations, U.S. Secretary of State Dean Rusk denounces the Soviet-led invasion of Czechoslovakia.

October 3–4   During negotiations in Moscow, where the Soviets complain that ''normalization'' is moving too slowly, the Czechoslovak leaders agree to end and take apart their reforms and to allow for a ''temporary'' occupation of the country.

October 16   Soviet Premier Kosygin flies to Prague to sign an agreement that formally allows Soviet troops to remain ''temporarily'' in Czechoslovakia after the Czechoslovak regime was forced to accept Soviet occupation on August 23–26. Two days later the National Assembly approves the treaty, which Gustáv Husák, the first secretary of the Slovak Communist party, calls a proper step toward ''normalization.''

October 25   East German troops leave Czechoslovakia to avoid comparisons with the 1939 German destruction of the country and possible Western Allied protests concerning the use of German troops outside Germany. Four days

later the forces of Poland, Hungary, and Bulgaria also depart.

October 27–30   On the 50th anniversary of the establishment of Czechoslovakia, celebrated for the first time since the Communist takeover in 1948, anti-Soviet demonstrations take place throughout Czechoslovakia.

October 30   President Svoboda signs into law one reform bill federalizing the country into two parts to take effect on January 1, 1969.

November 7   Anti-Soviet demonstrations erupt throughout the country on the 51st anniversary of the Bolshevik Revolution in Russia. Police intervene brutally to break them up.

November 14–17   The Central Committee of the Communist party elects an eight-man committee to handle the problems stemming from the occupation. The committee outlines a program to restrict many freedoms granted during the reform period. On November 18 the Communist party publishes excerpts from the three-day meeting emphasizing the need to prevent the same "mistakes" of the reform movement from reoccurring.

November 18–21 A three-day sit-in protesting the Soviet-led invasion and supporting the reform program takes place by university students throughout the country in conjunction with the International Student Day on November 17; the government denounces the sit-in.

November 25 The government announces travel restrictions to the West.

December 7–8 Czechoslovak and Soviet leaders end a secret summit meeting in Kiev, where the Czechoslovaks report on economic affairs, the agenda for the upcoming Central Committee meeting, and the federalization of the country on January 1.

1969

January 1 A new constitution makes Czechoslovakia a federal state with two republics: the Czech Socialist Republic composed of Bohemia, Moravia, and Silesia and the Slovak Socialist Republic. This step, proposed by the Dubček regime in 1968, creates two states with regional governments and legislatures, with the federal government responsible for the common defense, finance, foreign affairs and trade, the interior, and labor and welfare.

January 7 Josef Smrkovský is removed as the chair of the Federal Assembly that came about due to the new constitution, the successor to the National Assembly, the country's parliament.

January 13 Journalists agree to self-censorship in an attempt to end their conflict with the government over the occupation.

January 16 As a protest against the Soviet military occupation of Czechoslovakia and the abandonment of the reforms, philosophy student Jan Palach sets himself on fire in Wenceslas Square in Prague, and dies three days later from the burns.

January 19–24 Palach's death provokes mass demonstrations throughout Bohemia and Moravia. Similar manifestations are forbidden in Slovakia by Husák, the Communist leader of the region.

January 25 Peaceful crowds attend the funeral of Jan Palach in Prague.

January 26 After six days of remaining in the background, the police use tear gas to break up the crowds

Jan Palach, a promising young history student who burned himself to death in protest against the Soviet invasion. His burial on January 25, 1969 is a national day of mourning in Czechoslovakia.

around the statue of St. Wenceslas in Wenceslas Square and arrest about 200.

February 25 Another student, Jan Zajic, commits suicide by setting himself on fire in protest against the Soviet intervention in Czechoslovakia.

February 26 An article in the Soviet Communist party paper *Pravda* expresses great concern over Czechoslovak attempts to increase trade with the West.

March 28 The Czechoslovak ice hockey victory over the USSR in the world championships in Stockholm causes widespread jubilation and anti-Soviet demonstrations throughout Czechoslovakia, and in many cities riots erupt. In Prague rioters ransack the offices of the Soviet airline Aeroflot. In response the Soviets call for tighter restrictions including censorship.

April 1 A Soviet delegation visits the Czechoslovak leadership and demands that "normalization" speed up. They threaten to take matters into their own hands if the Czechoslovaks continue to take their time.

April 8 The government appoints Josef Havlín, a staunch supporter of the former Stalinist president Antonín Novotný as chief censor.

April 17 At a meeting of the Central Committee, Gustáv Husák replaces Alexander Dubček as first secretary of the Communist party. Dubček keeps his seat on the Presidium of the Communist party, but other reformers are removed. The Central Committee announces tough policies against anti-socialist elements in society.

April 28 Dubček is elected as the chair of the Federal Assembly.

May 1 Czechoslovakia celebrates May Day with civilian parades instead of the traditional military ones, although in Prague no ceremonies take place.

May 17 Purges of reformers begin in Moravia, marking the start of widespread purges on a local level.

May 27 In an effort to stem the tide of people leaving the country with and without travel visas and to entice others to return, President Ludvík Svoboda offers an amnesty to all who left the country "illegally" without visas. There are few takers by the time the amnesty ends on September 15, 1969.

May 29–30 The Central Committee of the Communist party adopts new hard-line Marxist-Leninist party guidelines and begins national purges.

August 10–15 Warsaw Pact forces hold joint maneuvers in Czechoslovakia.

August 14 The federal and regional governments ask the public to remain calm on the first anniversary of the invasion.

August 18–21 Mass demonstrations throughout Czechoslovakia mark the first anniversary of the Soviet-led Warsaw Pact invasion. Five people are killed in Prague and Brno when troops with fixed bayonets and police using tear gas and submachine guns disperse the crowds. Two thousand people are arrested in conjunction with the demonstrations.

August 22 In response to the demonstrations, the government announces emergency decrees and grants the police greater powers to preserve order.

August 27 Husák receives the Order of Lenin from the Soviet government for his role in the "normalization" of Czechoslovakia.

August 28 At celebrations marking the 25th anniversary of the Slovak National Uprising in Banská Bystrica, Slovak leaders characterize the Soviet-led invasion as "fraternal assistance."

September 25–26 The Communist Party Central Committee removes Alexander Dubček and Josef Smrkovský from the presidium and expels other reformers from the Central Committee.

September 27 Prime Minister Černík forms a new government with hard-line conservatives in control.

October 9 In an effort to keep people from emigrating from the country, the government cancels approximately 100,000 tourist visas to the West.

October 13 The driving force behind the 1968 economic revitalization of Czechoslovakia, Ota Šik, is expelled from the Communist party.

October 15 Alexander Dubček loses his position as chair of the Federal Assembly, while numerous other reformist delegates in parliament resign or are removed.

October 20–28 Husák, Černík, and Svoboda visit Moscow where an agreement is signed to supply equipment for a nuclear power plant and to increase Soviet raw materials shipments including crude oil, cotton, and iron ore. Furthermore, the two countries agree to strengthen political and social relations.

December 15 Ladislav Mňačko, the Slovak writer, is expelled from the Slovak Writers' Union (*see* April 26, 1968).

December 17 The government closes its investigation into the mysterious death of Jan Masaryk, the foreign minister in 1948, ruling out murder, but without any explanations or findings (*see* May 7, 1968).

December 18 The Federal Assembly extends indefinitely the emergency decrees from August 22.

1970

Mid-January The police raid homes, question thousands, and detain about 1,500 to prevent any demonstrations marking the first anniversary of the death of Jan Palach.

January 26 Alexander Dubček becomes Czechoslovakia's ambassador to Turkey. While there he is greeted enthusiastically by crowds. This is seen as a defeat for the hard-liners who wanted to make Dubček a scapegoat for 1968.

January 28 Lubomír Štrougal becomes premier of Czechoslovakia upon the resignation of Oldřich Černík, a major leader of the reform movement who is expelled from the Communist party in December.

Marking the one-year anniversary of the Soviet invasion, thousands of Czech demonstrators march down Wenceslas Square. Police, instructed to keep order by any means, arrest thousands; many are killed.

February 3 The Communist party announces that it will begin loyalty checks on its members, numbering about 1.5 million, with regards to the events in 1968. This leads to a new round of purges in all sectors of public life.

March 6 The Communist party reportedly suspends Dubček's membership after investigating his conduct during 1968.

March 19 The government introduces four mandatory working Saturdays in order to help fulfill the targets for the planned economy.

April 4 A gas explosion kills 29 miners near Ostrava.

May 6 In Prague for the 25th anniversary of the liberation of Czechoslovakia by the Red Army, Soviet leader Leonid I. Brezhnev signs a 20-year Soviet-Czechoslovak Treaty of Friendship. This treaty reaffirms the USSR's and Czechoslovakia's commitments to the Warsaw Pact and CMEA (Council of Mutual Economic Aid), permits Soviet troops to remain on Czechoslovak soil, and enunciates the Brezhnev Doctrine, which states that socialist countries

have the right to intervene in any nation whenever socialism is threatened.

June Czechoslovakia and West Germany sign an agreement that allows for an increase of trade between the two countries.

June 3 Štrougal takes the newly created position of deputy first-secretary of the Communist party, thereby strengthening the conservative wing within the party.

June 24 The government fires Alexander Dubček as ambassador to Turkey.

June 26 Dubček is expelled from the Communist party. The move is denounced by Communist parties in the West.

July 8 Dubček loses his seat in the Federal Assembly.

August 10–17 Czechoslovak and Soviet forces hold joint maneuvers in Czechoslovakia.

August 21 The second anniversary of the Soviet-led invasion of Czechoslovakia passes without incident.

August 28 In a speech, Husák claims that the crisis stemming from 1968 is over.

December 10–11 The Central Committee of the Czechoslovak Communist party characterizes the Prague Spring, the name given to the 1968 reform movement, as an imperialist-Zionist-Vatican conspiracy, which warranted the Soviet-led invasion. It also notes that over 326,000 have been expelled or have left the party since February.

December 20 The Federal Assembly approves a series of measures strengthening the federal government, which can now overrule many decisions made by the Czech and Slovak regional governments.

1971

January 1 The federal government receives powers, enacted in December, to override decisions of the separate Czech and Slovak republics, thereby maintaining a centralized political system. Constitutional amendments also go into effect that restore central planning and abolish separate Czech and Slovak citizenship for the respective halves of the country.

March 22 General Václav Prchlík receives a three-year prison term for criticizing the Soviet Union's domination of the Warsaw Pact; his sentence is subsequently reduced to 22 months in June (*see* July 15, 1968).

May The Czech Journalists' Union is revamped to become pro-government.

May 13–15 The congress of the Slovak Communist party announces that approximately 17.5 percent of its membership, or 40,000 persons, has been purged of right-wingers.

May 25–29 The Communist party holds its delayed 14th congress in Prague with Soviet leaders in attendance. Husák characterizes the 1968 invasion as international assistance and thanks the USSR for its help. The Soviet and Czechoslovak leaders agree that "normalization" has been achieved in the country.

Antonín Novotný, the former hard-line president, is readmitted to the Communist party.

November 26 Elections to the Federal Assembly and local governments are held. New electoral laws grant only the Communist-dominated National Front the right to choose the candidates and to control the elections, allowing the Communist party to retain complete control of the government. A reported 99.4 percent of the people vote, fearful of reprisals from the authorities if they do not, for a slate of unopposed candidates.

December 20 New constitutional changes gives the federal government exclusive control over a number of economic areas including fuel, power plants, transportation, and telecommunications. As a result, new federal ministries are created and the old state ones dissolved.

1972

Early January Journalist Jiří Lederer receives a two-year sentence after writing articles critical of the Polish Communist government.

March The Czechoslovak Journalists' Union announces that 40 percent of journalists in the country, or more than 1,200 individuals, have been dismissed since August 1968 because they refuse to follow the government line.

May The Austrian government cools its relations with Czechoslovakia after Czechoslovak border guards shoot a Czechoslovak émigré on the Austrian border, while with his mother, and drag him into Czechoslovakia. Austria lodges a complaint with the Council of Europe, which formally condemns Czechoslovakia for its actions.

June The Congress of Czech writers acknowledges that the government will not tolerate intellectual freedom like that offered in 1968.

September Warsaw Pact countries hold military maneuvers in Czechoslovakia.

October 27 A British clergyman, the Reverend David Hathaway, receives two years in prison for attempting to smuggle Bibles and other Christian literature into the country.

November 9 Czechoslovakia, along with 34 other nations, accepts an invitation to meet in Helsinki on November 22 to begin preliminary talks for a conference on European security.

1973

Mid-February Soviet leader Brezhnev visits Prague for the 25th anniversary of Communist rule and receives the Order of the White Lion from the Czechoslovak government. In conjunction with the observance, President Svoboda grants an amnesty for about 50,000 Czechs and Slovaks who fled the country after the August 1968 Soviet-led invasion, provided they are not political offenders and return before the end of the year.

March After protracted negotiations, the Vatican and Czechoslovakia agree on the appointment of four new bishops to fill positions left vacant for years.

March 22 The Federal Assembly unanimously reelects Ludvík Svoboda to a second five-year term as president.

April British Labour party leader, Harold Wilson, visits Czechoslovakia, during which time the authorities release the Reverend David Hathaway (*see* October 27, 1972).

April 19 The Soviets launch the *Intercosmos-Copernicus 500,* a joint endeavor of Czechoslovakia, Poland, and the USSR, that will measure the sun's radiation and the earth's ionosphere.

May 20 Czechoslovakia and West Germany begin the normalization of relations by agreeing that the Munich Agreement of 1938 is null and void.

July 9 Secretary of State William Rogers of the United States visits Prague and signs a consular agreement that regularizes trade and travel between the two countries. Rogers asks the Czechoslovaks to allow 31 citizens who had been denied emigration permits to leave the country to join their families in America.

August As a result of strained Soviet-Iraqi relations, the Czechoslovak cultural center in Baghdad is closed.

December 11 Czechoslovakia and West Germany sign a treaty normalizing relations and nullifying the Munich Agreement of 1938. The two countries exchange notes calling for further negotiations regarding West Germany's right to fully represent West Berlin.

1974

January 15 Josef Smrkovský, expelled Communist, former chair of the National Assembly during the Prague Spring, and one of the most popular of the 1968 reformers, dies from cancer in Prague at age 62. Police prevent numerous people from attending the funeral.

February 6 In an interview in Prague with Western German correspondents, dissident writer Pavel Kohout charges that the literary atmosphere in Czechoslovakia resembles that of Stalin's Soviet Union.

February 12 Czechoslovakia, Hungary, and Yugoslavia sign an agreement to build the Adria pipeline from the city of Omisalj on the Adriatic Sea to Bratislava.

March President Ludvík Svoboda, in office since 1968, becomes too ill to perform his duties as president, causing concern over succession.

The ashes of Jan Palach are buried in his village of Všetaty. The government exhumed Palach's body in 1973 from a cemetery in Prague and cremated it to prevent his grave from becoming a pilgrimage site (*see* January 16, 1969).

March 27 Amnesty International condemns Czechoslovakia for worsening prison conditions for political prisoners.

April 7 The archbishop of Litoměřice, Cardinal Štěpán Trochta, dies of a heart attack after a long meeting with a government official during which, Roman Catholics in the West assert, the government official threatened and browbeat him. The government denies the allegations.

May The first section of the Prague subway opens to the public with expected completion of the entire system by the year 2000.

July 1 A law comes into effect that allows security forces to ignore any civil liberties if socialism is endangered in the country.

July 15 The Federal Assembly ratifies the December 1973 treaty with West Germany, after which the Czechoslovak foreign minister visits Bonn.

July 18–20 During the official visit of the Czechoslovak foreign minister to West Germany, the two countries sign a treaty nullifying the Munich Agreement of September 1938 that ceded the Sudetenland to Germany.

October Alexander Dubček sends a letter to the Federal Assembly protesting his almost constant surveillance by the authorities and charging the current leadership with stagnation in the country.

December 19 Czechoslovakia and Austria sign an agreement settling the problem of compensation for property seized from Austrian citizens expelled from Czechoslovakia after World War II. This marks the beginning of normalized relations between the two countries.

1975

January 1 Increases in the prices of Soviet oil hurt the Czechoslovak economy, which depends heavily on it for its energy needs.

February Alexander Dubček's October 1974 letter to the Federal Assembly is made public. Gustáv Husák attacks Dubček suggesting that he should leave the country if he is not happy.

March The West German foreign minister Hans-Dietrich Genscher visits Prague, signaling an improvement in relations between the two countries.

May 29 After months of maneuvering, including amending the constitution and talks with the Soviets, Husák replaces the ailing Ludvík Svoboda as president of the republic. The constitution is amended but Svoboda cannot be persuaded to resign as there are no constitutional means to remove a president unable to perform his duties (*see* March 1974).

July 30–August 1 The Helsinki conference takes place. Thirty-three European countries, including Czechoslovakia, as well as the United States and Canada, sign the Final Act which includes respecting human rights and accepting the territorial changes caused by the end of World War II as final.

August Relations between West Germany and Czechoslovakia become strained after West German citizens violate Czechoslovakia's territorial integrity by trying to smuggle several East Germans out of Czechoslovakia by helicopter.

1976

February Austrian Chancellor Bruno Kreisky visits Czechoslovakia and signs an agreement on the relaxation of border travel procedures, economic cooperation, and cultural exchanges.

April 12–16 The Communist party meets and reelects Gustáv Husák as general secretary; the Central Committee is enlarged to 121 members from 115. The chief themes of the 15th party congress include unity, stability, continuity, and moderation, while proclaiming loyalty toward the USSR and attacking right-wing revisionists.

May Pope Paul VI appoints 21 new cardinals worldwide, including one *in petto* as the archbishop of Prague due to the poor relations between Czechoslovakia and the Vatican.

July 27 Czechoslovakia, East Germany, Sweden, and the Soviet Union launch *Intercosmos 16,* a cooperative satellite that will study the sun's ultraviolet and X-ray radiation and its effects on the earth's upper atmosphere.

July and September Seven members of the rock groups the Plastic People of the Universe and DG 307 receive prison sentences ranging from eight to 30 months for spreading anti-socialist ideas in their songs.

October 22–23 Elections are held for federal, state, and local representative bodies: the federal legislature, the Czech and Slovak National Councils, and the people's committees. Only candidates approved by the Communist-controlled National Front run and are elected.

December 10 Under pressure from West European Communists, the government releases four prominent dissidents imprisoned in 1972.

1977

January 6 Two hundred forty-two prominent persons sign Charter 77, a resolution that accuses the government of violating human rights that it agreed to uphold by signing the Final Act of the Helsinki Conference in 1975. The government arrests those signatories who unsuccessfully try to deliver the document to the Federal Assembly, the federal premier, and the Czechoslovak News Agency. The charter is then subsequently released to the foreign press. By word of mouth and foreign broadcasts, the Czechoslovak public learns about Charter 77, and several hundred more people sign the document in the coming months. Several people receive prison terms, including journalist Jiří Lederer who later in the year receives a three-year prison sentence for signing the charter.

January 26 The U.S. Department of State condemns Czechoslovakia for violating the 1975 Helsinki Agreement by arresting and harassing the members of Charter 77 earlier in the month.

July 1 The government increases the prices of certain foodstuffs up to 50 percent and up to 40 percent for some consumer goods.

October Czechoslovakia and East Germany sign a new 25-year treaty of friendship, cooperation, and mutual assistance.

Václav Havel, the dissident playwright and member of Charter 77, receives a 14-month prison sentence for his role in the charter movement, but he is released four months later.

1978

January Jiří Hájek, one of the official spokesmen for Charter 77, claims in an interview with the West German magazine *Der Speigel* that Charter 77 is not a movement, but it is rather an initiative by citizens in response to the Czechoslovak legal system.

After long negotiations with the Vatican, Slovakia becomes a separate ecclesiastical province with an archbishopric at Trnava, and Cardinal František Tomášek officially becomes the archbishop of Prague (*see* May 1976).

April Gustáv Husák visits West Germany, the first visit ever made by a Czechoslovak president. He and West German Chancellor Helmut Schmidt sign an agreement calling for closer relations between the two countries. A cultural agreement, signed by the foreign ministers of the two countries, calls for cooperation in science, culture, and education.

May–June A Soviet delegation, led by Leonid I. Brezhnev, visits Czechoslovakia and signs the Joint Declaration on the Further Development of Fraternal Friendship and All-Around Cooperation of Czechoslovakia and the USSR.

June The USSR chooses Captain Vladimír Remek of the Czechoslovak armed forces as the first foreign cosmonaut for a space shot as a reward for Czechoslovakia's contribution to *Intercosmos,* the joint space program of the USSR and the countries of the Eastern Bloc.

August 21 Charter 77 issues a statement on the 10th anniversary of the Warsaw Pact invasion, asserting that the invasion and the continued occupation of the country by Soviet troops are illegal.

October 16 The Czechoslovak media downplays the election of the Polish archbishop Karol Wojtyla as Pope John Paul II in an attempt to downplay the event.

November Charter 77 issues an open letter to the United Nations Secretary-General and the leaders of the countries who signed the 1975 Helsinki Agreements asking them to investigate human rights violations in the country.

The International Labor Organization based in Geneva publishes a document charging the Czechoslovak government with discrimination against the members of Charter 77 by denying them employment or arbitrarily removing them from jobs.

1979

May The authorities arrest 11 leading members of Charter 77, including the playwright Václav Havel, on charges of subverting the authority of the state.

July 20–23 The government steeply increases the prices on gasoline, electricity, fuel oil, telephone and postal rates, and children's clothes an average of 50 percent. The period before the price increases went into effect was marked by panic buying and hoarding.

September 20 General Ludvík Svoboda, president from 1968 to 1975, dies at the age of 83.

October Six of the Charter 77 members arrested in May, including Václav Havel, receive sentences ranging from two to five years.

December 31 Czechoslovakia, following the lead of the Soviet Union, abstains when the United Nations Security Council votes on a resolution calling for economic sanctions against Iran if it refuses to set free all American hostages it holds.

František Hrabal, a dissident and member of Charter 77, is released from prison after serving 14 months of a three-year sentence on charges of subversion stemming from distributing Charter 77 materials.

1980

January 3 Jiří Lederer, a leading dissident and signer of Charter 77, is released from prison after three years. In September he is forced to leave the country after being detained three times; he goes to West Germany where he seeks political asylum (*see* January 6, 1977).

March and April Increasingly worried by events in Poland concerning the independent Polish trade union Solidarity, the government cracks down on dissidents by breaking up lectures in private apartments, detaining some of the participants, and deporting non-Czechoslovak citizens including British scholars William Newton-Smith and Anthony Kenny.

May President Husák proclaims a general amnesty, excluding political prisoners, to honor the thirty-fifth anniversary of the liberation of the country from Nazi rule.

May 12 The International Labor Organization in Geneva again criticizes the Czechoslovak government for firing people who had signed Charter 77, which goes against an international agreement that Czechoslovakia had signed regarding the right to work and discrimination in the workplace (*see* November 1978).

May 22 The Federal Assembly reelects Communist hard-liner Gustáv Husák as president for a second term of five years.

June 2 The authorities arrest 15 signers of Charter 77 in a dissident's apartment in Prague on charges of holding an unauthorized meeting.

July 9 In a hail of bullets, three Czechoslovaks and a dog swim across the Morava River to freedom in Austria.

August 25 In an attempt to avoid strikes as in Poland, the Czechoslovak Communist party orders its factory committees and managers to become more attuned to the interests of workers and to be more sensitive to workers' complaints.

September The authorities detain and question about 30 of the most prominent members of Charter 77 concerning two letters: one of support for the Solidarity strike in

Poland and the other, addressed to the European Conference on Security and Human Rights to be held later in the year in Spain, detailing violations of human rights in Czechoslovakia.

October Czechoslovakia follows East Germany's example by closing its border with Poland to free travel in an attempt to keep Polish problems from spreading to Czechoslovakia.

Work stoppages are reported in Ostrava, where the population receives Polish television and is informed about events in that country.

November Husák pays a surprise visit to Ostrava, attempting to calm the reported uneasiness of the region.

November 13 Griffin Bell, the head of the U.S. delegation to the East-West Conference in Madrid called to discuss human rights and cooperation in Europe, denounces Czechoslovakia for harassing and imprisoning members of Charter 77.

December 12 Jaroslav Šabata, the former spokesman for Charter 77, is released after 23 months in prison, only to be rearrested the same day in Prague.

regime is undermined. He compares the Polish situation to events in East Germany in 1953, Hungary in 1956, and in his own country in 1968. The following day Brezhnev briefly addresses the congress in milder tones than Husák. Although the Soviet leader makes references to the 1968 invasion of Czechoslovakia by Soviet-led forces, he stresses that he has faith in the Polish government to solve its own problems, which surprises hard-line Communists. Overall, the congress presents no new initiatives or changes, stressing its ties to and support for the USSR.

May 3 In a dramatic escape, a Czechoslovak pilot and his family fly a crop duster to Austria and seek asylum.

May 7–8 As a result of continued unrest in Poland, the authorities crack down on the political opposition. Using the excuse that two French socialist lawyers were arrested in April and expelled on charges of trying to smuggle printed material, money, and a duplicating machine to the dissidents, the government begins a roundup of over 40 activists throughout the country, mainly members of Charter 77, including the former 1968 reformer foreign minister Jiří Hájek.

1981

Throughout 1981 The Czechoslovak government will take steps to insure that the problems in Poland will not spill over the borders. Some of the measures taken include not raising prices as earlier announced, making certain that goods are readily available in stores, making tourist visas to Poland extremely difficult to receive, restricting visits by Poles to Czechoslovakia, and being openly critical of Solidarity, the independent Polish labor union.

April Czechoslovakia cancels its June participation in an international cultural festival in Vienna because the play *The Castle,* by the imprisoned dissident playwright and co-founder of Charter 77, Václav Havel, is scheduled to be performed.

April 6–11 In an unexpected visit, Leonid I. Brezhnev, the Soviet leader, attends the sixteenth congress of the Czechoslovak Communist party in Prague. This marks his first appearance at a national party congress outside the Soviet Union since 1975, and thereby gives it an international flavor in light of the continued crisis in Poland. In the opening speech, Gustáv Husák, the president of the republic and Czechoslovak Communist party secretary general, harshly denounces the events in Poland and warns that Communist countries will not remain idle while the Polish

Gustáv Husák welcomes Soviet leader Leonid Brezhnev (l.) at Prague airport.

July Amnesty International calls for the release of eight persons still detained from the May roundup and the dropping of charges against over 20 others.

The trials of those detained in the May crackdown begin on charges of subversion of the government. Rudolf Battek, a former parliamentary deputy from 1968–1969, receives a sentence of seven-and-a-half-years after being convicted. This is the heaviest sentence for a political crime since the purge trials of the 1950s. On appeal his sentence is reduced in October.

The authorities also move against outspoken members of the Roman Catholic Church; in September six priests are sentenced to prison terms of up to three years for their activity.

July 10 A group of seven American playwrights, including Arthur Miller, sign an open letter to the Czechoslovak government urging it to release Václav Havel, who is in the midst of serving a four-and-a-half-year sentence (*see* October 1979).

November 6 In a speech to the Communist party Central Committee, Prime Minster Lubomír Štrougal notes that the Czechoslovak economy is not as healthy as earlier projected, with unfavorable balances of trade with both the East and the West, wastefulness of energy, a lag in agriculture and construction, and too great a reliance on imported fuels.

December U.S. Helsinki Watch Committee, an organization that monitors human rights in countries that signed the 1975 Helsinki Accords, offers free 1982 calendars that feature the photos of 12 Czechoslovak and Soviet dissidents and the names, birth dates, ages, occupations, length of prison sentences, and prison addresses of 68 others so that cards and letters can be sent to them.

December 28 The authorities arrest Jacques Derida, a French philosopher, on charges of drug smuggling, to keep him from participating in an unofficial Charter 77 seminar; the government expels him three days later.

1982

January 25–30 Czechoslovak, Hungarian, and Soviet forces hold joint maneuvers in western Czechoslovakia near the East German border.

January 29 Czechoslovakia, Great Britain, and the United States sign an agreement in which the United States and Great Britain will return about 18.5 tons of Czechoslovak gold, worth an estimated $250 million, captured by Allied forces from the Nazis in 1945. In return Czechoslovakia

agrees to pay approximately $130 million to British and American citizens whose assets were seized by the Communist government in Czechoslovakia in 1948. The issue had clouded U.S.-Czechoslovak relations since 1948, and negotiations to settle the problem failed in 1964 and 1974.

Mid-March Five Roman Catholic bishops, including Cardinal František Tomášek, the Archbishop of Prague, visit Pope John Paul II in the Vatican. The pontiff decries the poor Czechoslovak-Roman Catholic relations that have left seven dioceses without bishops and only two seminaries to function, thereby training an inadequate number of priests for the needs of Czechoslovakia.

May 31 The last of those detained from the May 1981 crackdown on dissenters, who did not go to trial, is released.

July 20 Wary of the power of the Roman Catholic Church in Poland, the authorities refuse to grant a travel visa to Polish Bishop Bogdan Sikorski so he can return to Poland after a visit to West Germany.

November Husák makes a state visit to Austria, the first by a Czechoslovak head of state, postponed since 1981 when a Czechoslovak agent had been discovered in Vienna.

1983

January 4–6 The Warsaw Pact countries meet in Prague, where they propose radical reductions of medium-range nuclear missiles in Europe, mutual reductions of conventional arms with NATO, and suggest a nonaggression pact with NATO.

March 4 Václav Havel, the jailed playwright dissident and co-founder of Charter 77, is released from a hospital to convalesce at his Prague apartment. He is granted a temporary suspension of his prison sentence until he gets well. The authorities moved him from prison to a hospital when he became seriously ill with pneumonia in February, fearing international repercussions if Havel died in prison.

June Czechoslovak authorities refuse to allow Roman Catholic Church leaders to go to Poland for Pope John Paul II's visit to his native country.

June 20 The government is shuffled to put a greater emphasis on economics and technological development. This, along with the death in April of Václav Hula, one of the strongest defenders of central planning, ushers in false hopes that changes might occur in the economy.

June 21 At a government-sponsored international peace conference, over 100 young Czechs chant for freedom at a rally marking the conference in Wenceslas Square in

Prague. The police quickly move in and disperse the first major protest in 14 years.

June 23 Since the government barred Charter 77 from participating in the international peace conference, members of the group hold a public meeting with West European human rights activists where about 20 people sign a declaration proclaiming that peace and human rights are one.

August 21 The fifteenth anniversary of the Soviet-led invasion of Czechoslovakia passes quietly throughout the country.

September 7 In a dramatic escape, a former member of the Czechoslovak national cycle team, his wife, and children fly in a hot air balloon made out of raincoats across the border into Austria, where they are granted asylum.

October 6 The Slovak Communist party newspaper, *Pravda,* blames Pope John Paul II for using religion to cause much of the political unrest in Poland, indicating that Czechoslovak relations with the Roman Catholic Church have reached a new low.

October 22 In an attempt to encourage private businesses, the Federal Assembly passes greater social security benefits for self-employed people such as hairdressers, auto mechanics, carpenters, and decorators.

December 2 The Czechoslovak foreign minister visits the pope in the Vatican in an attempt to smooth over the bitter relations between church and state that have become increasingly acrimonious in the past few months.

1984

February 29–March 3 The papal secretary of state returns the December visit of the Czechoslovak foreign minster. Little comes out of their talks over the stalled relations, except both sides agree to meet again. Talks resume in July.

Mid-May Czechoslovak authorities detain Miklós Duray, the acknowledged leader of the Hungarian minority in Czechoslovakia, to keep him from campaigning against plans to reduce instruction in the Hungarian language in Czechoslovak schools where Hungarians make up a sizable portion of the pupils.

May 25 Czechoslovakia agrees to partially settle American claims amounting to about $3 million on national and municipal government bonds issued in the 1920s to Czech and Slovak Americans, on which the government stopped paying the interest in 1952. Czechoslovakia began negotiations after an American public outcry arose over this bond issue, which threatened to derail the gold agreement in 1983 with the U.S. and Great Britain (*see* January 29, 1982).

June In response to reformer Mikhail Gorbachev's assumption of power in the Soviet Union in March, Gustáv Husák asserts at a Communist Party Central Committee meeting that no changes are in the works for Czechoslovakia.

Czechoslovakia orders two British diplomats to leave the country in retaliation for an earlier expulsion of two Czechoslovak diplomats from Great Britain.

August 4 A Czechoslovak student flies across the frontier in a motorized kite and seeks asylum in Austria.

August 16–17 On the eve of the sixteenth anniversary of the Soviet-led invasion of Czechoslovakia, the police interrogate, search the homes of, and detain some members of Charter 77.

August 21 On the anniversary of the Soviet-led invasion of 1968, Charter 77 calls for the withdrawal of all Soviet troops from the country and the right of Czechoslovakia to self-determination.

September 14 Ten Czechoslovak tourists defect from a Soviet cruise ship that stopped in Hamburg for a visit.

October The Austrian newspaper *Die Press* publishes a partial report commissioned by the Czechoslovak government in 1980 that notes that acid rain has affected more than four hundred thousand hectares of the country's forests, and that by the year 2000 more than a quarter of these forest lands may be irreversibly damaged.

The Budapest Cultural Forum, one of the follow-up meetings to the 1975 Helsinki Accords, receives an open letter from Charter 77 accusing the Czechoslovak government of repressive actions.

October 11 The 83-year-old poet and signer of Charter 77, Jaroslav Seifert, receives the 1984 Nobel prize for literature. Although the author is congratulated by the Communist party, it hints that Seifert is being used by the West to embarrass the government in Czechoslovakia. However, popular manifestations take place to mark the occasion.

November Charter 77 issues a joint resolution with East German peace activists for a ''missile free Europe.''

November 9 Czechoslovak police and border guards thwart a bus hijacker who attempted to force the driver at gunpoint to crash through the frontier into West Germany.

1985

March 11   The authorities round up about 45 political dissidents in a raid on a home in Prague. Eleven are detained including Jiří Dienstbier, the spokesman for Charter 77.

March 26   In a speech to the Federal Assembly, Prime Minister Lubomír Štrougal predicts that the country will be able to pay off its foreign debt estimated to be at $3 billion.

April 24   Pope John Paul II names Monsignor Jozef Tomko as the first Slovak cardinal.

April 26   Meeting in Warsaw, representatives of the Warsaw Pact sign a twenty-year extension of their treaty, with an option for a ten-year renewal in 2005.

May   An estimated 2,000 people now have membership in Charter 77.

Mid-May   The second highest ranking Czechoslovak diplomat in the United States defects in Washington D.C.

July 7   Some 150,000 pilgrims visit the reported site of St. Methodius's grave in Velehrad on the 1,100th anniversary of his death and celebrate an outdoor mass. It is the largest church rally since the Communists took power in 1948 despite severe government oppression of the church.

October   A Czechoslovak air force jet fires on an American army helicopter to keep it from crossing into Czechoslovak airspace. The United States protests this action, which is rejected by the Czechoslovaks.

October 24   Police overpower a gunman in Brno who took children and nurses as hostages in a bid to leave the country.

November 21   In an article in the Italian Communist party newspaper, *L'Unita,* Alexander Dubček, the leader of the Prague Spring in 1968, denies he signed a document in early August 1968 expressing concern that his country was threatened by counter-revolutionaries. This is Dubček's first public statement since he was removed from power, and it is in response to assertions by the Czechoslovak Communist party's ideologist Vasil Bil'ak in an interview with the West German magazine *Der Spiegel.*

1986

January 11   Jaroslav Seifert, the Czech Nobel laureate poet, dies at the age of 84. He is given a state funeral (*see* October 11, 1984).

May   Following the Soviet example, the Czechoslovak media plays down the Chernobyl nuclear power plant disaster.

May 2   Sweden expels five Czechoslovak diplomats on charges of collecting intelligence information. The following week, Czechoslovakia retaliates by ordering two Swedish diplomats to leave.

September 4–5   The authorities close the offices of the Jazz Section of the Union of Czechoslovak Musicians and arrest seven leading members of the group. The Jazz Section, founded in 1971, had become an independent cultural organization that advocated total freedom of the arts, and its uncensored newsletter, published 4,000 copies at a time, was read by an estimated 80,000 Czechoslovaks. Although the organization avoided political dissent, the police harassed the members, banned its concerts, cut off its telephone privileges, and seized its mailing lists.

October   Several Czech and Slovak dissidents sign a resolution, with other activists from East Germany, Hungary, and Poland, commemorating the thirtieth anniversary of the 1956 Hungarian Revolution. The statement proclaims that ideals such as pluralism, self-government, and independence from the 1956 revolt are still legitimate.

November 1   Sixteen Czechoslovak tourists defect from a Soviet cruise ship visiting Hamburg.

December 27   Two members of the Jazz Section detained since September are released due to poor health.

1987

January   On the tenth anniversary of the founding of Charter 77, the organization issues a document that urges Czechoslovaks to demand their educational, religious, media, and political rights, and denounces the Communist leadership as a privileged group.

January 27   In a major speech, Soviet leader Mikhail Gorbachev advocates economic and political reforms in the Soviet Union. Shocked by his proposals, the Czechoslovak Communist leadership refuses to print Gorbachev's remarks despite the fact that Soviet television is available throughout Czechoslovakia.

February   The police detain Václav Havel from meeting with Democratic representative Steny H. Hoyer of Maryland, who is chair of the congressional committee monitoring human rights.

March 11   Five remaining members of the Jazz Section detained since September are convicted on charges of unofficial commercial activity, but receive relatively light sentences. Western governments, human rights organizations, and internationally famous writers, artists, and musicians denounce the convictions as travesties of justice and violations of human rights.

March 13 About 30 members of Charter 77 meet publicly, without police interference, at the grave of Jan Patočka, to pay homage on the 10th anniversary of his death. Patočka, a founding member of the organization, died from a stroke after he had been intensely interrogated by the police about Charter 77. The current lack of police harassment is viewed as a result of Gorbachev's emphasis on openness and shows the uncertainty of the Czechoslovak government in the wake of Gorbachev's January speeches.

April 9–11 Mikhail Gorbachev arrives in Czechoslovakia for an official visit. The crowds enthusiastically greet him, but the Czechoslovak Communist leadership, which rejects Gorbachev's reforms, does not. The Soviet leader gives a speech in Prague encouraging change by suggesting that Soviet-style reforms would benefit the countries of the Eastern Bloc. Yet, Gorbachev states that the Soviet Union would not assert that its example be strictly followed. When journalists ask Gorbachev's spokesman to explain the difference between *perestroika* and the Prague Spring of 1968, he replies, "Nineteen years." In the coming months the Czechoslovak government makes it clear that it will follow its own path distinct from the Soviet example and does introduce some minor economic changes.

August 20 On the nineteenth anniversary of the Soviet-led invasion, Charter 77 issues a statement that includes the demands for amnesty for political prisoners and an end to controls in the political sector.

October Charter 77 sends a petition, signed by 50 people, to the Federal Assembly that expands upon its demands from August 20, including freedom of information and free access to public life.

In a speech, President Husák notes that the government needs to move slowly and cautiously in its reforms, with an emphasis on economic and not political change.

November 26 Both President Husák and his foreign minister wear "I Like Gorby" pins, given to them by West Germans, when they meet the West German foreign minister in Prague.

December 10 Despite an official ban, over 1,000 Czechoslovaks peacefully commemorate United Nations Human Rights Day in Prague.

December 17 Seventy-five-year old Gustáv Husák resigns as first secretary of the Communist party, but he retains the largely ceremonial office of president of the republic. He is replaced by Miloš Jakeš, the Central Committee secretary in charge of economic affairs. The 65-year-old Jakeš, who came to prominence in the 1970s by purging the supporters of the Prague Spring, is not a reformer, so there will be no change in domestic policies for Czechoslovakia. The move implies that the Communist party wants to establish greater unity in its leadership to oppose any reformist faction backed by the Soviet Union. Nonetheless, Mikhail Gorbachev sends Jakeš a congratulatory letter on his new position and urges him to restructure Czechoslovak economic and political life.

1988

January 1 In his New Years address, President Husák praises the political and economic transformations made by Gorbachev in the USSR, but he adds that change will not come soon to Czechoslovakia.

January 5 The USSR denies that its economic changes have anything in common with the 1968 Prague Spring, despite the fact that the Prague Spring leader, Alexander Dubček, states in an interview with the Italian Communist party newspaper *L'Unita* that he sees numerous similarities.

February 20 After the archbishop of Prague, Cardinal František Tomášek, urges Czechoslovak Roman Catholics to sign a petition to allow greater religious freedom in the country, more than 300 thousand do so. By November over 600 thousand will have affixed their signatures.

February 25 Czechoslovakia and East Germany begin removing short-range Soviet nuclear missiles from their countries in accordance with the arms treaty signed by the United States and the USSR in December 1987.

March 4 The authorities start rounding up dissidents, including the playwright Václav Havel, before a Catholic pilgrimage to demand religious freedom can take place.

March 25 After banning religious rallies, riot police attack and arrest hundreds of peaceful demonstrators in Bratislava who gathered to ask for greater religious freedom.

May 5 In an unprecedented move, the government allows two American doctors to visit one dissident and to perform an autopsy on another, Pavel Wonka, who died in prison at the age of 35 in late April. The government wants to dispel rumors that Wonka died from torture; the doctors who represent Physicians for Human Rights find no evidence of foul play.

June 17–18 Police in Prague break up an East-West human rights seminar organized by Charter 77. The Czechoslovak participants are detained while 32 foreigners from 15 countries are expelled. The seminar was a follow-up meeting to others held in Budapest, Warsaw, and Moscow, where no incidents took place.

June 28–29 The Voice of America (a broadcasting service sponsored by the United States) broadcasts interviews with the leader of the Prague Spring, Alexander Dubček. In these interviews, which were taped earlier in the month, Dubček calls for religious freedom and adds that the future looks positive for the country.

July Prime Minister Lubomír Štrougal admits that the country is in an economic slump and that changes are needed to get it going again. However, he does not outline any steps to take. The government then lowers its projected 1989 economic growth by one-third to 2.2 percent.

July 2–3 Approximately 280,000 Czechoslovaks make a pilgrimage to the fifteenth century shrine of the Virgin Mary and attend religious services in the Slovak city of Levoča. Since the government announced in May that it wanted better church-state relations, no incidents are reported.

August 18 About 12 Western demonstrators briefly display banners in Wenceslas Square in Prague calling for freedom, human rights, and the removal of Soviet troops. They are detained and expelled from Czechoslovakia.

August 21 On the 20th anniversary of the Soviet-led Warsaw Pact invasion that ended the Prague Spring, approximately 10,000 demonstrators rally in Prague demanding the withdrawal of Soviet forces and greater freedom.

Police in a Moscow park round up protestors before they can begin a rally marking the twentieth anniversary of the Soviet-led invasion of Czechoslovakia.

September 28 Czechoslovakia expels two British diplomats as spies. Six days later Great Britain retaliates by ordering three Czechoslovak diplomats to leave.

October 10 After a two-day meeting of the Communist Party Central Committee, Miloš Jakeš announces the resignation of his chief political rival, Lubomír Štrougal, as premier and as a member of the presidium, or ruling circle, of the Communist party. The conservative Communists view Štrougal, a popular leader and premier for 18 years, as the person who could take control of a reform wing within the Communist party. Since 1987 Štrougal worked with economists on plans for greater market economy strategies and a lessening of the planned economy. He also advocated a faster pace of economic change and criticized the government for the use of the police to break up the East-West

seminar in Prague in June. Jakeš and other hard-line Communists, feeling this to be a repetition of the 1968 Prague Spring, force Štrougal out.

The entire government submits its resignation in a move that is made to give the appearance that changes will be made. Ladislav Adamec, a moderate economist more in line with Jakeš, who favors gradual change, succeeds Štrougal as prime minister. Beyond these symbolic changes very little new is accomplished.

October 11 The entire government submits its resignation. Ladislav Adamec, a moderate economist more in line with Jakeš, who favors gradual change, succeeds Štrougal as prime minister.

October 27 Police throughout the country begin detaining dissenters on the eve of the first legal celebration of national independence since 1968.

October 28 In a move to appease the people, the government allows official celebrations marking the country's independence. On the 70th anniversary of the founding of the republic, some 5,000 people, representing Charter 77 and five other anti-government groups, rally in Wenceslas Square demanding democratization and greater freedom. Throughout the demonstration the name of Tomáš G. Masaryk, the founder and first president of the republic and also a symbol of democracy, is chanted. Police, wielding clubs and using water cannons, brutally disband the rally and detain more than 80 people. The police seal off the square on the following day to prevent another rally.

November Despite its statements in May that it wanted better church relations, the government cracks down on religious as well as other dissenters (*see* July 2–3, 1988).

November 11 Police break up a conference in Prague organized by Charter 77 to examine recent Czechoslovak history.

November 13 Alexander Dubček receives an honorary degree from the University of Bologna in Italy, where he defends his regime's policies in 1968.

December Czechoslovakia stops jamming the broadcasts of Radio Free Europe and the Voice of America.

December 9 French president François Mitterand meets with eight members of Charter 77 during an official visit to Prague, where he states that he advocates human rights in Czechoslovakia.

December 10 Thousands attend a government-allowed rally in Prague to mark the fortieth anniversary of the universal declaration of human rights.

1989

January 15–20   Several hours after Czechoslovakia signs the Vienna Agreement, a human rights document and a follow-up to the Helsinki Accords, police brutally attack peaceful demonstrators commemorating the twentieth anniversary of the death of Jan Palach, who set himself on fire to protest the Soviet-led invasion in 1968. As a result, six days of protests erupt demanding political freedom, with the police ruthlessly intervening at times. The authorities detain over 1,400 people including the playwright Václav Havel.

February 10   The editor of the Communist party's weekly cultural newspaper, *Tvorba* (Creation), is dismissed in an attempt to suppress dissent within the Communist party and intellectual circles.

February 21   Václav Havel, the Czech playwright and dissident, receives a nine-month prison sentence for his part in the January protests.

February 22   Seven other prominent dissidents are sentenced for illegal actions, receiving fines or sentences of up to one year.

April 17 and 26   Alexander Dubček, the leader of the 1968 reform movement, appears on Hungarian television despite complaints from the Czechoslovak government. Dubček describes the Prague Spring and his dealings with the Soviet leadership.

May 1   Approximately 2,000 young Czechoslovaks hold a pro-democracy counterdemonstration in Wenceslas Square in Prague following the traditional Communist May Day celebrations.

May 17   Havel is released early from prison for good behavior (*see* February 21, 1989).

May 26   Three British diplomats and one businessman are expelled on charges of spying shortly after Great Britain ordered the expulsion of four Czechoslovaks for the same reasons.

June 1   The United States announces that the child movie star, Shirley Temple Black, will become the ambassador to Czechoslovakia. She presents her credentials in August.

June 29   "A Few Sentences," a petition demanding political reforms, goes around the country.

June 30   In retaliation for an earlier expulsion of a Czechoslovak diplomat, Czechoslovakia expels an American diplomat on the charge that he took part in the January protests.

August 15   The Hungarian Communist party expresses regret over Hungary's participation in the 1968 invasion.

August 17   The Polish parliament passes a resolution condemning the 1968 invasion.

August 18   The Czechoslovak government criticizes Poland and Hungary for condemning the 1968 invasion and states that it is an internal matter of Czechoslovakia.

August 21   The police arrest 370, including several Poles and Hungarians, who demonstrate along with thousands on the anniversary of the 1968 invasion.

Late August   Attempting to calm the population, the government admits the necessity for "cautious" change and announces it will introduce some economic reforms in January 1990.

September   Radio Free Europe plays a secretly recorded tape of the leader of the Communist party, Miloš Jakeš, complaining at a closed meeting of the Communist party. He bemoans the lack of popular support for the government and the international fallout over the jailing of prominent dissidents such as Havel in February.

October 28   Over 10,000 people gather in Wenceslas Square on the seventy-first anniversary of the founding of the republic. The peaceful protestors, demanding freedom and the end of Communist rule, are attacked by police. Prominent dissidents are detained before October 28 to keep them from participating in the rallies.

Mid-November   Although the government continues to talk tough, it announces it will ease travel regulations, censorship, and restrictions on the church starting January 1, 1990.

November 17   To mark the 50th anniversary of a student killed by the Nazis, approximately 50,000 people, led by students, take part in a government-sponsored demonstration. This largest demonstration since August 1969 in Prague quickly turns anti-Communist when the students call for a new government. The police move in and brutally suppress the rally.

November 18   Smaller demonstrations continue. Theaters in Prague go on strike to protest the police violence from the day before.

November 19   The anti-government protests grow larger with police arresting leading dissidents. The Civic Forum, an unofficial political coalition of opposition groups including former Communist allies, led by the playwright Václav Havel, takes shape in Prague in the evening. The Civic Forum demands the resignation of the Communist party leadership, the end of the Communist monopoly on power, the democratization of the country, and freedom of the press. The government ignores the Civic Forum and its demands. Several days later in Bratislava, the Slovak equivalent to the Civic Forum, Public Against Violence, is formed.

November 20 Two hundred thousand marchers demand a new government and freedom. University students go on strike while protests spread to other large cities such as Bratislava, Brno, and Ostrava.

November 21–22 Prime Minister Ladislav Adamec holds informal talks with representatives of the Civic Forum while the demonstrations continue.

November 23 Alexander Dubček, the leader of the Prague Spring, addresses a crowd estimated at 70,000 people in Bratislava, stating he supports the anti-government rallies that are spreading to all parts of the country. In Prague, Václav Havel tells about 200,000 people in Wenceslas Square in Prague, "We are against violence."

November 24 In response to the unrest, the Communist Party Central Committee calls an urgent meeting of its membership. Unable to control the situation, Miloš Jakeš, head of the Communist party, and other top leaders resign, causing jubilation throughout the country. Alexander Dubček, the leader of the Prague Spring, makes an emotional speech to approximately 350,000 people in Prague.

November 25 The new Communist leadership promises reform and negotiations with the opposition. Havel and Dubček speak to thousands in Letenské Gardens in Prague since Wenceslas Square will no longer hold all the demonstrators; the protests are carried live by Czechoslovak television.

At the canonization ceremony of a medieval Czech princess, St. Agnes, the Archbishop of Prague, Cardinal Tomášek, calls for an end to the Communist regime.

November 26 With demonstrations keeping pressure on the government, Prime Minister Adamec meets again with opposition representatives. The Communist party announces a special party congress for January and conducts another shakeup in the Politburo, the chief decision-making and executive committee of the Communist party.

November 27 A two-hour long general strike called by the opposition starts at noon with millions walking off their jobs, showing that the Communist government has almost no support nationwide.

November 28 Under extreme pressure, the government agrees to share power with non-Communists and promises political and social reforms.

November 29 The Federal Assembly, the national parliament, deletes language from the constitution that

gives the Communist party the leading role in society, and abandons Marxism-Leninism as a basis for educational theory and instruction in all schools.

November 30 Members of the Communist government hold their first formal talks with the Civic Forum.

The government begins to dismantle fortifications along its 240-mile border with Austria.

East Germany officially states that its decision to invade Czechoslovakia in 1968 was a mistake.

December 1 The new Politburo of Czechoslovakia declares that the 1968 invasion was wrong. Two days later the government officially denounces the invasion.

December 3 In response to the demands of the demonstrators and the Civic Forum, a new government is formed consisting of five non-Communists and 16 Communists; the Civic Forum rejects the new government due to the small number of non-Communists in it.

Students demonstrate outside the Chinese embassy to mark the massacre of the pro-democracy protestors in Tiennamen Square in Beijing, China, in June 1989.

December 4 Dissatisfaction with the new government leads to renewed demonstrations in Prague. A general strike is called for December 11 if no change occurs in the government.

Five members of the Warsaw Pact, the USSR, East Germany, Poland, Hungary, and Bulgaria, jointly condemn the 1968 invasion of Czechoslovakia at a meeting of the Pact in Moscow, describing it as undue influence in the internal affairs of a sovereign country.

The Civic Forum announces it will endorse candidates when free elections are held, tentatively scheduled for June.

December 7 Prime Minister Ladislav Adamec and his government resign under intense pressure from the Civic Forum. He is replaced by the Slovak Communist Marián Čalfa, who announces that a new multi-party government will be formed with the Communists in the minority.

To dispel rumors of a military coup, the Communist minister of defense, General Miroslav Vacek, meets with Václav Havel and assures him that the military will remain neutral in the current crisis.

In a news conference, Havel announces that he is willing to become president.

December 8 The Communist-controlled government of the Czech Republic gives in to the demonstrators and accepts a minority position in a new government; the same occurs in Slovakia a couple of days later.

Czech students hold a solidarity march December 3, 1989 in support of the Chinese pro-democracy movement that was defeated in June.

December 9   In a conciliatory, televised speech, the hard-line President Gustáv Husák states he will resign upon the formation of a new government.

About 100,000 Czechs and Slovaks flock to Austrian cities on the first weekend of eased travel restrictions.

December 10   The first non-Communist government in 41 years, consisting of ten Communists and 11 non-Communists, is sworn in by President Husák, who resigns immediately afterward. Thus the last vestige of the "normalization" policies following the 1968 invasion leaves power. Čalfa, the Communist prime minister, announces that the main task of his government is to prepare for free parliamentary elections as soon as possible.

December 11   Instead of a planned strike, nationwide celebrations called for by the Civic Forum and Public Against Violence take place at noon for five minutes.

December 14   The new foreign minister and former leading dissident, Jiří Dienstbier, declares the agreement allowing Soviet troops to be stationed in Czechoslovakia as void since it was concluded under duress in 1968. He urges a radical transformation of CMEA (Council for Mutual

Economic Assistance), the economic equivalent of the Warsaw Pact that aimed at integrating the socialist economies of Eastern Europe and the USSR. He also states that all Czechs and Slovaks who fled the country for political reasons are welcome to return.

December 15   The Defense Ministry proposes dismantling the fortifications along the 150-mile frontier with West Germany, reducing compulsory military service to one year from two years, and reducing the number of total active reserves.

December 17   Thousands take to the streets to commemorate the November 17 beatings of students that led to the downfall of the Communist regime. These demonstrations quickly turn into rallies supporting Havel's bid for the presidency.

December 19   The Communist-dominated Federal Assembly approves a program for free democratic elections, changes from a planned to a free market economy, and schedules presidential elections for December 29.

December 20   Prime Minister Čalfa and Soviet leader Mikhail Gorbachev agree that special negotiations will take place to discuss the issue of Soviet troops on Czechoslovak soil.

December 21   In an attempt to reconstitute itself after two days of meetings, the Communist party votes to suspend the party membership of 32 former leaders, including Gustáv Husák and Lubomír Štrougal, and expel the former hard-liner party ideologist, Vasil Bil'ak, whom it accuses of inviting the Warsaw Pact to invade in 1968. It also agrees to disband the People's Militia, groups of armed workers who were instrumental in seizing power in 1948.

December 23   The authorities arrest the former Communist party chief of Prague, Miroslav Štěpán, for his part in brutally putting down the November 17 student protests.

December 28   After 21 years of political obscurity, Alexander Dubček, supported by the Civic Forum and Public Against Violence, is elected unanimously as chairman of the Federal Assembly, or national parliament.

December 29   The Federal Assembly elects Václav Havel as president of the republic. With this act the old Communist order ends in Czechoslovakia.

1990

January 1   In his televised New Years address, President Havel tells the country that it is in poor economic and environmental shape. He emphasizes that honesty in government and society, not lies as during the communist regime, will lead to recovery. He also urges mutual respect among the various nationalities of Czechoslovakia, and he issues an amnesty for about 20,000 prisoners who are serving sentences of two years or less.

January 2   In his first official state visit abroad, President Havel visits East and West Germany instead of the USSR or the United States, thereby showing the importance of Germany to Czechoslovakia.

January 4   The government devalues its currency, the koruna (Kčs), against the dollar to make it convertible in Western markets.

Mid-January   The government appoints Frank Zappa, the American rock musician and filmmaker and friend of Havel and many other members of the new government, as Czechoslovakia's representative of trade, culture, and tourism to the West. Several weeks later the government admits that it acted overzealously in its actions and reduces his role to an unofficial emissary for Czechoslovakia.

January 16   The city of Prague renames Red Army Square for Jan Palach, who, on this day 21 years ago, set himself on fire to protest the Soviet-led Warsaw Pact invasion.

January 18   The government announces that Prime Minister Čalfa has resigned from the Communist party, the third cabinet official to do so, thereby reducing the number of Communists in the government to seven.

January 30   As a result of an agreement worked out on January 23, the Communists in the Federal Assembly hand over more than 100 seats to the opposition, ending its 40-year control of the legislature.

February 6   The Communist prime minister of the Czech Republic, František Pitra, is replaced by Petr Pithart, a member of the Civic Forum.

February 6–7   On an official visit to Prague, U.S. Secretary of State James A. Baker III offers American economic and other aid to allow a smooth transfer from a Communist society to a democracy in Czechoslovakia.

February 9   Czechoslovakia and Israel resume diplomatic relations broken since the Arab-Israeli conflict in 1967.

February 20–22   President Havel visits the United States. While in Washington D.C., he answers students' questions at Georgetown University and meets with President George Bush, who promises freer trade and economic incentives for Czechoslovakia. Havel addresses a joint session of Congress and receives five standing ovations during his hour-long speech in which he urges the United States to help the USSR's fledgling democracy. In a visit to New York City, Havel receives an honorary law degree from Columbia University.

February 26–27   Havel meets with Soviet leader Mikhail Gorbachev in Moscow, where the two sign agreements. One treaty calls for cooperation in law enforcement, and the other starts the withdrawal of Soviet troops from Czechoslovakia, beginning immediately, and to be completed by July 1, 1991. While in Moscow, Havel has breakfast with the two surviving dissidents, out of an original seven, who publicly demonstrated on August 28, 1968, in Red Square against the Soviet-led invasion. The seven were quickly arrested and subject to brutal treatment and internal exile for many years.

March 10   The Slovak prime minister, Milan Čič, who came to power in mid-December, resigns from the Communist party.

March 23   The official name of the country changes from the Czechoslovak Socialist Republic (ČSSR) to the Czechoslovak Federative Republic (ČSFR).

President Václav Havel (r) meets U.S. president George Bush on a trip to Washington D.C. where Havel addresses a joint session of Congress.

April Martech U.S.A., an environmental service company, signs an agreement with Czechoslovakia to clear up polluted areas including former Soviet bases.

April 6 The United States and Czechoslovakia conclude a trade agreement to cut tariffs and increase business contacts and tourism.

April 18 Czechoslovakia rejoins the International Monetary Fund (IMF) and the World Bank.

April 19 The Vatican and Czechoslovakia restore diplomatic relations after forty years.

April 20 As a result of months of complaints from Slovaks who contend that the name of the country does not adequately convey its true identity, the Federal Assembly votes to change the official name of the country to the Czech and Slovak Federal Republic (ČSFR).

April 21–22 Pope John Paul II visits Czechoslovakia where he celebrates mass for thousands in Prague, Bratislava, and Velehrad, Moravia.

April 23 The campaign manager for the Civic Forum receives $25,000 at a fund raiser sponsored by American actress Jane Fonda.

Late April A six-day conference brings together European and North American legal and constitutional experts to discuss the drafting of a new constitution for the country. The main topic of discussion is how to divide power between the federal government and the two republics.

May 5–6 The city of Plzeň, in western Bohemia, celebrates for the first time since 1968 its liberation from the Nazis by American forces at the end of World War II. Under the Communist regime, credit was given to the Red Army, which supposedly freed the entire country.

May 7 Czechoslovakia signs a ten-year trade and economic cooperation agreement with the European Community, giving it associate status that will lead to full membership in that organization by the year 2000.

Mid-May Alexander Dubček visits the United States and Canada where he meets with officials and reminds them that Slovaks as well as Czechs participated in the Velvet Revolution in 1989 since many people in both countries assume that only Czechs took part. The 1989 revolution receives this characterization due to the lack of bloodshed in the peaceful change of the government.

May 12 Approximately 100,000 people rally in Prague to demand that the former Communist leaders be punished.

June 2 A week before national elections, a bomb explodes in the Old Town Square in Prague injuring 15 people. No group or people claim responsibility for it.

June 4 Slovak separatists heckle President Havel at two out of three public appearances and speeches in Nitra, Komárno, and Bratislava. Alexander Dubček scolds the protesters for a lack of respect. Since the Velvet Revolution, separatist feelings among the Slovaks has been growing for a division of the country.

June 8–9 Some 22 political parties, including the Friends of Beer party and the Romanies, who champion the rights of Gypsies, vie for seats in the Federal Assembly and the Czech and Slovak parliaments in the first free elections in 44 years. In the three ballot voting process, the Civic Forum and Public Against Violence win approximately 46 percent of the seats in both houses of the Federal Assembly; the Civic Forum also gains a majority in the Czech parliament, while Public Against Violence wins a plurality in the Slovak parliament. About 14 percent of the electorate votes for the Communist party.

June 27 The Slovak Marián Čalfa, the incumbent prime minister and former Communist, forms the first democratically elected government dominated by members of the Civic Forum and Public Against Violence. Alexander Dubček easily wins reelection as chairman of the Federal Assembly.

Vladimír Mečiar, a former boxer, an ex-Communist, and a member of Public Against Violence, becomes prime minister of Slovakia and forms a new government consisting of members from Public Against Violence, the Slovak Christian Democratic Movement, and the Slovak Democratic party.

June 29 Petr Pithart, the Civic Forum prime minister of the Czech Republic since February, forms a new government comprising members of the Civic Forum, the People's party, and the Movement for Self-Governing Democracy-Society for Moravia and Silesia.

July A plaque in memory of Father Jozef Tiso, the president of the Nazi puppet Slovak state during World War II, is placed on the wall of a former Catholic teachers college, which he helped to found. It will be quickly taken down after protests from Jewish organizations and moderate political leaders in the Slovak parliament.

July 4 The Group of 24, the foreign ministers of the 24 most advanced industrialized countries, meets in Brussels and agrees to provide economic aid for Czechoslovakia, Bulgaria, Yugoslavia, and East Germany.

July 5 An unopposed Václav Havel wins reelection as president for a two-year term.

July 9 Miroslav Štěpán, former Communist boss of Prague, receives a prison term of four years after being convicted of abusing his power during anti-government demonstrations in October 1988 and January 1989. He is the first Communist leader to be indicted and convicted (*see* December 23, 1989).

July 10 Czechoslovakia grants asylum to 51 Albanians who sought refuge in the Czechoslovak embassy in the Albanian capital of Tirana and flies them to Prague. They are among the approximately 5,000 people crowding into foreign embassies to escape the harsh economic and Stalinist political conditions in Albania.

August 14 The government puts aside $95 million in restitution for about 250,000 victims of Communist political oppression from 1948 to 1989, who have until the end of December 1990 to make their claims.

August 21 For the first time, Czechs and Slovaks commemorate the 1968 Soviet-led invasion without fear of reprisals.

August 26 More than 30,000 Slovak separatists rally in Ružomberok to pressure the Slovak government to declare its independence. However, public opinion polls show that only about 8 percent of the Slovaks favor such a move.

October 11 Thousands demonstrate throughout the country after the leader of the Communist party, Vasil Mohorita, states it is time to reassert the party's authority. The protesters want the party to be banned and its former leaders arrested. Since the Velvet Revolution the Communist party's membership has officially lost about 1 million members to now stand at about 750,000.

October 13 After deciding that the Civic Forum needs a more formal, structured organization, its members elect Václav Klaus, the federal finance minister who advocates a quick transformation to a free market economy, as its first chairman. Klaus announces that he will move the organization to the right.

October 17 Due to the backlash from October 11, General Miroslav Vacek, the Communist defense minister, is replaced by a civilian. Five days later Vasil Mohorita, the Communist party leader, loses his seat in the upper house of the Federal Assembly.

October 25 The Slovak parliament approves a law to make Slovak the official language of the state, allowing

Hungarians to use their language in official matters where they make up at least 20 percent of the population. The original bill, met by pro- and anti-demonstrations, does not make such provisions for the approximately 600,000 Hungarians who make up the largest minority in Slovakia at about 10 percent of the population.

The Federal Assembly passes a law allowing for the privatization of small businesses.

November 9 American President George Bush grants Czechoslovakia ''Most Favored Nation'' status, thereby removing most barriers to free trade between the United States and Czechoslovakia.

November 16 The Federal Assembly votes to confiscate the property of the Communist party, whose members walk out on the vote.

November 17 President Bush visits Czechoslovakia and presents a replica of the Liberty Bell on the first anniversary of the Velvet Revolution. He is the first American president to visit the country, and in honor of this occasion, the main train station in Prague is renamed for Woodrow Wilson who helped Czechoslovakia gain its independence in 1918.

November 23–24 Nationwide elections take place for reorganized municipal governments. The Civic Forum and Public Against Violence win 37 percent of the vote and the Communists win 17 percent. Under the former Communist regime, urban governments were controlled by loyal Communist appointees.

December 10 In response to the Slovak government's demand for greater autonomy, President Havel asks the Federal Assembly for unspecified temporary powers to keep the country together and the right to call a referendum on the subject of the continuation of Czechoslovakia. The Slovak government, led by Vladimír Mečiar, is becoming increasingly separatist due to fears that the federal government's moves to a quick free market economy will hurt the heavily subsidized Slovak economy.

December 12 The Federal Assembly approves new laws giving both republics greater control over internal affairs, thereby defusing the Slovak separatist drive for the moment.

1991

January 1 In a plan worked out with the International Monetary Fund (IMF), Czechoslovakia initiates the first stage of the transformation of the economy to a free market by removing price controls on 85 percent of goods sold, closing unprofitable, outdated state enterprises, privatizing small stores by auction, and making the currency, the koruna (Kčs), convertible.

January 7 As a result of implementing its January 1 plan, the IMF grants a $1.8 billion loan to Czechoslovakia. Czechoslovakia rejoined the IMF in the fall of 1990 after a 36-year absence.

January 17 The Persian Gulf War begins. To show solidarity with the U.S.-led coalition, 200 Czechoslovak soldiers take part by manning four chemical decontamination units in Saudi Arabia, where they have been posted since December 1990.

February A special commission begins investigations into the lives of about 1,000 top governmental officials, including parliamentary deputies and cabinet officers and their aides, to ascertain if any were informers for the secret police (S.T.B.) and to bring about their removal. A similar search takes place in the regional Czech government, while the regional government of Slovakia does not enact such a commission.

The government passes a law to restore businesses and other properties confiscated by the Communists after 1948 to the original owners or heirs. Persons have until the end of September to make their claims. An earlier law passed in the fall of 1990 allowed for the return of small shops and houses seized after 1955.

February 10 Civic Forum splits into two factions, one led by the federal minister of finance, Václav Klaus, which advocates a quick movement to a free market economy, and the other led by the foreign minister, Jiří Dienstbier, which consists of former Communists from 1968 and dissidents who were active in the Charter 77 movement. The Civic Forum's Slovak counterpart, Public Against Violence, falls apart in March into opponents of Slovak separatism, who support the policies of the Prague government, and advocates of Slovak separatism, who want the economic reforms to proceed slowly and greater political freedom away from Prague.

February 15 The leaders of Czechoslovakia, Poland, and Hungary meet in Hungary and sign an agreement that says that they will cooperate in transforming their planned economies to free market economies.

February 25 The Czechoslovak foreign and defense ministers, along with their counterparts from Bulgaria, Hungary, Poland, Romania, and the Soviet Union, sign an agreement in Budapest to dissolve the Warsaw Pact by March 31, 1991. However, it does not take place until July.

March In Bologna, Italy, the foreign ministers of the Pentagonale (Czechoslovakia, Austria, Hungary, Italy, and Yugoslavia) declare their support for the continued existence of Yugoslavia as a federal republic based on democratic reform.

March 11 Over 20,000 Slovak separatists, calling for independence, rally in Bratislava.

March 14 During a visit to coincide with the fifty-second anniversary of the independence of the Slovak Republic in 1939, President Havel urges the Slovaks not to secede from the country. He is jeered by crowds and his motorcade is mobbed. Public opinion polls show that 70 percent of the Slovaks want to retain a common country, down from 92 percent in August 1990.

March 22 Ten members of the Federal Assembly are publicly accused of being informants for the secret police. Many fear that this is the beginning of an inquisition since there are no criteria in place to judge the extent or severity of the informants' actions.

April 11 Volkswagen agrees to buy a majority share of the Czechoslovak automaker Škoda for $821 million. Volkswagen also promises to modernize and to increase the output of Škoda. This is the first major foreign investment into Czechoslovakia. In the coming months, other foreign corporations such as Dow Chemical, K-Mart, Mercedes Benz, Philip Morris, Conoco Oil, Rockwell, and IBM invest in Czechoslovakia by buying into large existing state concerns.

April 22 The Slovak parliament dismisses the separatist prime minister, Vladimír Mečiar, and seven other ministers when the government nearly ceases to function after the mid-March demonstrations. The new government, led by Ján Čarnogurský, a gradual separatist, supports the continued union with the Czechs until the country is admitted as a full member of the European Community. For this reason he is well received by Prague.

May 21 The Federal Assembly votes to restore farmland seized by the Communists to its original owners or heirs, but it delays action on the cooperative farms which control 90 percent of the farmland.

June 25 The USSR and Czechoslovakia sign an agreement formally ending the twenty-three-year Soviet occupation of the country. Four days later the last Soviet troops leave the country.

October The Federal Assembly passes a law prohibiting former officials of the Communist party and secret police informants from holding high governmental positions for five years.

A plaque in memory of Monsignor Jozef Tiso is placed at the house of his birth in the Slovak town of Bytča; no protests erupt over this event as they had earlier. Tiso was the president of the Nazi puppet Slovak Republic from 1939 to 1945 and was hung after being convicted by Czechoslovakia as a war criminal in 1946.

October 1 Coupon books go on sale, which are validated after paying 1000 crowns or koruny (Kčs) or about $36 on November 1, for an auction of state enterprises in a move toward private-owned businesses. On November 11 the coupon auction is delayed for two months (*see* February 29, 1992).

October 7 A Treaty of Good Neighborliness and Co-operation is signed with Germany, which affirms the inviolability of Czechoslovakia's borders and the continued existence of the country since 1918.

October 22–27 President Havel makes a state visit to the United States where he signs various political and trade agreements.

October 28 Returning from his visit to the United States, President Havel flies directly to Bratislava to show the importance of the Slovaks in the country. As Havel is about to address a rally marking the seventy-third anniversary of the country's independence, Slovak separatists jeer and throw eggs at him, ignoring his request for two minutes of silence in memory of Czechs and Slovaks who died defending freedom.

November 11 President Havel returns to Bratislava to spend a week fulfilling his presidential duties. He receives a better reception from the Slovaks this time.

November 18 Gustáv Husák, secretary general of the Czechoslovak Communist party from 1969 to 1987 and president of the republic from 1975 to 1989, dies in Bratislava at the age of 78 after a long illness. Before dying, the hard-line Communist receives the last rites of the Roman Catholic church.

November 21 Czechoslovakia signs an association agreement with the European Community (EC) that allows it a ten-year transition to full free trade.

December The Federal Assembly passes a law that imposes prison sentences of up to five years for persons supporting or promoting fascist or communist subversion.

1992

February 6 Vasil Bil'ak, former secretary of the Czechoslovak Communist Party Central Committee and Communist hard-liner, is indicted with several others on charges of illegally sending $10 million in Czechoslovak funds to the USSR to be used to support Communist movements in the West and the Third World.

February 27 Chancellor Helmut Kohl of Germany and President Václav Havel sign a treaty of friendship between their two countries in Prague. In the treaty Germany also agrees to support Czechoslovakia's entry into the European Community.

February 29 This is the last day of the government's program of "coupon privatization," which began in November 1991. All citizens 18 years and older, numbering about 11 million people, can purchase coupon books for 1,000 Kčs or approximately $35. The coupons can be redeemed for shares in over 2,000 state companies going over to the private sector or placed into mutual funds. Approximately 8.6 million people take advantage of the program for about 260 billion Kčs or $9.3 billion worth of enterprises. The purchases take place over the next few months.

March McDonald's opens its first restaurant in Prague and plans another 100 stores throughout the country over the next decade.

March 16 Volkswagen receives final approval from the Czechoslovak government to buy a percentage of Škoda, the Czechoslovak automaker, after an agreement worked out in 1991, (*see* April 11, 1991).

June 5 and 6 Approximately 86 percent of the eligible voters cast their ballots in the second and last free elections for a new Czechoslovak federal parliament and the two regional parliaments of the Czech Lands and Slovakia. About 80 different political parties are in the running. The proliferation of parties is a result of the fragmentation of the Civic Forum and its Slovak counterpart, People Against Violence, since the 1990 general elections in which they were the big winners. The results give pluralities in Slovakia to the leftist party, Movement for a Democratic Slovakia, led by Vladimír Mečiar, an ex-Communist and former boxer, and to the Civic Democratic party in the Czech Lands, led by Václav Klaus, a right-wing economist. Both parties receive about 33 percent of the vote for the federal parliament and 37 percent and 30 percent respectively for the republic parliaments. In the campaign Mečiar played on Slovak fears of continued Czech dominance in Slovakia and rapid privatization of the economy, which has resulted in an unemployment rate of 12 percent, or about four times higher than in the Czech lands, while espousing Slovak sovereignty. Klaus, on the other hand, advocates continued western-style market economy reforms. The third largest bloc in the federal parliament and the second in both

republic parliaments are leftists and Communists, who win 14 percent of the vote.

June 7 Mečiar declares he will work to unseat Václav Havel as president of the republic, while Klaus asserts he intends to keep Havel in that position. Havel allegedly offended Mečiar in a speech the day before the election, although he did not mention him by name.

June 20 After two weeks of intense negotiations on the future of Czechoslovakia, Mečiar and Klaus agree to form a new federal government and to begin the division of the country into two independent states. The federal government will be reduced from 13 ministries to five, with defense, finance, economics, interior, and foreign affairs remaining. The functions of the other ministries go to the respective republic governments, which are also instructed to work out the final arrangements by September 30 for the split of the country. Despite the agreement, a majority of Czechs and Slovaks do not approve of the dissolution of the country.

June 21 In his weekly radio address, President Havel states that the "only constitutional and moral way" for the division of Czechoslovakia to take place would be in a national referendum, which the constitution requires.

June 24 Mečiar forms a new government in Slovakia after being appointed prime minister.

June 25 In his opening address to the new Czechoslovak federal parliament, President Havel admits that the future of the country looks dim, but he appeals to the Czechs and Slovaks to remain together. He states, "Perhaps we must truly divide if we are to unite again." Furthermore, he notes that he would neither resign the presidency, nor would he preside over the dissolution of the country.

July 2 President Havel approves the new federal government that will oversee the breakup of the country.

July 3 Václav Havel's bid for his second term as president of the republic fails after the majority of the Slovak deputies in the Federal Assembly do not vote for him. Havel supporters mob and taunt the Slovak deputies after they leave the parliament building in Prague.

Mid-July Václav Klaus becomes the prime minister of the Czech republic.

July 16 A Russian representative presents two previously secret letters to President Havel. The notes, requesting Soviet aid, were written and presented to the Soviet leader Leonid I. Brezhnev in early August 1968 by five high-ranking Czechoslovak Communists who opposed the Prague Spring. Of the five Communists, only Vasil Bil'ak, the party ideology chief, remains alive, and claims that the letters could be forgeries.

July 17 As one of the first steps toward independence, the Slovak parliament declares the sovereignty of Slovakia. Shortly after Slovakia voted on its sovereignty, Václav Havel announces that he will resign the presidency on July 20 and not wait until the expiration of his term on October 5. He cites as reasons the loss of trust in him by a large portion of the Slovaks and an inability any longer to influence events in the country.

August Anticipating the dissolution of the country, the federal government announces that the second phase of the privatization program will occur in the individual republics, where the Czechs and Slovaks will be restricted to investment in their own republics.

August 4 Cardinal František Tomášek, the archbishop of Prague, who had become a symbol of the struggle for religious freedom in Communist Czechoslovakia, dies at the age of 93.

Late August After numerous negotiations between Vladimír Mečiar and Václav Klaus, the prime ministers of Slovakia and the Czech republic, the two men agree that the formal split of the country will take place on January 1, 1993.

October 26 The governments of the Czech republic and Slovakia agree to a customs union after the split on January 1, 1993. This is a condition for continued associated status in the European Community as the successors to Czechoslovakia. The two governments also acknowledge that the people of Czechoslovakia must choose citizenship in either republic before the January 1, 1993 split.

October 31 Over the vehement protests of environmental groups and Hungary, the Slovak government finishes the damming of the Danube River at Čunovo to supply water to the hydroelectric plant at Gabčíkovo. Negotiations between Hungary and Slovakia concerning the dam broke down earlier in the month. The original project, worked out 15 years earlier between Czechoslovakia and Hungary, is now viewed by the Hungarians as a relic of the Communist past. They claim it will cause an environmental disaster that will pollute the underground drinking water supply and lower the level of the river causing a hazard to shipping. The Slovak government counters that besides producing energy, the dam will improve navigation and control flooding along the Danube. It also views the dam as a symbol of their impending independence, as well as a source of extra revenue by selling surplus electricity to the West.

November The first private dental clinic opens in Prague. Under the former Communist regime, dental care was free.

November 3 The leaders and founders of the pro-democracy Charter 77, including Václav Havel, agree to disband the organization. The twelve-year-old dissident human rights organization, the oldest in Eastern Europe, fought against the Communist regime and was instrumental in its fall in Czechoslovakia. As a result, its members feel that it is no longer necessary in a democratic country.

November 7 Alexander Dubček, the leader of the Prague Spring, dies at the age of 70. Dubček, the leader of the Slovak Social Democrats at the time of his death, received multiple injuries in an automobile accident on September 1.

November 25 The Czechoslovak Federal Assembly passes a constitutional amendment that will allow the country to dissolve without requiring a referendum and stipulating that the split will occur at midnight on December 31, 1992. Until this amendment passed, there was no legal basis for the end of the country.

December 6 A masked man repeatedly stabs Jiří Svoboda, head of the Czech Communist party, at his home, severely injuring him.

December 31 During the past several weeks, over 30,000 Slovaks apply for citizenship in the Czech republic before the split occurs forcing them to remain in the poorer Slovakia.

1993

January 1 After 74 years Czechoslovakia ceases to exist at midnight December 31, despite the fact that opinion polls show that a majority of Czechs and Slovaks oppose the "Velvet Divorce," or the peaceful split into two independent parts: the Czech Republic and Slovakia. The Prague government holds no official celebrations in conjunction with the event, but instead it expresses regret over the breakup. Several hundred Czechs lay flowers before a Czechoslovak flag in front of the statue of St. Wenceslas in Wenceslas Square in Prague to mark the end of the country. In Bratislava over 50,000 people pack the main square in below freezing temperatures to sing the Slovak national anthem. The two countries will retain a common currency for the time being. Due to the separation, Slovakia stands to lose up to $1 billion in subsidies. The population of the new Czech Republic is 10.5 million, while that of independent Slovakia is 5 million.

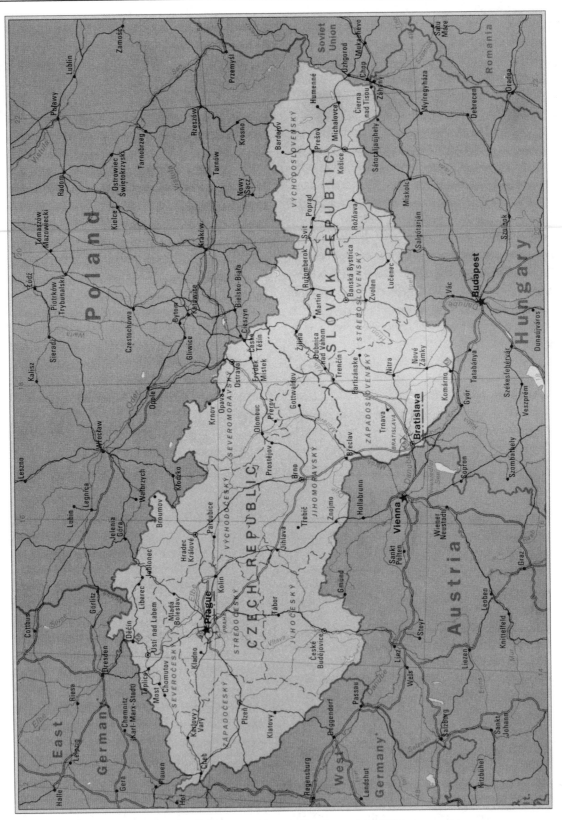

The former Czechoslovakia, which ceased to exist on January 1, 1993, is now two separate and independent states—Czech Republic and Slovakia.

Citizens in both the Czech Republic and Slovakia must now pay for their health care, which under the Communist regime was free.

The editor-in-chief of the largest Slovak opposition newspaper, *Smena,* is dismissed.

Prices rise in Slovakia 10 to 40 percent despite governmental assurances that the new valued added tax (VAT) would cause only a 5 to 6 percent increase. The government blames retailers for taking advantage of the VAT to hike prices and launches an investigation.

In his New Years address, Prime Minister Vladimír Mečiar of Slovakia rejects the ban on former Communists in governmental positions and a total free market economy, two items that are continuing in the Czech Republic. He also states that all members of the Slovak parliament should swear allegiance to the new constitution. His remarks are aimed at the deputies of the Christian Democratic Movement (KDH) and the Hungarian minority, who either voted against or abstained in the September vote. The KDH claim the constitution places too much power in the hands of the government and ruling party, while the Hungarians feel it does not recognize their right to autonomy in Slovakia. In the months since becoming Slovak prime minister in June, Mečiar has moved against his critics by renationalizing the company that prints all the newspapers in Bratislava; by blocking foreign investment, aimed at financial self-sufficiency, into the largest Slovak independent daily newspaper; by taking steps to increase the government's share in banks; and by returning the media to state control. He furthermore warns Hungary against interfering in the internal affairs of Slovakia.

January 2 A bomb causes minor damage at the Starý Hrozenkov checkpoint, one of the twenty new border stations between the Czech Republic and Slovakia. No one claims responsibility.

January 3 Many Slovaks begin withdrawing their money from banks fearing that the end to a common currency, the Czechoslovak koruna (Kčs), will result in a much devalued Slovak currency introduced in the next few weeks.

January 26 Václav Havel defeats two opponents in elections held in the Czech parliament to become the Czech Republic's first president. He is sworn in on February 2 to a five-year term.

Michal Kováč, Prime Minister Vladimír Mečiar's candidate for the presidency of Slovakia, does not receive the needed three-fifths majority vote of the Slovak parliament to become president. It is seen as a setback for Mečiar and further balloting is scheduled. However, Kováč, a former

Communist bank executive, is elected as president on February 15.

March 15 Jiří Svoboda, the head of the Communist party, resigns after the party rejects his proposal to rename the organization the Party of Democratic Socialism and in protest to the party's readmitting Miroslav Štěpán, the former party chief of Prague, who served more than a year in prison for his role in brutally suppressing the prodemocracy demonstrations in 1989.

April 13 The Czech Republic bans abortions for foreigners to prevent a rush of Poles seeking the operation after the Polish government adopted a strict abortion policy in March.

May Slovakia and Hungary go to the World Court in The Hague to decide the issue of the Čunovo dam on the Danube that has lowered water levels in Hungary threatening the water table and a protected wildlife sanctuary.

May 6 Czech police arrest five foreigners on charges of plotting to assassinate President Václav Havel.

June 15 In an attempt to improve its international credit rating, Slovakia signs an agreement with the International Monetary Fund (IMF) in which it agrees to hold its deficit spending to about 5 percent of the Gross National Product (GNP), to speed up the privatization of state owned business, and to preserve its hard currency reserves.

June 22 The European Community formally invites the Czech Republic, Slovakia, Bulgaria, Hungary, Poland, and Romania to apply for membership. It is not expected that the countries will become full members before the turn of the century.

Radio Free Europe announces it will end its foreign language broadcasts to the Czech Republic, Slovakia, Hungary, and Poland.

June 30 Slovakia begins collecting a 20 percent surcharge on import tariffs in an attempt to aid Slovak exports.

July 11 Under pressure since the Czech and Slovak currencies separated on February 8, the Slovak government devalues the Slovak crown by 10 percent.

July 17 The Czech Republic and Slovakia agree to tighten their common border controls in an attempt to reduce the number of illegal aliens passing through the two countries on their way to Western Europe.

August 13 The Czech government announces that employment remains low at 2.8 percent or 148,600 people.

August 26 In Prague to commemorate the 25th anniversary of the Prague Spring and the Soviet-led invasion of Czechoslovakia, Russian President Boris Yeltsin and Czech

President Václav Havel sign a treaty of friendship and agree to end past tensions. While in Prague, the Russian president condemns the 1968 Soviet led invasion of Czechoslovakia and places flowers on the grave of a Czech student killed during the invasion. During his visit, Yeltsin states that Russia has no objection if the Czech Republic joins NATO.

Yeltsin meets with Premier Mečiar in Bratislava and signs an accord with Slovakia that calls for military cooperation and closer economic ties.

September 30 The second round of the privatization of 770 state-owned enterprises, estimated to be worth $5 billion, begins in the Czech Republic. It is estimated that 60 percent of the large businesses in the Czech Republic are already privately owned (*see* February 29, 1992).

October 21 During a state visit to Warsaw, Czech President Havel states that the Czech Republic, Poland, Hungary, and Slovakia want full membership in NATO after the United States earlier proposed they receive associate membership. Havel notes that the relationship suggested by the United States would not guarantee the four countries' security, while at the same time he attempts to reassure Russia by stating that full membership would not endanger Russia.

November 2 French automaker Renault and Karosa, the Czech bus manufacturer, announce the formation of a joint company to produce busses and trucks. According to the plan, Renault will purchase an initial 31 percent of the business for about $10 million, after which its share will rise to 51 percent in five years.

November 10 After months of negotiations, the Movement for a Democratic Slovakia, the ruling party led by Prime Minister Mečiar, and the opposition Slovak National party agree to form a coalition thereby giving it control of the parliament with 80 seats.

November 24 President Havel signs a new criminal code into law despite his objections to the provisions that call for prison sentences of up to two years for slandering

the Czech Republic, government, and parliament. Havel expresses the hope that the constitutional court will find the slander clauses unlawful.

November 27–28 At the annual meeting of the Civic Democratic party, Václav Klaus, the premier of the Czech Republic, wins reelection as party leader.

December 1 Slovak Premier Mečiar accuses Slovakia's ethnic Hungarian minority of attempting to stir up trouble between Slovakia and Hungary.

December 8 The results of a poll conducted in November find that the most trusted politician in Slovakia is President Kováč, followed by Premier Mečiar.

Following the German example, the Czech parliament agrees to tighten asylum laws. Refugee status now will be granted only to people who fear persecution in their native country; economic reasons will no longer be valid for asylum.

December 14 In the wake of Russian national elections on December 12 in which the ultra-nationalists, led by Vladimír Zhirinovskii, have a strong showing, Czech Premier Klaus admits that the Russian election results are discouraging, but he urges calm. In Slovakia Premier Mečiar warns that fascism threatens Russia. He urges support of Russian President Yeltsin and the Russian government to counter the influence of Zhirinovskii.

December 15 Bowing to American pressure the Czech government agrees not to allow Škoda Plzeň, an engineering company that builds nuclear power plants, to export nuclear technology to Iran. The United States fears that Iran will use the technology to build atomic bombs.

Slovak President Kováč tells reporters that the only way for the political situation in Slovakia to stabilize is for Premier Mečiar to resign. Mečiar's political coalition holds a slim majority in parliament (*see* November 10).

December 28 It is reported that the official unemployment rate for the Czech Republic stands at 3.3 percent while inflation hovers at 10 percent.

Chapter Four

EAST GERMANY

Prior to the establishment of the German Democratic Republic (GDR), the territory composing the new state consisted of the provinces of Prussia, Saxony, Thuringia, Mecklenburg, and Silesia. Boasting a combination of agriculture and industry, it contained several historically important cities such as Potsdam, the home of Prussian kings such as Frederick the Great; Berlin, capital of Prussia and of the German Empire under the Hohenzollern dynasty; and Weimar, the namesake city of the German Republic that existed between the world wars. Other old and important cities such as Lübeck, Leipzig, Dresden, and Stettin were also included.

This area was considered the heart of "old Germany" and spawned the Hohenzollern empire that came to dominate Germany prior to World War I. Parts of Prussia and Silesia were lost to Poland as a result of Germany's defeat during World War I. Further losses to Poland occurred along the lines of the Oder and Neiße rivers following World War II.

During the course of World War II the Soviet Army pushed the German forces back across Poland and into the area that would become the GDR. The Soviets occupied the territory at the end of the war according to Allied occupation agreements reached at the Yalta and Potsdam conferences in 1945. When Germany was divided into four occupation zones, the Soviets maintained control over their occupied area and with the help of German Communists ran the zone as a one-party government until the GDR was formed in 1949.

The creation and development of the GDR was the work of Wilhelm Pieck and Walter Ulbricht. Ulbricht, a dedicated Stalinist, worked to achieve security and pros-

perity for his country and fought liberalism throughout his regime. By the late 1960s his country had grown to be the tenth industrial power in the world. His power peaked in 1968 when he influenced the Soviets to crush the "Prague Spring" in Czechoslovakia, a movement Ulbricht considered threatening to all Communist states in East Europe. Resisting the Soviet Union's desire for détente with the West and suffering from ill health, Ulbricht was forced into retirement in 1971.

Ulbricht's disciple, Erich Honecker, replaced him and moved the country toward a position more acceptable to the Soviets and to East Germans as well. While industrially advanced in East European terms, the East Germans suffered from outdated machinery and methods as well as environmental problems seldom seen in the West. Honecker was removed from office in the power shake-up in 1989 resulting from the onset of glasnost throughout Eastern Europe and the daily flight of thousands of East Germans to the West. It was clear that East Germany was ready to renounce its Communist past and reunite with West Germany in 1990.

1943

November 28 The Allied leaders meet at the Teheran Conference. U.S. president Franklin Delano Roosevelt, British prime minister Winston Churchill, and Soviet dictator Joseph Stalin issue a vague and general agreement to demilitarize, denazify, and democratize Germany and to set up three (American, British, and Soviet) occupation zones.

The former East Germany in relation to the size of the United States.

1945

February 4–11 Roosevelt, Churchill, and Stalin meet once again, at the Yalta Conference. They confirm the broad zones of occupation but create a fourth zone for France, with the Soviet zone being left essentially intact. They also agree that Berlin and Vienna are to be zoned, or divided, for occupation purposes.

April 25 U.S. and Soviet forces meet at the Elbe River at Torgau.

April 30 Led by Walter Ulbricht, Communist Party of Germany (KPD) functionaries return to Berlin from Moscow to organize the population as desired by the Soviets. Anton Ackermann and Gustav Sobottka do the same in Saxony and Mecklenburg.

May 1 The Battle of Berlin begins.

May 2 The German Berlin garrison is ordered to surrender to the Soviet general Vasili I. Chuikov.

May 7 Germany surrenders to the Americans at Reims.

May 8 Victory in Europe (VE) Day. Germany surrenders to the Soviets in Berlin.

June 5 The Allied Control Committee is established to administer the four occupied zones.

June 6 The Allied Control Committee meets to sign a declaration for joint assumption of control of occupied Germany.

June 9 The Soviet Military Administration is set up in the eastern zone.

June 10 General—soon to be Marshal—Georgi Zhukov pledges economic disarmament for Germany, and he announces his appointment as supreme head of the USSR military administrator of the eastern zone, with General Vasili D. Sokolovsky as first deputy.

The Soviet Military Administration in Germany allows the establishment of antifascist political parties and free trade unions.

June 11 General Zhukov announces concessions to anti-Nazi political parties and labor and formally abolishes all Nazi laws, decrees, and instructions.

The KPD issues its first public declaration since 1933, that argues for a parliamentary democratic republic based on a German, instead of a Soviet, model.

June 14 The USSR begins its occupation of U.S.-held territory in central Germany.

June 15 The Socialist Party of Germany (SPD) Central Committee publishes an appeal to the German people arguing for a relatively moderate, Weimar-style democracy that allows for multiparty participation in a democratic government.

June 22 Germans flee areas in the eastern zone to be occupied by the USSR.

June 26 The KPD bars a Soviet political system. It seeks a coalition parliamentary government and development of private enterprise. Wilhelm Pieck, a German Communist leader, heads the list of manifesto signers.

The Christian Democratic Union (CDU) is organized and publishes its appeal, giving its political philosophy and asking for support.

June 27 Thousands of Poles, awaiting repatriation, flee from the USSR zone to the West.

June 31 The Allied Control Council holds its first formal meeting in Berlin and begins the task of governing Germany.

July 3 At a party conference, Ulbricht appeals for agreement between Social Democrats and Communists to form antifascist youth groups.

American and British troops arrive to occupy their zones in Berlin. French forces arrive by the end of the month.

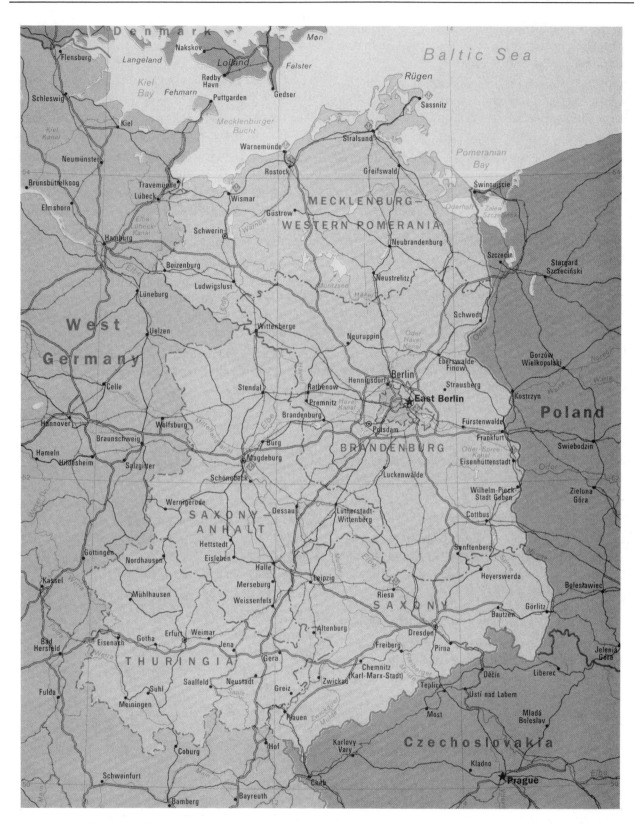

The former East Germany.

1946

July 5 The USSR begins removing machines and industrial equipment from its zone as described in the Yalta Agreement (*see* February 4–11, 1945).

The liberal Democrats (LDPD) organize and publish their appeal to the German people, supporting a less socialistic system. They are the most pro-capitalist party at this time.

July 8 Supreme Headquarters in Europe of Allied Forces (SHEAF) responsibilities are to be absorbed by the four-power council.

July 11 Moderate groups form the CDU political party in USSR-occupied Berlin.

July 14 The Front, an organization of the four major political parties (KPD, SPD, CDU, and LDPD) forms to work out a common program of action.

July 17 The Allied Reparations Committee in Moscow outlines eight principles to govern its program. It urges the removal of heavy industries and a ban on foreign loans to Germany.

The USSR announces it will break up big estates and begins to decentralize industry in its zone of occupation.

American president Harry S Truman and British prime ministers Winston Churchill and Clement Attlee meet with Soviet dictator Joseph Stalin at the Potsdam Conference to discuss the specifics of the occupation and the future of Germany.

August 1 Marshal Zhukov authorizes the creation of antifascist Youth Committees in the Soviet zone.

August 13 After forming the Front on July 14, the major political parties (KPD, SPD, CDU, and LDPD) hold a conference to discuss political cooperation.

September 6 The Soviets break up estates in Saxony.

September 10 Estates are expropriated in Mecklenburg.

September 13 The Soviets announce the establishment of a German government for their zone, consisting of 11 directors; three men named are Communists.

October 1 Schools open in the Soviet zone.

October 13 Ulbricht demands the end of Opel Motor Works in the Soviet zone.

November 4 The Berlin Antifascist Democratic Front (composed of the Berlin sections of the KPD, SPD, CDU, and LDPD) announces its policy on punishment of Nazis.

December 28 The Social Democrat and Communist parties appoint a joint committee to prepare for their merger into a single workers party.

1946

March 7 The Free German Youth (FDJ) is formed under the leadership of Communists Erich Honecker and Hermann Axen.

April 11 General Sokolovsky succeeds Marshal Zhukov as the Soviet member of the Allied Control Council.

April 20 The first German Communist party congress on the zonal level convenes in Soviet-occupied Berlin.

April 22 The Communist and Socialist parties in the Soviet zone officially merge into the new Socialist Unity party (SED). Party leader Wilhelm Pieck (KPD) and the Socialist leader Otto Grotewohl (SPD) clasp hands at a mass meeting to celebrate the merger.

May 14 The Allied Control Council orders the confiscation of German books glorifying militarism. Confiscation of books glorifying Nazism is ordered May 25. The Soviets compile a list of books to be seized.

May 21 Soviet Military Command recognizes the *Social Democratic* (SPD) and SED (Einheit) parties in Berlin.

May 29 The Allied Control Council recognizes both the SPD and SED parties, paving the way for citywide elections in Berlin.

June 23 The USSR announces that it will permit municipal and other local elections in the Saxony and Thuringia regions of the Soviet zone in September 1945.

June 30 The Soviets introduce bureaucratic measures to prevent Germans from moving across the demarcation line to the western zones.

July 6 The British and Soviet zones exchange 2.25 million homebound German refugees.

July 11 The USSR announces plans to expropriate 200 large business enterprises in its zone.

August 10 The Allies approve a temporary constitution for Berlin and schedule the first postwar city elections.

August 19 The USSR seizes all properties of alleged Nazi war criminals.

September 7 The U.S. secretary of state James Byrnes states that American policy urges a central German government under a federal constitution, zonal unification, and a cut in all occupation forces.

September 16 Election returns in the eastern zone show the SED winning in Saxony, Thuringia, Mecklenburg, and Brandenberg, but with strong opposition.

October 20 The SED is defeated in its bid for control of the four Allied occupied zones of Berlin. The SPD wins in all four zones in Kreis (county) and Länder (state) elections.

October 21 In the elections in Berlin the SED gets only 20 percent of the vote while the SPD wins, and the CDU comes in second. In the USSR zone, the SED party maintains a narrow lead. However, the combined votes of the opposition parties exceed the SED party numbers.

Operation Ossavakim begins when thousands of technical and managerial personnel and skilled workers and their families are removed to the USSR with their equipment.

November 17 Otto Grotewohl, co-chairman of the SED, offers a strongly socialistic draft for a national constitution for all of Germany.

December 2 The Berlin Municipal Assembly elects Otto Ostrowski as lord mayor to replace Acting Mayor Arthur Werner.

December 7 The Berlin City Administration is unable to start operations because of USSR objections to the mayoral election.

December 8 Werner ousts Ostrowski. Berlin now has two city governments resulting from USSR objections to the assembly's election of Ostrowski.

1947

January 16 Soviet troops invade and search the SPD party headquarters in the U.S. zone of Berlin for subversive materials.

February 9 The three democratic parties' representatives win the Berlin university student election despite Soviet support for the SED party candidates.

February 14 The Berlin parliament passes legislation to socialize essential industry, including electrical, steel, automotive, and coal.

February 26 The Allied Control Council unanimously approves a law abolishing the Prussian state.

March 11 The Democratic Women's Society of Germany forms under SED sponsorship. Soviet-zone women are pressured to join.

March 23 U.S. secretary of state George C. Marshall and Soviet foreign minister Vyacheslav M. Molotov offer different plans for a new German government to the Foreign Ministry Council of the four occupying powers. Marshall's plan envisions a freely elected democratic government, while Molotov wants a government more in line with Soviet thinking and control.

April 16 The Foreign Ministry Council clashes over the two plans in a general meeting called to discuss the issue.

May 8 Foreign Ministry Council president Ludwig Erhard, a CDU economist, calls for a conference of German state presidents from all zones to discuss the economic future of Germany and the two plans.

May 31 Erhard rejects the demand of German leaders from the Soviet zone to move the presidents' conference from Munich to Berlin.

June 6–8 Soviet-zone state presidents leave the Munich conference when the agenda is limited to economic issues.

October 9 The Soviet zone launches efforts to get its workers to speed output to gain superiority over western zones.

October 29 The USSR starts its purge of noncommunist public officials in its zone.

November 28 Marshall and Molotov agree on the need for a provisional central government for Germany.

1948

January 12 The USSR threatens to oust the Western Powers from their occupation zones in Berlin.

January 15 Reacting to the January 12 Soviet threat, American undersecretary of state Robert A. Lovett says U.S. troops will stay in Berlin.

January 25 Soviet sentries halt a British train carrying Germans to the British zone in Germany and force it to return to Berlin.

February 7 The British and Americans merge economic administration of their zones and establish the Bizonal Economic Administration.

February 14 General Sokolovsky, the Soviet commander, proclaims an economic administration for Soviet zone similar to that of merged American and British zones from February 7.

March 23 The USSR cancels sessions of Allied Control Council committee. American general Lucius Clay, the U.S. military commander in Germany, reaffirms the decision of the Western Powers to stay in Berlin.

April 1 The USSR imposes stringent highway and railway restrictions on shipments from the western zones to Berlin in an attempt to get the Allied powers to leave Berlin. This is the start of the Berlin blockade.

April 5 A Soviet fighter collides with a British European Airways airliner flying into Berlin at the start of the blockade.

June 15 The Soviets halt coal railway cars from the west and assume control over all outbound German rail travelers.

June 18 The Western Powers, over Soviet protest, send a new joint occupation currency (the west mark) into their Berlin sectors.

June 23 Soviet military administration decrees their own currency (the east mark) reforms in their zone and in all four sectors of Berlin.

June 24 The USSR bans all rail traffic between the western zones and Berlin.

June 26 The Western Powers begin airlift operations to West Berlin with thirty-two flights carrying eighty tons of food and medicine.

July 1 The Soviets withdraw from the Allied Kommandantura Berlin, the four Allied military commanders who collectively run the occupation of Berlin, and complete the division of the city between East and West.

July 6 The United States, Great Britain, and France demand that the USSR lift the rail blockade.

Soviet zone Communists form a committee to enforce a two-year recovery plan in the east zone.

July 14 The USSR rejects the Western Powers protest over the blockade. It hints that the siege will be lifted only if the Western Powers agree to reopen discussions on the question of German reunification.

July 20 General Clay and American ambassador Robert D. Murphy fly to Washington to discuss the German question with President Truman.

July 26 The Germans agree to proceed with the organization of a trizonal government for western Germany on the basis of the six-power London agreement of February 1948.

July 31 The envoys of Big Three Western Powers discuss currency and blockade situations with Soviet foreign minister Molotov in Moscow.

August 2 Western envoys have a two-hour meeting with Stalin at the Kremlin concerning Germany currency and Soviet restrictions.

August 26 Communists invade the city hall in Berlin, demanding the resignation of the city assembly dominated by non-Communists.

August 27 Molotov and his deputy, Andrei Y. Vishinsky, meet with three Western envoys in Moscow to discuss the blockade.

August 31 The four military governors of Germany meet in Berlin to work out the manner in which a Moscow decision reached the day before, to give the Soviet Union the right to issue Berlin's only currency, can be reconciled with the four-power rule of the city, and to discuss technical procedure by which the Soviet military administration can lift the blockade of Berlin.

September 1 A parliamentary assembly convenes in Bonn to draft a constitution for western Germany.

September 12 The USSR creates the German Committee to assure implementation of its industrial program. It receives wide powers in order to deal with saboteurs.

September 22 The three Western powers deliver identical notes to the Soviet Union designed to bring a showdown on the question of whether Stalin intends to recognize their rights in Berlin.

September 26 The foreign ministers of the United States, Great Britain, and France announce that the Berlin question will go to the Security Council of the United Nations for consideration.

October 4 The UN Security Council begins consideration of the Berlin dispute.

October 13 The Soviet military government refuses to end the blockade until western marks are withdrawn from Berlin and eastern marks are established in all sectors.

The United States reports it evacuated 1,200 children to western Germany from Berlin due to the hardships.

October 16 The United States and Great Britain unify their airlift efforts. As a result, the Western sectors' food rations are raised 15 percent.

October 20 The western German parliamentary council meets in Bonn to draft a constitution for western Germany.

October 22 Western parliamentary council members submit a resolution to the UN Security Council for "immediate removal" of all Berlin transportation restrictions.

October 22–25 Wilhelm Pieck, co-chairman of the SED, presides at a meeting of the All German People's Council (AGPC), which is a prelude to the establishment of an east German parliament. The AGPC meeting ends amid dwindling enthusiasm, but Pieck sees the council as the future government.

October 26 The United States, Great Britain, and France formally accept the United Nations Resolution to

An American C-47 brings food to blockaded Berlin as Berliners watch from the ruins at the edge of Templehof Airfield.

remove travel restrictions on Berlin, while the Soviet Union vetoes it.

October 27 Three Western governments state their willingness to accept the resolution despite the Soviet veto.

October 28 Stalin accuses the Western governments of deliberately refusing to abide by the Moscow agreement on currency from August 30 (*see* August 31).

November 7 General Clay asserts the Berlin airlift can maintain an average supply load of 4,000 tons a day in all types of weather.

November 11 The chief of staff of the Soviet military administration says the USSR intends to force down all American and British planes flying outside the corridors leading to blockaded Berlin.

November 17 President Truman bars all Big Four talks between the United States, Great Britain, France, and the USSR until the USSR lifts its blockade.

November 22 The USSR requires all sports groups in the Soviet zone to join the Free German Youth Organization (FDJ). It plans strict control for political indoctrination.

November 27 Ousted Socialist Unity party (SED) leader Ernest Gniffke flees to U.S. zone.

November 30 The SED calls a meeting in the Admiralpalast Theater and sets up a separate administration for East Berlin. Communist Friedrich Ebert is elected as the East Berlin mayor.

December 2 The Western Zonal City Assembly demands that the Ebert government resign. Allied liaison officers are withdrawn from city hall to avoid implying recognition; Deputy Mayor Friedensburg is barred from city hall.

December 4 The Ebert regime acknowledges the USSR as the sole authority in East Berlin.

December 5 Five thousand employees of the Soviet sector Bewag electric works defy Ebert regime by threatening to strike unless police guards are removed and the five arrested workers, who are held as political prisoners, are freed.

West Berlin holds elections, giving 64.5 percent to the German Social Democratic party (SPD), led by Ernst Reuter.

December 6 Eighty-six percent of eligible voters cast their ballots for a city assembly. In defiance of Soviet threats, voters give the SPD a win by a huge majority.

December 8 The newly elected city assembly, dominated by the SPD, names Ernst Reuter lord mayor.

December 22 The Western Allies reconstitute the Berlin (Allied) Kommandantura (Command Office) on a Three Power (United States, Great Britain, France) basis, but leaves the way open for USSR participation if it wishes.

December 31 The Western military governments announce the formal reconstitution of the Allied Kommandantura on a Three Power basis after the USSR refuses to participate.

1949

January The first two-year economic plan (1949–51) is announced. Using Soviet-style economic planning, it advocates the rapid expansion of the basic industries as critical to the building of socialism.

January 26 The Communist party congress opens in Berlin where leaders indicate that a purge of nationalist elements and curbs on minority parties are to begin.

February 2 Soviet Premier Stalin, answering a reporter, "sees no obstacles" to lifting the Berlin blockade if the Western powers remove their "counter-blockade" of East Berlin.

February 15 American and Soviet delegates to the United Nations confer on the Berlin issue.

February 27 The Communists take over the courts, the SED party, and the legislative committees by purging "unreliable elements" and by appointing new judges, prosecutors, etc., in an effort to move east Germany toward a satellite people's democracy.

March The All German People's Council (AGPC), the government in east Germany elected in March 1948, establishes a constitution setting up the German Democratic Republic (GDR), also called East Germany.

March 1 The SED party is admitted into the Cominform, the international Communist organization.

March 20 The AGPC, controlled by Communists, approves a constitution for all of Germany, setting up a totalitarian regime. It orders the election of a congress to ratify the constitution, but if it is not ratified, the constitution will apply to the Soviet zone anyway.

The Western Powers declare that the reformed West German mark will be the sole currency acceptable in their zones. West Berlin follows suit in a few weeks, but some shops accept East German marks at an eight-to-one ratio.

March 30 Soviet marshal Sokolovsky leaves as military governor; General Vasili I. Chuikov is named as his successor.

April 2 Due to the flight of great numbers of scholars and scientists to the West, East Germany offers special privileges to induce bourgeois, or middle-class, intellectuals to stay in East Germany.

April 4 The North Atlantic Treaty is signed in Washington D.C., establishing a defensive alliance, NATO, aimed at the Soviet bloc.

April 11 American and British airmen fly a record 8,240.1 tons of food and coal into Berlin.

April 12 The AGPC calls a congress to adopt the constitution approved on March 20.

April 19 The Soviet Military Administration in Berlin tells the German Economic Council in the Soviet zone that all interzonal barriers to rail, water, and highway traffic will be lifted by the middle of the year.

April 20 The USSR approves the elections for the AGPC.

April 26 The USSR demands a Foreign Ministers Council meeting on the political status of all of Germany as a condition for ending the Berlin blockade.

May 5 Big Four representatives reach an accord that ends the blockade on May 12. They agree to convene a Foreign Ministers Council on May 23 with the German problem on the agenda.

May 10 Soviet general Chuikov issues an order to lift the blockade on May 12.

May 12 The blockade is lifted after 328 days. Trains, cars, and buses reach the city and electricity is restored to Berlin.

May 16 AGPC elections take place. One slate of candidates is presented, nominated by Communists. Final election results show a crushing defeat for the USSR. The Soviet news bureau puts the no vote at 33.1 percent, while the Americans and West Germans put the vote against the Communist slate at over 50 percent.

May 26 Trains are halted again as a Soviet railroad administrator bars East Berlin workers from manning switch boxes to counter a strike over the workers' desire to be paid in western marks.

May 31 The AGPC adopts the constitution for the German Democratic Republic (GDR). Only one representative dissents, and American Communist leader Gerhart Eisler is elected to the AGPC in absentia.

July 11   The blockade is virtually reimposed as the USSR halts truck traffic.

July 13–15   The U.S. Army sends a 60-truck convoy from Helmstedt to Berlin to test new curbs. It arrives unhampered and, by July 15, truck traffic returns to normal.

August 24   A purge of state governments is announced.

October 1   The Berlin airlift ends with Lord Mayor Reuter greeting the last flight carrying some 277,264 people.

October 8   The Communists form a government in East Germany, which they claim represents all of Germany. The People's Council is renamed the People's Chamber and promulgates the constitution. Otto Grotewohl is named minister-president, and Johannes Dieckmann president of the People's Chamber. Elections are set for October 1950.

October 10   The USSR transfers to East Germany all functions that were previously the responsibilities of the Soviet military authorities in the Soviet occupied zone.

October 11–12   The GDR is inaugurated with Pieck being elected president by a joint session of both houses of parliament. Grotewohl becomes prime minister, and Ulbricht (KPD), Otto Nuschke (CDU), and Professor Hermann Kastner (LDPD) become deputy premiers.

October 17   The GDR and the USSR establish diplomatic relations.

The Chinese Communist leader Mao Tse-tung hails the new government.

October 22   West German chancellor Konrad Adenauer refuses to recognize the GDR.

A purge starts among non-Communist political leaders and Berlin radio staff.

December 5   The West Berlin government reports that 30,000 refugees have entered the sector since the first of the year.

December 9   The GDR government bans the Christmas holiday and Christmas school programs.

December 19   Pro-Tito Communists, who want a German state independent of the Soviets, form the Independent Workers party (UAP).

1950

January   The first five-year economic plan for the country is authorized by parliament and begins immediately.

January 8   The Socialist Unity party (SED) announces a drive to "liberate" Western sectors of Berlin from U.S. colonial control.

January 17   The USSR ends control of all East German concentration camps established in 1945 for Nazis and other enemies of the state. As a result about 15,000 inmates expect to be released.

January 18–February 3   The GDR begins a slowdown of rail and truck traffic to protest Western sector police seizing Soviet railroad administration headquarters in Berlin because of tax arrears and ousting East German guards from the building.

American major general Maxwell Taylor charges the USSR with attempting to blockade Berlin.

February 6   The SED begins a purge of provincial officials, causing some officials to flee to West Berlin.

February 9   Participants who are not members of the Communist-organized Free German Youth (FDJ) organizations are banned from sports and other activities.

The Ministry of State Security is created with the secret police (SSD) system at the core.

February 16   The East German Communist National Front adopts a plan for reunification under its domination.

March 1   American high commander John McCloy pledges U.S. support if democratic principles are guaranteed for reunification. He backs general elections on unity at time of East German elections in October.

March 7   Grotewohl rejects McCloy's proposal for nationwide elections.

March 23   The West German government outlines a reunification plan calling for a constitution drafted by an elected assembly and approved by a national referendum; Grotewohl rejects the plan.

April 22   A new East German law gives police control over the flow of goods into Berlin.

April 23   The Western commandants approve West Berlin's request for elections for a single city government.

April 24   Roman Catholic and Evangelical clergy of Berlin join in an attack on Communism. They charge the regime with trying to suppress religion.

May 1   Deputy Premier Ulbricht calls for Communist agitation in Western zones; youths amass at the border with the American zone but make no attempt to cross.

May 15   The East German Politburo, the main decision-making body in the country, calls on Communists to speed up the Bolshevization, or communization, of all Germany. It targets schools and private enterprise.

Wilhelm Pieck, Walter Ulbricht, and Otto Grotewohl.

Western foreign ministers renew their bid for free all-German elections under proper safeguards to ensure that they are truly democratic.

May 16   Stalin announces his government's decision to cut East Germany's war reparations balance of $6.432 billion by 50 percent.

May 20   The USSR withdraws the travel passes of the American and British military missions in Potsdam; the United States and Great Britain retaliate in kind for the Soviets in their respective zones.

May 24–30   An FDJ rally draws a crowd of 500,000 into East Berlin, where Ulbricht, Pieck, and Grotewohl address the crowd.

May 27   The United States, Great Britain, and France ask the USSR to join in forming an all-German election law; Ulbricht rejects the election proposal the next day, and Communist leaders urge the FDJ to banish Western powers from Berlin and all of Germany.

June 4   Three hundred eighty FDJ deserters plead to stay in West Berlin claiming they were coerced to join the rally held in May. Their wish to remain in West Berlin is eventually granted.

June 8   The USSR shifts its local control to East German civilians.

Ulbricht completes a series of trade and defense pacts with east bloc countries starting with Poland on June 8, Czechoslovakia on June 24, and Hungary on June 25. The East German parliament ratifies the pacts on June 29.

June 17   Grotewohl offers government protection to clergy who cooperate with the Communists. He warns church leaders who interfere in political activity that they are subject to arrest.

June 21   Ulbricht visits Prague and signs a treaty with Czechoslovakia stating that the current borders between the two countries are permanent.

July 1   The USSR cuts off electricity and water to the Western sectors of Berlin; however, electric power is kept running by a West Berlin plant.

July 6   East Germany signs a treaty with Poland that recognizes the Oder-Neiße line as the legitimate border between the two states and renounces claims to the former German territories now in Poland and the Soviet Union.

July 8   The USSR detains Berlin-bound trains and trucks at Helmstedt border crossing.

July 9 East Berlin restores water to Western sectors, while talks on power delivery resumption are set.

July 11 West Germany reports that the USSR and People's Police seized mail to and from Berlin, holding 40 mail cars.

July 21 The SED congress opens. President Pieck's speech to the group outlines party aims, admits membership decline, and urges a Titoist purge (party members not following the Soviet line but aligning themselves with the philosophy of Yugoslavian leader Josip Broz Tito).

July 22 The USSR gives the East German government control over foreign property pending a peace treaty.

July 24 Ulbricht outlines a new five-year economic plan announced for 1951. He orders German Communists to support the plan and indicates that the Soviet Union and Czechoslovakia will send the raw materials to help fuel it.

July 30 The SED Central Committee names Walter Ulbricht secretary general of the party.

August 26 East German Communists hold a national congress in Berlin to map out an anti-West protest.

August 30 East Germany joins the Council for Economic Mutual Assistance (CEMA, COMECON), a Communist bloc trading organization established in Moscow in 1949 consisting of Czechoslovakia, Bulgaria, Hungary, Poland, Romania, and the USSR.

September 8 Communists raze the Imperial Castle in Berlin for a Moscow-type Red Square; West Berliners protest the action.

September 19 The three Western foreign ministers announce that an attack on West Germany will be regarded as an attack on the United States, Great Britain, and France.

September 21 Soviet troops seize 150 yards of the British sector, but withdraw before British troops arrive.

East Berlin again stops electric power to the Western sectors. Supply, nonetheless, is kept near normal levels from Western sources.

September 26 Ulbricht signs a friendship pact with Bulgaria.

October 21 Seven Soviet bloc foreign ministers meet in Prague to discuss problems arising from the Western foreign ministers' September 19 decision.

October 22 The Western conference of September 19 issues its four-point plan to establish a sovereign, all-German government. It will be countered with a Soviet bloc plan from the Prague conference.

October 26 American secretary of state Dean Acheson rejects the Soviet bloc's plan for an all-German government.

President Pieck confirms the SED transformation into a Bolshevist or Soviet type party.

November 1 Marxism-Leninism courses become compulsory for SED party members.

November 9 After the October 15 election, newly elected People's Chamber, or lower house of parliament, meets and renames Otto Grotewohl minister president.

November 12 East Berlin officials tighten the blockade of secondary streets to West Berlin.

November 16 Grotewohl proclaims the transition to a ''workers state'' in a speech to the People's Chamber. He calls for a new administration, called the National Front government, consisting of the SED, Liberal Democrats (LDPD), Democratic Farmers (DBD), National Democrats (NDPD), and Christian Democrats (CDU).

December 4 Grotewohl proposes East and West German talks to form a unified government on the basis of the Prague proposals of October 22.

December 23 The United States rejects the USSR bid for Big Four talks on the future of Germany.

1951

January 2 A steel mill opening in Fürstenberg launches the new five-year plan.

January 6 Communist leaders reveal the forming of purge committees (*see* July 21, 1950).

January 16 West German chancellor Konrad Adenauer asks for political freedom for East Germans as a prerequisite for West German participation in unification talks.

February 11 Adenauer demands the release of political prisoners in East German concentration camps as the price for unity talks.

February 22 By decree GDR universities are brought under central control of the new *Staatssekretariat fur Hochschulwesen* (State Secretariat for University Organization).

February 23 The People's Police alert units get heavy weapons from the USSR and will join USSR military maneuvers in the spring.

March 15 Grotewohl rejects Adenauer's plan for simultaneous elections in all four zones under Big Four supervision. He wants a vote under German jurisdiction and urges election of a constitutional council with equal East and West German representation.

March 23 A partial accord on waterways traffic is reached in British/Soviet talks. The British release East

German barges held since March 13, while the Soviets grant permits for West German barges.

April 29 The USSR reorganizes People's Police alert units into 23 cadres for infantry divisions with Soviet military doctrine to be used exclusively.

The third purge of Communist members is completed with party loyalty required for attainment of rank.

May 25 The Communists begin a campaign to rename streets in the GDR currently named after emperors, kings, and generals.

June 3 Factory workers demonstrate in Berlin against excessive overtime and pay cuts.

June 28 An East German refusal to guarantee free traffic movement from West Berlin to West Germany breaks off talks on an interzonal trade pact.

July 18 The West halts talks with the USSR until a backlog, caused by the lack of an interzonal trade pact, of West Berlin transit permits is approved.

July 20 In a virtual ultimatum, West Germany tells East Germany that no trade pact will be signed until traffic interference ends.

August 4 The interim East/West trade accord expires. All trade between East and West stops until the West signs a new pact on September 21.

August 5–7 At the East Berlin Youth Festival, 100 youths seek asylum in West Berlin. Deputy Minister President Ulbricht addresses the festival and urges a united Germany.

August 12 President Grotewohl bars unity talks with West Germany.

August 15 Two thousand youths seek asylum in the West; 130 get provisional asylum, but most are urged to return to East Germany.

August 29 East Germany drops plans for the all-German constitutional assembly. It urges reunification talks instead.

September 2 East Germany imposes a road tax on West German and West Berlin vehicles crossing East Germany.

September 14 A riot between 3,500 civilians and 400 police breaks out in Leipzig, with many injured and over 100 arrested.

During a six-month purge, 170,000 are ousted from the SED. Membership now stands at 1.6 million.

September 16 The East German Volkskammer, or parliament, renews its bid for free all-German elections of a constitutional convention. Grotewohl invites West Germany, but West Germany rejects it.

September 21 East and West Germany sign an interzonal trade pact that the Allied powers approve. West Germany, however, bars implementation of the pact pending the end of the tax on West German traffic to Berlin.

Since a peace treaty is not forthcoming, the USSR turns over the administration of property owned by foreigners to East Germany (*see* July 22, 1950).

September 28 Chancellor Adenauer sets 14 conditions under which West Germany would agree to an all-German vote on reunification.

October 7 East Germany marks second anniversary of the founding of the GDR. Stalin sends perfunctory greetings, but only minor figures head the USSR delegation.

October 14 President Pieck says East Germany now wants talks on unification without conditions. Ulbricht backs this unity appeal as means to bar West Germany from rearming.

October 16 The Western Allies ask the United Nations to probe East and West German readiness for general elections preparatory to reunification.

October 19 People's Police seize Steinstücken, an isolated part of the U.S. sector near Potsdam.

October 24 The East Germans return Steinstücken, whose residents now seek a corridor to West Berlin.

November 3 East Germany threatens a new blockade by slowing truck traffic at the Helmstedt border crossing.

November 5 East Germany again rejects a UN pre-election investigation of existing freedoms. East Germany requests instead a Four Power supervision of the investigation.

November 6 The Western Allies ask the UN General Assembly to set up a committee to investigate the possibilities of a free vote in East Germany.

November 11 Ulbricht says East German laws will be based on the laws of the Weimar Republic (1918–33). He also states that East Germany is ready to accept Four Power control of an election committee, and he proposes an exchange of East and West German experts to study draft laws for elections and unification.

December 3 The USSR lengthens military airfield runways for jet planes and extends port installations throughout the Eastern zone.

December 5 The UN General Assembly committee votes 50–6 to invite representatives of East and West Berlin to take part in discussion of a proposal for a UN committee on German unification.

December 9 East Germany accepts the UN invitation, but Grotewohl reasserts his opposition to the UN survey that would be in all zones.

December 11 East Germans request, and receive, a delay for their UN appearance.

East Germany completes a rail circle around Berlin and announces plans for canals to do the same.

December 12 Foreign Minister Lothar Bolz charges West Germany with fomenting trouble and urges a UN inquiry to block the Unity Assembly Committee.

December 20 The UN committee votes 45–6 to form a five-nation committee to survey East and West Germany. Poland refuses to serve on committee, while the USSR and Israel oppose the plan. The next day the UN General Assembly approves the plan and forms a committee.

1952

January 3 East Germany completes a draft law for an all-German election and again declares its intention to bar the UN committee.

January 17 Ulbricht bars the UN survey of East Germany.

February 12 The UN committee holds its first meeting.

February 25 The UN committee on Germany invites East and West German representatives to conference on the possibility of free all-German elections.

March 11 The USSR submits a draft peace treaty outline to the United States, Great Britain, and France. It asks for a Four Power conference to be followed by a conference of all interested states, a united democratic Germany with Potsdam Declaration borders, and a withdrawal of foreign troops.

March 26 The Western Powers reject the Soviet proposal.

March 27 East Germany uses the 125th anniversary of composer Ludwig von Beethoven's death to advance their unification campaign through propaganda.

April 11 The USSR asks that the all-German elections be supervised by the occupying powers.

May 13 Ulbricht warns of new pressure from East Germany if West Germany joins the European Defense Community (EDC). The EDC—comprised of Belgium, France, Italy, Luxembourg, and the Netherlands—is formed to establish an integrated European army. The French parliament ultimately rejects this proposal in 1954.

May 14 The Western Allies propose an impartial committee, not necessarily the one from the UN, to investigate election conditions at once. They propose a Big Four conference on elections after the committee makes its report.

May 24 The government is reorganized with five "co-ordinators" created to function on the level between cabinet and deputy minister-president. A sixth deputy minister-president is created, and Grotewohl orders the newly created state prosecutors to be firm against West German agents.

May 28 East Berlin divides the city's telephone system, barring East and West Berlin contact, and cuts most West Berlin and West German lines.

May 31 The Western High Commanders ask the USSR to end travel and political curbs. East Berlin offers to install substitute phone lines through East Berlin centers, but the offer is rejected; East Berlin fells trees and digs trenches at sector borders.

June 1 East Berlin police order the residents of three West Berlin border communities to leave and orders the residents of Steinstücken and Klein-Machnow to end contact with West Berlin.

June 7 Grotewohl calls for a Socialist Unity party (SED) conference, while rumors of his purge subside.

June 11 Soviet marshal Chuikov denies the Western Allies the right to patrol the Berlin-West German Highway.

June 12 American and British patrols try to patrol the highway but are turned back by the Soviets.

June 21 The East German People's Police, led by Soviet officers, seize two farms inside West Germany.

June 23 Soviet troops and People's Police kidnap forty West German workers in a disputed border area at Hohnsleben.

June 26 East Germany bars West Berliners from commuting to work on property outside West Berlin.

June 28 The Western Allies prepare to tighten their patrolling of the border. They set up two new refugee camps to handle the influx from East German border zones.

July 5 It is reported that 8,000 East Germans fled to West Berlin in June.

July 10 In speech to the SED party congress, Ulbricht offers a plan to abolish provinces and divide East Germany into 15 districts.

July 24 In a special session, parliament approves a law abolishing provinces and divides the country into 14 districts and 217 counties. By August 13 the division of the country into districts is achieved, and political organizations are reorganized in accordance with new divisions.

August 3 Soviet troops and East German police seize 30,000 square yards of the West German border area, saying it was erroneously included in West Germany.

September 2 The education minister's message on the opening day of school lists the student's political tasks and duties for the strengthening of socialism.

October 2 The East German parliament (Volkskammer) votes to restore full civil rights to ex-Nazis not convicted as war criminals.

October 31 Claiming the load is too wide and too heavy, the USSR turns back two Berlin-bound trainloads of U.S. military equipment in the first such move since 1949. The shipment includes eight new Patton tanks.

November 1 The West German parliament (Bundestag) president gets an East German unification bid from Volkskammer president Johannes Dieckmann, the first direct East German move since September. West German chancellor Adenauer rejects bid on November 3.

November 28 Nonresidents of the Soviet zone of Berlin are barred from buying food and industrial products at government stores, a move officials claim is due to ''shortages.''

December 10 Ulbricht, Supply Minister Karl Hamann, and other Supply Ministry aides are suspended as the food shortage crisis worsens.

December 11 Several key officials in Saxon coal mining districts are held for sabotaging output.

December 12 Hamann is ousted as Liberal Party of Germany (LDPD) co-chairman.

1953

January 4 Ex-Minister Hamann's family surfaces in West Berlin, but he is reported held for attempting to flee.

January 5 A Communist party Central Committee resolution finds Titoism, Trotskyism, and Zionism active within the Party. A purge is planned.

January 8 The police force bars Jews from its ranks.

January 19 Police raid the homes of Jews in a hunt for Zionist spies. They seize papers and identity cards and then order Jews to stay close to home. Communist leader Hans Jendretsky calls them enemies of the state in an effort to bar them from public life.

East German president Pieck warns of a new USSR blockade if West Germany ratifies the EDC pact and contractual agreement.

January 20 The East Germans close the elevated train line to block those seeking refuge in West Berlin. Thirteen hundred East Germans, including 30 Jews, flee just before the line is blocked.

February 6 The Volkskammer approves the budget, which, for the first time, includes funds for defense.

February 14 The East Berlin government reorganizes along Communist lines and holds the first meeting of the People's Assembly, which votes to continue Mayor Friedrich Ebert in office.

February 22 A record 26,000 refugees have entered West Berlin since February 1. Some West Berlin property owners reap profits renting empty plants and warehouses to refugee officials.

February 23 The government dissolves the Jewish-dominated Leftist Union of Nazi Persecutees and forms a Committee of Antifascist Resistance Fighters to assume its functions.

February 25 All men ages 18–45 are asked to fill out forms in preparation for a possible draft.

March 5 The Bundestag asks the free world for aid for refugees who continue to stream into West Berlin.

Stalin dies, setting off an uncertain struggle for power in the Soviet Union, with change and reform anticipated in the German Democratic Republic (GDR) and the Soviet Bloc.

March 10 The communization drive hits small business. Many owners and employees flee to West Berlin as a result.

March 29 Secretary General Gerald Götting of the Christian Democratic Union (CDU) assails Christian youth groups in the GDR's opening round in the persecution of religious groups.

April 29 The leader of Berlin's Protestants, Pastor Otto Dibelius, tells Protestant groups to continue functioning; he assails Communist tactics.

May 3 Lutheran pastor Martin Niemoller asks Roman Catholic archbishop Boris of Berlin to aid Protestant clergy in their struggle.

May 5 The government renames the city of Chemnitz to Karl Marx Stadt.

May 28 Food rationing and threats against farmers cause 8,000 persons to flee to West Berlin in five days.

May 29 The USSR appoints Vladimir Semyonov, a civilian, as high commissioner in a surprise reorganization move that ends the Control Commission. Marshal Chuikov is now the only military commander in the group.

June 6 The USSR names Colonel General Andrei A. Grechko to replace Chuikov as commander.

June 9 As a result of Stalin's death, the Politburo of the SED announces a new course designed to correct mistakes and discriminations of the past Stalinist era.

June 10 A church–state agreement leads to decreasing pressure on the church. It lasts for a year before restrictions are reintroduced.

June 11 The Politburo eases the socialization effort and pledges to aid private enterprise and shift some output from capital to consumer goods. It also eases curbs to travel to and from West Germany and pledges reduced pressure on churchmen.

June 14 The government releases 4,000 political prisoners with the promise to release 1,500 more.

June 15 Building workers go on strike in East Berlin to bring about change in higher work "norms," or goals, established by the government for the same pay. Other isolated strikes take place throughout the GDR.

June 16 Demonstrations for lower "norms" begin with 300 workers in East Berlin, who also ask for free elections.

June 17 Thousands of workers demonstrate against an East German government order raising work "norms." The Politburo revokes the order but workers shift the attack to economic and political issues. Martial law is declared after 20,000 to 50,000 rioting workers try to swamp the police and seize the government.

Strikes extend to over 270 localities throughout the GDR, involving 5 percent of the work force. Twenty-one demonstrators die and many are injured as the government forcefully represses the strikes; economic demands are conceded but not political ones.

Soviet troops help to enforce martial law in East Berlin.

June 18 The USSR sends in a full armored division in a show of force.

June 19 The Allied commanders demand that the USSR end martial law. West Berliner Willi Göttling is executed as an alleged instigator. Rioting is reported spreading to other cities; 13,000 laborers battle police in Magdeburg.

June 24 Minister President Grotewohl promises changes but asserts that the government will not resign. The USSR commander eases martial law in East Berlin.

June 26 Grotewohl outlines a plan to reallocate $500 million to raise living standards by discarding most of the five-year plan and the rearmament program. Thirty-eight persons die and 278 are hurt in riots over the past several days.

June 30 The government backs an eased rearmament effort, starts giving back nationalized property, reports all factories are back at work, and frees hoarded food stocks.

July 10 The Soviet sector reopens to West Berliners for the first time since June 17.

July 12 Martial law ends in East Berlin.

July 15 East Germany (GDR) calls for a "German round table," wherein both the GDR and West Germany (BRD) meet to discuss the German problem of unification.

The four occupation powers propose a foreign ministers meeting to discuss free all-German elections and the establishment of an all-German government.

July 21 The government announces that the Soviet Union has extended credits of $57 million for the purchase of food in the second half of 1953.

July 23 Reports from trial accounts show that the uprisings occurred in rural areas as well as cities, sometimes involving SED members.

July 28 In an SED party shakeup, Wilhelm Zaißer is dropped from the Politburo post of party secretary general, but Walter Ulbricht, as first secretary of central committee, remains.

Food distribution starts in West Berlin. Almost 10,000 East Germans pour across border, but the East German police do not interfere.

August 12 Ulbricht charges SED leaders in Dresden, Magdeburg, Halle, and Karl Marx Stadt with treason in connection with June 17 riots.

August 15 Soviet Union proposes establishment of an all-German government elected by the parliaments of East and West Germany, leading to a neutral, democratic, and united Germany.

August 23 The Soviet government announces the signing of a USSR–East German protocol that cancels East German reparation payments on January 1, 1954, limits Soviet occupation costs, and will result in the return of some industrial plants seized by the Soviets.

September 20 Ulbricht says the government will try to end rationing and unify the price system in 1954.

September 25 The government renews its drive to raise output, while Ulbricht rejects worker's demand for shorter work week.

September 29 Ulbricht announces a new party reorganization of which an elite corps will exclude former Socialist-Democrats and elect new leaders.

Soviet High Commissioner Vladimir Semyonov becomes the first ambassador to East Germany from the USSR (*see* May 29).

October 3 The East German parliament (Volkskammer) votes to seize the property of farmers who have fled to West Germany unless they return.

October 8 Pieck is re-elected as president.

October 25 Grotewohl dissolves the Art Commission to form the Culture Ministry in order to provide better party control.

November 17 Hundreds are reported seized for spying, sabotage, and anti-Communist activity.

December 25 The government bars Lutheran bishop Dibelius from holding a Christmas service in a government building in Stalinstadt.

December 27 The USSR proposes a Berlin conference to begin on January 25, and the United States accepts.

December 29 Seven Liberal Democratic party (LDPD) leaders and eight German army officers are sentenced for espionage in Dresden.

1954

January 1–19 East Germany reopens some East–West phone lines to aid communication for the Foreign Ministers Council Conference (*see* May 31, 1952).

January 30 At the Foreign Ministers Council Conference, Anthony Eden presents the West's plan for unification supervised by a Four Power commission. It provides for free elections to pick an assembly to draft a constitution and to set up an all-German government, which would make a peace treaty and join the European Defense Community (EDC).

February 2 Soviet Foreign Minister Molotov submits a draft peace treaty calling for the neutralization, the withdrawal of occupied forces, and the end of Allied bases in West Germany.

February 4 Molotov proposes a referendum to let West Germany choose between his plan and the EDC.

February 13 Molotov links a peace treaty settlement of Germany with a demand for the continued occupation of Austria.

February 19 The Big Four admit failure in the settlement in a joint communique.

February 23 Western high commissioners and West Berlin Allied commandants ask their USSR counterparts to lift most East–West barriers for unity.

March 7 The USSR high commissioner and ambassador Vladimir Semyonov rejects the Western high commanders' bid for talks on lifting travel and communication barriers.

March 8 The Communists end the central command chairman post held jointly by Pieck and Grotewohl. Ulbricht remains as the party's first secretary, which is now the party's top position, which strengthens the party role in government and weakens rival parties.

March 15 The SED launches a drive against Western-oriented ''social democratism.''

March 26 The USSR grants the East German government the right to handle its own foreign affairs, declares East Germany a sovereign state, but will continue to occupy and insure development of a ''democratic peace-loving state.'' The United States refuses to recognize East Germany as a country.

March 30–April 7 At the Fourth Socialist Unity Party Day, speeches by Pieck, Ulbricht, and Grotewohl attack the bureaucracy and decry serious shortcomings and problems in planning but offer no new program for reform, thus spreading uncertainty throughout the government and the party. Pieck and Grotewohl quit as SED co-chairmen, leaving Ulbricht as sole head. The party congress also approves a reorganization along USSR Communist party lines, with party rolls set at 1.272 million plus 14,000 probationers. The SED elects an enlarged Central Committee of 125. In a speech given at an East Berlin workers' rally, Soviet vice premier Anastas Mikoyan says that the USSR seeks maximum rights and freedom for the East German regime.

April 8 The Western Allied High Commission declines to recognize the sovereignty of East Germany and declares that the USSR will continue to be regarded as the power responsible for the Soviet zone of Germany.

April 16 Semyonov notifies the military missions of non-occupying powers to deal with the East German government and not him. Visa applicants are now referred to the East German foreign office.

May 25 East Germany asks West Germany to cosponsor an all-German plebiscite to choose between a German peace treaty and the EDC.

June 20 the USSR chooses the high commissioner office to replace the office of the USSR representative

July 17 Georgi M. Pushkin replaces Semyonov as the high commissioner.

August 8 The Soviet high command closes the Berlin offices and merges them with the USSR embassy.

August 26 The government reports that various East German industries failed to reach output goals.

September 11 The Western Allies tell the USSR that it must agree to all German free elections before they will agree to a Big Four conference on the German issue.

September 20 The East German parliament (Volkskammer) presidium invites the West German parliament (Bundestag) to send representatives for a unification congress.

The USSR and East Germany sign a series of agreements that enhance the power and authority of the East German government.

October 7 Molotov proposes a Four Power conference for neutralization, reunification, and evacuation of foreign forces from Germany. But the next day British foreign minister Anthony Eden rejects the Molotov offer as a plan to subvert all Germany.

October 24 The USSR suggests November talks on ending the occupation of Germany.

West Germany agrees under protocols signed in Paris with the West not to seek reunification by force.

November 17 The SED names Grotewohl to continue as minister-president.

December 25 Two hundred thousand cross East–West German border to visit during the Christmas holiday.

1955

January 1 West Germany reports that only 2 percent of 105,000 East Germans going to West Germany in 1954 can be called refugees and does not dispute statistics that about 4,000 return to East Germany monthly.

January 26 The USSR formally ends its state of war with Germany and blames the West for the lack of reunification and a peace treaty.

February 7 Lutheran bishop Dibelius again attacks Communist youth consecration rites despite Communist press attacks on him and the Evangelical church.

February 21 The government makes Communist Youth Federation members overseers of all business transactions by increasing the use of members to check on all phases of political activity.

March 7 The Roman Catholic church labels participation in Communist youth initiation ceremonies a sin.

March 18 East and West German youth groups meet in Bad Godesberg where they agree to distribute both Communist and democratic propaganda in all parts of Germany.

March 19 The press and radio launch a drive to cut state-owned industry losses by raising output.

March 20 Erich Kleiber quits as the Berlin State Opera musical director, likening the curbs on freedom under the Communists to those under the Nazis.

March 29 Roman Catholic and Protestant leaders announce that confirmation and communion will be denied to youths who take the Communist pledge.

Walter Freund, chief of the Office for Church Questions, defects to West Berlin and asks for asylum.

March 31 East Germany raises heavy trucking tolls elevenfold on Berlin–West German roads. West Berlin has expected this move and has stocked supplies. West Germany suspends trade talks in retaliation.

May 14 East Germany joins the Warsaw Pact, a mutual defense alliance aimed at the West, by signing the East European Defense Treaty in Warsaw with Albania, Bulgaria, Czechoslovakia, Hungary, Romania, and the USSR.

May 16 Molotov stipulates that unarmed neutrality is the USSR's price for reunification.

May 19 Soviet high commissioner Georgi M. Pushkin agrees to a conference with the Western high commanders on the truck toll dispute. The conference takes place two days later and fails to achieve anything of value.

May 25 At a press conference, U.S. secretary of state John Foster Dulles rejects the idea of a reunified neutral Germany.

June 7 West German chancellor Konrad Adenauer is invited to visit the USSR to discuss relations with the Soviet Union and the reunification of Germany.

June 16 West Berlin seizes 127 demonstrators and breaks up three Communist-led demonstrations on the eve of the anniversary of the 1953 East German uprising; the demonstrators are reported to be from East Berlin.

July 25 Soviet Premier Nikolai A. Bulganin and Communist party chairman Nikita Khrushchev visit Berlin, where the next day Khrushchev denounces the "mechanical reunification" of Germany as "unreal." He says reunification can only be achieved within a system of European collective security.

September 21   The USSR grants full sovereignty to the German Democratic Republic (GDR) in a pact signed in Moscow. Some of the provisions of the agreement are that Soviet troops will remain but not intervene in internal affairs, the USSR agrees to end the Soviet high commissioner post and annul Allied Control Council laws, and orders East Germany to get full control over West German and Berlin traffic.

September 29   Western Big Three ministers tell the USSR it cannot unilaterally give up Four Power obligations to East Germany; they stress their refusal to recognize East Germany.

October 4   The Supreme Soviet Presidium (Executive Committee) approves the sovereignty pact. The Big Three challenge the USSR's right to give up West German–West Berlin border control and stress that Allied Control accords are still valid.

October 14   The West German foreign minister says West Germany will not agree to accredit the same Soviet ambassador to both East and West Germany.

October 24   Big Four Ministers Conference opens in Geneva on the unification issue, but the conference ends in mid-November when the Western Big Three ministers blame the USSR for failure on reunification.

November 27   The cabinet is reorganized: state security service is raised to ministerial rank under Ernst Wollweber; the number of deputy minister-presidents is increased from seven to nine, giving the SED party a majority on the Presidium; and the pre-1953 party organization is revived.

December 4   Walter Ulbricht receives a promotion to first deputy minister-president.

December 7   Higher education authorities ban student Christian groups from using university property for meetings.

December 9   The East German government announces that its own border guards have replaced the Soviet guards.

The West German foreign minister enunciates the Hallstein Doctrine, proclaiming that any government establishing diplomatic relations with East Germany (GDR) would forfeit the same with West Germany (BRD).

December 10   East Germans replace Soviet forces at the border.

December 15   Pushkin implies that the Four Power status has ended with East German sovereignty over East Berlin but reaffirms that the USSR retains responsibility for the Western Allies' traffic between West Germany and West Berlin.

1956

January 1   Defections to the West in 1955 are set at 271,000, the highest since 1953 with the four-year total set at 1 million.

Church magazines are banned from being sold in retail outlets. Later in the same month 13 members of the church railway missions are arrested as spies.

January 16   Fifteen thousand armed workers parade in East Berlin, demonstrating the power of ''fighting groups'' organized to safeguard the regime.

January 19   Parliament approves the creation of the post of defense minister with Army Deputy Minister-President Stoph to head it, while the People's Police will be converted into the People's Army.

February 11   Western Big Three protest the GDR's parades of armed civilians as provocative and as violating Big Four directives.

February 26   The SED party orders its members to make a careful study of points made at the Twentieth Congress of USSR Communist party.

March 4   Walter Ulbricht returns from Moscow and writes in a *Neues Deutschland* magazine article that ''Stalin cannot be regarded as one of the classical thinkers of Marxism.'' This leads to the acceptance by the Central Committee of the decisions of the Communist Party Soviet Union (CPSU) Twentieth Congress regarding Stalin later that month.

March 16   Big Four commandants meet for the first time in two years.

March 19   Following the USSR's new Communist line, Ulbricht assails Stalin's war record.

March 25   Ulbricht outlines new five-year plan at the SED party congress seeking to raise general production by 55 percent and to establish a nuclear power plant.

March 31   Armed forces members make their first public party appearance at the end of the SED party congress meeting. The congress also introduces modern techniques in industrial production and agriculture.

April 5   West German Social Democrats (SPD) reject the Communist bid for an alliance by saying that the two groups have nothing in common.

April 22   A U.S. Central Intelligence Agency (CIA) tunnel into East Berlin is stormed by Soviet officers and turned into a tourist and propaganda attraction.

May 1 The first new army regiment gets its colors and marches in a May Day review in traditional Prussian style, by goose-stepping in East Berlin.

June 3 Grotewohl reveals price cuts in state-operated stores.

June 23 East Germany eases East–West travel involving family emergencies.

July 17 Minister-President Grotewohl, Ulbricht, and representatives of other leading political parties visit Moscow in a move linked with the anti-Stalin drive.

August 1 With an SED Central Committee resolution, the government opens a long-term drive aimed at greater development of Communism.

August 14 Playwright Bertolt Brecht dies in East Germany. Brecht was East Germany's showcase intellectual.

August 26 The SED Central Committee publication *Neuer Weg* reveals that laborers and farmers are less willing to join the party than are white collar workers; it reports that membership is declining.

August 29 The East German paliament (Volkskammer) begins to study excessive centralization of the economy.

August 30 The Volkskammer session opens, for the first recorded time since the government was formed in 1949, and bills are debated in a procedure similar to Western parliaments.

October 26 Stalin's statue in East Berlin is removed.

October 27 Due to events in Poland and Hungary, the army cancels leaves and alerts 120,000 troops. Soviet troops are on a war footing, while East German Communists organize loyalty demonstrations.

November 4 Walter Ulbricht, in a Volkskammer speech, says a USSR troop withdrawal must await peaceful solution of German problem. At the same time he seeks to placate anti-USSR feeling among students.

November 25 The USSR stops U.S. and British trains crossing East Germany to West Berlin. It questions the right of Western railroads to transport any Western nationals they choose through the USSR zone.

November 27 USSR border guards stop a British military train, charging incorrect travel documentation.

November 29 In the wake of the October 1956 Hungarian revolution, Professor Wolfgang Harich of Humboldt University in East Berlin is arrested as a "revolutionist" intellectual. He is charged with establishing an antistate group and sentenced to ten years in jail.

December 3 As a result of the revolution in Hungary, the party organization warns youths of expulsion from schools and colleges if they join counterrevolutionary activities. As a result, students and workers at a Leipzig meeting affirm faith in party and government.

December 7 Soviet commanders suspend the truck check at the border. The next day U.S. convoys go through after complying with the new USSR clearance procedure.

December 13 Colleges purge "rebellious" students. In an open letter to student publications, Ulbricht warns of action against those who seek to preserve or restore capitalism (*see* December 3).

December 14 Minister-President Grotewohl announces that Five-Year Plan goals will be altered because of "revolutionary" events in Hungary and Poland.

December 29 The State Planning Bureau reveals that scheduled 1957 output will lag due to an alleged East European raw materials slump.

December 31 In a *Neues Deutschland* article, First Deputy Minister-President Ulbricht warns there is no room for opposition, no third way between communism and capitalism and deplores the "taint" of counterrevolutionary thinking.

1957

January 1–17 East Berlin reports 15,307 refugees and returnees from West Berlin during 1956, while West Berlin reports giving asylum to 156,377 from East Germany.

January 1–21 Seven youths receive prison sentences in Dresden for attempting a pro-Hungarian sympathy strike.

January 31 The government reports maneuvers being held near Magdeburg to train the armed forces in crushing any domestic revolt.

February 2–6 Ulbricht says the regime will not be swayed by Polish political experiments or disputes over Stalinism. He discloses that an alleged students' revolt, plotted for last November 2 by Professor Wolfgang Harich, was uncovered by Communist groups.

March 2–3 The reorganized and newly equipped army and navy are on display in parades.

March 3–10 Professor Harich (*see* February 2–6, 1957) receives a sentence of ten years of hard labor for allegedly conspiring to overthrow government; two of his aides get shorter prison sentences.

March 12–13 A treaty is signed with the USSR regulating the stationing of Soviet troops in the GDR, reportedly totalling 400,000. Soviet foreign minister Andrei

Gromyko and Soviet marshal Georgi K. Zhukov visit East Germany to sign.

April 22 Premier Grotewohl proposes that East and West Germany agree not to use atomic weapons. Six days later the USSR also proposes that East and West Germany agree not to use atomic weapons. On April 30 the West German foreign minister rejects these proposals.

June 22 Ulbricht and Polish premier Władysław Gomułka sign a statement of principles acknowledging the Titoist theory in Yugoslavia and that each nation must develop socialism according to historical and national characteristics of each country.

June 24 Local elections are held with National Front candidates getting 99.52 percent of the votes.

June 28 The USSR again warns West Germany that reunification will be barred forever if its forces are equipped with nuclear arms.

July 26 Ulbricht presses for a program of further industrial and administrative decentralization.

July 30 The Western Big Three and West Germany sign the Declaration of Berlin, reaffirming demands for reunification by free election.

August 10–14 In a speech at Leipzig, Soviet premier Khrushchev exhorts workers to surpass capitalist nations in living standards. However, the welcome to Khrushchev on his tour remains cool and attracts only thin crowds. Other speeches at market places and factories stress East German–USSR unity for peace. At the end of Khrushchev's visit, the Soviet and East German leaders sign a declaration pledging USSR political and economic support for East Germany.

October 2 The Rapacki Plan, a resolution supported by Czechoslovakia, East Germany, and Poland that calls for a nuclear free zone in Central Europe, is proposed to the United Nations (*see* April 1958).

October 8 The government votes a new term for President Pieck and marks the eighth anniversary of the country.

October 14 West German borders are closed and the military patrols East Berlin streets as East Germany suddenly calls in East German marks and issues new banknotes up to 300 marks. Grotewohl says the move is to curb West German speculators and spies.

October 25 East Germany begins border searches of civilian trucks going to West Berlin.

November 26 Soviet marshal Andrei A. Grechko is succeeded by Lieutenant General Matvei V. Zakharov as commander of USSR forces in East Germany.

December 2 Lutheran bishop Dibelius assails a government drive against religion in an East Berlin sermon.

December 29 East Germany announces that Western Big Three diplomats must get visas to cross from East Germany into West Berlin beginning January 1.

1958

January 2–3 West Berlin reports 129,579 persons seeking asylum in 1957, while West Germany reports the registration of 264,500 refugees in 1957.

January 6 The government blames high prices and austerity for workers' unrest. The government reportedly divides on the issue of whether to stress industrial buildup or meet consumer needs.

January 7 Forty-one thousand of the total Soviet forces in East Germany are demobilized and begin leaving the country in late February.

January 10 The East German parliament (Volkskammer) approves a plan for a 25 percent rise in industrial output over the next three years.

February 9 The magazine *Neues Deutschland* announces Karl Schirdewan, Ernest F. Wollweber, and Fred Oelßner have been expelled from the party central committee and the Politburo for their attempt to democratize and reform the party along anti-Stalinist lines in opposition to party chief Ulbricht.

February 11 Ulbricht offers a bill to disband eight economic ministries and two agencies in an attempt to decentralize industry and spur output.

February 16 Border guards are issued heavy arms such as submachine guns.

March 13 The United States, Great Britain, and France warn the USSR that flights by its craft may be barred over West Germany unless it permits Western flights over East Germany.

April The West rejects the proposed Rapacki Plan (*see* October 2, 1957).

June 15 Ulbricht urges the party to ease its pressure on intellectuals. He blames excessive zeal for driving too many abroad; for example, 400 doctors and dentists have fled since January alone.

July 7 In a protocol signed in Moscow, the USSR agrees to expand technical aid and raw materials shipments to spur industrial growth. The move is seen as a step toward East German and Soviet economic integration. Khrushchev stresses the role of chemical industry in a socialist economy, with Ulbricht predicting sharp output gains.

July 12 Premier Khrushchev says payments from East Germany for Soviet forces in East Germany will be canceled as of January 1, 1959.

July 13 The seventy-eighth German Catholic Conference is held in East Berlin, leading to a period of repression of those East Germans who attend the meeting.

July 16–17 At the SED congress the Central Committee purges the anti-Ulbricht faction.

July 25 The government signs a pact with Evangelical churches to settle the rift over religious instruction in schools and other issues.

September 27 On the twentieth anniversary of the signing of the Munich Agreement (*see* Czechoslovakia, September 1938), Czechoslovakia and East Germany issue a joint declaration denouncing the agreement as a shameful plot against the USSR.

October 20 In a pastoral letter, Roman Catholic priests denounce government persecution of the Church.

November 11 In a speech in Moscow, Khrushchev demands the end of Big Four occupation. He says the USSR is ready to turn its functions over to East Germany and calls the 1945 Potsdam Pact (*see* July 17, 1945) out of date. Khrushchev states that the West must negotiate with East Germany for entry rights to West Berlin.

November 21 Representatives from the USSR and East Germany meet to discuss the transfer of Soviet functions in the occupation of Germany to the East Germans.

November 27 Khrushchev threatens to sign a separate peace treaty with East Germany and hand over all administrative authority for East Berlin to the GDR.

November 28 The USSR proposes in notes to the West that West Berlin be demilitarized and become a self-governing free city. The USSR will withdraw troops and transfer access control to East Germany by June 1 regardless of Western decision. Furthermore, Khrushchev denies proposal is an ultimatum.

The United States says it will not abandon the city to hostile rule but will study the USSR's plan.

November 30 Deputy Premier Walter Ulbricht claims that de facto recognition of his country by many states already exists.

Big Four powers, including West Germany begin talks in Bonn to develop policy on the USSR proposal.

December 8–9 In a citywide—East and West—Berlin election, the 2 percent vote for Communists is seen as a rebuff of the USSR free-city plan. Final election returns are: Socialist Democrats (SPD) 52.1 percent of the vote; Christian Democrats (CDU) 37.3 percent. In a speech to the Volkskammer, Premier Grotewohl says the vote cannot determine the city's status.

The parliament approves a constitutional amendment to abolish its Länderkammer, or upper chamber.

December 30 The NATO Council approves the Three Power Western replies to the USSR, reaffirming the stand of the foreign ministers on the Soviet proposals on Berlin self-government.

1959

March 19 Khrushchev accepts in advance the Western bid for a foreign ministers conference on May 11, but limits the agenda to Berlin and peace treaty issues by barring any discussion of reunification.

March 26 The United States protests Soviet fighter planes buzzing a U.S. military cargo craft in a high-altitude flight along the Berlin corridor.

April 22 The Bitterfeld Conference is held to bring writers into line with the needs and direction of the SED party.

May 13 The Big Four foreign ministers conference opens in Geneva where in opening speeches, the American, British, and French representatives clash with Soviet foreign minister Andrei Gromyko.

May 15 Gromyko urges the West to postpone reunification and sign separate peace treaties with East and West Germany.

June 19 After the West rejects Gromyko's proposal of May 15, the Big Four ministers agree to recess the conference until July 13.

July 13 Geneva conference resumes but recesses on August 4 with no agreement.

September 21 The East German cabinet approves a design to make the East German flag different from that of West Germany by adding the socialist emblem of a hammer and compass.

October 1 The East German parliament (Volkskammer) agrees to establish a seven-year economic plan that replaces the 1956 five-year plan.

1960

January 25 Lutheran bishop Dibelius announces his intent to resign from Evangelical church posts to avoid a church schism caused by tensions with the government.

January 30 East Germany protests to the United States, Great Britain, and France over "provocations" caused by the visit of West German leaders to West Berlin as if it were part of West Germany.

February 1 In a letter to West German chancellor Konrad Adenauer, Khrushchev warns that a Western refusal to meet with an "understanding" for his "free city" plan for West Berlin will result in the Communist nations alone settling the German eastern border problems and a separate peace treaty being signed with East Germany.

February 4 Warsaw Pact nations warn that a West Berlin settlement may be forced by their signing a separate peace treaty with East Germany.

February 10 A twelve-member National Defense Council is formed to organize and streamline the security system. Ulbricht serves as its president.

March 24 The U.S. State Department cites the 1944 Allied–USSR pact defining German occupation zones and describing Berlin as separate from all zones to dispute East German and Soviet claims that Berlin is part of East Germany.

April 16 Colonel General Ivan I. Yakubovsky succeeds Marshal Matvei V. Zakharov as USSR forces commander.

June 1 Sixteen thousand five hundred East Germans have reportedly fled to West Berlin in May, the largest monthly total since 1953; the 1960 total is 54,000 to date.

August 3 An East German spokesman says Western Big Three powers have no original rights in Berlin, because their troops did not take part in its military conquest in 1945.

August 16 The free flow of traffic to and from West Berlin is stipulated in a new East–West German long-term trade pact, which provides for $130 million yearly barter. However, West Germany says that East German interference with traffic to Berlin will void the pact.

September 7 President Pieck dies and state mourning is decreed; Volkskammer chairman Johannes Dieckmann becomes acting president.

September 8 Deputy Premier Ulbricht offers three-phase disarmament plan for East and West Germany; Berlin is to be effected by 1965.

East Germany bars West Germans from East Berlin without special police permits, in violation of a Four Power accord. As a result, the West Berlin government holds an emergency meeting to discuss East Germany's actions and their implications for the city.

September 10 The Western Big Three order the withholding of special travel documents used by East Germans in lieu of passports for visits to Western nations.

September 11 The city of Guben is renamed Wilhelm Pieck Stadt.

September 12 Ulbricht is named Council of State Chairman, or head of state, by the parliament after it abolishes the council office of president, replacing it with a Council of State; Grotewohl becomes one of six deputy chairmen.

September 13 Ulbricht asks to be relieved of duties as deputy premier.

The Soviets reject Western protests over Berlin stemming from September 8 by stating that East Germany has legal sovereignty there. East Germany refuses to recognize West German passports held by West Berliners.

September 15 West German President Heinrich Lübke visits West Berlin; East Germany denounces the visit.

Poland and Czechoslovakia announce they will no longer recognize West German passports held by West Berliners.

October 4 In a speech to parliament, Ulbricht grants assurances on access to West Berlin but offers no conditions acceptable to the West. He says nothing of rescinding East German curbs on travel and disputes the Western claims of the four power status of the city.

October 7 Soviet Premier Khrushchev threatens to end the occupation status via a peace treaty with East Germany, unless the West agrees to a summit conference shortly after the U.S. presidential election.

December 4 Many political prisoners are freed under a general political amnesty.

December 29 East and West Germany agree to continue trade in 1961.

1961

January 1 In an unusual move, Ulbricht calls for a ten year "truce of God" between East and West Germany.

January 10 The Western Big Three agree to keep the ban on East German travel to the West that was applied in September in reprisal for East German curbs on West Berlin.

February 11   Doctor Margarete Wittkowski becomes a deputy premier. She is the first woman to get such a post in East Germany.

June 4   American president John F. Kennedy meets Khrushchev in Vienna concerning Berlin. The conference ends in sharp discord, particularly over the issue of Berlin, but the communiqué calls it useful.

June 8   The USSR protests to the Western Big Three and West Germany regarding West Germany's plan to hold a parliamentary session in West Berlin. It charges West Berlin with repeated "unlawful interference" endangering peace, stresses that West Berlin has never been part of West Germany, and complains that use of it is a base for "international provocations."

Soviet marshals Rodion Malinovsky and Andrei Grechko observe Soviet–East German maneuvers near West German border; Malinovsky pledges military support for East Germany.

July 1   East German leaders warn of hardship and sacrifices linked with the Berlin crisis.

July 5   Ulbricht announces major government reorganization by enlarging the cabinet to deal with economic problems due to unrest in the country.

July 11   The deputy minister of foreign affairs says East Germany will control Western access to Berlin directly, not as an agent of the USSR, after a peace treaty is signed.

July 15   East German refugees exceed 1,500 in a day, a record high since 1953.

August 1   East Germany curbs interzonal travel on the grounds that West Germany is allegedly spreading polio.

August 2   The USSR offers to negotiate a final German peace treaty that would recognize the division of Germany.

August 4   East Germany orders the registration of commuters to West Berlin and decrees that they must pay bills in West German marks.

August 7   During a televised speech in Moscow, Khrushchev remains adamant on ending the Allied occupation through a peace treaty. The speech is also telecast in East Germany and warns that Soviet troops may amass on Western borders.

August 9   Over 1,900 East Germans enter West Berlin in one day, equaling the record rate just before the 1953 uprising. East Germany stages "show trials" of captured escapees to discourage flights.

August 10   Marshal Ivan S. Konev is appointed as supreme commander of USSR forces in East Germany.

Council of State chairman Ulbricht stresses the need to strengthen border defenses against "Western militarists."

August 13   East Germany (GDR) seals border between East and West Berlin, posts troops at the Brandenburg Gate and other crossing points, and halts trains and subways between East and West Berlin. GDR troops begin sealing off East Berlin and erecting "the wall" in a move to stem the flow of refugees to the West, numbering 155,402 since January 1.

August 15   East Germans bar West Berlin traffic from crossing into East Berlin without special permits, charging espionage. The Brandenburg Gate is closed to all traffic to reduce incidents while East and West Berlin police clear both sides of the gate to bar violence. East Germans cut phone and other communications to West Berlin and West Germany and halt barge traffic. East Berlin is quiet, but West Berlin becomes angry, with some 5,000 marching on city hall, demanding strong countermeasures. Five hundred workers at the West German electric plant strike briefly to force dismissal of Communist workers. U.S. troops hold maneuvers and the NATO Council meets on the crisis.

The Western commandants formally protest to the USSR commandant against the border closing.

August 17   The Western Allies protest the August 13 Communist blockade of refugees trying to leave East Berlin.

In a personal letter to President Kennedy, Willy Brandt, the mayor of West Berlin, demands "political action," not just words, to counter the Communists. He announces the letter at a rally of 250,000 West Berliners protesting Allied inaction.

August 18   Communists erect a five-foot barrier of concrete at the border crossing at Potsdamer Platz.

August 19   In notes to the Western Allies, the Soviet Union rejects their protests of August 17.

President Kennedy orders 1,500 American battle troops to West Berlin from West Germany to reinforce the U.S. garrison. He also sends Vice President Lyndon Johnson, accompanied by General Lucius Clay, to Berlin to assure Germans of continued U.S. support in the crisis.

August 20   A U.S. battle group enters the autobahn (highway) through East Germany to West Berlin after receiving quick clearance at the Helmstedt checkpoint and keeps radio contact with the U.S. army headquarters in Heidelberg, West Germany.

The USSR rejects the Western protest over the border closing and it questions the legality of the Western occupa-

During the night of August 13, 1961 construction begins on the "Berliner Mauer," or Berlin Wall, dividing Berlin into east and west sectors and standing as the most graphic symbol of Communism in Eastern Europe.

tion of West Berlin and of rights to access to the city. Vice President Johnson arrives in West Berlin with General Clay and makes three speeches of support for the city.

August 21 The U.S. battle group reaches West Berlin without incident and is greeted by Vice President Johnson.

August 23 East Germans tighten curbs on travel to East Berlin by West Berliners and foreigners, including Western Allied troops, and they warn all persons to stay at least 110 yards away from the border on both sides.

August 27 The East German government, in an apparent move to stifle opposition, empowers local courts to restrict persons to a given area, deport them to another area, and impose forced labor terms. It decrees such sentences for imperiling public security and for succumbing to influence of "psychological warfare" by West Germany or West Berlin.

August 29 The East German government continues plugging possible escape routes by building barbed wire barricades along the autobahn leading from West Berlin to West Germany.

August 30 American and British troops hold maneuvers to test mobility in city streets and to show strength to West Berliners.

September 9 Large groups of East German students leave universities to politically "enlighten" farmers on Marxism-Leninism.

September 17 The government sets up a network of 124 relay towers to transmit political and military messages to outlying areas.

September 18 The USSR warns it will destroy any West German plane that strays over East Germany and refuses orders to land.

September 19 A conscription draft law is approved by the Council of State, under which all men ages 18–26 will be subject to the draft.

September 20 Since August 13 the armed forces have reportedly added 174,287 men, which puts their total strength at 350,000.

September 21 The East German parliament (Volkskammer) approves emergency mobilization powers including martial law and conscription.

September 25 East Berlin police evacuate about 500 people from border area houses, as over 30 have leaped from windows into West Berlin.

September 29 The East Germans clear a no-man's-land strip at the border.

October 3 Tourist travel to Yugoslavia is banned because the latter permitted some East Germans to go to West Germany and defect after their visits.

October 19 Council of State chairman Ulbricht urges the barring of nuclear arms from both East and West Germany.

A defecting East Berlin soldier leaps over a barbed-wire barricade into West Berlin and to freedom.

October 20 The East German government offers prizes to children who inform on would-be escapees.

October 23 Nine U.S. military police enter East Berlin to enforce the right of Allen Lightner, from the U.S. diplomatic mission in Berlin, to enter without showing identification.

October 26 Several Allied officials in civil dress test East German rules by refusing to show papers at a checkpoint; U.S. and British tanks and troops move to the border to back them up.

October 27 Thirty-three USSR tanks and accompanying troops move to within one mile of the border crossing.

October 28 USSR and U.S. tanks face each other 100 yards apart. In a conference with Soviet foreign minister Andrei Gromyko in Moscow, U.S. ambassador to the Soviet Union Llewellyn Thompson demands that the USSR restore the freedom of movement in East Berlin for U.S. citizens.

October 29 Tanks on both sides of Berlin pull back after a sixteen-hour confrontation.

November 3 Stalinism and Ulbricht's cult of personality are discussed for the first time publicly. The cult of personality was first used by Stalin and then copied by other East European Communist leaders. The cult entails unquestioned devotion to the leader no matter what the consequences. Stalin and others, like Ulbricht, who used the cult of personality are now being criticized for their excesses in governing that did not take into account the effects their actions would have on the country or the people.

November 14 The statue of Stalin is removed from Stalinallee, now renamed Karl-Marxallee.

November 15 The city of Stalinstadt is merged with Fürstenberg and renamed Eisenhueststadt, while all other references to Stalin are eradicated in the city.

November 18 East Berlin propaganda sound trucks are used at the border.

November 19 After two days of publication silence on Ulbricht, the East German press resumes the drive to clear him of charges related to his "personality cult."

November 20 The East Germans build antitank fortifications behind the wall and add a new section of concrete barriers on the western side of the Brandenburg Gate.

November 29 In a report to the party Central Committee, Ulbricht charges that the late Lavrentia Beria, leader of the Soviet secret police (the KGB), tried to prevent him from building communism; Ulbricht also denies he sought a personality cult.

December 4 The U.S. infantry is stationed near the Berlin Wall at Friedrichstraße. East Germans fill gaps in the wall and extend tank traps, leaving only a narrow crossing point at Mauer Straße.

December 22 East and West Berlin police engage in a teargas duel after East Germans throw rocks, grenades, and Christmas trees onto the West Berlin side.

December 24 A government drive against anti-Ulbricht elements in schools is reported.

December 31 Ulbricht announces that the flight of East Germans to West Berlin have cost the national economy about $1.5 billion, or 40 percent of the national economy.

1962

January 25 Twenty-eight East Berliners flee to West Berlin, the largest group to escape since the August 13, 1961, border closing. The West German government orders a news blackout on details, hoping to keep the route open.

The Volkskammer unanimously approves conscription, making all men ages 18–26 subject to 18 months of service in the armed forces (*see* September 19, 1961).

January 26   East German guards seize the entry to a tunnel used by the 28 Berliners who fled. The discovery of the secret tunnel is linked to a United Press International (UPI) escape report.

February 2   East Germany charges that West Germans built the tunnel under the wall to smuggle Western agents into East Berlin.

February 10–13   The USSR tries and fails to curb Western civilian and military air traffic in the air corridors to West Germany. On February 13 USSR officials back down from their attempt to curb Western use of air corridors and cancel scheduled flights of Soviet planes.

Registration for the East German draft begins.

February 16   Soviet fighters intensify harassment of Western planes. The Western Big Three protest the "aggressive and dangerous" Soviet harassment of West Germany and West Berlin flights.

February 27   The government razes houses and evacuates more families from the West Berlin border area.

March 1   The USSR announces that Soviet premier Khrushchev and Ulbricht have ended a two-day conference on a peace treaty that would end Western rights in West Berlin.

March 6   A trade and aid pact worth $825 million is signed with the USSR in Leipzig.

March 7   East Germany dismantles obstacles at the Friedrichstraße crossing in East Berlin.

The International Jurists Commission, an independent group of jurists headquartered in Geneva, declares that the East German wall has neither a moral nor a legal justification.

March 8   East Germany opens two customs stations at the border with West Berlin as an indication that it is now an international frontier.

March 11   The USSR resumes harassment of Western air traffic by dropping metal strips to confuse radar.

March 17   Khrushchev calls for a treaty to settle the Berlin issue.

March 18   Soviet diplomats in East Berlin say the harassment of Western air traffic will continue until a peace treaty is signed. East Germans fortify the Friedrichstraße check point.

March 25   East Germans complete the building of new obstacles and customs sheds along the East Berlin border.

April 23   West Germans are allowed to pass through the wall for Easter visits with East Berliners.

May 1   Rival May Day parades are held in East and West Berlin.

June 24   East Germans strengthen parts of the wall and extend it under the Spree River.

June 28   Ulbricht assails a Western proposal for Big Four talks on border violence as unneeded. He urges instead that the West Berlin government negotiate with his government.

July 5   The cabinet is reorganized to increase Willi Stoph's power by naming him sole first deputy premier.

July 17   The USSR rejects the Western proposal for a Four Power meeting on averting shooting incidents along the wall.

July 20   The East German government sets up a Baltic coast three-mile-wide forbidden zone along the Baltic coast to keep people from fleeing to the West.

August 1   The USSR warns that U.S. Army helicopters may be downed if they fly over East Berlin. Two days later a U.S. Army helicopter flies over East Berlin without incident.

August 7   The East German army minister orders the registration of 250,000 men in September for compulsory service.

August 23   The Soviet Union abolishes the office of USSR commandant of Berlin due to charges of interference with East German rights. The commandant's duties are transferred to the USSR commander in East Germany.

August 24   In a joint communiqué, the Western Big Three insist they will maintain their rights in Berlin. They deny that the USSR can curb their rights or its own responsibility.

October 7   The East German government offers to renounce nuclear arms if West Germany will.

October 20   The East German government defers parliamentary elections by one year because of the international tensions concerning Germany.

December 6   In a speech delivered in Cottbus, East German chairman Ulbricht says East Germany is ready to compromise with the West on unification. He urges "peaceful coexistence" of East and West Germany and numerous "compromises" leading to confederation and eventual reunification.

December 28   Replying to West German Chancellor Adenauer's August letter asking for an end to incidents along the wall, Khrushchev asks the Western powers for a "normalization of situation" in Berlin through a peace treaty.

1963

January 5   West Germany offers a $100 million, two-year trade credit to East Germany if West Berliners are allowed to enter East Berlin. The offer will be rejected by Ulbricht in a televised speech on February 9.

January 16–22   With Khrushchev and Polish president Władysław Gomułka in attendance to show their support, Ulbricht opens the East German Communist Party Congress with a verbal attack on Communist China.

Ulbricht is re-elected party first secretary.

February 9   Ulbricht rejects West Germany's two-year trade credit offer.

February 11   The government dismisses Professor Karl-Heinz Bartsch from the Politburo and from chairmanship of the Agriculture Council after the West Berlin Association of Free Jurists discloses his Nazi past.

April 14   Politburo member Erich Honecker urges ex-Nazis in the government to confess their pasts in order to become better communists.

June 16   A "worker and peasant" inspection system is set up to tighten control over the stagnant economy. It has wide disciplinary powers and replaces the State Control Commission.

June 27   American president John F. Kennedy arrives at Berlin's Tegel Airport and makes his *"Ich bin ein Berliner"* speech, greeted by over 1 million in West Berlin and telecast around the world. In his speech Kennedy gives notice that the Western powers will not abandon West Berlin and will defend it against communist encroachment.

June 29   In contrast to the Kennedy reception in West Berlin, Soviet premier Khrushchev and his wife receive a mild welcome in East Berlin.

August 29   East Germany increases mine-laying along the border as a means of foiling escape attempts.

September 3   The USSR suggests a peace treaty based on a "three-Germanies" concept, with walled West Berlin as a sovereign state.

October 21   Volkskammer elections are held. The National Front ticket, the only slate on the ballot, receives 99.95 percent of the vote, of a reported turnout of 99.25 percent of eligible voters.

December 18, 1963–January 6, 1964   East Germany and West Berlin sign an accord for West Berliners to visit relatives in East Berlin during the holidays until January 6. West Berlin mayor Brandt, however, says the accord does not imply recognition of East Germany which would mean the West would recognize East Germany as a sovereign state. With such sovereignity in hand East Germany could claim legitimacy as an independent country and expect full diplomatic relations. Sixty thousand permits are issued in one day, with 73,000 visitors entering East Berlin on Christmas Day and sixty thousand on New Year's Eve. The wall closes as the holiday accord ends. A record 290,000 visited East Berlin in one day, with 1.25 million crossing the wall in eighteen days.

1964

January 16   Ulbricht proposes to West German chancellor Ludwig Erhard that both Germanies renounce nuclear arms; West Germany rejects the proposal.

March 12   Under an agreement reached in mid-February, East Germany allows West Berliners traveling through East Germany to foreign nations stay in East Germany up to seventy-two hours to visit relatives.

April 21   Professor Robert Havemann is ousted from the Communist party for his attacks on it and for demanding more freedom.

April 25   East Germany orders tighter border controls.

June 12   Khrushchev and Ulbricht sign a twenty-year friendship pact following a three-hour rally in Moscow. The pact asserts the legal existence of the Communist party in East Germany and assures East Germany equal status with other communist bloc nations. Fourteen days later the United States, Great Britain, and France denounce the Soviet–East German treaty of friendship as an obstacle to bringing peace to divided Germany.

June 22   East Germans criticize Ulbricht for the USSR pact and his failure to win a peace treaty with the Western Big Three.

August 18   Ulbricht meets with the Evangelical bishop of Thuringia, D. Moritz Mitzenheim, which leads to a compromise by both the state and the church in an attempt to reach a working accommodation by the state of church activities.

August 22   The East German government abolishes the statute of limitations for the trying of Nazis and war criminals. The statute, set to expire in 1965, provided that the prosecution of crimes had to begin within 20 years of the criminal act.

August 27 East Germany reportedly releases many political prisoners, mostly West Germans and West Berliners.

August 28 East Germany seeks West German trade concessions in return for day-visitor passes to East Germany.

September 2 The Volkskammer adopts amnesty for refugees who left East Germany before August 1961 and now wish to return.

September 22 Premier Otto Grotewohl dies. Three days later Willi Stoph succeeds him and also becomes Ulbricht's deputy in the State Council.

September 24 The West German cabinet approves a pact to permit West Berliners to visit East Berlin five times in the next 11 months (*see* August 28).

September 27 The Volkskammer ratifies the 25-year friendship treaty with the USSR from June 12.

October 1 East Germany presses for large-scale West German economic aid as payment for easing political repression.

October 6 Fifty-seven East Germans flee through a tunnel to West Berlin in the largest mass escape since the wall was built. During the escape an East German guard is killed.

October 9 The Western press reveals that West Germany recently bought the release of 800 prisoners for millions of dollars in consumer goods and seeks a second trade agreement to allow East German children to join parents in West Germany. The first agreement was made before the August 27th East German amnesty.

October 19 After Soviet premier Khrushchev is removed from power on October 16, the East German government pledges full support to the new Brezhnev regime.

October 31 Visits to East Berlin begin with 20,000 West Berliners crossing through the wall (*see* September 24).

November 4 To show support for the new Soviet regime, East German chairman Ulbricht condemns Khrushchev in a speech given at a workers rally in Cottbus.

December 3 West Germany cancels plans to grant East Germany credits and concessions in retaliation for currency exchanges forced on visitors to East Germany.

December 6 Ulbricht retains the leadership of the Communist party after the Central Commission rejects the cult of personality charges brought against him (*see* November 19, 1961).

December 20, 1964–January 4, 1965 Christmas visits to East Berlin begin, but this time East Germany sets a fee for visitors. A reported 800,000 West Berliners pass through the wall.

1965

April 3–9 As a result of an announced West German parliament (Bundestag) meeting in West Berlin, East Germany begins reprisals. East Germany and the USSR close the main autobahn for four hours for the first time since 1949; Soviet commander marshal Andrei A. Grechko visits East Berlin to stress USSR support; the USSR warns Western planes to use high altitudes in the corridor, reserving low altitudes for USSR and East German military planes; and the Berlin-Hamburg section of Mittelland Canal closes. On April 7 the road is blockaded several times, forcing Allied vehicles to turn back, while Soviet planes fly low over Berlin, causing sonic booms. Nonetheless, the Bundestag meets as scheduled on April 8 in West Berlin as USSR jets buzz Congressional Hall during their session. Allied notes to USSR ask for the harassment to end.

June 2 East German demonstrators invade the U.S. military mission in Potsdam to protest the U.S. Vietnam policy. They tear down the American flag and damage the building.

October 12 The government claims dissatisfaction with a 98 percent voter turnout in local elections in which voters may reject candidates for first time. However, fewer than 1 percent vote against the official candidates.

December 25 Physics professor Robert Havemann is dismissed from the Science Academy after criticizing communists in the West German publication *Der Spiegel* (*see* April 21, 1964).

1966

January 3 The Christmas–New Years visiting period ends with about 840,000 crossing into East Berlin.

March 3 East Germany applies for UN membership and suggests that the membership of both Germanies would lead to reunification under a confederacy.

August 12 West Berlin police report 24,500 East Germans have escaped over the wall since 1961.

August 14 In an East Berlin speech, Ulbricht urges West Germany to extend long-term credits to East Germany to partly compensate for "heavy damages" it has inflicted due to economic and diplomatic restrictions.

September 11   Ulbricht makes a secret visit to the USSR, reportedly for economic concessions, linked to the West German refusal to extend credit as long as East Germany will not renew the current trade pact (see August 16, 1960).

October 11   East Germany demands from West Germany more than 100 million marks ($25 million) for communications services since 1949.

October 18   West German chancellor Erhard, West German cabinet members, and 300 others from the West German parliament gather in Berlin to underline its role as the past and future capital of Germany. However, the Western Allies bar a full-scale parliament meeting.

November 5   Ulbricht states that reunification remains impossible under present conditions in which West Germany refuses to grant recognition to East Germany, and that the two Germanies must adjust to a mutual peaceful status.

December 9   East Germany announces that it will not grant Christmas passes unless West Germany recognizes East Germany as an independent state. As a result no passes are granted until December 1971.

1967

January 1   Ulbricht offers an East German guarantee for West Berlin access routes as part of a program to relax tensions.

January 8   Ulbricht proposes that the East and West German governments help each other in obtaining diplomatic recognition by other nations; East Germany demands West Germany treat it as foreign country in postal and phone traffic.

January 31   East Germany launches a press attack on Romania after it establishes diplomatic relations with West Germany.

February 19   Ulbricht unsuccessfully suggests changing the name of the German Democratic Republic, saying it should reflect the concept of the "socialist fatherland."

March 16   Poland and East Germany sign a mutual aid pact aimed against a West German attempt to change their borders by force.

March 17–18   Ulbricht signs a defense treaty with Czechoslovakia in Prague, pledging mutual military aid if attacked by West Germany. He and Czechoslovak presi-

dent Antonín Novotný also sign a pact that will oblige West Germany to establish "normal relations" with East Germany if it wants to establish diplomatic ties with the rest of East Europe.

March 30   East German Communists renew pressure against churches to cut ties across the border into West Germany.

April 13–23   At the Socialist Unity (SED) Seventh Congress, East Germany appeals for a relaxing of tensions between East and West. Ulbricht proposes that West German chancellor Kurt Georg Kiesinger and East German premier Stoph negotiate an understanding between the two Germanies. He says, however, that unity can only be achieved through the seizure of power by the West German working class. In the congress closing session, Ulbricht is reappointed as first secretary of the Central Committee; Erich Honecker becomes second secretary.

June 16   East Germany rejects the West German proposal for mid-level talks by insisting on talks between Stoph and Kiesinger.

July 1   An auto crash in East Berlin kills four Chinese Communist diplomats, causing a major diplomatic incident. The Chinese label the East Germans as "murderers" and damage the seal of the East German embassy building in Peking.

July 3   The Communist-picked single slate of candidates for chamber of deputies and local governments wins over 90 percent of the votes.

July 14   As a result of the July 3 elections, parliament reappoints Ulbricht and Stoph to their posts; Ulbricht is also reappointed defense council chief.

August 8   East Germany orders $25 million worth of rolling stock and electric equipment from West Berlin. This marks the first successful step in West Berlin's search for new markets in East Germany.

September 19   Prime Minister Stoph contacts Kiesinger, calling for immediate talks to normalize relations between East and West Germany by saying he is willing to come to Bonn, the West German capital (*see* June 16).

November 30   In the continuing search for recognition, East Germany turns down West German overtures for arrangements on postal and transport services, declaring unacceptable any pact stopping short of official recognition.

December 2   Ulbricht, in a speech to parliament, says East Germany is ready to replace its constitution with a new code designed to establish the country as a "sovereign Socialist state." He continues by stating that reunification is possible only after a "Socialist upheaval" takes place in

West Germany. As a result of his speech, parliament sets up a constitution committee.

1968

January 22 Professor Wolfgang Harich, arrested in 1956 (see November 29, 1956) on charges of anti-regime activities and released in 1964, is allowed to publish an article in an East German periodical. This is viewed as a first step toward his full "rehabilitation" back into the academic community.

February 1 Ulbricht presents to parliament a new constitution that establishes East Germany as a socialist state, declares Berlin the capital of the German Democratic Republic, and calls for the unification of East and West Germany on the basis of democracy and socialism. The new constitution is adopted unanimously by parliament on March 27, while on April 6 a national referendum passes, stressing the socialist nature of the GDR instead of the old antifascist democratic constitution of 1949. On April 7, East Germany votes on the new constitution in a plebiscite; 94.54 percent of the electorate favors the new constitution. Ulbricht proclaims the constitution two days later and calls on Western nations to recognize his regime.

March 5 The West German parliament (Bundestag) defies East Germany's standard threats and holds meetings in West Berlin.

March 6 East Germany, fearing the possibility that demonstrations against the war in Vietnam may turn against the regime, bars marches in East Berlin and other major centers.

March 23 In Dresden, leaders of Bulgaria, East Germany, Hungary, Poland, and the Soviet Union warn the Czechoslovak leaders Alexander Dubček and others not to let their liberalizing program of the "Prague Spring" get out of hand.

April 14 East Germany bars the West German cabinet and other officials from access to West Berlin over land through East German territory.

May 8 Bulgarian, East German, Hungarian, and Polish Communist party leaders confer in Moscow about the "Prague Spring" reforms in Czechoslovakia.

June 12 East Germany introduces a new set of regulations on travel to West Berlin, further restricting access to the West.

June 14 Kiesinger flies to West Berlin in a show of solidarity in the face of new East German pressures.

June 19 West German foreign minister Willy Brandt goes to East Berlin to establish direct contacts with Soviet authorities on the issue of access to West Berlin.

June 20–July 2 Joint Soviet–Polish–Hungarian–East German military maneuvers take place near and then move into Czechoslovakia. All forces will be removed by August 3, one month later than scheduled, in an attempt to intimidate the Czechoslovaks into slowing down their reform program.

July 14–16 The Communist leaders of Bulgaria, East Germany, Hungary, Poland, and the USSR, fearful of the repercussions in their own countries from the Czechoslovak liberalizing movement, meet in Warsaw and send a virtual ultimatum to the Czechoslovak Communist party demanding an end to the reforms, including the banning of all non-Communist political organizations, controls on the media, and a strengthened military. The five countries back up their resolution with troop movements near the Czechoslovak borders.

July 28 East German army units move into regions bordering on Czechoslovakia.

August 10 East German chairman Ulbricht declares East Germany is prepared to negotiate with West Germany in renouncing the use of force between them.

August 12–13 Fearful of Czechoslovakia's liberalizing program spilling over into his country, Ulbricht meets with the Czechoslovak leader Alexander Dubček in Karlovy Vary, Czechoslovakia and demands that the reforms cease and the old ways be restored. Dubček refuses.

August 20–21 East German troops join with those of the USSR, Poland, Hungary, and Bulgaria in invading Czechoslovakia, ending the reforms there.

September 3 East German troops begin to leave Czechoslovakia with their withdrawal being complete by October 25.

September 18 The government discloses plans to extend compulsory military training to cover virtually the entire population.

October 22 Trials of dissidents who staged protests in August against the occupation of Czechoslovakia open.

October 27 In light of the events in Czechoslovakia, Ulbricht campaigns to tighten his rigid control and to develop a new "reliable young guard of revolutionaries."

December 14 East Germany is ranked among world's ten greatest industrial powers, with a gross national product of $14 billion and with a total output rising at a 6 percent annual rate.

1969

February 10 The East German Ministry of the Interior announces travel restrictions barring all members of the West German Bundestag from traveling to West Berlin across East German territory for the upcoming West German presidential election. If East Germany does nothing and allows the presidential elections in the city and West German parliamentary delegates to visit West Berlin, it would imply that East Germany recognizes West Berlin as part of West Germany.

February 13 East Germany sends notes to the United States, Great Britain, and France demanding that they prevent the West Berlin election, stating that it is illegal. Its pleas go unheeded.

March 1–6 Communist border guards seal the main autobahn access route to West Berlin as a large movement of Soviet and East German troops begin the first major harassment of Berlin traffic since 1965. East German troops close all roads leading out of Berlin during voting. Despite East German intimidation, presidential elections proceed in West Berlin and are not disturbed.

April 1 East German premier Stoph says West Germany must recognize East Germany ''as a sovereign state and equal partner'' prior to direct negotiations between the two nations.

April 4 Ulbricht reviews a 1968 proposal to relax tensions by naming a state secretary to negotiate with West Germany.

May 1 East Germany is the only Soviet bloc country to observe May Day with military parades.

October 1 East Berlin deputies to East German parliament (Volkskammer) vote for first time on a law approving the nuclear nonproliferation treaty.

October 6 Soviet Communist Party general secretary Leonid I. Brezhnev states a willingness to cooperate with West Germany during a speech marking East Germany's twentieth anniversary.

October 31 East Germany protests new West German chancellor Willy Brandt's plan to visit West Berlin.

December 14 Ulbricht says East Germany is ready to negotiate with West Germany on ''equal rights and nondiscrimination'' and insists that relations be based on mutual ''internal'' recognition; Ulbricht, however, says reunification is out of the question.

1970

January 19 Ulbricht now says East Germany is prepared—with no preconditions—to enter talks with West Germany on fundamental issues, including the renunciation of force.

February 12 Stoph sends a letter to Brandt urging that they confer later this month in East Berlin on a treaty establishing ''normal, equal relations'' between the two states.

March 19 Brandt and Stoph meet in Erfurt, East Germany. A crowd of about 2,000 people cheer Brandt as he and Stoph ride from the Erfurt railroad station to Erfurter Hof Hotel, where private talks are held.

March 22 In a Volkskammer speech, Stoph indicates that East Germany is ready to enter lengthy negotiations with West Germany.

April 19 In East Berlin, chairman Ulbricht unveils a sixty-two-foot-high monument to mark the 100th anniversary of Vladimir I. Lenin's birth.

May 5 In a letter to Brandt, East German prime minister Stoph sets new conditions for a May 21 meeting with Brandt in Kassel, West Germany. He asks that West Germany cease blocking East Germany's efforts to become a member of the European Economic Commission (EEC) and the World Health Organization (WHO) and abolish laws that ''discriminate'' against East Germans and to give East Germans at meetings all honors and protocol accorded representatives of a sovereign state.

May 15 Ulbricht and other East German leaders meet with Soviet leaders in Moscow to discuss East German and Soviet policies toward West Germany. Tass, the official Soviet news agency, reports they agree on ''all matters.''

May 21 Brandt and Stoph hold a second meeting in Kassel, West Germany. The talks are marred by the desecration of the East German flag by three West German youths and clashes between West German Communists and right-wing supporters of the National Democratic party. Brandt and Stoph apparently are far apart on the issues and do not issue a joint communique, but the two agree to pause until mid-autumn for reflection.

August 12 The USSR and West Germany sign a treaty on the renunciation of force. The treaty includes recognition of the Polish–East German border at the Oder–Neiße line.

August 14 The Council of Ministers endorses the renunciation of force treaty signed earlier in the month between Moscow and Bonn as part of Brandt's Ostpolitik, or political policies on good relations with the Communist bloc.

September 20   Communist Chinese ambassador Sung Chih-kuang arrives in East Berlin, filling the post left vacant since 1967 and marking formal resumption of full diplomatic relations between Communist China and East Germany (*see* July 1, 1967). Relations, however, remain cool until 1987.

September 30   The American, Soviet, British, and French ambassadors hold talks on easing tensions in Berlin.

November 25   Soviet foreign minister Andrei Gromyko and several other Soviet leaders meet with Ulbricht, Stoph, and Foreign Minister Otto Winzer in East Berlin, in an attempt to resolve Soviet and East German differences on Berlin and to aid negotiations with the West on the Berlin issue.

December 11   The East German Communist party Central Committee unanimously approves a declaration expressing hope that the Four Power talks will end in a ''mutually acceptable agreement,'' indicating that East Germany has yielded to Soviet pressure on the Berlin issue.

December 24   Several thousand West Germans visit friends and relatives in East Berlin on Christmas, but no West Berliners are allowed to enter.

1971

January 17   The centennial of the establishment of the second German empire (1871–1918) is marked in East and West Germany. In a nationally televised speech, Ulbricht says that the ''blood and iron'' policy of Germany's first chancellor, Otto von Bismarck, hurt the German nation.

January 25   East German officials and West Berlin postal authorities sign a pact reopening ten direct phone lines between East and West Berlin, which the East Germans disconnected in 1952. Limited phone service resumes between East and West Berlin on January 31.

February 25   In an apparent major East German government policy change, Premier Willi Stoph, in a letter to the West Berlin mayor, offers to allow West Berliners to visit East Berlin and East Germany for thirty days and agrees that Four Power talks take precedence over East German–West German talks. This letter, unlike previous East German offers, sets no preconditions.

East German guards discover and destroy a secret 390-foot-long tunnel running from West to East Berlin, foiling a planned escape of seventeen East Berliners.

May 3   Ulbricht resigns as Communist party head after experiencing Soviet hostility to his unwillingness to change his Stalinist, or hard-liner, position. The Central Committee names Erich Honecker as his successor.

June 15–19   In a speech opening the eighth Party Congress meeting, Honecker, in a sharp break with Ulbricht's Berlin policy, praises the Four Power talks. Party delegates re-elect Honecker as first secretary of the congressional session; Ulbricht, who does not attend the congress ostensibly because of illness, is re-elected to the Politburo and named honorary party chairman. However, he loses his post in the party secretariat but will continue as State Council chairman, a ceremonial post.

June 24   Walter Ulbricht loses his position as chairman of the National Defense Council; the Volkskammer unanimously appoints Honecker to succeed him.

August 13   East Berlin armed workers march in a parade marking the tenth anniversary of the Berlin Wall.

September 3   American, Soviet, British, and French representatives sign a Four Power Berlin agreement that will not go into effect until East and West Germany have reached a subsidiary agreement on details of its implementation and final four power agreement. In it commercial and cultural ties between West Berlin and West Germany will be maintained, but West German political activity in West Berlin will be limited.

September 4   Honecker contends that the Four Power Berlin agreement contains a binding acknowledgment by the West that East Germany is a ''sovereign state.''

September 30   East and West Germany sign a postal agreement under which West Germany will pay East Germany $75.5 million for additional services by East German postal authorities.

November 1   Brezhnev, at the end of two days of talks in Moscow with East German leaders, calls for the ''fastest possible'' conclusion of East and West Germany implementation talks. He says he received a pledge from Honecker to cooperate in the negotiations; Honecker says the talks can be concluded in the near future if all sides demonstrate goodwill.

November 26   The Volkskammer re-elects Walter Ulbricht as the chairman of the Council of State, the nominal head of state, and Willi Stoph as premier.

December 11   West Germany, East Germany, and West Berlin sign two accords that will make possible completion of the Four Power Berlin agreement. In this agreement, about 42 acres of East German territory will be exchanged for 38 acres in West Berlin. This major political agreement is formalized on December 17.

December 20   The East Germans and West Berliners sign an agreement permitting West Berliners to visit East Berlin for 30 days for the first time since 1966. The agreement also straightens out border anomalies.

1972

February 22   Honecker moves to wipe out all remnants of capitalism by forcing East Germany's few remaining private concerns to surrender their enterprises to the state in a drive to complete the socialization of East Germany.

March 29   The Berlin Wall is opened to allow West Berliners to visit East Berlin for first time in six years.

April 29   The East German government announces a far-reaching reform program to improve living conditions for the elderly and working class. It is designed to further the development of an egalitarian welfare state and to end private enterprise.

May 13   East German women rebel against stereotyped sexual roles of male supremacy and female subservience with encouragement from the Communist government through the showing of a film, "The Third," as well as classes on marriage and sex education.

June 2   The foreign ministers of the United States, USSR, Great Britain, and France sign the first comprehensive agreement on Berlin and vow it will end twenty-five years of periodic crises and uncertainty over the divided city. It lifts travel restrictions for West Germans visiting East Germany and is seen as a move toward normalization of East-West relations.

September 18   East and West Germany receive membership in the United Nations.

October 5   The East German Council of State announces an amnesty that is expected to bring release of thousands of criminals and political prisoners from jail. The program begins on October 31 with the release of 5,000 prisoners.

October 15   East Germany announces it is dropping all criminal proceedings against refugees and others who left the country "without permission" before January 1, 1972.

November 18   East Germany opens an indoctrination campaign and takes other protective steps designed to halt the spread of Western ideas in the wake of improved relations between East and West Germany.

December 20   East and West Germany sign a treaty on basic relations which opens the door to West Germany's removal of the Hallstein Doctrine, which forbade West German relations with foreign countries if they recognized East Germany (*see* December 9, 1955).

1973

January 3   East Germany moves toward seeking diplomatic relations with the United States. The issue is raised with American ambassador to the UN George Bush.

February 8   Great Britain and France formally recognize East Germany, leaving the United States as the last of the major Western powers without official ties with East Germany.

May 10   The West German parliament (Bundestag) ratifies the treaty that will establish formal relations between East and West Germany.

June 12   The East German parliament (Volkskammer) unanimously ratifies the treaty of normalization of relations to go into effect on June 21 after an exchange of documents of ratification at a West German ceremony on June 20.

July 31   State Council chairman Walter Ulbricht dies at the age of 80.

September 19   Both the East and West German foreign ministers, in initial speeches as members of the UN, renounce the use of force.

October 2   East German Premier Stoph is named chairman of the Council of State to succeed Ulbricht.

1974

March 7   East and West Germany agree to establish permanent diplomatic missions in each other's capitals.

April 28   The arrest of East German spy Günter Guillaume on West German chancellor Brandt's staff leads to Brandt's resignation in May.

June 20   East and West Germany open formal relations with exchange of permanent representatives.

July 14   The United States and East Germany begin talks in Washington D.C. aimed at establishing diplomatic relations.

August 7   The power of the Council of State (Staatsrat) is reduced as expressed in the Council of Ministers' Law of October 16, 1972, which increases the power of the Council of Ministers. The right to act for the Volkskammer between sessions was the key question in this move to give the Council of Ministers more authority.

September 3   The United States establishes diplomatic relations with East Germany to take affect in early December.

September 26   East Germany removes from its constitution all mention of the concept of eventual reunification of East and West Germany.

October 6   East Germany's twenty-fifth anniversary is celebrated with a visit by Soviet leader Brezhnev.

1975

May 20   East Germany enters into long-term cooperation agreements with the German firms of Fried, Krupp GmbH, and Hoechst Works that provide for new production capacities and for eventual joint marketing in third world countries.

June 9   The Vatican's secretary for foreign affairs arrives in East Germany to discuss the establishment of normal relations and the final disengagement of the Roman Catholic church in East Germany from church authorities in West Germany.

July 30   Speeches by West German chancellor Helmut Schmidt and East German party leader Honecker at the Europe Security and Cooperation Conference in Helsinki prove that East and West German relations are still far from friendly.

October 7   The Soviet Union and East Germany sign a revised treaty of friendship that no longer mentions the reunification of Germany.

December 18   East and West Germany reach a long-term agreement for improvement of road and rail connections that link West Berlin with the West.

1976

April 3   The press announces that East German Protestant and Roman Catholic churches have served as conduits for hundreds of millions of dollars in West German payments to the East over the last 15 years, leading to freedom of East German political prisoners, many of whom were allowed to leave for West Germany.

July 1   The prime minister of India, Indira Gandhi, arrives in East Berlin on the first official visit to East Germany by the leader of a noncommunist government.

July 27   East Germany, Czechoslovakia, Sweden, and the Soviet Union launch *Intercosmos 16,* a cooperative satellite that will study the sun's ultraviolet and X-ray radiation and its effects on the earth's upper atmosphere.

October 29   The Volkskammer unanimously elects Honecker as chairman of the State Council and chairman of the National Defense Council.

1977

January 26   U.S. vice president Walter Mondale visits the Berlin Wall to reaffirm the U.S. commitment to West Berlin.

March 2   An official announcement notes that the trade between East and West Germany increased by 13.3 percent in 1976.

April 14   The East German author Reiner Kunze "emigrates," or flees to West Germany, due to the repression of intellectuals and writers in a socialist environment.

May 9   The West German government announces the preparation of 80 East and West German cooperative projects to be submitted to East Germans on such practical matters as cleaning up polluted border waterways and electrical line construction.

June 16   The United States concludes new accords on trade and economics with East Germany, establishing joint trade and economic councils. Emphasis is on optics, petrochemicals, electrical and machine tools, and foodstuffs.

August 24   East Germany arrests dissident East Berlin Communist party official Rudolf Bahro, author of *The Alternative*, a critical assessment of communism in East Germany.

October   East Germany and Czechoslovakia sign a new twenty-five year treaty of friendship, cooperation, and mutual assistance.

October 5   East and West Germany agree to start formal negotiations on a series of proposed general normalization agreements.

November 8   East Germany discloses it is spending the equivalent of $20 billion in 1977 to subsidize food prices, rents, fares, and a wide range of other services.

1978

January 10   The West German magazine *Der Spiegel's* East Berlin office is forced to close by the authorities who feel that the magazine has published too much material critical of East Germany.

March 6   Erich Honecker meets with representatives of the *Bund der Evangelischen Kirchen in der GDR* (League of Evangelical Churches in the GDR), resulting in a loosening of restrictions on the churches in the GDR.

May   The Communist party excludes the most politically vocal authors from a national writer's conference to avoid dissent.

June 1   The United States claims East Germany is a "silent partner" in increased heroin traffic aimed at U.S. servicemen in West Berlin and West Germany.

July 18   East Germany announces its per capita income is $4,220 in 1977, the highest in the Soviet bloc and twenty-first in the world.

August 28   Sigmund Jähn, aboard the Soviet space craft *Salyut 6,* becomes the first East German in space.

September 1   Defense education is made a compulsory part of the curriculum for ninth and tenth grades to extend military control.

September 14   East Germany completes a 635-mile-long frontier fence begun in the early 1970s from the Czechoslovak border to the Baltic Sea at the cost of $500,000 a mile.

November 16   West Germany agrees to pay East Germany over $3 billion in the next 10 years in a pact to improve access to West Berlin with a four-lane Berlin-Hamburg highway planned by 1984.

1979

January 31   Eight regional Protestant churches form a united evangelical church, hoping to strengthen the position of organized religion within the Communist state.

July 28   The government enacts new laws penalizing citizens for unapproved contacts with Westerners.

September 4   The United States and East Germany sign a consular accord to open diplomatic offices after nearly two years of negotiations.

September 25   East Germany proclaims amnesty for hundreds of common criminals and political prisoners to mark its thirtieth anniversary.

October 5   Soviet leader Brezhnev and East German party leader Honecker sign an economic pact marking the thirtieth anniversary of the GDR.

1980

April 6   East Germany begins a national recycling program.

June 13   The GDR sets up a Martin Luther Committee, headed by Erich Honecker, to plan for the celebration of the 500th anniversary of Luther's birth.

September 14   Jews are allowed to celebrate the 100th anniversary of the founding of the largest Jewish cemetery in Europe at Berlin Weißensee.

October 17   Chief General Erich Mielke, leader of the East German secret police, promises maximum secret police activity against "subversive, counter-revolutionary, and antisocialist" movements both in East Germany and in the rest of the Soviet bloc.

December 13   Honecker orders the memorial equestrian statue of Frederick the Great, dismantled by the Communists in 1950, returned to its pedestal in East Berlin.

December 17   East Germany announces an 8.4 percent increase in military spending for 1981, which it attributes to threats to world peace and international security from the West.

1981

April 11   Honecker pledges East German solidarity with Polish Communists during the Polish labor crisis with the independent trade union Solidarity.

April 14   Premier Stoph, citing labor unrest in Poland, announces intensified political vigilance and party discipline to protect the country from either internal or external attack.

April 16   The Communist party, at the close of a six-day congress in East Berlin, re-elects Honecker as secretary general and pledges to strengthen the country's internationalist role by following the lead of the Soviet Union.

June 14   East Berlin elects delegates to the Volkskammer in defiance of the Four Power agreements. The United States, Great Britain, and France unseccessfully protest in Moscow.

December 11   West German chancellor Schmidt and Honecker hold the first full-scale talks between the leaders of their countries in more than a decade.

1982

June 21 The governments of East and West Germany agree to extend a controversial, interest-free credit arrangement used to finance bilateral trade.

August 24 The Soviet Union honors Honecker on his seventieth birthday with the title, "Hero of the Soviet Union," Moscow's highest state honor.

1983

June 29 The West German government agrees to guarantee $396.8 million in private bank loans to East Germany, the largest such credit ever underwritten by Bonn.

1984

January 14 Honecker allows Western television programming into East Germany.

May 17 Believing it is losing its best minds and trained citizens, East Germany closes off legal emigration to West Germany and orders the arrests of applicants to deter others from applying to leave.

July 28 The XXIII Summer Olympic Games open in Los Angeles, California. East Germany, Bulgaria, and the USSR refuse to participate because of "inadequate security." In actuality their refusal stems from the U.S. boycott of the 1980 games in Moscow.

August East Germany takes part in Friendship '84, the Soviet Union's sport festival for nations who pulled out of the summer Olympics.

October 5 The West German government reports that more than 80 East Germans have entered its Czechoslovak embassy in Prague, demanding asylum in West Germany. This incident is a major embarrassment for East Germany, whose Communist leadership is preparing for ceremonies commemorating establishment of East Germany in October 1949.

October 8 East and West Germany hold talks to discuss the East German refugees in the Prague West German embassy.

November East German peace activists issue a joint resolution with Charter 77, the Czechoslovak dissident organization, for a "missile free Europe."

November 9 About 180 people seeking emigration from East Germany take refuge inside West German embassies in four Eastern European capitals.

December 15 Forty East Germans who sought refuge in the West German Embassy in Prague start a hunger strike to dramatize their demand to be allowed to emigrate to the West.

1985

January 15 The four-month sit-in by East Germans at West Germany's Czechoslovak embassy ends when the last six, of some 150 people, return home.

March 12 West German chancellor Helmut Kohl and Honecker, in Moscow for the Soviet leader Konstantin Chernenko's funeral, talk for more than two hours and pledge to work toward better relations.

March 24 U.S. Army major Arthur D. Nicholson, Jr., on a reconnaissance mission in East Germany, is fatally shot by a Soviet guard near the Soviet military installation in Ludwigslust while he is observing Soviet tank sheds.

April 13 The ceremony in Weimar, East Germany, commemorating the fortieth anniversary of the liberation of the Buchenwald concentration camp, is filled with bitter attacks on the United States and accusations that the U.S. is destroying détente with the "policy of confrontation and arms buildup."

1986

February 19 Kohl greets Honecker on an official visit to East Berlin and invites him to visit Bonn which would be the first by the leader of East Germany.

August 13 Honecker and East German officials mark the twenty-fifth anniversary of the Berlin Wall with speeches and a nationwide celebration. Public sentiment, however, remains subdued.

October East German dissidents sign a resolution with other activists from Czechoslovakia, Hungary, and Poland commemorating the 30th anniversary of the 1956 Hungarian Revolution. The statement proclaims that ideals such as pluralism, self-government, and independence from the 1956 revolt are still legitimate.

October 21 Honecker, the first East German leader to visit China, receives a red-carpet welcome in Peking at the beginning of a six-day tour that formally ends an icy relationship after twenty years (*see* September 20, 1970).

1987

February 11 East Germany's Communist leadership strongly opposes Soviet leader Mikhail S. Gorbachev's calls for "openness" and "democratization" of *glasnost* and *perestroika* by stating it does not intend to initiate Soviet outlined reforms.

June 6–9 Thousands of East German youths skirmish with police after being barred from eavesdropping on rock concerts on the other side of the Berlin Wall. Their chants for Gorbachev reflect the popularity of the Soviet leader, and his calls for new openness have attracted East German youths and intellectuals.

June 12 American president Ronald Reagan, in West Berlin, challenges Gorbachev to tear down the Berlin Wall.

September 7–12 Honecker visits West Germany and is greeted by Kohl thereby becoming the first leader of East Germany to visit West Germany.

December 13 East Germany announces it has freed over 25,000 prisoners since July in the most comprehensive amnesty in its 38-year history.

A historical meeting: West German chancellor Helmut Kohl (r) welcomes Erich Honecker in Bonn to discuss issues of cooperation between the two countries. Never before has an East German leader visited West Germany.

1988

January 8 Honecker visits Paris and meets polite but firm disagreement on human rights and arms control from French leaders.

February 3 East Germany is facing increasingly assertive human rights movements among young, small independent groups who desire to stay and change things rather than flee to the West. As a result, the government attempts to crack down on them whenever possible.

February 25 East Germany and Czechoslovakia begin removing short-range Soviet nuclear missiles from their countries back to the USSR in accordance with the arms treaty signed by the United States and the USSR in December 1987.

March 15 About 300 protestors defy police orders and stage a march for freedom of expression and assembly in Leipzig, East Germany's second largest city.

August 13 West German protesters throw tomatoes and eggs at East German guards at the Berlin Wall, while Communist police haul away protesting East German youths, as both sides mark the barrier's twenty-seventh anniversary.

October 29 East German's chief ideologist, Kurt Hager, rejects the idea that East Germany should follow Moscow's restructuring programs, saying they are not transferable to other Communist countries.

December 17 Honecker criticizes Moscow for tolerating revisions of Soviet history and bans many Soviet publications.

1989

January 15 East German police detain 80 protesters from another major march in Leipzig who were demanding freedom of expression and assembly.

January 18 The Soviet Union and East Germany reject Western calls for the destruction of the Berlin Wall by calling it a "factor for stability" in Europe.

January 23 Honecker announces that East Germany will reduce its armed forces by 10,000 and cut military spending by 10 percent.

May 31 In a speech at Mainz, West Germany, American president George Bush calls for the demolition of the Berlin Wall as well as joint East and West efforts on common environmental problems and reductions of conventional military forces in Europe.

August 5 Hungary, opening a rift in the Soviet bloc, says it will weigh granting political asylum to some East Germans.

August 8 West Germany closes its embassy in East Berlin to slow the flow of East Germans seeking to emigrate.

August 13 West Germany thinks about closing its embassy in Budapest because it is filled with more than 180 East Germans trying to emigrate to the West. West Germany fears that if it allows these people to come to West Germany it will start an East German rush on all West German embassies in the Eastern Bloc overloading these embassies' ability to properly handle the situation.

August 19 Over 200 East Germans use a symbolic picnic on the Austrian–Hungarian border as cover to flee to the West, while Hungarian border guards turn a blind eye to the exodus. For years East Germans have been allowed to travel to other countries (mostly Eastern bloc) where their chances of fleeing to West Germany were slim. With the fall of communism in 1989 in Hungary the door is now wide open for "vacationing" East Germans to leave for West Germany.

September 1 Over 3,000 East German tourists wait in Budapest for permission from Hungary to cross into Austria on the way to West Germany.

September 11 Thousands of East Germans pour into Hungary, West Germany, and Austria. Some 16,000 reportedly cross into Czechoslovakia—which is allowing them transit—en route to Hungary. Sixty thousand East German vacationers are also in Hungary and could join the exodus; East Germans have automatic citizenship in West Germany and are welcomed by that country.

September 19 The New Forum, the largest of several new groups formed to campaign for change in East Germany, applies for field candidates in parliamentary elections next May, thereby becoming the first countrywide opposition organization.

September 26 About 8,000 people march through Leipzig, calling for democracy.

September 30 More than 6,000 East German émigrés arrive in West Germany after Honecker agrees to a face-saving arrangement to free the East Germans, most of whom had taken refuge in the West German Embassy compound in Prague. The arrangement involves a detour through East Germany before heading to West Germany, fulfilling the East German demand that they return home first.

October 3 East Germany allows thousands of East Germans who have swarmed into Prague to travel to West Germany through East Germany in East German trains, and then closes its borders in an attempt to halt the chaotic exodus.

October 4 Thousands of East Germans crowd rail stations and junctions along the route taking East German émigrés from Prague to West Germany in hopes of sneaking aboard.

October 6 Soviet President Gorbachev arrives in East Berlin to offer East German Communists a measured show of solidarity and to declare that Moscow will not interfere in East Germany's problems. However, he urges East German party leader Honecker to adopt a program of reform.

One hundred thousand members of the Free German Youth march in East Berlin in celebration of the fortieth anniversary of East Germany.

October 9 Honecker's deputy Egon Krenz cancels Honecker's October 7 order to security forces to shoot to enforce order in Leipzig.

Thousands march peacefully through Leipzig demanding freedom and democracy.

October 13 Honecker meets with the leaders of new minority parties and speaks of the need to change economic and social policies.

October 16 More than 100,000, demanding reforms, march through the streets of Leipzig. The demonstration is the largest since the 1953 uprising and is reported without condemnation for the first time by the East German press.

October 18 The East German Communist party ousts its leader, Honecker, and names his protege, Egon Krenz, to replace him.

October 19 In an attempt to quiet the country, Krenz visits a factory to hear workers' grievances and meets with senior church leaders to whom he pledges a "new chapter of constructive cooperation."

East German deputy foreign minister Harry Ott, speaking for the new Communist leadership, strongly rejects offers of Western economic help in exchange for East German political and economic liberalization.

October 20   Fifty thousand people hold a silent candle-light march in Dresden in a demonstration for change.

October 21   Thousands of East Berliners march through the center of the city in the first demonstration for more democracy since Krenz replaced Honecker.

October 23   Hundreds of thousands march peacefully in Leipzig demanding democratic changes, including legalization of opposition movements, independent labor unions, and a separation of powers between the Communist party and state. Smaller demonstrations take place in other cities.

October 24   The Volkskammer elects Krenz president.

October 27   East Germany announces amnesty for all citizens who had fled—or tried to flee—the country, as well as for most of those arrested in the recent wave of antigovernment demonstrations; and that East Germans can again travel to Czechoslovakia without a visa.

October 30   More than 300,000 march around Leipzig chanting demands that include free elections, ousting the secret police, and the legalization of the New Forum opposition movement.

October 31   Krenz visits Moscow, and upon his return to East Germany, he declares his support for the policy of *perestroika* (reconstruction).

November 2   Margot Honecker, the wife of the former East German leader, is dismissed as education minister, along with several other senior politicians.

November 4   Five hundred thousand demonstrate in East Berlin for further political change.

November 5   Thousands of East Germans emigrate to West Germany and are allowed, for the first time, to travel directly across Czechoslovakia.

November 7   The entire East German cabinet resigns in testimony to the scale of the crisis that has seized the state under pressure resulting from mass demonstrations and mass flight.

November 8   Most of the East German Politburo is forced to resign, and Hans Modrow, the party chief in Dresden with the reputation as an advocate of change, is brought into the Politburo and nominated to be the new head of government.

November 9   In an attempt to bolster the popular support of the new government, the authorities announce the opening of East Germany's border with West Berlin and West Germany. As a result, thousands of East Berliners

cross through the Berlin Wall and throng through the streets of the western sector.

November 10   The Communist party Central Committee announces a program of radical changes, including free, democratic, and secret elections, a socialist planned economy oriented to market conditions, freedom of assembly, and a new law on freedom of the press and broadcasting.

November 12   East German workers open the Berlin Wall at Potsdam Platz, the city's former center, where the West and East Berlin mayors meet.

Prime Minister-Designate Hans Modrow bluntly criticizes former party leader Honecker in a speech to the Communist party Central Committee.

November 13   The Volkskammer criticizes the Communist party while electing Modrow prime minister at Krenz's request.

November 17   Modrow announces a sweeping program of economic and political change and holds out the prospect of relations "on a new level" with West Germany.

November 18   More than a million East Germans surge into West Berlin and West Germany, jamming stores and markets from Lübeck to Hof.

November 25   The Communist party surrenders its constitutional monopoly on political power.

November 30   East Germany officially states that its decision to invade Czechoslovakia in August 1968 was a mistake.

December 1   The Volkskammer amends the constitution by eliminating the Communist party's leadership position.

December 3   Honecker and eleven other former leading officials are expelled from the party, and three former members of leadership are arrested on charges stemming from their abuse of power, while a fourth flees before arrest.

December 4   Tens of thousands again march through Leipzig, this time demanding German reunification and eradication of the crumbling Communist party. Public fury at revelations of gross corruption increase demands for the punishment of top officials, who have already resigned in disgrace.

Five members of the Warsaw Pact (East Germany, the USSR, Poland, Hungary, and Bulgaria) jointly condemn the 1968 invasion of Czechoslovakia at a meeting of the Pact in Moscow, describing it as undue influence in the internal affairs of a sovereign country.

Casually crossing over the Invalidenstraße checkpoint, East Berliners arrive home from a shopping trip to West Berlin.

December 5 Honecker and top members of his government are placed under house arrest.

December 6 Fallen Communist party leader Egon Krenz gives up his remaining state positions amid continuing political turmoil and is replaced as head-of-state, on an interim basis, by Manfred Gerlach, head of the small Liberal Democratic party (NPD).

December 9 The Communist party elects Gregor Gysi to the new post of chairman.

December 11 West German chancellor Helmut Kohl pledges his country will not move toward reunification without consulting with the Western alliance and the USSR.

December 14 Chairman Gysi unsuccessfully asks for help from the United States to keep his country separate from West Germany. He fears reunification will result in his country being absorbed by West Germany and says that the continued independence of East Germany is in the interest of European stability.

East and West German economic ministers meet and agree to set up a joint economic commission to guide intensified trade and investment cooperation in this new era of open borders.

December 19 Kohl and Modrow hold the first meeting between East and West German leaders since the upheavals began in Eastern Europe and, in a symbolic reconciliation, agree to reopen the famous Brandenburg Gate, the symbol of Germany, on December 22.

December 25 U.S. conductor Leonard Bernstein leads a performance of Beethoven's Ninth Symphony in East Berlin to celebrate the fall of the Berlin Wall.

1990

January 4 Six East German reform groups form a coalition against the Communist party, but it falls apart three days later.

January 12 East German prime minister Modrow bows to public opinion and opposition pressure and scraps plans to set up a new security service, or secret police, at least until after the May elections.

Germans from East and West ''occupy'' the Wall at Berlin's Brandenburg Gate to attain the opening of this barrier. On December 22, 1989 the gate opens.

January 15 Crowds of angry protesters invade the 3,000 room state-security headquarters in East Berlin, destroying files and furniture in expression of their fury with the hated secret police. Modrow, along with other government and opposition leaders, goes to the scene to appeal for calm during the transition period.

January 21 East German's Communist party purges Egon Krenz and 13 other former Politburo members.

January 28 The government and all major political groups in East Germany agree to hold the country's first democratic elections on March 18 instead of in May, and to form a coalition government until then. Modrow will remain as prime minister, but the cabinet will be jointly responsible for all decisions.

January 29 Disgraced former leader Honecker is officially arrested and charged with treason after leaving a Berlin hospital where he was being treated for cancer.

January 30 Soviet president Mikhail Gorbachev meets with Modrow and acknowledges that pressure is building for German reunification but cautions against undue haste.

February 5 The Volkskammer formalizes a power-sharing agreement by adding eight new cabinet ministers from the opposition.

Neo-Nazi skinheads goose-step through Leipzig, smashing windows and shouting anti-Semitic slogans. With East German authority collapsing, radical political groups now come out into the open, especially Neo-Nazis who, although not very numerous, are very vocal and attract a lot of attention.

February 13 Kohl meets with Modrow and announces that a joint committee will start immediate preparations for currency and economic union. This becomes the first major step in Kohl's drive toward rapid reunification.

February 17 West Germany's Christian Democratic party (CDU) founds a party organization in East Berlin with Eberhard Diepgen as the party leader.

February 20 Kohl, introduced to a cheering East German crowd as the ''Chancellor of our German fatherland,'' plunges into an intense political campaign for the East German elections in Erfurt.

February 24 Former West German chancellor and West Berlin mayor Willy Brandt is elected the East German Social Democratic party (SPD) honorary president for his past service to the German people.

March 17 East Germans vote in a nationwide free election. The Alliance for Germany, the East German conservative party coalition of Christian Democrats, ac-

tively supported by Kohl, is victorious in the first free elections defeating the former Communists.

March 23 Lothar De Maiziere, chairman of the CDU, ends five days of uncertainty by declaring his readiness to head East Germany's first freely chosen and non-Communist government.

April 3 East Germany's first freely elected Volkskammer holds its inaugural session in Berlin. Political parties agree to try to form the nation's first non-Communist government before April 15.

April 12 The Volkskammer installs the first democratic government and accepts, for the first time, joint responsibility for Nazi crimes against Jews. It expresses a willingness to pay reparations and seek diplomatic ties with Israel, and it condemns East Germany's participation in the 1968 invasion of Czechoslovakia. CDU chairman Lothar De Maiziere is chosen prime minister.

June 1 The Volkskammer orders the removal of the hammer and compass symbols from East Germany's government buildings.

June 11 U.S. President George Bush meets De Maiziere in Washington and reiterates the U.S. wish that united Germany be a part of NATO.

June 21 The parliaments of East and West Germany adopt matching resolutions guaranteeing Poland's existing borders and also adopt a treaty on monetary and economic union.

July 1 East Germany formally cedes its currency and economy to West Germany. Thousands of East Germans gather in the center of East Berlin to celebrate.

July 4 The Group of 24, the foreign ministers of the twenty-four most advanced industrialized countries, meet in Brussels and agree to provide economic aid for East Germany, Bulgaria, Czechoslovakia, and Yugoslavia.

September 12 The four wartime Allies who defeated Nazi Germany in 1945 sign a treaty relinquishing all their occupation rights, leaving the two German nations free to reunite.

September 20 Lawmakers of East and West Germany ratify a treaty that will formally unite their nations on October 3. The vote in the West German parliament is 442 to 47 in favor of reunification; in the East German parliament 299 to 80.

September 31 East and West Germany sign the Treaty of Union detailing the mechanics of reunification. Berlin is elected as the capital of the unified country.

October 3 Germany is officially reunited.

East German Neo-Nazis, or skinheads, are a small but powerful presence at a demonstration in Leipzig.

October 3   As a result of reunification, price controls in the former East Germany are removed, causing the cost of living to skyrocket.

October 19   Police raid the Berlin headquarters of the East German Communist party for transferring $63 million to Moscow.

November 9   Gorbachev asks for toleration of Soviet troops in Germany until they can be brought home.

December 2   Chancellor Kohl and the CDU win the first all-German election with strong support in eastern Germany. Kohl forms a coalition with the Free Democrats and includes East Germans.

December 3   Former East German party leader Erich Honecker enters a Soviet hospital near Berlin.

December 18   De Maiziere, the only non-Communist premier of the former German Democratic Republic, resigns from the Kohl cabinet due to reports that he was an alleged secret police spy for East Germany in the 1980s.

December 20   Germany's newly elected "unity" parliament holds its first meeting.

1991

January 16   Kohl names a 20-member cabinet, including three members from eastern Germany.

January 23   Postal workers strike in eastern Germany in the first of many job actions related to the changing and uncertain status of wages and benefits for east German workers. Throughout January unemployment rises in eastern Germany due to market forces. The government responds with unemployment checks, retraining programs, and unemployment agencies.

February 2   Numerous instances are reported of west Germans demanding the return of their former holdings in eastern Germany, which were confiscated by the GDR.

February 12   Kohl provides $3 billion in aid in an attempt to ease problems in eastern Germany. However, workers continue to call strikes and economic demonstrations later in the month and into March.

February 14   Honecker is taken to a hospital in the Soviet Union in spite of protests from the German government, which wants to prosecute him.

In the shadow of the former East German Reichstag (l) the Wall is dismantled; its remnants collectors' items for many passersby.

April 14   The first reports of neo-Nazi youths harassing foreigners surface. This becomes a major problem in the coming years with repeated incidents of non-German workers being attacked on the streets and in their homes. The Neo-Nazis feel that non-Germans are ruining the ethnic purity of Germany.

April 15   Honecker undergoes surgery in Moscow for liver cancer.

May 21   A number of former East German officials are arrested for crimes against the German people, chief among them is Willi Stoph, the former premier.

June 12   The German parliament votes to move the seat of government from Bonn to Berlin, but no date is set for the move.

August 11   Brigit Breuel, head of the agency (Treuhand) established to privatize government property in eastern Germany, is openly critical of West Germans, and western nations generally, for not investing in eastern Germany.

August 16   The remains of the former Prussian monarchs Frederich William I and Frederich II (the Great) are reinterred at Potsdam after being returned from west Germany, where they were moved at the end of World War II.

September 2   The Soviets announce plans for troop withdrawals that will be much slower than the Germans previously expected. All Soviet troops are expected to be out before the end of 1994, at a rate of 150,000 per year.

September 6   De Maiziere resigns his CDU party post as a result of continued allegations that he spied for the East German secret police in the 1980s (*see* December 18, 1990).

October 4   President Richard von Weizsacker speaks at an antiviolence rally in support of foreign workers and their hostels, which have been targets of neo-Nazi attacks.

November 13   Reflecting the struggle for power in the Soviet Union, Russian leader Boris Yeltsin says President Gorbachev is blocking Erich Honecker's return to Germany out of a sense of moral obligation. Gorbachev announces three days later that Honecker can stay in the USSR.

December 12   Following strong protests from Germany and because of the Yeltsin–Gorbachev feud, Honecker takes refuge in the Chilean embassy in Moscow.

December 15   The CDU elects Angela Merkel, from eastern Germany, to replace De Maiziere as deputy party leader under Chancellor Kohl.

1992

January 4   It is reported in the press that 200,000 East Germans have migrated to the west, seeking jobs and better living conditions.

January 20   A German court finds former East German border guards guilty of killing escapees at the Berlin Wall. They are given a suspended sentence February 4.

February 8   Former East German interior minister Erich Mielke is placed on trial for murder of two policemen in 1931.

February 24   In Moscow Honecker gives up his sanctuary in the Chilean Embassy to enter a Russian hospital. A spokesman for the Russian foreign ministry states that Honecker will be allowed to return to the embassy, but will be prevented if he attempts to board a plane to fly to Chile.

March 31   Former East German premier Hans Modrow is indicted on charges of election fraud.

April 20   Neo-Nazi demonstrators are arrested in Dresden in a government crackdown on antiforeign violence.

May 15   Honecker is formally charged with manslaughter for ordering border guards to shoot to kill escaping East Germans. On June 5, further charges of embezzlement and breach of trust are added. He returns to Germany from Russia on July 29 to stand trial.

August 25–26   Neo-Nazi violence flares up in Rostock in two nights of rioting against foreigners and quickly spreads in eastern Germany. Antiviolence demonstrations are held in Rostock on August 29, but the violence, including firebombing, spreads to 16 eastern German cities by September 5.

September 24   In a move to ease tensions concerning foreign workers in Germany the government signs an agreement with Romania enabling Germany to deport Romanian Gypsies back to Romania. Germany gives $20 million to the Romanian government earmarked for reintegrating the Gypsies into Romanian life.

November 8   Antiforeigner violence continues. President von Wiezsacker tries to speak at a rally of 350,000 in Berlin condemning the violence, but he is booed and pelted with eggs by anarchists. Chancellor Kohl is also the target of egg-throwing.

November 17   The trial of top East German leaders is suspended due to illness on the part of three of the leaders. Honecker has liver cancer, Willi Stoph collapsed at the trial from a heart attack, and Erich Mielke also has severe heart problems.

1993

January 12   A German court drops the trial of Erich Honecker due to his illness. He is released and leaves for Chile the next day to join his family.

January 21   Kohl announces a hike in taxes to pay for the cost of unification and the rebuilding of East Germany.

February 4   Violence continues with an attack on Turkish workers in Cologne and throughout Germany. In April, the government seeks to curb illegal workers and asylum seekers to help ease tensions.

March 10   Erich Mielke's trial resumes. However, the case will be postponed numerous times due to Mielke's poor health.

May 3   Thousands of steel and metal workers go on strike in east Germany after companies renege on earlier promises to increase wages to bring them more in line with west German workers. Two days later another 18,000 join the strike.

May 4   Markus Wolf, the head of the former East German spy service from 1953–1986, goes on trial on charges of treason and espionage.

May 14   A compromise is reached in the two-week-old metal workers' strike that effected over 40,000 workers with some 80 companies. Under the terms of the agreement, the companies agree to raise wages as much as 26 percent, but they extend the timetable, originally set for 1994, for wage parity with workers in west Germany.

May 27   Former East German prime minister Hans Modrow is found guilty of local election fraud from 1989. The court, however, refuses to sentence or fine him due to his role in helping German reunification.

May 28   The constitutional court rules that the abortion law is unconstitutional, which angers women particularly in the eastern part of the country where the procedure had been readily available for 20 years.

July 18   Wolfgang Vogel, a lawyer who was instrumental in exchanging spies and political prisoners between East and West Germany between 1964 and 1989, is arrested on tax evasion charges for not paying taxes on the money he

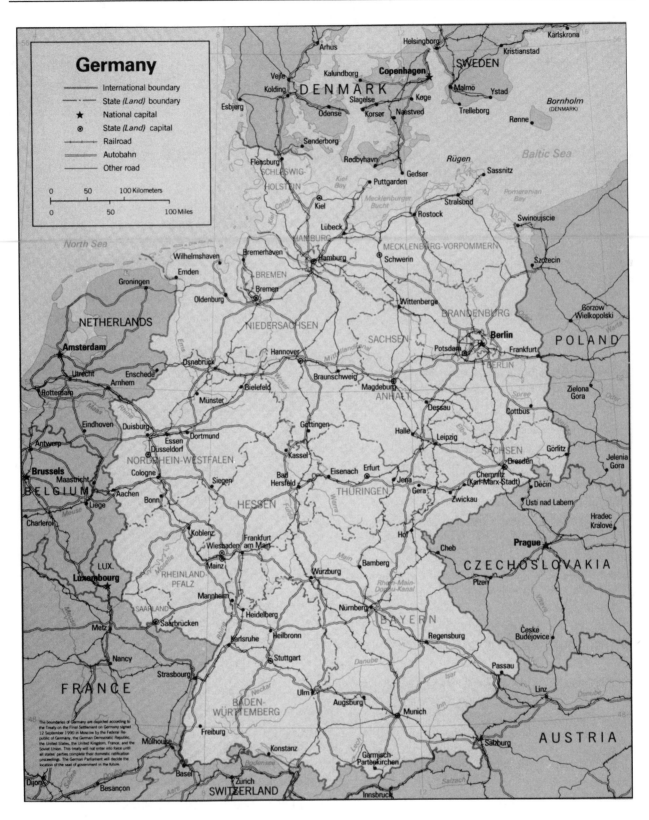

Germany after the reunification on October 3, 1990.

extorted from people wanting to leave East Germany. His wife, Helga, is also charged as an accomplice.

August 11–14 A meeting of the 13th of August Society, a private organization that monitored escapes from East Germany, raises the number of deaths in attempts to flee East Germany from the official governmental figure of 372 to 588 people. Included in this new figure are those who died while trying to escape via the Baltic Sea, into other Communist countries, and border guards who were killed while attempting to flee from August 13, 1961, when the Berlin Wall went up.

August 18 An official report notes that more than 75 percent of agricultural workers in the former East Germany have lost their jobs since reunification due to better mechanization and production standards from western Germany.

August 19 The Institute for the German Economy reports that former East German trade with the former nations of COMECON had fallen by more than 75 percent between 1989 and 1992.

September 16 After a ten month trial three former East German officials are convicted for their roles in the deaths of East Germans attempting to flee the country. Former Defense Minister Heinz Kessler receives seven and a half years in prison; former Deputy Defense Minister Fritz Streletz gets five and a half years; and former Communist party leader Hans Albrecht receives four and a half years. Kessler and Streletz had already served more than two years in prison, while Albrecht had remained free due to poor health.

October 12 The German government decides to move the capital from Bonn to the traditional site of Berlin by the end of the year 2000. In a compromise, some ministries, however, will remain in Bonn.

October 26 After a 20-month trial, 85 year old Erich Mielke, former head of the East German secret police (Stasi) from 1957 to 1987, receives a six year prison sentence for the murders of two policemen in 1931. He remains in prison awaiting the results of an appeal and possibly removal to house arrest due to age and poor health.

November 12 The mayor of the east German city of Rostock resigns after reports criticize him for the August 1992 anti-foreign violence in the city.

December 5 The Party of Democratic Socialism, the successor to the East German Communist party, comes in second in local elections in the east German state of Brandenburg. It wins 21.2 percent of the vote, up 10 percent from the last elections, as compared to the Social Democratic party's 34 percent and the ruling Christian Democratic party's 20.5 percent. The election results show that the former Communist party enjoys renewed support in eastern Germany due to the expectation that privatization will cause the loss of many jobs.

December 6 Markus Wolf, head of the former East German spy operations, receives a six-year prison sentence after being convicted on charges of treason against West Germany and bribery to West German officials. The sentence is suspended while Wolf appeals the decision.

Chapter Five

HUNGARY

The Hungarians, members of the Finno-Ugric people from northeastern Asia, known also as the Magyars, migrated from the area between the Volga River and Ural Mountains into the river valleys of the Don and lower Dnieper between 100–600 A.D. A semi-nomadic people, the Magyars migrated farther west from 600–900 into the Danube-Tisza river basin. A tribal leader, Árpád, was chosen chieftain in 895/896 and his heirs became the hereditary kings of Hungary. The Hungarian chieftain, Géza (972–997), was baptized into the Roman Catholic Church but Hungary did not became a Christian kingdom until Géza's son, István I's (Stephen I's), reign (997–1038). As the predominant power in Central Europe, the Magyars occupied Transylvania and Slavonia in the eleventh century and became the hereditary kings of Croatia in 1103. The Árpád dynasty's domination of the area was interrupted with the invasion of the Mongols in 1241–1242 when the country lost approximately half its population.

With the expiration of the Árpád line in 1301, conflicts erupted as various candidates supported by the Czechs, the Germans, and the Italians fought over succession. Charles I (the French Charles Robert of Anjou, 1308–42) emerged victorious, founding the Anjou line. Dynastic marriages linked Hungary to Poland, Naples, and Bohemia. As the Anjou line became increasingly distant from affairs in Hungary by ruling from outside the country, great nobles sought to usurp authority from the crown. One such noble, János Hunyadi, used his vast wealth in Transylvania to become regent to the infant Hungarian King László V who ruled from 1453 until his death in 1457 at the age of 17. Under Hunyadi's regency (1444–53), the Hungarians successfully fended off the Ottoman Turks. Hunyadi's son, Mátyás (Matthias Corvinus), was elected king of Hungary in 1458 by the nobility after László V died without any heirs in 1457. He broke the power of the great nobles and established Hungary again as the most powerful state in Central Europe. After Mátyás's death in 1490, his efforts were reversed and an oligarchy of great nobles took control, weakening the central imperial state and its successful military. As a result of the constant onslaught of the Ottoman Turks, the religious strife of the Protestant Reformation and the Catholic Counter-Reformation, and the infighting of the nobility, the Ottomans finally defeated the Hungarians at Mohács in 1526.

From 1526–1699, Hungary was partitioned between the Ottoman Empire and Habsburgs, who claimed the Hungarian throne in 1526. Upon suffering major defeats after 1683, the Ottoman sultan, Mustafa II, surrendered most of his Hungarian and all of his Croatian holdings to the Habsburgs in 1699 at the Treaty of Carlowitz. Vienna assumed control of Hungary's foreign affairs, defense, and tariffs, but treated Transylvania as separate from Hungary. In the eighteenth and nineteenth centuries, the Hungarian nobility tried to regain control over Hungary's domestic affairs from the Habsburgs. As a result of economic pressures and rising Hungarian nationalism, the lesser nobility, or gentry, played an increasingly important role in Hungarian affairs and began to press for independence from the Habsburgs. Hungarian discontent with Austrian rule exploded in the March 1848 revolution which broke down central authority in Vienna. The Habsburgs finally suppressed the revolt in 1849 with the help of Russian

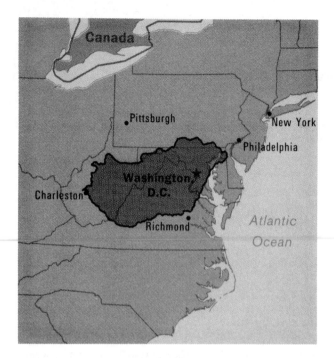

Hungary in relation to the size of the United States.

troops. The Habsburg emperor, Francis Joseph I, then introduced two decades of absolutism, or direct rule by the emperor.

In 1867, facing the possible disintegration of his multiethnic empire due to military defeats by the Italians and Prussians, Francis Joseph I negotiated a compromise with the Hungarians. Known as the *Ausgleich,* or Compromise of 1867, the Habsburg monarch accepted a "dual monarchy" which left the managing of foreign policy, defense, and finance to the Habsburgs in Vienna and granted the Hungarians control over their domestic affairs. The compromise returned Transylvania, Vojvodina, and the Croatian military frontier to Hungary's administrative jurisdiction, although Croatia gained autonomy from Hungary over its domestic affairs in 1868. Faced with restive ethnic minorities of Croats, Slovaks, and Romanians, the Hungarians introduced the Nationalities Law of 1868 which defined Hungary as a single nation comprising different nationalities whose members enjoyed equal rights in all areas except language. Many Hungarians thought this act was too generous; the minorities thought it was too restrictive. In the last third of the nineteenth century, the new government struggled to solve Hungary's ethnic and economic problems and attempted to renegotiate the dualist structure with Austria to the advantage of Hungary.

1896

The 1896 Millennium Celebration. Amid frenetic nationalism, throughout the year Hungarians celebrate the millennium of the Magyars' conquest of and settlement in the Carpathian Basin in 896. Hungary's non-Magyar populations decline to participate because of increasing pressure by the government to linguistically and culturally make them into Magyars, *i.e.,* "Magyarize" them.

1899

February 26   Kálmán Széll, the son-in-law of the nineteenth-century Hungarian nationalist and politician, Ferenc Deák one of the architects of the Compromise of 1867, is appointed prime minister by the crown and forms a government. He is a member of the Liberal party, which favors continued economic ties with the Austrian half of the empire. As prime minister, Széll must accommodate the highly nationalistic Independence party whose political platform focuses on wrestling more Hungarian economic and political power from the Austro-Germans, the Slavs, and especially the Czechs. As an opposition party, the Independence party, pressing for its platform, has successfully obstructed all legislation in the parliament since April 1898. Within hours of taking office, Széll, who is on good terms with the Independence party, promulgates legislation declaring Hungary an independent customs territory, thereby ending its commercial union with the Austrian half of the empire. The passage of this legislation forces the Independence party to halt its obstructionary tactics, and budget and military recruitment bills are passed.

1900

In Hungary and Croatia, 68 percent of the population engages in agriculture while industry employs 14 percent. Those employed in commerce and transportation constitute 5 percent.

Landownership in Hungary is varied. Small farms—usually inadequate to provide a family with even a modest standard of living—are owned by more than half (approximately 52 percent) of the agricultural population. Although the total population stands at more than 19 million, only four thousand individuals or institutions own almost half of the arable land. This disparity influences the political life of Hungary in favor of the large landowners.

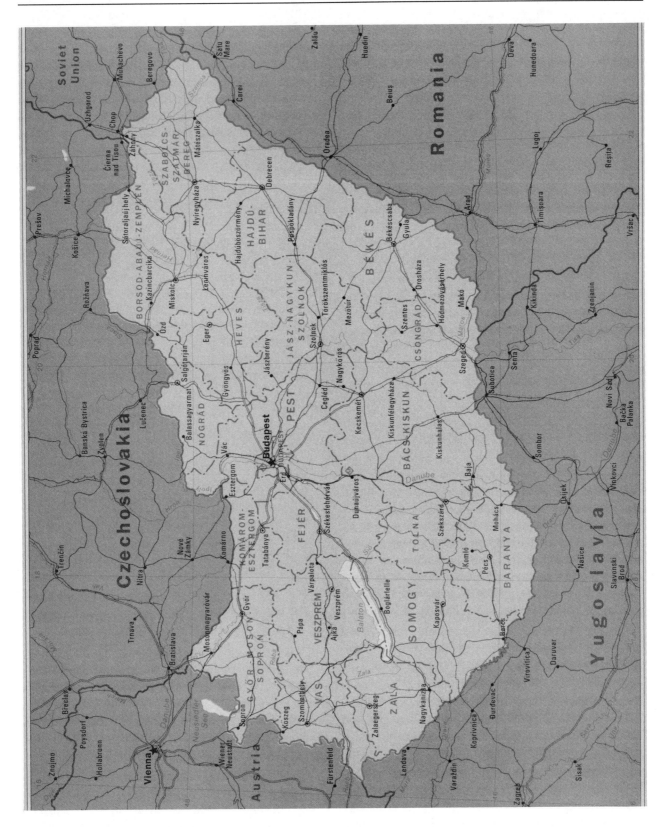

Furthermore, Hungary's manufacturing base is closely linked with agriculture, especially flour mills, sugar beet refineries, alcohol production, and agricultural machinery.

1901

The Social Science Association is established. The organization is soon referred to by its magazine's name, *Huszadik Század* (Twentieth Century), which has become an outlet for their ideas. Members of this group reject classical liberalism, promote the abolition of landed estates, explore ways to curb excesses of public officials, condemn the nationalist rhetoric of previous generations by advocating the granting of cultural and linguistic autonomy to Hungary's national minorities, and seek the answers to Hungary's internal problems in modern social sciences. This association has many Jewish members and becomes a political force during the first decade of the new century.

1903

January   Széll's government presents the draft law to reorganize the army to parliament. The law raises the yearly recruitment quota for the army in anticipation of possible conflicts in Europe. The opposition is led by the Independence party, whose goal is to weaken the connection with Vienna and whose leader is Ferenc Kossuth (the son of Lajos Kossuth, the leader of Hungary's nationalist revolt against the Habsburgs in 1848). The Independence party demands: the introduction of Hungarian as a language of command; regiments conscripted from the Kingdom of Hungary be led by Hungarian officers; the introduction of the Hungarian insignia; the flying of the Hungarian flag; and a reduction in the length of compulsory service.

June 27   As the opposition grows more critical of his regime, Széll resigns as prime minister. Count Károly Khuen-Héderváry, former *ban,* or governor, of Croatia, forms his first government.

September 17   During military maneuvers in Chlopy, Galicia (Austrian Poland), Emperor Francis Joseph I of Austro-Hungary reinforces his conviction that the army remains a common and uniform force and declares he will "never yield the rights and duties guaranteed to its supreme commander."

November 3   A storm of protest by Hungarian nationalists over the emperor's September 17 declaration forces Khuen-Héderváry—who is loyal to his ruler and now unacceptable as prime minister—to resign. Count István

Tisza forms a government, stepping in as prime minister after being appointed by the crown. Tisza, a career politician and nobleman, represents the Liberal party and its mercantilist wing which support capitalist development, industrialization, and close cooperation with finance capital. He is convinced the Dual Monarchy of Austria-Hungary still represents the best interests of Hungarians.

1904

November 18   Tisza convinces the opposition to accept German as the language of command in the army by introducing legislation that enables the government to enforce procedural rules in the Lower House of parliament and creates compulsory measures designed to censure obstructionists. Tisza's maneuvering, however, is done illegally. The left wing of the Liberals and its leader, Gyula Andrássy, leave the Liberal party in protest.

1905

January   The Liberal party is defeated in the elections after 30 years of rule. Francis Joseph I tries to appoint a new coalition government consisting of the Independence party, the Catholic People's party, and the Andrássy Liberals, provided these parties drop their demands to revise the Compromise of 1867, particularly their demand for a separate Hungarian army. This group, now referred to as the "Coalition," refuses. Francis Joseph I appoints Baron Géza Fejérváry, who was the minister of defense in 1902 and is loyal to Habsburg army traditions, to act as interim prime minister.

June 18   István Tisza resigns and Baron Fejérváry becomes prime minister of Hungary.

1906

Hungary's greatest lyric poet Endre Ady (1877–1919) publishes his collection of poetry, *New Poems.* His lyrics explore the faults and flaws in the Hungarian nation, in contrast to the praises sung a century before by Mor Jókai, a nineteenth-century nationalist writer.

February 19   Due to intransigence of the majority political parties over the army issue of 1903, the Habsburg army violates the constitution of Hungary and occupies the parliament. The parliament is dissolved by the government; no date is set for new elections. In an attempt to get parliament functioning again the minister of interior, József

Kristóffy, publishes the text of a bill on voting rights reform, and threatens to introduce the bill into the new parliament when it is elected. This reform advocates universal manhood suffrage (voting rights), which will draw many non-Magyars, small peasants, and agricultural and industrial workers into the political arena. Facing a social revolution that will destroy their political control of the country, the traditional ruling establishment of the landed gentry—the middle nobility and the nationalist intellectuals—back down from their demands on the army. Parliament is reinstated a short time later.

April 6 The "Coalition" of various political parties concedes to form a government under a non-Coalitionist, Sándor Wekerle. Wekerle is a member of the Budapest middle class and a former prime minister (1892–96) with expertise in economic issues. The "Coalition" also agrees to raise no military issues, revoke its attempts to break up the Dual Monarchy, and implement a bill for universal manhood suffrage. The "Coalition" responds negatively to demands by Hungary's national minorities—the Slovaks, Romanians, and Croats—for more political rights with increased forced Magyarization, further political, economic and social abuses, and additional administrative pressures to relinquish their ethnic identities. The height of its repressive policy is Apponyi's Education Law of 1907 (*see* 1907).

April 8 Sándor Wekerle, as prime minister, forms the new government.

April 11 Tisza dissolves the Liberal party after forty years of being the party in power, because it is now too fractionalized to be effective. The party has split into a mercantilist wing—supporting capitalist development, industrialization and close cooperation with finance capital—and an agrarian wing—supporting protectionism for agricultural goods, introduction of marketing and credit cooperatives, and control of "foreign" capital.

May Elections are held for the Hungarian parliament. The nationalist Independence party wins 59.9 percent of the vote, giving it 253 seats. The Slavic (Slovaks, Ruthenians, Serbs, and Croats) and Romanian minorities return 26 deputies to parliament who join together to form the Club of National Minority Deputies, an opposition bloc. Under Wekerle, the parliament passes laws on military recruits and payment of Hungary's share of the Habsburg military budget, negotiates with Austria on common economic agreements, and authorizes the collection of unpaid taxes during the years of resistance (1897–1906) to the crown when the Hungarians attempted to gain more freedom from Austria.

October 10 Massive demonstrations organized by the Social Democrats protest the withholding of universal suffrage. The Social Democrats advocate the education of workers, granting of voting rights to the working class, and active participation in organizing unions and workers' strikes.

1907

Pressured by Count Albert Apponyi, the minister of education, the parliament passes the Education Law of 1907. This law expresses the core of the "Coalition's" values. It makes governmental subsidies of the schools among non-Magyar national groups dependent on expanded use of the Magyar language by teachers and students. Teachers in church schools and state employees must demonstrate the ability to read, write, and teach Magyar adequately. Non-Magyar pupils must be able to express themselves orally and in writing in Magyar by the end of their fourth year or they will not receive diplomas and will be ineligible for government service.

Oszkár Jászi, a sociologist, historian, and future minister of nationalities under Mihály Károlyi's government (1918–19), makes public the program of the Twentieth Century Group in the article, "Toward a New Hungary" (*see* 1901). The important planks of the program call for the dissolution of large estates, establishment of a cooperative network for peasants, democratic local self-government, educational reform, graduated taxes, general health and social insurance, and the enforcement of the Nationalities Law of 1868.

1908

Nyugat editor Mihály Babits criticizes the gentry, his own social class, in his novel *Sons of Death*. This work attributes the problems of Hungary to the disintegration of the solid and virtuous gentry.

Frequent contributors to *Nyugat* include great writers and intellectuals Árpád Toth, Gyula Juhász, Dezsó Kosztolányi, Margit Kaffka, Frigyes Karinthy, Dezsó Szabó, and Zsigmond Móricz. Móricz excels at the exposition of peasant life and becomes one of the first writers to discuss the problem of anti-Semitism in Hungarian society.

The Independence party demands the creation of a Hungarian bank separate from the Austrian bank when the charter of the joint Austro-Hungarian bank expires in 1910. The Independence party draws up a plan for a new bank and submits it to Emperor Francis Joseph I, who declines to consider it because the Wekerle government did not implement the promised voting rights reform from 1906.

A radical faction within the Independence party, led by Gyula Justh, a wealthy member of the gentry and a staunch separatist, pushes for the extension of voting rights to the national minorities. This faction believes a democratized Hungary has the best chance of dealing with the non-Magyar nationalities. Other "Coalition" members like István Tisza, former leader of the Liberal party, believe true voting rights mean the end of a Magyar Hungary.

Nyugat (The West), a literary magazine, is founded by Baron Louis Hatvany. This magazine provides an outlet for a new trend in Hungarian literature. Inspired by Western Europe and reflecting the social changes brought about by industrialization, the contributors disavow the anachronistic writings of Mor Jókai, a nineteenth-century Hungarian nationalist writer, and his patriotic and romantic depictions of his fellow Hungarians *(see 1906)*.

October 6   The Austro-Hungarian monarchy proclaims the annexation of the Ottoman province Bosnia-Herzegovina under the terms of the Congress of Berlin (1878). Most Hungarians are not pleased at the addition of more Slavs to the empire's population.

1909

November 11   The Independence party formally splits in two *(see April 11, 1906)*. The nationalist wing, formally the mercantilist faction, supports the creation of an independent Hungarian bank, not as a viable economic institution, but as a symbol of the Hungarian nation's total independence from Vienna. The militant extremists, formally the agrarian faction, led by Gyula Justh, break away from the Independence party. His leadership weakened further by these acts, Prime Minister Wekerle resigns.

With Wekerle's resignation and the split of the Independence party, the political stalemate continues.

1910

January 17   Count Károly Khuen-Héderváry assumes the post of prime minister after being selected by Emperor Francis Joseph I.

February 19   István Tisza reconstitutes the Liberal party as the Party of National Work. Supported mainly by landowners and influential members of the middle class, this party fights to uphold the principles of the Compromise of 1867 that created the dualist state structure of Austria-Hungary.

June   Elections are held for parliament. The Party of National Work wins 258 seats and 47 percent of the vote. The nationalistic part of the Independence party, led by Ferenc Kossuth, wins 14.3 percent of the vote and 54 seats, and the Justh wing takes 15.8 percent and 41 seats. As a result, the Party of National Work gains an absolute majority in parliament. Headed by István Tisza, the new majority of the Party of National Work in parliament agrees to maintain the Dual Monarchy. One faction of the majority believes in voting rights reform, but the other faction defends the old system. Both agree Hungary must support the Dual Monarchy in foreign affairs.

From June 1910 through 1914, the paramount issues dominating domestic politics in Hungary are the joint-bank question, army issues from 1903, and widening of voting rights.

1911

The Germans act to protect their interests in Morocco when unstable domestic politics allow the French to occupy Morocco. As an ally of Germany, the Habsburg High Command calls up reserves and keeps men who are already in service under arms. The Hungarian parliament fails to vote on the annual contingent of troops because the parliamentary opposition resorts to filibustering and to counterdemands such as extending voting rights to the working class.

1912

April 22   Unable to secure support for the armed forces bill, Khuen-Héderváry resigns as prime minister and László Lukács, a member of the Party of National Work, heads the new government approved by parliament and appointed by the crown.

May 23   István Tisza, leader of the Party of National Work, is elected president of the Chamber of Deputies of the lower house of parliament, the most powerful parliamentary position. Because Tisza is considered unfriendly to industrial workers and an opponent of universal voting rights, the Social Democrats proclaim a general strike and ask for peaceful demonstrations. Subsequently, massive demonstrations take place in Budapest opposing Tisza's selection. Tisza sends the army against the demonstrators and the opposition deputies rallying outside the parliament building. Six people die when the demonstrations degenerate into a street fight. The day is known as "Bloody Thursday."

Shortly after May 23 Tisza proposes changes to the rules of parliamentary procedure, prevents parliamentary debate, and orders the police to eject any deputies who provoke violence. Under such restrictive conditions, parliament forces the military bill into law.

December 31 A new voting rights bill is passed in parliament. This bill extends the right to vote to more people but leaves Magyar predominance in government in effect. Restricted by occupational, property, and educational requirements, the bill denies the right to vote to almost all propertyless laborers, over half the farm owners, artisans, civil servants, and half the tradesmen.

1913

June 10 When Lukács' government is forced to resign under a cloud of financial scandal, Tisza, after intimidating the parliamentary opposition, is made prime minister. Tisza remains prime minister until June 5, 1917.

1914

June 28 Archduke Francis Ferdinand, the Habsburg crown prince, is assassinated in Sarajevo by Gavrilo Princip, a Bosnian Serb supporter of Serbian independence. The Serbian government is aware of the plot and does little to thwart the efforts of the Bosnian revolutionaries. Vienna, convinced of Serbia's complicity, acts decisively and believes war with Serbia is necessary.

July 12 Tisza, after several days opposition to war with Serbia, finally accepts Vienna's decision to issue an ultimatum to Serbia, and agrees, if necessary, to attack Serbia on the condition that Austria-Hungary does not annex Serbia after the war.

July 23 With assurances from Germany that it will back whatever decision Vienna reaches regarding Serbia, Austria-Hungary issues a ten point ultimatum to Belgrade, which would compromise the independence of Serbia.

July 25 The Serbian government accepts all points of the Austro-Hungarian ultimatum except the Habsburg demand that its government institute a judicial inquiry against every participant in the assassination conspiracy who may be found on Serbian territory. Serbia mobilizes for war.

Wishing to reassure Russia, Vienna declares no Serbian territory will be annexed in the event of war. However, Russia does not trust Austria-Hungary and will not risk the possibility of Serbia being reduced to a satellite state of Austria-Hungary and of Russian influence waning in the Balkans.

July 28 Austria-Hungary declares war on Serbia, beginning World War I. Russia will not allow Habsburg encroachment, so on the following day the Russian tsar, Nicholas II, agrees to general mobilization against Austria-Hungary. As a result of Russian actions, Vienna orders general mobilization on July 31.

August 1 France and Germany order mobilizations against one another; Germany declares war on Russia.

August 3 Germany declares war on France.

August 4 Great Britain declares war on Germany.

August 6 Austria-Hungary declares war on Russia.

Many Hungarians look forward to a chance to even the score with the Russians who, in 1849, had sent forces into Hungary to put down their fight for independence from the Habsburgs. The political parties (even the Social Democrats), the churches, and most Hungarians are firmly united behind the war effort.

Under Prime Minister Tisza the war aims of the Hungarian nationalists are focused on the preservation of the Magyars' dominant position in Hungary vis-à-vis the other nationalities. Hungarian nationalists are opposed to territorial gains of non-Magyar territories because they are afraid new territorial acquisitions will threaten their majority status.

As the war progresses, nationalities within Austria-Hungary agitate for independence and the breakup of the Dual Monarchy.

August 13 Austria-Hungary begins its invasion of Serbia.

September 13 The Russians, in the first year of war, concentrate their forces in Galicia in eastern Poland, the frontier with Austria-Hungary. After an initial victory on the eastern front, the Habsburgs are defeated by the Russians at Lemberg and the Austro-Hungarians abandon eastern Galicia.

September 24 Russia places forces at the fortress of Przemyśl and launches an attack upon the passes of the Carpathians leading into northern Hungary. The Russians are halted, but resume the invasion on November 15. Russia will not advance further than the foothills of the western side of the Carpathians during the war.

Archduke Francis Ferdinand and Archduchess Sophie leaving the town hall in Sarajevo a few minutes before their assassination on June 28, 1914.

December 2   The Habsburg army takes the Serbian capital of Belgrade, only to be driven out on December 15 by the Serbs.

1915

May 2   The great German and Austro-Hungarian offensive into Galicia begins. By June, Austro-German forces have recaptured the Habsburg provinces of Galicia and Bukovina from the Russians.

May 23   After the Allies promise Italy large sections of Austria-Hungary after the war, the country mobilizes and declares war on Austria-Hungary. The first two years of fighting between Italy and Austria-Hungary will be on the Isonzo, a river northwest of Trieste.

July 1   The second great offensive of the Germans and Austro-Hungarians begins. The Habsburgs advance and take the area from the southern part of Russian Poland to Lublin.

September 19   The Germans capture Vilna from the Russians. With this defeat, the Russians have lost all of Russian Poland and Lithuania.

October 6   Austria-Hungary begins an offensive into Serbia and captures Belgrade for the second time by October 9.

1916

The third year of war brings currency depreciation, food shortages especially in urban areas, realization of the war's futility, and growing discontent throughout Austria-Hungary. The Social Democrats and other opposition parties doubt the military leadership, question the government's attempts to justify the high cost of human life, and complain about the state of the economy.

June 4   The Brusilov Offensive starts. This Russian offensive, conceived by the Russian General Aleksey Brusilov, is designed to distract the Habsburgs from the Italians in Trentino. An assault on Austria's northernmost front surprises the Austro-Hungarians. By September, however, the Russians do not reach Lemberg and are stopped by the arrival of 15 German divisions from the western front. With losses totaling one million men, the Russian army becomes demoralized and discontented.

July 9 Watching the growing restlessness of Hungarians, the nobleman and politician Mihláy Károlyi leaves the Independence party and establishes the Party of Independence, which is democratic, anti-German, and advocates that Hungarians negotiate a separate peace with the Entente—the wartime alliance of the British, French, Russians, Italians, and Romanians.

August 27 The Romanians invade Transylvania hoping to annex this territory but are thwarted by the Central Powers. The Romanians are not alone in their hope of dismembering Austria-Hungary. Two Czech leaders, Prof. Tomáš Garrigue Masaryk and Edvard Beneš, campaign for an independent state consisting of the Czechs and Slovaks. In Croatia-Slavonia Croat leaders Ante Trumbić and Frano Supilo work for a South Slavic state. These independence movements threaten the integrity of Hungary in the event of an Entente victory.

November 21 Emperor Francis Joseph I dies. Charles succeeds his great uncle Francis Joseph and becomes King Charles IV of Hungary and Charles I of Austria. Charles's ideas pertaining to the Dual Monarchy are to placate the Slavs and Romanians at the expense of the Germans and Magyars. He favors giving concessions to the Czechs in Austria, and to the Croats, Serbs, and Romanians in Hungary. However, he is unable to put his ideas into effect when, upon coronation as King of Hungary, he agrees to abide by the terms of the Compromise of 1867.

1917

April 6 The United States enters World War I.

May 1 Large numbers of Hungarian workers demonstrate due to the continuing war, with trade union membership exceeding 200,000 for the first time. In the wake of demonstrations, Charles IV calls upon Tisza to resign.

June 5 With Hungarian discontent over the war continuing, István Tisza resigns the prime ministry.

June 15 As prime minister appointed by the crown, Count Móricz Esterházy—a member of the moderate opposition—forms a government that promises to be receptive to electoral reform.

July 1 Russian General Brusilov begins another Russian offensive on the Galician front but the Germans and

Austro-Hungarians drive the Russians back and regain Galician territory lost in 1916.

August 18 Count Esterházy's government falls after two months because it is unable to bring about the promised electoral reform, and Sándor Wekerle is appointed prime minister by the crown. Wekerle's government, his third (he was prime minister in 1892–95 and 1906–10), enacts electoral reform but does little to quiet revolutionary fires expressed in mass labor demonstrations and the formation of left wing groups such as the Revolutionary Socialists.

October 24–December 26 The Caporetto Campaign takes place. German and Austro-Hungarian forces attack the Italians at Isonzo and push them back to Piave, a river running north of Venice.

November 7 The Bolshevik Revolution in Russia brings the Communists to power under the leadership of Vladimir I. Lenin who states he will take Russia out of the war.

December 15 An armistice is signed between Germany, Austria-Hungary, and Bolshevik Russia on the Eastern Front.

1918

January 8 U.S. president Woodrow Wilson lists American war aims in his Fourteen Points to a joint session of Congress. Article X of the Fourteen Points states the nationalities of Austria-Hungary should be free to develop autonomously.

Mid-January Strikes and demonstrations over the continuing war that has brought food and fuel shortages spill over from Vienna into Hungary. The government forces the half million or more participants to go back to work after three days. To curb the radical forces, Wekerle's government bans left-wing publications and associations, creates special armed squads to maintain internal order, and arrests the leaders of the strikes.

May 1 The Slovak Social Democratic Party in Hungary issues a resolution including the right to self-determination for Slovaks in Hungary.

May 20 In the city of Pecs, Hungarian army units mutiny and are disarmed only after heavy fighting with other Habsburg units. Waves of strikes sweep through Hungary. On June 20, the army is deployed to squelch civil unrest. This prompts a nine-day general strike that ends only through mediation by the Social Democratic party.

June 15–24 The Battle of Piave takes place. The Austro-Hungarians advance across the Piave river in Italy, but are unable to maintain their position. They withdraw after losing 100,000 men. From this time onward, morale is a severe problem in the Habsburg army.

September 15   Due to its acute military and domestic situations and hoping to forestall the disintegration of its empire, the Austro-Hungarian government appeals to President Wilson for an informal peace conference; Wilson rejects the appeal, knowing that victory is not far away.

October 4   The Austro-Hungarians join the Germans in appealing for an armistice.

October 16   Emperor Charles I of Austria (Charles IV of Hungary) issues the October Manifesto promising a federal structure for the Austrian half of the empire only. This manifesto will transform Austria into a federation of national member states of Czechs, South Slavs, Poles, and Germans. To appease Hungary, the emperor promises the lands of the Hungarian crown will not be affected by the constitutional changes.

October 17   The Hungarian parliament replies to Emperor Charles's manifesto of October 16 by declaring complete independence from Austria, except in the form of the Habsburg monarch who will remain as king of Hungary.

October 24   Due to the dire position of Hungary in the war and because he continues to support the Compromise of 1867, Wekerle's government falls.

October 25   The Hungarian National Council is formed under the chairmanship of Count Mihály Károlyi. During the war, Károlyi has become the chief proponent of voting rights reform and negotiations with the minorities of Hungary. After breaking away from the Independence party in July of 1916, his left wing party (the Party of Independence) now demands national autonomy from Austria, general franchise, and the breakup of big agricultural estates.

October 27   The Romanians in Bukovina announce secession from Austria-Hungary.

October 28   The Czechs declare their independence from Austria-Hungary.

Protests against the war and in support of Hungarian independence from Austria are held on the Chain Bridge in Budapest. The protests end in bloodshed when government forces attempt to stop them, leaving three dead and 52 injured (*see also* October 30–31).

October 29   Croatia secedes from Hungary.

October 30   Slovakia proclaims it is leaving Hungary and joining Czechoslovakia. Hungarian forces, however, will remain in control of Slovakia until late in 1918. The

Galician Ukrainians announce their secession from Austria-Hungary.

October 30–31   The "Chrysanthemum Revolution" comes in the wake of bloodshed arising out of protests held on the Chain Bridge on October 28 in Budapest.

The protests on the Chain Bridge are significant because of the bridge's place in Hungarian history. This bridge was the first permanent suspension bridge connecting Buda and Pest over the Danube. Buda and Pest were at one time separate cities across from each other; they were unified in the late nineteenth century. The bridge was built under the patronage of István Széchenyi, a nineteenth-century Hungarian aristocrat who supported Hungary's cultural and economic renaissance. Finished in the mid-nineteenth century, the Chain Bridge symbolized Hungary's growing independence from Vienna, its rise as the commercial center for Hungary, and the abolition of the nobility's right to tax exemption because the Hungarian nobles had to pay the bridge toll just like everyone else.

The brutal, ineffectual actions of the government on October 28 spur reservist Hungarian units of the Territorial Army (Honvéd)—which has now sworn allegiance to Károlyi's National Council party—to seize public buildings, the post office, the telephone and telegraph exchanges, and the railway stations. The Budapest garrison of the Habsburg army, despite being headed by a staunch supporter of the monarchy, General Géza Lukachich, remains in its barracks due to the unpredictable loyalty of the Hungarian troops.

October 31   Count Mihály Károlyi is made prime minister by Charles IV in hopes of securing satisfactory peace terms from the Entente powers (*see* July 9, 1916) and attaining Hungary's independence from Austria while maintaining the Habsburg monarchy. Károlyi's new government includes members of his left wing faction of the Independence party, middle class radicals, and the Social Democrats.

After breaking into his Budapest home, a group of thugs murder Tisza, blaming him for Hungary's defeat in the war.

November   Revolt and violence break out in the countryside, primarily in the eastern regions and in lands inhabited by Romanians, Slovaks, Ruthenians, and Croats who no longer want to be under Hungarian control. The unrest follows the traditional pattern of village protest; the peasants chase away all representatives of the central government and destroy and pillage manor houses, stores, granaries, and state offices. The National Council, now the government of Hungary, uses force to put down the revolt.

November 3   Austria-Hungary and the Entente Powers agree on a cease-fire in Padua, Italy. The Hungarian government insists on concluding a separate armistice in the name of Hungary alone in order to press Hungary's newly gained independence and sovereignty.

November 16   In front of the houses of parliament, the National Council announces the creation of the Hungarian Republic by declaring its oath of allegiance to the crown as null and void.

November 24   The Hungarian Communist Party (HCP) is founded by Belá Kun, who has recently returned from Russian captivity as a prisoner of war. Kun began his career as one of the young leaders of the Social Democrats. He was a reserve officer during the war and was captured by the Russians. While a prisoner, he and other captured Hungarians observe the Bolshevik (Communist) Revolution and believe it is the model for the Hungarian socialist movement.

1919

January 11   Count Mihály Károlyi is elected provisional president of the Hungarian Republic by the National Council. He steps down as prime minister several days later when he is sworn in as president. Károlyi labors unsuccessfully to develop either a political organization or policies to deal with the social unrest caused by the end of the First World War, the dissolution of the Habsburg empire, and returning soldiers. Károlyi does not succeed in either the domestic or foreign realm. The proposed land reform and the new electoral law of November 22, 1918—extending voting rights to adult citizens literate in any language, including the majority of women over 21—are too radical for the majority of the landed gentry, the middle nobility, and nationalist intellectuals (*see* February 16, 1919).

Workers and returning soldiers agitate for government representatives of their interests and push for the appointment of more socialists to ministerial posts. The left wing of the Social Democrats refuses to participate in the provisional government. Balancing on the narrow base of a small, moderate middle class, Károlyi tries to broaden his political base by inviting the leader of the Independent Smallholders' party, István Szabó Nagyatadi, to accept a cabinet post.

January 18–March 20   Dezso Berinkey, an expert in international law, is appointed prime minister by Károlyi. Berinkey is apolitical and attempts to hold together a diverse coalition: Oszkár Jászi's Radical party, which represents modern intellectuals and the radical middle class but has little popular support; the Smallholders' party, whose political base rests on the program of universal suffrage, quick action on land reform, and abolition of inherited feudal privileges; the Social Democrats, who are the strongest party in the new coalition and who command the loyalty of the unions and skilled workers; and the left wing of Károlyi's party, the Party of Independence.

January 20   Czechoslovak forces take control of all of Slovakia (now part of Czechoslovakia) from Hungary after the victorious Allies pressure Hungary to evacuate it in December.

February 16   The land reform law is passed. All estates over 300 hectares (1 hectare=2.471 acres) are to be expropriated by the state and compensation paid to their owners at pre-war 1913 prices. Plots will then be parceled out to create a new economic structure based on small peasant farms. Neither the peasants, because of the reluctance of the government to expropriate more land from the large landowners, nor the large estate owners, because of the low level of compensation and breaking up of their estates, support the law.

February 20   In Budapest, a crowd excited by Communist speeches marches on the editorial offices of the socialist newspaper *Népszava* (The Voice of the People) in order to seize it. In the fight to restore order, six police officers are killed and several others wounded. The government arrests 42 prominent Communists, including Hungarian Communist Party (HCP) leader Béla Kun. Kun and several others are beaten while in custody.

February 22   One hundred thousand workers demonstrate against the Communists in a meeting called by the Social Democrats. The slogan of this meeting is "Down with the leftist and rightist counterrevolutions." Under pressure from the Social Democrats, the government arrests a few rightist politicians.

March   Peasants begin to seize land and distribute it themselves since the newly appointed governmental officials who have the responsibility of seizure and distribution have proven reluctant to confiscate land from the large landowners.

March 20   Lt. Col. Fernand Vyx, the head of the French military mission in Budapest, hands Károlyi a note demanding all Hungarian forces evacuate the region between the Tisza river and the Carpathian mountains on the eastern edge of the Hungarian plain. The Hungarians erroneously assume this line represents the country's new borders; these are actually to be military demarcation lines. The Hungarian government has 18 hours in which to accept

Vyx's terms. The government is in a quandary: if it accepts the terms, the public will be outraged; if it resists, the government has no real military means to back up its actions.

Károlyi's government rejects the Vyx note and hands power over to the Social Democratic party, which looks to the Communists hoping they can get Russian support. The Socialists conclude a pact with the Communists on March 21. Their joint manifesto declares the union of the two parties, the dictatorship of the proletariat (workers), the organization of a proletarian Red Army to repel the Romanians who had moved into Transylvania in 1918, and alliance with the Russian Bolsheviks. Thus, power virtually falls into the laps of Béla Kun and the Communists.

March 21   The Hungarian Soviet Republic is proclaimed and the Revolutionary Governing Council is created with Kun as Minister of Foreign Affairs although he is the real power in the government. The council draws its support from the unemployed, the returning veterans, and disgruntled workers. Its platform is simple: dictatorship of the proletariat; the nationalization of houses, lands, and factories without compensation; all power to councils composed of workers; and world revolution.

March 28   Hungary declares war on Czechoslovakia and proceeds to reconquer the area.

The Entente powers at the Paris Peace Conference perceive the new Hungarian Soviet Republic as a threat to the establishment of order and security in Central Europe and maintain their economic blockade of the country.

April 2   The provisional constitution and a new electoral law declaring universal suffrage are promulgated. Dozens of decrees are passed aimed at the introduction of socialism, the establishment of equality, and public ownership of industry, agriculture, trade, and finance. However, attempts to build socialism in Hungary become secondary after the Romanians attack on April 16.

April 3   Land reform decrees are enacted in which middle- and large-sized estates—together with livestock—are expropriated without compensation and taken into state ownership. Further, the government nationalizes church properties and forbids the division of the seized land into individual plots. Former estates are to be collectively managed by agricultural cooperatives.

April 7–10   Elections are held for the workers' council (soviet), a national legislature, on the basis of extended suffrage. A single list of candidates is introduced to ensure the Revolutionary Governing Council wins a majority.

April 16–August 1   Romanian troops invade Hungary to forestall Hungarian plans for the reconquest of Transylvania. Initially, the Hungarian Red Army does not halt the Romanian advance. However, in May and June the Hungarian Red Army, swelling with volunteers, begins its offensive against the Czechs and Slovaks in Slovakia and Ruthenia with great success. By the beginning of June, the Hungarian Red Army has driven a wedge between the Czechoslovak and Romanian forces. This success prompts Kun in mid-June to negotiate a Hungarian and Romanian pull-back to the former demarcation line at the Tisza river. However, the Romanians refuse to withdraw until Hungary disarms, prompting an attack by Hungarian forces on July 20. After several initial victories, the Hungarians fall back into a disorderly retreat and on July 31, only 60 miles separate the Romanians from Budapest. After 133 days, the Hungarian Soviet Republic falls due to military defeats and counterrevolution.

May 2   Hungarian anti-Communist white forces raid Kun's embassy in Vienna.

May 5   A rival Hungarian government is formed in Arad, Romania, by Count Gyula Károlyi (brother of Mihály), Count István Bethlen, Admiral Miklós Horthy, and Count Pál Teleki. Later in May, Gyula Károlyi transfers it to Szeged where French and Serbian occupation forces provide a friendlier atmosphere than that of the Romanian Army.

Capt. Gyula Gömbös—a former Habsburg general staff officer whose politics are based on radical right ideology and anti-Semitism—is also assembling counterrevolutionary forces. Bethlen and the Hungarian emigration in Vienna and eastern Austria supply Gömbös with funds and supplies. These forces never go into battle against the Communists, but remain in Szeged until Kun flees to Vienna on August 1. They then move against the trade unionist government of the Soviet Democrat leader Gyula Peidl (*see* below).

August 1   Given the hopelessness of the military situation with Romania, the Hungarian Soviet government resigns in favor of a moderate trade unionist government headed by Gyula Peidl and Ernő Garami, leaders of the Social Democratic party. Peidl becomes prime minister and Garami becomes the Minister of Justice. Béla Kun and some of his followers flee to Vienna in the face of the Romanian advance to Budapest. The counterrevolutionary right-wing forces of Captain Gyula Gömbös and the Szeged government move against the government of Gyula Peidl which succeeded the Communist regime.

August 4   The Romanians occupy Budapest.

August 6 A coup d'état supported by the Romanian army puts an end to the trade unionist government which is viewed as too left leaning. The Habsburg Archduke Joseph, acting as Charles IV's representative, asks István Friedrich to form a new government. Friedrich, a factory owner, is loyal to the House of Habsburg and leans to the right with a few liberal proclivities. Representatives from the Szeged government, representing the traditional Hungarian political elite, compete for places on Friedrich's cabinet.

November 14 Romanian troops leave Budapest after the Allies pressure them to do so.

November 16 The Szeged army enters Budapest, now led by Admiral Horthy, a nobleman and former Austro-Hungarian naval commander. This army has not fought a battle against either the Communists or the Romanians, instead has confined its heroics to attacks on the Jews and persecuting those who had sided or sympathized with the Communists.

The Szeged army quickly transforms itself into the national army and begins to act independently from the Friedrich government. Horthy's troops advance into areas between the Tisza and the Danube that are not under Romanian occupation and extend their control to areas west of the Danube. As these forces move into these areas, actual and alleged Communists are ruthlessly persecuted, brutalized, and murdered along with workers and peasants who have played an active part in implementing the Communist government's social program; a similar fate meets the Jews.

These acts of violence and retribution rage throughout the countryside during the fall of 1919 and cease slowly in the spring of 1920. Known as the "White Terror," the persecution by Horthy's forces bears no semblance of legality. The White Terror claims approximately 5,000 lives, puts 70,000 citizens behind bars, and forces many Communists, Socialists, moderate liberals, and intellectuals to flee abroad. Among those forced abroad are Béla Kun, literary theorist and philosopher György Lukács, leftist economist Jenő Varga, Social Democratic leaders Ernő Garami, and Mihály Károlyi, sociologists Oszkár Jászi and Károly Mannheim, physicist Károly Polányi, film director Alexander Korda, and artist László Moholy-Nagy.

November 25 Friedrich's government is not recognized by either the Allied or Entente powers, subsequently his ability to negotiate is minimal. As a result, Friedrich's government resigns and is succeeded by a more moderate and broader coalition government with Károly Huszár, leader of the Christian Social party, as prime minister.

December 1 Hungary is invited to send a delegation to Paris to take part in the peace conference following the First World War. In actuality it will be a dictated peace without any Hungarian input.

1920

January 25 Parliamentary elections for the National Assembly are held in the midst of the White Terror. Although the vote is by secret ballot and encompasses broad voting rights, the intimidation and fear of the White Terror render the elections farcical. The Social Democrats boycott the elections and other political factions display a lack of leadership, unity, and stability. The intimidated electorate votes in an overwhelmingly counterrevolutionary and agrarian parliament which professes "Christian" ideals.

March 1 Admiral Horthy is elected regent of Hungary, making him the most powerful person in the country and the head of state. Law I of 1920 stipulates that Hungary will remain a kingdom, maintaining historical continuity to the new republic and legalizing the country's claim to all lands of pre-war Hungary that Romania, Czechoslovakia, and Yugoslavia have taken. The restoration of Charles IV (who was pressured to abdicate in November 1918) to the throne worries Hungary's neighbors, who fear the installation of a Hungarian king will lead to the reestablishment of the territory of the old Hungarian kingdom and possibly even the Dual Monarchy of Austria-Hungary. Acknowledging these fears, the National Assembly revives the medieval office of regent to run the country in place of the king for the duration of the interregnum until a king, acceptable to all parties, can take the throne.

Supported by the great powers, primarily Great Britain, and by the national army, Horthy is the only possible candidate for regent. His powers are broadly defined and include the rights to dismiss parliament, act as commander in chief, and subordinate legislation to the wishes of the regent and of the prime minister, who is appointed by the regent. The election of Horthy is a temporary measure as far as the members of parliament are concerned, but, in actuality, these powers allow Horthy to rule in a longlasting, authoritarian manner until 1944.

March 13 Károly Huszár's government falls.

March 14 Sándor Simonyi-Semadam forms a government.

March 23 Regent Horthy officially proclaims Hungary a monarchy but with its throne vacant.

June 4 In the Trianon Palace at Versailles, the Hungarians sign the Trianon Peace Treaty. By the terms of the treaty, old Hungary is shorn of 70 percent of its territory and 60 percent of its inhabitants, including 28 percent of its Hungarian speakers. At this time 89.5 percent of the eight million people left are Hungarian; the Germans, the largest minority group, compose 6.9 percent of the population.

Czechoslovakia receives Slovakia and Ruthenia; the Kingdom of Serbs, Croats, and Slovenes (or Yugoslavia) takes Croatia-Slavonia and part of the Banat of Temesvar. Austria receives a western slice of Hungary, and Romania acquires the rest of the Banat, Transylvania, and part of the Hungarian plain. Hungary agrees to pay reparations to the Entente powers with the sum to be determined later, to keep an army of only 35,000 men, and to assume part of the old Austro-Hungarian debt.

As a result of the treaty, the economic structure of Hungary changes. The country retains only 11 percent of its iron production, 16 percent of its forests, 38 percent of its railroad network, and 56 percent of its food processing industry.

Hungary's government and people continue to firmly identify their dismembered state with the Hungary of the prewar period. Although representatives of the Hungarian government sign the treaty, the government remains irreconcilable to the terms of Trianon and rejects the possibility of ever accepting them. The slogan, *''Nem, nem, soha!''* (No, no, never!) expresses the attitude of the Hungarian people. Until 1945, each successive government adopts a virulent revisionist policy aimed at regaining the territories lost under the Treaty of Trianon.

June 27 Sándor Simonyi-Semadam's government— formed only four months prior—falls due to its signing of the Treaty of Trianon.

July 19 Count Pál Teleki forms a government as prime minister. Teleki is a member of an old Transylvanian family, and advocates territorial revision to restore Hungarian territories that belonged to Hungary before the Treaty of Trianon. His conservativism leads him to reject both the left and right extremists. His government ends the excesses of the army, bans the activities of certain rightist extreme groups, and outlaws the Communist party.

Legislation enacted by Teleki's government reflects the mood of interwar Hungary; the parliament passes the Numerus Clausus Act that sets religious quotas for admission to institutions of higher learning, thus cutting back on Jewish enrollments. This law is followed by Public Law xxvi/1920 which provides for the restoration of corporal punishment for certain types of criminal offenses. Addressing the pressing issue of land reform, Public Law xxvi/

1920 transfers 900,000 acres of land from large estates to peasant proprietors.

1921

March 26–30 King Charles IV returns to Hungary in his first restoration attempt and calls on Horthy to give up his powers. Owing to the threatening attitude of neighboring states who oppose restoration, the parliament votes against restoration and Charles is obliged to return to exile in Switzerland where he has lived since March 1919.

April 13 In reaction to the failed restoration attempt of King Charles IV, Count Pál Teleki's government falls.

April 14 Count István Bethlen forms a government as prime minister. Bethlen, a member of an old Transylvanian landowning family, seeks to reestablish the old economic, social, and political system of the prewar period and believes that a parliamentary government representing the old ruling classes (estate owners, important capitalists, and nationalists) and the majority of the middle class is the only possible political path. He wishes to provide safeguards making a turn to the left or extreme right impossible. His ascendancy is a period of consolidation and stability in the first decade after the First World War.

In July 1920, Bethlen engineered the merger of the Smallholders' party with the more conservative Legitimist Christian National Union. Calling this new party the Party of Unity, or the Government party, Bethlen steers a middle course between left and right extremism. Under Bethlen, the new government reaches an agreement with the Social Democrats who promise to refrain from organizing public officials and agricultural workers, and promise to avoid politically motivated strikes.

July–December The Burgenland dispute with Austria occurs. Burgenland, a strip of territory formally in Hungary, predominately German, and only 15 miles from Vienna, had been assigned to Austria by the Trianon Treaty peace treaty. Hungarian irregulars—soldiers acting without government or military sanction— occupy it and refuse to evacuate. Through Italian mediation a plebiscite, or referendum, is arranged for the city of Sopron, the capital of Burgenland, and its environs, both populated mostly by Hungarians.

October 20–24 King Charles IV makes his second restoration attempt. With an improvised military force Charles marches on Budapest. Czechoslovakia begins to mobilize in opposition to the restoration and Hungarian forces are obliged to capture the king and deport him. The

Entente powers intern Charles on the island of Madeira, where he dies six months later.

November 3 The National Assembly votes to officially remove the Habsburgs from the monarchy by passing the Dethronement Act of the House of Habsburg. The act placates some anti-Habsburg members of the Government party, mostly from the Smallholders' party, and is applauded by the great powers, who adamantly oppose restoration.

December 14 The plebiscite is held in Sopron and its environs, resulting in the return of this small slice of the Burgenland to Hungary (*see* July–December).

1922

June 2 Elections held under a system of restricted suffrage and open ballot voting in the rural areas give the government of Bethlen (the Party of Unity) a strong majority in parliament.

Under the restricted suffrage, only 28.4 percent of the population votes—primarily estate owners, industrialists, and the middle class. In rural areas, the vote is made public; only the capital and the 10 largest cities are granted secret balloting. Bethlen's Party of Unity gains 143 seats out of a total of 245.

Prime Minister Bethlen proceeds with a conservative policy designed to maintain the status quo. He governs for the remainder of the decade not only through the Government party but through control of other institutions such as the civil and military bureaucracies, the clergy, banks, the professions, and landowners. During this era, the traditional elites (estate owners, industrialists, and nationalists) dominate, sympathize, and collaborate with Bethlen; their policies are conservative, paternal, and indifferent to the problems of rural areas and the working class.

September 18 The League of Nations accepts the application of Hungary for membership. Hungary officially becomes a member on January 31, 1923.

October 28 Czechoslovakia and Hungary agree on a common boundary.

1923

May 4 Bethlen presents a plan to the League of Nations for the economic reconstruction of Hungary. He requests foreign loans to stabilize the currency and the budget; demands national assets sequestrated during the war and

Béla Kun's regime be returned; and reparations from the First World War be diminished, if not revoked.

December 20 The League of Nations adopts a plan for economic reconstruction of Hungary. The great powers grant a loan of 250,000,000 gold crowns ($50 million in 1923 U.S. dollars). An exact figure for reparations is finally negotiated, in which Hungary is obliged to pay 200,000,000 gold crowns ($40 million U.S.) over the next 20 years. National assets are returned.

With the credits, returned confiscated assets, and loans from the League of Nations, inflation comes to an end; the budget deficit disappears, and the reparations are deemed manageable. The new currency, the pengo, is introduced in 1927 and proves stable. From 1927, the Hungarian National Bank becomes the center of the Hungarian credit system.

The right-wing of the Government party, led by Gyula Gömbös, opposes the foreign credits and fights for anti-Semitic legislation (*see* May 5, 1919). However, Bethlen needs both foreign capital and the prosperous Jewish industrial and middle classes to rebuild the national economy. Horthy sides with Bethlen, his prime minister, causing Gömbös and his followers to defect from the Government party and form the racist Party of Hungarian Independence.

1926

November 11 The Upper House of the Hungarian parliament is reconstituted. The Upper House represents the landed aristocracy, whose House of Magnates had been abolished in 1919 or 1920. Bethlen argues for its reestablishment on the premise that the legislature needs a "safety brake," *i.e.,* to protect traditional ruling elites (estate owners, industrialists, and nationalists), and that only an upper house can play this role. With this legislation, Bethlen completes the last stages of consolidation and now concentrates on social reform and foreign policy.

1927

1927–31 Under Count Kunó Klebelsberg, the minister of education, a new health insurance program begins in 1927 for lower, middle, and working classes. The rural population is not insured. Those who are covered can draw benefits for a year instead of just 20 weeks. Sick pay is raised from 50 percent of wages and salaries to 60–70 percent, and accident insurance is also raised. In 1928 the government passes obligatory old age, disability, widow, and orphan insurances.

In education, Hungary establishes universities in the cities of Szeged and Pecs, and Klebelsberg enlarges the medical facilities and natural science institutes at Szeged and Debrecen. However, the most important of his reforms is the construction of approximately 3,500 new elementary school classrooms and 1,500 new homes for elementary school teachers in the rural areas of Hungary. This measure reinforces the fears of nationalistic "reformers" who see these schools as cornerstones for the state-sponsored ideology of "Hungarian cultural superiority" over all other peoples of Europe.

April 5 A treaty of friendship is negotiated with Italy. This treaty initiates a period of close relations between the two governments and ends Hungary's diplomatic isolation since the end of the World War I. Valid for 10 years, it declares "permanent and eternal peace" between the two countries and provides that future disagreements between the two signatories that cannot be settled diplomatically be submitted to arbitration. In an additional secret agreement, Italian fascist leader Benito Mussolini and Bethlen agree to consult on a regular basis concerning common interests. Both men consider the territorial settlements in Central Europe temporary and are hostile toward Yugoslavia, or the Kingdom of Serbs, Croats, and Slovenes.

1928

January At the border crossing of St. Gotthard between Hungary and Austria, Austrian customs officials discover five freight cars loaded with machine-gun parts shipped from Italy and destined for Hungary. The Little Entente powers of Czechoslovakia, Yugoslavia, and Romania protest to the League of Nations because of Hungary's known irredentist ambitions toward each member. These ambitions advocate the recovery of lands that the Hungarians lost under the terms of the Treaty of Trianon and that the Hungarians consider to be culturally and historically related to Hungary but now subject to foreign rule (*see* June 4, 1920).

April 2–5 Bethlen and Mussolini meet for the second time and agree to support the Heimwehr (the Austrian fascist movement encouraged by Italy) and the Croatian separatists who wish to secede from the Kingdom of Serbs, Croats, and Slovenes. Bethlen agrees to help Mussolini organize a pact between Italy, Greece, and Bulgaria in order to encircle Yugoslavia. Despite the meeting, little comes of these plans due to unwillingness of Greece and Bulgaria.

1929

Academics Gyula Szekfű and Bálint Hóman publish their seven-volume *Hungarian History* considered to be the most comprehensive and analytical survey of the history of Hungary from the earliest times through the end of the First World War.

Early July Relations between Czechoslovakia and Hungary become strained after Hungarian authorities arrest a Czechoslovak railway worker on charges of espionage. In reprisal, the Czechoslovaks close the Budapest-Kosice railway, which reopens on July 24, although the Hungarians continue to detain the alleged spy.

1930

October 13 A leading member of the Smallholders' party, Gaston Gáal—disgusted with the government's economic policy and agrarian reforms—forms a new party, the Independent Party of Smallholders which represents the interests of small farmers.

During the 1920s, agricultural production does not reach its pre-war levels and remains stagnant through the 1930s. During this time, its contribution to the national product declines from 50 percent to 32 percent and it no longer produces the large export surpluses to cover the import demands of industrialization. In addition, agriculture is unable to provide a steadily growing market for industrial products.

1931

May 1–July 13 The National Bank pays out 200 million pengos ($40 million 1931 U.S. dollars) in gold and foreign currency. The National Bank of Hungary is saved from bankruptcy only by an emergency loan from the Bank of International Settlements, an institution established in 1930 in Switzerland to aid in the transfer of international funds and to help central banks cooperate.

The recovery of the banking system is slow, and its assets never reach the pre-depression level until 1938. Losses are greatest in agriculture. After the crash, very little foreign capital is invested in the country.

Overall, Hungary's economic performance in the interwar period is modest. Its annual growth rate is 1.1 percent, compared to 3 percent in the prewar years. Population increases from 7.9 million in 1920 to 9.3 million in 1940, with a per capita yearly average close to .7 percent. Per capita national income is $120 (in 1938 U.S. dollars) in 1937–38.

June 14 Hungarian banks fail as a result of the collapse of the Viennese bank, Credit-Anstalt, which recalls its short-term credits and loans from Hungary. The entire banking system of Hungary collapses, and its foreign currency and bullion (uncoined gold or silver) reserves are depleted, causing a depression.

August 19 With the onset of the worldwide depression, Bethlen's supposed infallibility as government leader disappears. Due to pressure from resurgent agrarian interests and the reemergence of Gömbös (who dissolved his own party and returned to the Party of Unity first as undersecretary and then as minister of defense), Admiral Horthy wants to introduce summary justice (trials, conducted without pleadings and juries, used to speed up the process) and to control the growing unrest of the workers caused by the depression. Prime Minister Bethlen refuses to introduce such restrictive measures and resigns.

August 24 Count Gyula Károlyi, a close friend of Horthy, forms a government as prime minister (*see* May 5, 1919).

After Bethlen resigns, the Government party splinters into three factions. One faction, under Bethlen's leadership, represents the interests of the leading capitalists and the large modernized estates. Another faction speaks for the discontented agrarian population, while the final third follows the conservative fascist Gömbös.

As the depression sets in, national discontent increases. Public officials are disgruntled at the reduction of salaries and the elimination of unemployment compensation. Waves of strikes sweep over Hungary, even reaching the villages in 1931–32. In the countryside, mass arrests follow.

December The National Socialist Hungarian Workers' party is founded by Zoltán Böszörményi, a journalist. Founded on the principles of rabid anti-Semitism and extreme nationalism, this party's platform urges nationalization of the large estates of more than 250 hectares (1 hectare=2.471 acres), the exclusion of all "non-Christian Hungarian elements" from important governmental posts, and the restoration of Hungary's pre-1914 borders.

1932

Count Sándor Festetics founds the fascist Hungarian National Socialist party. Festetics is a member of the landed gentry looking to gain support of the rural and urban middle classes. The Hungarian National Socialist party

will later fuse with Ferenc Szálasi's party, the Party of the National Will, in August 1938 to form the Arrow Cross party, a radical fascist organization (*see* August 1938).

June In the wake of continued social unrest, four Communist leaders are arrested.

July 28 Imre Sallai and Sándor Furst, two Communist leaders arrested in June, are tried and executed on charges of social unrest.

September 21 Prime Minister Gyula Károlyi resigns. Bethlen, still active in the politics of his party, had become increasingly frustrated at Károlyi's government due to its foreign policy. Dissatisfied with Károlyi's management of the Government party, which has been fragmenting, Bethlen asked Károlyi to resign. After consultation with Horthy, Bethlen negotiates with and asks Gömbös to become the next prime minister.

October 1 Gyula Gömbös forms a government. Gömbös's appointment as prime minister rests upon the condition that he maintain the existing governmental system and refrain from propagating racist ideas. In contrast to Bethlen's regime, Gömbös' policies are totalitarian and attempt to gain the support of disgruntled parts of the population behind his government.

Gömbös is an old friend of Admiral Horthy's from the counterrevolutionary Szeged government. He is anti-Government party, hostile to the privileges of the upper aristocracy, and openly anti-Semitic. Yet, his aversion to democratic liberal ideas, hostility toward workers, hatred of leftwing radicalism, and extreme nationalism make him acceptable to the aristocratic ruling elite. Gömbös is also popular among the military officer corps and the bureaucracy.

Gömbös begins his tenure in office with the "National Work Plan." This plan proposes land and tax reforms, generous loans and concessionary arrangements for repaying agricultural debts, stepping up of agricultural exports, creation of new jobs, the holding of secret elections, and the introduction of social legislation. His real aim, however, is to establish a fascist-style dictatorship in Hungary. Shortly after becoming prime minister, Gömbös takes over the presidency of the Party of Unity from Bethlen. He renames it the Party of National Unity and establishes within its ranks a paramilitary organization called "vanguard fighters," comprising 60,000 men, to support his policies for creating a totalitarian fascist state. He even attempts to incorporate workers into the party by creating a labor section. Newspapers funded by the government and pro-Gömbös propaganda ensure him of some support. In addition, Gömbös has plans to control a new powerful economic ministry but these plans are thwarted because economic and business leaders realize these measures will increase his power and allow his interference in economic affairs.

During his term, Gömbös develops a foreign policy strategy centered on German, Italian, and Hungarian cooperation in the framework of an "axis of fascist states."

1934

January–February Germany and Hungary sign economic agreements in which the Germans lay the foundation for their future economic agreements in southeastern Europe (*see* September 1934). The German government undertakes to promote Hungarian exports by barter transactions and settlement of accounts through *clearing,* which allows Germany to buy from countries that do not stipulate payment in foreign exchange but will accept German goods instead.

March 16 Hungary, Italy, and Austria sign the Rome Protocols that provide for cooperation on matters of common policy between these three countries. Special emphasis is placed on economic cooperation. Italy promises to find markets for Austrian goods and Hungarian agricultural produce, and to allow the Hungarians and Austrians to use the port of Trieste for export trade.

September The Germans develop the Neuer Plan to overcome armament and foreign trade difficulties. The fundamental principle behind the Neuer Plan is *clearing* (*see* January–February 1934). Being debtors, the Hungarians do not have foreign currency to spend on imports; thus, Germany's offer of bilateral trade and barter gets around this obstacle.

By the Second World War, the Nazis' economic policies bring all the countries of East Central and Southeastern Europe under German influence. The Germans successfully make these countries into suppliers of food and raw materials for the German economy.

October 9 King Alexander I of Yugoslavia and French Foreign Minister Jean-Louis Barthou are assassinated at Marseilles by a Macedonian separatist (*see* Yugoslavia). The League of Nations implicates a number of Hungarian senior military officers in the assassinations and they are forced to resign from the military. Gömbös replaces them with new officers who are radically right and pro-German. Horthy grows increasingly more disenchanted with Prime Minister Gömbös due to Gömbös' politicization of the army, and his interest in rural social problems and their alleviation through land reform.

In addition, new polarization occurs in the Government party. On one side stands the fascist and mass-supported axis of Right-Radicalism; on the other stands the emerging coalition of the "old school" civil libertarian conservatives and liberals, Socialists, Jews, and others with vested interests in preserving or restoring traditional rule and in maintaining ties with Western democracies.

1935

March 1 Ferenc Szálasi, a former army staff officer, establishes the Party of the National Will. His creed is one of absolute anticapitalism, antisocialism, anti-Semitism, Magyar racism, and populist authoritarianism or totalitarianism of the masses. Szalasi makes contact with German fascist circles. He later joins the many new fascist parties organized along foreign models into one party, the party of National Will.

March 5 As the economy improves, Bethlen and his followers wish to reassert their control over the government and replace Gömbös, who is promoting the creation of a one-party state and dictatorship.

To preempt his opponents, Gömbös dissolves parliament and calls for new elections on April 11. He also leads a purge of Bethlen supporters from the Government party.

April 11 With a slate of pro-Gömbös Government candidates and with the rigging, intimidation, and influencing of voters, the Government party wins 43.6 percent of the vote and 170 seats. This majority is composed mostly of ex-military officers, the gentry, civil servants, and middle-ranking landowners.

1936

October 6 Prime Minister Gömbös dies from a prolonged kidney disease. In the next eight years, Admiral Horthy appoints seven prime ministers.

The growing power of the right and the popularity of Germany prevent the restoration of a moderate right government as led by Bethlen in the 1920s. Germany has facilitated Hungary's recovery economically and many on the right believe Germany is Hungary's best hope to revise the Treaty of Trianon (*see* June 4, 1920).

October 12 Kálmán Darányi, a conservative who is acceptable to most parties, forms a government as prime minister. Facing increasing pressure from the far right groups, Darányi's government practices concessionary politics. It attempts to quiet some of the more radical and vocal opponents, such as Szálasi, by restricting their activity while granting political, economic and cultural concessions to other groups.

1937

April Darányi's government arrests Szálasi on charges of "agitation against the political and social order and against religious toleration." He is tried and sentenced to three years imprisonment, making him a popular martyr since many Hungarians like his ideas. He is quickly released.

July 1 Hungary struggles to solve the problem of finding a successor to regent Admiral Horthy, who is 69 years old. The regent's powers are extended and include the right to suggest a successor.

1938

March 5 Darányi announces a rearmament program that will make 1,000 million pengos available for the modernization and expansion of the armed forces in the next five years. However, support for Darányi is dwindling. He is not regarded by the traditional ruling elite as strong enough to maintain governmental unity in the event of an external threat from Germany, or to ward off the danger from the extreme right groups in and around Szálasi.

March 11–12 German troops occupy Austria, uniting it with Germany, in what is called the *Anschluss*. German Chancellor Adolf Hitler shows no sign of awarding the Burgenland to Hungary, despite Hungarian hopes (*see* December 14, 1921).

May 13 Kálmán Darányi's government falls after regent Admiral Horthy and other conservatives feel it has moved too much to the right politically.

May 14 Béla Imrédy, president of the National Bank, is appointed prime minister by Admiral Horthy and forms a new government.

August The two principal extreme rightist parties, the Hungarian National Socialist party and the Party of the National Will, merge to form the Arrow Cross party. The Arrow Cross party preaches a combination of anti-Semitism and land reform. It has some success among students, unemployed workers, and some rural workers.

August 23 The Little Entente, an alliance of Czechoslovakia, Romania, and Yugoslavia to maintain the status quo in Central Europe, recognizes Hungary's right to rearm.

September 20 Adolf Hitler summons Imrédy and Kálmán Kánya, the Hungarian foreign minister, to Berchtesgaden where he informs them he has no claims on Slovakia or Ruthenia, provided the Hungarian government takes an active part in his plans for the destruction of Czechoslovakia.

September 29 The Munich Conference and Agreement (*see* Czechoslovakia). Hungarian claims to Slovakia are to be settled by negotiation between Hungary and Czechoslovakia, and delegates of the two countries meet October 9.

Prime Minister Imrédy, appointed by Horthy because of his pro-Western views and outright Anglophilism, unsuccessfully tries to win Britain's support for returning the Magyar-populated districts of Slovakia to Hungary.

October 9 Hungarian and Czechoslovak delegates meet to discuss the contested territory. An agreement proves to be impossible and clashes break out along the Hungarian-Slovak frontier.

November 2 German foreign minister, Joachim von Ribbentrop, and his Italian counterpart, Count Galeazzo Ciano, award to Hungary southern Slovakia and southern Ruthenia (Carpathian Ukraine) in the First Vienna Award. This encompasses 12,009 square kilometers (5000 square miles) with a population of 1,040,000, including 592,000 Magyars, 290,000 Slovaks, 37,000 Ruthenes, and 14,000 Germans. The Hungarians, however, are not successful in their demand to absorb all of Ruthenia.

November 23–28 Imrédy's government is forced to resign in the face of public attacks on the government's failure to secure all of Ruthenia. Unable to find a replacement for Imrédy, Horthy reappoints Imrédy as prime minister on November 28. In an attempt to appease the Nazis, ministerial posts are assigned to pro-German politicians acceptable to the German government. As a result, the government shifts further right politically. Count István Csáky, who is pro-German, is appointed foreign minister. Csáky believes Hungary can secure further revisionist successes and retain its independence only if it follows Berlin's advice. Throughout 1938, Hungary increasingly becomes more dependent on Germany.

1939

January 27 A universal conscription law is passed. Men and women between the ages of 14 and 70 are required to join the para-military Labor Service for the sake of national defense.

February 13 Prime Minister Imrédy has lost Admiral Horthy's confidence due to his government's failure to secure all of Ruthenia from the November 2, 1938 First Vienna Award. Even attempts at a new land reform and discriminatory anti-Jewish legislation modelled on the German example do not save Imrédy. On the dubious pretense that Imrédy's great grandmother was Jewish, he is dismissed.

February 16 Count Pál Teleki forms a government. Teleki, a former prime minister, recognizes that if Hungary is to realize its revisionist aims, Hungary must support Germany (*see* July 19, 1920). Yet, Teleki quietly harbors hope that the western democracies will gain the upper hand over the Axis powers of Germany, Italy, and Japan.

February 24 Hungary joins the Anti-Comintern Pact with Germany, Japan, and Italy. The signatories agree to fight against world communism, and secretly name the Soviet Union as their main opponent.

March 15 Germany invades rump Czechoslovakia, the territory of the country remaining after it loses land to Germany, Hungary, and Poland in the autumn of 1938. On March 14, Slovakia and Ruthenia declared their independence from Czechoslovakia. On March 16, the Czech provinces of Bohemia and Moravia become German protectorates (*see* Czechoslovakia).

Hungary occupies Ruthenia and annexes it after heavy fighting with its inhabitants who were able to enjoy only one day of independence. By possessing all of Ruthenia, Hungary now has its desired common border with Poland, its long-time ally.

Teleki, examining the possibility of German aggression toward Poland, informs Hitler that Hungary will not be part of any aggression toward Poland despite Hungary's many basic mutual interests with Germany. Teleki tries to keep Hungary nonaligned and adopts a policy of "armed neutrality."

April 11 Hungary leaves the League of Nations, signalling the government's willingness to subordinate Hungarian interests to Germany's leadership.

May 3 The parliament introduces anti-Jewish legislation that provides for rigorous limitation of Jews in the professions and business, expulsion of Jews from government service, and eventual Jewish emigration within five years.

August 8 The Hungarian foreign minister, István Csaky, the chief spokesman of the radical right clamoring for an equivocally pro-German foreign policy, meets with Hitler and German foreign minister Joachim von Ribbentrop at

Berchtesgaden and gives assurances to Germany of Hungary's unhesitating alignment to Germany. This assurance directly violates Teleki's policy of "armed neutrality", but he is unable to do anything.

September 1 Germany invades Poland, starting the Second World War. Teleki tries to have Hungary remain neutral by refusing passage of Slovak and German troops through Hungary to Poland, sheltering Polish refugees, and helping Polish soldiers move to France.

September 17 Soviet troops invade Poland from the east (*see* Poland).

September 29 The German and Soviet governments divide Poland. Russia now occupies the Ukrainian-inhabited portions of Poland. Instead of a border with Poland, Hungary now has one with the Soviet Union. The new border sends the Hungarian ruling circles, who fear communism, into a frenzy .

1940

June 26 The Soviets issue an ultimatum to Romania to surrender the territories of Bessarabia and northern Bukovina and the Bulgarians follow with a demand for southern Dobrudja, triggering Hungarian revisionist aspirations for taking Transylvania. Although Hitler favors the Romanians with regard to Transylvania, he is forced to arbitrate a settlement between the two countries (*see* Romania).

August 30 The Germans issue the Second Vienna Award by which Hungary regains 43,492 square kilometers of northern and eastern Transylvania, two-fifths of its Treaty of Trianon (1920) loss to Romania, and a population of 2.5 million, of whom over one million are Romanian. A half million Magyars are still left in Romania. Prime Minister Teleki is displeased these gains came from German arbitration and not through direct Hungarian military or diplomatic efforts.

September 18 Indebted to the Germans for the vast territorial acquisitions, Teleki releases from jail their ardent fascist supporter, Ferenc Szálasi, who had been sentenced to a three-year prison term in August 1938.

October 8 Under pressure from Germany, Prime Minister Teleki introduces further anti-Semitic legislation and makes concessions to Hungary's German minority.

November 20 Hungary joins the Tripartite Pact, a mutual assistance and cooperation agreement, which firmly allies Hungary with Germany, Italy, and Japan against Britain and France. Teleki is verbally attacked by his own supporters and his center-left supporters for signing the pact. They perceive his signature as an excessive compromise and a dangerous departure from Hungary's formal neutrality.

December 12 Teleki, seeking to prove Hungary is still nominally independent in foreign affairs, signs a Treaty of Eternal Friendship and Nonaggression with Yugoslavia.

1941

March 25–27 A crisis erupts in Yugoslavia (*see* Yugoslavia). On March 25, the pro-German Yugoslav cabinet signs the Tripartite Pact. This act provokes public outrage and a coup d'état ousts the government although the new government does not revoke the pact. Feeling betrayed and demanding retribution, Hitler demands Hungary's complicity in the partition of Yugoslavia due to its common border with Yugoslavia.

April 2–3 Prime Minister Teleki, unable to convince Great Britain that Hungary will honor its recent treaty with Yugoslavia, despairs at the failure of his policy of "armed neutrality" and commits suicide.

April 4 Admiral Horthy chooses career diplomat László Bárdossy as prime minister to head the government. Bárdossy, like his predecessor, bids for greater independence from Germany but is drawn into closer accommodation with Germany due to the Hungarians' dreams of regaining from the Kingdom of Yugoslavia, areas that had formerly belonged to Hungary.

April 6 Germany attacks Yugoslavia. The Hungarian civil military authorities enthusiastically welcome this action and join the invasion despite Hungary's treaty of friendship with Yugoslavia from December 12, 1940, hoping for territory.

April 11–14 Hungary occupies 11,475 square kilometers of Yugoslavia (approximately half of its 1920 Treaty of Trianon losses to Yugoslavia) with a population of approximately one million. Of the one million, one-third are Magyars and the remaining a mixture of Jews, Serbs, Romanians, and Germans. Hungary—due to its collaboration with Germany—has doubled its territory in three years.

New anti-Semitic laws outlaw marriage between Jews and gentiles, expropriate Jewish landholdings, and exclude Jews from the army.

June 22 Germany attacks the Soviet Union.

June 27 Now closely allied with Germany, Bárdossy, in agreement with the Hungarian general army staff, urges his cabinet to participate in Germany's war against the Soviets. Hungary declares war on the USSR.

November 29 Great Britain, an ally of the Soviet Union, sends an ultimatum to Hungary to withdraw from the Russian campaign. Hungary ignores the edict.

December 6 Hungary refuses to withdraw from the Russian campaign and Great Britain declares war on Hungary. Shortly thereafter, Báradossy proclaims that Hungary is at war with Great Britain.

December 12 Hungary declares war on the United States following the lead of its allies. However, the United States waits until June 5, 1942 to declare war on Hungary.

1942

January 21–23 The Hungarian army massacres over 2,000 Serbs and 1,000 Jews in Novi Sad, in the Hungarian occupied Yugoslav region of Vojodina.

March 6 Admiral Horthy, upset that Bárdossy's policies have isolated Hungary from the Western allies, dismisses him. Horthy appoints Miklós Kállay, an old-style gentry politician and supporter of Bethlen, as prime minister.

March 9 Kállay curbs the excessively Germanophile and radicalized Hungarian military by leaking news of its January massacre of over two thousand Vojvodinian Serbs and a thousand Jews.

May Kállay rejects German demands for more Hungarian troops on the Russian Front. In a variant on the Little Entente (the interwar alliance system of Romania, Czechoslovakia, and the Kingdom of Yugoslavia), Croatia, Romania, and Slovakia proclaim their anti-Magyar friendship; Kállay declares he needs Hungarian troops to fend off his neighbors.

June The Second Hungarian Army, composed of approximately 200,000 combat troops, 50,000 occupation troops, and a labor service corps of 40,000, supports the northern wing of the German advance toward Stalingrad.

October The Germans demand Hungarian Jews wear the Yellow Star of David and their deportation be organized; Prime Minister Kállay refuses to comply, realizing that Hungarian Jews are productive citizens and sensing that Germany is losing the war. Needing continued Hungarian support for the war effort, the Germans do not press the issue.

1943

January 12 The Second Hungarian Army is almost annihilated at Voronezh in the Soviet Union, about 290 miles southeast of Moscow, with 40,000 men killed and 70,000 taken prisoner, causing immense demoralization of Hungarian soldiers. Prior to this battle, 7,000 men have already frozen to death in the Russian winter.

April Kállay withdraws the remnants of the Second Army, leaving only occupation troops on the eastern front. Believing Hungarian troops have been senselessly sacrificed and the Axis powers are losing the war, Kállay increases contacts with the Allies.

Hitler accuses Kállay of defeatism and demands Admiral Horthy replace him, but Horthy stands by his prime minister. To bring about the government's downfall, the Germans try to mobilize Imrédy's National Socialist Party Union within the parliament. Imrédy's party is composed of military officers, ex-gentry bureaucrats, and members of the middle class who have profited from the economic elimination of the Jews and still fear communism.

May 4 Horthy suspends the parliament indefinitely to make the Nationalist Socialist Party Union attacks impossible. Prime Minister Kállay gains support of centrist and leftist parties with this move, but the Communists are still unimpressed.

July 25 Mussolini's fascist government falls in Italy.

September After secret negotiations with the British, Kállay, with Horthy's approval, agrees to order the withdrawal of all Hungarian forces from the Eastern Front. In exchange for British territorial guarantees of Hungary's Trianon (1920) borders, he concedes to reduce the supply of armaments to Germany, remove pro-German officers from the General Staff, and introduce social reforms. However, Kállay and Horthy back away from these agreements after meeting opposition from the Arrow Cross and National Socialist Party Union.

1944

March 17 Admiral Horthy is summoned to Germany where, under pressure from Hitler, he agrees to dismiss Kállay and appoint a right-wing puppet government led by Hungary's long-serving ambassador to Berlin, Lt. Gen. Döme Sztójay. Members of the National Socialist Party Union occupy key posts in the government. To ensure Hungary's continuing cooperation, Hitler orders the German occupation of the country.

March 19–August 24 When Miklos Kallay's government falls, Döme Sztójay, former ambassador to Berlin, forms a new government as prime minister. With the exception of the extreme right-wing parties, all political parties, including the Smallholders and Social Democrats, are banned. All leading politicians, journalists, academics, and even some of Horthy's close associates are arrested and sent to German concentration camps. At the "request" of Sztójay's government, eight German divisions move into Hungary. The German SS and the Gestapo follow.

Adolf Eichmann, German Nazi leader and specialist in Jewish evacuation and extermination programs, is dispatched to Budapest with the German army. Under his supervision and with the help of the Arrow Cross and the assistance of the Hungarian police, over 450,000 Hungarian Jews are deported to German extermination camps in Poland. Humanitarian concern about the fate of the Hungarian Jews reaches Admiral Horthy from a number of sources, including the Catholic and Protestant churches.

May The Hungarian Front, an organization named as illegal under the new laws in March, organizes a resistance movement against the Germans and their collaborators. Its members comprise the Peace party (in reality, the Communist party), the Social Democrats, the Smallholders, and the Brotherhood of the Legitimists.

August 29 Admiral Horthy dismisses Sztójay and appoints Col. Gen. Géza Lakatos as prime minister. The new government, under Prime Minister Lakatos, orders a halt to Jewish deportations. Most of the 200,000 Jews herded together in the Budapest ghetto are saved. The Germans protest, but they need Hungarian troops on the Eastern Front and are unable to force a change.

September 12 The Hungarian Communist party is refounded.

September 23 The Soviet Red Army moves into Hungarian territory.

October 10 The Communists sign an agreement with the Social Democrats for the creation of a united front against the government and a merger of the two organizations into a single party after the war.

October 11 Horthy, who after several months is unsuccessful in negotiating a cease-fire with the Western powers, sends a delegation to Moscow, where a provisional cease-fire is signed. This preliminary armistice agreement obligates Hungary to give up territories annexed from Czechoslovakia, Romania, and Yugoslavia, and to declare war on Germany.

October 15 After securing the armistice with the Soviet Union, Horthy proclaims an end to the fighting and calls for action to be taken against the German occupying forces. However, many officers of the Hungarian army and members of the Arrow Cross will not ally with the Soviets and, instead, they support the Germans. A division of the German army storms the Royal Palace in Budapest, kidnaps Horthy's son, and forces the regent to revoke the armistice and to appoint Arrow Cross leader Ferenc Szálasi, as prime minister.

October 16 Ferenc Szálasi becomes prime minister. Szálasi and the Arrow Cross conduct a reign of terror, with indiscriminate killings, on their former political opponents and the Jews who have not yet been deported. It is estimated that more than 85,000 Jews alone will perish between now and the end of the war in April 1945. In addition, the new regime promises to place 1.5 million soldiers at Hitler's disposal.

All protection for the Budapest Jews are removed. In the waning days of the war, the Arrow Cross subjects the remaining Jews to murder and torture. Only the activities of Swedish diplomat Raoul Wallenberg, who passes out thousands of Swedish passports to Jews, prevents even more deaths. At the end of the war, 70 percent of Hungary's Jewish population, some 450,000, are dead.

December 21 The Provisional National Assembly is created in Debrecen under the auspices of the Red Army. Also formed is the Provisional National Government led by Béla Dálnoki Miklós, a colonel in the Hungarian Army who had gone over to the Russians in October. Under Soviet supervision, elections have been held several weeks earlier in the eastern part of the country where the Communist party wins 72 of 230 contested seats, the Independent Party of Smallholders wins 57 seats, the Social Democratic party 35, and the National Peasants' party 12.

The provisional government is composed of three generals, three Communists who hold the ministries of agriculture, industry, and transport, two Social Democrats who take the justice and economic ministries, two Smallholders who hold the ministries of foreign affairs and finance, and a National Peasant who holds the ministry of interior. National Peasant party member, Ferenc Erdei, is sympathetic to the Communists and establishes the "Political Police Section," a secret police force (originally the AVO, later AVH) in the ministry of interior.

December 28 Under the scrutiny of the Red Army, the Provisional National Assembly renounces all treaties with Germany and declares war.

1945

January 20 The Allies and Hungary sign an armistice agreement in Moscow that fixes Hungary's borders at their December 31, 1937 position. In addition, Hungary must pay reparations to the Soviet Union in the sum of $200 million (1945 U.S. dollars) and $100 million compensation to Czechoslovakia and Yugoslavia.

February Veteran Communist and staunch Stalinist Mátyás Rákosi returns to Hungary from the Soviet Union, where he spent the war. Upon his return, Rákosi becomes General Secretary of the Communist party of Hungary. At this time, the Communist party claims only 30,000 members; by July, membership is 225,000, rising to almost 610,000 in January 1946, and peaking at 887,472 in June 1948. Membership in the party never totals more than 10 percent of the population.

February 13 Budapest falls to the advancing Red Army.

March 15 The Provisional Government decrees an expropriation and redistribution of the land promulgated under the dictation of Soviet Marshal Kliment Voroshilov, chairman of the Allied Control Commission for Hungary.

The principle of the land reform is to abolish the great estates and reallocate the land to the village poor. This reform has two major goals. One is the liquidation of the old landowner class, and the other is to win support of the landless peasantry and establish control over the agrarian population.

Land, owned by "traitors to the fatherland and Horthy fascists" and those who own estates of more than 575 hectares (1 hectare=2.471 acres), is expropriated within six weeks. Land owned by the church, banks, and other institutions is also confiscated. In all, 3.2 million hectares of Hungary's 8.3 million hectares of cultivable land (38.8 percent) is expropriated. The law provides for compensation, but in reality it is only paid in exceptional cases.

Two-thirds of rural households eventually possess plots between .575 hectares and 2.8 hectares. A fifth of the households will own between 2.8 hectares and 5.6 hectares, while a tenth of the peasantry will own between 5.6 and 11.2 hectares. Some 1.348 million hectares become state property.

By the end of the redistribution, approximately 95 percent of the peasantry owns small plots whose yields are still insufficient to feed its families.

April 4 German troops evacuate the country, and Hungary is now placed under Soviet military occupation. The

Soviet-sponsored provisional government extends its authority throughout Hungary.

Approximately 630,000 Hungarians, including Jews, have been killed in the Second World War. Direct property damage is estimated at 22 billion pre-war pengos, which is about four or five times the national income for 1938 and about 40 percent of the nation's entire wealth.

In addition, all the bridges over the Danube and Tisza rivers are destroyed, as is 35 percent of Hungary's railway installations, over 80 percent of its rolling stock, and the entire Danube military fleet. A quarter of all dwellings suffer from shelling and bomb damage. Fifty percent of the country's industrial installations and plants have been destroyed. Industrial production in May 1945 is only 30 percent of prewar levels.

Agricultural losses amount to half of the livestock and a third of the agricultural machinery. The harvest for 1945 is only 30 percent of the pre-war average.

October 7   Marshal Voroshilov, the Soviet chairman of the Allied Control Commission, supports the Hungarian Communists' wish to hold municipal elections in Budapest. The Smallholders' party obtains an absolute majority of the votes, shocking the Communists, who hoped for working class support.

November 4   General parliamentary elections are held in which the Communists poll 17 percent of the vote, whereas the Smallholders win 57 percent. Seats in parliament are divided as follows: Smallholders, 245; Communists, 70; Socialists, 69; Peasant party, 21; and the Civic Democratic party, 2 indicating weak Communist party support.

1946

January 9   Communists initiate the creation of a Supreme Economic Council in order to implement their economic views. This council is empowered to grant loans, distribute raw materials, and intervene in the decision-making process of large enterprises.

February 1   The first legislative act of the parliament declares Hungary a republic. The new constitution institutes the offices of the president and prime minister. Zoltán Tildy, the leader of the Smallholders' party, becomes the first president. He appoints Ferenc Nagy, another leading Smallholder, prime minister. The Communists pressure the governing party and obtain three ministerial posts, the most important of these being the minister of the interior. Imre Nagy becomes minister of the interior and is eventually replaced by Lázló Rajk.

Through the use of 50,000 secret police, controlled by the minister of the interior, the Communists are able to intimidate and eliminate actual or potential opponents. In addition, the Communists obtain an absolute majority in agencies such as radio, movies, and newspapers. The Soviet occupation forces, and then the Communists, allocate all newsprint, while the publication of newspapers is authorized through a Communist-controlled licensing system.

February 27   Despite earlier Slovak attempts to remove all Hungarians from Slovakia after the war, Czechoslovakia and Hungary now agree to a mutual exchange of populations that affects only about 68,000 out of a total Hungarian population of approximately 500,000 in Czechoslovakia.

March 5   Fearful of losing their power, the Communists—together with the Socialists, the Peasant party, and the Trade Union Council—establish the Left-Wing Bloc in the parliament which often browbeats the Smallholders in the name of the Hungarian people. Under pressure, the Smallholders' party is forced to expel 21 of its deputies who are accused of being "reactionaries" by the Communists. Politicians opposing the leftist demands are frequently derided as "fascists" and "enemies of the people."

June   In the continuing struggle for political control in Hungary the Smallholders' party, under the direction of Béla Kovács, hands the Communist party a list of demands. The most important among them are: proportional Smallholder representation in administration and the police; municipal elections in fall 1946; abolition of the People's Courts which are in the hands of the Communists dispensing summary judgments against so-called "enemies of the people" and collaborationists; and reestablishment of trial by jury.

August 1   Runaway inflation and continual devaluation, which have made the pengo worthless, forces the government to replace it with a new currency, the forint, in an attempt to stabilize the economy and help control inflation.

November 22   Using the power of the Supreme Economic Council, the Communists place Rimamurany Ironworks (the country's largest ironworks), Ganz and Company, and the Manfred Weiss Steel and Metalworks, under state ownership.

1947

February 10 The Hungarian Peace Treaty is signed at Paris. It requires Hungary to accept the frontiers of the Treaty of Trianon from 1920, (*i.e.,* the return of Transylvania to Romania), cessation of 40 square kilometers more in favor of Czechoslovakia near Bratislava, reparations of $300 million, and reduction of its armed forces.

The Smallholders feel betrayed by the Soviets' choice of supporting Romanian claims to Transylvania and stiffen their resistance to the Communists, especially their demand that their executive secretary Béla Kovács resign.

February 25 The Soviets arrest Kovács on charges of spying for Western intelligence services.

May 28 The Supreme Economic Council places all major banks under state control.

May 31 The Soviets announce that Béla Kovács has implicated prime minister Ference Nagy, who is on vacation in Switzerland, in a conspiracy against the state. Nagy resigns and in exchange the Soviets release his four-year-old son, whom they were holding hostage. Fearing arrest, Nagy does not return to Hungary and Lajos Dinnyés, a member of the left wing of the Smallholders' party, replaces him as prime minister.

August 1 The parliament launches a Three Year Plan, which calls for a planned economy and nationalization of industry, banking, and utilities.

August 31 A general election gives the Communists the largest number of seats in the parliament. Dinnyés continues as prime minister, presiding over a cabinet of 15 ministers, including five Communists. These elections, considerably less free than the prior elections, return only 22.3 percent of the votes to the Communists; 14.9 percent to the Social Democrats, 15.4 percent to the Smallholders, 8.3 percent to the National Peasants, 13.4 percent to the Independence party, and 16.4 percent to the Democratic Populists.

November 29 Dinnyés' government nationalizes the banks and 264 industrial and commercial enterprises.

1948

February 6 The parliament approves of legislation for the nationalization of all industrial firms employing more than 100 workers. This law nationalizes an additional 600 industrial firms. Now 85 percent of all employees work in state-controlled enterprises.

February 10 The Hungarians and Soviets sign a Treaty of Friendship, Cooperation, and Mutual Support. Each state pledges to support all efforts to maintain world peace and to resist any aggressive plans of Germany and its allies, meaning the United States, Great Britain, and France. This treaty also promotes close economic ties.

June 12–14 Forced to withdraw from the Socialist International in March, the international organization for Social Democratic parties, the Social Democrats purge and merge their party with the Hungarian Communist party. The merger creates the Hungarian Workers' party, in reality the Hungarian Communist party.

July 30 The president of the Republic of Hungary, Smallholder Zoltán Tildy, resigns in favor of Árpád Szakasits, the chairman of the Hungarian Workers' (Communist) party.

December 9 After completing another purge of their party, the Smallholders call for the resignation of Prime Minister Lajos Dinnyés. Dinnyés resigns and is replaced by István Dobi, another member of the Smallholders' party and a Communist sympathizer. Ten of the 15 ministers of his cabinet are Communists, including Mátyás Rákosi, who becomes deputy prime minister. János Kádár takes over the interior ministry, and László Rajk controls the foreign ministry.

December 27 The refusal of the Roman Catholic Church to give up control of its schools and to force the resignation of its Cardinal, József Mindszenty, leads to the Cardinal's arrest on charges of conspiracy to overthrow the government.

1949

January 25 Hungary joins the newly created Council for Mutual Economic Assistance (CMEA or Comecon). Directed by the Soviets, this organization coordinates the economies of its member states: the Soviet Union, Poland, Czechoslovakia, Hungary, Bulgaria, Romania, and Albania.

February 3–8 Cardinal József Mindszenty is tried and sentenced to life imprisonment on charges of anti-state activities.

April 16 Czechoslovakia and Hungary sign a treaty of friendship and mutual assistance.

May 15 General elections are held with open ballot voting. A single "Government list" is drafted by the Communists and gives them a complete victory with 95.6 percent of the vote.

June 16 The arrest of Communist foreign minister László Rajk on charges of conspiracy triggers violent purges within the Hungarian Workers'(Communist) party.

The general secretary of the party and deputy prime minister, Mátyás Rákosi, uses accusations of deviation from the pro-Soviet line to rid the party of any potential rivals. Rákosi leads the ascendancy to positions of power and authority of the ''Muscovites''—those Hungarian Communists who had spent the war years in the Soviet Union, and who include Ernő Gerő, Mihály Farkas, and József Révai.

By 1955, 2,000 Communists have been executed, 150,000 imprisoned, and 350,000 expelled from the party. The victims are predominantly wartime ''local'' resistance members, ''Westerners,'' veterans of the Spanish Civil War, former Social Democrats, and senior military personnel.

The secret police becomes increasingly important, thanks to the purges. The secret police is composed of 16 departments, keeps records on more than one million citizens, and relies on nearly 300,000 informers. It gradually becomes semi-autonomous and does not even answer to the Communist leaders.

August 20 The new assembly accepts a Soviet-style constitution and officially renames the Republic of Hungary as the Hungarian People's Republic.

September László Rajk is tried for conspiracy. He confesses to prolonged treasonable service for both fascists and capitalists, resulting in a death sentence.

October 15 Rajk is hanged for treason.

1950

January 2 The First Five Year Plan is introduced. It orders an increase in the output of heavy industry of more than 200 percent.

Late April–June The remaining ex-Socialists, among them President Árpád Szakasits, are dismissed from the government. Hungary is now fully under the control of the Communists.

1951

June 28 While more conciliatory than Cardinal Mindszenty, the new Catholic primate, Abp. József Grősz, continues the Catholic church's fight against the state's encroachment upon the church's rights. Grősz is tried and convicted of

The trial of Hungarian foreign minister László Rajk where he confesses to prolonged treasonable service for both fascists and capitalists, and is hanged. In 1956 he is posthumously cleared of these charges.

conspiring to overthrow the government. He is sentenced to 15 years in prison.

July 21 Having purged the Catholic church of its more vocal and resistive elements, the government pressures the remaining Roman Catholic priests and bishops to swear an oath of allegiance to the "people's republic" against the wishes of Rome.

1952

August 14 István Dobi resigns as prime minister and Deputy Prime Minister Mátyás Rákosi takes his place.

1953

March 5 The Soviet dictator Joseph Stalin dies. His successors in the Soviet Union opt for collective leadership, a "New Course," that targets the production of consumer goods versus heavy industrial output, and repudiation of the "cult of personality" which emphasizes unquestioned devotion to the leader. "The little Stalins" of the people's democracies, including Hungary's Rákosi, face challenges to their absolute authority by other party members.

June 27–28 Following the example of the "New Course" in the Soviet Union, the Central Committee, the ruling body of the Hungarian Workers' (Communist) party, meets in full session and decrees a new official party line that promotes better living standards, better consumption and wages, agricultural and light industrial investments, artisanal private enterprise, administrative decentralization, educational liberalization, socialist law and order, amnesty, and religious toleration.

July 4 Keeping with the tone of the Central Committee meeting, there is a shakeup in the upper echelons of the party. Rákosi is forced to resign as prime minister, and Imre Nagy is appointed prime minister by the moderate members of the party. The Stalinist Rákosi retains the general secretariat of the party and sets out to sabotage, in any way possible, Nagy's New Course which promotes disinvestment in heavy industry, investment in sectors of the economy producing consumer goods, relaxation of Hungary's collectivization drive, and a higher standard of living for workers.

1955

February 8 Georgi M. Malenkov, the last of the Soviet collective leadership that advocates the New Course and a

firm supporter of Nagy, is ousted, which has a profound effect on the new leadership in Hungary in the coming months. Malenkov is viewed as a reformer and his removal marks the beginning of the fall of Hungarian moderate Communists, like Nagy, in the coming weeks.

April 14 Without Malenkov's support, Imre Nagy is relieved of the prime ministry, his parliamentary seat, and of all party offices. He even resigns from his university lectureship and membership in the Academy of Sciences. As of November, he is considered persona non grata in Hungary.

April 18 András Hegedüs, the Communist deputy prime minister, replaces Nagy as prime minister.

May 11–14 The People's Democracies of Hungary, Poland, Czechoslovakia, Romania, Bulgaria, and Albania sign a multilateral military agreement on friendship, cooperation, and mutual support in Warsaw on May 14. Known as the Warsaw Pact Organization, Hungary is a founding member. As a result, Hungary accepts the continued presence of Soviet units as a force to preserve internal political order, and the Kremlin's right to intervene militarily.

September The Hungarian censor orders the confiscation of an edition of the weekly newspaper of the Writers' Federation, *Irodalmi Újság* (Literary Journal), because of an article criticizing of the government's cultural policy. The editorial board resigns and 59 well-known writers send a protest resolution to the Central Committee of the Hungarian Workers' (Communist) party.

December 14 Hungary joins the United Nations after the United States, due to warming relations, no longer blocks its application as it has done in the past.

1956

February 14–25 The Twentieth Party Congress of the Communist Party of the Soviet Union (CPSU) convenes. Nikita Khrushchev, general secretary of the CPSU, denounces the crimes of Stalin and approves of the possibility of different national paths toward socialism. In Hungary, Khrushchev's speech widens the split in the upper echelons of the party and encourages the liberal elements, reformers, and revisionists to unseat Rákosi, who is still the general secretary.

March As a result of Khrushchev's denunciation of Stalin, the Communist leadership allows the Petőfi Circle, a student discussion circle named after the poet of the 1848–49 revolution, to meet in Budapest.

March 29 László Rajk, the Communist foreign minister who was executed in October 1949, is posthumously cleared of treason and rightist deviationism by governmental and party decree.

June 30 After the Poznań riots (*see* Poland), Rákosi calls a meeting of the Central Committee and announces his decision to liquidate the "Nagy conspiracy," a coup d'état allegedly planned by 400 of Nagy's associates. He also announces the closing of three literary magazines that have been at the forefront of the anti-Rákosi struggle

July 17 The Soviets watch with increasing apprehension the rifts in the Hungarian Workers' (Communist) party. Two members of the Soviet Politburo—the executive committee of the Central Committee of the Soviet Communist Party—Anastas Mikoyan and Mikhail Suslov, go to Budapest and force Rákosi to resign in an attempt to quiet the situation.

July 18 Rákosi is replaced by Ernő Gerő as first secretary of the Hungarian Workers' (Communist) party. However, Gerő is too closely linked with Rákosi and Moscow and is a bitter opponent of Nagy's. It becomes obvious to the Hungarian population in the next three months that Gerő is not going to grant Hungary the much demanded political reforms. His reforms emphasize heavy industry, continued collectivization, battling domestic subversion, and condemning oppositional elements in the party.

October 6 László Rajk, posthumously cleared of treason charges that led to his execution in the purges of 1949, is given a funeral procession. Nagy leads the procession and embraces Rajk's widow, signaling an official end to the excesses of the Stalinist era in Hungary.

October 13 Imre Nagy is readmitted to the communist party.

October 22 Petőfi Clubs—offshoots of the Petőfi Circle consisting of revisionist intellectuals—issue a 10 point program that insists upon the reform of communism, the reappointment of Nagy as prime minister, factory autonomy, Rákosi's expulsion from the party, the trial of secret police chief Mihály Farkas, and equal economic and political links with the USSR.

University students' demands are less restrained. They want elections with multiple parties, evacuation of Soviet troops, and economic revisions. To show solidarity with the Poles, they call for street demonstrations to be held the next day.

October 23 Fearing violence, the government lifts the ban on demonstrations and Budapest students are able to demonstrate militantly at the statue of Gen. Józef Bem, a Pole who aided the Hungarians in the 1848–49 revolt against the Habsburgs. During the demonstrations, the students demand Nagy's reappointment to a position of power; the punishment of leaders who ruled during the Stalinist years; evacuation of Soviet troops; freedom of the press, speech, and religion; reappraisal of Soviet-Hungarian relationships; and party pluralism.

Within hours, the whole population of Budapest is demonstrating on the streets, and workers flood in from the suburbs to join the students. The police cannot contain the spontaneous outbursts of activity. Crowds destroy Stalin's statue, promote Nagy as prime minister, and hoist the national flag without its Communist symbols. The army remains neutral.

October 24 In the early morning hours, Hungarian Workers' (Communist) Party leader Gerő appoints Nagy as prime minister. Gerő retains the general secretary position. Gerő also appeals to the Soviet garrison to restore order.

Soviet armored vehicles appear on Budapest streets at 2 A.M. Since the Hungarian government has shown itself incapable of controlling the ferment in the streets, a Soviet delegation arrives, headed by Suslov and Mikoyan. The two Soviets dismiss Gerő, appoint János Kádár (a victim of Rákosi's purges) as general secretary, and then leave.

October 27 As the revolt spreads throughout the country, the Central Committee of the Hungarian Workers' (Communist) party promises to work for the withdrawal of Soviet troops as soon as the rioting ends. Prime Minister Nagy appoints members of the illegal anti-Communist Smallholders' party to his cabinet to make it more representative of the true political orientation of the country.

October 28 Hoping Nagy can quiet the rebellious forces, the Soviets halt their military intervention and Soviet troops begin to pull out. The Soviet press proclaims all is well in Hungary and that Nagy and General Secretary Kádár are now the legitimate leaders.

However, Nagy allows the events to sweep him along. He asserts that for Hungary to build socialism, it cannot exist as a pawn between East and West. He infers both NATO and the Warsaw Pact Organization should be dissolved.

October 29 Suslov and Mikoyan again return to Budapest and deliver the Soviet government's declaration that

A giant statue of Stalin being hauled by tractor from Stalin Square to the Hungarian National Theatre in the center of town.

reaffirms the Soviet position that the deployment of Soviet troops on October 24 was a mistake.

October 30 Soviet forces withdraw from Budapest. Prime Minister Nagy promises Hungarians free elections, a prompt ending of one-party rule, and "a system of government based on the democratic cooperation of coalition parties," *i.e.,* party pluralism. These declarations are unacceptable to the Soviets, who now plan intervention.

Nagy also releases Cardinal Mindszenty from prison. Mindszenty seeks asylum in the American embassy when

the revolution fails in early November, resulting in his confinement within the embassy after the suppression of the revolt.

November 2 Nagy denounces the Warsaw Pact, declares Hungarian neutrality, and requests the United Nations to take up the Hungarian situation. As of October 28, the United Nations had already voted to discuss the Hungarian problem.

November 4 Soviet artillery fire in Budapest signals the Soviet determination not to tolerate national commu-

A typical street scene in Budapest, October 1956.

nism in Hungary. Soviet forces reverse their withdrawal and move to smash the revolt. Nagy has failed to reign in the opposition like Władysław Gomułka (*see* Poland 1956) has done in Poland. He is ousted as prime minister and General Secretary János Kádár becomes prime minister.

The Yugoslav leader, Josip Broz (Tito), is sympathetic to Nagy's strong national Communist leanings and offers him refuge in the Yugoslav Embassy. Fearing retribution from the Soviets, Nagy accepts.

November 4–11   The "counter-revolution" is crushed by a massive deployment of Soviet troops. The official report on the uprising cites more than 3,000 deaths and 13,000 injured, with well over 4,000 buildings destroyed. Twenty thousand people are sent to prison and thousands are sent to Soviet forced labor camps. Two thousand are executed.

November 14   Resistance still survives in Budapest where the Greater Budapest Central Workers' Council is formed and a general strike is conducted. This council lasts for several weeks and acts as a second government. At the beginning of December, Prime Minister Kádár has the council's leaders arrested.

The Soviets seize Nagy as he leaves the refuge of the Yugoslav embassy in Budapest under a safe conduct pass. The Soviets force Nagy and his family to seek asylum in Romania where he is officially arrested in April 1957.

1957

March 20–28   In an attempt to make the Kádár regime more palatable to the Hungarians, the Soviet and Hungarian governments sign a pact in Moscow that attempts to balance the relationship between the two. Trade between the USSR and Hungary is to be on the basis of world market prices; the Soviets extend the period of repayment of loans; and the Soviets grant the Hungarians a long-term loan of 750 million rubles and consignment of goods and service to the value of 1.1 billion rubles.

April   Acting on behalf of the Hungarian government, Romanian security forces arrest former Hungarian prime minister Imre Nagy, Gen. Pál Maléter—who was Nagy's defense minister—and several others after they had been forced by the Soviets to seek asylum in that country in late 1956.

Cardinal Jozsef Mindszenty after Hungarian Prime Minister Nagy gets him released from a life sentence in prison for alleged anti-state activities.

May 27 A party and governmental delegation led by Kádár signs an agreement in Moscow to station Soviet troops in Hungary indefinitely.

1958

January 28 Ferenc Münnich, a Central Committee member of the Hungarian Workers' (Communist) party who supported the Soviet actions in 1956, becomes prime minister, replacing Kádár, who many thought was becom-

ing too powerful. Kádár remains party general secretary and becomes a minister without portfolio in the government.

June Imre Nagy pleads not guilty to charges of "conspiracy and creating a secret organization aimed at forcibly seizing power and overthrowing the Hungarian People's Democracy." Nagy, Maléter, and the others are found guilty of conspiracy and treason and are sentenced to death.

June 16 Imre Nagy, his defense minister Gen. Pál Maléter, and two others involved in the 1956 revolution are executed.

Patrons and clerks stand at the entrance of a shop watching as members of the Hungarian Revolutionary Army take aim against Red secret police in Budapest on October 31, 1956. Fighting flares up again on November 2 as Russian tanks and troops encircle Budapest and sweep West in an apparent drive to seal off Hungary's frontier with Austria.

December 7 The government announces coercive measures, *i.e.,* confiscation of land and property, use of force, and forced agricultural requisitions, against Hungarian peasants who refuse to enter the collective farms. By September 1961, 95.6 percent of all farmland is in the socialist sector.

Romania, Bulgaria, and Albania to create a division of labor among the members. Hungary is classified as an "industrialized agrarian country" and will focus its economic development on industry and agriculture with a special emphasis on agricultural production and food processing.

1959

November 30–December 5 The Hungarian Socialist Workers' party Seventh Party Congress convenes. This party is the successor to the Hungarian Workers' (Communist) party whose name was modified in October 1956 by former Prime Minister Kádár.

December 14 The Committee for Mutual Economic Aid (CMEA or Comecon) negotiates a treaty with the socialist states of Poland, Czechoslovakia, Hungary,

1961

September 12 The Central Committee approves the Second Five Year Plan. The targets set by this plan give priority to heavy industry, but also recognize the need for capital investment in the chemical industry, machinery, improved seeds, and fertilizers. Enterprises are given more freedom in decision-making, encouraging individual initiative, and tolerating the acquisition of private property.

September 13 Ferenc Münnich is replaced by János Kádár, who is now prime minister for the second time.

Red emblems are removed from a Communist party building in Budapest after revolutionaries take over.

Under the influence of Soviet leader Nikita Khrushchev's readopted policy of de-Stalinization, Kádár forces ideologically inflexible members of the party to resign. Kádár and his government begin a period of rehabilitation and clemency for victims of Rákosi and even some alleged "counter-revolutionaries" from 1956. Nagy's advisor, Ferenc Donáth, Hungary's first president Zoltán Tildy, and writers Tibor Déry and Gyula Hay are released from prison. Internment camps are closed and the summary courts abolished.

1962

March 30   The Central Committee announces the completion of the socialization of agriculture.

November 20–24   The Eighth Party Congress of the Hungarian Socialist Workers' (Communist) party announces the adoption of the conciliatory theme devised by Kádár: "He who is not against us is with us and welcomed by us."

1963

March   The parliament grants a final amnesty to ensure the release of the remaining prisoners from 1956 who are still waiting to be sentenced for their part in the uprising.

1964

October 15   Soviet leader Nikita Khrushchev is removed from power. The small remaining number of Stalinists left in Hungary hope this event will change Kádár's plans which they label as pragmatic revisionism.

1965

June 30   To allay the fears of the new Soviet leadership under Aleksey N. Kosygin and Leonid Brezhnev that Hungary will be susceptible to national communism, Kádár resigns his position as prime minister and dedicates himself to Communist party affairs by becoming first secretary. Kádár hands the reigns of government over to Gyula Kállai, his deputy prime minister.

1966

November 11   The parliament passes a new electoral law allowing more candidates to run than there are seats, thereby abolishing the single slate of candidates that had been employed since 1948.

November 23–December 3   The Ninth Party Congress of the Hungarian Socialist Workers' (Communist) party decides to introduce the New Economic Mechanism (NEM) on January 1, 1968. Under this new economic plan, producers are given considerable freedom in fixing prices, can determine wages and salaries according to company profits, and can participate in decisions on production targets and areas of investment.

The aftermath of the 1956 Hungarian Revolution: A Hungarian hero is buried.

1967

April 14 Gyula Kállai resigns as prime minister and is replaced by Jenő Fock, a member of the Hungarian Socialist Workers' (Communist) party and loyal supporter of Kádár who is in the midst of fighting for the implementation of his new economic program (*see* January 1, 1968).

September 6–9 Hungary and the Soviet Union prolong the Treaty of Friendship, Cooperation and Mutual Support for another 20 years—until 1987. Kádár, preparing the way for Soviet acceptance of Hungary's economic reforms, reiterates the view that any individual or state purporting to be Communist cannot hold anti-Soviet opinions.

1968

January 1 The New Economic Mechanism is implemented. Its most crucial measure is a new price system. Central planning is retained, but obligatory planning directives are abolished. The central plan still binds the government, but not each individual enterprise. The newly independent enterprises are regulated by the government through indirect economic means such as taxes, price regulations, and wage guidelines. Plants now have to concentrate on the profits made by selling their products on the market.

From the mid-sixties to the mid-seventies, Hungary's economy grows yearly by three to four percent. Prices only rise an average of two to three percent.

Agriculture also profits from the new reforms. Between 1968 to the early 1980s, the annual growth rate jumps to three to four percent.

June 14 Showing some understanding for the Czechoslovak reform program underway since January, Hungary renews its friendship treaty with Czechoslovakia (*see* Czechoslovakia).

July 14–16 The Communist leaders of Bulgaria, East Germany, Hungary, Poland, and the USSR—fearful of the repercussions in their own countries from the Czechoslovak liberalizing movement—meet in Warsaw and send an ultimatum to the Czechoslovak Communist Party. The ultimatum demands an end to the Czechoslovak reforms, including the banning of all non-Communist political organizations, controls on the media, and a strengthened military. The five countries back up their resolution with troop movements near the Czechoslovak borders. Despite Hungary's earlier sympathy, many Hungarian leaders feel that the Czechoslavak reform movement has gotten out of hand.

August 21 The Hungarian government, safeguarding its own advancements in the cultural and economic spheres, mobilizes two divisions for the military invasion of Czechoslovakia (*see* Czechoslovakia).

1970

November 23–28 The Tenth Party Congress of the Hungarian Socialist Workers' (Communist) party meets. Due to Kádár's tutelage, his realism, and his understanding of the realities of the power relationship between the Soviet Union and Hungary, Hungary wins the approval of its economic innovations from Brezhnev at this meeting.

1972

April 19 The parliament of the People's Republic of Hungary proclaims that Hungary is now a "socialist state." While insisting on the primacy of the Communist party, the government throughout 1972 passes reform legislation

conceding to citizens full legal rights and a guarantee of a judicial system divorced from the party. In granting these concessions, however, the government declares its determination to fight against "right" and "left" wing revisionism or any attempts to change the governing structure.

1973

March 15 On the 125th anniversary of the revolt against Habsburg rule in 1848, the party sets out to silence its critics. The philosophers János Kis and Mihály Vajda are expelled from the party in May on charges of "serious errors and lack of self criticism." Prominent social commentators and sociologists Agnes Heller, Maria Markus, and György Bencze leave the party. Cultural policy will now come under more careful scrutiny.

June 28 The Soviets grow wary of Hungary's reforms. To placate the Soviets, the government sets up a State Planning Commission chaired by György Lázár that reneges on some of the reforms of the New Economic Mechanism (NEM).

1974

February 12 Czechoslovakia, Hungary, and Yugoslavia sign an agreement to build the Adria pipeline from the city of Omisalj on the Adriatic Sea to Bratislava.

March 21 A shakeup in the Central Committee of the party, its executive council (the Politburo), and government signals an apparent change in the government's liberal economic and cultural policies. Central Committee secretary for economic affairs, Rezsö Nyers, is dismissed, as is the liberal secretary for culture and ideology, György Aczél.

1975

March 17–22 The Eleventh Party Congress of the Hungarian Socialist Workers' (Communist) party convenes. Reassuring the Soviets, First Secretary Kádár continues to emphasize Hungary's loyalty to the Soviet Union while the Congress makes sure the economic reforms, although not being advanced, will not be halted.

May 6 Cardinal Mindszenty, a symbol of Hungarian anti-communism and the 1956 uprising, dies in exile in Vienna, saddening many Hungarians. Mindszenty had left the American embassy compound in Budapest after the

Vatican, hoping to improve the position of the Catholic church in Hungary, relieved him of his offices as Primate of Hungary and Archbishop of Esztergom in 1974.

May 15   Prime Minister Jenő Fock resigns due to the faltering economy. György Lázár, regarded as a critic of the NEM, replaces Jenő Fock as prime minister and forms a new government.

November 13   Lázár is given a Vatican audience with Pope Paul VI.

1976

February 12   As a result of Lázár's meeting at the Vatican in November 1975 and the death of Cardinal Mindszenty in May 1975, László Lekai, a moderate in dealing with the government, is appointed Archbishop of Esztergom and Cardinal-Primate of the Catholic Church in Hungary.

1977

June 26   The plenum, or general assembly, for the executive meeting of the Central Committee decrees more cultural freedom will be permitted. Kádár and his regime agree a measure of pluralism and the freedom of party members to express their opinions is constructive and necessary.

1980

March 24–27   The Twelfth Party Congress of the Hungarian Socialist Workers' (Communist) party allows changes in the relationship between the trade unions and the party. Sándor Gaspar, the general secretary of the trade unions' National Council, makes clear his organization no longer regards itself as a broker between the workers and the party, but rather as a protector and representative of the workers' interests. Personnel changes also occur at this meeting. Kádár dismisses five of 15 Politburo members, blaming them for the faltering Hungarian economy affected by the worldwide recession.

December 12–14   The Twenty-Sixth Trade Union Congress passes a resolution stating trade unions must protect the workers' interests independently of the party and government thereby theoretically removing the trade unions from Communist control.

1981

January 2   The Sixth Five Year Plan aims to shift the emphasis of production in favor of more profitable goods for which there is an international demand to increase economic efficiency and to maintain the standard of living of the 1970s.

1982

May 6   Hungary joins the International Monetary Fund (IMF) as its foreign debt soars to almost $9 billion. During the 1980s, Hungary experiences a shortfall of foreign exchange necessary for repayment of interest and capital from Western loans.

July 7   Hungary becomes a member of the World Bank. With access to the resources of the IMF and World Bank, Hungary overcomes its immediate problems by short-term borrowing.

December 15   The apartment of László Rajk, Jr.—a leading dissident and son of the Communist leader executed in 1949—is raided because of his role in the distribution of underground literature known as Samizdat. In the early eighties, more dissident groups are formed which concentrate on social and cultural issues in Hungary.

One group is formed around the philosopher János Kis who was relieved of his post at the Academy of Sciences in the late seventies. Gábor Demzsky, whose magazine *Hormondo* (The Messenger) concerns itself with the events of the October 1956 Revolution, forms the nucleus of another group. János Vargha, a biologist and journalist, takes up ecological issues and succeeds in halting two major power stations planned to be built on the Danube.

1984

April–May   Having won the approval of the new Soviet leader, Yuri Andropov, First Secretary Kádár introduces a "regulated market" which combines the advantages of independent private initiative and market forces with state central planning over banking, pricing, balance of payments, and monetary policy. State companies are allowed more autonomy; ministerial intervention in planning is reduced; industrial deconcentration and establishment of small businesses are encouraged; competition is intensified; credit access is improved; and companies are forced to bear greater risks.

1985

March 25–28 At the Thirteenth Party Congress of the Hungarian Socialist Workers' (Communist) party, Kádár is barely able to retain his position as first secretary due to the declining economy. Two of Kádár's protégés, Károly Grász and Imre Pozsgay, emerge as leading figures. At this meeting, it is decided that more flexible economic measures must be developed for export-oriented goods, changes must be in price structures must occur, subsidies must be gradually eliminated, and changes made in managerial structure. However, it becomes clear to the reformist section of the party that any type of economic reform is impossible without social and political changes. Kádár does not agree.

July 8–22 Parliamentary elections are held. For the first time since the 1940s independent, non-Communist constituency candidates are allowed to run.

1987

May 25 János Kádár's 75th birthday. It becomes increasingly clear that Kádár needs to appoint a successor. In the running are the deputy prime minister, Károly Németh, as well as the Budapest Communist party secretary, Károly Grósz.

June Changes occur within the Hungarian Socialist Workers' (Communist) party and the government. Károly Grósz replaces György Lázár as prime minister and improves his chances to succeed Kádár.

1988

May 20–22 During a meeting of the Hungarian Socialist Workers' party, Kádár is replaced in the party by a quartet consisting of Károly Németh, the deputy prime minister; Grósz, the prime minister; Imre Pozsgay, a reform Communist; and Rezsö Nyers, the author of the New Economic Mechanism (NEM). Kádár will become the party president.

1989

March 15 For the first time ever, independence day in Hungary is declared a public holiday.

May 2 Hungary begins to dismantle the barbed wire fence along its border with Austria showing that commu-

nism is crumbling in the country and that Hungary wants to have open relations with the West; this action is applauded by the Hungarian people.

May 8 Viewed as a collaborator with the Soviet Union János Kádár loses his post as president of the Hungarian Socialist Workers' party.

June 16 Two hundred thousand people attend the reinterment of Imre Nagy and other executed leaders of the October 1956 revolution.

July 6 First Secretary János Kádár dies.

August 15 The Hungarian Communist party expresses regret over Hungary's participation in the 1968 invasion of Czechoslovakia.

September Returning from their annual vacations in Eastern Europe, East Germans flee over the Hungarian border into Austria, signifying that Hungary is no longer a member of the Soviet bloc.

The Hungarian opposition and leadership agree to hold multiparty elections in the spring of 1990.

October 9 The Hungarian Socialist Workers' (Communist) party disbands and reconstitutes itself as the Hungarian Socialist party.

October 23 Hungary officially becomes the Republic of Hungary, dropping the terms Peoples' Republic from its name.

1990

April 8 The final ballot for seats in the parliament takes place. The Hungarian Democratic Forum wins 42 percent of the vote; the Free Democrats win 24 percent; the reconstituted Independent Smallholders' party, 11 percent; the Hungarian Socialist party, 8.5 percent; Alliance of Young Democrats, 5.4 percent; and the Christian Democratic party, 5.4 percent.

The majority party, the Hungarian Democratic Forum, is a center-right party that favors a transition to a free market economy and, in some quarters, has nationalist overtones. The Free Democrats are composed mainly of individuals from the old dissident movement and see themselves as European-oriented. The Independent Smallholders' party, which was a major party in the interwar period, adopts a program promising to return land to its 1947 owners. Its base is primarily in the villages, particularly among the elderly.

Hungary's new coalition government is headed by prime minister, József Antall, the leader of the Hungarian Demo-

On March 15, 1989, independence day in Hungary is declared a public holiday; citizens demonstrate for more freedom before the Hungarian Parliament in Budapest.

cratic Forum (HDF). This coalition government is composed of the HDF, the Independent Smallholders' party, and the Christian Democratic party. The Free Democrats are thrown into opposition. Writer, Árpád Göncz, is made president of the republic.

May   Prime Minister Antall presents a reform program to the parliament that emphasizes privatization, foreign investment, and free prices.

June 21   A stock exchange opens in Budapest.

August 3   Árpád Göncz, is elected president.

1991

February 15   The leaders of Czechoslovakia, Poland, and Hungary meet in Hungary and sign an agreement pledging mutual cooperation in transforming their planned economies to free market economies.

February 25   Under continued insistence and pressure from Hungary, Czechoslovakia, and Poland, an agreement is signed providing for the dissolution of the Warsaw Pact.

March   In Bologna, Italy, the foreign ministers of the Pentagonale (Czechoslovakia, Austria, Hungary, Italy, and Yugoslavia) declare their support for the continued existence of Yugoslavia as a federal republic based on democratic reform.

April   The parliament passes the Law on Compensation, which is amended on June 26. This law partially compensates former property owners and provides legal recourse for those whose property had been confiscated under Communist rule. This law does not meet the expectations of the Independent Smallholders' party which ran on a platform of total land and property restitution.

May   Imre Pozsgay and Zoltán Bíró, influential former Communists, form the National Democratic Alliance. This party advocates a renewed socialism and warns workers of the dangers of uncontrolled capitalism.

June   The last Soviet troops depart from Hungary.

August 16–20   Pope John Paul II visits Hungary. In preparation for the Pope's visit, the parliament passes a law in July 1991 returning property to the churches that had been nationalized by the Communists.

Hungarian border guards cut part of the barbed wire fence as Hungary starts dismantling its 354 kilometers of "Iron Curtain" between Hungary and Austria and the free West.

September The Constitutional Court, founded January 1, 1990, favors limiting the power of the Hungarian president. Up until this point, the president, Árpád Göncz, and Prime Minister József Antall quarreled publicly over the role of the president.

October János Kis resigns as chairman of the Free Democrats. The new leader, Peter Tolygyessy, has difficulty gaining the support of the core of the party. This core has grown up around the samizdat (underground publication) journal, *Beszélő* (The Communicator), whose membership consists of well-known former dissidents such as Mátyás Eorsi, Peter Hack, Miklós Haraszti, Károly A. Soos, István Szent-Ivanyi, Gáspár M. Tamás, and Ferenc Wekler.

November 4 Parliament passes the Zetenyi-Takacs Law which suspends the statute of limitations for all crimes of murder, treason, and aggravated assault leading to the victim's death committed during the past 45 years that had not been prosecuted for political reasons.

November–December By the end of 1991, Hungary's economic situation has deteriorated. Most of the large state industries have yet to be privatized, the foreign debt remains high at some $20 billion, and the unemployment rate has reached 351,000 persons, or 7.3 percent of the work force, and is still rising.

Industrial production has declined over 16.6 percent in the first nine months of 1991 and will result in a decline in the gross domestic product of 7 to 8 percent for the year. The inflation rate is at 35 to 36 percent, surpassing the 28.9 percent inflation rate in 1990.

1992

March 1 Hungary becomes an associate member of the European Community (EC). Associate membership facilitates the entry of Hungarian exports, especially agricultural products, into EC markets.

March 25 The leader of the Independent Smallholders' party, József Torgyán, unhappy with Antall's tendency to make important political decisions without consulting his junior coalition partner, leads a march of 7,000 to 25,000 supporters through the streets of Budapest. The marches demand Antall's cabinet resign and be replaced by a cabinet of "experts." Torgyán's demands are ignored.

June 9 Fearing an ecological disaster if completed, the Hungarian parliament declares the 1977 Czechoslovak-Hungarian treaty on the Gabčíkovo-Nagymaros dam project invalid (*see* Czechoslovakia, October 31, 1992).

August 19 At the opening of the third world congress of Hungarians in Budapest, Prime Minister József Antall states that "it is the constitutional duty of the Hungarian government to take responsibility for Hungarians abroad." Antall is not promoting the redrawing of borders but is putting Hungary's neighbors, Slovakia and Romania, on alert that his government expects them to grant full ethnic rights to their Hungarians. He pledges to continue to speak out in defense of those rights.

December Árpád Göncz, the writer-turned-president of Hungary, and József Antall, the Hungarian prime minister, engage in a public debate over legislation about how to restructure the state-controlled media. Göncz wants an independent media, while Antall wants government scrutiny of programs, appointments, and budgets. Antall frequently complains television and radio news programs are too critical.

1993

January 8 The heads of Hungary's state radio and television resign, citing the many causes of their resignations: the prime minister's office's takeover of the budget process of the two networks; parliament's inability over the last two years to pass a law regulating the media; disciplinary action against the director of Hungarian television by the government; and an investigation into two of television director's deputies that they assert is politically motivated.

January 22 The congress of the ruling Hungarian Democratic Forum, the center-right party led by Antall, beats off an attack by the party's nationalist wing. Antall and the moderates of his party are able to keep a majority of moderates on the governing presidium.

István Csurka, former vice president of Antall's Democratic Forum and now the head of the nationalist wing, calls for Hungarians to rise up against a conspiracy of Jews, Communists, liberals, journalists, and western firms that are stifling the rebirth of Hungary. In addition, Csurka calls for a Hungarian version of *Lebensraum* (room in which to live, or expand); the word he uses is the direct Hungarian equivalent of Hitler's German term used to denote Nazi German expansion in the 1930s and 1940s. As a result, Antall's government feels compelled to respond and asks Hungary's neighbors to give their Hungarian minorities a large measure of local autonomy.

March 18 In an interview, Prime Minister Antall attacks his party's (HDF) right wing and its leader István Csurka by labeling them as anti-democratic and attempting to bring down his government.

April 14 The parliament passes a law banning the public display of fascist and communist symbols.

April 17 In an attempt to increase support, the Alliance of Young Democrats (AYD), Hungary's most popular liberal opposition party, agrees to open its membership to people over the age of 35.

June 7 The HDF expels four vocal rightist members so that it can maneuver into a coalition government with liberal parties that are predicted to win the 1994 general elections.

June 22 The European Community formally invites Hungary, Bulgaria, the Czech Republic, Poland, Romania, and Slovakia to apply for membership. It is not expected that the countries will become full members before the turn of the century.

July István Csurka is expelled from the Hungarian Democratic Forum and establishes the Hungarian Justice and Life Party (HJLP). Only a small number of HDF party members opt to join his new party.

September 4 The remains of Admiral Miklós Horthy are reburied in his hometown of Kenderes as thousands, including some former members of his government, turn out to commemorate the event. Horthy, the leader and regent of Hungary from 1919 to 1944, died in exile in Portugal in 1957 at the age of 89. Demonstrations were held the day before in Budapest to protest the government's decision to broadcast Horthy's reinterment on television. Many people view Horthy as a Nazi sympathizer.

October The Hungarian Constitutional Court approves the prosecution of former communist officials for actions taken during the 1956 Hungarian Revolution.

October 30 Approximately 10,000 people march through Budapest demanding freedom of the press and the media claiming that the government censors it.

November The largest party of the liberal opposition in Hungary, Alliance of Young Democrats (AYD), has three of its top leaders resign. They accuse the chairmen of AYD of turning the party toward the right. The other liberal opposition party, the Alliance of Free Democrats (AFD) seeking to shore up its popularity, which has sunk to 6 percent, replaces its leader Iván Petö with Gábor Kuncze. During 1993, Petö had moved toward closer cooperation with the former communist Hungarian Socialist Party (HSP). The AYD removes him in order to gain the support of the AYD.

The HSP increases its popularity steadily throughout 1993, presenting itself as the party of wage earners and the unemployed. It becomes the second most popular party after the AYD in the polls.

November 2 Hungary signs friendship and cooperation treaties with Slovenia and Croatia.

December 12 Prime Minister József Antall and leader of the HDF dies after a long bout with cancer. The HDF supports the Internal Affairs Minister, Péter Boross, as the replacement for Antall.

December 14 The HDF elects Péter Boross as its nominee for prime minister. Boross pledges to continue Antall's policies. Known for his authoritarian style and efficiency, his supporters in the HDF are confident that he will maintain stability and continuity leading into the 1994 national elections. Boross is sworn in on December 21.

December 19 The American and German telecommunications giants Ameritech Corporation and Deutsche

Bundespost Telekom announce in Budapest that a consortium of the two companies purchased a 30 percent share of the state owned telephone company Matav for $875 million. Experts consider this deal one of the largest privatization deals in Eastern Europe since the fall of communism.

Chapter Six

POLAND

Poland's origins can be traced to the mid-fifth century, when eastern Europe was gradually settled by Slavic tribes. One of these tribes was the Polonie, whose name means "people of the fields." By the middle of the tenth century, the Polanie and neighboring tribes had united in an elementary feudal system under Prince Mieszko, ruler and head of the Piast dynasty. In 966 he converted his people to Christianity and placed his country under the protection of the pope to counter the German military threat of the Holy Roman Empire.

Under succeeding Piasts, Poland gained and lost territory during endless wars and invasions. The power of the monarchy diminished, with a fractious nobility in actual control of the country by the twelfth century. Kazimierz III (the Great), the last Piast ruler, wrested control of the government back from the nobility, codified the law (giving protection to Jews and minority groups), and founded the University of Kraków during his rule from 1333 to 1370. He also increased Poland's territory to include Silesia, Galicia, and Pomerania.

In 1382 Jadwiga, Kazimierz's great-niece, became ruler. Four years later she married the Grand Duke Władysław Jagiełło of Lithuania uniting both lands into the Polish-Lithuanian Commonwealth, a state that stretched from the Baltic to the Black Sea, and included large sections of modern-day Ukraine and Belarus. For the next 200 years the Jagiełłonian dynasty ruled and prosperity reigned, culminating in Poland's Golden Age in the sixteenth century.

After the last Jagiełłonian king died in 1572, the monarchy became elective, and both foreigners and Poles served as king until the end of the eighteenth century. This paved the way for outside interference and destructive rivalries within an increasingly powerful nobility. In the mid-1600s the country became involved in costly wars, particularly with Russia and Sweden, and lost much territory along the Baltic and in the southeast. King Jan III Sobieski restored Poland's dignity somewhat when he lifted the Ottoman Turkish siege of Vienna in 1683, but he was unable to stop further foreign encroachment on Polish territory.

While Poland declined, its neighbors grew stronger. No longer content to control the country through its elected kings and nobility, Austria, Prussia, and Russia seized roughly one-third of Poland's territory in 1772, an event known as the First Partition. Disgraced by their powerlessness, the Polish government and nobility began a series of reforms. These reforms culminated in the May 3, 1791 liberal constitution, which restored a hereditary monarchy and abolished all vestiges of feudalism. But these moves came too late. In 1793 Prussia and Russia seized more land in the Second Partition. Tadeusz Kościuszko, already a hero in the American Revolution, led an unsuccessful revolt against this move by Prussia and Russia. The following year, the Third Partition between Russia, Prussia, and Austria wiped Poland off the map.

In 1807 Napoleon established the Grand Duchy of Warsaw, which he carved out of land taken from the three partitioning powers. This puppet state was to serve as a sentinel, protecting French interests in the east. With Napolean's fall, the territory was repartitioned by Austria, Prussia, and Russia in the Congress of Vienna. Only the city of Kraków, remained free. It was the center of Polish national life until its annexation by Austria in 1846.

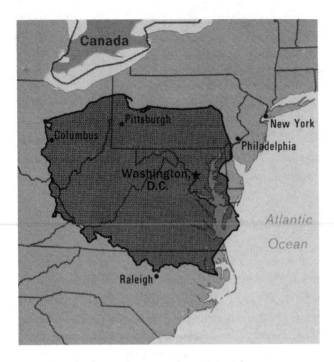

Poland in relation to the size of the United States.

After the Napoleonic era, the divided Poles continued to resist foreign domination, especially by the Russians, and dreamt of an independent Poland. In 1830 the Poles launched an unsuccessful rebellion in Russian Poland, after which Polish autonomy was revoked and many Polish intellectuals, like Chopin, fled to the West. In 1863 another revolt erupted. Brutal repression followed, and the Russian government began a policy of forced assimilation called Russification. A similar practice of Germanification was employed in Prussian Poland after German unification in 1871. Poles under Austrian rule, however, were much freer due to Vienna's need for their support in keeping the Austrian half of the Habsburg monarchy politically stable, and Galicia (Austrian Poland) became the focal point of Polish nationalism.

On the eve of World War I, Poland was a divided nation. Each section of the dismembered country had a different currency, economy, and no direct communications or rail lines linked the regions. Only in Galicia was there any kind of autonomous government. In spite of the partitions, political life in the Polish lands flourished toward the end of the nineteenth century. Parties and programs spanning the political spectrum could be found by the early 1890s; these parties would then blossom into the various political parties and factions of interwar Po-

land. The two most important politicians in the Polish lands were Józef Piłsudski and Roman Dmowski.

When the war erupted, Poles found themselves on both sides of the conflict with Austria and Germany part of the Central Powers, and Russia a member of the Allies. All recognized the necessity of Polish support for their war efforts, and pandered endlessly to nationalistic hopes, promising freedom and independence once the war was over.

1914

June 28 Archduke Franz Ferdinand, the heir-apparent of Austria-Hungary, and his wife are assassinated in Sarajevo, Bosnia.

July 28 Austria-Hungary declares war on Serbia. Soon all the major European powers are entangled in what becomes World War I: Germany and Austria-Hungary, as the Central Powers, battle Russia, France, Great Britain, and their allies as the Entente powers.

July 31 In order to muster the war support of Poles in Germany, German Emperor Wilhelm II decrees that after the ''imminent'' German victory, a Polish state should be created.

August 6 Austria-Hungary declares war on Russia.

Józef Piłsudski, a young patriot and member of the Socialist party, who had been working in Galicia (Austrian Poland) persuades the Austrian military to let him lead 200 riflemen into the Congress Kingdom of Poland (Russian Poland), hoping to incite an anti-Russian revolt. He is not successful in organizing a rebellion.

August 7 The Germans bombard and destroy Kalisz in Russian Poland.

August 8 Poles in the Russian Duma, or national parliament, offer loyal cooperation to the war effort.

Poles and Polish troops fight in large numbers in the armies of the partitioning nations, thus finding themselves fighting against one another.

August 14 Grand Duke Nicholas, the Russian commander in chief and an uncle of Tsar Nicholas II, issues a manifesto promising that a unified Poland will be restored under tsarist rule in an attempt to keep the Poles in the Congress Kingdom on the side of Russia during the war.

August 16 With Austrian permission, Piłsudski establishes the Supreme National Committee *(Naczelny Komitet Narodowy)* in Kraków to unite all Polish political parties in the area, and he recruits Special Legions to fight against the Russians. These regions form the basis of Piłsudski's

government in the 1920s and 1930s. This furthers Austrian ambitions to incorporate the Congress Kingdom into Galicia.

September 2   The Russian army occupies the Austrian Polish city of Lemberg (Lwów, Lviv).

November 25   Roman Dmowski, leader of the National Democrats *(Narodowa Demokracja)*—an anti-German, anti-Semitic, and extremely pro-Russian political group— in Russian Poland, forms the Polish National Committee *(Komitet Narodowy Polski)* in Warsaw, which supports the Russian war effort.

1915

April 3   In another attempt to gain further Polish support for its war effort, the Russian government grants autonomy to urban areas of the Congress Kingdom of Poland (Russian Poland).

May   A successful German-Austrian offensive eventually puts all Polish territory under the rule of the Central Powers.

June 22   Lemberg (Lwów) is recaptured by the Austrians *(see* September 2, 1914).

August 5   Warsaw falls to German forces.

December   Members of Polish Socialist Party *(Polska Partia Socjalistyczna)* and left-wing intellectuals found the Central National Committee *(Centralny Komitet Narodowy)* hoping to create a Polish republic with the aid of the Central Powers. Their hopes are dashed when Germany and Austria-Hungary agree to divide the Congress Kingdom between them.

1916

July 25   Piłsudski withdraws his Legions from the front and resigns his command, protesting Germany's failure to create a Polish state as promised. His Legions are then incorporated into Austro-Hungarian army.

November 5   The German and Austrian emperors proclaim the Kingdom of Poland as an hereditary constitutional monarchy in the vain hope that their actions will increase military enlistment among the Polish population. The new state comprises a fraction of the territory that had belonged to the old Polish Commonwealth at the time of the First Partition in 1772.

November 16   One of the greatest Polish Romantic novelists of the nineteenth century, Henryk Sienkiewicz, dies in exile in Switzerland.

November 26   A 25-member Council of State for the Polish Kingdom is appointed and begins functioning in January 1917.

December 5   Piłsudski becomes head of the council's military commission.

December 25   Hoping to sway Polish sympathies, a tsarist proclamation speaks vaguely about a free, united Poland. Two months later, the Russian government conspires with France, allowing Russia to expand its western borders into Poland.

1917

January 22   U.S. President Woodrow Wilson delivers his "Peace without Victory" speech in which he speaks of the necessity of a "unified, independent Poland." Wilson believes the resurrection of an independent Poland is a key to future European security and peace.

January 30   The Council of State adopts a constitution, drawn up by the Polish conservatives of the German-appointed Regency Council.

March 21   The Petrograd Soviet of Workers and Peasant Deputies issues a proclamation denouncing the partitions of Poland as a symbol of the decadent diplomacy of capitalism. This Bolshevik initiative is merely a "paper tiger," because the Bolsheviks have no way of actively supporting such a position. Also, the Bolsheviks only recognize Poland's right to exist and never clearly define what boundaries should be established for a restored Poland.

March 28   The Petrograd Soviet or Communist-led council and rival of the Provisional Government in Russia declares the right of national self-determination and recognizes Poland's right to independence.

March 30   Two days after the Petrograd Soviet's declaration, the Provisional Russian government—made up largely of Russian liberals rather than Communist Bolsheviks—accepts idea of an independent Poland, composed of those areas "where the population is majority Polish," in a military alliance with Russia.

April 6   The United States enters World War I.

Polish fraternal organizations in the United States agree to establish a Kościuszko Army (named for the Polish national who fought in the American Revolution) to fight alongside American forces for the creation of an independent Poland. The troops are to consist of soldiers who are not

U.S. citizens, and therefore not subject to the American draft (*see* October 12).

April 10   Austria-Hungary transfers the Polish Legions to the German army (*see* July 25, 1916).

May   Starting this month and continuing over the next year, three anti-Bolshevik Polish army corps are founded from the ranks of the Russian army in order to defend Polish towns and property in Belorussia and Ukraine against Bolshevik forces.

May 30   Polish deputies in the Austrian parliament unanimously demand a free and unified Poland with an outlet to the sea. This outlet is critical to Poland's economy as it will only thrive if given a port and the possibility to trade outside of eastern Europe.

June 5   French President Raymond Poincaré raises and equips a 100,000-man Polish army from Polish prisoners of war, émigrés, and volunteers in the French military.

June 22   Piłsudski is arrested by Germany because he refuses to take the oath of fealty to the German Emperor.

July 2   Piłsudski resigns from the Council of State to protest German interference in the nominally independent Kingdom of Poland.

July 9   Two-thirds of the Polish officers and men in the German army renounce their oath of loyalty to Germany.

July 22   Piłsudski is arrested by German authorities for his actions earlier in the month and his continued refusal to follow German orders and is imprisoned in the fortress of Magdeburg, Germany.

August 15   After leaving Russia, Roman Dmowski reestablishes the Polish National Committee in Lausanne, Switzerland. By the end of the year, the committee is recognized by the Allies as the official Polish delegation to the Paris Peace Conference. Dmowski is its president and Ignacy Jan Paderewski, the pianist, its representative to the United States.

August 25   Having lost the support of the Polish population who view it as a tool of the Germans, the rest of the members of the Council of State resign.

October 12   In the United States, recruitment for the Kosiuszko Army begins (*see* April 6).

October 15   The Central Powers appoint a three-member Regency Council to replace the Council of State. German advisors who closely supervise the council make sure it has very limited powers.

1918

January 5   British Prime Minister David Lloyd George publicly declares his support for an independent Poland.

January 8   American President Wilson's Fourteen Points speech names a free and independent Poland—with secure access to the sea—as the thirteenth of his famous fourteen points (*see* January 22, 1917).

February 9   In a treaty between the Central Powers and independent Ukraine, the Germans, hoping to secure Ukrainian support in the war, give the predominantly Polish Chelm province to Ukraine. Poles are infuriated and the government of the "independent" Kingdom of Poland resigns.

February 15   As a result of the February 9 treaty between the Central Powers and the Ukraine, most of the Polish military Auxiliary Corps under Józef Haller desert from the Austro-Hungarian army to join Polish forces in Russia.

March 3   The Treaty of Brest-Litovsk between the Central Powers and Communist Russia removes Russia from the war. Furthermore, Russia renounces all claims to Polish territory.

March 20   The Polish army in France is put under the direction of Dmowski's Polish National Committee.

May 6–11   At the Battle of Kaniów, Haller's troops are defeated by German forces; Haller escapes into Russia.

June 3   The Polish National Committee in Paris is recognized by the Allies as an "allied belligerent nation"—a major step toward Polish independence because from this point forward, the resurrection of the Polish state is officially accepted as an Allied war aim. The governments of Great Britain, France, and Italy state that "the creation of a united and independent Polish state with free access to the sea constitutes one of the premises of a lasting . . . peace."

September 21   The Polish army in France is put under the command of General Haller, who had come to France from Russia. The army, known as the "Blue Army," or "Haller's Boys," becomes an important stabilizing force after World War I.

Poland is governed as the Second Polish Republic from 1918 to 1939.

October 7   The Regency Council of the Polish Kingdom declares an independent Poland.

Polish deputies in the German parliament in Berlin demand an independent Poland that includes German-held Polish land.

October 12 Great Britain recognizes the Polish National Committee's control of the Polish army in France, hence it becomes a government-in-exile with its own army, marking another key step toward Polish independence.

October 15 Polish deputies in the Austrian parliament end all ties to Austria-Hungary by declaring that they are citizens of an independent Poland.

Austrian officials turn over control of Lublin and the surrounding provinces to the Poles.

October 19 A Polish National Council formed in Cieszyn, Poland (Těšín, Teschen) declares that the Cieszyn area belongs to Poland. This is an important mining region with a mixed Polish and Czech population.

October 27 A Polish Liquidation Commission is set up in Kraków upon the military collapse of Austria-Hungary. It is the first fully independent governing body in the Polish territories.

November 1 The Polish-Ukrainian war begins over possession of Galicia. The Ukrainians occupy Lwów.

November 2 Piłsudski is released from prison in Magdeburg, and returns to Warsaw (*see* July 22, 1917).

November 3 The Polish Republic is proclaimed in Warsaw by the newly established government of Józef Swiezynski, chairman of the Inter-Party Political Circle, which the National Democrats dominate. Meanwhile, a Polish army moves into Galicia.

November 5 The Poles and Czechs agree to divide the Cieszyn area along ethnic lines and await the final result of the impending peace conference, which will assign boundaries (*see* October 19).

November 7 A regional Polish administration—known as the "People's Government" of Lublin—establishes a government with Ignacy Daszyński as prime minister as an attempt by the pro-independence Left to take power in the rapidly forming state. Daszyński's program calls for nationalized industry and the expropriation of large noble estates.

November 10 Piłsudski returns to a hero's welcome in Warsaw, upon his release from prison.

November 11 The Second Republic is founded after German troops are disarmed and expelled from Warsaw. Piłsudski is made provisional head of state and granted full military power until an elected government can be formed. Regional independent administrations in Lublin and Kraków put themselves under Piłsudski's command, and Daszyński is entrusted to form a cabinet. The new republic consists of the Kingdom of Poland (1916 borders), the Duchy of Cieszyn, and West Galicia.

From 1918 to the German invasion in 1939, the Second Republic will go see 31 different cabinets or governments.

November 14 Piłsudski names Daszyński as premier, but the National Democrats boycott his appointment due to his leftist ideology, forcing Piłsudski to search for a more acceptable candidate.

Polish representatives in the German parliament and Prussian provincial assembly meet in Poznań and declare their independence from Germany and their attachment to Poland.

November 18 Jędrzej Moraczewski, a moderate socialist who is acceptable to Right-wing factions, replaces Daszyński as premier.

November 23 After three weeks of fighting, Lwów falls to the Poles (*see* November 1).

November 26 The Polish government mandates a working day of no more than eight hours.

November 28 The government grants suffrage to all Poles 21 years and older.

December 4 The Polish government issues an ultimatum ordering Germany to withdraw its troops from former German Poland which declared itself part of Poland on November 14. Germany refuses, and Poland severs diplomatic relations on December 15.

December 9 Due to problems between Poland and Bolshevik Russia over the now independent non-Russian areas of imperial Russia, Poland breaks off relations with Bolshevik or Communist Soviet Russia.

December 16 The Communist Worker's Party of Poland (*Komunistyczna Partia Polski-KPP*) is formed by the fusion of the Social Democratic Party of Poland and Lithuania (*Socjaldemokracja Królestwa Polskiego i Litwy*) and elements of the Polish Socialist Party. Supporting Marxist orthodoxy, the party rejects the idea of an independent Poland. By January 1919, the government outlaws the KPP for supporting the inclusion of the Polish state into Communist Russia.

December 27 The city of Poznań falls to Polish troops. By January 8, 1919, virtually the entire province of Poznańia is now in Polish hands, but fighting continues until late February 1919 (*see* December 4). Eventually, Poznańia is officially incorporated into the greater Polish state.

1919

January 4 An unsuccessful coup takes place in Warsaw, staged by right-wing National Democratic sympathizers.

January 17 Premier Moraczewski's cabinet is replaced with a more center-oriented or politically moderate coalition cabinet led by Ignacy Jan Paderewski. Piłsudski is appointed provisional president (*see* November 18, 1918).

January 22 The U.S. recognizes the Republic of Poland.

January 23 Fighting breaks out in Cieszyn between Poles and Czechs who no longer accept the November 5, 1918 agreement.

January 26 Elections for a constituent assembly are held.

The United States recognizes an independent Poland.

January 29 The Council of Ten at the Paris Peace Conference demands an explanation of the Cieszyn crisis from the Czech and Polish delegates.

January 31 The Supreme Allied Council, consisting of the chief ministers of the victorious allies, appoints a commission to investigate the Cieszyn crisis.

February 1 The Council of Ten forces Czech and Polish delegates to redivide the Cieszyn region along the lines drawn in 1918 until the dispute can be resolved by the conference (*see* November 5, 1918 and January 23, 1919).

February 5 Members of the high and middle nobility, a large percentage of the middle class, and elements of the wealthy independent farmer class form the People's Union (*Związek Ludowo-Narodowy),* trying to prevent extensive reform of landholding laws in the new state proposed by the leftists.

The Cieszyn crisis is temporarily resolved with Czechoslovak and Polish regions being defined (*see* February 1).

February 7 In an attempt to address rampant illiteracy, the government requires all children between 8 and 15 to attend school. Not until the mid-1920s, however, can the law be enforced.

February 14 After elections on January 26, the Sejm (parliament) constitutes itself, votes confidence in the Paderewski government, and elects the right-wing Wojciech Trampczyński as marshal (leader) of the Sejm. Piłsudski resigns as provisional head of state.

February 20 In a brief proclamation known as Little Constitution, the Sejm declares itself the "sovereign and legislative authority in the State of Poland." In the absence of a constitution, however, the representatives appoint Piłsudski chief of state, with authority to serve until a

formal government structure is drafted and ratified. Nearly three years will elapse before this occurs.

February 21 Fighting breaks out again between German and Polish forces in Poznań (*see* December 27, 1918).

February 24 France officially recognizes the independent Polish state; Great Britain follows suit three days later.

April General Haller's army, consisting of about 100,000 men, returns from France and is used to help stabilize the political situation in the country (*see* September 21, 1918).

May 19 The government requires medical insurance coverage for all workers.

June–July Polish troops occupy the West Ukrainian People's Republic, which had been established the previous November.

June 28 The Treaty of Versailles—the peace treaty between the Allied powers and Germany that ends World War I—is signed by Roman Dmowski and Ignacy Jan Paderewski, establishing Polish frontiers in the west. Poland receives an outlet to the sea (Polish Corridor) with the Pomeranian region of Germany and large parts of West Prussia and Poznańia. Danzig (Gdańsk) is made into an independent free city. The disposition of Silesia is to be determined by plebiscite in that region. Poland is also forced to accept a treaty protecting its minorities from attempts at forced polonization.

The disputes between Poland and Lithuania over Vilnius, and between Poland and Czechoslovakia over Cieszyn intensify.

July 10 The parliament passes a bill calling for the expropriation of large estates.

July 27 The demarcation line drawn between Poland and Lithuania by the Allies puts Vilnius (Wilno) on the Polish side.

August 16–17 Despite the promised plebiscite, Polish Silesians rebel against German control, and agitate for inclusion into Greater Poland in the first Silesian Uprising.

September 10 The Treaty of St. Germain between the Allies and Austria recognizes Poland as an independent state. Poland also signs two other treaties with the Allies: the first providing equal rights and protection for ethnic minorities in Poland under the protection of the League of Nations, and the second calling for it to pay a portion of the former Austro-Hungarian debt as a successor state.

December 8 The Supreme Allied Council, also known as the Allied High Council, suggests that the Polish-Russian border should run along a line corresponding to the

Bug and San rivers. Later, this border becomes known as the Curzon Line.

December 9 Paderewski's government falls, to be succeeded four days later by a centrist coalition headed by Leopold Skulski, who was supported by the main peasant parties and Christian Democrats (*see* January 17, 1919).

1920

January 28 Russia agrees to a border with Poland that is significantly further east than the Curzon line.

February 19 Poland and Czechoslovakia sign an armistice concerning Cieszyn and agree to a demarcation line drawn up by the Allies. The settlement is favorable to the Czechs (*see* February 5, 1919).

March 7–11 Fighting erupts again with the Czechoslovaks over Cieszyn.

March 19 Piłsudski is named First Marshal of Poland, a position created for him by the Polish military. It is the highest rank in the country's armed forces.

April 13 Piłsudski signs an agreement with Ukrainian Nationalist leader Semen Petlyura, allowing Polish aid to expel the Red Army from the Ukraine.

April 24 Poland agrees to an offensive with the Ukrainian Republic aimed at Communist Russia and attacks the Bolsheviks in the Ukraine.

The Poles end Bolshevik rule in Lithuania. Both incidents result in the Polish-Soviet War.

April 25–October 12 The Polish-Soviet War.

May 6 Polish troops, under General Śmigły-Rydz, take Kiev, the capital of the Ukraine.

May 18 Polish riots break out in the town of Cieszyn, held by Czechoslovakia.

May 19 Parliament passes a compulsory workmen's compensation law.

May 21 Polish miners strike in the Karvin district of Cieszyn.

May 22 Polish forces capture Riga, Latvia.

June 5 The cavalry army of the Bolshevik General Semyon Budenny breaks through the Polish front near Kiev, and by June 11 the Red Army regains control of the city.

June 28 Czechoslovakia and Poland sign another armistice in Paris regarding the disputed region of Cieszyn.

July–August The Red Army advances to the outskirts of Warsaw and Lwów.

July 4 Five Soviet Army groups to the north break through the Polish lines and drive toward Warsaw.

July 11 Plebiscites, called for in the Treaty of Versailles to determine the fates of Marienwerder (Kwidzyń) and Allenstein (Olsztyn) spell defeat for Poland; both areas vote to remain part of East Prussia, a province of Germany.

July 15 A conservative agrarian reform measure mandates the redistribution of roughly one-tenth of all arable land, with compensation to the owners.

July 23 Russia refuses a Polish demand for an armistice.

July 24 A new government takes shape under the leadership of the Piast Peasant party leader Wincenty Witos.

July 28 The Allied Ambassadorial Conference divides the Duchy of Cieszyn between Poland and Czechoslovakia, leaving a sizeable Polish minority in the Czech area. This situation will remain a constant source of friction between the new states throughout the interwar period. The conference also settles disputes in two small regions of Orawa (Orava) and Spisz (Spiš) on the border between Poland and Slovakia.

August 1 The Red Army takes Brest-Litovsk from Polish forces, and establishes a Polish Bolshevik government.

August 10 The New States Treaty between the Allies and Poland, Czechoslovakia, and Romania recognizes their independence and their borders.

August 13 Piłsudski launches a bold offensive that encircles the Red Army at the gates of Warsaw and throws the Soviets into complete retreat.

August 16–28 The Battle for Warsaw (called the Miracle on the Vistula) against the numerically superior Red Army results in Polish victory, thus eliminating further Communist encroachment into Central Europe.

August 19–20 The Second Silesian Uprising begins—prompted by the fact that the majority of the region was Polish and did not want to be under German rule.

October 9 Without the knowledge of the Polish government, a coup in Vilnius led by Gen. Lucjan Zeligowski, brings the entire province under Polish control until 1939.

October 12 An armistice ends hostilities between Poland and Russia.

1921

February 19–22 A French-Polish treaty of mutual aid and military cooperation is signed. Poland emerges as the cornerstone of France's *cordon sanitaire* policy against

Germany and Communist Russia in an attempt to isolate them.

March 3 Poland joins an alliance with Romania and Hungary promising mutual military aid in the event of Soviet aggression against any signatory.

March 17 A new constitution, modeled on the French and American systems, is adopted after a nearly three-year wait. It gives Poland a bicameral parliament, the National Assembly, consisting of the Senate and the Sejm. The Sejm holds all real political power; the Senate exercises only a weak veto. Representatives, chosen by their constituents, elect a president, who then appoints a prime minister and cabinet. These officials serve only with the Sejm's approval and can be removed from office by a majority vote, making governments extremely unstable.

March 18 The Peace of Riga ends the Polish-Soviet War, dividing Ukrainian and Belorussian areas between Poland and Russia. The Polish-Russian border now lies roughly 150 kilometers or 93 miles east of the Curzon Line (*see* December 8, 1919).

March 20 A plebiscite held in Upper Silesia by the League of Nations partitions the province between Poland and Germany. Six hundred eighty-two communes vote for inclusion in Poland; 792 for Germany. The southeastern area, with its heavy industry, votes for Poland.

May 4 The third Silesian Uprising under Wojciech Korfanty results in victory for the Poles and the occupation of large sections of Upper Silesia after several weeks of fighting.

September 10 Witos's government falls due to public economic hardship (*i.e.,* food prices have increased twelvefold in the past two years).

September 19 Antoni Ponikowski becomes premier and forms a new government.

October 20 The Conference of Ambassadors, consisting of diplomats meeting to work out the details of the Treaty of Versailles, draws the final boundaries in Upper Silesia. Poland receives the majority of steel works, coal mines, and blast furnaces (*see* March 20).

November 6 Czechoslovakia and Poland sign an agreement ending their bitter relations over Cieszyn.

1922

January 8 Poland officially receives Vilnius after a plebiscite. The Vilnius parliament ramifies this decision on February 24 (*see* October 9, 1920).

February 4 Poland and Czechoslovakia sign an agreement settling their border disputes as delineated in July 1920 (*see* July 28, 1920, November 6, 1921).

June 6 The Ponikowski government resigns (*see* September 19, 1921).

June 28 Artur Śliwiński forms a new government, which lasts until July 7.

July 31 A new government under the direction of Prof. Julian I. Nowak takes control.

September 26 Parliament passes a law standardizing local government from the three forms that existed prior to World War I and independence.

October 20 Czechoslovakia and Poland sign a commercial agreement to begin trade.

November 5–12 Representatives are elected to the Sejm and Senate. The right-wing National Democrats win a plurality of seats, about 40 percent; centrists, like the Piast Peasant Party, and leftists, including the Socialists each win another 20 percent. The remainder of the seats are divided among minority parties, especially those that represent Jews and non-Polish factions.

December 4 Piłsudski, declared chief of state *pro tem* by the Little Constitution, refuses to seek the presidency of the new government, a position he calls little more than a "gilded cage." He remains, however, First Marshal, chairman of the Inner War Council, and wartime commander in chief.

December 9 After five ballots, the National Assembly elects Gabriel Narutowicz—noted Polish scientist before World War I and a Socialist and associate of Piłsudski—president. Support from minority parties is crucial in giving him the election. A close friend of Piłsudski, Narutowicz is despised by the National Democrats, who view him as a virtual puppet. Others resent his minority support, and denounce him as "president of the Jews." His car is stoned as it travels to the inauguration.

December 16 Eligiusz Niewiadomski, a fanatical right-wing nationalist and anti-Semite, assassinates President Narutowicz at an art gallery. After his capture, Niewiadomski admits he would have preferred to kill Piłsudski. Many on the Right view Niewiadomski almost heroically, and the gulf between Piłsudski and the National Democrats widens.

December 17 A supra-party cabinet is formed by Gen. Władysław Sikorski. Piłsudski is appointed army chief of staff.

December 20 Stanisław Wojciechowski of Piast Peasant party is elected president by a coalition of center, left, and minority parties.

1923

March   Hyperinflation begins destroying the value of the Polish currency, the mark. By November it will take 2,300,000 Polisy marks to equal one U.S. dollar.

March 15   Despite Lithuanian protests, the Conference of Ambassadors recognizes Poland's eastern front—including Vilnius—as determined by the Treaty of Riga (*see* March 18, 1921; January 8, 1922).

April 15   The Sikorski government orders all Ukrainian refugees, who are fleeing from the Communists who had taken over Ukraine, to return to Communist Russia.

May 26   Sikorski's cabinet falls under the pressure of a crumbling economy.

May 28   Wincenty Witos of the Piast Peasant party forms a cabinet in coalition with the right.

May 29   Embittered by Narutowicz's murder, Piłsudski refuses to serve with the right-wing coalition. He resigns as commander in chief and retires to his manor at Sulejówek.

July 7   Anti-Semitic riots erupt in Vilnius.

October 27   A cabinet shakeup makes Wojciech Korfanty vice-premier and Roman Dmowski foreign minister.

November 6–8   The government uses the military to put down a general strike, caused by the economic chaos in the country, with much bloodshed.

December 14   Witos's cabinet falls.

December 19   Władysław Grabski forms a so-called government of experts, intended to be nonpartisan.

1924

January 3   The government is granted emergency powers to deal with the desperate economic situation in the country.

February 1   As a result of the January 3 emergency powers, the government replaces the mark with the złoty, a gold-backed currency. This is part of a broad-based economic reform policy.

February 17   General Władysław Sikorski becomes the new military minister.

May 23   The government enacts a law requiring military service for all males between the ages of 21 and 40.

Summer   As a result of inflation and catastrophic agricultural conditions, a wave of strikes sweeps the country. Over 360,000 are unemployed.

July 10   After to protests from the Soviet Union and Lithuania, the Polish parliament passes laws permitting the use of the Lithuanian, Ukrainian, and Belorussian languages in government administration and education where the population is large enough to mandate it.

July 18   The parliament passes a compulsory unemployment compensation law.

August 3   Soviet terrorists raid the border town of Stołbce.

1925

February 10   An agreement or concordat with the Vatican reorganizes the ecclesiastical administration of Poland, giving it five bishoprics: Gniezno/Poznań, Warsaw, Lwów, Kraków, and Vilnius. In return, the state promises to make instruction in religion obligatory in all schools.

March 9   Poland and the USSR open postal and telegraph communication relations. In July railway traffic between the two countries will commence.

April 23   Poland and Czechoslovakia sign a treaty calling for the peaceful resolution of all mutual disputes except those involving territory.

May 16   Polish postal service is established in the free city of Danzig (Gdańsk).

June 15   Germany launches a tariff war against Poland, undermining the economic achievements made by the Grabski regime.

October 16   The Locarno Conference. Germany, Poland, and Czechoslovakia agree to arbitration of mutual disputes, and France guarantees Poland's border with Germany.

November 13   Grabski resigns as prime minister after remaining in office for 23 months—a record in interwar Poland.

November 20   Grabski's foreign minister, Count Aleksander Skrzyński, forms a new cabinet; another nonpartisan coalition.

December 28   A law further redistributing land holdings passes parliament, but regional differences and rapid population increases combine to exacerbate agrarian difficulties such as small plots of land and antiquated farming methods, preventing any real reform.

1926

March 26 The Polish-Romanian-Hungarian alliance is renewed (*see* March 3, 1921.

March–April The currency fails, and runs on banks create more economic chaos.

April 24 The Berlin Treaty signed between Germany and the Soviet Union confirms Poland's general diplomatic isolation in the east between the two powers.

May 5 Skrzyński resigns as prime minister.

May 10 Wincenty Witos forms a new center-right coalition government, with Stanisław Vojciechowski as president; it lasts five days.

May 12–14 Piłsudski, with the support of Defense Minister General Lucjan Żeligowski, leads a coup in Warsaw. Heavy fighting ensues between government supporters and Piłsudski's forces. Important support comes from the Socialist party as railroad workers impede the advance of troops loyal to the government.

May 15 President Wojciechowski and Premier Witos resign. Piłsudski appoints Kazimierz Bartel, a professor at Lwów Technical University, as premier. He forms a supra-party cabinet of experts. Piłsudski's philosophy is encapsulated in the word *sanacja* (a cleansing) of political life from the inside out. Subsequent governments are built not on parliamentary support, but on their degree of personal loyalty to the Marshal himself.

June 1 Although he holds almost all political power, Piłsudski lets others run the government for him. The National Assembly elects him president, but he refuses the office, and supports instead the candidacy of Ignacy Mościcki, a well-known chemistry professor. Piłsudski serves in the cabinet as minister of war.

August 5 A revised constitution gives the president greater power than before.

August 26 The government establishes a council of 26 experts to study and approve/veto every bill submitted to parliament.

September 30 The Bartel government resigns after the Sejm refuses to pass the national budget.

October 2 Piłsudski takes the office of prime minister; Bartel serves as "deputy" prime minister and continues to run the government.

December 4 Under Dmowski's leadership, rightist political parties form a new oppositional organization characterized as the "New Right."

1927

March 25 Piłsudski adjourns the Sejm.

June 7 The Soviet ambassador is mortally wounded by a Russian monarchist in a Warsaw train station.

October 5 Claiming harsh treatment of Poles in Lithuania, the government arrests several Polish Lithuanians and closes numerous Lithuanian schools in the Vilnius region.

October 13 The government issues new złotys after reforming the currency.

November 28 The government dissolves the Sejm and arrests opposition deputies.

December Piłsudski asks Col. Walery Sławek, his closest confidante, to create a "governmental bloc" to give him the parliamentary support he wants. The result is the Non-Party Bloc for Cooperation with the Government (*Bezpartyjny Blok Współpracy Z Rządem*). This is not a true political party, but rather a group of individuals who agree to support the Marshal and his objectives.

1928

January 3 Poland and the USSR exchange political prisoners.

March 4–11 National elections give the Non-Party Bloc roughly one-quarter of all parliamentary seats. The Socialist Ignacy Daszyński, and not Piłsudski's candidate Bartel, is elected Marshal, or leader, of the Sejm. From now on, the Non-Party Bloc and the rest of the Sejm will be at loggerheads on almost every issue that comes before them, especially constitutional reform that would strengthen the executive branch.

June 27 Admitting his ill health, Piłsudski resigns as prime minister and Bartel takes his place. The Marshall remains minister of war.

1929

April 3 Amid a scandal over misappropriated government funds, Bartel's government resigns.

April 14 A new government takes control, led by Maj. Kazimierz Świtalski, a supporter of Piłsudski and former minister of education.

October 31 In an attempt to intimidate parliament, close to 100 army officers guided by Piłsudski's military chief of staff, pack the lobby of the Sejm building. Daszyński refuses to seat the assembly in the face of the military threat, and postpones parliament's opening until November 5. President Mościcki retaliates by adjourning parliament still further, until December 5.

November 1 In response to Piłsudski's increasingly dictatorial stance, the Polish Peasant party and other left-wing and centrist groups unite to form the center-left opposition *(Centrolew),* controlling roughly two-fifths of the delegates in the Sejm.

December 7 Centrolew's first act in the reconvened parliament is a no-confidence vote against the Świtalski government. The vote passes, and the government falls. This is the first time since Piłsudski's takeover that the Sejm has removed a cabinet. Piłsudski taps Bartel again as prime minister.

1930

March 14 Disgusted with the Sejm's continual recalcitrance, the Bartel government resigns.

March 29 Col. Walery Sławek, founder of the non-party Bloc and a staunch Piłsudski supporter, becomes premier and forms a new government; Piłsudski remains minister of military affairs.

June 20 With the Senate and the Sejm in recess, Centrolew forms an anti-government coalition with leftist and peasant party members and calls for the government's resignation.

June 29 Twenty-thousand people representing six political parties rally in Kraków protesting Piłsudski's dictatorship.

August 23 Sławek resigns as premier; he is succeeded two days later by Piłsudski who forms a largely military government.

August 30 Piłsudski dissolves the Sejm and sets the date for new elections at November 17.

September 10 Witos and other opposition political leaders are arrested illegally and imprisoned for months in the military fortress of Brześć (Brest Litovsk). They are released only after the November elections.

September 13 The government forbids all public political meetings. Numerous arrests follow in the next weeks. Other opposition leaders are beaten and harassed.

November 17–24 National elections result in an absolute majority for the Non-Party Bloc supported by Marshal Piłsudski.

November 28 Piłsudski resigns as premier and is succeeded by Sławek until December 29, when Bartel becomes prime minister again and forms a new government.

1931

January 12 Ten Centrolew politicians are convicted of antigovernment activity, receiving sentences of up to three years. Many intellectuals become disenchanted with Piłsudski and the government.

March All peasant parties unite in the People's party *(Stronnictwo Ludowe)* under the leadership of Witos.

November 2 Col. Józef Beck, a former member of Piłsudski's Legions and an active participant in the coup of 1926, is named foreign minister. He plans to make Poland less dependent upon France and to give it a more dominant position in east central Europe. Both policies are motivated by an overriding fear of the USSR. Beck will remain in this post until 1939, making him the longest-serving European foreign minister at the outbreak of World War II *(see February 19–22, 1921).*

1932

July 25 The Soviet Union and Poland sign a nonaggression pact guaranteeing their common border and agreeing not to engage in warfare against each other.

1933

February 16 The Senate of the Free City of Danzig (Gdańsk)—which is primarily German—unilaterally denounces its agreement with Poland regulating administration of the port. This agreement was made at Versailles in 1919; Danzig actions, prompted by German nationalists, foretell the poor relations between Poland and Nazi Germany in the late 1930s.

March 6 As a result of Danzig's actions, Polish infantry troops land at the Westerplatte depot to strengthen the garrison there. Ten days later, under pressure from the League of Nations, the troops are withdrawn.

1934

January 26 Poland signs a nonaggression pact with Germany as part of Foreign Minister Beck's strategy of avoiding entanglement in quarrels. Poland manages to retain its alliance with France, although relations are strained (*see* November 2, 1931; February 19–20, 1921).

September 13   Poland unilaterally renounces the "minority rights" provision of the Treaty of Versailles (*see* June 28, 1919).

1935

April 23   A new antidemocratic constitution is adopted, replacing the one from 1921. Presidential decrees are given the force of law, while actions by political parties are greatly limited. Poland's government is now authoritarian.

May 12   Marshal Piłsudski dies after being ill for some time. Gen. Edward Rydz-Śmigły becomes leader of the army.

July   A new electoral law, drafted by Premier Sławek, is enacted. It reduces seats in the Sejm by more than half, and organizes Poland into 104 districts, each of which elects two deputies. Nominations are proposed by an "electoral assembly" whose members are from professional and governmental associations—those most likely to preserve the status quo. In addition, each assembly is chaired by a government-appointed commissioner. Most of these assemblies are populated with Non-Party Bloc supporters, leaving opposition candidates little chance for nomination.

The Senate is even more tightly controlled under the new law. The number of seats is reduced, but now one-third are appointed directly by the president, and the remaining two-thirds are elected not by the populace but by special electoral assemblies in each province. These electors are even more pro-government than their Sejm counterparts; all are high-ranking civil servants, government honorees and dignitaries, or heads of professional organizations.

September 8 and 15   Elections for Sejm deputies and senators are held. The people show their disgust with the new election law from July. Fewer than half vote and many submit blank ballots while most opposition parties boycott the election. The Non-Party Bloc wins 75 percent of the seats in both the Sejm and the Senate, and Mościcki, as allowed by the new law, appoints 32 more pro-government senators. Mościcki appoints Marian Zyndram-

Koscialkowski, a Piłsudski supporter, as premier, replacing Sławek.

October 30   Sławek dissolves the Non-Party Bloc, causing the Piłsudski group to splinter into factions. Sławek is angry about not being reappointed premier and disgusted with power struggles within the bloc that developed after the September elections.

December   In an attempt to pacify his critics, Mościcki devises a power-sharing agreement with General Rydz-Śmigły. Although Mościcki is still in charge, Rydz-Śmigły is given a sizable amount of political power, and a media campaign is begun to convince the public that Rydz-Śmigły is, indeed, Piłsudski's military successor.

1936

May 15   As part of his power-sharing agreement, Mościcki replaces Premier Koscialkowski with Gen. Felicjan Sławoj-Składkowski, a close friend of Rydz-Śmigły's and a frequent member of Piłsudski cabinets. In this change of government, Rydz-Śmigły is allowed to choose five of the 12 cabinet ministers; Mościcki chooses another six, while Składkowski, the prime minister, is allowed to make only one appointment.

July   The government declares that Rydz-Śmigły is the "first person" of the country—after the president—and that as such he must be both respected and obeyed by the general population as well as the prime minister and the rest of the government.

November   With the public now saturated with the "legitimacy" of Rydz-Śmigły's succession, he is promoted to General, and, within a few days, granted Piłsudski's old title, Marshal of the Army.

Opposition to the Mościcki–Rydz coalition solidifies. The Polish Socialist party (PPS) stages a number of violent strikes, and in collaboration with the outlawed Polish Communist party (*see* December 16, 1918) wins a majority in the Łódź city council. The centrist Peasant party grows more strident in its demand for the breakup of large estates, and like the PPS also sponsors antigovernment protests, many of which are also bloody. The right-wing National Democrats remain staunchly conservative, anti-Semitic, and opposed to any part of Piłsudski's legacy; a more radically fascist branch of the party, the Falanga, emerges.

1937

March 1   Col. Adam Koc announces the birth of the Camp of National Unity (OZON), an organization designed to foster pro-government support. The party espouses a rigid and exclusionary view of Polish culture, rejecting foreign and Jewish influences. Although opposed by socialists, peasants, and some intellectuals, within a month OZON has two million members, mostly civil servants and former members of the military plus a few ultra-right radicals. Public and parliamentary resentment of both the Mościcki-Rydzthe clique and OZON grows. OZON succeeds, however, in legitimizing anti-Semitism, and its support from government workers paves the way for official discrimination against Jews.

June 9   Poland, Romania, and the USSR sign an agreement mutually guaranteeing their borders against invasion from one another.

August 15–27   The peasants, in open opposition to OZON stage a nationwide strike, refusing to supply the towns with food. The strike is brutally repressed, and both political opponents and the people remain hostile to the party.

October 10   A new opposition group, the Christian Democratic Party of Work (SP or Stronnictwo Pracy) is formed. It joins a growing number of groups aimed at the authoritarian government.

November 5   Germany and Poland draw up "guiding principles" for the reciprocal treatment of each other's minorities. To finalize the agreement, German Chancellor Adolph Hitler himself receives the Polish ambassador. During their meeting Hitler twice reassures him that Poland's claim to Danzig and the Polish Corridor will remain unchallenged.

1938

January 10   Adam Koc resigns as head of OZON. He is replaced by Stanisław Skwaraznski, an army general. With this change of leadership, OZON's political significance declines. The intolerance it unleashed, though, remains strong.

January 13   The Germans begin a series of discussions with Polish Foreign Minster Józef Beck concerning Poland's views on their plan to annex Austria. He assures them that his nation is neutral on the matter. In return, the Nazis insist that they will respect Poland's claim to Danzig and the Corridor. On March 12, the Germans annex Austria.

March   Soviet dictator Joseph Stalin orders the dissolution of the Polish Communist party, feeling the Soviets have lost control of it. Many Polish communists had been imprisoned during the Piłsudski years, and those who could have fled to safety in the USSR. There they encountered Stalin's purges, and were charged as spies, capitalists, or other enemies of the state. The highest-ranking were executed, the others sent to gulags or concentration camps. The only ones to escape this fate are those who remain in Polish jails. This wave of Stalinist action signals a new round of Soviet-Polish tension, as Moscow openly criticizes Polish foreign policies, resumes its border raids, and closes several Polish consulates.

June   The leader of the Sejm dies. The deputies select Walery Sławek, former prime minister and Mościcki's enemies to replace him. Mościcki sees this as a symbol of defiance from the old Piłsudski faction.

September 13   Mościcki, in retaliation for the Sejm's insubordination by refusing to cooperate with him, dissolves the parliament and calls for new elections on November 6 and 13.

September 15   Hitler threatens war unless the Sudetenland region of Czechoslovakia, whose population is mostly German, is annexed to Germany. British Prime Minister Neville Chamberlain agrees to mediate the matter.

September 21   Taking advantage of Czechoslovakia's isolation during the Sudetenland crisis, Poland demands that the Czechoslovaks cede the Cieszyn region to Poland.

September 23   The Soviet government threatens to renounce its nonagression treaty if Poland invades Czechoslovakia (*see* July 25, 1932).

September 29   To stop the outbreak of war between Czechoslovakia and Germany, the Munich Agreement—part of a larger western strategy known as "appeasement''—gives over the Sudetenland region to Germany (*see* Czechoslovakia; September 7–30, 1938).

October In a move designed to expatriate thousands of Polish Jews living in Germany, the Polish government mandates that all Poles living abroad must have their passports revalidated by a Polish Consul. The consulate, however, will almost certainly refuse to validate any Jewish passport, intentionally depriving its owner of the right to reenter Poland. The Nazis, irate over this unwanted infusion of Jews, round up all the Polish Jews they can find—17,000 men, women, and children—lock them in cattle cars and send them back to Poland (*see* November 5, 1937). One couple swept up in this repatriation describes their ordeal in a letter to their son, who lives in France. In an attempt to bring the plight of the Jews to the world, he assassinates a German diplomat whom he mistakes for the ambassador. Although persecution of the Jews, including marking with the Star of David and harassing, had begun under Hitler's regime, this murder—along with other factors cited by Nazi Germany—served as an impetus for the Kristallnacht, ''night of broken glass,'' retaliation against Jews in Germany. The name is derived from the shards of broken glass left in the streets when Germans destroyed Jewish businesses by smashing their glass storefronts. Kristallnacht is eventually considered a turning point in the blatant persecution of Jews, culminating with the Holocaust.

October 1 Yielding to a Polish ultimatum for the immediate surrender of Cieszyn (*see* September 21), the weakened Czechoslovakia has no choice but to comply (*see* November 6, 1921). Polish troops move into the area the next day.

October 24 Having acquired both Austria and the Sudetenland, Hitler now begins to look eastward. No longer interested in Polish support for German ventures, the Nazis now pressure Poland to return Danzig to the Third Reich (*see* January 13). They also propose new highway and rail lines under joint Polish-German control across the Polish Corridor to connect Germany and East Prussia, and encourage Poland to join Germany's Anti-Comintern Pact against the USSR. In return, the Germans offer to extend their nonaggression treaty with Poland for an additional 25 years, and to guarantee Poland's borders.

October 31 Polish Foreign Secretary Józef Beck rejects Germany's proposal, and cautions that Poland will fight any German attempt to annex Danzig.

November 2 A further concession from Czechoslovakia gives Poland two small disputed border regions in northern Slovakia (*see* July 28, 1920).

November 6 and 13 Elections for the Sejm are dominated by OZON candidates, netting the government 75 percent of all seats while OZON holds almost the entire Senate. Once again, opposition parties boycott the elections (*see* September 8 and 15, 1935).

November 26 Poland and the Soviet Union reaffirm their nonaggression pact of July 25, 1932.

1939

January 5–6 Hitler warns the Polish ambassador to Germany that Danzig belongs to Germany and must be restored to the Reich.

January 25–27 German Foreign Minister Joachim von Ribbentrop visits Warsaw, and is bluntly told that Poland will not give up its rights to Danzig, nor will it join the Anti-Comintern Pact or allow highway or rail construction across the Corridor (*see* October 24, 1938).

March 15 Hitler destroys Czechoslovakia and seizes Bohemia and Moravia. The next day, the remainder of the country, the nominally independent Slovakia, is placed under German ''protection.''

March 21 The Germans demand the port city of Memel, with its mostly German population, from Lithuania. Two days later the country agrees. The Poles are now bordered by German-held territory on three sides, and realize that Hitler cannot be appeased.

March 22 Germany demands the return of Danzig, along with the rest of the Polish Corridor. Poland rejects the ultimatum, and Hitler prepares to invade Poland. He begins negotiations with Stalin to secure his cooperation, and secretly forces Romania to repudiate its Polish alliance.

March 31 Both Great Britain and France warn Germany that they will lend Poland ''all support in their power'' should Polish independence be threatened.

April 6 Confidential orders instruct Hitler's armies to prepare for ''Case White,'' the invasion of Poland and the capture of the Corridor.

April 28 Using Great Britain and France's assured defense of Poland as an excuse, Hitler declares that the Poles have abrogated their nonagression pact with Germany and that it is no longer binding (*see* January 26, 1934).

May 10 The Soviet deputy commissar for foreign affairs assures Beck that the USSR will remain neutral if Poland were attacked by Germany.

May 19 France signs a military protocol in which it agrees to defend Poland against any German aggression, promising to send troops within 15 days of a French mobilization, and to assist the British in bombing raids on German cities should war break out.

August 23 The Nazi-Soviet Nonagression Pact—also known as the Molotov-Ribbentrop Pact, in which the two dictators agree not to interfere with each other is signed. This removes Hitler's only real obstacle to a Polish invasion, and seals Poland's fate. In a secret codicil, Stalin and Hitler also plan to divide eastern Europe, including Poland, between them after the invasion.

August 25 Great Britain and Poland formalize the British and French guarantee of March 31. As part of the pact, Britain promises to bomb German targets should Hitler declare war on Poland.

August 29 Western Soviet garrisons are reinforced in preparation for the Russian occupation of eastern Poland.

August 31 Poland announces a full military mobilization.

September 1 Germany attacks Poland at dawn without a declaration of war—beginning World War II. The invasion proceeds so rapidly that the inadequate Polish defenses are often overrun or destroyed before they even realize they are under attack. The Germans quickly capture Polish communications codes, allowing them to decipher messages and transmit false ones.

September 3 Following their March 31 agreement with Poland, Great Britain and France declare war on Germany. The promised bombing raids and military reinforcements never materialize, however, because both France and Britain fear that the Nazis will retaliate. Poland is left to defend itself against the German blitzkrieg.

September 7 Rydz-Śmigły and the headquarters command flee from Warsaw to a series of new cities. By the fifteenth, they are in Kolomyja, close to the Romanian border. Mościcki and the rest of the government also retreat to the southeast. They eventually stop in Kuty, about 10 miles from Kolomyja and the military command. The Germans, able to intercept communications, follow both groups, bombing them wherever they go.

September 10 Rydz-Śmigły orders all troops to retreat to the southeast.

September 16 Polish military communications cease, unable to locate or coordinate troops.

September 17 Two Soviet army corps invade Poland from the east, fulfilling the terms of the Molotov-Ribbentrop Pact. The invasion is justified under the guise of ''protecting'' Belorussians and Ukrainians living in Poland.

Mościcki and his ministers cross the border into Romania. Under extreme pressure from the Germans (*see* March 22), the Romanians imprison them, but allow them to ''escape'' several months later.

September 18 Cut off from his troops, Marshal Rydz-Śmigły leaves for Romania; from there he makes his way to France. His departure leaves Polish troops to fight a hopeless battle without a leader or even instructions for surrender.

German and Soviet forces meet in the Polish city of Brest-Litovsk, completing the invasion.

September 21 The assault on Warsaw intensifies. When a propaganda blitz fails to induce surrender, Hitler orders an all-out assault by air and ground artillery on the city.

September 27 Warsaw surrenders after a valiant defense.

Nearly 100,000 Polish soldiers escape from Poland and are reorganized under French and British commands. Those who remain in Poland form an underground resistance force.

September 29 Germany and the Soviet Union renegotiate the Molotov-Ribbentrop Pact (*see* August 23), in which the dividing line is pushed eastward to the Bug River. In this division of territory, sometimes called the Fourth Partition, the Soviets get the eastern half of Poland, the Germans take the western portion. The Soviets begin to deport many Poles to the German sector. More than 1,700,000 others are forced into Soviet labor camps, where many of them die.

September 30 The interned President Mościcki resigns his post, and Polish politicians—mostly Piłsudski

The city of Danzig greets Adolph Hitler and his troops soon after the occupation.

opposition—who had managed to reach Paris form a government-in-exile. Władysław Raczkiewicz becomes president; General Władysław Sikorski, a long time Piłsudski adversary, is premier. Their main task is to form an army, which they man from Polish escapees and expatriate volunteers.

October 1 In order to keep Great Britain from declaring war on the USSR, British politician Winston Churchill does not condemn Soviet actions in Poland as he realizes that Britain and France could not possibly fight both Germany and Soviet Russia.

Nazi authorities in occupied Poland begin issuing laws modeled after those in Germany to isolate the Jewish population.

October 4–5 The Germans' final victory over the remnants of the Polish military is won near the central Polish town of Kock. The Nazi takeover is completed in just 36 days.

October 12 The Germans reorganize the conquered Polish lands. Pomerania, Silesia, Poznańia, and the Łódż district are incorporated directly into the Reich. The central part of the country becomes a colony called the General

Gouvernement; the capital is Kraków. It is administered by Hans Frank, a Nazi who views both Poles and Jews as subhumans. During the occupation, 1,300,000 Poles will be transported to Germany as slave labor for factories; another 2,000,000 will be taken from the annexed provinces and forced into the General Gouvernement area. Three million are shot, hanged, or tortured to death; another three million Jews—more than 80 percent of the Jewish population—perish in concentration camps. Three-quarters of a million Germans are relocated to Polish territory.

October 22   The Soviets supervise plebescites in occupied eastern Poland, ostensibly to further protect the rights of Belorussian and Ukrainian minorities in those provinces. Election results show 90-percent majority favors inclusion in the Soviet Union.

October 25   Hans Frank conscripts all Jewish men from 14 to 60 for obligatory government work. Some work in or near their homes; others are forced into labor camps.

October 26   British Foreign Minister Lord Halifax, in an attempt to avoid conflict with the Soviet Union over Poland, justifies the newly expanded Soviet border as a close approximation of the Curzon line (*see* December 8, 1919). This rationalization becomes the basis for the redrawn Polish-Soviet border after the war.

October 27   In town of Torun, the Nazis post a list of rules for Polish citizens. Among them: Germans will be served first in shops and in the marketplace, Polish men must raise their hats to German soldier, and Poles must yield to any Germans they encounter on the street. Anyone who fails to abide by these rules will face severe punishment.

November 1   The Supreme Soviet admits Polish Western Ukraine into the Soviet Union; the following day it admits Polish Belorussia (White Russia).

November 23   Jews are required to wear a Star of David armband on their right sleeve; their identification papers also designate them as Jews.

For Christian Poles, only the most elementary education is permitted to continue. Heinrich Himmler, leader of the SS, states: "For the non-Germanic population of the East there must be no schooling higher than . . . simple arithmetic . . . writing one's own name . . . and the lesson that it is a divine command to be obedient to the Germans."

1940

January 5   French prime minister Edouard Daladier and Polish premier Sikorski reorganize Polish armed forces under French command.

January 25   Hans Frank orders a million Polish agricultural and industrial workers—at least 50 percent of them women—to be sent to the Reich as forced labor.

February 21   SS Chief Heinrich Himmler establishes a "quarantine camp" for Polish prisoners at an old Austrian cavalry barracks just outside Oświęcim, or Auschwitz. Here Poles arrested for even minor infractions are interned and work under the harshest conditions.

February 24   British Prime Minister Chamberlain promises that both Polish and Czechoslovak independence will be restored after the war.

February 27   Large numbers of Poles, including priests, are executed in Katowice.

April 1   Jews are forced to dig ditches in preparation for the walls that will enclose the Warsaw ghetto.

May   The Soviets massacre thousands of captured Polish officers held in the Kozelsk prison camp and bury their bodies in mass graves in the Katyń Forest. The graves will not be discovered for three years (*see* December 1941; April 12, 1943).

May 1   A Jewish ghetto is cordoned off in Łódź with one hundred sixty thousand people. Police shoot anyone who approaches the barbed wire fence surrounding the area.

June 30   Himmler outlines a plan to resettle the annexed Polish territories with "strong German stock." In this scheme, one-eighth of the Polish population, deemed "racially acceptable," will be transferred to Germany; the seven-eighths remainder will be forced from their homes and into the General Gouvernement area. Farms will be parceled out to German soldiers, who will work the land with the help of serf-like Polish laborers.

October 2   Warsaw's ghetto walls are almost complete (*see* April 1). The city's German governor orders all Jews confined to the area, which covers most of the old Jewish quarter. Before November 15, when it is finally sealed off, 80,000 Christians will be evicted and almost 140,000 Jews crowded in. By the following summer, more than 18,000 people will die from starvation in the Warsaw and Łódź ghettos. Ghettos are established in other Polish cities as well.

1941

June 22   "Operation Barbarossa:" Germany invades the Soviet Union, moving first through Soviet-held eastern Poland. As German troops advance, they slaughter the

One of the most notorious Nazi death camps, Auschwitz.

Jewish population. By the end of the year, they have killed 1.4 million people.

June 24   Soviet planes bomb Warsaw.

July 30   With Germany and the USSR now at war, the Soviets try to mend the bridges burned when they invaded Poland in 1939. Premier Sikorski and the Soviet ambassador to Great Britain Ivan Maisky sign an agreement restoring diplomatic relations between their two countries. In the pact, the Soviets repudiate their territorial gains of 1939 (*see* September 17, 1939), but refuse to promise that prewar borders will be restored. They also agree to support a Polish army on Soviet soil and to free all Polish prisoners, both military and civilian.

August 14   The Polish and Soviet governments organize an eastern Polish army. Gen. Władysław Anders is freed from a Soviet prison to command the force.

October 15   Twenty thousand Jews and five thousand Gypsies are deported from Germany and sent to the Łódź ghetto, by now a bastion of starvation and disease. In Warsaw, death sentences are prescribed for Jews who leave the ghetto without permission and for anyone found to be sheltering Jews.

November   A small group of Polish communists, including Władysław Gomułka, parachute into German-occupied Poland to help run the resistance.

December   Sikorski and Anders meet with Stalin and Molotov in Moscow to discuss the whereabouts of several thousand missing Polish officers captured by the Soviets in 1939. The Polish generals know that at least 15,000 officers were among the more than 200,000 troops captured by the Soviets, yet when Anders forms his Polish force, only about 450 officers can be found. The Soviets deny any knowledge about the rest of the officers. Still, Anders manages to assemble two Polish divisions (75,000 men) in the USSR.

December 1   A conference of pro-Soviet Poles meets in Saratov under the leadership of Alfred Lampe and Wanda Wasilewska, both prewar members of the Communist Party of Poland.

December 4   At Britain's prompting, Sikorski signs a treaty with Stalin that promises "in peacetime the relations between the two states will be based on the principles of good neighborly collaboration, friendship, and the honest mutual observance of obligations agreed upon by both

Polish women and children wait to be led off—many to concentration camps—by Nazi soldiers during the destruction of Warsaw.

sides.'' There is still no assurance, however, that Poland will regain its lost territory after the war.

December 16 Hoping to keep the territory he gained during the 1939 invasion, Stalin suggests that the Polish-Soviet border be drawn at the Curzon Line (*see* October 26, 1939).

December 24 Already starved and living in the most squalid conditions, Jews in Warsaw are further ordered to surrender their furs and boots to the Germans. During this month in western Poland, over 1,000 Jews (and many Gypsies) are taken each day to the town of Chelmno, where they are herded into vans and driven to a neighboring forest. During the drive the van compartment is flooded with a toxic gas, killing the occupants.

1942

January Nazi officials, meeting at the Wannsee Conference, decide to deport all European Jews to concentration camps in Poland, where they will either be gassed or

worked to death. Half of the six million Jews murdered in the course of Hitler's Final Solution will be Polish.

January 5 The Communist Party of Poland, dissolved by Stalin in March 1938, is now resurrected as the Polish Workers Party (Polska Partia Robotnicza, or PPR).

January 19 The Polish and Czechoslovak governments-in-exile agree to a postwar union of their countries that may also include other countries. Soviet opposition, fearing a large European state on their border, soon kills the plan.

February 14 The Home Army (Armia Krajowa) unites most underground groups, coordinating sabotage and counterintelligence activities, while planning for an eventual uprising against the German occupiers. The Communists will later form a separate military organization, the People's Guard (Gwardia Ludowa).

July 7 The Soviet Union, in an agreement with Churchill, transfers General Anders's army to the Near East and Mediterranean.

July 19 Himmler orders the General Gouvernement "cleansed" of Jews by the end of the year. German authorities begin the first large scale deportations of Jews from the Warsaw ghetto directly to death camps.

July 28 Desperate Warsaw ghetto residents form the Jewish Fighting Organization in a futile attempt to resist further deportations.

1943

January 16 Moscow announces that Poles in border regions are considered Soviet citizens and will be drafted into the Red Army.

January 18–21 Deportations provoke fighting with the Germans in the Warsaw ghetto during which six hundred die fighting. Despite these actions, another 6,000 will be deported and die in the gas chambers.

February 4 The Soviet government appeals to all Poles still on Soviet territory to join a new Polish army that will be formed in the USSR.

March The Polish government-in-exile in London flatly demands that the Soviets restore Poland's prewar borders. Stalin, however, ignores the Poles.

April 12 German troops discover the bodies of thousands of Polish officers buried in mass graves in the Katyń Forest (*see* May 1940). The dead, whose identities are discerned from papers still on their uniforms, had been held at Soviet prison camps. The Germans and Soviets accuse each other of the executions.

April 17 Polish authorities, who had been searching for the dead soldiers, ask the International Red Cross to investigate. Nine days later the Soviets use this situation as an excuse to sever diplomatic relations with the Polish government-in-exile, calling reports of Soviet guilt in the Katyń Forest massacre "a hideous Gestapo frameup." From this point on, Stalin ignores the London-based Poles and begins to establish instead a puppet government of pro-Soviet Polish communists that he will later install in Warsaw.

April 19 Another round of deportations causes the Warsaw ghetto to erupt in a courageous final revolt. Twelve hundred Jews, armed at first with only 17 rifles, fight the Germans in houses, streets, and sewers, capturing weapons as best they can. Despite their efforts, 7,000 are killed, and another 7,000 are deported. Ten thousand flee to Christian Warsaw, but many are later caught.

May 8 The Warsaw Ghetto Uprising is finally crushed, but sporadic fighting continues for another month. The Nazis order the entire ghetto destroyed and deport its remaining inhabitants to concentration camps. Ghettos in Białystok and Vilnius also organize armed resistances during spring and summer 1943, but they too are ultimately futile.

July 4 Prime Minister Sikorski, leader of the Polish government in exile, is killed in a plane crash at Gibraltar. Stanisław Mikołajczyk, head of the Peasant party, succeeds him.

July 12 German soldiers kill every man, woman, and child in the small village of Michniow, an act of terror designed to strengthen Nazi rule. The next day 48 Poles—including 14 children—are executed when their village fails to deliver its quota of foodstuffs.

November Władysław Gomułka becomes the leader of the Polish Communist Party.

November 28–December 1 The Tehran Conference convenes, bringing together U.S. President Franklin D. Roosevelt, British Prime Minister Winston Churchill, and Soviet leader Joseph Stalin to discuss war strategy and the future peace. Stalin insists that he will retain Polish territory up to the Curzon line. This constitutes one third of prewar Poland—including the cities of Lwów and Vilnius—and contains five million people. Roosevelt and Churchill pressure Poland to accept the plan, offering German territories in the west as compensation. Mikołajczyk and his cabinet refuse to yield. Despite their protest, however, Roosevelt and Churchill agree to Stalin's demand.

December 31 Stalin forms the National Home Council (Krojowa Rada Narodowa, or KRN) from the Polish Workers Party (PPR). This group becomes the government of the pro-Soviet Polish People's Republic. Bolesław Bierut, a trusted Comintern aide, heads the new group.

1944

January 1 Stalin creates a pro-Soviet provisional government, the Polish National Council, in defiance of the Polish government-in-exile in London. The People's Guard regroups as the People's Army (Armia Ludowa) under the command of General Michał Rola-Żymierski (*see* February 14, 1942).

January 6 Soviets capture the eastern Polish town of Rokitno, 12 miles inside the 1939 Polish border. The Polish government in London instructs underground forces not to impede the Soviet advance.

January 11 The Soviet Union guarantees Poland's postwar independence if the Curzon Line becomes the border between the two states.

January 14 The Polish government-in-exile offers to discuss outstanding problems with the Soviets if the United States and Britain act as intermediaries. The United States accepts the following day.

January 28 In Warsaw, Nazi authorities order the public hanging of 102 Roman Catholic Poles.

February 3 Three hundred citizens of Warsaw are executed by the Germans in reprisal for the assassination of a Warsaw SS commander.

February 12 The Union of Polish Patriots announces that it has organized a national government on Polish soil.

February 20 Churchill proposes that Poland be allowed to keep Lwów and Vilnius in any postwar settlement. Stalin calls the suggestion an ''insult.''

March A new Polish army, commanded by General Zygmunt Berling, is formed on Soviet territory (*see* February 4, 1943).

Polish troops under Allied command play a decisive role in the Battle of Monte Cassino, Italy.

June 10 The Germans launch Operation Hurricane, a search for Polish partisans. In the village of Pikule, where resistance fighters are found, more than 40 people are executed in reprisal.

June 18 A second Operation Hurricane kills 700 partisans in the Lublin region.

June 23 The Union of Polish Patriots repudiates the Polish government-in-exile in London.

July 7 Gen. Kazimierz Sosnkowski succeeds the deceased Sikorski and becomes commander in chief of the Polish armed forces. Foreseeing Nazi defeat and Soviet advance, he warns Gen. Tadeusz Komorowski-Bór, commander of the Home Army, that it is imperative to establish Polish control of critical areas and preempt a Soviet takeover.

July 17 Soviet troops reach the Curzon Line and cross the Bug River the next day.

July 21 Bolesław Bierut establishes the Polish Committee of National Liberation (Polski Komitet Wyzwolenia Narodowego, or PKWN) with help from the Union of Polish Patriots. Known as the Lublin Committee, the body declares itself to be ''the sole legal Polish executive power,'' a direct challenge to Mikołajczyk and the London Poles. The Lublin Committee is controlled by the Soviets and chaired by Edward Osóbka-Morawski, a Stalin puppet.

July 23 Soviet troops liberate Lublin and find the Majdanek death camp—the first to be discovered by Allied forces.

July 24 The Polish government in exile denounces the Lublin Committee.

July 25 As Soviet troops advance westward and Nazi defeat seems certain, Mikołajczyk informs general Bór that he has full power to order an uprising in Warsaw.

July 26 The Lublin Committee, at Stalin's behest, assumes civil leadership in Soviet-occupied Poland.

July 28 Marshal Konstantin Rokossovsky's Red Army troops advance toward Warsaw.

July 29 Mikołajczyk flies to Moscow, trying to reconcile the Soviets and the London Poles.

July 30 Radio broadcasts from Moscow announce that Soviet troops have reached the Warsaw suburb of Praga.

August 1 Sure of imminent Soviet support, General Bór orders the Home Army to recapture Warsaw from the Germans, despite warnings from General K. Sosnkowski, commander in chief or the London-based forces. The surprise revolt, known as the Warsaw Uprising, is initially successful, and within a few days the Poles control much of the city. When Stalin learns of the uprising, however, he orders Rokossovsky to halt his advance. The Germans, meanwhile, retaliate by pummeling Warsaw with massive artillery and bombing raids.

August 4 In an attempt to aid the insurgents, Churchill orders 13 planeloads of weapons and supplies to be flown from Italy to Poland. Only two of the planes make it to Warsaw, and half of the parcels intended for the Poles fall into German hands. Rokossovsky's army, on the other side of the Vistula, does nothing.

August 6 The remaining inhabitants of the Łódż ghetto are deported to Auschwitz.

August 16 Red Army leader Rokossovsky waits on the Vistula while Warsaw and the Home Army are destroyed. Stalin orders his troops not to enter the city until the Nazis have crushed all resistance, clearing the way for a Soviet takeover. To ensure the Poles' helplessness, Stalin orders nearby airstrips closed to Allied planes, which prevents any supplies from being delivered.

September 6 The Lublin Committee expropriates property in excess of 250 acres. Eventually, even property half that size will be seized, and businesses employing more than 50 people will be nationalized.

September 11 Bierut assumes the presidency of the new provisional government.

September 14 Rokossovsky liberates Praga (a Warsaw suburb on the eastern bank of the Vistula) but makes no attempt to cross the river as the Germans lay waste to Warsaw.

October 2   General Bór surrenders, and the Warsaw Uprising is over. Two hundred thousand civilians are dead, along with 15,000 Home Army troops and 10,000 Germans. Hitler orders the city completely destroyed and its remaining populace, some 700,000 people, evicted.

1945

January 1   The Lublin Committee declares itself the new provisional government of Poland.

January 4   Despite British and American protests, Stalin recognizes the Lublin Committee as the legitimate government of Poland, ignoring the exiled London Poles.

January 17   Warsaw is captured by the Soviets.

January 27   Soviet troops reach Auschwitz.

February 4–11   The Yalta Conference convenes. The Allies set Poland's eastern frontier at the Curzon Line and agree to add some German territory (to be determined later) in the west. Britain and the United States promise to endorse the Lublin Committee, provided it is expanded to include ''democratic elements . . . from within Poland and abroad.'' Stalin concurs, promising to ensure free elections. The Polish government in London protests.

March 6   The Soviets arrest and/or kill anyone active in the Home Army or suspected of loyalty to the exiled Polish government. Thousands are sent to Soviet labor camps.

March 27   Soviet secret police arrest 16 Polish underground leaders and deport them to the USSR for trial. Twelve will later receive prison terms ranging from four months to 10 years; the rest are acquitted.

April 22   Edward Osóbka-Morawski, the chairman of the Lublin Committee, signs a 20-year treaty of friendship, mutual assistance, and postwar cooperation with the Soviet Union.

April 23   American president Harry S Truman criticizes Soviet actions in Poland during a White House meeting with Soviet foreign minister Molotov.

May 7   Germany surrenders to the Allies signalling the end of World War II in Europe. Close to six million Poles are dead, three million of them Jews. Approximately 40 percent of Poland's industrial capacity and 35 percent of its agricultural potential is destroyed.

May 21   During a plenum of the Polish Workers Party (PPR), the first secretary complains that many Poles regard members of the PPR as foreign agents.

June 19   Polish troops seize Cieszyn. The Soviet Union invites representatives from Czechoslovakia and Poland to Moscow to discuss this and other matters affecting their mutual relations. Poland eventually returns the region.

June 28   Following Stalin's promise to enlarge the Lublin Committee, a new provisional government (Tymczasowy Rząd) is formed, this one a coalition of five parties: the PPR, the Polish Socialist Party, the Peasant Party, the Democratic Party, and the Labor Party. Of the 21 ministers in the cabinet, only five are from the government exiled in London. Bolesław Bierut is acting president; Mikołajczyk is vice premier. Free elections are promised for the future.

July 5   Britain and America officially recognize the new government and withdraw support from the London Poles.

July 17–August 2   The Potsdam Conference convenes with U.S. President Truman, British prime minister Clement Attlee, and Joseph Stalin. To compensate for Stalin's land appropriation in the east, Poland is given all German territory west of its 1937 border to the Oder-Neiße line, as well as the provinces of Pomerania and Silesia; East Prussia is divided between the Poles and the Soviets. The Allies also agree to deport the remaining three million Germans from Poland to Ally-controlled Germany (four million had already fled the approaching Soviet armies) and to relocate the millions of Poles in the Soviet sector to the newly acquired German territories.

August 16   A treaty between Poland and the USSR fixes their border at the Curzon Line (*see* November 28–December 1, 1943). In this westward shift Poland loses 69,290 square miles of territory in the east and gains 39,596 in the west. In addition, Poland will receive 15 percent of all reparations paid by Germany to the USSR.

August 22   Mikołajczyk establishes a new Peasant Party (Polskie Stronnictwo Ludowe).

September   Former members of the Home Army, hoping to prevent a communist takeover, form the Association of Freedom and Independence (Wyzwolenie i Niepodległość). The organization will fight the Communists until February 1947, primarily in the Lublin and Białystok regions.

1946

For a number of years following the war, resistance groups remain active. Many of these groups are composed of former Home Army units who refuse to accept the communist takeover of the country. Hiding out in remote corners of the country, these units constantly harass government

A battle-torn Warsaw—Poland's capital—in the aftermath of World War II.

troops. They are finally stamped out in 1948, and then only with the aid of special Soviet antiguerilla units sent in for the purpose.

It is estimated that from 1946 to 1949, more than six thousand Poles are executed by the Communists, due either to continued postwar resistance or mere membership in wartime resistance movements.

January 3 The government nationalizes all industries with over 50 workers.

February 14 Polish and British representatives of the Allied Combined Repatriation Executive in Berlin agree on the repatriation of millions of Germans to the West (*see* July 17–August 2, 1945).

May 12 Stefan Wyszyński becomes bishop of Lublin.

June 30 A national referendum takes place on the issues of the acquisition of the western territories, land distribution, industrialization, and the proposed abolition of the upper house in the Polish legislature. Contrary to the Communists, who want a resounding ''yes'' vote on each issue, Vice Premier Mikołajczyk advises his party's adherents to vote ''yes'' on all but abolishing the Senate. The results are 10 days late. Thirty-two percent voted against

abolishing the Senate; 92 percent approved the western border issue. Polish Communists now begin to characterize Mikołajczyk as a tool of foreign agencies bent on destabilizing Poland.

July 4 A pogrom kills 42 Polish Jews in Kielce. Since the end of the war Jews have been attacked throughout the country as they attempt to return to their homes.

August 5 Poland and the USSR sign an agreement ending the Soviet occupation of the Oder region and giving control to Polish officials.

October 16 Hans Frank, found guilty of war crimes and crimes against humanity, is hanged at Nuremberg. The following day his body, along with those of other war criminals, is taken to Dachau, and burned in the crematorium there; that night their ashes are dropped into a river on the outskirts of Munich.

1947

January 17–19 The first general elections are held, during which the police intimidate the non-Communist opposition. Although decried by the Western powers as undemocratic, Mikołajczyk's Peasant Party claims to have received 84 percent of all votes. Nonetheless, the Communist-controlled bloc is awarded 382 seats out of 444 in parliament, claiming almost 90 percent of the vote. The United States and Great Britain protest that the elections are not being carried out freely or fairly as agreed to in Yalta in 1945 (*see* February 4–11, 1945).

February 5–6 Bolesław Bierut is elected president, and the Socialist Józef Cyrankiewicz becomes premier.

February 19 The Communist government passes a new, democratic constitution, but it never goes into effect.

April 4 The vice minister of defense, General Karol Świerczewski, is killed by members of the Ukrainian Insurrection Army, an organization dedicated to a free and independent Ukrainian state. Świerczewski was a veteran Communist and soldier. His death leads the government to begin a series of reprisals against Ukrainian villages in the Bieszczady mountains and the forcible dispersal and deportation of many of the minority populations in the Lemko and Bojko areas.

April 30 The USSR and Poland sign a treaty recognizing their mutual borders.

July 7 Under Soviet pressure, Poland is forced to reject an invitation to participate in the Marshall Plan, a U.S.-sponsored economic program to help rebuild war-ravaged Europe. The plan did not include Soviet-dominated countries.

July 23 The United States ends its foreign aid—begun toward the end of World War II—to Poland.

September 14 Indicating that the Communists are in full control, Poland denounces its February 10, 1925, Concordat with the Vatican and begins a long campaign against the church.

October 5 Poland is a founding member of the Communist Information Bureau (Cominform), a Soviet-dominated organization that coordinates the international Communist movement and is a successor to the Comintern.

November 3 Mikołajczyk flees to London after having been falsely accused of treason on October 12. No significant internal opposition to the Communist takeover of power remains in Poland.

1948

January 26 The Soviet Union and Poland sign a five-year trade treaty that will increase trade between the two nations by 15 percent and provide Poland with credits of $450 million in the form of industrial equipment and machinery.

March Prime Minister Cyrankiewicz goes to Moscow to meet with Stalin to discuss formation of a united Polish Workers party.

May 3 The government bans the celebration of Constitution Day. This holiday, established in 1919, commemorates the 1791 liberal constitution, which was an attempt to revive the country, which had suffered a devastating seizure of land in 1773.

June The Plenum of the Polish Workers Party (PPR) Central Committee praises the historical trends of Polish communism and socialism, an act interpreted as open defiance of Moscow.

June 26 Another five-year trade agreement is signed with the Soviet Union. This agreement is meant as a counterbalance to the U.S. Marshall Plan, which Poland and other Eastern bloc countries were forbidden to join (*see* July 7, 1947). This new agreement is meant as a substitute for the aid that the Marshall Plan would have given Poland.

September 3 As part of an ongoing struggle within the PPR, Władysław Gomułka is forced to relinquish his post as general secretary of the party because of "nationalist deviation." He reportedly opposed agrarian collectivization, Soviet control of the Cominform, and espoused a national form of communism much like the Yugoslavs.

December 15–22 At a congress in Warsaw, the Polish United Worker's Party (Polska Zjednoczona Partia Robotnicza, PZPR) is formed as a result of the forced merger of the Socialists with the Communists; National Home Council (KRN) leader Bolesław Bierut becomes its first secretary (*see* March).

1949

January Bp. Stefan Wyszyński of Lublin becomes the archbishop of Warsaw and primate of Poland (*see* May 12, 1946).

January 11 German lands given to Poland after World War II are officially incorporated into Poland.

January 21 Gomułka is again demoted for deviating from the Communist party line (*see* September 3, 1948).

January 25 Poland becomes a founding member of the Council for Mutual Economic Assistance (CMEA, COMECON). This Soviet-dominated organization of Eastern bloc nations coordinates their economic cooperation with the USSR and themselves.

July 13   The pope excommunicates all Communist Party members from the Roman Catholic church.

August 5   The government enacts a law that guarantees freedom of religion with heavy penalties for people attempting to force religion on others or trying to use religion as a means to exert political pressure.

September 30   Following the USSR's lead in isolating Yugoslavia from the Communist world since it will not follow the party line dictated by Moscow, Poland revokes its 1946 treaty of friendship and mutual assistance with Yugoslavia.

October 28   The government expels the International Refugee Organization and the International Red Cross claiming that they are tools of the West.

November 7   At the "request" of the Polish government, Soviet marshal Konstantin Rokossovsky becomes the Polish defense minister and marshal of the Polish army. Rokossovsky is of Polish descent, being born in Warsaw in 1896, but he is completely Russified. He, in turn, appoints a large number of Soviet advisers and officers to positions in the Polish army. He imposes an organizational structure of the armed forces that copies Soviet model, even in the design of the uniform.

November 14   The PZPR expels Gomułka (*see* January 21).

1950

March 1   Poland withdraws from the International Monetary Fund (IMF), a United Nations affiliated agency that takes responsibility for stabilizing international exchange rates and payments.

April 14   The government and the Roman Catholic church sign an agreement providing for religious toleration and recognizing the pope as the head of the church in Poland. In return the Catholic church in Poland agrees to support the government in foreign affairs.

June 1   The number of Polish provinces *(wojewodztwo)* is increased from 14 to 17 by the creation of three new regions in the western territory taken from Germany.

July 6   The German Democratic Republic, or East Germany, signs a treaty with Poland that recognizes the Oder-Neiße line as the legitimate border between the two states and renounces claims to former German territories now in Poland and the Soviet Union.

July 21   The parliament passes a Six-Year Economic Plan (1950–55) that emphasizes heavy industry.

October 29   In a further attempt to control the Polish economy, the Soviets tie the Polish currency, the złoty, to the Soviet ruble, thereby reducing its convertability with western or hard currencies. Furthermore, all precious metals and foreign currencies are to be turned over to the authorities under threat of heavy penalties.

1951

February 15   Poland and the USSR exchange about 185 square miles of Polish territory in Lublin province for a Soviet area of similar size in the Carpathian mountains.

August 2   The authorities arrest Gomułka for "nationalist deviation." He spends three years under house detention (*see* November 14, 1949).

1952

January 5   Due to the excesses of Communism in Poland, the cancellation of the American Most Favored Nation status for Poland goes into effect, which raises tariffs and other duties on Polish goods imported into the U.S., making them more expensive.

July 22   A new constitution, based on the 1936 Soviet constitution, proclaims Poland to be a country building socialism. The office of the presidency is abolished and replaced by a Council of State; Bolesław Bierut becomes premier of the new Polish People's Republic (Polska Rzeczpospolita Ludowa) in late November.

August 1   A new law grants all citizens 18 years of age or older the right to vote, whereas anyone 21 years of age or older can run for an office.

October 26   Parliamentary elections take place that result in almost 99 percent of the votes being cast in favor of the single, Communist slate.

November 29   Abp. Stefan Wyszyński of Warsaw is elevated to cardinal (*see* January 1949).

1953

February 9   The government passes a law that gives it the exclusive right to make all appointments to religious offices.

March 5   Soviet dictator Joseph Stalin dies.

March 19   Following the example of the Soviet Union, which, since the death of Stalin, has had a collective leadership, Bierut resigns as premier to be succeeded by Józef Cyrankiewicz. Bierut retains the post of first secretary of the PZPR.

May 8   The Roman Catholic hierarchy protests the February 9 law in a letter to the government.

September 26   The government arrests Stefan *Kardynat* (Cardinal) Wyszyński, primate of Poland, for alleged conspiracy against the state and interns him in a monastery, where he remains until 1956.

December 17   In an attempt to end the government's campaign against the church, the Roman Catholic hierarchy takes an oath of loyalty to the Polish Communist regime and state.

1954

February 25   The United States orders Polish consulates to close in Chicago, Detroit, and New York due to poor relations between the United States and the Communist government in Poland.

February 27   In retaliation for the closure of three of its consulates in the United States, Poland orders the United States to close its consulate in Gdańsk.

March 10–17   The Second Party Congress of the PZPR meets to discuss the terrible condition of agriculture caused by collectivization.

December   The government abolishes the ministry of security following unsavory revelations in the West about its conduct by a former member of the ministry. Its former duties are split by the new ministry of home affairs and the committee of state security.

The government releases former Communist Party leader Władysław Gomułka from house arrest (*see* August 2, 1951).

1955

February 18   The government officially ends the state of war with Germany in existence since September 1, 1939.

May 14   The Warsaw Pact, a treaty of friendship, cooperation, and mutual assistance, is signed in Warsaw by Poland, Albania, Bulgaria, Czechoslovakia, Hungary, Romania, East Germany, and the Soviet Union. This Soviet-controlled defensive alliance is aimed at the Western alliance of NATO.

Poland ends diplomatic relations with the Vatican.

1956

March 12   First Secretary Bolesław Bierut dies in Moscow at the age of 64 after attending the Twentieth Congress of the Communist Party of the Soviet Union. Four days later, he is buried in Warsaw.

March 20   Edward Ochab, a veteran Communist, is elected first secretary of the Polish United Workers Party (PZPR) Central Committee, and he begins to prepare for the return of Gomułka to public life (*see* December 1954).

April 10   Gomułka is officially "rehabilitated;" all charges are dropped and he is readmitted to party membership.

June 28   Spontaneous riots erupt in Poznań over sudden price increases. Over fifty-thousand workers strike and demonstrate for better living conditions. A workers' procession clashes with the army, during which more than 70 die and hundreds are wounded. This represents the first major challenge to the legitimacy of the Communist system.

July   Due to the poor results, the government calls off its agrarian collectivization policy.

July 23–28   Edward Gierek is elected to Politburo of PZPR.

August 5   The PZPR restores the membership of Władysław Gomułka. Other party members purged in the early 1950s will also have their memberships returned.

August 25–26   More than one million Poles take part in a pilgrimage to Jasna Góra monastery in Częstochowa to mark the 300th anniversary of the defeat of the Swedes here, sometimes referred to as the Battle of Częstochowa. Not only is it a celebration of the military victory, but an expression of anti-communism.

September 18   The Soviet Union and Poland sign an agreement for large-scale Soviet aid to the Polish economy.

October 19   Gomułka meets with Soviet leaders Nikita Khrushchev and V. M. Molotov, who arrive in Warsaw uninvited to try to block Gomułka's election as first secretary. Gomułka convinces the Soviet leaders that he will keep Poland within the Communist orbit.

October 21   A "rehabilitated" Gomułka is elected as first secretary of PZPR. He replaces Ochab, regarded by Khrushchev as being "anti-Soviet." Strong Stalinists in Politburo are pushed aside, and Gomułka begins to introduce some liberal reforms. This reform era is eventually characterized as "Spring in October" to try to show the blossoming of a new age in the country.

October 22   Demonstrations in support of the Poles, and against the Soviets and Polish Stalinists take place in

First Secretary of the Polish United Workers Party,
Władysław Gomułka.

the Hungarian capital of Budapest, leading to the outbreak
of a revolution in Hungary (*see* Hungary; October 1956).

October 28   The authorities release Cardinal Wyszyński
from detention in a monastery (*see* September 26, 1953).

November 13   Marshal Rokossovsky, whose army put
an end to the June 28 Poznań demonstration, is relieved of
his posts of vice premier and defense minister. He and 32
other Soviet officers in the Polish army return to Moscow.
Rokossovsky will be appointed Soviet deputy minister of
defense later in the month.

November 14–18   Gomułka travels to Moscow, where
he signs the Five Point Declaration, putting Soviet-Polish
relations on a better footing by reaffirming the Soviet-
Polish friendship, cooperation, and mutual assistance alliance from April 22, 1945. Among other issues, the partners
swear to uphold Poland's western border with Germany.

November 21   In the United Nations the Polish delegation abstains from the vote condemning Soviet intervention
to suppress the Hungarian revolution.

December 17   Poland and the USSR sign an agreement permitting Soviet military forces to remain "temporarily" in Poland.

1957

January 20   Stalinist elements in the party win the
general elections.

February 27   A new government headed by Józef
Cyrankiewicz shows that the Stalinists are in control of the
country.

March 25   The USSR and Poland sign an agreement for
the further repatriation of Polish nationals from the Soviet
Union.

May   The Economic Advisory Council urges the government to grant state-owned business greater autonomy.

June 7   The United States grants two loans to Poland
totaling approximately $49 million.

October 2   In response to the growing strength of
"dogmatists," or Stalinists, within the party, Gomułka
decides to toughen his stand somewhat by ordering the
closing of the revisionist periodical *Po Prostu* (To Put It
Plainly). This action elicits street protests by the populace
in Warsaw over the next four days, which special riot
police brutally suppress.

Foreign Minister Adam Rapacki reveals a plan at the
United Nations to create a "nuclear free zone" out of the
two Germanies, Czechoslovakia, and Poland. It will be
rejected by the Western powers in April 1958.

1958

February   The lower house of Parliament (Sejm) announces the organization of a national celebration for the
1,000th anniversary of the founding of the Polish state.
This celebration is meant to counter a similar church-
sponsored celebration of the millennium of Polish Christianity, both scheduled for 1966.

1959

July 31   The government proclaims a "Meatless Mondays" campaign to deal with the shortage of meat that has
resulted due to problems with collectivization and poor
transportation problems resulting from bad central economic planning. People are asked to refrain from buying
meat on Mondays.

August 2–5   American vice president Richard M.
Nixon receives an enthusiastic welcome during an official
visit to the country.

1960

July 17   A celebration at Grunwald commemorates the 550th anniversary of the defeat of the Teutonic Knights by King Władysław Jagiełło at that site in 1410.

1961

January   The government decrees that religion can no longer be taught in public schools.

April 15   In elections to the Sejm, the populace reveals tremendous apathy by refraining from noting or casting blank ballots, reflecting doubts that the PZPR is actually capable of instituting meaningful reforms.

1962

February   The authorities close the Club of the Crooked Circle in Warsaw. The club had been a center for revisionist thinkers across the political spectrum. The three most important figures in the club were Witold Jedlicki, Jan Józef Lipski, and Aleksander Malachowski.

October 8   At a meeting of the Second Vatican Council in Rome, Pope John XXIII addresses the Polish bishops at the council and speaks of the "western territories regained by Poland after centuries." The Communist authorities in Poland make a great deal out of what is portrayed as Vatican support for Polish gains achieved by the PZPR.

1963

January 6   Cardinal Wyszyński protests against a plan to place government observers in religion classes.

March 7   Poland and the German Federal Republic, or West Germany, sign a trade treaty.

October   Three days of riots occur in Przemyśl after authorities close a convent school.

November 22   Poland orders an official mourning period for assassinated American president John F. Kennedy, who was very popular with the Poles.

December   The Polish government agrees to the nomination of Karol Wojtyła as bishop of Kraków.

1964

March 14   Thirty-four intellectuals, including writer Jerzy Andrzejewski and literary historian Julian Krzyżanowski, sign a complaint, the so-called "Letter 34," to Prime Minister Cyrankiewicz protesting a "change in Polish cultural policies" and stressing the need to adhere "to the spirit of the laws in the constitution" for greater freedom of expression. The government responds with a storm of denunciations in the press, radio, and television. The whole affair, however, has an electrifying effect on Polish youth, especially at the University of Warsaw, which, from this point on, becomes a center of revisionism.

November 14   The authorities arrest Karol Modżelewski and Jacek Kuroń after police raid the home of Modżelewski and find a manuscript critical of the regime written by both men. The two intellectuals, the sons of high party officials, are released awaiting trial.

November 24   The Polish Communist Party (PZPR) expels both Modżelewski and Kuroń from its ranks for their manuscript. As a result they write an "Open Letter" to the party, which is an in-depth, critical analysis of the functioning of the Communist bureaucracy; the "Open Letter" is also released to the public.

1965

April 8   Poland and the Soviet Union sign a 20-year treaty of friendship, cooperation, and mutual assistance, renewing their pact from April 22, 1945.

July   Modżelewski and Kuroń each receive three-year prison sentences for their manuscript criticizing the regime (*see* November 24, 1964).

1966

May 3   The millennium of Christianity in Poland is celebrated, but without the participation of Pope Paul VI, who does not receive government permission to enter the country (*see* February 1958).

October 21   The government makes no special attempt to celebrate the tenth anniversary of the "Spring in October," which brought Gomułka to power. However, students at the University of Warsaw hold a massive demonstration to mark the event, during which they demand the release of Modżelewski and Kuroń (*see* July 1965).

October 22   The PZPR expels from the party Leszek Kółakowski, a philosophy professor at the University of

Warsaw and former editor of *Po Prostu,* (Quite Simply) for giving the chief address at the October 21 rally.

1967

March 1 Poland and Czechoslovakia renew their friendship and mutual assistance pact from 1947 for another 20 years. The treaty, aimed at possible West German territorial claims against Poland and Czechoslovakia, furthermore declares the borders of both countries as inviolable.

June 5–11 The Arab-Israeli Six-Day War unleashes vigorous public opinion in favor of Israel, over what the Poles view as Soviet client states (the Arab countries). In an effort to appease Moscow, First Secretary Gomułka responds by breaking diplomatic relations with Israel and by starting an "anti-Zionist" drive after claiming there is a "Zionist fifth-column" in Poland. Gomułka's campaign drives thousands of the remaining Polish Jews out of the country.

1968

January 30 The police close down the play *Dziady* (Forefather's Eve) by Poland's greatest romantic poet of the nineteenth century, Adam Mickiewicz, due to its anti-Russian tone. Students respond by protesting at the statue of Adam Mickiewicz in Warsaw; several students are arrested.

March 2 The Writer's Union condemns the government's policy of repression in the arts.

March 8–11 University of Warsaw students protest the arrests of fellow students and the January 30 closing of *Dziady.* The peaceful demonstrations take on pro-Czechoslovak reformist ideals with a show of support for the liberalized Dubcek regime.

March 11 Police and worker "allies" attack the students at the University of Warsaw, resulting in an eight-hour battle that ends the student demonstrations.

March 13–July 9 Interior Minister Mieczysław Moczar, a conservative nationalist with strong connections to the officer corps and veteran's groups, leads an anti-Zionist campaign as part of a bid for power within the party and state. Roughly 10,000 Jews, many of them important members of the intelligentsia, emigrate permanently (*see* June 1967).

March 14 University students in Kraków go on strike in a show of solidarity with their fellow students in War-

saw. The student strikes quickly spread to other regions of Poland.

March 19 Although he initiated the anti-Zionist drive in June 1967, Gomułka attempts to curb "anti-Zionist excesses" of Moczar and his followers by appealing for peace in a nationwide radio address.

March 23 In Dresden, East Germany, the leaders of Bulgaria, East Germany, Hungary, Poland, and the Soviet Union warn Czechoslovak leaders not to let their liberalized regime get out of their control.

March 28 Student demonstrators at the University of Warsaw demand the reinstatement of six professors fired several days earlier, including Leszek Kółakowski (*see* October 22, 1966) and the dismissal of all charges against their fellow students arrested since January 30. They give the government until April 22 to fulfill their demands. In response over the next several days, the government closes down eight "potentially dangerous" departments of the university and forces more than one-thousand "suspicious" students to reapply to the school.

April Marshal Marian Spychalski becomes the head of state.

April 19 All classes at the University of Warsaw are told that if demonstrations take place on April 22 the school will be closed down for an unspecified amount of time.

April 21 The police arrest numerous students to prevent them from protesting on April 22, and the date passes quietly at the University of Warsaw.

May 8 Bulgarian, East German, Hungarian, and Polish Communist party leaders confer in Moscow about the liberalizing events in Czechoslovakia, which they fear may spread to their own countries.

July 14–16 The Communist leaders of Bulgaria, East Germany, Hungary, Poland, and the USSR meet in Warsaw and send a virtual ultimatum to the Czechoslovak Communist Party demanding an end to the reforms. The five countries back up their resolution with troop movements near the Czechoslovak borders.

August 3 The leaders of Bulgaria, East Germany, Hungary, Poland, and the Soviet Union meet in Bratislava to ratify the Čierna plan, a compromise worked out between Czechoslovakia and the USSR between July 29 and August 1, in which Czechoslovakia agrees to limit its reforms in relation to the media.

August 20–21 Polish troops take part in the Soviet-led invasion of Czechoslovakia, crushing the liberal program of the Prague Spring. Most ministers in the Polish cabinet are not informed or consulted about the decision.

September 8 A 59-year-old Polish bookkeeper, Ryszard Siwiec, sets himself on fire at a fall festival in a major stadium in Warsaw to protest the invasion of Czechoslovakia. He dies four days later. This event goes unnoticed until 1991, after the fall of communism in Eastern Europe, when a film about the incident, *Cry for Freedom,* is released.

October 20 The fiftieth anniversary of the founding of the Catholic university in Lublin, the only such institution in socialist lands, is celebrated. Since its establishment, the university has produced 21,000 graduates, among them 33 bishops and two cardinals.

October 29 Four days after East German troops leave Czechoslovakia, Poland, Bulgaria, and Hungary also depart.

November 11–16 In a power struggle, First Secretary Gomułka ousts Moczar from his post of interior minister. Nonetheless, the power struggle will continue into the next year.

1969

August 22 The burial of the popular historian/journalist Paweł Jasiennica gives Jerzy Andrzejewski the opportunity to publicly condemn the obscurantism of the regime.

December 22 After a unilateral West German diplomatic initiative, Poland agrees to hold talks with the German Federal Republic, or West Germany, on mutual outstanding problems.

1970

August 12 The Soviet Union and West Germany sign a treaty on the renunciation of force. The treaty includes recognition of the Polish-East German border at the Oder-Neiße line.

December 7 West German chancellor Willy Brandt signs a treaty with Poland provisionally recognizing the Oder-Neiße line as Poland's western border.

December 12 The government increases the prices of basic foodstuffs by approximately one-fifth, but reduces the prices on luxury items.

December 14–17 Rioting breaks out in Gdańsk and other Baltic coast cities, as well as in Łódź, in response to the price increases. In Gdańsk alone there are 48 dead and 1,165 wounded as the result of police attempts to restore order.

December 20 Party secretary from Katowice, Edward Gierek replaces Władysław Gomułka, who suffered a mild stroke two days earlier. Gierek rescinds the price increases.

Marshal Spychalski resigns as head of state.

December 23 Piotr Jaroszewicz replaces Józef Cyrankiewicz as prime minister; Cyrankiewicz becomes head of state.

1971

January 8 The Vatican takes the diocese of western areas of Poland away from German jurisdiction and puts it under Polish administration.

January 14 Gierek issues a proclamation for the reconstruction of the Royal Palace in Warsaw, destroyed in World War II.

January 22 Another worker strike takes place in Szczecin. Gierek meets with the strikers in a nine-hour session, which ends the strike with a feeling that the government of Gierek should be given a chance; Gierek meets with Gdańsk shipyard workers three days later.

February 7 Gomułka is suspended from the Central Committee of the Polish United Workers Party (PZPR) officially for health reasons, but in actuality due to his inability to foresee and to control the mid-December 1970 riots.

February 13 Łódź textile workers strike and demand an end to the price hikes from December.

March 3 A meeting between Primate Wyszyński and Premier Jaroszewicz takes place. This is the first meeting between the head of the Polish church and the head of the government in 25 years.

June 24 In an attempt to calm the population, Gierek announces a revision in the current five-year plan (1971–75), which will shift to the production of more consumer goods. This plan, however, relies on the influx of major loans from the West.

July 23 The government directly hands over 4,700 church buildings in the former German territories to church administration. Prior to this, such buildings were technically owned by the state and only rented to the church.

December 6–11 Both Cyrankiewicz and Moczar are forced out of the Politburo, and Gierek strengthens his position during the Sixth Congress of the PZPR.

1972

During 1972, Gierek begins a modernization program that requires large-scale borrowing of money from Western banks.

May 17 The West German parliament ramifies the Oder-Neiße treaty recognizing the western border of Poland (*see* December 7, 1970).

June 28 An apostolic constitution confirms the diocesan divisions in the former German western territories.

September 14 Poland and West Germany agree to establish diplomatic relations.

1973

April 19 The Soviets launch the *Intercosmos-Copernicus 500,* a joint endeavor of Poland, Czechoslovakia, and the USSR, to measure the sun's radiation and the earth's ionosphere.

October 6–24 The Yom Kippur War between Israel and several Arab states causes long lines for gasoline and price hikes for electricity and other forms of energy in Poland.

December In a move to please West Germany, the government agrees to permit 50,000 ethnic Germans to leave Poland and settle in West Germany.

1974

Throughout the year, workers strike in various parts of the country demanding wage increases, which the government grants.

1975

April 10 Karol Cardinal Wojtyła, archbishop of Kraków, delivers a sermon in the church in Nowa Huta, saying that one cannot "fight against religion in the name of the workers." Nowa Huta, a steel mill town just outside Kraków, was built without a church, until local initiative constructed one.

May 28 The government restructures the administrative divisions of the country according to the French model. The People's Republic now comprises 49 provinces (*wojewodztwo*) designed to reflect central government power rather than regionalism (*see* June 1, 1950).

August 1 Poland is one of 35 countries that signs the Helsinki Accord, which recognizes the postwar boundaries as permanent and guarantees basic civil rights in the signatory countries.

1976

June 24 Prime Minister Jaroszewicz announces price increases of up to 60 percent on staple items, due to poor harvests since 1974, without preparing the public beforehand. Workers in Radom and elsewhere threaten a general strike.

June 25 Jaroszewicz moderates the price increases and chooses to maintain costly price subsidies after demonstrations take place but orders the arrest of strike ringleaders.

September 23 A group of intellectual dissidents organize the Workers' Defense Committee (Komitet Obrony Robotników, KOR) to provide legal assistance and material support to families of imprisoned workers, after striking miners were arrested in Radom in late June. The Workers' Defense Committee receives a grant of $10,000 from an American union, the United Auto Workers.

1977

May Several members of KOR establish a clandestine publishing operation called *Nowa* (New), which produces works of literature banned by the Polish authorities.

December 1 In a meeting arranged by Cardinal Wyszyński, First Secretary Gierek meets with Pope Paul VI to speak about a possible new concordat with the Vatican (*see* September 14, 1947).

December 29–31 American president Jimmy Carter makes an official visit to Poland and praises Poland's respect for human rights and religious freedom. His visit is marred when his American translator mistranslates some of his remarks into Polish; although not derogatory, they sound quite ridiculous.

1978

February The beginnings of an independent trade union is formed in Katowice with the establishment of a Workers' Committee.

May The beginning of another free trade union takes place with the founding of the Committee of Free Trade

Unions for the Baltic Coast, with one of its leaders being an electrician from Gdańsk, Lech Wałęsa.

October 16 Cardinal Wojtyła is elected pope and takes the name John Paul II. The Polish media gives his election scant coverage; nonetheless, spontaneous celebrations take place throughout the country.

December 16 Lech Wałęsa and other members of the Committee of Free Trade Unions for the Baltic Coast hold a spontaneous memorial service for the victims at the site of the December 1970 massacre at the Lenin Shipyard in Gdańsk.

1979

June 2–10 Pope John Paul II visits his native country and delivers a speech in Victory Square, Warsaw. He is the first pope to visit a Communist country. Everywhere he goes he is greeted by hundreds of thousands of people.

December 16 Wałęsa and others again hold a memorial service for those killed in the 1970 massacre and demand that a monument be erected on the site of the massacre. Police break up the service and make several arrests.

1980

February Edward Babiuch, a senior party official, replaces Jaroszewicz as premier.

May 3 A small group publicly celebrates Constitution Day, banned since 1948. The police intervene and several people are taken into custody (*see* May 3, 1948).

June 18 An explosion at the Lenin Shipyard in Gdańsk kills eight and injures 60. Workers express concern over working conditions and the lack of safety standards. A similar incident occurred in October 1979, when more than 50 miners were killed in three explosions in Silesia.

July 1 The government raises meat prices to reflect actual cost, in some cases by almost 100 percent; strikes break out nationwide through mid-August as a result. Unofficial strike committees are formed to demand better living conditions and, later, political reforms.

August 1 On the 36th anniversary of the beginning of the Warsaw Uprising, a small rally takes place in Warsaw.

August 14–31 Waves of nonviolent strikes continue to spread all over Poland in response to price increases, eventually involving over 300,000 workers. In the Lenin Shipyard of Gdańsk, Lech Wałęsa begins organizing the union that will come to be known as Solidarity (Solidarność). The shipyard workers issue a list of economic and political demands.

August 22 The government arrests 24 leaders of the strikers.

In Rome, Pope John Paul II holds a special mass for the striking Polish workers.

August 23 The government agrees to hold talks with the strikers.

August 24 Due to the strike crisis, Babiuch is dismissed and Józef Pinkowski becomes premier. Gierek appoints Mieczysław Jagielski deputy premier in order to begin negotiations with strikers.

August 31 Jagielski and Wałęsa sign an agreement (henceforth known as the Gdańsk Agreement) in which the government recognizes the right to strike and the new self-governing trade unions (two of shipyard workers in Szczecin and Gdańsk, and one of miners in Silesia), and it agrees to adhere to the constitution, but the central role of the Polish United Workers Party (Communist Party, PZPR) is still recognized in society as the overall governing body in the country.

Arrested striking workers are released.

September 1 Striking workers in Gdańsk and Szczecin return to their jobs, but strikes continue elsewhere in Poland until mid-September.

September 6 PZPR apparatchik Stanisław Kania replaces the now ill Gierek as first secretary.

September 17 Solidarity is formed by the merger of 35 independent unions, resulting in the end of all the remaining strikes.

October 3 Solidarity organizes a one-hour strike to force the government to put into effect many of the August 31 concessions.

October 9 Polish poet Czesław Miłosz, living in exile in the United States, receives the Nobel Prize in Literature, although most of his works are banned in Poland.

November 10 The government officially recognizes Solidarity as an independent trade union.

December 1–15 The Soviet Union, unhappy with the ''antisocialist forces'' at work in Poland, makes moves towards invading Poland. On December 8, other Warsaw Pact nations mobilize on Poland's frontiers.

December 2 U.S. president Carter warns the Soviet government that relations between the two countries will be seriously affected by a Soviet invasion of Poland.

A crowd of striking Polish workers gathers outside of an administrative building in Gdańsk.

December 5   Members of the Warsaw Pact meet in Moscow to discuss the situation in Poland. Members express confidence that Poland will be able to solve its problems without damaging its socialist system of government.

December 12   The foreign ministers of NATO inform the USSR that an invasion of Poland would end East-West detente.

December 15   The USSR publicly states that Poland can handle its own affairs, easing tensions between East and West.

December 16   A memorial to the victims of the December 1970 Lenin Shipyard massacre is dedicated; members of Solidarity, the Roman Catholic church, and the government attend.

1981

January–February   Intermittent strikes take place across the country.

January 1   The government dissolves the government-controlled Central Council of Trade Unions formed on July 1, 1949.

January 15   Wałęsa meets with Pope John Paul II in Rome.

January 25   Gierek resigns from the Central Committee of the PZPR.

February 9   Pinkowski resigns as premier, and defense minister General Wojciech Jaruzelski becomes the head of a new government.

February 17   The government recognizes an independent university Student's Union.

March 8   A massive rally at the University of Warsaw commemorates the 1968 demonstration and condemns Polish anti-Semitism.

March 19   The beating by plain-clothes police of three Solidarity activists in Bydgoszcz leads to a crisis. Tensions are diffused a few days later when Solidarity's leaders are able to persuade its membership that a nationwide protest strikes might lead to a general insurrection or even civil war.

March 19–26 Warsaw Pact maneuvers—code named Soiuz 81—in Poland, East Germany, Czechoslovakia, and the Soviet Union are extended to April 7 in response to unrest in Poland.

March 27 Instead of a general strike, Poles observe a nationwide four-hour "warning strike" in protest over police attacks on members of Solidarity on March 19.

April 3 The first issue of Solidarity's newspaper, *Solidarność,* stresses the need "to tread a narrow path" between society's problems and Poland's geopolitical situation.

April 7 Czechoslovak Communist leader Gustav Husak, addressing a Czechoslovak Communist party congress, declares that the Warsaw Pact will not sit idly by while socialism is undermined in Poland. Soviet president Leonid Brezhnev addresses the congress and states that the USSR will not solve Poland's problems, which—on the surface—removes the threat of a Soviet invasion, although similar declarations have been followed by Soviet invasions (*see* Czechoslovakia, 1968; Hungary, 1956).

May 3 Huge rallies mark Constitution Day, a holiday that has been illegal since 1948 (*see* May 3, 1980). The rallies pass largely without incident.

May 12 Rural Solidarity, whose membership consists of agrarian workers, is legalized.

May 28 The primate of Poland, Stefan Cardinal Wyszyński, the symbol of Polish resistance to communism, dies at age 79. Thousands, including Communist party members, attend his funeral.

June 7 Czesław Miłosz, the 1980 Nobel laureate, is given an enthusiastic welcome on his return to Poland.

June 28 More than 150,000 people in Poznań attend services for those massacred in June 1956; several monuments are dedicated to mark the event.

July 7 Bp. Józef Glemp of Warmia is elevated to archbishop and succeeds the late Cardinal Wyszyński as primate of Poland.

July 14–18 During a congress of the PZPR, secret ballots with multiple candidates are used for the first time, resulting in the reelection of only four Politburo members.

August 5 A general strike takes place in response to food price hikes.

September 5–10 Solidarity holds its first national congress in Gdańsk with a membership estimated at over 10 million. In the following weeks, the USSR will condemn and denounce the congress as anti-socialist and anti-soviet.

September 28 The Workers' Defense Committee (Komitet Obrony Robotników, KOR) is officially disbanded at the Solidarity congress.

October 4 The government announces further price hikes on food.

October 19 Defense Minister Jaruzelski ousts Stanisław Kania as first secretary of the PZPR.

October 21 Riots break out over food shortages after price increases are announced on October 4. Solidarity stages a one-hour strike on October 28 in protest. Strikes will continue through November.

November 4 Wałęsa, Archbishop Glemp, and Jaruzelski meet to discuss the creation of a Council of National Understanding to try to solve Poland's political and economic problems. Very little results from the meeting.

November 10 Poland reapplies for membership in the International Monetary Fund (IMF)—an organization it left in 1950—hoping to get more loans from the West to pay off its existing debts.

November 11 For the first time since 1938, Poland holds nationwide celebrations in honor of the country's independence after World War I.

November 22 Jacek Kuroń, a founding member of KOR, forms the group "Clubs for a Self-Governing Republic: Freedom, Justice, Independence" (KRS-WSN), aspiring to the same basic goals as the now-defunct KOR.

November 29 In a closed meeting of the Central Committee of the PZPR, Jaruzelski states that Communism in the country is in imminent danger if strikes continue.

December 8 Archbishop Glemp appeals to Solidarity and the government to hold a second round of talks about ending the problems in Poland.

December 12 In Gdańsk, Solidarity leaders propose a nationwide referendum on a non-Communist government for Poland and redefinition of Poland's military relationship with the Soviet Union.

December 13 Due to economic and popular political pressure from Solidarity—which threatens the existence of Communism in Poland—Jaruzelski declares a state of emergency and imposes martial law, announcing: "Our country stands at the brink of an abyss. . . . In conformity with the provisions of the constitution, at midnight tonight the Council of State proclaimed martial law throughout the whole country." Jaruzelski bans Solidarity and establishes a Military Council of National Salvation to run the country. Wałęsa and other Solidarity leaders are rounded up and imprisoned, while others go into hiding.

December 14 Poland enforces a news blackout by cutting Western news cables.

Spontaneous strikes take place in protest over the imposition of martial law. The government moves quickly to suppress them over the next several days.

December 17 Despite Brezhnev's comments on April 7, U.S. president Ronald Reagan blames the USSR for the imposition of martial law in Poland.

December 20 The Polish ambassador to the United States defects over the imposition of martial law in his country. The Polish minister to Japan defects four days later.

December 29 The United States imposes economic sanctions against the USSR for the imposition of martial law in Poland. Great Britain does the same on February 5, 1982.

1982

January 11 North Atlantic Treaty Organization (NATO) foreign ministers meeting in Brussels condemn the Soviet Union for its role in "the system of repression in Poland." The ministers also call for European participation along with the U.S. in imposing economic sanctions against the Soviet Union.

April 22 Now-banned Solidarity leaders form an underground Temporary Coordinating Commission to keep in touch with each other and to organize and unify responses to martial law.

May 1 Police disperse antigovernment demonstrators during the traditional May Day celebrations.

May 3 Demonstrations take place in response to appeals from Solidarity's underground leadership.

August 31 Protests take place to mark the second anniversary of the Gdańsk Agreement.

September 1 Former Polish Communist party leader Władysław Gomułka dies at age 77.

October 8 The government dissolves all trade unions and outlaws Solidarity after demonstrations support the union.

November 13 The government releases Wałęsa from prison.

December 30 Jaruzelski suspends martial law.

1983

June 16 Pope John Paul II makes his second visit to Poland, his native country.

July 21 Martial law officially ends, and the Military Council of National Salvation is disbanded.

October 5 Lech Wałęsa, leader of the now illegal trade union Solidarity, is awarded the Nobel Peace Prize.

1984

June 24 Solidarity leads a boycott of local government elections.

July The government proclaims a general amnesty for all but political prisoners and criminals who committed serious crimes to mark the fortieth anniversary of the country's reestablishment after World War II.

October 19 Members of the secret police kidnap and murder pro-Solidarity priest Father Jerzy Popiełuszko of St. Stanisław Kostka parish in Warsaw.

December 1984–February 7, 1985 Four interior ministry functionaries are found guilty, by trial, of the murder of Father Popiełuszko.

1985

January The government announces new price hikes but has to revise the hikes after Solidarity threatens a nationwide strike.

April 26 Poland and the other nations of the Warsaw Pact sign a 20-year extension of the alliance (*see* May 14, 1955).

October 18 Solidarity urges a boycott of general elections where some multicandidate slates are allowed but are filled with Communists.

November 6 Zbigniew Messner, an economics professor, replaces Jaruzelski as prime minister; Jaruzelski remains as first secretary of the PZPR.

The police are called in when May Day celebrations are disrupted by antigovernment demonstrations, May 1982.

November 12 Jaruzelski takes the position of chairman of the State Council, thereby becoming the head of state.

1986

February Wałęsa goes on trial for publicly challenging the October 1985 election results. His case will eventually be dismissed.

Late April The Polish media reports on the Soviet Chernobyl nuclear power plant accident after the radioactive cloud passes over the country (*see* Soviet Union; April 26, 1986).

May The authorities arrest Zbigniew Bujak, a leader of Solidarity who had been in hiding almost five years. Spontaneous demonstrations erupt in protest over his arrest.

June 29 During a PZPR congress, General Jaruzelski states that Solidarity is finished.

July Parliament passes a law calling for the release of all political prisoners.

Charismatic leader of Solidarity, Lech Wałęsa, speaks to a crowd of striking workers.

September 11   The government grants a general amnesty for most political prisoners.

November 19   Although illegal in Poland, Solidarity becomes a member of the International Confederation of Free Trade Unions and the World Confederation of Labor.

1987

March   The government raises food prices 10 percent and fuel prices 40 percent.

May 1   Antigovernment demonstrations again mar traditional May Day celebrations; the authorities arrest over 150 protesters.

June 8–14   Pope John Paul II visits Poland for the third time, where he is greeted enthusiastically and meets with both General Jaruzelski and Solidarity leader Lech Wałęsa.

October   The government announces a November referendum to discuss economic and political reforms. Solidarity urges a boycott.

November   The referendum fails to pass due in large part to the Solidarity-backed boycott.

1988

January 30   Solidarity protests after the government announces price hikes.

April–May   Sporadic nationwide strikes take place.

June   Only about 55 percent of the people vote in local elections after Solidarity urges a boycott.

August 16   Miners in Silesia strike for higher pay and restoration of Solidarity. Strikes soon become nationwide.

August 23   Due to the national situation, Wałęsa calls for a discussion with the government and by August 31 calls for an end to the strikes.

September 19   Messner resigns as prime minister.

September 27   Mieczysław Rakowski, a senior party official and former editor of the journal *Polityka,* becomes prime minister.

October 31   Massive demonstrations take place after the government announces that the Lenin Shipyard in Gdańsk will close due to unprofitability.

November 30   Wałęsa appears on television for a 45-minute debate with the leader of the government-spon-

Students hang Solidarity banners on the University of Warsaw campus, preparing a demonstration in support of striking miners.

sored trade unions, Alfred Miodowicz. The government intends to show the people of Poland that, without his advisers around him, Wałęsa is nothing short of crude and unknowledgeable; but the debate turns into a solid victory for the electrician from Gdańsk. Wałęsa outwits and outargues Miodowicz, winning the debate decisively.

December 18 A group of over 100 intellectuals found the Citizen's Committee to assist Wałęsa as the head of the Solidarity union.

December 21 Six members resign from the Central Committee of the PZPR as part of a government attempt to reform itself in the wake of continued pressure from Solidarity.

1989

January 18 The PZPR Central Committee agrees to discuss legalizing Solidarity again.

January 27 Members of the Communist government, Solidarity, and the Roman Catholic church agree to begin talks in February on political and economic reforms.

February 6–April 15 A series of more than 90 sessions of roundtable talks takes place between Solidarity, Catholic, and government representatives. The highest level talks, between Wałęsa and Interior Minister General Czesław Kiszczak (with their advisers), begin on March 2 at the government retreat in Magdalenka.

February 9 A four-day-old miners' strike in Bełchatów is suspended for six weeks to await the results of the Wałęsa-Kiszczak talks.

March 7 Many years after the fact, the Polish government officially accuses the USSR of carrying out the 1940 Katyń Forest massacre (*see* April 12 and 26, 1943).

April 5 Government and Solidarity representatives sign an agreement dealing with economic reforms and free elections. It is agreed that the president will be the chief executive officer of the country. Furthermore, the government agrees to recognize Solidarity as a legal union.

April 7 As a result of the April 5 agreement, several constitutional amendments are enacted, including the creation of a bicameral national parliament consisting of the Sejm (lower house) and the Senate (upper house).

April 17   Solidarity is registered in Warsaw as a legal union.

American president George Bush announces economic aid totaling $1 billion for Poland.

April 27–28   Head of state Jaruzelski travels to Moscow for discussions with Soviet leader Mikhail Gorbachev.

May 16–17   A series of anti-Soviet protests erupt in Kraków.

May 17   Laws granting full political rights to Roman Catholics and freedom of religion go into effect.

June 4   In free elections, Solidarity-backed candidates win 99 of the 100 seats in the newly constituted Senate. In accordance with agreements made during the preceding months, the Communists are guaranteed 65 percent of the seats in the Sejm, in spite of the fact that Solidarity candidates win the majority of seats there too.

June 6   Solidarity refuses an invitation by Jaruzelski to take part in a coalition government.

July 4   The new bicameral parliament opens.

July 6   During a speech to the Council of Europe in Strasbourg, France, Gorbachev announces that the Soviet Union will not interfere with reforms in Poland or Hungary.

July 9–11   President Bush makes an official visit to Poland. He addresses a joint session of the Sejm and Senate and meets with Wałęsa in Gdańsk.

July 17   Poland reestablishes diplomatic relations with the Vatican.

July 19   A joint session of the Sejm and the Senate elects Jaruzelski president by a margin of one vote. He becomes Poland's first president since 1952.

July 25   Jaruzelski asks Solidarity to join a coalition government; Wałęsa rejects the plan.

July 29   Mieczysław Rakowski resigns as prime minister and becomes the head of the PZPR after Jaruzelski steps down.

August 1   In a move toward a free economy, the government ends all price controls on and rationing of food, causing steep price increases and panic buying.

August 2   Jaruzelski appoints General Czesław Kiszczak as prime minister. Within two weeks, Kiszczak announces that he will resign after he is unable to form a government.

August 15   Solidarity proposes that Wałęsa be named premier.

August 17   The Polish parliament passes a resolution condemning the 1968 invasion of Czechoslovakia, in which Poland took part (*see* August 20–21, 1968).

Tadeusz Mazowiecki, the Eastern bloc's first non-communist prime minister, after his election victory.

August 19   Kiszczak resigns, and President Jaruzelski offers the prime minister portfolio, on the suggestion of Lech Wałęsa, to Tadeusz Mazowiecki, a prominent Catholic intellectual, journalist, and adviser to Wałęsa.

August 24   The Sejm accepts Mazowiecki as premier, who then forms Poland's first non-Communist government in more than 40 years.

September 19   Poland and the European Economic Community (EEC) sign a trade agreement.

September 26   Finance Minister Leszek Balcerowicz meets with International Monetary Fund (IMF) officials to seek immediate aid.

November 19   During a state visit to the United States, Wałęsa addresses a joint session of Congress, where he asks for more economic aid for Poland.

November 25   A statement issued after a meeting between President Jaruzelski and Archbishop Glemp urges Poles to support the Mazowiecki government and its tough economic policies that would mean short-term hardship, but would eventually mean an end to state control of the economy and restore a free enterprise, capitalistic society.

December 4 At a meeting of the Warsaw Pact in Moscow, five members—the USSR, East Germany, Poland, Hungary, and Bulgaria—jointly condemn their August 1968 invasion of Czechoslovakia, describing it as undue influence in the internal affairs of a sovereign country.

December 8 The Solidarity-led government announces austere policies in an attempt to end Poland's severe economic problems.

December 28–29 First the Sejm and then the Senate approve economic reform measures. Changes in the constitution formally end the existence of the Polish People's Republic; the country now becomes the Republic of Poland. The PZPR's monopoly on power in Poland is ended, and the prewar flag of the country is restored.

1990

January 1 Economic reforms go into effect. As part of the program, the government raises prices sharply and devalues the złoty, the Polish currency.

January 16–19 Strikes over the government's economic policy break out in the Silesian coal mining region.

January 25 The PZPR officially votes itself out of existence at its eleventh and final congress. It is formed again the next day under the name Social Democracy of the Republic of Poland.

January 27 Lenin Shipyard in Gdańsk is given its prewar name of Gdańsk Shipyard.

February 15 Prime Minister Mazowiecki meets with a Solidarity delegation led by Wałęsa to discuss growing worker discontent in Poland. This marks the beginning of a split of Solidarity between the supporters of Mazowiecki and Wałęsa who cannot agree on the pace of political and economic restructuring reforms. Wałęsa's faction wants early free parliamentary and presidential elections and the removal of all Communists from positions of authority, while creating a jobs program for people who lose employment due to economic restructuring.

March In a concession of symbolic importance, the Soviet Union at last—after 50 years—admits that its secret police were responsible for the 1940 Katyń massacre of more than 4,000 Polish officers taken prisoner by the Red Army.

March 8 To put Polish worries at ease over the German reunification issue, the West German Parliament renounces all claims to German lands given to Poland after World War II.

March 9 France officially supports the Oder-Neiße line as the border of Poland and Germany.

April Wałęsa lets it be known that he will run for president, but he does not officially announce his candidacy until September 17.

April 3 The Soviet government takes responsibility for and expresses regret over the 1940 massacre of Polish prisoners-of-war in the Katyń Forest (*see* March 7, 1989).

April 19–25 The second congress of Solidarity reelects Wałęsa as its leader, although the rift between his and Mazowiecki's factions is publicly apparent.

May 2 On an official visit to Poland, the West German president states that Poland's borders are permanent.

May 21–25 Railway workers strike in Ślusk and Koszalin over government economic policies.

June 21 Both the West and East German Parliaments approve a resolution respecting Poland's borders.

July 13 The Parliament approves the Law of Privatization of State Enterprises.

November 14 The foreign ministers of Poland and united Germany sign a treaty guaranteeing Poland's post-World War II borders.

November 20 Miners strike in protest over the government's tough economic policy.

November 25 The presidential election matches Wałęsa, Mazowiecki, and an expatriate Canadian businessman, Stanisław Tyminski. Wałęsa wins with a plurality of 40 percent of the vote, forcing a runoff election between Wałęsa and Tyminski.

Mazowiecki resigns as prime minister.

December 9 Wałęsa wins the runoff election outright with 74 percent of the vote, defeating Tyminski.

December 22 Wałęsa takes the presidential oath of office.

December 29 Wałęsa nominates economist Jan Krzysztof Bielecki as prime minister. Bielecki promises to continue the reform measures pursued by Mazowiecki.

1991

January 5 A split forms in the Citizens Parliamentary Club, the Solidarity deputies in parliament, and one group becomes the Democratic Union party.

February 15 In Visegrad, Hungary, Wałęsa meets with President Václav Havel of Czechoslovakia and Hungarian Premier Jozsef Antall. Their discussion leads to the formation of the Visegrad triangle and the signing of an agreement that says they will cooperate in transforming their planned economies to free market economies.

February 23 Marian Krzaklewski is elected to succeed Wałęsa as the leader of Solidarity.

February 25 The Polish foreign and defense ministers, along with their counterparts from Bulgaria, Czechoslovakia, Hungary, Romania, and the Soviet Union, sign an agreement in Budapest to dissolve the Warsaw Pact by March 31, 1991. However, it will not take place until July.

March 9 In a rebuke to President Wałęsa, the Sejm refuses his call for immediate general elections to parliament.

March 15 Due to the fall of communism in Poland, 17 Western countries forgive $16.5 billion of Poland's $33 billion foreign debt.

April 4 The USSR begins to withdraw its troops from Poland; the withdrawal is expected to be complete by the end of 1993.

April 16 Company stocks are traded in Warsaw for the first time since 1939.

April 18 The International Monetary Fund (IMF) approves a $2.5 billion loan to Poland.

May 12 Three other political groups of former Solidarity politicians merge with the Democratic Union party.

May 16 The Sejm upholds legislation keeping abortions legal.

May 17 The government devalues the Polish currency, the złoty, by almost 17 percent. Three days later the government allows the złoty to become convertible into Western currencies by allowing its value to float.

May 22 Solidarity backs a day of protest against the government's austere economic policies.

June 17 Prime Minister Bielecki and German chancellor Helmut Kohl sign a treaty of friendship and mutual assistance in Bonn, Germany. In October, the Parliaments of both countries ratify the treaty.

June 27 The government announces plans to turn over about one-quarter of state-owned enterprises to every adult through a program of vouchers to begin later in the year. In October, the plan is reduced to about 7 percent of state-owned companies and then postponed until a later date.

July 1 The Warsaw Pact formally dissolves.

July 27 Poland joins Austria, Czechoslovakia, Hungary, Italy, and Yugoslavia as a member of the Hexagonal Group, which meets to discuss regional political issues and problems.

September 5 Poland and Lithuania establish diplomatic relations. Four days later Poland and Estonia restore relations.

October 27 Elections occur in which only 42.3 percent of the eligible electorate take part and candidates from 65 parties run. No party wins anything approaching a majority; the largest faction is the Democratic Union with 12.3 percent of the mandates. The former Communists receive 12 percent. All tolled, 29 separate groups are represented in the Sejm. Nonetheless, as a result of the elections, Premier Bielecki's government falls.

December 5 Jan Olszewski is appointed premier.

December 23 Olszewski assembles his cabinet.

1992

January 9 For economic reasons, Russia cuts gas deliveries to Poland in half.

January 13 In Vilnius, Lithuania, Poland signs a declaration of Polish-Lithuanian friendship.

January 21 Poland recognizes the independence of Slovenia and Croatia.

February 25 In an attempt to stimulate the economy, the government devalues the złoty by 12 percent, measured against major Western currencies.

March 25 The Vatican issues the papal bull *Totus tuus poloniae populus,* according to which the pope reorganizes church administration in Poland by creating new archdioceses and dioceses. In terms of numbers, the Polish episcopate is now the third largest in Europe.

April 23 The Polish and Belorussian premiers signs treaties of friendship in Warsaw.

May 6 At a summit in Prague, the presidents of Poland, Czechoslovakia, and Hungary express their strong desire to be linked to the West European security network. They also declare the formation of a free trade zone among the three countries.

May 18 In Warsaw Wałęsa and President Leonid Kravchuk of Ukraine sign a treaty of good neighborliness and cooperation.

May 22 Wałęsa and Russian president Boris Yeltsin sign a pact of cooperation between Poland and Russia, as well as an agreement on the removal of Russian troops still in Poland.

May 26 Feeling it to be effectual, Wałęsa officially withdraws his support of the Olszewski government, causing it to fall.

June 29 The remains of Ignacy Jan Paderewski—the pianist and former president who died of pneumonia on June 19, 1941 and was buried in the United States—arrive in Poland via a special flight from the United States. Paderewski had left Poland in 1919 never to return alive. He resumed his musical career while in the United States, but with the outbreak of World War II, he joined the Polish government-in-exile. Pres. Franklin Roosevelt ordered his body kept in the crypt of the Battleship Maine at Arlington Cemetery until it could be returned to Poland after the war. Following the war the Communists took power in Poland and would not allow Paderewski's body to be returned for burial. Only after the collapse of the Communists could Paderewski's body reenter the country.

July 10 Lawyer Hanna Suchocka of the Democratic Union, appointed premier by Wałęsa, forms a new government.

September 1 The 83-year-old former Communist prime minister Piotr Jaroszewicz and his wife are found murdered in their Warsaw home. Police have no clues, suspects, or motives.

October 14 Russian president Yeltsin sends President Wałęsa photocopies of documents dated March 5, 1940, proving that the Soviet Politburo gave the order to execute more than 20,000 Poles, including 5,000 senior army officers, whose bodies were dumped in mass graves in the Katyń Forest (*see* April 3, 1990). Wałęsa terms the gesture a "symbol of sincerity between our nations," marking a new era in Russo-Polish relations.

October 22 The Polish government announces that American automotive company General Motors will purchase a 70 percent share in the Polish automaker FSO.

October 28 The last Russian combat troops leave Poland. President Wałęsa states that with their departure Polish sovereignty has been restored.

November 24 Poland and the IMF sign an agreement in which Poland will receive a $700 million loan.

December 17 Thousands of coal miners go on strike over low wages and a government planned reorganization of the mining industry that would cut close to 180,000 jobs in 10 years. The government claims it will not back down and will import coal if necessary.

1993

January 2 Romania and Poland sign a treaty of cooperation in Bucharest that replaces the 1960 accord. The treaty calls for a system of permanent ties between the two countries.

February 15 Wałęsa signs the strictest antiabortion law in Eastern Europe, effective in March. The law bans abortions and provides prison sentences up to two years for doctors who perform them except in cases of rape, incest, genetic disorders, and when pregnancy is life-threatening to the mother. The Roman Catholic church is not satisfied with the law and vows to push for a total ban; many Poles, however, favor more liberal abortion policies. Starting in March, many Poles travel to the Czech Republic to have the procedure performed.

March 3 Former president Wojciech Jaruzelski states in an interview that he regrets declaring martial law on December 13, 1981.

March 30 Poland's telephone company, Telekomunikacja Polska, awards a $100 million contract to American Telephone and Telegraph to update Poland's telecommunications equipment.

April 21 A constitutional court rejects a case that questions compulsory religion classes and prayers in public schools, thereby strengthening the position of the Roman Catholic church in education.

April 30 After defeating similar legislation in mid-March, the Sejm approves a plan for the privatization of state-owned businesses in which a majority of shares in 600 companies would be turned over to twenty investment funds. It passes the Senate and is signed into law by President Wałęsa.

May 28 The coalition government of Hanna Suchocka falls after losing a no-confidence vote from the parliament by one ballot. Suchocka had been criticized for her conservative budget policies. The following day President Wałęsa refuses to accept her resignation, asking her to remain head of a caretaker government until a new one can be formed after elections scheduled for September 19.

June 1 In an attempt to reduce the number of political parties in parliament and thereby reduce the chances of cumbersome and ineffectual numerous party coalition governments, President Wałęsa signs a reform bill that denies representation in the Sejm to any party if it is unable to win a minimum of 5 percent of the vote.

June 22 The European Community formally invites Poland, the Czech Republic, Slovakia, Bulgaria, Hungary, and Romania to apply for membership. It is not expected that the countries will become full members before the turn of the century.

June 27 President Wałęsa disassociates himself from Solidarity, the independent trade union that brought him to

1993 marks the 50th anniversary of the Warsaw Ghetto Uprising. On the outskirts of the
Ghetto stands the monument to its victims, created several years back by a Jewish
sculptor.

prominence, after it refuses to endorse political candidates of a nonparty group supported by the president.

July 5 In an attempt to bring its finances up to Western standards, the government levies a value added tax (VAT) of 22 percent on most goods and adds numerous excise taxes on such items as gasoline, automobiles, alcohol, and tobacco.

August 16 The Polish government announces that employment stands at 15.2 percent or 2.8 million people of the work force.

August 25 In Warsaw, Russian President Boris Yeltsin signs a trade agreement with Poland that requires the two countries to regulate customs duties and to follow rules established by the General Agreement on Tariff and Trade (GATT). Another accord is signed which will allow for the construction of a natural gas pipeline from Russia through Poland to Western Europe.

While in Warsaw Yeltsin lays a wreath at a memorial in honor of the victims of the Katyń Forest massacre from 1940.

August 28 In an attempt to increase the marketability of Polish exports, the government devalues the złoty by 8 percent.

September 14 A Lufthansa flight with 70 people aboard crashes killing two while attempting to land in Warsaw during a rain storm.

September 17 The body of General Władysław Sikorski, the prime minister of the Polish government-in-exile and commander in chief of the Polish free forces during World War II, is reburied in Kraków. Sikorski was killed in a mysterious air crash in Gibraltar on July 4, 1943, and buried in England.

A minor earthquake in Silesia causes a mine shaft to collapse killing six miners and injuring others.

September 18 The last Russian (former Soviet) military personnel leave Poland (*see* October 28, 1992).

September 19 A reported 52.1 percent of the eligible population votes in nationwide general elections where only four parties win 5 percent or more of the vote thereby granting them seats in the parliament (*see* June 1). The Peasant party wins 132, the Democratic Left Alliance (the former Communist party) 171, and the Democratic Union party 74 seats out of 460 in the Sejm, the lower house of parliament.

September 23 The German electronics firm Siemens announces the purchase for $38.5 million of two state-owned Polish telecommunications companies: Zwut in Warsaw and Elwro in Wrocław. Siemens also plans to invest an additional $100 million in the two businesses over the next six years.

September 24 Trying to calm fears that its victory on September 19 means a return to communism, leaders of the Democratic Left Alliance assure the West that they are committed to financial reforms and budgetary constraints.

October 13 The World Bank reports that it has granted Poland $450 million, with $100 million going toward repaying the country's $12.3 billion international debt.

October 14 Thirty-four-year-old Waldemar Pawlak, the leader of the Peasant party, is named prime minister; he had been prime minister briefly in 1992. The Peasant party and the Democratic Left Alliance have held talks since late September, formed a coalition on October 13 in the Sejm, and named Pawlak their leader. This is the first government since the fall of communism in 1989 not to include a political party that sprang from the independent trade union Solidarity.

October 26 Pawlak and his government take office when the caretaker government of Hanna Suchocka resigns.

November 10 The Pawlak government weathers a no-confidence vote.

November 23 With the help of Polish authorities, British customs agents seize an armaments shipment smuggled from Poland aboard a Polish container ship. The weapons and ammunition were destined for Protestant extremists in Northern Ireland.

December 7 The deputy defense minister states that Russia has nothing to fear when Poland becomes a member of NATO.

December 13 After two years of negotiations, General Motors announces a joint business venture with Poland's second largest automaker F.S.O. Under the accord, GM will invest about $25 million to assemble initially 10,000 Opel automobiles at the Warsaw state-owned FSO plant, where GM will control management, beginning in the fall 1994.

December 14 In the wake of the Russian national elections on December 12 in which the ultra-nationalists, led by Vladimir Zhirnovskii, have a good showing, President Wałęsa in a television interview expresses hope that the West will not allow Russia to become a global policeman. Nonetheless, the mood in Poland concerning events in Russia remains somber.

December 16 The Sejm votes to raise personal income tax brackets from 20 to 21 percent, 30 to 33 percent, and 40 to 45 percent depending on the amount a person earns annually.

December 29   In a speech to the Sejm, Prime Minister Palwak reluctantly admits that the government will continue economic policies established by previous government despite his election promises to end them. He states that attempting to change the course of the economy now at this point could have dire consequences for the country.

Chapter Seven

ROMANIA

The Romanians trace their history back to the second century A.D. when the Romans defeated the Dacians—an Indo-European people living in the area of the modern day state of Romania—and incorporated them into the Roman Empire as the province of Dacia. During the next one-and-a-half centuries, the Romanians were born out of a mixing of Roman colonists and the native Dacians who accepted Christianity and Roman culture. Unable to hold the region against the onslaught of barbarian invasions, the Romans left around the year 270. What occurred after this date is difficult to ascertain. Romanians claim that the native population of Daco-Romans fled to the mountains where they maintained their culture, and moved back after the barbarian invasions. Others, particularly the Hungarians, argue that the Daco-Romans completely evacuated the area and, after the invasions ended around the tenth century, Latin-speaking people from the south moved north of the Danube River as colonists.

In the Middle Ages, Wallachia and Moldavia were established as feudal principalities ruled by native princes and nobility, called *boyars*. Starting in the late fourteenth century and continuing for about 100 years, the various Romanian rulers, including Vlad the Impaler (better known as Dracula), fought the Moslem Ottoman Turks in unsuccessful attempts to retain their independence. By 1500, both regions had come under Turkish control as tributary states. Occasional uprisings occurred against the Ottomans, and during the reign of the Wallachian prince Michael the Brave (r. 1593–1601), Moldavia, Wallachia, and the principality of Transylvania were briefly unified.

After this interlude, the Ottoman Turks placed Moldavia and Wallachia under the control of Greeks from Constantinople known as Phanariots, who for the most part mismanaged the two regions by exploiting them economically and repressing their populations.

Meanwhile, in 1699, the Habsburgs (rulers of the Holy Roman Empire and Central Europe for nearly 400 years) received Transylvania from the Turks, which remained part of the Hungarian crown until 1918. Due to Phanariot misrule in Wallachia and Moldavia, the Turks restored power to Romanian princes in 1821. The next 45 years saw the consolidation and unification of the two states, first in the person of the ruler and later administratively as the united principalities under great power support of France, Great Britain, and Russia, although still legally part of the Ottoman Empire.

In 1866 the German prince Carol (Charles, Karl) of Hohenzollern-Sigmaringen (1839–1914) became the ruler of an autonomous, unified Romania, technically still under the control of the Ottoman Empire. In 1878, as a result of the Congress of Berlin (an international meeting to reduce great power tensions that resulted from Russia's dictated peace after defeating the Ottoman Empire), the country received its independence and the region of Dobrudja; three years later Romania became a kingdom. In 1883 King Carol allied his country with Austria-Hungary and Germany with a secret defensive alliance. If publicly known, this treaty would have been quite unpopular for it effectively destroyed Romanias's desire to take the Austro-Hungarian province of Transylvania, where large numbers of Romanians

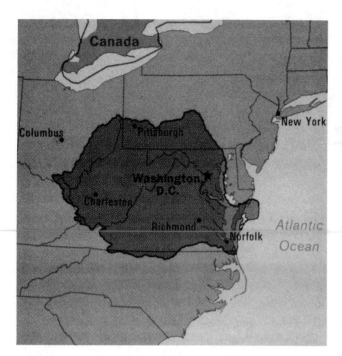

Romania in relation to the size of the United States.

lived. Although Carol granted a liberal constitution in 1866, the peasantry had almost no political rights, and Jews were not even considered citizens. Power remained with the landed interests and the slowly emerging middle class until well after World War I, and it was exercised by two predominant political parties, the Liberals and the Conservatives. Nonetheless, before the war, Romania was the most politically stable and the most advanced of the Balkan states.

The spelling of the country's name is rather irregular in Western historiography. There exist, at present, three variants: Rumania, Roumania, and Romania. There appears to be a tendency to use the latter form more frequently in recent Western works, and the Romanians prefer this version to emphasize their connections with ancient Rome.

Dating is also problematic when considering Balkan history. The Orthodox peoples, such as the Romanians, used the Julian calendar, while Roman Catholics and Protestants used the Gregorian calendar. In the nineteenth century, the Julian calendar lagged twelve days behind the Gregorian calendar, and in the twentieth century, that number increased to thirteen days. Dates in this chronology are given in the ''New Style'' or Gregorian variant, although this calendar did not become effective in Romania until October 1, 1924.

1902

June As a result of state-sponsored anti-Semitism, a steady number of Jews leave the country.

July Romania renews its secret defensive alliance from 1883 with Austria-Hungary and Germany.

September 17 Both the United States and Great Britain protest the treatment of Jews in Romania.

September–October Another round of anti-Semitism sweeps the country.

1904

April 24 Approximately 5,000 Romanian and Hungarian peasants demonstrate at Alesd, near the city of Oradea, over poor economic conditions and high rents. The government does nothing to help them.

1905

May 23 Romania threatens to rupture diplomatic relations with Ottoman Turkey if compensation demands are not met over the arrest of two school inspectors in Yunina on charges of spreading Romanian nationalism. The Romanians also demand full recognition of Vlach or Romanian communities in the Ottoman Empire, like that accorded to Greek and Bulgarian communities. The Ottoman Turks agree to the demands.

September 24 Romania breaks off diplomatic relations with Greece because Greeks living in Ottoman Macedonia are attempting to forcibly convert Vlachs or Romanians. Romania counters by attempting to convert Greeks on its soil.

1906

February 16 The government expels a number of Greeks who are allegedly members of a secret society seeking to expand the territory of Greece.

March 27 Rioting in Bucharest occurs over continuing economic problems.

May An exhibition opens to commemorate the fortieth anniversary of King Carol's arrival to accept the Romanian throne.

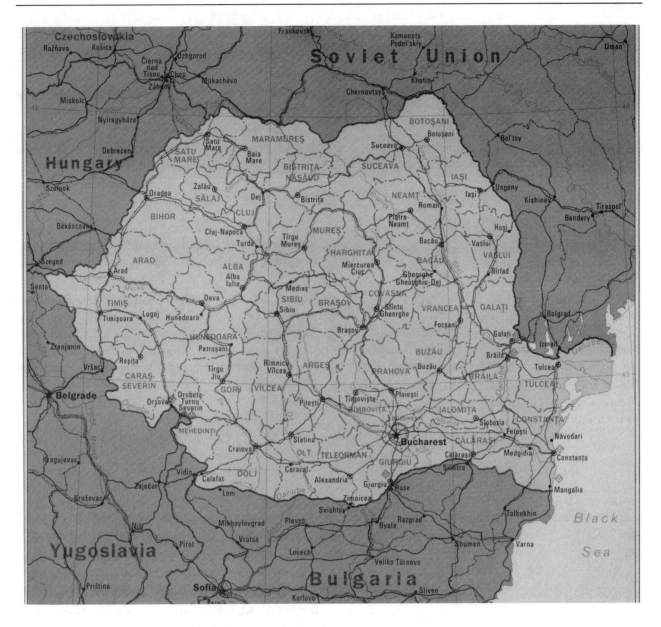

June 12   Romania again breaks off diplomatic relations with Greece, and will expel more Greeks in August and October (*see* September 24, 1905).

1907

March–April   A peasant rebellion breaks out in northern Moldavia that catches the government by surprise. Although the beginning of the revolt is caused by anti-Semitism, it quickly becomes anti-landlord as it spreads south. Many of the peasants seize the land of the great

estates and kill the owners. Their anger is caused by the fact that about 85 percent of the peasantry own no land or cannot support their families on the land they do own. The government declares martial law to quell the insurrection, calling out approximately 100,000 troops who, in the process of restoring order, kill over 10,000 peasants by the end of April.

December   As a result of the March–April rebellion, the parliament passes four laws to lessen the plight of the peasantry. They include regulating farm contracts to avoid exploitation of the peasants; creating a department to transfer land to the peasants; limiting leases of land to 4,000 hectares or less (1 hectare equals 2.47 acres); and establishing cooperatives for land rental.

1908

March 3 Sixty soldiers who refused to carry out orders and killed their commanding officer during the March–April 1907 peasant rebellion receive long prison sentences after their trial concludes in Bucharest.

April The most popular of the December 1907 laws goes into effect creating an institution called the "Rural House" that will buy land from large estate owners and sell it to the peasants in pieces no smaller than five hectares.

1911

March 1 Elections result in a victory for the Conservative party, already in control of the government.

June Diplomatic relations are resumed with Greece after several years of increasingly improving relations (*see* June 12, 1906).

1912

October 18 The First Balkan War begins with Bulgaria, Serbia, Montenegro, and Greece attacking the Ottoman Empire; Romania remains neutral.

1913

May 7 A great power peace conference in St. Petersburg, Russia marks the end of the First Balkan War and awards Romania the fortress of Silistra and a small piece of southern Dobrudja, which Romania demanded for its neutrality in the First Balkan War. Romania occupies the territory the same day.

June 29 The Second Balkan War begins when Bulgaria, feeling slighted by the territory it received as a result of the May 30 Treaty of London that officially ended the First Balkan War, attacks the Greeks and Serbs in Macedonia. Montenegro and Ottoman Turkey will also join the war against Bulgaria. Romania remains neutral for the time being.

July Romania renews its secret alliance with Austria-Hungary and Germany (*see* July 1902).

July 3 Romania mobilizes due to the Second Balkan War.

July 10 Romania declares war on Bulgaria and easily occupies the rest of Dobrudja.

July 31 An armistice is declared in the Second Balkan War resulting in peace negotiations in Bucharest.

August 10 As a result of the Treaty of Bucharest, Bulgaria surrenders a larger section of Dobrudja to Romania.

1914

January 14 A Liberal government led by Ion Brătianu is appointed by King Carol. The Brătianu cabinet focuses on agrarian reform.

March 27 Crown Prince Ferdinand, King Carol's nephew, officially visits the Russian capital of St. Petersburg. The Crown Prince is looking for support of an emerging policy that takes into consideration the interests of all Romanian communities, including those outside the country, especially those in Austria-Hungary. This marks an about-face in foreign policy to the secret alliance with Austria-Hungary and Germany renewed in July 1913.

June 14 Tsar Nicholas II of Russia and his family return the March visit of Crown Prince Ferdinand. The visit marks a warming in relations between the two countries that had been strained since 1878 after Russia received southern Bessarabia at the Congress of Berlin. During his visits to Bucharest and Constanța, the tsar and the Romanians agree to cooperate should the Dardanelles and Bosporus straits, linking the Mediterranean and Black seas, be closed in an event of a Greek-Turkish conflict.

June 28 The assassination of Archduke Franz Ferdinand, heir of the Austro-Hungarian empire, leads to the outbreak of the First World War in late July and early August.

July 30–31 Romania is offered Transylvania by Russia and Bessarabia by Germany in return for its neutrality in the wake of war between the Central Powers of Austria-Hungary and Germany and the Entente powers of Great Britain, France, and Russia.

August 3 At a government meeting, only the king and one minister wish to support the Central Powers in the World War due to the country's treaty with Austria-Hungary and Germany from 1883 (*see* July 1913). A majority of the cabinet votes for Romania to declare its neutrality.

October 1 Russia and Romania sign a secret treaty which in effect gives eventual Romanian support to the

Entente cause in return for promises of Transylvania and Bukovina.

October 10   King Carol, ruler of Romania since 1866, dies.

October 11   Ferdinand succeeds his uncle Carol as king. Unlike his uncle, who was pro-German, Ferdinand is pro-Entente and more easily influenced by the offer of territory from the Entente powers of Russia, France, and Great Britain.

1915

January 25   Romania is offered Transylvania from the Entente if it immediately joins the war against Austria-Hungary and Germany. Romania declines. Instead, the Romanian leaders are willing to remain neutral for as long as possible until they can be more sure that the outcome of the war will result in an Entente victory. Meanwhile, neutral Romania earns a large sum of money selling foodstuffs to the Central Powers.

February 6   The Romanians and Italians negotiate a mutual assistance treaty in case of Austro-Hungarian aggression.

May 23   Prime Minister Bratianu and King Ferdinand almost agree to enter the war on the side of the Entente following the lead of Italy earlier in the month. This decision comes after the Entente offers, in addition to Transylvania, Bukovina and the Banat regions of Austria-Hungary. However, Russian defeats in Galicia on the eastern front cause the prime minister and king to quickly change their minds.

1916

March 2   Queen Elizabeth, wife of King Carol, dies. She is better known as the author Carmen Sylva.

April 7   While still playing off both sides in the war, Romania signs an agreement with Germany, providing the Germans with grain and other Romanian domestic products.

August 17   Romania, seeing the initial victories of the Russian Brusilov campaign (the Russian military offensive against Germany and Austria-Hungary) and fearing it will receive nothing if the war ends, finally decides to join the Entente by signing a secret treaty with Great Britain, France, Russia, and Italy. The treaty guarantees Romania the Banat, Transylvania as far as the Tisza River, and Bukovina as far as the Prut River.

August 26   In compliance with the August 17 treaty, Romania declares war on Austria-Hungary and invades Transylvania.

August 29   Romanian armies enter the Transylvanian city of Braşov.

August 30   Germany declares war on Romania.

September 1   Bulgaria and Ottoman Turkey declare war on Romania.

September 25   Bucharest is bombed from the air by the Central Powers. The war is going poorly for Romania now, with the country being attacked on three fronts. In the next three months, the Romanian armies will be virtually destroyed.

December 3   The king and members of the government flee Bucharest and go to Iaşi, the capital of Moldavia.

December 6   The Central Powers occupy Bucharest.

1917

January 2   Due to the defeats at the hands of the Central Powers, Premier Brătianu restructures the government now in Iasi.

Mid-January   Over two-thirds of Romania is under Central Power occupation.

March 9   In an attempt to keep Romania in the war, Great Britain grants it a loan of 40 million pounds sterling.

May   Trying to keep the occupied population loyal, the government grants direct, universal suffrage (or voting) rights.

July 14   In further trying to retain the loyalty of its occupied population and to forestall Communist propaganda seeping in from Russia, the Brătianu government enacts the Agrarian Law. The law is to correct the unequal distribution of land by breaking up large estates and distributing the land among the peasants; owners are to be paid with state bonds and not allowed to retain more than 500 hectares.

December 2   Due to the anarchy following the Russian Revolution in February, the Democratic Moldavian Republic (Bessarabia) is proclaimed in the city of Kishinev as an autonomous entity of a federated Russia. Bessarabia, largely inhabited by Romanians, had been taken by Russia after the Congress of Berlin in 1878.

December 6   The Truce of Focşani is signed ceasing hostilities between the Central Powers and Romania.

December 23   The Democratic Moldavian Republic declares its independence and asks Romania for aid against Bolshevik, or Communist, Russians attempting to seize control.

1918

January 13   Romania sends troops to help Democratic Moldavia rid itself of Communists.

January 28   Bolshevik Russia breaks relations with Romania because of Romanian aid to Democratic Moldavia.

February 6   After waiting two months for Romania to sit down at the peace table, the Germans deliver an ultimatum to begin peace negotiations at once (*see* December 6, 1917).

February 9   Premier Ion Brătianu resigns rather than negotiate and sign a peace treaty with the Central Powers. King Ferdinand replaces him with the leader of the army, General Alexandru Averescu.

February 23   Central Power peace negotiators arrive in Bucharest for talks.

March 9   Romania agrees to withdraw its troops from Democratic Moldavia in an accord with Bolshevik Russia.

March 12   Unable to influence the peace negotiations with the Central Powers, the government of General Averescu resigns.

March 20   To receive better terms in the negotiations with the Central Powers, the pro-German Alexandru Marghiloman becomes prime minister and forms a new government.

April 9   Feeling its independence threatened by Ukrainians and Bolsheviks, despite agreements promised especially by the Bolsheviks, Democratic Moldavia votes in favor of a union with Romania.

April 23   Bolshevik Russia unsuccessfully protests the union of Democratic Moldavia with Romania.

May 7   Romania signs the Treaty of Bucharest with the Central Powers, in which Romania cedes Dobrudja to the Central Powers collectively and the Carpathian passes to Austria-Hungary; agrees to pay for the upkeep of an occupation army; allows the Central Powers to transport military goods and personnel through its territory; and leases Romanian oil fields to Germany for 99 years. In return, the Central Powers ''give'' Democratic Moldavia (Bessarabia) to Romania.

September 12   Crown Prince Carol elopes with the daughter of a Romanian general.

October 27   The Romanians in Bukovina announce their secession from Austria-Hungary.

November 8   Realizing that the Central Powers are losing the war, Romania acts to assert itself and get back into the war before it ends. King Ferdinand appoints General Coanda as premier; Coanda then voids all laws passed by the pro-German government of Marghiloman. The government furthermore repeals the direct, universal suffrage, or voting rights, granted in May 1917.

The government declares war against Germany and pushes enemy troops out of Wallachia.

November 10   Romanian forces invade Transylvania; most of this region is occupied by December 1.

November 11   World War I ends.

November 12   King Ferdinand dismisses General Coanda as premier and recalls Ion Brătianu to serve again as prime minister. Brătianu, however, waits a month until he takes office.

November 25   The king dissolves parliament.

November 27   The National Council of Bessarabia votes to join Romania (*see* April 9).

November 28   The National Council of Bukovina declares its bonds to Austria void and votes to join Romania (*see* October 27).

November 30   The Romanian government reestablishes itself in Bucharest, and King Ferdinand returns to the capital.

December 1   An assembly consisting of 100,000 Romanian delegates from Transylvania and the Banat meets in Alba Iulia and votes to leave Hungary and to join Romania.

December 2   A new government in Transylvania is constituted, headed by Iuliu Maniu, the leader of the Transylvanian Romanians.

December 3   King Ferdinand is acclaimed as a victor in Bucharest in celebrations marking the end of World War I.

December 14   Ion Brătianu becomes premier, signaling a return to power of the industrial and professional classes of Romania.

December 21   Another agrarian law goes into effect that orders the expropriation of even more estates.

December 27   King Ferdinand formally proclaims the annexation of the following lands of former Austria-Hungary: Bukovina, Transylvania, and the Banat.

1919

January 8 The government annuls the ''inappropriate'' marriage of Crown Prince Carol (*see* September 12, 1918).

January 21 An assembly of Saxons, or Germans, in Transylvania ratify the vote to join Romania (*see* December 1, 1918).

March 24 In a battle near the Dniester River, a Romanian force defeats a Russian Bolshevik army attempting to take back Bessarabia.

April 16–August 1 A Hungarian Soviet Republic is proclaimed in March that aims to retake all territory seized by Czechoslovakia, Yugoslavia, and Romania after the First World War. Romanian troops subsequently invade Hungary to forestall Hungarian plans for the reconquest of Transylvania. At first the Hungarian Red Army does not halt the Romanian advance. In May and June, however, the Hungarian Red Army, swelling with volunteers, begins a successful offensive against the Czechs and Slovaks in Slovakia and Ruthenia. By the beginning of June, a wedge between the Czechoslovak and Romanian forces has been created. This success prompts the Hungarian leadership to negotiate in mid-June a pullback to the former demarcation line at the Tisza River. The Romanians refuse to withdraw until Hungary disarms, which prompts an attack by Hungarian forces on July 20. After several initial victories, the Hungarians fall back into a disorderly retreat, and on July 31, only 60 miles separate the Romanians from Budapest. After 133 days, the Hungarian Soviet Republic falls.

May 2 The Romanian government ignores Bolshevik Russia's ultimatum to evacuate Bessarabia.

May 8 The Allies urge Romania to halt its invasion of Hungary.

May 18 Bolshevik Russia announces that a state of war exists between it and Romania due to Romania's refusal to leave Bessarabia. Involved in a civil war, however, Russia can do little against Romania.

May 28 Romanian Jews are granted emancipation by the king thereby becoming full citizens of the country. However, anti-Semitism continues to be strong.

June 13 The Allies decide that the Banat should be divided between Romania and Yugoslavia, much to the dissatisfaction of the Romanians.

Romanian officials announce that a common boundary with Czechoslovakia has been drawn.

July 28 The Allies award Romania the Danubian island of Ada Kaleh, formerly under the control of the Ottoman Empire.

August 4 Romanian troops occupy Budapest.

August 6 The Romanian army supports a coup d'état against the Hungarian trade unionist government that succeeded the Hungarian-Soviet government on August 1.

The Allies send a note requesting that Romanian forces evacuate Hungary.

September 10 The peace Treaty of St.-Germain between the Allies and Austria confirms the union of Bukovina with Romania. The Brătianu government resigns rather than sign what it considers an unfair treaty that does not give it more territory. Romania also refuses to sign a minority treaty that provides for equal rights and protection for ethnic minorities in Romania under the protection of the League of Nations.

November 7 The Allies send another note, in reality an ultimatum, to Romania demanding it withdraw from Hungary, sign the peace and minority treaties, and permit an Allied (rather than a Romanian) commission to decide on the amount of Hungarian reparations to Romania (*see* August 6, September 10).

November 8 In nationwide elections, the first where all adult males can vote, the Peasant and National parties defeat the Liberals of Ion Brătianu, who are blamed for the poor showing in World War I. The victors, however, have no real power to create effective change in the government as the power lies with the king who appoints and dismisses governments at will.

November 14 Romanian troops leave Budapest. As the Romanians slowly withdraw from Hungary, they take whatever they can.

November 27 The Treaty of Neuilly between the Allies and Bulgaria recognizes the old border established with Romania after the Second Balkan War in 1913; Romania also refuses to sign this treaty.

December 2 Following the results of the November elections, the Transylvanian Alexandru Vaida-Voevod, a leader of the National party, becomes prime minister.

December 3 The Allies threaten to break diplomatic relations with Romania unless it signs the St.-Germain, Neuilly, and minority treaties.

December 9 Caving into Allied pressure, Romania signs the peace treaties with Austria and Bulgaria and the treaty guaranteeing minority rights in Romania (*see* September 10, November 27, December 3).

1920

February 25 The last Romanian troops leave Hungarian territory.

March 2 An armistice is signed with Bolshevik Russia.

March 15 King Ferdinand, for the second time, appoints General Alexandru Averescu as prime minister after dismissing the Vaida-Voevod government, which wanted to enact major economic, political, and social reforms.

May 25 Nationwide elections, characterized by voting irregularities long ingrained in Romania, result in a victory for Averescu's People's party, giving it control of parliament. The party supposedly represents no social class or special interests but has strong leanings toward the Liberals.

June 4 In the peace Treaty of Trianon between the Allies and Hungary, Romania receives Transylvania, but divides the Banat with Yugoslavia.

August 10 The New States Treaty between the Allies and Czechoslovakia, Poland, and Romania recognizes each country's independence and borders.

August 17 Romania unofficially joins the Czechoslovak-Yugoslav alliance signed on August 14, a mutual defensive alliance against Hungary, by pledging to uphold the Treaty of Trianon. This marks the beginnings of the Little Entente, joined officially by Romania in 1921.

September 14 Romania joins the League of Nations.

October 18 The Council of Trade Unions calls a general strike to demand the right to freely join unions.

October 25 The Council of Trade Union's strike fails after the army intervenes, closes down all unions, and arrests their leaders, almost causing the destruction of the union movement in the country.

October 28. Great Britain France, Italy, and Japan recognize the union of Bessarabia with Romania.

December 8 A bomb explodes in the upper house of parliament killing two; no one claims responsibility.

1921

Throughout the year, almost all the lands of the Romanian Orthodox Church are expropriated.

February 27 In the tradition of using dynastic alliances to solidify political bonds, Romanian Princess Elizabeth marries Crown Prince George of Greece.

March 3 Romania, Poland, and Hungary form a defensive military alliance aimed at Communist Russia.

March 10 Crown Prince Carol "appropriately" marries Princess Helen of Greece (*see* January 8, 1919).

April 23 In response to ex-Emperor Charles's attempt to return to the Hungarian throne, Czechoslovakia and Romania form an alliance to uphold the Treaty of Trianon and to render mutual military aid in case of unprovoked attack by a third country, meaning Hungary (*see* June 4; August 17, 1920).

May 8 The Romanian Communist party is founded.

May 26 The government enacts a law that grew, in part, out of the October 18, 1920 general strike. It grants workers the right to organize unions and establishes procedures for resolving labor disputes.

June 7 The Romanian-Yugoslav alliance is signed, officially forming the Little Entente between Romania, Yugoslavia, and Czechoslovakia (*see* April 23).

June 8 Yugoslavia and Romania sign an agreement to demarcate their mutual borders in the Banat. This process will be complete by November 24.

October 25 The heir to the Romanian throne, Prince Michael, is born to Crown Prince Carol and Crown Princess Helen. Shortly after, Crown Prince Carol leaves his wife to live with his mistress, Magda Lupescu.

December 17 King Ferdinand dismisses Alexandru Averescu as prime minister. Two days later Take Ionescu, a former foreign minister and Conservative party leader, replaces Averescu.

1922

January 18 Due to the inability of Ionescu to form a stable government, the Liberal party comes back to power when Ion Brătianu again becomes premier.

March In fraudulent general elections, the Liberal party wins an overwhelming majority in parliament.

June 8 Romanian Princess Marie marries King Alexander I of Yugoslavia in another dynastic alliance.

October 15 King Ferdinand and Queen Marie are crowned as the rulers of greater Romania at a ceremony in Alba Iulia. However, no leaders from the territories added in 1918 to make a greater Romania attend the coronation in protest over centralized rule from Bucharest.

December 22 Germany refunds Romanian gold deposits seized after Romania entered the First World War against the Central Powers.

1923

January 10 Romanian and Hungarian troops battle in a border skirmish at Lokoshaza.

March 28 Parliament adopts a new constitution replacing, but based upon, the one from 1866; it goes into effect the next day. The new constitution, written by the Liberals to assure their hold on the government, includes the following provisions: all natural resources are nationalized, only Romanian citizens are permitted to own land, political centralization is retained, and the crown keeps extensive powers.

May 7 Romania and Czechoslovakia sign a three-year defensive military treaty.

July 7 Romania signs a defensive military treaty, much like that from May 7, with Yugoslavia.

October 18 The police uncover a fascist conspiracy to assassinate several members of the government.

December 26 Police and troops move on the campuses of the universities in Bucharest, Iaşi, and Cluj to restore order after anti-Semitic riots.

1924

March 23–April 2 Talks on the normalization of relations with the Soviet Union break down over the issue of Bessarabia (*see* April 9, 1918).

March 31 Anti-Semitism again flares up when students attack the Bucharest Economic Institute, hurting approximately 100.

April 15 Due to continued anti-Semitic violence in the universities, the government declares martial law in all university areas.

July 4 The government enacts a mining law requiring foreign companies operating in Romania to sell 55 percent of their stock to Romanian citizens in the next ten years.

October 1 The Gregorian calendar replaces the Julian calendar.

October 11 The Soviets create a Moldavian Autonomous Republic across the Dniester River from Bessarabia in anticipation of one day taking over this region.

December 18 In an attempt to end Communist influence in trade unions, the government bans the Romanian Communist party. The party, however, continues to exist underground.

1925

January 25 Iuliu Maniu, leader of the National party, calls for the unification of all political parties to bring down the government controlled by the Liberal party of Brătianu.

January 27 Following Maniu's appeal, the National and Democratic parties merge.

April 22 Romania agrees to pay all pre-World War I debts owed to Italy from the former areas of Austria-Hungary now part of Romania.

May 17 Approximately 15,000 people demonstrate in Bucharest against the Brătianu government.

June 13 The government replaces the existing local administrative structure with 71 centrally governed prefectures, or counties.

June 29 Romania and Hungary sign an agreement that sets the borders between the two countries.

September 1 Twenty-eight members of the illegal Communist party are arrested in Bucharest.

September 15 The Soviets launch an unsuccessful raid on Tatar-Bunar in Bessarabia.

October 7 The government reduces export duties on grain to help stimulate the export of Romanian grain after prices collapse worldwide.

November 1 Miron Cristea becomes the first patriarch, or leader, of the Romanian Orthodox Church.

December 1 Romania agrees to repay its $44,500,000 World War I debt to the United States during the next 62 years.

December 28 Crown Prince Carol renounces his right to succession in favor of his four-year-old son Prince Michael. He chooses to live in exile with his mistress, Magda Lupescu.

1926

January 4 Concern about King Ferdinand's health and Crown Prince Carol's lifestyle leads parliament to enact the Succession Act, which accepts Crown Prince Carol's renunciation of the throne, recognizes Prince Michael as the next in line to the throne, and establishes a regency council to advise Prince Michael. The Liberals are more than happy to exclude Carol from the throne, knowing that he did not care for them.

January 11 A regency council is appointed consisting of Patriarch Miron Cristea, the head of the Supreme Court, and Prince Nicolae, an uncle of Prince Michael.

February The Liberals do poorly in local elections.

March 16 Students stage a strike against allowing Jews to enter the University of Bucharest, forcing the school to close.

March 26 A treaty of alliance is signed with Poland, and on June 10, a similar treaty is concluded with France.

Former Crown Prince Carol takes the name Carol Caraiman.

March 27 Realizing that it has been alienating large sections of the country, Brătianu's government resigns and parliament is dissolved for new elections in May.

March 28 As a result of the poor showing in the February local elections, Brătianu designs a new electoral law to prevent due representation by peasant parties. The law allows for any party receiving 40 percent or more of the votes to receive over half of the seats in the lower house of parliament.

March 30 Alexandru Averescu becomes premier again.

May 25 In nationwide, blatantly fraudulent elections, Averescu's People's party wins a majority in parliament.

June 13 Romania, Czechoslovakia, and Yugoslavia renew the Little Entente treaties.

June 15 A treaty of friendship with Italy is signed that provides for the funding of Romania's World War I debt to that country and Italian resources for the development of the Romanian oil fields.

October 10 Iuliu Maniu's National party and Ion Mihalache's Peasant party unite to form the new National-Peasant party headed by Maniu.

November 30 King Ferdinand agrees to the Succession Act of January 4.

1927

January 1 Agrarian land reforms passed between 1917 and 1921 officially end. In all, the government states that over 6 million hectares have been taken from large estates, with over half of the land being distributed to landless or dwarf landowning peasants and the remainder being reserved for communal interests.

January 10 A combined Romanian-Hungarian commission is formed to rule on claims by Hungarian citizens that their land in the former Hungarian territories of Transylvania and the Banat was confiscated due to the land reform bill of December 21, 1918.

February 1 The National-Peasant party, as a supporter of former Crown Prince Carol, demands that the Succession Act of January 4, 1926 be repealed.

June 3 After the king removes his support, Alexandru Averescu's government falls. A temporary government headed by Prince Barbu Ştirbei is formed two days later.

June 22 The Ştirbei government resigns and the new government is lead once again by the leader of the Liberal party, Ion Brătianu, who also assumes the post of foreign minister.

June 24 A fascist, terrorist organization called the Legion of the Archangel Michael is formed by Corneliu Zelea Codreanu, a radical politician from Moldavia. In 1930 it changes its name to the Iron Guard, in 1935 the All for the Country Movement, and in 1940 the Legionnaire Movement; it is most commonly referred to as the Iron Guard. The program of this fascist and anti-Semitic group includes making Romania a Christian and racially pure country. Liberal use of violence and intimidation characterize the Iron Guard. Beginning in 1933 it becomes the outpost of the Nazi Germans in Romania.

July 7 In nationwide rigged elections, Brătianu's Liberal party scores an overwhelming victory.

July 20 King Ferdinand dies of cancer.

July 21 The five-year-old grandson of King Ferdinand becomes King Michael. According to the Succession Act of January 4, 1926, a regency consisting of Prince Nicolae, Patriarch Miron Cristea, and Gheorghe Buzdugan, the chief justice of the Supreme Court of Appeals, takes control to rule for the king until he becomes of age.

October 25 A government official is arrested upon his return from Paris for having in his possession letters written by former Crown Prince Carol to Romanian political leaders mentioning the fact that he should end his exile and ascend the throne. A court will acquit the government official of the charges in November.

November 24 Ion Brătianu dies unexpectedly causing a reshuffling of the government; Vintila Brătianu, the minister of finance, takes his brother's position as prime minister.

December 8 Students in Cluj, Oradea Mare, and Bucharest engage in anti-Semitic riots, causing the military to intervene.

1928

March 18 Over 100,000 peasants take to the streets of Bucharest to demand the resignation of the Brătianu government.

March 21 Romania signs a nonaggression treaty with Germany.

May 6 At a congress of the National-Peasant party, over 200,000 peasants meet in Alba Iulia and increase their pressure on the Brătianu government by demanding reforms including decentralization of the government or local autonomy and representative government.

May 8 British authorities expel former Crown Prince Carol on charges of using Great Britain as a base of operations to take the Romanian throne.

June 21 Princess Helen, the mother of King Michael, receives a divorce from former Crown Prince Carol.

July 26 Keeping up its pressure on the Brătianu government, Iuliu Maniu, leader of the National-Peasant party, creates a rival parliament in Bucharest.

November 3 Due to a bad harvest and pressure from the peasantry and regency council, the Brătianu government resigns.

November 9 Iuliu Maniu becomes premier with a program of purging the administration of Liberal party members, improving peasant life, and easing the way for foreign investment. He forms a new government two days later.

December 12 In the first free parliamentary elections in Romania, the National-Peasant party wins an overwhelming victory with 78 percent of the vote, thereby taking 349 seats out of 387 in the lower house.

December 22 The new parliament opens. Among its first acts are the abolition of censorship and martial law.

1929

February 11 Due to the depression, Romania receives a loan of over $100 million from 14 countries in an attempt to balance the country's budget, to stabilize its currency, the *lei,* and to get the economy going again.

March The Maniu government makes the highly bureaucratic and government subsidized state monopolies of ports, railroads, and roads semiautonomous enterprises that are run on a for-profit basis. Furthermore, it lowers or

ends tariffs on industrial and agricultural goods, and in an effort to attract foreign capital to mining, the law from July 4, 1924 is revised.

March 1 Police raid a Bucharest meeting of the illegal Communist party, making numerous arrests.

April 7 Police and Communists battle in Bucharest, leading to numerous arrests.

May 21 Romania, Czechoslovakia, and Yugoslavia renew the treaties of the Little Entente, adding a further agreement to peacefully settle all disputes between the three countries.

June The government introduces extensive decentralization by granting local autonomy. It will be revoked in 1931 by the Iorga government.

July 8 Forty members of the Iron Guard, some with ties to the military, are arrested on charges of plotting to seize the government. In their trial in mid-September, 26 are acquitted and the rest receive mild sentences. As a result, the National-Peasant party forms its own paramilitary organization.

July 14 To show their disapproval of the administrative reform from June, the Liberal's and People's deputies boycott sessions of parliament until November 15, 1930.

August 1 In an attempt to get the stalled economy moving, tariffs are reduced.

August 6 Communist-organized striking coal miners in Lupeni fight with police; the strike is brutally repressed by the army with much bloodshed.

October 5 An unsuccessful Communist assassination attempt takes place on the minister of the interior, Alexandru Vaida-Voevod.

October 7 Regent Gheorghe Buzdugan dies (*see* July 21, 1927). Prime Minister Maniu replaces him with a National-Peasant party representative, resulting in declining respect for the regency council.

December 14–17 Elections for the upper house of parliament, or the Senate, result in an overwhelming victory for the National-Peasant party.

1930

February 6 Local elections result in another victory for the National-Peasant party.

June 6 In a move engineered by the National-Peasant party, former Crown Prince Carol returns to Romania.

June 7 The Maniu government resigns. Gheorghe Mironescu, the foreign minister in the Brătianu cabinet, forms a new government.

June 8 Parliament repeals the Succession Act of January 4, 1926, abolishing the regency so that former Crown Prince Carol can take the throne.

June 9 King Michael is removed as king and his father is proclaimed King Carol II, with Carol's brother Prince Nicolae as his successor; former King Michael receives the title of Grand Voivode of Alba Iulia.

June 11 After the Mironescu government is dismissed by the king, Maniu forms a new government.

June 12 King Carol II signs a law naming his ex-wife, Princess Helen, queen of Romania. However, the king's mistress, Magda Lupescu, has enormous influence on the affairs of state (*see* October 25, 1921).

July 21 A student unsuccessfully attempts to assassinate the minister of the interior.

Carol II renounced the throne in favor of his four-year-old son, Michael, to live in exile with his mistress. Returning to Romania, he held the throne until 1940 when he was forced from power by the Iron Guard.

October 6 Claiming ill health, Prime Minister Maniu resigns. Gheorghe Mironescu succeeds him and forms a new government on October 10.

December 1 Anti-Semitic student riots erupt in Galaţi.

December 23 Vintila Brătianu, leader of the opposition Liberal party, dies. His place is taken by Ion Duca.

December 29 A government census reports the population of Romania at 14,280,729 of which 21.4 percent live in urban centers and 78.6 percent in rural areas.

1931

April 4 The Mironescu government falls. Nicolae Titulescu, a diplomat, becomes prime minister and unsuccessfully attempts to form a coalition government during the next 13 days.

April 18 King Carol II appoints a coalition government under Professor Nicolae Iorga, a historian and Carol II's former tutor.

May A new electoral law is announced that should make elections more representative.

June 1 Despite the May announcement, national elections are again manipulated. This causes a defeat for the National-Peasant party and a victory for the coalition government of Titulescu, which claims 49.88 percent of the vote. The Iron Guard participates for the first time in the elections but receives less than 2 percent of the vote.

1932

January–May Negotiations with the Soviet Union over the ownership of Bessarabia prove fruitless.

May 31 Due to its inability to handle the worldwide economic depression that also affects Romania, the Iorga government resigns.

June 6 The peasant leader Alexandru Vaida-Voevod, a former premier and minister of the interior, forms a new cabinet.

July 17 The National-Peasant party wins the nationwide elections, but Maniu, due to his disapproval of King Carol's affair with Magda Lupescu, refuses to form another government so Vaida-Voevod remains as prime minister.

October 17 After the king withdraws his support, the Vaida-Voevod government falls.

October 20   After the king appeals to Maniu to change his mind, the National-Peasant party leader forms another government.

1933

January 12   Maniu resigns as premier. He is succeeded by Vaida-Voevod four days later.

February   Communists organize a railway workers strike that the government brutally represses.

February 16   The Little Entente of Czechoslovakia, Romania, and Yugoslavia meets in Geneva and reorganizes the alliance with a permanent council to harmonize economic relations and to create a unified foreign policy in the wake of Nazi successes in Germany.

July   Romania signs a nonaggression pact with the Soviet Union.

November 14   Due to disunity in the National-Peasant party and the resignation of Vaida-Voevod on November 12, Ion Duca, leader of the Liberal party, forms a new government.

December 20   In rigged general elections, Duca's Liberal party claims almost 51 percent of the vote and thereby a majority of seats in parliament.

December 29   Members of the Iron Guard assassinate Duca, resulting in the proclamation of martial law and the arrest of the leaders of the Iron Guard. The assassins will be acquitted.

1934

January 3   King Carol II appoints Gheorghe Tătărescu of the Liberal party as prime minister to replace the late Duca.

February 8   The Balkan Pact is concluded between Romania, Yugoslavia, Greece, and Turkey. The plan, inspired by Nicolae Titulescu, the Romanian foreign minister, is an attempt to isolate Bulgaria and keep it in check.

March 16–17   Austria, Italy, and Hungary sign the Rome Protocols in which the three countries agree to cooperate in foreign affairs. The agreements are aimed against the Little Entente of Czechoslovakia, Romania, and Yugoslavia.

April 7   The government reduces all agricultural debts preceding December 1931 by 50 to 70 percent in an attempt to stimulate the economy.

May   The National-Peasant party supports the Liberal party in parliament and foils an attempt by King Carol II to establish a royal dictatorship.

June 9   Tensions between peasant groups and the monarchy mount but are soon overshadowed by a rise in fascism and anti-Semitism.

Romania, Poland, and the USSR sign an agreement mutually guaranteeing their borders.

1936

February   Elements from the National-Peasant party and the National Christian party combine to form the anti-Semitic Christian League.

August 29   Foreign Minister Nicolae Titulescu, who supported solid ties to France, the Soviet Union, and the Little Entente, is forced to resign by rightist groups who favor stronger relations with Nazi Germany.

1937

June 9   Romania, the Soviet Union, and Poland sign an agreement mutually guaranteeing their borders.

December 21   In nationwide elections, the National Liberal government is defeated, winning only about 36 percent of the vote due to a strong showing by the Iron Guard.

December 27   Tătărescu, in power since January 1934, resigns as prime minister.

December 28   King Carol II appoints Octavian Goga, an extreme anti-Semite and the leader of the right-wing Christian League, as premier. Anti-Semitic legislation soon follows laying the groundwork for the establishment of a dictatorship.

1938

January 18   Since the anti-Semitic policies of the Goga government (driving Jews out of businesses throughout Romania) have brought the country to a virtual economic collapse, King Carol II dissolves parliament, causing protests from non-fascist political parties.

February 10   Due to mainly British and French pressure, Goga is forced out of office which discredits him and the fascists, while King Carol II's position strengthens, allowing him to establish a royal dictatorship. A new government, consisting of seven former prime ministers and led by Patriarch Miron Cristea, the leader of the Romanian Orthodox Church, takes form and suspends the constitution and suppresses all political parties. A new constitution is written to give the king complete power.

February 24   A nationwide plebiscite, or referendum, approves King Carol II's constitution and actions from February 10. Over 4.2 million people vote favorably while only 5,400 people disapprove. The king furthermore decrees that the upper house of parliament will from now on be one-half appointive, that only the crown may initiate legislation, and that the king may govern by decree.

April 19   The government begins to attack the fascists by arresting and imprisoning hundreds of members of the Iron Guard. Corneliu Codreanu, leader of the Iron Guard, receives a six-month prison sentence that will be extended to ten years in May.

August 4   A new nationalities law grants ethnic minorities equal rights with Romanians in language, religion, and race.

August 23   Signaling the end of the alliance between Czechoslovakia, Romania, and Yugoslavia, the Little Entente recognizes Hungary's right to rearm.

Early November   King Carol II visits Great Britain and France in an attempt to receive more support in his moves to resist German influence in his country. He is not successful.

November 24   King Carol II meets with the Nazi leader Adolf Hitler at Berchtesgaden where the two agree to increase trade between their countries.

November 30   Prison guards garrote to death Corneliu Codreanu, the leader of the Iron Guard, along with 13 of his followers (*see* April 19). The government, however, announces that they were shot to death while trying to escape. The incident arouses the anger of the German Nazis, but the government continues its measures to stamp out the fascist movement in Romania.

December 15   The Front of National Renaissance is established by royal decree as the only political party in Romania. By mid-January 1939, it will have over 3 million members since political advancement is tied to the party.

1939

January 5   The Front of National Renaissance publishes its rules and regulations.

February 20   A standard uniform is adopted for members of the Front of National Renaissance; it will be modified in November.

March 6   Patriarch Miron Cristea dies; Armand Călinescu, a politician and government official, succeeds him as prime minister.

March 23   Romania signs a more extensive ten-year commercial agreement with Nazi Germany that allows German economic dominance by exploiting Romanian natural resources.

April 13   After the destruction of post-Munich Czechoslovakia by Nazi Germany in mid-March, and alarmed at increased German influence in Romania Great Britain and France guarantee Romanian independence and territorial integrity.

September 1   The Second World War begins when Nazi Germany invades Poland.

September 21   In retaliation for the death of the Iron Guard leader Corneliu Codreanu, the Iron Guard murders Prime Minister Armand Călinescu, setting off numerous arrests and murders of Guardists (*see* November 30, 1938).

November 24   King Carol II appoints Tătărescu as prime minister to replace the murdered Călinescu. Tătărescu forms a government that is half pro-Ally and half pro-German.

December   In an attempt to placate Hitler and the Iron Guard, King Carol II dismisses the heads of police and secret police under the pretext that they failed to protect Călinescu from assassins.

1940

January   In a further move to appease the Germans, numerous Guardists are released from prison; others will be allowed to return from exile during the coming months.

May 29   A new German-Romanian trade agreement is signed further tying Romania economically to Germany.

June 21   King Carol II reorganizes the only legal political party, the Front of National Renaissance, into the Party of the Nation, with membership required for all public officials.

June 26   Due to the secret Nazi-Soviet nonaggression pact from August 1939, which gave the USSR a free hand in the Balkans, the USSR issues a 24-hour ultimatum to Romania demanding the return of Bessarabia and the ceding of northern Bukovina. Romania, with no great power support, has no choice but to agree. Two days later

Soviet troops occupy the regions. Approximately 40,000 refugees leave the two regions for Romania proper. The Soviet success triggers Bulgarian demands for southern Dobrudja and Hungarian revisionist aspirations for Transylvania. Although Hitler favors the Romanians in regard to Transylvania, he is forced to arbitrate a settlement between the two countries (*see* August 21, 30).

July 1   Since neither Great Britain nor France did anything to help Romania in its crisis with the Soviet Union despite the British-French territorial guarantee from April 13, 1939, Romania renounces it. Instead, Romania turns toward Nazi Germany, causing the fall of Tătărescu on July 3. He is replaced by the pro-German businessman Ion Gigurtu, who proclaims Romania's willingness to join the Axis camp of Germany, Italy, and Japan.

July 10   Romania withdraws from the League of Nations.

August 9   A law forbids marriages between Jews and Christian Romanians marking the beginning of official anti-Semitic policy.

August 21   Under pressure from the Axis powers, Romania agrees to cede southern Dobrudja to Bulgaria (*see* June 26). The treaty is signed in early September.

August 30   Despite Romania's turn toward the Axis powers, Germany and Italy pressure the Romanian government to relinquish large sections of Transylvanian territory to Hungary in the Second Vienna Award. From June 26 to August 30, Romania lost about a third of its land and population. Nazi Germany and Italy guarantee Romania's new borders.

September 5   Due to the public outcry from the loss of Transylvanian land as a result of the Second Vienna Award, political reversals take place and General Ion Antonescu becomes premier with extensive powers.

September 6   Due to the territorial losses suffered in the previous months, the Iron Guard force King Carol II to flee the country and to abdicate in favor of his nineteen-year-old son Michael, who again becomes the ruler of the country. His government is led by Ion Antonescu, a popular general who is a conservative nationalist. Antonescu's former duties included military attaché in London and minister of war from 1934–1938. He has links to the Iron Guard, and after forming a National Legionary (Iron Guard) government, he adopts the title *conducător* or leader, something akin to *il duce* in fascist Italy or *Führer* in Nazi Germany.

September 14   At the instigation of the Nazis, Horia Sima, the Iron Guard leader, becomes deputy prime minis-

ter, and Romania is proclaimed a National Legionary state with the Iron Guard as the only legal political party.

October 10   General Antonescu permits German troops to enter Romania. They will eventually number about 500,000.

October 22   Germany and Romania sign an agreement that calls for the repatriation of approximately 77,000 Germans from southern Bukovina and northern Dobrudja.

October 26   Soviet troops occupy Romanian islands at the mouth of the Danube.

November 12   Soviet troops mass on the border with Romania.

November 23   Fearing Soviet intentions, Romania joins the German-Italian-Japanese Tripartite Pact aimed at the United States and the USSR.

November 27–28   In retaliation for the murder of Codreanu and other Guardists two years earlier, the Iron Guard massacres 64 prominent statesmen and generals, including former premiers Nicolae Iorga and Virgil Madgearu, the leader of the National-Peasant party. The massacres continue into January 1941 against other political opponents and Jews.

1941

January 14   General Antonescu meets with Hitler at Berchtesgaden, where Hitler seems to approve of a purge of the Iron Guard to end the turmoil it has caused since late November.

January 17–19   Unaware of the results of the January 14 meeting between Hitler and Antonescu, the Iron Guard holds rallies and organizes paramilitary groups in Bucharest in preparation for a coup attempt.

January 21–23   Thousands of Guardists are killed in pitched battles with the army in Bucharest. Antonescu disbands the National Legionary state and reshuffles his government in February to include only army officers and technocrats. Horia Sima and several other Iron Guard leaders flee to Germany where they are granted asylum, while about 8,000 others are arrested and receive heavy prison sentences.

February 10   Due to the continued presence of about 500,000 German troops in the country, Great Britain severs ties with Romania.

March 2–5   In a rigged plebiscite to legitimize his actions in January, Antonescu receives almost unanimous support.

June 22 In conjunction with Nazi Germany's invasion of the Soviet Union, Romania declares war on the USSR. Romania supplies more troops for the Russian campaign than all the other of German allies put together; Romanian armies cooperate with German forces during offensive maneuvers into Soviet territory.

Late June The Romanian army begins attacks on Jews starting in Iaşi and then in captured Soviet territories.

Late July The Romanians take back Bessarabia and northern Bukovina. For these actions of the Romanian army, General Antonescu is promoted to the rank of marshal in August.

August 6 Romania creates the Transnistria province out of captured Soviet territory, between the Dniester and Southern Bug rivers. Odessa becomes its capital, after its eventual capture on October 15.

December 6 Great Britain declares war on Romania after it does not respond to the British ultimatum of December 1 to withdraw back over the Dniester River. Later in the month, the British Commonwealth nations of Canada, New Zealand, Australia, and South Africa also declare war on Romania.

December 12 Holding true to its obligations under the Tripartite Pact from November 23, 1940, Romania declares war against the United States.

1942

September 14 Soviet bombers attack Bucharest and the Ploieşti oil fields north of the capital.

October Marshal Antonescu admits that Germany has lost the war after he is unable to convince the Germans that an attack on Stalingrad would prove fruitless.

1943

Throughout the year representatives of the illegal Liberal and National-Peasant parties hold secret negotiations with the Allies in Spain, Sweden, Egypt, and Turkey in an attempt to take Romania out of the war. The negotiations continue into 1944.

1944

March 26 The Soviet army, on the eastern bank of the Prut River, poises to invade Romania proper after taking northern Bessarabia.

April 2 In a move to allay Romanian fears, Soviet Foreign Minister V. M. Molotov declares that the USSR will not change the social structure, political system, or borders of Romania.

April 4 American and British bombers attack Bucharest.

May The Soviet army moves into northern Moldavia.

May 1 In a secret meeting, the blanket organization of trade unions, the General Confederation of Labor, agrees to reorganize its leadership into a committee of twelve members divided equally between the Socialists and the Communists. Furthermore, all leaders who supported the rule of former King Carol II are banned, thereby giving the Communists almost complete control of the labor movement in the country.

June 13–14 Royal, military, and political representatives create a plan to take Romania out of the war and present it to the Allies who do not respond.

August 20 The Red Army begins a major offensive in Romania.

August 23–24 Suffering defeats as Germany's ally and with Soviet troops capturing large sections of Romania, King Michael overthrows the government of General Antonescu, who is arrested, and appoints General Constantin Sănătescu to form a coalition government. In addition, Romania accepts an armistice offered by the Allies and declares war on Nazi Germany on August 25. In the war against the Soviet Union, approximately 130,000 Romanian soldiers died and another 180,000 were captured or missing in action. In its war against Germany until May 1945, Romania will lose another 160,000 troops.

August 24 King Michael flees Bucharest to avoid capture by the Germans; he returns on September 10.

Marshal Antonescu is handed over to members of the Communist party who lock him in a safe; they give him to the Red Army after it enters the capital in late August.

Horia Sima, the Iron Guard leader in exile in Germany since late January 1941, becomes head of a pro-German puppet Romanian government in Vienna.

The German air force bombs Bucharest while the German army attacks on land under orders from Hitler to destroy the traitors who betrayed his cause.

August 26 Allied bombers attack German positions outside Bucharest, lifting the German attack on the city. Numerous German soldiers surrender to Romanian forces in the city.

August 29 Soviet troops capture the Romanian Black Sea port of Constanţa.

Germany attacks its former ally: some of the first Romanian victims of Nazi bombings.

August 31 The Red Army enters and occupies Bucharest.

September People's Tribunals, dominated by Communists, begin trying war criminals but soon turn against political opponents.

September 1 The Communist-dominated General Confederation of Labor begins operating (*see* May 1).

September 6 Romanian troops invade Transylvania causing Hungary to declare war. Two days later Romania declares war on Hungary.

September 12 After waiting eight days in Moscow, Romanian representatives sign the armistice between Romania and the Allies that confirms Soviet control of Bessarabia and northern Bukovina. Romania agrees to officially join the Allies, pay the USSR for the cost of its occupation forces and $300 million in reparations, ban all fascist organizations, and repeal anti-Jewish laws.

Soviet military authorities begin censorship throughout the country.

October 9 Winston Churchill meets with Soviet leader Joseph Stalin in Moscow where the two divide up the Balkans. The Soviets are granted a 90 percent sphere of influence in Romania.

October 16 Actions orchestrated by Communists, supported by the Soviets, force General Sănătescu's government to resign. A new government is formed with more members from the Communist controlled National Democratic Front; Sănătescu remains as premier.

November 13 The Red Army takes complete control of northern Transylvania after claiming the need to preserve order.

December 6 Sănătescu's second government resigns. General Nicolae Rădescu puts together a new government with even more ministers from the Communist controlled National Democratic Front.

1945

January 21 Claiming that Romanian fascists abused the right to organize unions in the past, the government enacts a law that grants only the Communist-dominated Ministry of Labor the right to bestow legal status to any new labor unions.

February 4–12 Despite American and British ideals calling for the independence of, and free elections in,

Eastern Europe, the Yalta Conference puts Romania in the Soviet sphere of influence.

February 13 Communists demonstrate against the monarchy outside the royal palace in Bucharest.

February 19 Members of the Communist party and National-Peasant party fight each other in Bucharest.

February 24 In an attempt to discredit the monarchy and non-Communists in the government, Communists murder some pro-National Democratic Front demonstrators, claiming that the government carried out the killings.

February 26 Realizing the governmental instability due to the chaos caused by the Communists, Premier Rădescu schedules elections that he knows will result in a victory for the non-Communist parties.

February 28 Due to the events from two days before, Soviet Deputy Foreign Minister Andrei Vyshinsky demands in an audience with the king that Michael withdraw his support from the Rădescu government, claiming that the Rădescu government cannot restore order in the country. King Michael initially resists, but unable to get support from the Western Allies, the king gives in and the Rădescu government resigns.

March 6 A Communist-dominated government is formed under the leadership of Petru Groza, the leader of the Plowmen's Front, an openly pro-Communist and pro-Soviet party.

March 10 The Soviet Union agrees to allow Romania to reannex northern Transylvania; later in the day, Premier Groza announces that Romania has regained the region.

March 20 King Michael signs a bill expropriating all private property over 50 hectares without compensation. Furthermore, the government takes all farm machinery and livestock without paying.

May 8 Romania and the USSR sign an agreement in Moscow establishing Sovroms, joint Soviet-Romanian companies that work to the advantage of the USSR.

August 20 King Michael demands the resignation of the Groza government. Groza, with Soviet support, ignores the monarch's request.

August 21–January 7, 1946 Due to Groza's intransigence, the king refuses to sign any bills into law, whereby Groza's government rules by decree.

November 8 On the king's birthday, police open fire on peaceful anti-Communist demonstrators, wounding and killing many and making numerous arrests.

December 16–26 After the United States labels the Groza government as authoritarian and not representative of the Romanian political spectrum, representatives of Great Britain, the United States, and the USSR meet in Moscow where they decide that one member of the National-Peasant and Liberal parties will be added to the Groza government.

1946

January 7 Groza forms a new government with the inclusion of opposition parties as stipulated by the December Moscow agreement.

February 4 The United States and Great Britain recognize the Groza government on the condition that it holds free elections. With his government recognized, Groza moves to destroy the opposition.

May 7 A conference of the foreign ministers of Great Britain, France, the United States, and the USSR declare the Second Vienna Award as null and void thereby de facto recognizing the reunion of northern Transylvania with Romania (*see* August 30, 1940).

June 1 Marshal Ion Antonescu is executed as a war criminal after going on trial in May.

June 14 The United States, France, and Great Britain accept the Romanian-Soviet border at the Allied meeting of foreign ministers in Paris, allowing the USSR to retain northern Bukovina and Bessarabia.

July 15 A law abolishes the upper house of parliament, which consisted of strong opponents of the Communists.

November 19 Nationwide general elections are held preceded by a campaign of violence and intimidation against the opposition carried out by Communists and Soviet occupation forces. Amazingly, the initial results show that the Communists have been defeated, and then, there are no more election reports. After three days the ''updated'' outcomes appear with now an overwhelming majority of almost 90 percent for the Communist-led slate. A new unicarmel (one house) legislature is established to replace the bicarmel (two house) legislature that had been inactive since 1936.

November 29 Due to the findings of the elections, the government is reorganized granting a majority of positions to the Communist-controlled coalition. However, several seats will go to members from the Liberal party, with the most important, foreign minister, going to former premier Gheorghe Tătăarescu. The arrest of many former leaders of the opposition and their supporters begins.

1947

January 1 The Romanian National Bank is nationalized.

February 10 The Romanian peace treaty is signed in Paris. Its terms include reparations, armaments reduction, Red Army occupation without any timetable for withdraw, and territorial concessions: the return of northern Transylvania to Romania and Bessarabia and northern Bukovina to the Soviet Union. It becomes effective on September 15.

June 3 Former King Carol II finally marries his long-time companion Magda Lupescu in Brazil (*see* June 12, 1930).

July 18 Due to the post-war inflation, the government issues a 5 million lei note.

July 30 The National-Peasant party is dissolved.

August 12 The leader of the National-Peasant party, Iuliu Maniu, along with several hundred other party members are arrested on the charges of espionage and treason. As a result of the arrests, the government declares the National-Peasant party illegal.

August 15 After months of post-war inflation, the government begins to exchange the currency, the lei, at the rate of 1,000,000 old lei for 50 new lei, in an attempt to stabilize the economy.

September 20–28 The government issues food and ration cards to all citizens in an attempt to deal with the inflation.

September 22–27 At a meeting in Poland, the representatives of the Communist parties of Romania, Poland, Czechoslovakia, Hungary, Bulgaria, Yugoslavia, France, Italy, and the USSR agree to form the Communist Information Bureau or Cominform. The purpose of the Soviet led and inspired organization is to coordinate the activities of European Communists.

November 5 Foreign Minister Gheorghe Tătărescu, a member of the Liberal party, resigns from the government and is succeeded by the Communist Ana Pauker.

November 6 Premier Groza dismisses the other members of the Liberal party from his government claiming they are involved in subversive activity with the National-Peasant leader, Maniu.

November 11 After a 14-day trial, the 75-year-old Iuliu Maniu is found guilty and receives life at hard labor; he dies in prison in 1953. Others arrested along with Maniu in August receive long prison sentences.

November 12 King Michael leaves for Great Britain to attend the wedding of his cousin Princess Elizabeth to Philip Mountbatten. Much to the disappointment of the government, the king returns to Romania even though many British and American politicians advise him not to do so.

November 20 The government restructures the Romanian judicial system along the Soviet model.

December 9 The first store owned completely by the government opens in Bucharest.

December 15 The Allied Control Commission for Romania dissolves.

December 19 Romania signs a treaty of friendship and mutual assistance with Yugoslavia.

December 30 King Michael abdicates under Communist pressure. In place of the monarchy, Romania is proclaimed as a democratic republic with Constantin I. Parhon, a little known politician, as president of the provisional presidium of the Democratic Republic of Romania. He officially takes office on January 9, 1948.

1948

January 3 The 26-year-old former King Michael leaves for exile in Switzerland where, in March, he repudiates his abdication as being done under duress.

January 25 The government census reports that the population of Romania is 15,872,624 of which 23.4 percent live in urban areas and 76.6 percent in rural areas.

February 4 Romania signs a 20-year treaty of friendship, cooperation, and mutual assistance with the Soviet Union.

February 23 The Social Democratic party merges with the Communist party to form the Romanian Workers' party, a Communist dominated organization.

February 27 The People's Democratic Front, consisting of the legal political parties of the Romanian Workers' party, Plowmen's Front (a Communist front party for the peasantry), National Popular Front, National Popular party, and the Magyar Popular Union (a Communist front party for the large Hungarian population in Transylvania), is formed. In upcoming elections, these parties join together for a single slate of candidates under the name of the People's Democratic Front.

March In general elections the People's Democratic Front receives 91 percent of the votes or a total of 405 out of 414 seats in the parliament, the Grand National Assembly (Marea Adunare Nationala).

April 13 The new constitution, modeled along the lines of the 1936 Soviet constitution, is approved by the parliament. Romania is officially proclaimed a People's Republic with Constantin Parhon becoming the president of the unicarmel parliament. The number of ministries also rises to fifteen.

May The Romanian Orthodox Church begins to urge members of the Uniate, or Eastern Orthodox Church, to return to the Orthodox Church. Uniates practice the Orthodox religion but acknowledge the pope as their spiritual leader because of a break with the Orthodox Church in 1698.

June 11 The government nationalizes transportation, industrial firms, mining corporations, insurance firms, and the remaining banks.

Late June Since Yugoslavia refuses to follow the lead of the USSR in all foreign and domestic policies, the Cominform moves its headquarters from Belgrade to Bucharest.

July The government establishes a planning commission for control of a state-run economy.

August 3 The government remodels the education system along the lines of that in the Soviet Union.

A law is passed regulating religion in the country; no new denominations may be considered legal or function unless approved by the Presidium of the Grand National Assembly.

November 1 Private health-care facilities and movie theaters are nationalized.

November 13 The government limits the types of religious training schools to three: choirs, monastic orders, and secular clergy.

December 1 The government dissolves the Uniate Church, merges it with the Romanian Orthodox Church, and imprisons the Uniate hierarchy. It is estimated that approximately 1,400,000 Romanians are Uniates (*see* May).

December 27 The country's first one-year planned economic program receives parliamentary approval for 1949.

1949

January 22 The government establishes the militia, a state security organization based upon the Soviet model, to take the place of the police. It becomes more than just a police force by controlling the movement of Romanian citizens and keeping an eye on foreigners.

January 25 Romania becomes one of the founding members of the Council for Mutual Economic Assistance (COMECON, CMEA) in Moscow. This organization of the Soviet bloc countries of Eastern Europe coordinates economic cooperation with the USSR and among themselves.

Early March Collectivization of agriculture begins.

March 4 The Communist youth organization, the Union of Working Youth, based upon the Soviet model is established.

April 4 The government nationalizes health-related companies.

May 23 The government decrees that all radio sets must be registered with the authorities.

The Romanian Press Agency begins to censor the news.

June 11 The Romanian Workers' (Communist) party announces purges will take place that will reduce the number of members to make the party easier to control.

July 5 The formation of three joint Romanian-Soviet companies (Sovroms) to control coal and metal production and the building industry in Romania is reported (*see* May 8, 1945).

October 4 Following the Soviet lead from September 1948, Romania revokes its treaty of friendship and mutual assistance with Yugoslavia from December 19, 1947.

December 24 The parliament approves the second one-year plan for the 1950 economy.

1950

February Romania and the USSR agree to organize further joint companies (*see* July 5, 1949).

March 2 The government orders the closing of the American and British information offices in Bucharest claiming that they are centers of espionage.

March 24 The Ministry of Defense is purged of non-Communist employees.

April 20 The government nationalizes rental properties, as well as all buildings owned by wealthy business people.

May In order to more strictly control the labor force, all workers are now required to carry work books in addition to identification papers. These work books contain the employment history of the worker and must be presented when seeking a new job.

July The Romanian Workers' party announces that over 192,000 members have been purged from its ranks since June 11, 1949.

July 1 Any type of copying machines owned by people or corporate bodies must be registered with the militia or police.

September 7 The parliament agrees to redivide the country into economic/administrative districts to make the country more productive. From 71 departments, the country is divided into 28 regions (counties) supposedly based upon historic, economic, geographical, and ethnic factors.

December 3 Elections to people's councils, local organs of government, result in an overwhelming victory for the single slate of candidates of the People's Democratic Front.

December 15 After two "successful" one-year plans, the government approves its first five-year plan for the Romanian economy.

The government enacts a law establishing controls on freedom of speech. Violations such as speaking out against the regime, in favor of "enemies" of the government, or in favor of war can result in a five- to 25-year prison sentence or the confiscation of property.

1951

November 21 A law goes into effect to further control the labor force by requiring the written approval of supervisors or the Labor Conflict Board when a worker wants to change employment.

1952

Purges of the leadership continue. In March and May several members of the government lose their positions and are expelled from the Central Committee of the Workers' party, including Foreign Minister Ana Pauker.

June 2 Petru Groza becomes president of the parliament, while the staunch Stalinist Gheorghe Gheorghiu-Dej replaces him as premier.

July 4 Ana Pauker is removed as foreign minister.

September 11 Ana Pauker loses her position as vice premier.

September 23 The Grand National Assembly, the parliament, unanimously approves a new constitution, also based upon the 1936 Soviet constitution, since the country has made "great" changes moving toward socialism since the April 13, 1948 constitution was written. As a result of the new constitution, only working people, 18 years or

older, are allowed to vote and the number of ministries increases to 24.

November 30 The government announces that 98.4 percent of all votes cast in the fall general elections were for the single slate of People's Democratic Front candidates.

1953

January 24 Due to the reorganization of the government bureaucracy, the cabinet is shuffled.

April 3 Former King Carol II dies in exile in Portugal.

August 22 Premier Gheorghiu-Dej describes his plan for improved living standards in a speech.

September 5 The government grants major tax incentives and relief in an effort to help agricultural production stalled by collectivization.

October 16 Romania and Yugoslavia agree to mutually investigate border incidents and to prevent them in the future. This event, made possible by the death of the Soviet dictator Joseph Stalin in March 1953, marks a warming in relations between the two countries which had been strained since 1948 (*see* October 4, 1949).

November 21 Since the one-year plans for the economy have not been as successful as initially announced, the government grants major tax reductions to workers and employees not engaged in agriculture or agrarian-related fields.

December 20 Nationwide local elections to People's Councils, or local governments, result in a victory for the People's Democratic Front.

1954

April 8 In a purge trial, the former Communist minister of justice receives the death penalty on charges of treason and espionage with unnamed foreign elements. Other show trials will follow.

April 20 The government is reorganized along the lines of the new Soviet collective leadership that took control after the death of Stalin in 1953. The position of secretary general of the Workers' party, held by Prime Minister Gheorghiu-Dej, is replaced by a four-member secretariat.

September 25 The USSR sells Romania its interests in the joint companies with the exception of the one engaged in oil production (*see* July 5, 1949).

Romanian citizens gather in Bucharest for the Memorial Meeting commemorating the March 1953 death of Soviet leader Joseph Stalin.

October 2   Signaling a further reduction in tensions since the death of Soviet dictator Joseph Stalin in March 1953, Romania opens regular train traffic with Yugoslavia (*see* October 16, 1953).

October 10   In another purge trial, the Communist Vasile Luca, the former finance minister and vice premier until 1952, receives a life prison sentence after being convicted of rightist deviationism.

December 27   Rationing is abolished (*see* September 20–28, 1947).

1955

May 14   The Warsaw Pact treaty is signed between the Soviet Union and its Eastern European satellites. This Soviet-controlled defensive alliance aimed at the North Atlantic Treaty Organization (NATO) consists of Albania, East Germany, Bulgaria, Hungary, Poland, Romania, Czechoslovakia, and the USSR.

August 30   The government orders the military to reduce its forces by approximately 40,000 men.

September 30   At a plenary meeting of the Central Committee of the Workers' party, Gheorghiu-Dej is elected as first secretary, taking personal control of the party once more and becoming the most powerful person in Romania.

October 3   The Grand National Assembly appoints Chivu Stoica, a senior Communist party offical, as prime minister to replace Gheorghiu-Dej, who resigned to become first secretary of the Workers' party.

December 14   Romania becomes a member of the United Nations.

1956

January   The country is again administratively redivided in an attempt to make Romania more efficient economically. The number of regions (counties) is reduced from 28 to 16 (*see* September 7, 1950).

February 14–25   At the Twentieth Congress of the Soviet Communist party, Soviet leader Nikita Khrushchev gives a speech in which he denounces Stalin and the excesses of his regime. It takes the Romanian leadership by surprise.

February 21   The government census reports the population of Romania at 17,489,450 with 31.3 percent residing in urban areas and 68.7 percent residing in rural areas.

March 25   In line with Khrushchev's speech in February, Gheorghiu-Dej addresses the Central Committee of the Workers' party where he mildly criticizes Stalin, but at the same time he stresses his great accomplishments. This marks the beginning of de-Stalinization in Romania, which never goes very far.

Late October–early November   The Hungarian Revolution takes place. Imre Nagy, Hungary's prime minister during the revolution, is seized by the Soviets after he leaves the Yugoslav embassy under a safe conduct pass and is taken to a Romanian prison.

November   Citing the Hungarian Revolution and troubles in Poland as evidence that de-Stalinization causes problems, Gheorghiu-Dej begins purging the party of reformers or supporters of Soviet Premier Nikita Khrushchev; Gheorghiu-Dej's actions are complete by the summer of 1957 (*see* March 25).

1957

April 15   The USSR and Romania sign an agreement that defines the legal status of Soviet troops stationed in Romania.

1958

During this year Soviet occupation troops from World War II are finally withdrawn from Romania.

January 7   Petru Groza, president of the parliament and premier from 1945 to 1952, dies.

January 11   Ion Gheorghe Maurer becomes the president of parliament.

1961

March 21   Gheorghe Gheorghiu-Dej is named president of the State Council.

1962

During this year the government announces that the peasantry has become fully collectivized. However, Romanian economic planning still emphasizes industrialization on the Stalinist-Soviet model rather than agriculture for which the country is better suited.

1963

The beginnings of Romanian defiance to the Soviets occurs when Gheorghiu-Dej refuses to follow the Soviet lead in condemning the People's Republic of China. He also refuses to allow Romania to be completely bound by COMECON economic plans.

1965

March 19   Gheorghe Gheorghiu-Dej dies of cancer. Nicolae Ceauşescu succeeds him as first secretary of the Workers' party. During the next 24 years, Ceauşescu will parley his position and growing power into a virtual dynastic-style rule over Romania. Ceauşescu will use nepotism to fill key posts of his government and end up running the country as a personal, feudal-style holding, establishing what is sometimes referred to as dynastic socialism.

March 24   Senior party official Chivu Stoica becomes the president of the State Council.

May 10–13   Signaling Soviet approval for the new Romanian leadership, Soviet leader Leonid Brezhnev visits Bucharest.

July   In a speech to a Workers' party congress, Ceauşescu emphasizes Romania's political and economic independence and its determination to proceed with industrialization. The congress also elects Ceauşescu as general secretary of the party, and changes the name of the party back to the Romanian Communist party.

1966

May 10–13   Soviet General Secretary Brezhnev visits Bucharest, reportedly in response to Romanian General Secretary Nicolae Ceauşescu's declaration on May 7 that Romania will improve its relations with West European countries.

September 20 The census reports the population of Romania at 19,105,056 of which 38.2 percent live in urban areas and the rest in rural regions. The ethnic composition of the population is stated as 87.8 percent Romanian, 8.4 percent Hungarian, 2 percent German, and 1.8 percent other.

1967

January 31 Asserting its independence in foreign affairs, Romania establishes full diplomatic relations with West Germany. It is the first country, with the exception of the USSR, in the Eastern bloc to do so. As a result, East Germany launches a press attack on Romania.

May 7 In a speech, Ceauşescu implies that the USSR had tried to interfere into the internal affairs of the Romanian Communist party by attempting to have him and others removed from their positions.

June 9 Soviet and East European governments and Communist party officials meet in Moscow to discuss the Arab-Israeli Six Day War that broke out on June 5. They issue a declaration condemning Israeli aggression; Romania refuses to sign the statement and break off diplomatic relations with Israel.

July In several moves, the government enacts measures that increases its authority over the population, allowing for tighter controls for reasons concerning law and order and socialist "legality."

The government permits small private stores, restaurants, and boarding houses to be established.

July 17 Ceauşescu announces that the world would be better off if both NATO and the Warsaw Pact were dissolved. Moscow launches a media campaign against Romania for these remarks.

December 6 In a speech, Ceauşescu implies that the USSR had tried to put economic pressure on Romania and other countries to change their policies.

December 7 The Romanian Communist party approves an administrative reorganization that strengthens the one-man rule of Ceauşescu. The Grand National Assembly votes its acceptance of these proposals three days later. As a result, Ceauşescu, the general secretary of the party, now becomes the president of the State Council, a collective governing body, making him technically the head of state.

December 13–15 Ceauşescu pays an official visit to Moscow where the USSR and Romania discuss the renewal of the 1948 Treaty of Friendship, Collaboration, and Mutual Assistance due to expire on February 4, 1968.

1968

May 14–18 To show their independence of Moscow in foreign affairs, General Charles de Gaulle, president of France, is invited to visit Romania where he receives a warm welcome.

July 15 The leaders of Bulgaria, East Germany, Hungary, Poland, and the USSR send a warning note to Czechoslovakia concerning their fears about anti-socialist forces in Czechoslovakia due to the Prague Spring liberalizing program that loosened the Communist grip on the country. In response to the letter, Ceauşescu declares that the Warsaw Pact treaty does not allow any interference into the internal affairs of any member country. In addition, he gives his public support for the events in Czechoslovakia.

August 15–16 To show Romania's approval for the liberalizing policies of Czechoslovakia, Ceauşescu visits Czechoslovakia where, amidst an enthusiastic welcome, he renews a 24-year treaty of friendship. He furthermore assures the Czechoslovaks of Romanian backing for their program of change.

August 20–21 Without warning the Warsaw Pact forces, minus Romania, invade Czechoslovakia to put an end to its reforms. Ceauşescu denounces the invasion and stresses the need to respect the sovereignty and independence of every socialist country.

Romanian authorities meet with Yugoslav representatives to discuss possible plans for a common defense against intervention by Soviet and Bulgarian forces.

August 26 Ceauşescu, the Communist party, and the Romanian government all officially denounce the Soviet-led invasion of Czechoslovakia on August 20–21. Fearing Romania could be the next victim, a home guard, or army consisting of civilians, is established and armed.

August 29 Numerous speeches are given in the Grand National Assembly that not only denounce the invasion of Czechoslovakia but also note that the Romanian people will fight to protect their independence. However, in the coming months, Romania will tone down its attacks on the invasion after the other countries of the Eastern bloc issue warnings and exert pressure. Nonetheless, Romanians continue to express sympathy for Czechoslovakia.

1969

February 1–2 In light of the invasion of Czechoslovakia, Ceauşescu and President Tito of Yugoslavia meet in Timisoara, Romania, to discuss and agree on common policy.

June 9 During his speech to a meeting of Communist parties in Moscow, Ceauşescu restates that no country has the right to interfere the internal affairs of another.

August 2–3 In further defiance of the Soviet Union, Romania allows U.S. president Richard M. Nixon to visit. Nixon receives a warm welcome during his tour, where he emphasizes respect for national sovereignty and noninterference in the internal affairs of a country. His stop demonstrates Western interest in attempting to woo Romania from the Soviet camp by bestowing on it most-favored-nation status and other favorable economic enticements.

August 6–12 At the Tenth Congress of the Romanian Communist party, the last potential rivals to Ceauşescu are removed and replaced with staunch supporters of him and his policies. During the congress Ceauşescu states on numerous occasions that the party has exclusive control and responsibility for ensuring that socialism will be completed in the years to come. The Congress approves Ceauşescu's plans for Romania that include nationalism, independence in international affairs, and the supremacy of the Communist party in internal affairs.

September 20 In a joint statement issued at the finished Iron Gates hydroelectric dam on the Danube River between Romania and Yugoslavia, Ceauşescu and President Tito of Yugoslavia declare their respect for the independence and sovereignty of countries, equal rights between nations, and noninterference in the internal affairs of countries.

1970

May–June The worst floods in over a century inundate large sections of the country. Over 300,000 hectares of land and 1,500 communities are covered by the waters causing damage worth more than 10 billion lei in local currency. Aid amounting to 1.5 billion lei is promised by mostly non-Eastern bloc nations; the United Nations Development Fund provides $500,000 to its Food and Agricultural Organization to buy seed for planting and medicine for farm animals in Romania.

July 7 The Soviet-Romanian friendship, cooperation, and mutual assistance treaty that lapsed in February 1968 is finally renewed in ceremonies in Bucharest (*see* December 13–15, 1967). Its text somewhat emphasizes Romanian sovereignty in relation to the USSR.

October 19 Ceauşescu addresses the United Nations during celebrations to mark its silver anniversary. He is the only Communist head of state to do so.

1971

January 12 Romania joins the COMECON investment bank after refusing to do so at its founding in the summer of 1970.

March 22 The People's Republic of China signs a number of agreements to supply Romania with foreign aid. Thus Romania becomes the first Warsaw Pact member, with the exception of Albania which withdrew from the alliance in 1968, to receive Chinese aid.

April 1 In a speech to the Congress of the Communist party of the Soviet Union in Moscow, Ceauşescu states his views of sovereignty and equal relations between countries and Communist parties. He is neither criticized nor applauded for his speech.

May 8 In a speech to mark the golden anniversary of the establishment of the Romanian Communist party, Ceauşescu states that the population must make continued and greater sacrifices to build a true socialist society.

Early June Ceauşescu makes an official visit to the People's Republic of China where he is encouraged in his independent foreign policy. Upon returning to Romania, he begins his own version of the Chinese Cultural Revolution to carry out purges in the party, the media, and cultural organizations.

June 24 Relations between Romania and Hungary reach a low after the Hungarian Communist party criticizes Romania's treatment of Hungarians in Transylvania. The rift will be smoothed over after an exchange of delegations in October and November.

July 15 The American press announces that President Nixon will visit the People's Republic of China in 1972 and praises Ceauşescu for his role in helping this event to come about.

November 14 Romania becomes a member of GATT (General Agreement on Trade and Tariffs), although this West European organization is well aware that Romania has deep economic problems.

1972

February Unofficial reports state that a Romanian general was executed for treason after giving defense information to the USSR.

March 11–April 6 To continue his policy of independence, nonalignment, and as a mediator in foreign affairs, Ceauşescu visits eight countries in Africa.

July 20 A national congress of the Communist party begins where plans are drawn up for social, political, and economic reforms. Despite these grandiose ideas, very little comes of these schemes.

December 28 A new law passes which copies the Yugoslav defense system by establishing small, armed partisan groups throughout the country. This action is viewed as a warning to the Soviets to stay out of Romania. It becomes effective on March 31, 1973.

1973

June 18–19 A Central Committee meeting elects Elena Ceauşescu, the wife of Nicolae Ceauşescu, to the Communist party's executive committee.

June 26 Ceauşescu becomes the first leader of a Warsaw Pact country to visit West Germany, thereby once again asserting his independence in foreign affairs.

September 11 After a rightist coup topples the regime of Communist President Salvador Allende of Chile, Ceauşescu cancels his visit to that country during a tour of Latin America; Romania breaks off diplomatic relations with Chile on September 25.

December 4–7 President Nixon again visits Romania. He and Ceauşescu sign a treaty of cooperation in economic, industrial, and technical endeavors.

1974

March At a meeting of the Central Committee of the Communist party, Ion Maurer, prime minister since 1961, resigns for health and age reasons. In actuality, the 74-year-old Maurer is removed because he has become increasingly critical of Ceauşescu. Among other changes, the meeting also decides to create the position of president of the republic, thereby leaving the State Council, which formerly acted as a sort of collective head of state, as a largely honorific body; the prime ministry is also stripped of many of its powers which go to the presidency. The

Presidium of the Communist party is also replaced by the Permanent Bureau that includes both party and state leaderships.

March 28 The Grand National Assembly elects Nicolae Ceauşescu, currently general secretary of the Communist party and president of the State Council, as president of the Socialist Republic of Romania. Ceauşescu now becomes the one and only head of state of the country (*see* December 7, 1967).

November The Eleventh Congress of the Romanian Communist party takes place. Very little is achieved except establishing the membership of the Permanent Bureau created in March. The Permanent Bureau consists of five men, including Ceauşescu, thereby increasing his control of the country.

1975

July Floods again inundate large sections of the country causing more damage than those in May–June 1970. The flood covers over 800,000 hectares of farm land and kills hundreds of thousands of farm animals.

November During a speech to a meeting of the Union of Communist Youth, Ceauşescu urges an end to apathy in Romania.

Late December The government releases its new Five Year Plan (1976–80). Among its many ambitious objectives are the construction of a nuclear power station, the building of a steel mill complex at Călăraşi on the Danube River, an increase in wages for agricultural workers, and as a result of the disastrous July floods, dam and canal construction to control waterways.

1976

June At the Congress on Political Education and Socialist Culture, Ceauşescu attacks the failures of domestic propaganda by blaming the media and the educational system. As a result, the minister of education is sacked and other party leaders are demoted. After the end of the congress, a massive campaign begins throughout the country to indoctrinate the population on the values of socialism.

August After publicly stating in June that his country has no territorial designs on the USSR, Ceauşescu makes an official visit to Bessarabia, now the Moldavian Soviet Socialist Republic. This trip ends several months of statements made by the Romanian press stressing that the area is overwhelmingly Romanian in population and had decided democratically to join Romania in 1918 (*see* November 27, 1918). Furthermore, this paves the way for a return visit by Soviet leader Leonid Brezhnev in November.

Late November In a speech just before a meeting of the Warsaw Pact is to take place in Bucharest, Ceauşescu again states that his country would fight to maintain its independence, and urges the abolition of both the Warsaw Pact and NATO.

To emphasize its independence in foreign affairs during the meeting of the Warsaw Pact in Bucharest, the American secretary of commerce signs a trade agreement in Bucharest, while a high-ranking member of the Romanian defense ministry officially visits the People's Republic of China.

1977

January The Permanent Bureau, the ruling party and political body in the country, increases its membership from five to nine. One of the new appointees is Elena Ceauşescu, the wife of the president.

January 5 A government census reports the population of Romania to be 21,559,416, of which 47.5 percent dwell in urban areas and 52.5 percent still reside in rural regions. It lists the ethnicity of the people as follows: 88.1 percent Romanian, 7.9 percent Hungarian, 1.7 percent German, and 2.3 percent others.

February 8 Nine prominent Romanians, including the novelist Paul Goma, sign an open letter appealing for help in monitoring human rights in Romania. Ceauşescu immediately denounces them, and they are arrested.

March 4 An earthquake measuring nine points on the Richter scale strikes Romania destroying large sections of Bucharest, leaving over 5,000 dead, and causing millions of dollars in damage.

May 9 Nationwide celebrations mark the centennial of the country's independence. An amnesty issued to mark the event frees over 19,000 prisoners, including the dissident Paul Goma (*see* February 8).

June 28 Magda Lupescu, mistress and later wife of former King Carol II, dies at the age of 81 in exile (*see* June 3, 1947).

June 28–30 A meeting of the Central Committee of the Communist party decides to increase some wages during 1977–80, improve education, and abolish censorship hitherto under the control of the Censorship Board. In actuality, very little changes despite the pronouncement on censorship.

August Approximately 35,000 miners strike in the Jiu Valley. They demand better pay and food supplies and an improved standard of living. Ceauşescu personally promises to fulfill their demands. However, once he is back in Bucharest, he reneges on his promises and has some strikers arrested while others are forcibly removed to other regions; the leaders of the strike are murdered. Due to the strike, troops patrol the region for several months and the minister of mines is dismissed in mid-December.

November An amnesty is declared for all political and common crimes committed before November 1977, except in the cases of murder, grand theft, treason, war crimes, and espionage.

The Grand National Assembly passes a law forbidding the use of the titles of ''Mr.,'' ''Mrs.,'' and ''Miss'' in the workplace, replacing them instead with ''Comrade.''

Late November In an attempt to get rid of the dissident writer Paul Goma, the government allows him and his family to travel to France (*see* May 9). Other leading dissidents have also been given their passports with the understanding that they will leave the country permanently. Once in Paris, Goma attacks the repressive government and reads the names of the miners arrested or exiled after the August strike in the Jiu Valley.

December 8–10 A national conference of the Communist party endorses proposals by Ceauşescu for continued economic austerity and sacrifice by increasing industrial and agricultural production targets during the current Five Year Plan, establishing quality control to make Romanian goods more desirable on the world market, and canceling plans for reducing the work week by four hours to 44.

1978

July 6 Ceauşescu acknowledges at a Central Committee meeting that the country is experiencing shortages in all sectors of the economy.

July 28 General Ion Pacepa, deputy minister of the interior and in charge of security for President Ceauşescu, defects while on a trade mission to West Germany. In the coming months, numerous government, military, and diplomatic officials lose their positions due to the defection.

August 16 Hua Guofeng, the chairman of the Communist party and the premier of the People's Republic of China, arrives in Romania for a three-week official visit of Romania and Yugoslavia. His trip is criticized in the press of the other Eastern bloc nations.

August 30 In a speech to mark the thirtieth anniversary of the founding of the Securitate, the secret police, Ceauşescu urges it to be more diligent in its work to expose people willing to betray their country and socialism.

November 22–23 Ceauşescu attends a Moscow meeting of the Warsaw Pact where he refuses the Soviet demand that Romania increase its financial commitment to the alliance.

December 19 In a deliberate move to underscore Moscow's November request for more money for the Warsaw Pact, the Romanian government decides to increase its annual contribution to child welfare by 500 million lei annually taken from the military budget.

1979

January Ceauşescu condemns the Moscow-backed Vietnamese invasion of Kampuchea, or Cambodia.

March Over 2,000 people from Wallachia, Transylvania, and the Banat establish an independent labor union, the Free Union of the Working People of Romania. After several days, the government bans it and arrests its leaders, but it is an important step in the acceleration of growing resistance to the Communist regime of Ceauşescu and his dynastic socialism.

November At the Twelfth Party Congress, Constantin Pirvulescu, one of the founding members of the Romanian Communist party in 1921, attacks Ceauşescu's control of the country; Pirvulescu is expelled from the party.

1980

Early January After condemning the Soviet invasion of Afghanistan in late December, Romania urges the Soviet Union to withdraw its forces.

1981

March Due to a worsening standard of living causing people to flee the country, a law provides stiffer penalties for those caught attempting to cross the border illegally.

1982

February The government raises food prices 35 percent despite a good harvest in 1981. Nonetheless, food shortages and waiting in line for food items have become commonplace in Romania.

March West Germany refuses to lend Romania any more money claiming it is a bad credit risk.

May Due to the bleak economic situation in the country, the prime minister and several other ministers and deputy ministers are replaced; seven members of the executive committee of the Communist party are also removed.

June The government and Communist party issue a document that sets minimum daily consumption requirements for meat, dairy products, fruit, and vegetables for all people in Romania. Ironically, much of the food items listed are often unavailable for months at a time.

October Two members of the secretariat of the Communist party are removed as a result of the poor performance of the economy.

November In an attempt to slow down application rates for emigration due to the poor standard of living, the government orders that people wanting to leave must pay a fee in hard currency equal to the "estimated" value of one's education. Due to pressure from the West, the fee will be suspended in June 1983.

Talks take place between Hungarian and Romanian officials in Bucharest in an attempt to resolve the issue of Romania's treatment of its Hungarian minority. During the past year, a media war broke out over the issue between the two countries, which took on highly nationalistic overtones in Hungary. The talks fail to produce any result.

December In an attempt to raise money, the government allows people to purchase shares on the fixed assets of a factory. These shares grant no rights other than voluntary participation in factory worker meetings and 5 percent interest paid on the amount of the shares.

Due to the bleak economic situation, Romania's debt payment is postponed.

1983

June The United States extends most-favored-nation status for another year after Ceauşescu agrees in March not to enforce the law requiring emigrants to pay for their educations (*see* November 1982).

July The Grand National Assembly passes a law that ties salaries to the amount of work actually completed. Prior to this time, workers received a minimum of 80 percent of their salaries no matter how they performed in their jobs.

Nicolae and Elena Ceauşescu enjoy a show of support at a national youth rally. Ceauşescu was known for appointing family members to political office: his wife, Elena, was both a Communist party executive and a member of the Permanent (ruling body) Bureau.

Fall A severe drought strikes large areas of the country resulting in further food shortages, as well as power shortages, as many hydroelectric plants cannot function with the low water levels. The government reacts by cutting the amount of electricity and heat each household can use and reducing the length of the television broadcast day.

December 1 Celebrations, marking the sixty-fifth anniversary of the union of Transylvania with Romania, are marked by extensive nationalistic feelings aimed particularly at Hungary. This causes relations between the two countries to reach a new low since 1945.

1984

March In an attempt to increase the birthrate, the government issues a proclamation to reduce the number of abortions, even though the procedure has been banned since 1966, except in life-threatening cases.

July 28–August 12 Despite a Soviet boycott of the Los Angeles Summer Olympics, the Romanian team takes part.

Late December Due to "revisionist and irredentist" attacks on Romania in the Hungarian press, Ceauşescu makes a speech denouncing Hungarian brutality in Transylvania during World War II; relations between the two countries sink even further. Relations will continue to be exceptionally bad for the next several years.

1985

January–March An extremely cold winter hits Romania, virtually paralyzing the country and causing extreme economic and physical hardships. Heating is stopped in public buildings and greatly reduced in homes, only one electric light is allowed to be used in a home and the use of electric appliances is forbidden, private cars are banned, and public lighting is reduced over 50 percent.

April 26 Despite its estrangement from the Soviet Union, Romania signs a 20-year extension to the Warsaw Pact treaty.

August In an attempt to pay off the national debt, the government decrees that all employees must work six days annually for free.

October 17 The Communist party declares a state of emergency in the electricity sector, reflecting the severe energy crisis the country experienced in 1984–85. All fossil fuel power plants are taken over by the military and run along military lines. In the coming months, Romanians face continued cuts in electrical use and heating, forcing them to live and work in freezing conditions and almost near darkness. Furthermore, the regime encourages the use of draft animals on farms instead of tractors and other mechanized means, horses and carts instead of automobiles and trucks, oil lamps instead of electric lights, and urges its citizens not to use their refrigerators and washing machines.

1986

February–March Due to continued energy problems, the use of private automobiles is banned.

March In an attempt to stimulate the economy by encouraging tourism and by making Romanian exports less expensive, the lei is devalued by 17 percent against the American dollar.

Late April The accident at the Chernobyl Soviet nuclear power plant sends high levels of radiative fallout to the northeastern section of Romania. As a result, the European Economic Community bans the importation of Romanian foods in May.

May Romania extends its territorial waters zone in the Black Sea to 200 miles to protect its control of possible offshore oil drilling sites.

August 30 An earthquake registering 6.5 on the Richter scale, centered in the eastern Carpathian Mountains in the Vrancea region north of Bucharest, rocks the country causing damage and the loss of life.

November 23 In an orchestrated referendum, over 99 percent of the voters approve of Ceauşescu's plan to reduce the military budget by 5 percent.

1987

February The government orders further cuts in residential electrical consumption.

Ceauşescu attacks the authors of a history of Transylvania written in Hungary as "fascists" and "racists," leading to even tenser relations between the two countries. Talks between Romania and Hungary take place in June and tone down the polemics over the history, but relations still remain strained.

May 25–27 Soviet leader Mikhail Gorbachev visits Bucharest where he receives a chilly reception due to his policies of *glasnost* and economic reform in the USSR. Ceauşescu declares that Gorbachev's reforms are not suited for a socialist country.

October Pursuing the policy of nepotism or dynastic socialism, Ceauşescu's son, Nicu, is promoted to party secretary of Sibiu county.

November 15 Further power and food shortages provoke workers in Braşov, Romania's second largest industrial center, to go on strike. They ransack city hall and Communist party headquarters in protest of the harsh living conditions. The demonstration is violently suppressed by the military, using armored vehicles and dogs. Demonstrations are also reported in Sibiu and Braila.

December 14 At an extraordinary conference of the Romanian Communist party, Ceauşescu states that the trade and industrial output targets of the past two years have not been met and that new solutions must be found. However, his speech leaves no doubt that he still intends to continue with the Stalinist style of heavy industrialization accompanied by extreme belt tightening by Romanians in order to pay off foreign debts, despite the fact that the Romanian economy is already in desperate condition.

1988

January 26 Celebrations, including best wishes from the monarchs of Great Britain, Sweden, and Spain, mark the seventieth birthday of President Ceauşescu. The governments of the three countries protest that these greetings are fake.

March Ceauşescu revives a "systemization" plan to destroy over 8,000 villages and transfer the inhabitants to agrarian-industrial complexes by the year 2000. The program, meant to remove the inequalities between rural and urban life, is attacked worldwide as a way to systematically destroy Romania's cultural heritage and rural life.

June Romania closes the Hungarian consulate in Cluj after demonstrations occur in Budapest against Ceauşescu's "systemization" plan (*see* March). The Hungarians feel that Ceauşescu's program will cause the forcible assimilation of the large Hungarian population in Romania.

August 23 Elena Ceauşescu, the wife of the president, delivers the keynote speech during celebrations marking national day, thus showing that she has gained great power in the country.

October Soviet leader Mikhail Gorbachev unsuccessfully urges President Ceauşescu, during his visit to Moscow, to adopt some measures of reforms.

November In an attempt to placate the population, the government raises energy consumption quotas by almost 25 percent for households. However, this move does little to improve the bleak energy situation in the country.

1989

March 11 Western news organizations broadcast an open letter, issued on March 1, by six former leading figures in the Romanian Communist party, including Constantin Pirvulescu (*see* November 1979). The letter is addressed to Ceauşescu and criticizes him for many things including the cult of personality and family, violating human rights, and destroying the economy. The letter creates a political platform for potential opposition within the Communist party and is considered a serious challenge to Ceauşescu. The six signers are arrested by the secret police, the Securitate.

April 12 Romania announces that its foreign debt has been paid and that it will not borrow any money in the future. As a result of paying off its debt, the Romanian economy has declined enormously, but the government organizes nationwide celebrations honoring the event and praises Ceauşescu's role in it.

September An anonymous letter signed by the National Salvation Front (NSF) circulates among delegates to the November Communist party congress urging them to remove Ceauşescu as general secretary.

November 20–24 The Fourteenth Congress of the Romanian Communist party is nothing more than a series of speeches praising Ceauşescu and his wife, Elena, for supposed achievements. The fall of communism in other East European countries is denounced, and Ceauşescu is reelected unanimously to another five-year term as general secretary.

December 16 Attempts to move the Lutheran pastor, László Tőkés, an ethnic Hungarian, from Timişoara to another part of the country fail after several hundred protestors resist thereby sparking a revolution. Tőkés had been critical of the regime's treatment of its Hungarian citizens for several years.

December 17 Protests against repression and poverty grow in Timişoara; the Securitate fires on the crowds killing 71.

December 18–20 Unaware of the gravity of the situation in Timişoara and spreading discontentment in the country, President Ceauşescu makes an official visit to Iran.

December 20 Upon returning to Romania, President Ceauşescu addresses the country on the radio and television where he attacks the protestors in Timişoara and praises the Securitate and the military for its actions in putting down the uprising. He furthermore warns that harsh measures will be taken if demonstrations take place elsewhere.

After troops withdraw from Timişoara, revolutionaries seize the city and demand free elections.

December 21 In an attempt to show that he is still in control of the country, Ceauşescu arranges for a mass demonstration of support in Bucharest. As Ceauşescu addresses the rally on live television, people start to heckle, which stuns him. The broadcast is cut off and resumes about three minutes later, now showing Ceauşescu attempting to calm the people with vague promises. Antigovernment rallies and protests spring up throughout Bucharest and the rest of the country. Ceauşescu unsuccessfully calls on the military to restore order.

December 22 The Securitate attempts to restore order by attacking demonstrators; much blood is shed. The military mutinies and joins the demonstrators against the Securitate. Heavy fighting breaks out in Bucharest.

With the situation out of control in Bucharest, President Ceauşescu and his wife flee from the roof of the Central Committee building by helicopter. They are captured a short time later by the army.

The NSF, made up of "former" Communists and non-Communists alike, becomes the self-appointed government and announces the end to the Ceauşescu regime.

December 25 After a nine-hour secret military trial, Nicolae Ceauşescu and his wife Elena are found guilty of genocide against the Romanian people and sentenced to

A mass funeral held in the Házsongárd cemetery following the bloody revolution of 1989. It is estimated that during the week of the December 25 civilian and military uprising, Securitate secret police snipers killed 500 and wounded 2,500.

death; they are shot immediately. The proceedings are videotaped and broadcast to assure Romanians and the world that the Ceauşescus are truly dead. As a result, fighting by the Securitate slows and stops several days later.

December 26 The NSF names Ion Iliescu as president and Petre Roman as prime minister, and calls for free elections in April 1990. The new government is run by six former senior Communist party officials who abolish food rationing and Ceauşescu's plan of "systemization," legalize abortions, and place the Securitate under the tight controls of the military.

December 29 Fighting ends in Bucharest.

1990

January 1 The Securitate is abolished.

January 8 The government restores free travel and emigration.

January 12 The NSF outlaws the Communist party, but it cancels its decree the next day.

January 18 The NSF orders the seizure of all Communist party assets.

February 1 A provisional Council for National Unity is established. It is made up of 241 members representing new political parties, ethnic minorities, former political prisoners, and the NSF; Iliescu remains as president.

February 2 A series of show trials of former leaders of the Ceauşescu regime begins. Among those convicted are General Andruta Ceauşescu and Nicu Ceauşescu, the brother and son of the late president, who receive 15 and 20 years respectively in prison.

February 19 Several thousand miners travel to Bucharest to rally in support of the NSF and to break up anti-NSF demonstrations that have occurred since mid-February.

March 17–20 Clashes between ethnic Hungarians and Romanians over cultural autonomy and human rights in Transylvania leave three dead. The government declares a state of emergency in the region.

Elena and Nicolae Ceauşescu on the day of their execution. After fifteen years of austerity and suppression that earmarked the Ceauşescu regime, tensions are so high that the executions are videotaped and broadcast worldwide.

April 11 Fearing the potential political results of his visit, the National Salvation Front rescinds its approval for former King Michael to enter the country from exile in Switzerland. He will be refused again in December.

April 24 The Uniate Church is legalized after forty years underground, permitting the Vatican to reestablish relations with Romania in May (*see* December 1, 1948).

April 25 The government establishes the Romanian Intelligence Service to replace the Securitate.

May 20 Ninety-four percent of the eligible population votes in the first free presidential parliamentary elections since 1937. Iliescu is elected with 85 percent of the vote, while NSF members win over 66 percent of the vote for seats in the new Assembly and Senate. The main opposition parties, the National-Peasant party and the Liberal party (both reflecting their pre-war counterparts), receive a small percentage of the vote. Petre Roman remains as prime minister.

June 13–16 In an attempt to suppress the opposition, student-led anti-Communist/government demonstrations, which began on April 22 in the capital, are put down by a police raid and the "importation" of thousands of miners and workers loyal to the government.

June 15 Due to government actions against anti-Communist/government protestors, the United States calls a halt to economic aid to Romania. The European Community follows suit three days later.

August 22 Further anti-government protests break out in Bucharest causing the mayor to ban all meetings and demonstrations indefinitely. Sporadic student-led protests against the NSF and high prices have taken place since July.

August 31 The National Privatization Agency is established to return Romania to a market economy by selling off state industries and businesses.

November The Romanian currency, the lei, is devalued in an attempt to help exports.

November 15 Nationwide protests erupt against the early November massive price increases on various goods and services.

Students protest in an anti-communist demonstration.

1991

February 25   Bulgaria, Czechoslovakia, Hungary, Poland, Romania, and the Soviet Union sign an agreement in Budapest to dissolve the Warsaw Pact by March 31, 1991. However, it will not be dissolved until July.

April 1   The highest rises in food prices in over fifty years force Prime Minister Roman to change the composition of his government. He fails to establish a broad-base coalition government.

The Romanian currency is devalued again in an attempt to make it convertible with Western currencies (*see* November 1990).

September 25–27   Three days of rioting by miners and the citizens of Bucharest over political instability and economic problems force the government of Prime Minister Roman to resign.

October 1   Theodor Stolojan, an economist committed to creating a market economy, becomes prime minister and establishes a broad-base coalition government.

December 8   Seventy-seven percent of eligible voters approve of the new constitution in a nationwide referen-

dum that gives the presidency strong powers; the ethnic Hungarians largely reject the new document.

Late December   In the wake of the dissolution of the USSR, Romanian nationalists call for the unification of the newly independent Moldova, with its Romanian majority, with Romania. Moldova, the former Soviet republic of Moldovia or Romanian province of Bessarabia, had been annexed from Romania in 1940 by the USSR (*see* June 26, 1940).

1992

January 25   President Ion Iliescu meets with the president of Moldova in Moldova where the two agree to promote closer economic and political ties. The two stop short of advocating reunification.

February 24   The Democratic Convention, a coalition of 14 opposition parties, wins the mayoral races in Bucharest and other cities, showing a general dissatisfaction in the public with the ruling NSF.

April 25   Seventy-year-old former King Michael receives an enthusiastic welcome after finally being allowed to return to Romania for an Easter visit after 45 years in exile.

May   The Center for Urban and Regional Sociology in Bucharest interviews 1,117 Bucharest residents in a survey. Forty-one percent state that their life is now worse than under Ceauşescu.

June 25   Leaders from 11 countries of the Balkan Peninsula (Turkey, Greece, Romania, Bulgaria, and Albania) and the former Soviet Union (Russia, Ukraine, Georgia, Moldova, Azerbaijan, and Armenia) sign the Declaration of Black Sea Economic Cooperation in Istanbul, Turkey. During the session Russian President Boris Yeltsin and Ukrainian President Leonid Kravchuk meet for two hours with Presidents Mircea Snegur of Moldova and Ion Iliescu of Romania to discuss the conflict over the Moldovan area east of the Dniester River (Trans-Dniester region) where a Slavic majority seeks secession from Moldova, which is 65 percent Romanian.

July 21   Russia and Moldova agree to send a joint peacekeeping force into the Trans-Dniester region of Moldova. They also agree that the Slav-dominated region on the eastern side of the Dniester River can decide its own fate if Moldova reunites with Romania in the future.

August 19   At the opening of the Third World Congress of Hungarians in Budapest, Hungarian Prime Minister József Antall states that "it is the constitutional duty of the Hungarian government to take responsibility for Hungarians abroad.'' Antall is not promoting the redrawing of borders, but he is putting Hungary's neighbors, Slovakia and Romania, on alert that his government expects them to grant full ethnic rights to their Hungarians. He pledges to continue to speak out in defense of those rights.

September 18 Germany and Romania reach an agreement to return approximately 50,000 Gypsies to Romania in return for $20 million. The Gypsies left Romania after the fall of Ceauşescu in December 1989, with the hopes of a better life in Germany.

September 27 Parliamentary and presidential elections result in no clear winners. There is no majority party in parliament and a runoff election is held for president in mid-October with Iliescu winning reelection.

November 4 President Ion Iliescu announces the nomination of the economist Nicolae Văcăroiu to head the new government. On November 19, the new government is given a vote of confidence by the parliament in a secret ballot.

November 11 The government estimates that 942,500 persons are unemployed or about 8.5 percent of the total labor force in Romania.

November 20 Nicu Ceauşescu, the son of the late dictator, serving a long prison sentence for his role in suppressing demonstrations and the murder of protestors in 1989, is released early from prison due to poor health (*see* February 2, 1990).

1993

January 2 Romania and Poland sign a treaty of cooperation in Bucharest that replaces the 1960 accord. The treaty calls for a system of permanent ties between the two countries.

January 26 The Hungarian foreign minister arrives in Bucharest to start talks on a draft bilateral treaty. However, the Romanians insist on a clause stipulating that Hungary has no territorial claims on Romania.

Between 200–500 people mark Nicolae Ceauşescu's seventy-fifth birthday at his presumed grave site.

January 27 The Romanian and Hungarian defense ministries state that they want to cooperate on overcoming their differences and trouble spots between the two countries.

February 14 Romania and Greece sign a protocol on political, diplomatic, and economic cooperation. The accord provides for regular contacts between the two coun-

tries' foreign ministers, and the two countries agree not to use force in regional conflicts.

February 15 An estimated 3,000–10,000 people turn out for a demonstration put together by the largest umbrella organization of labor unions. Workers demand higher minimum wages, job security, and better social services.

March 3–4 Thousands of workers demonstrate in Bucharest demanding wage increases and job security.

March 5 A blizzard dumping sixteen inches of snow causes large sections of southern Romania to come to a standstill.

April 18 President Iliescu visits the United States in an attempt to improve relations that have become strained over Romania's treatment of its minorities, the oppression of political opponents, and state control of television.

May 2 Romania co-sponsors a four-day conference at Lake Snagov near Bucharest that discusses the increased violence against Gypsies throughout Europe since the late 1980s and asks for human rights for them.

June 10 Forensic experts report finding approximately 300 bodies over the last two years at a former Securitate interrogation center. Many of the victims unearthed at this camp, about 25 miles north of Bucharest, show evidence of being shot at a close range.

June 22 The European Community formally invites Romania, Bulgaria, the Czech Republic, and Slovakia to join.

June 30 Representatives of Romania, Bulgaria, Georgia, Russia, Turkey, and Ukraine meet in Varna, Bulgaria and agree to establish a program to protect the Black Sea from pollution.

July 1 The government introduces a value added tax (VAT) of 18 percent on most goods including food that had previously been exempted.

July 18 After three days of meetings between the government and representatives of the German and Hungarian minorities, Romania agrees to broader educational and linguistic rights for its ethnic minorities.

August 2 Approximately 45,000 coal miners in the Jiu Valley strike for better pay.

August 9 Polls report that only 7 percent of the population of Moldova favors unification with Romania.

August 11 Striking Jiu Valley coal miners return to work after an undisclosed settlement is reached.

Railway workers go on strike demanding raises. By August 13, the nation's railways are shut down despite a supreme court ruling that the strike is illegal.

August 18 Railway workers return to their jobs after the government threatens to fire and replace all the strikers.

September 20 The government reports that the unemployment rate stands at 9.1 percent of the working population.

Anti-Gypsy violence by Romanians and ethnic Hungarians in the Transylvanian town of Hadareni result in the deaths of four Gypsies and the destruction of 13 Gypsy homes.

October 12 Citing Romania's advances in human rights, the United States House of Representatives approves Most Favored Nation status for Romania; the Senate approves on October 21. As a result of this change, import tariffs on Romanian goods to the United States are lowered substantially.

November 18 Fifty thousand people march through Bucharest demonstrating against dismal living conditions and continued economic decline.

November 23 The price of gasoline increases by 20 percent. In the past two months the government has raised gasoline prices by a total of 60 percent.

November 29 Labor unionists march in Bucharest and throughout Romania demanding that the government resign.

December 1 In an attempt to quiet protests the government raises wages an average of 6.5 percent, with a minimum annual salary guaranteed at 45,000 lei.

December 8 Approximately 40,000 people, including trade unionists and students, march in Bucharest calling for the government's resignation.

December 9 In an attempt to slow inflation running reportedly at over 300 percent from January to October, the International Monetary Fund (IMF) agrees to lend Romania $696 million on the condition that the parliament will pass an IMF sponsored economic reform plan that includes the reorganization of industry.

December 13 Thousands of university students across the country boycott classes to protest substandard living conditions and a new examination system proposed by the government.

December 16 Over 10,000 demonstrators in Bucharest march to mark the beginning of the revolution that overthrew the Ceauşescu regime in 1989. They demand

Mourners pay tribute to former communist dictator Nicolae Ceauşescu at the presumed site of his grave in Bucharest.

that the government resign and that the monarchy be restored. Similar demonstrations take place throughout the country.

December 25 A number of people pay their respects at the presumed grave site of former Communist dictator Nicolae Ceauşescu, marking the fourth anniversary of his execution. Many of those present state that their lives were better under Ceauşescu's regime.

December 27 Over 100 prominent cultural personalities issue a letter to the government urging it to restore Romanian citizenship to former King Michael, who had his citizenship taken away by the Communists in 1948.

Chapter Eight

SOVIET UNION

The former Soviet Union was a huge country, extending 6,000 miles east to west and almost 3,000 miles north to south. It covered 11 time zones and one-sixth of the total land mass of the globe. For most of the twentieth-century, this immense country stood as the most powerful symbol of communism and oppression in the world through its domination of the nations of Eastern Europe, changing the fabric of those nations forever.

The Soviet Union's interest in Eastern Europe stemmed from the fact that it feared further devastating invasion of its territory—such as the invasions orchestrated by the Germans in both the First and Second World Wars. The United Soviet Socialist Republic (USSR), therefore, demanded a buffer zone of states along its borders at various meetings of the Allied war-time leaders. As the Red Army liberated these bordering eastern european countries during the waning days of World War II, the Soviets installed "friendly" regimes within these generally anti-communist, anti-Russian nations. Once in control, the Soviets engineered Communist takeovers in all the East European countries by the late 1940s, with the exception of Albania and Yugoslavia where local Communists had seized power during the latter phases of the Second World War.

While careful to avoid a war between the Soviet Union and the United States and its allies, the USSR kept these East European states under a tight reign and transformed them into near duplicates of itself. This polarization of Europe into East and West (along with its Allies, including the United States) led to the Cold War. By the 1980s the Soviet Union faced deep economic, political, and social problems that required fundamental changes that

began with glasnost and perestroika of the Gorbachev Era. As a result, the USSR was forced to abandon its domination of Eastern Europe and look inward, thereby permitting the largely peaceful revolutions of 1989 to occur in Eastern Europe which saw the fall of communism.

The history of the region of the former Soviet Union can be traced back thousands of years. In 878, the Slavic peoples of the area began to consolidate in Kievian Russia (present-day Kiev, Ukraine). The region of Great Russia was established around Moscow in the sixteenth century. A national assembly of clergy, nobles, and townspeople chose the Romanov family to rule the country in 1613 after nearly 30 years of a succession crisis known as the Time of Troubles. The Romanovs served as absolute rulers, or tsars, of the Russian empire until its collapse during World War I. Under the Romanovs' leadership the country greatly expanded its territory in the nineteenth century, annexing vast areas of Central Asia and emerging as a great European power. At the end of the nineteenth century, the territory of the Russian empire greatly resembled the territory of the former Soviet Union.

In the late 1890s, bad harvests caused the peasantry to starve, and the poor working and living conditions of the working class in the industrialized cities led to widespread discontentment causing Russians to form various political parties to attempt change. The most important were the Marxists who organized the Russian Social Democratic party that split in 1903 into the Mensheviks and Bolsheviks. The Bolsheviks, led by Vladimir Ilich Ulyanov—who later changed his surname to Lenin—believed that a revolution must be led by a single centralized party of a small number of professional revolutionaries who would seize power with the help of the proletariat or working class and the peasantry.

After an economic depression in 1899 that made living and working worse, the number of peasant uprisings, strikes, and student demonstrations grew. This discontentment increased rapidly when war broke out against Japan in 1904 leading to Russia's defeat in 1905. On January 22, 1905, thousands of peaceful, unarmed demonstrators marched on the tsar's Winter Palace in St. Petersburg to present Nicholas II a list of grievances and demands for reforms. Troops fired upon the crowd, killing more than 100 and wounding hundreds of others. This incident, known as "Bloody Sunday," touched off the Revolution of 1905, which resulted in military mutinies, further strikes, and great unrest in Russia.

In an attempt to quiet the country, Nicholas II agreed to summon an advisory body, but the disturbances continued, culminating in October 1905 with a general workers' strike that paralyzed Russia. As a result, the tsar conceded to share power with a parliament (the Duma) and to guarantee civil rights. The revolution, however, continued until December when the last remnants dwindled. Nonetheless, representative government did not function well as the tsar refused to give up very much power. Dissatisfaction with the government and Russia's poor military performance in World War I—coupled with food and equipment shortages on the home front—forced the tsar to abdicate in March 1917.

Note: Dates are given in the old style, 13 days' difference, up to February 14, 1918 when the Bolshevik Government adopted the Gregorian calendar.

1917

February 22–26   Riots break out and marches take place in Petrograd as a result of severe food shortages. Police fire on the people, and elite cavalryman, called Cossacks, disperse the crowds. However, soldiers begin to join the strikers and protesters, providing weapons for the demonstrators. The tsar suspends the Duma, the representative branch of the tsarist government, which he perceives to be supporting the strikers and demonstrators.

February 27   The Petrograd Soviet (council) of Workers' and Soldiers' Deputies, a kind of rival government consisting of anti-tsarist forces, is formed to overthrow the existing political system.

Prince Golitsyn, chairman of the Council of Ministers, and all members of the tsar's cabinet resign.

A provisional committee of the Duma, formed from the Progressive bloc of politicians, proclaims itself a committee of state and declares that it has replaced the tsarist government.

March 1   The Petrograd Soviet declares the army under its control, and issues Order No. 1 which creates soldiers' soviets, or councils, to replace the authority of officers.

March 2   Tsar Nicholas II abdicates and the Provisional Government is formed to lead the country. Prince Georgy Lvov, a social reformer, statesman and chairman of the All-Russian Union of Zemstvos (institutions of local self-government in Russia and Ukraine), heads the new government; the historian Pavel Miliukov serves as foreign minister; Alexander Guchkov serves as war minister; and a lawyer, Alexander Kerenskii becomes minister of justice.

March 4   Socialists in Kiev establish an independent government: the Ukrainian Rada (council).

April 3   Vladimir Ilich (Ulyanov) Lenin, leader of the Russian Social Democratic party (Bolsheviks or Communists), returns from exile in Switzerland to Petrograd on a "sealed train" provided by the German government. Lenin fled to Switzerland after taking part in the Russian Revolution of 1905, but continued to direct revolutionary movements in Russia through underground organizations.

May 3–4   Petrograd troops mutiny against pro-war ministers Guchkov and Miliukov, who resign.

May 5   Kerenskii becomes minister of war.

June 18   The Brusilov offensive, the last great Russian military campaign of World War I, begins on the Austrian front. After initial success the offensive fails and over 60,000 men are lost. On July 6, an Austro-Hungarian-German counteroffensive begins.

July 3–5   The Bolsheviks lead an unsuccessful uprising by servicemen and citizens of Petrograd, against the provisional government in Petrograd known as the "July Days." The provisional government issues warrants for the arrest of leading Bolsheviks; Lenin flees to Finland.

July 8   Kerenskii becomes premier and organizes a new cabinet to lead the Provisional Government.

August 24–28   Kerenskii suspects that troops moving towards Petrograd led by General Lavr Kornilov, the commander-in-chief of the military, will attempt a coup d'etat to establish a military dictatorship. Kerenskii orders the arrest of Kornilov and other generals. Workers and a Bolshevik military group, the Red Guard, defend Petrograd against Kornilov and his forces.

August 31   A majority of the members of the Petrograd Soviet support the Bolsheviks.

September 1 The Directory, a new government headed by Kerenskii, is formed.

October 23–24 With a Bolshevik majority in the Petrograd Soviet, Lenin calls for the Bolsheviks to take power.

October 25 The Bolsheviks forcibly come to power during the October Revolution in Petrograd; they organize the Council of People's Commissars to govern the country.

October 27–November 2 A Bolshevik victory ends fighting in Moscow.

November 6 The Ukrainian Rada declares Ukraine an independent republic.

November 15 Estonia declares its independence while Bolshevik rule is established in Belorussia.

November 21 Under the leadership of Bolshevik Felix Dzerzhinsky, the Special Commission for the Struggle Against Counter-Revolution and Sabotage (Cheka), the secret police, is established.

December 2 The Brest-Litovsk armistice stops the fighting with Germany; peace talks between Russia and Germany begin in Brest Litovsk on December 9.

December 6 General Kornilov and several other generals escape from Bolshevik imprisonment in Bykhov, Belorussia and make their way to the Don headquarters of the Volunteer Army, an anti-Bolshevik force.

December 14 All Russian banks are nationalized.

1918

January 5–6 The democratically elected Constituent Assembly convenes to organize a new government for Russia. Pro-Bolshevik supporters forcibly disperse the Constituent Assembly after the group refuses to recognize the Soviet government as the legal government of Russia.

February 8 Bolshevik troops occupy Kiev, Ukraine thereby taking over Ukranian Rada rule (*see* November 6, 1917).

February 9 Germany and Austria finalize a peace treaty with Ukraine, recognizing its independence.

February 16 Lithuania declares its independence.

March 2 German troops capture Kiev and reestablish Ukrainian Rada rule.

March 3 Russia and Germany sign the treaty of Brest-Litovsk giving up much of the former Russian empire to

German forces. The seventh Bolshevik party congress ratifies the treaty on March 15.

March 12 The Russian government is moved from Petrograd to Moscow to avoid potential German attacks.

March 25 The Belorussian Rada declares Belorussia a national republic.

April 5 Allied troops, consisting of British and American forces, land at Murmansk, allegedly to protect stores of Allied arms and ammunition.

April 13 Leon Trotsky, a leader of the Bolsheviks, becomes Commissar of War.

April 22 The Democratic Federal Republic of Transcaucasia, consisting of the regions of Georgia, Azerbaijan and Armenia, declares its independence.

April 23 The Russian government nationalizes all foreign trade.

April 29 After the Ukrainian Rada refuses to comply with German orders, German troops overthrow the Ukrainian Rada and form a puppet government designed to do whatever the Germans ask.

April 30 German troops take over the naval base of Sevastopol and establish a puppet government in the Crimea.

May 4 The Bolsheviks sign an armistice with German-controlled Ukraine.

May 26 Czechoslovak soldiers being transported eastward across Russia revolt when Trotsky orders that they be disarmed; the soldiers belong to the Czecho-Slovak Legion, a unit of former POWs in Russia organized to fight the Germans. The Civil War begins with this action as many rival factions now want to take advantage of the weak Bolshevik control of the country.

The Democratic Federal Republic of Transcaucasia ceases to exist when the Georgian Soviet Democratic Republic is created. On May 28, Azerbaijan establishes its own government, and on May 30, Armenia declares independence.

June 8 The Czecho-Slovak Legion takes Samara and allows the Socialist Revolutionaries, a political party based on socialist, revolutionary populism, to form a government under the authority of the Constituent Assembly.

June 28 The Bolshevik government nationalizes large industry.

July 6 Members of the Socialist Revolutionary party assassinate the German ambassador in Moscow to provoke Germany into renewing the war against Bolshevik Russia.

July 10 The Fourth All-Russian Congress of Soviets publishes the constitution of the Russian Soviet Federal Socialist Republic.

July 16 Ex-Tsar Nicholas II and his family are murdered in Ekaterinburg to prevent them from being rescued by anti-Bolshevik forces.

July 30 The German commander in Ukraine is murdered; the assassination is similar to the July 6 murder of the German ambassador in Moscow.

August 2 Allied troops, consisting of British and American forces, occupy Archangel.

August 14 British troops land at Baku.

August 30 A member of the Socialist Revolutionary party attempts to assassinate Lenin.

September 5 The Sovnarkom (Council of People's Commissars) issues broad powers to the Cheka, the secret police, starting the Red Terror, with massive arrests and executions of people opposed to Bolshevism.

September 10 The Red Army captures Kazan from the Czecho-Slovak Legion.

September 14 British troops withdraw from Baku, leaving anti-Bolshevik administrators in charge.

September 20 Twenty-six Bolshevik Commissars are taken from Baku and shot by anti-Bolshevik forces.

October 2 The Red Army captures Samara.

November 11 Germany and the Allies establish an armistice.

November 13 The Bolshevik government denounces the Treaty of Brest-Litovsk in response to the German Allied armistice.

November 17 Latvia declares its independence.

December 14 The German puppet regime in Ukraine collapses and the Ukrainian Rada again takes control.

1919

January 1 The Belorussian Soviet Socialist Republic is formed.

January 3 The Red Army captures Riga, Latvia.

January 16 The Ukrainian Rada declares war on Soviet Russia.

February 6 The Red Army captures Kiev and moves through southern Ukraine.

February 15 General Anton Denikin assumes command of the White (anti-Bolshevik) forces in southeastern Russia.

March 2–7 In an effort to facilitate the international spread of Communism, the Bolsheviks establish the Communist International (Comintern). The Comintern holds its first congress in Moscow.

April 1 British troops withdraw from Transcaucasia.

April 8 French troops leave Odessa. The Bolsheviks create the Ukraine Soviet Republic.

April 15 The Cheka opens labor camps, called Gulags, throughout the country for opponents of the regime.

April 24 The anti-Bolshevik Poles forcibly end Bolshevik rule in Lithuania, resulting in the Russo-Polish war.

April 30 French forces evacuate Sevastopol.

May 4 The Red Army defeats the White forces of Admiral Alexander Kolchak in the south of Russia.

May 22 Polish forces capture Riga, Latvia.

June 14 The Bolsheviks expel Mensheviks, or Social Democrats, and Socialist Revolutionaries from the Central Executive Committee of the Communist party.

August 23 Denikin's White forces capture Odessa.

August 31 Denikin's White forces capture Kiev.

September 19 Allied troops leave Archangel.

September 25 Anarchists bomb the Moscow Communist party headquarters.

October In an attempt to cause its fall and fearful that the Soviets might spread communism, the Allies impose an economic coastal blockade in an attempt to isolate Soviet Russia.

October 11–14 The White forces of Nicholas Iudenich reach the suburbs of Petrograd. Denikin captures Orel. This is the height of the White force's advances against the Bolsheviks.

November 14 The Red Army captures Omsk.

December 12 The Red Army takes Kharkov.

December 16 The Red Army captures Kiev and a reorganized Bolshevik government assumes power in Ukraine.

December 30 The Red Army takes Ekaterinoslav.

1920

January The Allies lift the economic coastal blockade of Soviet Russia after they realize it is not working.

January 3–8 The Red Army captures Tsaritsyn and Rostov on the Don.

January 4 Kolchak resigns as commander-in-chief of all White forces and is replaced by Denikin.

January 15 The Czecho-Slovak Legion, still making its way east across Siberia and acting as a bodyguard for Admiral Kolchak, turn the admiral over to the Bolsheviks in an effort to continue their journey unimpeded by the Red Army.

February 2 Estonia signs a peace treaty with the Soviet Russia.

February 4 Admiral Kolchak is executed by the Bolsheviks.

April 25 In an attempt to seize territory, Polish forces invade Ukraine.

May 6 Polish troops occupy Kiev.

June 12 The Red Army recaptures Kiev from the Poles.

July The peasants of the Tambov region revolt against Bolshevik rule. Their opposition ends after Lenin meets with a delegation from the region in February 1921.

July 8 Due to the ineffectual Allied coastal blockade of October 1919, the United States imposes a trade embargo against Communist Russia.

July 11 The Red Army captures Minsk.

July 12 Russia and Lithuania sign the Treaty of Moscow, which recognizes the independence of Lithuania.

August 1 The Red Army takes Brest-Litovsk from Polish forces.

August 11 Russia and Latvia sign the Treaty of Riga, which recognizes the independence of Latvia.

August 16 A Polish counteroffensive against the Red Army begins south of Warsaw.

August 26 The Kirghiz Autonomous Soviet Socialist Republic (ASSR) is established. The name is later changed to Kazakh ASSR.

October 9 Polish troops capture Vilnius, Lithuania; they control the city until 1939.

October 12 A Polish-Russian armistice is established.

October 14 Finland and Russia sign a peace treaty in Tartu, Estonia. An unofficial war existed between the two countries during the Finnish Civil War (January–May 1918) when Russian soldiers and aid supported the Finnish Red Guards. After May 1918, when the Bolsheviks were defeated by right-wing Finns, relations between Finland and Russia remained cool.

November 14 General Wrangel evacuates the Crimea, ending the Civil War.

November 23 Lenin introduces a policy of concessions with the capitalist world. Trade relations are established in an effort to rebuild the country.

November 29 The Bolshevik government establishes a new Soviet Armenian government.

December 28 The Bolshevik government signs a treaty of alliance with the Ukrainian Soviet Socialist Republic unifying their commissariats for war, foreign affairs, and the economy.

1921

January 16 The Belorussian Republic signs a treaty of alliance with Russia, similar to the Ukrainian treaty of December 28, 1920.

February 14 Lithuania and Russia sign a peace treaty.

February 16 Red Army troops enter Georgia; Joseph Stalin, Commissar of Nationalities, supervises the occupation.

February 22 GOSPLAN, the Soviet State Planning Commission, which coordinates economic activities, is established.

February 24 Due to a lack of food and fuel, factory workers in Petrograd go on strike. Three days later, the government declares martial law in the city.

March 1–17 Disillusioned with communism, sailors rebel against Bolshevik rule at Kronstadt, the chief base of the Russian Baltic fleet near Petrograd. The rebellion is unsuccessful.

March 16 In an effort to rebuild the country after years of international and civil war, Lenin initiates the New Economic Policy (NEP), intended to raise the level of the national income, it provides greater economic freedom and permits small businesses in agriculture, industry, and trade.

Joseph Stalin is elected to the Politburo (the leading council of the party) and Orgburo (concerned with organizational matters) of the party's Central Committee.

March 18 Russia and Poland sign the Treaty of Riga, giving Poland control of disputed western territories and establishing the Curzon Line, the line of the Polish-Soviet armistice, as the border.

July 23 Herbert Hoover, Chairman of the American Relief Administration (ARA), offers assistance to feed the starving people of Russia. The Bolshevik government accepts Hoover's offer.

August 20 Famine relief agreements are signed, the ARA and Red Cross feed over 11 million people in Soviet Russia over the next two years.

October 13 The Russian government signs the Treaty of Kars with Turkey, setting the borders between Turkey and the Soviet republics of Armenia, Azerbaijan, and Georgia.

1922

February The Cheka becomes the GPU, the State Political Administration. In 1934 it changes its name to NKVD (the People's Commissariat for Internal Affairs); in 1943 to NKGB (the People's Commissariat for State Security); in 1946 to MGB (Ministry for State Security); and in 1953 to KGB (Committee for State Security).

April 3 Joseph Stalin becomes general secretary of the Communist party.

The Orthodox Church Holy Synod, the governing body of the church, is dissolved and the leader of the Russian Orthodox Church is arrested.

April 16 Soviet Russia and Germany sign the Treaty of Rapallo. The treaty cancels economic claims from the tsarist era, calls for the initiation of trade, and establishes mutual diplomatic relations.

Vladimir Lenin and Joseph Stalin in Moscow's Gorky Park.

May 26 Lenin suffers a paralytic stroke, after which Stalin serves as an intermediary between Lenin and the Politburo.

December 16 Lenin suffers his second paralytic stroke which limits his public activities.

December 24 Lenin writes his "Testament," which evaluates his potential successors; he warns against giving Stalin too much power.

December 30 The Bolshevik government establishes the Union of Soviet Socialist Republics through the federation of the republics of Russia, Ukraine, Belorussia, Transcaucasia, Khorezm, Bokhara, and the Far Eastern Republic.

December 31 Azerbaijan joins the Union of Soviet Socialist Republics.

1923

January 4 Lenin advocates replacing Stalin as general secretary of the Communist party.

March 9 Lenin suffers his third stroke, after which he can no longer speak.

April 17–25 The Twelfth Soviet Communist Party Congress accepts Stalin's plan to reorganize the party by increasing the size of the Central Committee, thereby giving Stalin more control over the Communist party.

October 15 Forty-six Communist party leaders present the Central Committee with a declaration criticizing the ruling regime.

December 5 Leon Trotsky publishes a letter criticizing the party for appointing officials from above rather than electing them, thus ending democracy in the party. This makes his conflict with Stalin, who makes the appointments, public.

1924

January 21 Lenin dies.

The government establishes the Mongolian Peoples' Republic as a Soviet protectorate.

January 31 The USSR Constitution is ratified by the Second All-Union Congress of Soviets.

February 1 Great Britain recognizes the USSR, followed by Italy and Sweden two days later. France waits until October 28.

May 23–31 At the Thirteenth Soviet Communist Party Congress, the Central Committee suppresses Lenin's last "Testament," which called for the removal of Stalin as general secretary—the committee supports Stalin.

Petrograd is renamed Leningrad.

July 8 The Fifth Comintern Congress is held. Delegates decide that all Communist parties of the world should be modeled along Soviet lines.

1925

January 21 Japan recognizes the Soviet Union. The last of its troops leave the eastern USSR, ending the Japanese occupation of portions of Siberia since 1918.

January 26 Trotsky is dismissed as Commissar of War.

December 18–31 At the Fourteenth Soviet Communist Party Congress, Lev Kamenev and Grigori Zinoviev, one-time allies of Stalin, are defeated in their efforts to oppose Stalin's industrialization plan. Zinoviev is demoted in his Politburo rank and is expelled from the party in July 1926.

1926

October 25–26 During a meeting of the Politburo, Leon Trotsky and Lev Kamenev are removed from the Politburo. They are expelled from the party on November 12, 1927.

1927

May A raid on the Soviet trade office in London reveals that the Soviets had financially supported British general strikers. Great Britain breaks diplomatic relations with the USSR until 1929 and cancels its 1921 trade agreement.

December At the Fifteenth Soviet Communist Party Congress, Stalin scores a decisive ideological victory of building socialism in one country over Trotsky's and his supporters' ideas of permanent and world revolution. Many of Troskii's supporters are expelled from the party.

The policy of collectivization of agriculture is established which entails the pooling of individual peasant's land and resources into huge farms.

1928

January Stalin issues an order to seize grain by force from the peasants.

January 16 Stalin exiles Trotsky to Alma-Ata, in Soviet Kazakhstan.

January 27 Agricultural collectivization begins.

October 1 Stalin introduces his first Five-Year Plan of economic development.

1929

January 18 Leon Trotsky is exiled from the Soviet Union.

November Members of the "rightist opposition," including the leading Bolshevik theorist Nikolai Bukharin, are expelled from the Politburo.

December Stalin launches a campaign to further collectivize the peasantry and to eliminate the wealthy peasants called Kulaks.

December 5 Tadjikistan becomes a republic of the USSR.

1930

June 26–July 13 At the Sixteenth Soviet Communist Party Congress, Vyacheslav Molotov is appointed chairman of the Council of People's Commissars. Maxim Litvinov succeeds Georgy Chicherin as Commissar of Foreign Affairs.

1932

February 20 The Soviet government revokes Leon Trotsky's Soviet citizenship.

April 23 The Central Committee issues a decree abolishing all artists and writer groups; a new Writer's Union is subsequently formed.

June Ukraine suffers famine due to collectivization.

July 25 The Soviet Union and Poland sign a nonaggression pact guaranteeing their common border.

December The Soviet government creates a system of internal passports to keep track of its citizens. Collective farmers are not issued passports and cannot leave the collectives.

1933

January The Communist party suspends recruitment of new members and begins a purge of its current members: one out of every six members is expelled.

May 25 Half the people placed in labor camps as a result of opposition to collectivization are released.

November 16 The United States and the Soviet Union establish diplomatic relations.

1934

June 8 The Soviet government issues the "Betrayal of the Motherland" law making the death penalty obligatory for treason and holding family members collectively responsible for violations of the law.

July The State Political Administration (GPU) is reorganized as the People's Commissariat for Internal Affairs (NKVD). It is forbidden to pass death sentences without the approval of the Soviet Procurator, a position similar to the U.S. Attorney General.

September 18 The USSR joins the League of Nations.

November Food rationing is abolished.

December 1 The murder of Sergei Kirov, a popular Communist leader from Leningrad, sets off the Stalinist purges. There is strong evidence Stalin was involved in Kirov's murder.

1935

January 22 Zinoviev, Kamenev, and seventeen others are arrested in connection with the Kirov murder.

May 2 The USSR and France sign a five-year mutual assistance treaty in which they agree to come to each other's aid in the event either country is attacked.

May 16 The Soviet Union signs an assistance treaty with Czechoslovakia; the treaty is similar to the Soviet pact signed with France on May 2. However, this treaty would only take effect if France comes to the aid of either the USSR or Czechoslovakia when under attack.

August 31 Coal miner Alexei Stakhanov reportedly mines 12 tons of coal in one day in the Donbas mines. The "Stakhanovite movement," urging workers to achieve similar over-production, begins.

September 22 Conventional ranks are reintroduced for officers of the Red Army. Prior to this time the Red Army officially had neither officers nor non-commissioned officers.

1936

March 12 The Soviet Union and the Mongolian People's Republic sign a mutual assistance pact, warning to Japan stay out of Mongolia.

July 18 The Spanish Civil War begins. The Soviet Union provides financial aid to the Loyalists, who are fighting German- and Italian-backed Nationalists led by Francisco Franco.

August 19–24 The first "show trial" of the Stalinist purges is held. Sixteen defendants, including Zinoviev and Kamenev, are found guilty of assassinating Kirov and are executed.

September 26 The great purges begin throughout the USSR. Between 1936 and 1938, thousands of people are arrested and sent to labor camps or are executed, some without trials (*see* December 1, 1934).

November 25 Germany and Japan sign the Anti-Comintern Pact which prevents each country from signing treaties with the Soviet Union and pledges support if either country is threatened by the USSR. Italy joins a year later.

December 6 The Kazakh ASSR becomes a Soviet Republic (*see* August 26, 1920).

1937

January 23–30 Seventeen leading Communists are put on trial in Moscow for allegedly participating in a plot, lead by Leon Trotsky, to overthrow the Soviet regime and assassinate its leaders. The accused confess to the crimes and thirteen are sentenced to death and executed on February 1; the four others are sentenced to prison (*see* September 26, 1936).

May 11 The purge of the Red Army begins (*see* September 26, 1936).

May 21 A Soviet plane lands at the North Pole to establish a weather station. The next day, the USSR claims the North Pole as its permanent possession.

July 25 The purge of the Soviet Communist party is extended to all newspapers, journals, and publishing houses (*see* September 26, 1936).

August 6 The Soviet government agrees to buy $40,000,000 worth of goods from the United States in return for lower tariffs on Russian coal and other concessions.

September 6 The Soviet government accuses Italy of torpedoing two Soviet freighters in the eastern Mediterranean; the Italian government refuses to pay reparations.

December 12 The Supreme Soviet of the USSR, the highest legislative body of the country consisting of two chambers with equal legislative rights, is elected under the terms of the new ''democratic'' constitution. The candidates, headed by Joseph Stalin, run unopposed.

1938

March 11 Eighteen former Soviet government officials, including Nikolai Bukharin, are condemned to death for treason by a Moscow court (*see* November 1929; September 26, 1936).

March 13 Russian language becomes a required subject in all schools in the Soviet Union.

March 17 Soviet Foreign Commissar Maxim Litvinov promises help to Czechoslovakia in the event of an attack by Germany.

June 9 The Soviet Union, Poland, and Romania sign an agreement mutually guaranteeing their borders.

July 18 The Japanese government charges that Soviet troops fired on a Japanese border guard and occupied Changkufeng Hill in Manchuria, or Manchukuo, on July 15.

July 29 Soviet and Japanese troops clash over the disputed Manchukuo-Soviet border.

July 31 Soviet bombers attack Japanese targets in Korea and Manchukuo, while Soviet and Japanese troops again clash over the disputed Manchukuo-Soviet boundary.

August 10 Foreign Commissar Maxim Litvinov and Japanese Ambassador Shigemitsu Mamoru reach a cease fire agreement regarding the border dispute, effect August 11. A commission is later created to demarcate the border.

September 2 In response to German agitation against Czechoslovakia, the Soviets request that the French attend a joint-staff military conference on assistance to Czechoslovakia (*see* Czechoslovakia, September 7, 1938).

September 23 The Soviet government notifies Warsaw that it will renounce its nonaggression treaty with Poland if the latter invades Czechoslovakia (*see* July 25, 1932).

September 27 As a result of meetings between Hitler and British Prime Minister Neville Chamberlain, Stalin sends assurances to the Czechoslovak government that the Soviet Union will assist them against the Germans. Soviet troops mass in Ukraine, and Romania gives the Soviet Union permission to fly over its country. Poland, however, will not permit Soviet troops to cross its territory. As Polish troops gather on the Czechoslovak border, the Soviets warn them not to take any action against Czechoslovakia, stating that aggression against Czechoslovakia will be seen as aggression against the USSR.

October 5 After the Munich Agreement in which France supports giving Czechoslovak territory to Germany, the *Journal de Moscou* declares the Franco-Soviet alliance no longer valid.

November 26 The USSR and Poland reaffirm their nonaggression pact of 1932 (*see* September 23 and 27, 1938).

December 26 The Soviet Union and Finland approve the demarcation of their border.

1939

February 2 The Soviet government severs diplomatic relations with Hungary after Hungary joins the Anti-Comintern Pact (*see* November 25, 1936).

February 4 The Manchukuo government reports renewed clashes between Soviet and Japanese troops on the border near Manchuli (*see* July 18, 1938).

March 10–21 In his opening speech at the Eighteenth Soviet Communist Party Congress, Stalin accuses the West of attempting to provoke a German-Soviet war.

March 19 The Soviet government sends a note to Berlin declaring the destruction on March 15 of Czechoslovakia illegal. Although the Soviet government refuses to recognize the German occupation of Bohemia and Moravia and the independence of Slovakia, the USSR later establishes diplomatic relations with Slovakia.

May 3 Vyacheslav Molotov, President of the Council of Commissars, replaces Maxim Litvinov as Soviet Foreign Commissar.

May 11 Soviet and Japanese forces begin fighting near Manchuko (*see* February 4, 1939).

June 12 British Foreign Office officials arrive in Moscow to revive negotiations for an alliance with the Soviet Union due to the rising power of Germany. Talks do not begin until August 12.

July 16 Soviet planes bomb Fularki in Manchukuo. Japanese forces retaliate with a raid on Halunarshan, Siberia.

August 23 A secret Nazi-Soviet nonaggression pact is signed in Moscow. The pact binds each country not to attack the other, and prohibits either country from supporting a third power that attacks the other country. The pact also divides territory in the Baltic states and Poland, giving Germany a free hand to invade the region.

August 25   The Anglo-French military delegation leaves Moscow when negotiations break down.

August 29   Reinforcements are ordered for Soviet garrisons on the western border in preparation for the Soviet occupation of eastern Poland.

September 1   The German army invades Poland.

September 15   The Soviet Union and Japan agree to a truce regarding their border dispute in Mongolia and Manchukuo (*see* July 16, 1939).

September 17   Under the pretense of protecting its borders, the Soviet Union invades and occupies eastern Poland as specified in the secret nonaggression pact with Germany from August 23, 1939.

September 18   Soviet and German troops meet in the Polish city of Brest-Litovsk.

September 19   Soviet troops occupy the city of Vilnius and the Soviet navy blockades the Estonian coast.

September 22   The German government announces a Nazi-Soviet agreement on the military demarcation of Poland.

September 23   The Soviet Union resumes its severed diplomatic relations with Hungary (*see* February 2, 1939).

September 29   After the Soviets gather troops on its border, Estonia signs a treaty of mutual assistance with the Soviet Union allowing the USSR to lease military bases and station troops in the country. Similar pacts are signed by Latvia on October 5 and Lithuania on October 10.

October 1   British Prime Minister Winston Churchill condones Soviet actions in Poland and the Baltic states as necessary to its national interests.

October 7   Finland calls up reservists when the Soviet Union invites the Finnish government for talks in Moscow.

October 9   Finland gathers troops on the Soviet border as Finnish officials leave for Moscow. Four days later, the Finnish foreign minister states that his nation will not sign a Soviet-dictated agreement.

October 27   A Soviet-organized assembly in Lvov unanimously approves Soviet rule for the Western Ukraine, formerly eastern Poland, now occupied by Soviet troops.

October 29   Soviet troops enter Latvia to occupy military and naval posts.

October 31   Molotov describes the new Soviet foreign policy to the Supreme Soviet (the legislature). He defends the Soviet invasion of Poland and outlines the Soviet proposal to Finland to trade part of Soviet Karelia in exchange for Finnish islands in the Gulf of Finland, a naval base at the entrance to the gulf, and a strip of territory on the Karelian isthmus north of Leningrad.

November 1   The Finnish government announces that it will not agree to the Soviet proposal of October 31.

The Supreme Soviet unanimously approves admission of Polish Western Ukraine into the USSR. The next day, Polish Belorussia (White Russia) is granted similar approval.

November 26–28   The Soviet government demands Finnish troops move twenty to 25 kilometers behind the fortified border on the Karelian isthmus. The USSR alleges border incidents have killed Soviet troops.

November 30   Soviet troops invade Finland.

December 1   The Soviets set up a puppet Finnish ''People's Government'' at Terijoki, and recognize it as the legitimate Finnish government.

The Finns stop the advancing Soviet Army in the Karelian isthmus.

December 2   The ''People's Government'' of Finland signs a pact with the Soviet Union ceding bases and territory to the USSR.

The Finns report successful counter-attacks on the Karelian isthmus.

December 3   Finnish troops strongly resist Soviet advances on the eastern front.

December 4   The Soviet government rejects a proposal to negotiate peace with Finland.

December 6   An official journal of Comintern warns Romania to negotiate a nonaggression pact with the Soviet Union.

December 7   The Soviet government announces a blockade of Finland.

December 10   TASS, the official news agency of the Soviet Union, reports German shipments of weapons to Finland; the German government denies this claim.

December 11   The League of Nations asks the Soviet Union to suspend hostilities in Finland and submit the dispute to negotiations; the USSR rejects this request.

December 13   The League of Nations names the USSR as the aggressor in the Soviet-Finnish War and expels the Soviet Union from the League on December 14.

December 18 Soviet troops occupy the Finnish corridor to the Arctic ocean.

December 30 The Finns defeat the Soviets in a two-day battle north of Lake Kianta.

1940

February 11 The Red Army launches an attack on Finnish defensive positions known as the Mannerheim Line.

February 12 Germany and the Soviet Union enter into a trade agreement to exchange German machinery and metals for Soviet food and oil.

February 17 Soviet tanks bypass the Mannerheim Line and drive back Finnish troops.

March 12 The Soviet Union and Finland sign a peace treaty in Moscow in which Finland gives Viborg and the territory around Lake Lagoda to the USSR, and leases the Hango and Ribachi peninsulas for Soviet military bases.

June 9 The Soviet Union and Japan agree to a cease-fire on the Manchukuo-Mongolian border (*see* September 15, 1939).

June 15 Soviet troops move into Lithuania and take control of the country.

June 17 Soviet troops move into Latvia and Estonia, seizing the countries.

June 26 The Soviet government expands the work week from 7 hours five days a week to 8 hours six days a week to increase production of war munitions.

June 29 Soviet troops move into the Romanian possession of Bessarabia, now called Moldavia. King Carol II of Romania orders Romanian troops to mobilize.

July 14 The Soviets hold parliamentary elections in Estonia, Latvia, and Lithuania; the victors are overwhelmingly pro-Soviet.

July 21 The parliaments of Estonia, Latvia, and Lithuania declare their countries part of the Soviet Union.

August 20 Leon Trotsky is attacked by a Soviet agent in Mexico City. He dies the following day.

October 26 Soviet troops occupy Romanian islands at the mouth of the Danube.

December 18 Hitler issues orders for Operation Barbarossa—the invasion of the Soviet Union.

1941

January 10 The Soviet Union and Germany sign a trade agreement that includes the biggest grain deal in history.

February 25 The Soviet government approves its national budget, one-third of which is for national defense.

March 25 The Soviet Union and Turkey exchange a pledge of neutrality.

April 5 The Soviet Union and Yugoslavia sign a five-year nonaggression pact.

April 6 Yugoslavia is invaded by German troops; Hungary invades Yugoslavia on April 11.

April 12 The Soviet Union denounces Hungary, but not Germany, for invading Yugoslavia.

April 13 The Soviet Union and Japan sign a neutrality pact. The USSR recognizes Japan's rule over Manchukuo while Japan pledges to respect the Soviet-dominated Mongolian People's Republic (*see* June 9, 1940).

May 6 Vyacheslav Molotov resigns as the premier of the Soviet Union, but continues as foreign minister. Joseph Stalin assumes the post of premier or chairman of the Council of People's Commissars.

May 9 The Soviet government withdraws recognition of the governments-in-exile of Yugoslavia, Belgium, and Norway in London.

June 4 The commander of the Red Army in Belorussia reports German troop concentrations on the Belorussian border. On June 14, however, the official Soviet news agency TASS denies the danger of a German invasion of the USSR.

June 22 German armies invade the Soviet Union on three fronts stretching from the Baltic Sea to the Black Sea. Nazi Panzer tank divisions move through Soviet Poland.

British Prime Minister Winston Churchill promises aid to the Soviet Union and any other country fighting against Hitler.

Italy declares war on the Soviet Union.

June 23 German tank units capture Brest-Litovsk. German troops march through Lithuania and enter Latvia.

June 24 Soviet planes bomb Warsaw in German-occupied Poland.

U.S. President Roosevelt pledges U.S. aid to the Soviet Union and promises to release $40,000,000 in Soviet credits frozen earlier.

June 25 Roosevelt announces that the Neutrality Act will not be invoked against the Soviet Union, allowing the USSR to obtain supplies from the United States.

June 26 Finland enters the war on the side of Nazi Germany.

German forces move within 50 miles of Minsk.

Soviet planes attack German bases in Hungary and Romania.

June 27 Hungary declares war on the Soviet Union.

June 28 German and Finnish forces launch an attack aimed at capturing Leningrad and Murmansk. Minsk and Lvov fall to the Germans.

July 1 The Soviet government asks the U.S. for help and offers to pay for supplies.

The Germans capture Riga, Latvia.

July 3 In his first broadcast since the German invasion, Joseph Stalin calls on all Soviet citizens to defend their country using a scorched earth policy that entails the destruction of as much as possible before the enemy forces advance.

July 10 Stalin becomes chairman of the High Command (Stavka) of the Soviet military.

July 12 The Soviet Union and Great Britain sign a mutual aid pact; each government pledges full war aid assistance to the other and agrees not to sign a peace pact except by mutual consent.

July 18 The Soviet Union and the Czechoslovak government-in-exile in London and sign an agreement to work together on the conduct of the war.

July 19 Stalin assumes the post of defense minister.

July 25 German troops capture Smolensk.

July 30 The Soviet and Polish government-in-exile sign an agreement ending the state of war that has existed between the two countries since 1939. The USSR agrees to recognize Polish borders prior to the Nazi-Soviet pact of August 23, 1939.

August 16 Stalin accepts a proposal submitted by Roosevelt and Churchill to accept high American and British officials in Moscow to discuss long-term plans to defeat the Axis powers of Germany, Italy, Japan, and their allies.

August 20 With Nazi troops outside Leningrad, Marshal Voroshilov, commander of forces in the city, appeals to the citizens to defend the city to the death.

August 25 Soviet and British troops simultaneously march into Iran in an effort to keep German troops out.

August 26 The Soviet Union warns Japan that any effort to interfere with Soviet-American trade in the Far East would be considered an unfriendly act.

September 5 German forces use long-range artillery to shell Leningrad.

September 11 Soviet Foreign Minister Molotov formally charges Bulgaria with serving as a base for Axis forces.

September 18 Stalin orders all Soviet males between the ages of sixteen and fifty who are not in the armed forces to begin military training after working hours.

German forces enter Kiev.

September 21 German tank divisions reach the Sea of Azov, cutting off the Crimea from the rest of the Soviet Union.

October 1 The U.S. and British missions in Moscow agree to fill all Soviet needs for war supplies.

October 13 German troops capture Kalinin, 100 miles northwest of Moscow.

October 16 Romanian and German troops capture Odessa after a two-month siege.

October 20 German forces place Moscow under siege.

October 25 German troops capture Kharkov.

November 6 The U.S. State Department reveals that the U.S. will lend the Soviet Union one billion dollars in lend-lease aid to buy American war materials.

During a broadcast celebrating the 24th anniversary of the October Revolution, Stalin urges the creation of a second front by U.S. and British forces.

November 29 Soviet troops recapture Rostov.

December 6 Soviet forces start a counter-offensive along the entire Moscow front breaking through the German line at two points.

December 9 Soviet troops lift the Leningrad siege by reopening the road to Moscow.

December 15 Soviet troops recapture Kalinin, Petrovsk, and Volovo. The Soviet government announces the 9th German Army Corp has been destroyed.

1942

January 1 The Soviets sign the United Nations declaration in Washington DC.

January 8 Moscow radio reports that the German siege of Sevastopol has been lifted.

February 14 The Soviet government declares that all able-bodied men between the ages of sixteen and 65 who are not already mobilized or engaged in government work are liable to be called up to military work. Women between the ages of sixteen and fifty who do not have children under the age of eight are liable to be called up for work in industry or building as well. The number of days that members of collective farms have to work is increased from 100 to 150 days.

April 7 The Soviet government announces the rail line to Leningrad has reopened.

April 13 *Pravda* (which means ''truth''), the official newspaper of the Soviet Communist party, warns Japan to adhere to the Soviet-Japanese neutrality pact of April 13, 1941.

April 24 Soviet authorities at Khabarovsk, Siberia, intern the five-man crew of a U.S. bomber forced down after the Doolittle raid on Japan. They are interned by the Soviet government as a part of their neutrality in the U.S. war against Japan. In 1943, the interned airmen escape to Iran.

April 30 Joseph Stalin announces that the Soviet Union has no interest in making territorial gains; its only goal is to liberate Soviet lands from the German invaders.

May 12 German forces breach the Soviet line in the Kerch peninsula and drive toward the Sea of Azov.

May 13 Soviet forces launch a counterattack on Kharkov to relieve German pressure on the Kerch peninsula.

May 18 German forces open a strong counterattack on Kharkov.

May 20 German forces capture the town and harbor of Kerch.

May 26 The USSR and Britain sign a 20-year mutual assistance treaty banning a separate peace with Germany; both countries pledge not to seek territorial gains and to cooperate to preserve peace in the future.

June 28 German forces open a new offensive from Kursk, 280 miles south of Moscow.

July 3 After 25 days of siege, Sevastopol falls to the Germans.

July 27 The Soviets evacuate Rostov and Novocherkassk before the German drive toward the Caucasus oil fields.

July 28 German forces take Rostov.

July 30 Stalin issues his ''Not another step back'' order to the Army.

August 12–15 British Prime Minister Winston Churchill, U.S. Ambassador Avrill Harriman, and Joseph Stalin meet in Moscow to discuss the creation of a second front.

August 24 German forces begin the siege of Stalingrad on the Volga River.

September 4 Soviet bombers attack Budapest, Hungary for the first time during the war.

September 14 Soviet bombers attack Bucharest and the Ploeşti oil fields in Romania.

September 16 The battle for Stalingrad becomes more intense as civilians fight side by side with the Red Army to defend the city.

September 18 Soviet troops from Siberia help repel three Nazi shock forces penetrating the streets of Stalingrad; by September 24, however, German forces control most of the center of Stalingrad.

October 3 In a letter to a U.S. reporter stationed in Moscow, Joseph Stalin complains that Allied aid to the Soviet Union is inadequate and not equal to the Soviet contribution in the war against Germany.

October 6 The United States and Britain agree to increase their aid to the Soviet Union.

October 10 The Soviet government issues a decree abolishing political commissars in the Red Army. Army officers regain full military control.

November 19 Soviet forces begin an offensive in the Stalingrad area and surround over 300,000 German troops by November 22.

December 12–23 German forces unsuccessfully attempt to relieve German troops surrounded in Stalingrad.

December 24 Soviet forces open their fourth major offensive in the Caucasus.

1943

January 2 German forces begin to withdraw from the Caucasus.

January 18 The Soviet government announces that their troops eased the German siege around Leningrad by smashing through nine miles of fortifications and recapturing the Schlusselburg fortress.

January 26 Soviet forces liberate Voronezh.

February 2 The survivors of the German Sixth Army surrender in Stalingrad.

February 8 Soviet troops take Kursk.

February 14 Soviet troops take Rostov.

February 16 Soviet troops recapture Kharkov, the anchor of the German line on the southern Russian front.

April 18 Moscow radio reports that the Soviets killed 10,000 Polish prisoners-of-war captured after Soviet troops seized eastern Poland in 1939 at Katyn, near Smolensk, a "hideous Gestapo frame-up."

April 26 Angered at the Polish intimation that Soviet troops massacred 10,000 Polish prisoners at Katyn, the USSR breaks off relations with the Polish government-in-exile in London.

May 5 Despite the rupture of relations with Poland, Stalin desires to see a strong and independent Poland established after the war.

May 22 Conceding to Western allies, Stalin dissolves Comintern, the international Communist party organization run by the USSR (*see* March 2–7, 1919).

August 23 Soviet troops recapture Kharkov.

September 8 The Soviet government allows Orthodox ecclesiastical administrations and seminaries to be reestablished. Stalin meets with the leader of the church.

September 25 The Soviet army recaptures Smolensk and Roslavl and moves into the suburbs of Kiev.

October 7 The Soviet government announces that the Red Army has crossed the Dnieper river and established bridgeheads on the west bank.

October 9 Stalin announces that all German troops have been pushed out of the Caucasus.

November 1 The U.S. secretary of state, British foreign secretary, and Soviet foreign commissar meet in Moscow and agree to continue Anglo-American-Soviet cooperation after the war and to fight until the Axis forces surrender unconditionally.

November 6 Soviet forces recapture Kiev.

November 28–December 1 Stalin, U.S. president Roosevelt, and British prime minister Churchill meet in Tehran, Iran, to discuss wartime strategy and postwar issues such as the division of power in post-war Europe.

December 12 Soviet Foreign Commissar Molotov and Czechoslovak Ambassador Zdeněk Fierlinger sign a Soviet-Czechoslovak treaty of mutual assistance in Moscow.

1944

January 4 The Soviet government announces that one of its armies crossed the prewar Soviet-Polish border. The next day the Polish government-in-exile in London instructs underground forces in Poland not to impede Soviet advances into their country.

January 6 The pro-Soviet Union of Polish Patriots in Moscow calls on the Polish underground to rise up against the German occupation forces.

January 11 The Soviet Union offers to guarantee Poland post-war independence if it agrees to accept the Curzon Line, the 1920 Polish-Soviet armistice line, as its eastern border.

January 14 The Polish government-in-exile offers to discuss outstanding problems with the Soviet Union if the United States and Great Britain act as intermediaries.

January 15 The U.S. offers to mediate the Polish-Soviet border dispute.

January 18 The Soviets open a new offensive around Leningrad.

January 20 Soviet forces recapture Novgorod.

January 26 The Soviets refuse the U.S. offer to negotiate the Soviet-Polish border dispute.

January 27 Soviet forces end the 870-day siege of Leningrad in which over 750,000 of the city's citizens died.

February 1 The Supreme Soviet approves Molotov's proposal to amend the constitution to allow each republic to form its own army and have separate diplomatic representation abroad. Ukraine and Belorussia are thereby permitted to have delegates at the future United Nations.

February 2 Soviet troops cross the pre-war border of Estonia.

February 12 The pro-Soviet "Union of Polish Patriots" announces that it has organized a national council or government on Polish soil.

February 26 Six hundred Soviet bombers attack Helsinki, Finland.

February 29 The Soviet government reveals it has offered a peace treaty to Finland if the latter breaks its ties with Germany, withdraws to the 1940 borders, and helps the Red Army intern German forces in Finland.

March 21 Finland rejects the Soviet peace plan.

March 26 Soviet troops cross the Prut River into Romania.

April 2 Molotov announces that the USSR will not seek territory or change the social structure of Romania.

April 10 Soviet troops recapture the Black Sea port of Odessa.

April 13 Soviet troops capture the capital city of the Crimea, Simferopol.

April 16 The Soviets report the capture of Yalta.

May 1 Stalin calls for a joint American-British-Soviet blow against German forces; he asks the people of Bulgaria, Romania, and Hungary to overthrow their pro-German governments and seek Allied aid.

May 9 Soviet forces recapture Sevastopol.

May 16 The Soviet Union, United States, and Great Britain sign agreements with the exiled governments of Norway, the Netherlands, and Belgium regarding control of civilian affairs during the liberation of Europe.

June 10 Soviet forces open a new offensive against Finnish and German forces in the Karelian isthmus.

June 23 Soviet forces open the 1944 summer offensive against the Germans along a 300-mile line in Belorussia.

July 3 Soviet troops enter Minsk and capture about 100,000 German troops.

July 13 Soviet troops capture Vilnius, Lithuania.

July 17 Soviet troops enter Latvia; they also reach the Curzon Line in Poland.

July 18 Soviet troops cross the Bug River.

July 23 After the capture of Lublin, Soviet radio announces the creation of the pro-Soviet Polish Committee of National Liberation to administer areas of Poland captured by the Red Army.

July 24 The Polish government-in-exile denounces the new Polish Committee of National Liberation.

August 1 The Warsaw Uprising begins, led by the Polish Home Army; the Red Army is not far. The uprising hopes to take control of the city away from the Germans and counts on Soviet aid to achieve this goal.

August 3 Soviet troops break through the German line on the Vistula River.

August 16 The Soviet government tells Britain that it will not help the Polish Home Army and refuses to give British-American aircraft permission to land a supply-drop mission to aid the Poles. As a result, the uprising fails.

August 17 Soviet troops reach the East Prussian border along the Sesupe River.

August 20 Soviet forces begin an offensive in Bessarabia and Romania.

August 29 Soviet troops capture the Romanian Black Sea port of Constanţa.

August 30 Soviet troops enter Bucharest and Ploeşti.

September 1 Soviet troops reach the Bulgarian frontier.

September 2 The Finnish government announces that Finland will negotiate peace with the Soviet Union and asks German troops to leave the country by September 15. A cease-fire goes into effect on September 4.

September 5 The Soviet Union declares war on Bulgaria due to Bulgaria's reluctance to sign an armistice.

September 9 Bulgaria ends its four-day war with the Soviet Union by agreeing to an armistice.

September 10 Soviet troops capture the Warsaw suburb of Praga.

September 12 The Soviet government announces that Romania agrees to join the Allies, to pay $300 million in reparations to the Soviet Union, and to return Bessarabia and northern Bukovina, seized by the USSR in June 1940, to the Soviet Union.

September 13 The Soviets announce that their troops have reached the Czechoslovak border in a drive from southern Poland.

September 16 Soviet troops enter Sophia, Bulgaria.

September 19 Finland signs an armistice with the Soviet Union. They agree to accept the 1940 border, cede Petsamo and Porkkalla peninsula to the USSR, disarm all German troops in Finland, and pay $300 million in war reparations.

September 22 Soviet troops capture Tallinn, Estonia.

September 22–26 The Communist Yugoslav partisan military commander Joseph Broz Tito meets with Stalin in Moscow; Stalin promises him military aid.

September 28 The Soviets announce that Marshal Tito gave them permission to enter Yugoslavia in order to attack Hungary from the south.

September 29 The Soviet army enters Yugoslavia and launches an attack on Belgrade.

October 2 The last of the Polish Home Army in the Warsaw Uprising surrenders to the Germans (*see* August 1 and August 16, 1944).

October 6 The Soviet government announces that its army invaded Hungary.

October 9–20 Winston Churchill meets with Stalin in Moscow. During their meetings they divide Europe into hypothetical spheres of influence. They agree to pursue a joint policy in Yugoslavia.

October 13 Soviet troops capture Riga, Latvia.

October 18 The Soviet Army enters Czechoslovakia.

October 20 Soviet and Yugoslav troops capture Belgrade.

October 22 Soviet troops enter East Prussia.

November 5　Soviet artillery shells Budapest.

November 24　The Soviet Union, the United States, and Great Britain agree to coordinate their policies for the occupation and administration of Germany.

December 27　Soviet forces surround Budapest and enter the eastern part of the city on December 30.

1945

January 5　Pending the establishment of a permanent government for Poland, the Soviet Union recognizes the pro-Soviet Polish provisional government in Lublin.

January 17　Soviet forces liberate Warsaw.

January 19　Soviet troops capture Cracow and reach the border of German Silesia.

January 20　The provisional Hungarian government signs an armistice agreement with the Soviet Union, Great Britain, and the United States.

February 4–11　Roosevelt, Churchill, and Stalin meet at Yalta in the Crimea. They agree to destroy German militarism; to establish popular governments in the liberated countries of Eastern Europe, which become pro-Soviet; to make Germany pay war reparations; to set up occupation zones in Germany; to call a meeting of the United Nations on April 25; and to broaden the base of Polish and Yugoslav governments to include non-communists. Stalin also agrees to end the Soviet-Japanese neutrality pact of April 1941 and to declare war on Japan two or three months after Germany's surrender.

February 11　Soviet troops reach the Oder River and are 38 miles from Berlin.

February 13　Soviet troops capture Budapest after a 49-day siege.

March 10　The Soviet Union grants Romania the authority to take over the administration of northern Transylvania in accordance with the terms of the armistices.

March 25　Soviet and U.S. troops meet on the Elbe River in Germany.

March 29　Soviet troops in Central Europe enter Austria.

March 30　Soviet troops in the Baltic capture Danzig.

March 31　The United States and Great Britain reject a Soviet request to invite the pro-Soviet Polish Lublin provisional government to the United Nations conference in San Francisco.

April 2–June 26　The United Nations Conference on International Organization meets in San Francisco; the USSR attends.

April 5　The Soviet government denounces its neutrality pact with Japan stating that Japan's aid to Germany invalidated the pact (*see* February 4–11).

April 13　Soviet forces capture Vienna.

April 22　The Soviet government announces that it has concluded a treaty of friendship, mutual assistance, and postwar cooperation with the Polish Lublin provisional government.

April 23　Soviet troops enter Berlin.

April 27　The United Nations conference agrees to grant the Soviet Union three votes in the proposed world security organization: one each from the USSR, Belorussia, and Ukraine.

May 2　All fighting in Berlin stops.

May 5　Soviet Foreign Commissar Molotov announces that sixteen Polish underground leaders were arrested by Soviet authorities on charges of "diversionist activities against the Red Army."

May 7　The German High Command surrenders.

May 8　The Allies proclaim victory in Europe called VE Day.

June 2　The Soviet delegates at the UN conference insist that permanent members of the United Nations council have the right to veto discussion of international disputes.

June 5　Soviet, British, American, and French commanders in chief assume supreme authority over Germany in their respective zones.

June 21　A Soviet court sentences twelve of the sixteen Polish underground leaders to prison terms ranging from four months to ten years; three are acquitted and the trial of the fourth is postponed (*see* May 5).

June 29　Czechoslovakia cedes Ruthenia to the Soviet Union.

August 2　Stalin, U.S. President Harry S Truman, and British Prime Minister Clement Atlee issue the Potsdam Declaration. They agree to reduce German industrial power; to allow Poland and the Soviet Union to annex East Prussia and a large part of east Germany; and to establish reparation scales.

August 8　The Soviet Union declares war on Japan.

August 14　Japan agrees to surrender (which officially takes place on September 2, VJ Day).

(L–r) Winston Churchill, Franklin D. Roosevelt, and Joseph Stalin at the Yalta Conference.

August 16   The Soviet Union and Poland sign a treaty which assigns the new Soviet-Polish border and determines how the two countries will share German reparations.

September 2   Stalin announces that the defeat of Japan allows the Soviet Union to regain the southern half of Sakhalin Island and the Kurile islands which were given to Japan after the Russo-Japanese War of 1904–05.

1946

March 5   Winston Churchill delivers his "Iron Curtain" speech in Fulton, Missouri. The "iron curtain" refers to the heavily guarded border between Soviet bloc countries and the West.

June 14   The U.S., France, and Great Britain accept the Romanian-Soviet border at the Allied meeting of foreign ministers in Paris; the agreement allows the USSR to retain northern Bukovina and Besserabia.

July 26   The United States accuses the Soviet Union of stripping Hungary of its food supplies and industrial materials. The USSR denies this accusation.

1947

February 10   The signing of peace treaties in Paris formally terminates the state of war between the Allies and Italy, Finland, Romania, Bulgaria, and Hungary.

February 17   The United States begins broadcasting into the USSR in an effort to send factual information about the U.S. to the Soviet people.

March 12   In response to Soviet actions against Turkey and Iran, U.S. president Truman formulates the Truman Doctrine which supports the rights of nations to formulate their own destinies. As a result, the U.S. provides military assistance to Greece and Turkey.

October 5   Leaders of nine Communist nations meet in Poland and establish the Communist Information Bureau (Cominform), an organization designed to succeed Comintern in the leadership of the international Communist movement (*see* May 22, 1943).

December 10   The U.S. calls on the USSR to end its practice of seizing German assets in the occupation zone.

December 14   The USSR completes the evacuation of all Soviet troops from Bulgaria.

December 16 The British government charges that the USSR has taken "considerably more" than the agreed $7 billion worth of reparations from the Soviet occupation zone of Germany. The Soviets deny the charge.

1948

January 26 The Soviet Union and Poland sign a five-year trade treaty that will increase trade between the two nations by 15 percent and provide Poland with credits of $450 million in the form of industrial equipment and machinery.

January 28 The Soviet Communist party newspaper *Pravda* repudiates a plan for a federation of the Balkan nations of Yugoslavia and Bulgaria proposed by Georgi Dimitrov, the Bulgarian Premier.

February 4 The Soviet Union and Romania sign a treaty of friendship, cooperation, and mutual assistance.

February 13 Marshal Vasili D. Sokolovski, the Soviet commander in Germany, announces the creation of a new economic advisory commission in the Soviet zone of Germany similar to the American-British structure.

February 18 The Soviet Union and Hungary sign a mutual defense pact.

March 18 The Soviet Union and Bulgaria sign a 20-year treaty of friendship and alliance.

March 25 U.S. Secretary of State George C. Marshall announces that the United States will continue its joint occupation of Berlin. Any further effort of the Soviet delegation to disrupt the Allied Control Council will be considered action aimed against the reunification of Germany.

March 31 British and U.S. military officials reject a Soviet proposal to place all road and rail traffic into Berlin under Soviet control.

June 8 The Soviet Union reduces by half the war reparation payments due from Romania and Hungary.

June 18 Soviet occupation authorities ban all motor, railway, and pedestrian traffic between Berlin and the western zones of Germany. The Soviets hope that this economic blockade of the city will force the Western Allies from Berlin.

June 21 The United States and Great Britain begin a massive airlift to bring supplies into Berlin.

June 28 The Cominform accuses the Yugoslav Communist party and Marshal Tito, of not following Soviet foreign and domestic policies; it expels Yugoslavia from

the organization thereby alienating Yugoslavia from the Communist world.

July 1 Soviet representatives withdraw from the Allied Kommandatura (Command) for Berlin—the last allied governing body functioning in Germany.

July 3 After a brief meeting with other zone commanders, Sokolovski refuses to lift the Soviet blockade of Berlin.

July 6 Great Britain, France, and the United States send letters of protest to the Soviet Union concerning the blockade of Berlin.

July 8 The British Foreign Office reports that the U.S., France, and Britain have suspended all reparation shipments to the Soviet Union from the western zones of Germany.

July 14 The Soviet government rejects the joint Anglo-French-American protest over the blockade of Berlin. The Soviets claim that the western powers forfeited all legal status in Berlin by violating the 1945 Yalta and Potsdam pacts for four power rule in Germany.

August 2 Representatives of the U.S., Great Britain, and France meet with Stalin in Moscow to discuss the Berlin situation.

September 6 German Communists, supported by Soviet troops, force the Berlin city assembly to leave its quarters and move to the British sector of Berlin.

September 7 Negotiations of the Allied military governors are suspended due to the Soviet refusal to lift the Berlin blockade until the Communists are given complete control of the city.

September 9 Soviet troops fire on a crowd of 250,000 Germans who gathered in Berlin to protest Soviet activities.

September 25 The Soviet Union insists on control of all traffic between Berlin and western Germany, and virtual economic control of Berlin.

September 29 The U.S., France, and Great Britain formally refer the Berlin blockade to the UN Security Council as a risk to peace.

October 10 The Soviets test launch the first long-range guided missile.

October 11 Representatives of Great Britain, France, and the U.S. reaffirm their refusal to negotiate with the USSR until the Soviets lift Berlin blockade.

October 28 In an interview published in *Pravda*, Stalin states that the western powers have blocked a settlement of the Berlin dispute in pursuance of plans to start another war.

November 10 Soviet authorities in Berlin threaten to shoot down all British and U.S. planes flying outside of the air corridors leading to Berlin.

November 16 President Truman restates U.S. refusal to negotiate with the Soviets until they lift the Berlin blockade.

November 30 The creation of a Communist-controlled city council in the Soviet section of Berlin virtually completes the division of the city into Soviet and western sectors.

December 2 Soviet occupation authorities in Berlin promise complete support of the new Communist-controlled city council in East Berlin.

December 21 The U.S., France, Great Britain revive the Soviet-boycotted Allied Kommandatura in Berlin (*see* July 1).

1949

January 25 The Soviets announce the formation of a six-nation (USSR, Bulgaria, Czechoslovakia, Hungary, Poland, and Romania) Council for Mutual Economic Assistance (CMEA), also known by the acronym COMECON, to assist the economic development of the member states through coordinated efforts.

March 4 After a two-day blockade of its office by the U.S. Army, the Soviet repatriation mission leaves Frankfurt.

March 31 The Soviet Union denounces the North Atlantic Treaty Organization (NATO), a military alliance of non-communist countries, as an instrument of aggression aimed at the USSR and a violation of the UN charter.

April 4 NATO is officially formed when representatives of twelve western nations sign the agreement.

April 12 The Soviet Union agrees to send equipment and materials to Albania to compensate it for the loss of trade with Yugoslavia resulting from Yugoslavia's alienation from the Communist world (*see* June 28, 1948).

May 4 Representatives from the USSR, U.S., Great Britain, and France agree to lift the blockade and counterblockade of Berlin starting May 12, and to begin discussion of the German reunification question.

May 30 Soviet Foreign Minister Andrei Vishinsky rejects a western proposal for the unification of Germany by extending the western German constitution to all of Germany.

June 20 The Allied Council of Foreign Ministers, meeting in Paris since May 23, adjourns without reaching any

solution on the German question; however, the ministers approve a general outline of an Austrian peace treaty.

July 5 The formation of three joint Romanian-Soviet companies (Sovroms) to control coal and metal production and the building industry in Romania is reported.

July 9 Soviet authorities close all but one zonal crossing to truck traffic bound for Berlin from West Germany.

July 25 Soviet officials announce the reopening of closed inter-zonal road crossings into West Berlin.

August 12 Moscow radio broadcasts the text of a Soviet note charging Yugoslavia with acting as an enemy to the USSR.

September 2 The U.S. State Department accuses the Soviet Union of refusing to make any real concessions, except at the expense of Yugoslavia, in negotiating an Austrian peace treaty.

September 18 Acting Soviet Foreign Minister Andrei A. Gromyko agrees to resume negotiations for the conclusion of an Austrian peace treaty.

September 25 The Soviet news agency TASS reports the testing of the first Soviet atomic bomb.

October 10 The USSR transfers to the German Democratic Republic (East Germany) all functions that were previously the responsibilities of the Soviet military authorities in the Soviet occupied zone.

October 25 The Soviet government requests that Yugoslavia recall its ambassador to Moscow on the grounds that he is conducting espionage in the USSR.

November 7 Soviet Marshal Konstantin K. Rokossovsky is named Polish minister of defense and marshal of the Polish army.

December 3 The Inter-Allied Reparations agency decides to divide among its member nations dismantled German industrial equipment originally intended for the Soviet Union.

1950

February 18 The American, British, and French commandants in Berlin protest continued Soviet interference of truck traffic between Berlin and West Germany.

May 16 Stalin announces his government's decision to cut East Germany's war reparations balance of $6,432,000,000 by 50 percent.

June 14   The Yugoslav government charges the USSR with attempting to block its trade on the upper Danube River.

July 7   The UN Security Council votes to establish a United Nations military command in Korea; the Soviet Union has boycotted the Council since January 10 and therefore has no veto.

1951

January 20   The Soviet government asserts that French and British support of West German rearmament violates wartime treaties of friendship.

November 19   In a flight from Munich to Belgrade, Yugoslavia, a U.S. Air Force transport plane is forced down by a Soviet fighter plane over Hungary.

1952

January 16   The Soviet government orders foreign diplomats to stay within 25 miles of Moscow and bars them from 22 cities.

May 26   The foreign ministers of the U.S., France, and Great Britain and Chancellor Konrad Adenauer of West Germany sign treaties that end the Allied occupation and restore West German sovereignty.

June 1   USSR authorities bar the residents of West Berlin from entering the Soviet zone of Germany.

September 18   The U.S. State Department charges the USSR with creating a vast system of slave labor camps consisting primarily of political offenders.

September 30   The British Foreign Office official confirms the presence of Soviet technical troops in North Korea.

October 3   The Soviet government demands the recall of George Kennan, U.S. ambassador to the USSR. The U.S. rejects the demand five days later.

October 5–14   At the Nineteenth Soviet Communist Party Congress the Politburo is renamed the Central Committee Presidium and the term "Bolshevik" is dropped from the party's title.

December 10   In notes to the USSR and Hungary the United States government demands the return of or com-

pensation for a U.S. plane shot down by Soviet fighters in November 1951.

1953

January 13   Nine doctors are arrested and charged with plotting to kill Soviet political and military leaders and conducting espionage for American Jewish organizations. Two doctors die during the investigation of the "Doctor's Plot." This act is seen as the beginning of Stalin's next round of purges (*see* September 26, 1936).

March 5   Joseph Stalin dies. Georgii M. Malenkov succeeds him as premier and first secretary of the Communist party on March 6.

March 15   Malenkov states that all problems existing between the Soviet Union and the United States can be resolved through negotiations.

April 14   Seven surviving doctors accused in the "Doctors Plot" are exonerated.

May 28   The USSR abolishes its control commission in Germany and names V. S. Semenov high commissioner to represent Soviet interests in Germany.

June 8   Soviet authorities terminate control over movements in and out of the Soviet zone in Austria.

June 15   The USSR and Yugoslavia renew diplomatic relations broken since 1949.

June 17   Soviet troops help to enforce martial law in East Berlin after rioting workers threaten to take control of the East German government.

June 26   Lavrentii Beria, chief of the Soviet secret police, is arrested after losing a power struggle to succeed Stalin. He is tried, found guilty of crimes against the USSR, and executed on December 23.

July 21   The East German government announces that the Soviet Union has extended credits of $57 million for the purchase of food in the second half of 1953.

August 12   The Soviet Union test explodes a hydrogen bomb.

August 23   The Soviet government announces the signing of a USSR-East German protocol which cancels East German reparation payments on January 1, 1954, limits Soviet occupation costs, and will result in the return of some industrial plants seized by the Soviets.

September 13   Nikita S. Khrushchev becomes the first secretary of the Communist party.

September 15 The Soviet government announces the reorganization of the agricultural and industrial ministries in an effort to increase production.

1954

January 22 Khrushchev proposes that the Soviet Union improve its economy by using fallow land for increased grain production; the proposal is known as the Virgin Lands campaign.

March 26 The USSR announces that the German Democratic Republic (East Germany) has become a sovereign state; however, Soviet troops will remain stationed in the country.

April 8 The Allied High Commission declines to recognize the sovereignty of East Germany and declares that the USSR will continue to be regarded as the power responsible for the Soviet zone of Germany.

June 30 The Soviets announce the operation of the first atomic electric power plant in the USSR.

September 25 The Soviet Union and Romania announce the USSR's agreement to transfer to Romania its shares in twelve joint stock companies (Sovroms).

October 1 The Soviet Union and Yugoslavia sign a barter trade agreement for the first exchange of trade since 1948.

October 9 The USSR and Bulgaria sign an agreement providing for the Soviets to turn over to Bulgaria its holdings in three joint-stock companies.

1955

January 25 The Soviet government formally terminates its state of war with Germany.

February 8 Georgii M. Malenkov resigns as prime minister of the Communist party and is replaced by Nikolai Bulganin.

March 10 The Communist party issues a decree giving collective farm leaders more authority to decide local agricultural policy.

March 21 The Soviet Foreign Ministry announces an agreement between the USSR and six East European countries—Albania, Bulgaria, Czechoslovakia, Hungary, Poland, and Romania—for the creation of a unified military command if West Germany is rearmed.

May 9 West Germany is formally admitted into NATO.

May 14 The Warsaw Pact, the military organization of Soviet bloc countries is established. The USSR, Albania, Bulgaria, Czechoslovakia, Hungary, Poland, and Romania all join the organization (*see* March 21).

May 15 The Austrian State Treaty is signed and the Soviets withdraw their troops soon after.

May 26 Communist party General Secretary Khrushchev and Soviet Premier Bulganin arrive in Belgrade for talks with Yugoslav President Tito, marking a thaw in relations (*see* June 28, 1948).

June 2 The Soviet Union and Yugoslavia issue a joint declaration of friendship and cooperation.

June 14 Soviet radio announces that the USSR will assist Hungary and Bulgaria by supplying atomic research equipment, scientists, and technical information.

September 1 The USSR announces that it has granted loans of $84 million to Yugoslavia.

September 3 The Soviets and Yugoslavs sign an agreement reestablishing air service between the USSR and Yugoslavia.

September 9 The Soviet Union and West Germany establish diplomatic relations.

September 20 The USSR and East Germany sign a series of agreements that enhance the power and authority of the East German government.

September 27 Egypt announces that it will purchase Soviet arms.

October 13 Under the provisions of the Austrian State Treaty, the Soviet government delivers to Austria about 350 industrial enterprises seized by the USSR as German property (*see* May 15).

October 19 The Soviet government announces that it will continue to control Allied military traffic between West Germany and West Berlin.

December 6 The USSR, U.S., France, and Great Britain formally recognize the neutrality of Austria.

December 9 The East German government announces that its own border guards have replaced the Soviet guards.

1956

January 26 The Soviet government formally returns to Finland the Porkkala naval base south of Helsinki.

January 28 The Warsaw Pact nations accept East Germany into the alliance (*see* May 14, 1955).

February 9 A Soviet legal journal reveals the abolition of a secret police tribunal with the power to condemn persons to Gulags, or labor camps, without a trial.

February 14–25 The Twentieth Congress of the Soviet Communist Party meets in Moscow. During a closed session on February 24, the delegates unanimously approve the report of Khrushchev which repudiates one-man rule. Khrushchev's ''secret speech'' also condemns some of the excesses of Stalin's rule.

March 28 *Pravda,* the Soviet Communist party newspaper, denounces Joseph Stalin for having abused his power during the later years of his rule.

April 8 The Soviet government announces that agricultural production must be dramatically increased in order to improve the Soviet standard of living.

April 18 *Pravda* announces the dissolution of Cominform (Communist Information Bureau).

May 11 The Presidium of the Supreme Soviet abolishes the 1940 law prohibiting Soviet citizens from changing jobs without permission.

June 3 The Soviet government announces the transfer of all-union judicial and certain economic functions to the governments of the Soviet republics.

June 20 Khrushchev and President Tito sign a joint declaration of renewed relations between the Yugoslav and Soviet Communist Parties.

June 30 The long suppressed text of the last testament of Lenin from December 24, 1923, calling for the removal of Stalin as general secretary of the Communist party, is released in Moscow.

July 2 The Central Committee of the Soviet Communist party issues a decree criticizing Communist parties abroad who question the Soviet's criticism of Stalin.

August 11 The Soviet government announces its Virgin Lands project. It plans to irrigate vast new cotton-producing regions on the steppes of Uzbekistan and Kazakhstan (*see* January 22, 1954).

September 18 The Soviet Union and Poland sign an agreement for large scale Soviet aid to the Polish economy.

October 13 At the UN security council, the Soviets veto a key section of an Anglo-French resolution in the Suez Canal crisis.

October 19 The Soviet government and Japan sign a joint declaration ending the state of war between the two nations and establishing diplomatic ties.

October 22 Soviet army units reportedly begin new maneuvers in Poland.

October 23 Hungarian police cannot control a Budapest crowd demonstrating against the Hungarian government and the presence of Soviet troops in Hungary.

October 24 Soviet troops quell anti-Soviet rioting in Budapest. Imre Nagy becomes Hungarian premier.

October 29 Israeli forces invade Egyptian territory and move within 25 miles of the Suez Canal.

October 30 The Soviet government announces its willingness to examine its policy of stationing Soviet troops in satellite countries.

November 3 Israeli forces reach the banks of the Suez Canal.

November 4 Moscow radio announces the formation of a new Hungarian government headed by János Kádár.

November 5 The Soviet government announces that it is willing to use force to stop aggression in the Middle East. The U.S. warns that it will oppose any Soviet intervention in the Middle East.

November 10 The Soviet government announces that it will allow military ''volunteers'' to go to Egypt if British, French, and Israeli troops are not withdrawn.

November 13 The Polish government relieves former Soviet Marshal Konstantin Rokossovsky of his posts as vice premier and defense minister.

November 14 The Budapest Central Council of Workers votes to strike until Soviet troops withdraw from Hungary and former Premier Nagy is restored to power.

The Soviets seize Nagy as he leaves the refuge of the Yugoslav embassy in Budapest under a safe conduct pass. The Soviets force Nagy and his family to seek asylum in Romania where he is officially arrested in April 1957.

November 18 Poland is reported to have secured important military, economic, and political concessions from the Soviet Union in an agreement signed in Moscow.

November 19 The Soviet government announces the appointment of Konstantin Rokossovsky as a Soviet deputy minister of defense (*see* November 13).

December 12 The UN general assembly censures Soviet intervention in Hungary and calls for the withdrawal of Soviet forces under UN observation.

December 17 A Soviet-Polish accord defines conditions for the temporary stationing of Soviet troops in Poland under the Warsaw Pact.

December 23 The Soviet Communist party issues a statement denouncing Communists who place nationalism above unity with the USSR and other Communist nations.

1957

January 29 The Soviet Union and Czechoslovakia sign an agreement providing for the integration of production in key industries and full cooperation in economic planning.

February 15 Andrei Gromyko becomes Soviet Foreign Minister.

February 26 The Yugoslav government accuses the USSR of attempting to isolate and discredit Yugoslavia.

March 25 The USSR and Poland sign an agreement for the further repatriation of Polish nationals from the Soviet Union.

April 15 The USSR and Romania sign an agreement that defines the legal status of Soviet troops stationed in Romania.

June 6 Soviet leaders Bulganin and Khrushchev begin a state visit to Finland. During the visit Malenkov, Vyacheslav Molotov, and Lazar Kaganovich form a coalition in the Presidium to demand Khrushchev's resignation. Upon his return, Khrushchev convenes the Central Committee which supports him and removes the "anti-party" group from the Central Committee and the Presidium of the Central Committee on July 3.

July 4 The Presidium of the Supreme Soviet announces the dismissal of Molotov, Malenkov, and Kaganovich from their government posts.

August 26 The Soviet government announces that it has successfully tested an intercontinental multi-stage ballistic missile.

September 14 The UN General Assembly adopts a resolution, by a vote of 60 to 10, condemning the Soviet Union's armed intervention in Hungary in October 1956.

October 4 The Soviet Union launches the first successful space satellite, Sputnik.

December 29 The East German government announces that American, French, and British diplomats will have to obtain East German rather than Soviet visas to travel to Berlin.

1958

January 27 The American and Soviet governments announce an agreement to expand cultural, educational, and scientific exchanges.

March 27 Khrushchev removes Bulganin as prime minister and assumes the post himself. The Supreme Soviet subsequently elects Khrushchev to the post.

April 8 The USSR and West Germany conclude a general repatriation and trade agreement in which the Soviets promise to examine, "in good faith," the application of all Germans wishing to leave the Soviet Union.

April 21 The Soviet government officially reduces the work day in heavy industry to seven hours and in mining to six hours.

May 27 The Soviet government informs Yugoslavia of a five-year postponement of the $285,000,000 aid in credits promised by the USSR.

July 7 In a protocol, the Soviet government agrees to provide technical aid and increased delivery of raw materials to East Germany in exchange for finished goods.

October 23 The 1958 Nobel Prize for Literature is awarded to Boris Pasternak for his novel *Doctor Zhivago*, which will not be published in the Soviet Union until the end of the 1980s.

Khrushchev agrees to lend Egypt $100,000,000 and to supply technical assistance for the construction of the Aswan dam.

October 28 The Soviet Writers Union expels Boris Pasternak.

October 29 After previously accepting, Boris Pasternak "voluntarily" rejects the 1958 Nobel Prize for Literature.

November 21 Representatives from the USSR and East Germany meet to discuss the transfer of Soviet functions of the occupation of Germany to the East Germans.

December 26 Several judicial reforms are implemented, including raising the age of criminal responsibility from fourteen to sixteen years old, reducing the maximum sentence for imprisonment from 25 to 15 years, and giving more precise definition to grave political crimes.

1959

January 27–February 5 The Twenty-first Congress of the Soviet Communist Party. The nominal function is to approve the new seven-year plan, but in reality the conference is called to acknowledge Khrushchev's victory in the struggle for the succession of Stalin. Many strongly worded denunciations of the Malenkov-Molotov opposition group are read (*see* July 4, 1957).

March 26 The Soviet Union is formally invited to join the U.S., France, and Great Britain at a foreign ministers' meeting in Geneva to discuss the German question. On March 30, they agree to attend.

May 11 The conference of foreign ministers opens in Geneva to discuss the German question with East and West German representatives present as advisors.

July 11 The U.S. State Department rejects a Soviet proposal for a nuclear-free zone in the Balkans.

July 24 The "Kitchen Debate" takes place between Khrushchev and American Vice-President Richard Nixon at a U.S. exhibition in Moscow. They argue over American and Soviet political ideologies.

September 14 A Soviet rocket crashes into the moon.

September 15–27 Khrushchev visits the United States and meets with President Eisenhower.

November 30 First Secretary of the Hungarian Communist party János Kádár announces that Soviet troops will remain in Hungary until international tensions subside.

December 1 Twelve countries, including the Soviet Union, sign a treaty making Antarctica a military-free zone.

December 26 The Central Committee of the Soviet Communist party orders tighter party control over collective farms.

1960

May 1 Soviet forces shoot down a U.S. U-2 spy plane and capture its pilot Francis Gary Powers. The U.S. government later admits that the U-2 plane was equipped for reconnaissance purposes.

May 30 Poet and novelist Boris Pasternak dies (*see* October 29, 1958).

June 21 During a speech to the Romanian Communist Party Congress in Bucharest, Khrushchev states that war with the West is not inevitable.

July 12 Khrushchev pledges Soviet support for any Cuban efforts to eliminate the U.S. naval base at Guantanamo.

August Due to poor relations the Soviet Union begin withdrawing its technical experts from the People's Republic of China.

August 17 At a Soviet military tribunal in Moscow, Francis Gary Powers pleads guilty to flying a U.S. reconnaissance plane on an intelligence mission over the USSR. Two days later he is found guilty of espionage and sentenced to ten years in prison (*see* May 1, 1960).

1961

February 22 U.S. President Kennedy sends a message to Soviet Premier Khrushchev expressing his hope for improved American-Soviet relations.

March 23 The Soviet government abolishes prior censorship on outgoing news dispatches.

April 12 Soviet cosmonaut, Yuri Gagarin, becomes the first person to successfully orbit the earth.

April 18 After a further Soviet offer of assistance to Cuba, President Kennedy warns that the United States will not tolerate outside military intervention in Cuba (*see* July 12, 1960).

April 30 The Soviet Union awards the 1960 Lenin Peace Prize to Cuban Prime Minister Fidel Castro.

July 30 The Soviet Communist party issues a draft program reaffirming the need for East-West peaceful coexistence.

August 7 During a televised speech, Khrushchev declares that the USSR will sign a separate treaty with East Germany if France, Great Britain, and the United States refuse to negotiate.

August 13 East German troops close the border between East and West Berlin after over 13,000 refugees have crossed over to the West in August alone. Two Soviet divisions are reportedly guarding the border while the East Germans begin building a wall to prevent escapes.

Albania breaks off relations with the Soviet Union due to the USSR's denunciations of Stalin and Communist China.

August 15 France, Great Britain, and the United States formally protest to the Soviet Union against the closing of the border between East and West Berlin.

August 18 The Soviet commandant in Berlin rejects the protest by the major powers over the closing of the East-West Berlin border.

President Kennedy orders a 1,500-man battle group to West Berlin to reinforce the 5,000-man garrison already there.

August 23 In a communiqué, the Soviet government charges France, Great Britain, and the United States with "provocative actions" and "abuse" of Western rights of access to Berlin by flying in "revanchists, extremists, saboteurs, and spies."

August 25 U.S. Secretary of Defense Robert McNamara announces that 76,500 reservists are called to active duty due to the Berlin crisis.

August 26   France, Great Britain, and the United States declare in notes to the USSR that it has no jurisdiction over western flights into Berlin; they warn against any interference with these flights.

September 5   A conference of neutral nations meeting in Belgrade, Yugoslavia, call on the U.S. and USSR to begin negotiations to establish world peace.

September 25   In a speech to the UN General Assembly, President Kennedy declares that Western powers will stand firm in West Berlin.

October 19   During a speech to the Twenty-second Congress of the Soviet Communist Party, Chinese Premier Zhou Enlai criticizes Khrushchev's decision to expel Albania from the Communist bloc.

October 27   Soviet and American tanks face each other at the Friedrichstrasse crossing point between East and West Berlin; the U.S. insists on free access for American citizens into East Berlin.

October 30   The Soviet Communist Party Congress orders the removal of Stalin's embalmed body from public view in the Lenin mausoleum in Red Square.

November 6   First Secretary Enver Hoxha of the Albanian Communist party accuses Khrushchev of being personally responsible for the rift between Albania and the Soviet Union.

November 11   The Soviet city of Stalingrad is renamed Volgograd.

December 10   The Soviet government reportedly closes the Albanian embassy in Moscow and recalls Soviet diplomats from Albania.

December 25   In a special television broadcast, President Kennedy assures the people of West Berlin of continued U.S. support.

December 29   The U.S. military bars the Soviet commandant in East Berlin from entering the American sector in retaliation for refusing to allow an American advisor into the Soviet sector without an identification check.

1962

January 17   Twelve Soviet tanks stationed near the Berlin Wall since October 1961 withdraw after a similar withdrawal of American tanks two days earlier.

January 27   The Soviet government changes the names of all places honoring Vyacheslav M. Molotov, Lazar M. Kaganovich, and Georgi M. Malenkov, who attempted to remove Khrushchev on June 6, 1957, and who were all members of Stalin's government.

February 10   In Berlin the Soviet government releases U.S. U-2 pilot Francis Gary Powers in exchange for convicted Soviet agent Rudolf Abel (*see* August 17, 1960).

February 15   Great Britain, France, and the United States protest to the USSR against dangerous Soviet harassment of their flights into West Berlin.

February 23   The Soviet Communist newspaper *Pravda* reports the implementation of Khrushchev's plan of reorganizing the Soviet Union into seventeen major economic units.

April 5   American and Soviet army commanders in Berlin agree on the resumption of normal relations between their military liaison missions.

June 1   The Soviet government announces large increases in domestic food prices to fund agricultural development.

June 9   In Moscow, Soviet bloc nations announce the adoption of measures to speed up the limited integration of their economies.

June 19   The Soviet government lowers the registration age for military service from 19 to 17.

July 2   During a televised speech, Khrushchev warns that the Soviet Union will defend Communist China if it is ever attacked.

August 22   The Soviet government abolishes the office of Soviet commandant of troops in East Berlin.

President Kennedy confirms reports that several thousand Soviet technicians and supplies are being moved into Cuba.

September 7   Given the international situation in relation to Cuba, Kennedy asks the U.S. Congress for authority to call up 150,000 military reservists for active duty.

September 11   The Soviet government warns that any American attack on Cuban or Soviet ships bound for Cuba would result in war.

September 13   Kennedy announces that the U.S. will move against Cuba when and if it is necessary to defend U.S. security.

September 25   Cuban Prime Minister Fidel Castro announces that the Soviet Union will collaborate in building a Cuban port as headquarters of a joint fishing fleet.

October 22   During a televised address, Kennedy announces a naval and air ''quarantine'' on the shipment of military supplies to Cuba. He declares that the Soviet Union, contrary to its assurances, had been building missile and bomber bases in Cuba.

Soviet Premier Nikita Khrushchev.

October 23 The Soviet government challenges the right of the U.S. to blockade Cuba and states that Kennedy is risking nuclear war.

October 25 The U.S. states that the Cuban blockade will continue as long as the missile threat continues.

October 27 Khrushchev offers to remove the missile bases in Cuba if the United States gives assurances it will not invade Cuba; the U.S. agrees.

November 2 Kennedy announces that aerial photographs indicate that Soviet missiles in Cuba are being dismantled. The aerial surveillance will continue until a means of inspection is established.

November 7 Khrushchev announces that the USSR has removed all of its missiles from Cuba, thereby finally ending a very critical global situation known as the Cuban Missile Crisis.

November 9 U.S. naval ships stop a Soviet freighter and photograph material believed to be missiles being shipped back to the USSR.

November 15 The Chinese Communist newspaper *Jenmin Jih Pao* (*The People's Daily*) criticizes Khrushchev's compromise in Cuba.

November 20 Following assurances by Khrushchev that all Soviet jet bombers will be removed from Cuba within 30 days, Kennedy lifts the blockade of Cuba.

1963

January 7 In the first direct Soviet criticism of Communist China, Pravda accuses Beijing of "dogmatic, divisive views."

February 27 Khrushchev states that the USSR will come to the aid of any Communist country under attack.

March 13 The Soviet government announces the formation of the Supreme Council of National Economy to coordinate industrial management and planning.

June 16 Soviet cosmonaut Valentina Tereshkova becomes the first woman to travel in outer space.

June 20 The United States and Soviet Union agree to establish a "hot line," a direct phone line between the White House and the Kremlin (the fortress in Moscow housing the Soviet government) in an effort to improve communications between the two superpowers. It is installed on August 31.

July 2 During a six-day visit to East Berlin, Khrushchev calls for an East-West nonaggression pact and nuclear test-ban treaty.

July 21 Talks in Moscow aimed at ending the Sino-Soviet ideological conflict end in failure.

1964

January 2 Khrushchev sends a personal message to all countries with which the Soviet Union has relations calling for the renunciation of war for settling diplomatic disputes.

February 4 Communist China accuses Khrushchev of seeking world domination through cooperation with the United States.

March 2 The Soviet Communist party announces a renewed campaign to eliminate religion from Soviet life.

March 31 The Chinese Communist party calls on the international Communist movement to reject the leadership of Khrushchev.

April 3 The Soviet Communist party announces that V. M. Molotov, Georgi M. Malenkov, and Lazar M. Kaganovich have been expelled from the Party (*see* June 6, 1957).

April 20 American president Lyndon B. Johnson and Khrushchev issue a joint statement declaring their intention to reduce the production of materials used in nuclear weapons.

June 12 Khrushchev and East German President Walter Ulbricht sign a 20-year treaty of friendship that asserts the legal existence of the Communist party in East Germany. Fourteen days later the United States, Great Britain, and France denounce the Soviet-East German treaty of friendship as an obstacle to bringing peace to a divided Germany.

June 22 The Soviet Union protests the start of direct passenger air service to West Berlin by the United States.

October 14–15 Due to failures in agriculture and foreign affairs, especially the continuing quarrel with China and the 1962 Cuban Missile Crisis, Khrushchev is forced to resign as premier of the Soviet government and as first secretary of the Communist party. On October 14, the Presidium of the Soviet Communist party votes to remove Khrushchev. Leonid I. Brezhnev is appointed first secretary and Aleksei Kosygin, premier.

October 16 Soviet ambassador to the United States Anatolii Dobrynin assures Johnson that good Soviet-American relations will continue despite the change of leadership.

November 6 During a speech, Brezhnev declares that the Soviet government will seek improved relations with the West.

1965

January 30 The Soviet Union and United States sign an agreement providing for expanded cultural exchanges.

February 7 Soviet Premier Kosygin assures a rally in Hanoi that the Soviet Union will continue to supply North Vietnam with all types of aid.

February 9 Two thousand demonstrators attack the U.S. embassy in Moscow in protest of the February 7 U.S. bombing raids on North Vietnam. Soviet police guarding the embassy do not stop the attacks.

March 3 The Soviet government re-centralizes the management of its defense industries by removing them from the control of regional industrial councils.

March 4 Soviet, Asian, African, and Latin American students attack the U.S. embassy in Moscow to protest continued bombing raids on North Vietnam.

April 8 Poland and the Soviet Union sign a new 20-year treaty of friendship, cooperation, and mutual assistance.

May 6 A U.S. presidential commission calls for the relaxation of barriers to American trade in "nonstrategic goods" with Eastern Europe and the Soviet Union.

July 4 Citing increased defense expenditures in the United States, Brezhnev calls for rearmament.

August 28 The Volga Germans, whose ancestors were invited by Empress Catherine the Great to settle in the Volga region in the eighteenth century, are exonerated of treachery during World War II.

September 7 The Soviet government urges India and Pakistan to end their fighting (which started with the Indian invasion of Pakistan on September 6), and offers to mediate a settlement.

October 2 In an effort to revamp Khrushchev's system of regional economic councils, the Supreme Soviet approves a series of domestic economic measures that centralizes the administration of the economy.

October 15 Soviet author Mikhail Sholokov is awarded the Nobel Prize for Literature for 1965.

1966

January 3 Negotiations to settle the conflict between India and Pakistan begin in Tashkent, the capital of Soviet Uzekistan, and are mediated by Soviet Premier Kosygin. Seven days later the Indian prime minister and the Pakistani president sign the Declaration of Tashkent ending the four-month war between the two countries.

January 14 Upon the return of a high ranking delegation from Hanoi, the Soviet Union issues a communique stating that it will increase its aid to North Vietnam's war effort and will support Hanoi's position for peace.

February 3 The Soviet spacecraft Luna 9, launched on January 13, completes the first successful "soft" landing without damage on the moon and begins transmitting signals to earth.

February 14 Two Soviet writers, Andrei D. Siniavskii and Iuli M. Daniel, are sentenced by the Russian Supreme Court to five years of hard labor for publishing anti-Soviet works abroad.

March 5 The Soviet government newspaper *Izvestiia* (News) reports that the Communist party will allow collective farmers to maintain private ownership of farming plots that they develop in their free time.

May 4 The Soviet government and the Fiat Company of Italy reach an agreement on the construction of an automobile factory in the USSR that will produce 2,000 vehicles daily.

May 10–13   Brezhnev visits Bucharest, reportedly in response to Romanian General Secretary Nicolae Ceaușescu's declaration on May 7 that Romania will improve its relations with West European countries.

July 4–6   Leaders of Warsaw Pact countries meet in Bucharest and declare that military volunteers will be sent to North Vietnam if requested by Hanoi. The leaders also call for a general European conference on security in Europe and increased cooperation among nations.

October 1   Soviet bloc diplomats walk off the reviewing stand at the Communist Chinese National Day parade in Beijing after Defense Minister Lin Piao accuses the USSR of plotting with the U.S. over Vietnam.

October 7   The Soviet government orders the expulsion of all Chinese students from the USSR.

December 15   The Soviet government announces that it will increase spending on defense by 8.2 percent in 1967 due to ''aggressive U.S. policies.''

1967

January 27   During ceremonies in Washington, DC, London, and Moscow, representatives from sixty countries sign a treaty banning the orbiting of nuclear weapons. Upon ratification, the treaty will take effect on October 10, 1967.

January 28–29   Chinese soldiers take part in massive anti-Soviet demonstrations outside the Soviet embassy in Beijing.

March 6   While visiting India, Svetlana Alliluieva, the daughter of Joseph Stalin, seeks political asylum in the United States. She arrives in the U.S. on April 21.

May 18   Yuri V. Andropov, the Soviet ambassador in Hungary during the 1956 October uprising, becomes the chairman of the Committee of State Security (KGB), the secret police (*see* February 1992).

June 5   Israeli warplanes and troops attack Arab forces in the Sinai Peninsula and Jerusalem. Five days later, the Soviet Union breaks diplomatic ties with Israel and pledges assistance to the Arab states if Israel refuses to withdraw from conquered territory.

June 14   Israeli sources report that the Soviet Union has resumed sending military aid to Egypt and Syria.

June 18   The Soviet Union reportedly withdraws permission for Soviet Jews to emigrate to Israel.

June 23–25   U.S. President Johnson and Soviet Premier Kosygin meet at Glassboro State College in New Jersey to discuss the Middle East, Vietnam, and arms control. No agreements are reached.

August 24   The United States and the Soviet Union submit identical drafts of a nuclear nonproliferation treaty to the United Nations Disarmament Committee in Geneva.

October 18   The Soviet government announces that an instrument capsule ejected from the Verna 4 space probe landed on Venus.

October 30   The Soviet Union accomplishes the first unmanned docking of two satellites in space.

1968

January 12   After a five-day closed trial, a Soviet court convicts the writers Aleksandr Ginzburg, Yuri Galanskov, and two others of anti-Soviet activities.

February 21   A bomb explodes in the Soviet embassy in Washington, DC; no one claims responsibility.

March 6   The U.S. government protests the imprisonment of dissenting writers and the suppression of free speech in the Soviet Union.

March 7   The USSR, US, and Great Britain commit themselves to take action through the UN Security Council against an actual or threatened nuclear attack on any nation that renounces nuclear weapons.

March 23   A summit meeting of Eastern European leaders, excluding Romania, convenes in Dresden, East Germany; the meeting calls on Alexander Dubček, First Secretary of the Czechoslovak Communist party, to explain liberalizing changes taking place in his country which include a growing freedom of speech, the press, and the arts.

May 9   Joint Soviet-Polish military maneuvers take place in Poland near the Czechoslovak border.

June 20   Warsaw pact maneuvers, dominated by Soviet troops, begin in Czechoslovakia.

July 1   Sixty-two nations, including the Soviet Union, sign the nuclear nonproliferation treaty.

July 14   The USSR halts the withdrawal of Soviet troops from Czechoslovakia, where they participated in Warsaw Pact maneuvers.

July 14–23   The continuing liberalization programs of the ''Prague Spring'' in Czechoslovakia cause increased tension between Moscow and Prague.

July 15 Pan American World Airways and Aeroflot, the Soviet national airlines, open the first direct flights between the United States and the Soviet Union.

July 16 The USSR, Bulgaria, East Germany, Hungary, and Poland issue a joint letter to Czechoslovakia warning that its current course of liberalization is unacceptable.

July 23 The Soviet government announces that large-scale troop maneuvers are underway in the western part of the country near the Czechoslovak border.

July 29–August 1 Leaders of the Soviet and Czechoslovak Communist parties meet in Ĉierna and Tisou, Czechoslovakia, in an effort to resolve their differences.

August 3 The leaders of the USSR, Czechoslovakia, and four other East European countries meet in Bratislava, Czechoslovakia. The Czechoslovak leaders accept the Soviet position that Prague be allowed to continue its liberalization within limits.

The last Soviet troops are removed from Czechoslovakia.

August 10 The Soviet news agency TASS announces the start of new Warsaw Pact maneuvers along the Czechoslovak border.

August 20–21 Czechoslovakia is invaded by 200,000 troops from the Soviet Union, Bulgaria, East Germany, Hungary, and Poland. Several Czech leaders, including Dubček, are arrested. Within a week the number of Warsaw Pact troops in Czechoslovakia increases to 650,000.

August 21 The Soviet Union justifies its invasion by announcing that the Czechoslovak government requested assistance (*see* July 16, 1992).

August 23 The Soviet Union vetoes a United Nations Security Council resolution condemning the invasion of Czechoslovakia.

August 26 Czechoslovak officials, including President Svoboda and First Secretary Dubček, return from Moscow. Moscow indicates that Soviet troops will leave Czechoslovakia when the situation returns to ''normal.''

September 11 Some Soviet tanks and military units begin to withdraw from Czechoslovakia.

September 26 *Pravda* reports on the ideological doctrine used to justify the invasion of Czechoslovakia citing the need to protect socialist countries from outside attack. The article denies that the invasion violates Czechoslovakia's ''real sovereignty,'' and asserts that ''world Socialism is indivisible, and its defense is the common cause of all Communists.'' This doctrine subsequently comes to be known as the ''Brezhnev Doctrine.''

October 11 Five Soviet citizens are sentenced to exile or hard labor for protesting in Red Square against the Soviet invasion of Czechoslovakia.

October 16 In Prague, Soviet Premier Kosygin signs a treaty authorizing the ''temporary'' stay of Soviet troops in Czechoslovakia.

November 16 In response to events in Czechoslovakia and after a three-day meeting, the North Atlantic Treaty Organization (NATO) Council of Ministers issues a warning to the USSR that ''any Soviet intervention. . .in Europe or in the Mediterranean would create an international crisis.''

December 31 The Soviet Union conducts the first test of a commercial supersonic airliner.

1969

January 16 Two Soviet spacecraft dock in orbit and accomplish the first transfer of men from one craft to another.

Leonid Brezhnev.

March 1 Border guards seal the main access road to West Berlin for two hours. Soviet and East German tank convoys are seen along the road.

March 2 The Soviet Union declares that it will not guarantee the safety of air traffic to West Berlin.

Soviet and Chinese forces battle over Damanskii (Chenpao) Island, disputed territory in the Ussuri river. During 1969 there will be over four hundred skirmishes along the Sino-Soviet border resulting in no change of territory.

March 28 After the Czechoslovak hockey team defeats the USSR team in Stockholm in one round of the World Amateur Hockey Championship, anti-Soviet demonstrations erupt in Czechoslovak cities.

May 1 With the exception of East Germany, all Soviet bloc countries observe May Day, the Communist holiday in commemoration of labor and workers, with civilian celebrations rather than military parades.

October 6 Brezhnev states a willingness to cooperate with West Germany during a speech marking East Germany's twentieth anniversary.

October 13 Seven Soviet cosmonauts in three spacecraft simultaneously orbit the earth.

November In Helsinki, the U.S. and USSR begin the first round of Strategic Arms Limitations Talks (SALT).

November 12 It is confirmed that novelist Alexandr I. Solzhenitsyn was expelled from the Soviet Writers Union for writings critical of the Soviet regime.

November 24 In ceremonies in Moscow and Washington, DC, Soviet president Nikolai Podgorny and American president Richard Nixon sign the nuclear nonproliferation treaty.

1970

March 26 Representatives from the U.S., Great Britain, France, and the USSR meet in West Berlin to discuss problems of Berlin. This is the first such meeting in eleven years.

April 16 The U.S. and USSR reopen SALT talks in Vienna.

April 21 The Communist world celebrates the one hundredth anniversary of Lenin's birth.

June 19 The Soviet spacecraft Soyuz 9 returns to earth after a record-setting flight of seventeen days.

July 3 The Central Committee of the Soviet Communist party approves a report condemning the mismanagement of agriculture and calling for increased grain and meat production.

August 12 The Soviet Union and West Germany sign a treaty on the renunciation of force. The treaty includes recognition of the Polish-East German border at the Oder-Neisse line.

August 21 The Warsaw Pact endorses the new Soviet-West German treaty on the renunciation of force.

September 1 The Soviet Central Ministry of Justice, abolished in 1956, is restored.

September 24 Luna 16, an unmanned Soviet spacecraft, returns from the moon with rock samples.

October 8 Soviet novelist Alexandr I. Solzhenitsyn wins the Nobel Prize for Literature.

October 9 The Soviet Writer's Union calls the decision to award the Nobel Prize for Literature to Solzhenitsyn "deplorable."

October 15 The first successful hijacking of a Soviet plane occurs when two Lithuanians commandeer a Soviet airliner and force it to land in Turkey. Although they kill a stewardess, the Lithuanians are allowed to claim political asylum.

October 29 American and Soviet officials sign the first cooperative space effort agreement.

November 23 A Lithuanian seaman is returned to his Soviet fishing ship after seeking political asylum on-board a U.S. Coast Guard cutter off the coast of Martha's Vineyard, Massachusetts. The two U.S. Coast Guard officers who order the return of the seaman are reprimanded and allowed to retire on December 21. The Lithuanian seaman will receive a ten-year prison sentence in May 1971.

1971

March 10 Approximately 100 Jews demanding permission to emigrate to Israel occupy the Supreme Soviet office building in Moscow for several hours.

April 6 During the announcement of the next five-year-plan, Soviet Premier Kosygin calls for closer economic ties with Western Europe and improved Soviet living and cultural standards.

May 20 The USSR and U.S. announce at the SALT meetings that they have agreed to seek a treaty limiting offensive and defensive weapons.

June 30 Soyuz 11 cosmonauts are found dead in their reentry capsule after completing a new space endurance record.

September 11 Former Soviet leader Nikita S. Khrushchev dies in Moscow. His death in announced in a one-sentence announcement in *Pravda* and *Izvestiia*.

September 30 Soviet Foreign Minister Gromyko and U.S. Secretary of State Rogers sign agreements on preventing nuclear accidents and the modernization of the Moscow-Washington "hot line."

October 18 During his visit to Canada, Kosygin is assaulted on the parliament grounds in Ottawa.

1972

January 14 The Soviet government expels U.S. Representative James Scheuer (Democrat, New York) from the USSR for "improper activities": Scheuer met with Soviet Jews.

April 11 The U.S. offers to sell grain to the Soviet Union on three-year credit terms. American and Soviet officials also sign an agreement extending cultural, educational, and scientific exchange programs.

May 22–30 President Nixon arrives in Moscow for the first official visit of a U.S. president to the Soviet Union. Brezhnev and Nixon sign the first Strategic Arms Limitations Treaty (SALT I), limiting anti-ballistic missile systems and offensive missile launchers. During a speech on Soviet television, Nixon expresses his desire for peace between the Soviet Union and United States.

June 3 The Soviet Union, the United States, France, and Great Britain sign the "final protocol" of the Quadripartite Agreement on Berlin, expected to improve travel to and from West Berlin.

July 8 Nixon announces an agreement under which the Soviet Union will purchase at least $750 million worth of U.S. grain over the next three years.

July 18 As a result of the Soviet Union's reluctance to sell arms to Egypt, President Anwar Sadat expels all Soviet military advisors from the country and places all Soviet bases and equipment under Egyptian control.

October 2–3 Nixon and Gromyko meet in Washington, DC to sign documents implementing the SALT I treaty.

1973

April 2 The Soviet government announces a major industrial reorganization plan which calls for the consolidation of plants into large "production associations."

April 19 The Soviets launch the Intercosmos-Copernicus 500, a joint endeavor of Poland, Czechoslovakia, and the USSR, that will measure the sun's radiation and the earth's ionosphere.

June 22 During Brezhnev's visit to the U.S. June 16–25, Nixon and Brezhnev sign an agreement aimed at avoiding confrontations that could lead to nuclear war between the United States and the Soviet Union.

July 3 A Swedish newspaper publishes an article by Soviet physicist Andrei D. Sakharov, the father of the Soviet hydrogen bomb, in which he calls the Soviet one-party system "antidemocratic in its essence."

August 21 Dissident Sakharov warns that the West should beware of détente on Soviet terms. Shortly thereafter, the Soviet press begins a campaign denouncing the views of Sakharov.

September 9 In response to the Soviet press campaign against Sakharov, the U.S. National Academy of Sciences says that American scientists will not continue joint research with the Soviets unless the harassment is stopped.

October 15 The U.S. government announces that it is resupplying Israel with arms to counterbalance the Soviet "massive airlift" to Egypt during the Arab-Israeli Yom Kippur War.

October 20–21 U.S. Secretary of State Henry Kissinger meets with Brezhnev in Moscow to formulate a Middle East cease-fire proposal. The UN Security Council adopts the proposal on October 22.

October 25 A "precautionary alert" of all U.S. forces is ordered when it appears that the Soviet Union might send troops to the Middle East. The crisis ends when the USSR approves a UN Security Council resolution establishing a Middle East peace-keeping force; major powers are barred from the force.

1974

February 13 The Soviet government deports dissident novelist Alexandr Solzhenitsyn and issues a decree stripping him of his Soviet citizenship. It is the first forced deportation of a Soviet political dissident since January 18, 1929, when Joseph Stalin exiled Leon Trotsky.

June 2 Andrei Sakharov begins a hunger strike in support of amnesty for political prisoners held in Soviet jails.

July 2 Three major American TV networks are cut off when the reporters, broadcasting via satellite from Moscow, attempt to discuss the activities of Soviet dissidents.

November 23–24 At a meeting in Vladivostok, U.S. President Gerald Ford and Brezhnev reach a tentative agreement on the limitation of their countries' strategic nuclear weapons and delivery systems through 1985.

1975

July 16 The Soviet Union purchases 73 million bushels of wheat from the U.S.A. Later in the month it buys 177 million bushels of corn and 41 million bushels of barley from the U.S.

July 17–19 The Soviets and Americans conduct joint space maneuvers. An Apollo and Soyuz spacecraft link together on July 17.

August 1 Leaders of 33 European nations, the United States, and Canada sign the Final Act of the Conference on Security and Cooperation in Europe, known as the Helsinki Accords. It represents the formal acceptance of the European territorial changes made during World War II and guarantees respect for human rights, but the agreement does not have treaty status.

October 9 Andrei Sakharov wins the Nobel Peace Prize for his work in fighting for civil liberties and human rights. He becomes the first Soviet citizen to win the prize.

December 10 Yelena Bonner, wife of Sakharov, accepts his Nobel Peace Prize in Oslo, Norway. The Soviet government refuses to grant Sakharov permission to go to Oslo because he is familiar with state and military secrets.

1977

January 25 The Soviet deputy chief prosecutor warns Sakharov to cease "hostile and slanderous activities" after Sakharov accuses the KGB of exploding a bomb in the Moscow Metro to create an excuse for a crackdown on dissidents.

January 27 With U.S. president Jimmy Carter's approval, the U.S. State Department warns the Soviet government that efforts to silence Sakharov would conflict with the accepted standards of human rights.

March 15 After refusing him permission to emigrate, the Soviet government accuses dissident Anatoli Shcharanskii

of working for the CIA, arrests him, and charges him with treason in June. He will receive a three-year prison sentence in July 1978.

March 21 During a speech Brezhnev calls Carter's support of dissidents "unwarranted interference in our internal affairs."

June 4 The Soviet Union releases a draft of its new constitution, its fourth since the Russian Revolution in 1917. Although the new constitution is very similar to the Stalin constitution of 1936, it states for the first time the dominant role of the Communist party in ruling the country. It will be adopted on October 7.

June 16 The Supreme Soviet elects Brezhnev to the post of president (chairman of the Presidium of the Supreme Soviet, nominal head of state) to replace Nikolai Podgorny. Brezhnev becomes the first Soviet leader to hold both the post of party general secretary and president at the same time.

1978

April 10 The highest ranking Soviet official to the United Nations, Arkady N. Shevchenko, renounces his Soviet citizenship. Ten days later Shevchenko applies for political asylum in the United States.

April 20 Two people are killed and thirteen injured when the Soviets down a South Korean Boeing 707 airliner carrying 110 people. The plane violated Soviet air space by passing over the Kola Peninsula, a Soviet military area, and is forced to crash land on or near a frozen lake about 280 miles from Murmansk. Although the Soviet government denies it, passengers report that the Soviet plane fired on the airliner. The passengers are allowed to leave Murmansk on April 23, and the pilot and navigator are turned over to U.S. officials on April 29.

July 13 A Soviet court convicts dissident Alexandr Ginzburg of "anti-Soviet agitation and propaganda" and sentences him to eight years at a labor camp (*see* January 12, 1968).

July 18 In response to the recent convictions of Ginzberg and Anatoly Shcharanskii (*see* March 15, 1977), the United States cancels the sale of sophisticated computers and limits the sale of oil technology to the Soviet Union.

December 5 The Soviet Union and Afghanistan sign a 20-year treaty of friendship and cooperation which calls for military cooperation between the two countries.

1979

April 27 The United States exchanges two convicted Soviet spies, employed at the United Nations and convicted in October 1978 for espionage, for five Soviet dissidents. The five—Aleksandr Ginzburg (*see* July 13, 1978), Valentin Moroz, Georgy Vins, Mark Dymshits, and Eduard Kuznetsov—are exchanged at Kennedy International Airport in New York.

June 16–18 Soviet President Brezhnev and U.S. President Jimmy Carter hold a summit meeting in Vienna. On June 18, they formally sign the SALT II treaty that limits long-range bombers and missiles, but SALT II still needs to be ratified by the U.S. Senate.

September 16 Nur Muhammad Taraki, president of the Revolutionary Council in Afghanistan, is replaced by Hafizullah Amin, who promises closer relations with the Soviet Union due to rebellion in the country.

October 7 NATO confirms its support of the deployment of Pershing II cruise missiles in Europe to address a military imbalance which strongly favors the Soviet Union. The Soviet Union offers to withdraw 20,000 troops from East Germany if there is a missile deployment freeze, but the suggestion is rejected because the Soviets are upgrading current missile systems.

December 14 The Afghan government admits that large numbers of Soviet military experts are helping them, but denies reports that the Soviets are involved in combat against Afghan rebels.

December 27 The Soviet Union invades Afghanistan. Hafizullah Amin, who became president of Afghanistan in September, is ousted and murdered in a Soviet-backed coup. Babrak Karmal, a former deputy prime minister in exile in Czechoslovakia, is brought back and installed as president.

1980

January 3 As a result of the Soviet invasion of Afghanistan, President Carter formally requests the Senate to delay further consideration of the SALT II treaty (*see* June 16–18, 1979).

January 4 Carter announces that the United States will sell the Soviet Union only eight million metric tons of grain. Seventeen million additional tons of grain will not be sold due to the invasion of Afghanistan.

January 7 The USSR vetoes a resolution of the UN Security Council demanding the immediate withdrawal of all Soviet troops in Afghanistan.

January 12 In his first official statement on Afghanistan, Brezhnev states that "aggressive external forces of reaction" forced Soviet intervention.

January 14 The UN General Assembly approves a resolution calling for the immediate withdrawal of all Soviet troops in Afghanistan.

January 20 Carter calls the Soviet invasion of Afghanistan the "most serious threat to peace since the Second World War."

January 22 Andrei Sakharov and his wife Yelena Bonner are exiled to the Soviet city of Gorky due to their public opposition to Soviet policies. The Supreme Soviet also takes away Sakharov's 1975 Nobel Prize and all of his Soviet honors.

February 22 Soviet and Afghan troops are placed under joint Soviet command and martial law is imposed in Kabul.

July 19 The XXII Summer Olympic Games open in Moscow. Many nations, including the United States and West Germany, boycott the Games in protest of the 1979 Soviet invasion of Afghanistan.

August 14 Seventeen thousand workers go on strike at the Lenin Shipyard in Gdansk, Poland due to low wages, food shortages, and other complaints. As a result, on August 27, the Soviet government accuses "antisocialist forces" of attempting to disrupt Poland's socialist government.

October 21 During an address to a plenary session of the Communist party Central Committee Soviet President Brezhnev states that two consecutive poor harvests have created serious food shortages in the Soviet Union.

December 2 After the Soviets hold troop movements near the Polish border, President Carter warns the Soviet government that relations between the two countries would be seriously affected by a Soviet invasion of Poland. Soviets continue to criticize events such as the Polish government's many concessions to the Polish strikers in late August. The Soviets feel these concessions are undermining communism in Poland.

December 5 Members of the Warsaw Pact meet in Moscow to discuss the situation in Poland. Members express confidence that Poland will be able to solve its problems without damaging its socialist system of government.

December 12 The foreign ministers of NATO inform the USSR that an invasion of Poland would end East-West détente.

December 27   Five thousand Afghans attack the Soviet embassy in Tehran on the first anniversary of the Soviet invasion of Afghanistan.

1981

March 19–26   In response to unrest in Poland, Warsaw Pact maneuvers (code name Soiuz 81) in Poland, East Germany, Czechoslovakia, and the Soviet Union are extended to April 7.

April 7   Speaking in Prague at the Czechoslovak Communist party congress, Brezhnev states that the USSR will not solve Poland's problems, thus removing the threat of a Soviet invasion.

April 24   President Reagan lifts the U.S. embargo on the sale of grain to the Soviet Union imposed by President Carter following the Soviet invasion of Afghanistan (*see* January 4, 1980).

September 5–October 7   The Soviet Union condemns the Polish independent trade union Solidarity's National Congress of Poland and denounces it as a "anti-socialist, anti-Soviet orgy."

November 16   During a speech to a Central Committee Plenum, Brezhnev states that the Soviet food supply is the central problem of the country's economic development. He promises to develop a new food program that will include decentralized decision-making in agricultural economy, incentives for local initiatives, and expanded use of private plots.

December 17   Ronald Reagan blames the USSR for the imposition of martial law in Poland on December 13.

December 29   Reagan imposes sanctions against the USSR for the imposition of martial law in Poland, including closing all U.S. ports to Soviet vehicles, delaying the renegotiation of a long-term grain export agreement, and implementing a ban on U.S. gas and oil technology for the Siberian pipeline.

1982

January 11   NATO foreign ministers meeting in Brussels condemn the Soviet Union for its role in "the system of repression in Poland." The ministers also call for European participation with the U.S. in imposing economic sanctions against the Soviet Union.

February 5   Great Britain imposes economic sanctions against the Soviet Union.

November 10   Leonid Brezhnev dies of a heart attack.

November 12   In an emergency session, the Communist party Central Committee elects Yuri V. Andropov, the former KGB head, general secretary of the Communist party.

November 22   Andropov calls for more independence for manufacturing and agricultural enterprises; he also expresses his support for détente with the West and improved relations with China.

1983

June 16   Andropov is elected chairman of the Presidium of the Supreme Soviet, a position equivalent to president.

July 7   Mehmet Ali Agca, the Turk convicted of attempting to assassinate Pope John Paul II in May 1981, states that Soviet and Bulgarian agents assisted him in his assassination attempt.

July 26   In an effort to improve production quality, the Soviet government announces its intention to implement limited economic reforms by allowing some factory managers greater control over wages, bonuses, and technical developments. The reforms are scheduled to begin January 1, 1984.

August 25   The United States and Soviet Union sign a new five-year grain sale agreement in which the Soviets will buy nine million tons of U.S. grain per year, with the option to buy an additional three million tons.

September 1   Soviet fighter planes shoot down South Korean Airlines flight 007 after the plane strays off course and flies near a Soviet military base on Sakhalin Island. All 269 persons aboard the flight are killed. The USSR refuses to admit the fact until September 6.

1984

February 9   Yuri Andropov dies as a result of acute kidney problems.

February 13   Konstantin V. Chernenko becomes general secretary of the Central Committee of the Communist party.

March 2   Chernenko endorses Andropov's economic programs and expresses the Soviet Union's desire to improve relations with China and the West.

March 20   A Soviet oil tanker hits a mine outside of Puerto Sandino, Nicaragua. The leader of the American-backed Nicaraguan Democratic Force, attempting to overthrow the Marxist Nicaraguan regime, claims responsibility for mining the area. As a result the USSR charges the United States with violating the right to freedom of navigation.

April 11 Chernenko is unanimously elected chairman of the Presidium of the Supreme Soviet.

July 5 Vyacheslav M. Molotov, the last of Lenin's associates who had served as prime minister and foreign minister under Stalin, and was removed from power in 1957 by Nikita Khrushchev, is readmitted to the Communist party. He dies in 1986 at the age of 96 (*see* April 3, 1964).

July 17 The U.S. and the Soviet Union sign an agreement to upgrade the hotline between Moscow and Washington, DC.

July 28 The XXIII Summer Olympic Games open in Los Angeles, California. The Soviet Union, East Germany, and Bulgaria refuse to participate because of "inadequate security." In actuality their refusal stems from the U.S. boycott of the 1980 Games in Moscow.

August 18 Friendship '84, the Soviet Union's sport festival for nations who pulled out of the Summer Olympics, begins in Moscow.

Ushering in a new era: Mikhail Gorbachev vows before the Supreme Soviet to assume all responsibility for the success or failure of perestroika.

1985

February 21 The Soviet government signs a nuclear safeguards accord with the International Atomic Energy Agency, which allows for the international inspection of some civilian nuclear power plants.

March 10 Konstantin Chernenko dies in Moscow.

March 11 The Soviet government officially announces the death of Chernenko and the appointment of Mikhail Gorbachev as general secretary of the Communist party. Gorbachev announces that the economic improvement of the country is his primary goal; he also promises to continue the policies of Chernenko and Andropov.

March 24 A Soviet guard shoots and kills an American army major while he is observing a Soviet military installation in East Germany. President Reagan condemns the shooting as an "unwarranted act of violence."

April 7 General Secretary Gorbachev announces the suspension of the deployment of intermediate-range missiles in Europe until November. The Reagan administration responds by stating that the freeze will not affect the scheduled deployment of NATO missiles in Europe.

April 26 Representatives of Bulgaria, Czechoslovakia, Hungary, Poland, Romania, and the Soviet Union sign a 20-year extension of their Warsaw Pact treaty. Mikhail Gorbachev presides over the signing in Warsaw.

July 2 Eduard A. Shevardnadze replaces Andrei Gromyko as Soviet Foreign Minister. The Soviet government honors Gromyko by appointing him president (chairman of the Presidium of the Supreme Soviet) of the Soviet Union.

November 3 Vitaly Yurchenko, a top-ranking KGB official who defected to the United States, announces that he wants to return to the Soviet Union claiming that he was kidnapped by the U.S.; he is allowed to return to the Soviet Union three days later.

November 19–21 Mikhail Gorbachev and Ronald Reagan meet in Geneva, Switzerland for the first summit between American and Soviet leaders since 1979. They achieve no breakthroughs on major issues, but they do sign bilateral agreements that provide for the establishment of consulates in New York and Kiev, resumed civil aviation ties, improved air safety of the northern Pacific, and cultural and scientific exchanges.

December 24 Central Committee Secretary Boris Yeltsin becomes first secretary of the Moscow City Communist party.

1986

January 1 Reagan and Gorbachev each deliver five-minute speeches shown on television in each other's country. Both leaders express their hopes for peace.

February Gorbachev announces that Soviet Union must follow a policy of glasnost (openness). Glasnost entails a public discussion of issues stemming from accessibility of information on controversial matters. Prior to Gorbachev, these issues had been kept secret.

February 11 Anatoly Shcharanskii, a human rights activist, is set free by the Soviet government in West Berlin after spending eight years in Soviet labor camps and prisons (*see* July 18, 1978).

February 15 A letter by dissident physicist Andrei Sakharov to the president of the Soviet Academy of Sciences, dated October 15, 1984, is smuggled out of the Soviet Union and made public in the West. The letter details the mental and physical abuse the KGB agents inflicted on Sakharov during his four-month imprisonment in a Gorky Hospital in 1984.

February 25–March 6 During his keynote address to the twenty-seventh Congress of the Communist Party of the Soviet Union, Gorbachev indirectly criticizes the policies of the Brezhnev era and calls for economic reform. He advocates détente with the West, but rejects a U.S. arms reduction proposal. On the final day of the congress Gorbachev states that all Soviet citizens must be prepared for a "radical transformation of all spheres of life."

April 26 Just after 1:00 A.M. an accident at Chernobyl nuclear power plant, located approximately 130 km north of Kiev, Ukraine, kills twenty people. Thousands more will subsequently die as a result of the radiation leak. Radiation is detected worldwide, but Gorbachev, not following his own policy of glasnost, waits several days to announce the accident.

April 27 The Soviet government evacuates nearly fifty thousand people from a 6.2 mile radius around the Chernobyl nuclear power plant.

May 4 The evacuation zone around Chernobyl is widened to eighteen miles around the plant.

May 10 The European Community temporarily bans all fresh food imports from the Soviet Union and six East European countries due to radioactive fallout from Chernobyl.

May 14 Gorbachev gives a televised address on the Chernobyl nuclear disaster. He states that nine people have died and 299 are hospitalized. He denies that the Soviet government withheld timely information on the accident and accuses the West of using this event to fuel anti-Soviet propaganda.

August 21 The Soviet government releases a report on the Chernobyl nuclear disaster which asserts that the accident is primarily the result of human error. The Soviets estimate that 5,300 people will die as a result of direct radiation exposure over the next 70 years.

December 16 Politburo member Dinmukhamed Kunaev, an ethnic Kazakh, is replaced as party leader of Kazakhstan by the Russian Gennadii Kolbin; riots erupt the next day in Alma-Alta, the capital of Kazakhstan.

December 19 Gorbachev calls Andrei Sakharov to inform him that he and his wife, Yelena Bonner, are free to leave exile in Gorky and return to Moscow.

1987

January 27 Gorbachev addresses a plenary session of the Central Committee of the Communist party and states that changes have to be made to improve Soviet society and end the stagnation of the economy. Gorbachev assures the audience that he is committed to the basic principles of Communism, but he states that conservative sentiment and inertia contributed to the nation's stagnation.

February 14 During his speech to an international peace and disarmament forum held in Moscow, Gorbachev says that the Soviet Union desires international stability so that it can pursue domestic reforms.

April 6 It is announced that the new U.S. embassy in Moscow is "fully compromised" by Soviet electronic listening devices.

April 10 During a speech in Prague, Gorbachev states that the USSR does not expect Czechoslovakia and other East European countries to follow Soviet-styled reforms such as glasnost and perestroika, Gorbachev's attempts to revitalize the economy, Communist party, and society of the USSR.

May 23 The Soviet government stops jamming Voice of America radio broadcasts for the first time since 1980.

May 25–27 Due to his reforms, Gorbachev receives a cool reception during his visit to Romania.

May 30 The government relieves the commander of the Soviet Air Defense Command of his position after the

A specialist measures the level of radiation in the reactor hall after the accident at Chernobyl nuclear power plant in the Ukraine.

military allowed Mathias Rust, a West German pilot, to land a small aircraft on Moscow's Red Square—without being challenged—on May 29.

Marshal Sergei Sokolov, who does not support Gorbachev's reforms, resigns as minister of defense.

June 12 Elections for local soviets (local bodies of government) are held. Some races have more than one candidate, but all candidates are approved by the Communist party.

June 25 Gorbachev addresses the Communist party Central Committee on ''The Party's Tasks in Fundamentally Restructuring Management of the Economy.'' He states that products need to be sold at their true market value while wages and bonuses have to be earned by the workers.

October 21 During a meeting of the Central Committee of the Communist party, Boris Yeltsin, Moscow party chief, openly criticizes Gorbachev and other top officials for introducing changes too slowly.

November 11 The party dismisses Boris Yeltsin from his post as head of the Moscow Communist party organization.

December 8 In Washington, DC, Gorbachev and Reagan sign the INF (Intermediate Nuclear Forces) treaty abolishing intermediate-range nuclear missiles. The treaty allows for on-sight inspection of missile bases and for verification of the systematic destruction of specific missiles.

1988

February 8 Gorbachev announces on national television that if a settlement can be reached at the UN-sponsored peace talks, the Soviet Union will begin withdrawing troops from Afghanistan by May 15.

February 18 The Central Committee of the Communist party removes Yeltsin from the Politburo.

February 23 Armenians in the Nagorno-Karabakh Autonomous Oblast, an administrative division of the Azerbaijan Soviet Socialist Republic demand that the borders be redrawn so that they can be incorporated in the Armenian Soviet Socialist Republic. The Soviet government resists because it does not want to allow individual ethnic groups to dictate Soviet policy.

February 28 Riots stemming from Armenian ethnic protests in the Azerbaijan city of Sumgait result in Soviet troops enforcing a dusk-to-dawn curfew.

March 2 A Soviet official confirms that only seventeen people were killed in Sumgait. Several Soviet journalists maintain that the riots were pogroms against the Armenian minority in Sumgait that left hundreds dead. Observers believe that this is the most serious outbreak of nationalist unrest in the history of the Soviet Union.

April 8 The Soviet government agrees to withdraw all 115,000 Soviet troops from Afghanistan within nine months. The Soviets and Americans agree that the future of Afghanistan will be decided by the Afghans.

April 29 Gorbachev meets with Russian Orthodox Church leaders and grants them greater religious autonomy.

May 7–9 More than 100 people meet in Moscow to draft the charter of the Democratic Union, an independent political party. Five members of the group including the editor of the journal *Glasnost* are arrested on May 9 and ordered to leave Moscow.

May 15 Soviet troops begin to leave Afghanistan. During the eight-and-a-half-year war over 13,300 Soviet soldiers were killed, while over one million Afghans lost their lives (*see* February 15, 1989).

May 21 Tass reports that the two Communist party leaders of Armenia and Azerbaijan have been replaced in an attempt to calm the region.

May 23 The Central Committee of the Communist party calls for changes in the country's political system. The restructuring of the Soviet system would allow broad sections of the population to run for all state and public offices. The party would continue to formulate national policy but its involvement in the management of government offices and the daily lives of Soviet citizens would be greatly reduced.

May 27 The Supreme Soviet passes a law legalizing private cooperatives.

June 5 The Russian Orthodox Church begins a year-long celebration to commemorate its 1,000th anniversary which receives the official support of the Soviet government.

June 6 In an article published in *Novy Mir* (New World), historian Vasilii Seliunin criticizes Lenin for initiating the systematic use of terror to intimidate enemies of the Bolshevik party and to eliminate potential opponents. This is one of the first published attacks on Lenin, long believed to be beyond reproach in Soviet political and journalistic circles.

June 15 The Armenian Supreme Soviet, or government of Armenia, officially requests that Nagorno-Karabakh, the Armenian ethnic area within the borders of Azerbaijan, be reunited with Armenia.

June 28 Gorbachev addresses a special conference of the Communist party, the Nineteenth Party Conference, June 28–July 1, the first all union party conference since 1941. He states that basic restructuring of the Soviet political system is the only way to solve the country's economic problems. He proposes a new type of president who would be elected by a broad based congress. Gorbachev also proposes the creation of a more democratic national legislature—the Congress of People's Deputies. The 2,250-seat body would consist of 1,500 elected deputies and 750 appointed deputies. The congress would meet semi-annually and select a standing Supreme Soviet of 450 members. He rejects the idea of alternative political parties and redrawing republic borders to satisfy the demands of Armenians living in Azerbaijan.

July 1 Delegates to the party congress approve most of the changes proposed by Gorbachev at the Communist party conference.

July 23 Tens of thousands of protesters march in Tallinn, Riga, and Vilnius in officially sanctioned demonstrations to protest the annexation of Estonia, Latvia, and Lithuania by the Soviet Union in June 1940.

August 17 The U.S. and USSR conduct a joint nuclear test in Nevada.

September 21 As a result of continued ethnic unrest in Nagorno-Karabakh, the government declares a state of emergency. A curfew is imposed in Stepanakert, the capital of Nagorno-Karabakh, and troops are deployed on the streets of Yerevan, the capital of Armenia.

October 1 Gorbachev is unanimously elected chairman of the Presidium of the Supreme Soviet.

October 12 Gorbachev states that all agriculture should move in the direction of privately leased farms. However, he does not call for the end of state farms and collectives.

November 15 The USSR successfully launches the space shuttle Buran.

November 16 The Supreme Soviet of Estonia approves a constitutional amendment that allows Estonia to ignore any Soviet law it deems to be an infringement of its local authority. Ten days later the Presidium of the Soviet Union declares the Estonian constitutional amendment of November 16 unconstitutional. On December 7, the Supreme Soviet of Estonia votes 150 to 91 to reconfirm the constitutional amendment granting greater autonomy to Estonia.

November 22 Anti-Armenian riots in Baku leave eight dead.

December 7 During an address to the General Assembly of the United Nations in New York City, Gorbachev announces unilateral cuts in the Soviet military. He pledges to reduce the military by 500,000 men and 10,000 tanks over the next two years and to remove half of the tanks deployed in Eastern Europe; he also vows to withdraw many of the troops stationed on the Chinese border.

An earthquake measuring 6.9 on the Richter scale destroys several cities in Armenia SSR. Gorbachev cuts short his trip to the United States to visit the sight of the quake. The final, official death toll is 25,000.

1989

January 12 The Presidium of the Supreme Soviet of the USSR places the region of Nagorno-Karabakh under direct rule in an attempt to end the ethnic violence between Armenians and Azerbaijanes.

January 18 The Estonian legislature approves a law making Estonian the official language of the Republic. During the following week, Lithuania passes a similar but more restrictive law.

February 15 The last Soviet troops leave Afghanistan (*see* April 8 and May 15, 1988).

March 12 An estimated 200,000 Latvians stage an anti-Russian (Soviet) demonstration in Riga. The group protests in support of the People's Front, an organization seeking to establish Latvian as the dominant language of the republic. Although some protesters call for secession from the Soviet Union, the People's Front is committed to working with the Communist party to achieve its goals.

March 14 Ethnic Russians in Estonia protest, claiming that they are victims of discrimination.

March 16 The Central Committee of the Communist party endorses Gorbachev's plan to improve Soviet agriculture. Among other things, the plan sanctions the leasing of land from collective farms and abolishes the government's central agricultural agency.

March 26 The Congress of Peoples Deputies holds the first multi-candidate elections since 1917. Several Communist candidates are defeated including the first and

second most powerful Communist officials in Moscow, the party leader in Leningrad who ran unopposed, the two top officials in Kiev, both the president and premier in Lithuania, and the commander of the KGB in Estonia, to name a few. The former Communist Party head Boris Yeltsin wins by a landslide.

April 7 The Soviet government deploys troops and armored personnel carriers along the streets of Tbilisi, Georgia, in an attempt to end the peaceful demonstrations. Participants in the demonstrations demand greater political and economic independence from the central government.

April 9 Approximately 30 people are killed and 200 injured when Soviet troops end a demonstration in Tbilisi, Georgia.

April 14 The party leadership in Georgia resigns after accepting the blame for the killings in Tbilisi.

April 19 *Izvestiia,* the Soviet government newspaper, reports that an official investigation of the demonstrations and deaths in Tbilisi show that many of the victims were poisoned by chemical agents.

April 25 The USSR begins its military reduction in Eastern Europe by removing 31 heavy tanks from Hungary.

In an effort to hasten reforms, the Soviet Union's Communist party votes to remove 74 of the 301 members of the party's Central Committee. Thirty-six other high officials are also voted out of office. Generally, younger men are appointed to replace them. The overall size of the Central Committee is reduced to 251 members. Members removed are considered impediments to reform.

May 15–18 President Gorbachev becomes the first Soviet leader to visit China since 1959.

May 16 China and the Soviet Union announce the normalization of relations between the two countries.

May 18 The Lithuanian Supreme Soviet adopts the Declaration of State Sovereignty decreeing that in 1940 Lithuania was forcibly and illegally annexed by the Soviet Union.

May 25 The newly constituted 2,250 member Congress of People's Deputies elects Gorbachev president of the Soviet Union.

May 29 The Congress of People's Deputies allows Boris Yeltsin to accept a seat on the Supreme Soviet. Although Yeltsin was not elected to the body, a victorious candidate offered him his seat.

June 3 An estimated 400 persons are killed when a gas pipeline explodes near two passenger trains in the Ural Mountains.

June 3–15 Approximately ninety people die during ethnic riots in Uzbekistan; Soviet troops are sent to the region on June 4.

July 1 During a nationally televised speech Gorbachev warns that ethnic violence and nationalism threatens the success of his reform programs.

July 6 During a speech to the Council of Europe in Strasbourg, France, Gorbachev announces that the Soviet Union will not interfere with reforms in Poland or Hungary.

July 7 Leaders of Warsaw Pact nations meet in Bucharest where Gorbachev calls for the independent solution of national problems.

July 10 Coal miners in the Siberian city of Mezhdurechensk demanding better living conditions go on strike. Over the next few weeks the strike spreads to other areas and over 100,000 miners join the strike. Nine days later Siberian coal miners agree to return to work after the government promises higher wages, more worker control over the mines, and improved living and working conditions.

July 23 In a televised address Gorbachev tells the striking miners in Ukraine that he is inspired by their determination to bring about changes necessary for the success of perestroika. As a result of Gorbachev's address, many miners return to work.

July 24 20,000 people demonstrating in Tbilisi, Georgia, shout "Down with the Russian Empire!"

July 30 About 300 members of the Congress of People's Deputies form an opposition bloc called the Inter-Regional Group. The group wants to end central economic control and the communist monopoly on power.

August 22 A commission of the Lithuanian Supreme Soviet declares that the 1940 occupation and annexation of Estonia, Latvia, and Lithuania by the Soviet Union is invalid.

August 23 Two million people form a human chain across Estonia, Latvia, and Lithuania to commemorate the 50th anniversary of the Soviet occupation of the countries.

September 12 The ultra-conservative, pro-Russian nationalist group Pamyat holds a rally in Moscow condemning Gorbachev's reforms.

October 6 Gorbachev meets with East German leader Erich Honecker and urges him to adopt a program of reform.

October 26 Gorbachev abandons the "Brezhnev Doctrine"—the ideological justification for Soviet troops to invade other East European countries in an effort to maintain Communist rule—and states that the Soviet Union has no moral or political right to interfere with the events taking place in Eastern Europe.

October 31 Egon Krenz, leader of the East German Communist party and head of state, visits Moscow. Upon his return to East Germany, Krenz declares his support for the policy of perestroika.

November 9 The Berlin Wall, a symbol of the Cold War and Communist repression, is taken down, resulting in free travel between East and West Germany.

November 12 The Estonian Supreme Soviet passes a resolution annulling the decree of July 22, 1940 which proclaimed Estonia's "voluntary" entry into the Soviet Union. Several Communist party members walk out in protest of the resolution.

November 27 All members of the Soviet Politburo sign a statement vigorously condemning Lithuania's move toward greater freedom. Lithuanian Communist party efforts to organize a local Communist party independent of Moscow are called "illegal and undemocratic" because Lithuania is considered a constituent part of the Union of Soviet Socialist Republics. However, the Politburo is disposed to grant Lithuania, Latvia, and Estonia freedom to experiment with market economies.

December 1 Gorbachev visits Pope John Paul II in the Vatican. Gorbachev states that the Soviet Union would soon enact a law guaranteeing freedom of conscience so people could "satisfy their spiritual needs." They also discuss the possibility of establishing diplomatic relations between the two states.

Ukrainian officials announce that the Ukrainian Catholic Church could begin to register with authorities thereby gaining legal recognition after years of repression.

December 2–3 Gorbachev and U.S. President George Bush meet in Malta to discuss the events in Eastern Europe and arms limitations treaties.

December 4 Members of the Warsaw Pact, excluding Romania which did not take part, condemn their 1968 invasion of Czechoslovakia.

December 7 The Lithuanian Supreme Soviet passes a resolution abolishing the leading role of the Communist party in society.

December 14 Soviet dissident Andrei Sakharov, now a member of the Congress of People's Deputies, suffers a heart attack and dies in Moscow (*see* December 19, 1986).

December 20 The Lithuanian Communist party declares itself independent of the Communist party of the Soviet Union.

December 24 The Congress of People's Deputies declares the Nazi-Soviet nonaggression pact of 1939 invalid because the Soviet Union illegally conspired to occupy independent nations (*see* August 23, 1939).

1990

January 2 Soviet troops are sent to Azerbaijan to protect Armenians.

January 7 The Soviet government announces that troops have been sent to Georgia to prevent fighting between Georgians and Ossetians.

January 11–13 President Gorbachev visits Lithuania in an attempt to persuade Communist party officials to rescind their break with the Soviet Union.

January 13–14 Azerbaijanis in Baku attack Armenians resulting in the deaths of about thirty people.

January 15 The Supreme Soviet declares a state of emergency in Azerbaijan.

January 16 Gorbachev sends eleven thousand troops to Azerbaijan; the Kremlin announces it is taking this action to prevent civil war.

January 20 Gorbachev orders Soviet troops into Baku. Officially, 83 people are killed in the violence but Azerbaijani sources claim that up to 300 people are killed. Gorbachev states that the attack was necessary to prevent a coup.

January 22 The Azerbaijan Supreme Soviet unanimously endorses a resolution calling for the immediate withdrawal of all Soviet troops.

January 27 Azerbaijan officials offer to work with the Soviet government in an effort to solve the republic's ethnic problems; however, they will do this only after Soviet troops have been removed from the region.

February 2 Representatives of Armenia and Azerbaijan meet in Riga, Latvia, for peace talks. The representatives agree that they will not discuss the issue of control over Nagorno-Karabakh. The representatives nevertheless condemn the Soviet use of force.

February 4 More than 100,000 people participate in a pro-democracy rally in Moscow. It is the largest unofficial demonstration since the Bolshevik revolution of 1917.

February 5 Gorbachev tells members of the Communist party's Central Committee that there is an urgent need to restructure both the party and the government, and calls for the end of the party's monopoly of political power and legalization of other political parties.

February 7 After three days of debate, the Central Committee of the Communist party approves a platform that ends its monopoly of power encoded in Article 6 of the Soviet constitution.

February 12 Soviet Interior Ministry troops enter the city of Dushanbe, Tajikistan, in an effort to quell three days of anti-Armenian rioting taking place; 37 people are killed.

February 13 The Communist party adopts a new platform that limits the role of doctrine, commits the party to a market economy, supports the right of secession and self-determination, and allows for a multi-party system.

February 24 The Communist party wins only seven of ninety seats in the Lithuanian Supreme Soviet. The Sajudis nationalist movement wins a majority of the seats.

February 28 The Congress of People's Deputies passes a law allowing peasants to choose to be in *kolkhozes,* government-run farm collectives, or to receive their own allotment of land.

March 4 Reformers and nationalists dominate elections to republic legislatures in Russia, Belorussia, and Ukraine.

March 6 The Congress of People's Deputies passes another law on property allowing people to own assets and shares in enterprises.

March 11 Lithuania declares independence from the Soviet Union. The Lithuanian Supreme Soviet elects Vytautas Landsberg is president of the country.

March 13 Gorbachev calls the Lithuanian actions illegal and refuses to negotiate with the breakaway republic.

March 13–15 The Congress of People's Deputies votes to strengthen the presidency of the Soviet Union which will have power to veto legislation, declare war if the country is attacked, declare martial law, command the armed forces and the KGB, negotiate all international treaties, and dissolve the legislature. The congress elects Gorbachev who runs unopposed for the office; public elections for the office are scheduled for 1995. The congress also repeals Article 6 of the Soviet constitution which guaranteed the Communist party's monopoly of power.

March 18 In a show of strength against the breakaway republic, Soviet military forces begin maneuvers in Lithuania. Thirteen days later Gorbachev warns Lithuanian leaders to renounce their declaration of independence or suffer the consequences.

March 30 Estonia proclaims that it will work to leave the Soviet Union.

Hundreds of thousands of people march over the Moscow River demanding that the Communist party relinquish its stranglehold on power, February 1990.

April 3   The Soviet government takes responsibility for and expresses regret over the 1940 massacre of Polish prisoners-of-war in the Katyn Forest (*see* April 18, 26 1943).

April 18   The Soviet government cuts off the supply of oil and natural gas to Lithuania.

May 1   After the annual May Day parade in Moscow, thousands of demonstrators march in protest of Marxist-Leninist ideology and shout slogans denouncing Gorbachev and the Communist party.

May 4   Latvia begins to work for independence from the Soviet Union. In an effort to avoid an economic blockade, they declare that the Soviet constitution and laws will remain valid until independence is achieved.

May 9   The Estonian Soviet Socialist Republic changes its name to the Republic of Estonia and reinstates its prewar constitution.

May 16   As a result of Soviet pressure, the Lithuanian parliament suspends all laws implementing its declaration of independence. However, they do not withdraw the declaration itself.

May 29   Boris Yeltsin wins the election for president of the Russian Supreme Soviet of the Russian Soviet Federated Socialist Republic.

June 8   The Russian Supreme Soviet declares that its laws take precedence over Soviet laws.

June 10   Soviet troops are used in an effort to stop the violence between Turkic-speaking ethnic groups of Kirgiz and Uzbeks in Central Asia.

June 12   The Supreme Soviet passes a law that forbids censorship by the government and guarantees the freedom of the press.

June 19–23   The newly formed Russian Communist party holds its first congress. During the sessions, delegates, who are predominately conservatives, criticize Gorbachev's reforms.

June 29   The Lithuanian parliament agrees to suspend its declaration of independence for one hundred days if Moscow will negotiate and lift its economic blockade. The next day the Soviet government reopens the Lithuanian oil pipeline.

July 5–6 During a meeting in London, the leaders of NATO declare that the Cold War is over.

July 10 Gorbachev is reelected general secretary of the Communist party.

July 12 During the Congress of the Communist Party of the Soviet Union, Boris Yeltsin announces his resignation from the party.

July 13 The mayors of Leningrad and Moscow resign from the Communist party.

July 15–16 Gorbachev meets with German Chancellor Helmut Kohl to discuss German reunification. During these meetings Gorbachev accepts united Germany's membership in NATO. In exchange, Kohl promises to negotiate a treaty with the Soviet Union that covers political, economic, military, scientific, and cultural relations.

July 16 The Ukrainian parliament passes a motion of sovereignty, but stops short of declaring full independence.

September 24 The Supreme Soviet grants Gorbachev emergency powers so he can deal more effectively with the country's economic problems. The new powers allow him to implement by decree policies governing wages, prices, finances, and budgets. He is also empowered to strengthen law and order.

December 20 During a speech to members of the Congress of People's Deputies, Soviet Foreign Minister Eduard Shevardnadze resigns from his post. He states that reformers have gone into hiding and that "a dictatorship is approaching."

1991

January 2 Soviet troops seize buildings in Vilnius, Lithuania.

January 13 The Soviet army kills fifteen pro-independence protesters and over 200 people are wounded in Vilnius, Lithuania.

Yeltsin, president of the Russian Federation, and representatives of Estonia, Latvia, and Lithuania sign a mutual-security agreement.

February 18 In an unsuccessful effort to reach a settlement to avoid a ground war in Kuwait and Iraq, Mikhail Gorbachev meets with Iraqi Foreign Minister Tariq Aziz in Moscow.

February 19 During a nationally televised speech, Yeltsin urges Gorbachev to quit. He accuses Gorbachev of creating a dictatorship in the name of presidential rule, and criticizes Gorbachev's use of the army in inter-ethnic

relations and for his use of force in Lithuania. Yeltsin also blames Gorbachev for the failing Soviet economy.

February 25 The foreign and defense ministers of the USSR, Bulgaria, Czechoslovakia, Hungary, Poland, and Romania meet in Budapest to sign an agreement to disband the Warsaw Pact by March 31, 1991.

March 3 In non-binding votes, a majority of the voters in Estonia and Latvia vote for secession from the Soviet Union.

March 17 In a general referendum, 76 percent of Soviet citizens vote to maintain the union.

April 2 State controls over the economy are relaxed resulting in increased retail and food prices. Bread, milk, and other staple goods double and triple in price while other items, such as television sets, inflate in price by 1,000 percent.

April 23 Gorbachev and leaders of nine of the fifteen republics of the USSR sign an agreement to cooperate in trying to solve the nation's economic and political difficulties. Under the agreement, political power would be shared.

May 20 The Supreme Soviet eases restrictions on travel and emigration by Soviet citizens.

June The last Soviet troops withdraw from Hungary.

June 12 Yeltsin wins the first direct election of a Russian president with almost 60 percent of the vote.

June 20 During a meeting in Berlin, U.S. Foreign Secretary James Baker III warns Soviet Foreign Minister Alexander Bessmertnykh of a pending hard-line (staunch communist) coup against Gorbachev. During a telephone conversation with President Bush, Gorbachev ignores the warning.

June 25 Soviet and Czechoslovak representatives sign an agreement formally ending 23 years of Soviet military occupation of Czechoslovakia. Four days later the last Soviet troops leave the country.

July 17 The Group of Seven—leaders of the major industrial democracies—meet with Gorbachev in London. G7 leaders offer the USSR a plan of technical assistance but are unwilling to offer massive Western investment because they are not informed of how the Soviet Union plans to move to a market economy.

July 24 Gorbachev announces that he and the leaders of ten of the fifteen Soviet Republics reached an agreement on the basic provisions of a new union treaty that redefines the relationship between the central government and the republics. The treaty is scheduled to be signed on August 20, 1991.

Soviet citizens queue up to buy milk at a state-owned food shop as drastic price increases take effect.

July 30–31   Gorbachev and Bush meet in Moscow to sign the Strategic Arms Reduction Treaty (START).

August 19   The Soviet news agency Tass announces that Gorbachev, who is at his summer home in the Crimea is ill. The Soviet Vice-President Gennadi I. Yanayev and seven other members of a State Committee for the State of Emergency in the USSR take over the government. A state of emergency is declared, all civil rights are suspended, curfews are established, and a ban on opposition political parties is declared. Military units position themselves in Moscow. At the Russian parliament building, Boris Yeltsin addresses a crowd of over 150,000 people and declares the coup unconstitutional and the coup leaders traitors.

August 20   Yeltsin calls for a general strike. In response, tens of thousands of people around the USSR defy the rule of the new government and armed forces. Foreign ministers of the European Community condemn the coup and freeze all but humanitarian aid.

Estonia proclaims its independence from the Soviet Union.

August 21   The coup collapses. Gorbachev is released from house arrest, and the Presidium of the Supreme Soviet

voids all decrees of the emergency committee. Gorbachev talks to President Bush and assures him that "constitutional authorities have regained power in the USSR."

Latvia adopts a new constitutional law declaring its independence from the Soviet Union.

August 22   Gorbachev returns to Moscow and declares that he is again in full control of the country. Thousands of Muscovites, celebrating the coup's failure, cover KGB headquarters in graffiti and topple the statue of Feliks Dzerzhinsky, the KGB founder. One member of the emergency committee, Boris K. Pugo, the interior minister, commits suicide. The arrest of the other coup members, who will be charged with high treason, begins. Yeltsin declares in a speech, "The people have made their decision and they clearly have no intention of going back again."

August 23   Yeltsin begins to exercise his new-found power by suspending the publication of the Communist party newspaper *Pravda* and five other pro-Communist newspapers; he also rejects Gorbachev's appointments of the interim heads of the military and KGB. Gorbachev then names Air Force General Yevgeny I. Shaposhnikov, who

Russian president Boris Yeltsin.

did not support the coup, and Vadim V. Bakatin, a reformer, as defense minister and KGB chief, respectively. Gorbachev dismisses Foreign Minister Aleksandr A. Bessmertnykh, who claimed to be ill during the attempted coup.

August 24   Gorbachev resigns as general secretary of the Communist party. All party property is placed under the management of the Soviet parliament. Political activity by the party in public institutions is banned or curbed.

Ukraine declares independence.

August 25   The Communist party of Belorussia declares the republic's independence.

August 26   Gorbachev appeals to the republics to remain in the union.

August 27   In Moldavia, the parliament of the Grand National Assembly declares the independence of the republic. Georgia, Armenia, and the Central Asian republics soon follow.

August 29   The Supreme Soviet votes to reduce all activities of the Communist party.

August 30   The KGB chief announces plans to depoliticize and reorganize the KGB.

September 6   The USSR's State Council, the new Soviet provisional executive body, recognizes the independence of the three Baltic republics.

October 18   Gorbachev and the presidents of eight of the twelve remaining Soviet republics (the Baltic States no longer are part of the USSR) sign an economic union treaty which endorses the principles of private property, a free-market economy, free trade between the republics, and a unified banking system. The republics of Ukraine, Georgia, Moldova (formerly Moldavia), and Azerbaijan do not sign the treaty.

November 6   Yeltsin bans the Communist party in Russia.

November 19   Gorbachev reappoints Eduard Shevardnadze as foreign minister.

December 8   Yeltsin and the leaders of Ukraine and Belarus (formerly Belorussia) sign an agreement establishing the Commonwealth of Independent States to replace the Union of Soviet Socialist Republics. They agree that any of the former Soviet republics may join the CIS; that any member is free to leave with one year's notice; that the CIS will observe all treaties signed by the Soviet Union; that members will work to create a free-market economy; and that the old Soviet ruble will serve as the CIS's currency. Two days later leaders of eleven of the former Soviet republics meet in Alma-Ata, Kazakhstan, to sign an agreement creating the Commonwealth of Independent states. Georgia, Estonia, Latvia, and Lithuania do not join.

December 19   Yeltsin orders the Russian government to assume all powers of the central government except for the departments of defense and nuclear energy.

December 25   Gorbachev resigns as president of the USSR and the Soviet Union formally ceases to exist. The independence of 12 former Soviet republics—Armenia, Azerbaijan, Belarus, Georgia, Kazakhstan, Kyrgyzstan, Moldova, Russia, Tajikistan, Turkmenistan, Ukraine, and Uzbekistan—is announced by U.S. president Bush. Dates of declared sovereignty vary.

December 30   Members of the Commonwealth of Independent States agree that each republic may maintain its own army; strategic weapons, however, will be placed under a single command with policy jointly decided by the four republics with nuclear weapons on their territory (Russia, Ukraine, Belarus, and Kazakhstan). The members of the CIS also agree to honor the Soviet arms control treaties.

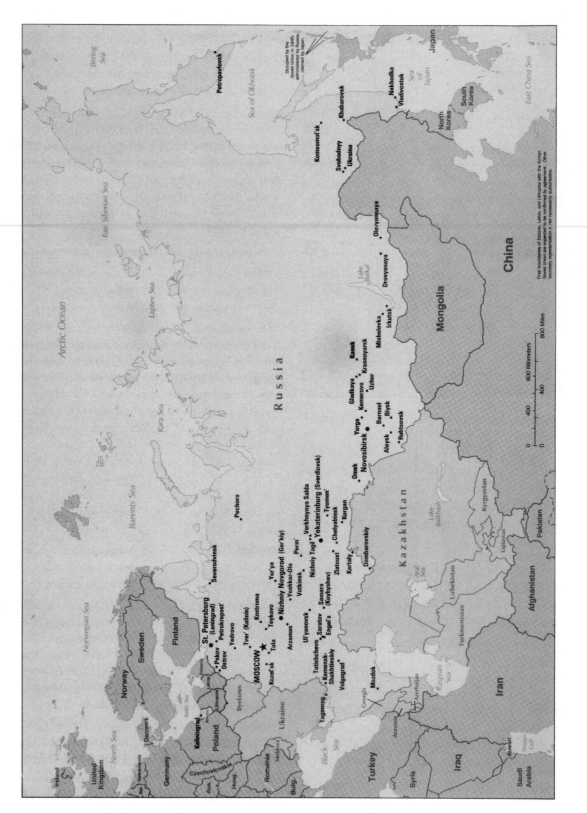

The former Soviet Union after the independence of the 12 republics on December 25, 1991.

1992

January 1 After a week of fighting, Georgian rebel forces opposed to the rule of the Georgian president meet to form an interim government. However, President Zviad K. Gamsakhurdia remains in power.

January 2 Yeltsin lifts most state price controls in an effort to encourage production and begin the transition towards a market economy.

President Ayaz Mutalibov of Azerbaijan imposes direct rule over most of Nagorno-Karabakh where ethnic conflict between Azeris and Armenians rages; the withdrawal of Russian troops in December intensified the conflict.

January 3 In Tbilisi, the capital of Georgia, opposition gunmen fire on people demonstrating in support of President Zviad K. Gamsakhurdia. Two people are killed and 25 are wounded.

January 4 The Ukrainian government orders the entire Black Sea Fleet and all ground forces in Ukraine to take an oath of loyalty to Ukraine. This order brings criticism from the Russian government.

January 5 Leaders of the Baltic states demand the immediate withdrawal of all former Soviet troops.

January 6 Georgian President Gamsakhurdia flees to Armenia as opposition forces storm the parliament building in Tbilisi.

January 8 The Central Military Command in Moscow reports that its primary communication link with 300,000 troops in Ukraine has been taken over by Ukrainian military officials attempting to nationalize the troops.

January 9 Despite early statements to the contrary, Yeltsin states that the Black Sea Fleet historically belongs to Russia, not Ukraine.

In Kiev, military officers meet with Ukrainian President Leonid M. Kravchuk to express their concerns over the proposed loyalty oath, control of nuclear weapons, and other issues of concern.

Russia cuts gas deliveries to Poland in half for economic reasons.

January 10 In an attempt to protect the limited goods available, Russia introduces a border embargo on basic consumer goods to prevent neighboring countries from taking products such as meat, butter, and vodka—as well as samovars and televisions—out of the country.

January 11 Officials from Russia and Ukraine meet in an effort to settle the dispute over the Black Sea Fleet. Both sides agree to abide by existing agreements calling for the joint control of the fleet by the Commonwealth of Independent States.

January 12 On Manezh Square, Moscow, approximately 10,000 pro-Communist supporters protest rising food prices and demand that the Russian government resign.

Officials negotiating the fate of the Black Sea Fleet announce that part of the fleet will be turned over to Ukraine.

January 14 Prosecutors officially charge twelve former high Soviet officials with conspiracy to seize power during last year's failed coup. Originally they were charged with treason, which carries the death penalty (*see* August 22, 1991).

January 16 Ousted Georgian President Gamsakhurdia returns to western Georgia in an effort to rally supporters. Two days later the Georgian Military Council states that it controls most of the western area where the ousted president is attempting to regain control.

January 16–17 Uzbek President Islam A. Karimov lifts price controls causing students to riot.

January 17 Five thousand officers of the former Soviet military gather in the Kremlin to demand that the armed forces remain intact. In a speech to the officers Russian President Yeltsin promises that 60 percent of the new military budget will be allocated to housing and other social services.

January 19 Over the objections of the Russian Central Bank and the Bush administration, Yeltsin's financial advisors push to create a convertible currency as soon as possible. Beginning today people are allowed to exchange rubles for "hard" or western currency.

In St. Petersburg (formerly Leningrad), Russia, an estimated 3,000 people, many members of the Russian Communist Workers party, protest the lifting of price controls by Yeltsin.

January 21 Russian prosecutors announce that they can find no evidence linking former Soviet President Gorbachev to last year's attempted coup (*see* August 22, 1991).

The Institute of Marxism-Leninism, renamed the Russian Center for the Study of the Documents of Modern History, opens its archives to scholars.

January 22–23 A 47-nation conference on aid to the former Soviet Union meets in Washington, DC and agrees to accelerate humanitarian assistance to the region. The U.S. announces it will fly 54 shipments of food and medical supplies to the region starting February 10.

January 25 Moldovan President Mircea Snegur meets with Romanian President Ion Iliescu to promote closer economic and cultural ties between the two nations.

January 27 At least sixty people are reported to have been killed in Nagorno-Karabakh on January 25 and 26. Fighting will continue into 1993.

January 30 Armenia, Azerbaijan, Belarus, Kazakhstan, Kirgizstan, Moldova, Uzbekistan, Tajikistan, Turkmenistan, and Ukraine are admitted into membership in the Conference on Security and Cooperation in Europe.

February 1 Meeting at Camp David, George Bush and Boris Yeltsin declare a formal end to the Cold War and agree to exchange visits by year's end.

February 6 The Ukrainian parliament adopts a resolution rejecting Russian demands to open the question of returning the Crimea to Russia. This resolution is in response to a demand by the Russian Parliament to examine the constitutionality of Khrushchev's gift of the Crimea to Ukraine in 1954.

February 8 The Russian government announces that the last ten political prisoners held have been released.

February 9 Two rallies are held in Moscow. Approximately 15,000 pro-Communist demonstrators march toward the Kremlin shouting that life was better under communism. About one mile away, at the Russian White House, about 25,000 people demonstrate in support of the Russian government.

February 14 Leaders of the Commonwealth of Independent States meet for eight hours in Minsk to discuss military affairs. The eleven leaders are divided over the question of command, some siding with Russia and joint command and others siding with Ukraine, which fears Russian dominance and seeks independent control over its own military. Despite differences concerning the military, the leaders sign several economic agreements and reconfirm their commitment to unified control over the nuclear arsenal on February 15.

February 16 Iran, Pakistan, and Turkey formally recognize the membership of Turkmenistan, Uzbekistan, Tajikistan, Kyrgyzstan, and Azerbaijan in the Economic Cooperation Organization they founded in 1963.

February 21 In a move to decrease Iranian influence in the region, Saudi Arabia establishes diplomatic ties with Uzbekistan.

February 23 Several thousand opponents of the Russian government in Moscow mark Armed Forces Day by protesting and calling for the restoration of the Soviet Union.

February 24 In Moscow former East German leader Erich Honecker gives up his sanctuary in the Chilean Embassy to enter a Russian hospital. A spokesman for the Russian foreign ministry states that Honecker will be allowed to return to the embassy; however, the Russian government prevents him from attempting to board a plane to fly to Chile.

March 7 Yeltsin removes remaining price controls on bread, milk, kefir (fermented milk), cottage cheese, sugar, salt, cooking oil, and matches.

March 10 Former Soviet Foreign Minister Eduard A. Shevardnadze is chosen to head the Georgian State Council, which has executive and legislative power.

March 12 Ukrainian President Kravchuk announces that he is halting the transfer of tactical nuclear weapons to Russia because there is no evidence that Moscow is destroying the weapons.

March 21 People in the Tatar region of southern Russia vote in favor of a referendum calling for autonomy for the region.

March 25 The Ukrainian parliament adopts a set of economic goals that includes replacing the ruble with a local currency by April 1.

March 28 After weeks of fighting between Romanian loyalists and Slavic separatists, Moldovan President Snegur imposes emergency rule in an area of eastern Moldova between Moldova and Ukraine called the Trans-Dniester.

March 31 The International Monetary Fund (IMF) endorses Russia's economic reform plan allowing Russia to receive up to $4 billion in IMF aid over the next year.

Eighteen out of twenty of Russia's main regions sign a federal treaty that forms the basis of the new Russian state.

April 1 Despite protests from the Moldovan minister of defense, Yeltsin takes command of the former Soviet army stationed in Moldova due to fighting in the Trans-Dniester region.

April 6 Ukrainian President Kravchuk issues a decree asserting Ukraine's legal authority over military forces on its territory.

April 9 Kravchuk and Yeltsin agree to create a commission to work out a plan for the distribution of the Black Sea Fleet.

April 11 The Russian Congress of People's Deputies passes a resolution requiring Yeltsin to give up his concurrent post as prime minister of Russia within ninety days in an effort to curb some of his powers.

April 13 Yeltsin's entire cabinet formally offers to resign unless the parliament halts its efforts to scale back economic reform. The next day, the parliament and cabinet reach a compromise and the cabinet members withdraw their resignations.

April 16 Members of the Russian Congress of People's Deputies vote to call their state Rossiia (Russia). It will not be called the Russian Federation or any other variation.

April 27 The World Bank and International Monetary Fund formally offer membership to Russia, Ukraine, and most of the other former Soviet republics.

May 3 The ruling Communist government in Tajikistan threatens to crack down on anti-government protesters in Dushanbe, the capital city. For the past five days thousands of demonstrators fill the two city squares and call for democratic reforms. Violence ensues.

May 5 The Crimean parliament votes to declare conditional independence from Ukraine. A referendum to confirm the vote will be held.

May 7 Yeltsin issues decrees forming a separate Russian Army with himself as commander-in-chief and acting minister of defense.

May 11 Due to the violence in Dushanbe, Tajikistan, President Rakhman Nabiyev agrees to a coalition government giving the opposition eight key ministries.

May 18 President Nursultan A. Nazarbayev of Kazakhstan signs a deal with Chevron Oil. According to the agreement, Chevron will invest more than $10 billion over the next 40 years to develop oil fields in Kazakhstan. It is one of the largest joint ventures between a Western company and a former Soviet republic.

May 21 The Russian parliament passes a resolution declaring that Khrushchev's 1954 gift of the Crimea to Ukraine—to mark the anniversary of the Ukrainian-Russian Union—unconstitutional and void. They agree that the issue needs to be resolved through negotiations (*see* February 6, 1992).

May 23 After agreeing in April to act as equal partners, Russia, Ukraine, Belarus, and Kazakhstan sign an agreement with the United States that opens the way for the ratification of the START (Strategic Arms Reduction Treaty); Ukraine, Belarus, and Kazakhstan also agree to turn over all, not just battlefield, strategic nuclear warheads to Russia.

June 7 Russia votes to join the United Nations sanctions against Serbia due to their aggression against the other ethnic groups in the former Yugoslavia; right-wing nationalists in the Russian parliament protest, claiming that they are betraying their Slavic brothers.

Azerbaijan holds its first multi-party presidential election. Voters elect Abulfez Elchibey, the leader of the nationalist Popular Front, who campaigned on the promise to keep the disputed Nagorno-Karabakh region and remove Azerbaijan from the Commonwealth of Independent States.

June 9 The Moldovan prime minister and most of his cabinet resign due to a failure to halt the bloodshed in the Trans-Dniester region.

June 15–19 Yeltsin attends a summit meeting with President Bush in the United States. On June 15, Yeltsin phones exiled Russian writer Alexander Solzhenitsyn. On June 16, Yeltsin and Bush agree to reduce stocks of long-range-missile warheads and eliminate all land-based multiple-warhead missiles. The reduction must be completed by the year 2003. On June 17, the U.S. grants Russia most favored trade status.

June 17 Over 5,000 people rally in Alma-Alta, Kazakhstan, to demand the resignation of the nation's Communist leaders.

June 22 Yeltsin and Ukrainian President Kravchuk meet in Sochi on the Black Sea, for talks aimed at easing tensions between the two nations. The main disputes are settled, including an agreement to divide the ships of the Black Sea Fleet and to share costs in the maintenance of the naval bases.

June 24 In Tbilisi, Georgia, approximately 300 backers of ousted President Zviad Gamsakhurdia attempt to stage a coup by seizing state TV and radio stations at 5 A.M. Government troops loyal to Eduard Shevardnadze put down the coup attempt. The government reports that two people, supporters of Gamsakhurdia, are killed and 27 people wounded in the attempted coup.

June 25 Leaders from the Balkan Peninsula (Turkey, Greece, Romania, Bulgaria, and Albania) and the former Soviet Union (Russia, Ukraine, Georgia, Moldova, Azerbaijan, and Armenia) sign the Declaration of Black Sea Economic Cooperation in Istanbul, Turkey. During the session Yeltsin and Kravchuk meet for two hours with Presidents Mircea Snegur of Moldova and Ion Iliescu of Romania to discuss the conflict over the Trans-Dniester region where a Slavic majority seeks secession from the republic of Moldova, which is 65 percent Romanian.

July 1 The value of the Russian ruble is determined by market forces, not government decree; it is therefore now convertible into "hard" or western currencies.

July 7 The Communist party of the Soviet Union goes on trial in Russia's Constitutional Court in Moscow. The case arose from the lawsuit by 37 pro-Communist members of Russia's parliament seeking to overturn Yeltsin's ban on the party (*see* November 6, 1991).

July 8 G7 leaders agree to provide Russia with $1 billion in economic aid.

July 10 Russia and Germany sign a treaty providing for the resettlement of about 2 million ethnic Germans along the Volga river. The treaty reestablishes an autonomous region for the Germans; such a region has not existed since World War II, when Stalin exiled the Volga Germans to Central Asia (*see* August 28, 1965).

July 14 Moscow announces that a joint peacekeeping force made up of 800 soldiers (200 Russian, 200 Georgian, 200 South Ossetian, and 200 North Ossetians) under the direction of the United Nations, took up positions near South Ossetia in Georgia in an effort to end the ethnic conflict.

July 16 A Russian envoy delivers letters to Czechoslovak officials; the letters are addressed to Leonid M. Brezhnev from five high ranking Czechoslovak Communist party officials who opposed the Prague Spring reforms and invited Soviet forces to enter Czechoslovakia in 1968 (*see* August 20–21, 1968).

July 17 Russian lawmakers adopt a resolution placing the newspaper *Izvestiia* under the control of the Congress of People's Deputies. Formerly the newspaper of the Soviet government, *Izvestiia's* staff declared the paper independent after the attempted coup of August 1991. Observers believe that the legislators' actions are a direct challenge to free press and the authority of Yeltsin who has publicly supported *Izvestiia*. On the following day, a spokesman for Yeltsin announces that Yeltsin will protect *Izvestiia* from a takeover by the Russian parliament.

July 21 Russia and Moldova agree to send a joint peacekeeping force into the Trans-Dniester region of Moldova. They also agree that the Slav-dominated region on the eastern side of the Dniester river can decide its own fate if Moldova reunites with Romania in the future.

August 3 Yeltsin and Ukrainian President Kravchuk meet near Yalta and agree to place the Black Sea Fleet under joint Russian-Ukrainian command until 1995. During this transition period Russia and Ukraine will work on a permanent division of the fleet.

August 9 Armenian President Levon Ter-Petrosyan appeals to the other nations in the Commonwealth of Independent States for help in fighting Azerbaijan.

August 12 Thousands take to the streets in Tbilisi, Georgia to show support for President Shevardnadze after the country's top police officials are kidnapped by militant supporters of ousted former President Gamsakhurdia.

August 14 Georgian troops fight with rebels in the breakaway region of Abkhazia. At least fifteen people are killed; the fighting continues for weeks despite a cease-fire announced in late August.

August 23 The Greek publishing company Akadumos announces that it has obtained majority control of the Russian daily newspaper *Pravda,* formerly the official paper of the Soviet Communist party.

September 7 Opponents of hard-line Communist President Rakhman Nabiyev of Tajikistan force him to sign a statement of resignation.

September 8 Russia agrees to withdraw all 20,500 former Soviet troops from Lithuania by the end of August 1993.

September 16 Russia and Cuba agree on the withdrawal of a former Soviet infantry brigade that has been in Cuba since the missile crisis of 1962. The 1,500 troops and their families will be removed in stages starting in 1993.

September 21 Russian officials announce that they are not willing to be liable for the entire Soviet debt of $70 billion.

September 22 Russian Foreign Minister Andrei V. Kozyrev asks the United Nations to consider setting up an international trusteeship to oversee the move to independence by the former non-Slavic Soviet republics to prevent them from discriminating against minorities. The Russians are particularly concerned about discrimination against Slavs in Latvia and Estonia.

September 30 Russian troops take control of the airport in Dushanbe, Tajikistan.

October 1 The Russian government issues vouchers worth 10,000 rubles to every man, woman, and child, to be used for the purchase of stock in state-owned enterprises. The vouchers become valid on December 1, 1992.

October 7 Apparently angered by Mikhail Gorbachev's refusal to testify at the Communist party trial (*see* July 7, 1992), Yeltsin signs a decree transferring the buildings and property of the Gorbachev Foundation, the International Foundation for Socioeconomic and Political Research, to a government academy. The following day armed police officers bar Gorbachev from entering his private offices.

October 14 The Russian government turns over documents to Polish President Lech Walesa proving that Stalin's Politburo in March 1940 specifically ordered the execution of more than 20,000 Poles including 5,000 senior Polish army officers whose bodies were dumped in a mass grave in the forests of Katyn (*see* April 18, 26, 1943).

October 20 Russian officials announce that they are temporarily halting the withdrawal of some former Soviet troops from the Baltic states because there is no place to house the soldiers in Russia.

October 28 Yeltsin signs a decree outlawing the National Salvation Front. This political opposition group, having held their first meeting only the week before, is made up of ultra-nationalists and former Communists.

The last Russian combat troops stationed in Poland leave.

October 29 Yeltsin charges that the Baltic states are not protecting the Russian minority living in each of the countries and suspends the withdrawal of Russian troops from the region.

November 10 Tajikistan's coalition government, which has been in power for only one week, resigns and leaves an interim council in control of the republic.

November 11 Yeltsin turns over to the Hungarian government a box of documents from the KGB archives pertaining to the Hungarian uprising of 1956. Russian and Hungarian officials also sign nine agreements including military and cultural cooperation.

November 13 Ukraine exchanges all Russian rubles for Ukrainian coupons, now the only legal tender in Ukraine. Russia also offers to take over Ukraine's share of the $70-80 billion Soviet debt in exchange for Ukraine giving up all claim to former Soviet assets in Russia.

November 15 Members of the former Communist party, now known as the Democratic Labor party, return to power in the Lithuanian parliamentary elections; the elections also witness the defeat of Vytautas Landsbergis, the leader of the independence movement. The Democratic Labor party holds at least 79 of the 141 seats in parliament. Voters are disenchanted with the failing economy, soaring prices, and the inability of elected officials to work together.

November 20 The Russian parliament passes a law giving property rights to owners of small plots of land—giving real property to about 100 million Russian people—thus opening a true real estate market.

November 21 The first 100 volunteers from the U.S. Peace Corps arrive in Russia.

November 30 The thirteen-member Russian Constitutional Court rules that Yeltsin's decree banning the Soviet and Russian Communist parties after the attempted August 1991 coup were basically legitimate; it further decides that the question of property rights will have to be decided in civil court, and finds that low level party organizations are legitimate (*see* July 7, 1992).

December 1 The Congress of People's Deputies, dominated by hard-liners elected before the collapse of the Soviet Union, meets in Moscow. The members of congress unsuccessfully attempt to impeach Yeltsin in an effort to slow his economic reforms. The vote fails 429 to 352.

December 4 Hard-line members of the Congress of People's Deputies unsuccessfully attempt to pass a constitutional amendment that would take away much of Yeltsin's power. Deputies vote 668 to 210 for a resolution condemning his economic reforms as "unsatisfactory."

December 13 Workers at Chernobyl nuclear plant restart a second reactor, damaged in 1986, calculating that Ukraine's need for energy outweighs the danger.

The first public auction of a state-owned enterprise, the bakery "Bolshevik," is held in Moscow. Shares in the company can only be purchased with the vouchers issued to all Russians over the past two months (*see* October 1, 1992).

December 17 German Chancellor Helmut Kohl, on his first visit to Moscow since the collapse of the Soviet Union, announces $11.2 billion of debt relief for Russia. Yeltsin and Kohl also agree to speed up the withdrawal of former Soviet troops from Germany to August 1994; in return, Germany will spend $318 million to build housing in Russia for the returning military personnel.

1993

January 6 The Russian government issues a decree limiting producers' profits on basic goods.

January 28 Due to poor health conditions, the World Health Organization reports that a diphtheria epidemic is sweeping Russia and Ukraine.

March 10–13 The Congress of People's Deputies, in an emergency session, passes resolutions limiting Yeltsin's power to implement economic reform. The congress also votes to cancel an April 11 referendum asking Russians to vote on whether the president or the parliament should govern the country. Congress ends its four-day emergency session by passing a resolution that accuses the president of asking for too much power.

March 20 In an attempt to consolidate his power, Boris Yeltsin declares emergency rule and calls for an April 25 referendum to decide whether the president or parliament should rule Russia.

March 22 Yeltsin issues a decree placing the media under his protection.

March 28 Hard-line (former Communist) lawmakers in the Congress of People's Deputies attempt to impeach Yeltsin. However, they fall 72 votes short of the 689 needed to impeach him.

April 3–4 U.S. president Bill Clinton and Yeltsin hold a summit in Vancouver, Canada. During the meeting Clinton promises Russia $1.6 billion in aid.

April 25 In a nationwide referendum, an estimated 65 percent of Russians vote in favor of Boris Yeltsin and his economic policies and for early elections to the Congress of People's Deputies, which has been Yeltsin's chief opponent in his economic reforms.

Late April Armenian troops overrun Azerbaijani forces and annex territory that separates Armenia from the disputed region of Nagorno-Karabakh.

May 1 In the first outbreak of violence since the August 1991 coup attempt, thousands of Communists fight with police in Moscow after they are barred from celebrating May Day in Red Square; dozens of injuries result, and several days later, a policeman dies from injuries received. The rest of the country remains quiet.

May 4 Supporters of ousted Georgian President Zviad Gamsakhurdia blow up a power station cutting off electricity to half the country.

May 5 The Russian government promises to commit troops to an international peacekeeping force to end the violence in the Bosnian civil war if a peace agreement is signed there.

May 14 Nine of the ten ex-Soviet republics that constitute the Commonwealth of Independent States sign an agreement of intent to form an economic union. The union will improve economic dealings and trade among the nations. Turkmenistan is the only nation of the CIS that does not sign.

May 18 The treason trial of 12 former Soviet officials accused of carrying out the coup of August 1991 is suspended indefinitely on the grounds that the prosecutors are biased. The charge of bias is based on the fact that the chief prosecutor Valentin G. Stepankov, and his deputy Yevgeny

Lisov wrote the book *The Kremlin Conspiracy* using state evidence. The book describes the defendants as criminals.

May 26 In Moscow, leaders of Armenia and Azerbaijan agree to a peace plan that could end five years of fighting in Nagorno-Karabakh. The plan, which calls for a 60-day cease-fire, was developed by Russia, the United States, and Turkey.

June 5 The Russian constitutional conference opens in Moscow. After a disagreement with President Yeltsin over the potential division of power between the presidency and the legislature, the chairman of the conference, Ruslan I. Khasbulatov, and about 50 delegates walk out of the meeting.

June 11 The Russian government refuses to commit more troops to the United Nation's peacekeeping force to defend six ''safe-havens'' in Bosnia.

June 12 Armenian forces in Nagorno-Karabakh attack the city of Agdam just hours after a deadline for the proposed cease-fire of May 26 passes.

June 18 Heydar Aliyev, a former K.G.B. official and currently chairman of the Azerbaijan parliament, takes control of the government of Azerbaijan as rebel forces move toward Baku. On June 24, the Azerbaijan parliament votes to strip President Abulfez Elchiby of his power.

June 25 The Russian government cuts the supply of natural gas to Estonia to protest Estonia's new residency laws that severely restrict the rights of non-Estonian-speaking inhabitants, which are viewed by the Russian government as violating the rights of ethnic Russians living in the Baltic state.

July 4 The last former Soviet troops leave Cuba. A brigade has been on the island since the 1962 Missile Crisis.

July 6 The United States signs a trade agreement with Russia worth over $2 billion to help bolster the sagging Russian oil and natural gas industries.

July 8 President Yeltsin arrives in Japan to discuss aid for Russia with the seven leading industrial nations (G7). He announces that he is also willing to meet with Japanese officials to discuss territorial disputes dating back to the end of World War II.

July 9 The Russian parliament passes a resolution declaring the Crimean port of Sevastopol, Ukraine, a Russian city. However, Ukraine has no intention of giving up the city and the resolution heightens tensions in the Black Sea

Fleet, which is claimed by both Russia and Ukraine. On July 10, Russian President Yeltsin denounces the resolution.

Using DNA testing, British scientists confirm that the remains unearthed two years previously are that of Tsar Nicholas II and his family, killed by the Bolsheviks on July 16, 1918.

July 14   The prime ministers of Belarus, Russia, and Ukraine decide to go ahead with an economic integration and trade agreement first discussed on May 14.

July 24   The Russian central bank announces that it is removing from circulation all banknotes printed before 1993 in an effort to control the money supply and inflation. Each Russian citizen can exchange 35,000 pre-1993 rubles (approximately $35) for new bills before August 7. On July 25, senior government financial officials complain to President Yeltsin about this course of action and Western bank officials criticize the plan saying that it could increase inflation. On July 26, President Yeltsin declares that by the end of August each Russian can exchange 100,000 pre-1993 rubles (approximately $100) and an unlimited number of 10,000 ruble notes printed in 1992.

August 13   While meeting with regional leaders, Yeltsin declares that he will not allow any territories to leave the Russian Federation, even if that means he would have to use force and declare a dictatorship.

August 18   The United Nation's Security Council calls for a complete withdrawal of Armenian forces from occupied areas of Nagorno-Karabakh in Azerbaijan since June 12.

The Lithuanian minister of defense announces that the Russians have suspended the withdrawal of 2,500 remaining former Soviet troops from his country scheduled to be completed on August 31. On August 22, the Russian foreign minister announces that the pullout would continue, but at a schedule convenient for Russia. The problem with the withdrawal arises over the Lithuanian government's demand of compensation for the five decades of Soviet occupation.

August 19   During a speech commemorating the coup of 1991, President Yeltsin warns that another reactionary putsch or coup is possible, but the Russian people will not allow the country to return to the past.

August 21   Health officials in Russia report there have been over 4,000 cases of diphtheria in 1993. As a result, a massive immunization program takes place.

August 26   While in Prague, the Czech Republic, to commemorate the 25th anniversary of the Prague Spring

and the Soviet invasion of Czechoslovakia, Russian President Yeltsin and Czech President Vaclav Havel sign an agreement aimed at ending past tensions. President Yeltsin condemns the Soviet invasion as ''an assault on the sovereignty of an independent state,'' but emphasizes that it was the Soviet Union, not Russia, who was responsible for the invasion.

August 30   The Russian government announces that it will immediately complete the withdrawal of troops from Lithuania, and the last troops leave on August 31, making Lithuania the first Baltic state free of former Soviet troops.

September 2   The United States and Russia agree to develop an international space station.

September 3   Ukrainian President Leonid M. Kravchuk agrees to allow Russia to purchase Ukraine's share of the disputed Black Sea fleet. However, on September 4, the Ukrainian parliament accuses Kravchuk of overstepping his authority; President Kravchuk then announces that parliament must approve the agreement.

September 18   A cease-fire between Georgia and its breakaway republic of Abkhazia crumbles as fighting resumes.

September 21   Stating that the large number of Communists in the Russian parliament are causing irreconcilable opposition to his reforms and ability to govern, President Yeltsin orders the parliament dissolved and calls for new elections on December 12. In response, the Russian parliament votes to remove Yeltsin and swears in Vice President Vladimir V. Rutskoi as acting president. The Russian Supreme Court upholds parliament's action.

September 22   When members of parliament refuse to leave, police officers barricade the Russian White House, home of parliament, and mount armed guards in the building. Several thousand anti-Yeltsin protesters rally at the White House. Although President Yeltsin receives support from the leaders of the police and military, he declares he will not use force to subdue his rivals.

September 23   President Yeltsin issues a decree taking control of all parliamentary newspapers, radio, and television. Yeltsin announces that he will call for early presidential elections to be held on June 12, 1994.

September 24   President Yeltsin orders the White House guards unarmed as police surround the building. Inside, a meeting of all the available Congress of People's Deputies is called but the meeting quickly adjourns after there a division over whether they should agree to Yeltsin's call for early presidential elections.

September 25 Russian troops take up positions around the White House.

September 26 A regional Russian leaders meeting in St. Petersburg calls for simultaneous elections for president and legislature. In Moscow, 15,000 people rally in support of President Yeltsin.

September 27 Yeltsin rejects the call for simultaneous elections for president and the parliament.

President Leonid Kravchuk takes direct control of Ukraine's government by eliminating the position of prime minister in an effort to speed up Ukraine's transition to a market economy.

September 28 The White House is sealed off.

September 29 President Yeltsin tightens the ring around the White House by deploying more troops who lay down concertina wire (a type of razor-sharp barbed wire). Moscow city officials and national officials order members of the Russian parliament to leave the White House by October 4.

October 1 In an effort to end the power struggle, Yeltsin and the leaders of parliament reach an agreement where the heat and power will be turned on in the White House if the members of parliament put their weapons in storage. A few hours later, however, the members of parliament reject the agreement.

Yeltsin sends a letter to President Clinton opposing any East European nations' membership in NATO.

October 2 While talks between the Russian president and members of parliament are taking place under the auspices of the Russian Orthodox Patriarch, supporters of parliament clash with riot police on the streets of Moscow. Russian Vice President Rutskoi calls for the people of Russia to resist the ''dictatorship'' in the Kremlin.

October 3 After continued rioting, which includes rioters breaking into radio and television stations, President Yeltsin declares a state of emergency in Moscow.

October 4 At 4 A.M. airborne troops enter Moscow. At 7 A.M. President Yeltsin orders troops in tanks and armored personnel carriers to oust the armed rebels from the White House. The tanks fire to disperse the crowds outside the building. After some fighting, the rebellion is crushed and the leaders, including Vice President Rutskoi and Ruslan Khasbulatov, are arrested. Russian government sources

report that 142 people were killed during the riots and subsequent attack on the White House.

October 5 Yeltsin begins to rule Russia by presidential decree. He bans all opposition organizations and newspapers; censorship is imposed on news critical of the government.

October 6 President Yeltsin appears on national television and appeals for calm. He promises there will be parliamentary elections on December 12 and lifts the censorship of the media. For the first time since Lenin's death in 1924, the honor guard is removed from his tomb on Red Square.

October 8 The Russian Justice Ministry suspends the right of organization for ten political parties including the main Communist party and Aleksandr Rutskoi's People's Party of Free Russia. Thirteen newspapers that were critical of Yeltsin are also suspended.

October 14 President Yeltsin permanently bans thirteen newspapers and television shows that were sympathetic to the legislature. *Pravda* is among the newspapers banned.

October 15 President Yeltsin orders a referendum on a new constitution, which has not yet been written, to take place simultaneously with the parliamentary elections on December 12.

October 21 Reversing a two-year-old decision to close the Chernobyl nuclear power plant at the end of 1993 due to safety concerns, the Ukrainian parliament votes to keep the reactors running to provide electricity for the country.

October 27 President Yeltsin signs a decree allowing farm workers to own and sell land. All workers and dependents on state-owned farms will receive shares which they can redeem for land, sell, or trade. Western analysts hail this move as an important step towards the privatization of the Russian economy.

November 3 Russian military officials confirm that the military doctrine adopted the day before no longer adheres to the old Soviet promise not to use nuclear weapons first in the event of a military conflict.

November 8 Yeltsin approves a draft of the first non-Soviet constitution for Russia. Voters will be asked to approve the constitution during the December 12 election for parliament. The constitution creates a two-chamber

Pro-communist demonstrators set a barricade on fire in downtown Moscow during the declared state of emergency.

parliament with members serving two-year terms. The office of president gains considerable power in appointing senior members of the executive and judicial members of the government.

November 12 Thirteen political parties in Russia receive permission to begin campaigning for the December 12 elections. Yeltsin focuses his attention on the new constitution and does not campaign for any candidates or political parties.

November 18 Ukrainian parliament approves the Strategic Arms Reduction Treaty (START), promising to destroy about half of their nuclear weapons. However, they do not approve a resolution to become a nuclear-free state. Ukraine's decision to retain 58 percent of their nuclear weapons upsets Russian leaders, who believe that this will destabilize the region.

November 29 After talking to President Clinton, Ukrainian President Leonid Kravchuk announces that the parliament will review its decision not to destroy all nuclear weapons.

December 12 Russian national elections are held to approve the new constitution and elect members of parliament. The constitution is approved by a majority of the voters and goes into effect on December 21. 54.8 percent of the eligible voters take part in the elections (out of a possible 106,170,335 eligible voters); 58.4 percent of the voters favor the constitution, and 41.6 percent vote against it. In general, candidates for reform parties do not have a strong showing in the election. The ultra-nationalist Liberal Democratic Party, led by Vladimir V. Zhirinovskii, and Russia's Choice Party, led by reformer First Deputy Premier Yegor Gaidar have the strongest showing in the elections.

December 22 Based on the performance of reform parties in the December 12 elections, President Boris N. Yeltsin announces he will form a presidential political party.

Chapter Nine

YUGOSLAVIA

When the now former Yugoslavia was formed in 1918 at the end of World War I out of the ruins of the Austro-Hungarian Empire and the independent states of Serbia and Montenegro, its peoples came from at least six separate legal entities: Austria, Hungary, Bosnia and Herzegovina, Montenegro, Serbia, and the Ottoman Empire. The nationalities encompassed by the Yugoslav state included Serbs, Croats, Slovenes, Hungarians, Turks, Macedonians, Albanians, Bulgarians, Romanians, Germans, Slovaks, Czechs, Russians, and Italians. Needless to say, this was a state with an extremely complex ethnic composition, whose peoples came into the new state with divergent experiences of government.

Serbs, the most numerous nationality in the new state, practiced the Serbian Orthodox religion. The first Serbian state was established in the 12th century but was defeated by the Ottoman Turks in 1389 at the Battle of Kosovo and became part of the Ottoman Empire for more than four centuries. By 1815, after a series of revolts Serbia had achieved virtual independence from the Ottoman Turks although still technically part of the empire; over the course of the next century, the state gradually expanded until it included all of today's Serbia (minus Vojvodina) and Macedonia, officially receiving independence in 1878. It was governed by a monarchy, which, after 1903, was limited by a fairly progressive constitution. Nonetheless, Serbia was an almost completely agrarian, peasant state. Its homogeneity gave it its strength and unity.

Croats were the next most numerous nationality in Yugoslavia in 1918. They were, for the most part, Roman Catholic, with a history radically different from that of Serbia. The Croats established their own kingdom in the early 10th century, and when the native dynasty died out they agreed to join Hungary in 1102. Until 1918, Croatia was a constituent part of Hungary, which in turn shared the spotlight in the Habsburg monarchy with Austria. Croats matured in the political atmosphere of ethnic conflict in the Habsburg monarchy. Croatia included a large Serbian minority which made it difficult for its people to develop a strong, self-centered identity, as Serbia had.

Among the other peoples of former Yugoslavia, the largely Roman Catholic Slovenes fell under centuries of Austrian domination, unable to assert their independence until 1918 when they broke away and joined Yugoslavia. Bosnia and Herzegovina was an independent kingdom in the Middle Ages with the elite belonging to the radical Christian Bogomil sect, which became the faith of the country. The Bogomils were attacked as heretics by both the Roman Catholic and Orthodox churches, so when the Turks conquered the region, the nobility easily converted to Islam to protect their property and wealth, but continued to speak Serbian. In 1878, the Congress of Berlin, where the great powers redrew the map of Southeastern Europe after the Russo-Turkish War of 1877–78, placed Bosnia and Herzegovina under the administration of Austria-Hungary, which annexed it in 1908. Montenegro, on the other hand, had been part of the Serbian kingdom until the Turks defeated Serbia in 1389. Thereafter, Montenegro remained virtually independent since the Turks were never able to establish a strong presence, until the 19th century when it gained its official independence under the Petrović dynasty despite repeated Ottoman attempts to conquer the area.

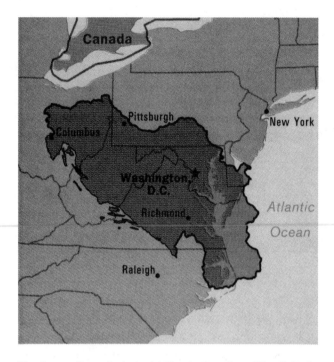

The former Yugoslavia in relation to the size of the United States.

From 1903 to 1914, an intellectual movement calling for the unity of Serbs and Croats (Yugoslavism) was in vogue in both Serbia and Croatia, reaching its height just before the First World War. Although the creation of Yugoslavia was an answer to the prayers of these intellectuals, beyond that stratum of Serbs and Croats who viewed Yugoslavia as the promised land, there were far too many historical and cultural traditions involved for coexistence to be easy. The conflicts of the 20th century emerged from that tension.

1914

June 28   In Sarajevo, Bosnia, Gavrilo Princip (a Bosnian Serb and Austro-Hungarian citizen) assassinates Archduke Franz Ferdinand, the heir to the Habsburg monarchy who is viewed as a threat to Serbian nationalism and expansionism. Princip is a member of Young Bosnia, a Serbian group that opposes Austrian control of Bosnia and whose ultimate goal is to see Bosnia united with Serbia. It receives considerable support, official and private, from within Serbia.

July 23   The Austro-Hungarian government delivers an ultimatum to the Serbian government, which the Austrians believe is behind the assassination of the archduke. The

Austrians have already decided to declare war on Serbia. The Serbian government agrees to all points of the ultimatum except one point requiring representatives of the Habsburg monarchy to participate in an investigation in Serbia of the assassination. Austria uses this Serbian refusal as a pretext to declare war. Unfortunately, Austria has not made the necessary diplomatic preparations with the great powers to assure that this local war will not escalate into a general European war.

July 28   The Habsburg monarchy declares war on Serbia. Russia, Serbia's ally, will not allow Habsburg encroachment in the Balkans, so the following day it orders general military mobilization. Soon all the major European powers become entangled in what develops as the First World War.

November 22   The Yugoslav Committee, with the aim of uniting the South Slavs in one state, is quietly established in Florence by Ante Trumbić, a Croatian deputy in the Austrian parliament, in consultation with the Serbian government. It is composed of émigrés from the South Slav lands (Serbs, Croats, Slovenes, Bosnian Serbs). Eventually it takes on the character of a representative body of South Slavs from the Habsburg monarchy, although the Serbian government views it only as an organization which will aid the Serbian propaganda effort in the Entente countries of England and France which are fighting against the Central Powers of Germany and Austria-Hungary. The Entente governments generally share the Serbian government view that it is a mere organization, which makes it exceedingly difficult for the Yugoslav Committee to exercise any influence on Entente policy for the formation of a south Slavic state.

December 7   The Serbian government issues its Niš Declaration, in which it announces its war aim—unification of all of the South Slavs in one state. The declaration is based on the vain belief that the war would soon end in an Entente victory. Thus Serbia declares its maximum political and territorial aims.

1915

April 26   The Entente and Italy sign the Treaty of London, which designates much of the Dalmatian coast and Istria as Italian in the event of a successful outcome in the war. The treaty is negotiated in order to bring Italy into the war on the Entente side. The treaty angers South Slavs, especially Croats, who view it as an unjust giveaway of Croatian territory.

The former Yugoslavia.

April 30 Trumbić publicly reveals the existence of the Yugoslav Committee to enable it to better fight the conditions contained in the Treaty of London. The committee issues a memorandum expressing its opposition to the treaty.

1917

May 30 The South Slav delegation to the Austrian Reichsrat, or parliament, declares its desire to see South Slav unity "under the scepter of the Habsburg dynasty."

This declaration affirms the loyalty of the signatories to the dynasty, but demands the creation of a South Slav political unit within the monarchy created out of Habsburg South Slavic lands.

July 20 Members of the Serbian government and the Yugoslav Committee negotiate the Corfu Declaration calling for a unified South Slav state, which will be a constitutional monarchy under the Karađorđević dynasty, the ruling dynasty in the Kingdom of Serbia. The declaration guarantees the equality of the languages, scripts—or the Latin and Cyrillic alphabets—religions, and flags of the three constituent peoples of the state-to-be, the Serbs, Croats, and Slovenes. The signatories leave the question of the future state's organization unsettled, which works to the advantage of the Serbs.

1918

October 5–6   With the political and military collapse of the Habsburg monarchy as their backdrop, Slovenian, Croatian, and Serbian politicians from Slovenia and Croatia form the National Council of the Slovenes, Croats, and Serbs. These men, led by Anton Korošec (Slovene), Ante Pavelić (Croat), and Svetozar Pribićević (Serb), all delegates of the Austrian Reichsrat or the Croatian *Sabor*, or parliament, now unanimously favor the creation of an independent state of Slovenes, Croats, and Serbs. Yet there is significant opposition to this move: the members of the Frankist Croatian Party of Right and the Croatian People's Peasant party make their disapproval known in the next month.

October 16   Habsburg Emperor Charles issues a proclamation stating that the Austrian lands of the Habsburg monarchy will be reformed as a federal state; he is too late to satisfy the nationalities of the monarchy who now look toward independence.

October 29   The Croatian Sabor declares Croatia an independent state. The Sabor invests the National Council of the Slovenes, Croats, and Serbs with its powers. Later, many members of the Sabor complain that the National Council overstepped its mandate and really never represented the desires of the parties in the Sabor at all.

November   The Serbian army attacks the Albanian population of towns in Kosovo, long considered the heartland of medieval Serbia, resulting in thousands of deaths.

November 1   The Serbian army, advancing with Entente armies from Thessaloníki, Greece, reaches and liberates Belgrade.

November 6–9   Members of the National Council, the Yugoslav Committee, and the Serbian government meet in Geneva to bring their disparate policies regarding the formation of a new state into line. Nicola Pašić, the Serbian premier, recognizes the National Council as the representative of the South Slavs in the Habsburg monarchy, and the various parties reach agreement on the formation of a new government representing all of the South Slav lands. Montenegro, without representation at the conference, is invited to join the state. But Pašić, who controls the situation in the new state, immediately abandons the provi-

sions of the Geneva agreement of November 9. Increasingly, Serbs in Serbia and Croatia (led by Pribićević) gain the leading role in the creation of the new state.

November 11   Emperor Charles of the Habsburg monarchy steps down from control of the government of Austria-Hungary, but does not abdicate.

November 16   The Dalmatian provincial government, afraid that Dalmatia will be occupied by the Italians as stated in the Treaty of London from 1915, requests that the National Council immediately seek union with Serbia and Montenegro.

November 24   Stjepan Radić, the charismatic leader of the Croatian People's Peasant party, speaks to the National Council, warning against unconditional unification with Serbia. Radić, whose party was not particularly influential before the war because his constituency of Croatian peasants could not vote, will become the single most powerful Croatian politician until 1928.

November 25   Serbs in Vojvodina proclaim their unification with Serbia. Radić speaks to his party at a rally in Zagreb where he openly attacks Pribićević and other centralists demanding that Croatia be established as a peasant republic.

November 26   The Great National Assembly of Montenegro, which was elected in the presence of the Serbian army, dethrones the native Petrović dynasty and chooses to unify with Serbia under the Karađorđević dynasty.

December 1   The National Council, represented by Pavelić and Pribićević in Belgrade, declares its desire to join Serbia. Serbian Crown Prince Aleksandar Karađorđević proclaims the union of Serbia, Croatia, and Slovenia, and the Kingdom of Serbs, Croats, and Slovenes, or Yugoslavia, is formed.

December 2   The Frankist Croatian Party of Right in Croatia announces its opposition to the declaration of December 1, noting that the declaration abolished Croatian sovereignty by placing all authority in the Karađorđević dynasty.

December 3   The National Council passes the act of unification of December 1 creating Yugoslavia, and agrees that the National Council's functions will end upon the formation of a new cabinet in Belgrade.

December 5   Croatian soldiers of the former Habsburg army who desire the independence of Croatia stage a violent demonstration on Zagreb's Jelačić square; it is put down with the loss of 13 lives by soldiers loyal to the National Council.

December 20 The first cabinet of the Kingdom of Serbs, Croats, and Slovenes is named by the king. Nine ministers are from Serbia, six are from Croatia, two each are from Bosnia and Slovenia, and one is from Montenegro. Stojan Protić is premier, Ante Trumbić is foreign minister, and Svetozar Pribićević is minister of the interior. Pribićević, the leader of Croatia's Serbs, will become a leader of the Democratic (and then the Independent Democratic) party, and will work to centralize the state as effectively as possible. Protić is a member of the Radical party in Serbia, the most powerful prewar party and the one that will dominate the governments of the new state until 1926 and beyond. Trumbić is the head of the Yugoslav Committee and will never accommodate himself to the new state because Croatia will receive none of the attributes of autonomy within the kingdom.

1919

January 3 Montenegrin rebels besiege Cetinje, the capital of Montenegro, in opposition to the unification of their state with Serbia.

January 6 A Christmas eve (according to the Orthodox calendar) battle in Cetinje between the Serbian army with its Montenegrin allies (''whites'') and Montenegrin rebels opposed to union with Serbia (''greens'') results in great loss of life, but victory for the whites.

January 7 After Pribićević, minister of the interior, demands the resignations of all regional governments, the resignations are received. The first step in the de facto centralization of the new state has been achieved.

February 2 Radić changes the name of his party from Croatian People's Peasant Party to the Croatian Republican Peasant party, reflecting its antimonarchist and federalist orientation.

February 25 A government decree abolishes serfdom as practiced in Bosnia and Herzegovina and Macedonia, institutes a land distribution of large estates in Croatia and Vojvodina, and promises indemnities to former owners.

March 16 The first meeting of a provisional parliament is held. The National Council, the Serbian Parliament, and other regional governing organizations choose the members of this parliament.

March 25 Stjepan Radić is arrested for appealing to the outside world to support Croatian independence, or, at the least, autonomy within Yugoslavia. He is held for nearly a year without trial.

April 21–23 The (Communist) Unification Congress is held in Belgrade. Here the Social Democratic and Communist parties of the pre-First World War period unify in the Socialist Workers' Party of Yugoslavia. It combines traditions inherited from the ''Austro-Marxists,'' the Communist International, and Serbian and Croatian socialism.

September 10 Yugoslavia signs the Treaty of St. Germain, the peace treaty with Austria after World War I. As a result, Yugoslavia officially receives Bosnia-Herzegovina, Slovenia, and Dalmatia.

1920

February 27 The new Protić cabinet frees Radić.

March 22 Radić is arrested again for anti-dynasty statements.

June 4 Yugoslavia signs the Treaty of Trianon, the peace treaty with Hungary after World War I. As a result Yugoslavia officially receives Croatia and the Vojvodina.

June 20–25 The Second Congress of the now renamed Communist Party of Yugoslavia (CPY) is held at Vukovar. The center moderate faction is defeated, leaving the party in hands of those who wish to undertake trade union activity, ignoring the agrarian nature of the state. The party's stand on the national question is clarified: the Serbs, Croats, and Slovenes are three tribes of a single nation. The party does not consider the national movements, especially that in Croatia, as having any relevance for the struggle for socialism; the Croatian nationalists are just as bourgeois as the Serbian ruling class, the focus of the CPY's struggle.

August 14 Czechoslovakia and Yugoslavia form a mutual defensive alliance against Hungary by pledging to uphold the Treaty of Trianon (*see* June 4). This marks the beginnings of the Little Entente alliance joined officially by Romania in 1921.

August 17 Romania unofficially joins the Czechoslovak-Yugoslav alliance.

September 3 The provisional parliament adopts a law governing the election of deputies to the Constituent Assembly, or national parliament, which will formulate a new constitution for the Kingdom of Serbs, Croats, and Slovenes. The law allows for universal suffrage for all males 21 years of age and over. Many complain the law is based on the 1910 census and inadequately deals with population changes since that year thereby giving the Serbs greater representation than they should receive since Serbia's population was devastated by World War I.

September 9   The government passes the Regulation on the Settlement of the Southern Regions, which results in Serbian colonization of Kosovo and Macedonia. The intent of the regulations is twofold: to exploit the resources of Kosovo and Macedonia, and to increase the Serbian population of the regions, which are largely Muslim in character.

November 28   Forty political parties take part in the elections for the Constituent Assembly, with the Democratic (92), (Serbian) Radical (91), Communist (58), and Croatian Republican Peasant (50) parties receiving the majority of the 419 seats.

December   The Communists lead a series of strikes in Slovenia and Bosnia.

December 7   Radić holds an outdoor rally in Zagreb attended by 100,000 Croats. He expresses the desire to see open and equal negotiations with Belgrade on the future organization of the new state, but also expresses the determination to see that Croatia's interests are not ignored. Radić refuses to acknowledge the Serbian monarchy. He refuses to accept the National Council's decision to join Serbia unconditionally in 1918.

December 8   The Radical party government of Milenko Vesnić issues standing orders for the conduct of the Constituent Assembly. The government requires members of the assembly to take an oath of allegiance to the king, provides that the government be the source of constitutional proposals and drafts, and determines that only a majority of one vote is required for passage of the new constitution. These rules guarantee a constitution favorable to the Serbian governing class will be promulgated. They enrage most non-Serbian parties, with the Croatian Republican Peasant party and the Communists the most offended.

December 29   The Vesnić government issues a decree prohibiting Communist political activity in Yugoslavia.

1921

January 21   The two main Serbian parties in the kingdom (Radical and Democratic) form a new government with Nicola Pašić as premier. These centralist parties dominate the negotiations on the new constitution. Pašić is the most powerful politician in Serbia, and as long as he lives, the Radical party will participate in governments.

March   The Organization of Yugoslav Nationalists (Orjuna) is formed in Split under the patronage of the

Pribićević faction of the Democratic party. It is a Serbian organization of thugs dedicated to the dynasty and Pribićević's unitary Yugoslavism. Other organizations with parallel programs and methods are organized for Serbian nationalists (Srnao) and Croats (Hanao).

March 21   The deposed King Nikola of Montenegro dies in France.

May 12   Mate Drinković, leader of the Croatian Union, a small Croatian party, announces its withdrawal from the Constituent Assembly to protest that the Serbian-dominated assembly is purposely ignoring the will of the South Slavs of the former Hapsburg monarchy.

May 21   The members of the Croatian Republican Peasant party, the Croatian Party of Right, and the Croatian Union issue a statement to the Croatian people explaining why these parties will not take part in the Constituent Assembly. They hope the Serbian government will agree to acknowledge the Croatian Sabor's decisions of October 29, 1918 to declare Croatia an independent state.

June 7   With the signing of the Romanian-Yugoslav alliance, the Little Entente is officially formed between Romania, Yugoslavia, and Czechoslovakia (*see* August 14, 17, 1920).

June 11   The Communist party leaves the Constituent Assembly to protest the imminent adoption of a centralistic constitution.

June 28   The new constitution of the Kingdom of Serbs, Croats, and Slovenes is passed by a 223 to 35 majority of the Constituent Assembly with 161 representatives boycotting the proceedings, which they believe are undemocratic. The constitution comes to be known as the Vidovdan Constitution after St. Vitus' day, on which it was promulgated.

June 29   Communists attempt to assassinate Crown Prince Aleksandar.

July 21   Communists kill Milorad Drašković, who had been minister of the interior in the Vesnić government and who had issued the December 29, 1920 decree criminalizing Communist political activity.

August   The Croatian Republican Peasant party, the Croatian Union, and the Croatian Party of Right form the Croatian Bloc led by Stjepan Radić of the Croatian Republican Peasant party.

August 2   The government enacts the Law for the Defense of Public Security in the State, which provides for absolute measures against Communist activity in the Kingdom of Serbs, Croats, and Slovenes.

August 16   King Petar Karađorđvić dies.

October 27 Czechoslovakia and Yugoslavia begin mobilization over the second attempted restoration of the last Habsburg Emperor Karl to the throne of Hungary. His earlier try failed in April 1921.

November 6 Prince Aleksandar Karađorđević is crowned King of the Kingdom of Serbs, Croats, and Slovenes.

1922

January 14 The Croatian Bloc demands that Croatia be recognized as a state within the "international community of Serbs, Croats, and Slovenes." They also demand a new constitution creating a federalized Yugoslavia. The government is not responsive to these demands and some Croatian newspapers are harassed. Radić appeals to the European powers for help in convincing Belgrade to reconsider Croatian demands. His petition is received poorly by the European powers; the Serbs are resentful of his action.

April 28 The government passes a law dividing the Kingdom of Serbs, Croats, and Slovenes into 33 centrally controlled districts which do not respect most of the historical borders existing before the First World War. The law is designed to help Belgrade maintain administrative control over the unequal territories that make up the state.

July 3–17 The Communist Party of Yugoslavia (CPY) holds its First Land Conference in Vienna. Sima Marković, leader of the party, believes the Serbs, Croats, and Slovenes are one nation. This view comes under attack by those who believe the revolutionary potential of the national question can be harnessed by the party to provoke revolution in the Kingdom of Serbs, Croats, and Slovenes.

August 31 Czechoslovakia and Yugoslavia sign a five-year alliance at Marienbad providing that the two countries will work jointly in foreign affairs on matters concerning their common interests, thereby strengthening the Little Entente.

1923

May The CPY holds its second conference in Vienna. Marković is again attacked for his views on the national question.

July 18 Radić appeals to Italy for help in establishing an independent Croatia. This action severely tries Belgrade's patience because the central government has been at odds with Italy for three years over the disposition of territories along the Dalmatian coast and in Istria. The Serbs resent championing Croatian territorial desires only to have the Croats turn to Italy.

July 21 Stjepan Radić leaves Yugoslavia under a false passport to travel to London, Vienna, and Moscow to plead the Croatian case.

August 18 Radić arrives in London, where he is ignored by the British leaders and the government.

December Radić returns to Vienna, where he plans a congress of oppressed nationalities as a forum for his cause of an independent Croatia; the Austrian authorities refuse to allow it.

1924

January The Third Conference of the CPY is held in Belgrade. The party finally approves a resolution identifying the national question as a source of strength in the struggle against the regime in Yugoslavia. This is a defeat for Sima Marković (*see* July 3–17, 1922; May 1923).

January 27 The Kingdom of Serbs, Croats, and Slovenes and Italy sign the Pact of Rome, finally settling the question of the ownership of the seaport of Rijeka, or Fiume, by granting it to Italy.

April 12 The Independent Democratic party issues its inaugural declaration, signed by Svetozar Pribićević and other ex-members of the Democratic party who had been expelled from that party. The new party is largely made up of *prečani* Serbs (Serbs who are not from Serbia proper). Pribićević prompted the formation of the new party because he feared the Democratic party was becoming too "Serbian," in the sense that it no longer represented the views of the prečani. Pribićević is gradually moving away from his exclusively Serbian orientation of the immediate postwar period. He hopes to make his new party a Yugoslav party of national unity; that is, an all-inclusive Yugoslav nationalist party with a statewide base.

June 3 Radić arrives in Moscow, where he attaches the Peasant party to the Communist Peasant International. Radić, although never sympathetic toward the Soviet regime, wants the Communist party of Yugoslavia to ally with his Peasant party but this does not occur. He also desperately needs international support for his opposition to the regime in Belgrade.

June 17–22 At the Fifth Congress of the Communist International, or Comintern, a international organization controlled by Moscow advocating Communist revolution, Sima Marković's views on the Yugoslav national question are rejected and the right to self-determination of the nations of Yugoslavia is recognized (*see* January 1924). This recognition is designed to gain the support of the Croatian Peasant party and the terrorist Internal Macedonian Revolutionary Organization (IMRO), both of which are viewed as strong enough to topple the Yugoslav regime.

August 11   Radić returns to Zagreb, having gained no foreign support for an independent Croatia. Operating within legal means, he immediately attacks the political position of Serbia that allows it to control the state, threatens to enlist Soviet support for an independent Croatia, and inflames the political environment again.

1925

January   Radić is arrested again and charged with treason for his association with the Comintern while in the Soviet Union.

March 27   In an attempt to work within the system Radić's nephew, Pavle Radić, announces that his uncle and the Croatian Republican Peasant party will accept the existence of the state, recognize the Karađorđević dynasty, and live with the Vidovdan Constitution. Pavle Radić agrees to change the name of his party to the Croatian Peasant party. Soon after, the Croatian Peasant party representatives are seated in the Skupština, the national parliament.

April 6   The Comintern tells Yugoslav Communists to utilize nationality conflicts in Yugoslavia to overthrow the rule of the Serbian bourgeoisie, the strength of the regime.

July 18   Charges against Stjepan Radić are dropped, and he and his party join a coalition government with the Radical party. As part of an agreement with King Aleksandar, Radić agrees his party will respect the state, constitution, and dynasty. The king and government allow the Peasant party to control administrative decisions affecting Croatia, promise to enact social legislation called for by the Peasant party, promise to implement land reform, and promise to standardize the tax system.

August 15   The royal family visits Zagreb. Thanks to Radić's position in the government, due to his reconciliation with the king, Aleksandar is received by the Croats with great enthusiasm.

November 17   Radić joins the government as minister of education.

1926

May 17–20   The Third Congress of the CPY meets in Vienna. The party recognizes the separate existence of the Macedonian nation or people and accepts the goal of eventual federalization of the Yugoslav state. The policy of supporting self-determination for the Croats, Slovenes, Macedonians, and Montenegrins is not popular.

June 13   Czechoslovakia, Romania, and Yugoslavia renew the Little Entente treaties.

December 10   Nicola Pašić, leader of the Radical party, dies. His death begins a period of unstable political maneuvering ultimately leading to the dictatorship of King Aleksandar in 1929.

1927

October 4   Radić and Pribićević exchange visits to each other's party headquarters. They attempt to resolve their differences in the hopes of forming a coalition between their parties and others.

November   With the atomization of the Radical party after Pašić's death, the Peasant party attempts to form a unified government with the Democrats, the Independent Democrats, the Agrarians, and others.

November 11   When the Democrats, under the leadership of Ljubomir Davidović, postpone their answer to Radić's invitation to join in a new political party, Pribićević and Radić agree to form an Independent-Peasant coalition. This alignment is significant: Pribićević and Radić have been mortal political enemies since 1905 with the former being a determined Serbian centralist, and the latter a confirmed Croatian federalist. Their coalition is based on an abrupt turn in Pribićević's politics: he is tired of allying with the Radicals, whom he feels only use him and his party when they wish to punish the Croats, who uniformly hate Pribićević. This coalition will outlive Radić and provide the most coherent opposition to centralism from this point on.

1928

May–June   Demonstrations break out in Croatia, Dalmatia, and Slovenia against ratification by the parliament of the Nettuno Conventions, which grant special privileges to property-owning Italian citizens in the Kingdom of Serbs, Croats, and Slovenes. Since most Italian property is in the northwestern parts of the country, Croats and Slovenes claim the conventions are colonial, and Belgrade is selling them and Croatia out. Nonetheless, the Nettuno Conventions will be ratified by parliament in November.

June In the Skupština, heated debates erupt as a result of the unrest in Croatia over the Nettuno Conventions. The subjects range from the use of the Cyrillic and Latin scripts, or alphabets, to the conventions themselves. Radić is involved in these debates and he provokes several Radicals to threaten him.

June 20 Stjepan Radić is shot and wounded by a Montenegrin deputy, Puniša Račić, in the Skupština. Two other Croatian representatives, including Pavle Radić, are killed immediately.

July 7 King Aleksandar recognizes Radić's impending death will give Croatia the martyr it needs, so he immediately offers Croatia its independence. Svetozar Pribićević and Vladko Maček, the new leader of the Peasant party, refuse the offer, fearing Italian and Hungarian partition of Croatia.

August 1 A new government under the Slovene Anton Korošec convenes in Belgrade; the Croatian Peasant party and Independent Democratic party hold a separate meeting in Zagreb and announce that the Skupština shootings mean the Vidovdan Constitution is dead and a new arrangement must be worked out.

August 8 Radić dies of wounds suffered in the June 20 attack in the Skupština.

October The Fourth Congress of the CPY meets in Dresden. Sima Marković, who least approved of the policy of supporting national self-determination in Yugoslavia, is excluded from the leadership (*see* June 17–22, 1924).

December 30 Korošec and his government resign due to increasing government paralysis, leaving only the Zagreb "parliament" of Peasants and Independent Democrats to negotiate the fate of the country. Maček demands virtual independence for Croatia, which the king refuses to grant.

1929

January 6 Since the Croatian and Serbian political parties refuse to cooperate with one another, thereby causing a paralysis in government, King Aleksandar proclaims a royal dictatorship and suspends the constitution, dissolves the Skupština, and abolishes all religious or ethnically-based parties. The king is now the source of authority in the land.

January 7 The Croat Dr. Ante Pavelić (not the same National Council member who declared Croatia's and Slovenia's willingness to join Serbia in 1918) goes to Italy to form a Croatian terrorist organization known as the Ustaša movement to work for Croatian independence. He establishes contact with all opponents of the Yugoslav regime, including the Internal Macedonian Revolutionary Organization (IMRO), a terrorist organization which seeks to bring about a union of Macedonia with Bulgaria. He receives subsidies from the Hungarian and Italian governments which have territorial aspirations in the Kingdom of the Serbs, Croats, and Slovenes.

October 3 The Kingdom of Yugoslavia is proclaimed by the king. The king has divided the kingdom into nine *banovine* (districts) which purposely do not respect historical and ethnic boundaries and which are given geographically-inspired names. The nine banovine are: the Dravska, the Savska, the Vrbaska, the Primorska, the Drinska, the Dunavska, the Zetska, the Moravska, and the Vardarska. The king hopes to instill a new Yugoslav loyalty in the people in place of their past ethnic/religious loyalties.

1930

April Members of the Croatian Peasant party and the *Ustaša* movement meet in Vienna, where they coordinate their strategies. Although the two groups are not technically linked politically or ideologically and they differ widely on political tactics, they agree that the Peasants will work among the American, British, and French to argue Croatia's case, whereas the *Ustaša* will work in Italy and Hungary to the same end.

1931

February 18 Milan Šufflay, an advisor to Maček, is murdered, probably by men in the service of the king.

Early July Svetozar Pribićević goes into exile in Czechoslovakia. He has spent much of the previous two years under house arrest in Brus, Serbia, due to his open opposition to the dictatorship of King Aleksandar.

September 3 The king proclaims a new constitution legitimizing his dictatorship. The constitution establishes a bicameral legislature, but the king, hoping to eliminate ethnic rivalries, also institutes restrictive electoral laws directing potential candidates to demonstrate their appeal in all of the banovine.

1932

November 7 In response to the declaration of the dictatorship, the Peasant-Democratic (Maček-Pribićević) coalition issues the "Zagreb Punctuation," which is unfavorable to the regime and which opposes King Aleksandar. Again the two parties demand Croatia be given a measure of autonomy.

1933

February 16 The Little Entente of Czechoslovakia, Romania, and Yugoslavia meet in Geneva to reorganize the alliance with a permanent council to harmonize economic relations and to form a unified foreign policy in the wake of Nazi successes in Germany.

1934

March 16–17 Austria, Italy, and Hungary sign the Rome Protocols in which the three countries agree to cooperate in foreign affairs. The agreements are aimed against the Little Entente of Czechoslovakia, Romania, and Yugoslavia.

October 9 King Aleksandar and the French foreign minister are assassinated by IMRO and *Ustaša* agents in Marseilles. Italy and Hungary assisted with the murder, and the French government, wanting better relations with Italy, does not undertake a thorough investigation. With King Aleksandar's assassination, the government continues to function as it had under the constitution of September 3, 1931. King Petar, the son of Aleksandar, must wait until September 6, 1941, his eighteenth birthday, to ascend the throne. In the absence of a king, the government decides not to undertake any constitutional revisions. The government does appoint a three-man regency, led by Prince Pavle, King Aleksandar's cousin, as called for in King Aleksandar's will.

1935

June 24 Prince Pavle calls upon Milan Stojadinović to form a government. Stojadinović is a member of the Radical party known for his expertise in economics. He governs for more than three years, which makes his gov-

ernment the longest-lasting in interwar Yugoslavia. His rule has some of the characteristics of fascism. He creates a government party (the Yugoslav Radical Union or YRU) which claims to be Yugoslav in orientation. Maček's opposition bloc refuses to participate in the government.

July 25 The Yugoslav government and the Vatican sign a concordat in Rome that places the Catholic Church on an equal footing with the Orthodox Church regarding matters of religion. Stojadinović does not submit the concordat to the Skupština, but hopes to submit it later when his government is more secure. Stojadinović sees the concordat as necessary for improving the relations between the Croats and the Yugoslav government. The Orthodox church opposes the concordat because it implies an outside agency would be involved in state decisions, and because it allows the Catholic church to interfere in areas the Orthodox church dominates—Niš, for instance, will gain a Catholic diocese. However, the Croats do not care that the concordat has been negotiated since there is significant anticlerical sentiment among them.

July–August At the Seventh Congress of the Communist International, the policy of supporting the breakup of Yugoslavia is abandoned. The Comintern now supports "popular fronts" to represent coalition opposition to fascism, and which would be hindered by the disintegration of Yugoslavia.

1936

March 6 A Serbian representative attempts to assassinate Stojadinović on the Skupština floor but Stojadinović is unhurt. His near martyrdom at the hands of the would-be assassin gives him greater public support and renders him politically stronger.

April The Central Committee or leadership of the CPY announces its opposition to the destruction of Yugoslavia and withdraws its support for a united and independent Macedonia.

September 15 Svetozar Pribićević, the former leader of the Independent Democratic party, dies in exile in Prague where he has lived since early July 1931.

September 26 Stojadinović decrees peasant debts should be repaid at half the actual level and authorizes a repayment period of 12 years at a relatively low interest rate. This move is popular, and results in the strong showing of the government party in the December elections. However, Maček's Peasant party still retains the loyalty of the Croatian regions.

1937

July 23 The YRU pushes through the concordat with the Vatican. The patriarch, the leader of the Orthodox church, dies the same day setting off rumors he has been murdered.

August 8 The Orthodox synod begins excommunication proceedings against those who ratified the concordat with the Vatican.

August 10 Maček announces he has no interest in the concordat, putting the government in the position of supporting a supposed concession to Croatian national feeling which does not matter to Croats.

September 10 At the Yugoslav Radical Union congress, Stojadinović gains tighter control of the party. The party assumes some of the pretensions of the Italian fascists, such as salutes, parades, and attempts to build a mass base. Stojadinović fails to match his models in this regard.

October 2 The Stojadinović government believes Yugoslavia's foreign policy and economic interests might require it to move away from France and toward Nazi Germany and hires the German firm Krupp to convert an old iron works into a steel mill in Zenica, Bosnia. Yugoslavia becomes dependent on the German economic relationship.

October 8 Five parties—the Independent Democrats, the Democrats, the Croatian Peasants, the Serbian Agrarians, and the Radicals—declare that they have formed a coalition designed to see the return of democratic government to Yugoslavia. The declaration elicits a strong popular reaction.

1938

February 1 Stojadinović announces he will not pursue implementation of the concordat with the Vatican. He had hoped it would make him more popular with Croats, but their disinterest gave him his most spectacular political defeat because it deeply wounded Serbian sentiments.

August 15 The Germans increase their pressure on Czechoslovakia which could result in a general war. Maček warns the government no Croats would defend Yugoslavia if it becomes embroiled in a European conflict.

August 23 The Little Entente recognizes Hungary's right to rearm, ending the alliance between Czechoslovakia, Romania, and Yugoslavia.

December 11 New elections are held, in which the YRU gains only 54 percent and the Croatian Peasants 45

percent of the vote. This is a major setback to Stojadinović, who had called the elections thinking that he would be able to consolidate his regime.

1939

January 15 The newly elected Croatian opposition meets in Zagreb and declares itself without responsibility toward the Yugoslav state, which it claims had been formed without its consent.

February 6 The regent, Prince Pavle, removes Stojadinović, replacing him with the minister of public health and social welfare, Dragiša Cvetković, with whom Maček has agreed to negotiate. The German and Italian governments are upset Stojadinović has been removed, but note the profascist Yugoslav ambassador to Germany, Aleksandar Cincar-Marković, has been named minister of foreign affairs.

April 2 Cvetković and Maček begin negotiations on the status of Croatia in Yugoslavia.

April 7 Italy occupies Albania. The Stojadinović government had earlier given secret approval to Italy to move into Albania in return for Italy's agreement to stop supporting the *Ustaša*.

August 26 The *Sporazum* (agreement) of Cvetković and Maček is announced. Croatia becomes its own *banovina* (province) within Yugoslavia; it will enjoy almost complete autonomy, with Belgrade controlling only foreign affairs, foreign trade, defense, transportation, and communications. The banovina encompasses the old Savska and Primorje banovine, with additions from parts of four others. Croatia will have its own *Sabor* (parliament) and a *ban* (governor) who will be appointed by the monarch. Maček and four other Peasant party leaders enter the Cvetković government, and Croat politician Ivan Šubašić is named ban of Croatia. In signing the *Sporazum*, Maček has abandoned many Serbian allies who oppose the dictatorship but he has also realized an old Croatian demand, so his popularity in Croatian areas of Yugoslavia is at its height. Yet, the Sporazum does not satisfy anyone completely. Serbs, Slovenes and others want the same sort of autonomy; the Serbs of the new banovina want guarantees of their civil rights.

1940

May 19 Local elections in Croatia demonstrate the appeal that the Ustaša has among nationalistic Croats.

October 19–23 The Fifth Congress of the Communist Party of Yugoslavia is held in Zagreb, the final congress before the Second World War. Josip Broz (Tito)'s position as head of the party is secured, as are those of the other leaders of the party: Aleksandar Ranković, Edvard Kardelj, and Milovan Djilas. As a result of the Sporazum, the party now demands the right of secession for Macedonians, Montenegrins, Albanians, and other national minorities; it views the Sporazum as a Croato-Serbian bourgeois plot to maintain control of the state.

1941

March 25 Yugoslavia joins the Tripartite Pact, no longer being able to resist the obvious pressure of German power in the Balkans. This military alliance directed against the United States and Great Britain includes Nazi Germany, Italy, Japan, Hungary, Slovakia, and Romania.

March 27 The adherence of Yugoslavia to the Tripartite Pact prompts Serbian officers and politicians to lead a coup against the regent Prince Pavle and the government of Cvetković and Maček. Prince Pavle is exiled, and King Petar II is proclaimed of age to rule. Dušan Simović, one of the leaders of the coup, is the new premier. Many leading Croats, including Maček, accurately interpret the coup as also being directed against the Sporazum, thus their support for the new government is difficult to win. Although Great Britain had a large role in encouraging the coup, the new government agrees to adhere to the Tripartite Pact in an attempt to appease Germany.

April 6 Despite Yugoslavia's continued adherence to the Tripartite Pact, Hitler feels he can no longer trust it so Germany strikes Yugoslavia with air attacks on Belgrade and a land offensive from Bulgaria into Macedonia. Within five days, Axis armies move from Bulgaria, Albania, Italy, Romania, and Hungary into Yugoslavia which is unable to defend itself.

April 10 The Independent State of Croatia, allied to Nazi Germany and with Dr. Ante Pavelić as its leader, is proclaimed by Croatian nationalists. The state is composed of Croatia, minus parts of Dalmatia, but all of Bosnia and Herzegovina. Maček issues a statement calling on Croats to cooperate with the new government and Archbishop Alois Stepinac of Zagreb gives his approval to the new state. From 1941 to 1945, the Ustaša regime of Pavelić institutes a policy of elimination of the Serbian Orthodox minority of Croatia through expulsion, conversion to Roman Catholicism, and extermination. Gypsies, Jews, and Croatian opponents of the regime are also exterminated.

April 12 Belgrade falls to Axis troops.

April 14–16 King Petar II and the royal Yugoslav government go into exile in Athens.

April 15 The CPY announces that it supports the self-determination of the peoples of Yugoslavia and offers them independence in a fraternal union of peoples to be reconstituted after the war.

April 17 German and Yugoslav representatives sign an armistice. Because all of Yugoslavia's official representatives have gone into exile, Aleksandar Cincar-Marković, a former foreign minister, and Radivoje Janković, a deputy chief of staff of the army, sign what many people nationally and internationally consider an invalid armistice.

April 21 The king and government of Yugoslavia arrive in Jerusalem.

April–May Members of the collapsed Yugoslav army band together in northern Bosnia under Colonel Dragoljub (Draža) Mihajlović to resist the Germans. These men, overwhelmingly Serbian, come to be known as Četniks and support the Yugoslav government-in-exile.

April 1941–October 1944 Nazi Germany occupies and administers the remainder of Serbia, first through the Serbian quisling, or collaborator, Milan Aćimović, and later through another quisling, Milan Nedić, the former chief of the Yugoslav general staff and minister of the armed forces.

May Germany, Italy, Albania, Bulgaria, and Hungary partition Yugoslavia while the Communists begin their own resistance to the occupiers.

May 12 The Četniks move to Ravna Gora, Serbia, where they are joined by others wishing to resist the Germans.

June 22 Germany invades the Soviet Union. The Communist Party of Yugoslavia meets and appoints Tito commander in chief of the Communist military forces, or Partisans. The Communists call for a popular uprising against the German invaders of Yugoslavia.

June 26 British Prime Minister Winston Churchill receives Premier Dušan Simović of the Yugoslav government-in-exile in London, thereby giving him de facto recognition.

July 4 The Communist Party of Yugoslavia again calls upon its members to resist the Germans and Italians after Germany invaded the Soviet Union in June.

July 13 An uprising in Montenegro ruins Italian plans for a puppet Montenegrin state. Montenegro will provide a high percentage of both Partisan and Četnik soldiers.

August 25 The CPY establishes a regional committee for Macedonia headed by Lazar Koliševski. The Yugoslav Communists stake out Macedonia as Yugoslav territory, although Bulgaria's Communists also have a stated interest in the region.

August 26 At its base in Serbia, the CPY establishes military commands for each region of Yugoslavia.

August 29 The quisling regime of Milan Nedić is officially installed in Serbia.

September 16 The German army orders that for every German soldier killed, one hundred Yugoslav hostages will be killed; for every wounded German, fifty hostages will be killed. This order leads directly to a confrontation between the Partisans, who do not allow the threat to limit their activity, and the Četniks, who fear the great loss in Serbian lives their activity may provoke.

September 19 The leaders of the Partisans and Četniks, Tito and Mihajlović, meet near Ravna Gora and agree to coordinate their resistance movements, although they realize that their methods and goals are completely at odds.

September 20 The Slovene Liberation Front announces it proposes to join the other peoples of Yugoslavia in a reconstituted state after the war on the basis of equality of nations.

September 26 The Central Committee of the Communist party meets in Stolice and establishes guidelines for the organization of Partisan military units, which have in fact been operating for several months. The Partisans adopt the five-pointed red star and the clenched fist as their symbols.

October The British military establishes a mission at the Mihajlović Četnik headquarters. Mihajlović's army is recognized by the Allies as the "true" resistance in Yugoslavia. Sporadic cooperation between the Četniks and the Partisans continues, but tension grows over whether to make the resistance active, as the Partisans wish, or to maintain their inactivity until the Allies give the signal for an uprising, as the Četniks want.

October 21 The German army massacres 7,000 men and boys in Kragujevac, Serbia, in retaliation for an attack on German soldiers. The Germans could not find enough adult male hostages to fill the quota, so schoolboys and their teachers were also executed.

October 27 Tito and Mihajlović meet again, but the idea of cooperation between the Partisans and the Četniks is dead.

November 1–2 Due to the failed talks of October 27, the Četniks attack the Partisans in Užice. The Četniks and

forces from Nedić's Serbia participate in the first Axis offensive against the Partisans, who are forced from their base in Serbia and move to the Sandžak and eastern Bosnia. The resistance to the Germans and Italians is no longer unified.

December 21 The Partisans establish their First Proletarian National Liberation Brigade. By November 1942, they will have 28 proletarian and shock brigades organized in the National Liberation Army of Yugoslavia.

December 24 The Partisan leader Tito reaches Rogatica, in eastern Bosnia, following the German offensive.

1942

January 11 The Četnik Mihajlović is appointed minister of the army, navy, and air force by the Yugoslav government-in-exile, now headed by the Serbian philosopher and historian Slobodan Jovanović.

January–February The second Axis offensive fails to encircle the Partisans, but does drive them south into Montenegro and Herzegovina. The Partisans begin to use terror tactics against their adversaries, which loses them support among the civilian population due to German retaliation.

February The Communist leadership orders the formation of national liberation committees to operate as parallel political apparatus to the Partisan proletarian brigades.

March 31 The third Axis offensive against the Partisans begins. It fails to destroy the Partisans, but does drive them into northwestern Bosnia where other guerrilla forces are fighting the occupying Italians.

June 24 The Partisans begin a march north after the third Axis offensive.

November 5 The Partisans reach Bihać in northwestern Bosnia.

November 26–27 The first meeting of the Antifascist Council of the National Liberation of Yugoslavia meets in Bihać, where the Partisans have set up their headquarters. Fifty-four representatives attend, but representatives from Macedonia and Slovenia cannot due to the war. AVNOJ, after the Serbo-Croatian title of the organization, is the main political body in the national liberation movement in Yugoslavia; it is dominated by the Communist party.

December 6–8 Various Partisan women's organizations form the Antifascist Front of the Women of Yugoslavia in Bosanski Petrovac. This component of the Partisan forces is of great military and organizational value during the war.

1943

January 20   The Axis forces begin Operation Weiss, a powerful sweeping attack of German, Italian, Četnik, and Ustaša forces driving the Partisans south again into southern Bosnia.

March   The Partisans are encircled by the Germans, Italians, and Četniks in a battle near the mouth of the Neretva river in Herzegovina, but escape with all of their accumulated wounded.

May 13   Mihajlović arrives near Čačak, Serbia, after narrowly escaping the Germans, who are no longer cooperating with the Četniks. Over the next year, he will constantly move around southern Serbia, avoiding the Germans but not fighting.

May 15   Operation Schwarz, the fifth and final Axis offensive against the Partisans, begins. Germans, Italians, and Bulgarians join the offensive but the Partisans again escape. The Partisans mount their own offensive into northeastern Bosnia and then move west.

May 18   Realizing the Partisans are a valuable tool against the Germans, the British government establishes a mission to the Partisan headquarters in Croatia.

May 28   F. W. Deakin and W. F. Stuart of the British army parachute into Montenegro and join Tito during the fifth Axis offensive. From this point, the Allies consider the Partisans a valuable resistance force, worth supporting. The reputation of the Četniks begins to suffer as the Allies realize the Četniks are not fighting the Axis enemy.

June 9   W. F. Stuart is killed in battle by the Germans, convincing Deakin the Partisans are indeed engaged in operations against the Germans.

June 10   In a dramatic escape, the Partisans cross the Sutjeska river after being pursued by Operation Schwarz; the crossing becomes one of the legends of Partisan mythology.

June 13–14   The Provincial Antifascist Council for Croatia (ZAVNOH), the Croatian branch of AVNOJ, meets in Otočac where it supports the formation of a unified Yugoslavia.

June 23   On the evidence provided by Captain F. W. Deakin, the British government changes its policy regarding the Partisans and authorizes air drops of supplies.

June 26   A new government-in-exile is formed by King Petar II in London with Serb politician Miša Trifunović as premier.

July 21   The Germans offer 100,000 marks each for the capture of Tito and Mihajlović.

August 10   Trifunović resigns as premier and a new government-in-exile, headed by Serb politician Božidar Purić, is appointed by King Petar II. The British government, however, expresses no opposition to the reappointment of Mihajlović as minister of the military.

September 9   With the collapse of Italy, the Partisans help disarm the Italian forces in Yugoslavia. The British begin a policy of giving equal aid to the Partisans and the Četniks. The Partisan forces become stronger, swelled by Italian munitions and new recruits.

November 29–30   The second session of AVNOJ meets in Jajce, central Bosnia. AVNOJ declares itself the government of Yugoslavia and the maintainer of Yugoslav sovereignty; it declares the claims of the government-in-exile to represent Yugoslavia at home and abroad null and void; it prohibits King Petar II from returning to Yugoslavia; and proclaims a renewed Yugoslav state organized as a federal state of equal nations.

December 1   Winston Churchill, U.S. president Franklin D. Roosevelt, and Joseph Stalin of the Soviet Union agree the Partisans will be given all possible aid in their struggle against the Axis powers.

1944

January   The Allies begin to cut off aid to the Četniks after the latter refuse to follow British orders without an Allied guarantee they would land in the Balkans. The Partisans now become the only viable resistance force in Yugoslavia.

January 25–28   Mihajlović hosts a congress of representatives of the anti-Communist resistance in Ba, Serbia, which calls for the creation of a federated Yugoslav state in an attempt to challenge the Partisan decisions at Jajce. The attempt fails as the Communists have the initiative (*see* November 29–30, 1943).

February   The British decide to withdraw their liaison officers from Mihajlović's headquarters.

February 23   A Soviet military and political mission joins the Partisans.

April 16   The United States bombs Belgrade, which is under Axis control.

May 24 The pro-Četnik government-in-exile of Božider Purić is dismissed by King Petar II.

May 25 The Germans launch an airborne attack on the Partisan headquarters in Drvar; the attack fails, barely.

June 1 A less pro-Četnik and a more moderate government-in-exile under Ivan Šubašić takes over. Hopes for a fusion of the government-in-exile and the AVNOJ government grow. Šubašić, and not Mihajlović, is named minister for the military; Mihajlović, however, remains the head of the supreme command of the Yugoslav army in occupied Yugoslavia.

June 3 Tito is evacuated to Bari, Italy, where he meets with Allied commanders.

June 8 Tito arrives on Vis, an island in the Adriatic Sea, where the Partisan headquarters had been moved after the unsuccessful German raid of May 25.

June 16 Tito and Šubašić sign the first agreement between the government-in-exile and the Partisans.

August 2 The Communist Party of Macedonia, which replaces the regional committee, holds the first meeting of its Antifascist Council for the National Liberation of Macedonia (ASNOM), which proclaims a Macedonian people's republic inside Yugoslavia.

August 12 Tito meets with the Supreme Allied Commander in the Mediterranean, General Henry M. W. Wilson, and Winston Churchill. Tito expresses his opposition to Allied plans to leave the fate of Istria to the peace conference following the war; he wishes it to be unconditionally annexed by Yugoslavia.

August 29 Realizing that the Četniks have no Allied support, King Petar II signs a declaration dissolving the supreme command of the army in Yugoslavia, thereby abandoning Mihajlović.

September 6 The Soviet Red Army reaches the Yugoslav border with Bulgaria.

September 12 King Petar II orders all Četniks to leave Mihajlović and join the Partisans. Remaining Mihajlović loyalists flee to northeastern Bosnia, where they are joined by the Montenegrin Četniks of Pavle Djurišić.

September 21 Tito leaves Vis for the Soviet Union to the surprise and alarm of the British.

September 22–26 Tito meets with Joseph Stalin in Moscow and agrees to allow the Soviet Army to enter Yugoslav territory as long as it is pursuing German troops.

October 1 The Soviet Army enters Yugoslavia.

October 15 Soviet and Partisan troops liberate Niš.

October 20 Soviet and Partisan troops liberate Belgrade.

October 23 Šubašić, the premier of the government-in-exile, arrives in Vršac, Yugoslavia, to discuss cooperative arrangements with Tito for the future of the country after the war.

November 1 Tito and Šubašić sign a final agreement, conditional on the approval of King Petar II. This agreement names AVNOJ the supreme legislative body for Yugoslavia. A united government of 18 members would be formed (12 would be from AVNOJ, six from the royal government in London). Yugoslavia would stay a monarchy, with the king remaining abroad and being represented in Yugoslavia by a regency until elections could be held to determine the type of government of the country.

November 22 In Moscow, Stalin meets with Partisan leader Edvard Kardelj and Šubašić to discuss the Tito-Šubašić agreement and the British government's fear that Tito is attempting to establish a Communist government. Stalin warns Kardelj and reassures the pro-West Šubašić that the Partisans have been moving too fast. Stalin also presses the Yugoslavs to form a federation with Bulgaria. Tito, who had been invited by Stalin to the meeting, refuses to attend. He realized Stalin intended to criticize the Partisans, so he sent Kardelj in his place.

December The Partisan-Yugoslav army begins operations to put down an uprising of Albanians in Drenica allied to the Balli Kombetar, an Albanian nationalist resistance group wishing Kosovo be joined to Albania. The operation lasts until mid-1945.

In Sofia, Bulgaria, discussions regarding the possible federation of Yugoslavia and Bulgaria are held between Kardelj and Traicho Kostov of the Bulgarian Communist party. Kostov does not like the plan, which would involve the cession of Bulgarian (Pirin) Macedonia to Yugoslavia. Nonetheless, a council is established in Belgrade to consider the plan further.

December 29 King Petar II expresses his dissatisfaction with the Tito-Šubašić agreement which keeps him from returning to Yugoslavia, but is unsuccessful in convincing the British to support him.

1945

January In Moscow, Bulgarian and Yugoslav Communist representatives meet with Stalin who urges a federation between the two states. The Yugoslavs want to add Bulgaria as a seventh republic, or at least unite Pirin (Bulgarian) and Vardar (Yugoslav) Macedonia within Yugoslavia. The Bulgarians favor a plan for a simple federa-

As commander in chief of the Communist forces in Yugoslavia, Marshall Tito conducts his campaigns against Nazi invaders from his secret mountain retreat; Tito is pictured at far right with members of his staff.

tion in which Bulgaria and Yugoslavia would be equal partners.

January 11 Despite unsuccessful attempts to gain British support to overturn the Tito-Šubašić agreements in late December 1944, King Petar II rejects them.

February 4–11 Churchill, Roosevelt, and Stalin meet at Yalta, where they declare AVNOJ should be enlarged to include representatives of other parties who had not collaborated with the Axis powers. They also declare a constituent assembly should ratify all acts passed by AVNOJ, and urge the Yugoslavs to implement the Tito-Šubašić agreement.

March 3 Realizing he can no longer ignore the Tito-Šubašić agreement, King Petar II appoints three regents to govern in his absence from Yugoslavia.

March 7 A unified provisional government is formed with Šubašić as foreign minister. Two other non-Communists are also included, but their influence within the government is small due to their numbers. Tito becomes prime minister.

April 6 The Partisans liberate Sarajevo.

April 11 The Yugoslav government signs a 20-year treaty of friendship and mutual aid with the Soviet Union.

April 12 The German/Croatian defenses collapse along the Sava river, and the liberation of Croatia and Slovenia begins.

April 25 The Partisans take the coastal city of Rijeka.

May 1 The Yugoslav army enters the port of Trieste two days before the Allies, who have decreed it an Allied occupation zone.

May 4 The government of the Independent State of Croatia flees Zagreb followed two days later by its leader, Ante Pavelić.

May 8 The German army unconditionally surrenders to the Allies, officially ending the European theater of the Second World War.

The Partisans liberate Zagreb.

May 15 The final German and Ustaša troops give themselves up to the Partisans after the British refuse to

An exiled King Petar and Queen Alexandra in Cannes.

accept their surrender. These and all members of the anti-Communist resistance (Četniks, Slovenian White Guards, Croatian Home Guards, and German Volksdeutsche) will be executed.

June 9   The Yugoslavs agree to allow the Allies to maintain the Allied occupation of Trieste, Pula, and the strip of coastline connecting these cities to Italy. The Yugoslavs maintain control of the remainder of Istria. Both sides agree the current disposition of forces will not compromise a future agreement on the possession of Istria and Trieste.

November 29   The Federal People's Republic of Yugoslavia (FPRY) is proclaimed by the Constituent Assembly, ending any hopes that the largely ignored Tito-Šubašić agreement would be put into effect. The Karađorđević dynasty is banished and the monarchy is abolished.

1946

January 31   The constitution of the FPRY is promulgated. The state will be governed according to the principle of "democratic centralism" based on the Marxist principle

of the "dictatorship of the proletariat" as practiced in the name of the working class by the CPY, and consists of the People's Republics of Slovenia, Croatia, Serbia, Bosnia and Herzegovina, Montenegro, and Macedonia. The autonomous province of Vojvodina and autonomous region of Kosovo are parts of the People's Republic of Serbia. The constitution is modelled on the Soviet constitution of 1936.

March 13   The Yugoslav government captures Dragoljub Mihajlović, the leader of the Četnik forces during the Second World War.

April 19   The United States formally recognizes Yugoslavia on the condition that the new government respect the international obligations of the interwar regime.

The politburo (executive committee) of the CPY decides Andrija Hebrang, a Croatian Communist who had been in control of the partisan political effort in Croatia, is out of line in his criticism of Tito; Hebrang had accused Tito of letting personal animosity get in the way of their official relationship. The real issue is Hebrang opposes some of the centralizing measures of the Communist party in the new Yugoslavia, and the party feels it must eliminate his voice. Hebrang is removed from his posts by 1947. In 1948, Tito accuses him of being loyal to Stalin when the Cominform, an information and propaganda service controlled by the Soviets, expels Yugoslavia.

June 10   Mihajlović's trial begins on charges of treason.

July 15   Mihajlović is executed after being found guilty.

August 19   Two American transport aircraft are shot down by the Yugoslav Air Force over Slovenia. Yugoslavia argues American planes had been regularly infringing on the sovereignty of the Yugoslav state, but apologizes for the loss of American lives.

October 11   In an attack on the power of the Roman Catholic church in Yugoslavia, Alois Stepinac, the Archbishop of Zagreb, is sentenced to 16 years of hard labor for collaborating with Germany and the Independent State of Croatia during the war.

December   The first nationalization law is passed, which calls for the nationalization of industries of national importance, banking, and transportation.

1947

February 10   Yugoslavia signs a peace treaty with Italy, Hungary, and Bulgaria in Paris. Yugoslavia gains control of the entire Dalmatian coast and the majority of Istria. The Free Territory of Trieste is established under United Nations control against the wishes of Yugoslavia.

April 28   The first Five-Year Plan for industry is implemented along the lines of the Soviet model.

August   Tito is visited by Georgi Dimitrov, the secretary of the Bulgarian Communist party, at Bled, Slovenia. They sign the Bled Agreement, which allows for a customs union between the two countries. Further, they discuss the possible union of Bulgaria and Yugoslavia, which would gradually take place. Tito presses the plan, while Dimitrov resists it.

September 9   The Communist Information Bureau (Cominform), an information and propaganda service, is formed in Poland. Edvard Kardelj and Milovan Djilas, two of the four leading Communists of Yugoslavia, are particularly aggressive in attacking any lack of support on the part of Western Communists for the Soviet Union and its policies. The seat of the Cominform will be Belgrade.

1948

January   Dimitrov of Bulgaria suggests a wider federation of Balkan states to include Romania, Greece, and possibly other states. Stalin is not pleased at this suggestion, which would imply a power base outside of the Soviet Union.

Djilas, in Moscow for one of his ''Conversations with Stalin,'' is told by the Soviet dictator that Yugoslavia should ''swallow'' Albania.

February 10   Stalin orders Yugoslavia to immediately form a federation with Bulgaria. The Yugoslav regime resists this suggestion, feeling that it is merely meant as a wedge to drive the Yugoslavs and Bulgarians apart. Stalin orders Kardelj to sign an agreement binding Yugoslavia to consult with the Soviet Union on all foreign policy issues. Further, Stalin accuses the Yugoslavs of pursuing an independent foreign policy, using as evidence the Bled Agreement with Bulgaria, about which the Soviet Union was not consulted.

March 1   The Central Committee of the Communist Party of Yugoslavia rejects Stalin's virtual ultimatum from February 10.

March 18   The Soviet Union recalls its military advisors from Yugoslavia; Tito protests this decision to Stalin.

March 27   The Soviet Union accuses the Yugoslav communists of ideological deviations and unbrotherly feelings toward the Soviet regime.

April   Industries not included in the nationalization law of December 1946 now are nationalized.

The first of three ''Dachau'' trials is held in Ljubljana. Thirty-seven Communists who had been interned at the Nazi concentration camp of Dachau are accused of having become Gestapo agents and tried for treason. The other two trials will be held in Ljubljana in August, 1948, and in Split in July, 1949. All of the accused confess; 11 are executed. It is widely accepted that the Dachau trials are show trials to purge the opposition. The convicted and the dead are rehabilitated, or exonerated of all crimes, in 1970–71 by the Communist party.

April 12–13   The Central Committee of the Yugoslav Communist party denies the Soviet accusations from March 27. Two committee members, Andrija Hebrang and Sreten Žujović, are accused by Tito of being ''Cominformists,'' meaning they are loyal to Stalin. Hebrang is a Croatian ''national'' Communist and Žujović a Serbian centralist and they have little in common, but their cases will come to symbolize the reaction against any who shows loyalty to Stalin. In fact, the accusation of disloyalty to Yugoslavia will often be used to purge members of the party that the leadership fears.

May 4   The Yugoslav response of April 13 draws an angry reply from the Soviet Union, in which Stalin and Soviet Foreign Minister Vyacheslav M. Molotov reassert their accusations of March 27 and add that the Yugoslav Partisans were not very effective as a resistance force against the Germans. Additionally, Stalin denies that Hebrang and Žujović ever betrayed the CPY to the Soviet Union.

May 9   At a meeting of the Central Committee of the CPY, Hebrang and Žujović are removed from the committee and the party.

June 28   The Yugoslav Communist party is expelled from the Cominform at a meeting in Bucharest. It is accused of nationalism, Trotskyist deviations (a label applied to those who do not follow Joseph Stalin's directives), and hostility toward the Soviet Union. The expulsion of Yugoslavia from the Cominform is often attributed to either (1) ideological differences between the Yugoslavs and the rest of the Communist bloc, (2) Yugoslav unwillingness to be under the control of the Soviet Union, or (3) Yugoslav ''pride,'' the Yugoslavian inability to recognize that the Soviet Union and Stalin demanded and deserved recognition as the first socialist state and leader. In fact, the Tito-Stalin split is a result of Tito's very independent foreign policy in the Balkans. Yugoslavia has attempted to follow an independent foreign policy in several arenas: Albania, Greece, Bulgaria, and Istria. Before the Second World War was over, Yugoslavia had already exhibited its independence by moving much faster than Stalin advised toward the imposition of a Communist regime in Yugoslavia. Stalin rejected Yugoslav independence for two reasons: it made his dealings with the British and Americans difficult due to the fragmentation of the Communist bloc, and he simply would not accept the creation of a sovereign state within the Communist bloc.

July 21–28 Tito reads the Cominform resolution at the Fifth Congress of the Communist Party of Yugoslavia and makes clear the party's rejection of the charges. A cold war between Yugoslavia and the Soviet Union and its Eastern European allies begins.

November Asserting its independence, Yugoslavia joins the European Coal and Steel Community.

1949

January At the Second Plenum of the Central Committee, the Communist leadership decides to work harder to implement the Five Year Plan; the party is attempting to out-Stalin the Soviets, hoping to impress them with their diligence. Collectivization of agriculture continues, in spite of agricultural experts advising against doing so.

July 27 In a move to draw it closer to the West, Yugoslavia closes its border with Greece and halts its aid to the Greek Communists who are fighting the British- and American-backed government in Athens.

September The United States loans Yugoslavia $620 million. This is the beginning of a relationship based solely on realism: the Yugoslavs need support from abroad against the Soviet Union, and the United States is happy to aid Yugoslavia in the interests of dividing the Soviet bloc.

September 28 The Soviet Union rejects the treaty of friendship that it had signed with Yugoslavia in April 1945. The governments of Poland, Hungary, Bulgaria, Romania, and Czechoslovakia do likewise with their agreements with Yugoslavia.

October Yugoslavia is elected to a seat on the United Nations Security Council.

December 23 The trade unions and the economic council of the federal government sign an agreement called the "Recommendation on the Founding and Work of Workers' Councils in State Economic Enterprises," which is the first step in formulating the idea of workers' self-management, the basis of Yugoslavia's claim of following a separate path to socialism.

1950

January The government retreats from collectivization of agriculture due to failures caused by peasant resistance (*see* July 27, 1949).

June 27 The Basic Law on the Management of State Economic Enterprises and Higher Economic Associations by the Working Collectives is passed by the national parliament, thereby establishing the basis of self-management. Self-management is part of the Yugoslav answer to the dilemma posed by the split with the Cominform: how can Yugoslavia justify its separation and independence within the Communist movement? The answer, formulated by Kardelj and Djilas with Tito's ultimate enthusiasm, is to address the relationship of the worker to his enterprise and the state. The Basic Law allows for workers' councils in enterprises. The councils will make decisions affecting the disposition of the income of the enterprise in which they work and the day-to-day management decisions in the enterprise. Self-management is envisioned as one Marxist approach to the state governed by the worker.

September Kardelj, representing Yugoslavia on the United Nations Security Council, opposes North Korea's aggression in South Korea and backs United Nations intervention there.

November 29 President Harry S Truman sends a letter to Congress in support of relief to Yugoslavia. He couches this letter in terms of realpolitik, or political, realism by not mentioning ideological differences between the two countries.

1951

January 6 The United States and Yugoslavia sign an agreement on aid to Yugoslavia.

November 14 The governments of Yugoslavia and the United States sign an agreement whereby the United States will provide Yugoslavia with military assistance. This is accomplished because of the threat the Soviet Union and its satellites are posing to the territorial integrity of Yugoslavia.

1952

November 7 At the Sixth Congress of the Communist Party of Yugoslavia, the name of the party is changed to the League of Communists of Yugoslavia (LCY). This cosmetic change implies a less dominant and threatening posture for the party. The congress opens the way for more openness within the party and Yugoslav society, a development that Tito will regret the rest of his life.

1953

January 13 The Yugoslav parliament adopts amendments to the 1946 constitution. These amendments, made in the spirit of self-management, envision the decentralization of decision making, and giving more power to the local communes over local economic, social, and political developments. At the federal level, a new structure is adopted: there will be a Federal Assembly, with two houses: the Federal Council and the Council of Producers. The Federal Council will be elected by delegates of the local workers' councils, and the Federal Executive Council will be elected by the Federal Assembly and operate as the government of the country. Tito is made the President of the Republic, a position abolished upon his death in 1980.

February 28 Yugoslavia, Turkey, and Greece sign a treaty of friendship and cooperation.

March 5 The Soviet leader Joseph Stalin dies, leading to an eventual easing of tensions between the Soviet Union and Yugoslavia.

March 29 Due to failures, collective farms are decreed to be voluntary. Peasants are allowed to leave them and return to their individual farms; cooperatives can be abolished by a majority vote of their members.

June At the Second Plenum of the LCY on the island of Brijuni, Tito complains the results of the Sixth Congress have not been positive; the party has not remembered its active role in the ongoing struggle for socialism, and the membership has become complacent.

October Milovan Djilas begins publishing articles in the Belgrade government daily *Borba* (Struggle) attacking the bureaucratization of the party and Yugoslav society. He hopes to spur the more rapid development of democratic socialism in the country. His sensibilities lead him eventually to propose that the development of the individual human spirit is more important than the achievement of communism.

December Djilas' *Borba* articles begin to attack the organization of the party, its Leninist and Stalinist attributes, and the general rigidity of the Communist experiment in Yugoslavia. His colleagues in the party elite are nervous.

1954

January 4 Djilas publishes an article calling for the immediate withering away of the party, which is unacceptable to his colleagues. In a subsequent article published in *Nova Misao* (New Thought), Djilas attacks the wives of the party leaders for their pretensions, which he believes in appropriate in a party of the revolution.

January 10 Acknowledging an easing in tensions between the two countries since the death of the Soviet dictator Joseph Stalin in March 1953, Yugoslavia and the Soviet Union exchange ambassadors.

Under orders from the government, *Borba* disowns Djilas and his views, which many had assumed came from the top government leadership. The newspaper also announces Djilas' writings will be considered by a party plenum, or a general meeting of the leadership, in the next week.

January 16–17 The Third Plenum meets at Brijuni and the party leadership denounces Djilas and his views. Djilas is stripped of his party and state offices and functions. Three months later he resigns from the party. Any threat the party might disappear and the state wither away have now been put to rest. Djilas will write numerous short stories, essays, and novels, but his memoirs and his studies of communism win him the most praise abroad and time in jail at home.

August 9 Yugoslavia, Greece, and Turkey sign the Balkan Pact, a military alliance strengthening the treaty of friendship and cooperation of February 1953.

October 1 The Soviet Union and Yugoslavia sign a limited trade agreement that further attempts to end the quarrel between the two countries that has been going on since 1948.

October 6 The Yugoslav and Italian governments negotiate an end to the crisis over Trieste. The Italians get the city itself, while Yugoslavia retains the outlying areas and the right to use the port.

December Serbian and Croatian cultural associations, including the two most important organizations for the Serbs and Croats, the Matica Srpska and the Matica Hrvatska, sign the Novi Sad Agreement for the production of a definitive Serbo-Croatian (or Croato-Serbian) dictionary for the entire country. The agreement authorizes experts from all sides of the issue to develop a single, generally-accepted orthography for the language, which will be known as Serbo-Croatian and/or Croato-Serbian.

December 26 Tito goes to India and meets with Indian Prime Minister Jawaharlal Nehru (*see* April 1955).

1955

January   After being arrested in late 1954 Djilas is tried for anti-state activities; he is sentenced to 18 months in jail; the sentence is suspended and he is placed on probation.

January 25   Tito visits Burma (*see* April 1955).

April   The Bandung Conference is held in Burma. This conference, coming on the heels of Tito's visits to Burma and India, convinces him and other leaders of nonaligned states of the potential power of a united movement of states independent of the Soviet or Western blocs in world politics. The nonaligned movement will emerge from Tito's contacts with leaders of countries, mostly from the underdeveloped world, which are not aligned with either the United States or the Soviet Union. Tito will become one of the three leaders of the movement along with Gamal Abdel Nasser of Egypt and Nehru of India. Tito will log hundreds of thousands of miles travelling around the world in the interests of the movement. The nonaligned movement will thrive during the 1960s, and although in theory it is not in either the East bloc or the West, it will often tilt toward the Communist world.

May 14   The Soviet Union announces its leaders Nikita Khrushchev and Nikolai Bulganin will visit Belgrade starting on May 26, surprising most observers.

The Warsaw Pact Treaty is signed by the USSR, Albania, Bulgaria, Czechoslovakia, Hungary, Poland and Romania. It is a military alliance designed to counter the existence of the North Atlantic Treaty Organization (NATO) of the West; Yugoslavia will not join either alliance.

May 15   The Soviet Union signs the Austrian State Treaty, ending the Allied occupation of Austria and establishing its neutrality to which the government of Yugoslavia adheres because the treaty guarantees minority rights for Austria's Slovene and Croat populations.

May 26   Soviet leaders Khrushchev and Bulganin arrive in Belgrade. Tito grudgingly accepts the apologies of the Soviet Union for its role in the ostracism of Yugoslavia in 1948. The visit is a propaganda coup for Tito because the Soviets came first to Yugoslavia.

June 2   Bulganin and Tito sign the Belgrade Declaration, which outlines the rapprochement of the states they represent. The Belgrade Declaration is considered a recognition of Yugoslavia's "separate road to socialism." The declaration makes no mention of party relations, only the normalization of the relations between the states.

1956

February 25   In his secret speech to the Twentieth Congress of the Soviet Communist party, Khrushchev reveals that Stalin thought he could simply "shake [his] little finger and Tito would be no more." This indicates that Stalin misjudged the strength of Tito's regime and expected the Yugoslav Communists to follow completely orders from Moscow.

April 17   As part of the reconciliation between the Soviet Union and Yugoslavia, the Cominform is dissolved.

June 1–20   Tito goes to Moscow, where he returns the Khrushchev/Bulganin visit to Belgrade the previous year.

June 20   Tito and Khrushchev sign the Moscow Declaration, which normalizes party relations and again affirms Yugoslavia's separate road to socialism.

July 16   The United States suspends aid to Yugoslavia as a result of the improvement of relations between Yugoslavia and the Soviet Union.

July 19   Tito, Nehru, and Nasser meet on the island of Brijuni and issue a declaration deploring the existence of two blocs in world politics.

September   Khrushchev meets with Tito on Brijuni to discuss the burgeoning move toward liberalization in Hungary and to get Tito's approval for the new Hungarian leadership of Erno Gero. Tito, however, argues unsuccessfully for the installment of Imre Nagy as the new Hungarian leader (*see* Hungary, July 1956). Tito goes to Yalta to meet the Hungarians where Khrushchev seems to accord Tito a special role in the Danubian region of Europe.

October 24   The Soviet garrisons in Hungary intervene when demonstrations favoring liberalization of Hungarian politics and society threaten Soviet influence in the country. Tito condemns this invasion as unnecessary, and says it is the Soviet Union's fault for supporting the Hungarian Stalinists and for picking a bad leader in Erno Gero. He also says the invasion is turning a progressive movement into a counterrevolution.

November   Milovan Djilas writes an article in the British press supporting the Hungarian revolutionaries, after which he is arrested again.

November 4   When the new Hungarian government of Imre Nagy and Janos Kadar is unable to stifle the movement that led to the actions of the Soviet army in October, the Soviets invade again and forcefully crush the revolution.

Tito, sympathetic to Nagy's strong national Communist leanings, offers him refuge in the Yugoslav embassy. Fearing retribution from the Soviets, Nagy accepts. He is seized by the Soviets when he leaves the Yugoslav embassy on a safe conduct pass on November 14, and is eventually executed.

November 11 In a speech in Pula, Tito reveals his opposition to the first Soviet invasion of Hungary on October 24; however, he believes that the second invasion on November 4 was necessary because the first opened the door to counterrevolution in the country. He is in an uncomfortable position because he had advised Khrushchev on the Hungarian situation. Additionally, there is much sympathy for Hungary in Yugoslavia.

December 12 Djilas is sentenced to three years in prison for his article in November supporting the Hungarian revolution and his interview with the French press denouncing the invasion of Hungary.

1957

February The Soviet Union cancels economic credits to Yugoslavia in retaliation for its "unfavorable" attitude toward the invasion of Hungary.

March 9 Due to the renewed tensions between Yugoslavia and the Soviet Union, the United States resumes limited aid to Yugoslavia, again isolated from the Soviet Union due to its behavior following the Soviet invasion of Hungary (*see* July 16, 1956).

August Tito and Khrushchev meet secretly in Bucharest to work out their differences, but they do not succeed. The effects of Tito's response to the Hungarian revolution will continue to be felt for some time in the icy relationship between Yugoslavia and the USSR.

A smuggled manuscript of *The New Class*, by Milovan Djilas, is published in the United States; Djilas, who is already in prison, gets six more years (*see* December 12, 1956).

November Tito refuses to attend the fortieth anniversary of the October Bolshevik, or Communist, Revolution in Moscow when he is told he will have to sign a document condemning revisionism as the greatest threat to the Communist movement. The Yugoslav leaders Kardelj and Aleksandar Ranković go to Moscow, but refuse to sign the document. These actions prompt another cold war period between Yugoslavia and the rest of the Soviet bloc.

1958

April 26 At the Seventh Congress of the LCY, a new program declares Yugoslavia is heading toward socialism down a different path than other socialist states. During the Congress, Tito praises the relations of the nonaligned states and downplays the renewed split with the Soviet Union. He says that relations between Communist states should be regulated by agreements such as the Belgrade Declaration of 1955 and not the Moscow Declaration of 1956, thus emphasizing their relationships as states not as parties.

1961

September 6 Fifty-one nonaligned states meet in Belgrade under the leadership of Tito. They denounce colonialism, condemn apartheid, and demand the ending of all armed action against dependent peoples.

November 1 Ivo Andrić, a Bosnian Serb writer, receives the Nobel Prize for literature.

1962

April 7 After being released in 1961, Milovan Djilas is arrested again because of his new book, *Conversations with Stalin*; on May 14 he is sentenced to over eight years in prison (*see* August 1957).

1963

April 7 A new Constitution is promulgated by the national parliament for Yugoslavia. The leadership acknowledges it is a transitional document and an attempt to demonstrate and regulate the workings of a society in which self-management is the guide. It is, according to Kardelj, an attempt to apply the lessons learned from workers' self-management during the past decade. The constitution divides the Federal Assembly, or national parliament, into five chambers. Election is indirect, by local assemblies. The unexpected result of this constitution's implementation is that political and economic debate is made easier, more open, and often confrontational.

August Khrushchev arrives in Belgrade on an official visit. The visit is seen as an attempt to eradicate the criticism Khrushchev has suffered in light of his recent relations with Communist China.

1964

September The first issue of the Zagreb magazine *Praxis* appears. The young philosophers behind its publication build a reputation as Marxist critics of the Communist system in Yugoslavia and throughout the world. Their orientation is intensely critical and characterized as "socialist humanist."

December 7–13 The Eighth Congress of the LCY meets in Belgrade. This meeting is the harbinger of decentralizing economic and political reform in Yugoslavia. The early 1960s have been a time of stagnation in the economy, and as a result demands will be made to rectify the imbalance between northwest and southeast. Croats and Slovenes complain that they are being exploited by the underdeveloped republics, which fear the end of strong centralization may mean they will be left further behind economically. The developed republics do not believe central planning is effective for their further development.

Nikita Khrushchev of the Soviet Union and President Tito in Belgrade. Tito, responsible for Yugoslavia's independence from the Soviet Union, is viewed by Soviet Communist leaders as a threat to the Soviet Communist bloc.

This congress marks the ascendancy of "liberals," including Vladimir Bakarić, who favor more decentralized decision-making in the economy.

1965

January The first international edition of *Praxis* appears, with articles in French, English, and German.

July 24 Mihajlo Mihajlov, a young Serbian academic, presents a proposal for an opposition journal to criticize the precepts of Yugoslav communism from within Yugoslavia. Mihajlov believes such a journal could only be positive for Yugoslavia, which he feels is headed toward a more pluralistic system. The authorities disagree, and Mihajlov is jailed for anti-state activity.

The reformists of the Eighth Congress emerge with several victories: economic decision-making will be moved from the federal government to the republics; the goal of economic self-sufficiency for each republic will be abandoned; and banking will be concentrated in the republics rather than in the federal government. More freedom is granted to the market, and decision-making is decentralized. Resistance to the reforms emanates from Aleksandar Ranković, Tito's vice president and the head of the state security service, and from other centralizing Serbs. This date will denote the beginning of real reform in Yugoslavia; all aspects of the social, political, and economic life of Yugoslavs will eventually be questioned.

1966

February 25 The Third Plenum of the LCY meets; Tito grants his approval of the reforms, and sends the delegates to discuss them with their home bases.

March 11 At a reconvening of the Third Plenum, those who opposed reform (Ranković and his supporters, all from Serbia) are forced to declare they favor the reforms and to attack the rise of Serbian nationalism in party relations and state decision-making. This plenum marks the victory of the reforms and the end of Ranković's notable prestige in the party.

July 1 At the Fourth Plenum of the LCY on Brijuni, Ranković is removed from his posts as vice president of the state and head of the state security service. He had established too much power through his leadership of the security service in Yugoslavia. Only Tito and Kardelj remain of the original four Partisan leaders that included Ranković and Djilas. Ranković's removal is necessary because the party wishes to lessen the influence of "unitarists," who oppose the liberal economic reforms. Furthermore, Ranković is a representative of the dominant Serbian influence in the leadership. His expulsion marks another victory for the reformists. Ultimately, his removal opens the door to Kosovo's democratic movement, because Ranković and the state security apparatus had been responsible for maintaining Serbian control of Kosovo and its party.

December 31   Milovan Djilas is released from prison due to a general amnesty (*see* April 7, 1962).

1967

March 17   Many Croatian cultural organizations object strenuously to the marginalization of the Croatian variant of the Serbo-Croatian language, as manifested in the first volumes of the common dictionary called for by the Novi Sad Agreement of December 1954. The dictionary relegated much of colloquial Croatian to "local" status, while the Serbian variant was presented as standard. This Croatian declaration does much harm to the Croatian cause because the response of the LCY is to condemn the declaration as not merely nationalist, but as a provocation to the nationalists among Serbs, who would now have good reason for response.

April 10   Ranković is expelled from the LCY.

1968

February   At a meeting of the Central Committee of the League of Communists of Bosnia, it is resolved that Bosnian Muslims are a separate nation or ethnic group, being neither Croatian nor Serbian. For 28 years, the Muslims of Bosnia and Herzegovina had been considered either Croats or Serbs, depending on whether one was a Croat or a Serb nationalist. With the fall of Ranković, who had been a proponent of the idea that they were all Serbs, the way was cleared for a new option. The declaration by Bosnian Muslims that they are a separate nation is met with intense disapproval in Serbia.

April   Tito travels to Moscow, where he expresses delight at developments in Czechoslovakia and warns the Soviets not to invade that country (*see* Czechoslovakia starting in January 1968).

May 29–30   At the Fourteenth Meeting of the Central Committee of the League of Communists of Serbia, Dobrica Ćosić and Jovan Marjanović express their dismay at the resurgence of Albanian and Hungarian nationalism in Kosovo and Vojvodina. They are also frustrated at the Bosnian claim of separate nationhood in Yugoslavia. Ćosić and Marjanović are removed from the Central Committee several months later. In the future, Ćosić is the main cultural representative of Serbian nationalism in Yugoslavia, a state where the national question had supposedly been solved. His trilogy, *Time of Death*, published over a period of years in the 1970s, is an ode to Serbian heroism in the First World War. He will become the president of the truncated Yugoslav state of Serbia and Montenegro in 1991.

June 2   During student demonstrations in Belgrade, the security forces use violence, which results in the occupation of university buildings by demonstrators. The students demand better conditions in the university, more opportunity for employment in Yugoslavia after graduation, the end of police brutality, and the end of social inequality in Yugoslavia. The demonstrations are part of a new trend in Yugoslavia and are a manifestation of national dissatisfaction. The trend will continue through the Croatian mass movement of the early 1970s.

June 12   Students in Belgrade end their occupation of university buildings after Tito promises to treat the students' grievances with care.

July 18   The League of Communists of Yugoslavia declares its support for the reformist program in Czechoslovakia. Four days earlier, President Tito expressed his support for the Czechoslovak reforms.

August 9–11   As a gesture of support for the Czechoslovak reforms, President Tito visits Czechoslovakia and receives a warm welcome.

August 20–21   The Soviet Union invades Czechoslovakia.

August 21   Tito pronounces his disapproval of the invasion of Czechoslovakia by the Soviet Union. When the West responds with mild warnings, Tito and the Yugoslav leadership fear the Soviet Union might attempt to bring Yugoslavia back into line in the same way—through invasion. They institute measures designed to show the Soviets they will not roll over as quickly and easily as the Czechs and Slovaks did. The fear of a Soviet invasion proves paranoiac.

November   The Central Committee of the League of Communists of Serbia allows the parties of Kosovo and Vojvodina to be renamed. Henceforth, they are the League of Communists of Kosovo (rather than the League of Communists of Serbia for Kosovo) and the League of Communists of Vojvodina. This move is part of a general relaxation of Serbian control of the two provinces.

November 29 On Kosovo Liberation day, (Yugoslav) Revolution day, and Albanian National Independence day (all on November 29), riots break out in Priština and other towns in Kosovo. The demonstrators demand that Kosovo receive republic status, be allowed the right of secession, and receive an Albanian university. They also demand that Kosovo, formally known as Kosovo-Metohija (the latter a region of Kosovo only recognized by Serbs), be officially called Kosovo. A party purge and mass arrests follow these demonstrations, which occur just as reforms are being implemented in Kosovo. Although republican status is not granted, Kosovo does receive an Albanian university and Metohija is dropped from its name.

1969

January 9–11 The Fifth Congress of the League of Communists of Bosnia endorses the granting of full nation status to Muslims. This status would make Muslims a constituent nation along with Serbs, Croats, Slovenes, Montenegrins, and Macedonians.

February 11 The government passes a law creating Partisan defense units in the countryside. These units are to implement guerilla warfare in case of invasion by the Soviets and their allies in the wake of events in Czechoslovakia in August 1968.

March 11 The Ninth Congress of the LCY meets in Belgrade. The only representative of a foreign party to attend is from Romania; the others protest Yugoslavia's lack of enthusiasm for the Soviet invasion of Czechoslovakia. Debate is relatively free and open for a communist society. One of the decisions of the Congress is that each republic should send its president and secretary to Belgrade to be members of an executive bureau, which would stand above the federal party presidency. Croatia sends Vladimir Bakarić, which leaves Savka Dabčević-Kučar and Miko Tripalo in charge in Zagreb. Other republics evade the requirement, sending less important representatives to Belgrade.

March 15 The first arrested demonstrators in the Kosovo riots of 1968 receive sentences of hard labor.

1970

January 15–17 The Tenth Meeting of the Central Committee of the League of Communists of Croatia meets in Zagreb. Attacks on the resurgence of Croatian nationalism had previously been heard, led by writers for the

Belgrade government daily *Borba* (Struggle). At the Tenth Meeting, Croatian Vladimir Bakarić rejects such accusations. The meeting represents the beginning of Croatian resistance to centralism. Bakarić appears to wish to make of Croatia an example of progressive democratic socialism as opposed to rigid centralized communism and one party rule. This "Croatian Spring," as it will come to be known, is a movement within and outside of the party. It is motivated by a desire of Croatians to see Croatia autonomous. It is also an expression of deep-seated unhappiness over what Croats view as Croatia's economic exploitation by the less-developed southern republics and provinces of Yugoslavia. After the Novi Sad dictionary debate, the Croatian cultural organization Matica Hrvatska is identified as a culprit of the "Croatian Spring" because of its cultural influence. Bakarić, who thinks the movement can be successfully accommodated within the LCY, does not realize the popularity it is assuming under the stewardship of Tripalo and Dabčević-Kučar in Zagreb.

August 28–29 In speeches in Split and Zadar, Tito vaguely attacks the growth of regionalism in the country and appears to refer to the Croatian meeting and other examples of dissatisfaction in individual republics.

September 21 Tito announces a plan for his succession, in which a collective leadership would be formed. All republics and provinces would be represented in this body.

1971

January The census for 1971 includes the designation Muslim. Although the catalyst for this change came from Bosnia and Herzegovina, Muslims in any republic qualified as members of the Muslim nation. This designation incites much opposition in Macedonia, where nationalists continue to insist that Muslims who speak Macedonian are part of the Macedonian nation. It is conceded by the government that Bosnia's Muslims have achieved nation status; other republics can deal with the Muslim issue as they wish. Latinka Perović, the secretary of the Serbian League of Communists, finally proposes that the issue of whether one is a Muslim or not be a matter of personal choice, where the matter rests.

March The first issue of the Matica Hrvatska publication, *Hrvatski Tjednik* (Croatian Weekly) appears. It favors autonomy for Croatia.

April Non-Communist nationalist supporters of the new autonomist line among Croatian Communist leaders take over the Student Federation of Zagreb University. Their leaders are Dražen Budiša and Ante Paradžik.

The party presidency meets on Brijuni, where the Croats discuss their fear that centralizing elements in the federal government are attempting to brand them as Ustaša, followers of the fascist independent Croatia during the Second World War, or at least accuse them of being in contact with émigré organizations. Tito opts to keep the dispute secret, but it emerges in public.

April 7 Croatian separatists assassinate the Yugoslav ambassador to Sweden, Vladimir Rolović.

May 14 After the Croatian leadership returns from Brijuni without being reprimanded, Miko Tripalo tells the Croatian Central Committee that the Socialist Republic of Croatia is now a "state."

June 30 Constitutional amendments giving more power to the republics in Yugoslavia are promulgated by the national parliament in Belgrade. Many Serbs fear decentralization may go too far; many Croats support it, and hope Croatia receives more freedom within the federation.

July 4 As the Croatian party, in association with the Matica Hrvatska, demands more freedom of action in Croatia, Tito explains to the leadership that nationalism is running wild in Croatia, and counterrevolution is a threat. He claims the threat of Soviet intervention hangs over Croatia and Yugoslavia, and says he would use his army to intervene before soviet intervention. The meeting ends on a high note, as Tito apologizes for being hard on the Croats. Dabčević-Kučar and Tripalo interpret the apology as Tito's general approval, and they continue on their course of action.

September Soviet leader Leonid Brezhnev visits Belgrade and reaffirms the Belgrade Declaration of 1955. The rift between the two nations caused by the Soviet invasion of Czechoslovakia is finally healed.

September 6 Tito comes to Zagreb and toasts the Croatian leadership for its enthusiasm, assuring it he senses no nationalist deviations in their work. Many interpret this as his endorsement of the Croatian strategy.

November 5 The Croatian Central Committee meets in Zagreb where Dabčević-Kučar reports favorably on the "mass national movement" in the republic. Bakarić, the head of the Croatian executive committee and an opponent of the mass movement, enlists Tito to finally put a halt to it.

November 15 Tito meets with Dušan Dragosavac, a Croatian Serb on the executive committee of the Croatian party, who expresses Bakarić's hope that Tito will not tolerate the mass movement any longer.

November 16 In a speech in Zagreb, Dražen Budiša, the head of the Student Federation and a leader in the nationalist movement, attacks Bakarić by name, warning the centralists among the Croatian party leaders that they ignore the mass movement at their own peril.

November 17 Tito goes to Timisoara, Romania, to meet Romanian President Nicolae Ceauşescu, unaware that in Zagreb, Budiša and his Student Federation are planning a student strike to begin the next day.

November 18 University students in Zagreb strike. They demand the end of economic exploitation of their republic and better conditions in their dormitories. Dabčević-Kučar and Tripalo call for an end to the student demonstrations knowing that they have gone too far for Tito to condone them, but the strike continues.

December 1 At a meeting called in Karađorđevo, Tito accuses the leadership of the League of Communists of Croatia of nationalism and counterrevolution. Tito says the Croatian leaders are catering to nationalism and counterrevolution will result. Tito does not specifically blame the Croats, but finds fault with the development of the Marxist education of all Yugoslavs; the other republics are warned to beware of nationalist deviations in their own regions.

December 12 In Zagreb, Budiša is arrested. The resignations of Dabčević-Kučar and Tripalo are announced.

December 23 Tito notes publicly he would not be reluctant to use force to end disturbances threatening the unity of Yugoslavia. He expresses his embarrassment that outsiders might involve themselves in Yugoslav affairs, referring, as always, to the Soviet Union's invasion of Czechoslovakia in August 1968.

1972

January 28 Croatian separatists claim responsibility for the crash of a Swedish airliner and the bombing of the Vienna-Belgrade express train.

July 4 Croatian émigré terrorists attempt to stir up rebellion in Bosnia among the Croatian population; little happens.

October 9 In Belgrade, Tito challenges the Serbian party leadership, which he views as too unwilling to respect the centralizing role of the Yugoslav party, to follow the line of LCY. The Serbian party responds aggressively, and the two sides reach a standoff. Tito is not pleased.

October 25 The leaders of the Serbian League of Communists, Latinka Perović and Marko Nikezić, resign. They are accused of liberalism, but their crime is probably "nationalist deviations."

October 30 The federal party presidency meets. Tito's desire to see a renewed centralization of the party is accepted.

1973

February 23 Dušan Makavejev is expelled from the League of Communists. Makavejev is the director of several films in Yugoslavia, including *Wilhelm Reich: Mysteries of the Organism*, which, although outwardly pornographic, is an assault on the power of the one-party state. Makavejev moves to Western Europe and continues his film-making career. His other films include *Man is Not a Bird* and *Sweet Movie*.

1974

February 12 Czechoslovakia, Hungary, and Yugoslavia sign an agreement to build the Adria pipeline from the city of Omis on the Adriatic Sea to Bratislava.

February 21 A new constitution is promulgated after over one year of preparation. It is the longest in the history of the world. Occupational and interest groups will elect members of the federal and local assemblies. The Federal Assembly now has two chambers, the Federal Chamber and the Chamber of Republics, which are elected by republican assemblies. Novelties in this constitution include writing the role of the military into the law of the land and providing that the League of Communists must be represented in the federal and republican presidencies. The army's role is the result of the Croatian events of 1971, when the party realized it should be bound to the army in case the state needs to intervene in regional affairs.

1975

March 13 The Nobel prize author Ivo Andrić dies (*see* November 1, 1961).

March Eight professors from the University of Belgrade, all leading members of the Praxis group, are expelled from their posts for advocation of a more humanistic socialism, which the regime cannot tolerate.

May The Tenth Congress of the LCY meets. It confirms the new constitution, which is more federalist than previous ones. However, it also endorses the trend toward centralization and strength in the party—republics and autonomous regions will be more internally autonomous of

the central government, but the party will gain more control than it had previously.

1979

September 3–9 Tito, the last of the three founders of the nonaligned movement, attends his last summit meeting of nonaligned nations hosted by Cuban dictator Fidel Castro, a staunch ally of the USSR, in Havana. Tito, in the spirit of nonalignism, argues for less emphasis on the Soviet Union in the resolutions of the summit, but he is only partially successful.

1980

January 5 Tito enters the hospital due to a series of illnesses.

May 4 President Josip Tito dies three days short of his 88th birthday.

1981

March–April Kosovo erupts as Albanian students and workers demonstrate and riot, eventually battling police. The students demand (1) their Albanian nationality be given equal status to that of the other constituent nations of Yugoslavia, (2) political prisoners be released from prison, and (3) social injustices be alleviated in Kosovo. Their rallying cry is ''Kosovo-Republic.'' A state of emergency is declared. One-third of the Yugoslav People's Army (JNA) is eventually deployed in Kosovo. The leadership of the LCY refuses to negotiate with the demonstrators, using a combination of force and the promise of economic progress to put an end to the unrest. Approximately 1,000 people die in the demonstrations. The demonstrations disturb authorities because the previous ten years have seen a concerted effort to speed the economic development of Kosovo, Serbia's and Yugoslavia's most backward province.

March 11 Albanian student demonstrations begin in Priština, Kosovo.

March 25 Riots break out in Prizren, Kosovo.

March 26 University students in Priština riot again.

March 31 Demonstrations occur in Obilić, Kosovo.

April 1 Battles between police and demonstrators break out in the streets of Priština. Workers join the students.

April 3 Kosovska Mitrovica and Uroševac erupt in violence.

December 29 Miroslav Krleža, Croatia's greatest writer, dies at the age of 88.

1982

June The Twelfth Congress of the League of Communists of Yugoslavia meets and designates itself the "Congress of Continuity," emphasizing its intention to maintain continuity after the death of Tito.

1983

January Vladimir Bakarić dies, ending the last major link with the LCY's Partisan past. Bakarić was Croatia's main contribution to the Communist leadership of post-Second World War Yugoslavia. Although he had been a candidate to succeed Tito, his political clout was limited outside of Croatia.

July 18 Thirteen Bosnian Muslims are put on trial for counterrevolution. They are accused of attempting to create a separate and pure Muslim state in Bosnia and Herzegovina. Authorities claim the basis of the charges is an "Islamic Declaration" which addresses all adherents of Islam and calls for the creation of an Islamic state. The charges are also related to unrest in Kosovo, where Muslim Albanians have been demonstrating for autonomy and/or independence. Alija Izetbegović, the future president of independent Bosnia and Herzegovina, is one of the defendants.

August 20 Eleven of the Muslim counterrevolutionaries are given sentences totalling 90 years. Izetbegović receives a 14-year sentence.

October Historians in Zagreb meet and call for a reassessment of Tito and his role in Yugoslav history.

December At a meeting of the Central Committee of the LCY, the party restates its refusal to negotiate with the Albanians of Kosovo.

1984

February The 1984 Winter Olympics are held in Sarajevo. Forty-nine countries participate in the first Games to be held in Eastern Europe.

April In Belgrade, 28 attendees of a meeting led by the dissident Milovan Djilas are arrested for engaging in hostile propaganda, but they are soon released.

May 15 The first new collective presidency since Tito's death takes office. The nine-member collective presidency consists of the leaders of the six republics, one each for the autonomous regions of Kosovo and Vojvodina, and the president of the LCY, who is a non-voting member. The president of the collective presidency revolves annually among the members.

July In Sarajevo, Vojislav Šešelj, a Serbian professor, is arrested and sentenced to eight years in prison for his nationalistic writings. He becomes known as the head of the renewed Serbian Radical party and a "Četnik" leader during the wars of Yugoslavia's collapse in 1991 and after.

1985

May In Kosovo, Djordje Martinović, a Serb, claims to have been impaled on a broken bottle by two Albanians. Others dispute this story, claiming he impaled himself on a bottle which then broke. The claim is used by Serbian nationalists as an example of Albanian persecution of Serbs in Kosovo. The incident illustrates the fears the Serbs of Kosovo have: they believe the Albanians are attempting to torture them, physically and socially, in the same ways the Turks did when the Ottoman Empire ruled the area. Accusations of mass rapes of Orthodox women by Muslim men continue to grow, as do claims that Albanians are engaging in a purposeful policy of Serbian genocide as reflected in their high birthrate.

The Serbian Academy of Arts and Sciences (SANU) commissions a committee of its members to formulate a memorandum to express the Academy's dissatisfaction with the lessening of the position of Serbs in Yugoslavia.

1986

January Over 200 Serbian intellectuals, doctors, and engineers send a petition to the national parliament protesting the alleged genocidal mentality of Albanians in Kosovo toward Serbs and Montenegrins.

March A deputation of Serbs from Kosovo comes to Belgrade to complain to the national parliament that Serbian communities in Kosovo are being driven out of the region by Albanians. They also complain that the justice system in Kosovo is biased toward Albanians, who the Serbs claim are not prosecuted for sex crimes and other offenses. The leader of this deputation, Kosta Bulatović, is arrested by Kosovo authorities when he returns to Kosovo.

May The career Communist Ivan Stambolić becomes President of Serbia. He is mentor to Slobodan Milošević who becomes President of the League of Communists of Serbia at its Tenth Congress meeting in Belgrade. Before entering politics in 1984, Milošević had been the director of the state-owned gas company, Tehnogas, and then president of Beogradska Banka (the Bank of Belgrade). He entered politics in 1984 after Stambolić became chairman of the Central Committee of the Serbian League of Communists.

July The federal government makes Albanian settlement in Serbian villages in Kosovo illegal, because homogenous Serbian villages are slowly disappearing due to Serbian immigration to Serbia.

September A group of prominent Serbian intellectuals, all members of the Serbian Academy of Arts and Sciences, publicly delivers a memorandum on the status of the Serbian people in Yugoslavia. This memorandum becomes the position from which Serbian nationalists and the Serbian government operate after 1987. The memorandum might say expresses Serbian displeasure over the marginalization of Serbian national aspirations in all sectors of economic, social, and political life in Yugoslavia. Its signers include Dobrica Ćosić (*see* May 1985).

1987

April 24–25 Slobodan Milošević makes his first foray onto the stage of popular politics in Serbia. He becomes a symbol for Serbian nationalism when he proclaims to a Serbian protest meeting in Kosovo that no one has the right to keep the Kosovo Serbs in an inferior position, and that the Serbs should fight for their rights in Kosovo.

September At the Eighth Session of the League of Communists of Serbia, Milošević successfully purges it of its less nationalistic (''Titoist'') members, who favor downplaying Serbian claims to Kosovo in keeping with Tito's attempts to keep the nationalisms of Yugoslavia in check. One of his first actions is to purge the editorial staffs of the daily *Politika* (Politics) and the weekly *Nedeljne Informativne Novine* (Weekly Informative News), which had enjoyed strong reputations for their balanced coverage. Milošević makes these publications his personal press organs for ethnic hatred and fear, especially between Serbs and Albanians in Kosovo. Milošević is now the most powerful political leader in Serbia.

December Milošević forces Stambolić, his former mentor, out of his position as president of Serbia after implicating Stambolić in corruption charges against one of Stambolić's protégés.

1988

July 9 One thousand Serbs and Montenegrins travel to Vojvodina to demonstrate for a reduction in the autonomy enjoyed by Vojvodina and Kosovo; the party apparatus in Novi Sad had been strongly opposed to such a reduction. Milošević denotes this action as an initial event in the ''anti-bureaucratic revolution,'' a term which refers to Milošević's claim that the party has grown away from the people and that party members are mere bureaucrats who have no connection to the people they serve. The various demonstrations Milošević will stage around the country will be called manifestations of the anti-bureaucratic revolution.

August 20 The anti-bureaucratic revolution comes to Montenegro, where 30,000 people march on the capital, Titograd.

August 29 Milošević takes the anti-bureaucratic revolution to Kosovo, where 17,000 Serbs and Montenegrins march on Priština.

October 6 With the help of manipulated street demonstrations, the leadership of Vojvodina is overthrown, and one obedient to Milošević is put into power.

October 7 The Montenegrin leadership resigns en masse and Milošević supporters take over the Montenegrin state and party leadership.

November The Albanian Communist leader Azem Vllasi is removed from the Central Committee of the Kosovo party. Vllasi has long been an obedient party stooge in Kosovo and aligned with the Serbian party until Milošević came to power. The Serbian leader Kolj Siroka is also forced from the Central Committee, and Milošević's puppet, Rahman Morina, becomes party president. With the elimination of the older generation of Serbian party leaders, Milošević is free to label the Kosovo Albanian leadership as nationalist—in the name of the anti-bureaucratic revolution.

1989

January Montenegro, following demonstrations similar to those in Vojvodina, installs a government obedient to Milošević (*see* October 7, 1988).

Slobodan Milošević, president of the Serbian Communist Party, and Dusan Ckrebic, Serbian member of the Yugoslav Politburo, during the opening session of Communist leaders meeting.

Ante Marković, a Croat known for his economic expertise, becomes the premier of Yugoslavia. Yugoslavs hope he will pave their way into the European Community.

February   Vllasi is expelled from the party, provoking an Albanian miners strike in Trepča, followed by a general strike. The government of Kosovo, now in the control of the Serbian party, continues its policy of occupation, arrest, and persecution that began in November 1988. The federal government proclaims a state of emergency.

February 27   The Yugoslav People's Army (JNA) deploys in Kosovo. The army will be a constant presence in Kosovo, although it does not actually take part in operations against Albanian demonstrators until February 1, 1990.

February 28   The Croatian Democratic Union party is founded in Zagreb. The group includes Franjo Tudjman, a former communist, ex-JNA general, and dissident. The Croatian Democratic Union is very nationalistic.

March   The Serbian government overwhelmingly passes a new constitution that virtually eliminates the autonomy enjoyed by Kosovo and Vojvodina; the puppet parliaments

of those two provinces also approve the new constitution. The Serbian government can now control four of the eight votes in the rotating federal presidency. This control will be useful to it in June of 1991 when Croatia and Slovenia secede. Milošević's revolution has now achieved its primary goal—Serbia can frustrate all action taken by the federal government. The Croats and Slovenes had feared this event, the final blow in their faith in the continuation of Yugoslavia.

June 28   Serbs celebrate the 600th anniversary of the Battle of Kosovo in which the Ottoman Turks ended Serbian independence. Hundreds of thousands travel to the Kosovo battlefield to listen to Milošević praise the Serbian nation and warn it of dangers ahead; his speech resounds with veiled and unveiled threats against Serbia's enemies.

July   To increase Serbian control, Milošević dismisses Kosovo's parliament, closes its Albanian-language television and radio programs, and bans the Albanian press of the province.

October   The Slovene parliament passes many amendments to its republican constitution, including one giving

Hundreds of thousands attend an anti-Albanian protest in Belgrade. The crowds are carrying portraits of Serbian Party leader Slobodan Milošević.

the republic the right to secede. The Slovenian amendment crisis will be a source of contention between the Slovene and Serbian parties.

In Kosovo, six Albanian protestors are killed while demonstrating against the trial of former Albanian leader Azem Vllasi.

November 21 After Serbian organizers plan a rally in Ljubljana to allegedly explain the Serbian position regarding Kosovo to the "unenlightened" Slovenes, they learn the Slovenian police will not allow the meeting. The police fear the rally is meant to cause trouble in the name of Milošević's anti-bureaucratic revolution.

November 29 The Serbian organizers of the Ljubljana rally cancel it. Milošević announces a boycott of Slovenian firms and business by Serbia.

December 12 Two new parties are formed in Serbia: the Democratic party, consisting mainly of university professors, and the Movement for Democratic Renewal, consisting mainly of students. The Democratic party is headed by Kosta Čavoški and Radoslav Stojanović; the government permits it to announce its founding. However,

the government refuses to allow the student party to continue, claiming it includes several people who have been involved in "anti-state" activity.

1990

January 1 The Marković federal government implements a currency reform and freezes wages and prices. The dinar is devalued such that 10,000 old dinars are equivalent to one new dinar. The dinar is now fully convertible and linked to the West German deutschmark.

January 5 The League of Communists of Yugoslavia announces that it will allow alternative groups and political parties to attend the LCY congress in two weeks.

January 6 The Serbian Renewal Movement is formed. Headed by the writer Vuk Drašković, the party is intensely nationalistic and rhetorically anti-Communist, and it will be the subject of the repressive measures by Serbia's Communist government.

January 6–7 For the first time since the Second World War, Serbs publicly celebrate Christmas (according to the

Orthodox calendar). The media gives wide coverage to the event.

January 17   DEMOS, Slovenia's democratic coalition, announces its participation in the coming free elections in Slovenia.

January 20   The Fourteenth Congress of the LCY meets in Belgrade. The meeting is held under the cloud of uncertainty following the fall of European Communist governments in general; Yugoslavia and Albania are the only two Communist governments remaining.

January 22   At the Fourteenth Congress, the party agrees to allow party pluralism, or multiparty elections, but the Slovenes walk out when further reforms are rejected. The Slovenes wish to see the party decentralized, while the Serbs wish just the opposite—a tightly unified Yugoslav party. All observers now agree the LCY is not a legitimate force in Yugoslav politics, that role being taken by the republican parties.

January 24   Albanian pro-democracy demonstrations begin again in Kosovo.

January 27   Five Albanian demonstrators are killed; the demonstrations continue.

February 1   The Yugoslav People's Army (JNA) deploys actively in Kosovo. The death count is now over 30, all Albanian.

February 4   The Slovenian League of Communists renames itself the Party for Democratic Renewal, while Slovenia pulls its police and army personnel from Kosovo.

February 11   After eight parties register for the free elections in Croatia, the League of Communists of Croatia changes its name to the Party of Democratic Change (LCC).

February 20   For the first time since 1981, the federal presidency orders the JNA to restore order in Kosovo.

March 4   In Petrova Gora, a region in central Croatia inhabited by both Serbs and Croats, 50,000 Serbs rally in opposition to perceived Croatian persecution of the Serbian minority in Croatia.

March 8   The Slovenian assembly passes amendments giving Slovenia near-independence economically. The assembly also requests countrywide negotiations begin for the creation of a confederation for Yugoslavia.

March 18   In Benkovac, a largely Serbian town in Croatia, a gunman attempts to kill Franjo Tudjman, now the leader of the Croatian Democratic Union and the favorite to win the Croatian presidential elections in April.

April 4   Croatia removes its members of the police force from Kosovo.

April 8   Multiparty elections are held in Slovenia. The coalition known as DEMOS, including the Christian Democrats, the Democrats, and the Social Democrats, wins the parliamentary elections, but the reform Communist Milan Kučan is elected president on May 20.

April 22   Multiparty elections are held in Croatia. The Croatian Democratic Union wins, led by Franjo Tudjman.

May 15   Borisav Jović, an ally of Milošević, takes over the presidency of Yugoslavia; he is the Serbian representative on the rotating presidency. The federal presidency now will be able to act as an arm of the Serbian government, or, barring that, at least immobilize the federation.

May 30   Tudjman is elected president of Croatia.

June 29   The federal premier, Ante Marković, implements a new economic reform package, including proposals to privatize government controlled businesses in an attempt to stop the continuing economic woes of the country. He notes the success of his program relies on the cooperation of all the republics.

July 1   A referendum is held throughout Serbia, including Kosovo and Vojvodina. The question is whether the voters wish to eliminate all vestiges of autonomy within Serbia for Kosovo and Vojvodina.

July 2   In view of the July 1 referendum, the reestablished Kosovo assembly declares Kosovo's independence from Serbia, but not from Yugoslavia.

July 4   The Group of 24, the foreign ministers of the 24 most advanced industrialized countries, meet in Brussels and agree to provide economic aid for Czechoslovakia, Bulgaria, Yugoslavia, and East Germany.

July 5   The Serbian assembly suspends the Kosovo assembly and executive council and purges all of the media in Kosovo.

July 16   The League of Communists of Serbia changes its name to the Socialist Party of Serbia. Milošević is elected president of the party.

August 18   The Serbs of Knin, Croatia, barricade their city. One of their leaders, Jovan Rašković, holds talks with Tudjman about the status of Croatia's Serbs, but they reach no agreement. A more radical leader, Milan Babić, a dentist from Knin, will soon take over leadership of the Serbs of western Croatia.

August 19   A referendum sponsored by the Serbian National Council of Knin is held to determine whether the Serbs of Croatia wish to remain in Croatia; they do not.

Babić is the head of the council, and will become the president of the territory called Krajina.

September 7 Prince Alexander Karađorđević, son of the late King Petar II of the exiled royal family, visits Belgrade. Eighty thousand persons turn out to see him.

October 1 The Serbian minority in Croatia declares the autonomy of its territory.

October 16 The statue of ban, or governor Josip Jelačić is returned to Zagreb's Republic square, which in turn is renamed Jelačić square. The statue of this Croatian governor during the 1848 revolution had been removed, and the square renamed, in 1947. The statue's sword points toward Bosnia and Herzegovina, denoting Croatian claims on this territory.

November 11 Multiparty elections are held in Macedonia.

November 18 Multiparty elections are held in Bosnia and Herzegovina, where ethnically-organized parties along Croatian, Serbian, and Muslim lines win.

December 8 Serbia holds free elections. Milošević receives 65 percent of the vote for president.

December 10 The Internal Macedonian Revolutionary Organization-Democratic Party of Macedonian Unity is declared the winner of a plurality of the seats (37 of 120) in the Macedonian parliament.

December 18 The federal government, responding to the Slovenian plans to hold an independence plebiscite, warns the Slovenian leadership not to hold the vote. The federal armed forces threaten to keep Slovenia in Yugoslavia by force.

December 20 Alija Izetbegović of the (Muslim) Party for Democratic Action is named president of Bosnia and Herzegovina. One Serb and one Croat are also named to top posts in the republic.

The federal government announces only economic measures will be taken against Slovenia if it votes to secede.

December 23 Eighty-five percent of eligible voters take part in the Slovenian referendum. Ninety-five percent of the voters wish to see Slovenia fully independent of Yugoslavia.

December 26 Slovenia declares its sovereignty and promises to secede if negotiations for the decentralization of Yugoslavia do not proceed immediately. Milan Kučan, Slovenia's president, gives the federal government six months to agree on changes in Yugoslavia's constitutional form to reflect the republic's demands.

1991

January 7 The federal government reveals that the Serbian parliament authorized the printing of 1.4 billion dollars worth of dinars without the approval of the federal government. It is rumored the money funded electoral graft in support of the Serbian Socialist party of Slobodan Milošević.

January 19 After unsuccessfully ordering all paramilitary groups in the country to voluntarily disarm on January 9, the federal presidency orders all such groups in Croatia and Slovenia to disband by January 21.

January 22 Croatian and Slovenian armed groups refuse to disband.

January 23 The JNA threatens to intervene in Croatia if the paramilitary units are not disbanded.

Macedonian parties agree to support Kiro Gligorov as president of the republic. Gligorov is a member of the League of Communists of Macedonia-Party for Democratic Transformation and an economist.

January 25 Tudjman and Milošević meet to discuss their differences. Their meeting is overshadowed by a spectacular broadcast on Belgrade TV which allegedly shows the Croatian minister of internal affairs negotiating an arms purchase from Hungary and threatening to kill JNA army personnel.

January 30 The federal government demands the arrest of the Croatian minister of internal affairs, Martin Špegelj, who has allegedly organized terrorist attacks on Yugoslav national Army members. The Croatian government refuses and takes Špegelj underground. On January 31, an emergency meeting of the federal government adjourns without finding a solution to the Špegelj affair.

February 2 Borisav Jović, the Serbian president of the rotating federal state presidency warns Croatia that it must surrender Špegelj and demobilize its republican police force or face military consequences. Croatia and Slovenia reject this threat and warn Jović he is speaking only for Serbs from his position as federal president. Špegelj, despite being indicted months later for his activities, remains underground.

February 10 An Albanian youth magazine in Kosovo publishes a poll showing that only 7 percent of respondents favor negotiations with Serbia while 93 percent favor unification with Albania.

February 20 The Slovenian parliament votes to give its laws superiority over the federal Yugoslav laws.

February 21 Following Slovenia's lead, the Croatian government votes to give its laws superiority over federal laws. Both Croatia and Slovenia have now laid the groundwork for secession.

February 28 In Knin, the Serbian National Council declares the independence of the Serbs in Croatia. The council represents an uncertain constituency at this point. Croatia shrugs off the declaration as a Belgrade provocation (*see* August 19, 1990).

March In Bologna, Italy, the foreign ministers of the Pentagonale group (Czechoslovakia, Austria, Hungary, Italy, and Yugoslavia) declare their support for the continued existence of Yugoslavia as a federal republic based on democratic reform.

March 1 Serbs take over the police station in Pakrac, Croatia. Croatian police retake the building. Federal President Jović orders the JNA into Pakrac; some of the Croatian police leave the police station on March 3.

March 9 Demonstrations against Milošević in Belgrade result in two deaths. Although the demonstrators desire Milošević's resignation in the name of democracy, all of the parties active in Serbia are as nationalistic as his. The specific demands of the protesters include the removal of the Serbian minister of internal affairs and changes in the editorial staff of Radio-Television Belgrade. These demonstrations seem to be the offspring of Milošević's anti-bureaucratic revolution, which was played out largely in the streets. Vuk Drašković, the head of the Serbian Renewal Movement and the inspiration to the students and opposition deputies in the parliament, is arrested.

March 12 Drašković is released as the protests continue. The federal presidency does not agree to the army's demand that a state of emergency be declared.

March 15 Jović resigns after he fails to convince the federal presidency to intervene against the demonstrators in Belgrade. For the last time, the presidency will show independence from Milošević: the member from Kosovo refused to go along with Jović.

March 16 As a result of the failed vote for a state of emergency on March 15, Milošević announces that Serbia will not necessarily respect decisions of the federal government.

The Serbian region of Croatia declares independence from Croatia; the region is now called the Serbian Autonomous Region of Krajina (*see* August 18, 1990).

March 18 The Serbian assembly orders the removal of Riza Sapundžija, Kosovo's representative on the federal presidency. This move is a result of Sapundžija's failure to authorize force in the Belgrade demonstrations.

March 25 Milošević and Tudjman again meet in Karadjordjevo to attempt to settle the differences between Serbia and Croatia. Tudjman agrees to respect Serbia's authority over Vojvodina and Kosovo and not to challenge Serbia's attempts to overthrow Marković; Milošević will not interfere in Croatia's handling of the Serbian Krajina. It is rumored Serbia promises not to act militarily in Croatia if Croatia allows it to deal with Slovenia. It is also rumored the two have agreed to the division of Bosnia and Herzegovina.

April 4 With JNA tanks and troop carriers on the roads around Osijek, Tudjman still refuses to acknowledge the threat the army will pose to Croatian independence.

April 18 The Serbian assembly passes a law giving confiscated property of the Serbian Orthodox church, seized after the Second World War, back to the church. This action further cements the relationship of the nationalist government of Milošević and the church.

April 30 Krajina establishes its own parliament and prepares for union with Serbia. In ongoing confrontations, Serbs challenge Croatian police officers in villages throughout the Serbian regions of Croatia (*see* March 16).

May 2 In Borovo Selo, Slavonia, in Croatia, 12 Croatian police officers and several Serbs are killed after the Croats fail to respect an agreement by which the village would be left alone by the Croatian territorial police. The JNA moves into Borovo Selo to "maintain peace." This event is considered the first battle of the coming war of Croatian secession. On the same day, violence is reported all around Croatia, with reports of very heavy fighting in Zadar on the Dalmatian coast. In the Plitvice Lakes region and Knin, the JNA separate combatants. The federal presidency, meeting on May 4 and 7 to discuss the crisis, considers whether the JNA should be used to quell disturbances all over Croatia or whether the Croatian government should be allowed to try to reestablish order in the republic.

May 9 Croatia agrees to demobilize its police reserves and disarm civilians, and Tudjman agrees to work with the JNA army. There is great confusion over who is considered police or civilian; Tudjman claims the Croatian police need not demobilize, but Serbian paramilitary groups must do so. The Serbs disagree.

May 12 Krajina Serbs hold a referendum on secession from Croatia to legitimize the action. According to authorities in Knin, 99 percent vote for secession.

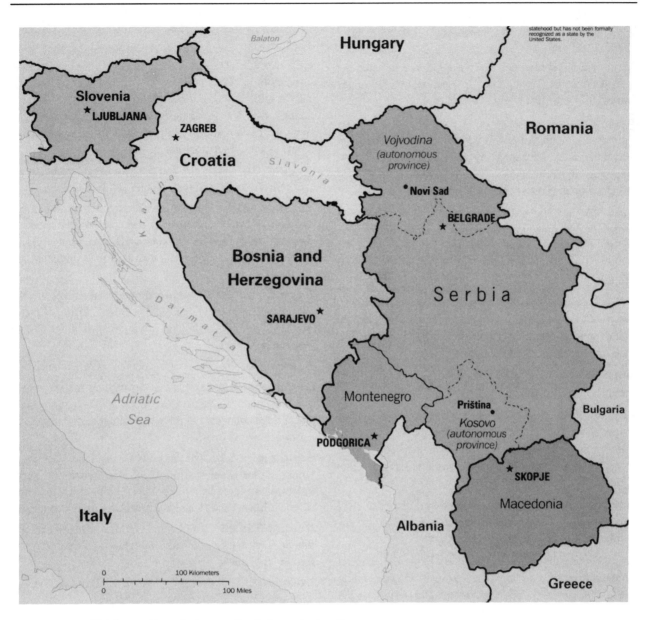

statehood but has not been formally recognized as a state by the United States.

The former Yugoslavia, now five independent nations.

May 13 The European Community foreign ministers declare they will only deal with a unified Yugoslavia.

May 15 Stipe Mesić, a Croat scheduled to become president in the rotating federal presidency, is not seated due to a deadlock in the voting among the eight representatives. Bosnia and Herzegovina, Slovenia, Croatia, and Macedonia vote to seat him; Serbia, Kosovo, and Vojvodina vote against him; Montenegro abstains. The country and its military have no leader. Milošević's control of the presidency, established in 1989, has now destabilized the federal government.

May 20 The United States suspends $5 million of aid to Yugoslavia because of ongoing human rights abuses in Kosovo and Serbia's destabilization of the federal presidency.

May 29 The Serbian parliament declines to accept Krajina's request to join Serbia, but demands the desires of Croatian Serbs be considered in any plan to reform Yugoslavia.

June 3 Bosnia and Herzegovina and Macedonia propose Yugoslavia be reformed as a unified state of sovereign nations, each possessing its own military and carrying on its own policies in foreign affairs and trade. The central government would have a joint parliament, an army, and a common currency.

June 15 Tudjman and Kučan agree to announce the independence of Croatia and Slovenia on June 26. They believe they must act together or not at all.

June 21 U.S. Secretary of State James A. Baker declares the United States will not recognize Croatian and Slovenian independence. Many believe Baker's statement gives the signal to the JNA and Serbian irregulars to militarily oppose the secessions.

June 25 Croatia and Slovenia vote to declare independence. The JNA secures Slovenia's international borders and the federal government announces police will patrol the Slovenian-Croatian border. The European Community and the United States announce they do not recognize the new states.

June 27 The JNA intervenes militarily to take the Ljubljana airport and all Slovenian border crossings. The JNA moves into Serbian regions of Croatia.

June 30 Mesić is finally elected president of the federal presidency (*see* May 15).

July 1 Josip Reichl-Kir, the Croatian police chief of Osijek, Slavonia is killed by a member of the local Croatian Democratic Union, presumably because he had been very successful in maintaining peace between Serbs and Croats in the region.

July 3 To great public acclaim, a huge column of JNA armored vehicles and troops leave Belgrade for the Croato-Serbian border and Bosnia and Herzegovina.

July 7 On the Adriatic island of Brijuni, European Community representatives negotiate an end to the fighting in Slovenia in return for a three-month moratorium on the independence declaration. Fighting ceases in Slovenia, but has only begun in Croatia. Slovenia is now virtually independent, as Serbia has announced that it has no intention of attempting to keep it in Yugoslavia because there are no Serbs in Slovenia.

July 21 The JNA begins to withdraw from Slovenia.

July 28 News reports say hundreds of Croats were killed by Serbian irregulars in villages in the Banija region of Croatia.

July 30 The Yugoslav air force attacks Kostajnica, a town on the Bosnian border in central Croatia.

July 31 Tudjman's Croatian government offers Krajina self-rule, but declines to negotiate with "terrorists"; this essentially rules out negotiations with the leaders of Krajina.

August 1 Leaders of Krajina refuse Tudjman's offer of self-rule.

August 22 Tudjman orders the JNA to leave Croatian territory or he will consider it an occupying army and will fully mobilize Croatian forces. Meanwhile, JNA and Serbian attacks on eastern Slavonian cities and towns increase, and the town of Pakrac is a battleground as Serbs attempt to create a band of territory across Slavonia.

August 24 The JNA and Serbian irregulars begin attacks on Vukovar, a Slavonian city south of Osijek.

September 4 The Conference on Security and Cooperation in Europe, a group of over 50 nations that meets to discuss European security, human rights, and trade, places an embargo on all arms shipments to the combatants in Yugoslavia.

September 7 A peace conference sponsored by the European Community opens at the Hague. Prime Minister Marković admits the federal government is powerless to stop the fighting.

September 8 Macedonia votes for independence.

September 12 Serbian forces capture the Maslenica gorge bridge near Zadar, Croatia, on the Dalmatian coast. This bridge connects Zagreb with Dalmatia; its capture is a serious blow to Croatia.

September 17 The Yugoslav navy blockades Pula, Rijeka, Zadar, Šibenik, Split, Ploče, and Dubrovnik. Serbs in Bosnia declare two autonomous regions and threaten to secede if Bosnia and Herzegovina declares its independence.

September 25 The United Nations Security Council places an embargo on arms shipments to all parts of the former Yugoslavia.

October 1 Vukovar and Vinkovci are besieged by JNA and Serbian paramilitary troops.

October 5 Prince Aleksandar Karađorđević again visits Belgrade; over 80,000 turn out to hear him (*see* September 7, 1990).

October 7 The Yugoslav Air Force attacks Zagreb, nearly killing Franjo Tudjman, Stipe Mesić, and Ante Marković.

October 8 After a three-month delay, Croatia and Slovenia resume their administrative movement toward full independence (*see* July 7).

October 14 The Croatian government offers autonomy to Serbian Krajina.

October 14–16 Milošević and Tudjman travel to Moscow, where they unsuccessfully ask Mikhail Gorbachev and Boris Yeltsin to negotiate a compromise.

October 17 The JNA besieges Dubrovnik while the siege of Vukovar continues.

October 22 Albania recognizes Kosovo as an independent sovereign state.

October 23 The Yugoslav navy bombards the old center of Dubrovnik, which dates back to Roman times.

October 26 The JNA completes its withdrawal from Slovenia.

November Fighting is reported between the forces of the Croatian army (HVO) and the Croatian Defense Forces (HOS), the paramilitary organization attached to the Croatian Party of Rights headed by Dobroslav Paraga.

November 9 Dubrovnik is heavily shelled by the Yugoslav navy and the JNA.

November 13 The United Nations explores the possibility of sending peacekeeping troops to Yugoslavia. Cyrus Vance of the United States is the United Nations' negotiator; the European Community's negotiator is Lord Peter Carrington of Great Britain.

November 18 Vukovar, which had a Serbian minority before the siege, falls to the JNA and Serbian irregulars. The city is totally destroyed.

November 21 The JNA begins to attack Osijek, the next goal following the fall of Vukovar.

December 4 The Croatian assembly passes a law giving Serbs control of the police, schools, and media in areas in which Serbs are the predominant ethnic group.

December 5 Mesić resigns as federal president and goes home to Zagreb.

December 6 The JNA breaks a local cease-fire in Dubrovnik and bombards the city for ten hours, breaching an agreement reached between Milošević, Cyrus Vance, and General Veljko Kadijević, the Yugoslav defense minister, for a permanent cease fire. The local commanders do not wish the cease fire to go into effect, highlighting the Serbian/Yugoslav central government's lack of full control of the army.

December 8 The European Community repeals its economic embargo on all republics of the former Yugoslavia except Serbia and Montenegro. The arms embargo remains in force for all of the republics.

December 9 The Yugoslav navy ends its blockade of Dubrovnik. The old center of the city is heavily damaged and many historic buildings are destroyed.

December 17 European Community foreign ministers agree to recognize Croatia and Slovenia by January 15. The two states must meet conditions set out by France and Germany that include respecting frontiers and recognizing the rights of minorities. They also must accept the Helsinki Accords, which guarantee human rights.

December 19 Ante Marković resigns as federal premier when he finds that 81 percent of the federal budget for 1992 is for defense. In reality, he no longer plays a constructive role in the crisis.

December 21 Serbian leaders in Bosnia and Herzegovina declare their intention to form a Yugoslav republic of the Serbian areas of Bosnia and Herzegovina.

1992

January 6 Macedonia amends its constitution to assure the European Community, and especially Greece, that it has no territorial ambitions in Greek Macedonia. Greece is opposing recognition of Macedonia since "Macedonia" is a geographical designation with deep roots in Greek history, and Greeks fear that the new state of Macedonia will mark the beginning of attempts to annex northern Greece. The issue causes an uproar in Greece, where it mobilizes the entire population. Greece eventually proposes the new Macedonia call itself the Republic of Skopje, after the capital of Yugoslav Macedonia (*see* April 8, 1993).

January 7 A Yugoslav Air Force fighter shoots down a clearly marked European Community observer helicopter, killing five. Ultimately, Veljko Kadijević, the defense minister of the Yugoslav government, resigns due to the provocative nature of the act, which he apparently did not approve.

January 9 The self-proclaimed Serbian Assembly of the Autonomous Region of Bosanska Krajina declares its independence of Bosnia and Herzegovina. On January 11, it declares the republic of Bosnia and Herzegovina no longer exists (*see* December 21, 1991).

January 15 Under pressure from Germany, the 12 European Community members recognize Croatia and Slovenia; other countries will follow. As a result, the break-up of Yugoslavia becomes official.

January 25 The Muslim and Croatian representatives in the legislature of Bosnia and Herzegovina vote to hold a referendum on the independence of the republic. Radovan Karadžić, the leader of the Serbian Democratic party in Bosnia and Herzegovina, labels this decision "the war option."

January 30 Marrack Goulding, the United Nations Under Secretary-General, says he fears the cease-fire negotiated in Croatia is breaking down.

February 3   Milan Babić, the leader of Serbian Krajina, refuses to disarm and accuses Slobodan Milošević of selling out the Serbs of Croatia. Other leading Croatian Serbs oppose Babić in this matter, wishing instead to place Croato-Serbian relations in Croatia on a better footing.

February 9   The Krajina parliament votes to accept a United Nations peace plan despite the opposition of Milan Babić.

February 17   Milan Babić is voted out as chief executive of the Krajina; he says the vote is meaningless.

February 26   In Borovo Selo, Milan Babić is voted out of office by the parliaments of the Serbian regions of Croatia. Goran Hadžić, the leader of the Slavonian Serbs, becomes president.

March 1   In Bosnia and Herzegovina, 63 percent of the electorate vote for independence; the Serbian population does not favor this course of action.

March 2   Serbs set up roadblocks in Sarajevo and other Bosnian cities. In Sarajevo, snipers kill several people demonstrating for peace.

March 11   Bosnian Serbs reject plans for the maintenance of a unified Bosnia and Herzegovina, claiming it would be ''the birth of a Muslim bastard on the land of our grandfathers.'' Talks continue on the future of the country.

March 16   Violence erupts between Serbian and Muslim fighters in Bosanski Brod. Serbs, Croats, and Muslims all erect barricades in Mostar, Herzegovina.

March 18   The European Community unveils a plan to which all ethnic groups in Bosnia and Herzegovina supposedly agree; the state would be cantonized, or divided, according to ethnicity, but borders are not yet settled.

April 1   Serbs are reported to be forming police units in Bosnia and Herzegovina.

April 2   Serbian paramilitary forces seize Bijeljina, a town in northeastern Bosnia; 27 Muslims are killed.

April 4–5   The war comes to Bosnia and Herzegovina. In Kupres, 200 people die. In Sarajevo, Serbian paramilitary troops capture a police academy and Serbian artillery fire on Sarajevo and its airport. Ten people are killed by masked Serbian gunmen in the city while they demonstrate for peace in Bosnia and Herzegovina.

April 7   In Banja Luka, the Assembly of the Serbian People of Bosnia and Herzegovina declares independence for the Serbs of the land.

April 9   After Serbian paramilitary troops conquer Zvornik on the Serbian border, Muslim refugees flee. Many fear this signals the beginning of Serbian attempts to link the Serbian enclaves of Bosnia by driving out the Muslim populations.

April 27   Serbia and Montenegro proclaim a new Federal Republic of Yugoslavia and claim the new state is the legitimate successor to the old Yugoslavia.

Alija Izetbegović, Muslim president of Bosnia and Herzegovina, demands the JNA leave the country.

May 2   Izetbegović is kidnapped at the Sarajevo airport by the JNA as he returns from European Community talks in Lisbon. He is exchanged for JNA prisoners the next day. May 2–3 is the most violent weekend yet in Sarajevo and the rest of the republic.

May 4   Franjo Tudjman, president of Croatia, declares Bosnia and Herzegovina cannot survive unless it is cantonized, with each ethnic group governing itself within the borders of its cantons in the republic (*see* March 18).

The Yugoslav government orders all JNA personnel who are not from Bosnia and Herzegovina to withdraw to rump Yugoslavia—Serbia, Montenegro, and the autonomous regions of Vojvodina and Kosovo.

May 6   Radovan Karadžić and Mate Boban, the leaders of Bosnia and Herzegovina's Serbs and Croats, negotiate an end to hostilities between their peoples and also agree on a partition of Bosnia and Herzegovina.

May 14   The first accusations of massacres surface. Serbs are said to have killed 500 Muslims in northern Bosnia, while Muslims are said to have massacred 200 Serbs in a Sarajevo suburb of Pofaliči.

May 21   Serbian forces consisting of the JNA and republican police are put on alert in the largely Albanian region of Kosovo before the presidential and legislative elections scheduled for May 24.

May 25   Reports in Kosovo state that a majority of voters voted for Ibrahim Rugova, the Albanian leader of Kosovo's Democratic Alliance party.

June 23   Serbian authorities block the opening of the Albanian-dominated parliament in Priština, Kosovo.

June 24   Dobrica Ćosić, the president of rump Yugoslavia, fails to find a prime minister for the federal government.

Five Albanian legislators elected on May 24 are arrested by Serbian authorities who do not recognize the validity of the elections. The charge against the Albanians is endangering the integrity and order of Serbia.

June 28   In a huge rally in Belgrade, Vuk Drašković, the leader of the Serbian Renewal Movement, Patriarch Pavle of the Serbian Orthodox church, and Prince Aleksandar

The death toll in Yugoslavia escalates daily; in a Bosnian cemetery, cellist Vedran Smalović mourns the loss of a friend.

Karađorđević call for Milošević to resign and a government of national salvation to be formed that will end the fighting.

July 2   Milan Panić, an American Serb millionaire born in Yugoslavia, announces he will return to Yugoslavia to become prime minister. Many people wonder if he is Milošević's puppet, or if he will act independently. Panić promises to end the war and warns Milošević to stay out of his way.

July 3   Croats in Herzegovina set up a region called Herzeg-Bosna, headed by Mate Boban, who favors the partition of Bosnia and Herzegovina between Serbia and Croatia. Boban appears to be allied with Tudjman, whereas other Bosnian Croat leaders, including Stjepan Kljuić and Jovan Dijvak, oppose Tudjman and the declaration for the partition of the region.

July 7   Tudjman states he does not support the formation of Herzeg-Bosna as a Croatian state. Rather, Tudjman says the Herzeg-Bosna will help administer the area in the midst of wartime chaos while the integrity of Bosnia and Herzegovina remains his chief concern.

July 19   Panić goes to Bosnia and Herzegovina where he meets with Alija Izetbegović, the president of Bosnia and Herzegovina. Panić blames all three nationalities for the war, while Izetbegović considers Serbs the villains.

August 4   Accusations of Muslim and Croatian massacres of Serbian civilians begin to circulate. Additionally, reports indicate the Muslims are operating concentration camps similar to those the Serbs are known to have.

September 6   Boban orders the Croatian Defense Forces (HVO) to stop cooperating with Muslim forces in the Sarajevo fighting because the Muslims have been attacking Croatian positions to take supplies.

September 25   The Zagreb weekly *Globus* reports the systematic rape of Muslim and Croatian women by Serbian forces in Bosnia and Herzegovina.

September 30   The president of the rump Yugoslavia, Dobrica Ćosić, and President Tudjman of Croatia sign an agreement in Geneva calling for the withdrawal of JNA forces from the Prevlaka peninsula in southern Dalmatia. The withdrawal will complete the formal removal of the JNA from Croatia and end threats to Dubrovnik.

October 2 Bosnian Serb leaders deny there has been a policy of raping Muslim women. There have been recent reports from Zagreb of rapes of dozens of women by Serbian ethnic cleansing operations aimed at making the areas ethnically Serbian.

October 6 Serbs take the town of Slavonski Brod, Croatia, a crucial link between Serbia proper and the Krajina regions of Croatia and Bosnia.

October 12–13 In Priština, 50,000 Albanian students demonstrate against the serbianization of the curriculum at the University of Priština.

October 22 President Izetbegović agrees to divide Bosnia and Herzegovina into eight to ten cantons.

October 29 Serbian forces capture Jajce from Croat and Muslim forces.

November 27 Milošević announces he will run again for Serbian president in the elections of December 20.

December 1 Prime Minister Panić announces he will face Milošević in the December elections for president of Serbia. The Serbian electoral commission, controlled by Milošević's followers, challenges Panić's right to run because he does not meet residency requirements.

December 3 The electoral commission rejects Panić's candidacy. Panić appeals to the Serbian Supreme Court, which is chaired by the same man who chairs the electoral commission—Časlav Ignatović.

December 9 In a surprise decision, the Serbian Supreme Court rules Panić can run for president.

December 10 The parliament of Macedonia debates whether to change the state's name to the Republic of Macedonia (Skopje) in the hopes of pacifying the Greek government. Kiro Gligorov, the president of Macedonia, hopes the new name will be an appropriate compromise leading to recognition of the state by the European Community. Ultimately, the parliament votes against the name change.

December 12–13 The European Community's foreign ministers refuse to recognize Macedonia. They endorse a United Nations proposal to send 700 troops to Macedonia, and approve $62 million in humanitarian aid.

December 17 Lawrence Eagleburger, the acting U.S. Secretary of State and a long time actor in power circles in Belgrade, releases the names of Serbs and Croats whom the United States believes are guilty of war crimes. The list includes Milošević; Radovan Karadžić, the leader of the Bosnian Serbs; General Ratko Mladić, the commander of Serbian forces in Bosnia and Herzegovina; Vojislav Šešelj, the head of the ultra-nationalist Radical party in Serbia and

the commander of the "Četniks"; and Željko Ražnjatović, also known as Arkan, an international criminal before the war but now a Serbian hero who is charged with many of the most sickening of the crimes.

In a huge outdoor rally in Belgrade, Milan Panić and Vuk Drašković try to convince Serbs to vote Milošević out of office. In Drašković's words, "Serbia has the chance to turn defeat into victory, disgrace into honor, war into peace, and destruction into reconstruction."

December 20 Voting is held throughout Serbia and results show Milošević and his Socialist party are victorious. The opposition asserts the elections themselves are seriously flawed, and the Socialists manipulated them and used persuasion at the polling places. Milošević receives approximately 56 percent of the vote, Panić 34 percent. In Montenegro, incumbent Momir Bulatović receives 42 percent, the challenger Branko Kostić 23 percent.

December 28 Final results of the voting in Serbia confirm that Milošević will remain president. The ultranationalist Serbian Radical party wins 73 of the 250 seats in the Serbian assembly (it had only one before the elections), and will continue its alliance with the Socialists of Milošević.

The United States warns Serbia not to bring the war to Kosovo, or it may face American military force.

1993

January Talks continue between Bosnian Muslims and Serbs in Geneva. The Vance-Owen plan under discussion would divide Bosnia and Herzegovina into ten cantons, each of which would be dominated by one nationality. The Croats sign the plan early in negotiations, since they have all the territory they desire. The Muslims feel that the plan rewards Serbian aggression, whereas the Serbs believe that it is in their interest to continue fighting because they can only lose territory if they accept the plan.

January 7 Vojislav Šešelj, the leader of the ultranationalist Serbian Radical party, attacks Yugoslav President Ćosić for urging the Serbs to accept the current peace plan for Bosnia and Herzegovina. Šešelj accuses Ćosić of being a fatalist and suggests that the writer turned politician return to writing novels.

January 9 In one of the more brazenly lawless acts of the war in Bosnia and Herzegovina, Serbian gunmen stop a United Nations vehicle carrying Bosnia and Herzegovina's Deputy Prime Minister Hakija Turajlić and murder him. The leader of the Bosnian Serbs, Radovan Karadžić, apologizes for the action, but other Serbian military leaders claim that Turajlić had insulted the gunman and therefore the murder was justifiable.

January 19 Bosnian Muslims and Croats intensify their battles in the Gornji Vakuf and Travnik areas, where they have been fighting each other all month.

January 20 Serbian representatives meeting in Pale, southeast of Sarajevo, vote to accept the Vance-Owen peace plan for the cantonization of Bosnia and Herzegovina.

January 22 Croatian forces initiate military action near Zadar, in the Serbian Krajina region of Croatia. This breaks a year-old cease-fire. The Croats quickly make gains around Zadar. The United Nations condemns the attacks, and the JNA threatens intervention. By January 29, the Croats have retaken the Maslenica bridge, the Peruča dam, and many villages in between as they push toward Knin, the heart of Serbian Krajina.

February 1 The Bosnian peace talks move to New York, where the negotiators hope pressure will be put on the Serbs and Muslims to agree to the plan.

February 11 Warren Christopher, the U.S. secretary of state, announces the United States' six-point plan for Bosnia and Herzegovina, including United States support for the peace negotiations; sanctions against Serbia; a war crimes tribunal; the availability of U.S. forces for enforcement of any peace agreement; and working together with Russia. Further, the United States will also contribute Reginald Bartholomew, its own negotiator, to the talks. These proposals are a significant disappointment to those who thought the new American president, Bill Clinton, would initiate a more active policy toward Bosnia and Herzegovina.

March 25 Bosnia and Herzegovina President Izetbegović signs the Vance-Owen agreement, leaving only the Bosnian Serbs as opponents of the plan (*see* January 20).

April 8 Macedonia becomes the 181st member of the United Nations and is called the Former Yugoslav Republic of Macedonia until an arbitration committee can choose a name acceptable to the Greeks, who kept the country out of the U.N., claiming its name implied territorial designs on northern Greece (*see* January 6, 1992).

April 12 Macedonia asks all countries to recognize it diplomatically after Albania and Great Britain have done so on April 12 and 8 respectively.

April 21 Canadian United Nations troops disarm the Muslim soldiers in Srebrenica and begin the creation of a "safe-haven" for Muslim refugees in the eastern Bosnian town.

April 22 Croatian President Franjo Tudjman is booed as he is introduced at the dedication of the Holocaust Memorial Museum in Washington D.C. because he had written in a 1988 book that deaths attributed to the Holocaust had been greatly exaggerated.

May 2 Karadžić signs the Vance-Owen plan in Greece.

May 6 In Pale, the Bosnian Serbian parliament votes to reject the Vance-Owen plan. Karadžić announces that on May 15–16, a referendum will be held for Serbs to vote on the plan directly.

May 9 Zepa falls to the Serbs; Muslim refugees numbering in the thousands are gone from the area.

May 10 Macedonia issues its own currency, the denar, replacing coupons that had been used since Macedonia proclaimed its independence in September 1991.

May 16 Up to 90 percent of Bosnian Serb voters reject the Vance-Owen plan.

June 1 The lower house of the Yugoslav parliament votes to remove Dobrica Ćosić as president of Yugoslavia by a 75 to 30 vote; the upper house concurs, voting 22 to 10 to remove him. Ćosić is under fire from more nationalistic Serbs for his moderation on the question of Bosnia's fate.

June 2 Following demonstrations against the Milošević regime, Vuk Drašković, a writer and one of the leaders of the opposition, and his wife are arrested and beaten in Belgrade.

June 7 Dražen Petrović, a member of the 1992 Croatian silver medal Summer Olympic basketball team and New Jersey Nets guard, dies in an automobile accident in Germany.

June 25 Serbs elect Zoran Lilić as president of Yugoslavia.

July 2 Žepče falls to Croats as the Bosnian army abandons the town.

July 9 At the order of Milošević, Drašković and his wife are released by Serbian authorities.

August 28 The Bosnian parliament, consisting mainly of Muslims, votes 65 to 0 against the new United Nations–European Community plan to divide Bosnia into three ethnic units. Bosnian Serbs in Pale accept the plan; Bosnia Croats in Grude also accept the plan and declare the independence of the Croat state of Herceg-Bosna in western Bosnia.

September 14 Due to daily hyperinflation of 15 percent, rump Yugoslavia issues a one billion dinar note.

September 27 Fikret Abdić, the leader of the Muslim enclave of Cazinska Krajina, declares the enclaves autonomy from Bosnia in Bihać.

Croatian soldiers in action against Muslim forces.

October 5 Croatia devalues its currency by 16 percent in an attempt to curb an annual inflation rate reported at 2,500 percent.

October 7 The Serbian Radical party of Vojislav Šešelj introduces a no-confidence motion in the Socialist government headed by Nikola Šainović. The motion is the result of increasing tension between the Socialists of Milošević and the Radicals, from whom Milošević is trying to distance himself.

October 16 Franjo Tudjman is reelected president of the Croatian Democratic Union. In addition, a more moderate executive committee is elected by the party which is attempting to soften its image.

October 20 Slobodan Milošević dissolves the Serbian National Assembly (Skupština), citing political obstruction of the opposition to his Socialist government. He announces elections to be held on December 19.

October 22 Fikret Abdić, leader of Cazinska Krajina in northern Bosnia, signs a peace treaty with Milošević and Radovan Karadžić in Belgrade. He is condemned by many Muslims loyal to Alija Izetbegović's government in Sarajevo.

October 25 Haris Silajdžić, until now the foreign minister in the Bosnian government, is named prime minister by Izetbegović.

October 31 Montenegrins in favor of the independence of their Orthodox church from the Serbian church declare Antonije Abramović their patriarch. This move reflects growing tensions between Montenegro and Serbia and is decried immediately by the Serbian church.

November 2 Hungary signs friendship and cooperation treaties with Slovenia and Croatia.

November 3 Croatian troops and citizens abandon the town of Vareš in central Bosnia; it is captured by the Bosnian army.

November 5 In Belgrade, the government announces the arrest of 18 members of the Četniks, the paramilitary arm of the Serbian Radical party led by Vojislav Šešelj. The move is interpreted as part of a plan to weaken the Radicals and offer up some of them as sacrifices to the war crimes tribunal in the Hague.

November 9 Croats destroy the famous bridge over the Neretva river in Mostar (Hercegovina). The bridge was built in the sixteenth century by the Ottoman Turks.

Bosnia, on the way to total destruction.

November 10 A number of ethnic Albanians are arrested in Macedonia on charges of planning an armed uprising. Among those arrested are the deputy defense minister and deputy health minister.

November 17 The Yugoslav war crimes tribunal meets for the first time at the Hague.

November 21–23 Serbian and Croatian intellectuals meet in Zagreb, the first such meeting since the wars began in 1991. The meeting is viewed as an opportunity to try to rebuild bridges in the intellectual community.

December 3 The Party for Democratic Action, which represents the Muslims of the Sandžak region of Montenegro and Serbia (as well as of Bosnia) declares its intent to boycott the December elections in Serbia.

December 12 In the Serbian Krajina region of Croatia, Serbs go to the polls to decide on representatives to a parliament and a president. Milan Babić, one of the contenders for the presidency, describes the election as a referendum on sovereignty, although almost all of the candidates reject Krajina's ties to Croatia.

December 15 It is announced that Babić has won 33,000 votes to Milan Martić's 23,000 in the race for

president of the Serbian Krajina. Martić had been the candidate of Slobodan Milošević. Babić is a voice against negotiation with Croatia.

December 16 Some members of the European Community announce that they plan to recognize Macedonian independence. Germany, Denmark, Britain, and the Netherlands reveal that they have taken steps already. The Greek government denounces the move.

December 19 Parliamentary elections are held in Serbia.

December 22 Election returns show that the Socialists of Slobodan Milošević win 123 seats in the Serbian assembly; three seats short of an absolute majority. Željko Ražnjatović (Arkan), the criminal who had been groomed by Milošević to take the place of Vojislav Šešelj as the coalition partner of the Socialists, fails to gain a seat in the assembly; his party also fails to gain representation in the parliament.

Representatives of the warring factions in Bosnia meet in Brussels and sign a Christmas cease-fire that is to last until January 15, 1994. Nonetheless, the fighting continues.

December 27 France recognizes Macedonia. As more countries establish diplomatic relations with Macedonia, Greece retaliates by closing its border with Macedonia hoping to cause economic ruin that will force Macedonia to change its name (*see* April 8).

Biographies

Ramiz Alia (1925–   )

First Secretary, Albanian Communist Party, 1985–1991

Ramiz Alia was born to a poor Muslim family in Shkodër (Scutari). His formal education was limited to secondary schooling, which he completed at the French Lyceum in Tirana. Alia joined the Albanian Fascist Youth League shortly after the country's occupation by the Italians in 1939. While still in school he switched his allegiance to the Communist-led resistance and joined the Albanian Communist Youth in 1942. In April 1943 he became a member of the Albanian Communist party, and in June of that same year he was dispatched by the party to the Berat region to organize the youth of that area for Communist activities. Alia's rise through the party ranks was rapid: in November 1944 he was assigned to the Communist resistance's Fifth Combat Division as its political commissar with the rank of lieutenant-colonel, and fought with distinction in Yugoslavia; in April 1945 he was made a member of the Central Committee of the Albanian Communist Youth.

Alia's wartime efforts and his intense loyalty to the Albanian Communist party's leader, Enver Hoxha, helped to accelerate his rise towards the top of the political hierarchy in Communist Albania. During the first decade of Communist rule Alia quickly leapt forward from one post to another, assuming more power with each advancement: in 1947 he became secretary general of the People's Youth of Albania; in 1948 he was elected to the party's Central Committee; in 1949 he was appointed president of the People's Youth; in 1950 Alia was elected as a deputy to

the People's Assembly, and became a member of the General Council of the Democratic Front; in 1952 he was appointed first secretary of the Union of Working Youth; in 1952 he was elected to the Presidium of the People's Assembly; and in June 1955 Alia was appointed Minister of Education and Culture. Alia left his ministry post to join the ideological staff of the People's Central Committee in 1958, at a time when Albanian-Soviet relations were deteriorating. He played a prominent part in the deliberations that led in 1961 to Albania's break with the Soviet Union and a shift of allegiance to China. In a purge of the pro-Soviet members of the party leadership in 1960, Alia was named one of the party secretaries under First Secretary Hoxha. After serving as a member of the Politburo for five years, Alia was elevated to a full, or voting, member in 1961.

Throughout the 1960s and 1970s, Alia acquired extensive experience in party matters and played a major role in Albania's ideological campaigns against Belgrade, Moscow, and, later, Beijing. Alia's ideological convictions and international outlook mirrored those of Hoxha. In his public pronouncements Alia echoed Hoxha's views on domestic and foreign policy issues and repeatedly defended Albania's adherence to Stalinism. Despite his close association with Hoxha, Alia's rise to the top was often blocked by Mehmet Shehu, a longtime member of Hoxha's inner circle. However, Shehu, whom Hoxha had been grooming as his successor for decades, fell from grace and was either killed or committed suicide in December 1981. With Shehu out of the way, Alia quickly emerged as Hoxha's most trusted adviser. Alia was elected chairman of the Presidium of the People's Assembly on November 22,

1982, making him the official head of state. In the following year Alia began filling in for the ailing Hoxha at official functions, and in the summer of 1984 he delivered a series of speeches throughout Albania, making a provincial tour that had been a classic Hoxha trademark.

On April 13, 1985, two days after Hoxha's death, Alia was elected party first secretary by the Central Committee. Initially it appeared that Alia would faithfully adhere to Hoxha's Stalinist platform. In his funeral eulogy to Hoxha, Alia pledged that he would preserve and keep the policies of his predecessor. However, shortly thereafter Alia began charting an altogether new course for Albania. Departing from Hoxha's policy of self-imposed isolation, Alia first began to reconsider Tirana's foreign relations in June 1985. Owing to the growing severity of Albania's economic problems, caused in part by the policy of isolation, Alia accepted the view that Tirana's opening up to the outside world could be appropriate if it were consistent with the country's interests. Consequently, during the five years after Hoxha's death Alia took diplomatic initiatives to break Albania from its isolation. He accelerated the process of diversifying the country's foreign ties, concentrating on normalizing and strengthening relations with Greece, Italy, and Turkey. Alia's domestic policies were also aimed at reform, but he ruled out the possibility of fundamental or systematic changes of the country's rigid political structure.

Despite Alia's determination to preserve the party's monopoly of power, his regime was overwhelmed by revolutionary events. Encouraged by the collapse of Communist governments elsewhere in Eastern Europe, Albanians demonstrated against the government in December 1989. Throughout the following year Alia attempted to quell the growing unrest through concession, but each concession served merely to promote further demands for substantive reform and, eventually, political liberalization. Initially the contest over Alia's policies was between reformist and hard-line Stalinists within the party, but following major public upheavals in July 1990 it became an open struggle against as well as within the party. Alia quickly discovered that the forces of reform, once unleashed, could not be easily controlled. Against a background of mounting pressure for reform to be accelerated, Alia proposed a multiparty system in November 1990. However, even this dramatic concession did not pacify the mounting unrest, and large anti-Communist demonstrations and riots erupted throughout the country's cities. Alia continued to preside over the collapse of communism in Albania following the country's first postwar multiparty elections in March and April 1991. Due in large part to

fraud and intimidation the Communists won a majority in the People's Assembly, and on April 30, 1991, Alia was, accordingly, confirmed as the country's President. Throughout the next year, however, Albania sunk deeper into economic crisis and public anarchy, and in national elections held in March 1992 the Communists were swept from power by their new opponents, the Democratic Party of Albania. On April 3, 1992, Alia resigned as president. Exacting revenge against their former oppressors, on September 15, 1992, the new government placed Alia under arrest on charges of corruption.

Ivo Andrić (1892–1975)
Serbo-Croatian writer

Andrić was one of the greatest Yugoslav writers of the twentieth century. He was born in Travnik and attended schools in Višegrad, Sarajevo, Zagreb, Vienna, and Krakow. He later utilized his youthful experiences in Bosnia in his novels. Before the First World War, Andrić was a member of nationalist youth organizations in Bosnia and Croatia. After the war, Andrić entered government service, eventually gravitating to the foreign service, where he served in several European capitals until the Second World War.

During the Second World War, Andrić lived in retirement in Belgrade, writing what would become his three most respected works: *The Bridge on the Drina*, *Travnik Chronicle*, and *Miss*, all of which were published upon the end of the war. The first two reflect Andrić's Bosnian background. *The Bridge on the Drina* presents Bosnian history with a bridge in Višegrad as the central "character." The huge panorama of four centuries of Bosnian history is the backdrop to Andrić's story of the town and its inhabitants. The bridge ages, but always provides evidence of the role of history in the activities of the animate characters. *Travnik Chronicle* presents a story from Bosnia's nineteenth-century history during the Napoleonic wars. With French and Austrian consuls coming to serve in Travnik, the town and its new foreign inhabitants learn about each other's ways. The novel shares a rich evocation of Bosnia's mixed cultural and historical heritage with *The Bridge on the Drina*. *Miss*, also called *The Woman from Sarajevo*, chronicles the bizarre and unfortunate life of a woman during World War I.

After the war, Andrić lived in near-seclusion in Belgrade. He never had been a Communist or even a left-oriented individual before the war, and his coexistence with the Communist regime was uncomfortable for him. He was awarded the Nobel prize for literature in 1961.

Yuri Vladimirovich Andropov (1914–1984)
General Secretary, Soviet Communist Party, 1982–1984

The son of a railway official, Yuri Andropov was born on June 15, 1914, in Nagutskaia, Stavropol Krai of the North Caucasus region of Southern Russia. In 1936 Andropov graduated from the Inland Waterway Transport College at Petrozavodsk State University in Rybinsk.

Andropov began his political career in 1936 as secretary, and then first secretary of the Iaroslav Oblast Committee of the All-Union Komsomol (Young Communist League). He joined the Communist Party of the Soviet Union in 1939, and in 1940 Andropov became the first secretary of the Komsomol in the Karelo-Finnish Autonomous Republic. In this position he organized partisan resistance behind German lines during World War II.

In 1947 Andropov became second secretary of the Karelian Communist party Central Committee, and held this position until the early 1950s when he was transferred to Moscow to work on the secretariat staff of the Communist party of the Soviet Union. In 1954 Nikita Khrushchev appointed Andropov ambassador to Hungary. During his tour as ambassador, Andropov was instrumental in suppressing the Hungarian uprising of 1956. Recalled to Moscow in 1957, Andropov supervised Soviet Communist party relations with other Communist parties from 1958-1962. He then went on to become secretary of the Central Committee of the Communist party.

In May 1967, Leonid Brezhnev, general secretary of the Communist party, appointed Andropov chairman of the State Security Committee (KGB). As chairman of the KGB, he became well known for his suppression of dissident movements. In June of the same year, Andropov became a candidate member of the Politburo, and in April 1973 he became a full member of the Politburo.

In 1982 Andropov resigned as head of the KGB to become a member of the Presidium of the Supreme Soviet, the ruling body of the Soviet government. On November 10, 1982, two days after Brezhnev's death, the Central Committee unanimously elected Andropov general secretary or head of the Communist party of the Soviet Union. During his fifteen months in office, Andropov unsuccessfully attempted to end government corruption. After August 18, 1983, he was not seen in public and he died on February 9, 1984 as a result of kidney failure.

József Antall (1932–1993)
Prime Minister of Hungary, 1990–1993

Antall was born in 1932 to a political family. His father was a founding member of the Independent Smallholder's party who briefly held government posts after the Second World War. Antall went to school in Budapest, later studied history at the University of Budapest, and became a school teacher. During the 1956 uprising, Antall became the chair of the Budapest school system and helped establish the Christian Democratic Youth Association, for which he was imprisoned after the collapse of the revolt. Prohibited from teaching after his release from prison, he became a librarian. In 1964 he went to work in the Semmelweis Medical Museum as an archivist, becoming its director ten years later. As the communist regime began to unravel in Hungary, Antall pursued a political career. In 1987 he attended the founding of the opposition group the Democratic Forum, and was elected its president in October 1989. In the spring of 1990, Antall became the first democratically elected prime minister of Hungary. He died in office in December 1993.

Ion Antonescu (1882–1946)
Prime Minister of Romania, 1940–1944

Ion Antonescu was born in Piteşti, Wallachia, on June 2, 1882. Prior to World War I, he received his education in French military academies. During the war he served with the Romanian army, after which he became the military attaché in both London and Rome. In the late 1930s, he was appointed chief of the general staff, but King Carol II removed him for being too critical of the king's policies. Antonescu was later reappointed, but again dismissed in 1940 for urging the king not to cede Bessarabia and Bukovina to the USSR. Antonescu, due to his popular stance against the Soviet Union, was appointed prime minister on September 5, 1940. Among one of his first acts, Antonescu forced King Carol II to abdicate. Antonescu then set about establishing a fascist state, although he did not care for the Nazis and suppressed the Romanian equivalent, the Iron Guard, in 1941. Nonetheless, feeling abandoned by the Western powers, he joined the Axis alliance in late 1940 and took part in the invasion of the USSR in June 1941, regaining for Romania the territories lost the year before, and taking additional land from occupied Soviet regions. For these exploits, he was promoted to marshal, and he was perhaps the only ally of Hitler who could openly criticize the German leader. However, after reversals on the Russian front, Antonescu's popular support faded, and on August 23, 1944, as Soviet forces were occupying Romania, he was overthrown in a coup led by King Michael. Antonescu was arrested and tried as a war criminal in May 1946. Found guilty by a military tribunal, he was executed on June 1, 1946 in Jilava.

Edvard Benes̆ (1884–1948)
President of Czechoslovakia, 1935– 1938, 1945–1948

Edvard Benes̆ was born on May 28, 1884, in Kožlany, Bohemia, and studied at universities in Prague, Paris, Dijon, and Berlin. Prior to World War I, he taught at the Commercial Academy in Prague. While in Prague, Benes̆ became a disciple of Tomás̆ G. Masaryk and joined his Realist party. With the outbreak of war, Benes̆ worked with Masaryk in an underground nationalistic liberation movement called the Maffia. In September 1915, Benes̆ escaped to Switzerland and worked in western Europe with Masaryk and Milan R. S̆tefánik, a Slovak, toward Allied recognition of an independent Czechoslovakia. Benes̆ became secretary of the Czechoslovak National Council, a quasi government-in-exile, headquartered in Paris.

In October 1918, when the Republic of Czechoslovakia was established, Benes̆ was named its first foreign minister. In that position he represented Czechoslovakia at the Paris Peace Conference of 1919, helped to set up the Little Entente (a loose alliance between Czechoslovakia, Romania, and Yugoslavia) in 1921, and established the French-Czechoslovak-Soviet defensive pact of 1935. He also served as a delegate to the League of Nations from 1923 until 1927. In 1935 Benes̆ succeeded Masaryk as president. He was soon faced with the rise of Nazi Germany and the failure of his earlier diplomatic triumphs. Under pressure from Great Britain and France in September 1938, Benes̆ was forced to accept the Munich Agreement, which ceded the Sudetenland of Czechoslovakia to Germany. Benes̆ resigned as president on October 5, 1938, and went into exile.

With the outbreak of World War II in September 1939, Benes̆ traveled to London, where he became president of the Czechoslovak National Committee, which was recognized by the Allies as the legal government of Czechoslovakia. During the war Benes̆ oversaw the activities of this government-in-exile and devised plans for the country upon its liberation from the Nazis. Realizing the need for a strong alliance with the Soviet Union, he traveled to Moscow in December 1943 and concluded a pact that would form the basis of Czechoslovak foreign policy.

Benes̆ returned to Prague as president in May 1945 and was reelected in 1946. He pursued a policy of democracy, limited nationalization of industry, and attempted independence in national as well as foreign affairs, hoping to make Czechoslovakia a bridge between the Western democracies and the Soviet Union. As president he headed a coalition of Communists and democrats until February 1948, when due to blatant illegal activity by the Communists, most of the non-Communist ministers resigned. The democrats mistakenly hoped Benes̆ would consequently call for general elections in which the Communists would lose their majority party status. Instead, the Communist leaders, led by Premier Klement Gottwald, pressured Benes̆ into accepting a new government dominated by the Communists and their allies. The president, in poor health and wanting to avert civil war or the intervention of Soviet forces, relented. After this coup, Benes̆ remained in office but resigned in June 1948 rather than sign the new Czechoslovak constitution giving control of the country to the Communists. Benes̆ died shortly thereafter of a stroke on September 3, 1948, in Sezimovo Ústí.

Count István Bethlen (1874–?1947)
Prime Minister of Hungary, 1921–1931

Count István Bethlen was born into one of Transylvania's most historic and influential families. Managing his family's extensive Transylvanian estates, Bethlen did not become involved in Hungarian politics until the dissolution of the Austro-Hungarian Monarchy in 1918.

Bethlen became a member of the Szeged counterrevolutionary government in 1919 which launched his career in interwar Hungarian politics. On April 14, 1921, the regent of Hungary, Admiral Horthy, appointed Bethlen prime minister, a post he held for the next decade. Under his leadership, Bethlen sought to reestablish the old economic, social, and political system of the prewar period. He believed a parliamentary government representing the old ruling classes (estate owners, important capitalists, and nationalists) and the majority of the middle class was the only possible political path. In July 1920, Bethlen engineered the merger of the Smallholders' party with the more conservative Legitimist Christian National Union. Calling this new party the Party of Unity or Government party, Bethlen hoped that this party would provide sufficient safeguards which would make a turn to the left or extreme right impossible. His ascendancy was seen by the Hungarians as a period of consolidation and stability in the first decade after the First World War.

Under Bethlen, the new government reached an agreement with the Social Democrats, who conceded to refrain from organizing public officials and agricultural workers, and promised to avoid politically motivated strikes. Bethlen proceeded, during his decade as prime minister, on a conservative path designed to maintain the status quo. He ruled not only through the Government party but through control of other institutions such as the civil and military bureaucracies, the clergy, banks, the professions, and through landowners who sympathized and collaborated with him. To ensure the landed gentry's influence, Bethlen, in November 1926, reconstituted the Upper House of the Hungarian parliament which represented the landed aristocracy, whose House of Magnates had been abolished in 1919/1920. Bethlen argued for its reestablishment on the premise that the legislature needed a ''safety brake,'' *i.e.*, to protect the needs of the traditional ruling elites (estate owners, industrialists, and nationalists), and that only an upper house could play this role. With the reconstitution of the Upper House, Bethlen completed the last stages of consolidation.

With the onset of the worldwide depression in 1929/1930, the period of stability Hungary enjoyed under Bethlen during the past decade disappeared. Feeling pressure from resurgent agrarian interests and the emergence of the far right, the regent of Hungary, Admiral Horthy, wished to introduce summary jurisdictional procedures and to control the growing unrest of the workers. Bethlen refused to introduce such restrictive measures and resigned on August 19, 1931.

After Bethlen resigned, the Government party splintered into three factions. One faction, under Bethlen's leadership, represented the interests of the leading capitalists and the large modernized estates. Another faction spoke for the discontented agrarian population, while the final third followed Gyula Gömbös. While out of the limelight, Bethlen for the next decade worked behind the scenes to keep Hungary on the course which he had charted. However, Bethlen was thwarted by the increasing power of the far right which wished to align itself with Germany to recover land lost in the Treaty of Trianon (1920). Bethlen, disgusted at the close alliance of Hungary with Germany during the Second World War, secretly negotiated with the Western Allies in 1942 to remove Hungary from the Axis powers, but failed. Bethlen returned to Hungary where he was captured by the Soviet Army in 1944 and taken to Moscow. He died in Soviet custody in 1947.

Bolesław Bierut (1892–1956)
Prime Minister of Poland, 1952–1953
Chairman, Polish United Workers Party, 1948–1952

Bolesław Bierut was born in 1892 near Lublin, the son of farmer. He became involved in leftist activities at an early age and was expelled from school in 1905 for participating in an anti-Russian strike. For the next seven years he worked in various jobs, then as a teenager became active in the Socialist party. Bierut joined the Communist party in 1919, and under a threat of arrest he went to the Soviet Union, returning to Poland in 1926. Arrested in 1927, he escaped to Moscow where he worked for the Comintern. After more clandestine activities in Poland he was arrested once more in 1933. Escaping again after the Nazi invasion in 1939, Bierut fled to the Soviet Union, returning to Poland via parachute in 1943. Enjoying the support of Stalin, he was made acting head of state in September 1944 and elected secretary general of the Communist party in 1948 after helping engineer Władysław Gomułka's fall. He reorganized the party to form the Polish United Workers Party (PZPR). In 1952 he dropped the presidency and became premier, a post he held until 1954. Bierut, sometimes called the ''Stalin of Poland,'' was in Moscow at the Twentieth Party Congress when he died.

Boris III (1894–1943)
King of Bulgaria, 1918–1943

The son of King Ferdinand of Bulgaria and Marie Louise of Bourbon, Boris completed his education in Sofia's military academy and university. Boris' relatively frivolous youth was spent on railroading, his most passionate devotion. Boris' fascination with railroad locomotives led him to become a member of the Bulgarian Railroad Engineers Union and he is supposed to have begged Ferdinand to allow him to go to the United States to become a railroad engineer.

The military defeat of Bulgaria in the First World War brought the abdication and flight of Ferdinand, who was succeeded by Boris on October 3, 1918. Boris began his reign in a precarious position. Only one week before his ascension the beleaguered government in Sofia had survived a republican rebellion led by members of the radical Agrarian party. Compounding Boris' problems, in October 1919 the Agrarian party leader, Alexander Stamboliiski, came to power as prime minister. Stamboliiski had been a personal enemy of King Ferdinand and he was openly hostile toward the monarchy. In addition, Stamboliiski threatened the kingdom's conservative status quo by launching a wave of liberal reforms. Boris was also frustrated by Stamboliiski's foreign policy which encouraged friendship and cooperation with the other Balkan countries. Stamboliiski's domestic and foreign policies antagonized the army and the powerful Internal Macedonian Revolutionary Organization (IMRO), and his acceptance of Bulgaria's territorial losses after the First World War stimulated a strong revisionist movement. Boris bided his time to take action against Stamboliiski. On June 9, 1923, conservative elements in the military along with the IMRO overthrew Stamboliiski and murdered him.

In the aftermath of the anti-Stamboliiski coup Boris' efforts to expand his personal power were limited in their success. Instead, the chief coup leaders organized their own coalition government and proceeded with a wave of terror against Stamboliiski's supporters. In response to the Rightist terror the Bulgarian Communist party launched an ill-fated uprising in September 1923. Violence in Bulgaria continued to escalate as the Communists launched a campaign of assassinations, as government forces clamped down on opposition, and as IMRO terrorized the entire country with attacks against opponents. In April 1925 King Boris narrowly escaped a Communist assassination attempt when a bomb exploded in the Cathedral of Sofia.

The combination of public disorder, political problems, and economic crises led to another coup in May 1934. Fearing that the new government leaders, Colonel Kimon Georgiev and Colonel Damian Velchev, were planning to abolish the monarchy, Boris resolved to undermine the new regime. Boris, accordingly, fomented disunity within the officer corps, the new regime's principal source of support. In January 1935 Boris succeeded in forcing Georgiev and Velchev out of power. A new government was subsequently formed under Boris' lackey, Pencho Zlatev. Boris in effect established a royal dictatorship. Thereafter he presided over a personal government administered through pliant officers and civilian dependents.

Committed to a policy of revisionism and territorial expansion, Boris led Bulgaria into a close relationship with Nazi Germany. In 1938 Boris' regime began the rearmament of the Bulgarian military. Despite Bulgaria's official neutrality, Boris assured the Germans of Bulgaria's support when the Second World War began in 1939. In March 1941 Boris' government officially joined the Axis. Although Boris was reluctant to commit Bulgaria's army to the Axis war effort, Bulgarian territory was made available to the German army as a staging area for its invasion of

Greece and Yugoslavia in April 1941. With the subsequent Bulgarian occupation of much of Greek and Yugoslav Macedonia and Western Thrace, Boris appeared to have realized Bulgaria's expansionist goals. Nevertheless, tension between Berlin and Sofia continued because of Bulgaria's limited military contribution to the war effort. Shortly after conferring with Hitler in mid-August 1943 King Boris died suddenly and mysteriously. He was succeeded by his seven-year old son, Symeon (born to Giovanna, the daughter of Italy's King Victor Emmanuel III, whom Boris had married in 1930) for whom a regency was formed.

Ion Brătianu (1864–1927)

Prime Minister of Romania, 1909–11, 1913, 1914–18, 1918–19, 1922–26, 1927

Ion Brătianu was born in Florica on August 20, 1864, to a leading Romanian statesman of the same name. He received his education in Paris, and upon returning to Romania, he became an employee of the state railways. In 1895 Brătianu was elected to parliament as a member of the Liberal party. He served in the government as minister of the interior in 1907, and two years later he assumed the prime ministry as the leader of the Liberal party. For the next eighteen years, Brătianu would serve as premier for a total of six times: 1909–1911, 1913, 1914–1918, 1918–1919, 1922–1926, and 1927. During his terms in office, he marshaled party support for the realization of a greater Romania through territorial expansion. Furthermore, he advocated agrarian reform to benefit the landless peasantry and small landholders. It was during his third premiership that he steered Romania into a course of neutrality while bargaining with both the Entente and Central Powers for territory in the early part of World War I. He finally agreed to join the Allies in 1916, a move which quickly saw the defeat of the country. After the war, Brătianu served as the chief Romanian representative to the Paris Peace Conference, where his country was officially granted large amounts of land to create greater Romania. Brătianu died on November 24, 1927, while serving again as prime minister.

Bertolt Brecht (1898–1956)

German playwright and poet

Probably the most important German playwright of the century, Brecht was born in Augsburg, Bavaria (now Germany) on February 10, 1898. He served in the German army during World War I but became disillusioned by the war, developing a skepticism that would become the hallmark of his later work in the theater. Brecht worked as poet, novelist, song writer, and stage director but was best known as a playwright and supporter of revolutionary causes.

He carried his political ideas, which were Marxist, over into his writing, developing a style known as epic or dialectical theater designed to involve the audiences and direct their political judgment. His most famous work, the ''Threepenny Opera'' (1928), is an excellent example of his skepticism as the individual struggled with modern society and the pressures it presented. While he regarded the Weimar government as his foe, he was especially hostile to the right-wing groups arising in Germany in the 1920s and 1930s, such as the Nazis.

When Hitler came to power in January 1933, Brecht's popularity and his Marxism put him on the Nazi persecution list. Brecht moved to Denmark, where he continued to write and produce until 1939 and the outbreak of World War II. He moved briefly to Sweden and Finland and finally to the United States in 1941, where he stayed for the duration of the war, writing anti-Nazi plays.

Following the end of World War II, Brecht returned to Germany and chose to live and work in the Soviet zone in Berlin. He was active in helping other intellectuals and artists remain in the eastern zone and was prominent in the 1949 effort to induce scholars and scientists to reject emigration. His work was recognized not only by the GDR but also by the Soviet Union, which awarded him the Stalin Peace Prize in 1954. Brecht died in East Berlin on August 14, 1956.

Leonid Ilich Brezhnev (1906–1982)
General Secretary, Soviet Communist Party, 1964–1982

The son of a steel worker, Leonid Ilich Brezhnev was born in Kamenskoie, now Dneprodzerzhinsk, Ukraine on December 19, 1906. He joined the Komsomol, the Communist Youth League, in 1923 while he was a student at a technical college in Kursk. After graduation, Brezhnev worked as an agricultural surveyor on collectivization farm projects.

In 1931 Brezhnev joined the Communist party of the Soviet Union. After serving in the Soviet Army he returned to Dneprodzerzhinsk to direct the Metallurgical Technical College. In 1938 he was appointed deputy chairman of the regional Communist party committee in Dneprodzerzhinsk

where his work impressed Ukrainian party boss Nikita Khrushchev.

During World War II, Brezhnev served as a political commissar, a Communist party officer who oversees the actions of the army officers and soldiers, and he attained the rank of major general. After the war, in 1950, Brezhnev was appointed party boss in Moldavia and was ordered to ''sovietize'' the Romanian population. Impressed by Brezhnev's work, Joseph Stalin appointed him as a candidate member of the Politburo and a member of the secretariat of the Central Committee of the Communist party; he became a member of the ruling elite. After Stalin's death in 1953, Brezhnev lost his seat on these bodies and was sent to supervise the ''virgin lands'' project aimed at converting more land into useable farm land in Kazakhstan. After some initial success with the project Brezhnev was again appointed to the Politburo and secretariat in 1957.

Brezhnev served as chairman of the Presidium of the Supreme Soviet, or president of the Soviet Union, from May 1960 to June 1964. After Nikita Khrushchev was removed from office in October 1964, Brezhnev was elected Communist party first secretary, or head of the party and leader of the country. After 1966 this position was called General Secretary.

After Warsaw Pact troops invaded Czechoslovakia in 1968 to end the reforms, Brezhnev issued the ''Brezhnev Doctrine'' as an ideological justification for the invasion; the doctrine allowed the Soviet Union to intervene in another socialist country when that country threatened to leave socialism. With the West, Brezhnev pushed for detente and peaceful coexistence and he worked to normalize relations with West Germany. Under his rule, the Soviet Union emerged as a political and military superpower. But at home Soviet citizens suffered during an extended period of economic stagnation. Brezhnev died on November 10, 1982.

Josip Broz (Tito) (1892–1980)
President of Yugoslavia, 1953–1980

The career of Tito is difficult to encapsulate, given the mythology surrounding his character. It may be enough to say that his personal history is littered with the most important dates in postwar Yugoslav history. Tito, whose mother was a Slovene and father a Croat, was born in Kumrovec, Croatia, and in 1907 went to work as a locksmith's apprentice in Sisak. In 1913, he joined the Habsburg army and was captured by the Russian army in 1915. He came back to Croatia in 1920 and joined the Communist party. By 1927, he was the secretary of the Communist Party of Yugoslavia Zagreb committee; in 1929 he was in jail for his work in the party. In 1934, he was released from prison and went to Moscow to work for the Comintern. Surviving the Stalinist purges he returned to Yugoslavia in 1936, and he headed the CPY from 1937 forward. From 1941 to 1945, he and his Partisans led a Communist resistance to the Germans and Italians; they also fought the Croatian Ustaša and the Serbian royalist Četniks. From 1945 until his death, he was the Marshal or the leader of Yugoslavia.

Tito laid claim to more than just the leadership of a medium-sized Balkan state; he aspired to be a world leader, and he succeeded to some extent. After his split with Stalin, Tito steered Yugoslavia between the East and West blocs and actually created a bloc of his own—the nonaligned movement, which grouped underdeveloped states wishing to be associated neither with the East nor the West. Another one of Tito's goals was self-management, the Yugoslav twist on Marxist economics. Self-management assumed the workers should make decisions for themselves in their enterprises; the ultimate goal of a workers' state, after all, could only mean worker control of the economy.

Tito's influence within the Communist world was transitory and variable, and depended on the attitude and needs of the Soviet Union, but he certainly carved for himself a niche in the iconography of the Communist movement. Ultimately, he can be held responsible for both the prosperity that Yugoslavia enjoyed after 1945 and the nationalist eruptions that followed his death in 1980.

Nicolae Ceauşescu (1918–1989)
President of Romania, 1974–1989
General Secretary, Romanian
Communist Party, 1965–1989

Ceauşescu was born to a poor peasant family in Scornicesti, in the Oltenia region of Wallachia. In the 1930s he worked for the Communist party, being imprisoned for his activity in 1936 and again in 1940. In 1936 he received a two-and-a-half year prison sentence during which he was the cell mate of Gheorghe Gheorghiu-Dej, who would rule Romania from 1952 until 1965. Ceauşescu quickly became his protege and eventually his successor in 1965. In 1939 Ceauşescu married Elena Petresu, who would later help him rule the country. Imprisoned again in 1940 for his activity within the illegal Communist party, he escaped in August 1944 with Gheorghiu-Dej and several

other Communists shortly before the coup against Marshal Antonescu. From 1944 to 1945, he served as the secretary of the Union of Communist Youth and was elevated to full membership in the party in 1948. After the Communists took control of Romania in late 1947, Ceauşescu was appointed deputy minister of agriculture in 1948, and during the same year he was elected a full member of the Central Committee of the party. Two years later he became the deputy minister of the armed forces, with the rank of major general. With the accession to power of Gheorghe Gheorghiu-Dej in 1952 after a power struggle, Ceauşescu received important positions in the ruling structures of the Romanian Workers' (Communist) party and became the number two man in Romanian politics. When Gheorghiu-Dej died of cancer in 1965, Ceauşescu succeeded him as first secretary, and two years later he became the Romanian head of state. Ceauşescu continued the policies of his predecessor that stressed industrialization over agriculture in domestic policy and independence in foreign affairs. Pursuing this course in international relations, Romania virtually ended active participation in the Warsaw Pact, emphasized friendly ties with Western nations, the People's Republic of China, and nonaligned countries, and denounced the invasions of Czechoslovakia in 1968 and Afghanistan in 1979. As a result of his independent, nationalistic course which challenged the dominance of the Soviet Union, he won widespread popular support at home. However, his intransigence forced him to behave rather forcefully in domestic policy, where he kept tight controls over his people. Ceauşescu stifled opposition while establishing a cult of personality and family with his dynastic socialism, appointing his wife and other family members to important leadership positions. Due to his policy of industrialization and a poorly planned economy, Romania was forced to borrow large amounts of money causing a huge national debt. Ceauşescu's determination to pay off this debt resulted in drastic shortages of food, fuel, energy, medicines, and other basic necessities for the Romanian population. Although the debt was paid off in 1989, the people were the edge of rebellion when a spark in the city of Timişoara ignited the tense situation in December 1989. Ceauşescu unsuccessfully attempted to keep control of the country by ordering the army to restore order. The army however, joined the protestors on December 22. On the same day, Ceauşescu and his wife fled the capital by helicopter but were captured a short time later by the military. After a quick military trial on December 25, both Ceauşescu and his wife Elena were executed by firing squad after being found guilty of genocide against the Romanian people.

Konstantin Ustinovich Chernenko (1911–1985)

General Secretary, Soviet Communist Party, 1984–1985

Konstantin Chernenko was born into a peasant family on September 14, 1911, in Bolshaia Tes, Krasnoiarsk region, Siberia. In his youth, Chernenko worked as a farm laborer and had very little time for a formal education. However, later in life he studied at the Higher Party School in Moscow and at the Kishinev Pedagogical Institute in Moldavia. He joined the Komsomol or Young Communist Youth League in 1926 and the Communist party of the Soviet Union in 1931. Starting in 1933, Chernenko served as a party official in the Krasnoiarsk region and became regional secretary or director of the party in 1941.

The turning point in Chernenko's career came in 1948 when he was sent to Moldavia to serve as head of the propaganda and agitation department of the Central Committee of the Moldavian Communist party. During his stay in Moldavia, Chernenko formed a close working relationship with the first secretary of the Moldavian Communist party, Leonid Brezhnev.

In 1956 Chernenko moved to Moscow to work as sector head of the propaganda and agitation department of the Central Committee of the Soviet Communist party. In 1960, when Brezhnev became chairman of the Presidium of the Supreme Soviet, Chernenko became head of the secretariat of the Presidium—in essence, he became Brezhnev's chief assistant. In 1971 Chernenko was elected as a member of the Communist Party Central Committee; in 1976 he became secretariat of the Central Committee; and in 1978 he was elected as a member of the Politburo. During this period he continued to work closely with Brezhnev, often traveling abroad with him on important diplomatic missions such as the signing of the SALT II Treaty (Strategic Arms Limitations Treaty) in Vienna in 1979. He also succeeded Mikhail Suslov as Central Committee Secretary in Charge of Ideology in 1982.

Although Brezhnev was grooming Chernenko as his heir apparent, Yuri Andropov succeeded Brezhnev in 1983. However, after Andropov died in February 1984, the Central Committee unanimously elected Chernenko as general secretary or leader of the Communist party of the Soviet Union on February 13, 1984. On April 11, 1984 the Supreme Soviet elected Chernenko chairman of the Supreme Soviet (President). Less than a year later, Chernenko died, on March 10, 1985.

Otto Dibelius (1880–1967)

German religious leader

The Lutheran church leader and opponent of both the Nazis and the Communists, Dibelius was born in Berlin, Germany, on May 15, 1880. Trained as an Evangelical theologian, he began as a pastor in Berlin in 1915. He became an advisory member of the Protestant church in the early 1920s, and as his popularity grew he became, in 1925, general superintendent of the Lutheran church in Prussia.

Dibelius was an early opponent of the Nazis and was removed from his position as superintendent when Hitler came to power in 1933. Dibelius continued to oppose state interference in church affairs, and he was brought before one of Hitler's special courts but was acquitted.

At the end of World War II Dibelius was appointed Evangelical Bishop of Berlin, serving all four zones of occupation. He was in conflict with the Communists almost immediately. The ban by the new East German government in 1949 of the Christmas holiday and Christmas school programs brought a joint response from the Catholic and Evangelical clergy the following spring, charging the German Democratic Republic (GDR), or East Germany, with trying to suppress religion.

In 1953 Dibelius was denied an entry permit into the GDR during a period of repression of religion because he told churches to continue to function and do their duties in spite of the repression. That summer he met with Otto Grotewohl and received a pledge that the pressure on the churches would ease. The pledge was short-lived and he was personally banned from holding Christmas services in Stalinstadt the same year. Dibelius was especially opposed to the Communists in their attempts to influence German youth in 1955, and along with the Catholics he refused the sacraments to any youth who took the Communist party pledge. He was active, and once again banned in the GDR, during the 1957 drive against religion. The same thing happened again in 1959. He offered to resign to prevent a schism within the Evangelical church in the GDR and the Federal Republic, or West Germany, but this was rejected by the Evangelical Synod.

Though he was chairman of the board of the Evangelical Church and one of five presidents of the World Council of Churches, he still was not allowed entry into the GDR after 1960. He remained bishop of Berlin until 1966, resigning shortly before his death in Berlin on January 31, 1967.

Georgi Dimitrov (1882–1949)
Prime Minister of Bulgaria, 1946–1949

The son of Mihail Dimitrov, a poor peasant who emigrated from Ottoman Macedonia to Bulgaria to become a factory worker, and of Paraskeva (Doseva) Dimitrov, Georgi Dimitrov was born in Kovachevtsi, Bulgaria, on June 18, 1882. He left school at the age of twelve and went to work for a printer two years later. Soon after he was hired Dimitrov organized a printers union. In 1902 Dimitrov joined the Social Democratic party (SDP) and that same year he was elected a representative to the Sofia City Council. When the SDP split into socialist and socialist-democratic factions in 1903 Dimitrov remained in the left wing of the party, becoming a member of its Central Committee in 1909. Dimitrov was elected to the Subranie in 1913, a position he held for the next ten years. He was imprisoned for a short time in 1918 for his antiwar activities.

Dimitrov was one of the leading organizers of the Bulgarian Communist party (BCP) in 1919. In 1921 he traveled to the Soviet Union where he was elected a member of the Executive Committee of the Communist International (Comintern). While engaged in furthering his position in the world Communist movement, Dimitrov led an ill-fated uprising against King Boris III in September 1923. In April 1925 Dimitrov led another abortive uprising in Bulgaria. He fled across the border to Yugoslavia and was sentenced to death in absentia. As a result, Dimitrov was unable to return to Bulgaria until after the Second World War. In the next years he served as a representative of the Comintern, traveling on various missions to Berlin, Paris, Prague, Vienna, and cities in the Balkans. Dimitrov gained world attention in 1933 when he was arrested by the Nazi authorities and accused of complicity in the burning of the German Reichstag, or parliament building. Pressure from public opinion and the intervention of the Soviet Union, which granted Dimitrov Soviet citizenship, resulted in his acquittal and release in 1934; he left immediately for Moscow.

Once in the Soviet Union Dimitrov returned to prominence as an important figure in the international Communist movement, as well as the *de facto* leader of the émigré BCP members, the "Muscovites." From 1935 to 1943 Dimitrov served as the Secretary General of the Comintern's Executive Committee in Moscow. In that capacity it became his task to outline and promote the popular front Soviet policy throughout Europe—calling for cooperation between Communists and liberals against fascism. Dimitrov was also, from 1937 to 1945, a deputy of

the Soviet Supreme Council elected from the Kostroma area of the USSR.

After Hitler attacked the Soviet Union Dimitrov directed from Moscow the Bulgarian Communist underground against the Germans. In June 1942, under Dimitrov's guidance from Moscow, the Fatherland Front was founded in Bulgaria as a Communist-led resistance coalition. On September 9, 1944, the Fatherland Front staged a coup and the Communists seized power in Bulgaria. The BCP, supported by Soviet occupation authorities, proceeded vigorously to consolidate its dominant political position and to destroy both its real and imagined enemies.

Dimitrov returned to Bulgaria in April 1945, after twenty-two years of exile, to assume the leadership of the BCP. With Dimitrov's arrival, the communization process was accelerated, and in September 1946 the monarchy was abolished and Bulgaria was proclaimed a people's republic. The subsequent rigged elections in October 1946 placed the BCP firmly in control of the state, and in November Dimitrov became Bulgaria's prime minister. Following the adoption of a new constitution in December 1947, shaped by Dimitrov and modeled on the Soviet constitution, the BCP launched a terror campaign which eliminated the remaining independent political and labor associations in Bulgaria. This liquidation policy was also extended to the ranks of the BCP. Under Dimitrov's orders hundreds of BCP members were executed or imprisoned in 1948–1949 as the "native" faction of the party (those who had remained in Bulgaria during the Second World War) was purged by the "Muscovites" (those leaders of the party who spent the war years in the Soviet Union). At the height of the party purges Dimitrov fell ill and died while in Moscow on July 2, 1949.

Milovan Djilas (1911–   )
Yugoslavian writer and dissident

Djilas is from Montenegro, and like Ivo Andrić, his youth in his native land provides much of the inspiration for his literary work. However, he was originally known as one of the four leading Communists in Yugoslavia along with Tito, Kardelj, and Ranković. He joined the Communist Party of Yugoslavia in 1932. Djilas belonged to the left faction of the party and participated with enthusiasm in the ideological conflicts within the party throughout the thirties (his experiences are documented in *Memoir of a Revolutionary* (1973). In the interwar period, he spent considerable time in prison for his Communist activities. During and after the Second World War, he served as the party's chief ideologist, and worked for the intellectual pursuit of a classless society. After the war, he made several trips as Tito's emissary to Stalin. These trips became the subject of his riveting *Conversations with Stalin* (1962).

By 1954, Djilas had concluded that the freedom of the human spirit was the highest goal to which one could aspire; however, this goal could not be accommodated within the context of the Communist movement. His writings of the period, which ultimately assumed the immediate withering away of the party and the state as desirable, resulted in his removal in 1954 from all of his positions in the state and party; he later resigned from the party altogether. He spent much of the next decade in prison as a result of his writings, which included the influential *The New Class* (1962) and his four volumes of memoirs (including *Land without Justice* (1958), *Wartime* (1977), and *Rise and Fall* (1983), in addition to *Memoirs of a Revolutionary*, noted above).

Djilas now lives in Belgrade in forced but literarily active retirement.

Roman Dmowski (1864–1939)
Polish statesman

He was born into the gentry class on August 9, 1864, near Warsaw in Russian Poland. Dmowski graduated from Warsaw University in 1891 with a degree in the sciences, but he took a liking to politics. From 1895 he worked with other Poles in Austrian and Prussian Poland for a reunification of the country. As a member of the National Democratic party from 1897, he was elected to the Russian Duma, or legislature, in 1907, serving until 1912, and he espoused the idea of an autonomous Poland under czarist Russia. With the outbreak of World War I, Dmowski supported the Russian war effort, but, becoming increasingly disillusioned with Russian policy toward Poland, he left for the West in 1915. From 1917 to 1919 he was a member of the Polish National Committee in Paris, which the Allies eventually recognized as the spokesman for Polish national interests. After the war, he was the Polish representative to the Paris Peace Conference along with Ignacy Jan Paderewski, where he stood for the incorporation into the new Polish state of Upper Silesia, Pomerania with Danzig, Mazuria, Warmia, Lithuania, and parts of Belorussia, and Ukraine; both signed the Treaty of Versailles on June 28, 1919. From 1919 to 1922 Dmowski sat as a delegate in the Sejm and served briefly as foreign minister in 1923. In 1926 he helped establish an opposition group to Marshal Piłsudski's

dictatorship, although he had retired from active politics after his stint as foreign minister. Dmowski, an integral nationalist, was known for his policies of anti-Semitism and assimilationism especially for the Belorussians and Ukrainians in Poland. He died in Drozdów on January 2, 1939.

Alexander Dubček (1921–1992)
First Secretary, Czechoslovak Communist Party, 1968–1969

Alexander Dubček was born on November 27, 1921, in Uhrovec, Slovakia. Four years later the Dubček family moved to Kirghizia, a republic in the Soviet Union, where Dubček's father helped build an industrial cooperative. Until 1938, when the family returned to Czechoslovakia, Dubček attended various local schools in the USSR. He joined the outlawed Czechoslovak Communist party in 1939, and during World War II he worked in an armaments factory. Dubček joined the Slovak National Uprising against the Nazis and the Slovak fascist regime in August 1944, during which he was wounded twice.

After the war he rose slowly through the local ranks of the Communist party until 1949 when he became the party secretary of the Trenčín district of Slovakia. From 1949 to 1951 Dubček held various positions of leadership in Slovakia and served as a deputy in the National Assembly from 1951 to 1955. In 1955 he travelled to Moscow where he studied for three years at the political school of the Communist Party of the Soviet Union, graduating with honors. Upon returning to Czechoslovakia, he held various leadership positions in Slovakia and Czechoslovakia. In 1960 he regained his seat in the National Assembly and was also elected as the secretary of the Central Committee of the Czechoslovak Communist party. Three years later he became the highest official in the Slovak Communist party and the top Slovak in the Czechoslovak Communist party. Due to cultural repression and a declining economy, Dubček attacked Antonín Novotný's control of the country at a Central Committee meeting in October 1967, forcing Novotný to resign as the chief Communist official on January 5, 1968. Dubček took over as first secretary of the party on the same day. In the weeks that followed, he embarked on a series of economic, cultural, and political reforms known as the Prague Spring to bring about "socialism with a human face." The USSR and other East European countries grew alarmed at the pace and scope of Dubček's liberalization, fearing it could spread. On August 20 and 21, they invaded Czechoslovakia, which put an end to the reforms. Although briefly arrested and taken to Moscow by Soviet authorities, Dubček returned to Czechoslovakia where he was forced to accept the Soviet occupation. Starting in 1969, he was slowly removed from his positions of power. In 1970, while serving as ambassador to Turkey, Dubček lost his membership in the party and was recalled to Czechoslovakia. From 1970 to 1989 Dubček lived the life of a political nonentity in Bratislava, where he was kept under constant surveillance. During the November 1989 Velvet Revolution that ended communist rule in Czechoslovakia, Dubček reemerged as a popular figure by addressing demonstrators both in Prague and Bratislava. In December he was appointed chairman of the Federal Assembly, the national parliament. Dubček held this position until his death on November 7, 1992, as the result of injuries received in an automobile accident two months earlier.

Ferdinand of Saxe-Coburg-Gotha (1861–1948)
King of Bulgaria, 1908–1918

Ferdinand-Maximilian-Charles-Leopold-Marie of Saxe-Coburg-Gotha was born to Prince Augustus of Saxe-Coburg-Gotha and Princess Clementine of Orleans, the daughter of King Louis Philippe of France, in the massive Coburg Palace in Vienna on February 26, 1861. While a young officer in the Habsburg army Ferdinand was offered the Bulgarian crown by the Subranie, the parliament of Bulgaria. On August 14, 1887 Ferdinand was unanimously elected prince of Bulgaria by the Subranie without the sanction of the Great Powers. Between 1887 and 1894 Ferdinand aspired to create a personal government under his absolute control. By exploiting rivalries between various political leaders he succeeded in becoming the actual as well as the titular ruler of Bulgaria during the late 1890s. In 1896 Ferdinand also succeeded in winning recognition from the Great Powers. On October 5, 1908, Ferdinand assumed the title King of the Bulgarians.

Although Ferdinand realized his domestic political goals, his foreign policy blunders led to his own downfall. Ferdinand's objective was to expand Bulgaria's territorial frontiers to encompass the borders of the San Stefano Treaty and beyond. He found great allure in the mystique of a resurrected medieval Bulgarian Empire modeled on the Byzantine Empire and dominant in the Balkans. Towards these goals Ferdinand's government led Bulgaria into the First Balkan War against the Ottoman Empire in 1912 and the Second Balkan War against Bulgaria's former allies Greece, Serbia, and Montenegro in 1913; the Second Balkan War ended in disaster for Bulgaria. His expansionist ambitions frustrated, Ferdinand committed Bulgaria to a policy of revisionism. In October 1915 Ferdinand's government brought Bulgaria into the First World War on the side of the Central Powers. Despite initial successes Bulgaria's involvement in the war ended in defeat in September 1918. Under the combined pressures of military catastrophe, economic disruption, political instability, and an abortive republican rebellion, Ferdinand abdicated the throne on October 3, 1918, leaving his son Boris III to succeed him. Ferdinand died on September 10, 1948, in Coburg, Germany, thirty years after his abdication.

Gheorghe Gheorghiu-Dej (1901–1965)
First Secretary, Romanian Workers Party, 1955–1965
Prime Minister of Romania, 1952–1955

Gheorghiu-Dej was born in Birlad, Moldavia, on November 8, 1901, to working-class. He attended school briefly before going to work as a shoemaker. After World War I, he became active in leftist political movements and joined the Communist party in 1926. In 1931 after a brief imprisonment in Dej, he added this place name to his surname. During the 1933 Grivita railway strike, Gheorghiu-Dej took a leadership role, and as a result he received a twelve-year prison sentence. Shortly before Romania left the Axis camp in August 1944, he escaped from prison and quickly became the secretary general of the Romanian Communist party. After the August 23, 1944 coup against the Antonescu government, Gheorghiu-Dej became the minister of communications. In the November 1946 general elections, he won a seat in the parliament. Between 1944 and 1948, Gheorghiu-Dej played an increasingly important role in the Communist subversion of Romania, while from 1946 to 1952, he held various positions for economic planning, including minister of economy. During the 1949-1951 power struggle, he successfully led his group of national Communists against that of the Moscow oriented Communists led by Ana Pauker, eliminating it by 1952 when he became prime minister. Although initially adopting policies that followed the Soviet model in the mid-1950s, he gradually pursued methods that were in the best interests of Romania. In 1954 he resigned as secretary general of the party, but in 1955 he resumed this position, now renamed first secretary, after quitting the premiership. In 1961 Gheorghiu-Dej became the president of the State

Council of a reorganized government, after which he followed a policy of industrialization and a independent course in foreign affairs by establishing friendly relations with non-Communist countries and the People's Republic of China. He died in Bucharest on March 19, 1965, of cancer, to be succeeded by his protege Nicolae Ceauşescu.

Edward Gierek (1913–   )
First Secretary, Polish United Workers Party, 1970–1980

Edward Gierek was born in the village of Porałka in Austrian Poland on January 6, 1913. At the age of ten, after his father died in a mining accident, his family moved to France, where he became employed as a miner. In 1931 he joined the French Communist Party and was deported back to Poland by French authorities after he helped organize a strike in 1934. Three years later he moved to Belgium and joined the Belgian Communist Party. Gierek remained in that country through World War II and became active in the underground movement against the Nazi occupiers. He returned to Poland in 1948, becoming the party boss of Silesia in 1951. Several years later he was elevated to the Politburo, and on December 20, 1970, he replaced Władysław Gomułka as first secretary of the Polish United Workers party (PZPR), a post he held until his downfall on September 6, 1980. In 1981 he was expelled from the party; he now lives in retirement. Gierek's decade in office can be characterized by fateful decisions in the economic sphere—especially to invest in heavy industry to the detriment of agriculture—that ultimately led to the creation of the independent trade union Solidarity and the downfall of not only Gierek but of Communist rule itself.

Władysław Gomułka (1905–1982)
First Secretary, Polish United Workers Party, 1956–1970

Władysław Gomułka, the son of a skilled oil worker, was born near Krosno in Austrian Poland on February 6, 1905. Trained as a locksmith, he worked actively in leftist movements, joining the Polish Communist Party in 1926, wherein he was known by the pseudonym "Wiesław." In the 1930s he helped organize unions and strikes for which he was arrested and imprisoned during 1932–34 and again in 1936–39. Between his prison terms, Gomułka attended the International Lenin Institute in Moscow. In September 1939 he was released from prison to help fight the Nazi invasion, and he organized a Communist resistance move-

ment against the Germans in 1941. During the war he rose through the ranks of the Communist Party, becoming its secretary general in 1943, and in 1944 joined the pro-Soviet Lublin government. In 1945 he became deputy premier and the official responsible for administering the lands in the west taken from Germany. Later that year he was elected to the Politburo and became secretary general of the Central Committee. During a purge of Polish Communists after 1948, Gomułka lost his positions within the party and government, being arrested in 1951 for "nationalist deviation." Gomułka was released in 1955 and officially "rehabilitated" the next year. After the June 1956 riots in Poznań, he became first secretary in October and introduced a number of reforms that were in part adopted. However, his popular support waned by the late 1960s, due to growing economic stagnation. Unable to address the growing economic difficulties of Poland, Gomułka was forced out of office on December 20, 1970, after which he remained a member of the Council of State until 1971 and continued to hold his seat in the Sejm until 1972, when he retired. Throughout his career, Gomułka was known as a nationalist, as evidenced by his pamphlet *O co walczymy? (Why Do We Fight?)* in which he stressed the equal importance of national independence and social revolution. Gomułka died on September 1, 1982.

Mikhail Sergeevich Gorbachev (1931–   )
General Secretary, Soviet Communist Party, 1985–1991

Mikhail Sergeevich Gorbachev was born into a Russian peasant family in Privolnoe, Stavropol territory, Russia, on March 2, 1931. As a teenager Gorbachev worked on farms driving agricultural machinery.

In the early 1950s Gorbachev joined the Communist party of the Soviet Union and attended Moscow University to study law. Upon his graduation in 1955 Gorbachev returned to Stavropol to head the regional Komsomol or Young Communist League. In 1962 he became regional agricultural secretary, and, in 1970, after completing a degree at the Stavropol Institute of Agriculture, Gorbachev assumed the post of first secretary of the Stavropol Region party committee, a position equivalent to a United States governor.

Gorbachev moved to Moscow in 1978 to become agricultural secretary of the Communist party Central Committee. In 1980 he was elected as a full member of the Politburo, the ruling body of the Communist Party. When

Iurii Andropov became General Secretary, Gorbachev was appointed second secretary to oversee the economy.

In March 1985, after Konstantin Chernenko's death, the Communist party leaders quickly appointed Gorbachev general secretary of the party. Gorbachev became the first, and last, Soviet leader to be educated and rise through the ranks of the party in the post-Stalinist era. Gorbachev embarked on a program of social, political, and economic reform for the country referred to as glasnost, or openness, and perestroika, or restructuring. In foreign affairs, Gorbachev allowed the East European countries to follow their own course of reform and government, allowing Germany to reunite in 1990. But at home he attempted to keep the republics of the Soviet Union united. However, he did allow reforms in government; in 1989 he established an elected legislative body, the Congress of People's Deputies, and in 1990 he pushed for the Communist party to give up its monopoly of political power. Under Gorbachev's rule the Soviet government became more tolerant by easing travel restrictions, allowing increased artistic freedom, and granting more religious tolerance.

Although he was seen as a great reformer in the West, many Soviet citizens did not support Gorbachev. Conservatives believed his reforms went too far, while some reformers felt that the pace of his liberalization policies was too slow. In August 1991, on the eve of signing a new union treaty that redefined the relation of the republics to the central government, a group of conservatives, headed by the Soviet vice-president, attempted to oust Gorbachev from power. Gorbachev stayed in power thanks to the efforts of Russian Federation President Boris Yeltsin and Leningrad Mayor Anatoli Sobchak, both of whom opposed the coup.

Although Gorbachev did briefly return to head the Soviet Union after the coup, it quickly became clear that government power was now in the hands of the leaders of the Soviet Republics. After leaders of most of the remaining Soviet republics (excluding Georgia and the Baltic States) agreed to create the Commonwealth of Independent States, Gorbachev resigned on December 25, 1991, and the Soviet Union ceased to exist.

Klement Gottwald (1896–1953)

President of Czechoslovakia, 1948–1953

Klement Gottwald was born into a peasant family in the Moravian village of Dĕdice u Vyskova, and at the age of twelve he was apprenticed to a woodworker in Vienna. In 1915, Gottwald was drafted into the Austro-Hungarian army, and he served on both the Italian and Russian fronts before deserting shortly before the end of the war. After the war, Gottwald joined the Czechoslovak Social Democratic party and allied with the left wing. In 1921 he and other leftist members of the Social Democrats resigned and formed the Czechoslovak Communist party. Gottwald soon became the editor of the Slovak party newspaper *Hlas L'udu* (Voice of the People) and later *Pravda* (Truth). In 1925 he was elected to the Central Committee of the Czechoslovak Communist party, becoming general secretary four years later. In 1929 he was also elected as a deputy to the National Assembly in Prague, where in his first speech, he reportedly said in reference to the non-Communist government and deputies, "You gentlemen ask me what we are here for. My answer is simple. We are here to break your necks, and I promise you most solemnly, we will do it."

In 1934 Gottwald was utterly defeated by Tomáš G. Masaryk in a bid for president of the republic during a joint session of the National Assembly. Later that year he fled to the USSR when the authorities sought to arrest him as an agitator, but he returned two years later. In 1938, due to the Munich Agreement that placed Czechoslovakia under Nazi German influence, he again went to the USSR where he organized a group of exiled Czechoslovak Communists who became the core of the party after the war. During World War II, Gottwald broadcasted to the underground urging resistance in the occupied Czech Lands and Slovakia. When the Czechoslovak government returned in April 1945, Gottwald received the position of deputy prime minister. After the general elections in May 1946 gave the Communists a plurality and thus the most seats in the parliament, President Edvard Beneš appointed Gottwald as prime minister of a coalition government. Gottwald then played a chief role in the subversion of democracy in the country. When it became apparent in early 1948 that the Communists would lose in the next general elections in the spring, Gottwald engineered a coup in February. By threatening President Beneš with civil war, Gottwald forced him to appoint a government with a Communist majority. When Beneš resigned in June rather than sign the new Communist-oriented constitution, Gottwald succeeded him. Gottwald then ran the country along the lines of the USSR, including a series of show purge trials in 1952. Gottwald died in Prague on March 14, 1953, of pneumonia, which he received while attending the funeral of Soviet dictator Joseph Stalin several days earlier.

Otto Grotewohl (1894–1964)

Premier of German Democratic Republic, 1949–1964

Otto Grotewohl was born in Brunswick Republic (now Germany) on March 11, 1894. He attended the Leibniz Academy in Hanover and the Institute of Politics in Berlin. He worked as a printer and an insurance administrator serving briefly as president of the Brunswick State Social Insurance Institute. He became prominent in the Social Democratic party (SPD) and in the 1920s served in city and state government positions and as state party chairman for the SPD in Brunswick. He was elected to the Reichstag, the national parliament, in 1925 and became a writer on social and union topics for newspapers and periodicals, in which he advocated a single Marxist Labor party in Brunswick.

An early opponent of the Nazis, Grotewohl was arrested in 1933 and spent time in prison. He was released and went underground following the assassination attempt on Hitler on July 20, 1944. Following the end of the war the SPD was reorganized in Berlin on June 17, 1945, and Grotewohl was elected chairman of the central committee. He resumed his advocacy of "a united working class front" and proposed a union merger between his and the Communist parties, but the SPD party membership in the western zones of the city voted 82 percent against it and in April 1946 voted to expel Grotewohl and his central committee.

On April 22, 1946, the Soviet zone SPD formally merged with the Communist party (KPD) to form the Socialist Unity party (SED). Wilhelm Pieck, the KPD leader, and Grotewohl were elected co-chairmen of the new organization, which had over a million members. Along with Pieck and Walter Ulbricht, he made the SED into a faithful supporter of Moscow, which in 1948 announced a two year economic plan to increase industrial production. By this time the SED was in almost complete control of politics in the Soviet zone and launched a party purge to transform the SED into a well trained cadre of political workers, encompassing all aspects of life—social, educational, religious, and political.

With the creation of the Federal Republic of Germany, or West Germany, the east responded with the new German Democratic Republic (GDR), or East Germany, which was created, with assistance from Grotewohl, on October 7, 1949, with Pieck serving as president and Grotewohl as premier or minister-president. The two-year economic plan was successful in orienting the GDR toward the USSR, with Grotewohl supportive of the Moscow position concerning the Berlin blockade in 1948 and hostile toward the Western powers.

Like Walter Ulbricht, Grotewohl sought to bring every phase of life in the new state under party control. In June 1950 he offered government protection to church leaders who cooperated and threatened those who did not. By the end of the year he proclaimed the GDR a "worker's state" and said he was willing to discuss reunification along those lines. The Western Allied powers responded by suggesting in 1951 that the United Nations supervise a poll to determine what the people wanted, and Grotewohl refused to agree.

Grotewohl survived the 1952 purges, but he refused to resign after the worker's strikes, demonstrations, and riots of June 1953, following the death of Soviet leader Joseph Stalin. As a result of the turmoil, he scrapped most of the current five-year plan and agreed to reallocate a larger portion of the budget to help raise living standards. The party was reorganized for tighter control, and in October Grotewohl dissolved the Arts Commission to form a new Culture Ministry, more closely controlled by the government.

Change was in the wind, however, and in April 1954 both Pieck and Grotewohl stepped down as co-chairman of the SED, leaving Ulbricht in sole control. Grotewohl was allowed to continue as premier or minister-president of the government. He continued to ally himself closely to Moscow and followed the new anti-Stalinist line after 1956, proposing in 1957 that both Germanies agree not to use atomic weapons.

Following Pieck's death in 1960, Ulbricht reorganized the government, setting up a Council of State to replace the minister-president and making Grotewohl one of six deputy chairmen under himself. For the next four years Grotewohl served in a government and party clearly dominated by Walter Ulbricht. Grotewohl died on September 22, 1964.

Václav Havel (1936–   )

President of Czechoslovakia, 1989–1992

Václav Havel was born on October 5, 1936, into a wealthy Prague family. After the Communists took power in 1948, the family lost its properties and businesses, and since Havel was a member of the "upper bourgeois" class, he had a difficult time in finishing his formal education. After being forced to leave school at the age of fifteen to become a laboratory technician, Havel attended night classes, slowly working his way to the Academy of Arts in Prague. After serving a two-year stint in the military, he returned to Prague in 1959 and took a job as a stagehand, eventually rising through the ranks to become a producer. Although he wrote his first book at the age of nineteen, he was not noticed until the 1960s when his plays *The Garden Party* (1963), *The Memorandum* (1965), and *Increased Difficulty of Concentration* (1968) were performed. During the 1968 Prague Spring, Havel traveled to the United States where several of his plays opened. After the Soviet-led invasion later that year, the authorities banned his works, although he continued to write until the Velvet Revolution in 1989.

Havel refused to bend to the repressive regime after 1968, and he became one of the leading dissidents in Czechoslovakia. In the mid-1970s he helped form and lead Charter 77 and the Committee for the Defense of the Unjustly Persecuted, both human rights organizations. As a result, he spent time in prison from January to April 1977, and received a fourteen month suspended sentence in October 1977. Havel was arrested again in October 1979 and received four-and-a-half years in prison, but he was released early due to a serious illness since the authorities feared an international backlash if he died in prison. Despite these arrests and other harassments, Havel continued to advocate human rights and democracy in Czechoslovakia. Arrested as a ringleader of demonstrations in Prague in January 1989, he received another prison sentence in February. In November, due to nationwide peaceful demonstrations against the regime, Havel helped to establish the Civic Forum, an unofficial political coalition of opposition groups. In 1989 the Civic Forum under Havel's leadership forced the downfall of communism in Czechoslovakia in what became known as the Velvet Revolution. On December 29, 1989, Havel succeeded the hard-line Communist Gustáv Husák as the first non-Communist president of Czechoslovakia in forty-one years; he was reelected in July 1990. From this point until his resignation in the summer of 1992, Havel attempted to keep Czechoslovakia together, but realizing his moves were futile, he stepped down rather than preside over the country's demise. In January 1993, Havel easily won the presidency of the new Czech Republic.

Erich Honecker (1912–   )
Chairman, Council of State, German Democratic Republic, 1973–1989

Honecker was born outside Neunkirchen on August 25, 1912. His father was a coal miner who taught his five children Marxist theory much as other children learned nursery rhymes. Honecker accompanied his mother as she delivered Communist newspapers after the First World War and became a member of the Communist Young Pioneers when he was ten and the Communist Youth League four years later. He proved to be a gifted speaker and became absorbed in politics, joining the Communist party (KPD) in 1929. In 1930, after rejecting a career in the roofing business, he was sent to Moscow for a year to attend the school of the Communist Youth International.

When Honecker returned to Germany in 1931 he was appointed secretary of the Communist Youth League for the Saar and worked to expand the youth organization. Honecker opposed the Nazis and helped organize resistance groups in the Ruhr and the Saar. He was arrested by the Nazis, tried and convicted on charges of high treason, and imprisoned in Brandenburg prison, where he remained until freed by Soviet troops in April 1945.

Shortly after the war ended, Honecker contacted the Ulbricht group of the KPD, and on instructions from Wilhelm Pieck he organized the Free German Youth, a paramilitary group used to intimidate democrats out of the Berlin city administration in 1948 and to help suppress the workers' revolt in Berlin in 1953. He became popular with the party leaders because of his administrative talents and his loyalty to Walter Ulbricht. In 1949 he became a member of the East German parliament (Volkskammer) and the next year a member of the Politburo, helping Ulbricht survive a purge attempt in 1953. In 1956 he returned to Moscow for two years of advanced training at the Institute of Higher Political Studies. In 1958 he became secretary of the Central Committee of the SED.

As Central Committee secretary he had responsibility for security affairs and the armed forces. In this capacity Honecker supervised the building of the Berlin Wall. He rapidly became the heir apparent to Ulbricht and oversaw much of the prosperity that developed in the 1960s after the building of the wall. He maintained a healthy suspicion of the technocrats who made the prosperity possible, feeling that they were more concerned about results and less about ideological purity.

Honecker was an opponent of reunification and often called for a "fencing off" of the GDR from the Federal Republic, or West Germany, and for closer cooperation with the other Soviet satellite states in East Europe. Honecker replaced the aging Ulbricht on May 3, 1971. As first secretary of the central committee of the SED he was now in charge of the most powerful of the east bloc nations. His policies were at first not at odds with the new, more flexible Soviet approach of detente with the West. Rejecting West German chancellor Willy Brandt's concept of two states within one German nation, he stressed the permanent separation of Germany into a socialist and a bourgeois nation. He worked to bring about an end to economic shortages and mindless bureaucracy, though with little success.

Honecker was resistant to changes brought on by Soviet leader Mikhail Gorbachev sweeping the Soviet Union and Eastern Europe, seeing them as ultimately being at odds with socialism. His unwillingness to change in the face of massive demonstrations and personal visits from Gorbachev urging reform ultimately brought about his removal from party and state offices in October 1989. He was arrested and charged with treason and manslaughter in 1990. He was able to flee to Moscow, where he sought asylum in the Chilean Embassy. With the disintegration of the Soviet Union, he was returned to Germany and put on trial. In late 1992 a court held that he was too ill to stand trial. He was released with charges still pending and migrated to Chile to be with his family.

Miklós Horthy de Nagybánya (1868–1957)
Regent of Hungary, 1920–1944

Miklós Horthy was born into a family of lesser nobility in Kenderes, a small community on the Great Hungarian Plain (puszta). In an unusual act, Franz Joseph I appointed Horthy's father, who was a member of the lesser nobility, to the House of Magnates. When Horthy was ten, his father sent him to school in Sopron, a city on the Hungarian-Austrian border, to learn German. At the age of eighteen, Horthy attended the Habsburg Naval Academy at Fiume where he was commissioned into the Austro-Hungarian navy as a midshipman. At 41, Horthy, then a captain, went to the Habsburg court in Vienna and several years later was appointed the commander in chief of the Navy of the Habsburg Monarchy. At the end of the First World War, Horthy returned after a 40-year absence to his native Hungary, essentially a foreign country to him since he had lived in non-Hungarian, German-speaking surroundings for most of his life.

On May 5, 1919, Horthy became the minister of war for the counterrevolutionary government at Szeged. This counterrevolutionary government, formed to oppose the Communist government of Béla Kun, was led by Count Gyula Károlyi (brother of Mihály), Count István Bethlen, and Count Pál Teleki. When Kun's government fell on August 1, 1919, this government became the nucleus of the

new regime. On November 16, 1919, Horthy led an armed force into Budapest where it quickly transformed itself into the national army. Horthy's troops advanced into areas between the Tisza and the Danube which were not under Romanian occupation and extended its control to areas west of the Danube. As Horthy's forces moved into an area, they ruthlessly persecuted real and alleged Communists along with workers and peasants who had played an active part in implementing the soviet government's social programs. A similar fate met the Jews. These acts of violence and retribution raged throughout the countryside during the fall of 1919 and died away slowly in the spring of 1920. Known as the "White Terror," these acts bore no semblance of legality. The White Terror claimed approximately 5,000 lives, put 70,000 citizens behind bars, and forced many to flee abroad.

On March 1, 1920, Horthy was elected regent of Hungary. Supported by the great powers, primarily Great Britain, and by the national army, Horthy was the only possible candidate. His powers were broadly defined: he had the power to dismiss Parliament, act as commander in chief, and subordinate legislation to the wishes of the regent and those of the prime minister who was appointed by the regent. The election of Horthy was a temporary measure as far as the members of parliament were concerned, but in actuality these powers allowed Horthy to rule in an authoritarian manner until 1944.

During the Second World War, Horthy attempted to steer Hungary toward greater independence from Germany but was forced into closer accommodation with Germany due to Hungarian wishes to regain lands lost under the terms of the Treaty of Trianon (1920). In 1943 and 1944, Horthy began to make overtures to the Allies while still accommodating the Nazis. In September 1943, in secret negotiations with the British, the Hungarian government agreed to order the withdrawal of all Hungarian forces from the eastern front. In exchange for British territorial guarantees of Hungary's Trianon (1920) borders, the government agreed to reduce the supply of armaments to Germany, remove pro-German officers from the General Staff, and introduce social reforms. Meeting opposition from the Arrow Cross, a fascist party, and the National Socialist Party Union, Horthy backed down.

In March 17, 1944, Horthy was summoned to Germany. There, he was forced to agree to appoint a right-wing puppet government under Hungary's long-serving ambassador to Berlin, Lieutenant-General Döme Sztójay. Under Sztójay and with the help of the Arrow Cross and the willing assistance of the Hungarian police, over 450,000

Jews, including most of Hungary's provincial Jews, were deported to German extermination camps in Poland. Concern about the fate of the Hungarian Jews reached Horthy from a number of sources, including the Catholic and Protestant churches. Most of the 200,000 Jews of Budapest, herded together in the Budapest ghetto, were saved when Horthy dismissed Sztójay in late August. The new government of Géza Lakatos ordered a halt to the deportations but these deportations resumed after Horthy was forced by the Nazis to resign on October 16, 1944. After his resignation, Horthy was placed under house arrest and then transported to the German concentration camps of Dachau and Buchenwald in late October 1944. Liberated by Allied troops in 1945, Horthy went into exile and died in 1957.

Enver Hoxha (1908–1985)
First Secretary, Albanian Workers Party, 1954–1985
Prime Minister of Albania, 1944–1954

Son of a Muslim land-owner, Enver Hoxha was born in the town of Gjirokastër (Argyrokastro). Hoxha's father had emigrated to the United States, where he had worked for a time before returning to Albania, and his family was as a result relatively affluent. The individual who exerted the greatest influence on Hoxha during his childhood was his uncle Hysen Hoxha, a xenophobic atheist and determined Albanian nationalist. Hoxha finished primary school in Gjirokastër and graduated from the National Lyceum in Korcë (Koritsa). In 1930 he received a scholarship from Zog's government to study abroad. Hoxha attended the University of Montpellier, France, but his scholarship was discontinued because of failure in his studies and he did not return to the university after his first year. In 1931 he proceeded to Paris in search of work, and from 1933 to 1936 he served as the private secretary to the Honorary Consul of Albania in Brussels. While in Belgium Hoxha studied law but received no degree. Hoxha was introduced to Marxism during his years in Belgium and France, and it was during that time that he developed his ideological leanings. Hoxha returned to Albania in 1936 and was appointed teacher of French at the State Gymnasium in Tirana; after four months he was transferred to the National Lyceum in Korcë to teach the same subject. Because of his political agitation in Korcë, he was arrested in January 1939 on a charge of conspiracy, for which he served a brief term in prison.

Hoxha's career took a dramatic turn after Albania was occupied by the Italians in April 1939. At the time of the invasion, Hoxha was again teaching at the National Lyceum in Korcë and working secretly against Zog's rule. Unwilling to take a demotion from the new Italian educational authorities, Hoxha was dismissed from his teaching position. He then made his way to Tirana and began organizing underground resistance against the Italians. As a front for his activities he opened a tobacco shop, with a Communist cell in its back room. Hoxha was one of the founders of the Albanian Communist party which was established in Tirana on November 8, 1941. At the time of the party's founding, Hoxha was not Albania's most renowned Communist. However, because the most prominent Communists were involved in bitter rivalries, Hoxha quickly emerged as the only acceptable compromise personality to lead the party. At the First Party Conference in March 1943, Hoxha was elected general secretary. He simultaneously directed the growing Communist-controlled resistance against the Axis occupiers, and, beginning in October 1943, led his forces in a civil war against the non-Communist Albanian resistance groups. By October 1944 the Communists were able to form a provisional government headed by Hoxha, and a month later, as the Germans completed their withdrawal from Albania, Hoxha took control of the entire country.

With the Communist seizure of power in late 1944, Hoxha took immediate action to consolidate the party's domination. Remnants of the nationalist parties, the prewar political elite, and other opponents were eliminated, while the party nationalized all industrial assets and launched a radical agricultural collectivization program. On January 11, 1946, the newly elected Constituent Assembly proclaimed Albania a people's republic, and in March of that same year a new constitution legitimized the Communist party's control of the country. Hoxha also consolidated his personal authority during 1946 by becoming the Minister of Defense, Minister of Foreign Affairs, and Commander-in-Chief of the Armed Forces concurrently. Nevertheless, Hoxha's regime was faced with serious domestic and foreign policy problems. The Albanian Communists emerged from the war under the strong influence of Yugoslavia. The party itself was divided over Tirana's relations with Belgrade: one faction, led by Hoxha's principal rival, Koci Xoxe, advocated a close alliance with Belgrade as a precursor to Albanian integration into the Yugoslav federation; the other faction favored Albanian independence and was opposed to the adoption of radical economic and social policies similar to those being carried out in Yugoslavia. Hoxha was able to survive the intense struggle within the party from 1946 to 1948 through a combination of humility, cautious moderation, and adroit diplomatic and political maneuvering. Hoxha seized the Soviet-Yugoslav dispute and break in June 1948 as the opportunity to eliminate Xoxe, the party's pro-Yugoslav faction, and other remaining opponents.

Following Tirana's rupture with Belgrade in 1948, Hoxha led Albania into a close and dependent relationship with Moscow. However, when Khrushchev succeeded Stalin and attempted a rapprochement with Yugoslavia, Hoxha turned from the Soviet Union, ousting it from Albanian naval bases, condemning Khrushchev at the Moscow meeting of the International Conference of Communist Parties in 1960, and turning to China as Albania's protector. In the meantime, Hoxha survived a domestic challenge in 1956 to his Stalinist policies and a Soviet-sponsored attempt to topple his regime in 1960. From 1960 Albania became an anti-Soviet Chinese satellite, but, although Chinese assistance proved indispensable for Albania's economic development, by the mid-1960s Hoxha's regime was faced with popular dissatisfaction and major domestic problems. In order to eliminate the perceived threats to his power, Hoxha launched Albania's "Ideological and Cultural Revolution" in February 1966. Hoxha's Cultural Revolution targeted the bureaucracy, the intelligentsia, the military, and the party, and was aimed at removing from these centers any potential alternative forces that might threaten the stability of his regime and its control over all aspects of Albanian society. Hoxha felt confident enough to bring the Cultural Revolution to a close in December 1969, by which time he had clearly reaffirmed his absolute authority over the party and the state. Between March 1973 and November 1976 Hoxha again implemented a widespread series of purges to eliminate officials who represented real or imagined threats to his Stalinist policies.

With the absence of either domestic or foreign threats to his power, Hoxha was able to realign Albania's international position. Hoxha bitterly opposed Beijing's opening to the West in 1971, and, after seven years of deteriorating relations between the two countries, the Albanian-Chinese alliance ended in 1978. Left completely isolated in the international community, Hoxha resorted to a policy of national self-reliance. However, Albania's self-imposed isolation proved to be disastrous as the country's economy declined in the 1980s. Nevertheless, until his death in 1985 First Secretary Hoxha's absolute political authority remained unchallenged. After his death Hoxha left behind him a powerful legacy. He had governed Albania for more than four decades, making him the world's longest-ruling Communist leader, and although he presided over much of the country's postwar progress, his ruthless dogmatism was also responsible for Albania's intense economic, cultural, institutional, and social impoverishment.

Gustáv Husák (1913–1991)
President of Czechoslovakia, 1975–1989
General Secretary, Czechoslovak Communist Party, 1971–1987

Gustáv Husák was born in Bratislava, Slovakia, on January 10, 1913. While studying law at Comenius University in Bratislava, he joined the Czechoslovak Communist party in 1933. After receiving his law degree in 1937, Husák worked for the law firm of Vladimir Clementis, a Communist and later the Czechoslovak foreign minister who perished in the Stalinist purges in the early 1950s. Husák continued his party activity even after it was banned in 1938. Two years later, the Nazi puppet Slovak Republic arrested him for his association with the Communist party, and he remained in prison until 1943. After his release, he became a deputy chairman of the Slovak Communist party and the party's representative to clandestine meetings of all political parties united in opposition to the fascist regime. Husák was instrumental in the organization and later a leader in the ill-fated Slovak National Uprising against the Slovak Republic in 1944.

After the end of World War II, Husák became a member of the Central Committee of the Czechoslovak and Slovak Communist parties, a delegate to the National Assembly, and the chairman of the Slovak regional government, the Board of Commissioners. During 1950 and 1951 he lost his various positions as a victim of the Stalinist purges in Czechoslovakia. The authorities arrested him on charges of treason in 1951, and subjected him to intense mental and physical torture before sentencing him three years later to life imprisonment for "bourgeois nationalism." A general amnesty in May 1960 freed Husak, and the government exonerated him of all charges three years later. From 1960 to 1963 he wrote about the Slovak National Uprising. For the next five years he worked as a researcher at the Slovak Academy of Sciences.

During the 1968 Prague Spring, Husák reentered politics by becoming a deputy prime minister. His chief work centered on the federalization of Czechoslovakia. After the Soviet-led invasion ended the reforms, he advocated compromise with the Soviets, and as a result they tapped him to run the country. Husák quickly rose through the ranks becoming first secretary of the Slovak

Communist party in late August 1968, first secretary of the Czechoslovak Communist party in April 1969, and president in 1975. Under Husak's control the majority of the Prague Spring reforms were revoked under a policy of "normalization," which included hard-line repressive measures against the reformers and other opponents of the regime. His rule also saw a decline in the Czechoslovak economy in the 1980s, and little agreement with the reforms of Soviet leader Mikhail Gorbachev. In December 1987 Husák was removed as the head of the Czechoslovak Communist party, but he retained the largely ceremonial presidency until December 10, 1989. On that day he resigned after swearing in the new government that came to power as a result of the Velvet Revolution that ended Communist rule. Husák returned to Bratislava where he died on November 18, 1991, after a long illness, but not before the hard-line Communist could receive the last rites of the Roman Catholic church.

Ion Iliescu (1930–)
President of Romania, 1990–

Iliescu was born on March 3, 1930, in Oltenita. He received his education at the Bucharest Polytechnic Institute and in Moscow. He became a member of the Union of Communist Youth after the overthrow of Marshal Antonescu in 1944, and a member of the Communist party in 1953. He served in various leadership positions of the Union of Communist Youth as a member of its Central Committee from 1949 to 1960, and its secretary from 1956 to 1960. In other leadership roles in Romania, Iliescu worked in the propaganda department of the Central Committee of the Communist party, and later as a member of the Central Committee itself from 1968 to 1984. After this he became the director of a technical publishing house until 1989, when he emerged during the December revolution against Nicolae Ceauşescu as the president of the National Salvation Front. From February to May 1990, he was the president of the Provisional Council of National Unity, and since June 1990, he has been the president of Romania.

Nicolae Iorga (1871–1940)
Romanian historian and politician

Iorga was born in Botoşani on June 17, 1871. He studied philology in Paris and Berlin before receiving his doctorate at the University of Leipzig in 1893. The following year, Iorga occupied the chair of history at the University of Bucharest, after which he published copiously on Romanian history, including the two volume *Geschichte des rümanischen Volkes* (History of the Romanian People, 1905) and the ten volume *Istoria Românilor* (History of the Romanians, 1936–1939). Furthermore, it is estimated that Iorga established and edited several journals and wrote over 800 books and thousands of articles. His writings had a strong nationalistic flavor that were very influential in Romanian life. Iorga is considered one of the best historians in the Balkans for his time. In 1911 he became a member of the Romanian Academy of Sciences, and over the years he received a variety of honorary doctorates from institutions abroad. Iorga was elected to parliament in 1907 as a member of the nationalistic National Democratic party, which he founded the year before. In 1931–1932 he served as prime minister and minister of education in a coalition government appointed by King Carol II. Interestingly, Iorga had served as Carol's private tutor many years before, and from 1938 until his death in 1940, he advised the king. Iorga was murdered by members of the Iron Guard on November 28, 1940, for opposing them and the regime of General Antonescu.

Wojciech Jaruzelski (1923–)
President of Poland, 1989–1990
First Secretary, Polish United Workers Party, 1981–1989

A member of the gentry class, Wojciech Jaruzelski was born in Kurów in eastern Poland on July 6, 1923. After Poland was partitioned by the Nazis and Soviets in September 1939, the Jaruzelski family found itself under Soviet authority, which ordered it deported to the USSR. In 1943 Jaruzelski joined the Soviet-sponsored Polish army, and saw action against the Germans. He joined the Polish United Workers party (PZPR) in 1947, steadily rising through the ranks of both the party and the army; by 1971 he was a member of the Politburo. Already minister of defense, Jaruzelski was elevated to the premiership on February 11, 1981, and made first secretary of the PZPR in October. On December 13, 1981, he declared martial law intending to destroy the independent trade union Solidarity while at the same time attempting to end the country's economic problems. He resigned as prime minister in 1985 and became president of the Council of State but retained control of the PZPR. Unable to solve Poland's economic woes, Jaruzelski was forced by circumstances into negotiations with Solidarity which led, eventually, to the restoration of the union, free elections, and the fall of communism. After a brief stint as president from July 1989 to December

1990, Jaruzelski resigned from political life; he lives in Warsaw.

János Kádár (1912–1989)
First Secretary, Hungarian Socialist Workers Party, 1956–1988
Prime Minister of Hungary, 1956–1958, 1961–1968

Janos Kádár was born in 1912 in the Adriatic port city of Fiume (Rijeka), at the time Hungary's outlet to the Adriatic Sea. His mother, Borbala Czermanik, was a Slovak peasant who was working as a maid in Fiume when she met and became pregnant by János Knessinger, a young Hungarian soldier. Registered at birth as János József Czermanik, Kádár and his mother returned to Slovakia after his father refused to take them in. Kádár and his mother moved to Budapest in 1918 where he was apprenticed as a mechanic at the age of fourteen. Unemployed during the depression years, Kádár joined the youth section of the illegal Communist party in 1931 where he received the name of János Barna. He was arrested by the Hungarian government in 1937 and spent three years in prison. In 1940, he joined the Social Democratic party and rose in its ranks, becoming a member of its executive committee in 1943. During the Second World War he adopted the name János Kádár. In 1944, he was captured by the Germans, but escaped. After the war, Kádár became the deputy chief of police in Budapest and closely allied himself with László Rajk, then the minister of the interior. During the purges of 1949, Kádár cosigned the order of execution for his close friend, Rajk.

During another purge in 1951, Kádár was arrested. He confessed to charges of deviationism and was imprisoned until July 1954. From his release to November 1956, Kádár built his reputation in the party as anti-Stalinist and anti-Rákosi, but he did not align himself with Imre Nagy. When the Soviet Red Army invaded Hungary in November 1956, Kádár established a Soviet-sponsored Revolutionary Worker-Peasant Government and promised to work for Hungarian national independence and sovereignty and to institute certain economic, administrative, and industrial reforms. He began to work on his promises in 1957 when he arranged for the Soviet and Hungarian governments to sign a pact which attempted to balance the relationship between the two countries: trade between the USSR and Hungary was to be on the basis of world market prices; the Soviets extended the period of repayment of loans; and they granted to the Hungarians a long term loan of 750 million rubles and consignment of goods and services to the value of 1.1 billion rubles. However, Kádár acquiesced to the stationing of Soviet troops in Hungary indefinitely.

In the 1960s, Kádár embarked upon a path of economic liberalization known as the New Economic Mechanism (NEM). Under the new economic plan, producers were given considerable freedom in fixing prices, could determine wages and salaries according to company profits, and could participate in decisions on production targets and areas of investment. While quietly shelving orthodox central planning, Kádár also fostered relations with the West, Israel, and the Roman Catholic Church. Most important, Kádár achieved social consensus among the 10 million Hungarians who relished their enhanced living standards and freedoms.

By the mid-eighties, Kádár was perceived by the more liberal quarters of the Hungarian Communist party as blocking badly needed changes in Hungary's increasingly stagnant economy. Hoping to control change, Kádár supported two of his proteges, Károly Grósz and Imre Pozsgay, for influential positions within the party. In May 1988, Kádár was replaced by a quartet containing his two proteges, Grósz, now prime minister, and Pozsgay, a reform Communist, as well as Károly Németh, the deputy prime minister, and Rezsö Nyers, the author of the NEM. Kádár was shuffled into the newly created post of party president, but due to his recalcitrance to change, he was removed from his new post and from the Central Committee in early 1989. He died on July 6, 1989.

Aleksandar I Karađorđević (1888–1934)
King of Yugoslavia, 1922–1934

Aleksandar was born in Montenegro, the second son of Petar Karađorđević, King of Serbia from 1903 until his death in 1921. Aleksandar became the heir to the throne in 1909, when his older brother Djordje abdicated his right to succeed his father. From 1914, was prince-regent of Serbia, exercising the royal authority after his father declined an active role. Aleksandar became the prince-regent of the Kingdom of Serbs, Croats, and Slovenes in 1918, and in 1921 he officially became king when Petar died.

Aleksandar was an exponent of Serbian power in Yugoslavia. He and Nikola Pašić were rivals for power in the state, although they shared a desire to see Serbia dominate it. In 1929 he suspended the Vidovdan Constitution and declared a royal dictatorship. In 1931 Aleksandar proclaimed a new centralistic constitution intended to solidify his power in the state. He claimed his dictatorship to be the first step in the creation of a truly "Yugoslav" state. However, he faced opposition from major Croatian and Serbian politicians and their parties, which made it impossible for Aleksandar to implement his vision, which was flawed in any case. His two most vocal and effective opponents were Vladko Maček of the Croatian Peasant party and Svetozar Pribićević of the Independent Democratic party. Aleksandar was assassinated in 1934 by a Macedonian working with the Ustaša.

Edvard Kardelj (1910–1979)
Yugoslav economist and politician

Kardelj, a Slovene, was born in Ljubljana. He was an active member of Communist organizations from his youth. In 1928, he became a member of the Ljublijana city committee of the Communist youth organization, and a year later he was a member of the Slovene Communist youth committee. In the same year he was arrested for the first time for his Communist activities. In 1934 he met Tito for the first time, and travelled to France and later the Soviet Union, where he remained until 1936. From 1937 Kardelj was a close confidant of Tito.

Kardelj's domain was economic theory and administration. He and Djilas were leading ideologists of the Yugoslav Communist party until the latter's fall in 1954. Where Djilas excelled at polemical writing and Ranković became the security expert in postwar Yugoslavia, Kardelj formulated social and economic policies, including the idea of self-management. After Ranković's demotion in 1966, Kardelj was the only remaining member of the close-knit wartime group around Tito. He died in 1979. Had he lived, it is conceivable he would have inherited Tito's position as the head of the state.

Mihály Károlyi (1875–1955)
President of Hungary, 1919
Prime Minister of Hungary, 1918–1919

Mihály Károlyi was born into one of Hungary's most historic and wealthiest families. Raised by his maternal grandparents after the death of his mother, Károlyi spent his early years being tutored at his grandparents estate, Foth castle. Károlyi attended the University of Budapest where he developed an interest in modern agricultural techniques. His concern for agricultural issues propelled him into public life as the president of Omge, the Hungarian Agricultural Society, in 1909. In addition, Károlyi

unsuccessfully ran for Parliament in 1902 as a delegate of the Liberal party, the traditional party of the Hungarian landowning class. In 1905, he won a seat as a delegate of the opposition party, the Independence party. Despite his early reactionary politics to the Habsburgs, Károlyi took no part in the opposition's conflict with the crown in 1905/1906.

Gradually, Károlyi became an important voice in parliament for broadening the franchise, or voting rights, and establishing secret balloting, but he was not an advocate of universal suffrage. Károlyi developed a theory that if Hungary introduced political and social justice toward the Hungarian minorities (Slovaks, Romanians, Ruthenians, and Croats) it would not only be righting a historic wrong but it would be guaranteeing its own internal stability.

Watching the growing restlessness of the population in 1916, Károlyi left the Independence party and established the Party of Independence, which was democratic, anti-German, and advocated that the Hungarians negotiate a separate peace with the Entente, the wartime alliance of the British, French, Russians, the United States, Italians and Romanians. When Hungary declared its independence from Austria in October, 1918, Károlyi formed the Hungarian National Council which acted as a provisional government. On October 31, Károlyi became the official prime minister of the new republic of Hungary. The Hungarians hoped that Károlyi could secure satisfactory peace terms from the Entente powers.

On January 11, 1919, Count Mihály Károlyi was elected provisional president of the Hungarian Republic by the National Council. Károlyi labored unsuccessfully to develop either a political organization or policies to deal with the social unrest caused by the end of the First World War, the dissolution of the Austro-Hungarian empire, and returning soldiers. Károlyi did not produce any successes in either the domestic or foreign realm. The proposed land reform which struck at the privileges and wealth of the landowning gentry and the new electoral law of November 22, 1918, which extended voting rights to adult citizens literate in any language, including the majority of women over 21, were too radical for the majority of the old ruling elements, the landed gentry, the middle nobility, and nationalist intellectuals.

On March 20, Colonel Fernand Vyx, the French military attaché representing the Entente, handed to Károlyi a note which demanded that all Hungarian forces evacuate the region between the Tisza river and the Carpathian mountains on the eastern edge of the Hungarian plain. Károlyi's government rejected the Vyx note and handed power over to the Social Democratic party which looked to the Communists for support. The Social Democrats concluded a pact with the Communists on March 21. As a result, power virtually fell to Béla Kun and the Communists. After the fall of the Hungarian Soviet Republic in August 1919, Károlyi was forced into exile by the authoritarian regime of Admiral Horthy and István Bethlen. After the Second World War, Károlyi returned to Hungary and served as the Hungarian ambassador to France until 1949 when he resigned in protest over the arrest of László Rajk. Once again he went into exile, and died in 1955.

Nikita Sergeevich Khrushchev (1894–1971)
General Secretary, Soviet Communist Party, 1953–1964

Nikita Sergeevich Khrushchev was born on April 17, 1894 in Kalinovka near Kursk in southern Russia. The son of a miner, Khrushchev worked as a sheepherder before serving as an apprentice mechanic in Iuzovka. After completing his apprenticeship, Khrushchev worked as a mechanic in the coal mines and coke plants of the region.

In 1918 Khrushchev joined the Russian Communist party and enlisted in the Red Army. After fighting in the Civil War, Khrushchev returned to Iuzovka to work as an assistant manager of a mine. During this period he also attended classes at the Donets Industrial Institute, graduating in 1925. In 1927 Khrushchev continued his education by studying industrial administration at the Industrial Academy in Moscow. He left the academy in 1931 when he was appointed secretary of a district party organization in Moscow. By 1935 Khrushchev was first secretary of the Moscow region. As part of his duties he helped to supervise the construction of the Moscow subway system.

Khrushchev's career continued to develop successfully during the purges, when Stalin removed thousands of people from the party because he perceived them as a threat; in 1938 Khrushchev was appointed first secretary of the Ukrainian Communist party. In 1939 he also became a full member of the Politburo, the ruling body of the Communist Party, and a member of the Presidium of the Supreme Soviet, the ruling body of government.

During World War II Khrushchev served in the Red Army in Ukraine and at the southern front at Stalingrad advancing to the rank of lieutenant general. After the war he supervised the reconstruction of Ukraine.

In 1949 Khrushchev moved to Moscow when he was appointed to the party's Secretariat, directed by Stalin. After Stalin's death in 1953, Khrushchev was one of eight men ruling the country. Within a few months he became first secretary or leader of the Communist Party.

As first secretary, Khrushchev appointed his supporters in key party positions; by 1955 he was the key political figure in the country. In 1958 Khrushchev succeeded Bulganin as chairman of the Council of Ministers, the head of the government. With this appointment he became the most powerful person in the Soviet Union.

Khrushchev encouraged a policy of de-Stalinization, that is, an opening up of Soviet society. Although the country continued to by ruled by the Communist party, living conditions improved considerably for Soviet citizens. At the Twentieth Party Congress in 1956 Khrushchev took the first steps toward denouncing Stalinism during his "Secret Speech," which was officially published in the Soviet Union for the first time in 1989.

Although Khrushchev believed in peaceful coexistence with the West, he brought the Soviet Union to the brink of war with the United States during the Cuban Missile Crisis of 1962. In October 1964, when Khrushchev was out of Moscow, top Communist Party officials united to force Khrushchev into retirement. They were unhappy with the way Khrushchev handled the Cuban Missile Crisis and did not like the quarrel he had with the Chinese over economic policy and ideology. After this Khrushchev lived in retirement outside of Moscow until his death on September 11, 1971.

Egon Krenz (1937–   )
Chairman, Council of State, German Democratic Republic, 1989

Krenz was born in Kolberg, Prussia (now Poland) on March 19, 1937. His father was a tailor who moved his family west to the Rostock area when the German population of Kolberg was expelled and replaced by Poles following World War II. Only twelve when the German Democratic Republic (GDR) was founded, Krenz became active in Communist youth organizations such as the Young Pioneers and the Free German Youth. From 1953 to 1957 he was enrolled in the Teacher Training Institute, followed by two years as an army officer. In 1955 he joined the Socialist Unity party (SED) and the Confederation of Free German Trade Unions. He spent three years in the Communist party staff college in Moscow, emerging as a prototype apparatchik. He was active in various leadership positions in the Ernst Thalmann Pioneer Organization from 1967 to 1974, where he became a protege of Erich Honecker.

Krenz became a member of the national council of the National Front in 1969 and a member of the Central Committee of the SED in 1971 and of the Politburo in 1976. He became secretary of the Central Committee and general secretary of the Politburo in 1989. He held almost all major leadership positions in both the SED and the GDR government including head of the Stasi (State Security Agency). He was a loyal follower of Erich Honecker and his intransigent hard-line approach to party rule, often deputizing for Honecker when he was ill or on vacation.

Krenz was held responsible for the mass arrest of dissidents who sought sanctuary in Protestant churches in January 1988 and was accused of rigging elections in May 1989. He sided publicly with China's leadership following the Tiananmen Square massacre and generally distanced himself, along with Honecker, from the liberalizing trends sweeping eastern Europe in 1988 and 1989.

In September 1988 thousands massed in the streets of Leipzig and other East German cities. Krenz claims he countermanded Honecker's order to fire on the people and tried to move toward moderation. In October Soviet premier Mikhail S. Gorbachev stated the Soviet Union's intention to stay out of East Germany's problems, thus withdrawing Soviet support of Honecker.

The Central Committee chose Krenz to replace Honecker on October 18, 1989, as party leader, head of state, and chairman of the National Defense Council, which did little to quiet the masses in the streets. Krenz was regarded as a continuation of Honecker's position. He attempted to make cosmetic reforms that kept the party in power, but under pressure from the people and changing events, Krenz was replaced by Hans Modrow on November 13, 1989.

Miroslav Krleža (1893–1981)
Yugoslavian writer

Krleža was Croatia's most famous novelist and writer of the twentieth century. He graduated from the Hungarian Royal Military Academy in Budapest and served in the Austro-Hungarian army during the First World War. After the war, he became a Marxist and wrote and edited leftist journals. He produced his best work in the 1930s as an independent writer in Zagreb. He utilized every form in his writings: prose, poetry, essays, plays. After the Second World War, he served on the Central Committee of the Communist party and as head of the Yugoslav Writers Union. Nonetheless, he maintained an independence that eventually brought him into conflict with the party in the

1970s. Krleža's most famous novel is *The Return of Philip Latinovicz* (1932), the story of an artist who returns to his Croatian home after a long absence. His other works include *The Croatian God Mars* (1922), *The Glembays* (1932), and *On the Edge of Reason* (1938). Where the writer Ivo Andrić drew upon the rich heritage of Bosnia and its simpler people, Krleža wrote in a style and of subjects more appealing to the intellectual. His early works, including *The Croatian God Mars*, portray his profound disillusion with Europe following the slaughter that was the First World War. *On The Edge of Reason* dissects the hypocrisy of conformity in the modern world. He and Andrić are recognized as Yugoslavia's best writers. As several commentators have noted, neither produced any of his best work after the Second World War, although the regime was happy to boast of their membership in the party and their acceptance of the system.

Béla Kun (1886–?1939)
Premier of Hungary, March 21–August 1, 1919

Béla Kun was born into a Jewish family in the small Transylvanian village of Lele in the Szilágycsehi district, Szilágy county. Influencing Kun was his father, a village clerk who idolized Lajos Kossuth (1802–94), the nineteenth-century nationalist and leader of the Hungarian revolt against the Habsburgs in 1848–49, and the poet, Endre Ady (1877–1919), who tutored ten-year-old Kun.

Kun joined the Hungarian Social Democratic party in 1902, and enrolled in the Kolozsvar Law Academy two years later, where Kun not only worked part-time at the local Workers' Insurance Bureau but began to write essays for a small radical newspaper, *OR* (Guardian). This experience launched his career as a journalist, and he worked his way to a position with the prestigious Budapest daily, *Budapesti Napló* (Budapest Post). After several years in Budapest, Kun returned to Kolozsvar and the Workers' Insurance Bureau. In 1913, he married a middle class Christian woman, Iren Gal.

Kun volunteered for the army in 1915 after it was alleged he misappropriated funds from the Insurance Bureau. He was captured by the Russians in 1916 and imprisoned in the city of Tomsk. In spring 1917, Tomsk fell under the control of the Bolsheviks, or Communists, and Kun applied to the local governing board (soviet) for a release from the prisoner of war camp. The local officials granted his release because of his socialist activities while in the camp. In April 1917, Kun joined the Tomsk Bolshevik organization. He gained a reputation as an organizer of prisoners of war and as a propagandist for the Bolshevik cause. Officially freed in late 1917, Kun went to Moscow and successfully established himself as one of the most influential foreign socialists in Petrograd and Moscow. In November 1918, Kun, with a number of Hungarian former prisoners of war, Jószef Rabinovics, Ernő Seidler, László Vántus, and Ernő Pór, formed a provisional Central Committee and established the Hungarian Communist party. Returning to Budapest the provisional Central Committee officially founded the Hungarian Communist party which included members of the Social Democratic party and several other revolutionary leftists.

During the short-lived rule of Mihály Károlyi's National Council (October 1918–March 1919), Kun, now general secretary of the Hungarian Communist party, and the Communists attacked the government for its neglect of issues such as economic inequalities, the slow implementation of agrarian reform, and its inability to secure from the Entente (France, Great Britain, and the United States) assurances of Hungary's territorial integrity. The final blow for Károlyi's government was the Vyx note which designated unfavorable postwar boundaries for Hungary. On March 19, 1919, Károlyi resigned and handed authority over to the Socialists who in turn offered a political alliance to Kun and the Communists. The Communists and socialists formed a united party, the Socialist-Communist Workers' party. At the same time, the Communists proclaimed a Hungarian Soviet Republic. Kun's name now became synonymous with the entire revolutionary experience in Hungary from March 21 to August 1, 1919.

After the fall of the Hungarian Soviet Republic on August 1, 1919, Kun fled to Austria where he was interned by the Austrians. The Austrians subsequently deported him to Soviet Russia. Kun spent the rest of his life in the Soviet Union working first as a political commissar in the Soviet Red Army, then as the coordinator of the translation and publishing of Lenin's work into foreign languages. He also became a high ranking official in the Communist International. In 1937, Kun was tried by the Presidium of the Communist International for a "disrespectful attitude" toward the Soviet leader Joseph Stalin and unwanted sympathies toward foreign Communists. Kun disappeared after this meeting. According to one source, he died on November 30, 1939. Different sources suggest that Kun was tortured for more than two years by the Soviet secret police in their prison, Lublianka, and then died in 1941.

Vladimir Ilich Lenin (1870–1924)
Russian Communist leader, 1918–1924

Vladimir Ilich Lenin was born as Vladimir Ilich Ulyanov in Simbirsk on April 10, 1870. The son of a tsarist official in the education bureaucracy, Lenin received a traditional Russian education given to the children of nobility, and earned a law degree from the University of Kazan in 1891.

Arrested in 1895 for revolutionary activities, Lenin was exiled to Siberia for three years in 1897. Upon his return from exile, Lenin moved to western Europe and became the leaders of the Bolshevik faction of the Russian Social Democratic Party after it split over ideological differences in 1903. Lenin returned to Russia during the 1905 revolution but moved to Switzerland after the revolution's failure in 1907.

Lenin once again returned to Russia after the February 1917 Revolution which overthrew the tsar (Nicholas II). In October, the Provisional Government, established after the fall of the tsar, collapsed and the Bolsheviks, under the leadership of Lenin, came to power. During his brief rule, Lenin had to negotiate with the Germans to end World War I, which had been a disaster for the Russian empire, then led the country through a brutal civil war as anti-Bolshevik forces attempted to overthrow the new socialist government. In 1922, after the Civil War, Lenin implemented the "new economic policy" (NEP) of limited free enterprise in an effort to rebuild the country. Lenin did not live to see the successful completion of this policy. He died on January 21, 1924, and his body was embalmed and placed on display in a mausoleum in Red Square in the center of Moscow.

Iuliu Maniu (1873–1953)
Prime Minister of Romania, 1928–30, 1932–33

Iuliu Maniu was born in Simleul-Silvaniei, Transylvania, then part of Austria-Hungary, on January 8, 1873. Following his father's footsteps, Maniu studied law at various universities in the Habsburg empire before being elected to the Hungarian parliament in 1906. During his four-year stint in the Hungarian diet as one of a handful of Romanian representatives, he championed the cause of his co-nationals against a repressive regime. After World War I erupted, he was drafted into the Austro-Hungarian army. With the collapse of the Habsburg monarchy in 1918, Maniu became the leader of Transylvania, and, along with the regional assembly at Alba, Iuliu proclaimed the union of Transylvania and the Banat with Romania. In 1919 he sat in the lower house of the Romanian parliament as a deputy from the Peasant party. In 1926 he engineered the union of the National and Peasant parties into the National-Peasant party, which he led until its dissolution in 1947. From November 1929 until October 1930, Maniu was prime minister, during which he helped former Crown Prince Carol gain his throne in June 1930. Forced to resign in October 1930, he returned to the premiership a second time in October 1932, but his government fell three months later. From 1933 until 1944, Maniu first opposed the royal dictatorship of King Carol II and then the pro-Axis-oriented government of General Ion Antonescu, although Maniu initially supported the country's effort against the USSR to regain Bessarabia and Bukovina. During World War II, he was considered Romania's chief resistance leader and helped organize the August 1944 coup against Antonescu. After the end of the war, Maniu continually opposed the Communist dominated government until he was arrested in July 1947, on false charges of espionage and treason. Convicted of these crimes in November 1947, and sentenced to life at hard labor, Maniu died in prison in 1953 at the age of 80.

Tomáš G. Masaryk (1850–1937)
President of Czechoslovakia, 1918–1935

Masaryk was born to a Czech mother and a Slovak father on March 7, 1850, in Hodonín, Moravia, a small city on the border of Slovakia in the Austrian half of the Habsburg Empire. After earning a doctorate in philosophy at the University of Vienna, he continued his education at the University of Leipzig in Germany, where he met an American music student, Charlotte Garrigue, whom he married in the United States in 1878. Masaryk taught at the University of Vienna until accepting a position at the newly established Czech University in Prague in 1882. Here he became a very popular professor who influenced not only Czechs but also other Slavs of the empire. In addition to teaching, Masaryk wrote numerous books and articles that at one time or another alienated various groups of Czech society. Nonetheless, in 1891, Masaryk was elected to the Austrian parliament as a member of the Young Czech party. In 1901 he established his own political party, the Realists, and was reelected to parliament in 1907.

While still a parliamentary deputy in 1914, Masaryk, with the outbreak of war, began to work secretly for the unification of the Czechs and Slovaks into one state. Upon learning he would be arrested for his activities, he fled the empire in December. Once outside Austria-Hungary, Masaryk eventually became the leader of the liberation movement, working with Edvard Beneš, another Czech, and the Slovak Milan R. Štefánik. During the war he travelled throughout England, France, Switzerland, Russia, and the United States on a propaganda campaign to convince the Allies of the feasibility of his plan. In 1916 he established a quasi government-in-exile, the Czechoslovak National Council, headquartered in Paris. In spring 1917, Masaryk traveled to Russia where he was instrumental in establishing the Czecho-Slovak Legion, a unit of the Russian army consisting of former Czech and Slovak prisoners of war. After the Communists seized power in Russia, he negotiated the transfer of the Legion to the Western Front via Siberia, and by May 1918, he arrived in the United States. Here Masaryk worked in the Slovak and Czech immigrant communities to gain support for a unified Czechoslovakia, and wrote the Pittsburgh Pact, an agreement that recognized a common country of both peoples. Furthermore, he worked to gain official recognition of Czechoslovakia in Washington, D.C., and eventually won over the United States, Great Britain, and France in the summer of 1918. On October 28, 1918, the Republic of Czechoslovak was established, with Masaryk, the writer of the Czechoslovak Declaration of Independence, installed as president. Masaryk triumphantly returned to Prague in December 1918, and he was reelected president in 1920, 1927, and 1934. The "liberator-president" retired from politics due to age in 1935, after choosing Beneš as his successor. Masaryk died on September 14, 1937.

Erich Mielke (1907–)
East German politician

Mielke was born in Berlin, Germany, on December 28, 1907. He worked as a shipping clerk and joined the Communist Youth League in 1921 and the Communist party (KPD) in 1925. He worked in the military wing of the KPD and served in the Emigration Spain International Brigade during the Spanish Civil War, where he was active in helping purge non-Communist Republicans. In 1939, with the Nazis in control in Germany, he emigrated to the Soviet Union where he stayed until the end of World War II.

When Mielke returned to his country after the war, it was to the new German Democratic Republic (GDR), or East Germany, where he worked to establish the East

German political police (SBZ). He joined the ministry of state security in 1950, where he served as state secretary from 1950 to 1960 and as deputy state secretary for state security in the Ministry of Interior from 1953 to 1955. From 1955 to 1957 he was state secretary and deputy minister for state security. He became a member of the East German parliament (Volkskammer) in 1958 and served until 1989. He attained the rank of colonel general in the army in 1959 and of full general in 1980.

Mielke presided over the secret police during some of the most repressive years of the GDR. He was responsible for the deaths of thousands of Germans who sought to leave the GDR. Mielke was removed from office and stripped of his party membership in 1989 and charged with numerous crimes and arrested in 1990. His trial began in February 1992, but he was released due to poor health.

Dragoljub (Draža) Mihajlović (1893–1946)
Yugoslavian soldier and politician

Mihajlović was born in Ivanjica, Serbia, in 1893. He fought for Serbia in the Balkan Wars of 1912–13, and during World War I. Mihajlović was a colonel in the Yugoslav army when the Second World War came to Yugoslavia in 1941. As a Serbian monarchist, he established the Četnik resistance organization which sporadically fought the Germans, Italians, and the Partisans, the largely Communist dominated resistance group led by Josip Broz (Tito). His organization was "Great Serbian" indicating he hoped to recreate a Yugoslav state to include all Serbs and as few others as possible. From late 1941 to 1944, Mihajlović was a member of the Yugoslav government-in-exile, serving as minister of the armed forces.

Mihajlović's Četniks and Tito's Partisans had conflicting views of how to execute resistance against the invader. Mihajlović feared reprisals, which were a trademark of German occupation; Tito, on the other hand, favored fighting despite reprisals. Mihajlović's approach was allegedly the result of his fear of the great losses that the Serbian nation would suffer since most of the resistance activity was centered in Serbia. In practice, Mihajlović probably cooperated with the Germans and Italians regularly; his fighters certainly engaged the Partisans more than the invaders after the first year of the war. Mihajlović was captured after the war and executed in July 1946 by the Communist authorities of the Yugoslav state.

Slobodan Milošević (1941–   )
President of Serbia, 1989–

Milošević was born in Požarevac, Serbia, where he went to school. His parents both committed suicide when he was young; the circumstances of those deaths are not clear. He studied at the University of Belgrade, where he first became active in politics and met his future mentor, Ivan Stambolić, a long time Communist and later president of Serbia. In 1968, he joined Tehnogas, a state-owned energy company. In 1969, he joined the League of Communists, in 1973, he became the head of Tehnogas, and in 1978, he became the president of Beobanka (Belgrade Bank). In 1984, he left the business world to become the head of the Belgrade city committee of the League of Communists of Serbia. In 1986, he followed Stambolić into the position of chairman of the Central Committee of the League of Communists of Serbia. Finally, after purging Stambolić and his followers, Milošević became president of Serbia in May 1989.

Milošević's career was built on his use of Serbian nationalism, especially after 1986. He is an example of the change in the Serbian party in the eighties when it went from being a Titoist organization to embracing the nationalistic mood in Serbia. Milošević built his reputation upon Serbian dissatisfaction with the status of Serbs in Yugoslavia and especially in Kosovo. Although no final judgment has passed on events in Yugoslavia since 1989, it can be safely said that Milošević has manipulated and even orchestrated events in the former Yugoslavia and must be held responsible for the wars that followed the country's collapse in 1991. His encouragement of excessive Serbian nationalism and his use of the media assured that the breakup of the country would not be peaceful.

Hans Modrow (1928–   )
Premier, German Democratic Republic, 1989–1990

Modrow was born into a working class family on January 27, 1928, in Jasenitz. He attended public schools and became an apprentice locksmith in 1942. He served in the German army and was captured by the Red Army. After his release by the Soviets in 1949 he returned to Germany and joined the Socialist Unity party (SED). He was elected a member of the East Berlin City Committee, serving as its first secretary from 1953 to 1961. He was a member of the East Berlin City Council from 1953 to 1971. After attracting the attention of party leaders he was sent to SED Party School from 1954 to 1958.

Modrow became a candidate member of the SED Central Committee in 1958 and was admitted to full membership in 1967. He served as a deputy to the East German parliament (Volkskammer) from 1958 to 1990. From 1961 to 1967 he was the first secretary of the SED Berlin-Köpernick district committee and as head of the department of agitation and propaganda for the SED Central Committee from 1967 to 1971. From 1973 to 1989 he was first secretary of the SED Dresden district committee, where he established a reputation as an honest party leader who worked hard and lived modestly, unlike many of his colleagues on the Central Committee. Modrow was viewed by rank-and-file party members as one of those who would lead in changing the party after the older leaders passed from the scene a reputation that did not endear him to the Honecker group.

Change came quicker than expected. Egon Krenz replaced Honecker as prime minister in October 1989 and Modrow replaced Krenz on November 13, 1989. Amid chaos, Modrow stayed with the SED when others were resigning in January 1990 and attempted to bring about reform. After meeting with Soviet leader Mikhail Gorbachev in February, he set up a commission to facilitate currency and economic union with West Germany and worked for a smooth transition toward unification. Modrow remained popular during the transition and was elected a member of the united Germany's parliament (Bundestag) in 1990. Although convicted of local election fraud from 1989 in the spring of 1993, he was neither imprisoned nor fined.

Imre Nagy (1896–1958)
Prime Minister of Hungary, 1953–1955, 1956

Imre Nagy was born into a poor peasant family in Kaposvár in the county of Somogy in southwest Hungary between Lake Balaton and the Yugoslav border. Although from a poor family, Nagy went to elementary school and to the gymnasium. After finishing school, Nagy's father apprenticed him to an agricultural machinery manufacturer in Slovakia. Later, Nagy found work at the Mavag foundry on the outskirts of Budapest.

When the First World War broke out in 1914, Nagy was conscripted into the Hungarian infantry. He was first sent to the Italian Front, and then was transferred to the Eastern Front, where the Russians captured him. In 1917/1918, Nagy was released from his prisoner of war camp and immediately joined the Russian Communist (Bolshevik) party and its Red Army. He fought for the Bolsheviks

in the Russian civil war and it was his involvement in this war which kept him out of Hungary during Kun's ill-fated Hungarian Soviet Republic.

Nagy returned to Hungary in 1921 as a member of the Hungarian Communist party, which had been outlawed in Hungary since August 1919. He was arrested in 1927 along with other members of the Hungarian Communist party, sentenced to two years in prison, and was released in 1929. He returned to the Soviet Union in 1930, where he studied agricultural economy at the International Agrarian Institute in Moscow. Nagy spent the Second World War in the Soviet Union and returned to Hungary with the Red Army in 1944. In the postwar period, Nagy served first as minister of agriculture and supervised the Communists' land reform. He was then appointed minister of the interior, where, after only four months, he was replaced by László Rajk in March 1946. During the late 1940s, Nagy remained an influential member of the Communist party, serving on the Political Committee of the Central Committee and as president of the National Assembly. During the purges of the Communist party in the late 1940s, Nagy was stripped of his governmental and party posts but was allowed to teach agronomy at Karl Marx University in Budapest.

After Mátyás Rakósi was pressured into resigning by the new Soviet leadership, Nagy reemerged on the political scene on July 4, 1953, as prime minister of the government. Nagy wanted to end the police state and one-person rule, and to govern the country by laws not arbitrarily administered. Nagy also wanted to relax economic controls, disband collective farms, and allow the return of small-scale private enterprise. In April 1955, however, the Stalinists, led by Rákosi, forced Nagy to resign as prime minister. He also was relieved of his parliamentary seat and all party offices. Nagy even voluntarily resigned from his university lectureship and membership in the Academy of Sciences. Rákosi, however, found it difficult to return to the former Stalinist path. In July 1956, following Nikita Khrushchev's February denunciation of Stalin and the East European Stalinists at the Twentieth Party Congress of the Communist Party of the Soviet Union (CPSU), Anastas Mikoyan, the Soviet representative to the Hungarian Communist party, engineered the election of Ernő Gerő as the new Hungarian party chief. Gerő, however, proved unacceptable to the moderates who favored more liberalization and the return of Imre Nagy, who had been readmitted to the Communist party on October 13. On October 23, the students took to the streets demanding liberalization as well as Nagy's reappointment to positions of power. In the early morning hours of October 24, Gerő appointed Nagy as prime minister; Gerő retained the general secretary position. As head of the government, Nagy unsuccessfully tried to control the population's desire to rid itself of Soviet control and Communist domination. On November 4, 1956, Soviet troops entered Hungary, and János Kádár ousted Nagy as prime minister.

The Yugoslav leader, Josip Broz Tito was sympathetic to Nagy's strong national Communist leanings and offered him refuge in the Yugoslav Embassy. Fearing retribution, Nagy accepted Tito's offer. On November 14, the Soviets seized Nagy as he left the refuge of the Yugoslav embassy in Budapest under a safe conduct pass. The Soviets forced Nagy and his family to seek asylum in Romania where he was officially arrested in April 1957. In June 1958, Nagy pleaded not guilty to charges of "conspiracy and creating a secret organization aimed at forcibly seizing power and overthrowing the Hungarian People's Democracy." Nagy was found guilty of conspiracy and treason and was hanged. Nagy was unceremoniously buried in an unmarked grave in the Rakoskeresztur cemetery in Budapest. In a public ceremony attended by 200,000 people, Nagy's remains were reinterred on June 16, 1989, 31 years to the day of his hanging.

Nicholas II (1868–1918)
Tsar of Russia, 1895–1917

The eldest son of Alexander III, Nicholas II has the dubious distinction of being the last member of the Romanov dynasty to rule the Russian empire. His rule is marked by a disastrous war with Japan which caused discontent at home. This, combined with the people's dissatisfaction with Nicholas II's autocratic rule, led to the Revolution of 1905, which resulted in the establishment of the Duma, a representative government assembly. However, even with the creation of the Duma, Nicholas II continued to rule as an autocrat.

Nicholas II took command of the Russian military forces at the outbreak of World War I, in which Russia fought against the military might of the Central Powers of Germany and the Austro-Hungarian empire. Once again, dissatisfaction with the war and the way the country was being governed led to revolution in March 1917. Forced to abdicate on March 17, 1917, Nicholas II and his entire family were executed by Red Guards, the pro-Bolshevik military forces, in July 1918.

Fan Stylian Noli (1882–1965)
Bishop of the Albanian Orthodox Church of America, 1918–1965
Prime Minister of Albania, 1924

Born Theophanus Stylianos Mavromatis in Imbrik-Tepe, a predominantly Albanian settlement in Thrace, then part of the Ottoman Empire, Fan Stylian Noli was educated in the Greek Gymnasium of Edirne (Adrianople). He began his career as a journalist for the Athenian newspaper, *Acropolis*. After leaving Athens he went to work for the Albanian-language periodical, *Dituria* (Knowledge), in Bucharest. In 1903 Noli moved to Alexandria, Egypt, where he found employment in a Greek community school. While in Egypt, Noli became actively involved in the nationalist movement then gaining momentum within the Albanian diaspora. Encouraged by a number of Albanian businessmen in Cairo, who provided him with financial support, Noli immigrated to the United States in 1906.

Noli's objective in the United States was to organize the Albanian American community for the advancement of the nationalist cause. Toward this end, in March 1908 Noli secured ordination (and appointment as bishop of the newly created Albanian Orthodox Church of America ten years later) from the Russian Orthodox Archdiocese of New York. From his headquarters in Boston, Noli used his pulpit to promote the nationalist movement throughout New England, the home to most Albanian American communities. With the aid of another prominent nationalist recently arrived in Boston, Faik Konitza, Noli was instrumental in establishing the Albanian-language newspaper, *Dielli* (Sun), in February 1909. The *Dielli* became the official organ of the Pan-Albanian Federation of America, called Vatra (Hearth), which Noli organized with Konitza and other community leaders in April 1912. Through his Church, newspaper, and federation, Noli exercised enormous influence over the Albanian American community. Noli was easily able to garner considerable financial support for the nationalist cause, and his efforts went so far as organizing émigré military bands in the United States for deployment in the Balkans. From Albania's liberation in November 1912 to the end of the First World War and the postwar peace conferences, Noli campaigned forcefully in Paris and the United States on behalf of an independent Albania, and in the meanwhile found time to graduate with a degree in divinity from Harvard University.

Due to the prominence he gained as the diaspora's leading nationalist advocate, Noli was assured an influential role in Albanian politics after the First World War. Vatra, at its Boston convention in July 1920, unanimously elected Noli deputy representing émigrés in the United States to the Albanian National Legislative Assembly. Noli arrived in Albania determined to uproot the old social order with its traditions of corruption and exploitation. Imbued with American democratic principles, he hoped to lead a reform movement to modernize and Westernize Albania. Noli, however, had only once before been in Albania, briefly in 1914, and he was detached from the realities of Albanian society and he had little understanding of the country's political complexities. Nevertheless, as one of the leading members of the Popular party, or Reform party, Noli became Albania's foreign minister in a Popularist government formed in December 1921.

By early 1922 Noli, for personal and political reasons, concluded that he could no longer cooperate with Albania's emerging leader, Ahmed Bey Zog. In March 1922 Noli resigned from his post as foreign minister in protest against Zog's drift towards dictatorship. Immediately after his departure from the Ministry of Foreign Affairs, Noli returned to the National Assembly to lead the democratic wing of the Popular party in a parliamentary fight against Zog and his supporters. Noli's opposition to Zog became fierce when he and his supporters in the National Assembly broke ranks with the Popular party in December 1922 and organized an anti-Zog coalition in parliament. Despite repeated attempts throughout 1923 by Noli to check Zog's power, he failed to dislodge him from his position as prime minister. Beginning in the summer of 1923 Noli became involved in revolutionary activity aimed at overthrowing Zog's government, which he regarded as an obstacle to reform, a threat to democracy, and a pawn of Yugoslav influence.

By the spring of 1924 Zog's policies had alienated enough Albanians to ensure Noli's rise to power. In May a revolt broke out against Zog's rule, and by June it succeeded in driving him out of office and into exile in Yugoslavia. On June 16, 1924, Noli became prime minister of a liberal government in Tirana. Three days later he announced an ambitious reform program which called for, among other things, the eradication of the feudal land-tenure system, establishment of democratic institutions, emancipation of the peasantry, judicial reform, tax reform, simplification of the state bureaucracy, and reorganization of education. Noli's premiership, however, was short-lived and he did not realize his reform goals. Although Noli's government was united with him against Zog, it was seriously divided over his reform program. Noli's policies, therefore, floundered as they were stifled by his own political allies. Compounding his domestic problems, Noli alienated most of his supporters by extending diplomatic recognition to

the Soviet Union—many of his friends and enemies alike feared what they perceived to be Noli's ideological affinities for Bolshevism. Encouraged by Noli's waning support, Zog struck back. From positions in Yugoslavia, Zog invaded Albania with a small force in mid-December 1924. On December 24, 1924, only six months after becoming prime minister, Noli fled Albania as his government collapsed in the face of Zog's invasion.

After failing to organize effective resistance from abroad to Zog's seizure of power, Noli ended his exile in Vienna and returned to the United States. By the early 1930s Noli had abandoned all opposition to Zog, and in 1933 he endorsed Zog's regime. Thereafter Noli's activities were limited to religious concerns and scholarly pursuits. Until his death in 1965, and despite strong dissension against him in a number of parishes and the establishment of a rival bishopric in the 1950s, Noli continued to be recognized as the head of the Autocephalous Albanian Orthodox Church of America. To Noli's intellectual credit, he devoted much of his time to the translation of Shakespeare, Ibsen, and other classic playwrights into Albanian. In 1947 Noli published a biographical study of his hero, *George Castrioti Scanderbeg (1405-1468)*, and in 1960 he completed, *Fiftieth Anniversary Book of the Albanian Orthodox Church in America, 1908-1958*, a commemorative history of his ecclesiastical charge.

Antonín Novotný (1904–1975)
President of Czechoslovakia, 1957–1968

Antonín Novotný was born in Letňany, Bohemia, on October 12, 1904. After attending school, he became a machinist and took an interest in the Communist party. In 1929, at the age of twenty-five, he became the chairman of the Karlin branch of the Communist party, which was led by Klement Gottwald. Until 1935 Novotný worked in various factories in Prague, Vysočany, and Libáň, where he espoused Communist ideology. In 1935 he served as a Czechoslovak delegate to a Comintern (the Communist International) conference in Moscow. After the Nazis destroyed Czechoslovakia in 1939, Novotný became a member of the resistance in Prague and a leader of the underground Communist party until his arrest in September 1941. He was eventually sent to Mauthausen concentration camp, where he remained until the end of the Second World War.

After his release, he became a regional Communist party secretary, and in 1946, a member of the Central

Committee. In May 1948, after the Communist coup, he was elected to the National Assembly. When Antonín Zápotocký became president of Czechoslovakia upon the death of Klement Gottwald, Novotný took the position of deputy prime minister. He first ran the Central Committee and then assumed its leadership in September 1953, thereby becoming the real power in Czechoslovakia. For the next sixteen years, Novotný ran the country along strict Stalinist lines while maintaining one-man rule that resulted in cultural repression and economic decline. His hardline stances resulted in his removal from the presidency, which he assumed in 1957, and a revocation of his membership in the Communist party by a group of reformers led by Alexander Dubček in early 1968. Although his membership in the Communist party was restored in 1971, he never regained any positions of authority. Novotný died on January 28, 1975.

Ignacy Jan Paderewski (1860–1941)
Polish pianist, composer, and statesman

Ignacy Jan Paderewski was born on November 18, 1860, in Russian Poland. His early life was devoted to music and included concert tours in Vienna, Paris, London, and New York, as well as on the continents of Africa, South America, and Australia. In 1910 Paderewski presented the Grunwald monument to the city of Kraków, commemorating the 500th anniversary of the defeat of the Teutonic Knights by King Władysław Jagiełło. As a member of the Polish National Committee during World War I, he was appointed that body's representative to the United States. During the war, Paderewski donated the proceeds from his concerts to aid Polish war victims. Through Colonel Edward M. House, Paderewski exercised influence over American president Woodrow Wilson in support of the cause of Polish independence. In postwar Poland, Paderewski briefly held the premiership and the portfolio of minister of foreign affairs from January 1919, all the while maintaining a nonpartisan political stance. He remained at his posts until his departure from Poland in November 1919, when he traveled to France to represent Poland at the Paris Peace Conference. He never returned to his native land after that date, retiring from politics in 1920 and resuming instead his musical career. He served briefly in the Polish government-in-exile during the Second World War but died on June 29, 1941, in the United States, where he was buried in Arlington National Cemetery. In 1992 his remains were returned to Poland for a ceremonial reinterment in a free Poland.

Nicola Pašić (1845–1926)
Serbian statesman and politician

Pašić was born in Zaječar, Serbia, and went to school in Belgrade, Kragujevac, and Negotin before attending university in Zurich where he received a degree in civil engineering. In Zurich, he travelled in circles with Mikhail Bakunin, the Russian anarchist and writer, whose teachings, however, did not leave much of an impression on him. He returned to Serbia in 1873, and in 1881, he became one of the founders of the Radical party.

Pašić's era in Serbian politics really began in 1903, when King Aleksandar Obrenović and his wife were murdered and Petar Karađorđević was installed as king, beholden to the Radicals, who had sponsored the coup with other parties. The Radical party became the most powerful party in Serbia, and Pašić was its leader. Until 1926, Pašić and his party were in or near power in Serbia and then the Kingdom of Serbs, Croats, and Slovenes.

During the First World War, Pašić directed Serbia toward its war aims. Although history will probably never arrive at a balanced judgment, his primary goal appears to have been to unify all Serbs in a single Serbian state. However, circumstances conspired to force the creation of a much larger and more diverse state including Slovenes, Croats, and numerous other nationalities. After the First World War, Pašić and his Radicals assured the new state would be dominated by Serbia. The new kingdom was unified on Serbia's terms which guaranteed Serbia would dominate the Kingdom of Serbs, Croats, and Slovenes.

Pašić's legacy is mixed: he was admired for his political ability and his power, but he was loathed by his enemies in and out of Serbia for the same qualities.

Ana (Rabinovici) Pauker (1893–?)
Romanian Communist politician

The daughter of a rabbi, Ana Pauker, was born in rural Moldavia. She became a teacher before joining the Communist party in 1921. After the party was outlawed in 1924, she worked intensely in its underground activity, rising to a position of leadership. The authorities arrested her in 1936, and sentenced her to ten years in prison for her work with the illegal party. Four years later the government exchanged her in a prisoner swap with the Soviet Union, where she remained during World War II. Once in the USSR, she took a position in the Executive Committee of the Comintern, an international organization of Communist parties dominated by the Soviets, until it was disbanded in 1943. When the Soviets occupied Romania in the summer of 1944, Pauker returned with the Red Army and became one of the top Communist leaders, becoming a member of the Central Committee and the secretariat in 1945. Two years later, she replaced a member of the Liberal party as foreign minister, adding the position of vice prime minister in 1949. In 1952 she and other Moscow-oriented Communists lost their jobs and memberships in the Romanian Workers' (Communist) party after an intense power struggle with the national Communists led by Gheorghe Gheorghiu-Dej. Gheorghe Gheorghiu-Dej then pursued a series of purges and show trials against his opponents of "non-Romanian" backgrounds such as Hungarians and Jews. Although Pauker was never brought to trial, she faded into political oblivion working as a minor bureaucrat.

Wilhelm Pieck (1876–1960)

President, German Democratic Republic, 1949–1960

Wilhelm Pieck was born into a working-class family in Gubin, Prussia (now Poland) on January 3, 1876. After attending public school, he became a carpenter at age fourteen and worked at self-education. In 1894 he joined a union and the Social Democratic party (SPD), where he quickly became active as a union organizer and a strike leader. In 1905 Pieck was elected to the national parliament (Reichstag), from Bremen, Germany, and the next year was elected secretary of the Bremen SPD. In 1910 he became secretary of the SPD's national central educational committee, serving as director of its educational activities.

While working in the Bremen organization Pieck worked with the leftist socialists Karl Radek and Rosa Luxemburg and was greatly influenced by them. In 1915 Pieck was an original organizer of the Spartacus League (Spartakusbund), a forerunner of the Communist party, which was led by Karl Liebknecht and Rosa Luxemburg. His activity in the antiwar movement led to his arrest and drafting, which resulted in his being sent to the front. Pieck deserted and fled to Holland, where he published a pacifist newspaper that was smuggled into Germany. He returned to Berlin in October 1918 and took an active part in the November revolt to establish a Communist government. Pieck escaped to Russia after the revolt failed.

Returning to Germany in 1919, he and other Spartacus survivors founded the German Communist party (KPD). Pieck was elected to the Prussian parliament in 1921 and

became chairman of the Red Help movement to aid revolutionary fighters. Between 1922 and 1933 he worked actively with Moscow and grew influential in the Comintern, the international communist movement. Pieck served on both the Comintern's and the KPD's executive committees. He was elected during this time to the Reichstag as a delegate from Prussia, to the Berlin city assembly, and the Prussian State Council.

As a member of the Reichstag, Pieck often attacked the Nazis and was forced to go underground after the Reichstag fire in 1933. He organized the cell and cadre organization of the Communist underground and, under orders from Moscow, fled to the USSR. He took an active role in Comintern leadership, replacing Georgi Dimitrov of Bulgaria as the last secretary general of the organization, which was dissolved in 1943.

During World War II Pieck served as secretary of the National Committee for Free Germany, working under Walter Ulbricht's direction to induce mass desertions of German troops. He returned to Germany at the end of the war and was the "chief architect" of the Berlin Antifascist Democratic Bloc (KPD, SPD, Christian Democrats, and Liberal Democrats).

In 1946 Pieck worked with Otto Grotewohl, the expelled SPD chairman, and Walter Ulbricht, organizing a merger of the East German SPD and the East German KPD into the Socialist Unity party (SED), with Pieck and Grotewohl serving as co-chairmen. In 1949 Pieck and Ulbricht were the primary organizers of the new German Democratic Republic (GDR). Pieck was elected president, Grotewohl as premier, and Ulbricht as deputy premier.

Pieck, like Ulbricht, had survived the purges of the 1940s and remained loyal to Moscow. In July 1950 he urged a purge of Titoist elements in the party and the adoption of a five-year plan that would communize industry and bring the GDR and the USSR closer together in economics and industry. He was not as opposed as Ulbricht was to discussing reunification, but Pieck objected to the West's formation of the North Atlantic Treaty Alliance (NATO) and the European Defense Community (EDC). In 1953 he warned of another Soviet blockade if the West were to ratify the EDC pact. Later that year he was re-elected GDR president.

Pieck's administration was marked by shortages, the rise of a police state, and repression of the people. In March 1954 he spoke to delegates at the Fourth Party Day, attacking the bureaucracy and calling for reform. On April 6, 1954 he resigned along with Grotewohl, leaving Ulbricht as the sole leader. Pieck died on September 7, 1960.

Józef Piłsudski (1867–1935)
Polish general and statesman

Józef Piłsudski was born on December 5, 1867, near Wilno (Vilnius) in Russian Poland to a noble family. He received his education in Wilno and Kharkov. In 1887 he was falsely arrested and sentenced to five years exile in Siberia, after which he returned to Wilno in 1892. He joined the Socialist Party and became the editor of its newspaper and its leader before being arrested again in 1900; the following year he fled to Galicia, or Austrian Poland. During the Russo–Japanese War in 1904–05, Piłsudski unsuccessfully plotted a Polish insurrection against the czarist regime. In 1912 Piłsudski was named commander of a paramilitary organization in Austrian Poland, out of which grew the Polish Legion, active in the First World War against the Russians. From 1917 to 1918 he was imprisoned by the Germans for defying them. After the conclusion of the war, Piłsudski became the head of state in November 1918 and, in 1920, marshal of Poland. During the Russo–Polish War in 1920, he won the Battle of Warsaw (the Miracle on the Vistula), which assured Polish independence and stopped the spread of communism into East Central Europe. Piłsudski is often identified with the idea of creating Poland as something of a federal state composed of Poles, Ukrainians, Belorussians, Jews, and Germans, as opposed to the integral nationalist ideas of Roman Dmowski. Piłsudski also liked to be pictured as a symbol of Polish nationhood who stood above the fray of partisan politics. In May 1926 Piłsudski carried out a coup against a government he had come to believe incapable of addressing the country's most serious problems; he twice held the premiership, in 1926 and again in 1930, although he was the real holder of political and military power in Poland until his death on May 12, 1935. Piłsudski, a politician, patriot, head of state, marshal of Poland, and one of the most powerful figures in Polish history, remains a strong symbol to Polish patriots to this day.

Stjepan Radić (1871–1928)
Croatian politician

Radić was born near Sisak, in Croatia. He attended university in Paris, and spent considerable time in Prague where he educated himself at the intellectual knee of Tomáš G. Masaryk. Radić and his brother Antun founded the Croatian People's Peasant party in 1904. The Radićs hoped to realize their vision of a Danubian federation of peoples through the cultivation of the most important segment of Croatian society: its peasantry. The party had little influence in Croatia before 1918 because its constituency could not vote. After the First World War, however, Radić found a place in the spotlight and became increasingly popular among the Croats.

Harnessing all of the disillusion in Croatia after its unconditional unification with Serbia, Radić expressed the legitimate desires of Croats for home rule: either independence or considerable autonomy within the Kingdom of Serbs, Croats, and Slovenes. The fact that Serbia so clearly dominated the new state gave his political position considerable power. However, he was not a conventional politician; he took his oppositional politics to ludicrous and often dangerous extremes. He and his party, for instance, boycotted the Constituent Assembly that gave the new kingdom a new constitutional order in 1921 to show their displeasure with the proposed constitution and thereby allowed it to pass by an overwhelming majority. Radić's unpredictability and criticisms of Serbia and its leaders only made him the object of derision and hatred outside of Croatia.

Radić died after he was shot in the Skupština by Puniša Račić, a Montenegrin deputy whom Radić had offended.

Mátyás Rákosi (1892–1971)
General Secretary, Hungarian Socialist Workers Party, 1945–1956

Born in 1892 in southern Hungary, Mátyás Rákosi was one of several children of a small village shopkeeper. In 1909, Rákosi left home for Budapest where he enrolled at the Oriental Academy of Commerce. Rákosi worked for a commercial firm in Hamburg and later worked in London from 1912–14. He joined the Hungarian Social Democratic party in 1910 and while abroad remained active in socialist circles.

In 1914, Rákosi joined the Sixth Infantry Regiment of the Hungarian army and was captured by the Russians in 1915. In 1917, Rákosi escaped from a prisoner of war camp and reached Petrograd in early 1918 where he met up with Hungarian Socialists and Communists and joined the Russian Bolshevik, or Communist, party. He returned to Hungary in the spring of 1918. When Béla Kun and the Communists seized power in March 1919, Rákosi served as Deputy People's Commissar of Commerce and as political commissar to the Sixth Division of the Hungarian Red Army. After the fall of Kun's government in August 1919, Rákosi fled abroad and did not return to Hungary until 1925. Upon his return, he was arrested, tried, and sentenced to eight-and-a-half years in prison. Shortly after his release he was rearrested and retried in 1935 and sentenced to fifteen-years imprisonment. In 1940, Rákosi was deported to the Soviet Union, where he spent the next five years, and returned to Hungary with the Soviet Red Army in February 1945.

Upon his return to Hungary, Rákosi became general secretary of the Communist Party of Hungary. He led the ascendancy to positions of power and authority of the ''Muscovites''—those Hungarian Communists who had spent the war years in the Soviet Union and who included Ernő Gerő, Mihály Farkas, and József Révai. During the late 1940s, Rákosi used accusations of deviation from the pro-Soviet line to rid the party of any potential rivals. The minister of the interior, László Rajk, was tried and sentenced to death in a show trial engineered by Rákosi. In addition, another one of his potential rivals, János Kádár, was tried and sentenced to prison in 1951.

Rákosi kept an iron grip on the Hungarian Communist party until the death of Soviet dictator Joseph Stalin on March 5, 1953. Stalin's successors in the Soviet Union opted for collective leadership, a ''New Course'' which targeted the production of consumer goods versus heavy industrial output, and repudiation of the ''cult of personality'' which emphasizes unquestioned devotion to the leader. Rákosi, considered one of the ''the little Stalins'' of Eastern Europe, faced a new challenge to his absolute authority over other party members.

On June 27–28, 1953, following the example of the ''New Course'' in the Soviet Union, the Central Committee (the ruling body of the Hungarian Workers' (Communist) party) met in full session and decreed a new official party line which promoted better living standards and wages, agricultural and light industrial investments, artisanal private enterprise, administrative decentralization, educational liberalization, socialist lawfulness, amnesty, and religious toleration. Rákosi, showing reluctance to accept the ''New Course,'' was forced to resign as prime minister of Hungary. Imre Nagy, who had recently been released from prison and whose membership to the Hungarian Workers' (Communist) party had been restored, was appointed prime minister. Rákosi remained as General Secretary of the Party and deliberately set out to sabotage Nagy's New Course.

In 1955, Rákosi attempted to reassert his power when Nagy's patron in the Kremlin, Georgi M. Malenkov, the last of the Soviet collective leadership which advocated the New Course, was ousted and Nagy fell out of favor. Rákosi's resurgence was short-lived when Nikita Khrush-chev denounced Stalin, and by association all of the East European Stalinists, in a speech in February 1956 to the Twentieth Congress of the Communist party of the Soviet Union. In July 1956 Ernő Gerő replaced Rákosi as the General Secretary of the party. Rákosi went into exile in Soviet Central Asia, was formally expelled from the Hungarian Socialist Workers' (Communist) party in 1962, and died in exile in 1971.

Aleksandar Ranković (1909–1983)
Yugoslavian politician

Ranković was born in 1909 in Draževac, Serbia. Ranković, like Tito, Kardelj, and Djilas, was an active Communist from his youth. He was accepted in the party in 1928 after several years of working in the Yugoslav Communist youth organization. He spent several years in the 1930s in prison in Sremska Mitrovica, where he and Djilas became ideologically close. In 1940 he was elected to the politburo of the Communist Party of Yugoslavia. During the Second World War, he was captured by the Gestapo but freed almost immediately by his comrades, after which he became one of the Partisan leaders.

After the war, Ranković established himself as the internal security expert in Yugoslavia. He administered the UDBa, the internal state security organization, or secret police, and was a leader of the Serbian party organization. In 1966 he was removed from his positions in the party and the state as a result of his opposition to the liberalizing economic reforms enacted during the previous two years. Ranković's opposition to the reforms was perceived to be a result of his Serbian orientation. After his fall, strong central control of Kosovo became weaker, resulting in ethnic Albanians beginning to agitate for democratization in their region. Rankovic died in 1982 without ever publicly bemoaning his fate or telling all of what he knew as the head of the secret police.

Władysław Sikorski (1881–1943)
Minister of war of Poland, 1924–1925
Prime minister of Poland, December 1922–May 1923

Sikorski was born on May 20, 1881, in Austrian Poland and educated in Lwów. He joined the Austro-Hungarian army and later served in Piłsudski's Polish Legion during the First World War, rising to a leadership position. After the war he fought against the Russian Communists in the Russo–Polish War. Sikorski served as prime minister from 1922 to 1923 and later as minister of military affairs from 1924 to 1925, during which he urged the modernization of the Polish military forces. Neutral during Marshal Piłsudski's coup in 1926, Sikorski joined the opposition in 1928 after being fired from his command, after which he wrote on military matters. In 1939 he became premier and war minister of the government-in-exile that established diplomatic relations with the Allied powers. His request that the International Red Cross investigate the Katyń Forest mass graves of Polish officers and soldiers in 1943 gave Soviet dictator Joseph Stalin the excuse he needed to break off relations with Sikorski's London Poles. Sikorski died in an airplane crash at Gibraltar on July 4, 1943, under what some consider to be suspicious circumstances.

Joseph Vissarionovich Stalin (1879–1953)

General Secretary, Soviet Communist Party, 1929–1953

The son of a cobbler, Stalin was born Joseph Vissarionovich Dzhugashvili on December 21, 1879 in Gore, Georgia. As a teenager Stalin attended the theological seminary in Tiflis, Georgia, but was expelled in 1899 for expounding revolutionary views.

Stalin was active in the Russian Social Democratic Party, and after the party split because of ideological differences in 1903, Stalin joined the Bolshevik party under the leadership of Vladimir Lenin. As a result of his revolutionary activities, from 1903 to 1912 Stalin was arrested, and managed to escape, several times. He was exiled to Siberia from 1913 to 1917, returning to Petrograd only after the fall of the tsar.

After the Bolsheviks came to power in October 1917, Stalin was appointed Commissar of Nationalities. During the Russian Civil War, Stalin distinguished himself as a military commander. Elected general secretary of the Central Committee of the Communist party, Stalin succeeded Lenin as chairman of the Politburo in 1924. By placing his supporters in key party posts, Stalin ousted Leon Trotskii from the party and became the uncontested leader of the Soviet Union by 1928.

At the end of the 1920s Stalin instituted a plan of collectivization of agriculture, forcing peasants to give up private farms to join state-run farms. This collectivization resulted in famine partly as a result of peasants' resistance to the plan and partly due to the fact that the state-farms were poorly managed. In 1928 Stalin also instituted the

first five-year industrial and economic development plan for the Soviet Union which forced the country to develop as an industrial nation. During the 1930s Stalin instituted the great purges which removed all "perceived" enemies from the party and government.

After defeating Nazi Germany in World War II, Soviet armies occupied Eastern Europe. This allowed Stalin to spread the Soviet Union's sphere of influence over these countries. They developed Soviet-type governments that served as "satellite states" to the Soviet Union.

Stalin's policies forced the Soviet Union to industrialize and thus allowed them to defeat Germany. However, this success was achieved at great cost. Millions of people died during collectivization, the purges, and World War II. Stalin died on March 5, 1953.

Alexander Stamboliiski (1879–1923)

Prime Minister of Bulgaria, 1919–1923

Born in Slavovitsa, Bulgaria, on March 1, 1879, Alexander Stamboliiski completed his education in an agricultural college in Germany. Stamboliiski turned to journalism and became editor of the newly formed Bulgarian Agrarian National Union's organ in 1902. By 1908 he had become the dominant figure within the Agrarian party and that same year he entered the Subranie, the Bulgarian parliament, as head of his party.

An ardent advocate of peasant interests, Stamboliiski's political ideology was founded on the idea that society was divided not into classes but into estates. According to Stamboliiski, an estate comprised a group of people whose shared occupation gave them common interests, regardless of different social background or economic status. He defined the estates as the agrarian, the artisan, the wage-laborer, the entrepreneurial, the commercial, and the bureaucratic. Of these estates Stamboliiski regarded the agrarian to be the most important because it supposedly guaranteed freedom from exploitation and insured other personal liberties. He consequently feared industrialization and urbanization as breaks from the noble, fulfilling life of the peasant farmer. Stamboliiski also ridiculed other institutional manifestations of the modern state, in particular the bureaucracy, the military, and, above all, the monarchy and its court.

Stamboliiski's repeated disputes with King Ferdinand finally climaxed in 1915, when Bulgaria prepared to enter the First World War on the side of the Central Powers. Stamboliiski, who personally favored the Entente or Allied cause, and who publicly advocated neutrality, threatened the king. Arrested and imprisoned for life, he was freed in September 1918. Stamboliiski was released from prison by a new government that hoped he would participate in a broad coalition to calm the nation after its defeat in the war. A few days following Stamboliiski's release, one of his Agrarian party subordinates proclaimed a republic and led an attack on Sofia. Although the Agrarian rebellion was defeated and the monarchy survived under Ferdinand's son, Boris, Stamboliiski became a cabinet member in January 1919 and prime minister of a coalition government on October 6 of that year. In May 1920, after new elections in March, Stamboliiski was able to form an Agrarian majority government.

Despite his democratic idealism, Stamboliiski's government was personally authoritarian. His emotional attachment to his fellow peasants was matched by his enthusiastic hatred for the city and the people who lived and worked there. Stamboliiski's domestic reforms were intended to make Bulgaria a model agricultural state in twenty years, and he hoped to ultimately create a strong peasant-based republic. Toward these ends, Stamboliiski redistributed land to the peasantry, reformed the judicial system, promoted universal suffrage, limited the bureaucracy, and furthered local self-government.

In the area of foreign affairs, Stamboliiski's policies were founded on the principle of peaceful coexistence with Bulgaria's neighbors and international cooperation through the Agrarian movement. With the support of Czechoslovak and Polish Agrarian leaders, Stamboliiski organized an International Bureau of Agriculture, the Green International. With offices in Prague the Green International sought to coordinate the Agrarian parties of Europe. Towards the goal of Balkan harmony, Stamboliiski signed the Treaty of Neuilly in 1919 officially ending the First World War hostilities with Greece, Romania, and Yugoslavia at the cost of a considerable loss of Bulgaria's territory. In order to improve relations with Yugoslavia, and with the hope of establishing the foundations for a South Slav federation, Stamboliiski signed the Treaty of Nish in March 1923. Despite his popularity, Stamboliiski's domestic policies, pacifist leanings, rapprochement with Yugoslavia, and advocacy of a militia alienated both the army and the terrorist Internal Macedonian Revolutionary Organization (IMRO). A military coup overthrew Stamboliiski's government on June 9, 1923. Captured near his native village, Stamboliiski was brutally tortured and killed by IMRO henchmen.

Willi Stoph (1914–)
Premier, German Democratic Republic, 1964–1973, 1976–1989

Stoph was born the son of a manual laborer in Berlin, Germany, on July 8, 1914. He attended public elementary schools and went to an apprentice program as a mason. He eventually became a building foreman and technical architect. He joined the Communist youth movement when he was fourteen and the Communist party (KPD) three years later, in 1931. He became a "party machine" and worked at setting up a courier system, linking the KPD with the Soviet Union. He was drafted into the German army at the start of World War II and was captured by the Soviets.

Stoph returned to Germany at the end of the war, and in 1945 he became an adviser in the military section of the KPD and its successor the Socialist Unity party (SED). He became a member of the East German parliament (Volkskammer), and the SED central committee, moving up to the Politburo in 1953.

A cold, reserved man, Stoph began to build the muscles of an army by using the Peoples Police (KVP), but actual command of the KVP was in the hands of the Soviets. In 1952 Stoph was named minister of the interior, and the next year he increased border and transport security forces and formed militia units in factories and trade unions. He became deputy premier in 1954; as defense minister in 1956 Stoph was in charge of building the new East German Peoples Army, in which he held the rank of full general. He became a member of the State Council in 1963, deputy chairman and premier in 1964, and chairman in 1973.

Stoph first received serious attention in the West when he met with West German chancellor Willy Brandt in Erfurt in March 1970 to discuss the possibility of recognition and reunification as part of Brandt's Ostpolitik, or relations with East Europe. Like his boss, Honecker, Stoph was not seriously interested in reunification except on Communist terms, so the meeting was fruitless. He continued to follow the hard line and resist liberalization until change began to sweep across eastern Europe in 1989. Stoph was removed from office following the mass demonstrations of fall 1989 and expelled from the party, along with Honecker, in December. He was arrested and accused of a variety of crimes in 1991 but was released without trial due to poor health.

Franjo Tudjman (1922–   )

President of Croatia, 1990–

Tudjman was born in Croatia and fought for the Partisans in the Second World War. He became the youngest general in the Yugoslav People's Army before retiring from active service in 1961. He then became a historian, although he is not known as a great historian, and eventually became a dissident. He spent several years in the early 1980s in prison for his Croatian nationalism. After his release from prison, he created a political party known as the Croatian Democratic Union. This party quickly became the most popular in Croatia and won the elections of 1990. Tudjman is now the president of Croatia and his party the governing party.

Walter Ulbricht (1893–1973)

Chairman, Council of State, German Democratic Republic, 1960–1973
First Secretary, Socialist Unity Party, 1953–1971

Walter Ulbricht was born on June 30, 1893, in Leipzig, Germany, the son of a tailor. His parents introduced him at an early age to socialism. As a youth he handed out Socialist Youth League leaflets and joined the Social Democratic party (SPD) in 1912. He became very active in the party, and following World War I he associated himself with the left wing of the party that was to form the Communist Party of Germany (KPD). During the early 1920s he traveled to the Soviet Union to undergo extensive training in party organization. After returning to Germany Ulbricht was in charge of establishing Stalin's cell system within the KPD. In 1928 he was elected to the Reichstag representing South Westphalia and was active in opposition to the Nazis.

In 1933, after Hitler came to power and began his persecution of the KPD, Ulbricht obtained false identity papers and fled to France. In Paris he headed a group of exiled Communists called the Auslandskomitee, where he perfected his technique of getting rid of party rivals. He then left to fight in the Spanish Civil War, in which he served the Soviets as a hatchetman, removing possibly disloyal party members.

With the outbreak of World War II, Ulbricht returned to the Soviet Union, where he followed the Moscow line in blaming Great Britain and France for the start of the war and encouraged German Communists to oppose col-laboration with the Allied powers. This policy ended with the German invasion of the USSR in 1941, when he worked as a leader with the National Committee for Free Germany, indoctrinating captured German soldiers and urging them to oppose the fascists. In 1945, with the rank of colonel in the Red Army, he returned to Germany with Soviet forces.

In the summer and fall 1945 Ulbricht worked to reorganize the KPD in the Soviet zone of occupation. With Wilhelm Pieck he helped bring about a merger of the SPD and the KPD to form the Socialist Unity party (SED), and he served as a deputy premier of that group. As a member of the SED's general secretariat he worked to remove non-Communists from positions of government leadership on all levels.

As deputy premier under Otto Grotewohl, Ulbricht worked to develop a plan to revive German industrial production and to communize industry. In 1950 he announced a five year plan to continue this work and to closely integrate the GDR with the USSR and Eastern Europe. A devoted Stalinist, Ulbricht reorganized the party to exclude Social Democrats from leadership positions in the SED in 1953, and in April 1954 he remained as sole party leader after the resignations of co-chairmen Pieck and Grotewohl.

By 1961, due to shortages and police state repressions, over 2,000 refugees a day were fleeing from the GDR to the West. As a result, Ulbricht ordered the erection of the Berlin Wall to stem the flow and bring some measure of social and economic stability to the GDR. Although the wall brought worldwide condemnation, it also served its purpose in promoting stability.

Ulbricht opposed reunification efforts with the Federal Republic, or West Germany, and in 1968 drew up a new constitution establishing the GDR as a socialist state with Berlin as its capital and stressing the separation between the two Germanies. That same year he was the loudest voice for strong action to contain the "Prague Spring" reforms going on in Czechoslovakia and sent forces to support Soviet repression of the Czechoslovaks in late August.

In the early 1970s Ulbricht refused to go along with the policy of detente being advocated by Soviet leader Leonid Brezhnev and American president Richard Nixon, and he was a thorn in the side of the Soviets over the status of Berlin. Age, illness, and an unwillingness to change, even under pressure from the Soviets, provoked Ulbricht's resignation as party head in May 1971. He was replaced by Erich Honecker and died in East Berlin on February 1, 1973.

Nicolae Văcăroiu 1943–   )
Prime Minister of Romania, 1992–

Nicolae Văcăroiu was born in Bolgrad, Bessarabia, in 1943. In 1969 he graduated *magna cum laude* from the Department of Finance at the Academy for Economic Studies in Bucharest. Under Ceauşescu, he worked in the State Planning Committee, which directed the planned economy of Romania. He was later promoted to head the Directorate of Economic and Financial Synthesis. After the December 1989 revolution, he received an appointment as a deputy minister in the Ministry of National Economy. After the reorganization of the government in May 1990, Văcăroiu became secretary of state at the Ministry of Economy and Finance. In November 1992 President Ion Iliescu appointed him as prime minister.

Lech Wałęsa (1943–   )
President of Poland, 1990–

Wałęsa was born the son of a carpenter on September 29, 1943, near Włacławek. He began work as an electrician at the Lenin shipyard in Gdańsk in 1967. As a result of the crushing of a strike in 1970 at the shipyard, Wałęsa became committed to the idea of a free trade union. On August 14, 1980, he climbed over the wall during protests at the shipyard and was soon elected the head of a strike committee. By August 31, with the signing of the Gdańsk Agreement, the strike committee became the trade union Solidarity (Solidarnose) with Wałęsa as chairman. Wałęsa was imprisoned for almost one year under martial law proclaimed in December 1981, and he was harassed by the authorities after his release. After the announcement that he had been awarded the Nobel Peace Prize in 1983, Wałęsa, fearful that he might not be allowed to reenter Poland should he leave the country, chose to remain at home; his wife accepted the prize on his behalf. During 1988–89 Wałęsa was at the forefront of the roundtable talks that culminated in the restoration of Solidarity to legal status and free elections to the Sejm. In 1990 Wałęsa won Poland's first free presidential elections by a landslide after a runoff election.

Stefan Wyszyński (1901–1981)
Primate of Poland, 1949–1981

Wyszyński was born on August 3, 1901, near Łomża in Russian Poland. He studied in Warsaw and elsewhere before being ordained in 1924. Wyszyński later received a doctorate from the Catholic University in Lublin in sociology and canon law, and after further studies abroad in France, Belgium, and Italy, he founded the Christian Workers University in 1935. Having survived World War II, in 1946 he was appointed bishop of Lublin and in 1948 he was made archbishop of Gniezno, and hence primate of Poland. In 1952 Wyszyński was elevated to the rank of cardinal, although he was prevented from going to Rome until 1957 to receive his cardinal's hat. A staunch anti-Communist, Wyszyński was arrested in 1953 for allegedly engaging in "anti-government activities." After Władysław Gomułka came to power in 1956, he was released and concluded an agreement with the government allowing for religious instruction in public schools. In later years, Wyszyński lent tacit support to the Workers' Defense Committee (Komitet obrony Robotników, KOR) and to rural Solidarity. One of his personal triumphs was helping organize the official visit to Poland of Polish Pope John Paul II in 1979. A symbol of Roman Catholic resistance to communism, Cardinal Wyszyński died in Warsaw on May 28, 1981.

Boris Nikolayevich Yeltsin (1931–   )
President of Russia, 1991–

Boris Nikolayevich Yeltsin was born into a Russian peasant family on February 1, 1931 in Sverdlovsk in the Urals. In 1955 he graduated from the Urals Polytechnical Institute and began a career in the construction industry.

Yeltsin joined the Communist Party in 1961 and became a full-time party worker in 1968. In 1976 he was appointed first secretary of the Communist party of the Sverdlovsk district, equivalent to a U.S. governor. Yeltsin became a full member of the Central Committee of the Soviet Communist party in 1981, and served as secretary of the Central Committee from June 1985 to February 1986. In December 1985 Yeltsin also became first secretary of the Moscow city Communist party committee, or mayor of Moscow. He became a candidate member of the Politburo in February 1986. After criticizing the slow pace of reforms during a speech to the Central Committee in 1987 Yeltsin was relieved of his duties in the Politburo and removed as first secretary of Moscow.

In March 1989 Yeltsin was elected to the Congress of People's Deputies, or Soviet legislature, and was later elected to the Supreme Soviet of the USSR, another legislative body. In 1990 he was also elected a member of the Russian Republic Supreme Soviet, and in May he was elected chairman of this body, equivalent to president of the Russian republic.

During the attempted overthrow of Gorbachev on August 19, 1991, Yeltsin opposed the coup leaders and helped to return Gorbachev to power. However, after Gorbachev's return, Yeltsin continued to operate independently of the central Soviet government. On December 8, 1991, Yeltsin, along with the presidents of Ukraine and Belarus, proclaimed the creation of the Commonwealth of Independent States. On December 21, eleven of the twelve remaining Soviet republics joined the Commonwealth of Independent States (the Baltic States had already left the Soviet Union, and Georgia refused to join the Commonwealth). This resulted in the resignation of Gorbachev as leader of the Soviet Union on December 25, 1991.

Yeltsin continues to serve as president of Russia and faces many problems economically and politically.

Antonín Zápotocký (1884–1957)

President of Czechoslovakia, 1953–1957
Prime Minister of Czechoslovakia, 1948–1953

Antonín Zápotocký was born on December 19, 1884, in Zákolany, Bohemia, and later became a stone mason. In 1907 he joined the trade union movement in Kladno, and in 1911 he served on its town council, being arrested several times for his political activity. During World War I Zápotocký served in the Austro-Hungarian army, after which he returned to Kladno, where he resumed his work in politics. He was arrested for his activity during the 1920 general strike of Kladno smelters and miners, and received a two-year prison sentence, but he was released a short time later. In 1921 Zápotocký helped to establish the Communist Party of Czechoslovakia, becoming its secretary general two years later. In 1925 he was elected as a deputy to the National Assembly, and four years later he became the head of the Revolutionary Trade Union Organization in Czechoslovakia.

Arrested by the Germans in 1939 after they destroyed Czechoslovakia, Zápotocký was sent to the Sachsenhausen concentration camp where he remained for the duration of World War II. After his release in 1945, he again took command of the trade union movement and once more served as a deputy to the National Assembly. For using his union members to support the Communist coup in February 1948, Zápotocký became deputy prime minister, and after Prime Minister Klement Gottwald be-

came president in June, Zápotocký succeeded him as premier. Under his prime ministry, Czechoslovakia moved against the church, free enterprise, and civil liberties, and became a staunch supporter of Soviet policies both domestically and internationally. In 1950 he resigned as the leader of the Czechoslovak trade union movement, and with the reorganization of the Czechoslovak Communist party in 1951, Zápotocký was elected to its two most important bodies: the secretariat and the presidium. Zápotocký became president of the republic upon the death of Gottwald in 1953, and he held the position until his own death on November 13, 1957.

Todor Zhivkov (1911–   )

General Secretary, Bulgarian Communist Party, 1981–1989
First Secretary, Bulgarian Communist Party, 1954–1981

Todor Hristov Zhivkov was born into a poor peasant family in Pravec, Bulgaria, on September 7, 1911. He moved to Sofia as a youth in the late 1920s and worked as a printer. There he joined the outlawed Bulgarian Communist party (BCP) in 1931 and held various minor offices in it during the early 1930s while continuing his printing work. In 1937, however, he became head of the BCP committee in Sofia, and he rose to great prominence as a partisan fighter in the Communist-led Fatherland Front during the latter part of the Second World War. He was entrusted by the BCP in organizing the successful Fatherland Front coup in Sofia on September 9, 1944. After the war Zhivkov served as party boss in Sofia and as commander of the People's Militia, which was at the forefront of the Communist campaign of repression against political opposition in Bulgaria. In recognition of his loyalty to Stalin, Zhivkov was appointed as a full member of the BCP Politburo in 1951.

Zhivkov took advantage of the internal power struggles in the BCP in the wake of Stalin's death and came out on top. Through the clever exploitation of the de-Stalinization issue, and the support of Stalin's successor, Nikita Khrushchev, Zhivkov emerged as the dominant figure in the BCP. In 1954 Zhivkov became first secretary of the BCP, and, after years of consolidation and maneuvering, he enhanced his position further in 1962 by taking over the position of prime minister. Although the sudden fall of Khrushchev in 1964 removed Zhivkov's most important patron, he maintained himself in power. Nevertheless, Zhivkov's authority did not remain unchallenged—between 1964 and 1971 he had to put down six different coups attempted by dissident BCP members and army officers.

Zhivkov's long tenure in office, however, began to be threatened by worsening domestic problems during the 1980s. Despite reforms introduced in the 1970s, the Bulgarian economy began to stagnate seriously during the early 1980s. In an effort to distract public attention from economic problems and in order to benefit from nationalist sentiment, the Zhivkov regime launched a major campaign of repression against Bulgaria's large Turkish minority during the mid-1980s. Nevertheless, in the second half of the 1980s Zhivkov's position began to deteriorate—economic performance declined, relations between Zhivkov and Soviet leader Mikhail Gorbachev were strained, and Zhivkov was confronted with increasing domestic demands to adopt economic, political, and social reforms like those introduced by Gorbachev in the Soviet Union. Adding to Zhivkov's problems, BCP unity collapsed as reformist factions in the party were alienated by the worsening economic situation and Bulgaria's rapidly expanding foreign debt, the disastrous diplomatic effects of Zhivkov's policy towards ethnic Turks in Bulgaria, and by his blatant nepotism and corruption. In the autumn of 1989 Zhivkov tried to reach some accommodation with the reformist wing of the party but his overtures came too late. On November 10, 1989, Zhivkov was forced to resign as party and state leader and expelled from the BCP as reformists attempted to prevent a repetition of the anti-Communist upheavals in the other East European states. Zhivkov was placed under house arrest and the new reformist Communist government scapegoated him for the preceding years of repression. In 1991 the new regime announced that Zhivkov would stand trail for a host of abuses allegedly committed during his long period in office. The trial was concluded in September 1992 and Zhivkov was sentenced to seven years in prison on charges of corruption. During the summer of 1993 the government moved him to house arrest on an estate outside Sofia.

Ahmed Bey Zog (1895–1961)
King of Albania, 1928–1939

Ahmed Bey Zog, originally Zogolli (Zogu), son of the most powerful Muslim chieftain in northern Albania, the head of the Mati tribe, was born in the village of Burgayet. His formal Ottoman education was limited to three years of study, first at the Galata-Serail Lyceum for notables and later at a military school in Bitola (Monastir). Following his training, Zog resided briefly in Constantino-

ple. In 1911 he was called back to Albania to lead his tribe in a revolt against the increasing authority of the Young Turks. The following year he distinguished himself in a campaign against the invading Serbian army. During that conflict Zog fought in defense of Albanian autonomy, and when Albania's independence was proclaimed in the marketplace of Vlorë on November 28, 1912, Zog was among the eighty-some notables present.

Zog was one of the first supporters of the new Albanian state. In March 1914 a German prince, William of Wied, was selected by the Great Powers as Albania's ruler. Despite Zog's considerable military backing, Prince William was not able to suppress an Italian-sponsored rebellion against his government and he thus fled Albania in September 1914. Having returned to their northern district, Zog and his tribesmen joined the Austrians who penetrated Albania during the early stages of the First World War. Initially the Austrians rewarded Zog with the title of Imperial and Royal Colonel and the Order of Francis Joseph, but later, suspecting him of plotting to restore Albanian independence, they interned him in Vienna until the end of the war. Zog returned to Albania in November 1918 to discover a country overwhelmed by crisis. The nation had been physically devastated by the preceding conflict, central authority was non-existent, and most of Albania was under foreign occupation. In February 1920 an Albanian provisional government was formed in order to organize resistance against the French, Greek, Italian, and Yugoslav plans for the partition of Albania. Zog was appointed interior minister and commander-in-chief of the Albanian armed forces. Due to international diplomatic conditions, and in no small part to Zog's military leadership, Albania succeeded in preserving its territorial integrity, and by November 1921 all foreign occupation forces had withdrawn from Albania.

Taking advantage of his countrymen's admiration of his organizational skills and his proven determination to rid Albania of foreign troops, Zog pursued parliamentary politics as a means to promote his ambitions. In the politically unstable period from 1921 to 1924 Zog advanced his influence at every opportunity through the Albanian military and the national Legislative Assembly. After exploiting a series of political crises as his pretext, Zog entered the capital of Tirana at the head of the army in December 1921 and proclaimed martial law. During the following year Zog attempted to crush his opponents which condemned him for governing as a dictator, but opposition to his regime expanded under the leadership of his former parliamentary ally, Fan Stylian Noli. Nevertheless, Zog became prime minister in December 1922. That same month Noli and his supporters left Zog's Popular party to organize an opposition bloc in parliament. After a series of electoral crises, mounting parliamentary and popular opposition, and an assassination attempt against him, Zog resigned from the premiership in February 1924. A new government was formed without Zog, but it was made up of his cronies and it was apparent that Zog continued to rule using the government as his front. Dissatisfaction with Zog's policies was great enough to produce a rebellion against his government. On June 10, 1924, Zog fled to Yugoslavia as insurgents entered Tirana. Zog's rival, Noli, took command of the state and formed a new liberal government. However, in December 1924, with the military backing of the Yugoslavs, Zog returned to Albania and forced Noli into exile.

With the overthrow of the Noli government and the emergence of Zog as Albania's dominant political personality, prospects for the survival of a democratic parliamentary system dimmed. A newly convened parliament under Zog's control proclaimed him president at the close of January 1925. In March of that same year a new constitution was approved which invested the president with virtually dictatorial powers. Despite at least five different uprisings, Zog continued to solidify his authority. On September 1, 1928, Zog realized his ultimate ambition—the parliament unanimously proclaimed Albania a hereditary monarchy and Zog assumed the title of "Zog I, King of the Albanians." Zog's royal dictatorship was characterized by a combination of despotism and Western reform. Although Zog continued to practice oppressive policies, his regime enacted a substantial number of reforms. Western-style civil, commercial, and penal codes were adopted while some modern facilities and technology were introduced into Albania for the first time. A major land-tenure reform law was approved in 1930, but was never effectively implemented.

Although Zog succeeded in centralizing his regime's political authority, he was incapable of developing Albania's primitive economy with the domestic resources at his disposal—his policies in this sphere eventually led to his downfall. Zog turned to Italy for assistance. Accordingly, in March 1925 Rome and Tirana concluded a far-reaching economic agreement which quickly drew both countries closer together politically as well. By 1927 Italian economic and political influence so dominated Albania that Rome had assumed responsibility for the training and equipping of the Albanian army. During the 1930s Zog attempted on several occasions to lessen Rome's tightening grip on Albania. However, in April 1939, angered by Zog's refusal to transform Albania into an Italian protectorate, Mussolini's forces invaded Albania. The Italian army was met with little resistance, and Zog fled to Greece on April 8, 1939, to join his wife, Geraldine Apponyi of Hungary, whom he had married a year earlier, and his newborn son, Leka. Zog's monarchy came to a formal end on April 12, 1939, when the Albanian parliament abolished the 1928 constitution and proclaimed Albania's union with Rome by offering the crown to the Italian monarch, Victor Emmanuel III. Zog's wartime attempts to gain Allied recognition, organize a provisional government, and lead an Albanian resistance movement against the Axis from abroad ended unsuccessfully. Until his death outside Paris in 1961, Zog spent most of his very private years in exile in Britain, Egypt, and France. Although Zog's regime ended in failure, it was significant for having established the foundations for a cohesive and centralized Albanian state.

Selected Bibliography

Albania

Amnesty International. *Albania: Political Imprisonment and the Law*. London: Amnesty International, 1984.

Biberaj, Elez. *Albania and China: A Study of an Unequal Alliance*. Boulder, Colorado: Westview Press, Westview Special Studies in International Relations, 1986. Thorough and well documented analysis of Tirana's relations with Beijing. Includes a solid history of Albanian foreign relations before the break with Moscow, as well as a clear assessment of Tirana's foreign policy in the post-Chinese period up to 1985.

————. *Albania: A Socialist Maverick*. Boulder, Colorado: Westview Press, 1990. Comprehensive examination of the major issues determining Albania's domestic development and foreign relations. Also examines the country's economy, prospects for the future, and the Albanian population in the former Yugoslavia.

Chekrezi, Constantine A. *Albania, Past and Present*. New York: The Macmillan Company, 1919.

Federal Writers' Project of Massachusetts. *The Albanian Struggle In the Old World and New*. Boston: The Writer, Inc., Publishers, 1939. Although the book contains some valuable information, it is largely unimaginative and anecdotal rather than critical history.

Fischer, Bernd Jürgen. *King Zog and the Struggle for Stability in Albania*. Boulder, Colorado: East European Monographs, 1984. Scholarly work covering the pre-Communist era.

Frasheri, Kristo. *The History of Albania (A Brief Survey)*. Tirana: n.p., 1964.

Griffith, William E. *Albania and the Sino-Soviet Rift* Cambridge, Massachusetts: The M.I.T. Press, 1963. Contains reprints of 34 Albanian and Soviet documents, over 200 pages of primary materials.

Halliday, Jon, ed. *The Artful Albanian: The Memoirs of Enver Hoxha*. London: Chatto and Windus, 1986. Provides insight into the influences that helped determine Hoxha's ideological outlook and policies.

Hamm, Harry. *Albania—China's Beachhead in Europe*. Translated by Victor Andersen New York: Frederick A. Praeger, 1963. Excellent discussion of Albania's position in the Chinese-Soviet dispute and the background to the Albanian-Soviet break.

Keefe, Eugene K., et al. *Area Handbook for Albania*. Washington, D.C.: United States Government Printing Office, 1971. Brief survey of Albania's past and a wealth of multifarious data on the country.

Logoreci, Anton. *The Albanians: Europe's Forgotten Survivors*. Boulder, Colorado: Westview Press, 1977.

Marmullaku, Ramadan. *Albania and the Albanians*. Translated by Margot Miloslavjević and Boško Miloslavjević. London: Hurst, 1975.

Minnesota Lawyers International Human Rights Committee. *Human Rights in the People's Socialist Republic of Albania*. Minneapolis: Minnesota Lawyers International Human Rights Committee, 1990.

Pano, Nicholas C. *The People's Republic of Albania*. Baltimore: The Johns Hopkins Press, 1968. Examines the role of Albania in the world Communist system through the late 1960s.

Pipinelis, M. P. *Europe and the Albanian Question*. Chicago: Argonaut, Inc., Publishers, 1961.

Pollo, Stefanaq, and Arben Puto. *The History of Albania*. Translated by Carol Wiseman and Ginnie Hole. London: Routledge and Kegan Paul, 1981.

Prifti, Peter R. *Socialist Albania Since 1944: Domestic and Foreign Developments*. Cambridge, Massachusetts: The M.I.T. Press, 1978. Survey of the Hoxha regime's policies up to the decline of Albanian-Chinese relations.

Robinson, Vandeleur. *Albania's Road to Freedom*. London: George Allen and Unwin, 1941. Journalistic narrative covering the pre-Communist era.

Schnytzer, Adi. *Stalinist Economic Strategy: The Case of Albania*. New York: Oxford University Press, 1982. Thorough analysis of Albania's economy.

Sinishta, Gjon. *The Fulfilled Promise: A Documentary Account of Religious Persecution in Albania*. Santa Clara, California: H and F Composing Service Printing, 1976.

Skendi, Stavro. *The Political Evolution of Albania, 1912–1944*. New York: Mid-European Studies Center of the National Committee for a Free Europe, Inc., Mimeographed Series, Number 19, 1954. Though narrowly focused, it is a useful survey of the major currents in Albania's political development from independence to the rise of the Hoxha regime.

———, ed. *Albania*. New York: Frederick A. Praeger, 1956. Published as part of Robert F. Byrnes' *East-Central Europe Under the Communists* series. The most thorough study of Albanian institutions during the first decade of the Hoxha era.

———. *The Albanian National Awakening, 1878–1912*. Princeton, New Jersey: Princeton University Press, 1967. The definitive examination of the national renaissance and movement toward Albanian independence.

Stickney, Edith Pierpont. *Southern Albania or Northern Epirus in European International Affairs, 1912–1923*. Stanford, California: Stanford University Press, 1926.

Swire. Joseph. *Albania, the Rise of a Kingdom*. London: Williams and Norgate, 1929. Journalistic narrative covering the pre-Communist era.

———. *King Zog's Albania*. London: Robert Hale, 1937. Journalistic narrative covering the pre-Communist era.

Winnifrith, Tom, ed. *Perspectives on Albania*. New York: St. Martin's Press, 1992. Compilation of nine brief but interesting essays by as many experts on Albanian history past and present.

Zavalani, T. "Albanian Nationalism." In *Nationalism in Eastern Europe*, edited by Peter F. Sugar and Ivo J. Lederer. Seattle: University of Washington Press, 1969, pp. 59-92. Important work dealing largely with pre-Communist Albania. Invaluable interpretation of the development of Albanian national identity.

Bulgaria

Bell, John D. *Peasants in Power: Alexander Stamboliski and the Bulgarian Agrarian National Union, 1899–1923*. Princeton, NJ: Princeton University Press, 1977. An indispensable study of the important Agrarian movement.

———. *The Bulgarian Communist Party from Blagoev to Zhivkov*. Stanford, California: Hoover Institution Press, Histories of Ruling Communist Parties, 1986. Traces the origins of the party from 1917 through the Zhivkov era of the mid-1980s. The most comprehensive history of the Bulgarian Communist party.

Boll, Michael M. *The Cold War in the Balkans: American Foreign Policy and the Emergence of Communist Bulgaria, 1943–1947*. Lexington, Kentucky: Kentucky University Press, 1984. Argues that the Communist takeover of Bulgaria was not a Soviet plot, but the result of the Bulgarian Communist party's unilateral actions.

———, ed. *The American Military Mission in the Allied Control Commission for Bulgaria, 1944–1947: History and Transcripts*. Boulder, Colorado: East European Monographs, Number 176, 1985. An interesting source book discussing Bulgaria immediately after World War II.

Brown, J. F. *Bulgaria Under Communist Rule*. New York: Praeger Publishers, 1970. An indispensable study of Bulgaria's development from the death of Stalin to the late 1960s. Provides an expert analysis of Bulgaria's political currents and economic, cultural, and foreign policies.

Chary, Frederick B. *The Bulgarian Jews and the Final Solution*. Pittsburgh: University of Pittsburgh Press, 1972.

Clarke, James F. *Bible Societies, American Missionaries, and the National Revival of Bulgaria*. New York: Arno Press and New York Times, 1971.

Constant, Stephen. *Foxy Ferdinand, 1861–1948. Tsar of Bulgaria*. London: Sidgwick and Jackson, 1979. Thorough and well-illustrated biography of King Ferdinand. Particularly useful as a political history of Bulgaria during Ferdinand's reign.

Crampton, Richard J. *Bulgaria 1878–1918: A History*. Boulder, Colorado: East European Monographs, Number 138, 1983. Most important and detailed study of its kind for the first four decades of Bulgaria's independence. Discusses the main political, economic, and social developments in Bulgaria from independence to the end of the First World War.

———. *A Short History of Modern Bulgaria*. Cambridge: Cambridge University Press, 1987. The most recent and authoritative survey of modern Bulgarian history.

Dellin, L. A. D. *Bulgaria*. New York: Praeger Publishers, for the Free Europe Committee, Mid-European Studies Center's Series, East-Central Europe under the Communists, 1957. A useful book on Bulgaria under Communist rule. This collection of articles covers, among other things, government structure, society, and economic policy. Although published in the 1950s, this work still contains an enormous amount of information on the postwar Communization of Bulgaria.

Devedjiev, Hristo. *Stalinization of the Bulgarian Society, 1949–1953*. Philadelphia: Dorrance, 1975. A good discussion of the political purges in Bulgaria in the late 1940s.

Dimitroff, Pashanko. *Boris III of Bulgaria: Toiler, Citizen, King*. Lewes, Great Britain: Book Guild, 1986. An uncritical and eulogistic account of Boris III.

Durman, Karel. *Lost Illusions: Russian Policies Towards Bulgaria in 1877–1887*. Stockholm: Acta Universitatis Upsaliensis, Uppsala Studies on the Soviet Union and Eastern Europe, 1988. Discussion of Russia's crucial role in the early development of the Bulgarian state.

Groueff, Stephane. *Crown of Thorns: The Reign of King Boris III of Bulgaria, 1918–1943*. Lanham, Maryland; London: Madison Books, 1987. An important book both for its extraordinary construction of Boris' life and for its detailed assessment of Bulgarian political currents.

Hall, William W. *Puritans in the Balkans: The American Board Mission in Bulgaria, 1878–1918*. Sofia: Cultura Printing House, 1938.

Isusov, Mito, ed. *Problems of Transition from Capitalism to Socialism*. Sofia: Bulgarian Academy of Sciences, 1975. A useful collection of essays assessing the problems encountered in the early period of Communization.

Johnson, Stowers. *Agents Extraordinary*. London: Robert Hale, 1975. A discussion of the activities of the British military mission to the Bulgarian partisans.

Kosev, Dimitar, H. Hristov, and D. Angelov. *A Short History of Bulgaria*. Sofia: Foreign Languages Press, 1963. Diminished by its commitment to the then official Marxist state view of Bulgarian national development.

Lampe, John R. *The Bulgarian Economy in the Twentieth Century*. London; Sydney: Croom Helm, 1986. Concise and scholarly economic history of Bulgaria

Lang, David Marshall. *The Bulgarians From Pagan Times to the Ottoman Conquest*. London: Thames and Hudson Limited, Ancient Peoples and Places Series, Volume 84, 1976. A solid survey of Bulgaria's pre-Ottoman history.

Macdermott, Mercia. *A History of Bulgaria, 1393–1885*. London: George Allen and Unwin Limited, 1962. Examines Bulgaria under Ottoman rule and concentrates on the cultural revival and the nationalist movement toward liberation. Very detailed yet regrettably marred by an uncritical and laudatory approach.

McIntyre, Robert J. *Bulgaria: Politics, Economics and Society* London; New York: Frances Pinter, Marxist Regimes Series, 1988.

Miller, Marshall Lee. *Bulgaria During the Second World War*. Stanford, California: Stanford University Press, 1975. The definitive study of Bulgaria in the Second World War, with emphasis on political and diplomatic developments.

Nestorova, Tatyana. *American Missionaries Among the Bulgarians: 1858–1912*. Boulder, Colorado: East European Monographs, Number 218, 1987.

Oren, Nissan. *Bulgarian Communism: The Road to Power, 1934–1944*. New York: Columbia University Press, 1971. A solid study of the Communist movement in Bulgaria in the decade before its assumption of power.

———. *Revolution Administered: Agrarianism and Communism in Bulgaria*. Baltimore: John Hopkins University Press, Integration and Community Building in Eastern Europe, Number 8, 1973. Explores the rivalry between the Agrarians and the Communists, and concludes with an analysis of the new constitution and Communist party program introduced in 1971.

Perry, Duncan M. *The Politics of Terror: The Macedonian Liberation Movements 1893–1903*. Durham, North Carolina: Duke University Press, 1988. This excellent study traces the revolutionary activities of the ethnic Bulgarian leadership in Ottoman Macedonia during the decade leading to the ill-fated Ilinden uprising.

Rothschild, Joseph. *The Communist Party of Bulgaria: Origins and Development, 1883–1936*. New York: Columbia University Press, 1959. The standard reference work on the early years of socialism and the Communist party in Bulgaria.

Sherman, Laura M. *Fires on the Mountain: The Macedonian Revolutionary Movement and the Kidnapping of Ellen Stone*. Boulder, Colorado: East European Monographs, Number 62, 1980. Interesting account of one of the Internal Macedonian Revolutionary Organization's most notorious escapades.

Simsir, Bilal N. *The Turks of Bulgaria, 1878–1985*. London: Rustem Brothers, 1988. An exhaustive and authoritative historical study of Bulgaria's Turkish minority.

Swire, Joseph. *Bulgarian Conspiracy*. London: Robert Hale, 1939. Detailed treatment of the Internal Macedonian Revolutionary Organization (IMRO) during the interwar period.

Tamir, Vicki. *Bulgaria and Her Jews: The History of a Dubious Symbiosis*. New York: Sepher-Hermon Press for Yeshiva University Press, 1979. The most comprehensive study on the history of Bulgarian Jewry.

Vassilev, Kiril. *Fatherland Front in Bulgaria*. Sofia: Sofia Press, 1982. Brief account tracing the social origins of the Fatherland Front before the Second World War in addition to outlining its key wartime activities.

Czechoslovakia

Beneš, Edvard. *My War Memoirs*. London: Allen and Unwin, 1928. Written by Tomáš Masaryk's right-hand man and successor as president, this is a condensed version of Beneš's three-volume work in Czech that fills in many of the gaps left by Masaryk's memoirs.

———. *Memoirs of Dr. Edvard Beneš: From Munich to New War and New Victory*. Boston: Houghton Mifflin, 1954.

Czechoslovakia's Blueprint for "Freedom": Dubček's Statements—The Original and Official Documents Leading to the Conflict of August, 1968. Washington, D.C.: Acropolis Books, 1968. Presents documents from the 1968 Prague Spring translated into English.

Eubank, Keith. *Munich*. Norman, OK: University of Oklahoma Press, 1963. A fine work on the Munich Crisis and Munich Agreement of 1938.

Gawdiak, Ihor, ed. *Czechoslovakia: A Country Study*. Washington D.C.: U.S. G.P.O., 1989. This area handbook gives an excellent overview of all aspects of Czechoslovakia from history and society to economics and politics. A good starting point for learning more about the country.

Golan, Galia. *Reform Rule in Czechoslovakia: The Dubček Era 1968–1969*. Cambridge: Cambridge University Press, 1973.

Jesina, Cestmir, ed. *The Birth of Czechoslovakia*. Washington D.C.: Czechoslovak National Council of America, Washington D.C. chapter, 1968. Presents the major documents of the liberation movement from 1915–1918, along with some interesting photographs.

Journalist M. [pseud.] *A Year Is Eight Months*. Garden City, NY: Doubleday, 1970.

Kalvoda, Josef. *The Genesis of Czechoslovakia.* Boulder, CO: East European Monographs, 1986. This exhaustive study examines the liberation and creation of Czechoslovakia from all angles.

Korbel, Josef. *The Communist Subversion of Czechoslovakia, 1938-1948: The Failure of Coexistence.* Princeton, NJ: Princeton University Press, 1959. Remains one of the best sources on President Edvard Beneš's unsuccessful attempts to make Czechoslovakia a bridge between the capitalistic West and the Communist East.

Kusin, Vladimir V. *From Dubček to Charter 77: A Study of 'Normalization' in Czechoslovakia.* New York: St. Martins, 1978.

Lettrich, Jozef. *A History of Modern Slovakia.* New York: F. A. Praeger, 1955. Surveys the history of Slovakia between the years 1918–1948.

Littell, Robert, ed. *The Czech Black Book.* New York: Praeger, 1969. This volume prepared by the Institute of History of the Czechoslovak Academy of Sciences gives a day-by-day account of the events from August 21 to 27, 1968. The book is the response to the Soviet "Whitebook" published to justify the invasion.

Loebl, Eugen. *My Mind on Trial.* New York: Harcourt Brace Jovanovich, 1976. A vivid personal account of a dedicated Czechoslovak Communist falsely accused, tried, and imprisoned during the purges of the 1950.

Luža, Radomír. *The Transfer of the Sudeten Germans: A Study of Czech-German Relations, 1933–1962.* New York: New York University Press, 1964.

Mamatey, Victor S., and Radomír Luža, eds., *A History of the Czechoslovak Republic 1918–1948.* Princeton, NJ: Princeton University Press, 1973. Contains seventeen first-rate essays by experts in their respective fields divided into three parts: 1918–1938, 1938–1945, and 1945–1948.

Masaryk, Tomáš G. *The Making of a State: Memories and Observations, 1914–1918.* New York: Stokes, 1927. The leader of the liberation movement abroad and the first president of Czechoslovakia presents remembrances of his global travels.

Mastney, Vojtech, ed. *Czechoslovakia: Crisis in World Communism.* New York: Facts on File, 1972. A balanced, almost journalistic account of the events of the 1968 Prague Spring and the "normalization" process through 1971.

Mnacko, Ladislav. *The Seventh Night.* New York: Dutton, 1969. A highly readable personal account of the Prague Spring reform movement.

Pelikán, Jiří, ed. *The Czechoslovak Political Trials 1950–1954: The Suppressed Report of the Dubček Government's Commission of Inquiry, 1968.* Stanford, CT: Stanford University Press, 1971. An intriguing official investigation into the purge trials, as well as an attempt to right the injustices and abuses after twenty-five years.

Perman, Dagmar. *The Shaping of the Czechoslovak State: Diplomatic History of the Boundaries of Czechoslovakia 1914–1920.* Leiden, Netherlands: J. Brill, 1962. An account of the frontier problems caused by the fall of the Austro-Hungarian Empire and the rise of Czechoslovakia. Also includes an overview of France's hand in the negotiations for the establishment of the post-war borders.

Prochazka, Theodore. *The Second Republic: The Disintegration of Post-Munich Czechoslovakia.* New York: East European Monographs, 1981. Presents an almost day-to-day account of the ill-fated rump Czechoslovakia from October 1938–March 1939.

Ripka, Hubert. *Czechoslovakia Enslaved: The Story of the Communist Coup d'Etat.* London: Gollancz, 1950. Written by one of the non-Communist government ministers who resigned in 1948, this book focuses on the events of the February Communist coup.

Seton-Watson, R. W. *A History of the Czechs and Slovaks.* London: Hutchinson, 1943. A standard work on the history of the Czechs and Slovaks that covers approximately one thousand years.

Shawcross, William. *Dubček.* New York: Simon & Schuster, 1971. Presents a fair evaluation of Alexander Dubček, the man behind the Prague Spring.

Skilling, H. Gordon. *Czechoslovakia's Interrupted Revolution.* Princeton, NJ: Princeton University Press, 1976. One of the definitive sources on the Prague Spring movement.

Smelser, Ronald M. *The Sudeten Problem 1933–1938: Volkstumspolitik and the Formation of Nazi Foreign Policy.* Middletown, CT: Wesleyan University Press, 1975.

Sterling, Claire. *The Masaryk Case: The Murder of Democracy in Czechoslovakia.* New York: Harper & Row, 1969. A gripping story about the end of democracy in Czechoslovakia. It also explores the mysterious death of the democratic foreign minister Jan Masaryk in 1948, and the reopening of the case in 1968.

Táborský, Edward. *President Edvard Beneš: Between East and West.* Stanford, CA: Hoover Institution Press, 1981. A fair portrayal of President Edvard Beneš by his personal secretary.

Taylor, Telford. *Munich: The Price of Peace.* New York: Doubleday, 1979. Focuses on the great power perspective of the Munich Crisis and Agreement of 1938.

Thomson, S. Harrison. *Czechoslovakia in European History.* Princeton, NJ: Princeton University Press, 1943. Along with Seton-Watson's *A History of the Czechs and Slovaks* this book has remained a classic source since the 1940s.

Valenta, Jiri. *Soviet Intervention in Czechoslovakia, 1968: Anatomy of a Decision.* Baltimore, MD: Johns Hopkins University Press, 1991. A very well written and documented view of the Soviet attempt to deal with the 1968 reform movement.

Wallace, William. *Czechoslovakia.* Boulder, CO: Westview Press, 1976. Provides an overview of the Czechs and Slovaks, concentrating on the period between 1849 and 1970.

Wheaton, Bernard, and Zdeněk Kavan. *The Velvet Revolution: Czechoslovakia, 1988–1991.* Boulder, CO: Westview, 1992. A timely work with a summary of the major events surrounding the fall of communism in 1989 through the free elections of May 1990.

Winter in Prague: Documentation on Czechoslovak Communism in Crisis. Cambridge, MA: MIT Press, 1969. Translation of documents from the 1968 Prague Spring.

Wiskemann, Elizabeth. *Czechs and Germans: A Study in the Historic Provinces of Bohemia and Moravia*. London: Oxford University Press, 1938. An excellent introduction to the subject of the Czech-German conflict.

Zauberman, Alfred. *Industrial Progress in Poland, Czechoslovakia, and East Germany, 1937–1962*. London: Oxford University Press, 1964. An interesting comparative study on the early postwar years.

Zeman, Z. A. B. *Prague Spring*. New York: Hill & Wang, 1969. A basic overview of the Prague Spring based on personal observations after a twenty-year absence.

Zeman, Zbyněk. *The Masaryks: The Making of Czechoslovakia*. New York: Barnes & Noble Books, 1976. Concentrates on the first president of the republic, Tomáš G. Masaryk; however, some material is also devoted to Masaryk's son Jan, an ambassador and foreign minister.

East Germany

Allen, Bruce. *Germany East: Dissent and Opposition*. Montreal: Black Rose Books, 1989.

Backer, John. *The Decision to Divide Germany*. Durham, NC: Duke University Press, 1978.

Bahro, Rudolf. *The Alternative in Eastern Europe*. London: NLB, 1978. Dated but readable.

Baring, Arnulf. *Uprising in East Germany*. Ithaca: Cornell University Press, 1972.

Baylis, Thomas. *The Technical Intelligentsia and the East German Elite*. Berkeley: University of California Press, 1974.

Childs, David. *The Changing Face of Western Communism*. London, St. Martin, 1980. Very good as a comparative study of East and West communism.

———. *The GDR: Moscow's German Ally*. London: Allen & Unwin, 1983. This source is strong on social, economic, and foreign relations as well as a good short look at how the military and security forces of the GDR were developed.

———, ed. *East Germany*. Nations of the Modern World Series. New York: Praeger, 1969. A good overall view of the first two decades of the GDR.

———, ed. *Honecker's Germany*. London, Routledge Chapman & Hall, 1985.

Childs, David, Thomas Baylis, and Marilyn Rüschemeyer, eds. *East Germany in Comparative Perspective*. London: Routledge, 1989. A very usable study of the comparative aspects of the two German states and their neighbors.

Cookridge, E. H. *Gehlen: Spy of the Century*. London: Hodder & Stoughton, 1972. Reinhard Gehlen, a former Nazi, headed West Germany's intelligence operations in the 1950s and ran a network of spies in East Germany.

Dennis, Mike. *German Democratic Republic: Politics, Economics, and Society*. London: Pinter, 1988.

Dornberg, John. *The Other Germany*. New York: Doubleday, 1968. A study of the GDR economy in the 1960s.

Dorpalen, Andreas. *German History in Marxist Perspective: The East German Approach*. London: Allen & Unwin, 1985.

Edwards, G. E. *GDR Society and Social Institutions*. London: Macmillan, 1985. A good place to start when studying East German society. Very readable.

Esslin, Martin. *Brecht: A Choice of Evils*. 4th ed. London: Methuen, 1984.

Flores, John. *Poetry in East Germany*. New Haven, CT: Yale University Press, 1971.

Forster, Thomas M. *The East German Army: The Second Power in the Warsaw Pact*. 5th ed. London: Allen & Unwin, 1980.

Fritsch-Bournazel, Renata. *Confronting the German Question*. Oxford: Berg, 1988.

Fulbrook, Mary. *The Divided Nation: A History of Germany 1918–1990*. New York: Oxford University Press, 1992.

Gehlen, Reinhard. *The Service: The Memoirs of General Reinhard Gehlen*. New York: World Publishing, 1972.

Glaeßner, Gert-Joachim, and Ian Wallace, eds. *The German Revolution of 1989: Causes and Consequences*. New York, Berg Publishers, 1991.

Goeckel, Robert F. *The Lutheran Church and the East German State: Political Conflict and Change under Ulbricht and Honecker*. New York: Cornell University Press, 1989.

Grosser, Alfred. *Germany in Our Time*. London: Praeger, 1971.

Günther, Karl-Heinz, et al. *Education in the German Democratic Republic*. Leipzig: n.p., 1962.

Hearndon, Arthur. *Education in the Two Germanies*. Oxford: Blackwell, 1974.

Heitzer, Heinz. *GDR: An Historical Outline*. Dresden: Zeit Im Bild, 1981. An official pictorial and historical outline of the GDR.

Herspring, Dale Roy. *East German Civil-Military Relations: The Impact of Technology 1949–1972*. New York: Praeger, 1973. A study of how industry and technology functioned in the environs of a semi-military state.

Heuttich, H. G. *Theater in the Planned Society*. Chapel Hill: University of North Carolina Press, 1978. A study of how the state controls the arts in East Germany.

Iggers, Georg. *Social History in the GDR: New Orientations in Recent East European Historiography*. New York: n.p., 1989. Very useful for the serious social historian.

Jeffries, Ian, and Manfred Melzer. *The East German Economy*. London: Croom Helm, 1987. Primarily a study of production but useful as a measure of the development of the GDR.

Joint Economic Committee of the Congress of the United States. *East European Economies Post-Helsinki*. Washington, DC: Government Printing Office, 1977.

Keesing's Research Report. *Germany and Eastern Europe since 1945*. New York: Scribner, 1973. A good source for documents.

Krejci, Jaroslav. *Social Structure in Divided Germany*. London: Croom Helm, 1976. Useful though dated.

Krisch, Henry. *German Politics under Soviet Occupation*. New York: Columbia University Press, 1974.

———. *The German Democratic Republic: The Search for Identity*. Boulder, CO: Westview, 1985.

Larrabee, F. Stephen. *The Two German States and European Security*. New York: St. Martin's, 1989.

Leptin, Gert, and Manfred Melzer. *Economic Reform in East German Industry*. London: Oxford University Press, 1978.

Lippmann, Heinz. *Honecker and the New Politics of Europe*. London: n.p., 1972.

Ludz, Peter C. *The GDR from the Sixties to the Seventies*. Harvard Center for International Affairs: Occasional Papers in International Affairs, no. 26. Cambridge, MA: Harvard Center for International Affairs, November 1970. A limited but useful study of social, political, and economic progress in the GDR in the decade of the 1960s.

———. *The Changing Party Elite in East Germany*. Cambridge, MA: MIT Press, 1972. Useful in following the leadership of the Socialist Unity party (SED).

Marshall, Barbara. *The Origins of Post-War German Politics*. London: Croom Helm, 1988. A very good source on the formative years of the party system in the GDR.

McAdams, A. James. *East Germany and Detente: Building Authority after the Wall*. Cambridge: Cambridge University Press, 1985. A good study on policy development.

McCauley, Martin. *Marxism-Leninism in the GDR*. London: Macmillan, 1979. Dated but still useful.

———. *The GDR since 1945*. London: St. Martin's, 1983.

Mellor, Roy E. H. *The Two Germanies: A Modern Geography*. London: Harper & Row, 1978.

Moore-Rinvolucri, Mina J. *Education in East Germany*. Newton Abbot, England: David & Charles, 1973.

Moreton, N. Edwina, ed. *Germany between East and West*. Cambridge: Cambridge University Press, 1987.

Myagkov, Aleksei. *Inside the KGB: An Expose by an Officer of the Third Directorate*. London: n.p., 1976.

Nettl, J. P. *The Eastern Zone and Soviet Policy in Germany, 1945–1950*. London: Oxford University Press, 1951. Quite helpful in understanding the relationship between the GDR leadership and the Soviet Union.

Ostow, Robin. *Jews in Contemporary East Germany: The Children of Moses in the Land of Marx*. London: Macmillan, 1989.

Phillips, Ann L. *Seeds of Change in the German Democratic Republic: The SED-SPD Dialogue*. Washington, DC: n.p., 1989.

Plock, Ernest D. *The Basic Treaty and the Evolution of East-West German Relations*. Boulder, CO: Westview, 1986.

Prins, Gwyn, ed. *Spring in Winter: The 1989 Revolutions*. Manchester: Manchester University Press, 1990.

Rüschemeyer, Marilyn. *Professional Work and Marriage: An East-West Comparison*. New York: St. Martin's, 1981.

———. *The Quality of Life in the German Democratic Republic*. Armonk, NY: M. E. Sharpe, 1989. An excellent overview.

Sanford, Gregory W. *From Hitler to Ulbricht: The Communist Reconstruction of East Germany, 1945–1946*. Princeton, NJ: Princeton University Pres, 1983. An excellent study of the origins of the German Democratic Republic.

Scharf, C. Bradley. *Politics and Change in East Germany*. Boulder, CO: Westview, 1984.

Shaffer, Harry G. *Women in the Two Germanies*. New York: Pergamon, 1981. Limited in scope but contains useful data.

Silnitsky, Frantisek, ed. *Communism and Eastern Europe*. New York: Karz, 1979.

Sodaro, Michael J. *Moscow, Germany, and the West from Khrushchev to Gorbachev*. Ithaca, NY: Cornell University Press, 1990.

Solberg, Richard W. *God and Caesar in East Germany*. New York: Macmillan, 1961.

Sontheimer, Kurt, and Wilhelm Bleek. *The Government and Politics of East Germany*. London: St. Martin's, 1975.

Spotts, Frederic. *The Churches and Politics in Germany*. Middleton, CT: Wesleyan University Press, 1973. Dated but useful.

Steele, Jonathan. *Socialism with a German Face: The State that Came in from the Cold*. London: J. Cape, 1977.

Stern, Carola. *Ulbricht*. London: Pall Mall Press, 1965.

Stolper, Wolfgang, and K. W. Roskamp. *The Structure of the East German Economy*. Cambridge, MA: Harvard University Press, 1960.

Thomanek, J. E. A., and James Mellis, eds. *Politics, Society, and Government in the German Democratic Republic: Basic Documents*. Oxford: Berg, 1988.

Tokes, Rudolf, ed. *Opposition in Eastern Europe*. Baltimore, MD: Johns Hopkins University Press, 1979.

Turner, Henry A., Jr. *The Two Germanies since 1945*. New Haven, CT: Yale University Press, 1987; rev. ed. published as *Germany from Partition to Reunification*. New Haven: Yale University Press, 1992.

Ulbricht, Walter. *Social Development in the German Democratic Republic up to the Completion of Socialism*. Dresden: n.p., 1967. The official word on the subject.

von Beyme, Klaus, and Hartmut Zimmermann, eds. *Policymaking in the German Democratic Republic*. Brookfield, VT: Gower, 1984.

von Oppen, Beate Ruhm, ed. *Documents on Germany under Occupation, 1945–1955*. London: Oxford University Press, 1955.

Wallace, Ian. *The GDR under Honecker, 1971–1981*. Dundee, NY: n.p., 1981.

———, ed. *East Germany: The German Democratic Republic*. World Bibliographical Series, vol. 77. Oxford: Clio, 1987.

Wettig, Gerhard. *Community and Conflict in the Socialist Camp: The Soviet Union, East Germany, and the German Problem 1965–1972*. New York: St. Martin's, 1975.

Woods, Roger. *Opposition to the GDR under Honecker, 1971–1985*. London: St. Martin's, 1986. Most useful on the period of change after détente and the GDR relationship to the Soviet Union.

Wyden, Peter. *Wall: The Story of Divided Berlin*. New York: Simon & Schuster, 1989.

Zauberman, Alfred. *Industrial Progress in Poland, Czechoslovakia, and East Germany, 1937–1962*. London: Oxford University Press, 1964. An interesting comparative study on the early postwar years.

Hungary

Aczel, Tamas, and Tibor Meray. *The Revolt of the Mind*. London: Thames and Hudson, 1960. Recounts the intellectual ferment that took place between 1953 and 1956 and its contribution to the events leading up to the revolution.

Barber, Noel. *Seven Days of Freedom: The Hungarian Uprising 1956*. London: Macmillan, 1973. Personal account on the actual events of the 1956 revolution.

Batt, Judy. *Economic Reform and Political Change in Eastern Europe*. New York: St. Martin's Press, 1988. Compares the economic policies and reforms of Hungary and Czechoslovakia in the postwar period.

Berand, Ivan T. *The Hungarian Economic Reforms, 1953–1988*. Cambridge: Cambridge University Press, 1990. Focuses on the politics of economic policy-making in postwar Hungary.

Berand, Ivan T., and Gyorgy Ranki. *The Hungarian Economy in the Twentieth Century*. London: Croom Helm, 1985. Details the dramatic restructuring of the Hungarian economy during the interwar years and the reconstruction of that economy under the Communists.

Bozoki, Andras, Andras Koroseny, and George Schopflin, eds. *Post-Communist Transition: Emerging Pluralism in Hungary*. New York: St. Martin's, 1992. Examines Hungary's emerging political culture and institutions.

Brada, Josef C., and Istvan Dobi, eds. *The Hungary Economy in the 1980s*. Greenwich, CT: JAI Press, 1988. Explores both the successes and failures of Hungary's economic reforms.

Burawoy, Michael. *The Radiant Past: Ideology and Reality in Hungary's Road to Capitalism*. Chicago: University of Chicago Press, 1992. Investigates the impact of Hungary's emergent capitalism on labor, class consciousness, and industrial efficiency.

Congdon, Lee. *Exile and Social Thought: Hungarian Intellectuals in Germany and Austria, 1919–1933*. Princeton, NJ: Princeton University Press, 1991. A discussion of Hungarian intellectuals and artists in exile during the Horthy era.

Deak, George. *The Economy and Polity in Early Twentieth Century Hungary*. East European Monographs, no. 288, New York: Columbia University Press, 1990. A discussion of the role of the National Association of Industrialists in Hungary's early twentieth century economic development.

Felkay, Andrew. *Hungary and the USSR, 1956–1988*. New York: Greenwood Press, 1989. Analyzes Hungary's precarious and often volatile relationship with the Soviet Union.

Fenyo, Mario D. *Hitler, Horthy, and Hungary: German-Hungarian Relations, 1941–1944*. New Haven, CT: Yale University Press, 1972. An impassioned study on this period based predominately on German documentation.

Gati, Charles. *Hungary and the Soviet Bloc*. Durham, NC: Duke University Press, 1986. Describes the Communist takeover and Hungary's dynamic relationship with the Soviet Union and its socialist neighbors.

Hankiss, Elemer. *East European Alternatives*. New York: Oxford University Press, 1990. Analyzes the evolutionary nature of Hungarian socialist society and compares it to the other East European states.

Hoensch, Jorg K. *History of Modern Hungary, 1867–1987*. New York: Longman, 1988. While lacking analysis of Hungary's social and cultural history, this volume is a valuable, concise, somewhat dry presentation of political and economic facts.

Janos, Andrew. *The Politics of Backwardness in Hungary, 1825–1945*. Princeton, NJ: Princeton University Press, 1982. An analytical treatment of Hungarian political history up to 1945 detailing the different strands of conservativism which ran through the ideology of the Hungarian ruling classes.

Jaszi, Oszkar. *Revolution and Counter-revolution in Hungary*. London: King and Son, 1924. Examines Hungary's revolutionary progression from the perspective of one who was there.

Kallay, Miklos. *Hungarian Premier: A Personal Account of a Nation's Struggle in the Second World War*. London: Oxford University Press, 1954. Kallay's memoirs lend credence to the contention that Hungarian leadership was irresolute in its dealings with the Germans.

Kecskemeti, Pal. *The Unexpected Revolution: Social Forces in the Hungarian Uprising*. Stanford, CA: Stanford University Press, 1969. Argues that class-consciousness of the participants—students, workers, and intellectuals—was a key motivating force in 1956 revolution.

Kiraly, Bela, and Paul Jonas, eds. *The Hungarian Revolution of 1956 in Retrospect*. East European Monographs, no. 40., New York: Columbia University Press, 1978.

Kis, Janos. *Politics in Hungary: For a Democratic Alternative*. Boulder, CO: Social Science Monographs, 1989. Suggests that Hungary should travel a path between socialism and western democracy.

Kornai, Janos. *The Road to a Free Economy. Shifting from a Socialist System; The Case of Hungary*. New York, Norton, 1990. Reflections on the transformation of socialist economies from one of Hungary's most astute economists.

Kovrig, Bennett. *The Hungarian People's Republic*. Baltimore, MD: John Hopkins Press, 1970. The seventh in a series published by John Hopkins Press examining the Communist states of Eastern Europe. A tedious but informative introduction to Communist Hungary.

————. *Communism in Hungary from Kun to Kadar.* Stanford, CA: Hoover Institution Press, 1979. Traces the evolution of communism in Hungary and details the histories of the various ruling Communist parties.

Lasky, Melvin J. *The Hungarian Revolution: The Story of the October Uprising as Recorded in Documents, Dispatches, Eyewitness Accounts, and World-wide Reactions.* London: Martin Secker and Warburg, 1957.

Lomax, Bill. *Hungary 1956.* London: Allison and Busby, 1976.

————. *Hungarian Workers' Councils in 1956.* Boulder, CO: Social Science Monographs, 1990. Contends that the working class and the revolutionary councils were principal actors in the events of 1956.

Lukacs, John. *Budapest 1900.* New York: Weidenfeld and Nicolson, 1988. Explores Budapest's rich cultural and artistic traditions at the turn of the century.

Macartney, C. A. *Hungary and her Successors: The Treaty of Trianon and its Consequences, 1919–1937.* London: Oxford University Press, 1937. Describes the territorial disputes existing between Hungary and the other "successor states." Although written in 1937, this book has lost little of its topicality.

————. *October Fifteenth: A History of Modern Hungary, 1929–1945.* 2 vols., Edinburgh: Edinburgh University Press, 1956–57. A rare objective study of Hungary's revisionist aspirations and its turn toward the radical right.

Marer, Paul. *East West Technology Transfer: Study of Hungary.* Paris: Organization for Economic Cooperation and Development, 1986. Examines Hungary's economic reforms and provides detailed analyses of Hungary's major economic sectors and its trade with the COMECON countries and the West.

Pastor, Peter. *Hungary between Wilson and Lenin: The Hungarian Revolution and the Big Three.* East European Monographs, no. 20, New York: Columbia University Press, 1976. Explores the reaction of the American, British, French, and Soviet governments to the "Chrysanthemum Revolution" in October 1918.

Seton-Watson, R. W. *Treaty Revision and the Hungarian Frontiers.* London: Eyre and Spottiswood for the School of Slavonic and East European Studies, 1934. Discussion of Hungarian revisionism.

Shawcross, William. *Crime and Compromise: Janos Kadar and the Politics of Hungary since Revolution.* New York: Dutton, 1974.

Sugar, Peter, ed. *A History of Hungary.* Bloomington: Indiana University Press, 1990. An up to date and comprehensive general history on Hungary. Includes an excellent bibliography of western language works for all of Hungarian history.

Tokes, Rudolf. *Béla Kun and the Hungarian Soviet Republic: The Origins and Role of the Communist Party of Hungary in the Revolutions of 1918–1919.* New York: Praeger, 1967. Discusses Béla Kun's and the Communists' brief tenure in the spring and summer of 1919.

Toma, Peter A. *Socialist Authority: The Hungarian Experience.* New York: Praeger, 1988. Provides a journalistic, urban overview of Hungary's social and economic conditions in the postwar era.

Vali, Ferenc A. *Rift and Revolt in Hungary: Nationalism versus Communism.* Cambridge, MA: Harvard University Press, 1961. Examines the tensions and rifts that existed between the "homegrown Communists" and the "Moscow Communists" within the Hungarian Communist party.

Vardy, Steven Bela. *Modern Hungarian Historiography.* Boulder, CO: East European Quarterly, 1976. Comprehensive view of the development of Hungarian historical studies from the 11th to the 20th century.

Volgyes, Ivan, ed., *Hungary in Revolution, 1918–1919.* Lincoln, NE: University of Nebraska Press, 1971. Presents nine essays by specialists on Hungarian history and politics who dissect the series of events leading to the upheavals of 1918–1919.

World Bank. *Hungary: Reform of Social Policy and Expenditures.* Washington: World Bank, 1992. Examines the social policies of post-Communist Hungary.

Poland

Ash, Timothy G. *The Polish Revolution.* New York: Random House, 1985. An interesting, popular presentation on the beginnings of Solidarity in the early 1980s.

Ascherson, Neil. *The Struggles for Poland.* New York: Random House, 1987.

Bethell, Nicholas. *Gomułka: His Poland and His Communism.* Marmondsworth, England: Pelican, 1962. Although dated, Bethell presents a very thorough record of the establishment of Communism in Poland. The account of the "October Spring" in 1956 that brought a disgraced Gomułka back to power is exceptionally detailed. Particularly useful for a background understanding of the turbulent decades of the 1970s and the 1980s.

Brumberg, Abraham, ed. *Poland: Genesis of a Revolution.* New York: Vintage Books, 1983.

Davies, Norman. *God's Playground: A History of Poland,* 2 vols. New York: Columbia University Press, 1982. A standard, though unusual, work. Rather than a straight narrative along a traditional chronological line, chapters are arranged thematically within an overall chronology. At times, this organization leads to factual errors and/or repetition, which may be confusing.

————. *Heart of Europe: A Short History of Poland.* Oxford: Oxford University Press, 1986. A condensed history, sporting an even more unusual organizational framework. Davies begins his account in the present, and then works backward. One result is that this book may often be confusing for readers with no prior knowledge of Polish history.

Dziewanowski, Marian Kamil. *Poland in the Twentieth Century.* New York: Columbia University Press, 1977. Concise. Valuable in that it presents a unified, easily understood interpretation of modern Polish history. The major drawback is the lack of precise dates.

Gieysztor, Aleksander, et al. *History of Poland.* Warsaw: Polish Scientific Publishers, 1979. An official work covering the period from the beginning of the Polish state up to 1939. Despite its official views, this work is quite valuable, especially in the chapters dealing with the earlier periods of Polish history.

Halecki, Oskar. *History of Poland.* Chicago: Henry Regnery, 1966. Available in various editions by numerous publishers. Another standard, older work exhibiting a clear ideological stand. Its greatest usefulness is helping people to understand nationalist and patriotic views of Polish history.

Kanet, Roger E., and Maurice D. Simon, eds. *Background to Crisis: Policy and Politics in Gierek's Poland.* Boulder, CO: Westview Press, 1981. A collection of essays that cover a wide range of topics concentrating on the end of Edward Gierek's rule in the late 1970s, shortly before the establishment of Solidarity.

Kaufman, Michael. *Mad Dreams, Saving Graces; Poland: A Nation in Conspiracy.* New York: Random House, 1989. Explains how Solidarity continued to function and grow despite the imposition of martial law in 1981. Extremely well written with numerous humorous stories.

Marer, Paul, and Włodzimierz Siwinski, eds. *Creditworthiness and Reform in Poland: Western and Polish Perspectives.* Bloomington: Indiana University Press, 1988. A collection of essays concentrating on the economic side of Polish history during the 1980s and late 1970s. Including perspectives from both the East and West, this work examines what happened to the economy and how it eventually led to the fall of communism.

Milosz, Czesław. *The Captive Mind.* New York: Vintage International, 1990. Written by the Polish Nobel Laureate and available in various editions since it was first published in 1953. Examines how four Polish intellectuals are able to rationalize their acceptance of communism after its imposition in 1945.

Reddaway, William F., ed. *The Cambridge History of Poland*, 2 vols. Cambridge: University Press, 1950–1951. Considered the definitive work for the study of Polish history. Although dated, it is still useful, especially on the earlier periods of Polish history.

Weschler, Lawrence. *The Passion of Poland, from Solidarity through the State of War.* New York: Pantheon Books, 1982.

Zauberman, Alfred. *Industrial Progress in Poland, Czechoslovakia, and East Germany, 1937–1962.* London: Oxford University Press, 1964. An interesting comparative study on the early postwar years.

Romania

Braun, Aurel. *Romanian Foreign Policy Since 1965.* New York: Praeger, 1978. One of a small number of books devoted to the period when Romania ventured out on its own in international affairs.

Eidelberg, Philip Gabriel. *The Great Rumanian Peasant Revolt of 1907: Origins of a Modern Jacquerie.* Leiden, the Netherlands: E.J. Brill, 1974. An in-depth look at the massive peasant revolt at the beginning of the twentieth century.

Fischer-Galati, Stephen. *20th Century Rumania.* 2d ed. New York: Columbia University Press, 1991. Indispensable source for understanding Romania in this century.

Georgescu, Vlad. *The Romanians: A History.* Edited by Matei Calinescu and translated by Alexandra Bley-Vroman. Columbus: Ohio State University Press, 1991. A broad, general history that gives excellent, objective coverage to all areas of Romania's history from earliest times.

Ionescu, Ghita. *Communism in Romania.* London: Oxford University Press, 1964.

Jowitt, Kenneth, ed., *Revolutionary Breakthroughs and National Development: The Case of Romania, 1944–1965.* Berkeley: University of California Press, 1971.

———. *Social Change in Romania, 1860–1940.* Berkeley: Institute of International Studies, University of California Press, 1978.

Markham, Reuben H. *Rumania Under the Soviet Yoke.* Boston: Meador, 1949. An account of the war years and the Communist takeover of Romania by a journalist who spent many years in the country

Mitrany, David. *The Land and the Peasant in Romania: The War and Agrarian Reform, 1917–1921.* London: Oxford University Press, 1930. A classic on the agrarian problem and land reform that resulted from the 1907 uprising.

Oldson, William O. *The Historical and Nationalistic Thought of Nicolae Iorga.* Boulder, CO: East European Quarterly, 1973. A solid biographical work on one of Romania's most notable cultural and political personalities.

Pascu, Stefan. *A History of Transylvania.* Detroit: Wayne State University Press, 1982. A Romanian version of the history of this multiethnic region, with a Marxist slant.

Roberts, Henry L. *Rumania: Political Problems of an Agrarian State.* New Haven, CT: Yale University Press, 1951. Monograph that covers the first half of the twentieth century

Seton-Watson, R. W. *A History of the Rumanians from the Roman Times to the Completion of Unity.* Cambridge: Cambridge University Press, 1934. Considered one of the classics; provides one of the first overviews of Romanian history and presents a useful narrative of the country's activities during the First World War and the acquisition of new territories.

Shafir, Michael. *Romania: Politics, Economics and Society.* Boulder, CO: Lynne Rienner, 1985.

Soviet Union

Billington, James. *Russia Transformed: Breakthrough to Hope: Moscow, August 1991.* New York: Free Press, 1992. Examines the August 1991 attempted coup.

Butson, Thomas G. *Gorbachev: A Biography.* New York: Stein and Day, 1985.

Cohen, Stephen, ed. *Voices of Glasnost: Interviews with Gorbachev's Reformers.* New York: W.W. Norton, 1989.

de Mobray, Stephen. *Key Facts in Soviet History.* London: Pinter Publishers, 1990–. An excellent chronology of important events in Soviet history, presenting concise, easy-to-understand explanations of the events listed.

Gorbachev, Mikhail. *The August Coup: the Truth and the Lessons.* New York: Harper Collins, 1991. An interesting work by a key figure in this event.

Joyce, Walter, and Stephen White. *Gorbachev and Gorbachevism.* London: F. Cass, 1989.

Kaiser, Robert G. *Why Gorbachev Happened: His Triumphs and Failures.* New York: Simon & Schuster, 1991.

Khrushchev, Sergei. *Khrushchev on Khrushchev: An Inside Account of the Man and His Era.* Boston: Little, Brown, 1990.

Kort, Michael. *The Soviet Colossus: the Rise and Fall of the USSR,* 3rd ed. Armonk, NY: M.E. Sharpe, 1993. For readers who are interested only in the Soviet period of history.

Loory, Stuart H., and Ann Imse. *CNN Reports: Seven Days that Shook the World.* Atlanta, GA: Turner Publishing, 1991. Examines the August 1991 attempted coup.

———. *Putsch: Three Days that Collapsed the Empire: the Diary: Text and Photographs.* Oakville, Ont.: Mosaic Press, 1992. Examines the August 1991 attempted coup. Includes an introduction by Boris Yeltsin,

MacKenzie, David, and Michael W. Curran. *A History of Russia, the Soviet Union, and Beyond,* 4th ed. Belmont: Wadsworth Publishing Co., 1993. Examines society, politics and culture during each major period of Russian and Soviet history. This work also provides an extensive bibliography for further study.

Mastro. Joseph P. *USSR Calendar of Events.* Gulf Breeze, FL: Academic International Press, 1988–. A detailed chronology of Soviet history from 1987 on. Each volume is divided into three parts; part one is a straight chronology, part 2 is divided by subject, and part three consists of the indexes.

McCauley, Martin, ed. *Khrushchev and Khrushchevism.* Houndsmills, Basingstoke: Macmillan, 1987.

Medvedev, Roy Aleksandrovich. *Khrushchev.* Garden City, NY: Anchor Press, 1983.

———. *Let History Judge: The Origins and Consequences of Stalinism.* Revised and expanded edition. New York: Columbia University Press, 1989.

Morrison, John. *Boris Yeltsin: From Bolshevik to Democrat.* New York: Dutton, 1991.

Murphy, Paul J. *Brezhnev, Soviet Politician.* Jefferson, NC: McFarland, 1981.

Paxton, John. *Companion to Russian History.* New York: Facts on File, 1983. Using a dictionary format, key events, terms, and characters of Russian and Soviet history are described and explained.

Riasonovsky, Nicholas. *A History of Russia.* New York: Oxford University Press, 1992.

Service, Robert. *Lenin, a Political Life.* 2 vol. Bloomington: Indiana University Press, 1985–.

Slusser, Robert M. *Stalin In October: the Man Who Missed the Revolution.* Baltimore: Johns Hopkins University Press, 1987.

Smith, Hedrick. *The New Russians,* revised ed. New York: Random House, 1991. Based on the author's experience of living in the Soviet Union, this work provides an interesting account of everyday life in the former Soviet Union. The revised edition also includes a chapter on the demise of the Soviet Union.

Solovyov, Vladimir and Elena Klepikova. *Boris Yeltsin: A Political Biography.* New York: G.P. Putnam's Sons, 1992.

Tolz, Vera. *The USSR in 1989: A Record of Events.* Boulder, CO: Westview Press, 1990.

———. *The USSR in 1990: A Record of Events.* Boulder, CO: Westview Press, 1992.

Volkogonov, Dmitri Antonovich. *Stalin: Triumph and Tragedy.* New York: Grove Weidenfeld, 1991.

White, Stephen. *Gorbachev and After.* 3rd ed. Cambridge: Cambridge University Press, 1992.

Wieczynski, Joseph L., ed. *The Modern Encyclopedia of Russian and Soviet History.* Gulf Breeze, FL: Academic International Press, 1976–. Written by specialists in Russian and Soviet studies, each entry gives an overview of the event or person in question and provides a short bibliography for additional readings on the topic.

Yeltsin, Boris Nikolaevich. *Against the Grain: An Autobiography.* New York: Summit Books, 1990.

Yugoslavia

Banac, Ivo. *The National Question in Yugoslavia: Origins, History, Politics.* Ithaca, NY: Cornell University Press, 1984. Banac's study analyzes the formation of the Yugoslav state from 1918 to 1921 through the eyes of all of the nationalities in the new state. His book is considered essential reading for all students of Yugoslavia.

———. *With Stalin against Tito: Conformist Splits in Yugoslav Communism.* Ithaca, NY: Cornell, 1988. Describes in great detail the Tito-Stalin split and its aftermath in Yugoslavia.

Burg, Steven L. *Conflict and Cohesion in Socialist Yugoslavia: Political Decision Making Since 1966.* Princeton, NJ: Princeton University Press, 1983.

Dedijer, Vladimir. *The Battle Stalin Lost: Memoirs of Yugoslavia, 1948–1953.* New York: Viking Penguin, 1971. A useful account of the Tito-Stalin split.

———, et. al. *History of Yugoslavia.* New York: McGraw-Hill, 1974. History of the South Slav peoples through 1973.

Djilas, Aleksa. *The Contested Country: Yugoslav Unity and Communist Revolution, 1919–1953.* Cambridge, MA: Harvard University Press, 1991. Discusses the relationship between communism and nationalism in Yugoslavia; also covers the prewar period.

Djilas, Milovan. *Conversations with Stalin.* New York: Harcourt, Brace, Jovanovich, 1962. An intriguing look into the mind of Stalin immediately before the split with Tito.

———. *Wartime.* New York: Harcourt, Brace, Jovanovich, 1977. An honest and engaging memoir of the author's experiences during the war. The other three volumes of Djilas' memoirs are also excellent evocations of the times in which he grew up and was a member of the Communist movement in Yugoslavia.

———. *Tito: The Story from the Inside*. New York: Harcourt, Brace, Jovanovich, 1980.

Djordjević, Dimitrije, ed. *The Creation of Yugoslavia*. Santa Barbara, CA: ABC-Clio, 1980. A very good collection of essays by an international group of scholars including an article on the postwar economy by John Lampe and a trio of articles by Gale Stokes, Alex Dragnich, and Milorad Ekmečić that present divergent points of view on Serbia's role in the formation of the new state.

Dragnich, Alex. *The First Yugoslavia*. Stanford, CA: Hoover Institution Press, 1983. An account of interwar Yugoslavia; defensive and apologetic toward Serbia.

Glenny, Misha. *The Fall of Yugoslavia*. New York: Viking Penguin, 1992. An evocative, readable, and disturbing look at the last two years of Yugoslavia and the war that is currently tearing the region apart.

Hoptner, Jacob. *Yugoslavia in Crisis, 1934–1941*. New York: Columbia University Press, 1962. Covers Yugoslavia's critical foreign policy decisions of the late 1930s.

Johnson, A. Ross. *The Transformation of Communist Ideology: The Yugoslav Case, 1945–1953*. New York: Cambridge University Press, 1972. A solid account of the ideological gyrations of Yugoslav Communism after the Tito-Stalin split.

Lampe, John, and Marvin Jackson. *Balkan Economic History, 1550–1950*. Bloomington: Indiana University Press, 1982. Covers economic developments in Yugoslavia until 1950.

Lederer, Ivo. *Yugoslavia at the Paris Peace Conference*. Northford, CT: Elliots Bks, 1963. A solid study of the Yugoslav delegation to the Paris conference.

Pavlowitch, Stevan K. *The Improbable Survivor: Yugoslavia and Its Problems, 1918–1988*. Columbus: Ohio State University Press, 1988. Covers the Tito era in great detail. Pavlowitch's critical approach is novel among postwar historians, who have been notably soft on the Communist regime.

———. *Tito: Yugoslavia's Great Dictator, A Reassessment*. Columbus: Ohio State University Press, 1992.

Peasants, Politics, and Economic Change in Yugoslavia. Stanford, CA: Stanford University Press, 1955. An encyclopedic study of the agrarian economy in Yugoslavia before 1941.

Petrovich, Michael. *History of Modern Serbia, 1804–1918*. New York: Harcourt, Brace, Jovanovich, 1976.

Ramet, Pedro. *Nationalism and Federalism in Yugoslavia, 1963–1991*. Indiana: n.p., 1992.

Remak, Joachim. *Sarajevo*. London: n.p., 1959. Analyzes the background to and formation of the Yugoslav state after the First World War.

Roberts, Walter. *Tito, Mihailović, and the Allies, 1941–1945*. New Brunswick, NJ: Rutgers University Press, 1973. It is a detailed analysis of the tangled goals and policies of Tito's subjects.

Rubinstein, Alvin. *Yugoslavia and the Nonaligned World*. Princeton, NJ: Princeton University Press, 1970.

Rusinow, Dennison. *The Yugoslav Experiment, 1948–1974*. California: n.p., 1977. A standard history of the postwar period; extremely detailed.

Shoup, Paul. *Communism and the Yugoslav National Question*. New York: Columbia University Press, 1968. Discusses the Communist party's policies toward the national question, specifically its approach to Macedonia, as well as the relationship of economic developments in Yugoslavia to the national question after the war.

Singleton, Fred. *A Short History of the Yugoslav Peoples*. New York: Cambridge University Press, 1985.

Tomasevich, Jozo. *War and Revolution in Yugoslavia, 1941–1945: The Četniks*. Stanford, CA: Stanford University Press, 1945. Discusses the role of the Serbian royalist resistance under Draža Mihailović.

Vucinich, Wayne, ed. *Contemporary Yugoslavia*. California: n.p., 1969. Short articles about the interwar period and the Second World War.

West, Rebecca. *Black Lamb and Grey Falcon*. New York: Viking Penguin, 1982. One woman traveler's account of Yugoslavia in the thirties.

General

Berend, Iván T., and György Ránki. *Economic Development in East Central Europe in the Nineteenth and Twentieth Centuries*. New York: Columbia University Press, 1974.

Cipkowski, Peter. *Revolution in Eastern Europe*. New York: John Wiley & Sons, Inc., 1991. Examines the political and personal forces behind the fall of Communism in the Warsaw Pact countries.

Drachkovitch, Milorad M., ed. *East Central Europe: Yesterday, Today, Tomorrow*. Stanford, CA: Hoover Institution Press, 1982.

Echikson, William. *Lighting the Night: Revolution in Eastern Europe*. New York: William Morrow and Co. Inc., 1990. First-hand accounts from the author, who witnessed the collapse of communism in Poland, Czechoslovakia, East Germany, Bulgaria, Hungary, and Romania as a reporter for *The Christian Science Monitor*.

Fischer-Galati, Stephen. *Eastern Europe in the Sixties*. New York: Praeger, 1963.

Haraszti, Miklos. *The Velvet Prison: Artists under State Socialism*. New York, Farrar, Straus, & Giroux, 1977. Conveys the bleakness of life and society under the Communists.

———. *A Worker in a Workers' State*. New York, Universe Publishing, 1977. Conveys the bleakness of life and society under the Communists.

Held, Joseph, ed. *The Columbia History of Eastern Europe in the Twentieth Century*. New York: Columbia University Press, 1992. A comprehensive history that begins with a chronology of events in Eastern Europe from 1918 to 1990.

Herz, Martin F. *Beginnings of the Cold War*. New York: McGraw-Hill, 1966.

Jelavich, Barbara. *History of the Balkans: Twentieth Century*. Volume 2. Cambridge: Cambridge University Press, 1983.

Jelavich, Charles and Barbara Jelavich. *The Establishment of the Balkan National States, 1804-1920*. Seattle: University of Washington Press, 1977.

Keegan, John., ed. *World Armies*. New York: Facts on File, 1979.

Lampe, John R., and Marvin R. Jackson. *Balkan Economic History, 1550–1950*. Bloomington: Indiana University Press, 1982. This work traverses three centuries; gives a good overview of economic development and industrialization in Romania, Bulgaria, and Yugoslavia.

Leonhard, Wolfgang. *Child of the Revolution*. London: n.p., 1957. Helpful in understanding the early 1950s.

Maier, Charles, ed. *The Origins of the Cold War and Contemporary Europe*. New York: New Viewpoints, 1978.

McCauley, Martin. *The Origins of the Cold War*. London: Longman, 1983.

Rakowska-Harmstone, Teresa, and Andrew Gyrorgy, eds. *Communism in Eastern Europe*. Bloomington, Indiana: Indiana University Press, 1984.

Revesz, Gabor. *Perestroika in Eastern Europe*. Boulder, CO: Westview Press, 1990. Considers the impact of perestroika in a historical context.

Rothschild, Joseph. *East Central Europe Between the Two World Wars*. Seattle: University of Washington Press, 1990.

Seton-Watson, Hugh. *The East European Revolution*. New York: Frederick A. Praeger, 1951.

Seton-Watson, R. W. *Eastern Europe Between the Wars, 1918–1941*. Cambridge: Cambridge University Press, 1946.

Stavrianos, Leften S. *The Balkans since 1453*. New York: Rinehart and Company, Inc., 1958.

Toma, Peter A., ed. *The Changing Face of Communism in Eastern Europe*. Tuscon, AZ: University of Arizona Press, 1970.

White, Stephen, ed. *Handbook of Reconstruction in Eastern Europe and the Soviet Union*. London: Longman Group UK Limited, 1991.

Wolf, Robert Lee. *The Balkans in Our Time*. New York: Norton, 1978.

Glossary

alliance A close connection of friendship between two or more governments, often made by formal written pact or treaty.

Allied Powers Those nations—namely the United States, Soviet Union, Great Britain, and France—united against the Axis powers in World War II.

anarchy A state of lawlessness or political disorder due to the absence of governmental authority.

armistice A temporary suspension of hostilities by agreement between the opponents; a truce.

autonomous regions Ethnically-based territorial units designated as national homelands for non-nationals inhabiting lands within a country not their own.

Axis Powers Those nations—namely Germany, Italy, and Japan—united against the Allied Powers in World War II.

Balkans Countries occupying the Balkan Peninsula: Albania, Bulgaria, Greece, Romania, the former Yugoslavia, and Turkey (in Europe).

Baltic States The former Soviet, now independent, republics of Estonia, Latvia, and Lithuania on the east shore of the Baltic Sea. Established as independent states in 1917 and forcibly annexed by the Soviet Union in 1940.

bloc A group of nations united by treaty or by agreement for mutual support or joint action; for example, the Soviet bloc.

Bolshevik Party A wing of the Marxian Russian Social Democratic party that seized power in Russia during the

1917 Revolution. Led by the Russian revolutionary Vladimir Lenin.

bolshevism Russian communism advocating the violent overthrow of capitalism.

bourgeoisie Of, or relating to, the social middle class.

BRD Federal Republic of Germany (West Germany).

Brezhnev Doctrine The ideological doctrine used to justify the Warsaw Pact invasion of Czechoslovakia in 1968 by citing the need to prevent socialist countries from leaving the socialist sphere. The doctrine asserts that ''world Socialism is indivisible, and its defense is the common cause of all Communists.'' Named for Soviet leader Leonid Brezhnev.

Bundestag Formerly the West German parliament, now united Germany's parliament.

capitalist economy A type of economy in which individuals, not the government, own industries and resources.

central planning Concept imposed under communism whereby the government plans everything economically for its people without taking into account market need or supply and demand. These predetermined quotas frequently led to gross excesses, but more often shortages, of products, especially food products (*see also* Five-year plan).

Cheka Soviet secret police.

CMEA *See* Comecon

cold war A conflict over ideological differences carried on by methods short of overt military action or violence. Used to describe the tensions that developed after World

War II between the democratic nations of the West and the Soviet Union and its allies.

collectivization Stalinist agricultural policy in which peasant-held land was nationalized by force and administered by the government. Peasants who had previously operated out of their own villages were resettled onto large communal farms and directed to work cooperatively, pooling their labor and resources.

Comecon Council for Mutual Economic Assistance. A seven-nation (USSR, Albania, Bulgaria, Czechoslovakia, Hungary, Poland, and Romania) organization formed to assist the economic development of the member states through coordinated efforts.

Cominform Communist Information Bureau. An organization designed to succeed Comintern (see below) in the leadership of the international Communist movement.

Comintern Communist International. An organization formed by the Bolsheviks to facilitate the international spread of Communism. Later succeeded by Cominform.

Commonwealth of Independent States (CIS) A loose confederation of former Soviet republics established in December 1991 to coordinate inter-republic policies, especially economic and military affairs.

communism A theory in which private industry and property are eliminated and economic goods are equally distributed. Under Communist rule the government owns and/or controls the goods and the means of producing them.

coup d'état The violent overthrow or alteration of an existing government by a small group.

cult of personality First used by Stalin and then copied by other East European Communist leaders. Entails unquestioned devotion to a leader no matter what the consequences. Those who used the cult of personality were known for their excesses in governing that did not take into account the effects their actions had on the country or the people.

de-Stalinization The process of removing Stalin's strict and oppressive controls.

despotism A system of government in which the ruler has unlimited power, usually exercised abusively.

détente A relaxation of strained relations or tensions (as between nations).

dictator An absolute ruler, especially one who suppresses a democratic government.

dictatorship A government in which a person or small group of people has complete power to rule.

dualism The state of being dual or consisting of two parts; division into two.

duchy The territory of a duke or duchess; a special domain.

duma The principal legislative body, or national parliament, in czarist and post-Communist Russia

EDC European Defense Community. Comprised of Belgium, France, Italy, Luxembourg, and the Netherlands. Formed to establish an integrated European army. The French parliament ultimately rejected this proposal in 1954.

EEC European Economic Community. An intergovernmental organization—established in 1957—of 12 Western European nations with its own institutional structures and decision-making framework. The aim of the EEC was to construct a united Europe through peaceful means and create conditions for economic growth, social cohesion among the European peoples, and for greater political integration and cooperation among governments. Now called the European Community (EC), its member nations are Belgium, Denmark, France, Germany, Greece, Ireland, Italy, Luxembourg, the Netherlands, Portugal, Spain, and the United Kingdom.

empire A group of lands and people ruled over by an emperor or other powerful sovereign or government.

entente An international understanding providing for a common course of action.

ethnic cleansing A sometimes questionable term referring to one ethnic group's quest to "clean out" another ethnic group or groups by any means possible. Forced removal or extermination of one or more ethnic groups by another group.

ethnic group A group of people who share a language and similar customs.

Five-year plan Basic organizing principle of centralized planning within the Soviet bloc. Used to guide state investment, economic growth, and development (*see also* Central planning).

free enterprise In a capitalist economy, the freedom to own property and run a business largely free of governmental control.

führer Leader (German).

G7 Group of Seven. A trade and economic organization headed by the leaders of the major industrial nations—Canada, France, Germany, Great Britain, Italy, Japan, and the United States.

GDR German Democratic Republic (East Germany).

Gestapo The Nazi secret police organization operating against those persons suspected of treason or resistance to authority, often using underhanded or terrorist means of control. From the German phrase *gehime staatspolizei.*

glasnost Policy of openness and freedom of expression. Embraced by Mikhail Gorbachev in the 1980s as part of his attempt to reform the Communist system.

Gulag A system of work camps and prisons located primarily in Siberia and the far north of Russia.

gypsy One of a nomadic caucasoid people originally migrating from India and entering Europe in the 14th or 15th centuries.

hegemony Superior influence or authority of one nation over another.

Helsinki Accord Signed by the leaders of 35 nations, this agreement recognizes post World War II boundaries as permanent and guarantees basic civil rights in the countries that sign.

Holocaust Historically known as the genocidal slaughter of more than six million European Jews by the Nazis during World War II. Other targets included Slavs, gypsies, and members of opposition groups from German-occupied countries.

IMF International Monetary Fund. A United Nations affiliated agency that takes responsibility for stabilizing international exchange rates and payments.

iron curtain A term coined by Winston Churchill in 1946 to describe the drastic philosophical divisions between the Soviet bloc and the West. A second meaning was attributed to the barbed wire ''iron curtain'' barricades dividing the borders of many Eastern European countries from the West.

KGB (Committee of State Security) Served as the police surveillance arm of the ruling Communist Party. The KGB was represented at every level of Soviet government activity and in each of the former republics. Its network of informers numbered in the hundreds of thousands adding to the repression of Soviet citizens. Now renamed the Ministry of Security.

kolkhozes Government-run farm collectives in the USSR.

Kremlin Formerly the Soviet Union's, now Russia's, main seat of government in Moscow.

Kristallnact ''Night of broken glass'' that took place in October 1938. The name is derived from the shards of broken glass left in the streets when Germans destroyed Jewish businesses by smashing their glass storefronts.

Kulaks A class of independent freeholding peasants destroyed during the Bolshevik drive to collectivize agriculture in the late 1920s and 30s.

land redistribution The taking of land from large landowners in order to give it to landless farmers.

League of Nations An organization established after World War I to promote international peace. The United States, though key in setting it up, was never a member of the league. An important instrument of diplomacy in the 1920s, the league was unable to fulfill its chief aims of disarmament and peace-keeping in the 1930s and fell into disuse before World War II. The league was formally terminated in 1946 when it was succeeded by the newly formed United Nations.

Little Entente A mutual defensive alliance formed by Czechoslovakia, Romania, and Yugoslavia in 1920 against Hungary by pledging to uphold the Treaty of Trianon.

Magyar A member of the dominant people of Hungary; of Finno-Ugric descent.

market economy An economy that is based on profit and private enterprise.

Marshall Plan A program of U.S. economic and technical assistance to 16 European countries after World War II. Its objectives were to restore the war-ravaged West European economy and to stimulate economic growth and trade among the major non-Communist countries. First announced by Secretary of State George C. Marshall, the plan was formally known as the European Recovery Program.

martial law The law administered by military forces, acting on orders from the government, in an emergency when non-military police agencies are unable to maintain public order and safety.

May Day First of May. The traditional workers' holiday in Communist Eastern European countries.

Mensheviks The larger of the two factions of the Russian Social Democratic Workers' Party, the other faction being the Bolsheviks. Mensheviks supported the development of the mass workers' party, breaking with Lenin in 1902 over the direction and organization of party authority and discipline.

monarchy Undivided rule by a single person with powers varying from nominal to absolute.

nationalism A feeling of intense loyalty and devotion to one's ethnic identity.

nationalize To place control or ownership of an industry in the hands of the national government.

NATO (North Atlantic Treaty Organization) A mutual defense alliance established in 1949 among Belgium, Canada, Denmark, France, Great Britain, Iceland, Italy, Luxembourg, the Netherlands, Norway, Portugal, and the United States; and later joined by Greece, Turkey, and West Germany. Its mission was to safeguard the Atlantic community, particularly against Soviet aggression.

Nazism Doctrines held by the National Socialist German Workers' party in the Third Reich including: totalitarian rule of government, state control of industry, the predominance of groups assumed to be racially superior, and supremacy of the führer. The Nazi party controlled Germany from 1933–45 under the leadership of Adolph Hitler.

oblast An administrative region comparable to, but often far larger than, a U.S. county. An "autonomous" oblast, however, may serve as the homeland for a particular ethnic group.

oligarchy A government in which a small group exercises control, often for corrupt or selfish purposes.

papertiger A person or entity that is outwardly powerful or dangerous but inwardly weak or ineffectual.

perestroika Broadly used to denote Mikhail Gorbachev's policies in the 1980s for the restructuring and revitalization of Soviet society through limited political and economic reform.

plebiscite A vote by which the people of an entire country or district express an opinion for or against a proposal, especially on a choice of government or ruler. Referendum.

plenum A full meeting (assembly) of all the members of a governing body.

pogrom Organized destruction of a chosen group of people. Often random acts of racist violence visited against Jewish persons and property.

politburo The highest and most powerful group of policymakers in each of the Communist bloc countries, chosen from the membership of the Central Committee of the Communist Party.

polonization To impose the language, culture, and customs of the Poles onto non-Polish peoples living in Poland.

Prague Spring Name given to the growing liberalizing reforms occurring in Czechoslovakia from January to August 1968 when Warsaw Pact nations invaded the country to end the reform.

privatization The process of turning state-owned industries into private ownership.

proletariat The lowest social or economic class of a community; the laboring class.

proxy The authority or power to act for another.

puppet government A "dummy" government that sits as a figurehead while other factions hold the real power.

purges A series of persecutions and trials resulting in exile or execution of citizens, both Communist Party members and others, who were accused of anti-socialist, and/or anti-Soviet behavior in the USSR and other Communist nations.

PZPR Polish United Workers' Party

recognition Formal acknowledgement of the political existence of a government or nation.

revisionism A recurrent movement in socialism to revise Marxist theory by favoring evolutionary rather than a revolutionary spirit.

SALT Strategic Arms Limitations Treaty. Leonid Brezhnev and Richard Nixon sign the first treaty (SALT I), limiting anti-ballistic missile systems and offensive missile launchers, in May 1972. SALT II, limiting long-range bombers and missiles, was never ratified by the U.S. Congress and died out in 1979.

Securitate Romania's secret police.

Sejm Poland's lower house of parliament.

Senate Poland's upper house of parliament.

separatist An advocate of independence or autonomy for a part of a political unit (such as a nation), racial or cultural group.

socialism An economic system in which land and industry is controlled by the government rather than by individuals or private companies.

Solidarity *(Solidarnosc)* Independent Polish trade union founded by Lech Wałęsa in 1980.

Soviet The word *soviet* in Russian means "council." The term first took on its twentieth-century political meaning during the 1905 Russian Revolution when "councils of workers' deputies" (the Soviets) organized the events leading to a general strike in October of that year. The Bolshevik government employed the term Soviet as an integral part of the new state's name, the Union of Soviet

Socialist Republics. The term "Soviet" also came to be used loosely as an adjective referring to the Soviet Union.

Sputnik   Built by the Soviet Union and launched in October 1957, *Sputnik* was the first successful man-made satellite ever sent into space. Marked the beginning of the "space race" between the U.S. and USSR and also heightened Cold War tensions.

SS   (Schutzstaffel) Elite military corps of the Nazi party.

Stalinism   Communism as developed by Soviet leader Joseph Stalin. Characterized by rigid authoritarianism, widespread use of terror and emphasis on Russian nationalism.

START   Strategic Arms Reduction Treaty. In May 1992, Russia, Ukraine, Belarus, and Kazakhstan sign an agreement with the United States that opens the way for the ratification of START. Ukraine, Belarus, and Kazakhstan also agree to turn over all, not just battlefield, strategic nuclear warheads to Russia.

Stasi   East Germany's secret police.

Subranie   Bulgarian parliament.

suffrage   The right of voting and also the exercise of such right.

TASS   Soviet news agency.

Third Reich   Adolph Hitler's Nazi regime in Germany (1933–45). This designation was chosen to identify the Nazi Reich, or empire, as third in succession to the Holy Roman Empire and the German Empire of 1871–1918.

Titoism   Following Communist policies and practices independently of, and often in opposition to, the Soviet Union. Named for Yugoslav leader Josip Broz Tito.

totalitarian   A government that controls all aspects of people's lives and which is led by a dictator or a small group of people.

Trotskyism   A radical form of mainstream communism championing immediate worldwide revolution as opposed to socialism in one country. Named for Russian Communist leader Leon Trotsky.

tsar   The supreme ruler of Russia until the Russian Revolution in 1917.

tyranny   Oppressive or cruel exercise of power by a single ruler or government.

United Nations   A general international organization established at the end of World War II (October 1945) to promote international peace and security. The UN's aims are to develop friendly relations among nations; cooperate in solving international economic, social, cultural, and humanitarian problems; and promote respect for human rights and fundamental freedoms.

USSR   Union of Soviet Socialist Republics.

Velvet Revolution   Term used to refer to the non-violent overthrow of communism in Czechoslovakia. Similarly, "Velvet Divorce" refers to the peaceful split of Czechoslovakia into two independent nations: the Czech Republic and Slovakia.

Volkskammer   East German parliament.

Warsaw Pact   (or Warsaw Treaty Organization) A mutual defense alliance established in 1955 among Albania, Bulgaria, Czechoslovakia, East Germany, Hungary, Poland, and the Soviet Union; it was the Soviet bloc's equivalent of NATO.

Zionism   An international movement supporting the Jewish national and religious community.

zomos   Polish police guards who used violence to break up demonstrations during martial law.

Central Europe, 1865–71.

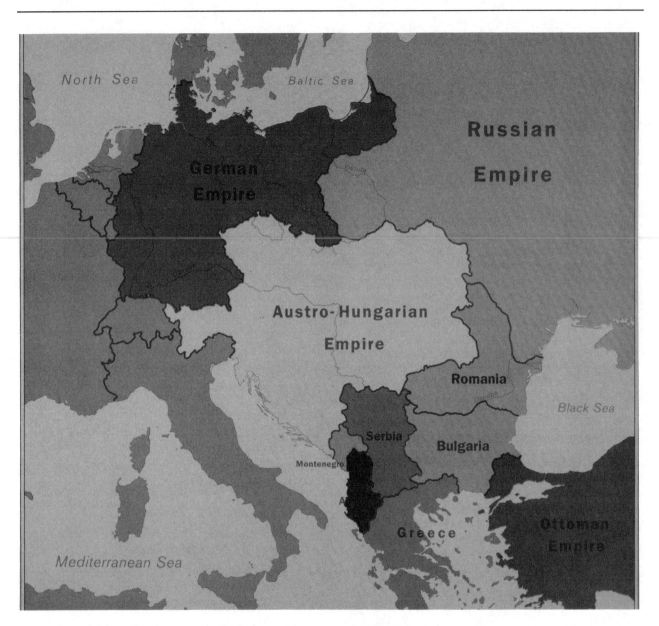

1914: Central Europe and the Balkans on the eve of World War I.

1919–37: Central Europe between the World Wars.

Eastern Europe, 1990.

Eastern Europe, 1993.

Index

B